The Penguin
DICTIONARY OF
ENGLISH
SYNONYMS

Bloomsbury Books
London

PENGUIN BOOKS

Published by the Penguin Group
Penguin Books Ltd, 27 Wrights Lane, London W8 5TZ, England
Penguin Books USA Inc., 375 Hudson Street, New York, New York 10014, USA
Penguin Books Australia Ltd, Ringwood, Victoria, Australia
Penguin Books Canada Ltd, 10 Alcorn Avenue, Toronto, Ontario, Canada M4V 3B2
Penguin Books (NZ) Ltd, 182–190 Wairau Road, Auckland 10, New Zealand

Penguin Books Ltd, Registered Offices: Harmondsworth, Middlesex, England

First published in the USA, under the title *Soule's Dictionary of Synonyms*, 1871
First published in Great Britain,
under the title *A Dictionary of English Synonyms and Synonymous Expressions*,
by Frederick Warne and Co. Ltd 1938
Published under the present title by Omega Books Ltd,
under licence from the proprietor, 1986
This edition published by Bloomsbury Books, an imprint of
Godfrey Cave Associates Ltd, 42 Bloomsbury Street, London WC1B 3QJ,
under licence from Penguin Books Ltd, 1991
1 3 5 7 9 10 8 6 4 2

Copyright © Frederick Warne & Co. Ltd, 1938

Printed in England by
BPCC Hazell Books
Aylesbury, Bucks, England
Member of BPCC Ltd

ISBN 1 8547 1060 5

PREFACE TO THE THIRD EDITION

In the thirty years and more since the former revision of this work much has been added to the resources for preparing a manual of expressively rich word-lists. The great *Oxford English Dictionary* has been completed, and offers not only an unsurpassed treasury of words but abundant dated quotations to help one's judgment as to their expressive values. The revisions of *Webster's New International Dictionary* have made use of newly amassed evidence from systematic studies in every field of literary and technical English. In revising *Soule's Dictionary of Synonyms*, therefore, the present editor has profited not only by consulting these works on points of doubt but by making critical comparisons between the synonym-lists in books that have been enriched by these works: notably *Allen's Synonyms and Antonyms* and the recent revisions of *Roget's Thesaurus*.

It has been possible to make the numerous additions of words in the descriptively important lists without adding greatly to the total bulk, by making certain omissions of unimportant or irrelevant matter. The older book contained numerous lists of local names for all sorts of plants, animals, and even minerals. A word-group of this sort does not have the value of a literary *synonym*-list, since the words are not expressive of nice alternatives of by-sense, feeling, and tone. For example, the word-group *couch grass, quitch grass, quick, scutch, twitch,* etc., all designate an identical grass — *Agropyron repens* — without offering any choices for descriptive precision. Another kind of matter now generally omitted is the mere *defining* of word-senses for which no synonyms are offered. The usefulness of this book requires that the stock words of the language shall be ranged alphabetically as title-words, each with numbered lists of words for *such* of its senses as have synonyms. Other senses, however important historically, are not relevant to the consulter at this point, since he has turned to the title-word as an approach to some *better* word — better, that is, for his immediate purpose. The present book, therefore, has sought to strengthen its distinctive values as a handbook of synonyms, without running inappropriately into the field of a historical dictionary.

The editor wishes to make a special acknowledgment for the assistance rendered in this task by Miss Evelyn K. Wells, who made the primary revision of more than half of the text. Her discriminating sense of word-values and her care have greatly lightened the labor of final revision.

A. D. S.

CAMBRIDGE, *August, 1937*

PREFACE TO THE FIRST EDITION.

THE main design of this Dictionary is to provide a ready means of assistance when one is at a loss for a word or an expression that best suits a particular turn of thought or mood of the mind, or that may obviate an ungraceful repetition. Even practised and skilful writers are sometimes embarrassed in the endeavor to make a sentence more clear, simple, terse, or rhythmical, by the substitution of one form of diction for another. It is presumed that they, as well as novices in composition, will find the present work useful in overcoming difficulties of this sort.

As to the method of using it: Whenever a doubt arises in regard to the fitness of any word, and a better one is not readily suggested, let the writer turn to this word in its alphabetical place. Under it will be found the words and phrases, or some clew to the words and phrases, which, in any connection, have the same meaning as itself, or a meaning very nearly the same. That one of them which comes nearest to expressing the exact shade of thought in the writer's mind will be likely to arrest the attention and determine the choice.

In most cases, all the words that belong to any group will be found in that group. But in some instances, as when the same word falls into two or more groups that are near to each other, or when there are so many synonymes for a word that a repetition of every one of them under each in its alphabetical place would seem to be too formal and prolix, the inquirer is referred to some prominent word among them for a view of the whole. Under the word *Blockhead*, for example, reference is made to the word *Dunce*, under which will be found all the words that are synonymous with it. This example is given because it is the most marked one in our language of a multiplicity of terms for the same idea.

FACSIMILE OF PREFACE TO FIRST EDITION

Many nouns ending in-*ness*, and adverbs ending in-*ly*, have been omitted in their alphabetical places, for the reason that their synonymes are sufficiently indicated by the corresponding adjectives.

The aim has been to present at a single glance the words or modes of speech which denote the same object, or which express the same general idea, with only slight shades of difference. There has been no attempt at elaborate discussion of the nice distinctions that obtain between words apparently synonymous; but hints of such distinctions have been given whenever it was practicable to give them briefly in a parenthetical remark.

In preparing this Dictionary, free use has been made of the following works: Roget's Thesaurus of Words and Phrases; the Quarto Dictionaries of Webster and of Worcester; Crabb's Synonymes; Graham's Synonymes; Whately's Synonymes; Platt's Synonymes; the Dictionaries of Synonymes by Fenby, Sherer, Mackenzie, and Smith; the Medical Dictionaries of Dunglison and of Thomas; and the United States Dispensatory by Wood and Bache. It contains much, however, that has been gathered from a wide field of miscellaneous reading during a long series of years.

The author is under special obligations to his friends, Mr. JUSTIN WINSOR, Mr. WILLIAM A. WHEELER, and Mr. LOOMIS J. CAMPBELL, for the interest they have manifested in the progress of the work, and for their valuable suggestions and criticisms.

BROOKLINE, MASS., 1871.

FINDING THE BETTER WORD

This book is the writer's cabinet, displaying his resources of diction in arrangements that make them most usably "on tap." His accomplishment with its listed words, however, will be much enhanced if he can approach them with a mind that has been made aware of certain discriminated *kinds* of meaning which may figure in the peculiar expressiveness of any word; also of certain *relations* of meaning which may bring quite different words within the same cluster of possibilities for choice. These clues to the right choice are here explained : —

1. The value of a word for use in a given connection is not a matter merely of its precise reference to some object of thought which we may call THE meaning of that word. It has a "meaningfulness" which takes in several kinds of significance. Let us first recognize and then examine these. A word shows its expressive value —

a. In what it *refers to :* in what we call its "sense." Thus the word *chuckle* refers to a particular sort of laugh.

b. In our *emotional response* to that which it names. Thus the word *giggle* not only refers to a particular sort of laugh but stirs a *feeling about* that way of laughing — as a way of silly young things we do not wish to be like.

c. In the *plane of discourse* upon which the speaker or writer is using his words: in what I. A. Richards[1] calls the "tone" of an utterance — solemn, bookish, chatty, and so on. Thus the word *chortle* is definitely colloquial in tone, suggesting a jocose attitude of its user towards the speech-occasion. In contrast, the word *cachinnation* is consciously bookish.

d. In the word's sensuous qualities as a sound entering into a desired phrase-pattern. Thus in "a ghastly, mirthless *grin*" the last word rounds out a rhythm-pattern ($\acute{-} \cup - \cup \acute{-}$) with a needed stressed syllable; it completes a suggestive progression of vowel-sounds (ah — erh — ĭ); and it helps to unify the phrase by alliterating its start and close.

[1] The expressive values here summarized were given their most effective statement for study by Dr. Richards in his *Practical Criticism.*

The two last-mentioned elements in expressive speech should remind us that not words but *utterances* are the real units of choice in diction, and that a word's value is always conditioned by its *context* — by what is being said in its whole immediate connection. This latter is what carries the "sayer's" controlling *intention*, and the rightness of any one word will appear in the response which the whole utterance is meaning to make happen. Thus, taken by itself, the verb *thrid* (an old variant of *thread*) seems merely odd, and so does *boskage*, improvised from *bosk*, a thicket; but in Tennyson's *Dream of Fair Women* these words interplay with others to stir certain desired feelings for the daughter of Jephthah : —

> "Glory to God," she sang, and past afar,
> *Thridding* the sombre *boskage* of the wood
> Toward the morning star.

2. The whole body of English words may be viewed against a sort of star map which shows the distinguishable "tone"-constellations and suggests their outer limits of usability. A large nucleus of the vocabulary is of course neutral in tone, comprising words (like *man*, *proud*, *strike*, *different*) which have no restrictive associations with any one level or field of discourse. Around this nucleus, however, appear groupings which affect one's judgment as to *where* (in what sort of writing) the proffered word will be "in good use." Thus —

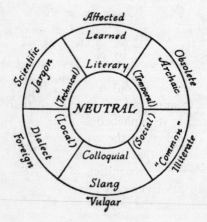

Here the vertical series of "tone"-distinctions forms a scale of dignity, moving from "neutral" up through "literary" (*e.g.: ingenuous, deprecate*), "poetic" (*e.g.: eventide, froward*), over the line — for most occasions — into "affected" (*e.g.: eleemosynary*); and moving down through "colloquial" (*e.g.: cocky*), "slang" (*e.g.: boob, galoot*), over the line into "vulgar" (*e.g.: bum doodads*). Next we have restrictive time-associations, moving through "archaic" (*e.g.: hostel, wroth*), over into "obsolete" (*e.g.: maumetry*); and place-associations which move through "dialectic" (*e.g.: mawk* for "maggot") over into what is out-and-out "foreign." Finally we have restrictive "technicality", moving through what is felt as "jargon" (*protasis, volplane*) over into the special nomenclatures of science (*maxilla, pomiform*); and restrictive feelings as to what is cultivated and well-bred, moving through the banal and "common" (a *gripping show*) over into the "illiterate" (*e.g. infer* for "imply").

3. Words can be displayed together as a synonym cluster to be chosen from when they share a basic meaning such that each synonym can be felt as offering this "core-sense" expressively enriched by further distinctions of sense, feeling, or tone. Thus the words *clothing, garments, garb, habiliments, vestments, apparel, attire, togs*, etc. have in common the core-sense "covering of fabric for the body", which makes them a set of variations on one theme. *Clothing*, perhaps, means just this core-sense and nothing more; but *garb* adds the "by-sense" of "special style distinctive of social or occupational class" (as the *garb* of a monk); *vestments* are liturgical, worn by those officiating in a church service; *attire* suggests that one is being impressed by elegance; *apparel* and *togs* offer contrasts of "tone."

In seeking the best word one naturally starts with some other word that comes to mind but is not felt as satisfying. One then turns to that word in its alphabetical place as a title-word in this book, expecting to find either the synonym list with the right word or a cross-reference to that list under another title-word. One needs, in this process, a recognition of the right *core-sense*, since the title-word will very commonly have two or more historic meanings, each of which links the word with a different synonym-cluster around a distinct core-sense. Thus if one thinks of *abandoned* when groping toward *profligate*, one should recognize the core-sense, "given over to depraved conduct", that will guide one to the *second* list under *abandoned*, where the first list gives synonyms for its earlier meaning : "given up, forsaken."

With the recognized core-sense and the right list before one, a judgment as to the best word is quickened and made precise if one has formed a habit of noting the *presumable kinds* of "by-sense" which given core-senses invite. For example, when one has found the synonym list *irritable, irascible, testy, choleric, ireful, waspish*, and so on, with the core-sense, "temperamentally disposed to displays of anger", one is helped toward the best choice by a little prevision of the variations to be expected. Displays of an emotion may be violent or weak, settled or transient, and their occasions may be serious or petty. These "categories" for the by-senses suggest comparisons by which one quickly sees, for example, that *irascible* means something less serious than *ireful*, more "flash-in-the-pan" than *choleric*, and more violent than *snappish*.

4. In looking for a desired word one can look beyond the limits of the synonym group which one naturally first consults. That group, one should remember, is a part-of-speech grouping as well as a core-sense grouping. Its words are a noun list or an adjective list, and so forth. One looks there first because one commonly starts with some grammatical pattern of phrase in which the wished-for word should fit. Thus one looks under *perplexed* for an adjective to describe somebody as deeply hesitant over a decision in a baffling situation. The right word for this may not appear among the adjectives *doubtful, puzzled, nonplussed*, and so on ; but by turning to the noun list under *perplexity* one will find *quandary*, with which, of course, one can either form an adjective phrase, or re-form the sentence pattern that one began with. So with the nouns *probity, integrity*, one may supply adjective and adverb equivalents (a man *of probity*, acting *with integrity*) that bring in elements of by-sense and feeling which are missing in the list under *upright*.

The worker with words may note with profit that "Basic English", the system of 850 words scientifically chosen to compose an inter-

national language,[1] gets its surprising efficiency — quite adequate
for all ordinary communication — from this possibility of improvising phrase-equivalents for adjectives and verbs. With only
sixteen verbs (*be, do, have, get, keep, give, take, come, go, let, make, put,
seem, say, see, send*), it makes thousands of good verb-substitutes.
With *put* alone it can, instead of *ask, kill, move, terminate, correct,
inform,* give us *put a question, put to death, put in motion, put an end
to, put right,* "*put (him) wise*" — all with nouns or adjectives. In
addition, these "operator verbs" combine with "directive" particles (*at, by, down, in, off, on, out, up, with,* and so forth), to give us
pithy idioms which do expressive duty as verbs. Thus, *put away*
(childish things), *put forward* (a suggestion), *put* (work) *before*
(play), "*put over*" (a stratagem), *put* (a boy) *up to* (mischief), *put
up with* (an annoyance). The present book includes such idioms
in its synonym lists, since they are really on a par with notional
words as units of expression. And it marks the peculiar importance
of the 850 "Basic" words by printing them in **BOLD FACE**.

Another source for the word one is seeking may be among the
antonyms of the word group one is consulting. That is, we can
get a new by-sense for the common idea in *sympathetic, pitying,
compassionate, commiserative* by using a negative with its opposite,
e.g. — *not indifferent, far from ruthless.* Notice here that for many
ideas there are two sets of antonyms: one expressing the simple
negative of lack or contradiction, the other expressing what is
negatively opposite or contrary. Thus the idea of "solicitude
shown for the misfortune of another" has one contrasting negative
in the *lack* of such feeling and another in the extreme *opposite,* or
"a brutal callousness towards others in misfortune." As core-
senses, these can be viewed as falling at plus, zero, and minus points
along a scale; thus —

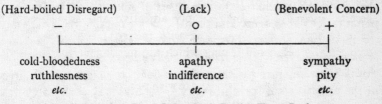

(Hard-boiled Disregard)   (Lack)   (Benevolent Concern)

cold-bloodedness	apathy	sympathy
ruthlessness	indifference	pity
etc.	*etc.*	*etc.*

[1] See C. K. Ogden, *The A B C of Basic English,* **Kegan Paul,** 1932.

5. The word that turns out to be best for one's purpose may be *made* best by one's management of its present context in writing. Any word — even such as "hiss with sibilants, or scrunch with lumps of grinding consonants, or dribble off into weak trickles of unaccented syllables" — may be so placed that it is caught up into a redeeming rhythm, or contributes its dissonance to some patterned contrast; as where the *salt-caked smokestack* of Masefield's "dirty British coaster" —

> Butting through the Channel in the mad March days,

comes with telling vigor after the *quinquireme of Nineveh*,

> Rowing home to haven in sunny Palestine.

It is not necessarily the finding of some exceptional word that counts. With the choices before one, one can often contrive, for a quite ordinary word, a phrasing which, as C. E. Montague says, will "re-impregnate" it with a "super-normal expressiveness" such as Shakespeare achieves in

> the tide of pomp
> That beats upon the high shore of this world.

But such a wizardry of expression with seeming-simple words only goes to show that any word has latencies of meaning beyond the meaning a dictionary gives it — however full and precise the definition may be. Its actual meaningfulness in a given context may represent an outreach from the sense and feeling stamped by its *average* uses to some implication, emotion, and hint of relationship that *emerges* in *this* use. This fact suggests that a dictionary of synonyms can make a unique contribution to the consultant's power with words. By simply displaying in each list the words that offer the *recognized variations of meaning* which accrue to one core-sense, the synonymy intimates the *variations of context* that invite fresh permutations of imagery and phrase. For example, the synonymy for the notion "brevity of speech" offers us *brief, concise, succinct, laconic, pithy, terse, epigrammatic, sententious, curt, short*. These words conspire, just by their collocation, to suggest possibilities in the experience of speech-brevity — such as may changeably link it with simple pressure of time, or with taciturn habit, or artistic economy, or rudeness, or rebuke.   These are all facets of by-sense, hinting metaphorical turns which will put a new complex matter in just the right light.   The user of a book which thus sets words, group by group, to mutual elucidations will find with pleasure that his progress in diction is being surprisingly speeded up.

A. D. SHEFFIELD

POINTS OF EXPLANATION AND ADVICE

The numbered synonym-groups under each title-word answer to different meanings of that word. Thus under the title-word *Stupid* —

List 1 answers to its meaning "not sensible or bright" — as applied to persons.

List 2 answers to its meaning "uninteresting" — as applied to talk, reading matter, activities.

List 3 answers to its meaning "torpid" — as applied to persons or higher animals under *physical* stupefaction.

When a satisfying word does not appear in the synonym-group consulted (*e.g.*, in the group *Stupid, a.* 3), look in the adjacent groups, first of the same title-word (*e.g.*, *Stupid, a.* 1 and 2), and then of nearby title-words with *part-of-speech* variations (*e.g.*, *Stupefy, v. t.*, *Stupidity, n.*, *Stupor, n.*). Thus the satisfying word might be *numb*, which does not appear at *Stupid, a.* 3, but is suggested by *numbness*, to be found at *Stupor, n.*

Remember that most, and sometimes all, synonyms for a *derivative* word can be supplied from the synonyms under its simpler variant. Thus the synonyms *tearing, rending* for the derivative noun *laceration* (not entered) can be supplied from *tear, rend*, given under the verb *lacerate;* and the desired synonym for *monstrously, adv.*, can be had simply by adding *-ly* to the right word under *monstrous, a.* By trusting the consultant to look across these part-of-speech divisions, the author and the present editor have omitted many entries which would have amounted to mere repeated matter.

The following abbreviations are used:

a. . . . . . . adjective	*Geom.* . . Geometry	*p.* . . . . . participle
adv. . . . . adverb	*Gram.* . . Grammar	*Phys.* . . Physics
Alg. . . . . Algebra	*Gr.* . . . . Greek	*pl.* . . . . . . plural
Arch. . . . Architecture	*interj.* . . interjection	*prep.* . . . . preposition
Arith. . . Arithmetic	*It.* . . . . . Italian	*pron.* . . . . pronoun
Bot. . . . . Botany	*L.* . . . . . Latin	*sing.* . . . singular
Colloq. . . Colloquial	*Log.* . . . Logic	Sp. . . . . Spanish
Com. . . . Commerce	*Math.* . . Mathematics	*Theol.* . . Theology
conj. . . . conjunction	*Med.* . . . Medicine	*U.S.* . . United States
Dial. . . . Dialectic	*Mil.* . . . Military	*v.t.* . . . . verb transitive
Eccl. . . . Ecclesiastical	*Mus.* . . Music	*v.i.* . . . . . verb intransitive
Fr. . . . . . French	*Naut.* . . Nautical	
Geol. . . . Geology	*n.* . . . . . noun	

Colloquial and slang words (the latter sparingly admitted) are put in quotation marks.

In entering compounds — such as *horse sense, horse-laugh, horseplay* — where two elements must be written either as separate, as hyphened, or as solid, the present editor has tended to retain the hyphened forms which predominate in the former edition. American practice (as standardized in the new Webster) favors the solid forms in numerous instances where British practice (as given in the *Shorter Oxford Dictionary*) favors hyphening. The writer will often feel his own preference to be affected by the context within which he uses the word, since the looseness or closeness of its union may answer to nuances of meaning that he should be free to convey. It will be understood, therefore, that the hyphened compounds in this book do not represent *a preferred usage* but are simply the *intermediate* form, which may be made separate or solid in response to expressive considerations.

THE PENGUIN DICTIONARY OF
ENGLISH SYNONYMS

A

Aback, *adv.* Back, backward, rearward, regressively, to the rear.

Abaft, *prep.* (*Naut.*) Behind, back of, in the rear of.

——, *adv.* (*Naut.*) Aft, astern, behind, back, rearward, in the rear.

Abandon, *v. t.* 1. Leave, relinquish, quit, forsake, desert, evacuate, drop, abjure, forswear, give over, cast off, retire from, withdraw from.

2. Surrender, cede, yield, resign, forego, renounce, waive, vacate, deliver up, give up, part with, let go, lay down, demit. See ABDICATE.

Abandoned, *a.* 1. Relinquished, deserted, forsaken, cast away, outcast, derelict, rejected, discarded, given up, given over, cast off, cast aside, thrown overboard, demitted.

2. Depraved, corrupted, corrupt, profligate, vicious, wicked, dissolute, reprobate, graceless, shameless, unprincipled, lost, obdurate, hardened, impenitent, incorrigible, irreclaimable, demoralized, lost to shame, dead to honor.

Abandonment, *n.* 1. Relinquishment, desertion, dereliction.

2. Renunciation, surrender, cession, resignation, abnegation, abjuration, rejection, demission. See ABDICATION.

Abase, *v. t.* 1. Depress, detrude, lower, reduce, drop, sink, cast down, let down, throw down, let fall.

2. Degrade, depose, humble, disgrace, dishonor, humiliate, debase, bring low, take down.

Abasement, *n.* 1. (*The act or process.*) Depression, detrusion, reduction, lowering, fall, deterioration, degradation, debasement, degeneration, vitiation, perversion, depravation.

2. (*The condition or state of being.*) Abjectness, abjection, vileness, baseness, degeneracy, contemptibleness, despicableness, ignominy, turpitude, infamy.

3. (*The attitude.*) Humiliation, submission, submissiveness, resignation, humility, meekness, humbleness, lowliness, self-abasement.

Abash, *v. t.* Shame, mortify, confuse, confound, dash, disconcert, discompose, humiliate, humble, snub, put to shame, make ashamed, put out of countenance, take down. See DISCOUNTENANCE.

Abashment, *n.* Confusion, shame, mortification, embarrassment.

Abate, *v. t.* 1. Lessen, diminish, decrease, reduce, lower, relax, slacken.

2. Remit, allow, bate, rebate, deduct.

3. Moderate, assuage, mitigate, soothe, soften, qualify, alleviate, mollify, allay, appease, pacify, compose, tranquillize, temper, attemper, quiet, quell, calm, dull, blunt.

4. Batter down, beat down, demolish, raze, lay low.

5. (*Law.*) Remove, suppress, terminate, put an end to.

——, *v. i.* 1. Decrease, diminish, lessen, subside, sink, wane, decline, fall away, fall off, fade, fade away, ebb, intermit, slacken.

2. (*Law.*) Be defeated, frustrated, *or* overthrown, fail.

Abatement, *n.* 1. Diminution, decrease, decrement, lessening, mitigation, moderation, assuagement, extenuation, remission.

2. Subsidence, decline, lowering, sinking, settling, wane, fading, evanishing, evanishment, ebb.

3. Discount, allowance, rebate, deduction, reduction, drawback.

Abbey, *n.* Monastery, convent, cloister, priory, nunnery.

Abbreviate, *v. t.* Shorten (*by cutting off*), curtail, clip, prune, reduce, contract, retrench, condense, compress, epitomize, cut short, cut down. See ABRIDGE.

Abbreviation, *n.* Shortening (*by cutting off*), curtailment, contraction, reduction, condensation, compression, brief, compend, compendium, abstract, epitome. See ABRIDGMENT.

Abdicate, *v. t.* Resign (*an office or dignity*), surrender (*a right*), cede, forego, renounce, relinquish, abandon, quit, vacate, give up, part with, lay down, renounce all claim to.

——, *v. i.* Resign, relinquish office (*especially that of a sovereign*), vacate the throne, retire to private life, go into retirement.

Abdication, *n.* Abdicating, resignation, surrender, renunciation, abandonment.

Abdomen, *n.* Belly, paunch, ventral region, visceral region, visceral cavity.

Abdominal, *a.* Ventral, visceral, hemal.

Abdominous, *a.* Large-bellied, great-bellied, big-bellied, pot-bellied, tun-bellied, paunchy.

Abduct, *v. t.* Take away (*surreptitiously* or *forcibly*, or both), kidnap, carry off, run away with, run off with, spirit away, drag away.

Abduction, *n.* 1. Withdrawing, withdrawal, withdrawment, drawing away.
2. Kidnapping, etc. See ABDUCT.

Aberrance, *n.* Aberrancy, roving, roaming, error. See ABERRATION.

Aberrant, *a.* 1. Deviating, wandering, rambling, diverging, divergent, devious, erratic, out of the right way.
2. Irregular, abnormal, unnatural, unusual, singular, peculiar, anomalous, unconformable, exceptional, strange, anomalistic, eccentric, erratic, out of the way, disconnected, inconsequent, idiotic, monstrous, preternatural.

Aberration, *n.* 1. Deviation, divergence, wandering, rambling, departure.
2. Irregularity, eccentricity, singularity, peculiarity, strangeness, unconformity, anomaly, abnormity, monstrosity.
3. Illusion, delusion, hallucination, monomania, self-deception.

Abet, *v. t.* 1. Aid, assist, help, support, succor, second, sustain, uphold, back, co-operate with, take part with, give support to, embolden, subsidize.
2. Favor, encourage, sanction, countenance, advocate, connive at, be *or* become subsidiary to.
3. (*Law.*) Instigate (*to commit a crime*), stimulate, incite, foment.

Abettor, *n.* 1. Assistant, helper, aider, coadjutor, co-operator, ally, auxiliary.
2. Advocate, adviser, promoter, instigator.
3. Confederate, accomplice, accessory, *particeps criminis, socius criminis.*

Abeyance, *n.* 1. (*Law.*) Expectation, prospect, expectancy, waiting, anticipation, calculation, contemplation.
2. Suspense, suspension, suspendedness, reservation, intermission, remission, dormancy, quiescence, suppression, sublation.

Abhor, *v. t.* Hate, abominate, detest, loathe, nauseate, shrink from, recoil from, revolt at, shudder at, view with horror.

Abhorrence, *n.* Abomination, horror, detestation, hatred, loathing, disgust, antipathy, aversion.

Abhorrent, *a.* 1. Hating, detesting, abominating, loathing.
2. Odious, offensive, shocking, repugnant, hateful, loathsome, revolting, nauseating, horrifying, horrible, repellent, repulsive.

Abide, *v. i.* 1. Stay, sojourn, tarry, lodge, rest, keep, take up one's quarters, pitch one's tent.
2. Dwell, reside, live, inhabit, settle, plant one's self, get a footing, get a foothold.
3. Remain, continue, persist, persevere, go on, keep on, be steadfast, be constant. See SUBSIST.
4. Endure, last, be enduring, be indestructible, be permanent, be immutable.
——, *v. t.* 1. Await, attend, wait for, be in readiness for, be in store for.
2. Endure, tolerate, bear, brook, suffer, bear with, put up with, sustain.

Abide by. Act up to, conform to, persist in, keep, fulfil, discharge (*of promises, and the like*).

Abiding, *a.* Permanent, lasting, durable, enduring, constant, continuing, stable, changeless, unchangeable, immutable.

Ability, *n.* 1. Power (*to execute anything*), ableness, force, potency, might, vigor, efficiency, efficacy, strength, energy, skill, skilfulness, dexterity, address, adroitness, cleverness, ingenuity, talent, aptitude, aptness, knack, expertness, facility, quickness, readiness.
2. Qualification, competency, sufficiency.
3. Capability, capableness, faculty, gift, parts, genius, endowment, calibre, forte, turn. See CAPACITY.

Abject, *a.* Base, vile, mean, low, despicable, contemptible, beggarly, paltry, dirty, grovelling, pitiful, ignoble, degraded, worthless, poor, servile, slavish, menial, cringing, sneaking, hangdog, sordid, shabby, scurvy, miserable, wretched, low-minded, base-minded, base-born, earth-bred.

Abjectness, *n.* Meanness, servility, vileness, baseness, abasement, abjection, contemptibleness. See ABJECT.

Abjuration, *n.* 1. Renunciation (*upon oath*), relinquishment, rejection, abandonment, abnegation, repudiation, discarding, disowning.
2. Recantation, retraction, revocation, repeal, reversal, recall, disavowal, disclaiming, disclaimer.

Abjure, *v. t.* 1. Renounce (*upon oath*), relinquish, forego, reject, forswear, abandon, give up, cast off, discard, repudiate, disown.

2. Retract, revoke, recant, recall, withdraw, disavow, disclaim, take back, go back on (*a promise*), "renig."

ABLE, *a.* 1. Clever, accomplished, talented, adroit, ingenious, expert, dexterous, adroit, apt, quick, skilful, efficient, proficient, good, versed, practical, *au fait*.

2. Qualified, fitted, competent.

3. Capable, gifted, powerful, strong, mighty, highly endowed, of talent, of great talents.

4. Masterly, effective, telling, vigorous.

Ablution, *n.* Washing (*especially of the body, as a religious rite*), lavation, bathing, wash, purification, cleansing, baptism.

Abnegation, *n.* Denial, renunciation, rejection, abandonment, surrender. See ABJURATION.

Abnormal, *a.* Irregular, anomalous, anomalistic, unusual, unnatural, singular, peculiar, unconformable, exceptional, heteroclite, aberrant, divergent, eccentric, erratic, strange, monstrous, preternatural.

Abnormity, *n.* Abnormality, irregularity, unconformity, anomaly, peculiarity, idiosyncrasy, singularity, deformity, monstrosity.

Aboard, *adv.* On board, in the ship, in the vessel, on, inside, within.

Abode, *n.* 1. Habitation, dwelling, lodging, domicile, home, house, seat, place, quarters, headquarters, place of residence, residency.

2. (*Rare.*) Continuance (*in a place*), stay, sojourn, residence.

Abolish, *v. t.* 1. Abrogate, annul, disannul, repeal, rescind, revoke, cancel, nullify, quash, vacate, invalidate, set aside, make void.

2. Destroy, overthrow, subvert, obliterate, extirpate, eradicate, annihilate, extinguish, suppress, do away, put an end to, make an end of, batter down, raze to the ground, leave not one stone upon another, crush out, stamp out, "squelch." See DISESTABLISH.

Abolition, *n.* 1. Abrogation, annulment, annulling, nullification, rescinding, revocation, cancellation, cancelling, repeal, rescission.

2. Destruction, overthrow, subversion, obliteration, extirpation, eradication, annihilation, extinction, extinguishment, suppression. See DISESTABLISHMENT.

Abominable, *a.* 1. Hateful, odious, detestable, horrid, horrible, execrable,

nefarious, damnable, cursed, accursed, hellish.

2. Loathsome, loathly, offensive, obnoxious, foul, nauseous, nauseating, disgusting, sickening, repulsive, revolting, shocking.

3. Vile, wretched, sorry, scurvy, shabby, utterly bad.

Abominate, *v. t.* Abhor, detest, execrate, hate, loathe, be nauseated by, shrink from, recoil from, revolt at, shudder at, view with horror.

Abomination, *n.* 1. Abhorrence, detestation, execration, hatred, loathing, disgust, nauseation, antipathy, utter aversion.

2. Contamination, pollution, defilement, taint, uncleanness, impurity, foulness, loathsomeness, odiousness, corruption, corruptness.

3. Nuisance, annoyance, plague, infliction, torment, curse, great evil, hateful thing.

Aboriginal, *a.* Primitive, primeval, primordial, pristine, primary, prime, original, first, native, indigenous, autochthonal, autochthonous, of eld.

Aborigines, *n. pl.* Natives, aboriginals, primitive inhabitants, autochthones, indigenes, indigenous population.

Abortion, *n.* 1. Miscarriage, premature labor, premature delivery.

2. Failure, disappointment, want of success, vain effort *or* attempt.

Abortive, *a.* 1. Miscarrying, failing, untimely, immature, incomplete, stunted, rudimentary, rudimental.

2. Unavailing, vain, fruitless, useless, bootless, ineffectual, ineffective, inoperative, unsuccessful, profitless, futile, unprofitable, idle, nugatory, in vain, of no account.

Abound, *v. i.* 1. Teem, swarm, superabound, swell, flow, increase, multiply, be in a great plenty, be numerous, be very prevalent.

2. Exuberate, luxuriate, revel, wanton, be well furnished, be well supplied.

ABOUT, *prep.* 1. Around, round, encircling, surrounding.

2. Near, near to, not far from.

3. Concerning, touching, respecting, anent, relating to, relative to, with respect to, with reference to, in regard to, with regard to, *re* (*Latin*).

4. Through, over, all over, in all parts of.

——, *adv.* 1. Around, hind part before, end for end, in an opposite direction.

2. Hither and thither, here and there, from one place to another, in various places, helter-skelter.

3. Nearly, near, approximately, not far from, almost, well-nigh.

4. Ready, on the point, on the eve.

Above, *prep.* 1. Higher than, on top of, atop of.

2. Over, exceeding, more than, greater than.

3. Beyond, superior to.

4. Too high for, too proud for, of rectitude too great for, too magnanimous for.

——, *adv.* 1. Overhead, aloft, on high, in a high place, in heaven, in the heavenly heights, *in excelsis.*

2. Before, in a former part, previously.

3. Of a higher rank *or* order.

Above-board, *adv.* Openly, candidly, ingenuously, frankly, sincerely, fairly, in open sight, without artifice, without concealment, without equivocation, without guile, without disguise, without mental reservation.

Abrade, *v. t.* Wear away, wear off, rub off. See SCRAPE.

Abrasion, *n.* Friction, attrition, rubbing, disintegration, wearing away, wearing off, rubbing off, rubbing down, wearing down.

Abreast, *adv.* 1. Alongside, side by side, in one line, in alignment, aligned, bow to bow, stem to stem.

2. Against, off, on a line with, opposite to.

Abridge, *v. t.* 1. Shorten, epitomize, condense, compress, make an abstract of, summarize.

2. Diminish, reduce, contract, curtail, lessen, retrench, cut down. See ABBREVIATE.

3. Deprive of, dispossess of, divest of.

Abridgment, *n.* 1. Shortening, compression, epitomizing, condensation, compacting, contraction, diminution, reduction, curtailment, retrenchment. See ABBREVIATION.

2. Compendium, compend, epitome, summary, précis, abstract, digest, synopsis, syllabus, breviary, brief, conspectus, outline, bird's-eye view.

3. Deprivation, dispossession, limitation, restriction.

Abroad, *adv.* 1. Widely, at large, expansively, in all directions, unrestrainedly, ubiquitously.

2. Forth, out of the house, out of doors, in the open air.

3. In foreign lands, away from one's country, over sea, beyond seas, on one's travels.

4. Extensively, before the public, publicly.

Abrogate, *v. t.* Annul, disannul, repeal, revoke, rescind, cancel, abolish, nullify, quash, vacate, invalidate, overrule, set aside, do away, void, make void.

Abrogation, *n.* Repeal, rescission, rescinding, abolition, annulment, annulling, revocation, voidance, voiding, making void. cancelling, cancellation, setting aside.

Abrupt, *a.* 1. Broken, cragged, craggy, rough, rugged, jagged.

2. Steep, precipitous, acclivous, acclivitous.

3. Sudden, out-of-hand, unexpected, unanticipated, precipitate, hasty, unseasonable, ill-timed, unlooked for, unannounced.

4. Short, blunt, unceremonious, curt, brusque, rude, rough, inconsiderate, uncomplaisant, discourteous.

5. Inelegant (*as style*), stiff, cramped, harsh, jerky, disconnected, unconnected.

Abscess, *n.* Sore, ulcer, fester, imposthume, pustule, gathering, boil.

Abscond, *v. i.* 1. Withdraw, flee, fly, decamp, escape, elope, retreat, bolt, make off, steal away, slink away, slip away, run away, run off, sneak off, pack off, effect one's escape, make off with one's self, give the slip, take French leave, give leg bail.

2. Hide, secrete one's self, lie concealed.

Absence, *n.* 1. Non-attendance, non-appearance, "cut."

2. Inattention, abstraction, preoccupation, distraction, revery, musing, brown study, absent-mindedness.

3. Want, deficiency, lack, privation, default, defect.

Absent, *a.* 1. Away, gone, not present, abroad, otherwhere.

2. Abstracted, preoccupied, inattentive, dreaming, musing, lost, napping, absent-minded, in a brown study.

Absolute, *a.* 1. Independent, unrestricted, unqualified, unlimited, unconditional, unconditioned, complete, perfect, self-existent, self-determined, ideal, supreme, *causa sui.*

2. Despotic, arbitrary, tyrannical, tyrannous, imperious, imperative, authoritative, autocratic, dictatorial, irresponsible.

3. Positive, actual, real, veritable, determinate, decided, genuine, categorical, unequivocal, unquestionable, certain.

Absolutely, *adv.* 1. Completely, unconditionally, without limit, definitely.

2. Truly, actually, positively, downright, indeed, really, in fact, in reality, in truth, unquestionably, indubitably, beyond peradventure, infallibly.

Absoluteness, *n.* 1. Despotism, arbitrariness. See ABSOLUTISM.

2. Positiveness, reality, actuality, perfection, ideality, supremeness, etc. See ABSOLUTE.

Absolution, *n.* Acquittal, remission, discharge, release, liberation, deliverance, clearance, forgiveness, pardon, shriving, shrift. See INDULGENCE, JUSTIFICATION.

Absolutism, *n.* Absoluteness, arbitrariness, despotism, tyranny, autocracy, personal government, Cæsarism, the "man on horseback."

Absolve, *v. t.* Acquit, clear, release, liberate, free, discharge, loose, deliver, exculpate, exonerate, excuse, forgive, pardon, shrive, set free. See JUSTIFY.

Absorb, *v. t.* 1. Imbibe, take in, take up, suck in, suck up, drink in, appropriate, assimilate.

2. Consume, exhaust, destroy, engorge, devour, engulf, swallow up.

3. Engross, engage, immerse, occupy, arrest, fix, rivet.

Absorbent, *a.* Absorbing, imbibing.

Absorption, *n.* 1. Absorbing. See ABSORB, 1 and 2.

2. Engrossment, occupation, engagement, immersion.

Abstain, *v. i.* Refrain, forbear, desist, deny one's self, hold *or* keep one's self back, withhold, stay one's hand, keep one's self from indulgence.

Abstemious, *a.* Abstinent (*by habit*), sober, moderate, habitually temperate, sparing in diet. See ABSTINENT.

Abstinence, *n.* 1. Abstaining, refraining, keeping aloof, avoidance.

2. Abstemiousness, soberness, temperance, moderation, non-indulgence, self-restraint, self-denial.

Abstinent, *a.* 1. Abstaining, fasting.

2. Abstemious, sober, temperate, self-restraining, self-denying, not indulgent of appetites.

Abstract, *v. t.* 1. Separate, disunite, disjoin, dissociate, isolate, detach, disengage, take out of context, take out of its proper whole, regard without reference to relations, consider in bare thought, think without the definiteness of sense-perception, think vaguely.

2. Take, seize, appropriate, steal, purloin.

3. Abridge, abbreviate, epitomize, make an abstract of, outline, make synopsis of.

Abstract, *a.* 1. Separate, isolated, not concrete, out of context, unrelated, simple, by itself, *per se.*

2. Occult, recondite, subtle, refined, abstracted, vague. See ABSTRUSE.

——, *n.* Abridgment, epitome, summary, précis, conspectus, compend, compendium, synopsis, syllabus, outline, digest, brief, breviary, sum and substance, concise statement, gist, drift, general contents.

Abstracted, *a.* 1. Subtle, refined, abstract, abstruse.

2. Inattentive, preoccupied, lost, dreaming, musing, absent, absent-minded, in a revery, in a brown study.

Abstraction, *n.* 1. Separation, disconnection, disjunction, isolation, severing from context, ignoring of relations, blindness to the proper whole.

2. Preoccupation, inattention, revery, musing, muse, absence, absence of mind, brown study.

3. Taking, abduction, seizure, appropriation, stealing, purloining, pilfering.

Abstruse, *a.* Recondite, remote, occult, profound, hidden, transcendental, obscure, difficult, dark, vague, indefinite, enigmatical, mysterious, mystic, mystical, high, abstract, abstracted, subtle, refined, attenuated, rarefied.

Absurd, *a.* Unreasonable, irrational, foolish, fantastic, nonsensical, ridiculous, incongruous, senseless, ludicrous, silly, stupid, preposterous, egregious, ill-judged, ill-advised, contrary to common sense, self-contradictory, self-annulling, nugatory, self-cancelling, patently fallacious.

Absurdity, *n.* 1. Unreasonableness, irrationality, foolishness, folly, foolery, extravagance, absurdness, nugacity, fatuity, idiocy, drivelling.

2. Absurd thing, drivel. See PARADOX.

Abundance, *n.* Flow, flood, overflow, exuberance, luxuriance, fertility, copiousness, profusion, richness, largeness, ampleness, amplitude, wealth, affluence, opulence, store, more than enough, plenty, plenteousness, plenitude.

Abundant, *a.* Abounding, flowing, overflowing, plentiful, plenteous, copious, much, exuberant, luxuriant, replete, full, large, ample, good, liberal, bountiful, lavish, rich, teeming, thick.

Abuse, *v. t.* 1. Misuse, misemploy, misapply, pervert, prostitute, desecrate, dishonor, profane, pollute, make an ill use of, deceive, impose on, betray, cajole, seduce by cajolery.

2. Maltreat, harm, injure, hurt, ill-treat, ill-use, mishandle.

3. Revile, reproach, vilify, slander, traduce, defame, asperse, inveigh against, carp at, malign, blacken, disparage, berate, rate, betongue, upbraid, calumniate, lampoon, satirize, lash, "bullyrag," rail at, sneer at, treat with contumely, pour contumely on. See VITUPERATE.

4. Violate, outrage, ravish, deflower.

Abuse, *n.* 1. Misapplication, misuse, misemployment, dishonor, dishonoring, profanation, prostitution, desecration, pollution, perversion, ill-use.

2. Maltreatment, outrage, ill-treatment, bad treatment.

3. Corrupt practice, malfeasance, malversation.

4. Vituperation, railing, reviling, vilification, defamation, aspersion, disparagement, rating, upbraiding, contumely, obloquy, opprobrium, insult, scurrility, ribaldry, foul invective, rude reproach, billingsgate, tongue lashing.

Abusive, *a.* Reproachful, opprobrious, scurrilous, ribald, contumelious, vituperative, condemnatory, vilificatory, damnatory, invective, carping, calumnious, denunciatory, injurious, offensive, reviling, insulting, insolent.

Abut upon. Meet (*end to end* or *side to side*), be contiguous, adjoin, be adjacent to, terminate at *or* upon, be conterminous with, be juxtaposed.

Abutment, *n.* 1. Abutting, being contiguous *or* adjacent, adjoining, adjacency, contiguity, juxtaposition.

2. Shore-pier, end-pier, terminal pier, terminal support.

Abuttal, *n.* 1. Adjacency, contiguity, nearness, juxtaposition, being next, boundary, terminus, limit, termination.

2. Terminal land, adjacent ground, contiguous estate, next holding, adjoining property.

Abyss, *n.* 1. Gulf, gorge, great depth, deep pit, abysm, depth, deep, chasm, profound.

2. Hell, limbo, purgatory, the pit, bottomless pit, the nadir, gehenna.

Academic, *a.* 1. Scholastic, literary, lettered, collegiate, of the college, of the university.

2. Platonic, of Plato, platonistic.

Academy, *n.* School, seminary, institute, gymnasium, high school, college, scientific body, association of artists, *littérateurs,* or *savants.*

Accede, *v. i.* 1. Consent, agree, assent, acquiesce, comply, yield assent, give assent.

2. Be joined, be added, unite itself.

Accelerate, *v. t.* Hasten, expedite, hurry, quicken, speed, precipitate, despatch, urge forward, push forward, push on, press on, urge on.

Acceleration, *n.* Hastening, increase of velocity. See preceding verb.

Accent, *n.* 1. Intonation, cadence, tone, inflection, modulation of voice.

2. Stress (*on a certain syllable*), ictus, emphasis, force of utterance, beat.

——, *v. t.* Accentuate, lay stress upon, pronounce with accent, put the ictus on.

Accentuate, *v. t.* 1. Mark with accent, put the mark of accent upon.

2. Accent, lay stress upon, pronounce with accent, put the ictus on, emphasize.

Accept, *v. t.* 1. Take (*what is offered*). See RECEIVE.

2. Admit, assent to, agree to, accede to, accord recognition to, acquiesce in, accommodate one's self to, approve, embrace, acknowledge, avow.

3. Estimate, regard, value, interpret, construe, put a sense upon.

Acceptable, *a.* Welcome, pleasing, pleasant, agreeable, grateful, gratifying.

Acceptance, *n.* 1. Accepting, taking, reception, receipt, acknowledgment.

2. Favorable reception, approbation, approval, gratification, satisfaction.

Acceptation, *n.* 1. Meaning, signification, significance, sense, import, interpretation, construction, mode of explanation, understanding.

2. Approval, adoption, currency, vogue, cordial reception, favorable regard.

Access, *n.* 1. Avenue, approach, passage, way, passage-way, way of approach, entrance, entrance-way, adit, entry.

2. Admission, admittance, means of approach, liberty to approach, audience, interview, entrance.

3. Accession, addition, increase, aggrandizement, enlargement, gain, increment, more.

4. Attack (*of disease, etc.*), onset, fit, paroxysm, recurrence.

Accession, *n.* 1. Addition, increase, enlargement, augmentation, extension.

2. Coming into power (*as a new dynasty*).

Accessory, *a.* Assisting, aiding, abetting, helping, contributory, appurtenant, subsidiary, ancillary, auxiliary, additional, additive, adjunct, supplemental, supplementary, subordinate, of detail, of minor importance, concerning minutiæ.

——, *n.* 1. Confederate, accomplice, abettor, assistant, helper, coadjutor, associate (*in a crime*), *particeps criminis, socius criminis.*

2. Detail, minor particular, minor parts, subordinate element, subsidiary, accompaniment, attendant, concomitant, supporting member, minutia.

Accidence, *n.* Inflection, grammatical variation of stems, case-endings *and* conjugation-endings.

Accident, *n.* 1. Casualty, chance, fortuity, mischance, misadventure, calamity, mishap, miscarriage, misfortune, hap, hazard, contingency, unforeseen *or* fortuitous event. See CONTRETEMPS.

2. Property, quality, modification, affection, mode, condition, state, change, alteration, attribute, contingent attribute, modalization.

Accidental, *a.* 1. Casual, fortuitous, contingent, happening by chance, unintended, chance, undesigned.

2. Incidental, adventitious, non-essential, immaterial, dispensable, not absolutely requisite, *de facto* but not *de jure*, that has merely happened to be.

Acclamation, *n.* Applause, plaudit, shouting, cheer, cry, outcry, *éclat*, acclaim, shout of applause, loud homage, gratulation, salutation, hosanna, *te deum*, *gloria in excelsis*.

Acclimate, *v. t.* Acclimatize, inure *or* habituate to a climate, season.

Acclimation, *n.* Acclimature, acclimatization, inurement to climate, adjustment to climate.

Acclivity, *n.* Ascent, upward slope, rising ground, steep, hill, height, up-hillway.

Accommodate, *v. t.* 1. Oblige, serve, supply, furnish, do a service for, supply the wants of, minister to the convenience of, make comfortable, contain, hold, furnish room for.

2. Fit, suit, adapt, make conform, make conformable, make consistent, make correspond.

3. Reconcile, adjust, settle, compose, harmonize.

Accommodation, *n.* 1. Advantage, privilege, convenience, supply of wants, provision of conveniences. See EASEMENT.

2. Agreement, adaptation, fitness, suitableness, conformity.

3. Reconciliation, adjustment, pacification, settlement, harmony, harmonization, harmonizing.

Accompaniment, *n.* Appendage, concomitant, attendant, adjunct, attachment, appurtenance.

Accompany, *v. t.* Attend, escort, chaperon, convoy, follow, wait on, be associated with, keep company with, go with, go along with, consort with, go hand in hand with.

Accomplice, *n.* Confederate, accessory, abettor, associate (*in a crime*), *particeps criminis, socius criminis*.

Accomplish, *v. t.* 1. Complete, achieve, effect, execute, perform, do, consummate, compass, carry, carry into effect, carry through, carry out, get through, bring about, work out, turn out, turn off, fulfil, realize, effectuate, bring to pass.

2. Finish, end, conclude, terminate.

Accomplished, *a.* 1. Completed, etc. See ACCOMPLISH.

2. Instructed, educated, practised, experienced, finished, consummate, ripe, versed, qualified, proficient, able, apt, adroit, expert, skilful.

3. Polished, refined, polite, elegant, fashionable, fine.

Accomplishment, *n.* 1. Completion, performance, execution, achievement, consummation, fulfilment. See ACCOMPLISH.

2. Acquirement, attainment, proficiency, stock of knowledge, mental resources, embellishment (*of mind* and *manners*), ornamental acquisition, ornament, adornment, grace.

Accord, *v. t.* Grant, concede, yield, give, allow, vouchsafe, deign.

——, *v. i.* Harmonize, correspond, agree, tally, quadrate, be in unison, be harmonious, square.

——, *n.* Accordance, concord, agreement, concurrence, consensus, concordance, conformity, conformation, harmony, unison, unanimity.

Accordant, *a.* Agreeable, agreeing, suitable, in accord (with), consonant, congruous, symphonious, harmonious.

Accordingly, *adv.* 1. Agreeably, suitably, conformably, consistently.

2. Consequently, therefore, hence, wherefore, whence, thence, then, thus, so, and so, as a natural consequence, as proper to the circumstances *or* the occasion.

According to. By, in accordance with, conformably to, agreeably to.

Accost, *v. t.* Come alongside, confront, approach, draw near, address, salute, greet, speak to, make up to.

Accouchement, *n.* [Fr.] Child-bearing, child-bed, child-birth, delivery, confinement, lying-in, parturition, labor, travail, being in the straw.

Accoucheur, *n.* [Fr.] Man-midwife, obstetrician.

Accoucheuse, *n.* [Fr.] Midwife, howdy (*or* howdie).

ACCOUNT, *n.* 1. Record, register, inventory, score.

2. Bill, charge, registry of debt and credit.

3. Reckoning, computation, calculation, enumeration, tale, tally, count, score.

4. Description, statement, narration, recital, rehearsal, relation, narrative, chronicle, history, story, delineation, representation, portrayal, detail, word, tidings, report.

5. Explanation, exposition, clearing up, elucidation, exhibition of causes, reference to grounds, exploration into principles, philosophy.

6. Consideration, regard, motive, reason, ground, sake.

7. Consequence, importance, worth, distinction, dignity, repute, reputation, note.

8. Profit, advantage. See BENEFIT.

Account, *v. t.* Esteem, regard, deem, judge, believe, take for, think, hold, consider, view, reckon, rate, estimate, look upon.

——, *v. i.* [With *with* or *to* before persons, and *for* before things.] 1. Render an account, answer in judgment, answer responsibly.

2. Explain, elucidate, expound, trace to causes, give the philosophy of, clear up, exhibit the grounds, give a reason, show the reason, render a reason, assign the cause, make explanation of.

Accountability, *n.* Accountableness, responsibility, liability, obligation, bond of duty, the having to answer for, amenability.

Accountable, *a.* Responsible, answerable, amenable, liable, in duty bound.

Accountant, *n.* Book-keeper, expert in accounts, auditor, controller.

Accoutre, *v. t.* Dress, equip, furnish, fit out, arm and equip, array in military harness, harness, array for the field.

Accoutrements, *n. pl.* [Written also *Accouterments.*] Dress, equipage, equipments, trappings, gear, harness, array.

Accredit, *v. t.* Credit, give trust *or* confidence to, give credit *or* honor to, receive as an envoy, receive as commissioned, empowered, *or* authorized, authorize, empower, commission, depute, send with credentials.

Accretion, *n.* Growth (*by accession of parts*), accumulation, increase by adhesion, concretion.

Accrue, *v. i.* Result, proceed, come, arise, inure, issue, follow, flow, redound, ensue, be added, be derived, be gained, be got, come in, accumulate (intrans.), be due.

Accumbent, *a.* Leaning, reclining.

Accumulate, *v. t.* 1. Pile, amass, aggregate, agglomerate, collect, collect together, gather up, pile up, heap up, bring together, heap together, scrape together.

2. Store, garner, husband, treasure up, garner up, lay up, lay by, lay in, set by. See HOARD.

——, *v. i.* Increase, grow, be accumulated, be heaped up, accrue.

Accumulation, *n.* Collection, pile, heap, aggregation, mass, accretion, amassment, agglomeration, conglomeration, amount accrued, store, hoard, hoarding.

Accuracy, *n.* Accurateness, exactness, exactitude, correctness, precision, niceness, nicety, truth, accurateness, fidelity, faithfulness, carefulness, correctness, closeness, strictness.

Accurate, *a.* Exact, correct, precise, true, truthful, faithful, strict, close, rigorous, severe, just, nice, unerring.

Accursed, *a.* 1. Cursed, unsanctified, unholy, diabolic, devilish, hellish, infernal, doomed, damned.

2. Detestable, execrable, hateful, abominable, odious, horrid, horrible, damnable, revolting. See ABOMINABLE.

Accusation, *n.* Crimination, impeachment, arraignment, indictment, charge. See ACCUSE.

Accuse, *v. t.* Charge, impeach, arraign, indict, criminate, incriminate, inculpate, tax, inform against, call to account, take to task, blame, censure.

Accuser, *n.* Informer, informant, plaintiff, complainant, libellant, prosecutor.

Accustom, *v. t.* Habituate, inure, use, harden, familiarize, train, discipline, drill, break in. See ADDICT.

Accustomed, *a.* Usual, habitual, wonted, habituated, customary, familiar, common, frequent, regular, ordinary, everyday.

Ace, *n.* 1. Single point (*in cards* or *in dice*), single pip, single spot, one-spot, head of suit.

2. Particle, item, atom, jot, iota, bit, tittle, whit, grain, scrap, mite, corpuscle, scintilla, trifle, fig.

Acerbity, *n.* 1. Sourness, astringency, roughness, acidity, acidness, tartness, acridity, acridness, bitterness.

2. Acrimony, acrimoniousness, severity, harshness, sternness, asperity, bitterness, venom, rancor, crabbedness, churlishness, moroseness, sullenness, illtemper.

Ache, *n.* Aching, dull pain, continued pain, pain, anguish, agony.

——, *v. i.* 1. Be in pain, feel *or* suffer pain.

2. Be painful, give pain, be anguished, sorrow, grieve, suffer.

Achieve, *v. t.* 1. Accomplish, perform, execute, do, complete, finish, compass, consummate, effect, realize, bring about, bring to pass, carry through, carry out, work out, bring to a close, bring to conclusion, bring to consummation *or* perfection, actualize, fulfil.

2. Obtain, acquire, procure, gain, win, get.

Achievement, *n.* 1. Performance, accomplishment, completion, attainment, realization, consummation.

2. Exploit, feat, deed, work.

Achromatic, *a.* Colorless, uncolored, untinged, hueless, free from color, perfectly transparent.

Achromatism, *n.* Absence of color, want of color, freedom from color, perfect transparency, freedom from iridescence.

Achromatize, *v. t.* Deprive of color, render non-iridescent, make perfectly transparent, render purely translucent.

ACID, *a.* Sour, tart, sharp, pricking, stinging, pungent.

Acidity, *n.* Acidness, sourness, tartness, sharpness.

Acidulous, *a.* Sourish, somewhat acid, slightly acid, sub-acid, somewhat sour.

Acknowledge, *v. t.* 1. Recognize, take cognizance of, be aware of, hold in remembrance.

2. Admit, grant, concede, allow, accept, indorse, subscribe to, agree to.

3. Confess, own, avow, profess.

4. Express gratitude for, give thanks for.

5. Own *or* admit the validity of.

Acknowledgment, *n.* 1. Recognition, recognizance.

2. Admission, avowal, concession, allowance, acceptance, indorsement.

3. Expression of thanks *or* gratitude.

Acme, *n.* Summit, top, apex, vertex, zenith, peak, pinnacle, utmost height, highest point, culmination, culminating point, climax.

Acolyte, *n.* Follower, attendant, underclergyman, satellite, henchman, retainer, acolythe, acolyth. See ADHERENT.

Acquaint, *v. t.* 1. Familiarize, make familiar.

2. Inform, apprise, tell, notify, make aware, make known to, mention to, communicate to, signify to, give notice to, send word to, advise of, advertise of, send advices to.

Acquaintance, *n.* 1. Familiarity, familiar knowledge.

2. Friend (*with whom one is not inti-*

mate), circle known, visiting circle, round of one's social intercourse, person *or* persons known.

Acquainted with. 1. Familiar with, versed in, *au fait* in.

2. A friend of (*without being intimate with*), in social relations with, knowing personally.

Acquiesce, *v. i.* 1. Yield, comply, submit, bow, rest, resign one's self, be reconciled, be resigned, be satisfied, rest satisfied, repose, rest content.

2. Assent, consent, agree, accede, concur, yield assent, give consent, fall in, go with the stream, go with the current.

Acquiescence, *n.* 1. Compliance, submission, resignation, satisfaction, contentment.

2. Assent, consent, agreement, concurrence.

Acquiescent, *a.* Complying, yielding, submitting, etc. See ACQUIESCE.

Acquire, *v. t.* 1. Gain, obtain, achieve, attain, procure, earn, win, get, secure, have, make, get possession of, get into one's hands. See PURCHASE.

2. Master, learn thoroughly, make one's self master of.

Acquirement, *n.* 1. Acquiring, gathering, gaining, mastery.

2. Accomplishment, attainment, acquisition, stock of knowledge, mental resources.

Acquisitive, *a.* Acquiring, disposed to acquire, eager for gain, greedy, avid.

Acquisitiveness, *n.* Love of acquiring, avidity, desire to acquire, eagerness for gain.

Acquit, *v. t.* Discharge (*from an accusation*), clear, release, absolve, exonerate, exculpate, excuse, pardon, forgive, quit, set free.

Acquittal, *n.* Discharge, release, deliverance, liberation, exoneration, exculpation, clearance, absolution, acquittance.

Acquittance, *n.* 1. Discharge. See ACQUITTAL.

2. Receipt, receipt in full, quittance.

Acrid, *a.* 1. Sharp, biting, mordicant, pungent, hot, burning, poignant, caustic, corrosive, bitter.

2. Severe, harsh. See ACRIMONIOUS.

Acridness, *n.* 1. Acridity, sharpness, pungency, poignancy.

2. Severity, harshness, hardness. See ACRIMONY, 2.

Acrimonious, *a.* 1. (*Rare.*) Corrosive, caustic, sharp.

2. Severe, harsh, hard, acrid, sarcastic, bitter, virulent, malignant, censorious, crabbed, snarling, snappish, testy, pet-

tish, petulant, cross, sour, tart, splenetic, peevish, ill-tempered, ill-natured, rancorous, spiteful, envenomed, galling, grinding, biting, mordacious, vitriolic.

Acrimony, *n.* 1. Sharpness, corrosiveness, causticity.

2. Severity, harshness, hardness, sourness, tartness, acridity, acridness, asperity, virulence, bitterness, acerbity, rancor, venom, crabbedness, moroseness, churlishness, ill-temper, spite, spitefulness, abusiveness.

Acrobat, *n.* Rope-dancer, funambulist, high-vaulter, tumbler, flying-trapezist, equilibrist, aerosaltant.

ACROSS, *prep. and adv.* Athwart, over, from one side of to the other, thwart, transversely.

Act, *v. i.* 1. Work, move, carry anything into effect, execute a purpose, be in action, be active, be in process, keep going, energize.

2. Behave, conduct one's self, demean one's self, acquit one's self, deport one's self.

3. Operate, have influence, be efficient, be efficacious, work, have effect, be operative, function.

4. Play a part, play, feign, dissimulate, pretend, make believe, dissemble.

——, *v. t.* 1. Do, perform, execute, carry into execution.

2. Personate, impersonate, represent, play, simulate, mimic, mime, enact, play the part of.

3. Be, realize, actualize, do the duties of, function as, display the qualities of.

ACT, *n.* 1. Deed (*viewed as a single exertion of power*), performance, proceeding, exploit, feat, achievement, turn. See ACTION, 2.

2. Statute, enactment, ordinance, edict, decree, law, bill.

3. Fact, reality, actuality, real existence.

Acting, *n.* 1. Deed, performance, action.

2. Personation, representation, simulation, rendition.

Action, *n.* 1. Activity, spontaneous process, exercise, motion, movement, play.

2. Deed (*viewed as requiring a continued exertion of power*), doing (*esp. in pl.*), performance, feat, exploit, achievement, procedure, proceeding, course, acting, turn.

3. Agency, operation, force, energy, influence, instrumentality, process, measure.

4. Battle, engagement, conflict, contest, combat, rencontre, encounter, skirmish, brush, affair.

5. Acting, performing, performance, enacting, representing, representation, putting on the boards, playing.

6. Subject, fable, plot, series of events.

7. (*Law.*) Suit, lawsuit, process, case, prosecution.

Active, *a.* 1. Operative, operant, influential, efficient, effective, effectual, efficacious, living, vigorous, in action, in operation, in actual process, in force.

2. Busy, bustling, "rustling," diligent, assiduous, industrious, indefatigable, unremitting, laborious, sedulous, at work, diligently employed, busily engaged.

3. Alert, nimble, agile, supple, brisk, dapper, stirring, smart, quick, prompt, ready, lively, sprightly, spirited. See SPRY.

4. Enterprising, energetic, strong, efficient, in earnest, vigorous, full of life, animated, ebullient, fervent.

5. Drastic (*as medicine*), powerful, potent, effective, efficacious.

Activity, *n.* 1. Action, exercise, mode of action, mode of exercise.

2. Alertness, agility, nimbleness, smartness, briskness, sprightliness, spryness, etc. See ACTIVE, 3.

3. Intensity, energy, strength, force, power, vigor.

4. Enterprise, efficiency, alert endeavor.

Actor, *n.* 1. Doer, operator, agent, participant.

2. Player, performer, comedian, tragedian, stage-player, dramatic artist, "histrion," mime, mummer, impersonator.

Actual, *a.* 1. Real, veritable, true, substantial, objective, determinate, decided, categorical, positive, absolute, certain, genuine, very, not imaginary, not merely supposed or fancied, not fictitious, that exists in deed and in truth, *de jure* as well as *de facto, bona fide.*

2. Present, now existing, now in being, sensibly real, sensible, perceptible, tangible, *de facto,* in hard fact, at this moment, here and now, just this present, un-ideal, in act, *in actu,* in process, energizing, energic.

Actually, *adv.* Really, truly, absolutely, positively, veritably, verily, indeed, in fact, in reality, as a matter of fact, in truth. See ACTUAL.

Actuary, *n.* Agent, superintendent, supervisor, overseer, clerk, registrar, computing manager, manager, executive agent.

Actuate, *v. t.* Induce, impel, move, prompt, instigate, persuade, incite, act upon, activate, prevail upon, work upon, urge, drive, dispose, incline.

Act upon. Influence, effect, have influence upon.

Acumen, *n.* Acuteness, shrewdness, sagacity, astuteness, sharpness, ingenuity, perspicacity, discernment, penetration, mother-wit, quick parts.

Acuminate, } *a.* (*Bot.*) Sharp, acute,
Acuminated, } pointed, cuspidate, cuspidated.

Acute, *a.* 1. Sharp, pointed, acuminate, cuspidate.

2. Keen, shrewd, discerning, knowing, quick, sharp, smart, bright, sage, sagacious, intelligent, astute, ingenious, subtle, penetrating, piercing, clear-sighted, sharp-witted, long-headed.

3. Severe, violent, intense, poignant, distressing, fierce, piercing, exquisite, pungent.

4. High, shrill, high-toned.

5. (*Med.*) Sudden, violent, temporary, limited, not chronic.

Acute-angled, *a.* Oxygonal.

Acuteness, *n.* 1. Sharpness, pointedness.

2. Acumen, shrewdness, penetration, sagacity, sagaciousness, astuteness, sharpness, brightness, perspicacity, discernment, ingenuity, mother-wit, quick parts.

3. Severity, intensity, poignancy, violence.

4. Highness, shrillness.

Adage, *n.* Proverb, saying, saw, dictum, aphorism, apothegm, maxim, by-word, sententious precept.

Adamantean, *a.* Adamantine, hard as adamant, very hard, infrangible, indestructible, imperishable, unyielding.

Adamantine, *a.* 1. Made of adamant.

2. Adamantean, very hard, hard as adamant.

Adapt, *v. t.* Adjust, accommodate, co-ordinate, suit, proportion, qualify, prepare, fit, temper, fashion, match, make, conform, make conformable *or* suitable, square.

Adaptation, *n.* 1. Fitness, suitableness, appropriateness, aptness, adaptability, conformableness, conformability, accommodation, harmony.

2. Fitting, process *or* act of fitting, adjustment, accommodation, suiting, etc. See ADAPT.

Add, *v. t.* 1. Join, subjoin, annex, affix, adject, adjoin, append, superadd, tag, tack on, connect, put with, attach, say further.

2. Sum, sum up, cast up, add together, aggregate, reckon up, count up, foot up.

Addendum, *n.* Addition, appendix, appendage, adjunct, appurtenance, attachment.

Addict, *v. t.* Accustom (*commonly in a bad sense*), habituate, dedicate, devote, apply (*habitually*), give, give up.

Addiction, *n.* Addictedness, habit, habituation, absorption, absorbedness, surrender, devotion, devotedness, enslavement, immersion.

ADDITION, *n.* 1. Adding, joining, etc. See ADD.

2. Accession, increase, augmentation, enlargement, extension. See ADD TO.

3. Appendage, adjunct, appendix. See ADDENDUM.

Additional, *a.* Superadded, adscititious, supplemental, supplementary, extra, more, further.

Additive, *a.* To be added. See ADD, 1.

Addle, *a.* 1. Addled, spoiled (*as eggs*), rotten, putrid, corrupt.

2. Barren, unfruitful, fruitless, abortive, unproductive, unprolific, unfertile, sterile, infecund, addled.

——, *v. t.* 1. Corrupt, spoil, render barren. See preceding.

2. Accumulate gradually, earn, lay up, save.

Addle-headed, *a.* Foolish, stupid, dull, muddled, doltish, brainless, shallow, soft, sappy, witless, blockish, weak-headed, muddle-headed, weak-minded, feeble-minded, half-witted, short-witted, shallow-brained, dull-witted, thick-skulled, addle-pated.

Address, *v. t.* Direct (*words, etc.*), accost, salute, speak to, apply to, invoke, memorialize, court, pay court to, make suit to.

——, *n.* 1. Appeal, invocation, petition, memorial, entreaty, request, imploration, application, solicitation, suit.

2. Discourse, speech, oration, lecture, sermon, harangue. *Specif.*, inaugural, valedictory, eulogy, etc.

3. Skill, art, adroitness, readiness, dexterity, expertness, cleverness, ingenuity, ability, tact, management.

4. Superscription, direction.

Add to. Increase, augment, enlarge, greaten, make greater, aggrandize.

Adduce, *v. t.* 1. Advance, offer, present, allege, assign, give, bring forward.

2. Name, mention, cite, quote, instance, introduce.

Adept, *n.* Master, proficient, expert, genius, veteran, virtuoso, master hand, doctor, "dab," "dabster."

——, *a.* Skilled, versed, experienced, practised, proficient, good, at home, *au fait.*

Adequacy, *n.* Adequateness, sufficiency, sufficingness, completeness, competence, competency, enough.

Adequate, *a.* Sufficient, sufficing, enough, commensurate, proportionate, correspondent, equal, suitable, fit, competent, adapted.

Adhere, *v. i.* 1. Stick, cling, cleave, hold, cohere, take hold, be firmly fixed.

2. Belong, pertain, appertain, be appurtenant, be intimately related.

3. Be faithful, be devoted, be attached, stand by, be true.

Adherence, *n.* 1. Tenacity, fixedness.

2. Attachment, constancy, fidelity, devotion, adhesion.

Adherent, *a.* Adhering, sticking, clinging.

——, *n.* Follower, partisan, disciple, sectary, votary, supporter, dependant, vassal, retainer, henchman, satellite, acolyte.

Adhesion, *n.* 1. Adhering, sticking, clinging, tendency to adhere.

2. Attachment. See ADHERENCE.

Adhesive, *a.* 1. Sticking, clinging, tending to adhere.

2. Sticky, tenacious, viscid, viscous, glutinous, gummy.

Adieu, *n.* Farewell, valediction, leave-taking, parting, good-by.

Adipose, *a.* Fat, fatty, unctuous, oily, sebaceous, greasy.

Adjacence, } *n.* Nearness, vicinity, jux-
Adjacency, } taposition, neighborhood, proximity, contiguity.

Adjacent, *a.* Adjoining, conterminous, neighboring, near, close, bordering, contiguous, abutting, juxtaposed.

Adjective, *n.* Qualifying word *or* term, attributive, attribute, adjunct, connotative name, adnoun. See EPITHET.

Adjoin, *v. t.* Be contiguous to, touch, abut, lie close to, border upon, be adjacent to, march on *or* with, lie next, be juxtaposed to.

——, *v. i.* Border together, lie near together, lie close together, be contiguous, be adjacent.

Adjourn, *v. t.* 1. Postpone, defer, delay, procrastinate, put off.

2. Suspend, interrupt, close, end, prorogue, dissolve.

——, *v. i.* Suspend *or* postpone session, take recess, dissolve.

Adjournment, *n.* 1. Postponement, delay, putting off.

2. Prorogation, etc. See ADJOURN, 2.

Adjudge, *v. t.* 1. Award (*judicially*), assign, allot.

2. Determine, settle, decide, decree (*by judicial authority*), adjudicate.

Adjudicate, *v. t.* Determine. See ADJUDGE.

——, *v. i.* Judge, decide, determine, arbitrate, umpire, pass judgment, sit in judgment.

Adjudication, *n.* 1. Act of deciding judicially. See ADJUDICATE.

2. Sentence, decision, determination, decree, award, arbitrament.

Adjunct, *n.* Addition, appendage, appurtenance, dependency, attachment, addendum, something added, modifier, subordinate part, accessory.

Adjuration, *n.* Entreaty (*as if to one bound by oath*), solemn charge, act of adjuring, adjuring, solemn appeal, oath.

Adjure, *v. t.* 1. Entreat (*as if under oath*), conjure, obtest, beseech, pray, supplicate, beg, implore, invoke, enjoin solemnly.

2. Swear by, invoke (*by oath*), take oath upon.

Adjust, *v. t.* 1. Arrange, dispose, rectify, trim, put *or* set in order, put *or* set to rights, put in tune, put in good *or* proper trim.

2. Regulate, set.

3. Settle, compose, pacify, reconcile, harmonize, make up.

4. Fit, adapt, suit, proportion, accommodate, measure, make conform, make conformable (followed by *to* or *with*).

ADJUSTMENT, *n.* 1. Arrangement, adjusting, putting in order, putting in good trim, setting to rights, disposal.

2. Regulation, setting, putting right, state of regulation, good order, accurate arrangement.

3. Settlement, reconciliation, pacification, agreement, understanding, mutual understanding.

4. Fitting, adapting, accommodation, making suitable *or* conformable, conformity, suitedness.

Adjutant, *n.* 1. (*Rare.*) Assistant, helper, aid, adjurant.

2. (*Mil.*) Order-aide, subordinate in charge of orders, subordinate through whom orders are issued and reports received.

Administer, *v. t.* 1. Dispense, give, distribute, supply, contribute, deal out, give out, afford, furnish.

2. Direct, manage, conduct, control, superintend, preside over.

——, *v. i.* 1. Contribute, conduce, be helpful. [With *to.*]

2. (*Law.*) Act as administrator. [With *upon.*]

Administration, *n.* 1. Dispensation, distribution, giving.

2. Management, conduct, direction, control, superintendence.

3. Executive department (*of a government*), President (or *other chief magistrate*) and cabinet, the Government, the ministry, the cabinet.

4. (*Law.*) Management of an estate (*of an intestate*).

Admirable, *a.* 1. (*Rare.*) Wonderful, surprising, striking, astonishing.

2. Excellent, praiseworthy, astonishingly good, fine, rare, superb, worthy of admiration.

Admiration, *n.* 1. (*Rare.*) Wonder, surprise, astonishment, amazement.

2. Liking, love, high regard, warm approbation.

Admire, *v. t.* 1. (*Rare.*) Wonder at, be surprised at, be astonished *or* amazed at.

2. Esteem great, regard with pleasure, think fine, count brilliant, like much, think highly of, have a high opinion of, prize *or* value highly.

Admirer, *n.* 1. Appreciator, one that esteems another great *or* excellent, one that greatly values.

2. Lover, gallant, suitor, sweetheart, beau.

Admissible, *a.* Permissible, allowable, lawful, proper, justifiable, warrantable, possible, probable, quite likely, not unlikely, not impossible.

Admission, *n.* 1. Admittance, introduction, access, entrance, initiation, *entrée*.

2. Allowance, avowal, concession, acknowledgment, assent, acceptance.

Admit, *v. t.* 1. Receive, grant entrance to, let in, take in, open the door to, give access to.

2. Concede, accept, grant, acknowledge, own, confess, take for granted, agree to, accede to, acquiesce in.

3. Permit, allow, bear, admit of, be capable of.

Admit of. Admit, permit, allow, bear, be capable of.

Admittance, *n.* 1. Admission, entrance, introduction, *entrée*.

2. Access, means of approach, liberty to approach, permission to enter, lodgment, acceptance, reception, welcome.

Admixture, *n.* 1. Mixture, mingling.

2. Spice, dash, infusion, leaven, sprinkling, touch, seasoning, smack, taste, tincture, tinge, hint, suggestion, flavor, suspicion, *soupçon*.

Admonish, *v. t.* 1. Reprove (*gently*), censure, warn of a fault, rebuke.

2. Advise, counsel, caution, forewarn, warn, enjoin.

3. Instruct, inform, teach, apprise, acquaint, notify, make acquainted, make aware, remind.

Admonition, *n.* 1. Hint of a fault, gentle reproof, mild censure, slight rebuke, remonstrance.

2. Advice, counsel, caution, warning, monition, instruction, reminder.

Admonitory, *a.* Admonishing, monitory, cautionary, warning, counselling, admonitive.

Ado, *n.* 1. Trouble, difficulty, travail, toil, labor, pains.

2. Bustle, stir, flurry, fuss, hubbub, noise, tumult, turmoil, pother, bother, botherment, "botheration," confusion, commotion, excitement, "to-do."

Adolescence, *n.* Youth, juvenility, minority, juniority, nonage, teens, springtime of life, dayspring of life, growing time, bloom of life.

Adolescent, *a.* Youthful, juvenile, young, growing, in the teens, etc. See ADOLESCENCE.

Adopt, *v. t.* 1. Appropriate, take to one's self, take *or* select as one's own, assume.

2. Approve, accept, avow, espouse, support, maintain.

3. Affiliate, father, take as one's own child.

Adoption, *n.* 1. Appropriation.

2. Approval, acceptance, avowal, espousal, support, maintenance.

3. Affiliation, adopting, fathering.

Adorable, *a.* 1. Divine, to be adored, worthy of adoration, worshipable, deserving divine honors.

2. Estimable, venerable, worthy of love *or* honor, admirable, worthy of the utmost love, supremely good.

Adoration, *n.* 1. Worship, devotion, act of adoring, adoring.

2. Homage, reverence, veneration, exalted regard, idolizing, idolatry, incense.

Adore, *v. t.* 1. Worship.

2. Revere, venerate, idolize, honor, pay homage to.

Adorer, *n.* 1. Worshipper.

2. Idolater, great admirer.

Adorn, *v. t.* Embellish, decorate, enrich, beautify, ornament, deck, bedeck, emblazon, set, beset, set round, stick, bestick, stud, bestud, gild, trim, betrim, grace, crown, garnish, array, set out, set off, varnish, bedizen, trick out, dress out, dress up, dress.

Adroit, *a.* Dexterous, expert, skilful, apt, handy, ready, quick, clever, able, masterly. See ADEPT.

Adscititious, *a.* Supplemental, supplementary, superadded, adventitious, superfluous, redundant, alien, artificial, spurious, smuggled. See ADDITIONAL, ACCESSORY.

Adulation, *n.* Flattery, cajolery, honeyed words, flummery, excessive praise, extravagant compliment, fulsome praise, over-laudation, blandishment, blandiloquence, fawning, sycophancy, incense.

Adulatory, *a.* Flattering, smooth, oily, full of compliments, servile in compliment, fawning, cringing, obsequious, unctuous, sycophantic, blandishing, cajoling.

Adult, *a.* Mature, grown up, full grown, of age, of mature age, ripe, ripened.

Adulterate, *v. t.* Debase, corrupt, contaminate, vitiate, deteriorate, make impure, sophisticate, "doctor," alloy, dash with, mix *or* mingle with.

Adulteration, *n.* Debasement, corruption, deterioration, sophistication, etc. See ADULTERATE.

Adulterous, *a.* Guilty of adultery, committing adultery, impure, debased, illicit, spurious, corrupt, unchaste, rakish, dissolute.

Adultery, *n.* Violation of the marriage-bed, infidelity, breaking of the marriage-vows, advoutry, criminal conversation, *crim. con.*

Adumbrate, *v. t.* 1. Shadow, foreshadow, shadow out, shadow forth, dimly outline, indicate, hint at, approximate, represent approximately, suggest, trace vaguely, faintly delineate.

2. Typify, represent, symbolize, show, denote, stand for, image, figure, prefigure, allegorize, image forth, be a parable of.

3. Darken, bedarken, dim, bedim, obscure, hide, conceal, overcast, overshadow, enshade, enshadow, disillumine, obumbrate, becloud, send into partial eclipse, send into a penumbral light.

Adumbration, *n.* 1. Shadowing forth, faint sketch, faint representation, indistinct image, shadowy outline, dim approximation.

2. Type, image, shadow, symbol, premonition, dark prophecy, foreshadowing, prefiguring, presage, prototype, mystery.

Advance, *v. t.* 1. Push, send, *or* set forward *or* onward, propel, shove, bring forward, move toward the front.

2. Promote, aggrandize, exalt, elevate, dignify, raise to preferment, raise to higher rank.

3. Forward, further, promote, improve, strengthen, benefit, make better, encourage the progress of.

4. Allege, adduce, propose, offer, assign, propound, bring forward, lay down.

5. Increase (*as price*), enhance, augment, raise, make greater, make higher.

——, *v. i.* 1. Proceed, progress, make progress, make way, get forward, go forward, get on, go on, get along, come on, gain ground, march, rise.

2. Improve, grow, thrive, prosper, make improvement.

——, *n.* 1. Progress, progression, procedure, movement to the front, march, way, moving forward, forwarding, headway.

2. Improvement, growth, advancement, rise, enhancement, progress, promotion, preferment.

3. Tender, offer, proposal, proposition, proffer, overture, addresses.

4. Increase (*of price*), enhancement, rise, appreciation.

Advancement, *n.* 1. Progress, progression, proficiency.

2. Promotion, preferment, elevation, furtherance, exaltation, aggrandizement.

3. Improvement, advance, growth. See ADVANCE.

Advantage, *n.* 1. Favorable opportunity, odds, vantage-ground, superior situation *or* condition, best estate, best plight.

2. Superiority, ascendency, precedence, pre-eminence, upper-hand.

3. Benefit, avail, profit, gain, emolument, return, utility, expediency, good, weal, service, blessing.

4. Behalf, behoof, account, interest.

5. Privilege, prerogative, convenience, accommodation. See EASEMENT.

——, *v. t.* Benefit, profit, serve, help, avail, advance the interest of, be of advantage to, be of service to.

Advantageous, *a.* Beneficial, profitable, helpful, useful, convenient, serviceable, salutary, favorable, expedient, good, well, gainful, opportune, for one's advantage, interest, *or* good.

Advent, *n.* Arrival, coming, approach, visitation, appearing, accession.

Adventitious, *a.* Accidental, incidental, supervenient, fortuitous, extrinsic, extraneous, foreign, non-essential. See ADSCITITIOUS.

Adventure, *n.* 1. Chance, hazard, fortuity, contingency, risk, venture, stake, experiment, trial.

2. Hazardous enterprise, bold undertaking.

3. Event, incident, occurrence, transaction, passage, crisis, contingency.

——, *v. t.* Hazard, venture, risk, peril, imperil, put to hazard, put at risk, put in danger, expose to peril *or* risk.

——, *v. i.* Dare, venture, take the risk, incur the hazard.

Adventurous, *a.* 1. Bold, daring, courageous, venturesome, adventuresome, venturous, chivalrous, doughty, enterprising.

2. Rash, reckless, precipitate, headlong, foolhardy, full of hazard.

3. Hazardous, dangerous, exposed to danger, perilous, full of peril, uncertain, full of risk.

Adversaria, *n. pl.* Notes, memoranda, remarks, note-book, journal, commonplace-book, *index rerum*, diary.

Adversary, *n.* 1. Enemy, foe, antagonist, opponent, opposer, counter-litigant, adverse party.

2. [With *The* prefixed.] Satan, Apollyon, the Tempter, the Evil One, the Devil, the Deuce, the Fiend, the Foul Fiend, the Old Serpent, the Prince of Darkness, Beelzebub. See DEVIL.

Adverse, *a.* 1. Contrary, opposing, counteracting, conflicting, head (*as head wind*).

2. (*Cf.* AVERSE). Hostile, inimical, antagonistic, unpropitious, unfavorable, injurious, harmful.

3. Unprosperous, untoward, unlucky, unfortunate, calamitous, disastrous.

Adversity, *n.* Misfortune, calamity, affliction, trouble, suffering, woe, disaster, distress, misery, ill-luck, bad luck, broken fortunes, hard life, frowns of fortune, reverses, hard times, ill-fate, ills of life, a sea of troubles.

Advertence, } *n.* Attention, heed, regard,
Advertency, } observance, observation, notice, consideration, heedfulness, mindfulness.

Advertise, *v. t.* 1. Announce, publish, declare, promulgate, trumpet, blazon, placard, proclaim, make known, spread abroad, noise abroad, give notice of, lay before the public, bring to public notice, make proclamation of.

2. Apprise, inform, give notice to, notify.

ADVERTISEMENT, *n.* Announcement, notification, information, notice, proclamation, promulgation, trumpeting.

Advert to. 1. Observe, remark, regard, heed, consider, notice, mark, view, give heed to, take notice of, pay attention to, attend to, look to, see to, give heed to, have an eye to, give a thought to, look after.

2. Refer to, allude to, mention, touch upon.

Advice, *n.* 1. Counsel, suggestion, instruction, recommendation, admonition, advisement, "rede," warning, caution, exhortation, earnest persuasion.

2. Intelligence, information, notice, notification, tidings, word.

3. Deliberation, care, counsel, aforethought, forethought, considerate purpose.

Advisability, *n.* Expediency, advisableness, propriety, judiciousness, prudence, desirability, desirableness.

Advisable, *a.* Expedient, proper, fit, prudent, desirable, fit to be advised, judicious, advantageous.

Advise, *v. t.* 1. Counsel, admonish, suggest, recommend to, give counsel to, give advice to.

2. Inform, acquaint, apprise, notify, make known to, give notice to, send word to, write word to.

——, *v. i.* Confer, consult, deliberate, take counsel, hold a conference.

Advisedly, *adv.* Deliberately, heedfully, purposely, by design, with consideration. See ADVICE, 3.

Advisement, *n.* Consultation, deliberation, consideration.

Adviser, *n.* Counsellor, instructor, guide, director, mentor, monitor.

Advocacy, *n.* Defence, vindication, support, countenance.

Advocate, *v. t.* Defend, support, vindicate, justify, countenance, uphold, maintain, favor, plead in favor of, stand up for, promote, propagate.

——, *n.* 1. Counsellor, counsel, barrister, lawyer, attorney, solicitor, attorney-at-law, limb of the law.

2. Defender, vindicator, supporter, upholder, maintainer, propagator, promoter, countenancer, favorer, apologist, pleader, friend, patron.

3. Intercessor, comforter, paraclete, Holy Spirit, Spirit of Truth.

Ægis, *n.* 1. Shield, buckler.

2. Defence, protection, safeguard, shelter.

Aerate, *v. t.* Aerify, fill with air, infuse air into, permeate with air *or* gas.

Aerial, *a.* 1. Atmospheric.

2. Aeriform, gaseous, vaporous, ethereal, airy, light, empyreal, empyrean.

3. High, lofty, empyreal, empyrean, aery.

Aerie, *n.* 1. Nest (*of a bird of prey*).

2. Brood (*of birds of prey*). See EYRIE.

Aeriform, *a.* Gaseous, ethereal, vaporous, airy, aerial, air-like.

Aeronaut, *n.* Balloonist, aerial navigator.

Aeronautics, *n.* Aerostation, ballooning, aerostatics.

Æsthetic, *a.* Tasteful, gratifying to taste, "tasty," beautiful, becoming, fit, appropriate, in good taste, referring to taste, concerning æsthetics, founded on the idea of beauty.

Afar, *adv.* Far away, far off, a long way off, afar off, wide away, a great way off, at a distance, to *or* from a distance, remote, remotely.

Affability, *n.* 1. Sociability, sociableness.

2. Courtesy, courteousness, complaisance, graciousness, condescension, accessibility, approachableness, conversableness, conversability, ease, easiness, civility, politeness, urbanity, comity, amenity, suavity, amiability, good manners, good-breeding, obliging manner.

Affable, *a.* 1. Conversible, communicative, free, frank, unreserved, open, accessible, approachable, familiar, easy, free and easy, sociable, social, cordial.

2. Courteous, complaisant, civil, polite, obliging, urbane, debonair, benign, gracious, mild, condescending, well-bred.

Affair, *n.* 1. Business, concern, function, duty, office, matter, circumstance, question, subject.

2. Event, occurrence, incident, transaction, proceeding, performance.

3. Battle, engagement, combat, conflict, contest, encounter, rencontre, collision, skirmish, brush.

Affairs, *n. pl.* 1. Administration, public business, matters of state, relations, practical concerns, active relations, matters of action.

2. Finances, estate, business, property, pecuniary relations.

Affect, *v. t.* 1. Influence, act upon, work upon, modify, alter, change, transform.

2. Concern, interest, regard, relate to, bear upon.

3. Touch, move, impress, melt, subdue, overcome, pierce.

4. Crave, yearn for, aspire to, aim at, desire, like, be drawn toward, be attracted by, take pleasure in.

5. Assume, adopt, take on, feign, arrogate, put on, make a show of, pretend to.

Affectation, *n.* Pretension, airs, affectedness, mannerism, assumed manners, affected manner, pretence, artificiality, unnaturalness, finical air, mincingness, foppery.

Affected, *a.* 1. Assumed, feigned, unnatural, artificial, insincere, canting, stagey, theatrical.

2. Assuming, pretending, pretentious, conceited, vain, coxcomical, foppish.

Affecting, *a.* Moving, touching, pathetic, piteous, impressive.

Affection, *n.* 1. Feeling, passion, inclination, propensity, proclivity, disposition, predisposition, bent, bias, turn of mind, cast *or* frame of mind.

2. Attribute, quality, property, character, characteristic, mark, note, accident, modification, mode.

3. Love, heart, attachment, kindness, partiality, fondness, liking, tenderness, endearment, regard, good-will, devotion, tender passion.

4. (*Med.*) Disorder, malady, disease.

Affectionate, *a.* Loving, fond, "spoony," attached, devoted, warm, tender, kind, sympathetic, tender-hearted, warm-hearted.

Affiance, *v. t.* Betroth, engage, plight.

Affidavit, *n.* Testimony (*in writing, signed and sworn to before a magistrate, but given without cross-examination*), evidence. See DEPOSITION.

Affiliate, *v. t.* 1. Adopt, take *or* treat as one's own child.

2. Connect, associate, unite, join, annex, graft in *or* upon, incorporate, bring into close relation, make resemble.

Affinity, *n.* 1. Relationship (*by marriage*), propinquity, connection. See KIN, CONSANGUINITY.

2. Resemblance, likeness, relation, correlation, analogy, connection, similarity, similitude, parallelism, correspondence, parity, sympathy, attraction.

3. (*Chem.*) Attraction.

Affirm, *v. t.* 1. Declare, aver, assert, maintain, asseverate, avouch, vouch, allege, say, profess, protest, pronounce, predicate, state, depose, testify, bear witness to.

2. Confirm, ratify, approve, establish, indorse.

——, *v. i.* Make solemn declaration, make asseveration, make averment, pledge one's word. [*Distinguished from* SWEAR, make oath, *which see*.]

Affirmable, *a.* Predicable.

Affirmation, *n.* 1. Assertion, declaration, asseveration, word, averment, protestation, avowal, allegation, saying, statement, pronouncement, announcement, predication, testimony, deposition.

2. Confirmation, ratification, approval, establishment, indorsement.

3. (*Law.*) Solemn declaration (*instead of oath*), solemn avowal *or* averment, legal pledge.

Affirmative, *a.* 1. That affirms, assertory, assertorical, declarative, declaratory, asseverating, avouching.

2. Confirmative, confirmatory, ratifying, approving, establishing, indorsing.

3. (*Alg.*) Positive, not negative, additive, not subtractive.

Affix, *v. t.* Join, subjoin, annex, attach, fasten, connect, set to, unite to the end.

Affix, *n.* Postfix, suffix.

Afflatus, *n.* Inspiration, supernatural influence, theopneusty, beatific vision, ecstasy.

Afflict, *v. t.* Grieve, distress, trouble, try, torment, agonize, plague, pain, hurt, harass, wound, exercise, grind, persecute, smite, make sorrowful.

Afflicting, *a.* Grievous, painful, troublous, tormenting, harassing, harrowing, sorrowful, piteous, distressing, calamitous, disastrous, afflictive, sad, unhappy, unfortunate, unlucky, wretched, dire, deplorable, sore, woful, severe, hard, trying, hard to bear.

Affliction, *n.* 1. Calamity, adversity, misfortune, disaster, visitation, stroke, ill, reverse, reverse of fortune.

2. Grief, sorrow, distress, woe, depression, tribulation, trial, plague, scourge, trouble, heartache, heartbreak, broken heart, heavy heart, bitterness, misery, wretchedness.

Affluence, *n.* Wealth, riches, opulence, fortune, plenty, abundance, exuberance, affluency, ample store, ample means.

Affluent, *a.* 1. Abundant, exuberant, plenteous, bounteous, abounding.

2. Opulent, wealthy, rich, moneyed.

——, *n.* Tributary, feeder, branch, confluent.

Afford, *v. t.* 1. Supply, furnish, yield, produce.

2. Confer, impart, grant, bestow, offer, lend, give, communicate, spare.

3. Bear (*the cost* or *expense of*), endure, support.

Affray, *n.* Brawl (*in a public place*), quarrel, conflict, personal conflict, struggle, contest, strife, row, fray, tussle, scuffle, set-to, fisticuffs, fracas, scrimmage, encounter, collision, broil, fight, *mêlée*, tumult, disturbance, outbreak, riot, *émeute*, breach of the peace, "rumpus," "mill," skirmish, rencontre, etc. See AFFAIR, 3.

Affright, *v. t.* Frighten, terrify, alarm, affray, scare, daunt, appall, dismay, shock, confound, dishearten, dispirit, fright, intimidate, startle, overawe, put in fear.

——, *n.* Terror, fear, fright, alarm, dismay, consternation, panic.

Affront, *v. t.* 1. Insult, abuse, outrage.

2. Offend, displease, irritate, provoke, chafe, fret, vex, annoy, pique, nettle, anger, gall, "miff," give offence to, make angry, put to shame, confound, bring to confusion, put out of countenance, shame.

3. Meet, strike upon, strike, come in contact with, smite, smite upon.

——, *n.* 1. Insult, abuse, contumely, indignity, outrage, injury, wrong, ill-treatment, ill-turn.

2. Provocation, offence, vexation, irritation, annoyance.

3. Shame, disgrace, degradation, sense of shame.

Aflow, *a.* On tap, flowing, running.

Afoot, *adv.* 1. On foot.

2. Preparing, forthcoming, in preparation, in course of preparation, on the carpet, on the tapis, on the anvil.

Aforesaid, *a.* Said before, aforementioned, beforementioned, fore-named, above-mentioned, above-named.

Aforethought, *a.* Premeditated, prepense, deliberate, considerate, well-considered, with forethought, sober, collected, calm, reflective.

Afraid, *a.* Fearful, haunted with fear, frightened, affrighted, aghast, terrified, scared, "scary," timid, timorous, panicky, shrinking, dreading, apprehensive, distrustful, anxious, alarmed.

Afresh, *adv.* Anew, newly, again, over again, *de novo.*

Aft, *adv.* (*Naut.*) Abaft, astern, behind, back, rearward, in the rear.

AFTER, *prep.* 1. Subsequent to, later than.

2. Following, behind, in the rear of.

3. About, in relation to, for.

4. In imitation of, in the pattern of, on the model of, for, from.

——, *adv.* Afterward, afterwards, subsequently, later.

——, *a.* 1. Succeeding, subsequent, following later.

2. Hind, hinder, posterior, rear, back.

After all. Eventually, finally, ultimately, upon the whole, when all has been considered, when all is said, at last, in the end, notwithstanding, in spite of that.

After-birth, *n.* Secundines, placenta, afterburden.

Aftercrop, *n.* Second crop of the year, aftergrowth, etc. See AFTERMATH.

Aftergrowth, *n.* Later growth, outgrowth, consequence, etc.

After-life, *n.* 1. Subsequent life, later life.

2. Future state, the hereafter, eternity.

Aftermath, *n.* Lattermath, rowen, rowett, eddish, arrish, earsh, eagrass, etch, fog, after-crop, after-growth.

Aftermost, *a.* Hindmost, sternmost, rearward.

Afterpiece, *n.* Postlude.

After-thought, *n.* After-wit, subsequent reflection, later *or* too late meditation.

Afterward, } *adv.* Subsequently, after,
Afterwards, } "eftsoons," later, thereafter, in the sequel.

AGAIN, *adv.* 1. Afresh, anew, once more, another time, *de novo.*

2. Moreover, besides, further, furthermore, in addition.

3. On the other hand, on the contrary, contrariwise.

4. In return, back, in restitution, in answer.

AGAINST, *prep.* 1. Opposed to, in opposition to, contrary to, adverse to, counter to.

2. Facing, fronting, off, opposite to, over against, close up to, in contact with.

3. In provision for, in expectation of, in preparation for, in anticipation of, for.

4. In compensation for, to counterbalance, in countervail to, in equalization of, to counterpoise, to match, in requital for *or* of.

Agape, *adv.* 1. Yawning, with mouth wide open, with open chasm, wide asunder.

2. Wondering, gazing eagerly, staring with open mouth, amazed, dumfounded, dazed, stupefied, thunderstruck.

Age, *n.* 1. Duration of existence, time of life, period of life, stage of life.

2. Period, date, epoch, æon, time.

3. Old age, decline of life, vale of years, senectitude, senility.

4. Oldness, antiquity, eld, ancientness.

Aged, *a.* 1. Old, elderly, stricken in years, senile, advanced in life, with one foot in the grave.

2. Having lived, of the age of, old.

Agency, *n.* 1. Intervention, instrumentality, mediation, means, action, operation, force, influence, procurement.

2. Charge, direction, management, superintendence, supervision.

Agent, *n.* 1. Actor, doer, operator, performer, executor.

2. Active element, cause, force, modifying cause *or* force, power, effective principle.

3. Deputy, attorney, factor, intermediary, broker, representative, substitute, proxy, go-between, procurator, middle-man, commissioner, vicegerent.

Agglomerate, *v. t.* Mass, mass together, gather in a ball *or* mass, gather together, lump together, heap up, pile up.

Agglomeration, *n.* Conglomeration, accumulation, lump, heap, pile, mass, aggregation.

Agglutinate, *v. t.* Unite, glue, cement, fasten together, attach to each other, conglutinate.

Agglutination, *n.* Cohesion, union, sticking together.

Aggrandize, *v. t.* Exalt, dignify, honor, elevate, promote, make great, raise to higher rank. See ADVANCE.

Aggrandizement, *n.* Exaltation, elevation, promotion, advancement, preferment. See ADVANCEMENT.

Aggravate, *v. t.* 1. Heighten (*in evil*), increase, make worse, worsen, render more serious.

2. Exaggerate, overstate, magnify, color.

3. (*In loose usage.*) Provoke, irritate, exasperate, enrage, tease.

Aggravation, *n.* 1. A heightening (*of something evil*).

2. Exaggeration.

3. (*In loose usage.*) Provocation, irritation.

Aggregate, *v. t.* Amass, collect, accumulate, pile, bring together, gather up, sum up, pile up, heap up, scrape together.

——, *a.* Collected, total.

——, *n.* Whole, total, totality, gross, lump, sum, amount, body, mass, gross amount, sum total, footing.

Aggregation, *n.* 1. Aggregating, act *or* process of collecting *or* combining *or* collocating. See AGGREGATE, *v.*

2. Collection, composite, mass, pile, heap, accumulation.

Aggress, *v. i.* Make the first attack, be the first to attack, be the aggressor, encroach.

Aggression, *n.* Attack, assault, invasion, intrusion, hostile encroachment, provocation, offence.

Aggressive, *a.* 1. Attacking, assaulting, assailing, assailant, invading, offensive.

2. Pushing, self-assertive.

Aggressor, *n.* Assailant, assaulter, attacker, assailer, invader, first offender.

Aggrieve, *v. t.* 1. Pain, grieve, afflict, wound the feelings of, cause sorrow to.

2. Wrong, injure, oppress, maltreat, abuse, bear hard upon, ill-treat, ill-use, impose upon.

Aghast, *a.* 1. Horror-struck, dismayed, horrified, appalled, terrified, frightened, panic-stricken, struck with horror.

2. Amazed, astounded, startled, astonished, dumfoundered, dumfounded, thunderstruck.

Agile, *a.* Lively, nimble, brisk, smart, active, quick, ready, prompt, alert, sprightly, supple, winged. See SPRY.

Agility, *n.* Liveliness, nimbleness, briskness, smartness, activity, quickness, readiness, promptness, promptitude, alertness, sprightliness, suppleness.

Agitable, *a.* 1. Movable, capable of being shaken, that can be disturbed.

2. Debatable, that can be discussed, investigable.

Agitate, *v. t.* 1. Shake, jar, toss, betoss, rock, disturb, trouble (*by brisk motion*), convulse.

2. Excite, ruffle, rouse, ferment, disturb, disquiet, trouble, perturb, betoss, toss, stir up, work up.

3. Fluster, flutter, flurry, hurry, confuse, disconcert.

4. Discuss, controvert, canvass, debate, dispute, investigate, revolve, consider on all sides.

——, *v. i.* Engage in discussion, keep discussion going.

Agitation, *n.* 1. Agitating, shaking, shake, concussion, succussion, succussation.

2. Disturbance, jarring, commotion, convulsion, ferment, storm, tumult, turmoil.

3. Excitement, emotion, ferment, perturbation, trepidation, discomposure, distraction, disquietude, ruffle, flutter, flurry, hurry, tremor, fever, fret.

4. Discussion, disputation, debate, controversy, canvassing, ventilation.

Agitator, *n.* 1. Urgent advocate, active reformer, exciter of active discussion.

2. Incendiary, firebrand, stirrer up of strife, demagogue.

Agnostic, *n.* Sceptic, doubter, Pyrrhonist, phenomenalist, sceptical idealist, unbeliever in the absolute reality of knowledge, empiricist, positivist.

——, *a.* Sceptical, phenomenalistic, etc.

Agnosticism, *n.* Scepticism, Pyrrhonism, negative idealism, empiricism, positivism.

Ago, *adv.* Past, gone, agone, since.

Agog, *a.* Eager, impatient, excited, wrought up, worked up, on tiptoe, with open mouth.

Agoing, *adv.* In motion, moving, in operation, at work, in action.

Agonize, *v. t.* Torment, torture, rack, wring, distress, excruciate, pain severely, put in great pain.

——, *v. i.* Be tormented, be tortured, suffer great pain, struggle (inwardly *or* outwardly) with pain *or* sorrow, writhe with pain.

Agony, *n.* Anguish (*especially of the body*), pangs, torture, torment, distress, rack, throe, severe pain, extreme suffering. See ANGUISH.

Agree, *v. i.* 1. Accord, harmonize, concur, unite, be in unison, be of one mind, come to the same conclusion.

2. Assent, consent, accede, acquiesce, comply, subscribe, yield assent, give consent, fall in with.

3. Stipulate, bargain, covenant, promise, engage, undertake, contract, make an agreement, pledge one's word, give assurance, take upon one's self, bind one's self.

4. Compromise, compound, come to an understanding, come to an agreement.

5. Suit, match, tally, correspond, chime, coincide, cohere, comport, conform, square.

Agreeable, *a.* [With *to*.] 1. Suitable, fitting, fit, proper, meet, appropriate, befitting, conformable, correspondent, accordant, concordant, consonant.

2. Pleasing, pleasant, pleasurable, grateful, gratifying, acceptable, welcome, good, goodly, delightful, charming, delectable, delicious, dulcet, sweet, to one's taste, to one's mind, after one's fancy.

AGREEMENT, *n.* Contract, pact, mutual promise, understanding. See ACCORD.

Agree with. 1. Chime in with, fall in with, tally with.

2. Be wholesome for, be healthful for, be good for.

3. Make a bargain with, strike hands with, be reconciled to.

Agriculture, *n.* Tillage, husbandry, farming, culture, cultivation, geoponics.

Agriculturist, *n.* Husbandman, farmer, tiller of the ground, cultivator of the soil, agriculturalist.

Aground, *adv.* 1. Ashore, not afloat, stranded.

2. Stranded, brought to a stop (for ideas, means, etc.), exhausted in resources, run out.

Ague, *n.* 1. Chilliness, cold, chill, shiver, shivering, shivering-fit, shakes.

2. Intermittent fever, fever and ague, chills, chills and fever.

Ahead, *adv.* 1. Onward, forward, in advance, in front.

2. (*Naut.*) In opposition (*said of the wind*), against us, in our teeth.

Aid, *v. t.* 1. Assist, help, support, serve, speed, second, back, befriend, bestead, encourage, bolster, "boost," prosper, abet, co-operate with, take part with, give support to, minister to, relieve. See SPELL.

2. Succor, relieve, do kindness to, supply the necessities of, give alms (to).

3. Further, advance, promote, facilitate.

Aid, *n.* 1. Assistance, help, furtherance, co-operation, patronage, support, helping hand, good offices. See LIFT.

2. Succor, relief, alms, bounty, subsidy.

3. Helper, assistant. See AIDER.

4. Aide-de-camp.

Aider, *n.* Helper, helpmate, assistant, associate, coadjutor, co-operator, ally, auxiliary, abettor, subordinate, accessory, retainer, henchman, follower, satellite, acolyte.

Ail, *v. t.* Pain, trouble, afflict, distress, be the matter with.

——, *v. i.* Suffer, be in pain, feel pain, be ill, peak, pine.

Ailing, *a.* Sickly, sick, ill, indisposed, unwell, diseased, feeble, infirm, weakly, poorly, delicate, languishing, unhealthy, in a feeble *or* bad way, out of sorts, on the sick list, peaked, pining.

Ailment, *n.* Disease, ail, illness, sickness, ailing, indisposition, malady, distemper, disorder, complaint, infirmity, weakness.

Aim, *v. t.* Direct, level, point, train.

——, *n.* 1. Direction, course, bearing, tendency, bent, proclivity.

2. Intention, intent, purpose, design, scheme, reason, view, object, objective, end, scope, drift, target, mark, goal, point, final cause, endeavor, effort, attempt, undertaking.

Aim at. 1. Take aim at, point at, level at, direct toward.

2. Intend, purpose, design, mean, be at.

3. Crave, desire, want, wish, long for, seek, look after, affect, yearn for, aspire to, aspire after, endeavor after, be after, drive at, propose to one's self, have in view, have in one's eye, have an eye to, strive for, attempt to reach.

Aimless, *a.* Purposeless, objectless, random, chance, hap-hazard.

AIR, *n.* 1. Atmosphere, aerosphere.

2. Breeze, zephyr, gentle wind, breath of air, current of air.

3. Appearance, aspect, mien, manner, look, cast, demeanor, conduct, carriage, bearing, deportment, behavior, port.

4. Tune, melody, song, treble *or* soprano.

——, *v. t.* 1. Expose to air, ventilate, change the air of.

2. Expose, display, spread abroad, make ostentation of.

Air-bubble, *n.* Bleb, blob.

Airiness, *n.* 1. Openness, exposure to air.

2. Lightness, buoyancy, grace, gracility, gracefulness, flexibility, pliancy, litheness.

3. Gayety, levity, sprightliness, vivacity, liveliness, etc. See AIRY, 3.

Airing, *n.* 1. Ride, drive, walk, promenade, stroll, excursion, out-door exercise.

2. Exposure to air, admission of air, ventilation.

3. Display, ostentatious exhibition, free exposure, diffusion.

Air-pipe, *n.* Vent, spiracle, blow-hole, air-tube.

Airs, *n. pl.* Pretension, mannerism, affectedness, affected manner, assumed manner. See AFFECTATION.

Air-tight, *a.* Hermetic, hermetical, impenetrable to air, impervious to air.

Airy, *a.* 1. Unsubstantial, aerial, ethereal, aeriform, thin, rare, tenuous.

2. Light, subtile, sublimated.

3. Sprightly, buoyant, vivacious, volatile, jocund, jolly, jovial, lively, gay, wanton, merry, blithe, light, light-hearted, light of heart, in spirits, in good spirits, of good cheer.

4. Light, buoyant, graceful, flexible, pliant, lithe.

5. Showy, gaudy, flaunting, jaunty, garish, fine.

Aisle, *n.* Passage, walk.

Ajar, *adv.* Partly open (*as a door*), on the turn.

Akin, *a.* 1. Kin, related, allied, kindred, cognate, of one blood, of the same stock, consanguineous, consanguineal.

2. Similar, congenial, analogous, parallel, like, corresponding, of a piece, cognate, connected, related.

Alack, *interj.* Alas, lackaday, alackaday, welladay, woe's me.

Alacrity, *n.* 1. Readiness, promptitude, eagerness, alertness, agility, activity, quickness.

2. Sprightliness, gayety, cheerfulness, hilarity, vivacity, liveliness, high spirits, good spirits.

À la mode. [Fr.] Fashionable, in the fashion, in vogue.

Alarm, *n.* 1. Alarum, larum, tocsin, summons to arms, alarm-bell, alarm-gun, beat of drum, sound of trumpet, notice of danger, signal of distress.

2. Fear, apprehension, terror, fright, affright, consternation, dismay.

——, *v. t.* 1. Call to arms, summon to arms.

2. Terrify, frighten, affright, startle, scare, daunt, appall, put in fear.

Albeit, *adv.* Although, notwithstanding.

Alchemy, *n.* Magic, black art, thaumaturgy.

Alcoholic, *a.* Spirituous, ardent.

Alcove, *n.* Recess.

Alert, *a.* 1. Watchful, awake, vigilant, circumspect, wary, heedful, on the alert, on one's guard, on the watch, on the lookout, on the *qui vive*.

2. Active, brisk, nimble, agile, smart, lively, sprightly, spirited, supple, quick, ready, prompt. See SPRY.

Alertness, *n.* 1. Watchfulness, vigilance, circumspection, wariness.

2. Activity, agility, nimbleness, briskness, smartness, sprightliness, quickness, spryness, promptness, readiness.

Alien, *a.* 1. Foreign, not native, not naturalized.

2. Estranged, differing, remote, unallied, separated, unconnected, strange, inappropriate, irrelevant, not pertinent.

——, *n.* Foreigner, stranger.

Alienate, *v. t.* 1. Abalienate, transfer, demise, consign, assign, convey, devolve, make over, deliver over.

2. Estrange, disaffect, wean, withdraw the affections of, make unfriendly.

Alienation, *n.* 1. Abalienation, transfer, demise, conveyance.

2. Estrangement, disaffection, variance, division, rupture, breach.

3. Insanity, aberration, derangement, hallucination, delusion, lunacy, madness, frenzy, craziness, delirium, mania, imbecility.

Alight, *v. i.* 1. Stop *or* rest (*after flight*), perch, drop, settle, lodge.

2. Dismount, descend, get down, land.

Alike, *a.* Similar, like, resembling, resemblant, identical, selfsame, twin, duplicate, analogous, allied, equal, of a piece.

——, *adv.* Equally, in the same manner, form, *or* degree, together, in common, both. See AKIN.

Aliment, *n.* Nourishment, nutriment, food, sustenance, subsistence, provision, fare, diet, regimen, victuals, meat, meat and drink, viands, cheer, pabulum, rations, feed, provender, fodder, forage, "prog." See FOOD.

Alimentary, *a.* Alimental, nourishing, nutritious, nutritive.

Alimentation, *n.* Nutrition, nourishment, sustentation.

Alive, *a.* 1. Living, breathing, live, animate, not dead, in life, above ground, quick.

2. Sensitive, susceptible, responsive, aware, with keen perceptions.

3. Active, in force, in existence, in operation, operative.

4. Cheerful, sprightly, lively, joyous, brisk. See ALERT.

ALL, *a.* Whole, entire, total, complete.

——, *adv.* Altogether, entirely, totally, completely, wholly, quite.

——, *n.* Whole, total, totality, aggregate, everything.

Allay, *v. t.* 1. Repress, restrain, check, subdue, lay, silence, appease, pacify, compose, calm, quiet, still, lull, hush, tranquillize, smooth.

2. Assuage, alleviate, soothe, soften, mitigate, solace, moderate, mollify, temper, attemper, lessen, lighten, abate, qualify, relieve, ease, dull, blunt, palliate.

Allegation, *n.* 1. Declaration, affirmation, averment, assertion, statement.

2. Excuse, plea.

Allege, *v. t.* 1. Declare, affirm, assert, aver, predicate, profess, asseverate, maintain, say. See AFFIRM.

2. Adduce, assign, advance, plead, produce, cite, quote, bring forward, lay down.

Allegiance, *n.* Fealty, fidelity, loyalty, homage, duty, obligation, obedience.

Allegorical, *a.* Figurative, typical, metaphorical, not literal.

Allegory, *n.* Fable, parable, apologue, story, tale, myth. See PARABLE.

Alleviate, *v. t.* Lighten, mitigate, assuage, moderate, soothe, soften, mollify, quiet, still, quell, abate, lessen, diminish, relieve, palliate, ease, dull, blunt. See ALLAY.

Alleviation, *n.* Mitigation, palliation, relief, etc. See preceding.

Alley, *n.* 1. Walk, passage, aisle.

2. Lane, narrow street, back-passage, by-way, slum.

All-Hallows, *n.* See ALL-SAINTS' DAY.

Alliance, *n.* 1. Intermarriage, affinity, family connection, relation, relationship.

2. Confederation, confederacy, league, union, treaty, combination, coalition, federation, copartnership, compact.

3. Affiliation, connection, similarity, relationship.

Allied, *a.* 1. Related, alike, similar, analogous, cognate, paronymous, kindred, of a piece. See AKIN.

2. United, confederated, co-operating, in league, in co-operation.

Allodial, *a.* Independent, freehold, not feudal, free of rent *or* service.

Allot, *v. t.* 1. Distribute, divide, measure, apportion, deal, dispense, parcel out, deal out, give out, mete out, portion out.

2. Assign, specify, fix, prescribe, appoint, destine, destinate, grant, give.

Allotment, *n.* 1. Apportionment, distribution, partition, dole.

2. Assignment, appointment, grant, gift.

3. Share, part, portion, lot, quota, contingent.

Allow, *v. t.* 1. Admit, acknowledge, confess, own, concede, grant.

2. Permit, let, authorize, grant leave to, give permission to.

3. Suffer, tolerate, endure, bear, put up with, bear with.

4. Grant, give, yield, relinquish, spare.

5. Approve, sanction, justify.

6. Remit, abate, bate, deduct.

Allow, *v. i.* Make allowance *or* provision; — followed by *for.*

Allowable, *a.* Permissible, admissible, lawful, proper, justifiable, warrantable.

Allowance, *n.* 1. Permission, leave, license, permit, authorization, connivance, sanction, authority, approval, approbation, sufferance.

2. Admission, acknowledgment, concession, assent.

3. Grant for support, stated maintenance, ration, stated quantity (*of food or drink*), commission.

4. Qualification, modification, extenuation, limitation, exception.

Alloy, *n.* 1. Combination (*of metals*), metallic compound, amalgam (*in case mercury is one metal*), alloyage.

2. Baser metal (*mixed with finer*), pinchbeck.

3. Baser element *or* ingredient (*in anything*), admixture, adulteration, deterioration, depreciation, impairment, debasement, detraction, disparagement.

——, *v. t.* 1. Admix (*a metal with a baser*), reduce the value, debase.

2. Admix, deteriorate, etc. See preceding noun.

All-powerful, *a.* Almighty, omnipotent, all-sufficient.

All-Saints' Day. All-Hallow, All-Hallows, All-Hallowmas, Hallowmas, the first of November, All-Saints.

Allude to. Refer to, glance at, make allusion to, intimate, suggest, insinuate, hint, imply. See ADVERT TO.

Allure, *v. t.* Entice, tempt, beguile, seduce, decoy, troll, lure, lead, solicit, invite, attract, engage, persuade, ensnare, coax, inveigle, cajole, toll, over-persuade, prevail upon, draw on, bring over, win over.

Allurement, *n.* 1. Enticement, temptation, seduction, seducement, solicitation, attraction, witchery. See ALLURE.

2. Lure, decoy, bait.

Allusion, *n.* Reference, hint, intimation, suggestion, insinuation, implication, passing mention, innuendo.

Allusive, *a.* Hinting, suggestive, innuent, emblematic, typical, symbolical, figurative.

Allusively, *adv.* By implication, by indirect reference, by way of allusion, by insinuation, suggestion, *or* innuendo.

Alluvium, *n.* Sediment, deposit, silt.

All-wise, *a.* Omniscient, all-knowing, all-seeing.

Ally, *v. t.* 1. Unite, join, league, confederate, connect, combine, marry, connect by marriage, bring into affinity.

2. Make similar, make analogous, bring into resemblance, raise into close relationship.

——, *n.* 1. Confederate, coadjutor, co-operator, assistant, helper, aider, auxiliary, associate, friend, colleague, partner.

2. Abettor, accomplice. See ACCESSORY.

Almanac, *n.* Calendar, ephemeris, register of the year.

Almighty, *a.* Omnipotent, all-powerful, all-sufficient.

ALMOST, *adv.* Nearly, toward, towards, well-nigh, all but, for the most part, not quite, within a little.

Alms, *n.* Charity, benefaction, gratuity, gift, dole, bounty, charitable donation, eleemosynary aid.

Almsgiving, *n.* Charity, beneficence, benefaction, benevolence.

Almshouse, *n.* Poorhouse.

Aloft, *adv.* Above, overhead, on high, in the air, in the sky, skyward, heavenward, in heaven.

Alone, *a.* 1. Single, solitary, only, sole, lone, lonely, isolated, unaccompanied, forsaken, deserted, companionless, by one's self, *solus.*

2. Of one's self, of one's own power, without help.

——, *adv.* Singly, etc. See preceding adjective.

Along, *adv.* 1. Lengthwise, longitudinally, in a line.

2. Onward, forward.

3. Together, in company, beside, side by side, at the same time, simultaneously.

——, *prep.* By *or* over, by the side of, on the border, bank, *or* shore of, through, alongst.

Alongside, *adv.* (*Naut.*) By the side of, side by side.

Aloof, *adv.* Apart, at a distance, away, off.

Aloud, *adv.* 1. Audibly, in a clear voice, with full voice.

2. Loudly, vociferously, sonorously, clamorously, obstreperously, at the top of the voice, with a loud voice.

Alphabet, *n.* Elements (*of a subject*), rudiments, the A B C, first steps.

Alpine, *a.* 1. Among the Alps, in the region of the Alps, on the Alps.

2. Mountainous, high, elevated.

Already, *adv.* 1. Even now.

2. Before that time.

Also, *adv.* Likewise, too, besides, withal, furthermore, moreover, in addition, in like manner.

Altar, *n.* 1. Shrine, sacred place, place of worship, sanctuary, Holy of Holies, *sanctum sanctorum*, inmost *adyta*, inner *penetralia*.

2. Communion-table, holy table, Lord's table.

Alter, *v. t.* Change, vary, modify, shift, turn, transmute, metamorphose, transform, convert, make some change in.

——, *v. i.* Vary, change, be changeable, become different.

Alterable, *a.* Changeable, variable, mutable. See ALTER.

Alteration, *n.* Change, variation, modification, deviation, variance, turn, mutation, vicissitude.

Altercation, *n.* Dispute, controversy, contention, strife, difference, jangling, jangle, jarring, rupture, quarrel, sparring, bickering, wrangle, wrangling, dissension, war of words.

Alternate, *a.* 1. Reciprocal, one after another, in turn.

2. Every other, separated by one, succeeding each other with intervals of one, discontinuous by omission of one.

3. On different sides successively.

——, *v. i.* Reciprocate, act interchangeably, rotate.

——, *v. t.* Perform reciprocally, *or* by turns, *or* responsively, *or* by strophe and antistrophe.

Alternation, *n.* Reciprocation, interchange, rotation

Alternative, *n.* Choice (*between two things*), other (of two), option, preference.

Although, *conj.* Though, albeit, notwithstanding, grant that, for all that, be it so, even if, even supposing.

Altitude, *n.* Height, elevation, loftiness.

Alto, *n.* (*Mus.*) Counter, counter-tenor, second, contralto.

Altogether, *adv.* 1. Wholly, quite, completely, entirely, totally, utterly, thoroughly, throughout, fully, perfectly, *in toto*, out and out, to the full.

2. Conjointly, in the aggregate, in sum total, in a body, in a mass, *en masse*.

Altruism, *n.* Devotion to others, love of others, philanthropy, unselfishness, public spirit.

Altruistic, *a.* 1. Referring to altruism, marked by the theory of devotion to others.

2. Devoted to others, philanthropic, unselfish, friendly to man, attached to the common weal.

Alumnus, *n.* [L. *pl. Alumni.*] Foster-child (*of an institution of learning*), graduate, pupil, disciple.

Alveary, *n.* Beehive.

Alveolate, *a.* Cellular, favose, honey-combed.

Alveole, *n.* Socket, cell, cavity, alveolus.

Always, *adv.* Ever, evermore, perpetually, continually, eternally, unceasingly, everlastingly, for ever, for aye, at all times, to the end of time, through all ages. See AYE.

Amain, *adv.* 1. Violently, forcibly, furiously, headlong, with force, with might and main.

2. (*Naut.*) Suddenly, all at once.

Amalgam, *n.* 1. Mercurial compound, mixture (*of other metals*) with quicksilver.

2. Mixture, composite, compound, combination, alloy.

Amalgamate, *v. t.* Mix, commix, commingle, unite, combine, blend, incorporate, compound.

Amalgamation, *n.* 1. Mixture, combination, compound, commixture, union, blending, commingling, intermingling, intermixture, junction, conjunction.

2. Intermarriage (*of different races*). See MISCEGENATION.

Amanuensis, *n.* Scribe, secretary, copyist, scrivener, transcriber, writer.

Amaranthine, *a.* 1. Unfading, fadeless, imperishable, undecaying, undying, deathless, immortal, perennial, ever-blooming, ever-vernal.

2. Purplish, purpureal, amethystine.

Amass, *v. t.* Accumulate, gather, aggregate, pile up, heap up, scrape together, collect together, rake up, gather into a heap *or* pile.

Amateur, *n.* Dilettante (*pl. dilettanti*), nonprofessional, desultory cultivator.

Amatory, *a.* Amorous, lovesome, erotic, tender, passionate, Anacreontic.

Amaze, *v. t.* Astonish, astound, confound, confuse, perplex, bewilder, daze, stagger, stupefy, dumfound, dumfounder, surprise, take by surprise, strike with wonder, strike with astonishment, petrify with wonder.

Amazement, *n.* Astonishment, confusion, perplexity, stupefaction, bewilderment, marvel, wonder, surprise.

Amazing, *a.* Astonishing, astounding, confounding, confusing, perplexing, bewildering, stupendous, wonderful, surprising, marvellous, prodigious, portentous, miraculous, strange, striking, very extraordinary.

Amazon, *n.* Virago, termagant, shrew, scold, vixen, Tartar, Xanthippe.

Ambages, *n. pl.* 1. Windings, turnings, sinuosities.

2. Circumlocution, periphrasis, verbosity, verbiage, wordiness, diffuseness, circuit of words.

3. Subterfuges, evasions, indirections, quirks, tortuous courses, devious ways.

Ambagious, *a.* 1. Tortuous, sinuous, serpentine, winding, devious.

2. Tortuous, indirect, evasive, full of subterfuges.

3. Round about, circumlocutory, circuitous, diffuse, disjointed, dull, tedious.

Ambassador, *n.* Minister (*of the highest rank*), plenipotentiary, envoy, legate, deputy.

Ambient, *a.* Surrounding, investing, encompassing, enfolding, embosoming, encircling, circling, circumjacent, circumambient.

Ambiguity, *n.* 1. Doubtfulness, dubiousness, doubt, uncertainty *or* equivocalness (*as respects the meaning of a term*), indefiniteness, vagueness, obscurity, amphiboly.

2. Ambiguous expression, double meaning, equivoke (*or* equivoque), *double entendre.*

Ambiguous, *a.* Doubtful, dubious, uncertain *or* equivocal, enigmatical, indefinite, indistinct, vague, indeterminate, not plain, not clear, susceptible of more than one meaning, quibbling.

Ambition, *n.* 1. Desire of superiority, desire of distinction, hunger for fame, love of glory.

2. Longing, yearning, aspiration, emulation.

Ambitious, *a.* 1. Aspiring, emulous, eager for superiority, eager for distinction *or* fame.

2. Eager, strongly desirous, intent, avid; — followed by *of.*

3. Showy, pretentious, aiming at effect.

Amble, *v. i.* 1. Pace, move, *or* go at an easy pace, jog-trot.

2. Walk affectedly, dawdle.

——, *n.* Pacing, pace.

Ambrosial, *a.* 1. Delicious, luscious, savory, palatable, dainty, nice.

2. Ambrosian, fragrant, balmy, odorous, aromatic, odoriferous, sweet-scented.

Ambulatory, *a.* Walking, moving.

Ambuscade, *n.* Ambush, cover, retreat, hiding-place, lurking-place.

Ameliorate, *v. t.* Improve, amend, mend, better, meliorate, elevate, raise, promote, make better.

Amelioration, *n.* Improvement, amendment, melioration, bettering, elevation, promotion.

Amen, *adv.* So be it, be it so, let it be so.

Amenability, *n.* Accountability, liability, responsibility, answerableness, amenableness.

Amenable, *a.* 1. Accountable, liable, responsible, answerable.

2. Open (to), within the reach (of), able to be influenced (by), impressible (by), pliant (to).

Amend, *v. t.* Improve, mend, correct, rectify, redress, reform. See AMELIORATE.

——, *v. i.* Improve, mend, become better.

Amendment, *n.* 1. Improvement, reformation, change for the better.

2. Alteration, change, correction.

Amends, *n.* Compensation (*for loss* or *injury*), recompense, indemnification, indemnity, reparation, restitution, redress, atonement, expiation, satisfaction.

Amenity, *n.* 1. Pleasantness, agreeableness, mildness, softness.

2. Suavity, affability, gentleness, refinement, civility, comity, courtesy, politeness, urbanity, complaisance, amiability, geniality, blandness, graciousness, obliging manner, good manners, good-breeding.

Amerce, *v. t.* Fine, mulct, impose a fine upon, deprive of, strip of.

Amercement, *n.* Fine, mulct, forfeiture, pecuniary penalty, deprivation.

Amiability, *n.* Loveliness, kindliness, kindness, amiableness, benignity, amenity, affability, obligingness, winsomeness, attractiveness, kind-heartedness, fellow-feeling, good feeling, good-humor, sweet temper, sweetness of disposition.

Amiable, *a.* Lovable, lovely, sweet, engaging, charming, winning, winsome, attractive, benignant, benign, sweet-tempered, kind-hearted, tender-hearted, worthy of love, of friendly disposition.

Amicable, *a.* Friendly, harmonious, cordial, peaceable, kind, kindly, amiable.

Amicableness, *n.* Amity, harmony, harmoniousness, peacefulness, peaceableness, kindliness, friendliness, friendship, cordiality, friendly feeling, good understanding, good-will.

Amid, } *prep.* 1. Among (*without being*
Amidst, } *part of*), amongst, in the midst of, in the middle of, surrounded by.

2. Jointly, together, some of.

Amiss, *a.* Wrong, improper, faulty, erroneous, incorrect, inaccurate.

——, *adv.* Wrong, wrongly, improperly, faultily, erroneously, incorrectly, inaccurately.

Amity, *n.* Friendliness. See AMICABLENESS.

Ammunition, *n.* Munition, military stores, supplies of projectiles, propellants, etc., powder and shot.

Amnesty, *n.* Forgiveness (*granted to whole classes of persons*), general pardon (*by proclamation*), act of oblivion, freedom from penalty.

AMONG, } *prep.* Amid (*while making part*
Amongst, } *of*), amidst, in the midst of, mixed *or* mingled with.

Amorous, *a.* 1. Full of sexual passion, erotic, ardent, full of desire, prone to sexuality.

2. Fond, enamoured, passionate, loving, longing, ardent, tender.

3. Amatory, erotic, tender, passionate, impassioned, Anacreontic.

Amorphous, *a.* 1. Irregular, shapeless, formless, unshapen.

2. Structureless, non-crystalline.

3. Characterless, misshapen, vague, unorganized, disorganized, chaotic, confused, clumsy. See ACEPHALOUS.

AMOUNT, *n.* 1. Aggregate, sum, total, sum total, net quantity, whole, footing, footing up.

2. Effect, substance, purport, result.

Amount to. 1. Aggregate, come to, be in the aggregate, be in the whole, be in all, foot up to, sum up to, total.

2. Be equivalent to, be in effect, be substantially.

Amour, *n.* Affair of gallantry, love intrigue, love affair, illicit relation, *liaison*.

Ample, *a.* 1. Large, great, capacious, wide, extended, extensive, spacious, broad, roomy.

2. Plentiful, plenteous, abundant, abounding, overflowing, copious, full, liberal, rich, unstinted, exuberant, luxurious, lavish, bountiful, generous, liberal, handsome, munificent.

3. Diffusive, unrestricted, not contracted, not condensed, not concise, copious, grandiose.

Amplification, *n.* 1. Enlargement, greatening, extension, dilation, expansion, broadening, development.

2. Full detail, fulness, diffuseness, prolixity, diffuse narrative, copious discourse.

Amplify, *v. t.* 1. Enlarge, greaten, extend, augment, magnify, dilate, expand, widen, develop, increase.

2. Make copious *or* diffuse, present in all *or* many aspects, dilate, expand.

——, *v. i.* Go into detail, be copious, speak with fulness of illustration.

Amplitude, *n.* 1. Bulk, size, bulkiness, largeness, bigness, greatness, volume, capaciousness, width, breadth, extent, spaciousness, roominess, dimensions, mass.

2. Range, reach, sweep, compass, extent, scope, swing.

Amputate, *v. t.* Sever, separate, cut off, prune, lop, curtail, clip, remove.

Amulet, *n.* Talisman, charm, phylactery, protection, safeguard.

Amuse, *v. t.* 1. Entertain, divert, please, charm, gladden, cheer, enliven, solace, beguile, relax, recreate.

2. Beguile, deceive (*by inspiring false hopes*), delude, cheat, inveigle, mislead, impose upon.

AMUSEMENT, *n.* Entertainment, diversion, *divertissement*, sport, play, fun, frolic, merriment, pleasure, merry-making, recreation, relaxation, pastime, game.

Amusing, *a.* Entertaining, diverting, pleasing, lively, laughable, risible, ludicrous, droll, comic, mirth-provoking, comical, funny, farcical, ridiculous.

AN, *art.* 1. One, any, some.

2. Each, every.

Anachronism, *n.* Misdate.

Anacreontic, *a.* Amatory, amorous, erotic, convivial.

——, *n.* Erotic *or* amatory poem, madrigal, drinking-song, wine-song.

Anæmic, *a.* Indicating anæmia, anæmied, deficient in blood, thin-blooded, bloodless.

Anæsthesia, *n.* (*Med.*) Insensibility (*as that produced by the inhalation of sulphuric ether, chloroform, etc.*), unconsciousness of pain, suspended sensibility, suspended consciousness.

Anæsthetic, *a.* Producing insensibility, destructive of pain.

Analect, *n.* [*pl. Analects* or *Analecta.*] Selection, extract, selected piece, select piece. In *pl.*, collection of literary fragments.

Analeptic, *a.* Restorative, strengthening, invigorating, comforting.

Analogical, *a.* Having analogy, resembling, by analogy, corresponding, similar.

Analogous, *a.* Similar (*in relations* or *uses*), resembling, alike, like, cognate, parallel, corresponding, correlative, allied, of a piece.

Analogue, *n.* Correspondent, parallel, counterpart, similar feature *or* trait, correlate.

Analogy, *n.* Similarity (*in relations* or *uses*), resemblance, likeness, parallelism, similitude, parity, correspondence.

Analysis, *n.* Resolution, decomposition, dissection, separation (*of elements*).

Analytic, } *a.* Separative, solvent, re-
Analytical, } solvent.

Analyze, *v. t.* Decompose, decompound, dissect, resolve.

Anarchical, *a.* Lawless, disordered, ungoverned.

Anarchist, *n.* Jacobin, turbulent demagogue, anarch.

Anarchy, *n.* Disorder, misrule, confusion, want of government, lawlessness, reign of violence.

Anathema, *n.* Curse, malediction, denunciation, imprecation, fulmination, execration, malison, proscription, ban, excommunication.

Anathematize, *v. t.* Curse, maledict, denounce, imprecate, execrate, fulminate against, proscribe, ban, excommunicate.

——, *v. i.* Curse, utter anathemas, fulminate, ban.

Anatomatize, *v. t.* 1. Dissect, vivisect, anatomize.

2. Scrutinize, analyze, sift, probe, examine, lay open.

Anatomy, *n.* 1. Dissection.

2. Structure, structural form, structural plan, structural details.

3. Skeleton, bony structure.

Ancestor, *n.* Forefather, forebear, progenitor, father.

Ancestral, *a.* Hereditary, patrimonial.

Ancestry, *n.* 1. Lineage, family, race, house, line of ancestors, line.

2. Pedigree, stock, genealogy, descent, progeniture.

3. High birth, noble blood, gentle blood, nobility, hereditary rank.

Anchor, *n.* 1. Ground tackle (*of a ship*).

2. Sure protection, security, stay, hold, defence.

——, *v. t.* Secure by anchor, secure, fasten, fix securely.

——, *v. i.* Cast anchor, come to anchor, keep hold, take firm hold.

Anchorage, *n.* Roadstead, road, port, harbor, resting-place.

Anchorite, *n.* Hermit, recluse, solitary, anchoret, eremite, *solitaire.*

Ancient, *a.* 1. Old, primitive, pristine, of eld, of old time, not modern. See OLDEN.

2. Of great age, of long duration.

3. Antiquated, antique, archaic, obsolete, by-gone, old-fashioned, out of fashion, out of date, gone by.

Anciently, *adv.* Formerly, of old, in the olden time, in ancient times, in days of yore, long ago, a long while ago, in days long gone.

Ancillary, *a.* 1. Helping, helpful, auxiliary, accessory, contributory, instrumental.

2. Subservient, subordinate, subsidiary.

AND, *conj.* (*Basic Eng.*)

Anecdote, *n.* Story (*of private life*), biographical incident.

Anew, *adv.* Newly, afresh, again, over again, *de novo.*

Anfractuous, *a.* Winding, meandering, crooked, serpentine, devious, tortuous, sinuous, intricate, ambagious.

Angel, *n.* Spirit, supernatural being, seraph, cherub.

Angelic, } *a.* 1. Seraphic, cherubic,
Angelical, } heavenly, celestial, adorable, angel, saintly.

2. Transporting, enrapturing, ravishing, rapturous, entrancing.

Anger, *n.* Wrath, rage, fury, frenzy, resentment, ire, indignation, exasperation, choler, gall, bile, spleen, "dander," "huff," dudgeon, passion, displeasure, vexation, irritation, offence, bad temper, ill temper, hot temper. See TEMPER.

——, *v. t.* Irritate, displease, offend, provoke, exasperate, rouse, chafe, gall, vex, nettle, incense, enrage, inflame, madden, infuriate, make angry.

ANGLE, *n.* 1. (*Geom.*) Difference of direction (*of two lines*), divergence, opening, flare.

2. Corner, bend, elbow, knee, crotch, cusp, point (*where two lines meet*).

3. Hook, fish-hook.

——, *v. i.* Fish (*with a rod*), bob.

Angle for. Fish for, scheme for, plot for, try to get by artifice.

Angler, *n.* Fisherman, fisher.

Anglican, *a.* English (*said of the Church*), Episcopalian.

Anglicism, *n.* English idiom, thorough English quality.

Anglicize, *v. t.* Give an English form to, introduce into English.

Angling, *n.* Fishing (*with a rod*). See also ANGLE FOR.

ANGRY, *a.* Provoked, exasperated, irritated, incensed, piqued, galled, chafed, indignant, moody, sulky, irate, ireful, wroth, wrathful, "wrathy," rabid, storming, infuriate, infuriated, furious, raging, resentful, hot, "huffy," "riled," inflamed, mad, passionate, in a passion, in a pet, in the tantrums, out of humor, out of temper, out of tune.

Anguish, *n.* Agony (*especially of the mind*), torment, torture, rack, pang, severe pain, extreme suffering, acute distress. See AGONY.

Angular, *a.* Pointed, with angles, with corners.

Anile, *a.* Aged, imbecile, senile, doting, decrepit, superannuated, old-womanish.

Anility, *n.* Imbecility, dotage, senility, decrepitude, superannuation, weakness.

Animadversion, *n.* 1. Notice, observation, perception, act of noticing, etc., remark, comment.

2. Reproof, stricture, censure, blame, aspersion, reflection, condemnation, reprobation, reprehension, severe criticism.

Animadvert upon. 1. Remark, notice, note, take notice of, mention, consider.

2. Censure, disapprove, find fault with, object to, take exception to, protest against, criticise severely.

ANIMAL, *n.* 1. Creature, living being, created being, sentient being. *Collective:* fauna.

2. Beast, irrational creature, dumb creature, beast of the field, fowl of the air, denizen of the deep. See BRUTE.

——, *a.* 1. Pertaining to living beings, living, sentient.

2. Derived from animals, composed of flesh, consisting of meat.

3. Carnal, physical, natural, fleshly, sensual, unspiritual, beastly, brutal, brutish.

Animal spirits. 1. Nervous fluid, the nervous force, vital principle, life.

2. Energy, vigor, life, spirit, buoyancy of mind, lightheartedness, impulsiveness, spiritedness. See ANIMATION.

Animate, *v. t.* 1. Quicken, inform, make alive, vitalize, give life to, vivify.

2. Invigorate, fortify, revive, give vigor *or* energy to.

3. Stimulate, waken, enliven, activate, rouse, whet, incite, impel, excite, fire, heat, urge, provoke, warm, goad, stir, kindle, prompt, work up, set on.

4. Encourage, inspire, inspirit, embolden, enhearten, hearten, exhilarate, gladden, elate, elevate, flush, erect.

Animated, *a.* Lively, vigorous, sprightly, brisk, vivacious, buoyant, spirited, jocund, blithe, gay, elated, full of life, full of spirit.

Animating, *a.* Cheering, inspiring, enlivening, encouraging, exhilarating, stimulating, exciting, elevating, spirit-stirring, heart-stirring.

Animation, *n.* 1. Act of enlivening *or* making alive, vitalization, vivification, inbreathing of life, inspiration, stimulation, etc., as below.

2. Life, vitality, breath, vital power, vital spark, breath of life.

3. Liveliness, spirit, spiritedness, vivacity, sprightliness, buoyancy, elasticity, airiness, vigor, ardor, courage, force, strength, energy, exhilaration, cheerfulness, gayety, cheer, animal spirits, high spirits, good spirits.

Animosity, *n.* Malignity, virulence, bitterness, rancor, hostility, hatred, hate, enmity, grudge, rankling, spleen, ill-will, heart-burning, violent hatred, active enmity, persistent hostility.

Animus, *n.* [L.] 1. Hostile feeling, malice, partisan feeling.

2. Disposition, spirit, temper, general tone, tone of mind.

Annals, *n. pl.* Records (*in the order of years*), chronicles, registers, rolls, archives, historical accounts.

Anneal, *v. t.* Temper (*as glass, by slow cooling*), toughen.

Annex, *v. t.* 1. Affix, attach, subjoin, superadd, append, tag, tack. See ADD.

2. Join, unite, connect.

Annexation, *n.* 1. Affixing, attaching, attachment, addition, adding, appending, annexment.

2. Junction, joining, connection, conjunction, union.

Annihilable, *a.* Utterly destructible, capable of being blotted out of existence, reducible to nonentity.

Annihilate, *v. t.* Destroy, extinguish, quench, dissolve, kill, exterminate, extirpate, raze, blast, ruin, nullify, annul, put an end to, put out of existence, blot out, blot from being, obliterate.

Annihilation, *n.* 1. Utter destruction, eradication, extermination, obliteration, abolishment.

2. Non-existence, non-being, oblivion, eternal blank, Nirvâna.

Anniversary, *n.* Day of annual celebration, fêteday, annual festival, *fête*.

Anno Domini. [L.] In the year of our Lord, in the year of grace, in the year of human salvation, *anno salutis*.

Annotate, *v. t.* Comment on, make notes on, make comments *or* remarks upon, supply with notes, gloss, gloze, elucidate, explain, illustrate.

——, *v. i.* Comment, make notes, act as an annotator.

Annotation, *n.* 1. Note, comment, commentary, remark, observation, gloss, scholium, marginalia, explanation, elucidation, illustration.

2. Supplying with notes, making notes, commentation, commenting, illustrating, illustration, elucidating, elucidation.

Announce, *v. t.* Publish, proclaim, blazon, bruit, promulgate, declare, report, trumpet, advertise, communicate, set forth, give out, blaze abroad, noise abroad, herald abroad, spread abroad, give notice of, make proclamation of, lay before the public, bring to the notice of the public.

Announcement, *n.* Advertisement, bulletin, notice, notification, proclamation, declaration, promulgation, annunciation, pronunciamento, manifesto.

Annoy, *v. t.* Molest, trouble, vex, wound, pain, plague, worry, irritate, fret, irk, chafe, incommode, disturb, disquiet, pester, bother, tease, infest, embarrass, harass, harry, hector, badger.

Annoyance, *n.* Vexation, molestation, discomfort, trouble, plague, nuisance, bore, torment, infliction, irritation, scourge, thorn, bitter pill, gall and wormwood.

Annual, *a.* Yearly, occurring once a year, occurring every year, lasting a year, recurring with the year, anniversary.

——, *n.* Yearly publication, year-book, yearly record, yearly report, yearly transactions, annals (*of science* or *letters*).

Annually, *adv.* Yearly, by the year, every year, once a year, year by year, *per annum.*

Annul, *v. t.* 1. Cancel, abrogate, repeal, revoke, recall, countermand, reverse, rescind, abolish, disannul, vacate, quash, nullify, supersede, invalidate, overrule, make void, set aside.

2. Reduce to nought, obliterate. See ANNIHILATE.

Annular, *a.* Ring-shaped, in the form of a ring, ring-like.

Annulet, *n.* 1. Little ring.

2. (*Arch.*) Fillet, listel, list, cincture, tenia.

Annulment, *n.* Annulling, nullification, abrogation, repeal, rescission, cancelling, revocation, abolition. See ANNUL.

Annunciation, *n.* 1. See ANNOUNCEMENT.

2. [With *The*] Salutation of the Virgin, *Ave Maria.* Also, anniversary of the Annunciation, 25th of March.

Anodyne, *n.* Opiate, sedative, palliative, lenitive, narcotic.

Anoint, *v. t.* 1. Smear, rub over with oil *or* unctuous matter.

2. Consecrate by unction, anele, inunct.

Anomalous, *a.* Irregular, abnormal, anomalistic, unconformable, preternatural, unnatural, unusual, singular, peculiar, exceptional, aberrant, eccentric, erratic, monstrous, out of the way.

Anomaly, *n.* Irregularity, abnormity, singularity, peculiarity, unconformity, eccentricity, monstrosity.

Anon, *adv.* Soon, quickly, shortly, immediately, forthwith, on the instant, directly, in a short time, ere long, at another time, again, afterward.

Anonymous, *a.* Nameless, without the name of the author, of unknown authorship, unacknowledged (*of writings*).

Another, *a.* 1. Some other, any other, not the same, a different.

2. One more, second.

Answer, *v. i.* 1. Reply (*especially to a question*), rejoin, respond, say in reply, make answer, reply, *or* response, retort.

2. Be accountable, be responsible *or* liable, be security, go surety.

3. Correspond, be correlated, be counterpart, be like, be similar.

4. Do, pass, serve, suit, be sufficient, be enough, do well enough, pass muster, be of use.

——, *v. t.* 1. Reply to, respond to, make answer to.

2. Refute, meet by argument *or* explanation, rebut.

3. Satisfy, fulfil, be suitable to, be sufficient for.

ANSWER, *n.* 1. Reply, response, rejoinder, replication, retort, counterstatement.

2. Refutation, rebuttal, confutation, defence, plea.

Answerable, *a.* 1. Refutable, that may be answered.

2. Accountable, responsible, amenable, liable.

3. Corresponding, correspondent, correlative, proportionate, suitable, suited, fit.

ANT, *n.* Pismire, emmet.

Antagonism, *n.* Opposition, contrariety, repugnance, contradiction, clashing, incompatibility, inconsistency, incongruity, discord, discordance, discordancy, disharmony, dissonance, conflict, hostility, enmity, feud.

Antagonist, *n.* Opponent, adversary, rival, competitor, enemy, foe, adverse party.

Antagonistic, *a.* Antagonist, opposing, adverse, opposite, hostile, inimical, contrary, contradictory, repugnant, conflicting, incompatible, inconsistent, incongruous, discordant, dissonant.

Antagonize, *v. t.* Oppose, contend against, counteract, conflict with, be hostile to, tend to annul, check.

——, *v. i.* Struggle together, contend with each other, be at feud, tend to annul each other.

Antecedence, *n.* Priority (*in time*), anteriority, precedence.

Antecedent, *a.* Preceding, precedent, previous, prior, anterior, foregoing, precursory, forerunning, going before.

——, *n.* Precursor, forerunner, first term.

Antecedents, *n. pl.* Previous history (*of an individual*), previous course, incidents of one's past life, record.

Antedate, *v. t.* 1. Date before the true time, date back, date earlier than the fact, predate.

2. Anticipate, forestall, foretaste, experience beforehand.

Anterior, *a.* 1. Preceding, prior, previous, foregoing, going before. See ANTECEDENT.

2. Fore, front, in front.

Anteriority, *n.* 1. Priority (*in time*), precedence, antecedence.

2. Position in advance, situation in front.

Ante-room, *n.* Vestibule, lobby, hall, antechamber.

Anthem, *n.* Hymn, divine song.

Anthropoid, *a.* Manlike, resembling man, anthropomorphic, having a human *or* manlike form.

Anthropophagi, *n. pl.* Cannibals, maneaters.

Antic, *a.* Odd, fanciful, fantastic, grotesque, merry, ludicrous, wild, ridiculous.

——, *n.* 1. Prank, trick, freak, gambol, caper, vagary.

2. Buffoon, fool, merry-andrew, scaramouch, mountebank, harlequin, punch, clown, zany, jester, jack-pudding, pickleherring.

Anticipate, *v. t.* 1. Go before, get the start of.

2. Take up beforehand, consider in advance, meet *or* pay in advance.

3. Foretaste, forestall, antedate, experience beforehand.

4. Expect, forecast, foresee, look forward to, count upon, reckon upon, calculate upon, prepare one's self for.

Anticipation, *n.* 1. Expectation, expectance, contemplation, prospect, hope, trust. See also ABEYANCE.

2. Foretaste, prelibation, antepast, presentiment, forestalling, foreseeing, foresight, prescience, prevision, forethought, forecast, preconception, experience beforehand, prior realization.

Anticlimax, *n.* Bathos, come-down.

Antidote, *n.* 1. Counterpoison, anti-poison, counteractive, corrective.

2. Remedy, cure, specific, restorative.

Antipathy, *n.* Repugnance (*natural* or *constitutional*), disgust, abhorrence, detestation, hatred, hate, loathing, aversion, horror.

Antipodal, *a.* Opposite, over against, diametrically opposite, contrary in the utmost.

Antiquarian, *n.* Antiquary, archæologian, archæologist.

Antiquated, *a.* Obsolete, unfashionable, antique, superannuated, bygone, archaic, ancient, grown old, out of use, out of fashion, out of date, old-fashioned, gone by.

Antique, *a.* Old, ancient, archaic, old-fashioned, bygone.

Antiquity, *n.* 1. Remote times, the olden time, ancient times, days of yore, early times, days of eld, hoary eld.

2. Ancients, people of old times, ancient life and practice.

3. Ancientness, great age.

4. [*pl.*] Relics of old times, early remains, ancient manners and customs, archæology.

Antistrophe, *n.* Counter-song, response.

Antithesis, *n.* (*Rhet.*) Contrast, opposition.

Antithetic, } *a.* Contrasted, placed in
Antithetical, } contrast, strongly *or* extremely opposed.

Anxiety, *n.* Solicitude, concern, care, uneasiness, disquiet, disquietude, apprehension, fear, misgiving, foreboding, perplexity, worry, vexation, trouble, pain.

Anxious, *a.* Solicitous, uneasy, restless, unquiet, apprehensive, greatly concerned. See CAREFUL.

ANY, *a.* 1. A single one (*of many*), any one.

2. Some (*indefinitely*).

——, *adv.* Somewhat, at all, in any degree.

Anyhow, *adv.* In any manner, in any way, in any case.

Apace, *adv.* Quickly, speedily, swiftly, rapidly, hastily, post-haste, with speed, with quick pace.

Apart, *adv.* 1. Separately, aloof, aside, by one's self, by itself.

2. Asunder, into two parts, to *or* in pieces.

Apartment, *n.* Room, chamber, hall.

Apathetic, *a.* Unfeeling, passionless, impassive, passive, inert, stoical, unimpressible, unsusceptible, insensible, senseless, soulless, phlegmatic, dull, listless, lethargic, lackadaisical, obtuse, cold, sluggish, torpid, tame, lukewarm, indifferent, unconcerned, unresponsive, callous, dead, cold-blooded, without sensibility, destitute of feeling.

Apathy, *n.* Insensibility, impassibility, dispassion, dulness, torpor, lassitude, inertness, hebetude, sluggishness, coldness, phlegm, indifference, unconcern, unfeelingness, stoicism, want of feeling, pococurantism.

Ape, *n.* 1. Simian, troglodyte, tailless monkey.

2. Mimic, servile imitator.

3. Imitation, image, type, likeness.

Ape, *v. t.* 1. Mimic (*in good sense*), imitate, counterfeit, take the form *or* appearance of.

2. Mimic (*in bad sense*), copy with servility, affect, imitate with effort, imitate futilely.

Aperient, *a.* (*Med.*) Laxative, deobstruent, loosening.

Aperture, *n.* Opening, hole, perforation, gap, cleft, rift, slit, chasm, orifice, passage, eye, eyelet, loop-hole.

Apex, *n.* Top, summit, acme, zenith, pinnacle, highest point, culminating point, utmost height.

Aphorism, *n.* Maxim, adage, proverb, saying, dictum, saw, apothegm, byword, sententious precept.

Apiarist, *n.* Bee-breeder, bee-keeper, keeper of an apiary, bee-master, apiarian.

Apiary, *n.* Bee-house, beehive-frame, bee-stand, bee-shed.

Apiece, *adv.* Severally, for each, each.

Apish, *a.* 1. Imitative (*in a servile manner*), mimicking.

2. Affected, foppish, trifling.

Aplomb, *n.* [Fr.] Self-possession, self-balance, self-confidence, collectedness, self-poise, assurance.

Apocalyptic, *a.* Prophetic, mystical, revelatory of mysteries.

Apocryphal, *a.* Unauthentic, legendary, uncanonical, of doubtful authority, fictitious, fabulous, false, dubious, spurious.

Apodeictic, } *a.* Necessarily universal, absolutely certain, demon-
Apodictic, } strative, unquestionable, infallibly so, beyond contradiction, beyond peradventure.

Apollyon, *n.* The Destroyer, Satan, the Arch-fiend, the Devil, Abaddon, the Fiend, the Arch-enemy, Beelzebub, the Prince of Darkness, the Prince of the Power of the Air.

Apologetic, *a.* 1. Excusatory, exculpatory.

2. Defensive, by way of defence, vindicative, repelling *or* refuting allegations.

Apologist, *n.* Defender, vindicator, supporter, advocate.

Apologize, *v. i.* Make an apology, offer an excuse, plead in defence *or* extenuation.

Apologue, *n.* Fable (*founded on the supposed action of brutes* or *of inanimate things*), parable, tale, story. See ALLEGORY.

Apology, *n.* 1. Defence, vindication, justification.

2. Excuse, plea, explanation, extenuation, acknowledgment, reparation, *amende honorable*.

3. Makeshift, mere excuse, poor excuse, temporary substitute.

Apostasy, *n.* Defection, desertion, traitorous defection, perfidious desertion, backsliding, dereliction, fall.

Apostate, *n.* Renegade, backslider, deserter, turncoat, pervert.

——, *a.* Treacherous, perfidious, traitorous, disloyal, false, faithless, untrue, recreant, backsliding.

Apostatize, *v. i.* Become an apostate, backslide, secede, foreswear one's faith *or* fealty, be a traitor, etc.

Apostle, *n.* Messenger, missionary, devoted proclaimer, first preacher, founder and interpreter.

Apostolic, *a.* Taught, founded, *or* authorized by the Apostles, derived from the Apostles, of the Apostles.

Apothecary, *n.* Pharmacist, pharmaceutist, pharmacian, druggist.

Apothegm, *n.* Maxim, saying, dictum, saw, proverb, aphorism, byword, sententious precept. See ADAGE.

Apotheosis, *n.* Deification.

Appall, *v. t.* Terrify, frighten, affright, dismay, daunt, horrify, shock, put in great fear, strike with terror, petrify with fear, palsy *or* paralyze with fear.

APPARATUS, *n.* Tools, instruments, utensils, means, mechanism, appliances, contrivances, *materiel*.

Apparel, *n.* Clothes, clothing, dress, raiment, attire, array, costume, toilet, habit, habiliments, garb, guise, gear, garments, garmenture, vesture, vestments, robes, outfit, accoutrement, equipment, suit, trappings, wardrobe, rig.

——, *v. t.* Dress, clothe, attire, habit, vest, array, robe, accoutre, equip, fit out, rig, rig out, trick out.

Apparent, *a.* 1. Visible, discernible, perceptible, in view, in sight, to be seen.

2. Manifest, obvious, patent, open, clear, evident, indubitable, plain, conspicuous, legible, unmistakable, in plain sight.

3. Seeming, specious, ostensible, semblable, external, superficial, not real, *quasi*.

Apparently, *adv.* 1. Evidently, obviously, clearly, manifestly, plainly, indubitably, unmistakably.

2. Seemingly, ostensibly, *quasi*, on appearance, at the first blush, in semblance, in show.

Apparition, *n.* 1. Appearing, appearance, manifestation, coming to view, epiphany.

2. Form, being, thing appearing.

3. Ghost, spectre, phantom, phantasm, spirit, double-ganger, bogy, sprite,

hobgoblin, shade, chimera, illusion, vision, preternatural appearance. See WRAITH.

Appeal, *v. i.* 1. (*Law.*) Seek reference of the case *or* cause (*from one court to another*).

2. Sue to another (*in any controversy*), apply *or* turn (to), plead (with), petition.

——, *v. t.* 1. (*Rare.*) Summon, challenge, accuse, indict.

2. (*Law.*) Refer, transfer by appeal (*from one court to another*).

——, *n.* 1. Address, invocation, petition, plea, request, entreaty, imploration, application, solicitation, suit.

2. Resort, recourse.

Appeal to. Address, invoke, implore, petition, entreat, solicit, sue to, refer to, call upon, make application to.

Appear, *v. i.* 1. Emerge, be in sight, come in sight, be visible, come into view, loom, present itself, crop out, show itself, turn up, come upon the stage, see the light, heave in sight (*naut.*).

2. Open, dawn, break.

3. Arise, occur, offer.

4. Stand in judgment, be present to answer, come into court.

5. Be manifest, be obvious, be open, be known.

6. Seem, look, show, wear the appearance, present the appearance, have the appearance, strike one as being.

Appearance, *n.* 1. Coming, arrival, advent, apparition.

2. Appearance, what is seen, form, being, apparition.

3. Semblance, seeming, show, face, pretence, color, pretext, guise, fashion, feature.

4. Mien, air, aspect, look, complexion, figure, manner, demeanor, personal presence.

Appeasable, *a.* Placable, forgiving, reconcilable.

Appease, *v. t.* 1. Pacify, calm, quiet, soothe, tranquillize, allay, assuage, mollify, alleviate, slake, mitigate, abate, ease, compose, still, hush, lull, dull, quell, quench, blunt, temper, attemper, lessen, qualify.

2. Propitiate, reconcile, satisfy, placate, make propitious, make favorable.

Appellation, *n.* Appellative, name, title, epithet, cognomen, denomination, style, description, designation, descriptive term.

Append, *v. t.* 1. Hang, attach, fasten.

2. Add, subjoin, join, annex, affix, superadd, tag, tack.

Appendage, *n.* Attachment, addition, adjunct, appurtenance, appliance, appen-

dix, appendant, tail-piece, concomitant, accompaniment, attendant.

Appendant, *a.* Annexed, attached, hanging, concomitant, attendant.

Appendix, *n.* 1. Adjunct, addition, appurtenance, appendage, appendant, addendum, codicil.

2. Supplement, excursus.

Appertain to. 1. Belong to, pertain to, be incident to, be proper to, be part *or* characteristic of, inhere in, adhere to.

2. Regard, concern, touch, relate to, refer to, bear upon.

Appetence, } *n.* 1. Appetite, strong desire,
Appetency, } craving, longing, passion.

2. Tendency, inclination, leaning, bent, disposition, propensity, proclivity, fondness, liking, *penchant.*

Appetite, *n.* 1. Desire, longing, craving, hankering, pruriency, appetency, passion, lust.

2. Liking, relish, stomach, gusto, gust, zest.

3. Hunger, stomach, desire of food.

Appetizer, *n.* Zest, relish, sauce.

Appetizing, *a.* That whets the appetite, stimulating to the appetite, inviting.

Applaud, *v. t.* 1. Cheer, clap.

2. Praise, commend, laud, approve, compliment, extol, magnify, cry up.

Applause, *n.* Acclamation, acclaim, plaudit, *éclat,* clapping of hands, shout of approbation, huzza, loud praise, burst of approbation.

APPLE, *n.* (*Basic Eng.*) Pome.

Apple-pie order. (*Colloq.*) Perfect trim.

Appliance, *n.* 1. Application, applying, use, exercise, practice.

2. Tool, instrument, appurtenance, appendage, adjunct.

3. Expedient, means, instrumentality, resource.

Appliances, *n. pl.* 1. Means, expedients, instrumentalities, resources, steps, measures, ways and means.

2. Appointments, appurtenances, attachments, adjuncts, tools, instruments, appendages, equipments.

Applicable, *a.* 1. To be applied *or* fitted *or* put on, adjustable, adaptable.

2. Suitable, fit, fitting, befitting, appropriate, adapted, apt, proper, pertinent, relevant, apposite, germane, to the point, to the purpose, bearing on.

Applicant, *n.* Petitioner, solicitor, suitor, candidate.

Application, *n.* 1. Applying, putting on.

2. Thing applied (emollient, irritant, stimulant, *or* rubefacient), lotion, wash, ointment, poultice.

3. Appliance, use, exercise, practice.

4. Solicitation, petition, appeal, request, suit.

5. Assiduity, industry, perseverance, persistency, constancy, diligence, sedulousness, intense study, close attention.

6. Reference to practice, use in detail, putting into practice, turning upon particulars, exemplification.

Apply, *v. t.* 1. Lay upon, put *or* place upon, bestow.

2. Appropriate, use, employ, exercise, ply, convert to use, put to use.

3. Execute, carry out, put in practice.

4. Devote, dedicate, addict, address, direct, engage, turn attentively, bend with diligence.

5. Refer, make pertain, give direction upon.

——, *v. i.* 1. Hold, hold good *or* true, fit *or* hit the case, come into play, be in point, be pertinent.

2. Make formal request, enroll one's self as a candidate, make suit, become a candidate.

Apply to. 1. Suit, fit, be adapted to, be suitable to, be applicable to, hold true of, hold of, bear upon, refer to.

2. Solicit, petition, request, appeal to, call upon, make application to, have recourse to.

Appoint, *v. t.* 1. Fix, determine, prescribe, set, establish.

2. Direct, ordain, enjoin, require, command, decree, order, bid, impose, insist on.

3. Assign, allot, depute, delegate, detail, designate, destine, settle.

4. Nominate, name, constitute, create.

5. Furnish, equip, supply.

Appointment, *n.* 1. Appointing, designation to office, assignment.

2. Station, position, office, place.

3. Assignation, agreement (*as to time and place of meeting*), stipulation, arrangement. See TRYST.

4. Decree, bidding, command, order, ordaining, ordainment, ordination, ordinance, direction, prescription, precept, mandate, edict, enactment, law, requirement.

5. *Usually pl.* Equipment, equipage, furniture, outfit, accoutrement, appliance.

Apportion, *v. t.* Allot, allocate, allow, distribute, assign, divide, partition, part, measure (out), share, deal, dole, dispense, parcel out, deal out, portion out, mete.

Apportionment, *n.* Distribution, allotment, assignment, partition, division.

Apposite, *a.* Apt, pertinent, relevant, fit, fitting, befitting, suitable, appropriate, seasonable, germane, *apropos*, "pat," to the purpose, to the point, well applied, well put.

Appraise, *v. t.* Value, estimate, prize, rate, set a value on, fix a price for, estimate the worth of, form an estimate of.

Appraisement, *n.* Appraisal, valuation, estimation, estimate, judgment.

Appreciate, *v. t.* 1. Estimate justly, set a just value on, form a correct estimate of, value rightly, perceive the worth of, value, esteem, prize.

2. Estimate, esteem, value, rate.

3. Raise the value of, make of greater value.

——, *v. i.* Rise in value, be worth more.

Appreciation, *n.* 1. Valuation, estimation, appraisal, appraisement.

2. Just estimate, correct valuation, esteem, sense of one's worth.

3. Rise in value, rise, increased value *or* price.

Apprehend, *v. t.* 1. Seize, arrest, take, catch, detain, capture, take prisoner.

2. Conceive, imagine, look at, regard, view.

3. See (*mentally*), perceive, realize, understand, take in, appreciate, take the meaning *or* point of.

4. Fear, forebode, have a presentiment of.

——, *v. i.* Think, suppose, imagine, conceive, fancy, hold, ween, presume, be of opinion, take it. See OPINE.

Apprehension, *n.* 1. Seizure, arrest, capture.

2. Understanding, intellect, intelligence, mind, reason.

3. Notice, simple taking in, mere reception, taking the point, getting the meaning, understanding.

4. Conception, the mind's eye. See IMAGINATION.

5. Knowledge, intellection, discernment, perception, sense.

6. Opinion, belief, fancy, supposition, judgment, sentiment, idea, notion, view.

7. Fear, distrust, suspicion, anxiety, solicitude, care, concern, dread, foreboding, presentiment, misgiving, uneasiness, alarm.

Apprehensive, *a.* 1. Quick to understand, of quick perceptions.

2. Fearful, afraid, distrustful, suspicious, anxious, uneasy.

Apprentice, *n.* Learner (*of a trade*), indentured, bound, *or* articled assistant.

——, *v. t.* Indenture, bind, article.

Apprise, *v. t.* Inform, acquaint, notify, tell, make acquainted, make aware, give notice, disclose to, make known to, advise, admonish, warn.

Approach, *v. i.* 1. Come, draw near, draw nigh, come near, be at hand.

2. [With *to*.] Approximate, come nearly up, be nearly equal.

——, *v. t.* 1. Bring near, carry toward, advance, push forward.

2. Come *or* draw near *or* nigh (to), go near.

3. Broach (*a subject*) to, address confidentially, make overtures to.

4. Resemble closely, come very near to, be much like, almost equal.

——, *n.* 1. Advance, advent, coming, drawing near.

2. Approximation, nearing, tendency, convergence.

3. [In *pl.*] Wily addresses, insidious overtures, advances.

4. Entrance, way, adit, path. See ACCESS.

5. Access, admittance, admission.

Approachable, *a.* Accessible.

Approbation, *n.* 1. Approval, praise, commendation, good opinion, favorable opinion, liking.

2. Support, concurrence, assent, consent, sanction, ratification, indorsement.

Appropriate, *v. t.* 1. Adopt, take to one's self, take as one's own, apply to one's own uses.

2. Assign, apportion, allot, set apart, devote.

3. Apply, use, employ, convert.

——, *a.* Adapted, fit, fitting, befitting, meet, apt, "pat," suitable, proper, becoming, due, seemly, agreeable, conformable, congruous, germane, convenient, pertinent, apposite, felicitous, happy, applicable, *apropos*, to the point, to the purpose.

Appropriateness, *n.* Suitableness, fitness, propriety, aptness, appositeness, pertinency, relevancy, felicity, applicability. See PERTINENCE.

Appropriation, *n.* 1. Seizure, capture, taking, taking to one's self.

2. Application (*to a particular use*), assignment, devotion, allotment.

APPROVAL, *n.* See APPROBATION.

Approve, *v. t.* 1. Commend, recommend, praise, like, appreciate, value, prize, think well *or* favorably of, think highly of, speak well of, be pleased with.

2. Sanction, countenance, confirm, justify, ratify, uphold, sustain, make valid, assent *or* consent to, concur in, indorse.

Approximate, *a.* 1. Proximate, approaching, coming near. [Followed by *to*.]

2. Nearly correct, nearly accurate *or* true, inexact, almost exact, rough.

——, *v. t.* Approach, come near, closely resemble, nearly rival.

Approximately, *adv.* Near, nearly, about, not far from.

Approximation, *n.* Approach, gradual convergence.

Appurtenance, *n.* Adjunct, accessory, dependency. See APPENDAGE.

Appurtenant, *a.* Belonging, pertaining, appertaining.

A priori. [L.] 1. Theoretically, before experience, before trial, from assumed principles.

2. From pure reason, from the nature of the case, independently of all experience, necessarily, absolutely, apodictically, primordially, aboriginally, constitutionally.

Apropos, *a.* [Fr.] Opportune, seasonable, timely, fit, suitable, apt, "pat," to the point, to the purpose, just the thing, quite the thing. See APPOSITE.

——, *adv.* 1. Opportunely, seasonably, to the purpose, etc. See preceding.

2. By the way, by the bye, speaking of that, that reminds me, while the matter's up, in that connection.

Apt, *a.* 1. Apposite, pertinent, suitable, fit, fitting, meet, befitting, germane, applicable, appropriate, felicitous, *apropos*, to the point, to the purpose.

2. Inclined, liable, likely, prone, disposed, subject.

3. Quick, sharp, ready, prompt, expert, dexterous, able, clever, happy, adroit, handy, skilful.

Aptitude, *n.* 1. Turn, disposition, genius, gift, knack, endowment, talent, faculty, capacity, capableness, tendency, inclination, bent, bias, proclivity, proneness, propensity, forte, aptness.

2. Readiness (*at learning*), quickness, cleverness, ability, aptness.

Aptness, *n.* 1. Fitness, suitableness, appropriateness, appositeness, pertinence, pertinency, point, pointedness, felicity, felicitousness, adaptation, applicability.

2. Turn, tendency, inclination. See APTITUDE, 1.

3. Quickness, readiness, expertness, skill, facility, knack, adroitness, tact, address, ability, happy faculty.

Aquatic, *a.* On *or* in the water, water (*as water vegetation*).

Aqueous, *a.* Watery, waterish, moist, wet, humid, damp.

Aquiline, *a.* Hooked (*like an eagle's beak*), Roman (*applied especially to the nose*), bent, curved, curving.

Arab, *n.* 1. Arabian, Saracen, Moor.

2. Street Arab, gamin, hoodlum.

Arabesque, *a.* Moorish, moresque.

Arabian, *a.* Arabic, Arab, Saracenic, Moorish.

Arabic, *a.* Arabian, Arab.

Arable, *a.* Tillable, cultivable, cultivatible, fit for tillage, that may be ploughed, fit for the plough, suitable for cultivation.

Aramaic, *a.* Aramæan, Chaldaic, Chaldean.

——, *n.* The Aramæan language, Chaldee, Chaldaic.

Arbiter, *n.* 1. Arbitrator, umpire, judge, referee.

2. Determiner, controller, master, lord, ruler, governor, sovereign.

Arbitrament, *n.* 1. Determination, decision, settlement, judgment, test, trial, umpirage.

2. (*Law.*) Award, adjudication, determination, decision, decree.

Arbitrariness, *n.* 1. Despotism, absoluteness, absolutism, tyranny, autocracy.

2. Capriciousness, wilfulness, absence of principle, unreasonableness.

Arbitrary, *a.* 1. Irresponsible, despotic, autocratic, unlimited, unrestrained, uncontrolled, absolute, tyrannical, tyrannous, imperious, dictatorial, overbearing, peremptory, domineering, bound by no law.

2. Capricious, wilful, whimsical, fanciful, determined by no rule or principle.

Arbitrate, *v. t.* Decide, determine.

——, *v. i.* 1. Mediate, interpose, intervene.

2. Judge, decide, determine, adjudicate, give judgment, pass judgment.

Arbitration, *n.* 1. Mediation, intervention, intercession, interposition.

2. Adjudication, arbitrament, umpirage, test, trial, judgment, decision, determination.

Arbitrator, *n.* 1. Arbiter, umpire, judge, referee.

2. Arbiter, determiner, controller, ruler, master, sovereign, lord, director, governor.

Arbor, *n.* 1. Bower, shady recess, shady retreat.

2. Spindle, axis, shaft.

Arboreal, *a.* 1. Arboreous, arborescent, arboriform, dendriform, tree-like, in the form of a tree.

2. Frequenting woods, living among *or* on trees.

Arborescence, *n.* Arborization, branching, ramification.

Arborescent, *a.* Arboreal, arboreous, tree-like, dendriform, dendrite, dendritic, arboriform, branching.

Arcade, *n.* Colonnade, loggia.

Arcanum, *n.* [L. *pl. Arcana.*] Secret, mystery.

ARCH, *n.* 1. Curved structure, cove, fornix.

2. Curve, bend, curving, bending.

——, *v. t.* 1. Vault, cover with an arch, arch over, span.

2. Bend (*into the form of an arch*), curve.

——, *a.* 1. Chief, principal, consummate, first-rate, of the first class.

2. Roguish, waggish, mirthful, frolicsome, sportive, merry, playful, sly, shrewd, cunning, knowing.

Archæological, *a.* Antiquarian.

Archæologist, *n.* Antiquarian, antiquary, archæologian.

Archæology, *n.* Science of antiquities, antiquities.

Archaic, *a.* Old, ancient, obsolescent, antiquated, antique, bygone, out of use, out of date, out of fashion, old-fashioned.

Archaism, *n.* Antiquated term *or* expression, obsolete idiom.

Archbishop, *n.* Primate, metropolitan.

Archduchy, *n.* Archdukedom.

Arched, *a.* 1. Vaulted, bowed, camerated, concave, forniciform, fornicated, fornicate.

2. (*Bot.*) Fornicate.

Archer, *n.* Bowman, sagittary.

Archetype, *n.* Pattern, model, type, prototype, original, exemplar, example, protoplast, mirror, paragon.

Arch-fiend, *n.* [With *The* prefixed.] Satan. See APOLLYON.

Arching, *a.* Vaulted, curving, bending.

Architect, *n.* 1. Designer (*of buildings*).

2. Contriver, maker, former, author.

Architecture, *n.* 1. Science *or* art of building, decorative building-art.

2. Style of building.

3. Workmanship, framework, frame, structure, construction, fabric.

Archives, *n. pl.* Records, rolls, documents, registers, muniments.

Archway, *n.* Arched passage.

Arctic, *a.* Northern, boreal, septentrional.

Arcuate, *a.* (*Rare.*) Curved, bent, bowed, hooked, crooked, aduncous.

Arcuation, *n.* 1. (*Rare.*) Curvature, incurvation, curvity, flexure, bend, crook.

2. Layering, propagation by layers.

Ardency, *n.* 1. Heat, warmth, glow.

2. Warmth, ardentness. See ARDOR, 2.

Ardent, *a.* 1. Hot, burning, fiery.

2. Warm, passionate, fervent, impassioned, eager, intense, keen, sharp, vehement, fierce, fiery, earnest, fervid,

perfervid, glowing, zealous, devoted, enthusiastic, strenuous, sanguine.

3. Alcoholic, spirituous.

Ardour, *n.* 1. Heat, warmth, glow, ardency, hotness.

2. Zeal, fervor, fervency, flame, glow, excitement, sharpness, earnestness, eagerness, feverishness, heartiness, devotion, enthusiasm, soul, spirit, vehemence, impetuosity, intensity, heat, hotness, fierceness, passion.

Arduous, *a.* 1. Steep, high, lofty, uphill.

2. Hard, difficult, laborious, onerous, troublesome, Herculean, toilsome, tiresome, wearisome, fatiguing, beset with difficulties, full of difficulties.

Area, *n.* 1. Region, sphere, realm, territory, field, range, tract, domain, district, circuit, circle, definite space.

2. Superficial contents, superficies, surface, expanse.

Arena, *n.* 1. Ring, amphitheatre.

2. Scene of action, theatre, field, stage, place of contest, scene of conflict, battlefield, cock-pit, lists.

Arenaceous, *a.* Sandy, arenose, arenarious.

Areometer, *n.* Hydrometer.

Argent, *a.* 1. Of silver, silver.

2. Silvery, bright, resplendent, shining, radiant, brilliant, beaming, effulgent, refulgent, fair, white, snowy.

——, *n.* Whiteness, fairness, snowiness, silveriness, brilliancy, resplendence, radiance, effulgence, refulgence.

Argosy, *n.* Carack, galleon.

Argue, *v. i.* 1. Reason, plead, offer reasons, use arguments.

2. Dispute, debate, chop logic, try conclusions, bandy words *or* arguments, hold *or* carry on an argument.

——, *v. t.* 1. Show, indicate, evince, denote, imply, mean, betoken, prove.

2. Debate, discuss, sift, contest, controvert, moot, reason upon.

Arguer, *n.* Reasoner, debater, controversialist, disputant, disputer.

ARGUMENT, *n.* 1. Reason, ground, proof, evidence, reasoning, chain of reasoning, process of reasoning.

2. Controversy, dispute, disputation, discussion, debate.

3. Subject, topic, matter, theme, thesis, question, subject-matter, matter in hand.

4. Summary, abstract, epitome, outline, general contents.

Argumentation, *n.* Reasoning, ratiocination, process of reasoning.

Argumentative, *a.* 1. Containing argument, concerned with argument, for advocacy, apologetic.

2. Controversial, polemical.

3. Disputatious, given to controversy, addicted to argument.

Argus-eyed, *a.* Vigilant, watchful, alert, all-observant, discerning, perspicacious, sharp-sighted, quick-sighted, lynx-eyed, hawk-eyed.

Arid, *a.* 1. Dry, dried up, parched with heat, parched, unfertile, barren, sterile.

2. Dry, uninteresting, dull, pointless, jejune, unsuggestive, barren, infecund.

Aridity, *n.* 1. Dryness, aridness, parchedness, siccity, want of moisture, sterility, barrenness, unfertility.

2. Dryness, want of interest, dulness, pointlessness, jejuneness, unsuggestiveness, barrenness, infecundity, sterility.

3. Dulness, insensibility, indifference, torpidity.

Aright, *adv.* Rightly, without error *or* mistake.

Ariose, *a.* Melodious, of a melodious character, characterized by melody (*as distinguished from harmony*).

Arise, *v. i.* 1. Ascend, mount, soar, tower, go up.

2. Get up, get out of bed, leave one's couch, start up, stand up, rise, rise from one's seat.

3. Rise, appear, emerge, come in sight, come into view, present itself, show itself, discover itself, make its appearance, reveal itself, come to light.

4. Begin, originate, spring, spring up, be excited, come into action, come into existence *or* being, enter upon life.

5. Rise, rebel, revolt, rise in sedition, rise in force, violence, *or* with threatening.

6. Accrue, result, proceed, issue, flow, follow, come, ensue, originate, be derived.

Aristocracy, *n.* 1. Government of nobles *or* a privileged order, rule of the higher classes, patriciate.

2. Nobility, noblesse, gentry, peerage, body of nobles, the quality, persons of rank, *élite*, patricians.

3. (*Colloq.*) Upper classes, upper ten thousand, upper ten.

Aristocrat, *n.* 1. Patrician, gentleman, chevalier, grandee, magnifico.

2. Haughty *or* overbearing person, person of supercilious feeling.

Aristocratic, *a.* 1. Noble, princely, patrician, titled, gentle, of gentle blood, high-born, of high rank, high-bred, courtly.

2. Of *or* by the privileged, vesting power in the nobility, belonging *or* pertaining to the aristocracy.

Aristotelian, *a.* Peripatetic.

ARM, *n.* 1. Anterior limb, anterior member.

2. Branch, bough, limb, projection, projecting part.

3. Inlet (*of the sea*), estuary, firth, frith, fiord, cove, creek.

4. Power, might, strength, puissance.

5. Weapon, instrument of warfare.

——, *v. t.* 1. Equip, array, furnish, provide, *or* supply with arms.

2. Fortify, put in a state of defence.

3. Cover, protect, clothe, guard, strengthen.

——, *v. i.* Take arms, be fitted *or* provided with arms, make warlike preparations, gather an army, collect munitions of war.

Armada, *n.* Fleet (*especially that of Spain against England in* 1588), squadron, flotilla.

Armament, *n.* 1. Body of forces.

2. Guns, cannon, arms, munitions of war.

Arm-chair, *n.* Elbow-chair, armed chair.

Armistice, *n.* Truce, suspension of hostilities, cessation of arms, temporary peace.

Armor, *n.* Defensive clothing, coat of mail. See ARMS.

Armorial, *a.* Heraldic.

Armory, *n.* Arsenal, depository of arms, magazine of arms.

Armpit, *n.* Axilla.

Arms, *n. pl.* 1. Weapons, means of offence and defence, armor, harness, accoutrements, muniments, array, panoply, mail, martial array.

2. War, warlike exploits, warfare, heroic achievements, deeds of valor, deeds of arms.

3. Escutcheon, scutcheon, shield, ensign armorial, armorial bearings, blazonry, device, crest, coat of arms, heraldic emblem.

ARMY, *n.* 1. Host, force, troops, legions, battalions, armed force, military force, body of troops.

2. Host, multitude, throng, vast assemblage.

Aroma, *n.* 1. Fragrance, perfume, redolence, sweet scent, pleasing scent, grateful odor, *bouquet*, delicate savor.

2. Subtle essence, supreme quality, ethereal spirit, fine flavor.

Aromatic, *a.* Fragrant, redolent, balmy, spicy, odoriferous, aromatous, ambrosial, high-scented, strong-scented, sweet-scented, sweet-smelling.

Aromatize, *v. t.* Scent, perfume, spice, fill with fragrance.

Around, *adv.* Round, on every side, on all sides, in a circle, right and left.

——, *prep.* About, round, encircling, encompassing, surrounding, on every side of.

Arouse, *v. t.* Incite, excite, animate, stimulate, warm, kindle, inspirit, provoke, instigate, awaken, rouse, raise, whet, stir up, wake up, summon up, set on, hurry on.

Arraign, *v. t.* 1. Prosecute, bring to trial, bring before a court.

2. Accuse, charge, denounce, impeach, indict, criminate, tax, censure, call to account, take to task.

Arraignment, *n.* 1. Prosecution, bringing to trial.

2. Accusation, indictment, impeachment, denunciation, calling to account, taking to task.

Arrange, *v. t.* 1. Dispose, array, class, classify, group, rank, marshal, array, distribute, place, range, put *or* bring into order, set in order, reduce to order, systematize, organize, set out, assign places to, allocate.

2. Adjust, settle, determine, fix upon.

3. Plan, devise, contrive, project, mature, concoct, construct, prepare, lay out.

——, *v. i.* Agree, come to terms, settle.

Arrangement, *n.* 1. Disposition, classification, method, distribution, grouping, allocation, collocation, placing, array, reducing to order, organization, systematization.

2. Structure, make, make-up, form, mode of building, manner of making.

3. Adjustment, settlement, agreement.

4. Regulation, management, economy.

5. Preparation, plan, scheme.

Arrant, *a.* Notorious, utter, gross, downright, consummate, rank, thoroughgoingly bad.

Arras, *n.* Tapestry, hangings.

Array, *n.* 1. Order, disposition, arrangement, collocation, marshalling.

2. Dress, fine clothes, elegant attire, rich garments. See APPAREL.

3. Exhibition, show, display.

4. Marshalled force, soldiery, troops, army, hosts, battalions.

——, *v. t.* 1. Rank, range, arrange, place, dispose, marshal, set in order, draw up, draw out, set in line, set in line of battle.

2. Dress, habit, attire, equip, accoutre, betrap, enrobe, robe, vest, invest, wrap, clothe, bedeck, deck, adorn, embellish, betrim, decorate, garnish, prank, bedizen, trick out, set off.

Arrears, *n. pl.* Arrearage, deficiency, unpaid dues, amounts due, but unpaid.

Arrest, *v. t.* 1. Stop, stay, check, interrupt, obstruct, hinder, delay, detain, restrain, hold, withhold, keep back.

2. Seize, apprehend, take, capture, catch, take up, take into custody, take prisoner.

3. Catch, secure, fix, engage, engross, occupy, rivet.

——, *n.* 1. Stay, staying, stopping, stoppage, check, checking, interruption, delay, detention, restraining, restraint, hindrance, obstruction.

2. Seizure, apprehension, capture, detention.

Arrival, *n.* Advent, access, coming, reaching one's destination.

Arrive, *v. i.* 1. Come, get here, reach this place.

2. Get there, reach that place, get to one's destination, get to the end of one's journey.

Arrive at. Reach, attain, come to, get to, touch at.

Arrogance, *n.* Haughtiness, pride, effrontery, assumption, superciliousness, disdain, contumely, lordliness, loftiness, self-assertion, assurance, self-assurance, self-conceit, conceitedness, self-importance, self-sufficiency, self-assumption, egotism, *hauteur*.

Arrogant, *a.* Haughty, proud, supercilious, lordly, disdainful, contumelious, insolent, cavalier, overbearing, overweening, assuming, magisterial, dogmatic, imperious, swelling, pompous, blustering, big, high, lofty, top-lofty, self-conceited, self-sufficient, self-assuming, self-important, self-asserting, egotistic, self-assured, uppish.

Arrogate, *v. t.* Assume, usurp, claim unduly, make unjust pretensions to.

Arrow, *n.* Dart, shaft, bolt, reed.

Arrow-headed, *a.* Wedge-shaped, cuneiform, sagittate.

Arrowy, *a.* 1. Slender, delicate, reed-like, gracile, graceful.

2. Swift, darting, rushing, lithe, sinuous.

Arsenal, *n.* Armory, magazine of arms, repository of military stores.

ART, *n.* 1. Trade, craft, business, calling, employment, exercise of skill.

2. Skill, address, adroitness, readiness, dexterity, tact, sagacity, aptitude, aptness, cleverness, ingenuity, knack.

3. Cunning, astuteness, artfulness, shrewdness, artifice, deceit, subtlety, finesse, craftiness, craft, duplicity, wiliness, guile.

Artful, *a.* Cunning, crafty, wily, subtle, insidious, designing, intriguing, politic, diplomatic, Machiavelian, deceitful, trickish, tricky, sly, foxy, snaky.

Article, *n.* 1. Part, portion, branch, division, member, clause, paragraph, head, heading, item, particular, count, point.

2. Essay, piece, paper.

3. Thing, substance, commodity.

——, *v. t.* Bind, indenture, apprentice.

Articulate, *a.* 1. Jointed, articulated, formed with joints.

2. Distinctly uttered, distinct, clear, clearly audible, intelligible.

——, *v. t.* 1. Join, unite by joints, unite, connect, fasten together.

2. Utter distinctly (*as respects the elementary sounds*), speak, enunciate. See Pronounce.

Articulation, *n.* 1. Distinct utterance.

2. Joint, hinge, juncture, connection, point of junction, mode of union.

Artifice, *n.* 1. Contrivance, invention, effort, art.

2. Cunning, deceit, deception, imposture, fraud, trickery, device, duplicity, guile, subtlety, finesse, stratagem, shift, trick, feint, manoeuvre, subterfuge, wile, ruse, doubling, Machiavelism, diplomacy, machination, cheat, shuffle, double-dealing, "dodge," hocus-pocus, crafty device, artful contrivance.

Artificer, *n.* 1. Maker, contriver, plotter, machinator.

2. Craftsman, mechanic, artisan, artist in handicraft, superior artisan, skilled workman.

Artificial, *a.* 1. Factitious, made by art, not natural.

2. Fictitious, feigned, counterfeit, counterfeited, sham, spurious.

3. Assumed, affected, forced, labored, strained, constrained.

Artillery, *n.* 1. Ordnance, cannon, "enginery," mounted guns.

2. Gunnery, theory of ordnance, art of handling artillery.

Artisan, *n.* Mechanic, craftsman, handicraftsman, artificer, workman, laborer, operative.

Artist, *n.* 1. Designer, contriver, projector, adept, skilled workman, artificer.

2. Painter, limner, sketcher, colorist, pastellist, etc.

3. Sculptor, carver, modeller.

4. Master, master-hand, consummate performer.

Artistic, *a.* 1. Skilful, masterly, workman-like.

2. Tasteful, marked by knowledge of art, displaying taste, showing skill in applying the principles of beauty.

Artless, *a.* 1. Ignorant, unlearned, un-taught, unskilful, rude. [Usually followed by *of*.]

2. Inartificial, simple, natural, plain, unadorned, without marks of art.

3. Unaffected, plain, honest, frank, fair, open, candid, *naive*, guileless, simple, sincere, true, unsophisticated, ingenuous, undesigning, truthful, trustful, unsuspicious, confiding, single-minded, simple-hearted, simple-minded, open-hearted, straightforward.

AS, *adv.* and *conj.* 1. In the manner that.

2. Like, similar to, for example, of the same kind with, in the same manner with.

3. Viewed like, taken in the character of, considered in the state of.

4. While, during the time that, at the same time that.

5. Because, since, for the reason that.

6. To the degree that, in the same proportion that.

7. Being of the kind which, being of the class who.

Ascend, *v. i.* 1. Rise, arise, mount, soar, aspire, tower, climb, clamber, go up.

2. Go backward (*in the order of time*).

——, *v. t.* Scale, go up, get up. See CLIMB, *v. t.*

Ascendancy,) *n* Power, authority, sway,
Ascendency,) control, superiority, government, mastery, masterdom, command, dominion, rule, sovereignty, supremacy, domination, predominance, controlling influence, advantage over, upper-hand.

Ascendant, *n.* Superiority, supremacy, predominance, ascendency, superior influence, commanding influence, controlling influence.

——, *a.* 1. Rising, above the horizon.

2. Superior, predominant, prevailing, prevalent, ruling, surpassing.

Ascension, *n.* Rising, rise, ascent, ascending, mounting, moving upward.

Ascent, *n.* 1. Rising, rise, ascension, ascending, mounting, moving upward.

2. Ascending, climbing, scaling, voyage up.

3. Acclivity, rising ground, rise, ascending path, upward slope, gradient.

4. Elevation, height, eminence.

Ascertain, *v. t.* 1. Determine, establish, fix, settle, define, certify, verify, make certain, make sure.

2. Discover, find out, get at (*with precision*).

Ascetic, *a.* Austere, rigid, severe, stern, puritanical, over-renunciatory, over-self-denying, abstemious, self-mortifying, over-abstinent.

——, *n.* Recluse, hermit, anchoret, anchorite, solitary, *solitaire*, eremite, devotee, yogi, mortifier of the flesh.

Asceticism, *n.* Austerity, abstemiousness, mortification, excessive abstinence, over-renunciation, renunciation.

Ascribable, *a.* Attributable, traceable, chargeable, imputable, referrible, owing.

Ascribe, *v. t.* Attribute, assign, arrogate, refer, charge, lay, set down. See IMPUTE.

Ascription, *n.* 1. Ascribing, attributing, arrogation, referring, charging, laying, setting down, imputing.

2. [*pl.*] Praises, adorations, magnifyings, extollings, homage, *Magnificats*, *Glorias*, *Te Deums*.

As far as. To the extent that, to the degree that.

As good as. The same as, equivalent to, equal to, tantamount to.

Ashamed, *a.* Abashed, confused, (put) out of countenance.

Ashen, *a.* 1. Ash, made of ash.

2. Ashy, pale, pallid, blanched, hueless, colorless, gray, ash-colored.

Ashes, *n. pl.* 1. Remains (*of what is burned*).

2. Corpse, remains (*of the human body*), dead body.

Ashore, *adv.* 1. On shore, on land.

2. To the shore.

3. Aground, not afloat.

4. (*Colloq.*) Stranded, aground, in difficulties, run out, come to grief, hard up.

Ashy, *a.* 1. Cineraceous, cineritious, cinereous, favillous, like ashes.

2. Pale, pallid, whitish, gray, ash-colored, cineraceous, cineritious, cinereous. See ASHEN, 2.

Aside, *adv.* 1. Laterally, to the side, to one side, on one side, bye.

2. Away, off, out of mind, out of thought, out of the heart, out of the character.

3. Out of the straight course, out of the true course.

4. Apart, separately, away, aloof.

As if. As though.

Asinine, *a.* 1. Of an ass, ass-like.

2. Doltish, stupid, blockish, foolish, senseless, dullard, duncical, duncish, dunderheaded, thick-headed, thick-skulled, muddle-brained.

As it were. So to speak, as it would seem, as it seems.

Ask, *v. t.* 1. Question, interrogate, inquire of, put the question to.

2. Inquire, make inquiry about, seek information regarding.

3. Invite.

4. Request, solicit, dun, sue, petition, seek, beseech, implore, supplicate, crave, beg, adjure, conjure, desire, entreat, importune, pray for, prefer a petition for, make application for.

5. Require, claim, demand, exact, challenge, call for.

Ask, *v. i.* 1. Petition, plead, appeal, beg, pray, sue, make suit.

2. Inquire, question, make inquiry.

Askance, } *adv.* Obliquely, sideways, side-
Askant, } wise, askew, awry, aslant, asquint, on one side, out of the corner of one's eye.

Asker, *n.* Inquirer, petitioner, solicitor, solicitant, suitor.

Askew, *adv.* Awry, obliquely, skewed, atwist, askile, aside, askance, askant, aslant, asquint, to one side.

Aslant, *adv.* Obliquely, askance, aslope. See ASKEW.

——, *a.* Oblique, inclined, slanting, sloping.

Asleep, *a.* 1. Sleeping, fast asleep, slumbering, dormant, in slumber, in repose, in a sound sleep, in the arms of Morpheus.

2. Dead, in the last sleep, at rest with God.

Aspect, *n.* 1. Air, mien, look, bearing, countenance, expression, visage, feature.

2. Appearance, view, light, condition, situation, position, state, phase, attitude, posture.

3. Direction, bearing, angle, outlook, prospect, relative position.

Asperity, *n.* 1. Roughness, ruggedness, unevenness.

2. Acrimony, tartness, sourness, sharpness, causticity, corrosiveness.

3. Harshness, moroseness, sternness, severity, virulence, crabbedness, bitterness, churlishness, acerbity, sullenness, ill-temper. See ACRIMONY.

Asperse, *v. t.* Vilify, slander, calumniate, traduce, defame, disparage, discredit, slur, censure, impugn, malign, revile, lampoon, backbite, attack, abuse, blacken, blemish, besmirch, bespatter, befoul, defile, run down, detract from, speak ill of, accuse falsely, reflect upon, cast reflections upon, animadvert upon, cast reproach upon, vituperate, cast obloquy upon.

Aspersion, *n.* Calumny, detraction, censure, slander, defamation, abuse, vituperation, obloquy, reproach, reflection, backbiting, reviling, traducing. See preceding verb.

Aspirant, *n.* 1. Aspirer, ambitious person.

2. Candidate, seeker, solicitor, solicitant, suitor, competitor.

Aspiration, *n.* 1. Pronouncing or pronunciation with the rough breathing.

2. Longing, yearning, craving, ardent wish *or* desire, spiritual elevation, upward looking, yearning after excellence.

Aspire, *v. i.* 1. Desire (*earnestly*), long, yearn.

2. Ascend, rise, soar, tower, mount.

Aspire to. Aim at, indulge an ambition for, entertain hopes of, seek, venture to make suit for, make bold to seek.

Aspiring, *a.* Ambitious, high-reaching, of high *or* lofty purpose, striving after excellence, etc. See the verb.

Asquint, *adv.* Askance, askant, awry, askew, obliquely, to one side.

Ass, *n.* 1. Jackass, donkey.

2. Dolt, fool, blockhead, simpleton, numskull, ninny. See DUNCE.

Assail, *v. t.* 1. Assault, attack, invade, oppugn, fall upon, set upon, fly at, bear down upon, make aggression on.

2. Attack, impugn, maltreat, malign, etc. See ASPERSE.

3. Set upon (*with arguments* or *entreaties*), ply, pelt, storm. See ATTACK and IMPORTUNE.

Assailable, *a.* Open to attack, censurable, vulnerable, not impregnable, sensitive.

Assailant, *n.* Aggressor, assaulter, attacker, invader, assailer.

——, *a.* Attacking, invading, assaulting.

Assassin, *n.* Murderer, killer, slayer, cutthroat, assassinator, bravo, thug.

Assassinate, *v. t.* Kill (*by secret assault*), murder, slay, despatch, murderously assail *or* assault.

Assassination, *n.* Murder (*by secret assault*), murderous assault.

Assault, *n.* 1. Attack, onset, onslaught, aggression, invasion, incursion, charge, thrust, assailing with blows, threatening with blows.

2. Storming, storm.

——, *v. t.* Assail, attack, invade, charge, storm, fall upon, fly at, bear down upon, make aggression on, assail with blows, batter upon, threaten with blows.

Assay, *n.* Trial (*to determine the quality of metals, alloys,* or *ores*), test, examination, analysis.

——, *v. t.* Analyze (*metallic substances*), test, make an assay of.

Assemblage, *n.* 1. Collection, group, aggregate, body, bunch, cluster, clump, mass, congeries, pack.

2. Assembly, concourse, company, crowd, rout, throng, congregation, gathering, mustering, meeting.

3. Collecting, gathering, congregating, assembling, meeting.

4. Combination, union, conjunction, association.

Assemble, *v. t.* Collect, muster, convene, convoke, congregate, gather, levy, call, summon, call together, bring together, get together.

——, *v. i.* Convene, congregate, meet, gather, meet together, gather together, come together.

Assembly, *n.* 1. Company, concourse, rout, throng, congregation, gathering, collection, assemblage, meeting.

2. Congress, parliament, legislature, lower house, legislative body, convention, convocation, conclave, synod, diet, meeting, council, conventicle, caucus.

3. Ball, dance, dancing-party.

Assent, *v. i.* Agree (*as to a matter of opinion*), concur, acquiesce, subscribe, yield, yield assent, accede, give consent, fall in, go with the current. See CONSENT.

——, *n.* Consent, agreement, concurrence, acquiescence, allowance, approval, approbation, accord.

Assent to. Consent to, agree to, give assent to, acquiesce in, concur in, approve, accept.

Assert, *v. t.* 1. Affirm, declare, maintain, pronounce, express, say, aver, allege, asseverate, protest, avouch, avow, predicate, lay down.

2. Vindicate, defend, claim, maintain, uphold, put forward, insist upon, press, emphasize, make felt.

Assertion, *n.* 1. Affirmation, declaration, asseveration, protestation, position, statement, word, averment, allegation, predication, remark.

2. Vindication, defence, maintenance, support, pressing, emphasizing, insistence on.

Assertive, *a.* Positive, decided, confident, unconditional, peremptory.

Assertory, *a.* Declarative (*either affirmatively or negatively*), declaratory, maintaining, affirming.

Assess, *v. t.* 1. Tax, charge with one's share, assign one's share to, impose one's share on.

2. Value, appraise, compute, estimate, rate.

3. Fix, assign, determine, impose, levy.

Assessment, *n.* 1. Assessing, valuation.

2. Tax, impost, charge, rate.

Assets, *n. pl.* Property (*particularly as compared with liabilities*), effects, possessions, estate.

Asseverate, *v. t.* Aver, affirm, declare, protest, maintain, avow. See ASSERT.

Assiduity, *n.* Industry, diligence, assiduousness, sedulousness, activity, persever-

ance, persistence, patience, devotedness, devotion, care, carefulness, close application.

Assiduous, *a.* Industrious, sedulous, diligent, indefatigable, active, busy, untiring, unwearied, unremitting, unintermitting, persevering, persistent, constant, patient, devoted, careful, attentive, laborious, studious, zealous, never-tiring, tireless, painstaking.

Assign, *v. t.* 1. Apportion, allot, appoint, appropriate, cast.

2. Fix, specify, determine, designate.

3. Adduce, allege, advance, offer, show, give, present, bring forward.

4. (*Law.*) Transfer, convey, make over.

Assignation, *n.* 1. Designation. See AsSIGNMENT, 2.

2. Guilty appointment, illicit *or* clandestine appointment, appointment for criminal *or* illicit converse.

Assignment, *n.* 1. Appointment, allotment, apportionment.

2. Designation, specification, fixing, determination.

3. Offer, offering, showing, giving, presentation, alleging, adducing.

4. (*Law.*) Transfer, conveyance.

Assimilate, *v. t.* 1. Make like, bring into resemblance.

2. Digest, turn to one's own substance, take into the organism, thoroughly appropriate, absorb into the system, incorporate, make part and parcel of one's being.

Assimilation, *n.* See preceding verb.

Assist, *v. t.* 1. Help, aid, support, befriend, patronize, serve, speed, second, further, promote, abet, back, sustain, subsidize, co-operate with, take part with, give support to, minister to.

2. Succor, relieve, aid, give alms to.

3. Alternate with, relieve, spell.

Assistance, *n.* 1. Help, aid, succor, furtherance, support, patronage, lift, helping hand, good offices.

2. Alms, aid, succor, relief, help, lift.

Assistant, *n.* 1. Coadjutor, helper, aider, co-operator, co-aid, ally, auxiliary, abettor, adjuvant, collaborator.

2. Subordinate, subaltern, aid, clerk, underworker, agent, underling.

Assizes, *n. pl.* Sessions (*of the superior courts in the counties of England*).

Associate, *v. t.* Join, conjoin, unite, connect, combine, affiliate, yoke, couple, link, bring into close relation.

——, *v. i.* Fraternize, sort, consort, mingle, keep company, be in familiar intercourse.

——, *n.* 1. Companion, mate, fellow, familiar, chum, crony, yokefellow, comrade, peer, compeer, consociate, follower, consort.

2. Partner, copartner, coadjutor, confederate, ally. See COLLEAGUE.

Association, *n.* 1. Union, connection, conjunction, combination.

2. Society, fraternity, fellowship, partnership, copartnership, sodality, company, band, corporation, body, guild, firm, house, confederacy, confederation, league, combine, lodge, club, coterie, clique, joint concern.

Assort, *v. t.* Class, classify, rank, group, arrange, distribute, sort.

——, *v. i.* Agree, consort, suit, be adapted, be suitable.

Assorted, *a.* Of various sorts, various, varied, diverse, divers, miscellaneous.

Assortment, *n.* 1. Assorting, arranging, allotment, distribution, arrangement.

2. Class, group, set, batch, lot, parcel, stock, store, collection, pack, package.

3. Variety of sorts, many kinds.

Assuage, *v. t.* Mitigate, moderate, appease, soothe, soften, mollify, pacify, compose, tranquillize, quiet, still, quell, allay, abate, temper, attemper, lessen, qualify, relieve, ease, dull, blunt, lull. See ALLEVIATE.

Assuagement, *n.* Mitigation, pacification, easing, abatement. See preceding verb, and ALLEVIATION.

Assuasive, *a.* Soothing, assuaging, emollient, lenitive, lenient, mitigating, mitigative, mild, moderating, softening, mollifying, pacifying, composing, tranquillizing, quieting, stilling, quelling, allaying, abating, easeful, tempering, relieving, lulling.

Assume, . *v. t.* 1. Take, undertake, take on, take upon one's self, be willing to bear, become responsible for.

2. Affect, feign, counterfeit, simulate, pretend to, put on, sham.

3. Arrogate, usurp, claim unduly, make unjust pretensions to.

4. Beg, suppose, presuppose, postulate, hypothesize, imply, consider as true, take for granted, posit.

Assuming, *a.* 1. Presuming, presumptuous, forward, audacious, bold, "nervy," shameless, frontless, unblushing, brazen, brazen-faced.

2. Lofty, haughty, supercilious, overbearing, overweening, conceited, consequential, self-conceited, self-sufficient. See ARROGANT.

Assumption, *n.* 1. Assuming, taking, taking on, taking up, accepting, becoming responsible for.

2. Assuming, arrogating, usurpation.

3. Presumption, supposition, conjecture, hypothesis, postulate, premise, theory.

4. Haughtiness, loftiness, superciliousness, lordliness, stateliness, conceit, pride, conceitedness, self-conceit, self-importance, vain-glory, insolence, *hauteur.* See ARROGANCE.

Assurance, *n.* 1. Assuredness, security, certainty, conviction, persuasion, pledge of certainty, ground of confidence, surety, certification, warrant.

2. Promise, engagement, pledge, word of honor.

3. Protestation, asseveration, averment, earnest *or* solemn declaration.

4. Intrepidity, courage, confidence, audacity, firmness, self-reliance.

5. Arrogance, boldness, effrontery, brass, "nerve," cocksureness, impudence, impertinence, presumption, face, front.

Assure, *v. t.* 1. Make certain *or* sure, free from doubt *or* uncertainty.

2. Embolden, encourage, enhearten, hearten, make confident.

3. Declare to (*confidently and earnestly*), vouch to, vow to, protest to, aver to, solemnly promise, pledge, guarantee, warrant.

4. (*Law.*) Insure, agree to indemnify for loss, secure against loss.

Assured, *a.* 1. Certain, indubitable, unquestionable.

2. Confident, self-confident, sure, secure, unquestioning, sanguine.

Assuredly, *adv.* Certainly, indubitably, undoubtedly, unquestionably, truly, surely, sure, without doubt.

Astern, *adv.* (*Naut.*) 1. Behind, back.

2. Backward, rearward, abaft, aft.

Asteroid, *n.* Small planet, planetoid.

Asthenia, *n.* Debility, debilitation, prostration, exhaustion, feebleness, weakness, languor, loss of power, loss of strength, atonicity, atony.

Asthenic, *a.* Weak, feeble, debilitated, prostrated, exhausted.

Asthmatic, *a.* Wheezing, wheezy, short-breathed, short-winded.

Astir, *a.* and *adv.* On the move, in motion, stirring, active, alert, roused, excited.

Astonish, *v. t.* Amaze, surprise, startle, astound, confound, stagger, stupefy, daze, stun, dumfounder, overwhelm, astony, strike dumb, strike with wonder, petrify with wonder.

Astonishment, *n.* Amazement, wonder, surprise.

Astraddle, *adv.* Straddle, astride, straddling.

Astral, *a.* Starry, stellar, sidereal, star-like.

Astray, *adv.* Out of the right way, wandering, in error, lost, at fault, on the wrong scent, abroad, confused, dazed, at the end of one's wits, quite confounded, aside of the mark, off the course without the least clew.

Astringent, *a.* Binding, contracting, styptic.

Astute, *a.* Shrewd, penetrating, eagle-eyed, keen, cunning, deep, sagacious, acute, sharp, quick, discerning, ingenious, perspicacious, intelligent, long-headed, keen-sighted, clear-sighted, quick-sighted.

Astuteness, *n.* Shrewdness, penetration, sagacity, perspicacity, discernment, acuteness, sharpness, subtlety, ingenuity, mother-wit, quick parts, long-headedness, keen-sightedness, quick-sightedness, power to fathom wiles.

Asunder, *adv.* and *a.* Apart, into two parts, in two, divided, separated, divergent, discordant.

Asylum, *n.* 1. Sanctuary, shelter, retreat, refuge, place of refuge.

2. Charitable institution, retreat (*for the afflicted*).

AT, *prep.* (*Basic Eng.*)

At all. In any manner, in any degree, in the least degree, in the least, in any case, ever, under any circumstances.

At all events. At any rate, in any case, in the worst case, at least, in any event, whatever be the case, happen what may, come what may, let it be as it will.

At a loss. Puzzled, perplexed, embarrassed, staggered, posed, nonplussed, aground, ashore, stranded, cornered, out, at one's wits' end, hard pressed, hard up, at a stand, in doubt, in difficulty, put to it, put to one's trumps, put to one's shifts, out of one's depth, beyond one's depth, in a quandary, at fault, in a dilemma, not knowing what to do.

At any rate. See AT ALL EVENTS.

At ease. Untroubled, comfortable, free from pain, at rest.

At first. In the beginning, at the commencement, at the outset, at the start.

At hand. Near, nigh, drawing near, approaching, almost come, close by, hard by, close at hand, within reach.

At heart. 1. In principle, in one's true character, in reality, really, at the core, inwardly, at bottom.

2. In esteem, in true regard, held dear, for matter of concern.

Atheistic, *a.* Godless, given to atheism.

Athirst, *a.* 1. Thirsty, dry.

2. Eager, keenly desiring, with fierce desire.

Athlete, *n.* Combatant, champion, trained contestant, gymnast.

Athletic, *a.* 1. Strong, stout, robust, sturdy, brawny, muscular, lusty, sinewy, stalwart, powerful, strapping, Herculean, able-bodied, made of iron.

2. Gymnastic, acrobatic.

Athletics, *n. pl.* Gymnastics, out-door exercises, open-air sports, games of strength, muscular contests.

Athwart, *prep.* Across, over, from one side to the other of.

——, *adv.* 1. Across, crosswise, sidewise, obliquely, awry, askant, askew.

2. Wrong, wrongfully, unseasonably, unsuitably, *malapropos*.

At last. 1. Finally, in the end, in the up-shot.

2. At length, after a long time, after so long a time.

At length. 1. After a long time, after a long while, at last, in the end.

2. In full, to the full extent, *in extenso*, with full detail, with fulness.

3. Along, in one's whole stature, in entire dimensions. [With *stretch* or *lie*, and the like.]

Atmospheric, *a.* Aerial, of the atmosphere.

At odds. Quarrelling, bickering, at variance, disputing, in dispute, at loggerheads.

Atom, *n.* 1. Molecule, monad, ultimate particle (*of any element*), indivisible particle.

2. Corpuscle, scrap, mite, bit, grain, jot, iota, tittle, whit, ace, scintilla.

Atomic,) *a.* 1. Of atoms, referring to
Atomical,) atoms.

2. Small, minute, infinitesimal, inappreciable.

At once. 1. Immediately, directly, forthwith, straightway, without delay.

2. At the same time, together, in one body.

Atone for. Expiate, make expiation for, make amends for, make reparation for, make satisfaction for, do penance for, answer for, pay for.

Atonement, *n.* Expiation, propitiation, satisfaction, reparation, amends, peace-offering, atoning sacrifice.

Atonic, *a.* 1. Marked by atony, asthenic, showing languor *or* exhaustion.

2. Unaccented, without any accentual mark.

3. Aspirate, aspirated, surd, non-sonant, merely breathed.

——, *n.* See preceding adjective.

Atrabilious, *a.* Melancholy, hypochondriacal, hipped, hyppish, dejected, dispirited, depressed, gloomy, sad, sorrowful, blue, desponding, down-cast, down-hearted, chop-fallen, low-spirited, cast down, in the blues, in the dumps, with a long face.

At random. By chance, without choice, without selection, just as it happens, haphazard, as may chance, at hazard.

At rest. 1. Resting, reposing, quiescent, in repose.

2. Untroubled, comfortable, at ease, free from pain.

3. Dead, asleep, in the last sleep, in the bosom of God.

Atrocious, *a.* Infamous, villanous, flagitious, heinous, felonious, flagrant, outrageous, enormous, grievous, nefarious, diabolical, monstrous, infernal, hellish, horrible, black, very wicked, excessively cruel.

Atrocity, *n.* 1. Heinousness, atrociousness, horrible cruelty, enormity, flagrancy, villany, flagitiousness, depravity, wickedness, savagery, ferocity.

2. Atrocious crime, flagitious villany, horror, enormity, act of ferocity.

Atrophy, *n.* Emaciation (*from want of nourishment*), consumption, marasmus, decline, gradual wasting.

At stake. 1. Hazarded, risked, pledged, in danger, at hazard.

2. At risk, in jeopardy, at the caprice of fortune.

Attach, *v. t.* 1. Fasten, tie, join, connect, engraft, cement, affix, fix, append, subjoin, tack, pin, annex, hitch, make fast, set to.

2. Attract, captivate, enamour, endear, charm, win, engage, gain over.

3. (*Law.*) Take, seize, distrain, distress.

Attachment, *n.* 1. Love, liking, regard, affection, friendship, fondness, predilection, devotedness, devotion, adhesion, adherence.

2. Fastening, appending, affixture, etc. See the preceding verb, 1.

3. Adjunct, appurtenance, addition, addendum. See APPENDAGE.

4. (*Law.*) Seizure, distress.

Attack, *v. t.* 1. Assail, assault, storm, encounter, invade, charge, engage, oppugn, tackle, have at, set upon, fly at, run at, make a run at, rush upon, spring upon, have a fling at, have a cut at, bear down upon, make aggression on, ride full tilt against.

2. Impugn, censure, criticise, reflect upon, pass censure on. See under ASSAIL.

——, *n.* Assault, offence, onset, onslaught, charge, thrust, encounter, invasion, aggression, raid, surprisal, descent. See ASSAULT.

Attacker, *n.* Assailer, assailant, assaulter, invader, aggressor.

Attain, *v. t.* 1. Procure (*by effort*), acquire, get, obtain, gain, win, secure, achieve, compass, accomplish, effect.

2. Reach, arrive at, come to, attain to.

Attainable, *a.* Compassable, achievable, practicable, feasible, possible.

Attainment, *n.* 1. Attaining, getting, acquisition, achieving, winning, gaining, accomplishing, securing.

2. Acquirement, accomplishment, erudition, learning, information, enlightenment, wisdom, stock of knowledge, mental resources.

Attaint, *v. t.* Taint, corrupt, stain, disgrace, pollute, cloud with infamy.

Attemper, *v. t.* 1. Temper, moderate, allay, alleviate, soften, mollify, soothe, qualify, appease. See ASSUAGE.

2. Adapt, suit, fit, proportion.

Attempt, *v. t.* 1. Try, essay, make trial *or* experiment of, venture.

2. Undertake, go about, set about, take in hand, endeavor to accomplish.

3. Assail, attack, assault, etc., which see.

——, *v. i.* Try, strive, endeavor, seek, aim, make an attempt, make essay, do one's best, do all that in one lies, strain every nerve, leave no stone unturned.

ATTEMPT, *n.* 1. Effort, trial, essay, endeavor, experiment, undertaking, enterprise, venture.

2. Attack, assault, onset.

Attend, *v. t.* 1. Accompany, escort, follow, go with, go along with, keep company with.

2. Guard, watch, protect, have in keeping.

3. Serve, minister to, wait on, dance attendance on, lackey.

4. Be present at, frequent.

——, *v. i.* 1. Listen, hearken, hear, give ear, give heed, pay attention.

2. Tend, serve, wait, be attendant.

Attendance, *n.* 1. Presence, being there, going to.

2. Number present, attendants, persons attending, persons present.

3. Persons attending *or* ministering, train, retinue.

4. Service, ministration, waiting on.

Attendant, *a.* 1. Accompanying, attending, concomitant, following, consequent.

2. Ministrant, ministrative.

——, *n.* 1. Follower, satellite, companion, fellow, associate, escort, attender.

2. Attender, frequenter, person present.

3. Servant, vassal, servitor, dependant, retainer, squire, page, acolyte, domestic, footman, lackey, valet, waiter, flunky, underling, menial, orderly, understrapper, tender.

4. Accompaniment, concomitant, attendant circumstance, consequence.

Attend on. Accompany, serve, wait on, be in waiting upon, be within call of.

Attend to. 1. Mind, heed, notice, regard, observe, mark, be attentive to, pay regard to, give heed to, take heed of, take notice of, give or pay attention to, give a thought to, be mindful of.

2. Look after, look to, see to, oversee, overlook, superintend, supervise, take care of, provide for.

3. Practise, pursue, follow.

ATTENTION, *n.* 1. Care, heed, regard, heedfulness, mindfulness, notice, observation, observance, consideration, advertence, circumspection, watch, watchfulness, alertness.

2. Application, reflection, study.

3. Civility, courtesy, politeness, deference, respect, regard.

4. [Esp. in *pl.*] Court, courtship, suit, *devoirs*, devotion, addresses, wooing.

Attentive, *a.* 1. Mindful, heedful, observant, careful, thoughtful, regardful, considerate, awake, alive, alert, wide awake, on the alert, on the lookout, wary, circumspect, watchful.

2. Sedulous, assiduous, studious, diligent, careful, respectful, deferential.

Attenuate, *v. t.* Thin, rarefy, make thin, make rare, make slender, slim, or spare, render thread-like, draw out, lessen, diminish, reduce.

Attenuation, *n.* 1. Thinning, diminishing, rarefying, making thin, thread-like, or slender, fine-drawing.

2. Thinness, thread-likeness, slenderness, emaciation, slender elongation, extreme slenderness.

Attest, *v. t.* 1. Witness, certify, indorse, confirm, ratify, corroborate, support, authenticate, seal, vouch for, bear out, set one's hand and seal to, bear witness to.

2. Adjure, invoke, call to witness.

3. Prove, show, exhibit, manifest, display, confess, give evidence or signs of.

Attestation, *n.* Attesting, authentication, confirmation, testimony, witness, proof, evidence, voucher, seal.

Attic, *a.* 1. Of Attica, of Athens, Athenian.

2. Chaste, classic, classical, pure, correct, refined, elegant, polished, in good taste.

3. Pointed, delicate, subtle, penetrating, pungent.

——, *n.* Garret, loft, cockloft, upper story.

Atticism, *n.* Attic idiom or phrase, elegant or concise expression, happy phrase.

Attire, *v. t.* Dress, clothe, array, apparel, rig, robe, enrobe, accoutre, equip, fit out, trick out. See APPAREL, *v.*

——, *n.* Dress, clothes, clothing, apparel, raiment, habit, garb, gear, costume, habiliment, vesture, vestment, outfit, suit, accoutrement, equipment, toilet, rigging, trappings, wardrobe. See APPAREL, *n.*

Attitude, *n.* 1. Posture (*with reference to the expression of some sentiment*), position, pose.

2. Situation, aspect, phase, standing, state, condition, posture, position, predicament, conjuncture, juncture.

3. Disposition of mind, state of feeling, mind set.

Attitudinize, *v. i.* Pose affectedly, strike attitudes.

Attorney, *n.* 1. Agent, factor, proxy, deputy, substitute.

2. [*U. S.*] Attorney-at-law, lawyer, counsellor, counsel, solicitor, advocate, member of the bar, limb of the law.

Attract, *v. t.* 1. Draw, pull, bring into proximity, cause to approach.

2. Allure, invite, entice, tempt, decoy, engage, win, captivate, fascinate, endear, charm, enamour.

ATTRACTION, *n.* 1. Attracting, drawing, affinity, pull.

2. Allurement, lure, charm, fascination, enticement, witchery, magnetism, seduction, attractiveness.

3. [In *pl.*] Attractive qualities, charms, graces.

Attractive, *a.* 1. Alluring, inviting, enticing, seductive, fascinating, captivating, charming, winning, winsome, bewitching, enchanting, engaging, interesting, prepossessing, taking, pleasing, pleasant, lovely, sweet.

2. Magnetic, magnetical.

Attributable, *a.* 1. Ascribable, imputable, referrible, chargeable, traceable, owing, due, to be charged, to be attributed, to be imputed.

2. Predicable, ascribable, belonging, adhering, inhering or inherent (in), true (of).

Attribute, *v. t.* Ascribe, assign, refer, impute, consider as due.

——, *n.* Quality, property, characteristic, peculiarity, mark, note, predicate.

Attrition, *n.* Abrasion, friction, rubbing, wearing away, rubbing away.

Attune, *v. t.* 1. Tune, accord, harmonize, modulate, put in tune.

2. Bring into accord *or* agreement, harmonize, adjust, adapt, attemper, accommodate.

Auburn, *a.* Nut-brown, chestnut-colored, reddish-brown.

Auction, *n.* Vendue, cant (*chiefly Irish*), public sale, auction sale.

Audacious, *a.* 1. Bold, daring, fearless, courageous, intrepid, venturesome, dauntless, undaunted, valiant, stout-hearted.

2. Presumptuous, assuming, forward, impudent, insolent, shameless, unabashed, brazen, impertinent, full of effrontery.

Audacity, *n.* 1. Boldness, daring, fearlessness, courage, intrepidity, venturesomeness, hardihood.

2. Impudence, insolence, effrontery, presumptuousness, presumption, assurance, face, front, brass, impertinence, sauciness.

Audience, *n.* 1. Hearing, formal reception.

2. Auditory, assembly of hearers, congregation, assemblage, gallery.

Audit, *v. t.* Examine (*as accounts, to ascertain whether they are correct or not*).

——, *n.* 1. Examination of accounts.

2. Final account.

Auditor, *n.* 1. Hearer, listener.

2. Examiner of accounts.

Au fait. [Fr.] Skilful, skilled, expert, at home, in one's element.

Augment, *v. t.* Enlarge, increase, swell, magnify, add to, make larger.

——, *v. i.* Increase, grow larger.

Augmentation, *n.* Increase, enlargement, extension, addition, accession.

Augur, *n.* Soothsayer, seer, prophet, fortune-teller.

——, *v. i.* 1. Prophesy, conjecture, predict, guess.

2. Portend, prognosticate, give token.

——, *v. t.* Portend, forebode, presage, foreshow, foreshadow, prognosticate, betoken, signify, foretell, predict, prophesy, be ominous of.

Augury, *n.* 1. Prognostication, soothsaying, prediction, prophecy, vaticination.

2. Omen, sign, auspice, portent, presage, prognostic, precursor, forerunner, harbinger, herald.

August, *a.* Imposing, awful, awe-inspiring, solemn, venerable, majestic, stately, grand, regal, kingly, noble, dignified, princely.

Aura, *n.* Effluence, exhalation, expiration, effluvium, aroma, odor.

Aureate, *a.* Golden, yellow, gold-colored.

Aureola, *n.* [L.] Halo, glory, aureole, effulgence, irradiance.

Aurora, *n.* 1. (*Mythol.*) Goddess of Morning.

2. Daybreak, dawn, morning, sunrise, break of day, opening of day, peep of day, first blush of the morning. See MORN.

Auspice, *n.* Omen, augury, sign, portent, presage, prognostic.

Auspices, *n. pl.* Favor, influence, patronage, protection, support, benign *or* favoring influences.

Auspicious, *a.* 1. Prosperous, successful, fortunate, lucky, happy, red-letter.

2. Propitious, promising, favorable, seasonable, opportune, golden, bright, "rosy."

Austere, *a.* Severe, rigid, strict, formal, rigorous, harsh, stern, difficult, hard, uncompromising, unrelenting, relentless, ascetic, straight-laced, stiff.

Austerity, *n.* Severity, rigor, sternness, harshness, asceticism, rigidity, rigidness, strictness, formality, stiffness, inflexibility.

Authentic, *a.* 1. Genuine, real, true, veritable, pure, uncorrupted, unadulterated, not false, not spurious, not fictitious, not apocryphal, what it purports to be.

2. Trustworthy, reliable, authoritative, veritable, true, accurate, according to the facts, accordant with fact, not garbled, not tampered with, from competent and trustworthy sources, from the original data, of approved authority, to be depended on, worthy of belief.

Authenticate, *v. t.* Verify, certify, avouch, countersign, seal, attest, give credit *or* validity to, prove to be genuine.

Authentication, *n.* Verification, attestation, seal, confirmation.

Authenticity, *n.* 1. Genuineness.

2. Trustworthiness. See AUTHENTIC, 1 and 2.

Author, *n.* 1. Originator, first cause, original, maker, creator, father, former, contriver, inventor.

2. Writer, composer.

Authoritative, *a.* 1. Official, commanding, imperative, by authority, *ex cathedra*.

2. Standard, orthodox, canonical, valid.

3. Dictatorial, imperious, magisterial, oracular, peremptory, dogmatic. See ARROGANT.

Authorities, *n. pl.* 1. Magistrates, rulers, the government, officials, persons in office, "powers that be."

2. Precedents, decisions, judgments.

3. Persons cited as vouchers, commanding scholars *or* men of science.

AUTHORITY, *n.* 1. Power, sovereignty, dominion, jurisdiction, empire, government.

2. Rule, sway, ascendency, supremacy, control, influence, interest.

3. Permission, warrant, warranty, liberty, permit, precept, order, authorization, sanction.

4. Witness, testimony.

5. Credibility, weight of evidence or commanding attestation.

6. Respectability, dignity, weight of character.

7. Person of commanding knowledge, leading expert, connoisseur, master, master-mind.

Authorize, *v. t.* 1. Sanction, justify, warrant, legalize, support by authority.

2. Empower, commission, permit, allow, license, enable, give permission to, give leave to, give authority to.

Autochthonous, *a.* Original, primitive, primeval, pristine, primary, first, native, indigenous. See ABORIGINAL.

Autocracy, *n.* Dictatorship, absolutism, czarism, despotism, absolute monarchy, arbitrary power.

Autocrat, *n.* Dictator, despot, czar, unlimited monarch, absolute ruler.

Autocratic, *a.* 1. Absolute, despotic, unlimited.

2. Tyrannous, tyrannical, oppressive, overbearing, disdainful, magisterial. See ARBITRARY, ARROGANT.

AUTOMATIC, *a.* 1. Self-moving, self-acting, self-regulating.

2. Reflex, mechanical.

Autonomy, *n.* Self-government, independence, self-legislation.

Autopsy, *n.* Post-mortem examination, *post-mortem.*

Autumn, *n.* Fall, fall of the year, fall of the leaf, harvest-time.

Auxiliary, *a.* Aiding, helping, assisting, ancillary, subsidiary, helpful, subserving.

——, *n.* Helper, assistant, coadjutor, adjuvant, co-operative, ally, confederate. See ACCESSORY.

Avail, *v. t.* Benefit, profit, be of advantage to.

——, *v. i.* Be of advantage, do good, be of use, answer the purpose.

——, *n.* Profit, advantage, benefit, use, utility, service.

Available, *a.* 1. To be availed of, to be turned to account.

2. Serviceable, useful, profitable, advantageous, beneficial.

3. Suitable *or* fit (*for some purpose*), likely to answer the end.

Avail one's self of. Use, employ, take advantage of, turn to account, make use of.

Avails, *n. pl.* Proceeds, profits, returns.

Avarice, *n.* Cupidity, covetousness, sordidness, graspingness.

Avaricious, *a.* Grasping, greedy (of gain), sordid, close, close-fisted, hard-fisted, eager for gain (*for the sake of hoarding it*). See COVETOUS.

Avast, *interj.* (*Naut.*) Hold, stop, stay, enough.

Avaunt, *interj.* Hence, begone, away, be off, get you gone.

Avenge, *v. t.* 1. Take satisfaction for, award just punishment for.

2. Revenge, vindicate (*by punishment of an offender*), inflict punishment in behalf of.

——, *v. i.* Take vengeance, retaliate.

Avenue, *n.* 1. Passage, entrance, entry, access, way of approach, passage-way. See under ACCESS.

2. Alley, walk, street, road, path.

3. Channel, route, way, pass.

Aver, *v. t.* Assert, declare, asseverate, protest, avouch, allege, say, pronounce, predicate. See AFFIRM.

Average, *n.* 1. Medium, mean proportion, medial sum *or* quantity.

2. Mediocrity, medium grade, mean standard, "the run."

——, *v. t.* 1. Equate, reduce to an average, reduce to a mean.

2. (*Com.*) Proportion, distribute proportionally.

——, *v. i.* Amount to, *or* result in (*when the mean is taken*).

—— *a.* 1. Medial, medium, mean.

2. Middling, ordinary, passable, moderate, tolerable, well enough, pretty well, not bad.

Averment, *n.* Affirmation, declaration, assertion, remark, asseveration, protestation, avowal. See AVER.

Averse, *a.* Unwilling, disinclined, indisposed, reluctant, loath, backward, adverse, opposed.

Aversion, *n.* 1. Dislike, distaste, disrelish, disinclination, reluctance, unwillingness, repugnance.

2. Antipathy, hatred, loathing, disgust, detestation, abhorrence, horror, repulsion.

Avert, *v. t.* 1. Turn aside, turn away, turn off.

2. Prevent, divert, preclude, ward off, parry, keep off. See FOREFEND.

Avid, *a.* Eager, greedy.

Avidity, *n.* 1. Eagerness, longing, yearning, intense desire.

2. Greediness, craving, voracity, voraciousness, rapacity, ravenousness, canine appetite.

Avocation, *n.* 1. Vocation, calling, business, occupation, trade, employment.

2. Occasional business (*business that calls aside*), distraction, hindrance, interruption, by-business, by-concernment.

Avoid, *v. t.* 1. Shun (*in a negative sense, or denoting care only without positive exertion*), eschew, escape, elude, keep away from, dodge, keep aloof from, keep out of the way of, withdraw from, keep clear of, fight shy of, have nothing to do with.

2. Forbear, refrain from, help (after *cannot*).

Avouch, *v. t.* Assert, asseverate, declare, protest, allege, say, maintain. See AFFIRM.

Avow, *v. t.* 1. Acknowledge, confess, own, admit.

2. Declare. See AFFIRM.

Avowal, *n.* Acknowledgment, confession, declaration, profession.

Avowedly, *adv.* Confessedly, as freely acknowledged.

Await, *v. t.* 1. Expect, abide, wait for, stay for, look for, be in readiness for.

2. Attend, be in store for, be prepared for, be ready for.

AWAKE, *a.* 1. Not asleep.

2. Attentive, watchful, vigilant, alive, on the alert.

Awaken, *v. t.* 1. Awake, wake, rouse from sleep.

2. Arouse, excite, kindle, spur, incite, stimulate, provoke, stir up.

——, *v. i.* 1. Wake, waken, be awakened, be roused from sleep.

2. Begin, become active, be aroused, be excited, return to life, come to life.

Awakening, *n.* 1. Waking, awaking, coming out of sleep.

2. Arousing, kindling, quickening, coming to life, revival.

Award, *v. t.* Adjudge, decree, assign, allot, grant, bestow.

——, *n.* Judgment, decree, adjudication, determination, decision, assignment, allotment, bestowal, gift.

Aware, *a.* Mindful, conscious, cognizant, observant, apprised, sensible, percipient, convinced, persuaded.

Away, *adv.* 1. Absent, gone, off, from home, at a distance, not present.

2. Begone, let us go. See AVAUNT.

Awe, *n.* 1. Reverence, veneration, reverential fear, abashment.

2. Dread, fearfulness, terror, fear.

3. Solemn exaltation, admiring solemnity, adoring wonder.

——, *v. t.* Inspire with awe, overawe, intimidate, daunt, cow. See AFFRIGHT.

Aweless, *a.* 1. Destitute of awe, irreverent, unrevering.

2. Inspiring no awe, unsolemn, unvenerable, unimposing, unmajestic, unstately.

Awe-struck, *a.* 1. Awed, inspired with awe, solemnized, solemn, reverent, revering, filled with solemn exaltation.

2. Dismayed, abashed, horrified, appalled, terrified, frightened, awestricken, horror-struck, overwhelmed.

Awful, *a.* 1. Dread, awe-inspiring, awesome, reverend, venerable, august, grand, stately, imposing, solemn, majestic.

2. Dreadful, fearful, horrible, horrid, horrifying, terrible, dire, direful, frightful, appalling, tremendous, overwhelming, alarming, portentous.

Awhile, *adv.* For a time, for some time, some time, for a while.

Awkward, *a.* 1. Unskilful, bungling, unhandy, maladroit, inapt, inept, clumsy, without dexterity.

2. Unwieldy, lumbering, unmanageable, inconvenient, unfit.

3. Uncouth, unrefined, unpolished, uncourtly, *gauche*, rude, rough, clumsy, coarse, wooden, inelegant, ungainly, untoward, ungraceful, stiff, constrained, uneasy, rustic, boorish, clownish, loutish, gawky, lubberly, slouching.

Awning, *n.* Canopy, tilt, baldachino, baldaquin.

Awry, *adv.* 1. Obliquely, asquint. See ASKANCE.

2. Perversely, wrong. See ATHWART, 2.

——, *a.* Oblique, slanting, distorted, wry, crooked. See ASKANT and ATHWART.

Axiom, *n.* 1. Truism, self-evident proposition, intuitive truth, necessary truth.

2. Postulate, settled principle (*not of necessity true*), proposition commonly received, assumed truth.

Axiomatic, *a.* Self-evident, certain, positive, absolute, necessary, apodictic, *a priori*.

Axis, *n.* 1. Shaft, spindle, arbor.

2. Central line, line of symmetry, line of rotation, line of revolution.

Ay, *adv.* (*Poetical.*) Always, forever, evermore, continually, ceaselessly, unendingly, changelessly, unchangingly, immutably.

Azure, *a.* Blue, cerulean, sky-colored, sky-blue.

——, *n.* 1. Blue, sky-color, cerulean.

2. (With *The* prefixed.) The sky, heaven, welkin, empyrean, arch *or* expanse of heaven, blue expanse, expanse, depths of space, the cerulean vault.

B

Babble, *v. i.* 1. Prattle, jabber, blather, chatter, gibber, talk inarticulately.

2. Prate, chat, gossip, palaver, tattle, be loquacious, talk idly *or* thoughtlessly. See PRATE.

3. Tell secrets, tattle, blab, let the cat out of the bag.

——, *v. t.* 1. Tell (*foolishly*), prate, utter, prate about.

2. Blab, let out, blab about (*hither and thither*).

——, *n.* Prattle, palaver, chit-chat, gabble, twaddle, chatter, patter, balderdash, platitude, flummery, fustian, wish-wash, stuff, drivel, blather, moonshine, fudge, trash, nonsense, gibberish, gibble-gabble, small talk, idle talk, childish *or* foolish talk, frothy discourse. See PRATTLE, *n.*

Babbling, *n.* 1. Prattle. See BABBLE.

2. Garrulity, loquacity, loquaciousness, talkativeness.

Babel, *n.* Confusion, disorder, tumult, din, discord, jargon, clamor, hubbub, pother, hurly-burly.

BABY, *n.* Babe, infant, baby, nursling, suckling, chit, brat, bantling (*bairn*), little one.

Babyhood, *n.* Infancy, babehood.

Babyish, *a.* Infantile.

Bacchanal, *n.* 1. Reveller, carouser, bacchanalian, roysterer, debauchee, bacchant, maenad.

2. [*pl.*] Revelry, revels, orgies, carousal, debauch, drunken frolic, potation, compotation, wassail, Saturnalia, drunken feasts.

——, *a.* Riotous, revelling, noisy, bacchanalian.

BACK, *n.* Hinder part, posterior portion, rear, end.

——, *a.* 1. Remote, on the frontier, away from the thicker settlements.

2. Hindmost, in the rear.

——, *adv.* 1. To the place of starting.

2. Backward, rearward, abaft, in the rear, toward what is behind.

3. Again, in return, in recompense.

——, *v. t.* 1. Aid, second, support, countenance, favor, sustain, abet, side with, stand by, take part with, give support to, co-operate with, back up. See ASSIST.

2. Move backward, push backward, cause to go backward.

——, *v. i.* Move *or* go backward, retire, retreat, resile, withdraw, draw back.

Backbite, *v. t.* Defame, traduce, malign, slander, revile, calumniate, libel, asperse, vilify, blacken, abuse, scandalize, speak ill of.

Backbiter, *n.* Slanderer, defamer, traducer, calumniator, libeller, maligner, reviler, vilifier, detractor.

Backbiting, *n.* Detraction, defamation, aspersion, slander, calumny, contumely, abuse, obloquy.

Backbone, *n.* 1. Spine, spinal column, vertebral column, chine.

2. Firmness, nerve, resolution, courage, pluck, hardihood, constancy, steadfastness, stability, decision, moral determination, stamina.

Backhanded, *a.* 1. Inclining to the left hand (*as writing*), sloping backward.

2. Outward and backward (*as a stroke*), with the back of the hand.

3. Indirect, unfair, unfavorable, backhand.

Back out. (*Colloq.*) Withdraw from a bargain, not keep a promise, not stand to an engagement, retract, retreat, withdraw, resile, renege.

Backslide, *v. i.* Apostatize, tergiversate, fall off, fall away, break faith.

Backslider, *n.* Apostate, deserter, renegade.

Backsliding, *n.* Apostasy.

Back up. Support, sustain. See BACK, *v. t.*

Backward, *a.* 1. Unwilling, reluctant, loath, disinclined, indisposed, wavering, hesitating. See AVERSE.

2. Dull, sluggish, slow, stupid, stolid. See DULL.

3. Regressive, retrograde, reversionary.

Backward, } *adv.* Regressively, rearward,
Backwards, } aback, behind. See ABAFT.

BAD, *a.* 1. Evil, ill, baneful, baleful, deleterious, pernicious, mischievous, noxious, harmful, hurtful, injurious, detrimental, unwholesome.

2. Wicked, depraved, abandoned, corrupt, unprincipled, immoral, sinful, dishonest, unfair, disingenuous, rascally, naughty, villanous.

3. Unlucky, unfortunate, unhappy, miserable.

4. Unwelcome, sad, saddening, disappointing, untoward, depressing, discouraging, distressing.

5. Vile, wretched, sorry, mean, shabby, scurvy, abominable.

6. Poor, inferior, imperfect, defective, incompetent, ill-qualified, unsuitable.

7. Serious, severe, hard, heavy.

Bad blood. Ill-will, malice, hatred, hate, venom.

Bad faith. Perfidy, perfidiousness, traitorousness, dishonesty, unfairness, faithlessness, lack of fidelity, want of good faith, breach of faith, Punic faith, *fides punica*.

Badge, *n.* 1. Token of office, shield of office, official star *or* emblem.

2. Emblem of membership, cognizance, device.

3. Emblem (*of anything*), sign, symbol, mark, token, stamp, brand.

Badger, *v. t.* Persecute, tease, worry, harry, bait, annoy, vex, plague, harass, torment, pester, trouble, bother, hector.

Badinage, *n.* [Fr.] Raillery, banter, asteism, *persiflage*, light talk, small talk, trifling *or* playful discourse.

Baffle, *v. t.* 1. Frustrate, foil, balk, block, thwart, defeat, mar, upset, check, neutralize, checkmate, undermine, circumvent.

2. Confound, bewilder, perplex, disconcert, out-general, out-manœuvre.

BAG, *n.* Sack, pouch, "poke," wallet, reticule, "scrip."

Bagatelle, *n.* [Fr.] Trifle, small matter, thing of no consequence or importance.

Baggage, *n.* Luggage, personal effects, travelling effects, traps, impedimenta.

Bagnio, *n.* 1. Bath, bathing-house.

2. Brothel, stew, bawdy-house, house of prostitution, house of ill-fame.

Bail, *n.* Security, surety.

Bailiff, *n.* 1. Deputy-sheriff, deputy-marshal, deputy-constable, "catchpoll."

2. Overseer, under-steward, factor, manager, supervisor.

Bait, *v. t.* Worry, harry. See BADGER, *v.*

——, *n.* Lure, decoy, allurement, enticement, temptation.

Bake, *v. t.* 1. Harden (*by heat*), dry up, parch, stiffen.

2. Cook (*in the oven*).

BALANCE, *n.* 1. Pair of scales.

2. Equipoise, equilibrium, libration, equiponderance, equality of weight.

3. Comparison, comparative estimate, weighing.

4. Excess, overplus, surplus, residue, remainder. (*Used of accounts.*)

5. Counterpoise, counterweight, makeweight, equalizing agency, equalizer.

6. Moral *or* mental equilibrium, equipoise, poise, self-control, self-possession, all-sidedness, good proportion.

——, *v. t.* 1. Poise, keep in equipoise, equilibrate, trim (*naut.*), hold in equilibrium.

2. Weigh (*mentally*), compare, estimate comparatively.

3. Counterpoise, counteract, neutralize, countervail, counterbalance, compensate, make up for.

4. (*Com.*) Equalize, make equal, square, adjust, clear.

——, *v. i.* 1. Be in equipoise *or* equilibrium, counterpoise each other, neutralize each other.

2. Cast accounts, keep accounts, reckon, make balances.

Bald, *a.* 1. Without hair (*on the head*), hairless, depilated, glabrous, destitute of hair.

2. Bare, treeless, verdureless, uncovered, unsheltered, naked.

3. Unadorned, inelegant, prosaic, dull, meagre, vapid, tame.

4. Literal, unabated, unmitigated, undisguised, unvarnished, naked, bare.

5. Unsupported, bare, mere, uncorroborated, glaring.

Balderdash, *n.* Verbiage, rodomontade, gasconade, rant, bombast, fustian, froth, palaver, twaddle, chatter, trash, stuff, bosh, platitude, flummery, fudge, senselessness, jargon, nonsense, prate, prating, jabber, gibberish, gibble-gabble, gabble, drivel, frothy discourse, idle talk.

Baldric, *n.* Shoulder-belt, bawdrick.

Bale, *n.* 1. Bundle, package.

2. Harm, injury, hurt, bane, ruin, mischief, calamity, misery.

Baleful, *a.* Hurtful, injurious, noxious, mischievous, pernicious, calamitous, baneful, ruinous, deadly, fraught with evil, sinister.

Balk, *v. t.* Disappoint, frustrate, defeat, foil, baffle, disconcert, thwart.

Balky, *a.* Perverse (*said of a horse*), unruly, refractory, wayward, contrary, stubborn, obstinate.

BALL, *n.* 1. Globe, sphere, orb, round body, globule, pellet, "sphericle," drop, marble, round *or* rounded part.

2. Missile (*of fire arms*), bullet, shot, projectile.

3. Dance, entertainment of dancing, assembly, dancing-party.

Ballast, *n.* 1. Weight (*for steadiness*), ballasting, filling, packing.

2. Steadiness, consistency, stability, equipoise, balance, self-control, prudence, discretion, judgment, good sense, sound sense.

Ballooning, *n.* Aeronautics, aerostation, balloonery.

Balloonist, *n.* Aeronaut, aerial navigator.

Ballot, *n.* 1. Voting-ticket, ticket, voting-ball.

2. Vote, total vote, number of voters, votes cast.

Ballot, *v. i.* Vote, cast votes, take a vote, take a ballot.

Balm, *n.* 1. Ointment, fragrant *or* precious ointment, unguent.

2. Healing, soothing, mitigant, assuager, anodyne, cure.

Balmy, *a.* 1. Soothing, refreshing, healing, easing, assuaging, lenitive, sedative.

2. Fragrant, odoriferous, odorous, aromatic, aromatous, ambrosial, spicy, sweet-smelling, sweet-scented, sweet.

Bamboozle, *v. t.* Deceive, cheat, dupe, beguile, mislead, inveigle, gull, trick, chouse, overreach, circumvent, defraud, mystify, hoax, impose on, practise upon, mislead.

Ban, *n.* 1. Proclamation, edict.

2. Curse, malediction, excommunication, denunciation, execration, anathema.

3. Interdiction, interdict, prohibition, outlawry, prohibitory penalty.

——, *v. t.* 1. Curse, execrate, anathematize, maledict.

2. Interdict, imban, outlaw, put under ban *or* prohibition.

BAND, *n.* 1. Tie, ligature, ligament.

2. Cord, chain, fetter, manacle, gyve, shackle, trammel, bond.

3. Bandage, fillet, binding, tourniquet, cincture, girth, belt.

4. Company (*especially of instrumental musicians*), troop, gang, crew, horde, party, body, cohort, club, junto, coterie, clique, society, sodality, association.

Bandage, *n.* Fillet, band, binding, cincture, belt.

Bandit, *n.* Outlaw, robber, brigand, freebooter, footpad, highwayman, marauder, gangster.

Bandy, *v. t.* Toss, toss about, toss to and fro, agitate, dispute about, interchange (*words, names, etc.*).

——, *a.* Crooked, bent, bow-(*legged*).

Bane, *n.* 1. Poison, venom.

2. Pest, scourge, curse, ruin, destruction, harm, injury. See BALE.

Baneful, *a.* 1. Poisonous, venomous.

2. Destructive, noxious, hurtful, injurious, pernicious, mischievous, deadly, ruinous, fraught with evil. See BALEFUL.

Bang, *v. t.* 1. Beat, thump, pound, strike, knock, maul, pommel, thrash, cudgel, thwack, handle roughly, deal roughly with.

2. Slam, shut with a bang.

——, *v. i.* Ring, rattle, resound, re-echo, clatter.

——, *n.* 1. Clang, clangor, whang.

2. Blow, thump, whack, thwack, lick, knock.

Banish, *v. t.* 1. Exile, expatriate, ostracize, expel from the country.

2. Exclude, expel, dismiss, dispel, shut out, drive away, put out of mind.

Banishment, *n.* Exile, expatriation, ostracism, expulsion, proscription.

Bank, *n.* 1. Mound, knoll, rising ground, ridge, heap, pile, tumulus, dike, embankment, escarpment.

2. Shore, brim, brink, margin, marge, levee, border, bound, rim, rivage, strand.

3. Shoal, shallow, bar, sandbank, syrtis.

4. Row, tier, course.

——, *v. t.* 1. Embank, dike, surround with a bank.

2. Deposit (*in the bank*), lay up, put in the bank.

Bankrupt, *a.* Insolvent, "broke."

——, *n.* Insolvent debtor.

Bankruptcy, *n.* Insolvency.

Banner, *n.* Flag, standard, streamer, ensign, gonfalon, oriflamme, pennon, colors.

Banquet, *n.* Feast, entertainment, regalement, treat.

——, *v. i.* Feast, be regaled with good eating and drinking.

——, *v. t.* Treat with a banquet *or* feast, regale, entertain festally, feast.

Banter, *v. t.* Jeer, joke, rally, quiz, chaff, "jolly," ridicule, twit, deride, mock, make fun of, make sport of, make merry with, play upon, make a butt of.

——, *n.* Raillery, ridicule, mockery, derision, *persiflage,* pleasantry, *badinage,* asteism, joking, jesting, quizzing, chaff.

Bantling, *n.* Infant, babe, baby, chit, brat, nursling, suckling, *bairn,* little child, little one, young one.

Baptize, *v. t.* 1. Administer baptism to.

2. Christen.

Bar, *n.* 1. Rod, pole, grating, cross-piece, rail, railing.

2. Obstacle, hindrance, obstruction, barrier, barricade, stop, estoppel, impediment.

3. Tribunal, judgment-seat.

4. Shoal, sand-bank, shallow, bank, sandbar, spit.

——, *v. t.* 1. Fasten with a bar.

2. Hinder, obstruct, stop, prevent, prohibit, restrain.

3. Exclude, shut out.

Barb, *n.* 1. Beard (or *excrescences like a beard*), wattles.

2. Guard (*of a hook, etc.*), beard, point, guarded *or* bearded point.

——, *v. t.* Point, fit with barbs, beard.

Barbarian, *n.* 1. Savage.

2. Brute, ruffian, brutal monster.

——, *a.* 1. Uncivilized, rude, savage, barbarous, barbaric.

2. Inhuman, brutal, cruel, unfeeling,

ruthless, truculent, ferocious, fierce, fell, bloody, brutish. See BARBAROUS.

Barbaric, *a.* 1. Barbarian, barbarous, uncivilized, rude, savage, untamed.

2. Gaudy, uncouth, coarse, coarsely showy, outlandish, unrefined, wild, untamed, unregulated, capricious, riotous, coarsely luxuriant.

Barbarism, *n.* 1. Savagism, savage state, savagery, barbarous state, uncivilized condition.

2. Rudeness, roughness, brutality, savageness, harshness, destructiveness, vandalism.

3. Solecism, impropriety.

4. Atrocity, outrage, act of cruelty *or* barbarity, brutality.

Barbarity, *n.* Cruelty, savageness, barbarousness, brutality, brutishness, ferociousness, ferocity, inhumanity, truculence, hardness of heart.

Barbarous, *a.* 1. Uncivilized, rough, coarse, rude, untutored, ignorant, unlettered, uncultivated, untamed, savage, barbarian, barbaric, Gothic, Hunnish.

2. Cruel, inhuman, brutal, brutish, unfeeling, ferocious, ruthless, fell, truculent, fierce, bloody, savage.

3. Uncouth (*as a word* or *an expression*), harsh, rugged, vulgar, contrary to good usage.

Barbed, *a.* 1. Bearded.

2. Clad in armor (*said of horses*), mailed, in barbes, furnished with barbes.

Barber, *n.* Tonsor.

Bard, *n.* Harper, minstrel, poet.

Bare, *a.* 1. Naked, nude, denuded, uncovered, unclothed, undressed, exposed, stripped, unprotected, unsheltered, unshielded.

2. Simple, sheer, mere, alone.

3. Unadorned, bald, plain, undecorated, unfurnished, meagre.

4. Poor, destitute, indigent, ill-supplied, empty.

——, *v. t.* Strip, uncover, make bare, unsheathe, denude, depilate. See preceding adjective.

Barebacked, *a.* Unsaddled.

Barefaced, *a.* 1. Undisguised, unreserved, unconcealed, palpable, conspicuous, glaring, notable, notorious.

2. Impudent, presumptuous, brazen, shameless, audacious.

Barely, *adv.* 1. Poorly, meagrely, slenderly, meanly.

2. Merely, simply, only, just, hardly.

Bargain, *n.* 1. Compact, agreement, stipulation, covenant, contract, convention, concordat, treaty, indenture, transaction.

2. Purchase, getting, proceeds, result.

3. Cheap purchase, purchase on favorable terms, good bargain.

——, *v. i.* Contract, agree, stipulate, covenant, make a bargain.

——; *v. t.* Sell, transfer, convey. [With *away*.]

Barge, *n.* 1. Vessel of state, pleasure-boat, barque.

2. Boat of burden, transport.

Bark, *v. i.* Yelp, bay.

Bark at. Clamor at, decry, cry down, carp at, asperse. See ASPERSE.

Barren, *a.* 1. Unprolific, sterile, childless, infecund, incapable of bearing offspring.

2. Destitute of fruit, sterile, acarpous.

3. Infertile, unproductive, sterile, poor, bare.

4. Ineffectual, uninstructive, unsuggestive, infecund, leading to nothing, unproductive, unfruitful.

Barricade, *n.* Obstruction (*as in the streets of a city to serve as a fortification*). See BARRIER.

——, *v. t.* Obstruct, block up, stop up, fortify hastily.

Barrier, *n.* Obstruction, obstacle, hindrance, bar, barricade, stop, impediment.

Barrister, *n.* Advocate (*admitted to plead at the bar*), counsellor, counsel, lawyer, attorney at law, limb of the law, member of the bar.

Barrow, *n.* 1. Wheelbarrow, handbarrow.

2. Mound, hillock.

3. Hog (*especially a castrated hog*).

Barter, *v. i.* Make exchanges, traffic by exchanges, traffic, trade, bargain.

——, *v. t.* Give in exchange, barter away, bargain away, traffic away, trade off, "swap."

——, *n.* Exchange, traffic by exchange.

Base, *a.* 1. Inferior, of little or no worth, cheap, worthless.

2. Debased, spurious, counterfeit, false.

3. Plebeian, vulgar, untitled, nameless, lowly, humble, unknown, unhonored, base-born, bastard, of low birth.

4. Mean, despicable, contemptible, degraded, beggarly, sordid, servile, slavish, menial, sorry, worthless, pitiful, low-minded, rascally, abject, grovelling, low, venal.

5. Shameful, disreputable, disgraceful, discreditable, dishonorable, scandalous, infamous, vile, villanous.

BASE, *n.* Basis, foundation, ground, groundwork, lowest part, bottom, foot.

——, *v. t.* Found, ground, rest, establish. [Followed by *on* or *upon*.]

Basement, *n.* Ground-floor, lowest story, basement story.

Base-minded, *a.* Mean, low, vile, grovelling, beggarly, pitiful, despicable, abject, low-minded, mean-spirited.

Baseness, *n.* 1. Meanness, despicableness, contemptibleness, abasement, worthlessness, abjectness.

  2. Disgrace, ignominy, infamy, shame, dishonor, turpitude, villany, perfidy.

Bashful, *a.* Shy, timid, timorous, coy, diffident, shrinking, sheepish, shamefaced, over-modest, not self-possessed.

Bashfulness, *n.* Shyness, timidity, coyness, diffidence, self-distrust, excessive modesty.

BASIN, *n.* Shallow receptacle; dish-shaped depression.

Basis, *n.* Base, foundation, fundamental, ground, groundwork, lowest part, bottom.

Bask, *v. i.* 1. Lie warming, warm one's self joyously, luxuriate.

  2. Rejoice, be shone upon, be bathed, revel, prosper.

BASKET, *n.* Wicker container.

Bass, *a.* (*Mus.*) Low, deep, grave.

Bastard, *n.* Love-child, whoreson, illegitimate child, natural child.

——, *a.* 1. Illegitimate, natural, spurious, base-born, misbegotten, whoreson.

  2. Spurious, false, counterfeit, not genuine, pretended, sham, supposititious.

Baste, *v. t.* 1. Beat (*with a stick*), cudgel, cane, drub, thrash, buffet, pound, pommel. See BEAT, 1.

  2. Moisten with fat.

  3. Sew (*with long stitches*), stitch (*loosely*).

Bastinado, *v. t.* Cudgel, baste, beat (*esp. on the soles of the feet*).

Bat, *n.* Stick, club, cudgel, walking-stick.

Batch, *n.* Quantity (*as of bread, ore, etc., treated at one time*), amount, lot, collection, crowd.

Bate, *v. t.* Abate, lessen, diminish, decrease, reduce, rebate, remit, suppress, suspend, hold in, repress.

BATH, *n.* 1. Receptacle for bathing-water.

  2. Ablution, washing, bathing.

Bathe, *v. t.* 1. Wash, lave, immerse.

  2. Flood, cover, suffuse, enwrap, infold.

Bathos, *n.* Anticlimax, false sublime, sham exaltation *or* pathos, the step from the sublime to the ridiculous.

Baton, *n.* Staff, truncheon, wand, rod, sceptre, staff of office.

Batten, *v. t.* 1. Fasten with battens.

  2. Fatten, make fat.

——, *v. i.* Grow fat, fatten, thrive.

Batter, *v. t.* 1. Beat, smite, pelt, dash against.

  2. Bruise, break, shatter, shiver, smash, demolish, destroy, strike down, knock down, shake to pieces, shiver to pieces.

  3. Indent, wear, wear away, abrade, deface, mar, disfigure.

——, *v. i.* 1. Attack by battering, employ battery.

  2. (*Masonry.*) Incline, slope, recede, retreat, slope backward.

——, *n.* 1. Paste, liquid paste.

  2. Batsman, striker.

  3. (*Masonry.*) Slope backward.

Battle, *n.* Combat, engagement, action, conflict, contest, fight, fray, affray, rencontre, skirmish, brush, collision, affair.

——, *v. i.* Contend, struggle, strive, do battle, fight, contest, desperately endeavor. [Usually with *for.*]

Battled, *a.* Embattled, battlemented, bristling with battlements.

Bauble, *n.* Trinket, gewgaw, toy, trifle, plaything, gimcrack, knick-knack.

Bavin, *n.* Fagot, twig, bough, brushwood.

——, *a.* Brushy, fagot-like, twiggy.

Bawd, *n.* Procurer *or* (*more commonly*) procuress, pander, pimp, whoremaster.

Bawdry, *n.* 1. Pandering, playing pimp *or* procuress.

  2. Fornication, whoredom, whoring, lechery, licentiousness, illicit intercourse.

  3. Obscenity, impurity, lewd talk, smut, indecency, filthy language.

Bawdy, *a.* Obscene, filthy, indecent, impure, lascivious, lewd, smutty, unchaste.

Bawdy-house, *n.* Brothel, stew, bagnio, house of prostitution, house of ill-fame.

Bawl, *v. i. and v. t.* Clamor, vociferate, yell, howl, roar, shout, hoot, cry, squall.

Bay, *a.* Reddish-brown.

——, *n.* 1. Bight, inlet of the sea.

  2. Recess (*as in a room*), opening, compartment.

  3. Laurel-crown, chaplet, laurel, garland; fame, renown, glory, honor, plaudits, praise, applause.

  4. Bark, barking, baying, yelp.

——, *v. i.* Bark, yelp.

——, *v. t.* Bark at, pursue with baying.

Bays, *n. pl.* 1. Crown, garland, wreath, chaplet, honorary distinction.

  2. Renown, fame, honors, plaudits, glory, praise, applause.

Bazaar, *n.* 1. Market-place, exchange, market, mart.

  2. Fancy fair, fair, charity fair.

BE, *v. i.* [*In its substantive sense.*] Exist (*whether in fact or in imagination*), subsist, have existence, have being.

Beach, *n.* Strand, sands, margin, marge, rim, shore, sandy shore, shingly margin.

Beach, *v. t.* Run ashore, put aground, strand.

Beacon, *n.* 1. Signal-fire.

2. Mark, sign, signal.

——, *v. t.* Illumine, light, illuminate, enlighten, guide, signal.

——, *v. i.* Give light, signal, shine, gleam, brighten, flame.

Bead, *n.* 1. Globule, pellet (*perforated for stringing*).

2. Drop, droplet, pearly drop, bubble, blob.

3. Moulding, astragal.

——, *v. t.* 1. Mould, decorate with a moulding.

2. Deck with beads, raise into beads.

Beadle, *n.* 1. Court crier, servitor, apparitor, summoner.

2. Bedell, university mace-carrier.

3. Church servitor, parish petty-constable.

Bead-roll, *n.* Roll (of honor), list, catalogue, roster.

Beads, *n. pl.* Rosary.

Beak, *n.* 1. Bill, mandible, neb.

2. Prow, bow, stem.

Beaker, *n.* Drinking-cup, goblet, bowl, cup.

Beam, *n.* 1. Girder, piece of timber, joist, balk, scantling, stud.

2. Ray, pencil, streak, gleam. See GLIMMER.

——, *v. i.* Shine, emit rays, gleam, glisten, glitter, beacon.

——, *v. t.* Shoot forth, emit in rays *or* beams.

Beamy, *a.* 1. Radiant, beaming, gleaming, shining, glancing.

2. Joyous, gladsome, gladdening, radiant, sparkling.

3. Beam-like, huge, ponderous, sturdy, thick, unwieldy.

Bear, *v. t.* 1. Uphold, support, sustain, hold up.

2. Carry, transport, convey, waft, deport.

3. Endure, suffer, undergo, brook, stand, tolerate, abide, put up with, bear with, take patiently, submit to.

4. Admit, permit, allow, admit of, be capable of.

5. Maintain, keep up, carry on.

6. Entertain, cherish, harbor.

7. Be answerable, accountable, *or* responsible for, be charged with.

8. Produce, yield, bring forth.

9. Give birth to, drop (*of animals*), cast, spawn.

——, *v. i.* 1. Suffer, submit, endure.

2. Press, push, be oppressive.

3. Be fruitful, be prolific.

4. Act, take effect, operate, work, succeed.

5. Tend, relate, refer, be pertinent, concern, affect.

——, *n.* 1. Bruin.

2. Growler, grumbler, snarler, surly old fellow, bundle of irritability.

Bearable, *a.* Tolerable, endurable, supportable.

Beard, *n.* 1. Whiskers, imperial, Vandyke, goatee, hirsute appendage.

2. Guard. See BARB.

——, *v. t.* Defy, bid defiance to, oppose to the face, confront boldly.

Bearded, *a.* 1. Whiskered, wearing a beard.

2. Barbed, pointed.

3. (*Bot.*) Aristate, awned, bristled, bristly.

Bear down. 1. Overcome, crush, put down, repress.

2. Overthrow, overwhelm, crush, overbear.

Bear down upon. 1. Attack, assail, assault, charge, advance upon, move upon, march upon, march against, set upon, rush upon.

2. (*Naut.*) Sail toward, approach, move to close quarters with.

Bearing, *n.* 1. Deportment, demeanor, behavior, conduct, carriage, mien, air, port.

2. Relation, dependency, connection.

3. Endurance, suffering, enduring, patience, long-suffering.

4. Direction, course, aim, aspect, point of compass.

5. Import, effect, force, meaning, scope, compass.

6. Producing, bringing forth, yielding fruit *or* increase.

7. Socket, bed, receptacle.

Bearings, *n. pl.* Charges (*in coats of arms*).

Bearish, *a.* Rough, rude, coarse, savage, boorish, uncivil, uncourteous, discourteous, impolite, ungentlemanly.

Bear out. Maintain, support, defend, uphold, justify, make good, vindicate, corroborate, confirm, sustain.

Bear up. 1. (*Active.*) Support, uphold, sustain, keep from falling.

2. (*Passive.*) Stand firm, show fortitude.

Bear witness. Testify, depose, state, affirm, declare, aver, avow, say, swear.

Beast, *n.* 1. Brute, irrational animal, quadruped.

2. Brutal *or* bestial person, brute, savage, sensualist.

Beastly, *a.* Brutish, brutal, bestial, sensual, coarse, repulsive, inhuman, abominable, vile, swinish, filthy, loathsome.

Beat, *v. t.* 1. Strike, knock, hit, thump, bethump, belabor, drub, maul, hammer, pommel, baste, thrash, thwack, bang, whack, pound, punch, cudgel, cane, whip, buffet, lay blows upon.

2. Pound, bruise, pulverize, comminute, bray, break in pieces.

3. Batter, smite, pelt, dash against.

4. Conquer, overcome, subdue, vanquish, overpower, defeat, checkmate.

5. (*Colloq.*) Excell, surpass, outdo, cut out, "scoop."

——, *v. i.* 1. Pulsate, throb.

2. Dash, strike.

——, *n.* 1. Stroke, striking, blow.

2. Pulsation, throb, beating.

3. Round, course.

Beat back. Repulse, repel, drive back.

Beat down. 1. Batter, overturn, destroy, break, throw down.

2. Subdue, overpower, overcome, crush, put down.

Beaten, *a.* 1. Worn by use, much travelled.

2. Hackneyed, trite, threadbare, common, common-place.

3. Defeated, baffled, dispirited.

Beatific, *a.* Ravishing, enchanting, enrapturing, rapturing, enravishing, enravished, raptured, enraptured, rapturous, ecstatic, transporting, enchanting, enchanted, transported, rapt.

Beatification, *n.* Bliss, blessedness. See BEATITUDE.

Beatify, *v. t.* Enrapture, rapture, enchant, transport, enravish, ravish, make supremely happy.

Beating, *n.* 1. Striking, drubbing, flogging, thrashing, cudgelling, pommelling, caning, flagellation, pounding, thumping, basting, bastinadoing.

2. Beat, pulsation, throb, throbbing.

Beat into. (*Colloq.*) Teach (*by laborious effort*), instil, inculcate, implant.

Beatitude, *n.* Bliss, felicity, blessedness, blissfulness, beatification, holy joy, solemn ecstasy, heavenly joy, peace that passeth understanding, ecstasy serene.

Beat out. Flatten (*by hammering*), attenuate.

Beat the air. Make vain efforts, waste one's efforts, try in vain, lash the waves, plow the sands.

Beau, *n.* 1. Fop, dandy, coxcomb, exquisite, macaroni, popinjay, jack-a-dandy, carpet knight, ladies' man.

2. Gallant, lover, admirer, suitor, sweetheart, *cicisbeo*.

Beau ideal. [Fr.] Ideal beauty or excellence, ideal standard, realized ideal, perfection, consummation, consummate flower.

Beauties, *n. pl.* 1. Beautiful traits, features, *or* characteristics, attractions, charms.

2. Beautiful women, belles, fair ones.

BEAUTIFUL, *a.* Handsome, comely, pretty, fair, fine, elegant, charming exquisite, lovely, graceful, beauteous.

Beautify, *v. t.* Adorn, decorate, embellish, deck, bedeck, ornament, emblazon, gild, array, garnish, grace, set, trick out, set off, make beautiful.

Beauty, *n.* 1. Elegance, grace, symmetry.

2. Comeliness, seemliness, fairness, loveliness, pulchritude, attractiveness.

3. Fine part, special grace, particular excellence, beautiful trait, feature, *or* characteristic, attraction, charm.

4. Beautiful woman, belle.

Becalm, *v. t.* 1. Quiet, soothe, still, calm, tranquillize, pacify, appease, make calm, make tranquil.

2. Detain by a calm (*as a ship*), affect, overtake, *or* surround by a calm.

BECAUSE, *conj.* For, since, as, forasmuch as, for the cause that, for the reason that, on this account that, inasmuch as.

Because of. On account of, by reason of, by cause of, by virtue of, on the ground of, owing to, due to, for, from, through, by.

Beck, *n.* 1. Nod, bow, beckon, knowing look *or* gesture, gesture of invitation *or* command.

2. Brook, brooklet, rill, run, runlet, runnel.

——, *v. t.* Beckon, nod to, signal to come, invite by signs.

——, *v. i.* Nod, beckon, gesture invitingly *or* commandingly.

Beckon, *v. i.* Make a sign, give a signal, call *or* invite by gesture.

——, *v. t.* Call by a sign *or* signal, invite, wave toward one.

Becloud, *v. t.* Dim, bedim, obscure, darken, bedarken, cloud.

Become, *v. i.* Get, go, grow, "wax," turn to, change to, be changed to, be converted into, be turned into, be transformed into, get to be, come to be.

——, *v. t.* Suit, befit, adorn, set off, be suitable to, beseem, grace, be proper for, be appropriate to.

Become of. Be the fate of, be the end of, be the final condition of, befall, bechance, happen to, be the place *or* whereabouts of.

Becoming, *a.* 1. Fit, proper, suitable, meet, appropriate, congruous, right, seemly, decorous.

2. Comely, graceful, neat, pretty.

Be confined. 1. Be restrained, be shut up, be shut in.

2. Be brought to bed, lie in, be in child-bed, be delivered, come to labor, be in travail, be in the straw.

BED, *n.* 1. Couch, berth, "bunk," cot, cradle, trundle-bed, resting-place.

2. Channel, hollow, depression.

3. Receptacle, resting-place, foundation, base, support, underlayer.

4. Layer, stratum, seam, vein, deposit, accumulation.

——, *v. t.* Embed, set, lay.

Bedaub, *v. t.* Smear, daub, besmear, soil, daub over.

Bedeck, *v. t.* Adorn, decorate, embellish, beautify, ornament, deck, emblazon, gild, array, garnish, grace, bedizen, prank, set out, set off, trick out. See ARRAY.

Bedew, *v. t.* Moisten, wet, damp, dampen, sprinkle, besprinkle.

Bedim, *v. t.* Darken, bedarken, dim, obscure, cloud, becloud.

Bedlam, *n.* Madhouse, lunatic hospital, lunatic asylum, hospital for the insane.

Bedlamite, *n.* Madman, lunatic, maniac, crazy person, insane person, deranged person.

BEE, *n.* (*Basic Eng.*) The honey-making insect.

Bee-house, *n.* Apiary, beehive.

Beetle, *n.* Mallet, maul.

——, *v. i.* Protrude, project, jut, jut out, hang over.

Beetle-head, *n.* Simpleton, fool. See DUNCE.

Beetle-headed, *a.* Dull. See STUPID.

Befall, *v. t.* Betide, overtake, bechance, happen to.

——, *v. i.* Happen, chance, betide, supervene, occur, take place, come to pass.

Befit, *v. t.* Suit, fit, become, be suitable *or* proper for, be appropriate for, comport with, be in keeping with.

Befitting, *a.* Becoming, suitable, fit, proper, right, meet, seemly, appropriate, congruous, decorous.

Befog, *v. t.* 1. Cover with fog, shroud in fog, wrap in mist, obscure.

2. Confuse, mystify, muddle, obfuscate, puzzle, perplex, embarrass, bewilder.

Befool, *v. t.* Infatuate, fool, dupe, deceive, delude, cheat, chouse, trick, hoax, stultify, hood-wink, circumvent, over-reach, beguile, impose upon, practise upon, play upon, make a fool of. See BAMBOOZLE.

BEFORE, *prep.* 1. Preceding, in advance of, ahead of, in front of, in the van of.

2. Prior to, previous to, "ere."

3. In the presence of, face to face with, in the sight of.

4. Near the front of, in front of.

5. Under the jurisdiction, judgment, control, *or* notice of.

——, *adv.* 1. Toward the front.

2. In advance, farther onward, ahead.

3. Formerly, in time past, of old, already, previously, earlier, antecedently, sooner.

4. Hitherto, up to that time.

5. Above, in a former part, in a previous place *or* passage.

Beforehand, *adv.* Previously, in anticipation, in advance. Cf. BEFORE, *adv.* 3.

——, *a.* Forehanded.

Befoul, *v. t.* Soil, pollute, daggle, draggle, foul, bemire, dirty. See BEDAUB.

Befriend, *v. t.* Favor, encourage, patronize, countenance, help, aid, benefit, act as a friend to, do a good turn for, be kind to. See ASSIST.

Beg, *v. t.* 1. Crave, solicit, beseech, pray, implore, supplicate, entreat, adjure, conjure, importune, petition, request, ask, pray for, petition for, seek by petition, sue for, ask earnestly.

2. Crave permission, solicit leave, desire earnestly, take leave, take the liberty, demand.

3. Assume, take for granted, assume without proof *or* without warrant.

——, *v. i.* Solicit charity, ask alms.

Beget, *v. t.* 1. Generate, procreate, engender, breed, get, be the father of.

2. Produce, originate, give rise to, lead to, bring about.

Beggar, *n.* Mendicant, pauper, starveling, poor *or* indigent person, wretch, tatter-demalion, ragamuffin, vagabond, bezonian, scrub, *sans culotte*, Pariah.

——, *v. t.* 1. Impoverish, ruin, render poor, reduce to poverty, bring to want.

2. Exhaust, surpass, exceed, baffle, go beyond, be above, put at fault, show to be inadequate.

Beggarly, *a.* 1. Destitute, indigent, needy, poor.

2. Sorry, mean, abject, base, low, paltry, shabby, vile, scurvy, miserable, contemptible, despicable, pitiful, pitiable, servile, slavish, grovelling, mean-spirited, niggardly, stingy, scant, wretched, miserly, stinted.

Beggary, *n.* Poverty, indigence, penury, destitution, want, distress, mendicancy, mendicity.

Begin, *v. i.* Originate, arise, take rise, start, enter, open, commence, make a beginning, take the first step, break ground, break the ice.

——, *v. t.* Commence, initiate, inaugurate, institute, originate, start, enter upon, set about, set on foot, set in operation, set going.

Beginner, *n.* 1. Originator, starter, author, initiator, inaugurator, prime mover.

2. Tyro, novice, learner, neophyte.

Beginning, *n.* 1. Commencement, outset, opening, start, initiation, inauguration, inception, rise, arising, dawn, emergence.

2. Origin, source, rise.

Begird, *v. t.* 1. Gird, bind with a girdle.

2. Surround, encompass, environ, encircle, enclose, engird.

Begone, *interj.* Depart, avaunt, go away, haste away, be off, get thee gone.

Begrime, *v. t.* Defile, befoul, besmirch, bedaub, pollute, cover with filth.

Begrudge, *v. t.* Grudge, envy the possession of.

Beguile, *v. t.* 1. Delude, cheat, deceive. See BEFOOL.

2. Divert, amuse, entertain, cheer, solace, while away.

Behalf, *n.* Benefit, advantage, convenience, profit, interest, account, behoof, support, defence.

Behave, *v. i.* Act, conduct one's self, deport one's self, demean one's self, acquit one's self, behave one's self.

BEHAVIOR, *n.* Deportment, comportment, bearing, demeanor, carriage, manner, mien, air, port. See CONDUCT.

Behead, *v. t.* Decapitate, decollate, guillotine, deprive of the head.

Behest, *n.* Command, commandment, mandate, order, precept, injunction, direction, charge, bidding, hest.

Behind, *prep.* 1. Abaft, at the back of, in the rear of.

2. After, following.

——, *adv.* 1. Backward, back.

2. Abaft, aft, astern, rearward, in the rear, at the back.

Behindhand, *a.* 1. Backward, late, tardy, after the usual time, behind time, too late.

2. In arrears (*with work*), behind time, not well enough advanced, in a backward state, behind one's dues, not up.

3. In arrears (*as to money*), burdened with liabilities, in debt, embarrassed.

Behold, *v. t.* See, observe, contemplate, eye, survey, consider, regard, view, scan, descry, discern, look upon, set one's eyes on.

——, *interj.* See, look, observe, mark, lo.

Beholden, *a.* 1. Obliged, indebted, bound, in debt, obligated, under obligation.

2. Obliged, grateful, thankful, devoted.

Beholder, *n.* Observer, spectator, onlooker, looker-on, by-stander, witness.

Behoof, *n.* Advantage, benefit, profit, interest, account. See BEHALF.

Behoove, *v. t.* 1. Become, befit, beseem, be fit for, be proper for, be meet for.

2. Be necessary *or* needful for, be binding *or* obligatory on, be one's duty.

Being, *n.* 1. Existence, subsistence, reality, actuality.

2. Essence, essential being, inmost nature, substance, inner reality, life, vital principle, root, core, heart, centre of life.

3. Sentient, conscious, *or* personal agent, living thing, creature, living being.

Be it so. 1. Suppose it to be so, granted, grant it, admit it.

2. Amen, so be it, let it be so.

Belabor, *v. t.* Thump, bethump, strike, knock, drub, lay blows upon. See BEAT.

Belated, *a.* 1. Delayed, retarded, hindered, made late.

2. Overtaken by night, out late in the night, overtaken by darkness, caught in *or* by the dark.

Belaud, *v. t.* Overlaud, overpraise, cover with laudations, load with praises, praise lavishly.

Belay, *v. t.* (*Naut.*) Fasten, make fast.

Belch, *v. t.* 1. Eject from the stomach, throw up, eject, emit, expel.

2. Throw out violently, cast forth, discharge, emit, vomit, eject, expel, hurl forth.

——, *v. i.* 1. Eructate, eruct, eject wind from the stomach.

2. Be ejected violently, rush forth, gush.

Belching, *n.* Eructation.

Beldam, } *n.* Hag, Jezebel, virago, vixen,
Beldame, } fury, old hag.

Beleaguer, *v. t.* 1. Besiege, invest, beset, blockade, lay siege to.

2. Beset, encompass, encumber, block up, environ, surround, obstruct.

Bel-esprit, *n.* [Fr. *pl. Beaux-esprits.*] Wit, man of wit, man of genius.

Belfry, *n.* Campanile, bell-tower.

Belial, *n.* Satan. See APOLLYON.

Belie, *v. t.* 1. Falsify, misrepresent, calumniate, slander, defame, represent falsely.

2. Contradict, controvert, go counter *or* contrary to.

BELIEF, *n.* 1. Believing (*the active phase of the fact*), persuasion, conviction, confidence, trust, reliance, assurance, feeling of certainty. See FAITH.

2. Being believed (*the passive phase*), credence, credit, acceptance, assent, currency.

3. Creed (*the thing or things believed*), doctrine, tenet *or* tenets, dogma, opinion, view, article of faith, profession of faith.

Believe, *v. t.* Credit, give credence to, accept, think to be true, give faith to, put faith in, rely upon, make no doubt of, put confidence in, be persuaded, convinced, confident, *or* sure of, assent to, trust, confide in.

——, *v. i.* 1. Exercise faith, have faith, have a firm persuasion.

2. Think, suppose, conceive, fancy, apprehend, imagine, hold, be of opinion, entertain the idea, take it. See OPINE.

Believe in. 1. Trust, have confidence in, place reliance on.

2. Be convinced of, be for, be in favor of, approve of, go in for.

Belike, *adv.* Probably, perhaps, perchance, peradventure, mayhap, it may be, it is likely.

BELL, *n.* Cup-shaped metallic instrument to ring when struck, tintinnabulum.

Belle, *n.* Beauty, toast, fair damsel.

Belles-lettres, *n. pl.* [Fr.] Polite letters, belletristic writings.

Belligerent, *a.* 1. Carrying on war, engaged in war, waging war, contending, in conflict, at war, in arms.

2. Warlike, hostile.

3. Bellicose, pugnacious, contentious, quarrelsome, full of fight.

——, *n.* Belligerent state *or* nation, party to war, contending party, antagonist, rival, combatant, opponent.

Bellow, *v. i.* 1. Roar (as a beast).

2. Vociferate, clamor, yell, howl, cry, bawl, make a loud outcry.

Bell-shaped, *a.* (*Bot.*) Campanulate.

Belly, *n.* 1. Abdomen, paunch.

2. Convexity, swell, swelling, bulge, protuberance.

3. Concavity, hollow, deep, depth *or* depths, recesses, womb, bosom, bowels, cave, cavernous depths, *penetralia.*

——, *v. i.* Swell, swell out, fill, round out, protrude, be protuberant.

Belonging, *n.* 1. Property, goods and chattels, estate, possession.

2. Appendage, appurtenance, appliance, accessory (*which see*).

Belong to. 1. Be the property of, be possessed by, be owned by.

2. Be an attribute *or* quality *or* characteristic *or* mark of, characterize, pertain *or* appertain to, inhere in, be the prerogative *or* right of, be the privilege of.

3. Regard, relate to, refer to, have reference to.

4. Be appendant to, constitute a part of, be connected with.

5. Behoove, concern, be incumbent on, be the duty of, devolve on, be the business *or* concern of.

Beloved, *a.* Dear, darling, much loved.

Below, *prep.* 1. Under, beneath, underneath.

2. Unbecoming, unworthy of.

——, *adv.* 1. Under, beneath, underneath.

2. On the earth, in this world, in the present life, in time, in the world of sense.

3. In hell, in the lower regions, in the under world, among the shades, in Hades, in the regions of the dead.

Belt, *n.* 1. Girdle, cincture, cestus, band, zone, girth.

2. Strip, zone, stretch, long and narrow piece *or* region.

Bemire, *v. t.* Daggle, draggle, bedaggle, bedraggle, besmirch, mire, muddy, befoul, foul, dirty, soil.

Bemoan, *v. t.* Bewail, lament, deplore, moan over, mourn over, express sorrow for.

Bemused, *a.* Stupefied, confused, bewildered, muddled, muzzy, tipsy, half-seas-over, half-drunk.

Bench, *n.* 1. Long seat, seat, form, settle.

2. Work-bench.

3. [With *The.*] Judge's seat, woolsack.

4. Court, tribunal, body of judges.

Bend, *v. t.* 1. Curve, crook, bow, incurvate, flex, make crooked, deflect, draw.

2. Direct, turn, incline.

3. Exert, apply (*earnestly*), direct (*attentively*).

4. [*Usually in the passive.*] Incline, determine, resolve, set.

5. Subdue, cause to yield, bring to submission, make submissive, persuade, influence, mould, dispose, bias.

6. (*Naut.*) Fasten, make fast.

——, *v. i.* 1. Crook, deflect, deviate, swerve, diverge, incline, be crooked, be bent, be curved.

2. Lean, incline, turn, deflect, deviate, diverge.

3. Bow, stoop, lower *or* lour, hang low.

4. Yield, submit, bow, stoop, kneel, give way.

5. Condescend, stoop, deign, be gracious.

——, *n.* 1. Curve, curvity, curvature, flexure, angle, elbow, crook, incurvation, turn, turning, arcuation.

2. Bight, coil.

Beneath, *prep.* 1. Under, underneath, below.

2. Unbecoming, unbefitting, unworthy of, below the level of.

——, *adv.* See BELOW, *adv.*

Benedick, } *n.* Newly married man, neog-
Benedict, } amist.

Benedictine, *n.* Blackfriar.

Benediction, *n.* 1. Blessing, benison, invocation of happiness, beatitude.

2. Benefit, blessing, grace, favor, boon, benison, beatitude.

Benefaction, *n.* Gift, donation, gratuity, grant, offering, contribution, boon, favor, present, alms, charity.

Benefactor, *n.* 1. Succorer, well-doer, savior, beneficent friend.

2. Patron, favorer, supporter, upholder, contributor, friend.

Benefice, *n.* Ecclesiastical living.

Beneficence, *n.* Charity, bounty, liberality, generosity, alms-giving, active goodness, kind action, doing of good.

Beneficent, *a.* 1. Bountiful, benevolent, kind, liberal, generous, bounteous, princely, munificent.

2. Benign, favorable, beneficial, benignant, salutary.

Beneficial, *a.* Useful, profitable, advantageous, helpful, serviceable, salutary, wholesome, favorable, good for one's advantage, for one's good, for one's interest.

Benefit, *n.* 1. Favor, service, act of kindness, good turn, kind office.

2. Advantage, profit, avail, gain, good, utility, behalf, behoof, account, interest.

——, *v. t.* 1. Befriend, help, serve, do good to, be useful to, advance the interest of, confer a favor on, do a good turn *or* kind office to.

2. Profit, advantage, avail, be of advantage to.

Benevolence, *n.* 1. Kindness, benignity, kind-heartedness, humanity, humaneness, philanthropy, tenderness, charitableness, good-will, altruism, unselfishness, disposition to do good, milk of human kindness.

2. Charity, benefaction, beneficence, alms-giving, charitable effort(s).

Benevolent, *a.* Kind, benignant, benign, kind-hearted, obliging, humane, tender, charitable, generous, liberal, philanthropic, altruistic, unselfish, disposed to do good, full of good-will.

Benighted, *a.* 1. Overtaken by night, belated, out in the dark.

2. Involved in darkness, profoundly ignorant, sunk in ignorance, unenlightened.

Benign, *a.* ' 1. Kind, kindly, benevolent, gracious, complaisant, humane, obliging, benignant, good, amiable, gentle, friendly, kind-hearted, tender-hearted, of a gentle disposition.

2. Beneficent, most salutary, most propitious, most favorable, benignant, most wholesome, most beneficial.

Benignant, *a.* Kind. See BENIGN.

Benignity, *n.* Kindness, graciousness, benevolence, complaisance, humanity, amiability, gentleness, amenity, friendliness, kind-heartedness, fellow-feeling, good feeling, good-humor, good temper, obliging manner.

Benison, *n.* Blessing. See BENEDICTION.

Bent, *n.* 1. Disposition, inclination, tendency, turn, *penchant*, learning, bias, propensity, proclivity, predisposition, predilection, partiality, liking, fondness, proneness, appetency.

2. (*Archaic.*) Wild land, hill, moor, wild.

BENT, *a.* Crooked, hooked, bowed, embowed, curved, flexed, deflected, aduncous, arcuate, incurvate.

Bent on. Resolved, determined, fixed, *or* set on.

Benumb, *v. t.* Stupefy, paralyze, deaden, blunt, hebetate, make torpid, render insensible.

Bequeath, *v. t.* 1. Leave, demise, devise, will, give by will.

2. Transmit, hand down, impart.

Bequest, *n.* Legacy, devise.

Berate, *v. t.* Scold, chide, reprimand, rate, reprove, betongue, rail at.

Bereave, *v. t.* 1. Deprive (*of something that cannot be restored*), dispossess, rob, divest, strip, despoil, spoil, take away from, make destitute of.

2. Deprive of friend *or* kindred, afflict with personal loss, render lorn.

Bereaved, *p.* and *a.* Deprived of friend *or* kindred, desolate, lorn.

Bereft, *p.* and *a.* Stripped, deprived, destitute, despoiled.

Bernardine, *n.* Cistercian.

BERRY, *n.* (*Basic Eng.*) Small fruit.

Berth, *n.* (*Naut.*) 1. Ship's station.

2. Bed, place to sleep in.

3. Situation, office, post, appointment, employment, place.

Beseech, *v. t.* 1. Entreat, beg, implore, supplicate, petition, conjure, importune, pray to. See ADJURE.

2. Solicit, ask, entreat, beg, implore, importune, plead for, crave, petition for, pray for, beg for.

Beseem, *v. t.* Become, befit, behoove, be proper for, be appropriate for, be meet for.

Beset, *v. t.* 1. Surround, encompass, environ, encircle, enclose, besiege, hem in. See BELEAGUER.

2. Embarrass, perplex, entangle.

3. Set, bestud, bestick, set about, engirdle, encircle, decorate, ornament, embellish, garnish.

Beshrew, *v. t.* Execrate, curse, wish evil to, implore a curse upon.

Beside, *prep.* 1. Near, close to, at the side of, by the side of.

2. Aside from, out of the way of, out of the course of, not according to.

3. Out of, not in possession of.

Besides, *prep.* Except, save, over and above, in addition to, distinct from.

Besides, ⎫ *adv.* 1. Moreover, too, also,
Beside, ⎭ furthermore, more than that, over and above, in addition, yet.

2. Else, more, further, beyond that, in addition.

Besiege, *v. t.* Surround (*with a military force*), encompass, beset, invest, lay siege to. See BELEAGUER, and cf. BLOCKADE.

Besmear, *v. t.* 1. Bedaub, daub, smear, bespatter, beplaster, beslime, daub over.

2. Defile, soil, foul, befoul, besmirch, pollute, contaminate.

Besot, *v. t.* 1. Intoxicate, steep, drench, soak.

2. Stupefy, make sottish, make foolish *or* stupid.

3. Infatuate, stultify, befool, intoxicate, delude.

Bespatter, *v. t.* Spatter (*usually with something filthy*), bedaub. See BESMEAR.

Bespeak, *v. t.* 1. Order, speak for beforehand, engage.

2. Solicit, speak for.

3. Address, speak to, accost.

4. Indicate, imply, proclaim, declare, betoken, evince, show.

Besprinkle, *v. t.* Sprinkle, bedew, bestrew, sprinkle over, scatter over, cover with drops *or* spray.

Best, *a.* Most good, most excellent, superlatively good, good in the highest degree. See the various meanings of GOOD.

——, *adv.* 1. Most of all, in the highest degree, beyond all others.

2. With most propriety, most profitably *or* advantageously, to the greatest advantage.

3. With the highest qualification, by the clearest title.

——, *n.* 1. Highest perfection, highest good, greatest good.

2. Utmost, highest endeavor, whatever in one lies, all that one can, the most that can be done.

3. Choice, pick, flower, cream, *élite*.

Bestial, *a.* 1. Beastlike, brutal, brutelike, brute, irrational.

2. Beastly, brutal, brutish, vile, low, depraved, degraded, degrading, sensual.

Bestow, *v. t.* 1. Put, place, stow, store, deposit, dispose, lay away, lay up in store.

2. Give, accord, grant, impart. See CONFER.

Bestowal, ⎫ *n.* 1. Putting, placing,
Bestowment, ⎭ stowing, stowage, storing, storage, disposing.

2. Giving, grant, granting, imparting, impartation, conferring.

Bestower, *n.* Giver, disposer, donor (*law*), donator.

Bestrew, *v. t.* Strew, sprinkle, scatter, bescatter, besprinkle, spread, bespread.

Bestride, *v. t.* 1. Straddle, stride over.

2. Ride astraddle upon.

3. Bespan, arch over.

Bet, *n.* Wager, stake.

——, *v. i.* Wager, lay a wager, make a bet.

——, *v. t.* Stake, pledge, wager, lay, wage.

Betake one's self. Resort, repair, apply, have recourse.

Bethink one's self. Consider, reflect, ponder, rouse one's thoughts, take thought.

Betide, *v. t.* Befall, overtake, bechance, happen to, come to.

——, *v. i.* Happen, befall, bechance, come to pass, occur, take place.

Betimes, *adv.* Seasonably, in season, in good season, in time, in good time, before it is too late, early, soon.

Betoken, *v. t.* 1. Signify, denote, indicate, represent, typify, imply, prove, evince, show, argue, betray.

2. Prefigure, foreshow, foreshadow, foretell, presage, portend, augur, presignify.

Betray, *v. t.* 1. Deliver up (*by breach of trust*), give up treacherously, give over to the foe.

2. Violate, break, prove recreant to, let perish, be false to.

3. Violate the confidence of, disclose the secrets of, deceive by treachery.

4. Divulge, reveal, discover, expose, tell, blab, show, make known.

5. Display, exhibit, manifest, show, indicate, imply, betoken, argue, evince, expose, reveal, uncover.

6. Mislead, lure, ensnare, entrap, beguile, delude, inveigle.

7. Seduce, ruin, corrupt, undo, lead astray.

Betroth, *v. t.* Affiance, plight, pledge in marriage, engage to marry.

Betrothal, *n.* Engagement, betrothing, affiancing, plighting.

Better, *a.* 1. More good, more excellent, good in a higher degree.

2. More useful, more valuable.

3. Preferable, more desirable, more acceptable.

4. More fit, more appropriate, more suitable. See various meanings of GOOD.

——, *n.* 1. Superiority, advantage, victory, upper hand.

2. Improvement, greater good.

3. Superior.

Better, *adv.* 1. In a superior manner, in a more excellent way, more fully, more completely.

2. With greater advantage, more usefully *or* profitably.

3. More, in a higher degree.

——, *v. t.* Improve, amend, emend, meliorate, ameliorate, reform, correct, rectify, advance, promote, make *or* render better.

——, *v. i.* Grow, get, *or* become better, improve, advance, mend, come up.

Bettering, *n.* Improvement, amendment, melioration, amelioration, betterment.

BETWEEN, *prep.* Betwixt. Cf. AMONG.

Bevel, *n.* Chamfer, slope, inclination.

——, *v. t.* Chamfer.

Beverage, *n.* Drink, potion, potation.

Bevy, *n.* 1. Flock, covey, swarm, flight.

2. Company (*especially of women*), group, throng, flock, party.

Bewail, *v. t.* Bemoan, lament, deplore, rue, grieve for *or* over, mourn for, mourn over, express sorrow for.

——, *v. i.* Mourn, moan, lament, sorrow, grieve.

Beware, *v. i.* Mind, take care, be cautious, be wary, be careful, look out.

Bewilder, *v. t.* Perplex, confound, confuse, distract, embarrass, puzzle, stagger, pose, nonplus, mystify, entangle, daze, befog, muddle, bemuddle.

Bewilderment, *n.* Perplexity, embarrassment, confusion, entanglement, mystification, daze, maze, muddle.

Bewitch, *v. t.* Charm, fascinate, spellbind, enchant, captivate, transport, enravish, enrapture, entrance.

Beyond, *prep.* 1. On the farther side of, over, across, on the other side of, past.

2. Before, at a distance before.

3. Remote from, out of the reach of, out of the grasp of.

4. Farther than.

5. Above, superior to, exceeding, in advance of.

——, *adv.* Yonder, at a distance.

Bias, *n.* Inclination, bent, leaning, slant, tendency, predilection, prepossession, proclivity, proneness, propensity, partiality, prejudice, disposition, predisposition, turn, *penchant.*

——, *v. t.* Influence, incline, prejudice, dispose, predispose, bend.

Bible, *n.* [Used with *The* prefixed.] The Scriptures, the Old and New Testaments, the sacred volume, the Book of books, the Word of God.

Biblical, *a.* Scriptural.

Bibulous, *a.* 1. Spongy, porous, absorbent, imbibing.

2. Drinking, intemperate, tippling, fond of drink, cup-loving, soaking.

Bicephalous, *a.* 1. Bicipital, bicipitous, two-headed, double-headed.

2. (*Anat.*) Double-attached, bicipital, bicipitous, biceps, with two origins.

Bicker, *v. i.* 1. Wrangle, dispute, quarrel, spar, spat, jangle, squabble, have words, have an altercation.

2. Quiver, tremble, vibrate, play, be tremulous.

Bickering, *n.* Dispute, quarrel, wrangle, wrangling, jangle, jarring, jangling, sparring, altercation, dissension, contention, strife, war of words.

Bicorn, } *a.* Two-horned, crescented,
Bicorned, } crescent-shaped, crescentic,
Bicornous, } bicornute.

Bicuspid, } *a.* Two-pointed, two-fanged,
Bicuspidate, } two-pronged, double-pronged.

Bid, *n.* Offer (*of a price*), bidding, proposal.

——, *v. t.* 1. Command, order, require, charge, enjoin, direct, summon.

2. Invite, ask, request, call, solicit, pray.

3. Offer, propose, proffer, tender.

Bidding, *n.* 1. Command, order, dictate, direction, injunction, precept, behest, requisition, mandate, decree, appointment.

2. Offer (*of a price*), bid, proposal.

Biddy, *n.* 1. Housemaid, domestic, maid, servant-girl.

2. Chicken, chick, chickabiddy.

Bide, *v. t.* 1. Endure, suffer, tolerate, bear, put up with, submit to, abide.

2. Abide, await, wait for.

——, *v. i.* 1. Dwell, abide, stay, have one's home.

2. Remain, abide, wait, stay, lie still.

Bidental, *a.* Two-toothed, bidentate, bidentated, bidented, bidential.

Bid fair. Promise, seem likely, offer a good prospect, present a fair prospect, make a fair promise.

Bifurcate, } *a.* Forked, two-pronged, two-
Bifurcated, } branched, bifurcous.

Bifurcation, *n.* Forking, branching, diverging, divergence.

Big, *a.* 1. Great, large, bumper, huge, bulky, hulking, monstrous, "whopping," massive, massy.

2. Imposing, important.

3. Distended, swollen, inflated, tumid, full.

4. Pregnant, *enceinte*, with child, in the family way, on the increase.

5. Full, teeming, fecund, fruitful, productive.

Big-bellied, *a.* Pot-bellied, tun-bellied, abdominous, paunchy.

Bight, *n.* 1. (*Naut.*) Bend, coil, round, loop.

2. Bay, inlet, cove.

Bigot, *n.* Zealot, fanatic, dogmatist.

Bigoted, *a.* Prejudiced, intolerant, obstinate, opiniative, hidebound, dogmatical, narrow-minded, over-zealous, creed-bound, wedded to an opinion.

Bigotry, *n.* Prejudice, intolerance, blind zeal, obstinacy, opiniativeness, dogmatism, zealotry, fanaticism.

Big-sounding, *a.* High-sounding, magniloquent, altiloquent, tumid, perfervid, inflated.

Big-wig, *n.* (*Colloq.*) Person of consequence, high official, great personage.

Bijou, *n.* [Fr.] Jewel, trinket, elegant ornament, little gem.

Bilateral, *a.* Two-sided, with two sides, in two sides.

Bilboes, *n. pl.* Shackles, fetters, gyves, chains, stocks.

Bile, *n.* 1. Hepatic excretion.

2. Ill-nature, gall, venom. See ACRIMONY.

Bilk, *v. t.* Deceive (*by not fulfilling an engagement*), disappoint, frustrate, thwart, balk, leave in the lurch, elude.

Bill, *n.* 1. Beak, mandible, neb.

2. Bill-hook, hedge-bill, hedging-knife, brush-cutter.

3. Account, charges, reckoning, score.

4. Placard, poster, broadside, advertisement.

——, *v. i.* Kiss, caress, fondle, toy, exchange kisses and caresses.

Billet, *n.·* 1. Note, short letter.

2. Stick, small piece, fagot, splitting.

——, *v. t.* Assign (*to a lodging-place, as soldiers, by a billet*), apportion, allot, distribute, quarter, place in lodgings.

——, *v. i.* Be quartered, lodge, have one's quarters.

Billing and cooing. Caresses, toying, dalliance. See BLANDISHMENT.

Billingsgate, *n.* Ribaldry, foul language. See ABUSE, *n.*

Billow, *n.* Wave, surge.

——, *v. i.* Surge, swell, roll, heave, roll in great surges.

Billowy, *a.* 1. Surging, rolling, heaving, full of surges *or* billows.

2. Fluctuating, rising and falling, heaving, undulating.

Bimonthly, *a.* Coming every two months, appearing once in two months, bimensal, bimestrial.

Bin, *n.* Bunker. crib, box, frame, receptacle.

Binary, *a.* Dual, double, twofold, binal, consisting of two.

Bind, *v. t.* 1. Confine, restrain, restrict, fetter, gyve, enchain, put bonds upon.

2. Bandage, wrap, put a bandage round, wrap up, tie up.

3. Tie, fasten, lash, pinion, secure, truss.

4. Engage, oblige, obligate, pledge, hold, make responsible, lay under obligation.

5. Indenture, apprentice, place under indenture.

6. Confirm, ratify, sanction.

——, *v. i.* 1. Contract, harden, stiffen, shrink.

2. Be obligatory, be binding, be valid, hold.

Binding, *n.* Bandage, band, fillet.

——, *a.* 1. Astringent, contracting, styptic.

2. Obligatory, incumbent, mandatory, valid.

Biography, *n.* Life, memoir, personal history.

Birch, *n.* Rod, lash, whip, rattan, ferule.

BIRD, *n.* Fowl, fowl of the air.

Bird's-eye view. 1. View from above, airview.

2. General survey, rapid glance over, conspectus, synoptical view.

BIRTH, *n.* 1. Nativity, coming into life, origin, beginning, rise.

2. Lineage, extraction, descent, race, family, line, ancestry, blood.

3. Offspring, progeny, creation, creature, production, being.

Bisect, *v. t.* Cut *or* divide into two equal parts, cut in halves, halve, hemisect.

Bisexual, *a.* Hermaphrodite, androgynous.

Bishop, *n.* Prelate, metropolitan, suffragan, patriarch.

Bishopric, *n.* Diocese, see, jurisdiction *or* charge of a bishop, episcopate.

BIT, *n.* 1. Mouthful, morsel, crumb, fragment, scrap, piece, small piece.

2. Whit, tittle, jot, iota, particle, atom, grain, mite, ace, scintilla.

3. Boring-tool, borer.

——, *v. t.* Bridle, get the bits on.

Bitch, *n.* Slut, female dog, "brach."

Bite, *v. t.* 1. Gnaw, chew, champ, crunch.

2. Pierce with the teeth, tear, rend, nip, nibble.

3. Sting, burn, cause to smart, make smart, make tingle.

4. Grip, grasp, catch, grapple, clutch, cling to, catch hold of, take firm hold of.

5. Defraud, deceive, cheat, dupe, trick, gull, overreach, jockey, cozen, chouse,

outwit, bamboozle, impose upon, beguile, mislead, inveigle, gammon.

Bite, *v. i.* See 1, 2, 3, 4, and 5, under preceding.

BITE, *n.* Mouthful, nip; portion bitten out.

Biting, *a.* 1. Pungent, piquant, hot, sharp, peppery, burning, stinging, high-flavored, high-seasoned.

2. Severe, sarcastic, cutting, caustic, mordant.

3. Cold, freezing, nipping, piercing, blasting, blighting.

BITTER, *a.* 1. ʹAcrid, tasting like wormwood, like gall.

2. Cruel, merciless, relentless, virulent, fell, ruthless, dire.

3. Severe, harsh, acrimonious, stern.

4. Distressing, painful, grievous, galling, intense, sore, sorrowful, afflictive, poignant, calamitous.

Bitterness, *n.* 1. Bitter taste, acridity, acridness.

2. Intensity, poignancy, grievousness, severity.

3. Spleen, gall, rankling, rancor, heartburning, animosity, hatred, malice, malignity, spite, enmity, ill-will, bad blood.

4. Asperity, acerbity, severity, harshness, acrimony, ill-temper, tartness.

5. Distress, pain, grief, sorrow, affliction, heaviness, regret, despondency.

Bivalve,
Bivalved, } *a.* Two-valved, bivalvular.

Bizarre, *a.* [Fr.] Odd, fantastic, strange, singular, whimsical, incongruous, extravagant, outlandish.

Blab, *v. t.* Betray, disclose, reveal, divulge, let out, speak out, prate abroad, tattle abroad.

——, *v. i.* Tattle, prattle, prate, blow, blabber, tell tales, tell a secret, let the cat out of the bag, tell tales out of school.

Blabber, *n.* Prater, tattler, babbler, telltale, blab.

BLACK, *a.* 1. Dark, ebon, inky, jet, sable, atramentous, swarthy.

2. Murky, dusky, pitchy, dingy, Cimmerian, lowering.

3. Dismal, sullen, forbidding, gloomy, dark, depressing, doleful, sombre, mournful, disastrous, calamitous.

4. Wicked, atrocious, villanous, infamous, nefarious, heinous, flagitious, diabolic, infernal, hellish, fiendish, devilish, outrageous, monstrous, horrible.

——, *n.* 1. Black color, nigritude.

2. Mourning, black garments.

3. Negro, blackamoor, black man, Moor, blackey.

Black art. Magic, conjuration, sorcery, diabolic art, necromancy, witchcraft, witchery, black magic (*in contrast to white, or innocent*), magical art.

Blacken, *v. t.* 1. Darken, make black, nigrify.

2. Sully, deface, soil, defile, darken, stain.

3. Vilify, defame, slander, calumniate, asperse, traduce, malign, besmirch, revile, besmut, run down, speak ill of. See ABUSE.

——, *v. i.* Grow black, darken, gloom.

Blackfriar, *n.* Benedictine, Dominican, predicant, jacobin, preaching friar, *frère prêcheur.*

Blackguard, *n.* Scurrilous *or* abusive fellow, low fellow, vile fellow, scamp, scoundrel, villain, rascal, rogue, rapscallion, loon, lown.

——, *a.* 1. Scurrilous, abusive, contumelious, insulting, ribald, vituperative, opprobrious, black-mouthed, foul-mouthed.

2. Vile, low, worthless, base, villanous, scoundrel, scoundrelly, rascally, rascal, dishonorable, blackguardly.

Blackguardism, *n.* 1. Ribaldry, scurrility, indecency, obscenity, foul language, billingsgate.

2. Scoundrelism, rascality, baseness, villany, villanousness, low ways, vile behavior, worthlessness.

Black-jack, *n.* Black flag, piratical ensign, skull and cross-bones.

Blackleg, *n.* Gambler, sharper, swindler.

Blackmail, *n.* 1. Tribute (*paid for immunity from robbery*), brigand-tax.

2. Hush-money, bribe to keep silence.

3. Extortion by threats.

Black man. Negro, blackamoor, black, blackey, Moor.

Black-sheep, *n.* Scapegrace, disgrace to the family.

BLADE, *n.* 1. Leaf.

2. Flat part (*as of a knife* or *an oar*).

3. Buck, gallant, spark; gay, dashing fellow.

Blain, *n.* Pustule, blister, blotch, sore.

Blamable, *a.* Culpable, censurable, delinquent, remiss, reprehensible, faulty, blameworthy. Cf. GUILTY.

Blame, *v. t.* Censure, condemn, disapprove, reprehend, reproach, reflect upon, lay *or* cast blame upon, find fault with, accuse.

——, *n.* 1. Censure, reprehension, animadversion, disapproval, disapprobation, reproach, reproof, condemnation, imputation of fault, dispraise.

2. Fault, wrong, misdeed, misdoing, ill-desert, guilt, shortcoming, sin, reproach, defect, demerit.

Blameless, *a.* Irreproachable, unimpeachable, irreprehensible, inculpable, faultless, guiltless, unblemished, unspotted, unsullied, undefiled, spotless, stainless, innocent.

Blanch, *v. t.* Bleach, whiten, etiolate, make *or* render white.

——, *v. i.* Bleach, whiten, pale, etiolate, become white, fade.

Bland, *a.* 1. Soft, mild, gentle, balmy, soothing, demulcent.

2. Affable, suave, kindly, mild, amiable, mild-mannered, complaisant.

Blandishment, *n.* Fascination, flattery, cajolery, cajoling compliment, artful caresses, coaxing, wheedling.

Blank, *a.* 1. Void, empty, bare, vacuous.

2. Astonished, confounded, confused, dumfounded, disconcerted, nonplussed. See AMAZED.

3. Utter, pure, simple, unmixed, unmingled, unadulterated, perfect, entire, complete, absolute, unabated, unqualified, unmitigated, mere, the merest.

——, *n.* 1. Void, vacancy, empty space, unfilled room.

2. Blank form, form.

3. Unwrought piece (*of metal*), block.

Blare, *n.* Blast, peal, clang, clangor.

——, *v. i.* Blow, peal, sound loudly.

——, *v. t.* Sound forth, blazon, proclaim, trumpet.

Blarney, *n.* Flattery, adulation, smooth phrases, cajolery, gammon.

Blasé, *a.* [Fr.] Surfeited, cloyed, satiated, palled, incapable of enjoyment (*in consequence of excesses*), worn out, exhausted.

Blaspheme, *v. t.* 1. Speak impiously of.

2. (*Rare.*) Revile, calumniate, defame, traduce, malign, speak evil of.

——, *v. i.* Utter blasphemy, speak impiously of God *or* of sacred things, be impious, utter sacrilege.

Blasphemous, *a.* Impious, sacrilegious, profane.

Blasphemy, *n.* 1. Impiousness, sacrilege.

2. Profanity, swearing, cursing.

Blast, *n.* 1. Gust, squall, sudden burst, blow.

2. Peal, blare, clang.

3. Explosion, outbreak, burst, discharge.

——, *v. t.* 1. Blight, kill, destroy, ruin, annihilate, wither, shrivel.

2. Rend by explosion, burst, explode, split.

Blatant, *a.* 1. Bellowing, braying.

2. Clamorous, obstreperous, vociferous, noisy.

3. Offensively assertive *or* obtrusive.

Blatherskite, *n.* (*Colloq. U. S. and Scotland.*) Blusterer, vaporer, prater, vapid talker, voluble dunce, noisy fool. Cf. BLUSTER.

Blattering, *a.* Blustering, swaggering, noisy.

Blaze, *n.* Flame, flaming light, flare, flash, bright burning, glow.

——, *v. i.* Flame, burn with a flame, glow.

——, *v. t.* Publish, proclaim, blazon, make known, noise abroad, spread abroad, blaze abroad.

Blazon, *v. t.* 1. Emblazon, emblaze, adorn with ensigns armorial.

2. Display, exhibit, set forth, make a show of, show off.

3. See BLAZE, *v. t.*

——, *n.* 1. Blazonry.

2. Exhibition, show, pompous display.

Blazonry, *n.* Emblazonry, heraldry.

Bleach, *v. t.* Whiten, blanch, etiolate, make *or* render white.

——, *v. i.* Whiten, blanch, etiolate, grow *or* become white.

Bleak, *a.* 1. Unsheltered, exposed, bare, unprotected, wind-swept, stormbeaten.

2. Cold, chill, chilly, raw, biting, piercing, desolating.

3. Desolate, drear, dreary, ungenial, cheerless, comfortless.

Blear, *v. t.* Dim, make rheumy, make watery (*as of the eyes*).

Bleary, *a.* Dim-sighted, blear-eyed.

Bleb, *n.* Blister, vesicle, little tumor.

Bleed, *v. i.* 1. Lose blood, drip blood, be dropping with blood.

2. Exude sap *or* juice, drip sap.

——, *v. t.* 1. Take blood from.

2. Exude, secrete, give forth, drop.

Bleeding, *n.* Phlebotomy, venesection, blood-letting.

Blemish, *v. t.* 1. Stain, sully, blur, spot, tarnish, mar, injure, taint.

2. Defame, vilify, traduce, asperse, calumniate, slander, malign, revile, run down, speak ill of. See ABUSE.

——, *n.* 1. Stain, spot, defect, disfigurement, speck, blot, blur, soil, tarnish, flaw, fault, imperfection.

2. Disgrace, dishonor, reproach, taint, stain, spot, blot.

Blench, *v. i.* Shrink, flinch, start back, give way, yield, weaken.

——, *v. t.* Shrink from, evade, shirk, avoid.

Blend, *v. t.* and *v. i.* Mingle, mix, intermingle, coalesce, commingle, amalgamate, unite, fuse, interfuse, make confluent, combine.

Bless, *v. t.* 1. Delight, gladden, make happy, beatify.

2. Glorify, exalt, celebrate, magnify, praise, extol, give thanks to, adore, gratefully adore.

Blessed, *a.* 1. Happy, beatified, blissful.

2. Holy, hallowed, sacred.

Blessedness, *n.* Bliss, blissfulness, happiness, felicity, beatitude, joy.

Blessing, *n.* 1. Benediction, benison, invocation of happiness.

2. Good, benefit, advantage, profit, gain, boon, service.

3. Glory, honor, praise, thanksgiving, gratitude.

Blight, *n.* Pestilence (*among plants*), mildew, blast, withering.

——, *v. t.* 1. Blast, wither, shrivel, kill, destroy, taint with mildew, cause to decay.

2. Disappoint, frustrate, blast, destroy, crush, annihilate, annul, bring to naught.

Blind, *a.* 1. Sightless, visionless, eyeless, unseeing, stone-blind.

2. Ignorant, undiscerning, unperceiving, purblind, unenlightened, benighted, without insight, injudicious, incapable of judging.

3. Concealed, hidden, remote, obscure, dim, unlucid, involved, intricate, labyrinthine, confused, mazy, dark, private.

4. Indiscriminate, heedless, careless, thoughtless, inconsiderate, headlong, rash.

5. Closed, shut, issueless, blank, without exit, leading nowhere.

——, *v. t.* 1. Make blind, deprive of sight, blear, darken.

2. Hoodwink, blindfold.

——, *n.* 1. Screen, cover, shade, shutter, curtain.

2. Blinder, blinker.

3. Concealment, disguise, pretext, misleader, subterfuge, pretence, ruse, feint, stratagem.

Blind-alley, *n.* Cul-de-sac.

Blinder, *n.* Blind, blinker.

Blindfold, *v. t.* Blind, hoodwink, cover the eyes of, hinder from seeing (*by a bandage over the eyes*).

——, *a.* 1. Blinded (*by a bandage over the eyes*), blindfolded.

2. Blind, headlong, rash, heedless, inconsiderate.

Blindman's-buff, *n.* Hoodman-blind, blindman-buff.

Blindside, *n.* Weakness, foible, failing, defect, weak side, weak point.

Blink, *n.* 1. Glance, glimpse, sight, view, wink.

2. Glimmer, gleam, sheen, shimmer, twinkle.

——, *v. i.* 1. Wink, nictitate, nictate, see obscurely.

2. Flicker, flutter, intermit, shine fitfully, twinkle, glitter, gleam.

——, *v. t.* Overlook (*purposely*), disregard, avoid, evade, ignore, pass over, gloss over, gloze, shut out of sight, make no account of, pretend not to see.

Blinker, *n.* Blinder, blind.

Bliss, *n.* Happiness, felicity, blessedness, blissfulness, beatitude, beatification, joy, transport, rapture, ecstasy, heavenly joy, heaven.

Blissful, *a.* 1. Transported, enraptured, in raptures, in ecstasies, very happy, full of joy, highly blessed.

2. Transporting, enrapturing, delightful, happy, joyful, rapturous, ecstatic, ravishing, blessed, conferring bliss.

Blister, *n.* 1. Vesicle, pustule, blain, bleb, blob.

2. Puffy film, bleb, blob, air-bubble.

3. Vesicatory, vesicant, blistering plaster, sinapism.

——, *v. t.* Raise blisters on, vesicate.

——, *v. i.* Rise in blisters, form vesicles *or* blebs.

Blithe, *a.* Cheerful, gay, sprightly, lively, animated, elated, vivacious, joyous, joyful, merry, mirthful, jocund, sportive, airy, buoyant, debonair, blithesome, of good cheer, in high spirits, in good spirits, full of life, full of spirit.

Bloat, *v. t.* Swell, inflate, distend, dilate, puff up, blow up, make turgid.

——, *v. i.* Swell, dilate, be swollen, be inflated *or* distended, be·puffed *or* blown up, become turgid.

Bloating, *n.* Swelling, dilatation, tumefaction, expanding, expansion. See DILATION.

Blob, *n.* Bubble, blobber, bleb, blister, vesicle.

Block, *v. t.* 1. Obstruct, close, blockade, stop, bar, check, choke, jam, impede, hinder, arrest, shut up, stop up, block up, fill up.

2. Mould, shape, form (on a block).

3. Make steady *or* firm, stiffen, brace.

——, *n.* 1. Thick and heavy piece (*as of wood or stone*), mass.

2. Mould (*on which objects are made*).

3. Simpleton, fool, blockhead. See DUNCE.

4. City block, square.

5. (*Naut.*) Pulley, tackle.

6. Executioner's block (*in fig. sense*), scaffold, execution.

7. Stoppage, obstruction, jam, pack.

Blockade, *v. t.* Close (*as ports, so as to prevent egress or ingress*), block, barricade,

shut up, stop up. See BESET and BE-
LEAGUER.

Blockade, *n.* Closure (*as of a port*), shutting up, blocking up.

Blockhead, *n.* Simpleton, fool. See
DUNCE.

Blockish, *a.* Stupid, stolid, heavy, doltish,
unintelligent, dull, stockish. See BEE-
TLE-HEADED and STUPID.

Block up. Obstruct. See BLOCK.

Blond, ⎫
Blonde, ⎬ *a.* Fair, light, flaxen.

BLOOD, *n.* 1. Vital fluid, vital current,
life-blood, life-current; cruor, gore.

2. Posterity, descendants, offspring,
children, progeny.

3. Kin, kindred, relations, family,
house, line.

4. Lineage, descent, kinship, kindred,
consanguinity, relationship, common
derivation, common ancestry.

5. High birth, noble extraction.

6. Temper, disposition, feelings, spirit,
courage, passion, mettle.

7. Hotspur, madcap, fiery fellow, hot
spark, blade.

Blood-letting, *n.* Bleeding, phlebotomy.

Bloodshed, *n.* Slaughter, carnage, butchery, massacre, murder, bloodshedding,
homicide, bloodspilling.

Blood-stained, *a.* 1. Bloody, stained with
blood, ensanguined.

2. Blood-guilty, murderous, homicidal.

Blood-sucker, *n.* Leech.

Blood-thirsty, *a.* Cruel, savage, ferocious,
tigerish, inhuman, barbarous, barbarian,
fell, truculent, ruthless, bloody, murderous, bloody-minded, sanguinary.

Bloody, *a.* 1. Sanguinary, ensanguined,
gory. See BLOOD-STAINED.

2. Murderous, cruel. See BLOOD-
THIRSTY.

Bloom, *n.* 1. Efflorescence, flower, blossom, blow.

2. Efflorescence, florescence, flowering,
blossoming, blow.

3. Flush, freshness, vigor, prime, heyday, delicate newness, delicacy, innocence.

4. Flush, glow, carnation, rose, roseate
hue.

5. Powdery film, delicate furze, down.

——, *v. i.* 1. Flower, blossom, put forth
blossoms, blow.

2. Prosper, thrive.

Bloomy, *a.* 1. Flowery, full of blossoms.

2. Fresh, glowing, roseate.

3. Downy, covered with bloom.

Blossom, *n.* Flower, bloom, blow, efflorescence.

——, *v. i.* Flower, bloom, blow.

Blot, *v. t.* 1. Efface, obliterate, erase,
cancel, expunge, rub out, blot out, scratch
out, strike out.

2. Spot, stain, blur, disfigure, deface,
sully.

3. Tarnish, sully, disgrace, dishonor,
blur, spot, stain.

——, *n.* 1. Obliteration, erasure, blotting,
blur.

2. Blur, spot, stain, blemish.

3. Disgrace, cause of reproach, blur,
spot, stain, dishonor.

Blotch, *n.* 1. Pustule, eruption, pimple,
blain, bleb, blemish.

2. Spot (*of any kind, especially irregular*), stain, smudge, patch, splotch.

BLOW, *n.* 1. Stroke, knock, punch,
"slug," "swipe," "smack," rap, pat,
thump, dab, beat, lick, thwack, bang,
slam, wallop, buffet, impact.

2. Calamity, disaster, misfortune,
affliction.

3. Gale, blast, gust.

——, *v. i.* 1. Move *or* flow in currents (*as
the wind*).

2. Pant, puff, lose breath, breathe
hard, gasp.

3. (*Colloq.*) Boast, brag, gasconade,
talk large, bluster.

4. Spout (*as a whale*).

——, *v. t.* 1. Drive (*by blowing*), impel.

2. Force wind upon, blast, puff, direct
a current of air upon.

3. Sound, wind, sound upon, wind a
blast upon.

Blown, *a.* 1. Swollen, inflated, puffed up.

2. Stale, worthless, discredited, past
its prime.

3. Out of breath, exhausted, fatigued,
tired out.

Blow up, *v. t.* 1. Inflate, fill with air.

2. Burst, explode, blast, burst in
pieces, shatter, scatter by explosion,
cause to explode.

3. Kindle.

4. (*Low.*) Scold, rate, berate, chide,
reprimand, censure, reprove, blame,
scold at.

——, *v. i.* Explode, burst, be scattered by
explosion.

Blowzed, *a.* Ruddy, blowzy, tanned,
ruddy-faced, high-colored, sun-burnt.

Blubber, *v. i.* Cry (*so as to swell the cheeks*),
whine, whimper, weep.

Bludgeon, *n.* Club, cudgel.

BLUE, *a.* 1. Azure, cerulean, sapphirine,
amethystine, sky-colored, cobalt, indigo,
ultramarine.

2. Livid, ghastly, pallid.

3. (*Colloq.*) Melancholy, dejected,
dispirited, depressed, sad, glum, gloomy,

mopish, downcast, desponding, down-hearted, hypochondriac, hipped, chap-fallen, low-spirited, cast down, in the dumps, with a long face, in the blues, down in the mouth.

4. (*Colloq.*) Dismal, depressing, dole-ful, gloomy, dispiriting, melancholy, disheartening.

——, *n.* Azure, sky-color, cerulean, ame-thystine, sapphirine.

Blues, *n. pl.* [With *The.*] Melancholy, dejection, depression, despondency, hy-pochondria, dumps, megrims, vapors, low spirits, blue-devils, the dismals.

Blue-stocking, *n.* Pedantic woman, sapient female.

Bluff, *a.* 1. Broad and full, hearty and open. (*Said of the countenance.*)

2. Rough and hearty, blunt and frank, roughly good-natured.

3. Steep, abrupt, precipitous, like a bluff.

——, *n.* Precipitous bank (*especially on the margin of a river* or *the sea*), cliff, height, headland.

Blunder, *v. i.* 1. Mistake (*grossly*), err (*from want of care*).

2. Flounder, stumble, go bungling.

3. Bungle, be awkward, "boggle," "foozle," miss the mark, miss the point, be stupid, inaccurate, *or* at loose ends.

——, *n.* Mistake (*gross*), error (*from thoughtlessness*), bull, solecism, "howler," gross mistake, piece of stupidity.

Blunderbuss, *n.* 1. Short gun (*with a large bore*).

2. Blunderer, blunderhead, stupid fellow, dolt.

Blunderer, *n.* Blunderhead, blunderbuss, stupid fellow, dolt.

Blunt, *a.* 1. Dull, obtuse, pointless, edge-less, unsharpened.

2. Dull, thick-witted, obtuse, insensi-ble, stolid.

3. Abrupt, bluff, plain, plain-spoken, outspoken, downright, uncourtly, un-ceremonious, without formal civility.

4. Brusque, rough, harsh, uncourte-ous, ungracious, impolite, rude.

——, *v. t.* 1. Dull, make dull.

2. Benumb, paralyze, deaden, stupefy, obtund, hebetate, make insensible, cal-lous, *or* obtuse.

3. Moderate, allay, assuage, mitigate, quiet, alleviate, soften.

Blunt-witted, *a.* Dull, stupid, stolid, dolt-ish, blockish, obtuse, unintelligent, un-intellectual.

Blur, *n.* 1. Blot, stain, spot, blemish, soil, tarnish, defect.

2. Confusion (*of vision*), dim and un-certain spot, confused glimmer.

3. Blot, stain, disgrace, spot, smear, blemish, blotch.

——, *v. t.* 1. Obscure, darken, dim, bedim, partially erase.

2. Tarnish, stain, blot, sully, spot, blemish.

Blush, *v. i.* Redden (*in the cheeks*), color, flush, glow.

——, *n.* Reddening (*of the cheeks*), suffusion of the face.

Bluster, *v. i.* 1. Roar (*as the wind*), make a loud noise.

2. Vapor, swagger, bully, vaunt, swell, domineer, gasconade, play the bully. See BOAST.

3. Make a great ado.

——, *n.* 1. Boisterousness, noise, tumult, turbulence.

2. Boasting, swaggering, bullying, blattering, bravado, vaporing, gasconade, fanfaronade.

3. Great ado, much ado about noth-ing.

Blusterer, *n.* Swaggerer, bully, boaster, braggart, vaunter, roisterer, braggadocio, drawcansir, fire-eater, fanfaron, noisy fellow, "bouncer."

Blustering, *a.* 1. Windy, stormy, tem-pestuous, squally, gusty, tumultuous, turbulent, noisy, roaring.

2. Swaggering, boasting, bragging, braggart, blattering, pompous, assuming, important, arrogant, swelling, big, bully-ing, overbearing, vaporing, self-sufficient.

Board, *n.* 1. Plank (*thin*), deal, panel.

2. Food, diet, provision, fare, victuals, entertainment, meals.

3. Conclave, council, committee, cabinet.

Boast, *v. i.* Brag, vaunt, gasconade, vapor, bluster, crow, crack, flourish, exalt one's self, magnify one's self, give one's self airs, talk big, ride a high horse.

——, *v. t.* Magnify (*unduly*), make much of, boast of, brag of.

——, *n.* 1. Vaunt, brag, braggadocio, bombast, gasconade, rodomontade, va-poring, bravado, boasting, blustering, swaggering, fanfaronade, magniloquence, flourish of trumpets, much cry and little wool.

2. Cause of pride *or* laudable exulta-tion.

Boaster, *n.* Braggart, braggadocio, rodo-mont. See BLUSTERER.

Boastful, *a.* Boasting, vaunting, bragging, braggart, vaporing, blustering, exulting, triumphant, Thrasonical, vain-glorious, cock-a-hoop.

BOAT, *n.* Bark, craft, skiff, vessel, ship.

Boat-shaped, *a.* Navicular, scaphoid.

Bob, *v. t.* 1. Move with a jerk.

2. Strike (*suddenly and lightly*), rap, knock.

3. Clip, cut short.

——, *v. i.* 1. Play back and forward, have a jerking motion.

2. Angle (*with a jerking motion*), fish.

——, *n.* Pendant, hanging appendage.

Bode, *v. t.* Betoken, portend, foreshow, foreshadow, prefigure, presage, augur, foretell, predict, forebode, prophesy, be ominous of.

——, *v. i.* Forebode, presage, be ominous.

Bodice, *n.* 1. Corset, stays.

2. Waist (*of a dress*), corsage.

Bodiless, *a.* Incorporeal, without a body.

Bodily, *a.* 1. Of the body.

2. Corporeal, physical, carnal, fleshly.

——, *adv.* 1. Corporeally.

2. Entirely (*as respects the body or mass*), completely, wholly, altogether.

BODY, *n.* 1. Material substance, material part (*as distinguished from the spirit or life*).

2. Carcass, corpse, dead body, "remains."

3. Visible form *or* frame.

4. Trunk (*as distinguished from the limbs*), soma, torso; stem, bole.

5. Bulk, corpus, mass, aggregate, main part (*as distinguished from subordinate parts*), greater part.

6. Person, being, individual, mortal, creature.

7. Company, assemblage, band, corps, force, troop; party, coterie, society, association, corporation.

8. System, summary, general collection.

9. Consistency, thickness, substance.

Bog, *n.* Morass, quagmire, slough, fen, marsh, swamp, moss.

Bogey, } *n.* Hobgoblin, bugaboo.
Bogy, }

Boggle, *v. i.* Hesitate, vacillate, waver, falter, demur, shrink, hang back, shrink back, hang fire, be in suspense.

Bogus, *a.* Counterfeit, false, fraudulent, spurious, sham.

Boil, *v. i.* 1. Be agitated by heat, be in ebullition.

2. Be in violent agitation, seethe, effervesce, foam, froth.

3. Bubble, rise in bubbles.

4. Be ardent, be hot, be wildly turbulent, rage.

——, *v. t.* Seethe.

——, *n.* Furuncle, pustule, gathering, inflamed tumor.

BOILING, *a.* Bubbling; at temperature to vaporize.

——, *n.* Ebullition, ebullience.

Boisterous, *a.* 1. Roaring, loud, stormy.

2. Noisy, tumultuous, turbulent, rampageous, violent, vociferous, clamorous, obstreperous, "rough-housing," loud.

Bold, *a.* 1. Fearless, dauntless, daring, valiant, valorous, doughty, undaunted, hardy, intrepid, courageous, brave, heroic, audacious, adventurous, venturesome, gallant, spirited, mettlesome, manful, manly, stout-hearted, bold-spirited.

2. Confident, assured, self-reliant, self-possessed, self-poised, free from bashfulness.

3. Impudent, insolent, "nervy," rude, impertinent, saucy, forward, pushing, assuming, brazen-faced, bold-faced.

4. Conspicuous, striking, projecting, prominent, standing out to the view.

5. Steep, abrupt, precipitous, prominent.

Boldness, *n.* 1. Fearlessness, dauntlessness, intrepidity, courage, bravery, doughtiness, dauntlessness, adventurousness, gallantry, spirit, mettle, valor, audacity, daring, pluck, heroism, hardihood, spunk.

2. Confidence, assurance, self-reliance, self-possession, self-poise, confident mien, freedom from bashfulness.

3. Impudence, insolence, sauciness, rudeness, impertinence, assurance, effrontery, presumption, brass, face, front.

4. Prominence, striking character *or* quality.

5. Steepness, abruptness, precipitousness, prominence.

Bole, *n.* 1. Body (*of a tree*), stem, trunk.

2. Bolus, large pill.

Boll, *n.* Pod, capsule, pericarp.

Bolster, *n.* Supporting cushion.

——, *v. t.* Support (*something weak or undeserving*), prevent from falling, hold up, prop up, defend, maintain.

Bolt, *n.* 1. Arrow, dart, shaft, missile.

2. Thunderbolt, stroke of lightning.

3. Metal pin *or* fastening.

4. Sieve.

——, *v. t.* 1. Fasten with a bolt *or* bolts.

2. Swallow (*without chewing*), gulp down, swallow whole.

3. Sift, pass through a sieve.

——, *v. i.* 1. Bounce, start suddenly, spring out abruptly.

2. Abscond, make off rapidly, run away, leave suddenly.

Bolt-upright, *a.* Perpendicular, quite upright.

Bolus, *n.* Bole, large pill.

Bombard, *v. t.* Attack with bombs, shell, cannonade; pelt.

Bombardment, *n.* Attack with bombs.

Bombast, *n.* Fustian, rodomontade, rant, altiloquence, magniloquence, sesquipedalianism, grandiloquence, mouthing, turgid talk, inflated style, swelling *or* pompous phraseology.

Bombastic, *a.* Inflated, turgid, tumid, swelling, stilted, grandiloquent, magniloquent, altiloquent, sesquipedalian, pompous, high-flown, "highfalutin."

Bona fide. [L.] Really, truly, actually, sincerely, in good faith, upon honor.

Bonbon, *n.* Sugar-plum, sweet, confection, sweet-meat.

Bond, *n.* 1. Band, ligature, cord, ligament, fastening, link, nexus.

2. [*In pl.*] Fetters, chains, shackle, bondage, captivity, constraint, durance, imprisonment, prison.

3. Tie, connection, coupling, attraction, link, union, attachment, uniting, influence.

4. Obligation, compact, binding, contract.

——, *a.* Enslaved, slave, in bonds, in bondage, captive, destitute of freedom.

Bondage, *n.* Servitude, slavery, thraldom, helotry, serfdom, peonage, captivity, imprisonment, confinement, bond-service, bonds, restraint of personal liberty.

BONE, *n.* (*Basic Eng.*) Osseous substance; part of skeleton.

Bonhomie, *n.* [Fr.] Good-nature, easy humor.

Bon-mot, *n.* [Fr.] Jest, joke, witticism, witty repartee.

Bonne-bouche, *n.* [Fr.] Titbit, delicacy, nice bit, delicate morsel, choice morsel, delicious mouthful.

Bonny, *a.* 1. Handsome, beautiful, fair, fine, pretty.

2. Cheerful, blithe, sprightly, buoyant, airy, gay, merry, joyous, jolly, jocund, winsome, buxom, playful, sportive, jocose, in good spirits, in high spirits.

3. Plump, round, chubby, in good health.

Bonus, *n.* [L.] Premium, reward, honorarium, gift, subsidy.

Bon-vivant, *n.* [Fr.] Luxurious liver, high liver, epicure.

Booby, *n.* Simpleton, fool. See DUNCE.

BOOK, *n.* Work, volume, brochure, monograph, tract, pamphlet, treatise, handbook, manual, textbook, booklet, chapbook, compendium.

Bookish, *a.* Given to reading, fond of books, fond of study, very studious.

Book-keeper, *n.* Accountant.

Book-making, *n.* Betting, laying of odds.

Bookseller, *n.* Bibliopole, bibliopolist.

Bookworm, *n.* Great reader *or* student (*without discrimination and without definite purpose*), "grind."

Boom, *v. i.* 1. Roar, resound, drone, hum, rumble.

2. Rush, bound, dash forward.

——, *n.* Resounding noise, roar, booming, droning, deep and hollow humming.

Boon, *n.* 1. Gift, present, benefaction, grant, favor.

2. Benefit, blessing, advantage, good, privilege.

——, *a.* 1. Kind, bountiful, generous, benign, benignant.

2. Gay, merry, jovial, jolly, convivial

Boor, *n.* Rustic, clown, hind, lout, lubber, swain, peasant, bumpkin, clodpole, clodhopper.

Boorish, *a.* Rustic, rude, clownish, clodhopping, loutish, bearish, awkward, clumsy, ungainly, coarse, rough, unrefined, uncourtly, ungraceful, uncouth, gawky, lubberly.

Boost, *v. t.* (*Colloq.*) Recommend, cry up, eulogize.

BOOT, *n.* Buskin, cothurnus, bootee, oxford.

——, *n.* Profit, advantage, gain, premium.

——, *v. t.* [*Generally used impersonally.*] Profit, benefit, advantage, avail, make difference.

Bootee, *n.* Bootikin, half-boot, short boot.

Bootless, *a.* Useless, unavailing, fruitless, futile, unprofitable, profitless, valueless, worthless, ineffectual, abortive, vain, idle, without avail.

Booty, *n.* Plunder (*to be used for any purpose*), loot, spoil, pillage. See PREY.

Boozy, *a.* Tipsy, bemused, inebriated, fuddled, disguised, maudlin, mellow, half-drunk, half-seas-over, in liquor.

Border, *n.* 1. Edge, rim, brim, verge, brink, margin, marge, skirt, hem, fringe, edging, selvedge.

2. Limit, boundary, confine, frontier, march, outskirts, bounds.

——, *v. t.* Put a border upon, adorn with a border, make a border for, rim, skirt, fringe.

Border on. 1. Adjoin, be in contact with, be coterminous with, touch at the side *or* end of, be contiguous to, lie adjacent to, be in juxtaposition with, border upon.

2. Approach, come near to, approximate, almost reach, want but little of, border upon.

Bore, *v. t.* 1. Perforate, pierce, drill.

2. Weary (*by tedious repetition*),

fatigue, tire, tire out, plague, trouble, vex, worry, annoy.

Bore, *n.* 1. Hole, calibre.

2. Proser, button-holer.

3. Eager, great tidal flood.

Boreal, *a.* Northern, northerly, arctic.

Boredom, *n.* 1. Realm of bores, domain of bores, land of bores.

2. Bores, the aggregate of bores, all the bores.

3. Being bored *or* "fed up," *ennui*, tedium, weariness, dulness.

Born again. Regenerated, regenerate, converted, renewed in spirit.

Borough, *n.* Town (*in England, a town represented in Parliament*), township, corporate town, corporation.

Borrow, *v. t.* 1. Take *or* receive as a loan, get on credit, obtain on trust.

2. Take, appropriate, adopt, imitate, make use of.

3. Take on, simulate, dissemble, feign.

Bosh, *n.* Nonsense, trash, twaddle. See BALDERDASH.

Bosk, *n.* Thicket, grove, bushes.

Boskage, *n.* 1. Thicket, grove, shrubbery.

2. Foliage, leafage, shrubbiness, leafiness.

Bosky, *a.* Shrubby, woody, leafy, bushy, sylvan, shady.

Bosom, *n.* 1. Breast, heart, affection.

2. Hollow, deep, depth, depths, midst, inmost recesses.

3. Retirement, quiet, retreat, inner mystery, intimate privacy.

Bosom-friend, *n.* Confidant, intimate friend, dear friend, inseparable companion.

Boss, *n.* 1. Protuberance, knob, stud, protuberant part.

2. Superintendent, overseer, master-workman, foreman, master, employer.

——, *v. t.* Stud, cover with bosses, bestud, emboss.

Bossy, *a.* Full of bosses, covered with studs.

Botch, *n.* 1. Pustule, blotch, blain, sore.

2. Failure, miscarriage, bad job, clumsy performance, bungling piece of work.

——, *v. t.* 1. Mend awkwardly, patch clumsily.

2. Put together unskilfully, construct in a bungling manner.

Both, *a.* The two, the one and the other, one as well as the other, the pair, the couple.

——, *conj.* [*Preceding a word or phrase which is followed by* and: Both — and.] As well — as; not only — but also; not only — but; not alone — but.

Bother, *v. t.* Perplex, worry, harass, trouble, annoy, tease, vex, plague, molest, incommode, disturb, pester, pother.

——, *n.* (*Colloq.*) Perplexity, vexation, annoyance, plague, trouble, pother.

BOTTLE, *n.* Phial, carafe, carboy, canteen, cruet, cruse, decanter, demijohn, flagon, flask.

Bottom, *n.* 1. Lowest part, base, foot.

2. Foundation, basis, groundwork, base, footing.

3. Dale, valley, meadow, alluvial land.

4. Fundament, seat, buttocks.

5. Stamina, native strength, power of endurance.

6. Grounds, lees, dregs, sediments.

——, *v. t.* Found, establish, build.

——, *v. i.* Rest (*for support*), be based.

Bottomless, *a.* Abysmal, unfathomable

Boudoir, *n.* [Fr.] Cabinet, private room, retired apartment, bower.

Bough, *n.* Branch, limb, shoot, offshoot.

Bouillon, *n.* [Fr.] Broth, soup.

Bounce, *n.* 1. Knock, thump, sudden blow.

2. Bound, leap, jump, spring, vault.

——, *v. i.* 1. Bolt, leap, *or* spring suddenly.

2. Rebound, recoil.

3. Knock, thump. See BEAT.

——, *v. t.* Thrust, drive against.

Bouncer, *n.* (*Colloq.*) 1. See BLUSTERER.

2. Falsehood, lie, "bounce," "whopper."

3. Giant, strapper, "whaler," huge fellow, huge specimen.

Bouncing, *a.* (*Colloq.*) Stout, lusty, strong, portly, burly, huge, great, strapping.

Bound, *n.* 1. Limit, bourn, border, compass, confine, pale, range. See BOUNDARY.

2. Leap, jump, spring, bounce.

——, *v. t.* Limit, delimit, demarcate, border, terminate, circumscribe.

——, *v. i.* 1. Jump, leap, spring.

2. Rebound, spring back.

——, *a.* [Followed by *to* or *for*.] 1. Destined, tending, going, on the way.

2. Obligated, committed.

Boundary, *n.* Limit, border, confine, march, bourn, bound, periphery, circuit, circumference, verge, term, termination.

Bounden, *a.* Obligatory, binding, appointed.

Boundless, *a.* Unbounded, unlimited, unconfined, undefined, immeasurable, illimitable, limitless, vast, endless, infinite.

Bountiful, *a.* 1. Liberal, munificent, beneficent, generous, princely, bounteous.

2. Abounding, abundant, overflowing, plenteous.

Bounty, *n.* 1. Liberality, munificence, beneficence, generosity.

2. Present, gift, benefaction.

3. Premium (*for encouragement*), reward, bonus, subsidy.

Bouquet, *n.* [Fr.] 1. Nosegay, bunch of flowers, posy, *boutonnière*, garland.

2. Aroma, delicate odor and flavor, redolence.

Bourdon, *n.* 1. Walking-staff, pilgrim's staff.

2. Bagpipe-drone, drone; bass-stop.

Bourgeoisie, *n.* [Fr.] Middle classes (*especially such as depend on trade*), tradespeople, townsfolk.

Bourn, *n.* 1. Bound, limit, confine, border. See BOUNDARY.

2. Brook, torrent, rivulet, rill, beck, runnel, runlet, burn.

Bourse, *n.* [Fr.] Exchange.

Bout, *n.* 1. Turn, twist, flexure, curve, curvature. See BEND.

2. Conflict, contest, round, match, set to, trial.

Bow, *v. t.* 1. (*Pron.* bō) Bend, inflect, crook, incurvate, curve, make crooked.

2. (*Pron.* bou) Incline, turn downward, bend, bend down, prostrate, droop, drop.

3. Depress, sink, cast down, bring down, crush, subdue.

——, *v. i.* (*Pron.* bō) Bend, buckle, be inflected, be bent, give way.

2. (*Pron.* bou) Incline (*in token of respect, reverence,* or *submission*), bend the head, make a bow, nod; stoop.

——, *n.* 1. (*Naut.*) Fore part (*of a ship*), prow, beak, stem, fore-foot.

2. Bob, nod, curtsy, obeisance.

——, *n.* (*Pron.* bō) Arc, curve, crescent.

Bowels, *n. pl.* 1. Intestines, entrails, viscera, inwards, guts.

2. Inside, interior, interior parts, midst.

3. Compassion, pity, tenderness, mercy, mercifulness, feeling, fellow-feeling, sympathy.

Bower, *n.* 1. Arbor, grotto, shady recess, shady retreat, summer-house.

2. Bow-anchor, working-anchor.

3. Knave (*of the trump color*).

Bowl, *n.* 1. Goblet, beaker, basin, crater, (*antiq.*), porringer.

2. Hollow, depression, receptacle.

Bowman, *n.* Archer, sagittary.

Bow-window, *n.* Bay-window.

BOX, *n.* 1. Case, receptacle, chest, cabinet, carton, casket.

2. Driver's seat, coachman's seat.

3. Enclosed seat *or* seats (*in a theatre*), loge, compartment.

4. Blow, stroke, cuff, buffet.

——, *v. t.* 1. Enclose in a box, case, put in chests *or* cases.

2. Strike (*with the hand* or *fist, as the ears*), buffet, cuff.

——, *v. i.* Spar, practise pugilism, play at fisticuffs, practise with the gloves.

BOY, *n.* Lad, stripling, male child, youth.

Boycott, *v. t.* Shun, ostracize, blackball.

Boyish, *a.* 1. Of boyhood.

2. Childish, puerile.

Brace, *v. t.* 1. Tighten, draw tight, make tense, strain up.

2. Strengthen, fortify, reinforce, buttress, shore, support, prop, give strength to, stiffen, truss.

——, *n.* 1. Couple, pair.

2. Prop, support, clamp, girder, stay, shore, strut, truss, tie.

3. Bit-stock.

Braces, *n. pl.* 1. Suspenders, gallowses.

2. Straps (*on which a carriage rests*).

Bracing, *a.* Strengthening, invigorating, stimulating, tonic.

Bracket, *n.* Corbel, console, brace.

Brackish, *a.* Saltish, somewhat salt.

Brag, *v. i.* Boast, vaunt, gasconade, bluster, vapor, flourish, exalt one's self, magnify one's self, talk big.

——, *n.* Boast, vaunt, gasconade, bluster, bravado, vaporing, blattering, braggadocio, great cry and little wool.

Braggadocio, *n.* 1. Boaster, blusterer, vaunter, braggart, bouncer, vaporer, blatterer, gascon, vain-glorious fellow.

2. Brag. See BOAST, *n.*

Braggart, *n.* See BOASTER.

Brahman, } *n.* Hindoo priest.
Brahmin, }

Braid, *v. i.* Plait, plat, intertwine, interweave, interlace, weave together.

BRAIN, *n.* (*Basic Eng.*) Cerebral organ.

Brain-fever, *n.* Phrenitis, meningitis.

Brain-pan, *n.* Skull, cranium.

Brains, *n. pl.* Understanding, sense, mentality, mind, reason, intellect, capacity, intellectual faculties.

Brain-sick, *a.* Demented, alienated, fantastic, disordered, crotchety, crazed, crazy.

BRAKE, *n.* 1. Checking mechanism on vehicles, clog, block, drag, skid.

2. Thicket, brushwood, jungle.

Bramble, *n.* Brier-bush, brier, prickly shrub, bramble-bush.

BRANCH, *n.* 1. Bough, limb, shoot, offset, twig, sprig.

2. Off-shoot, ramification, arm, projecting part, fork, spur.

3. Section, department, subdivision, part, portion, article, member.

4. Tributary, affluent, tributary stream.

5. Derivative line, cognate line, member of a stock.

——, *v. i.* Diverge, ramify, furcate, fork, spread in branches, shoot off, branch off, radiate.

Branching, *n.* Ramification, arborescence.

——, *a.* Arborescent, arboriform, dendriform, dendroid, dendritic.

Brand, *n.* 1. Fire-brand, flambeau, torch.

2. Thunderbolt, lightning-flash, bolt.

3. Mark (*of a hot iron*), stamp, cachet, tally.

4. Kind, quality, grade, make.

5. Stigma, stain, reproach. See BLOT.

——, *v. t.* 1. Mark (*with a hot iron*), mark as a criminal.

2. Stigmatize, denounce, gibbet.

Brandish, *v. t.* Flourish, wave, shake.

Brand-new, *a.* Quite new, fire-new, spick and span new, span new.

Brash, *a.* 1. Hasty, rash, impetuous.

2. (*Local, U. S.*) Brittle, fragile, easily broken.

BRASS, *n.* 1. Alloy of copper and zinc.

2. Assurance, boldness, impudence, impertinence, pertness, effrontery, presumption, audacity, forwardness, face, front.

Brassy, *a.* (*Colloq.*) Bold, pert, assuming, forward, brazen, brazen-faced, saucy, impudent.

Brat, *n.* [*Term of contempt.*] Child, urchin, bantling, infant, bairn.

Bravado, *n.* Boast, boasting, brag, bluster, storming, furious bombast.

Brave, *a.* 1. Fearless (*from temperament*), courageous, intrepid, daring, undaunted, dauntless, valiant, bold, chivalrous, chivalric, gallant, "game," valorous, doughty, heroic, hardy, spirited, mettlesome, manful, manly, stalwart, stout-hearted, high-spirited, high-hearted, Spartan, lion-hearted.

2. Gay, brilliant, fine, effective, showy, splendid, gorgeous.

——, *v. t.* Defy, dare, challenge, set at defiance.

Bravery, *n.* Fearlessness, intrepidity, audacity, valor, gallantry, daring, boldness, spirit, mettle, pluck, manhood, heroism, spunk. See COURAGE.

Bravo, *n.* Bandit, assassin, assassinator, murderer, cut-throat, daring villain, desperado.

——, *interj.* Well done!

Brawl, *v. i.* 1. Quarrel (*noisily*), dispute

(*angrily*), wrangle, brangle, jangle, squabble, bicker.

2. Roar, resound.

——, *n.* Quarrel, wrangle, brangle, jangle, squabble, dispute, uproar, broil, altercation, fracas, scuffle, fray, feud, tumult, disturbance, row, mêlée, "rumpus," outbreak. See AFFRAY.

Brawny, *a.* Muscular, sinewy, stalwart, sturdy, athletic, powerful, strong, vigorous, lusty, robust, strapping, Herculean, able-bodied.

Bray, *v. t.* Pound (*into small pieces* or *powder*), bruise, crush, grind, comminute, triturate.

——, *n.* 1. Ass's cry, hee-haw.

2. Harsh sound, blare, roar, crash, blatant voice.

——, *v. i.* 1. Utter a harsh cry (*like the ass*).

2. Make a harsh sound, clamor, vociferate.

Braying, *a.* Blatant, bellowing, clamorous, vociferous.

Brazen, *a.* 1. Made of brass.

2. Bold, brazen-faced. See BRASSY.

Brazier, *n.* 1. Worker *or* artificer in brass.

2. Pan for coals, firepan, mangal.

Breach, *n.* 1. Break, fracture, rupture, disruption, opening, chasm, gap, crack, flaw, fissure, rent, rift.

2. Infraction, violation, infringement, nonobservance.

3. Quarrel, difference, variance, disagreement, dissension, schism, misunderstanding, alienation, disaffection, rupture, split, falling out.

BREAD, *n.* Food (*especially food made of grain*), sustenance, aliment, nutriment, nourishment, subsistence, fare, diet, regimen, victuals, viands, provisions.

Breadth, *n.* 1. Width, broadness, wideness, expanse.

2. Largeness, openness, freedom, liberality, broadmindedness, catholicity, generosity, tolerance, width of view.

Break, *v. t.* 1. Rend, sever, part, dispart, disrupt, rive, fracture, tear asunder.

2. Shatter, shiver, smash, batter, burst, splinter, dash to pieces.

3. Discard, dismiss, discharge, degrade, cashier.

4. Violate, infringe, transgress, disobey, set at nought.

5. Lessen the force of (*as a fall*), mitigate. See ASSUAGE.

6. Interrupt, stop, intermit, cut short.

7. Disclose, open, unfold, lay open.

——, *v. i.* 1. Be shattered, burst, crack, crash, disrupt, splinter, be shivered, be dashed to pieces.

2. Open, dawn, appear.

3. Decline, lose health *or* strength.

Break, *n.* 1. Breach, opening, aperture, gap, fissure, rent, rift, chasm, rupture, disruption, fracture.

2. Crash, break-up, debacle.

3. Interruption, pause, cæsura.

Break away. 1. Escape (*against resistance*), break loose.

2. Be scattered, be dissipated.

Break down, *v. t.* Crush, overwhelm, overcome.

——, *v. i.* Fail, give out.

Breakdown, *n.* Crash, fall, ruin, downfall, failure, collapse.

Breaker, *n.* Rock-broken surge, comber, "whitehorse."

Breaking, *n.* Rupture, fracture. See BREAK, *n.,* 1.

Break of day. Dawn, dawning, daybreak, morning, cockcrowing, dayspring, peep of day, prime of day, first blush of the morning. See MORN.

Break off. 1. Be ruptured.

2. Desist, cease, stop, leave off.

Break out. Issue, break forth, burst out.

Break the ice. Make a beginning, prepare the way, open a way.

Breakwater, *n.* Jetty, pier, mole.

Break with. Fall out, part friendship with, separate from, give up association with.

Breast, *n.* 1. Bosom, thorax, chest.

2. Heart, conscience, affections.

3. Pap, mammary organ, *mamma*, udder, dug.

——, *v. t.* Face, stem, withstand, oppose, resist, bear the breast against.

Breast-bone, *n.* Sternum.

Breastwork, *n.* (*Fort.*) Parapet.

BREATH, *n.* 1. Breathing, respiration, suspiration, inhaling, exhaling, sigh, pant, whiff.

2. Life, existence, animation, breath of life, vital spark.

3. Respite, pause, rest.

4. Moment, instant, breathing-space.

Breathe, *v. i.* 1. Respire.

2. Live, exist.

3. Pause, rest, take breath, have a respite.

——, *v. t.* 1. Respire.

2. Exhale, emit, give out, throw out.

3. Whisper, utter softly.

4. Indicate, manifest, express, show, send forth, diffuse.

Breathing, *n.* Respiration, spiration.

——, *a.* Living, alive, live.

Breathless, *a.* 1. Out of breath, "blown."

2. Dead, lifeless, defunct.

Breech, *n.* Hinder part, after part, butt.

Breeches, *n. pl.* 1. Small-clothes, knee-breeches, knickerbockers.

2. Trousers, pantaloons, "pants."

Breed, *v. t.* 1. Bring forth, bear, conceive and bring to birth, beget, hatch, produce, engender.

2. Nourish, nurture, foster, bring up, rear, raise.

3. Discipline, educate, instruct, train, teach, school, bring up, nurture, rear.

4. Originate, occasion, beget, produce, engender, generate, be the occasion of, give rise to, be the cause of.

——, *v. i.* 1. Bring forth young, produce offspring.

2. Be born, be produced, have birth, arise, take rise, grow, develop.

——, *n.* Race (*of animals*), lineage, pedigree, progeny, stock, family, line, extraction, strain.

Breeding, *n.* 1. Procreation, having *or* begetting offspring, bearing, bringing forth; stirpiculture.

2. Nurture, education, discipline, instruction, training, schooling, rearing, upbringing.

3. Deportment, manners, gentility, gentilesse.

Breeze, *n.* 1. Zephyr, air, gentle gale, gust, moderate wind, light wind.

2. (*Colloq.*) Quarrel, disturbance, commotion, noise, tumult, uproar, stir, agitation.

Breviary, *n.* 1. Abridgment, epitome, compend, compendium, summary, synopsis, syllabus, abstract, digest, brief, conspectus, outline, sum and substance.

2. Prayer-book.

Brevity, *n.* 1. Briefness, shortness, momentariness, transiency.

2. Conciseness, terseness, compression, curtness, succinctness, pithiness.

Brew, *v. t.* 1. Prepare by fermentation.

2. Contrive, plot, devise, project, hatch, concoct, foment, excite, stir up.

Bribe, *n.* Reward of treachery, price of corruption, corrupting gift, subornation, graft, boodle, *douceur*.

——, *v. t.* Suborn, gain by a bribe, give a bribe to.

BRICK, *n.* (*Basic Eng.*) The building material.

Bridal, *a.* Nuptial, connubial, hymeneal, matrimonial, conjugal.

——, *n.* Marriage, wedding, nuptials, nuptial festival.

Bridewell, *n.* Prison, jail, penitentiary, workhouse, house of correction.

BRIDGE, *v. t.* [*The noun is Basic Eng.*] Span, traverse, overcome, surmount.

Bridle, *n.* Restraint, curb, check, snaffle.

Bridle, *v. t.* 1. Put a bridle on, bit.

2. Restrain, check, curb, control, govern.

——, *v. i.* Ruffle, rustle, bristle, toss the head, be incensed, put on an air of offended dignity.

Brief, *a.* 1. Concise, succinct, compendious, laconic, pithy, terse, epigrammatic, sententious, curt, short.

2. Short, transitory, fleeting, momentary, passing, transient, temporary, short-lived, ephemeral.

——, *n.* 1. Epitome, compendium, summary, synopsis, syllabus, abstract, breviary, abridgment, conspectus.

2. Pontifical letter, papal rescript.

3. (*Law.*) Writ, precept.

Briefly, *adv.* Concisely, in short, in brief, in a few words.

Brigand, *n.* Robber, highwayman, footpad, freebooter, marauder, outlaw, bandit, gangster, thug.

BRIGHT, *a.* 1. Luminous, shining, resplendent, glaring, glowing, lustrous, beamy, gleaming, glittering, glimmering, glistening, glistering, twinkling, beaming, shimmering, sparkling, scintillating, scintillant, coruscating, flashing, flaming, blazing, dazzling, radiant, brilliant, fulgent, effulgent, refulgent, splendid, luminiferous, luciferous, light, vivid, nitid, sheeny, glossy, burnished, sunny, noon-day, meridian, noontide, silvery, argent.

2. Clear, transparent, lucid, pellucid, lucent, lambent, cloudless, untroubled, limpid.

3. Illustrious, glorious, famous.

4. Acute, ingenious, discerning, keen. See INTELLIGENT.

5. Auspicious, cheering, promising, propitious, encouraging, favorable, enlivening, inspiriting, exhilarating, inspiring.

6. Merry, lively, cheerful, cheery, happy, sprightly, genial, smiling, pleasant, animated, vivacious.

Brighten, *v. t.* 1. Polish, burnish, furbish, make bright, illuminate, illumine, illume, irradiate.

2. Make cheerful, make joyous, cheer, animate, enliven, encourage, hearten, exhilarate, inspirit, inspire.

——, *v. i.* Grow bright *or* brighter, clear, clear up, improve, grow better, become more encouraging.

Brightness, *n.* 1. Lustre, splendor, brilliancy, radiance, resplendence, effulgence, refulgence, shine, light, sheen, luminousness, luminosity, shine, glow, glare, glitter, dazzle, blaze, gloss, burnish, gleam,

gleaming, beam, beaming, flash, flashing, flame, flaming, sparkle, sparkling.

2. Clearness, transparency, lucidity, lucency, translucency, limpidity, cloudlessness, uncloudedness.

3. Acuteness, ingenuity, sagacity, brilliance, acumen, astuteness, discernment, mother-wit, quick parts.

4. Cheerfulness, cheeriness, merriment, liveliness, happiness, sprightliness, vivacity, vivaciousness, animation, geniality, lightness.

Brilliancy, *n.* 1. Splendor, lustre, brightness, effulgence, refulgence, radiance, shine, sheen, gloss, glister, glitter, gleam, sparkle, sparkling, brilliance.

2. Fame, illustriousness, renown, distinction, eminence, celebrity, prominence, excellence, pre-eminence, force.

Brilliant, *a.* 1. Sparkling, glittering, splendid, lustrous, shining, bright, beaming, radiant, effulgent, refulgent, resplendent, glistening, gleaming. See BRIGHT, 1.

2. Illustrious, glorious, celebrated, famous, renowned, distinguished, eminent, admirable.

3. Clever, keen, intellectually outstanding.

4. Striking, prominent, decided, unusual, impressive, signal, dazzling.

——, *n.* Diamond (*cut into facets*).

Brim, *n.* 1. Edge, border, rim, verge, margin, skirt, brink.

2. Shore, bank, border, margin, marge, rim, sands, coast.

Brimful, *a.* Quite full, full to the brim, choke-full, *or* chock-full, *or* chuck-full, full to overflowing.

Brimstone, *n.* Sulphur.

Brinded, } *a.* Tabby, party-colored.
Brindled, }

Brine, *n.* 1. Salt water, pickle.

2. Sea, ocean, deep, main.

Bring, *v. t.* 1. Convey, bear, fetch.

2. Conduct, convey, lead, guide, attend, accompany, convoy.

3. Produce, gain, get, procure, obtain, occasion, bring about, be the cause of, be the means of.

4. Draw, lead, induce, prevail upon.

Bring about. Effect, achieve, accomplish, bring to pass.

Bring back. 1. Recall, call to mind, recover, recollect.

2. Restore, return.

Bring down. Humble, abase.

Bring forth. 1. Give birth to, bear.

2. Produce, exhibit, show, expose, bring out, bring to light, make manifest.

Bring forward. Introduce, propose, bring in.

Bring on. Originate, give rise to, occasion.

Bring out. Produce, expose, show, exhibit, bring forth, bring to light.

Bring over. 1. Bear across, fetch over.

2. Convert, win over.

Bring to. 1. Check the course of (*said of a ship*).

2. Resuscitate, revive.

Bring under. Subdue, repress, restrain, conquer, get the better of.

Bring up. Educate, instruct, rear, nurse, breed, nurture.

Brink, *n.* 1. Edge, border, margin, verge, brow.

2. Shore, bank, brim, rim, margin, marge, sands, border.

Briny, *a.* Salt.

Brisk, *a.* Active, lively, perky, quick, agile, nimble, smart, alert, spry, spirited, vivacious, sprightly.

Bristle, *v. t.* Make bristly, roughen, erect in bristles, corrugate, bethorn, bespine, ruffle.

——, *v. i.* 1. Stand on end, stand up like bristles, be horrent.

2. [With *up*.] Become irritated, show anger, take offence, ruffle, bridle.

Bristly, *a.* Setaceous, hispid, scrubby.

Brittle, *a.* Fragile, crisp, crumbling, shivery, splintery, frail, frangible, brash, easily broken (*into pieces*), easily shivered, shattery, delicate.

Broach, *v. t.* 1. Pierce, tap, set running, open (*for the first time*).

2. Open (*a subject*), suggest, hint, approach one on, break.

3. Utter, publish, proclaim, give out.

Broached, *a.* Tapped, abroach, on tap.

Broad, *a.* 1. Wide.

2. Large, ample, extensive, expanded, extended, vast, wide-reaching, sweeping, spacious, capacious.

3. Liberal, uncontracted, large, large-minded, catholic, enlarged, hospitable, tolerant, free from narrowness.

4. Spread, diffused, open.

5. Gross, indelicate, vulgar, indecent, unrefined, coarse.

Broadcast, *v. t.* Disseminate, spread by radio.

Broaden, *v. t.* Widen, make broad, enlarge, liberalize.

Broadside, *n.* 1. Cannonade (*from all the guns on the side of a ship*).

2. Placard, bill, poster, hand-bill.

Brochure, *n.* [Fr.] Pamphlet.

Broil, *n.* Affray, fray, quarrel, contention, feud. See BRAWL.

BROKEN, *a.* 1. Shattered, shivered, rent, fractured, ruptured, torn, severed, interrupted, separated.

2. Weakened, impaired, feeble, enfeebled, shattered, shaken, spent, wasted, exhausted, run-down.

3. Imperfect, defective, hesitating, stammering, halting, stumbling.

4. Humble, lowly, penitent, contrite.

5. Abrupt, craggy, steep, precipitous, rough.

Broken-hearted, *a.* Disconsolate, inconsolable, comfortless, cheerless, sad, sorrowful, melancholy, woe-begone, forlorn, undone, crushed, broken-down, despairing, hopeless, quite dispirited, heart-broken, in despair.

Broker, *n.* Factor, agent, middleman, go-between.

Bronze, *n.* 1. Alloy of copper, tin, and zinc.

2. Brown, brown color.

——, *v. t.* Brown, embrown, embronze.

Brooch, *n.* Pin, clasp, broach, fibula.

Brood, *v. i.* 1. Incubate, sit.

2. Lie outspread, lie incumbent, lie low.

——, *n.* 1. Offspring, progeny, issue.

2. Breed, sort, kind, line, lineage, strain, extraction.

Brood over. Dwell upon, think anxiously upon, morbidly meditate.

Brook, *n.* Rivulet, streamlet, creek, run, runnel, runlet, rill, burn, beck, small stream.

——, *v. t.* Endure, bear, abide, tolerate, suffer, put up with, submit to, bear with, take patiently *or* easily.

Broth, *n.* Soup (*in which meat has been macerated*).

Brothel, *n.* Bagnio, stew, bawdy-house, bordel, house of prostitution, house of ill-fame.

BROTHER, *n.* *Frater*, kinsman, mate, "buddy," pal, companion, fellow, comrade.

Brotherhood, *n.* 1. Brotherliness, mutual kindness, fellowship, friendliness, fraternal feeling, brotherly love.

2. Fraternity, association, sodality, society, clique, coterie, clan, junto.

Brotherly, *a.* Fraternal, affectionate, kind, amicable, friendly, cordial.

Brow, *n.* 1. Eyebrow, forehead.

2. Edge (*as of a precipice*), brink, border.

Browbeat, *v. t.* Bully, overbear, beat down, treat insolently.

BROWN, *a.* Auburn, bronze, bay, beige, chocolate, ecru, russet, mahogany, maroon, tan, tawny, fawn, khaki, chestnut, sorrel, henna, roan.

——, *v. t.* Embrown, tan.

Brown study. Reverie, musing, abstraction, preoccupation, absence, absence of mind.

Browse, *v. t.* Nibble, crop, feed upon.

——, *v. i.* Feed on browse *or* tender twigs, graze.

Bruise, *v. t.* 1. Crush, squeeze, contuse.

2. Break, batter, maul, pound, bray, pulverize, comminute, triturate, break to pieces.

3. Indent, batter, deface.

——, *n.* Contusion.

Bruit, *n.* Rumor, fame, report, hearsay, town-talk.

——, *v. t.* Report, noise, blaze, blazon, *or* spread abroad.

Brunt, *n.* Shock, heat of onset.

BRUSH, *n.* 1. Skirmish, engagement, rencounter, encounter, contest, fight, conflict, collision, action, affair.

2. Thicket, bushes, shrubs, scrub, chaparral, underwood, brushwood.

Brushwood, *n.* Underwood, shrubs, bushes, brush.

Brusque, *a.* Rude, rough, blunt, unceremonious, curt, short, abrupt, bluff, gruff, ungentle, uncivil, ungracious, bearish, discourteous, uncourteous, impolite.

Brutal, *a.* 1. Savage, ferocious, cruel, inhuman, unfeeling, barbarous, barbarian, fell, barbaric, ruthless, truculent, bloody, brutish, brute.

2. Churlish, gruff, bearish, harsh, uncivil, rude, rough, impolite, unmannerly, brusque, ungentlemanly.

3. Gross, coarse, sensual, carnal, brutish, beastly, bestial.

Brutality, *n.* Savageness, inhumanity, barbarity, cruelty, brutishness, ferocity, truculence, hardness of heart.

Brute, *n.* 1. Beast (*in a wild state*), quadruped, dumb animal, ferocious animal.

2. Ruffian, barbarian, brutal monster.

——, *a.* 1. Irrational, void of reason.

2. Dumb, speechless, inarticulate, silent, voiceless, destitute of language.

3. Bestial, savage, barbarous. See BRUTAL.

4. Rough, rude, uncivilized.

Brutish, *a.* 1. See BRUTAL.

2. Brute, irrational.

3. Stupid, dull, insensible, stolid, unreasoning.

4. Gross, carnal, sensual, bestial, beastly.

Bubble, *n.* 1. Bleb, blob, fluid vesicle, bead, globule.

2. Trifle, bagatelle, small matter.

3. Cheat, delusion, hoax, false show.

——, *v. i.* Effervesce, foam, boil.

Buccaneer, *n.* Pirate, corsair, sea-rover, sea-robber, freebooter, picaroon.

Buck, *n.* 1. Male (*of the deer, sheep, goat, rabbit, and hare*).

2. Blade, spark, gallant, blood, fop, dandy, beau; gay, dashing fellow.

BUCKET, *n.* Pail, scoop, tub.

Buckle, *n.* 1. Clasp, brooch, broach, fibula.

2. Curl, crimp, crimpage; warp, bend, twist.

——, *v. i.* Bend, bow, double up, curl, shrivel, warp.

Buckler, *n.* 1. Shield, ægis.

2. Defence, protection, safeguard.

Bucolic, *n.* Eclogue, pastoral, idyl, pastoral poem.

——, *a.* Pastoral, rustic, countrified.

Bud, *n.* Germ, gem, gemmule, bourgeon, sprout, shoot.

——, *v. i.* Sprout, shoot, push, bourgeon, gemmate, germinate, vegetate, pullulate, put forth, burst forth, shoot forth.

Buddy, *n.* (*Colloq.*) Chum, comrade, "pal."

Budge, *v. i.* Stir, move, go, move the least, flinch.

Budget, *n.* 1. Bag (*with its contents*), pack, packet, parcel, package, bundle, roll.

2. Stock, store, batch, lot, set, assortment, collection.

3. Governmental estimate, fiscal estimate.

Buff, *a.* 1. Light yellow.

2. Made of buff *or* buff-skin.

Buffalo, *n.* [*U. S.*] Bison.

Buffer, *n.* Buffing-apparatus, guard, bumper, cushion, fender, concussion-guard.

Buffet, *n.* 1. Slap, box, knock, stroke, rap, blow, cuff.

2. (*pron.* boo-fā) Cupboard, sideboard.

3. Refreshment-counter, luncheon-board.

——, *v. t.* 1. Beat, box, slap, strike, smite, cuff.

2. Struggle against, contend against, resist.

Buffoon, *n.* Mountebank, harlequin, jester, droll, merry-andrew, punch, punchinello, clown, zany, scaramouch, fool, antic, jack-pudding, pickle-herring.

Buffoonery, *n.* Jesting (*of a low sort*), clownery, mummery, foolery, tomfoolery, harlequinade, horseplay, low pranks, vulgar tricks.

Bugbear, *n.* Hobgoblin, spectre, ogre, bogey, bugaboo, Gorgon, hydra, frightful object, raw head and bloody bones, object of baseless terror.

Bugle, *n.* 1. Hunting-horn, bugle-horn.
2. (*Mil.*) Call-bugle, key-bugle.

Build, *v. t.* Construct, erect, raise, rear, establish, fabricate, fashion, model.

——, *n.* Make, form, shape, construction, model, figure.

BUILDING, *n.* 1. Construction, fabrication, erection.
2. Structure, edifice, house, fabric, pile, construction, substructure, superstructure.

Build up. Establish, settle, preserve, increase, strengthen.

Build upon. Depend on, rest on, repose on, rely upon, calculate upon, reckon upon, count upon.

BULB, *n.* 1. (*Bot.*) Scaly bud (*like those of the onion and the tulip*), tuber, corm.
2. Protuberance, knob, bulge.

Bulbous, *a.* 1. (*Bot.*) Like a bulb, having bulbs, bulb-like, bulbiform.
2. Round, roundish, protuberant, swelling out.

Bulge, *n.* Protuberance, bilge, belly, bulge, swell, swelling.

——, *v. i.* Protrude, bag, jut out, swell, be protuberant.

Bulk, *n.* 1. Magnitude, size, volume, mass, dimensions.
2. Largeness, bulkiness, great size, bigness, massiness, massiveness, greatness, amplitude.
3. Majority, mass, body, generality, major part, most, main part, greater part, principal part.

Bulky, *a.* Large, great, big, huge, vast, massive, massy, of great size *or* bulk.

BULL, *n.* 1. Male (usually of bovine animals), bullock, bovine.
2. Edict (*issued by the Pope*), rescript.
3. Blunder (*involving a contradiction*), gross mistake.
4. (*Astron.*) Taurus.
5. Speculator on a rise, stimulator of the stock-market.

Bulletin, *n.* Report, statement, newsitem.

Bully, *n.* Blusterer, swaggerer, roisterer, hector, fire-eater, Hotspur, mock hero, swash-buckler, browbeater, bulldozer, tyrant.

——, *v. t.* Browbeat, overbear, hector, bullyrag, haze, domineer over, intimidate with threats, treat insolently.

Bullying, *a.* Blustering, swaggering, vaporing, vaunting, hectoring, bluff, gruff, bearish.

——, *n.* Bluster, swagger, fanfaronade, gasconade, vaporing, hectoring, fire-eating, mock-heroics, browbeating, domineering.

Bulwark, *n.* 1. Rampart, redoubt, fortification, parapet, wall, barrier,
2. Security, safeguard, palladium, protection, main reliance, chief defence.

Bump, *n.* 1. Thump, knock, blow, shock, jar, jolt.
2. Swelling, protuberance, lump.

——, *v. t.* Knock, thump, strike, collide with, hit.

——, *v. i.* Come in contact, strike together, strike, thump, collide.

Bumper, *n.* Full glass, flowing bowl, glassful, bowlful, brimmer, brimming beaker, brimmed goblet.

Bumpkin, *n.* Rustic, peasant, clodpoll, clown, boor, hind, lout, lubber, swain, ploughman, country-fellow.

Bumptious, *a.* (*Colloq.*) Conceited, vain, egotistical, self-opinionated, self-conceited, self-assertive, froward.

Bunch, *n.* 1. Protuberance, hunch, knob, lump, bulge, hump, bump.
2. Cluster (*as of grapes*), hand (*of bananas*), fascicle.
3. Batch, assortment, lot, set, parcel, collection, group.
4. Tuft, knot.

Buncombe, *n.* (*Colloq.*) "Blah," claptrap.

Bundle, *n.* Package, pack, packet, parcel, budget, roll.

Bungle, *v. t.* Botch, do clumsily, mismanage, blunder, foozle, muff, make a botch of, make a mess of.

——, *v. i.* Work clumsily, botch, foozle, muff.

Bungler, *n.* Botcher, lout, mismanager, lubber, muddler, "duffer," fumbler, clumsy workman, bad hand (*at anything*).

Bungling, *a.* 1. Clumsy, awkward, botchy, unhandy, unskilful, maladroit, inapt.
2. Ill-done, botched.

Bunk, *n.* (*Colloq.*) Berth, bed.

——, *v. i.* (*Colloq.*) Lie (*in a bunk*), sleep; lodge.

Bunker, *n.* 1. Bin, crib.
2. Hazard.

Buoy, *n.* Float (*to indicate shoals, anchoring-places, etc.*).

Buoyancy, *n.* 1. Lightness, levity, specific lightness.
2. Vivacity, liveliness, sprightliness, cheerfulness. See GAYETY.

Buoyant, *a.* 1. Tending to float, light; resilient.
2. Cheerful, hopeful, lively, sprightly, vivacious, animated, spirited, joyful, joyous, gay, blithe, blithesome, jocund, sportive, elated, jubilant, in good spirits, in high spirits, full of life, full of spirit.

Buoy up. 1. Float, keep afloat, bear up, keep on the surface.

2. Encourage, sustain, keep up, keep in spirits, keep in heart, hearten, embolden, reassure.

Burden, ⎫ *n.* 1. Load, weight; cargo,
Burthen, ⎭ freight, lading.

2. Capacity, carrying capacity, tonnage.

3. Encumbrance, clog, impediment, incubus, onus, charge, incumbency; grievance, trial, trouble, sorrow, affliction, drag weight, dead weight.

4. Chorus, refrain.

5. Main topic, drift, tenor, point, substance, reiterated doctrine.

Burden, *v. t.* Load, encumber, saddle, overload, overlay, oppress, surcharge, put a burden upon, grieve, try, afflict.

Burdensome, *a.* 1. Heavy, oppressive, onerous.

2. Troublesome, grievous, afflicting, hard to bear.

Bureau, *n.* 1. Chest of drawers, dresser.

2. Office, counting-room, place of business.

3. Department (*of Government*).

Burgher, *n.* Townsman, citizen, freeman, dweller in the town.

Burglar, *n.* House-breaker, robber, porch-climber, "cracksman," "yegg."

Burglary, *n.* House-breaking.

Burial, *n.* Interment, sepulture, inhumation, entombment, burying.

Burial-ground, *n.* Cemetery, grave-yard, burying-ground, church-yard, necropolis, God's Acre.

Burin, *n.* Graver, style.

Burke, *v. t.* 1. Suffocate, murder by suffocation, smother to death.

2. Smother, suppress, shelve, bury, shuffle aside.

Burlesque, *a.* Caricaturing, travestying, mock-heroic, parodying, parodical, ridiculing.

——, *n.* Caricature, travesty, parody, farce, extravaganza, take-off, ludicrous representation, piece of ridicule.

——, *v. t.* Caricature, travesty, make ludicrous *or* ridiculous.

Burly, *a.* Stout, lusty, brawny, portly, bulky, strong, strapping, "bouncing."

Burn, *v. t.* 1. Consume (with fire), reduce to ashes, cremate, incinerate.

2. Calcine, char, scorch, toast, parch, bake, broil.

3. Injure by fire *or* heat, sear, singe.

4. Shrivel, cause to wither.

5. Tan, bronze, brown, embrown.

BURN, *n.* Burning; burned spot.

——, *v. i.* 1. Flame, be on fire, smolder, glow, blaze.

2. Glow, warm, be excited.

3. Tingle, be hot, be feverish.

——, *n.* [*Scotch.*] Brook, rivulet, streamlet, runnel, runlet, rivulet, rill, beck, small stream.

Burning, *a.* 1. Fiery, flaming, aflame, hot, scorching, consuming.

2. Glowing, ardent, fervent, fervid, impassioned, intense, earnest, vehement.

3. Feverish, fevered, hot.

Burnish, *v. t.* Polish, furbish, brighten, make bright, make glossy, make glisten *or* glistening.

Burrow, *v. i.* Mine, tunnel, excavate.

Bursar, *n.* Treasurer, cashier (*of a college* or *monastery*).

Bursary, *n.* Treasury, pay-office.

Burst, *v. i.* 1. Break open (*from internal pressure*), fly open, be rent asunder, explode, blow up, split, split open, crack, "bust."

2. Break (out *or* forth *or* upon) suddenly.

——, *v. t.* Rend asunder, break open, shatter, split apart.

BURST, *n.* 1. Explosion. See BURSTING.

2. Sudden rush, outpouring, gust, breaking forth.

Bursting, *n.* Explosion, disruption, eruption, outburst, blast, blasting, burst.

Bury, *v. t.* 1. Cover (*with earth, etc.*), cover up.

2. Inter, inhume, entomb, inurn, inearth, lay in the grave.

3. Hide, conceal, secrete, shroud.

4. Immure, confine, plunge into retirement.

5. Cover with oblivion, utterly forget, hide beyond remembrance, lay aside forever, cancel, compose, hush.

Burying, *n.* Interment, sepulture, inhumation, entombment, burial.

Burying-ground, *n.* Cemetery. See BURIAL-GROUND.

Bury the hatchet. Make peace, be reconciled, sheathe the sword, put up the sword.

Bush, *n.* Shrub, brushwood.

BUSINESS, *n.* 1. Calling, employment, occupation, pursuit, vocation, profession, craft, avocation, walk of life.

2. Trade, commerce, traffic, dealing.

3. Concern, matter, affair, undertaking, transaction.

4. Office, duty, function, task, work.

Buskin, *n.* 1. Half-boot (*especially one with high soles, worn by the ancient tragedians*), cothurnus.

2. Tragedy, tragic drama.

Buss, *n.* Kiss, smack.

Bustle, *v. i.* Fuss, stir about, busy one's self, hustle, flurry, bestir one's self, be in a fidget, make much ado about trifles.

——, *n.* Stir, fuss, hurry, flurry, hustle, tumult, pother, commotion, ado, to-do.

Busy, *a.* 1. Engaged, employed, occupied, at work, hard at work.

2. Diligent, assiduous, industrious, sedulous, engrossed, active, working, hard-working.

3. Brisk, stirring, bustling, nimble, agile, spry, constantly in motion.

4. Meddling, officious.

——, *v. t.* Occupy, employ, make busy.

Busybody, *n.* Meddler, intermeddler, talebearer, officious person, quidnunc.

BUT, *conj.* 1. On the other hand, on the contrary.

2. Yet, still, however, howbeit, nevertheless, moreover, further.

3. Unless, if it were not that, if it be not that.

4. But that, otherwise than that.

——, *prep.* Except, excepting.

Butcher, *n.* 1. Slaughterer, flesher.

2. Murderer, slayer, assassin, cut-throat, thug, bravo.

——, *v. t.* 1. Slaughter, kill for food, kill for the market.

2. Murder barbarously, massacre, slaughter.

Butchery, *n.* 1. Murder, slaughter, massacre.

2. Great slaughter, wholesale killing, carnage, enormous bloodshed.

Butt, *n.* 1. Mark, object, target, point aimed at.

2. Laughing-stock.

3. Thrust, bunt, push, "buck."

4. Cask, pipe.

——, *v. i.* Strike (with the head *or* the horns), push, "bunt."

BUTTER, *n.* (*Basic Eng.*)

Buttery, *n.* Pantry.

Buttock, *n.* Rump, fundament, breech, "bottom," hind quarters.

BUTTON, *n.* (*Basic Eng.*)

Button-hole, *v. t.* Persuade importunately, hang about, prose at, bore.

Buttress, *n. and v. t.* Shore, prop, support, stay, brace.

Buxom, *a.* Healthy, vigorous, plump, hearty, well-fed, rosy, ruddy, comely, fresh, fresh-looking, in high health.

Buy, *v. t.* 1. Purchase.

2. Bribe, corrupt, pervert with money *or* gain.

Buzz, *v. i.* 1. Hum, make a humming sound (*as bees*).

2. Whisper, murmur.

——, *n.* 1. Hum, humming noise.

2. Whisper, murmur.

BY, *prep.* 1. Through (*as the cause,* or *the remote agent*), by the agency of, by means of, by dint of. See WITH.

2. At, on, by way of.

3. From, according to.

4. Near to, close by, near.

5. Past.

6. Along, over, through.

7. In proportion to, in the quantity of, per, a.

——, *adv.* Near.

By and by. 1. Presently, soon, before long, in a short time.

2. After a while, hereafter, some time hence.

By chance. 1. Perhaps, perchance, possibly, haply, peradventure, maybe, it may be, as luck may have it.

2. As it happened, as luck would have it, it so happened that, accidentally, it so chanced that.

By degrees. Gradually, step by step, little by little, by little and little.

By dint of. By, by force of, by means of, by the agency of.

By far. Very much, in a great degree, greatly, exceedingly.

Bygone, *a.* Past, gone by.

By hook or by crook. Somehow *or* other, one way *or* other, in one way *or* another, some means *or* other.

By-path, *n.* 1. By-way, side-path.

2. Private way, secret path, devious way, indirect course, crooked means.

By-road, *n.* Private road, unfrequented road.

By rote. Mechanically, perfunctorily, parrot-like, by mere repetition, without any exercise of the understanding, with no attention to the meaning.

Bystander, *n.* Spectator, looker-on.

By the bye. In passing, *en passant, apropos* of the matter in hand, by the way.

By-way, *n.* By-path, private way, side-path, secluded road, out-of-the-way path.

Byword, *n.* 1. Saying, saw, maxim, adage, proverb, aphorism, apothegm, dictum, sententious precept.

2. Object of contempt, mark for scorn.

C

Cabal, *n.* 1. Clique (*for some sinister purpose*), junto, coterie, set, party, gang, faction, combination, league, confederacy, *camarilla*.

2. Intrigue, plot, complot, conspiracy, machination.

——, *v. i.* Intrigue, plot, conspire, complot, machinate.

Cabalistic, *a.* Occult, secret, mysterious, mystic, mystical, dark.

Cabaret, *n.* Tavern, inn, wine-shop, public-house, house of entertainment.

Cabbage, *v. t.* (*Colloq.*) Steal, purloin, filch, pilfer, make off with.

Cabin, *n.* Hut, hovel, shed, cot, cottage, humble dwelling.

Cabinet, *n.* 1. Closet, boudoir, by-room, small room, private room, retired apartment.

2. Case, set of encased drawers.

3. Ministry, council, body of advisers.

Caboose, *n.* Cookroom (*of a ship*), galley.

Cabriolet, *n.* Cab, hansom, brougham.

Cachinnation, *n.* Laughter (*loud* or *immoderate*), laugh, guffaw, horse-laugh.

Cackle, *v. i.* 1. Laugh (*with a sound like the cackling of a goose*), giggle, titter, snicker.

2. Chatter, prattle, babble, gabble, palaver, talk idly. See PRATE.

——, *n.* Prattle, twaddle, idle talk, small talk. See PRATE.

Cacophonous, *a.* Harsh, grating, discordant, raucous.

Cacophony, *n.* Discord, jarring, jar, harsh sound.

Cadaver, *n.* Corpse, dead body, body, remains, subject (*for dissection*).

Cadaverous, *a.* Pale, pallid, wan, ghastly, deathlike.

Cadence, *n.* 1. Fall of the voice.

2. Tone, intonation, modulation of the voice.

Cæsura, *n.* Pause (*in a verse*), break.

Café, *n.* [Fr.] Restaurant, coffee-house.

Caitiff, *n.* Villain, wretch, miscreant, coward, sneak, traitor, knave, rascal, scoundrel, mean fellow, vagabond, bezonian.

Cajole, *v. t.* 1. Coax, wheedle, flatter, "jolly," blandish.

2. Deceive (*by flattery*), delude, beguile, inveigle, entrap, impose upon.

Cajolery, *n.* 1. Flattery, wheedling, fawning, coaxing, adulation, blandishment, blarney.

2. Deceit (*by flattery*), beguilement.

CAKE, *v. i.* [*The noun is Basic Eng.*] Harden, solidify, concrete, become firm *or* solid.

Calamitous, *a.* Disastrous, unlucky, unfortunate, adverse, untoward, unhappy, unprosperous, hapless, ill-fated, ill-starred, deplorable, ruinous, catastrophic, miserable, wretched, dreadful, distressful, distressing, baleful, severe, afflictive, sad, grievous.

Calamity, *n.* Disaster, misfortune, catastrophe, ruin, mishap, mischance, reverse, visitation, trial, blow, stroke, trouble, affliction, adversity, distress, misery, evil, ill, hardship, casualty, ill-luck, ill fortune.

Calcine, *v. t.* Burn, reduce to ashes, powder.

Calculable, *a.* Computable. Cf. also CALCULATION, 2.

Calculate, *v. t.* Compute, reckon, estimate, count, rate, cast.

——, *v. i.* Tell, estimate, make a calculation, make a computation, cast accounts.

Calculated, *a.* Adjusted, adapted, fitted, suited.

Calculate upon. Anticipate, contemplate, foresee, expect, look forward to, look out for, reckon upon, count upon, rely upon, depend upon, prepare one's self for.

Calculating, *a.* 1. Scheming, crafty, designing, self-considering, selfish.

2. Wary, cautious, careful, guarded, politic, circumspect, far-sighted, far-seeing, sagacious.

Calculation, *n.* 1. Computation, reckoning.

2. Expectation, expectance, anticipation, contemplation, prospect.

3. Forethought, foresight, circumspection, wariness, caution, cautiousness, discretion, deliberation, prudence.

Calculous, *a.* Stony, gritty, calculose.

Calculus, *n.* 1. (*Med.*) [L. *pl. Calculi.*] Morbid concretion, stone, gravel.

2. [*Eng. pl. Calculuses.*] Fluxions, differential and integral calculus.

3. Computation, method of computation, computative method, computative art.

Caldron, } *n.* Boiler, kettle, copper.
Cauldron, }

Caledonian, *a.* Scottish, Scotch.

——, *n.* Scotchman, Scot.

Calefacient, *a.* 1. Warming, heating.

2. Rubefacient, vesicatory, tending to blister.

——, *n.* Rubefacient, vesicant, vesicatory.

Calefaction, *n.* 1. Heating, warming.

2. Incalescence, hotness, warmth, becoming warm.

Calefy, *v. t.* Heat, warm, make warm *or* hot, cause to incalesce.

Calendar, *n.* 1. Almanac, ephemeris, register of the year.

2. List, schedule, catalogue, register.

——, *v. t.* List, catalogue, register, enroll, enter, place upon the calendar.

Caliber, *n.* 1. Diameter (*of a cylindrical body*).

2. Bore, diameter of bore, capacity.

3. Capacity, scope, talent, ability, faculty, endowment, parts, gifts, compass of mind.

Caliber-compasses, *n. pl.* See CALLIPERS.

Calico, *n.* 1. [*Eng.*] Cotton cloth.

2. [*U. S.*] Print, printed cotton cloth.

Call, *v. t.* 1. Name, term, denominate, entitle, style, phrase, designate, dub, christen.

2. Bid, invite, summon, ask to come, send for.

3. Convoke, assemble, convene, muster, call together.

——, *v. i.* Exclaim, cry, cry out, speak aloud, make appeal.

——, *n.* 1. Cry, outcry, voice.

2. Invitation, summons, appeal.

3. Demand, claim, requisition.

4. Appointment, election, invitation.

Calling, *n.* Occupation, business, profession, pursuit, trade, craft, employment, vocation, avocation, walk of life.

Callipers, *n. pl.* Calibers, cannipers, caliber-compasses, calliper-compasses.

Call on. 1. Invoke, appeal to, pray to, call upon.

2. Solicit, apply to.

3. Make a visit to, pay a visit to.

Callous, *a.* 1. Indurated, hardened, hard.

2. Insensible, unfeeling, apathetic, obtuse, thick-skinned, unsusceptible, unimpressible, sluggish, dull, torpid, indifferent, dead.

Callow, *a.* 1. Unfledged, unfeathered, naked.

2. Inexperienced, unsophisticated, immature, silly, unfledged, green, soft, sappy.

Calm, *a.* 1. Tranquil, placid, quiet, still, smooth (*of water*), unruffled, peaceful, serene, reposeful, mild, halcyon.

2. Undisturbed, imperturbed, untroubled, impassive, composed, self-possessed, sedate, unruffled, cool, collected, controlled.

——, *n.* 1. Fall of the wind, wind-lull, lull.

2. Peace, serenity, tranquillity, placidity, quiet, stillness, repose, equanimity. See CALMNESS.

——, *v. t.* 1. Still, compose, hush, smooth, allay, lull, becalm, tranquillize.

2. Tranquillize, pacify, appease, assuage, quiet, soothe, soften, mollify, moderate, alleviate.

Calmness, *n.* 1. Quietness, tranquillity, serenity, repose, peace, peacefulness, stillness, calm, placidity, lull.

2. Mildness, sedateness, composure, self-possession, coolness, quiet, tranquillity, serenity, serenitude, placidity, peace, equanimity, repose.

Calorific, *a.* Heating, heat-producing.

Calumet, *n.* Indian pipe, pipe.

Calumniate, *v. t.* Slander, malign, traduce, defame, vilify, revile, abuse, libel, blacken, blemish, accuse falsely. See ASPERSE.

Calumniator, *n.* Slanderer, maligner, traducer, defamer, vilifier, reviler, blackener, backbiter, libeller, detractor.

Calumnious, *a.* Slanderous, abusive, defamatory, contumelious, opprobrious, vituperative, scurrilous, insulting.

Calumny, *n.* Slander (*known to be false*), defamation, aspersion, backbiting, detraction, abuses, scandal, obloquy, false accusation, malicious lying.

Calyx, *n.* Flower-cup.

Camarilla, *n.* [*Sp.*] Clique, cabal, junto, ring, secret cabinet, power behind the throne.

Camber, *n.* Convexity, arch, arching, rounding up, swell, curve.

——, *v. t.* Arch, bend, curve (*especially a ship's planks*).

Cambrian, *n.* Welshman, Cambro-Briton, Cymro.

Camel-backed, *a.* Hump-backed.

CAMERA, *n.* (*Basic Eng.*) Kodak.

Camp, *n.* Encampment, bivouac, cantonment.

——, *v. i.* Encamp, pitch one's tent, pitch a camp.

Campaign, *n.* Crusade, "drive."

Campanile, *n.* Belfry, bell-tower.

Campanulate, *a.* Bell-shaped.

Can, *v. i.* 1. Be able to, have power to.

2. Be possible to.

Canaille, *n.* [*Fr.*] Populace, rabble, mob, riffraff, the vulgar, the crowd, vulgar herd, the ignoble vulgar, the multitude, the million, scum of society, dregs of society, *ignobile vulgus*, rag-tag and bob-tail.

Canakin, *n.* Drinking-cup, pot.

Canal, *n.* 1. Artificial water-way.

2. Channel, duct, pipe, tube.

Canard, *n.* [*Fr.*] Hoax, groundless story, false rumor, fabrication.

Cancel, *v. t.* 1. Obliterate, efface, erase, expunge, blot, blot out, cross out, rub out, scratch out, wipe out.

2. Abrogate, annul, repeal, rescind, revoke, abolish, nullify, quash, set aside, make void.

Cancellated, *a.*   Cross-barred, reticulated.

Candelabrum, *n.*   [L. *pl. Candelabra; Eng. pl. Candelabrums.*]   Chandelier, lustre, branched candlestick.

Candid, *a.*   1. Impartial, fair, just, unprejudiced, unbiassed.

2. Open, free, ingenuous, artless, frank, sincere, honest, plain, honorable, *naïve*, guileless, straightforward, openhearted, frank-hearted, above-board.

Candidate, *n.*   Aspirant, solicitant, probationer.

Candle, *n.*   Taper, light, dip.

Candle-ends, *n. pl.*   Scraps, savings, scrapings, fragments, worthless trifles, petty savings.

Candle-holder, *n.*   Inferior, subordinate, assistant.   See AID.

Candor, *n.*   1. Fairness, impartiality, justice, freedom from prejudice, freedom from bias.

2. Openness, ingenuousness, artlessness, frankness, guilelessness, truthfulness, honesty, sincerity, straightforwardness, simplicity, *naïveté*.

Canker, *n.*   1. Mordent ulcer, gangrene, rot.

2. Corrosion, erosion, blight.

3. Corruption, infection, blight, bane, bale, irritation.

——, *v. t.*   1. Corrode, erode, eat away.

2. Infect, corrupt, blight, envenom, poison, sour, embitter, fill with gall.

——, *v. i.*   Be blighted, grow embittered, become malignant, become infected *or* corrupted.

Cannibals, *n. pl.*   Anthropophagi, maneaters.

Cannonade, *v. t.*   Attack with cannon, attack with heavy artillery, bombard.

Canon, *n.*   1. Rule (*especially in ecclesiastical matters*), law, formula, formulary, standard.

2. Received books of Scripture, canonical books.

Canonical, *a.*   1. Received, authorized, according to the canon.

2. Regular, stated.

Canonize, *v. t.*   Declare a saint, make a saint of, enroll in the canon, exalt.

Canopy, *n.*   Awning, tilt, baldaquin, tester.

Canorous, *a.*   Musical, tuneful.

Cant, *n.*   1. Whining talk, pious prating, sanctimonious phrases.

2. Hypocrisy, affected piety, sham holiness.

3. Peculiar form of speech, professional parlance, shibboleths of sect, jargon, lingo.

4. Slang, thieves' vocabulary, argot.

5. Turn, tilt, slant, bevel.

——, *a.*   Set, partisan, routine, current, rote, popular, bandied by the crowd.

——, *v. i.*   Whine, affect piety.

Cantankerous, *a.*   (*Colloq.*)   Crabbed, perverse, stubborn, obstinate, unyielding, refractory, contumacious, headstrong, wilful, dogged, intractable, heady, obdurate, stiff, cross-grained.

Canter, *n.*   1. Whiner, sanctimonious prater, pious twattler, Pharisee.

2. Easy gallop, gentle gallop.

——, *v. i.*   Gallop gently.

Canting, *a.*   1. Affected, whining, affectedly pious, sanctimonious.

2. Hypocritical, insincere, hollow.

Cantonment, *n.*   Quarters.   Cf. CAMP.

CANVAS, *n.*   Burlap, scrim, tarpaulin.

Canvass, *v. t.*   1. Debate, discuss, dispute, agitate.

2. Investigate, examine, scrutinize, sift, study, consider, follow up, inquire into.

3. Bespeak the votes of, solicit votes from.

——, *n.*   1. Discussion, debate, dispute.

2. Examination, scrutiny, sifting.

3. Solicitation of votes.

Canyon, *n.*   [Sp. *Cañon.*]   Gorge, ravine, gulch.

Cap, *n.*   1. Head-cover, head-dress, beret, chaco, coif, coiffure, caul, fez, kepi, tam-o'-shanter.

2. Acme, crown, head, summit, pitch, peak, top, chief, perfection.

——, *v. t.*   1. Cover, surmount.

2. Crown, complete, finish.

3. Exceed, surpass, transcend, overtop.

4. Match, pattern, parallel.

Capability, *n.*   Capableness, capacity, ability, power, skill, competency, efficiency, calibre, faculty, force, scope, brains.

Capable, *a.*   1. Susceptible, open (to), admitting.

2. Qualified, suited, fitted, adapted.

3. Able, competent, intelligent, clever, skilful, efficient, ingenious, sagacious, gifted, accomplished.

Capacious, *a.*   Spacious, ample, large, wide, broad, extensive, roomy, expanded, comprehensive.

Capaciousness, *n.*   Spaciousness, amplitude, largeness, roominess, vastness, openness, freedom, breadth, extent, extensiveness, expansiveness, comprehensiveness.

Capacitate, *v. t.*   Qualify, enable, make able, make *or* render capable.

Capacity, *n.* 1. Containing power, magnitude (*in reference to contents*), volume, dimensions, amplitude, extent of room *or* space.

2. Power (*of apprehension*), faculty, talent, genius, gift, turn, forte, parts, brains, aptness, aptitude, discernment, wit, mother-wit, calibre.

3. Ability, cleverness, skill, competency, efficiency. See CALIBRE, CAPABILITY.

4. Office, post, position, sphere, province, character, function, service, charge.

Caparison, *n.* Trapping (*for a horse*), housing, barde, barbe.

Cape, *n.* Headland, promontory.

Caper, *v. i.* Leap (*in a frolicsome mood*), hop, skip, jump, bound, romp, gambol, frisk, dance, prance.

——, *n.* Leap (*in frolic*), skip, hop, spring, bound, gambol, romp, prank, frisk, caracole.

Capillary, *a.* Fine (*like a hair*), slender, minute, delicate, filiform.

Capital, *a.* 1. Chief, principal, leading, essential, cardinal, first in importance.

2. Fatal, forfeiting life, involving death.

3. (*Colloq.*) Excellent, good, prime, first-rate, first-class.

——, *n.* 1. Metropolis, chief city, seat.

2. Stock, sum invested.

Capitulate, *v. i.* Surrender (*by treaty*), yield on conditions.

Capitulation, *n.* Surrender (*by treaty*).

Caprice, *n.* Whim, freak, fancy, humor, crotchet, maggot, quirk, vagary, whimsey, phantasy.

Capricious, *a.* Whimsical, fanciful, fantastical, crotchety, humorsome, wayward, odd, queer, fitful, freakish, puckish, changeable, uncertain, fickle, variable.

Capsize, *v. t.* Upset, overturn.

Capsule, *n.* 1. Case, wrapper, envelope, covering, shell, sheath.

2. (*Bot.*) Pod, pericarp, seed-vessel.

Captain, *n.* Commander, leader, chief, chieftain, master.

Captious, *a.* 1. Censorious, caviling, carping, hypercritical, disposed to cavil, given to faultfinding.

2. Crabbed, snappish, testy, touchy, waspish, splenetic, cross, snarling, acrimonious, "cantankerous," contentious.

3. Ensnaring, insidious.

Captivate, *v. t.* Charm, fascinate, enchant, enthrall, bewitch, enamour, infatuate, win, catch, lead captive.

Captive, *n.* Prisoner.

Captivity, *n.* 1. Imprisonment, confinement, duress, durance.

2. Bondage, thraldom, enthralment, servitude, subjection, slavery, vassalage.

Capture, *n.* 1. Seizure, arrest, apprehension, catching, catch, taking captive, making prisoner.

2. Prize, bag.

——, *v. t.* Sieze, catch, apprehend, arrest, take by force, take possession of, make prisoner.

Capuchin, *n.* Franciscan, Minorite, Gray Friar.

Caracole, *v. i.* Wheel, prance, curvet.

Caravansary, *n.* Tavern (*in the East*), khan, inn, public-house, house of entertainment.

Carcass, *n.* Dead body (*of an animal*), corpse, corse.

CARD, *n.* Pasteboard, ticket.

Cardinal, *a.* Principal, chief, main, leading, most important, essential, capital, central, vital.

CARE, *n.* 1. Anxiety, solicitude, concern, trouble, perplexity, worry.

2. Caution, heed, regard, attention, circumspection, carefulness, wariness, watchfulness, vigilance.

3. Charge, oversight, superintendence, guardianship, ward, custody, keep.

4. Object of care, charge, burden, responsibility, concern.

——, *v. i.* 1. Be anxious, be solicitous, feel concerned, be troubled, worry one's self, reck.

2. Be inclined, be disposed, like, feel interested.

3. Have regard, heed, bethink oneself.

Careen, *v. i.* Lean to one side, incline to one side.

Care for. 1. Have regard for, pay heed to, attach value to, ascribe importance to.

2. Be interested in, like, be fond of, be attached to.

Careful, *a.* 1. (*Rare.*) Anxious, solicitous, concerned, troubled, uneasy.

2. Heedful, attentive, thoughtful, mindful, regardful. See PROVIDENT.

3. Watchful, cautious, circumspect, vigilant, "canny," "leery," discreet, wary.

Careless, *a.* 1. Unperplexed, undisturbed, untroubled, unapprehensive, at ease, carefree, nonchalant, without anxiety, unsolicitous.

2. Heedless, thoughtless, inattentive, unconcerned, unmindful, incautious, unthinking, unobservant, remiss, disregardful, regardless, neglectful, negligent, unconsidered, inconsiderate.

Carelessness, *n.* Thoughtlessness, heedlessness, inattention, inadvertence, inconsiderateness, remissness, slackness, negligence, neglect, unconcern.

Caress, *v. t.* Fondle, embrace, hug, pet, kiss, coddle, cosset, treat with fondness.

——, *n.* Embrace, kiss, expression of affection.

Caressing, *n.* Fondling, endearment, blandishment, dalliance, billing and cooing.

Cargo, *n.* Lading, freight, load, burden *or* burthen.

Caricature, *n.* Travesty, parody, farce, burlesque, ludicrous representation, "take-off."

——, *v. t.* Burlesque, travesty, parody, "take off."

Carious, *a.* Ulcerated (*as a bone*), decayed, mortified, rotten, putrid.

Cark, *v. t.* Fret, worry, perplex, harass, grieve, annoy.

Carking, *a.* Distressing, worrying, grievous, wearing.

Carl, *n.* Churl, clown, boor, lout, clumsy rustic, bumpkin.

Carnage, *n.* Slaughter, butchery, massacre, blood-shed, havoc.

Carnal, *a.* 1. Fleshly, sensual, lustful, libidinous, lecherous, lascivious, lickerish, lubric(al), lubricous, concupiscent, salacious.

2. Natural, unspiritual, bodily, unregenerate, earthly, temporal.

Carnality, *n.* Sensuality, grossness (of mind), sensual appetites, fleshly lusts.

Carnivorous, *a.* Flesh-eating.

Carol, *n.* Song, lay, ditty.

——, *v. t.* Sing, warble, chant, hum.

Carousal, *n.* 1. Feast, festival, entertainment, jovial banquet, merry-making, regale.

2. Revelling, revelry, revel, bacchanals, saturnalia, debauch, compotation, wassail, orgy, carouse, cups, drinking-bout, "spree," "jamboree," jollification.

Carouse, *v. i.* Revel, tipple, guzzle, "booze."

Carouser, *n.* Reveller, tippler, toper, drunkard, debauchee, bacchanal, bacchanalian.

Carp at. Cavil at, find fault with, pick flaws in.

Carping, *a.* Cavilling, censorious, captious, hypercritical.

——, *n.* Censure, cavil, fault-finding, hypercriticism, captious criticism.

Carriage, *n.* 1. Vehicle, conveyance.

2. Bearing, manner, demeanor, air, mien, front, port, behavior, deportment, conduct.

Carrion, *n.* Putrefying flesh, putrescent *or* putrid meat.

Carry, *v. t.* 1. Convey, bear, transport, transfer, transmit.

2. Urge, impel, push forward.

3. Accomplish, effect, gain, secure, compass, bring about.

4. Support, sustain, bear up.

5. Imply, import, signify, infer, involve.

Carry off. 1. Remove, take away.

2. Destroy, kill.

Carry on, *v. t.* Conduct, manage, transact, prosecute, continue, help forward.

——, *v. i.* [*Colloq.*] Frolic, cut capers, play tricks, behave wildly *or* rudely.

Carry one's self. Conduct, behave, demean, deport, quit, *or* acquit one's self.

Carry out. Apply, execute, put in practice, carry into detail, complete.

Carry through. Accomplish, consummate, finish, complete, work out, bring to a close, bring about, bring to pass.

CART, *n.* Vehicle, wagon, conveyance, tumbrel, van.

Carte-blanche, *n.* [Fr.] Unlimited authority, full powers.

Cartilaginous, *a.* Gristly.

Carve, *v. t.* 1. Sculpture, chisel, cut, grave engrave, incise.

2. Form, shape, fashion, mould.

3. Cut in pieces *or* slices, slice, divide

——, *v. i.* 1. Exercise the trade of a carver.

2. Cut meat at table.

Carving, *n.* Sculpture (*in wood or ivory*).

Cascade, *n.* Cataract, waterfall, fall.

Case, *n.* 1. Covering, sheathe, capsule

2. Box, receptacle, holder, container, cabinet.

3. State, condition, situation, plight, predicament.

4. Instance, particular occurrence, example, specific instance.

5. Circumstance, condition, contingency, event.

6. Suit, action, cause, process, trial.

7. Question, matter of inquiry, subject of discussion.

——, *v. t.* 1. Cover (*with a case*), protect, wrap, encase, enclose, envelop.

2. Box, put in a box *or* case, pack, pack up.

Casehardened, *a.* and *p.* 1. Hardened (*on the outside*), steeled, converted into steel (*on the surface*), indurated.

2. Conscience-seared, obdurate, reprobate, dead to duty, lost to shame, brazen, brazen-faced.

Caseous, *a.* Cheesy, of the nature of cheese.

Cash, *n.* 1. Coin, specie, currency.

2. Money, ready money.

Cash, *v. t.* Turn into money, pay in money.

Cashier, *v. t.* Break, discharge, discard, dismiss from office, cast off, turn away, send away.

Casino, *n.* [It.] 1. Cottage, small house, lodge.

2. Club-house, gaming-house, dancing-hall, dancing-saloon.

Cask, *n.* Hooped, wooden vessel (*as a hogshead, butt, pipe, tun, barrel, keg, etc.*).

Casket, *n.* Little box, jewel box, reliquary.

Casque, *n.* [Fr.] Helmet, cask, helm, morion.

Cast, *v. t.* 1. Throw, fling, hurl, send, toss, pitch, sling, "shy."

2. Drive, impel, force, thrust.

3. Shed, put off, lay aside.

4. Compute, reckon, calculate.

5. Impart, communicate, throw, shed, diffuse.

——, *n.* 1. Throw, fling, toss.

2. Tinge, tint, shade, touch.

3. Manner, style, air, mien, look, turn, tone, character.

4. Mould, form.

Cast about. Consider, revolve in the mind, ponder, search, seek, inquire.

Cast away. 1. Reject, discard. See CAST OFF.

2. Throw away, waste, squander, fling away.

3. Wreck, strand, founder, shipwreck.

Castaway, *n.* Outcast, reprobate, vagabond, abandoned wretch, moral shipwreck, moral wreck, derelict, lost soul.

——, *a.* Rejected, discarded, abandoned, cast-off.

Cast down. Dejected, depressed, discouraged, melancholy, sad, downcast, disheartened, chapfallen, downhearted, desponding, despondent, blue, dispirited, low-spirited, in low spirits.

Caste, *n.* 1. Permanent hereditary order (*among the Hindoos*), Varna, fixed class.

2. Social order (*generally*), class-distinction, class, rank, grade of society, status.

Caster, *n.* 1. Thrower, hurler.

2. Calculator, computer.

3. Founder, moulder.

4. Cruet, cruse, phial.

Cast forth. Eject, emit, throw out.

Castigate, *v. t.* 1. Chastise, whip, beat, thrash, punish with stripes *or* the lash, lash, flog, "lambaste."

2. Discipline, correct, punish, chasten.

3. Upbraid, flagellate, fall foul of, dress down, take to task, haul over the coals, censure bitterly, criticise severely, trim out, call to account.

Castigation, *n.* 1. Whipping, beating, lashing, thrashing, flagellation, drubbing, flogging, chastisement.

2. Punishment, chastisement, discipline, correction, chastening.

3. Upbraiding, taking to task, lashing, flagellation, trimming, hauling over the coals, dressing down, invective, censorious assault, berating, denunciation, objurgation.

Castle, *n.* Fortress, citadel, stronghold, fortified residence.

Cast off. 1. Reject, discard, abandon, forsake, renounce, repudiate, lay aside, cast by, cast away, throw away, throw by, get rid of.

2. (*Naut.*) Loose, untie, let go, let slip.

Cast off, *a.* Discarded, castaway, cast-aside, thrown aside, worn, worn out.

Cast out. 1. Eject, expel, oust, turn out of doors.

2. Send forth, throw out, eject, hurl out *or* forth.

Castrate, *v. t.* 1. Geld, emasculate, caponize (*a cock*), glib, deprive of virility, make a eunuch.

2. Deprive of vigor, mortify, suppress, subdue, weaken, take the life out of.

Castration, *n.* Orchotomy, gelding, emasculation, glibbing.

Cast up. 1. Compute, calculate, reckon, cast.

2. Eject, throw up, vomit, spew, puke.

Casual, *a.* Accidental, fortuitous, random, incidental, contingent, that happens by chance.

Casualty, *n.* 1. Chance, fortuity, contingency, hap, unforeseen event.

2. Accident, disaster, misfortune, calamity, mischance, catastrophe.

CAT, *n.* Kitten, grimalkin, puss, tabby.

Cataclysm, *n.* Inundation, deluge, overflow, flood.

Catacomb, *n.* Crypt, vault, tomb.

Catalogue, *n.* List (*arranged in a certain order*), index, enumeration, register, roll, record, schedule, invoice, inventory.

Cataract, *n.* Waterfall, fall, cascade.

Catastrophe, *n.* 1. Upshot, issue, consummation, conclusion, termination, *dénouement, finale*, winding up, finishing stroke, final event.

2. Disaster, cataclysm, *débâcle*, misfortune, mishap, mischance. See CALAMITY.

Catch, *v. t.* 1. Grasp, seize, snatch, clutch, gripe, grasp, lay hold of, fasten upon, "nab."

2. Arrest, apprehend, capture.

3. Overtake, come up with.

4. Ensnare, entrap, entangle, enmesh, net, lime.

5. Captivate, charm, enchant, fascinate, bewitch, win.

6. Take unawares, surprise, come suddenly on.

Catch, *v. i.* 1. Lay hold, take hold, hold.

2. Get entangled, hitch.

——, *n.* 1. Seizure. See CAPTURE.

2. Clasp, hook, detent, pawl, click, ratchet. See HASP.

3. Quantity (*of fish caught*), amount caught, catching, take, haul, draft.

Catch at. Grasp at, try to seize, snatch at, snap at, be eager to get.

Catching, *n.* 1. Seizure, capture, arrest, apprehension.

2. Catch, take.

——, *a.* 1. Infectious, contagious, communicable, pestilential, pestiferous.

2. Captivating, taking, charming, attractive, winning, winsome, enchanting, fascinating.

Catchword, *n.* 1. Cue, clew-word, marginal clew.

2. Party cry, shibboleth.

Catechise, *v. t.* Question, interrogate, examine, quiz, put questions to.

Catechumen, *n.* Pupil (*in Christian doctrine*), neophyte, convert, proselyte.

Categorical, *a.* Positive, absolute, unconditional, unqualified, unreserved, downright, express, explicit, direct, emphatic.

Category, *n.* 1. Class, head, division, order, rank.

2. Ultimate form of conceiving, predicable, universal aspect, basic distinction, primitive *or* elemental relation.

Catenation, *n.* Connection, union, conjunction, linking together, continuous junction, concatenation, intimate connection.

Cater, *v. i.* Purvey, provide food, procure provisions.

Cathartic, *a.* Purgative, laxative, evacuant, abstergent, aperient, cleansing.

——, *n.* Purge, purgative, laxative, aperient, physic, purgative medicine.

Catholic, *a.* 1. Universal, general, worldwide.

2. Liberal, tolerant, unbigoted, unsectarian, unexclusive.

3. Roman Catholic, Romish, papal.

——, *n.* Papist, Roman Catholic.

Catholicism, *n.* 1. Universality, catholicity.

2. Liberality, tolerance, largeness of mind, catholicity.

3. Roman Catholic religion, Romanism, papistry.

Catholicity, *n.* 1. Universality, generality, world-wideness.

2. Liberality, tolerance, largeness of mind, freedom from prejudice, bigotry, *or* narrowness, generosity.

Cat's cradle, *n.* Scratch-cradle, cratch-cradle.

Cat's-paw, *n.* Dupe (*in serving another's purpose*), gull, cully.

Cattle, *n. pl.* 1. Bovine quadrupeds, beeves, neat, dumb beasts.

2. Human trash, rabble, riff-raff. See CANAILLE.

Cattle-plague, *n.* Murrain, rinderpest.

Causal, *a.* See CAUSATIVE.

Causality, *n.* Causativeness, causativity, causation, causal system, interdependence of events.

Causation, *n.* 1. Production, bringing about, creation.

2. See CAUSALITY.

Causative, *a.* Causal, generative, productive, conducive, inducing.

CAUSE, *n.* 1. Origin, original, source, spring, mainspring, efficient cause.

2. Ground, reason, motive, consideration, account, inducement, incentive, incitement.

3. Purpose, object, aim, end, final cause.

4. (*Law.*) Suit, action, case, trial.

——, *v. t.* 1. Produce, create, originate, breed, bring into existence, bring into being.

2. Effect, effectuate, produce, bring about, lead to, occasion, give rise to.

Caustic, *n.* Catheretic, mordent, erosive.

——, *a.* 1. Erosive, mordent, corrosive, corroding, catheretic, consuming, acrid, virulent, eating.

2. Burning, scalding, scathing, stinging, biting, sharp, cutting, bitter, severe, sarcastic, satirical.

Cauterize, *v. t.* Sear, burn with a hot iron, burn with cautery.

Caution, *n.* 1. Wariness, heed, heedfulness, circumspection, care, carefulness, watchfulness, vigilance, forethought, providence, prudence, discretion.

2. Warning, admonition, injunction, advice, counsel.

——, *v. t.* Warn, admonish, forewarn, put on one's guard.

Cautious, *a.* Prudent, wary, careful, heedful, chary, circumspect, discreet, watchful, vigilant.

Cavalcade, *n.* Procession (*of mounted men*).

Cavalier, *n.* 1. Knight, equestrian, horseman, chevalier, horse-soldier.

2. Beau, attendant (*on a lady*), partner (*in a dance*).

——, *a.* Disdainful, haughty, arrogant, supercilious, scornful, insolent, curt.

Cavalry, *n.* Horse-soldiers, horse, mounted soldiers, dragoons, hussars.

Cave, *n.* Cavern, den, grotto, grot.

Cavernous, *a.* Hollow.

Cavil, *n.* Frivolous *or* specious objection, captious criticism, carping, censoriousness, hypercritical censure.

Cavil at. Censure captiously, carp at, wilfully find fault with, pick flaws in, raise frivolous *or* specious objection to.

Caviler, *n.* Carper, censurer, captious disputant, frivolous censor, specious objector.

Caviling, *a.* Captious, censorious, carping, critical, hypercritical, disposed to cavil, given to fault-finding.

Cavity, *n.* Hollow, empty space, pocket, vacuole, void, vacant place.

Cease, *v. i.* 1. Desist, refrain, intermit, pause, stop, stay, break off, leave off, give over.

2. Fail, be extinct, be wanting.

3. Terminate, discontinue, quit, end, be at an end, come to an end, blow over.

——, *v. t.* Leave off, stop, desist from, give over, end. See also preceding.

Ceaseless, *a.* 1. Incessant, unceasing, uninterrupted, continual, continuous, unintermitting, unremitting.

2. Perpetual, eternal, endless, everlasting, never-ending, interminable.

Cede, *v. t.* 1. Surrender, relinquish, yield, abandon, resign, deliver up, give up.

2. Grant, convey.

Celebrate, *v. t.* 1. Praise, extol, laud, applaud, magnify, glorify, emblazon, trumpet, bless, commend, give praise to, make famous.

2. Commemorate, honor, keep, observe.

3. Solemnize, perform with due solemnities.

Celebrated, *a.* Famous, renowned, distinguished, illustrious, eminent, famed, far-famed.

Celebration, *n.* 1. Honor, praise, commendation, laudation.

2. Commemoration, observance.

3. Solemnization, reverent performance.

Celebrity, *n.* 1. Fame, renown, glory, honor, credit, reputation, eminence, distinction, repute.

2. Person of note, notable, lion.

Celerity, *n.* Speed, quickness, swiftness, rapidity, fleetness, velocity (*of inanimate objects*).

Celestial, *a.* 1. Of *or* in the firmament, of *or* in the visible heavens, empyrean, empyreal.

2. Heavenly, supernal, angelic, seraphic, god-like, divine.

Celibacy, *n.* Single life, unmarried state, abstinence from marriage.

Celibate, *n.* Bachelor, unmarried person, virgin.

——, *a.* Unmarried, single.

Cell, *n.* 1. Small room, confined apartment.

2. Solitary abode; squalid, lonely dwelling.

3. Enclosed space, small cavity.

4. Elementary corpuscle, organic unit, simplest organism.

Cellular, *a.* Alveolate, favose, honeycombed.

Cement, *n.* 1. Mortar, glue, paste, solder.

2. Bond of union, bond.

——, *v. t.* Unite, connect, attach, join.

——, *v. i.* Unite, cohere, stick together.

Cemetery, *n.* Graveyard, burying-ground, burial-ground, church-yard, necropolis, God's Acre.

Censor, *n.* 1. Inspector, critic of morals.

2. Censurer, caviller, faultfinder.

Censorious, *a.* Captious, carping, hypercritical, severe, condemnatory, faultfinding, hard to please, prone to find fault, apt to blame *or* censure.

Censurable, *a.* Blamable, reprehensible, culpable, blameworthy, faulty, worthy of censure.

Censure, *n.* Blame, disapprobation, disapproval, condemnation, reproof, reproach, reprehension, rebuke, reprimand, animadversion, stricture.

——, *v. t.* Blame, reproach, reprove, chide, reprobate, condemn, reprehend, reprimand, find fault with, pass censure on.

Censurer, *n.* 1. Censor, critic.

2. Caviller, carper.

Centenary, *n.* 1. (*Rare.*) Century, a hundred years.

2. Hundredth anniversary, centennial celebration.

Center, *n.* Middle, midst, middle point, midmost point.

Centesimal, *a.* Hundredth, by the hundred.

Central, *a.* Focal, midmost, middle, nuclear, pivotal.

Centralize, *v. t.* Concentrate (*powers or functions*), delocalize.

Centralization, *n.* Concentration, delocalization, nationalization.

Centuple, *v. t.* Increase a hundred-fold, centuplicate.

Century, *n.* 1. Hundred.

2. Centenary, centennium, hundred years.

Cereals, *n. pl.* Edible grains.

Cerement, *n.* Cerecloth, graveclothes.

Ceremonial, *a.* Ritual, formal.

——, *n.* 1. Ritual, rites, system of rites, ritual system.

2. Formalities, established forms, system of ceremonies, etiquette.

3. Grand ceremony, stately rites, prolonged ceremony.

Ceremonious, *a.* 1. Full of ceremony, stately, lofty, courtly.

2. Formal, studied, according to due form, observant of all the punctilios.

3. Formal, punctilious, stiff, precise, starched, observant of conventionalities.

Ceremony, *n.* 1. Rite, form, formality, ceremonial, solemnity, observance.

2. Parade, pomp, show, stateliness.

CERTAIN, *a.* 1. Indubitable, unquestionable, indisputable, undeniable, incontestable, incontrovertible, unquestioned, undisputed, undoubted, absolute, positive, plain, sure, past dispute, beyond all question, clear as day.

2. Sure, assured, confident, undoubting, fully convinced.

3. Unfailing, infallible, never-failing.

4. Actual, real, existing.

5. Settled, determinate, fixed, stated, constant.

6. Known but unnamed, sort of, some, indeterminate.

Certainty, *n.* 1. Surety, indubitableness, unquestionableness, inevitableness, inevitability.

2. Certitude, assuredness, assurance, absolute confidence, complete conviction, inability to doubt, certain knowledge.

3. Truth, fact, fixed fact, accomplished fact, thing beyond question.

Certificate, *n.* 1. Voucher, written evidence.

2. Testimonial, attestation, credential.

Certify, *v. t.* 1. Attest, testify to, vouch for.

2. Verify, ascertain, determine, make certain.

Cerulean, *a.* Azure, blue, sky-colored, sky-blue.

Cessation, *n.* Stoppage, stop, intermission, remission, suspension, pause, rest, respite, discontinuance, ceasing.

Cession, *n.* 1. Surrender, relinquishment, yielding, ceding, renunciation, abandonment.

2. Grant, conveyance.

Cestus, *n.* [L.] 1. Girdle (*especially the girdle of Venus*), belt, cincture, band.

2. Gauntlet, boxing-glove.

Chafe, *v. t.* 1. Rub, injure by rubbing, wear by rubbing.

2. Irritate, vex, annoy, fret, tease, gall, chagrin, provoke, ruffle, offend, nettle, incense, enrage, exasperate, anger, make angry.

——, *v. i.* 1. Be rubbed, be worn by rubbing.

2. Rage, fret, fume.

Chaff, *n.* 1. Husks, hulls, glumes.

2. Refuse, worthless matter.

——, *v. t.* Ridicule (good-naturedly), mock, scoff, deride, jeer, banter, rally, make fun of, poke fun at.

Chaffer, *v. i.* Higgle, haggle, bargain, negotiate.

Chagrin, *n.* Mortification, vexation, annoyance, humiliation, displeasure, disquiet, ill-humor.

——, *v. t.* Mortify, vex, irritate, chafe, annoy, displease, provoke, put out of temper.

CHAIN, *n.* 1. Fetter, manacle, shackle, bond.

2. Connected series, succession, congeries.

——, *v. t.* 1. Fasten with a chain.

2. Confine, restrain, fetter, shackle, trammel.

3. Enslave, hold in bondage.

Chains, *n. pl.* Fetters, bonds, irons, shackles, manacles, bondage, captivity, thraldom, durance, duress, prison, constraint.

Chair, *n.* 1. Seat.

2. Seat of justice, seat of authority.

Chairman, *n.* Chair, presiding officer.

Chalice, *n.* Cup (*especially the communion cup*), bowl, goblet.

CHALK, *n.* (*Basic Eng.*)

Chalky, *a.* Cretaceous.

Challenge, *v. t.* 1. Defy, dare, brave, invite to contest, call to combat, call to answer.

2. Demand, require, lay claim to, call for.

3. (*Law.*) Object to, take exceptions to.

——, *n.* 1. Defiance, summons to contest, call to combat, call to answer.

2. (*Law.*) Exception, objection.

Chamber, *n.* 1. Apartment, room, hall.

2. Cavity, hollow, hollow place.

Chamber-fellow, *n.* Chum, room-mate.

Chambers, *n. pl.* 1. Lawyer's quarters.

2. Lodgings, hired apartment.

Chamfer, *v. t.* 1. Bevel.

2. Channel, flute, groove, cut furrows in, cut channels in.

——, *n.* 1. Bevel.

2. Fluting, channel, furrow.

Champ, *v. t.* Bite, chew, gnaw.

Champaign, *n.* Flat, open country, plain.

Champion, *n.* 1. Defender, protector, vindicator (*by arms*).

2. Defender, protector, vindicator, promoter (*by word and deed*).

3. Hero, victor, winner, acknowledged chief, belt-holder, challenger of all comers.

CHANCE, *n.* 1. Accident, hap, fortuity, fortune, luck, cast.

2. Possibility, contingency.

3. Opportunity, occasion, opening.

4. Uncertainty, contingency, fortuity, peradventure, gamble, "toss-up."

5. Risk, hazard, peril, jeopardy.

——, *v. i.* Happen, occur, befall, betide, take place, fall out, turn up, come to pass.

Chancery, *n.* 1. Court of equity, Court of Chancery.

2. [*U. S.*] Equity, proceedings in equity.

Change, *v. t.* 1. Vary, modify, make different, make some change in. See ALTER.

2. Shift, remove for other, replace by other.

3. Exchange, barter, commute, give in exchange.

——, *v. i.* Alter, vary, shift, veer, turn, undergo change, change about.

CHANGE, *n.* 1. Alteration, variation, variance, mutation, transition, transmutation, turning, revolution.

2. Vicissitude, variety, novelty, innovation.

Changeable, *a.* 1. Variable, alterable, variant, modifiable, inconstant, unsteady, unsteadfast, unstable, unsettled, mutable, uncertain.

2. Fickle, wavering, vacillating, fitful, capricious, volatile, flighty, mercurial, giddy, like a weathercock.

Changeful, *a.* [Same as CHANGEABLE, but referring properly to inanimate objects.]

Changeless, *a.* Unchanging, immutable, abiding, unvarying, permanent, invariable, constant, fixed, unalterable.

Changeling, *n.* 1. False-child (*left in place of another taken*).

2. Oaf, simpleton, fool, dunce.

3. Waverer, shifter, person of fickle mind.

4. Substitute, fraudulent shift.

Channel, *n.* 1. Passage, duct, conduit, canal.

2. Water-course, canal, trough, drain, aqueduct, flume, chute.

3. Gutter, furrow, fluting, chamfer, groove.

4. Avenue, route, way.

——, *v. t.* Groove, flute, chamfer, cut furrows in, cut channels in.

Chant, *v. t.* and *v. i.* 1. Sing, warble, carol.

2. Intone, recite in musical monotone.

——, *n.* Song, canticle.

Chaos, *n.* 1. Primeval matter, primordial confusion.

2. Disorder, confusion.

Chaotic, *a.* Disordered, utterly confused.

Chap, *v. i.* Crack, open in slits.

——, *n.* 1. Cleft, crack, opening.

2. Boy, youth, fellow.

Chapfallen, *a.* [Sometimes spelled *Chopfallen.*] Dejected, dispirited, depressed, discouraged, melancholy, sad, downcast, cast down, disheartened, downhearted, desponding, despondent, blue, crestfallen, low-spirited, in low spirits.

Chaplet, *n.* Garland, wreath, coronal.

Chaps, *n. pl.* Mouth, jaws.

Char, *v. t.* 1. Burn on the surface, burn partially, scorch.

2. Reduce to charcoal, carbonize.

Character, *n.* 1. Mark, figure, sign, symbol, ideograph, hieroglyph, emblem, letter.

2. Constitution, quality, nature, disposition, cast, turn, bent.

3. Moral qualities, personal traits, habitual conduct.

4. Marked traits, strongly marked personality, striking qualities.

5. Person, personage, individual, "original."

6. Reputation, repute.

Characteristic, *a.* 1. Special, peculiar, distinctive.

2. In keeping with one's character, thoroughly illustrative.

——, *n.* Peculiarity, marked feature *or* quality, lineament, distinguishing trait.

Characterization, *n.* Designation (*of properties*), specification.

Characterize, *v. t.* 1. Distinguish, designate, mark.

2. Describe, set forth the character of, specify the peculiarities of.

Charge, *v. t.* 1. Load, burden, freight, lade, encumber.

2. Intrust, put in care of.

3. Ascribe, impute, lay, lay at one's door, lay to one's charge.

4. Accuse, arraign, impeach, inculpate, criminate, indict, tax, call to account, take to task, inform against.

5. Command, order, bid, require, enjoin, commission.

6. Attack, assault, fall upon, bear down upon, set on.

——, *v. i.* Make an onset, rush.

——, *n.* 1. Load, lading, cargo, freight, burden.

2. Care, custody, keeping, ward, management.

3. Commission, duty, office, trust, employment.

4. Trust, intrusted object, intrusted cause, object of responsibility.

5. Order, injunction, direction, mandate, precept, command.

6. Instruction, exhortation.

7. Accusation, crimination.

8. Cost, expense, outlay, debit, expenditure.

9. Price, sum charged.

10. Onset, onslaught, assault, attack, encounter.

Chargeable, *a.* 1. Attributable, imputable, referrible, traceable, owing, to be charged, to be ascribed.

2. Liable to be accused.

Charger, *n.* 1. Dish, platter.

2. War-horse, officer's mount, steed.

Charily, *adv.* Cautiously, warily, heedfully, carefully, circumspectly, with caution, with circumspection.

Charitable, *a.* 1. Benevolent, beneficent, benignant, kind, benign, liberal, bountiful, generous, open-handed.

2. Considerate, lenient, mild, candid.

Charity, *n.* 1. Benevolence, kindness, benignity, tender-heartedness, kind-heartedness, fellow-feeling, good-will, good-nature, milk of human kindness.

2. Beneficence, liberality, generosity, bounty, humanity, philanthropy, alms-giving, active goodness, doing of good.

3. Benefaction, gift, alms.

Charlatan, *n.* Quack, empiric, mountebank, pretender, impostor, cheat.

Charlatanic, *a.* Empirical, quackish.

Charlatanry, *n.* Quackery, empiricism, trickery, deceit.

Charm, *n.* 1. Spell, enchantment, incantation, witchery, magic, sorcery, necromancy, magical power.

2. Amulet, talisman.

3. Attraction, fascination, allurement, attractiveness.

——, *v. t.* 1. Subdue by a charm, enchant, cast a spell upon, allay by enchantment.

2. Fascinate, enchant, enchain, becharm, delight, attract, captivate, catch, transport, enravish, enrapture, enamour, bewitch, allure, win, please highly, lead captive.

Charmer, *n.* 1. Enchanter, magician, sorcerer.

2. Sweetheart, loved one, darling, dear.

Charming, *a.* Fascinating, captivating, enchanting, enrapturing, bewitching, delightful, lovely.

Charnel-house, *n.* Ossuary, tomb. See GRAVE.

Charter, *n.* 1. Act of incorporation, patent of rights and immunities.

2. (*Rare.*) Right, privilege, prerogative, immunity, franchise, liberty.

——, *v. t.* 1. Incorporate, establish by charter, grant by charter.

2. Let *or* hire (*a ship* or *other means of conveyance*).

Chary, *a.* 1. Cautious, wary, careful, shy, circumspect.

2. See FRUGAL.

Chase, *v. t.* 1. Pursue, hunt, track, run after, follow, give chase to.

2. Emboss, enchase.

——, *n.* 1. Hunting, hunt, course, field-sport.

2. Pursuit, race.

Chasm, *n.* Opening, cleft, fissure, gap, hiatus, cavity, hollow.

Chaste, *a.* 1. Pure, undefiled, virtuous, pure-minded, modest, continent, clean, innocent.

2. Uncorrupt, pure, unaffected, simple, neat, free from barbarisms, in good taste, chastened.

3. Refined, elegant, classic.

Chasten, *v. t.* 1. Discipline by affliction, correct, humble, bring low.

2. Purify, refine, render subdued, toned down.

Chastening, *n.* Chastisement, correction, discipline, humbling.

Chastise, *v. t.* 1. Castigate, punish (*with stripes*), whip, flog, beat, lash, correct.

2. Punish (*by whatever means*), correct, chasten, discipline, humble, subdue, bring to duty, render obedient.

Chastisement, *n.* Punishment, chastening, correction.

Chastity, *n.* 1. Purity, virtue, modesty, pure-mindedness, continence, innocence.

2. Purity, cleanness, decency, freedom from impurity *or* obscenity.

3. [*Rare.*] Chasteness, chastened character, unaffectedness, simplicity, restrainedness, sobriety, refinement, purity, freedom from extravagance.

Chat, *v. i.* Prattle, prate, chatter, babble, gossip, confabulate, talk freely, talk lightly and unceremoniously, have a free and easy talk.

——, *n.* Prattle, gossip, confabulation, chit-chat, *causerie,* easy conversation, free and easy talk, rambling and informal talk, "confab."

Chattels, *n. pl.* Goods, effects, movables, property other than freehold.

Chatter, *v. i.* Prattle, chat, babble, confabulate, have a free and easy talk, gossip, talk idly, talk freely. See PRATE.

——, *n.* Chat, prattle, babble, gabble, patter, jabber. See PRATE and BALDERDASH.

Chatterer, *n*. Prater, prattler, tattler, gossip, babbler, gadder, gadabout, rattlehead, gibberer, jabberer, cackler, blabber, blatterer, blatherskite.

CHEAP, *a*. 1. Low-priced, inexpensive.

2. Common, paltry, poor, mean, indifferent, inferior, meretricious.

Cheapen, *v. t.* 1. Depreciate, reduce in value, lower the price of, lower in price.

2. Depreciate, belittle, reduce in esteem.

Cheat, *v. t.* Defraud, trick, deceive, dupe, gull, overreach, jockey, cozen, "chouse," outwit, bamboozle, circumvent, delude, hoodwink, beguile, mislead, cajole, inveigle, gammon, impose upon, take in, swindle, victimize, practise on, entrap, ensnare, hoax, fool, befool, play false.

——, *v. i.* Deceive, practise fraud, act dishonestly, shuffle, dissemble, cozen, juggle.

——, *n*. 1. Trick, deception, beguilement, imposture, imposition, juggle, stratagem, fraud, wile, blind, catch, swindle, snare, trap, pitfall, artifice, deceit, chouse, piece of finesse, bit of knavery, piece of chicanery.

2. False show, delusion, illusion, deception, mockery, sham, counterfeit, make believe, tinsel, paste.

3. Trickster, impostor, rogue, knave, swindler, sharper, cheater, artful dodger, shuffler, render, seizer, tearer, taker, biter, misleader, beguiler, cozener, jockey, charlatan, mountebank.

Cheater, *n*. Trickster. See CHEAT.

Check, *n*. 1. Restraint, curb, clog, block, bridle, hindrance, stop, obstacle, impediment, obstruction, bar, barrier, damper, interference, rebuff, repression, stopper, brake, control.

2. Mark, symbol, sign, tally.

——, *v. t.* 1. Restrain, curb, block, bridle, hinder, obstruct, repress, counteract, control, put a restraint upon, hold in check, put a damper upon, nip in the bud.

2. Reprove, chide, reprimand, rebuke.

Checker, *v. t.* Variegate, diversify.

Checkmate, *v. t.* Beat (*at chess*), conquer, vanquish, put in check, corner, entirely thwart.

Cheek by jowl. Close (*as in familiar intercourse*), face to face, side by side, *tête-à-tête*, in close proximity.

Cheep, *v. i., v. t.,* and *n*. Pipe, peep, chirp, squeak, creak.

Cheer, *n*. 1. Gladness, joy, gaiety, jollity, hilarity, glee, mirth, merriment. See CHEERFULNESS.

2. Entertainment, provisions, food, repast, viands, victuals.

3. Acclamation, shout of applause, huzza, hurrah.

——, *v. t.* 1. Gladden, exhilarate, inspirit, enliven, animate, incite, encourage.

2. Comfort, console, solace, make cheerful.

3. Applaud, clap, salute with cheers.

Cheerful, *a*. 1. Glad, lively, sprightly, animated, joyful, joyous, happy, lighthearted, lightsome, blithe, merry, mirthful, buoyant, gleeful, gay, cheery, airy, sunny, jocund, jolly, in good spirits, of good cheer, in high feather.

2. Gladdening, gladsome, cheery, cheering, enlivening, encouraging, glad, jocund, pleasant, grateful, hope-inspiring, inspiriting, animating.

Cheerfully, *adv.* 1. Gladly, joyfully, etc.

2. Willingly, gladly, with pleasure, with alacrity, ungrudgingly.

Cheerfulness, *n*. 1. Cheer, good spirits, gladness, gladsomeness, happiness, contentedness, joyfulness, joy, animation, liveliness, lightsomeness, light-heartedness, blithesomeness, mirth, mirthfulness, sunshine, gleefulness, buoyancy, buoyancy of spirits, flow of spirits.

2. Willingness, glad alacrity, ungrudging consent, pleased promptitude.

Cheerless, *a*. Dreary, gloomy, sombre, dark, melancholy, sad, dismal, joyless, spiritless, lugubrious, mournful, dejected, despondent, discouraged, low-spirited, doleful, woe-begone, rueful, disconsolate, forlorn, desolate.

Cheery, *a*. 1. Blithe, hearty, gay, lightsome, sprightly, lively, buoyant, sunny, joyous, merry.

2. Cheering, heartening, animating, enlivening, brightening.

CHEESE, *n*. (*Basic Eng.*)

Cheesy, *a*. Caseous, cheese-like, of the nature of cheese.

Chef-d'œuvre, *n*. [Fr.] Master-piece, master-work, master-stroke, paragon, capital performance.

Chemical, *a*. Alchemical; pertaining to chemistry.

Chemise, *n*. Shift, smock, slip.

Cherish, *v. t.* 1. Nurture, foster, nourish, nurse, sustain, support, comfort, care for.

2. Hold dear, count precious, care greatly for, treasure, protect anxiously, coddle, protect tenderly.

3. Harbor, entertain, indulge, encourage.

Cherub, *n*. 1. [*pl. Cherubim.*] Angel, power, angel of knowledge.

2. [*pl. Cherubs.*] Beautiful child.

CHEST, *n.* 1. Box, case, packing-box, coffer.

2. Breast, thorax, trunk (*of the body*).

Chevalier, *n.* Knight, horseman, cavalier.

Chew, *v. t.* and *v. i.* 1. Masticate, manducate, munch, crunch.

2. Champ, bite, gnaw.

3. Meditate, ruminate, muse on, reflect upon, chew the cud upon.

Chicanery, *n.* Trickery, duplicity, chicane, sophistry, sophistication, deception, intrigue, intriguing, wire-pulling, stratagems, wiles, tergiversation.

Chide, *v. t.* Rebuke, reprimand, censure, reprove, blame, upbraid, admonish, scold, scold at.

——, *v. i.* Scold, clamor, fret, fume, chafe.

CHIEF, *a.* 1. Leading, headmost, first, supreme, arch- (*in compounds*), foremost, master, "top," supereminent, most eminent.

2. Principal, main, prime, vital, essential, capital, especial, great, grand, cardinal, master, supreme, paramount, most important.

——, *n.* 1. Chieftain, commander.

2. Leader, head, corypheus, principal person.

Chiefly, *adv.* 1. Principally, eminently, mainly, capitally, cardinally, especially, particularly, above all.

2. Mostly, for the most part.

Chieftain, *n.* Leader (*of a clan* or *of troops*), chief, commander, captain.

Chiffonnier, *n.* [Fr.] Side-board, cabinet.

Child, *n.* [*pl. Children.*] 1. Infant, babe, baby, nursling, suckling, chit, brat, bantling, *bairn*, little one.

2. Offspring, issue, progeny.

Childbirth, *n.* Parturition, delivery, travail, labor, childbed, child-bearing.

Childhood, *n.* Infancy, minority, pupilage, nonage.

Childish, *a.* 1. Puerile, infantile, juvenile, young, tender.

2. Foolish, silly, weak, trifling, frivolous, "kiddish."

Childlike, *a.* 1. Docile, meek, submissive, dutiful, obedient, gentle.

2. Simple, innocent, ingenuous, uncrafty, guileless, trustful, confiding.

Chill, *n.* 1. Cold, coldness, chilliness, frigidity.

2. Shiver, ague, shivering-fit, ague-fit, rigor.

3. Depression, damp, depressing influence.

——, *a.* Cold, frigid, gelid, chilly, bleak.

——, *v. t.* 1. Make chilly, make cold.

2. Depress, discourage, deject, dampen, dishearten.

Chilly, *a.* Cool, somewhat cold. See CHILL.

Chime, *n.* Consonance, harmony, correspondence of sound.

——, *v. i.* Harmonize, accord, sound in harmony.

Chimera, *n.* Illusion, hallucination, delusion, fantasy, phantom, dream, crotchet, idle fancy, creature of the imagination, air-castle.

Chimerical, *a.* Imaginary, fantastic, fanciful, unfounded, delusive, visionary, illusory, shadowy, wild, Quixotic, Utopian.

CHIN, *n.* (*Basic Eng.*) Lower jaw.

China, *n.* Porcelain, chinaware.

Chine, *n.* Backbone, spine.

Chink, *n.* Opening, gap, crack, cranny, crevice, cleft, rift, fissure, narrow aperture.

——, *v. t.* and *v. i.* Jingle, clink, ring.

Chip, *v. t.* Hew, cut chips from.

——, *n.* Fragment, flake, paring, scrap, small piece.

Chirography, *n.* Handwriting, hand, penmanship, style of penmanship.

Chiromancy, *n.* Palmistry.

Chirp, *v. i.* Cheep, peep, chirrup, twitter.

Chirrup, *v. t.* Encourage, animate, inspirit, cheer, urge on.

Chisel, *v. t.* Cut, carve, sculpture, gouge.

Chit-chat, *n.* Prattle, gossip, chat, *causerie*, easy conversation, familiar talk, idle talk, free and easy talk.

Chivalrous, *a.* 1. Gallant, adventurous, valiant, brave, warlike, bold, knightly, chivalric.

2. High-minded, generous, gallant, magnanimous, knightly.

Chivalry, *n.* 1. Knighthood, knight-errantry.

2. Valor, gallantry.

Chock-full, *a.* Choke-full, brim-full.

Choice, *n.* 1. Election, selection, option, alternative.

2. Preference, pick, favorite.

——, *a.* 1. Select, exquisite, precious, valuable, rare, uncommon, *recherché*, excellent, superior, unusual.

2. Frugal, careful, chary, sparing.

Choke, *v. t.* 1. Suffocate, stifle, smother, strangle, throttle, gag.

2. Suppress, overpower, overcome, stifle, smother, keep down.

3. Obstruct, close, block, stop, bar.

——, *v. i.* Be choked, strangle, suffocate.

Choler, *n.* 1. Bile.

2. Anger, wrath, ire, fury, rage, spleen, exasperation. See ANGER.

Choleric, *a.* Irascible, irritable, hasty, testy, touchy, petulant, waspish, hot, fiery, passionate.

Choose, *v. t.* Select, elect, coöpt, prefer, cull, pick, pick out, single out, fix upon, pitch upon, make choice of.

Chop, *v. t.* 1. Cut (*with a quick blow*), hack, hew.

2. Mince, cut into small pieces.

——, *v. i.* Shift, veer, change suddenly.

——, *n.* 1. Slice, piece cut off.

2. Brand, quality.

3. Jaw, chap.

Chopfallen, *a.* See CHAPFALLEN (the preferable spelling).

Chop-house, *n.* Restaurant (*of a low class*), eating-house.

Choral, *n.* Psalm-tune, hymn-tune.

Chord, *n.* 1. String (*of a musical instrument*).

2. Harmony, consonance.

Chore, *n.* Small job, light task.

Chouse, *v. t.* Deceive, cheat, trick, delude, defraud, swindle, dupe, gull, bamboozle, cozen, overreach, circumvent, beguile, hoodwink, victimize, take in, impose upon, put upon, practise upon, play upon.

——, *n.* 1. Dupe, tool, gull, simpleton, cully.

2. Trick, cheat, wile, ruse, imposture, imposition, fraud, deception, circumvention, deceit, double-dealing, stratagem, artifice, delusion, crafty device, piece of knavery, bit of finesse.

Christ, *n.* The Anointed, The Messiah, Jesus, Immanuel, The Saviour, The Redeemer, The Mediator, The Intercessor, The Advocate, The Judge, The Son of God, The Son of Man, The Lamb of God, The Word.

Christen, *v. t.* 1. Baptize.

2. Denominate, name, term, designate, style, call, dub, entitle, title.

Christian, *n.* 1. Disciple of Christ.

2. Inhabitant, native, or member of Christendom.

Christian name. Baptismal name (*as distinguished from the family name or surname*), given name, prænomen.

Chronic, *a.* Inveterate, deep-seated, rooted, confirmed, continuing, of long duration.

Chronicle, *n.* 1. Register (*of events in the order of time*), diary, journal.

2. Record, history, annals, narration, narrative, recital, account.

——, *v. t.* Record, register, narrate.

Chronicler, *n.* Historian.

Chronometer, *n.* Time-keeper, time-piece.

Chrysalis, *n.* Pupa, aurelia, nympha.

Chubby, *a.* Plump, buxom, chubbed, short and thick.

Chuck, *v. t.* 1. Tap *or* pat (*under the chin*).

2. Throw, pitch, hurl, toss, thrust, push.

——, *n.* 1. Tap *or* pat (*under the chin*).

2. Throw, toss, thrust, push.

Chuckle, *v. i.* Giggle, titter, laugh (*quietly, with satisfaction*).

——, *n.* Giggle, titter, laughter (*half suppressed*), chuckling.

Chum, *n.* Chamber-fellow, room-mate, "pal," "buddy."

Chump, *n.* Thick piece *or* block.

CHURCH, *n.* 1. Temple, fane, kirk, chapel, house of worship, house of God, meeting-house.

2. Body of Christians, ecclesiastical body, denomination.

Churchman, *n.* 1. Ecclesiastic, clergyman, minister, pastor, divine, priest.

2. Episcopalian, Conformist.

Churchyard, *n.* Burying-ground, burial-ground, graveyard, cemetery, necropolis, God's acre.

Churl, *n.* 1. Rustic, peasant, countryman, clodhopper, bumpkin, ploughman, clown.

2. Ill-bred man, boor, surly fellow.

3. Niggard, miser, skinflint, scrimp, curmudgeon, hunks, mean fellow.

Churlish, *a.* 1. Rude, harsh, brusque, uncivil, impolite, rough, brutish, surly, cynical, snarling, snappish, waspish.

2. Crabbed, morose, sullen, ill-tempered.

3. Niggardly, miserly, close, close-fisted, sordid, penurious, stingy, mean, illiberal.

Churlishness, *n.* 1. Rudeness, incivility, roughness, brutishness.

2. Crabbedness, moroseness, sullenness, tartness, acrimony, acerbity, asperity, harshness, bitterness, ill-temper.

3. Niggardliness, stinginess, penuriousness, closeness, meanness, miserliness, sordidness, close-fistedness.

Churn, *v. t.* Agitate, jostle violently, cause to foam.

Cicatrice, } *n.* Scar, seam.
Cicatrix, }

Cicatrize, *v. t.* Heal, cover with a scar, cause to heal up.

——, *v. i.* Heal, scar over.

Cicisbeo, *n.* [It.] Gallant (*of a married woman*), beau, gigolo, dangler about women.

Ci-devant, *a.* [Fr.] Former, late, quondam, old-time.

Cimeter, *n.* Falchion, scimeter.

Cimeter-shaped, *a.* Acinaciform.

Cimmerian, *a.* Black, very dark, intensely dark, midnight.

Cincture, *n.* Band, belt, girdle, cestus.

Cinctured, *a.* Girded, belted, girdled, girt, engirt.

Cinders, *n. pl.* 1. Embers.
   2. Slag, dross, scoria.

Cinereous, *a.* Ashy, ashen, cineritious, like ashes.

Cipher, *n.* 1. Zero, naught *or* nought, nothing.
   2. Character, symbol, device, monogram.
   3. Secret character, private alphabet, cryptogram.
——, *v. i.* Use figures, figure, compute arithmetically.

Circean, *a.* Magical, enchanting, spellbinding, brutifying.

CIRCLE, *n.* 1. Round, plane figure; rondure, gyre, circlet, corona, hoop, ring.
   2. Circumference, periphery, cordon.
   3. Orb, sphere, globe, ball.
   4. Compass, enclosure.
   5. Company, society, class, fraternity, coterie, clique, set.
   6. Range, sphere, province, field, compass, bounds, circuit, region.

Circuit, *n.* 1. Revolution, circular course, circumambience, ambit, turn, cycle.
   2. Space, region, tract, district, province, range, sphere, field, compass, bounds.
   3. Boundary, compass, boundary line, distance round.
   4. Course, tour, round, perambulation, detour.

Circuitous, *a.* Tortuous, devious, turning, winding, indirect, roundabout.

Circular, *a.* Round, annular, ring-shaped, orbed, orbicular, cycloid, discoid.

Circulate, *v. i.* 1. Move round, move in a circle.
   2. Spread, be diffused, have currency.
——, *v. t.* Spread, diffuse, disseminate, promulgate, propagate, give currency to, spread abroad.

Circulation, *n.* 1. Motion in a circle.
   2. Diffusion, dissemination, promulgation, propagation, spread, spreading.
   3. Currency, money, circulating medium.

Circumambient, *a.* Surrounding, encompassing, encircling, circling, circumjacent, ambient.

Circumference, *n.* Periphery, perimeter, girth, circuit, bound.

Circumjacent, *a.* Surrounding, encompassing, encircling, ambient, circumambient, environing, enfolding, enclosing, lying around.

Circumlocution, *n.* Periphrasis, periphrase, ambage, indirect expression, roundabout mode of speech.

Circumlocutory, *a.* Periphrastical, periphrastic, ambagious, roundabout, indirect.

Circumscribe, *v. t.* 1. Bound, encircle, surround, enclose.
   2. Confine, restrict, limit, keep within bounds.

Circumspect, *a.* Cautious, wary, careful, watchful, heedful, considerate, judicious, vigilant, attentive, discreet, prudent, observant.

Circumspection, *n.* Caution, wariness, watchfulness, thoughtfulness, care, vigilance, attention, prudence, discretion, forecast.

Circumstance, *n.* 1. Incidental, accidental, *or* subsidiary fact.
   2. Event, fact, incident, occurrence.

Circumstances, *n. pl.* 1. Situation, condition, position, state of affairs.
   2. Surroundings, environment, attendant conditions.
   3. Pecuniary standing, moneyed condition.

Circumstantial, *a.* 1. Particular, minute, detailed.
   2. Indirect, inferential, presumptive, founded on circumstances.

Circumvent, *v. t.* 1. Thwart, check, checkmate, outgeneral.
   2. Deceive, cheat, defraud, trick, cozen, over-reach, delude, hoodwink, dupe, gull, bamboozle, chouse, outwit, beguile, mislead, inveigle, impose upon.

Circumvention, *n.* Fraud, deception, imposition, imposture, deceit, cheat, cheating, trick, trickery, indirection, crooked ways, chicanery, wiles.

Cirrus, *n.* [*pl. Cirri.*] 1. (*Bot.*) Tendril, filament.
   2. (*Meteor.*) Curl-cloud, cat's-tail, mare's-tail.

Cistern, *n.* Reservoir, tank.

Citadel, *n.* Castle, stronghold. See FORTRESS.

Citation, *n.* 1. Summons, official call *or* notice.
   2. Quotation, extract, excerpt, quoted passage.
   3. Enumeration, mention, quoting, quotation, bringing forward.

Cite, *v. t.* 1. Summon, send for.
   2. Quote, adduce, extract.
   3. Enumerate, mention, bring forward.

Citizen, *n.* Inhabitant, resident, dweller, burgess, burgher, townsman.

City, *n.* Incorporated town; metropolis.

Civic, *a.* Civil (*as distinguished from military*), municipal, political.

Civil, *a.* 1. Municipal, political, civic.
   2. Intestine. domestic.
   3. Courteous, polite, refined, complaisant, urbane, suave, obliging, affable,

debonair, easy, gracious, well-bred, courtly.

Civilities, *n. pl.* Acts of courtesy, attentions.

Civility, *n.* Courtesy, courteousness, urbanity, politeness, affability, complaisance, amiability, suavity, good-breeding, elegance of manners.

Civilization, *n.* Culture, cultivation, refinement.

Civilize, *v. t.* Refine, cultivate, educate, polish, enlighten, improve, humanize, reclaim from barbarism.

Clack, *n.* 1. Click, clink, tick, beat.
2. Prate, prattle, babble, babbling, gossip, palaver, cackle, gabble, gab, idle talk, small talk. See PRATE.
——, *v. i.* 1. Click, clink.
2. Prate, prattle, babble, gabble, chatter, jabber, clatter, gossip, talk idly.

Claim, *v. t.* Require, ask, demand, challenge, call for, lay claim to, assert as one's right.
——, *v. i.* 1. Derive a right, obtain a title.
2. Assert a claim, put forward the claim.
——, *n.* 1. Demand, call, requisition, lien.
2. Right, pretension, title, privilege.

Clairvoyance, *n.* 1. Seeing without eyes, seeing in a mesmeric state, trance-vision, second sight.
2. Insight, divination.

Clairvoyant, *a.* Able to see without eyes, seeing by mesmeric influence, seeing in trance.

Clamber, *v. i.* Climb (*with difficulty*), scramble.

Clammy, *a.* Viscous, glutinous, gummy, viscid, sticky, slimy, ropy, adhesive, dauby, smeary.

Clamor, *n.* Outcry, vociferation, exclamation, noise, hullabaloo, hubbub, uproar, blare, din.
——, *v. i.* 1. Vociferate, cry out, shout, make uproar, make outcries.
2. Cry importunately, demand importunately.

Clamorous, *a.* 1. Vociferous, noisy, boisterous, obstreperous, uproarious, blatant.
2. Importunate.

Clan, *n.* 1. Race, tribe, family, phratry.
2. Clique, coterie, set, gang, brotherhood, fraternity, sodality.

Clandestine, *a.* Concealed (*for an illicit purpose*), secret, hidden, private, underhand, underhanded, furtive, stealthy, covert, surreptitious, *sub rosa*, sly.

Clang, *n.* Clangor, clank, clash, clashing.
——, *v. i.* Clank, clash.

Clangor, *n.* Clang, clank.

Clank, *v. i.* Clang, clash.

Clap, *v. t.* 1. Pat, strike gently, slap.
2. Thrust, force, slam.
3. Put hastily, put hurriedly, slap.
4. Applaud (*by striking the hands together*), cheer.
——, *n.* 1. Blow, knock, slap.
2. Explosion, burst, peal, slam, bang.

Clap-trap, *n.* Trick (*for the sake of effect, as on the stage*), stage-effect, stage-trick, *coup de théâtre, tour de force.*
——, *a.* Stage-tricky, *ad captandum*, spectacular, theatrical, histrionic.

Clarify, *v. t.* Purify, clear, make clear, strain, depurate.

Clash, *v. i.* 1. Collide, crash together, come into collision, strike against each other.
2. Clank, clang, crash, clatter, rattle.
3. Disagree, contend, interfere, be mutally opposed, act in a contrary direction.
——, *n.* 1. Collision.
2. Clang, clank, clangor, clashing, crash, clatter, rattle.
3. Opposition, contradiction, interference, clashing, jar, jarring, disagreement.

Clashing, *n.* 1. Clang, clank, clangor, clash, crash.
2. Opposition, interference, clash, jar, jarring, disagreement, contradiction, hostility, enmity.

Clasp, *v. t.* 1. Grasp, grip, clutch, grapple, seize, entwine, put the fingers around, lay hold of, fasten upon.
2. Embrace, hug, fold, enfold.
——, *n.* 1. Hook, catch, buckle. See HASP.
2. Embrace, hug.

Class, *n.* 1. Rank *or* order (*or persons*), social *or* official status, form, grade.
2. Group (*as of pupils pursuing the same studies*), seminar.
3. Scientific division (*of animate or inanimate objects, including orders, genera, and species*), kind, sort, breed.
4. Category, division, head, group, collection, denomination.
——, *v. t.* Arrange, rank, range, classify, dispose, distribute, form into classes.

Classic, *n.* First-rate work (*of literature*), work of the first class, standard work, model production, master-piece, *chef d'œuvre.*

Classic, } *a.* 1. First-rate, of the first
Classical, } class (*in literature*), standard, model, master, masterly.
2. Greek *or* Latin, Greek and Latin, Grecian and Roman.
3. Elegant, polished, refined, chaste, pure, Attic.

Classification, *n.* Arrangement, assortment, disposition, distribution, grouping, reducing to order.

Classify, *v. t.* Arrange, class, categorize, distribute, dispose, group, form into classes, pigeonhole, reduce to order.

Clatter, *v. i.* 1. Rattle, clash.

2. Prate, prattle, babble, clack, gabble, clatter, jabber, talk loudly.

——, *n.* Rattling, clattering, clutter, confused noise.

Clause, *n.* Article, provision, proviso, condition, stipulation.

Claviform *a.* (*Bot.*) Clavate, clavated, club-shaped.

Clavis, *n.* [L. *pl. Claves;* Eng. *pl. Clavises.*] Key, explanation, clew, guide.

Claw, *n.* Talon, ungula.

——, *v. t.* Tear (*with the claws*), scratch, lacerate, laniate.

Clay, *n.* [*Scriptural* or *poetic.*] Flesh (*of man, as perishable*), mortal part, earthly part, earthly substance, perishable substance.

CLEAN, *a.* 1. Unstained, unspotted, spotless, unsmirched, unsoiled, unsullied, immaculate, cleanly, white.

2. Unadulterated, unmixed, pure, purified, clarified.

3. Neat, delicate, shapely, graceful, light, dexterous, adroit, free from bungling.

4. Entire, complete, perfect, whole, free from defect, faultless, unblemished, unimpaired, without abatement, unabated.

5. Pure, innocent, free from moral impurity, undefiled in heart, chaste, free from lust.

6. Ceremonially pure, ritually just, according with ceremonial.

——, *adv.* Entirely, completely, perfectly, quite, altogether, wholly, thoroughly, fully, in all respects, in every respect, out and out.

——, *v. t.* Cleanse, purify, purge, wash, scour, make clean, free from dirt.

Cleanly, *a.* Neat, tidy. See CLEAN, *a.*

——, *adv.* Neatly, in a clean *or* neat manner.

Cleanse, *v. t.* 1. Purify, clean, elutriate, make clean, free from dirt.

2. Purify, free from sin.

3. Remove, purge away.

Cleansing, *n.* Purification, purifying.

——, *a.* 1. Purifying, purgative, abstergent, cathartic.

2. Purifying, regenerating, regenerative, redemptive.

CLEAR, *a.* 1. Transparent, crystalline, bright, light, luminous, pellucid, limpid.

2. Unmixed, pure, unadulterated.

3. Unobstructed, unencumbered, free, open.

4. Serene, fair, cloudless, unclouded, sunny, unobscured, undimmed.

5. Net, without deductions.

6. Perspicuous, lucid, luminous, distinct, plain, intelligible.

7. Apparent, visible, palpable, evident, obvious, manifest, distinct, conspicuous, patent, unequivocal, unmistakable, indisputable, undeniable, unambiguous, unquestionable, not to be mistaken.

8. Innocent, unspotted, spotless, guiltless, sinless, irreproachable, unblemished, unsullied, undefiled, immaculate, clean.

9. Unobstructed, unimpeded, unhampered, free from hindrance *or* obstruction *or* impediment.

10. Musical, silvery, liquid, fluty, sonorous, mellifluous, euphonious.

——, *v. t.* 1. Clarify, refine, purify, cleanse, make clear.

2. Free, loose, liberate, emancipate, disinthrall, set free.

3. Acquit, absolve, exonerate, discharge, justify, vindicate, set right.

4. Extricate, disengage, loosen, disentangle, disembarrass.

5. Free from obstructions, sweep, scour, clean up.

6. Net, get *or* gain over and above expenses.

——, *v. i.* 1. Clear away, up, *or* off, become free from clouds, fog, *or* mist, break, break away, become fair.

2. Balance accounts, settle balances, settle at the clearing-house.

Clearance, *n.* 1. Discharge, release, exoneration, acquittal.

2. (*Com.*) Permission to leave port, permission to sail.

Clear-cut, *a.* Sharply outlined, sharp-cut, delicately and cleanly outlined, well-defined, exact, definite, precise.

Clear-headed, *a.* 1. Free from confusion *or* confused thought, lucid, luminous, clear-thoughted, clear-thinking.

2. Discerning, clear-sighted, clear-seeing, keen-sighted, shrewd, sagacious, perspicacious, penetrating, acute, long-headed. See INTELLIGENT.

Clear off. 1. Become fair, clear away, clear up, break, break away.

2. Remove, clear away *or* off, cancel, pay, pay off *or* up, liquidate.

Clear-sighted, *a.* Discerning. See CLEAR-HEADED, 2.

Clear up, *v. i.* See CLEAR OFF.

——, *v. t.* Explain, expound, make out, make plain, satisfactorily account for, relieve from suspicion, explain away, relieve from doubt.

Cleave, *v. i.* 1. Adhere, cohere, stick, hold, cling, be attached, united, *or* joined.

2. Attach one's self, unite one's self, take the side (of), take sides (with), take part (with).

3. Remain devoted to, be devoted to, be true to, cling.

4. Separate, divide, part, open, split, crack, be divided, sunder, be sundered, sever, be severed.

——, *v. t.* Split, rive, rend, sever, sunder, cut *or* hew asunder, tear asunder.

Cleft, *a.* Cloven, forked, bifurcated.

——, *n.* Crevice, chink, fissure, rift, break, breach, gap, cranny, crack, interstice, opening, fracture, chasm.

Clemency, *n.* 1. Lenity, lenience, leniency, mildness, mercifulness, mercy, gentleness, forgivingness, compassion, tenderness, kindness, fellow-feeling, long-suffering, freedom from vindictiveness, disposition to mercy.

2. Softness, mildness. (*Said of weather, etc.*).

Clement, *a.* Lenient, merciful, mild, forgiving, compassionate, kind, indulgent, tender, gentle, humane, kind-hearted, tender-hearted.

Clench, *v. t.* 1. [Written also *Clinch.*] Secure, fasten, rivet, and *fig.*, confirm, establish, fix, secure.

2. Set, set firmly, clasp firmly, double, double up tightly.

3. Grasp firmly, clutch, seize and hold.

——, *n.* Clinging grasp, clutch, persistent hold.

Clergy, *n.* Ministers, clergymen, the cloth, body of ecclesiastics (*in distinction from the laity*).

Clergyman, *n.* Minister, divine, priest, pastor, parson, ecclesiastic, churchman.

Clerk, *n.* 1. Recorder, registrar, scribe, scrivener, secretary.

2. [*U. S.*] Assistant (*in a place of business*), accountant, salesman, saleswoman.

3. [*Archaic.*] Scholar, man of letters, lettered man.

Clever, *a.* 1. Dexterous, skilful, apt, ingenious, handy, ready, quick, smart, expert, adroit, capable.

2. Able, gifted, talented, apt.

Cleverness, *n.* Dexterity, adroitness, ingenuity, skill, aptness, aptitude, readiness, quickness, smartness, expertness, ability.

Clew, *n.* Guide, guidance, direction, key, *clavis*. See CLUE.

Click, *v. i.* Tick, clack, clink, beat, vibrate with a click.

——, *v. t.* 1. Move with a click, make click.

2. Sound with a click, utter with a click.

——, *n.* 1. Tick, clack, clink, beat.

2. Pawl, detent, catch, ratchet.

Client, *n.* 1. Dependant, henchman, retainer.

2. (*Law.*) Retainer (*of counsel*), person represented (*by counsel*).

Clientage, *n.* 1. Clientship.

2. Clientelage, clientele, body of clients, all one's clients.

Cliff, *n.* Precipice, crag, precipitous rock, palisade, rocky headland, steep, scar (*Eng.*).

Climacteric, *n.* Crisis, critical point, critical period.

Climate, *n.* Meteorological character *or* habit, usual weather, clime.

Climax, *n.* 1. Gradual culmination, successive increase of effect.

2. Acme, culmination, top, summit, crowning point.

Climb, *v. t.* Struggle up, go up, mount, surmount, ascend, scale.

——, *v. i.* 1. Clamber, scramble, ascend gradually, come slowly up.

2. Creep, twine, clamber. (*Said of plants.*)

Clime, *n.* Region, place, country, climate.

Clinch, *v. t.* 1. Grasp, grip, clasp, clutch, clench, grapple, lay hold of.

2. Fasten, secure.

3. Confirm, fix, establish.

——, *n.* 1. Catch, grip, clutch, grasp.

2. Clincher, cramp, holdfast, clamp.

Clincher, *n.* 1. Cramp, clinch, holdfast, clamp.

2. Conclusive argument, unanswerable argument, poser, "settler," "closer."

Cling, *v. i.* 1. Adhere, stick, cleave, be attached, hold, hold fast. Also *fig.*

2. Twine round, throw tendrils about.

3. Embrace, clasp.

Clink, *v. i.* 1. Ring, jingle, tinkle, chink.

2. Rhyme, jingle, chime.

——, *v. t.* Ring, jingle, chink.

Clinker, *n.* Scoria, slag, incombustible refuse (*of furnaces*).

Clip, *v. t.* 1. Cut, shear, snip.

2. Prune, trim, pare, curtail, dock, cut short.

——, *n.* 1. Shearing, cutting.

2. (*Colloq.*) Blow (*with the hand*), rap, knock, lick, whack, thwack, thump.

Clique, *n.* [Fr.] [*Generally used in a bad sense.*] Coterie, club, brotherhood, sodality, clan, junto, cabal, *camarilla*, party, gang, set, ring, private *or* exclusive association.

Cloak, *n.* 1. Mantle, surcoat.

2. Mask, veil, cover, blind, pretext.

——, *v. t.* Mask, hide, veil, cover, conceal, dissemble.

CLOCK, *n.* 1. Timekeeper, timepiece, horologe.

2. Beetle, scarab, scarabee, scarabæus, coleopter.

Clod, *n.* 1. Lump (of earth).

2. Ground, earth, turf, sod.

3. Clodpoll, clown, dolt. See DUNCE.

Clodhopper, *n.* Rustic, peasant, countryman, boor, swain, hind, bumpkin, ploughman, clown, churl, clod-breaker.

Clog, *v. t.* 1. Trammel, shackle, hamper, fetter, put a clog on.

2. Obstruct, choke, choke up, stop up.

3. Encumber, hinder, impede, hamper, embarrass, cumber, restrain, trammel, burden, load.

——, *n.* 1. Trammel, fetter, shackle, drag-weight, dead-weight.

2. Impediment, encumbrance, hindrance, obstacle, obstruction, check, drawback.

Cloister, *n.* 1. Convent-walk, abbey-walk, arched ambulatory.

2. Convent, monastery, abbey, nunnery, priory.

3. Arcade, colonnade, colonnaded court, piazza.

Cloistral, *a.* Recluse, solitary, secluded, sequestered, monastic.

Close, *v. t.* 1. Shut, shut up, occlude, seal.

2. Stop, obstruct, estop, choke, stop up, clog.

3. Conclude, finish, terminate, end, cease, complete, bring to a period.

——, *v. i.* 1. Unite, coalesce, come together, be brought together.

2. Terminate, end, be concluded, cease.

3. Grapple, come to close quarters, clinch.

4. Agree, come to terms, accept the offer.

——, *n.* 1. [Pron. *cloze.*] End, conclusion, termination, cessation.

2. [Pron. *close.*] Cathedral *or* abbey precinct.

3. Enclosure, inclosure, inclosed place, yard, grounds.

——, *a.* 1. Tight, closed, shut fast, confined, snug.

2. Hidden, secret, private.

3. Reserved, taciturn, reticent, secretive, incommunicative.

4. Retired, withdrawn, concealed, secluded, pent up.

5. Confined, stagnant, motionless.

6. Oppressive, stale, stifling, stuffy.

7. Dense, compact, solid, compressed, firm, thick.

8. Near, approaching nearly, adjoining, adjacent, immediately, neighboring.

9. Intimate, confidential, devoted, strongly attached, dear.

10. Intense, intent, unremitting, earnest, fixed, assiduous.

11. Faithful, accurate, precise, exact, strict, nice.

12. Parsimonious, stingy, penurious, miserly, niggardly, close-fisted, close-handed, mean, illiberal, ungenerous, churlish, curmudgeonly.

Close-fisted, *a.* Parsimonious. See CLOSE, *a,* 12.

Closet, *n.* 1. Cabinet, private room, retiring-room.

2. Store-room, clothes-room.

——, *v. t.* Admit to intimate interview, put into concealment, admit to secret conference.

Closeting, *n.* Clandestine conference, secret conference.

Close with. 1. Accede to, consent to, agree to.

2. Agree with, make an agreement with.

3. Grapple with.

Clot, *n.* Concretion, coagulation, crassament, lump, clout.

——, *v. i.* Concrete, coagulate.

CLOTH, *n.* 1. Woven fabric.

2. [With *The* prefixed.] Clergy, clerical profession, clergymen, ecclesiastics.

Clothe, *v. t.* 1. Dress, attire, apparel, array, deck, "rig," robe, put garments upon.

2. Provide garments for, provide with clothes, habilitate, furnish with raiment.

3. Invest (with), cover, endue, endow enwrap, envelop, swathe.

Clothes, *n. pl.* Garments, raiment, apparel, attire, vesture, vestments, dress, clothing, garb, costume, habiliments, habits, wearing apparel, array, gear, "rig," "things."

CLOUD, *n.* 1. Nebulosity, haze, mist, fog, vapor, scud, cumulus, cirrus, nimbus, stratus.

2. Throng, multitude, dense mass, vast number, host, army, horde, vast assemblage.

3. Blue, blurred spot, dark spot *or* blotch.

4. Darkness, obscurity, gloom, obscuration, eclipse.

——, *v. t.* 1. Overspread, overcast, cover with clouds, becloud, obnubilate.

2. Darken, obscure, dim, befog, begloom, shade, shadow.

Cloud-built, *a.* 1. Cloud-piled, cloud-formed, made of clouds.

2. Illusive, illusory, unstable, fanciful, imaginary, chimerical.

Cloudy, *a.* 1. Clouded, nubilous, foggy, filmy, hazy, murky, lowering, lurid, overcast.

2. Obscure, dark, dim, confused.

3. Gloomy, dismal, depressing, sullen.

4. Varied with dark spots, mottled, clouded.

5. Blurred, dimmed, lustreless, muddy.

Clown, *n.* 1. Rustic, peasant, swain, ploughman, countryman, clodhopper, clod-breaker, husbandman, hind, churl, lubber.

2. Bumpkin, lout, boor, churl, fellow, ill-bred and uncouth man.

3. Dolt, blockhead, clodpoll, clodpate, simpleton, thickhead, dunderhead, numskull. See DUNCE.

4. Buffoon, fool, harlequin, jester, droll, punch, zany, scaramouch, merry-andrew, jack-pudding, pickle-herring, mime, pantaloon, jack-a-dandy, wearer of the motley, *farceur.*

Clownish, *a.* 1. Rustic, boorish, loutish, coarse, rough, awkward, clumsy, ungainly.

2. Rude, impolite, uncivil, ill-bred, ill-mannered, churlish.

Cloy, *v. t.* Satiate, glut, surfeit, pall, sate.

Club, *n.* 1. Bludgeon, cudgel, bat, truncheon, hickory, shillalah.

2. Association, society, company, set, fraternity, sodality, coterie.

——, *v. i.* 1. Form a club, unite in a club.

2. Co-operate, unite together, act in concert, club together.

3. Contribute, unite to share expenses, make a common purse.

——, *v. t.* 1. Combine, unite, add together, aggregate.

2. Average, defray by shares, lump.

3. Beat (with a club), cudgel, bludgeon.

Clue, *n.* 1. Ball of thread.

2. Thread, string, twine, tie, fastening.

3. Guiding-thread, guide, guidance, direction, hint, indication, key, *clavis,* clew.

Clump, *n.* Cluster, bunch, tuft, patch, group, assemblage, collection.

Clumsy, *a.* 1. Unwieldy, ponderous, heavy, cumbrous, lumbering, ill-shaped, ill-made, botched.

2. Awkward, unhandy, bungling, blundering, maladroit, inapt, unskilful, heavy-handed, elephantine.

Cluster, *n.* Clump, bunch, group, assemblage, collection.

——, *v. i.* Grow in bunches, grow in clusters, agglomerate, collect together, crowd together, throng.

Clutch, *v. t.* Grasp, gripe, grip, grapple, clasp, clench, seize, catch, snatch, lay hold of, fasten upon.

——, *n.* Grasp, gripe, grip, clasp, clench, seizure.

Clutches, *n. pl.* 1. Paws, talons, claws.

2. Hands (*implying rapacity* or *cruelty*), power, cruel power.

Clutter, *n.* 1. Bustle, clatter, clattering, racket, confused noise.

2. Confused mass, disorder, disarray, confusion.

——, *v. t.* Disarrange, throw into disorder, lumber, fill full of confused materials, heap into disorder.

Coadjutor, *n.* Helper, collaborator, *collaborateur,* co-operator, auxiliary, colleague, partner, aider, ally, abettor, co-aid. See ASSISTANT and ACCESSORY.

Coagulate, *v. t.* and *v. i.* Curdle, clabber, concrete, thicken, clot.

Coagulation, *n.* 1. Curdling, concretion.

2. Clot, coagulum.

Coagulum, *n.* Clot, coagulation.

COAL, *n.* (*Basic Eng.*) The black mineral.

Coalesce, *v. i.* 1. Unite, combine, blend, come together, become consolidated.

2. Concur, fraternize, come to an agreement.

Coal-hod, *n.* Coal-scuttle.

Coalition, *n.* Union, alliance, confederacy, federation, confederation, league, combination, co-partnership, compact.

Coal-mine, *n.* Colliery, coal-pit.

Coarse, *a.* 1. Of large size.

2. Of large fibres *or* particles.

3. Crude, rough, impure, unpurified.

4. Gross, broad, ribald, indelicate, indecent, vulgar.

5. Rude, unpolished, uncivil, impolite, gruff, boorish, bluff, bearish, brutish, loutish, clownish, churlish.

6. Crass, inelegant.

Coast, *n.* Shore, beach, strand, seaboard, seaside, sea-coast.

COAT, *n.* 1. Outer garment (*of men*), jacket, frock, cutaway.

2. Cover, covering, coating.

3. Layer, covering layer.

——, *v. t.* Cover, spread a covering over, spread.

Coating, *n.* Covering, coat, covering *or* protecting layer.

Coat of arms. Escutcheon, arms, armorial bearings, armorial ensigns, device, crest, coat-armor.

Coat of mail. Suit of armor, suit of mail, armor, mail, hauberk, cuirass, habergeon, *lorica, thorax.*

Coax, *v. t.* Wheedle, cajole, flatter, cog, persuade by fondling, prevail upon by flattery.

Cob, *n.* 1. Sea-mew, sea-cob, gull, mew.

2. Horse (*short-legged and stout*), cob-horse.

Cobble, *v. t.* 1. Botch, tinker, patch up, mend clumsily.

2. Bungle, botch, do clumsily, make clumsily.

——, *v. i.* 1. Do cobbler's work, mend shoes.

2. Be a bungler, bungle, botch, do bungling work.

——, *n.* Cobble-stone, cobstone, small round stone.

Cobbler, *n.* 1. Mender of shoes.

2. Clumsy workman, bungler, botcher.

3. Iced-sangaree, sherry-cobbler.

Cobweb, *n.* 1. Spider's web.

2. Entanglement, snare, meshes, toils, insidious intricacy.

3. Flimsy or frail thing, piece of flimsiness.

——, *a.* Flimsy, slight, gauzy, worthless, thin.

Cochleate, *a.* Cochleated, cochlean, cochleary, cochleous, spiral, spiry, screw-shaped.

Cock, *n.* 1. Chanticleer, rooster [*U. S.*].

2. Faucet, turn-valve, stop-cock, spout, tap.

3. Turning-up, turn, toss, perking.

4. Pile (*of hay, etc.*), rick.

5. Yawl, ship's boat, small boat, cock-boat.

——, *v. t.* 1. Set, set up, set the cock or hammer of.

2. Perk, perk up, toss.

3. Pile, make into cocks or ricks.

4. Point, sharpen, calk (*said of a horse-shoe*).

——, *v. i.* Bridle, perk, hold the head high, look big or pert or menacing.

Cock-a-hoop, *a.* Boasting, boastful, bragging, vaunting, vaporing, blustering, exulting, triumphant, vain-glorious.

Cockatrice, *n.* Basilisk.

Cocker, *v. t.* (*Rare.*) Indulge (*unduly*), fondle, pamper.

Cock-eyed, *a.* Squint-eyed.

Cockle, *v. t.* Wrinkle, pucker, corrugate, gather into folds.

Cock-loft, *n.* Garret, loft, attic, upper story.

Cockney, *n.* [*Term of slight ridicule.*] Londoner, native or resident of London.

Cocksure, *a.* (*Colloq.*) Very sure, quite sure, quite certain, very confident.

Coddle, *v. t.* Humor, nurse, pamper, cocker, indulge, fondle, caress, pet, treat with fondness, make much of.

Code, *n.* Digest, collection of laws, codex, formulary.

Codger, *n.* 1. Miser, niggard, churl, curmudgeon, lick-penny, skinflint, scrimp, hunks, screw, muckworm.

2. (*Colloq.*) Queer old fellow, eccentric chap, odd stick.

Codicil, *n.* Supplement or postscript (*to a will*).

Codify, *v. t.* Digest, systematize, reduce to a code or digest.

Coequal, *a.* Co-ordinate, of like rank, of the same rank, of equal dignity or power, on a level, on a par.

Coerce, *v. t.* 1. Restrain, curb, check, repress, put under restraint.

2. Compel, force, drive, constrain.

Coercion, *n.* 1. Restraint, check, curb, repression.

2. Compulsion, constraint, force.

Coercive, *a.* 1. Coercing, checking, restraining, curbing, repressing, repressive.

2. Constraining, compelling, compulsory.

Coeval, *a.* Coetaneous, of the same age.

Coexist, *v. i.* Exist together, exist at the same time.

Coexistent, *a.* Simultaneous, synchronous.

Coffer, *n.* 1. Chest, box, casket, trunk.

2. Money-chest, strong-box, safe.

3. (*Arch.*) Sunk panel, caisson, lacunar.

Coffin, *n.* Burial chest, casket, cist (*archaeol.*), sarcophagus.

——, *v. t.* 1. Put or enclose in a coffin.

2. Confine, shut up, imprison, crib.

Cog, *v. t.* 1. Wheedle. See COAX.

2. [With *in* or *upon*.] Thrust slyly, intrude deceitfully, push craftily, insert by wiles.

3. Furnish or fit with cogs.

——, *v. i.* Deceive. See CHEAT.

——, *n.* 1. Trick, deceit, fraud, cheat.

2. Tooth (*of a wheel*).

Cogency, *n.* Force, strength, power, conclusiveness, convincingness, convincing power, persuasiveness, potency.

Cogent, *a.* Forcible, effective, trenchant, powerful, urgent, potent, irresistible, resistless, persuasive, convincing, conclusive.

Cogitate, *v. i.* Meditate, think, reflect, consider, ponder, weigh, deliberate, ruminate, muse.

Cogitation, *n.* Meditation, contemplation, thought, thinking, reflection, deliberation.

Cognate, *a.* Allied, akin, kin, related, affiliated, affined, connected, kindred, similar, analogous, alike, of a piece.

Cognition, *n.* 1. Knowledge, cognizance.

2. Knowing, (*the*) act of knowing, cognitive process, cognizing.

3. Cognitive act, (*some one*) act of knowing, piece of knowledge.

Cognizance, *n.* Knowledge, cognition, knowing, observation, notice.

Cognizant of. Aware of, acquainted with, familiar with, conversant with, having knowledge of, possessed of knowledge concerning.

Cognize, *v. t.* (*Psych.*) Take knowledge of, notice, know, recognize, beware of, take in as object, observe, be conscious of.

Cognomen, *n.* Surname, family name.

Cohabit, *v. i.* Live together (*as husband and wife*), live in sexual intimacy.

Co-heir, *n.* Joint heir, parcener.

Cohere, *v. i.* 1. Adhere *or* cleave to each other, stick together, hold together.

2. [With *with.*] Suit, fit, agree, square, tally, coincide, comport.

3. Be consistent, be rationally connected, make sense, tally *or* agree *or* comport with each other.

Coherence, } *n.* 1. Cohesion, union, con-
Coherency, } nection, dependence.

2. Consistency, congruity, correspondence, harmony, agreement, unity, rationality, intelligibility, intelligible meaning.

Coherent, *a.* 1. Connected, united, adherent, sticking together.

2. Consistent, congruous, logical, intelligible.

Cohesion, *n.* 1. Coherence, sticking together.

2. Cohesive force *or* attraction.

Cohort, *n.* [*In pl., usually poetic.*] Bands, battalions, squadrons, lines.

Coiffure, *n.* Head-dress.

Coign, *n.* Corner, quoin, coin.

Coil, *v. t.* Gather into a coil, lay into a spiral, wind, loop, curl, convolute.

——, *v. i.* Make coils, form spiral rings.

——, *n.* 1. Convolution, circular heap, spiral ring, spiral.

2. Perplexities, entanglements, tumult, bustle, care, turmoil, clamor, confusion, uproar.

Coin, *n.* 1. Corner, quoin, coign.

2. Prop, wedge, plug, key, quoin.

3. Specie, cash, money, metallic money, hard money, stamped money.

——, *v. t.* 1. Convert (*metal*) into money by stamping, convert into coin, mint, stamp.

2. Invent, fabricate, devise, create, form, mould, stamp.

Coinage, *n.* 1. Coin.

2. Invention, fabrication, creation.

Coincide, *v. i.* 1. Be identical (*in place or time*), fall exactly together, be conterminous, fill identical spaces *or* times, fit exactly, cover each other exactly.

2. Correspond, square, tally, cohere.

3. Agree, concur, harmonize, be of the same mind.

Coincidence, *n.* 1. Exact overlapping, identical size *or* duration, exact equality, precise falling together, conjunction.

2. Correspondence, coherence.

3. Agreement, concurrence, consistency.

Coincident, *a.* 1. Exactly conterminous, exactly overlying, identical in extent *or* duration, concurrent, concomitant.

2. Correspondent, tallying, squaring.

3. Agreeing, concurring, concurrent.

Coition, *n.* Copulation, sexual conjunction, sexual congress, sexual intercourse.

COLD, *a.* 1. Devoid of warmth *or* heat, chilled, frigid, gelid, cool, cooled.

2. Bleak, raw, biting, cutting, nipping, chill, chilly, boreal, arctic, polar, frosty, icy, glacial, gelid, "frore," wintry, hyemal, brumal.

3. Chilly, chill, shivering, frost-bitten.

4. Apathetic, unsympathetic, unresponsive, phlegmatic, stoical, unfeeling, unsusceptible, unimpressible, passionless, cold-blooded, sluggish, torpid, lukewarm, dead, indifferent, unconcerned, frigid, freezing, stony.

5. Unaffecting, uninteresting, spiritless, uninspiring, dull, dead.

——, *n.* 1. Absence of warmth, want of heat.

2. Coldness, chilliness, "coolth."

Cold-blooded, *a.* 1. Having cold blood.

2. Unfeeling, apathetic, cold-hearted. See COLD, 4.

3. Deliberate, calculating, calculated, heartless, unrelenting, relentless, remorseless, cruel.

Cold-hearted, *a.* Unfeeling. See COLD, 4.

Cole-slaw, *n.* Cabbage salad, sliced cabbage.

Colic, *n.* Spasmodic pain in the bowels, intestinal cramp, gripes, "bellyache."

Collapse, *n.* 1. Falling together, falling in (*as the sides of a flue*), "cave-in."

2. (*Med.*) Prostration, exhaustion, sinking, extreme depression.

3. Break-down, downfall, dead failure.

——, *v. i.* 1. Fall together, fall in.

2. Break down, come to nothing, fail utterly, go out in smoke, vanish in thin air.

COLLAR, *n.* 1. Neck-band, collarette, gorget, ruff, torque.

2. Ring, fillet, belt, band, guard.

——, *v. t.* 1. Seize by the collar *or* throat.

2. Put a collar on, fit with a collar, fillet, belt.

Collar-bone, *n.* Clavicle.

Collate, *v. t.* Comparing, bring into comparison, compare critically, estimate relatively.

Collateral, *a.* 1. Indirect, subordinate, not directly to the point.

2. Corroboratory, confirmatory, concurrent.

Collation, *n.* 1. Comparison.

2. Meal (*less than a feast*), light repast, simple entertainment, luncheon.

Colleague, *n.* Associate (*in office*), coadjutor, co-operator, assistant, collaborator, *confrère*, co-laborer, helper, aider, co-aid, partner, ally.

Collect, *v. t.* 1. Gather, assemble, muster, compile, bring together.

2. Accumulate, amass, aggregate, garner, heap up, scrape together.

Collection, *n.* 1. Assemblage, group, cluster, gathering, crowd, aggregation, drove, pack.

2. Accumulation, heap, mass, hoard, store, pile, lot, congeries, conglomeration.

College, *n.* 1. Society (*of persons engaged in common pursuits*), corporation, guild, association, community, body.

2. Institution of scholarship *or* seminary of higher learning.

Collide, *v. i.* 1. Come into collision, strike forcibly against each other, run into each other, encounter with a shock, crash together.

2. Clash, interfere, be antagonistic *or* in antagonism, be at variance.

Collier, *n.* 1. Coal-miner, coal-digger.

2. Coal-dealer, coal-merchant, dealer in coals.

3. Coal-transport, coaling vessel.

Colliery, *n.* Coal-mine, coal-pit.

Colligate, *v. t.* 1. Unite, combine, fasten together, bind.

2. Bring into unity, form into a logical whole, combine, unite, unify.

Collision, *n.* 1. Clash, shock, impact, impingement, concussion, crash.

2. Opposition, interference, crashing, conflict.

Collocate, *v. t.* (*Rare.*) Place, set, dispose, arrange.

Collocation, *n.* Arrangement, disposition, grouping.

Colloquial, *a.* Conversational, familiar in tone.

Colloquy, *n.* Dialogue, conversation, conference, talk, (mutual) discourse.

Collude, *v. i.* Participate in fraud, conspire fraudulently, act in secret concert, connive, play into each other's hands.

Collusion, *n.* 1. (*Law.*) Covin, participation in fraud.

2. Secret understanding *or* agreement (*for fraud*), connivance.

Collusive, *a.* Deceitful, fraudulent, deceptive, dishonest, covinous.

COLOR, *n.* 1. Hue, tint, tinge, shade, tone.

2. Pigment, paint, stain.

3. Redness, ruddiness, rosiness, freshness of complexion.

4. Complexion, hue of skin.

5. Plea, pretext, pretence, excuse, guise, disguise, semblance, appearance, make-shift, false show.

——, *v. t.* 1. Tinge, dye, paint, stain, discolor, tint.

2. Disguise, varnish, gloss over, make plausible.

3. Distort, pervert, garble, misrepresent.

——, *v. i.* Redden, blush, flush, show color.

Color-blindness, *n.* Daltonism.

Colorless, *a.* 1. Uncolored, untinged, achromatic.

2. Pale, pallid, blanched, hueless, livid.

3. Dull, monotonous, characterless, blank, expressionless, inexpressive.

Color-sergeant, *n.* Ensign, standard-bearer.

Colors, *n. pl.* Flag, standard, ensign, banner.

Colossal, *a.* Gigantic, huge, monstrous, immense, enormous, vast, prodigious, Cyclopean, Herculean.

Colt, *n.* Foal, filly.

Coltish, *a.* Frisky, rampant, playful, frolicsome, sportive, gay.

Column, *n.* 1. Round pillar, rounded pillar.

2. File, line, row.

Coma, *n.* 1. (*Med.*) Lethargy, stupor.

2. (*Astron.*) Envelope, hairy envelope, nebulous sheath.

3. (*Bot.*) Tuft, cluster, bunch, clump.

Comatose, } *a.* Lethargic, stupefied, stuporous.
Comatous, } like.

COMB, *n.* 1. Toilet-comb, dressing-comb.

2. Card (*for wool, hair, flax, etc.*), ripple, hatchel.

3. Caruncle, head-tuft (*of a cock or bird*).

4. Top, crest (*of a wave*).

——, *v. t.* Dress (*with a comb*), disentangle.

——, *v. i.* Curl, roll over, break in foam.

Combat, *v. i.* Fight, contend, struggle, contest, war.

——, *v. t.* Oppose, resist, withstand, contend against, battle with, struggle with, war against.

Combat, *n.* Battle, fight, conflict, engagement, action, contest, encounter, rencounter, skirmish, brush, affair.

Combatant, *n.* Contestant, participant in fight, fighter, fighting-man.

Combative, *a.* Contentious, belligerent, pugnacious, militant. Cf. QUARRELSOME.

Combination, *n.* 1. Union, conjunction, connection, association.

2. Alliance, coalition, confederacy, consolidation, syndicate, cartel, merger, league.

3. Complot, conspiracy, cabal, ring, junto, clique, faction.

4. Mixture, compound, amalgamation.

Combine, *v. t.* 1. Unite, join together, merge, pool.

2. Mix, blend, incorporate, amalgamate, compound, put together.

——, *v. i.* Coalesce, become united, unite, blend, mingle, mix, amalgamate.

Combustible, *a.* Inflammable, consumable.

Combustion, *n.* Burning, consuming.

COME, *v. i.* 1. Approach, advance, advene, draw near, tend hitherward.

2. Arrive, get to, reach *or* attain any place *or* point.

3. [With *from.*] Proceed, issue, arise, result, follow, flow, ensue, originate, be derived, be due *or* owing, take rise.

4. Happen, occur, befall, betide, take place, come to pass, fall out, come about.

Come about. Happen, come to pass. See preceding.

Come at. Reach, obtain, get at.

Come by. Get, obtain, gain, get possession of.

Come in. 1. Enter.

2. Accrue (*as gain*).

Comeliness, *n.* 1. Propriety, fitness, suitableness, seemliness.

2. Symmetry, grace, gracefulness, beauty.

Comely, *a.* 1. Becoming, fitting, suitable, seemly, decorous, decent.

2. Symmetrical, graceful, pretty, handsome, fair, beautiful, personable.

Come near. Approximate, approach.

Come of. Proceed, issue, grow out of, originate from, arise from, be derived from.

Come on. 1. Advance.

2. Succeed, thrive.

Come-outer, *n.* [*U. S.*] Radical, radical reformer, repudiator of established usages.

Come round. Change, veer.

Come short. Fail, be deficient, be wanting.

Come to a head. 1. Mature, suppurate, fester.

2. Come to a crisis, mature, be consummated.

Come to grief. (*Colloq.*) 1. Fail, result disastrously.

2. Be ruined, meet with disaster, come to a bad end.

Come to one's self. Recover one's senses, come to, return to consciousness.

Come to pass. 1. Happen, chance, occur, befall, betide, fall out, come about.

2. Be fulfilled.

Come up. 1. Rise, ascend.

2. Shoot (*as a plant from the earth*), sprout, spring up.

Comfit, *n.* Sweetmeat (*dry*), confection, confect, conserve, preserve.

Comfort, *v. t.* Solace, console, cheer, gladden, encourage, inspirit, enliven, animate, revive, refresh, invigorate, relieve, strengthen.

COMFORT, *n.* 1. Support, assistance, aid, help, succor, countenance.

2. Solace, consolation, encouragement, relief.

3. Ease, enjoyment, satisfaction, peace.

Comfortable, *a.* 1. Agreeable, pleasant, pleasurable, grateful, gratifying, acceptable, welcome.

2. Snug, convenient, easeful, adapted for comfort.

3. At ease, free from pain.

Comforter, *a.* 1. Consoler, solacer.

2. Paraclete, Holy Spirit, Spirit of Truth.

3. [*U. S.*] Stuffed coverlet, wadded quilt, comfort, comfortable, puff.

Comfortless, *a.* 1. [*Said of places.*] Forlorn, cheerless, desolate, wretched, miserable, dreary, drear, bleak.

2. [*Said of persons.*] Inconsolable, disconsolate, woe-begone, heart-broken, broken-hearted, forlorn, desolate, wretched, miserable.

Comic, } *a.* Droll, funny, farcical, bur-
Comical, } lesque, ludicrous, laughable, diverting, sportive, humorous.

Coming, *n.* Approach, advent, arrival.

——, *a.* Future, to come, approaching, ensuing, forthcoming, nearing, imminent.

Comity, *n.* Courtesy, civility, amenity, politeness, suavity, urbanity, affability, good breeding, good manners.

Command, *v. t.* 1. Order, direct, bid, charge, require, enjoin.

2. Rule, govern, sway, control, dominate, lead, preside over, have authority over.

3. Claim, challenge, exact, compel, demand.

Command, *v. i.* Govern, rule, lead, have sway, exercise authority, have control, take the lead.

——, *n.* 1. Order, direction, injunction, mandate, behest, hest, bidding, charge, requirement, requisition, commandment, word of command.

2. Rule, sway, authority, power, dominion, government, control, ascendency, supremacy.

Commander, *n.* Chief, chieftain, leader, head, captain, commandant.

Commandment, *n.* Mandate, precept, charge. See COMMAND.

Commemorate, *v. t.* Celebrate, solemnize.

Commemoration, *n.* Celebration, solemnization.

Commemorative, *a.* Memorial.

Commence, *v. i.* 1. Begin, originate, take rise.

2. Begin, open.

3. Take the first step, make a beginning, break ground, break the ice.

——, *v. t.* Begin, institute, inaugurate, initiate, originate, open, start, enter upon, set about, set on foot, set in operation.

Commencement, *n.* 1. Beginning, outset, opening.

2. Graduation day, day of conferring degrees.

Commend, *v. t.* 1. Recommend, bespeak, regard for.

2. Commit, intrust, yield.

3. Praise, extol, applaud, laud, eulogize, cry up, speak well of, say a good word for, sing *or* sound the praises of.

Commendable, *a.* Laudable, praiseworthy, to be commended.

Commendation, *n.* 1. Recommendation, approval, approbation, good opinion.

2. Praise, encomium, eulogy, panegyric, good word.

Commendations, *n. pl.* Regards, compliments, respects.

Commendatory, *a.* Commending, laudatory, eulogistic, complimentary, encomiastic, panegyrical.

Commensurable, *a.* Commeasurable, commensurate, measurable by a common unit.

Commensurate, *a.* 1. Commeasurable, commensurable.

2. Equal, coextensive, conterminous.

3. Adequate, proportionate, proportioned, due, appropriate, on a proper scale, corresponding, on a scale suitable.

Comment, *v. i.* Annotate, make notes, remark, make remarks or observations, animadvert.

——, *n.* 1. Annotation, note, gloss, explanation, elucidation, illustration, exposition, commentary.

2. Remark, observation, animadversion.

Commentary, *n.* 1. See COMMENT.

2. Book of comments.

3. Memoir, familiar narrative.

Commentator, *n.* Annotator, expositor, expounder, commenter *or* commentor, writer of comments.

Commerce, *n.* 1. Dealing, trade, traffic, business, exchange, mercantile relations, system of exchanges.

2. Intercourse, communication, communion.

Commercial, *a.* Trading, mercantile, engaged in traffic, relating to traffic, arising from traffic, skilled in commerce.

Commination, *n.* Threatening, threat, menace, denunciation.

Commingle, *v. t.* and *v. i.* Blend, mix, commix, mingle, intermingle, intermix, combine, unite, amalgamate, mingle together, run together.

Comminute, *v. t.* Pulverize, triturate, levigate, powder, grind, bruise, bray, break to pieces, break *or* separate into fine particles, reduce to powder.

Comminution, *n.* Pulverization, trituration, levigation, powdering, reduction to powder.

Commiserate, *v. t.* Pity, compassionate, have pity or compassion for, sympathize with, feel for, feel sorry for, condole with.

Commiseration, *n.* 1. Pitying, compassionating, etc.

2. Compassion, sympathy, pity, condolence.

Commission, *n.* 1. Perpetration, doing (*of something bad*).

2. Warrant of authority.

3. Trust, charge, office, care, duty, task, employment, errand.

4. Allowance, fee, compensation, "rake-off."

5. Delegation, body of commissioners.

——, *v. t.* 1. Authorize, empower, give a commission to.

2. Depute, delegate, send on a commission.

Commissioner, *n.* 1. Agent, delegate, deputy.

2. Member of the commission.

Commissure, *n.* Seam, joint, closure, suture, conjunction, juncture.

Commit, *v. t.* 1. Intrust, consign, remand, delegate, confide, give in trust.

2. Deposit, consign, resign, give over, relegate, put, place, lay.

3. Perpetrate, enact, do, perform.

4. Imprison, send to prison, put in custody, place in confinement.

5. Engage, pledge, implicate.

Commitment, *n.* 1. Delivering, intrusting, consignment, placing in charge.

2. Imprisonment, committal, placing in confinement, putting in custody.

3. Giving in adhesion, unreserved adherence, pledged relation.

Committal, *n.* Intrusting, depositing, perpetrating, etc. See COMMIT, in all its senses,

COMMITTEE, *n.* (*Basic Eng.*) Organized group for deliberation.

Commix, *v. t.* and *v. i.* Blend, mingle, commingle, intermingle, combine, unite, compound, mix, amalgamate.

Commixture, *n.* 1. Intermingling, blending, mingling, commingling, combination, union, compounding, mixing, intermixture, admixture, mixture, amalgamation.

2. Intermixture, admixture, mixture, composition, compound, amalgamation, amalgam.

Commodious, *a.* Convenient, comfortable, roomy and convenient, spacious and comfortable, useful, advantageous, suitable, fit, proper.

Commodities, *n. pl.* Merchandise, wares, goods, produce.

COMMON, *a.* 1. Public, collective, belonging to all, for the use of all.

2. General, universal, used by all.

3. Usual, frequent, familiar, habitual, customary, everyday, often met with.

4. Trite, stale, banal, threadbare, hackneyed, common-place, worn out.

5. Ordinary, indifferent, inferior, vulgar, popular, plebeian, low, undistinguished (*by high birth, attainments* or *character*).

Commonalty, *n.* The common people (*below the orders of nobility*), the lower classes, commoners, the commons.

Commoner, *n.* 1. One of the commons, *or* common-people, untitled person.

2. Student not on a foundation, gentleman-commoner (*Oxford*), pensioner (*Cambridge*).

Commonplace, *a.* Trite, stale, hackneyed, ordinary, common, threadbare, not new, worn out.

Commons, *n. pl.* 1. Commonalty, the common people, untitled class, commoners.

2. Provisions, food, fare.

Common-sense, *n.* 1. Natural sagacity, good sense, sound sense *or* understanding, plain sense, good judgment, practical discernment.

2. Ordinary sense, ordinary judgment, common view of things, usual way of looking at things.

——, *a.* Sober, practical, matter of fact,

sagacious, sensible, free from fanciful views, free from vagaries, keeping to facts, proceeding from mother wit.

Commonwealth, *n.* 1. State, nation, republic, body politic, public interest, the people.

2. The public, the people, the community, body of the people.

Commotion, *n.* 1. Agitation, disturbance, perturbation, ferment, welter.

2. Turmoil, turbulence, tumult, disorder, "hurly-burly," violence, bustle, disturbance, pother, ado, to do.

Commune, *v. i.* Converse, communicate, discourse, speak, talk, hold intercourse.

Communicant, *n.* Partaker, sharer, participator.

Communicate, *v. t.* 1. Impart, give, bestow, convey, transmit. See CONFER.

2. Disclose, reveal, divulge, declare, announce, make known.

——, *v. i.* 1. Have a connection (*by a passage*), be connected, connect.

2. Hold intercourse *or* converse, interchange thoughts, commune, converse, correspond.

Communication, *n.* 1. Imparting, giving, conveyance, transmittal.

2. Intercourse, conversation, converse, conference, commerce.

3. Message, despatch, information (*by letter, wire,* or *by word*).

4. Connection (*by a passage*), passage, connecting passage.

Communicative, *a.* Free, unreserved, open, sociable, social, affable, "chatty," conversable.

Communion, *n.* 1. Participation, fellowship, converse, intercourse.

2. Eucharist, Sacrament, Lord's Supper, Holy Communion.

Community, *n.* 1. [With *The* prefixed.] Commonwealth, people, public, society, body politic.

2. Association, society, brotherhood, college.

3. Sameness, likeness, identify, similarity, participancy.

Commute, *v. t.* 1. Exchange.

2. Replace (*a greater punishment by a less*).

Compact, *n.* Agreement, contract, covenant, stipulation, bargain, treaty, concordat, convention, pact, arrangement.

——, *v. t.* 1. Press together, condense, compress.

2. Consolidate, join firmly, knit together, bind, unite.

——, *a.* 1. Close, dense, solid, imporous, firm, compressed, pressed together, closely put together, snug, of firm texture.

2. Pithy, terse, concise, laconic, sententious, short, brief, compendious, succinct, pointed, full of meaning.

Companion, *n.* 1. Comrade, associate, mate, fellow, consort, compeer, boon companion.

2. Partner, partaker, participator, participant, sharer.

Companionship, *n.* Fellowship, friendship, association, intercourse, company, society.

COMPANY, *n.* 1. Assemblage, assembly, body, gathering, collection, group, circle, troop, crew, crowd, gang, rout, herd, bevy, flock, set concourse, congregation.

2. Party, meeting of friends, social meeting.

3. Visitor, visitors, guests.

4. Fellowship, companionship, society.

5. Corporation, association, partnership, copartnership, firm, house, joint concern.

Comparative, *a.* 1. Comparing, able to compare.

2. Judged by comparison, relative.

3. Founded in comparison, general.

Compare, *v. t.* 1. Collate (*followed by* with), bring into comparison, estimate relatively, balance, parallel.

2. Liken (*followed by* to), declare similar, represent as resembling.

——, *v. i.* Bear a comparison, admit of comparison, present a resemblance.

COMPARISON, *n.* 1. Collation, compare, relative estimate, comparative estimate.

2. Simile, similitude.

Compartment, *n.* Division, section, cell, pigeonhole, bay, separate part.

Compass, *v. t.* 1. Encompass, environ, surround, encircle, enclose, engird, embrace, compass about, stretch round.

2. Besiege, invest, beset, beleaguer, block, blockade, hem in, hedge in, wall in, lay siege to.

3. Attain, obtain, procure, accomplish, effect, perform, achieve, consummate, realize, carry, bring about, bring to pass.

4. (*Law.*) Meditate, contrive, plot, purpose, intend, devise.

——, *n.* 1. Stretch, reach, extent, range, gamut, register, scope, limit, bound, boundary.

2. Circuit, round, circular course.

3. Mariner's *or* surveyor's compass, ship's compass, needle.

Compassable, *a.* Attainable, to be attained.

Compassion, *n.* Pity, commiseration, sympathy, rue, ruth, tenderness, kindness, kindliness, clemency, fellow-feeling, heart, tender-heartedness, kind-heartedness, mercy, bowels of compassion, melting mood.

Compassionate, *a.* Tender, pitying, sympathetic, commiserative, ruthful, merciful, benignant, gracious, clement, kind, inclined to pity, full of compassion.

——, *v. t.* Pity, commiserate, feel pity for, be moved with sympathy for.

Compatible with. Consistent with, consonant with, congruous with, accordant with, agreeable to, suitable to, in keeping with, reconcilable with, in harmony with.

Compatriot, *n.* Fellow-countryman, countryman.

Compeer, *n.* Companion, mate, equal, peer, associate, fellow, comrade.

Compel, *v. t.* 1. Force, oblige, constrain, coerce, drive, necessitate.

2. Subject, subdue, bend, bow.

Compend, *n.* Abridgment, compendium, conspectus, summary, abstract, epitome, digest, précis, synopsis, syllabus, breviary, brief, sum and substance.

Compendious, *a.* Brief, concise, short, abridged, summary, succinct, comprehensive.

Compendium, *n.* Abridgment. See COMPEND.

Compensate, *v. t.* 1. Counterbalance, counterpoise, countervail, make up for, offset, recoup.

2. Recompense, remunerate, reimburse, reward, guerdon.

3. Requite, indemnify, reimburse, make good, make amends to.

——, *v. i.* Atone, make compensation, make amends.

Compensation, *n.* 1. Recompense, pay, remuneration, reward.

2. Requital, satisfaction, indemnity, atonement, indemnification, reparation, amends.

3. Counterpoise, balance, equalization, offset.

Compete, *v. i.* Contend, strive, struggle, cope, enter the lists, be rivals.

Competence, } *n.* 1. Ability, capableness, **Competency,** } capacity, qualification, suitableness, fitness.

2. Sufficiency, adequateness, adequacy, enough.

3. Sufficient fortune, adequate income, independent support, means of independence.

Competent, *a.* 1. Able, capable, qualified, endowed.

2. Adequate, sufficient, adapted, convenient, suitable, fit.

COMPETITION, *n.* Rivalry, rivalship, emulation, contest (*for the same object*).

Competitive, *a.* Competing, prompted by emulation, based on competition.

Competitor, *n.* Rival, antagonist, contestant, opponent, rival candidate.

Compilation, *n.* 1. Compiling, selecting and combining, selection and combination (*of literary matter*), book-making.

2. Selection (*of literary matter*), book of selections, *or* excerpts *or* extracts; anthology.

Compile, *v. t.* 1. Write (*by selecting from other works*), prepare, compose, draw up, get up.

2. Select and arrange, collect together, combine.

Complacence, } *n.* 1. Satisfaction, gratifi-
Complacency, } cation, pleasure, content, contentment.

2. Complaisance, civility, courtesy, politeness.

Complacent, *a.* 1. Pleased, satisfied, gratified, contented.

2. Complaisant, civil, polite, courteous, affable, easy, obliging, urbane, gracious.

Complain, *v. i.* Murmur, lament, bewail, grumble, croak, find fault, grouch, repine, whine.

Complainant, *n.* Plaintiff, accuser.

Complainer, *n.* 1. Murmurer, censurer, grumbler, croaker, fault-finder, "grouch."

2. Moaner, groaner.

Complaining, *a.* Querulous, murmuring, querimonious, fault-finding.

Complaint, *n.* 1. Murmur, lamentation, plaint, lament, wail.

2. Malady, disease, ailment, ail, illness, indisposition, disorder, distemper, sickness.

3. [With *against*.] Accusation, charge, information.

Complaisance, *n.* Obligingness, compliance, yieldingness, affability, graciousness, civility, courtesy, politeness, urbanity, suavity, condescension, good-breeding, complacence.

Complaisant, *a.* Obliging, compliant, yielding, affable, gracious, courteous, polite, civil, debonair, familiar, easy, well-bred, suave, "smooth."

Complement, *n.* 1. Full number, full quantity, quota, full tale, tale.

2. Completeness, fulfilment, fulness, perfection, consummation.

3. Deficiency, deficit, shortage, amount lacking (to make some fixed amount).

COMPLETE, *a.* 1. Perfect, full, thorough, consummate, clean, without fault *or* blemish *or* flaw, out and out.

2. Total, entire, whole, undivided, unbroken, undiminished, unimpaired, integral.

3. Completed, finished, concluded, consummated, ended.

——, *v. t.* 1. Finish, perfect, consummate, accomplish, achieve, perform, effect, effectuate, execute, terminate, end, conclude, bring to a close, give the finishing touch to, put the finishing hand to, put the seal to.

2. Fulfil, realize, come up to, bring to pass.

Completion, *n.* 1. Consummation, perfecting, accomplishing, achieving, effecting, effectuation, termination, ending, accomplishment, performance, execution, conclusion, finishing, finishing touch.

2. Fulfilment, realization, achievement, attainment, consummation.

COMPLEX, *a.* 1. Compounded, compound, composite, mixed, mingled, manifold, composed of several elements.

2. Complicated, complicate, tangled, entangled, intricate, involved, knotty, mazy.

——, *n.* Network, complexus, complication, tangle, tangled skein, compages, compage, intricate web, webwork.

Complexion, *n.* 1. Color, hue, tint (*of the face*).

2. Appearance, aspect, look.

Complexity, *n.* Intricacy, complication, entanglement, involved character, involution.

Compliance, *n.* 1. Concession, submission, obedience.

2. Acquiescence, assent, consent, agreement, concurrence.

3. Compliancy, yieldingness, yielding disposition, compliant temper. See COMPLAISANCE.

Compliant, *a.* 1. Yielding, submissive, obedient, obsequious.

2. Yielding, obliging, accommodating, conformable. See COMPLAISANT.

Complicate, *v. t.* Involve, entangle, make complex, make intricate.

Complication, *n.* 1. Complexity, intricacy, entanglement, confusion.

2. Mixture, combination, complexus. See COMPLEX, *n.*

Complicity, *n.* Criminal participance, being privy, partnership (*in wrong*), sharing (*of crime*).

Compliment, *n.* 1. Praise, commendation, encomium, laudation, good word, eulogy, tribute.

2. Formal praise, hollow commendation, empty encomium, flattering remark, ceremonious phrase *or* flattery.

Compliment, *v. t.* 1. Praise, commend, flatter (*by expressions of civility*), eulogize.

2. Congratulate.

Complimentary, *a.* Commendatory, laudatory, encomiastic, flattering (*in the good sense*).

Complot, *n.* (*Rare.*) Conspiracy, machination, intrigue, cabal, plot, combination.

Comply with. 1. Observe, perform, fulfil, discharge, meet, satisfy, complete, adhere to, be faithful to, carry into effect.

2. Yield to, consent to, assent to, accede to, agree to, çonform to, acquiesce in, give consent to.

Component, *a.* Composing, constituting, constituent.

——, *n.* Constituent, element, ingredient, component part.

Comport, *v. i.* Agree, accord, harmonize, tally, correspond, square, fall in, chime in.

Comport one's self. Behave, act, conduct one's self, demean one's self, quit one's self.

Comport with. Suit, fit, become, agree with, accord with, square with, chime in with, be suitable to.

Compose, *v. t.* 1. Constitute, form, make, build, compound, compact, synthesize, put together, make up.

2. Indite, write, frame, invent, contrive, imagine, create, draw up, put *or* set down in writing, express by writing.

3. Adjust, settle, regulate.

4. Tranquillize, assuage, soothe, appease, pacify, calm, still, quiet, quell.

Composed, *a.* Calm, quiet, unruffled, undisturbed, unmoved, tranquil, placid, sedate, collected, self-possessed, imperturbable, cool.

Composite, *a.* Compounded, complex.

Composition, *n.* 1. Constitution, formation, framing, construction, making.

2. Compound, mixture.

3. Union, conjunction, combination, arrangement (of parts), make-up, synthesis.

4. Writing, literary work, invention (*esp. in music, painting, or sculpture*), production, opus, piece.

5. Compromise, agreement, arrangement.

Compost, *n.* Manure, fertilizer, fertilizing mixture.

Composure, *n.* Quiet, tranquillity, calmness, sedateness, placidity, coolness, equanimity, self-possession.

Compotation, *n.* 1. Pot-companionship, tippling in company, drinking together, symposium.

2. Reveling, revelry, conviviality, ca-

rousing, wassailing, frolicking, jollification.

3. Revel, debauch, bacchanals, saturnalia, wassail, orgies, carouse, carousal, drinking-bout, wassail-bout, merry frolic, jolly time, "jollification," "spree."

Compound, *v. t.* 1. Mix, mingle, intermix, intermingle, blend, combine, unite, amalgamate (*either physically or mentally*).

2. Compromise, settle, adjust, compose.

3. Commute, pay with an abatement, pay by substitution.

4. Connive at, bargain with.

——, *v. i.* Compromise, agree, come to terms, come to an agreement, make an arrangement.

——, *a.* Complex, composite, compounded.

——, *n.* 1. Mixture, composition, combination.

2. Medley, olio, farrago, hodge-podge, hotch-potch *or* hotchpot, "mess," jumble.

3. [*In the Orient.*] Yard (*round a building*), enclosure.

Comprehend, *v. t.* 1. Comprise, include, involve, enclose, embrace, contain, embody, take in.

2. Grasp (*mentally*), understand (*fully*), apprehend, conceive, imagine, see, discern, perceive, enter into the idea of, catch the idea of.

Comprehension, *n.* 1. Inclusion, comprising, embracing.

2. Scope, reach, sweep, range, compass, embrace, field, sphere, limits, domain, province.

3. (*Log.*) Intension, connotation, force, depth, etc. (*of a notion*).

4. Grasp (*of our understanding*), power to understand, conception, understanding, intelligence.

5. Intellect, mind, reason, mental capacity, understanding, intelligence.

Comprehensive, *a.* Extensive, wide, broad, large, capacious, compendious, full, sweeping, wide-reaching, all-embracing, of great scope, of extensive application.

Compress, *v. t.* 1. Press together, close tightly, shut firmly.

2. Bind tightly, wrap closely.

3. Squeeze *or* press together *or* into smaller compass, condense.

4. Squeeze, force, crowd, press.

5. Make brief, abbreviate, condense, make terse *or* pithy.

——, *n.* (*Surg.*) Bandage, compressing pad.

Compression, *n.* 1. Condensation, pressing together, squeezing, pinching, confining.

2. Tight closure, close shutting, firm closing.

3. Brevity, terseness, succinctness, pithiness, condensation, conciseness.

Comprise, *v. t.* Comprehend, include, involve, enclose, embrace, contain, embody, take in.

Compromise, *n.* Agreement, composition, adjustment, settlement, mutual concession, abatement of differences.

——, *v. t.* 1. Adjust, arrange by mutual concessions, settle, compose, compound.

2. Jeopardize, imperil, bring into danger, put at hazard, expose the repute of, prejudice.

3. Engage, pledge, implicate, commit.

——, *v. i.* Agree, compound, come to an agreement, come to an understanding, settle *or* compose *or* compound differences *or* disputes.

Compulsion, *n.* Coercion, constraint, forcing, application *or* employment of force.

Compulsory, *a.* 1. Compelling, constraining, coercive.

2. Binding, obligatory, enforced, necessary, imperative, unavoidable, not to be evaded.

Compunction, *n.* Repentance, remorse, contrition, penitence, sorrow, regret, misgiving, qualm, reluctance, reproach of conscience, sting of conscience.

Compunctious, *a.* Repentant, penitent, contrite, remorseful, sorrowful, conscience-stinging, conscience-stung.

Computable, *a.* Calculable, reckonable, numerable.

Computation, *n.* Reckoning, calculation, estimate, account, score, tally.

Compute, *v. t.* Reckon, calculate, estimate, figure, count, number, rate, cast, cast up, sum up.

Comrade, *n.* Companion, associate, mate, fellow, crony, chum, "pal," compeer, boon companion.

Con, *v. t.* Study, read over carefully, consider minutely, fix in the mind, commit to memory, learn by heart, con over.

Con amore. [It.] With love, with delight, with delighted interest, with pleasure, with zeal, zealously, with zest, with inclination, with predilection, with fondness.

Conation, *n.* Voluntary activity, desire and will, wishing and willing, want and volition.

Conative, *a.* Voluntary, pertaining to conation.

Concatenate, *v. t.* Connect, unite, join, link together.

Concatenation, *n.* 1. Connection, linking-together, intimate relationship.

2. Series, chain, succession, sequence, congeries, successive series.

Concave, *a.* Hollow, hollowed, depressed.

Concavity, *n.* 1. Hollowness, hollow shape, hollowed condition, state *or* degree of incurvation.

2. Hollow space, hollow, depression.

Conceal, *v. t.* 1. Hide, secrete, cover, screen, bury, cover up.

2. Disguise, dissemble, keep secret.

Concealment, *n.* 1. Concealing, secreting, secretion, hiding, covering, screening, burying, covering up, keeping secret.

2. Secrecy, dissembling, disguises, indirection, dark ways, secret methods.

3. Privacy, secrecy.

4. Retreat, shelter (*from observation*), hiding-place.

Concede, *v. t.* 1. Surrender, yield, grant, give up.

2. Allow, admit, grant.

Conceit, *n.* 1. Conception, image, notion, thought, fancy, imagination, idea, belief.

2. Whim, vagary, illusion, freak of fancy, caprice.

3. Opinion, estimate, estimation, judgment, impression.

4. Vanity, conceitedness, egotism, self-conceit, self-complacency, self-esteem, self-sufficiency, priggery, priggishness, priggism.

5. Quip, quirk, point, odd thought, odd turn, crotchet, affected witticism, far-fetched fancy.

Conceited, *a.* Vain, egotistical, opinionated, overweening, opinionative, self-conceited, self-sufficient.

Conceitedness, *n.* Vanity, conceit, egotism, opinionatedness, self-conceit, self-complacency, self-sufficiency, priggery, priggishness, priggism.

Conceivable, *a.* 1. Imaginable, picturable, capable of being sensibly represented.

2. Thinkable, intelligible, comprehensible, capable of being understood, cogitable, rational.

3. Imaginable, supposable, possible, perhaps so.

Conceive, *v. t.* 1. Be *or* become pregnant with, bear in the womb.

2. Form (*in the mind*), devise, contrive, plan, purpose.

3. Imagine, form a distinct image of, image, make sensibly real.

4. Think, realize in the mind, comprehend, understand, fathom.

5. Imagine, suppose, suppose possible, assume as a possible case.

6. Apprehend, take, view, look at, regard, fancy.

——, *v. i.* 1. Become pregnant.

2. Think, imagine, have an idea, form a conception.

3. Suppose, apprehend, think, imagine, fancy, take it.

Concentrate, *v. t.* 1. Condense, bring into a small compass, bring toward a central point, concenter, compact, consolidate.

2. Boil down, reduce by evaporation, rectify, reduce to extreme purity and strength, intensify.

Concentration, *n.* 1. Condensation, compression into a small compass, collection upon a single point.

2. Reduction by evaporation.

Concept, *n.* Universal, general *or* abstract notion, conception. See IDEA.

Conception, *n.* 1. Conceiving.

2. Apprehension, the mind's eye. See IMAGINATION.

3. Notion, idea, thought, fancy, conceit, impression.

4. General notion, generic idea. See CONCEPT.

Concern, *v. t.* 1. Affect, interest, touch, regard, relate to, belong to, pertain to, bear upon, be of importance to.

2. Trouble, disturb, disquiet, make anxious, make uneasy.

——, *n.* 1. Matter, business, affair, transaction.

2. Importance, interest, moment, consequence, weight, concernment.

3. Anxiety, solicitude, worry, care, carefulness.

4. Firm, house, establishment.

Concerning, *prep.* Respecting, regarding, about, relating to, with relation to, with regard to, with reference to.

Concert, *v. t.* Contrive, plan, plot, devise, design, concoct.

——, *n.* 1. Agreement, concord, concordance, co-operation, harmony.

2. Musical entertainment.

Concession, *n.* 1. Yielding, assent, compliance, acquiescence, cession.

2. Grant, boon, allowance.

Conciliate, *v. t.* 1. Propitiate, reconcile, pacify, appease.

2. Win, gain, engage, secure, draw over, win over.

Conciliation, *n.* Propitiation, pacification, reconciliation, reconcilement, peace.

Conciliatory, *a.* 1. Reconciling, pacifying, pacific, pacificatory.

2. Winning, persuasive.

Concise, *a.* Brief, short, laconic, summary, compendious, succinct, terse, pithy, pregnant, sententious, comprehensive, pointed, compact, condensed, compressed, crisp.

Conclave, *n.* Secret council, private assembly.

Conclude, *v. t.* 1. End, finish, terminate, close, bring to an end.

2. Gather (*as a consequence*), infer, judge, deduce.

3. Determine, judge, decide.

4. Settle, arrange, complete, bring to a successful issue.

5. (*Law.*) Stop, estop, bar, hinder, restrain, cut off.

——, *v. i.* 1. Determine, resolve, decide, make up one's mind, come to the conclusion *or* decision.

2. End, close, come to a conclusion *or* close, terminate.

3. Draw inferences, make deductions, reason, syllogize.

4. Settle opinion, come to a final decision.

Conclusion, *n.* 1. Deduction, inference.

2. Determination, decision, judgment.

3. Termination, end, completion, upshot, close, finale, issue, event.

4. Settlement, arrangement, effecting, closing, establishment.

Conclusive, *a.* 1. Decisive, convincing, unanswerable, irrefutable, clinching *or* clenching.

2. Final, ultimate, without appeal.

Concoct, *v. t.* Devise, plan, plot, contrive, design, invent, project, brew, frame, mature, prepare, hatch.

Concomitant, *a.* Accompanying, concurrent, coincident, accessory, attendant, attending, conjoined.

——, *n.* Attendant, accessory, accompaniment, attending *or* accompanying circumstance, accessory fact.

Concord, *n.* 1. Agreement, amity, friendship, peace, harmony, unanimity, unity, union, good understanding.

2. Consonance, concordance, harmony, accord, agreement, adaptation.

Concordance, *n.* Agreement, harmony. See CONCORD.

Concordant, *a.* Agreeing, accordant, harmonious, agreeable.

Concordat, *n.* Compact, convention, covenant, agreement, bargain, stipulation, treaty.

Concourse, *n.* 1. Confluence, conflux, congress, flocking together.

2. Meeting, assemblage, assembly, collection, gathering, throng, crowd, multitude.

Concrete, *v. i.* Solidify, harden, cake, become firm *or* solid, be consolidated, coagulate, congeal, thicken.

——, *a.* 1. Firm, solid, solidified, consolidated, compact.

2. Concreted, formed by admixture, complex, compound, agglomerated, conglomerated.

3. Completely real, individualized, total, entire, free from abstraction.

Concrete, *n.* (*Pron.* con'crete.) 1. Concretion, mixture, compound.

2. Cemented stones and gravel.

Concretion, *n.* 1. Solidification, concrescence.

2. Concreted mass, calculus.

3. Concrete, mixture, admixture, firm combination, compound, complex.

Concubine, *n.* Mistress, paramour, hetaira.

Concupiscence, *n.* 1. Inordinate desire, morbid longing, sinful craving, extravagant passion, depraved appetite.

2. Lust, lewdness, lechery, lasciviousness, pruriency, carnal desire, animal appetite.

Concupiscent, *a.* 1. Full of ill-regulated passion, inordinately desirous, morbidly passionate, depraved in appetite *or* cravings.

2. Lustful, lecherous, libidinous, lascivious, salacious, lickerish, prurient, rampant, carnal.

Concur, *v. i.* 1. Be conjoined, be combined, unite, meet.

2. Agree, acquiesce, approve, coincide, harmonize.

3. Co-operate, help, combine, conspire, contribute jointly.

Concurrence, *n.* 1. Conjuncture, combination, coincidence, consistence, consilience.

2. Agreement, union, alliance, consent, joint approval *or* approbation.

3. Co-operation.

Concurrent, *a.* 1. Agreeing, harmonizing, meeting, uniting, coincident.

2. Conjoined, united, associate, associated, attendant, concomitant.

3. Joint and equal, of equal authority.

Concussion, *n.* 1. Shaking, agitation, quassation.

2. Clash, shock, crash, violent collision.

Condemn, *v. t.* (Cf. CONTEMN.) 1. Sentence, doom, adjudge.

2. Pronounce guilty, utter (judicial) sentence against.

3. Disapprove utterly, proscribe, reprobate.

4. Censure, blame, disapprove, deprecate, reprehend, frown on, reprove, upbraid, pass censure on.

5. Confiscate, declare (to be) forfeited.

Condemnation, *n.* 1. Act of condemning, sentencing, dooming.

2. Sentence of punishment, judgment, conviction, penalty.

3. Utter disapproval, proscription, banning.

4. Guilt, sin, wrong, ground of condemnation, condemning fact, ill-desert, what deserves condemnation.

5. Blame, censure, reproof, disapproval, disapprobation, reprobation.

Condemnatory, *a.* 1. Condemning, conveying sentence, dooming, conveying *or* expressing condemnation.

2. Reproachful, censuring, deprecatory, damnatory, blaming, disapproving, severely disapproving.

Condensation, *n.* 1. Compression.

2. Reduction, abridgment, contraction.

Condense, *v. t.* 1. Compress, consolidate, concentrate; make dense, compact, *or* close, densify, thicken; press together.

2. Abridge, abbreviate, shorten, epitomize, reduce, diminish, contract, curtail.

3. Reduce to a liquid state, liquefy.

——, *v. i.* 1. Grow dense.

2. Become liquid, liquefy.

Condescend, *v. i.* 1. Deign, vouchsafe, graciously stoop.

2. Stoop, descend, degrade one's self, lower one's self, so forget one's self.

Condescension, *n.* Graciousness, affability, gracious favor, gracious temper *or* disposition.

Condign, *a.* [*Said only* or *chiefly of punishment.*] Deserved, merited, suitable, adequate.

Condiment, *n.* Seasoning, relish, appetizer, sauce.

CONDITION, *n.* 1. Situation, state, case, plight, predicament, circumstances.

2. Rank (*of life*), estate, grade, class *or* order of society, station.

3. Consideration, provision, proviso, stipulation, arrangement, article of agreement, rule of proceeding.

4. Prerequisite, precondition, necessity, necessary antecedent *or* attendant, postulate, *sine qua non.*

——, *v. t.* Subject to conditions, put under limits, assign terms, conditions, *or* limits to, limit, restrict, make contingent, put as contingent *or* dependent, cognize under conditions *or* limits.

Conditional, *a.* 1. Depending on conditions, dependent, modified by conditions, contingent, provisional, provisory.

2. Expressing conditions *or* a condition, limiting, limitative.

Conditions, *n. pl.* Stipulations, provisions, terms.

Condole with. Sympathize with, share one's sorrow, express sympathy for, feel grief *or* sorrow in common with.

Condolence, *n.* Sympathy, expression of sympathy *or* common sorrow.

Condonation, *n.* Pardon, forgiveness, overlooking.

Condone, *v. t.* Pardon, forgive, overlook, excuse, let go *or* pass.

Conduce, *v. i.* Contribute, tend, redound, lead, have a tendency.

Conduce to. Serve, subserve, promote, advance, forward, contribute to *or* towards, tend to, be subsidiary to.

Conducive, *a.* Conducing, contributing, subservient, instrumental, subsidiary, promotive.

Conduct, *n.* 1. Management, direction, administration, guidance, leadership.

2. Convoy, escort, guard.

3. Deportment (*in general*, or *as a matter of habit*), demeanor, carriage, bearing, manners, career, manner of life, course of life, actions, ways, mode of action. See BEHAVIOR.

——, *v. t.* (*Pron.* conduct'.) 1. Lead, direct, guide, escort, convoy.

2. Command, lead, govern, preside over, superintend.

3. Manage, regulate, operate, carry on, direct.

4. Lead (*in music* or *ceremonial*), direct, take the lead in.

5. (*Phys.*) Carry, transmit, propagate.

Conduction, *n.* (*Phys.*) Transmission, propagation, carrying.

Conduct one's self. Behave, act, comport one's self, demean one's self, acquit one's self.

Conductor, *n.* 1. Leader, guide.

2. Manager, director, leader.

3. (*Phys.*) Transmitter, propagator.

Conduit, *n.* Channel, canal, duct, passage, pipe, tube.

Cone-shaped, *a.* Coniform, conical.

Confection, *n.* Sweetmeat, confect, comfit.

Confectionery, *n.* 1. Sweetmeats, confections, confects, comfits, candies.

2. Confectioner's shop.

Confederacy, *n.* Confederation (*especially of independent states*), federation, league, coalition, alliance, union, federal compact.

Confederate, *v. t.* Ally, league, combine, unite.

——, *v. i.* Unite, be leagued, be allied.

——, *p.* and *a.* Confederated, leagued, federated, allied, united in federal compact.

——, *n.* Accomplice, abettor, accessory, associate, ally.

Confederation, *n.* League. See CONFEDERACY.

Confer, *v. i.* Converse, discourse, parley, advise, talk, hold a conference, talk together, compare notes, interchange views.

——, *v. t.* Bestow, give, grant, vouchsafe.

Conference, *n.* Meeting for consultation, interview, colloquy, parley, "powwow."

Confess, *v. t.* 1. Acknowledge (*as a crime* or *fault*), own, avow, admit.

2. Admit, grant, concede, recognize.

3. (*Poetical.*) Attest, prove, show, exhibit, manifest, be proof of.

4. Receive *or* hear one's confession (*as a priest*), shrive.

——, *v. i.* Acknowledge one's sins (*to a priest*), go to the confessional.

Confession, *n.* Acknowledgment, admission, avowal.

Confessional, *n.* Confession-chair, confessionary, shriving-pew, stall.

Confessor, *n.* 1. Persecuted saint, faithful believer.

2. Shriver, confessing priest, ghostly *or* spiritual adviser.

Confidant, *masc.* } *n.* Bosom-friend, inti-
Confidante, *fem.* } mate, dear, *or* confidential friend.

Confide, *v. t.* Trust, intrust, commit, consign, give in trust.

Confide in. Trust, depend upon, rely upon, put faith in, have confidence in, repose confidence in.

Confidence, *n.* 1. Trust, faith, belief, certitude, reliance, dependence.

2. Boldness, courage, intrepidity, assurance, aplomb, firmness, self-reliance, cocksureness.

3. Secret, private *or* confidential communication.

4. Intimacy, confidential relations.

Confident, *a.* 1. Assured, certain, sure, positive, fully convinced, "cocksure."

2. Bold, presumptuous, sanguine, undaunted.

Confidential, *a.* 1. Private, not to be disclosed, not to be communicated.

2. Trusty, faithful, to be trusted.

Confidentially, *adv.* Privately, in confidence, under the rose, between ourselves, between you and me, *sub rosa*, *entre nous*.

Configuration, *n.* Form, figure, shape, conformation, outline, Gestalt.

Confine, *n.* Boundary, border, limit, frontier.

——, *v. t.* (*Pron.* confine'.) 1. Restrain, shut up, shut in.

2. Imprison, immure, incarcerate, jail, mew, impound.

3. Limit, circumscribe, bound, restrict.

Confinement, *n.* 1. Restraint.

2. Imprisonment, incarceration, immurement, captivity, duress, durance.

3. Lying-in, childbed, delivery, parturition, childbirth.

Confines, *n. pl.* Boundaries, borders, edges, limits, marches, frontiers, precincts, remote regions.

Confirm, *v. t.* 1. Establish, fix, settle, assure, make firm.

2. Strengthen, add strength to.

3. Corroborate, substantiate, verify, avouch, endorse, countersign, authenticate.

4. Ratify, sanction, bind.

Confirmation, *n.* 1. Settlement, establishment.

2. Corroboration, substantiation, verification, proof.

3. Ratification, sanction, seal.

Confirmatory, *a.* Corroborating, corroborative.

Confiscate, *v. t.* Appropriate, seize, cause to be forfeited, condemn to public use.

Conflagration, *n.* Great burning, general fire.

Conflict, *v. i.* Clash, interfere, be inconsistent *or* inharmonious, be contrary, be opposed.

——, *n.* (*Pron.* con'flict.) 1. Struggle, encounter, contest, combat, battle, fight, collision, strife in arms.

2. Clashing, interference, inconsistency, antagonism, opposition, disagreement, discord, inharmony.

Confluence, *n.* 1. Meeting, junction, conflux, union, flowing together.

2. Concourse, assembly, assemblage, congregation, multitude, crowd, collection, throng, army, host, swarm, horde.

Confluent, *a.* Meeting, blending, commingling, mingling, flowing together.

Conflux, *n.* 1. Confluence, meeting, union, flowing together.

2. Collection, multitude, concourse, crowd, throng. See CONFLUENCE, 2.

Conform, *v. t.* Make conformable, bring into compliance, adjust, adapt, accommodate.

——, *v. i.* 1. Comply, yield, assent.

2. Agree, harmonize, tally, square, correspond, comport.

Conformable to. 1. Resembling, similar to, corresponding to, like.

2. Agreeable to, suitable to, consistent with.

3. Compliant with, submissive to, obedient to, obsequious towards.

Conformation, *n.* 1. Accordance, compliance, agreement, conformity.

2. Configuration, structure, form, figure, shape, manner *or* mode of formation.

Conformity, *n.* 1. Accordance, agreement, congruity, harmony.

2. Correspondence, likeness, similitude, resemblance.

3. Yielding, submission, obedience, compliance with the will of.

Confound, *v. t.* 1. Mingle confusedly, confuse, crowd together in disorder.

2. Confuse with each other, mistake one for another, mistake between.

3. Perplex, bewilder, baffle, embarrass, mystify, pose, nonplus, flurry.

4. Surprise, amaze, astonish, astound, stupefy, bewilder, stun, startle, dumfounder, paralyze, take by surprise, strike with wonder, strike dumb, petrify with wonder.

5. Destroy, overthrow, ruin, overwhelm, cast down, demolish, annihilate, bring to nought.

6. Abash, confuse, disconcert, discompose, shame, mortify.

Confounded, *a.* (*Colloq.*) 1. Miserable, horrid, shameful.

2. Exceeding, excessive, enormous, great, monstrous.

3. Odious, detestable, hateful, abominable, cursed.

Confront, *v. t.* 1. Face, stand in front of, stand over against, be opposite to.

2. Oppose, stand opposed, challenge, threaten, encounter, stand athwart the path of, rise in hostility before.

3. Bring face to face, bring into the presence of, contrapose.

Confuse, *v. t.* 1. Mingle, intermingle, mix, blend, confound.

2. Disorder, disarrange, derange, disturb, jumble, throw into disorder *or* confusion, muddle, mess.

3. Perplex, obscure, darken, render uncertain.

4. Mystify, embarrass, pose, nonplus, bewilder, flurry, fluster, "flabbergast," befuddle.

5. Abash, shame, mortify, discompose, disconcert, confound.

Confusion, *n.* 1. Confusedness, disorder, disarrangement, muddle, "muss," clutter, derangement, disarray, jumble, chaos, anarchy.

2. Tumult, turmoil, commotion, ferment, stir, agitation.

3. Distraction, perplexity, embarrassment, fuddle, fluster, bewilderment, astonishment.

4. Shame, mortification, abashment, embarrassment.

5. Overthrow, destruction, defeat, ruin, annihilation, demolition.

Confutation, *n.* Refutation, disproof.

Confute, *v. t.*   1.   Overthrow (*by argument*), overcome (*in debate*), convict of error, put to silence, silence.

2.   Disprove, refute, prove to be false.

Congeal, *v. t.*   Freeze, turn *or* convert to ice, solidify, curdle.

——, *v. i.*   Freeze, be *or* become frozen, turn *or* be converted into ice.

Congelation, *n.*   Freezing.

Congenial, *a.*   1.   Kindred, similar, sympathetic.

2.   Suited, adapted, proper, suitable, natural, agreeable.

3.   Favorable, agreeable, genial (*said of climate, etc.*).

Congenital, *a.*   Connate, connatural, inborn, coeval with birth, existing at *or* from birth.

Congeries, *n.*   Aggregate, aggregation, agglomeration, conglomeration, compages, compage, crowd, cluster, crowded series.

Congratulate, *v. t.*   Felicitate, compliment, gratulate, wish joy to, rejoice with.

Congratulation, *n.*   Felicitation, gratulation.

Congratulatory, *a.*   Gratulatory.

Congregate, *v. t.*   Assemble, collect, muster, gather, convene, convoke, bring together.

——, *v. i.*   Assemble, meet, collect, muster, gather, convene, throng, swarm, come *or* crowd together, come together, meet together.

Congregation, *n.*   Assembly, assemblage, gathering, meeting, collection.

Congress, *n.*   Meeting, assembly, convention, council, conference.

Congruity, *n.*   Suitableness, agreement, fitness, consistency, conformity.

Congruous, *a.*   1.   Accordant, agreeing, suitable, consistent, consonant, compatible.

2.   Proper, fit, befitting, appropriate, meet, seemly.

Conical, *a.*   Coniform, cone-shaped.

Conjectural, *a.*   Presumptive, surmised, hypothetical, theoretical, suppositional, supposititious.

Conjecture, *n.*   Supposition, surmise, guess, hypothesis, theory.

——, *v. t.*   Surmise, guess, suppose, divine, suspect.

——, *v. i.*   Surmise, guess, presume, suppose, suspect, fancy, dare say, take it, hazard the conjecture.

Conjoin, *v. t.*   Join, unite, combine, connect, associate, join together.

Conjoint, *a.*   Joined, united, combined, connected, associated.

Conjugal, *a.*   Matrimonial, connubial, nuptial, bridal, hymeneal.

Conjunction, *n.*   Union, association, combination, connection, conjoining.

Conjuncture, *n.*   1.   Combination, concurrence.

2.   Crisis, emergency, exigency, juncture, critical occasion.

Conjuration, *n.*   1.   Adjuration, solemn summons *or* imploration, conjuring.

2.   Magic, sorcery, incantation, enchantment, spell, magic spell.

Conjure, *v. t.*   1.   Beseech, supplicate, beg, pray, entreat, implore, enjoin solemnly, invoke.   See ADJURE.

2.   Charm, enchant, bewitch, fascinate, affect by magic arts.

——, *v. i.*   Juggle, practise magic *or* sorcery, play tricks.

Conjurer, *n.*   Juggler, enchanter, sorcerer, magician, necromancer, diviner, seer, wizard, charmer, exorcist.

Conjure up.   1.   Summon by enchantment, raise up by magic.

2.   Raise by effort, produce by artificial effort, bring forward by pretence.

Connate, *a.*   Congenital, connatural, inborn, coeval with birth, existing at *or* from birth.

Connect, *v. t.*   Join, unite, combine, conjoin, associate, couple, link together, interlink, hyphenate.

——, *v. i.*   1.   Join, unite, cohere, be joined, interlock, have relation.

2.   Be connected, communicate, lead into each other.

Connected, *a.*   1.   Joined, united, associated, coupled.

2.   Related, akin, allied.

3.   Communicating, leading one into the other.

CONNECTION, *n.*   1.   Union, alliance, junction, association, dependence.

2.   Intercourse, communication, commerce.

3.   Affinity, relationship.

4.   Kinsman, relative, relation, kindred.

Connivance, *n.*   1.   Voluntary blindness (*to an act*), pretended ignorance, forbearance of disapproval, winking at, blinking.

2.   Tacit consent, secret approval, collusion, indirect *or* underhand *or* remote participation, secret and indirect abettal.

Connive at.   1.   Purposely overlook, make light of, pretend not to see, shut one's eyes to, forbear to censure, wink at, blink.

2.   Be knowing *or* consenting to, secretly and indirectly promote, allow by inaction.

Connoisseur, *n.*   Critic, critical judge, expert, virtuoso, man of good taste (cf. *dilettante, one who merely pretends to good taste*).

Connotation, *n.* (*Log.*) Meaning, intension, comprehension, depth, intent, force, sum of attributes expressed *or* implied.

Connotative, *a.* (*Log.*) 1. Comprising as attributes, expressing, implying.

2. Attributive, descriptive.

Connote, *v. t.* (*Log.*) Express *or* imply as attributes, include in its meaning, comprise among its attributes, imply.

Connubial, *a.* Matrimonial, conjugal, nuptial, hymeneal, bridal.

Conquer, *v. t.* 1. Vanquish, subdue, overcome, subjugate, defeat, discomfit, overthrow, overpower, beat, rout, quell, checkmate, master, subject, reduce, humble, crush, get the better of, put down, prevail over, get the upper hand of, get the whip hand of, have on the hip.

2. Surmount, overcome.

3. Gain by effort, win by victory.

——, *v. i.* Prevail, overcome, succeed, win, triumph, be triumphant, win success, gain the victory.

Conqueror, *n.* 1. Vanquisher, subjugator, subduer, humbler.

2. Victor, victress, superior, winner, successful contestant.

Conquest, *n.* 1. Subjugation, subjection, mastery, reduction, overthrow, rout, defeat, discomfiture.

2. Victory, triumph.

3. Winning, victorious establishment.

Consanguinity, *n.* Relationship (*by blood*), kindred, kin, blood-kindred, blood-relationship, affinity.

Conscience, *n.* Moral sense, moral faculty, the still small voice.

Conscientious, *a.* Scrupulous, exact, upright, honest, just, honorable, fair, uncorrupt, incorruptible, faithful, careful, high-minded, straightforward.

CONSCIOUS, *a.* 1. Knowing, sentient, percipient, intelligent.

2. Thinking, intellectual, reflecting, self-conscious, rational, reasoning.

3. Sensible, aware, awake, cognizant, apprised, percipient.

4. Inwardly known, clearly felt, self-admitted, self-accusing.

Conscription, *n.* Compulsory enrolment *or* registry *or* registration (*for service in war*), draft, impressment.

Consecrate, *v. t.* 1. Dedicate, devote, ordain, set apart as sacred, appropriate to sacred uses.

2. Hallow, sanctify, make *or* render venerable *or* reverend.

Consecration, *n.* Dedication, devotion.

Consecutive, *a.* Successive, uninterrupted, continuous, succeeding regularly, following in a series.

Consecutive to. Following, succeeding, coming after, following upon.

Consensus, *n.* Agreement, unanimity, concord, consent, unison, according *or* consenting judgment.

Consent, *n.* 1. Concurrence, assent, approval.

2. Concord, accord, agreement, unison, consensus, co-operation, harmony, coherence.

3. Acquiescence, compliance.

——, *v. i.* 1. Agree (*as to a matter of conduct*), assent, concur, yield assent, give consent.

2. Yield, comply, acquiesce, accede.

Consequence, *n.* 1. Effect, result, issue, event, end.

2. Deduction, inference, conclusion.

3. Connection, concatenation, consecution, chain of cause and effect, dependence of cause and effect.

4. Importance, moment, weight, distinction, standing, influence, interest, concern.

Consequent, *a.* 1. Following, consequential, resulting.

2. Deducible, inferable *or* inferrible.

——, *n.* 1. Following *or* succeeding event, second *or* after term.

2. Deduction, conclusion, inference.

Consequential, *a.* 1. Following, consequent, sequential, resulting.

2. Pompous, conceited, self-sufficient, vainglorious, self-important.

Conservation, *n.* Preservation, maintenance.

Conservative, *a.* 1. Preservative, conservatory.

2. Opposed to change, unprogressive, Tory, reactionary.

Conservator, *n.* Preserver, protector, guardian.

Conservatory, *n.* (*Rare.*) 1. Repository, storehouse, receptacle.

2. Greenhouse.

3. School, institute, *conservatoire.*

Conserve, *v. t.* Preserve, save, keep, protect, maintain, sustain, uphold.

——, *n.* (*Pron.* con'serve.) Preserve, confection, comfit, sweetmeat, jam.

Consider, *v. t.* 1. Contemplate, ponder, study, examine, weigh, mind, heed, mark, reflect upon, brood upon, revolve, be attentive to, give *or* pay attention to, give heed to, take into consideration, give a thought to, keep in view.

2. Respect, regard, envisage, consult, care for, have regard to, have reference to, take into account.

3. Cf. *v. i.* 2.

——, *v. i.* 1. Deliberate, reflect, meditate,

ponder, ruminate, muse, cogitate, think, take thought, cast about.

2. Opine, believe, think, deem, hold, judge, account.

Considerable, *a.* 1. Respectable, worthy of consideration.

2. Moderately large, not small, sizable, goodly, not little, a good deal of.

Considerate, *a.* 1. Thoughtful, deliberate, serious, discreet, prudent, provident, circumspect, judicious, sober, staid.

2. Thoughtfully kind, forbearing, charitable, patient.

Consideration, *n.* 1. Attention, notice, heed, regard, reflection, deliberation, meditation, cogitation, pondering, serious thought, contemplation.

2. Importance, consequence, weight, moment, import, significance.

3. Reason, motive, ground, account, score, sake, cause.

Considering, *prep.* Taking into account, allowing for, making allowance for.

Consign, *v. t.* 1. Transfer, deliver over, hand over, remand, resign.

2. Intrust, commit, give in trust, *or* charge.

Consignee, *n.* Agent, factor, receiver (*of goods shipped*).

Consigner, ⎫ *n.* Sender, shipper, trans-
Consignor, ⎭ mitter.

Consignment, *n.* 1. Sending, shipping.

2. Goods shipped, amount shipped.

Consilience, *n.* Concurrence, coincidence, conjuncture.

Consistence, *n.* 1. Consistency, body, degree of density.

2. (*Rare.*) Structure, combination, organization.

Consistency, *n.* 1. Consistence, degree of density.

2. Congruity, agreement, compatibility, conformableness, consonance, correspondence.

Consistent, *a.* Compatible, suitable accordant, conformable, congruous, harmonious, correspondent.

Consist in. Lie in, be contained in, be comprised in, be constituted by.

Consist of. Be made of, be composed of, be formed of, be made up of, be constituted of.

Consist with. Suit, become, befit, agree with, be compatible with, be in accordance with, be consistent with.

Consolation, *n.* Solace, comfort, encouragement, alleviation of sorrow, relief from distress.

Consolatory, *a.* Consoling, comforting.

Console, *v. t.* Solace, comfort, cheer, encourage, soothe, relieve from distress.

——, *n.* (*Arch.*— *pron.* con′sole.) Bracket, ancone, corbel.

Consolidate, *v. t.* 1. Condense, compact, compress, harden, solidify, make solid, make firm.

2. Conjoin, combine, unite into one.

Consolidation, *n.* 1. Solidification.

2. Union, combination.

Consonance, ⎫ *n.* 1. Concord, accord, har-
Consonancy, ⎭ mony.

2. Consistency, congruity, congruence, agreement, unison, accord, accordance.

Consonant, *a.* 1. Accordant, according, harmonious, in harmony.

2. Consistent, congruous, compatible, accordant, in harmony.

——, *n.* Articulation, letter-sound.

Consort, *n.* Companion (*esp. a wife or a husband*), partner, associate.

Consort with. Associate with, keep company with.

Conspectus, *n.* [L.] Outline, epitome, abstract, summary, compend, compendium, synopsis, syllabus, digest, brief, breviary, general view.

Conspicuous, *a.* 1. Visible, discernible, perceptible, apparent, noticeable, plain, clear, in plain sight, glaring, striking.

2. Eminent, pre-eminent, prominent, distinguished, remarkable, noted, celebrated, marked, signal, outstanding, famed, famous, illustrious.

Conspiracy, *n.* Plot, combination, collusion, cabal, complot, intrigue, machination.

Conspire, *v. i.* 1. Co-operate, conduce, tend, concur.

2. Combine (*for some evil design*), plot, scheme, confederate, intrigue, cabal.

——, *v. t.* Plot, contrive, devise, project, compass.

Constancy, *n.* 1. Stability, immutability, unchangeableness, permanence.

2. Uniformity, regularity.

3. Inflexibility, steadiness, steadfastness, firmness, resolution, determination, decision, tenacity of purpose.

4. Fidelity, faithfulness, loyalty, truth, trustiness, devotion.

Constant, *a.* 1. Stable, fixed, abiding, unalterable, enduring, immutable, unvaried, invariable, invariant, unchanging, permanent, perpetual.

2. Uniform, regular, stated, certain.

3. Resolute, firm, steady, steadfast, stanch, determined, unmoved, unswerving, undeviating, unshaken, unwavering.

4. Persevering, assiduous, unremitting, tenacious, diligent, sedulous.

5. Incessant, uninterrupted, unbroken, perpetual, continuous, continual, sustained.

6. Faithful, true, trusty, loyal, devoted.

Constellation, *n.* 1. Group of stars.

2. Collection, assemblage, cluster, galaxy.

Consternation, *n.* Alarm, amazement, terror, horror, fright, dismay, panic, sudden fear.

Constipated, *a.* Costive.

Constipation, *n.* Costiveness.

Constituent, *a.* 1. Forming, composing, constituting, component.

2. Appointing, electoral.

——, *n.* 1. Component, element, principle, ingredient, component part.

2. Elector, voter.

Constitute, *v. t.* 1. Form, compose, make, make up, enter into the composition of.

2. Appoint, depute, empower.

3. Set up, establish, enact, fix.

Constitution, *n.* 1. Formation, organization, structure, make-up.

2. Quality, character, temper, temperament, spirit, humor, peculiarity, characteristic.

3. Charter of government, fundamental law, organic law.

Constitutional, *a.* 1. Natural, inherent, inbred, inborn, innate, connate, congenital, organic.

2. Legal, lawful, legitimate, consistent with the constitution.

Constrain, *v. t.* 1. Compel, force, drive, oblige, coerce.

2. Confine, restrain, inthrall, hold, curb, put under restraint, keep down, keep under.

3. Urge, impel, draw, draw urgently *or* irresistibly.

Constraint, *n.* 1. Compulsion, force, necessity, obligation, coercion, pressure.

2. Confinement, restraint, imprisonment, incarceration, inthralment, durance, duress, captivity.

Constrict, *v. t.* Cramp, contract, compress, squeeze, tighten.

Constriction, *n.* Contraction, compression, constraint.

Construct, *v. t.* 1. Fabricate, build, erect, raise, set up, put together.

2. Organize, institute, originate, invent, arrange, make, form, frame.

Construction, *n.* 1. Fabrication, erection, building.

2. Structure, formation, conformation, configuration, form, figure, shape, mode of constructing.

3. Interpretation, explanation, version, rendering.

Construe, *v. t.* Interpret, explain, expound, translate, render, put an interpretation upon.

Consubstantiation, *n.* Impanation (*the Lutheran doctrine of the Eucharist*).

Consuetudinary, *a.* (*Rare.*) Usual, common, wonted, customary, accustomed, conventional.

Consulate, *n.* Consulship, consular office, consular government, consular term.

Consult, *v. i.* 1. [Followed by *with*.] Confer, advise, seek counsel, take counsel, deliberate.

2. Take counsel (together), confer, deliberate together.

——, *v. t.* 1. Ask advice of, seek information from.

2. Consider, regard, care for, have reference to, have regard to, take into account.

Consultation, *n.* 1. Consulting, making inquiry, seeking the advice.

2. Conference, deliberation, colloquy, interview, parley.

3. Council, meeting for deliberation.

Consume, *v. t.* Destroy, waste, spend, expend, exhaust, devour, lavish, squander, dissipate, use up.

——, *v. i.* Waste away, be exhausted, perish, decay, vanish out of being.

Consummate, *v. t.* Complete, finish, perfect, accomplish, compass, effect, perform, achieve, execute, do, carry out, bring about, work out.

——, *a.* (*Pron.* consum'mate.) Complete, perfect, finished, supreme.

Consummation, *n.* Completion, termination, finishing, close, accomplishment, fulfilment, achievement, realization, last stroke, finishing stroke, last finish, final touch, crowning touch.

Consumption, *n.* 1. Use, using up, destruction, waste, expenditure.

2. Phthisis, marasmus, atrophy, decline, tabes, gradual wasting, progressive emaciation.

Contact, *n.* Touch, tangency, taction, juxtaposition, junction, contiguity, close union.

Contagion, *n.* 1. Infection, communication of disease (*by contact, direct or indirect*).

2. Contagious matter, disease-germs, virus, contagium.

3. Contamination, taint, corruption, infection.

4. Pestilential influence, poisonous exhalations, pestilence, poisoned air.

Contagious, *a.* 1. Infectious, catching.

2. Pestilential, pestiferous, poisonous, deadly.

Contain, *v. t.* 1. Comprehend, comprise, embrace, include, embody.

2. Hold, have capacity for.

3. Restrain, keep in check.

Contaminate, *v. t.* Defile, pollute, corrupt, taint, infect, poison, vitiate, sully, tarnish, soil, stain.

Contamination, *n.* 1. Contaminating, polluting, pollution, defiling, defilement, etc. See the verb.

2. Taint, stain, infection, impurity, foulness, uncleanness, abomination, pollution, defilement.

Contemn, *v. t.* Despise, disdain, scorn, scout, spurn, slight, hold in contempt, look down upon, turn a cold shoulder upon, turn up one's nose at, snap one's fingers at, laugh to scorn, point the finger of scorn at.

Contemplate, *v. t.* 1. Gaze upon, view attentively, look abroad upon, survey.

2. Study, ponder, survey, meditate on, dwell on, think about, reflect upon, muse on, consider attentively, revolve in the mind.

3. Intend, purpose, design, think of, have in view, have in contemplation, look forward to.

Contemplation, *n.* 1. Reflection, meditation, cogitation, deliberation, study, thought, speculation, pondering.

2. View, prospect, prospective.

3. Expectation, prospect, view.

Contemplative, *a.* Thoughtful, studious, given to contemplation, meditative, musing, pensive.

Contemporaneous, *a.* Contemporary, coexistent, concomitant, simultaneous, synchronous, coeval, coetaneous, coincident.

Contempt, *n.* 1. Disdain, scorn, mockery, derision, contumely, disregard, slight, despite, misprision, mean opinion.

2. Shame, disgrace, confusion.

Contemptible, *a.* Despicable, vile, low, mean, base, pitiful, abject, worthless, paltry, sorry, scurvy.

Contemptuous, *a.* Insolent, scornful, contumelious, sneering, disdainful, supercilious, haughty.

Contend, *v. i.* 1. Strive, struggle, combat, contest, battle, fight, vie.

2. Debate, dispute, argue, join issue.

3. Maintain, affirm, assert, claim.

Content, *a.* Satisfied, contented, easy in mind.

——, *n.* Satisfaction, ease, contentment, peace.

——, *v. t.* Satisfy, appease, suffice, gratify, make easy, make contented.

Contented, *a.* Satisfied, content, easy in mind, at peace.

Contention, *n.* 1. Strife, discord, dissension, wrangling, wrangle, quarrel, squab-

ble, feud, rupture, falling out, high words.

2. Dispute, debate, bickering, altercation, controversy, contest, litigation, logomachy, war of words, strife of words.

Contentious, *a.* 1. Quarrelsome, cross, petulant, perverse, pugnacious, litigious, wrangling, belligerent.

2. Disputatious, captious, cavilling.

Contentment, *n.* Satisfaction, ease, content.

Contents, *n. pl.* 1. What is contained, filling, filling up.

2. Solid dimensions, capacity, volume, solid contents.

3. Topics, matters treated, subjects considered, table of contents.

Conterminous, *a.* 1. Adjoining, adjacent, contiguous, bordering upon.

2. Identical in limits, of identical boundaries, co-extensive, coincident, commensurate.

Contest, *v. t.* 1. Dispute, controvert, argue, debate, litigate, contend against, call in question.

2. Strive to hold, struggle to defend.

3. Contend for, strive to carry, compete for, make the object of competition *or* rivalry *or* emulation.

——, *v. i.* Contend, strive, struggle, vie, fight, compete, cope.

——, *n.* (*Pron.* con'test.) 1. Dispute, altercation, debate, controversy, contention, quarrel, difference, high words, strife of words, war of words.

2. Struggle, battle, bout, tussle, match, "scrimmage," affray, conflict, fight, combat, encounter, rencounter, strife in arms.

3. Competition, rivalry, contention.

Context, *n.* Words immediately preceding *or* following, adjoining matter, connection, connected thought *or* thoughts.

Contexture, *n.* Constitution, structure, framework, texture, composition, mode of formation.

Contiguity, *n.* 1. Contact, touching, meeting, juxtaposition, proximity, nearness.

2. Continuity, continuous stretch, expanse, unbroken extent.

Contiguous, *a.* Touching, meeting, conterminous, adjacent, adjoining, in contact.

Continence, *n.* 1. Chastity, restraint of sexual appetite.

2. Self-command (*in general*), self-control, moderation, temperance.

Continent, *a.* 1. Chaste, temperate in sexual passion, free from lust.

2. Temperate (*in general*), moderate, self-commanding, self-controlled, restrained.

——, *n.* Mainland, great tract of land.

Contingency, *n.* 1. Accidentalness, fortuity, uncertainty, chance.

2. Casualty, accident, incident, occurrence, event.

Contingent, *a.* 1. Accidental, fortuitous, adventitious, incidental, casual, happening by chance.

2. Conditional, uncertain, dependent on circumstances.

——, *n.* Quota, proportion, share, proportional part.

Continual, *a.* 1. Perpetual, uninterrupted, unceasing, incessant, unremitting, constant, continuous.

2. Perpetual, endless, everlasting, eternal, perennial, permanent, unending, interminable.

3. Oft-repeated, very frequent, perpetual, constant, constantly recurring.

Continuance, *n.* 1. Continuation, duration, stay, abiding, endurance, lasting, persistence.

2. Prolongation, continuation, extension, perpetuation, protraction.

3. Sequence, succession, connection, concatenation.

4. Perseverance, persistence, constancy, endurance.

Continuation, *n.* Extension (*in time* or *space*), prolongation, protraction, continuance, perpetuation. See CONTINUITY.

Continue, *v. i.* 1. Remain, endure, last, subsist, be permanent, be durable.

2. Abide, stay, tarry, remain, linger.

3. Persist, persevere, endure, perdure, hold out, go on, keep on, be steadfast, be constant, "stick."

——, *v. t.* Extend (*in time* or *space*), prolong, perpetuate, protract.

Continuer, *n.* Continuator.

Continuity, *n.* 1. Cohesion, close union, intimate connection.

2. Unbroken extent, contiguity, uninterrupted connection, uninterrupted continuance *or* duration, ceaselessness, constant flow.

Continuous, *a.* Connected, continued, unbroken, uninterrupted, unintermitted.

Contort, *v. t.* Twist, writhe, distort.

Contortion, *n.* Twist, distortion, wryness, deformity.

Contour, *n.* Outline, profile.

Contraband, *a.* Prohibited, forbidden, illegal, unlawful, illicit.

——, *n.* 1. Illegal traffic.

2. Prohibited articles.

Contrabandist, *n.* Smuggler.

Contract, *v. t.* 1. Lessen, shorten, narrow, diminish, abridge, reduce, epitomize, draw together.

2. Incur, make, get, take, catch, absorb, take in.

——, *v. i.* 1. Shrivel, shrink, shrink up, constrict, narrow, draw in.

2. Agree, stipulate, bargain, covenant, engage, pledge, make a bargain.

——, *n.* (*Pron.* con'tract.) Compact, bargain, stipulation, covenant, convention, concordat, treaty, agreement, pact, arrangement.

Contraction, *n.* 1. Shrinking, shrivelling, corrugation, drawing together, drawing in.

2. Reduction, shortening, diminution, lessening, abridgment, abbreviation.

Contradict, *v. t.* 1. Deny, gainsay, dispute, controvert, impugn, traverse.

2. Oppose, contravene, counteract, annul, belie, disallow, negative, counter, abrogate, traverse, thwart, be contrary to, run counter to.

Contradiction, *n.* 1. Gainsaying, denial, controversion.

2. Opposition, contrariety, incongruity, antagonism, antinomy, clashing.

Contradictory, *a.* Opposite, negating, contrary, inconsistent, repugnant.

Contradistinction, *n.* Distinction (*by opposite qualities*), opposition.

Contrariety, *n.* Opposition, repugnance, antagonism, contradiction, clashing, contrast.

Contrary, *a.* 1. Opposite, opposing, adverse, opposed, counter.

2. Antagonistic, conflicting, contradictory, counteracting, retroactive, repugnant.

3. (*Colloq.*) Perverse, humorsome, wayward, obstinate, stubborn, headstrong, refractory, unruly, froward.

Contrast, *n.* 1. Exhibition of differences, contrasting, antithesis.

2. Opposition, difference, striking difference, contrariety.

——, *v. t.* (*Pron.* contrast'.) Set off by opposition, exhibit the differences of.

——, *v. i.* Show difference, exhibit a contrast, stand out in opposition.

Contravene, *v. t.* Oppose, contradict, counteract, countervail, thwart, nullify, abrogate, annul, cross, traverse, obstruct, defeat, hinder, go against, clash with, run counter to, militate against.

Contravention, *n.* Contradiction, opposition, obstruction, violation, abrogation, transgression, traversal.

Contretemps, *n.* [Fr.] Mishap, mischance, accident.

Contribute, *v. t.* 1. Give (*in common with others*), grant *or* bestow (*as a share*).

2. Furnish, supply, afford.

Contribute, *v. i.* Conduce, minister, conspire, serve, redound, co-operate, concur, bear a part, be helpful, tend.

Contribution, *n.* 1. Grant *or* bestowment of a share.

2. Gift, donation, offering, subscription.

Contributory, *a.* Conducive, helpful, instrumental, accessory.

Contrite, *a.* Penitent, repentant, humble, broken in spirit.

Contrition, *n.* Penitence, compunction, remorse, repentance, sorrow, regret, self-condemnation, self-reproach, stings of conscience, sorrow for sin.

Contrivance, *n.* 1. Design, designing power, inventiveness, invention.

2. Invention, device, enginery, piece of mechanism, "contraption," "gadget," machine.

3. Device, scheme, plan, plot, artifice, shift, stratagem, complot, machination.

Contrive, *v. t.* Devise, plan, design, invent, project, hatch, brew, form, frame, concoct, fall upon, hit upon, strike out, chalk out.

——, *v. i.* 1. Scheme, plot, plan, consider, set one's wits to work, rack one's brains, cudgel one's brains, strain one's invention, cast about.

2. Manage, make out.

CONTROL, *n.* Ascendency, sway, command, rule, regulation, "regiment," disposition, dominion, government, mastery, superintendence, direction.

——, *v. t.* 1. Direct, dominate, order, manage, regulate, govern, sway, rule, reign over, command, superintend, have the direction of, have charge of.

2. Hinder, check, repress, curb, restrain, bridle.

Controversial, *a.* Polemical, eristic.

Controversialist, *n.* Disputant, arguer, debater, disputer, "polemicist."

Controversy, *n.* 1. Discussion, dispute, disputation, debate, polemics, altercation, logomachy, war of words, strife of words.

2. Lawsuit, suit at law, process in law.

Controvert, *v. t.* Dispute, contest, debate, argue, canvass, contend against, call in question.

Contumacious, *a.* Insolently disobedient, wilfully disrespectful, obstinate, perverse, stubborn, headstrong, heady, dogged, intractable, refractory, cross-grained, stiff-necked, pertinacious, obdurate.

Contumacy, *n.* 1. Obstinacy, stubbornness, doggedness, perverseness, pertinacity, headiness, obduracy.

2. Disobedience, insubordination, insolence, disrespect.

Contumelious, *a.* Abusive, calumnious, contemptuous, insolent, insulting, opprobrious, rude, supercilious, overbearing, arrogant, scornful, disdainful.

Contumely, *n.* Obloquy, reproach, opprobrium, abuse, contemptuousness, insolence, rudeness, superciliousness, arrogance, scorn, contempt, disdain.

Contuse, *v. t.* Bruise, crush, squeeze.

Convalescence, *n.* Recovery (*of health*), recuperation.

Convalescent, *a.* Improving (*in health*), recovering, recuperating.

Convene, *v. i.* Meet, assemble, muster, congregate, come together, hold a session.

——, *v. t.* Convoke, summon, assemble, collect, muster, bring together, gather together, call together.

Convenience, *n.* 1. Suitableness, fitness, propriety.

2. Commodiousness, accommodation, handiness, accessibility, serviceableness, satisfaction, ease, comfort.

3. Cause of satisfaction, source of comfort.

4. Suitable opportunity, comfortable occasion.

Convenient, *a.* 1. Fit, suitable, proper, appropriate, adapted, suited.

2. Commodious, advantageous, useful, handy, serviceable, helpful, beneficial, comfortable, favorable.

Convent, *n.* Monastery, cloister, abbey, priory, *or* nunnery (*as the case may be*).

Convention, *n.* 1. Assembly, meeting. See CONVOCATION.

2. Contract, compact, agreement, stipulation.

3. Conventional *or* arbitrary arrangement, usage, formality, custom.

Conventional, *a.* 1. Stipulated, agreed on, bargained for.

2. Usual, customary, standard, orthodox, approved, traditional, common, habitual, wonted, accustomed, ordinary, regular, every-day.

3. Resting on mere custom *or* arbitrary agreement, stereotyped.

Conventual, *a.* Monastic.

Converge, *v. i.* Tend to the same point, approach, draw gradually together.

Convergent, *a.* 1. Converging, gradually approaching.

2. (*Math.*) Tending to a limit.

Conversable, *a.* Sociable, social, communicative, affable, free, unreserved, open.

Conversant with. Acquainted with, familiar with, versed in, skilled in, proficient in.

Conversation, *n.* Converse, talk, colloquy, parley, conference, dialogue, chat, palaver, confabulation, interlocution, familiar discourse.

Conversational, *a.* Colloquial, chatty.

Converse, *v. i.* 1. Commune, hold intercourse.

2. Talk, chat, confabulate, discourse familiarly, gossip, parley, hold a conversation.

——, *n.* (*Pron.* con'verse.) 1. Communion, intercourse, commerce.

2. Talk, colloquy, conversation.

3. Reverse, opposite.

Conversely, *adv.* Reciprocally, by conversion.

Conversion, *n.* 1. Transmutation, transformation, reduction, resolution, change.

2. Interchange, transposition, reversal.

3. Change of religion; change of heart, regeneration, new birth.

4. Application, appropriation, employment.

Convert, *v. t.* 1. Transmute, transform, change.

2. Change the heart of, regenerate, create anew, re-create, renew.

3. Interchange, transpose, reverse, turn about.

4. Appropriate, apply.

Convertible, *a.* Interchangeable.

Convex, *a.* Gibbous, protuberant, rounding (*outwardly*).

Convey, *v. t.* 1. Carry, bear, bring, transmit, transport, waft, fetch.

2. Transfer, alienate, abalienate, consign, demise, devolve, cede, grant, devise, sell, deliver over, make over.

Conveyance, *n.* 1. Transfer, demise, alienation, cession, transferrence.

2. Transfer, conveying, carrying, carriage, transmission.

3. Carriage, vehicle.

Convict, *v. t.* 1. Prove *or* find guilty.

2. Convince (*of sin*), make sensible, rouse to a sense.

——, *n.* (*Pron.* con'vict.) Malefactor, criminal, felon, culprit, condemned person.

Conviction, *n.* 1. Proof of guilt, detection in guilt.

2. Confutation, refutation.

3. Persuasion, convincing.

4. Firm persuasion, settled belief, assured belief, ascertained principle.

Convince, *v. t.* Satisfy (*by proof* or *evidence*), persuade.

Convivial, *a.* Festal, festive, social, jovial, jolly, gay, symposiac.

Conviviality, *n.* Festivity, joviality, jollity, gayety, merry-making.

Convocation, *n.* 1. Calling together, convoking, gathering, convening, assembling, summoning.

2. Meeting, assembly, convention, congress, diet, synod, council.

Convoke, *v. t.* Convene, assemble, summon, muster, call together, bring together.

Convolution, *n.* 1. Rolling together.

2. Coil, curl, volute, fold, bight.

Convoy, *v. t.* Accompany (*for protection*), escort, attend, keep company with, go along with.

——, *n.* 1. (*Pron.* con'voy.) Attendance (*for the purpose of protection*), escort.

2. Escorting force, escort, guard (*esp. at sea*).

3. Charge (*of a convoying force*), ships under escort, train under escort.

Convulse, *v. t.* 1. Throw into spasms.

2. Agitate, shake, disturb.

Convulsion, *n.* 1. Spasm, cramp.

2. Agitation, disturbance, tumult, commotion.

COOK, *v. t.* [*The noun is Basic Eng.*]

1. Prepare (*food*) for the table. Specifically, bake, boil, fry, roast, etc.

2. Dress up, tamper with, color, give a color to, garble, falsify.

Cool, *a.* 1. Somewhat cold, a little cold, moderately cold, rather cold.

2. Unimpassioned, dispassionate, collected, composed, self-possessed, calm, unruffled, undisturbed, sedate, unexcited, placid, quiet, staid.

3. Indifferent, unconcerned, lukewarm, cold-blooded.

4. Frigid, chilling, apathetic, freezing, repellent.

5. (*Colloq.*) Impudent, shameless, selfishly self-possessed.

——, *v. t.* 1. Refrigerate, chill, ice, "infrigidate," freeze, make cool, reduce the heat of.

2. Allay, calm, quiet, temper, attemper, moderate, abate, damp.

——, *v. i.* 1. Grow cool, lose heat.

2. Grow lukewarm *or* indifferent *or* less furious, lose ardor, be less zealous.

Coop, *v. t.* Confine, cage, incage, imprison, shut up.

Co-operate, *v. i.* 1. Work together *or* in unison, take part, act jointly, act in concert.

2. Conspire, conduce, contribute, concur, coact, collaborate, unite, work together.

Co-operation, *n.* 1. Joint action, concurrent effort.

2. Concurrence, concert, coaction, collaboration, "synergy," joint operation, pulling together.

Co-operator, *n.* Coadjutor, assistant, helper, aider, auxiliary, ally, abettor, joint operator.

Co-ordinate, *a.* Equal, co-equal, of the same rank.

Copartner, *n.* Sharer, partaker, partner, associate.

Copartnership, *n.* 1. Association, fraternity, partnership, joint stock.

2. Firm, house, establishment, concern, company, joint concern.

Cope with. 1. Encounter, engage with, contend with, compete with, struggle with, strive with.

2. Encounter successfully, combat on equal terms, manage, hold at bay, hold one's own with.

Copier, *n.* Transcriber, copyist.

Copious, *a.* Abundant, plentiful, plenteous, ample, profuse, rich, full, exuberant, overflowing.

Copiousness, *n.* Abundance, exuberance, plenty, profusion, richness.

COPPER, *n.* [*Basic Eng. as designating the metal.*] 1. Cent.

2. [*pl.*] Small change, copper money.

3. Large boiler, cauldron (*esp. in a ship's kitchen*).

Copse, *n.* Grove (*of small trees or shrubs*), thicket, coppice.

Copulation, *n.* Coition, sexual congress, coupling, venereal act.

Copulative, *a.* Uniting, connecting.

COPY, *n.* 1. Transcript, reproduction, replica, counterscript, offprint, facsimile, duplicate.

2. Original, model, pattern, archetype.

3. Manuscript (*to be printed*), typescript.

——, *v. t.* 1. Transcribe, make a transcript of, reproduce, duplicate, trace, make a copy of.

2. Imitate, follow as a pattern, pattern after, follow.

Copyist, *n.* 1. Transcriber, copier.

2. Imitator.

Coquet, *v. i.* Flirt, philander, make love, make a show of love, affect to be in love, play at courtship.

Coquetry, *n.* Flirtation, affectation of love.

Coquette, *n.* Flirt, jilt.

Coranach, *n.* See CORONACH.

CORD, *n.* String, line, small rope, braid, gimp.

Cordate, *a.* Cordiform, heart-shaped.

Cordial, *a.* 1. Hearty, warm, ardent, affectionate, earnest, sincere, heartfelt.

2. Grateful, pleasant, refreshing, invigorating, restorative.

——, *n.* 1. Stomachic, stomachal, stimulating medicine.

2. Liqueur, aromatized spirit.

Cordiality, *n.* Heartiness, sincerity, ardor of affection, warmth of feeling, affectionate regard.

Core, *n.* Heart, inner part, inmost part, essential part, essence, centre.

CORK, *n.* 1. Bark of the *Quercus suber*, or cork-tree, epiphlœum.

2. Stopple *or* stopper (*made of cork*).

Cormorant, *n.* Glutton, greedy fellow, belly-god, greedy-gut.

——, *a.* Greedy, rapacious, all-devouring.

Corn, *n.* 1. Cereal grain.

2. Maize, Indian corn.

——, *v. t.* 1. Salt moderately, sprinkle with salt.

2. [*U. S., Scotch, and provincial.*] Intoxicate, fuddle, muddle, inebriate, make drunk, make tipsy.

Corneous, *a.* Horny, corny.

Corner, *n.* 1. Angle, bend, elbow, crotch, knee, cusp, "coign."

2. Nook, recess, niche, retired place, secret place.

——, *v. t.* (*Colloq.*) 1. Drive into a corner.

2. Nonplus, pose, confound, confuse, puzzle, perplex, put to a stand.

Corner-wise, *adv.* Diagonally.

Corollary, *n.* Inference, conclusion, consequence, deduction.

Coronach, *n.* Dirge, funeral song.

Coronal, *n.* Crown, garland, wreath, chaplet, laurel, bays.

Coronation, *n.* Crowning.

Corporal, *a.* 1. Bodily.

2. Material, physical, corporeal, not spiritual.

Corporate, *a.* Incorporated.

Corporation, *n.* Incorporated body, company, association.

Corporeal, *a.* Material, physical, corporal, non-spiritual.

Corps, *n.* [Fr.] Body of troops, division of an army.

Corpse, *n.* Remains, dead body (*of a human being*), body, corse, carcass (*used in disrespect*).

Corpulence, ⎫ *n.* Obesity, fleshiness, fat-
Corpulency, ⎭ ness, plumpness, *embonpoint*, rotundity.

Corpulent, *a.* Fleshy, fat, stout, portly, plump, pursy, obese, rotund.

Corpuscle, *n.* Atom, particle, molecule, mite, monad, scrap, bit, grain, jot, iota, tittle, whit, ace, scintilla.

Corpuscular, *a.* Molecular, atomic.

Correct, *v. t.* 1. Rectify, amend, mend, reform, remedy, improve, redress, reclaim, make right, set right.

2. Punish, chasten, discipline.

3. Change the quality of (*by something of an opposite character*), modify, redress.

Correct, *a.* Faultless, exact, precise, accurate, right, true, proper, free from error, not faulty.

Correction, *n.* 1. Amendment, improvement, redress.

2. Chastening, punishment, discipline.

3. Change (*in quality, by something opposite*), modification, alteration.

Corrective, *a.* Rectifying, reformatory, reformative, alterative, emendatory, modifying, improving, correctory, counteractive.

Correctness, *n.* Accuracy, exactness, nicety, precision, truth, propriety, faultlessness, rightness, rectitude.

Correlate, *n.* Correlative, counterpart, complement, complemental term.

Correlative, *a.* Reciprocal, complemental, complementary.

Correspond, *v. i.* 1. Agree, suit, fit, answer, accord, harmonize, tally, square, comport, cohere, conform, match, be accordant.

2. Answer, correlate, belong, stand counter, be complemental.

3. Communicate (*by letter*), write letters.

Correspondence, *n.* 1. Coincidence, concurrence, congruity, fitting relation, reciprocal adaptation, conformity, accord.

2. Correlation, complemental relation, counterposition.

3. Intercourse *or* communication by letters, epistolary intercourse.

4. Letters.

Correspondent, *a.* 1. Adapted, suited, suiting, fitted, suitable, fitting, agreeable, conformable, answerable, corresponding.

2. Corresponding, answering, correlative, belonging, counterposed, complemental, complementary.

Corridor, *n.* Gallery, passage.

Corroborate, *v. t.* Strengthen, confirm, establish, sustain, support.

Corroborative, *a.* Confirmatory, corroborating.

Corrode, *v. t.* 1. Erode, canker, eat away.

2. Consume, waste, wear away, prey upon, impair.

3. Blight, poison, envenom, embitter.

Corroding, *a.* Caustic, catheretic. See CORROSIVE.

Corrosion, *n.* 1. Erosion, eating away.

2. Wasting, wearing away, consuming, gnawing away.

3. Blighting, poisoning, embittering.

Corrosive, *a.* 1. Corroding, consuming, eroding, erosive, catheretic, caustic, acrid, virulent, eating away.

2. Corroding, wasting, consuming, gnawing, mordant, wearing.

3. Blighting, poisoning, envenoming, embittering, carking, cankerous.

Corrosiveness, *n.* Causticity, acridness, virulence, acrimony.

Corrugate, *v. t.* Wrinkle, cockle, furrow, pucker, contract into wrinkles.

Corrugation, *n.* 1. Wrinkling, cockling, puckering.

2. Wrinkle, fold, plait.

Corrupt, *v. t.* 1. Putrefy, render putrid.

2. Contaminate, taint, defile, pollute, infect, vitiate, spoil.

3. Deprave, degrade, demoralize, vitiate, pervert.

4. Debase, falsify, adulterate, sophisticate.

5. Bribe, entice.

——, *a.* 1. Corrupted, impure, rotten, infected, spoiled, tainted, putrid, contaminated, unsound.

2. Depraved, wicked, vicious, dissolute, debauched, profligate, reprobate, abandoned.

3. Open to bribes, given to bribery, dishonest, false to one's trusts.

Corruption, *n.* 1. Putrefaction, putrescence, rottenness.

2. Defilement, contamination, pollution, perversion, infection, vitiation, adulteration, debasement.

3. Depravity, depravation, wickedness, demoralization, immorality, laxity, looseness of morals, want of principle.

4. Bribery, dishonesty, abuse of public trusts.

Corsair, *n.* Pirate, buccaneer, picaroon, sea-rover, sea-robber.

Corset, *n.* Bodice, stays.

Cortège, *n.* [Fr.] Train.

Coruscate, *v. i.* Shine, glisten, glitter, gleam, sparkle, twinkle, flash, scintillate.

Coruscation, *n.* Flash, sparkle, glitter, gleam, scintillation.

Corypheus, *n.* [L.] Leader, chief, guide, director.

Cosmopolite, *n.* Citizen of the world, cosmopolitan.

Cosmos, *n.* Universe.

Cosset, *v. t.* Fondle, caress, pet, coddle, make a pet of, make much of.

Cost, *v. t.* Require to be paid *or* undergone, take away from.

——, *n.* 1. Expense, charge, price, outlay.

2. Costliness, preciousness, richness, sumptuousness, splendor.

3. Loss, detriment, damage, pain, suffering.

Costly, *a.* 1. Expensive, dear, high-priced, of great price.

2. Rich, sumptuous, precious, splendid, gorgeous.

Costume, *n.* Style of dress.

Cot, *n.* 1. Hut. See COTTAGE.

2. Low bedstead.

Coterie, *n.* Club, association, society, sodality, brotherhood, circle, set (*especially an exclusive one*).

Cottage, *n.* Cot, lodge, hut, *casino*, chalet, small house.

Cottager, *n.* Cotter.

COTTON, *n.* Cotton-wool, raw cotton.

Couch, *v. i.* 1. Lie, recline, lie down.

2. Crouch, squat, lie flat.

3. Stoop, bend down.

——, *v. t.* 1. Express, utter, set forth, clothe in words.

2. Conceal, hide, cover up.

3. Lay (*a spear*) in rest, put in posture of attack, level.

——, *n.* 1. Bed, place for rest.

2. Sofa, lounge, divan, settee, davenport.

COUGH, *n.* Tussis [L.], hack, hem.

Council, *n.* 1. Cabinet, ministry, body of advisers.

2. Assembly (*for consultation*), meeting, husting, congress, diet, synod, convocation, convention.

Counsel, *n.* 1. Consultation, interchange of opinion.

2. Advice, opinion, suggestion, recommendation, instruction, admonition, caution.

3. Deliberation, forethought.

4. Design, plan, scheme, purpose.

5. Counsellor, lawyer, barrister, advocate.

——, *v. t.* Advise, admonish, give advice to.

Counselor, *n.* 1. Adviser.

2. Lawyer, barrister, counsel, advocate.

Count, *v. t.* 1. Enumerate, number, score.

2. Calculate, reckon, compute, estimate, cast, cast up.

3. Consider, esteem, regard, deem, hold, judge, think, account, look upon.

——, *v. i.* Add to the number, swell the number, tell.

——, *n.* Reckoning, tally.

Countenance, *n.* 1. Aspect, look, mien, expression of the face.

2. Favor, encouragement, patronage, support, aid, assistance, sanction, approbation, approval.

——, *v. t.* Approve, sanction, support, aid, abet, assist, favor, encourage, patronize, befriend, stand by, side with, take the side of.

Counter, *n.* Reckoner, calculator, computer.

——, *adv.* Contrary, contrariwise, in opposition to.

Counteract, *v. t.* 1. Oppose, contravene, resist, cross, thwart, hinder, check, defeat, frustrate, traverse, run counter to, act against, clash with.

2. Neutralize, destroy the effect of, annul.

Counteraction, *n.* Opposition, contravention, resistance, frustration.

Counteractive, *n.* Corrective, antidote, cure, remedy, restorative, medicine, counter-agent.

Counterbalance, *v. t.* 1. Counterpoise, balance.

2. Countervail, compensate, set off, make up for.

Counterfeit, *v. t.* 1. Forge, make a spurious copy of, imitate *or* copy fraudulently.

2. Feign, simulate, sham, fake, put on the appearance of.

3. Imitate, copy.

——, *a.* 1. Forged, spurious, fraudulent, fake, supposititious.

2. Feigned, false, simulated, sham, mock, spurious, hypocritical, put on, make-believe.

3. Imitated, copied, resembling.

——, *n.* Forgery, fraudulent copy, sham.

Counterfeiter, *n.* 1. Forger, falsifyer.

2. Pretender, feigner, impostor.

Countermand, *v. t.* Revoke, rescind, recall, abrogate, annul, make void.

Countermarch, *v. i.* March back, reverse the direction of a march.

Counterpane, *n.* Coverlet, coverlid.

Counterpart, *n.* 1. Corresponding part.

2. (*Law.*) Duplicate, copy.

3. Correlative, correlate, complement, supplement, reverse (*to obverse*).

4. Match, fellow, mate, tally, twin, the very image.

Counterpoise, *v. t.* Counterbalance, balance, equilibrate, countervail, counteract, offset.

——, *n.* Equal weight, balance, counterweight, neutralizing force.

Countersign, *n.* Watchword, password.

Countervail, *v. t.* Balance, counterbalance, compensate, make up for.

Count on. Depend on, depend upon, rely on, rely upon, count upon.

Countrified, *a.* Rustic, rude, country.

COUNTRY, *n.* 1. Region, land, geographical division, political division.

2. Rural parts (*as distinguished from city*), countryside.

3. Native land, fatherland, nation, home, abiding habitation.

4. Nation, people, population, inhabitants.

——, *a.* 1. Rustic, rural.

2. Rude, rough, unrefined, unpolished, uncultivated, countrified.

Countryman, *n.* 1. Compatriot.

2. Rustic, peasant, swain, farmer, husbandman, clown, hind, boor, "hayseed."

County, *n.* Shire.

Coup-d'état, *n.* [Fr.] Master stroke of policy, stroke of statesmanship, stroke of sudden and forcible usurpation.

Coup-de-grace, *n.* [Fr.] Death-blow, decisive blow, finishing stroke, mercy-stroke.

Couple, *n.* 1. Brace, pair, two (*of the same kind*).

2. Man and wife, married pair.

3. Link, bond, tie, coupling, leash.

——, *v. t.* 1. Join, conjoin, connect, unite, pair, link together, yoke.

2. Marry, wed.

——, *v. i.* 1. Unite, pair.

2. Copulate, embrace.

Couplet, *n.* Two verses (*especially that rhyme*), pair of rhymes, distich.

Courage, *n.* Fearlessness, dauntlessness, derring-do, bravery, valor, gallantry, prowess, intrepidity, heroism, spirit, resolution, fortitude, hardihood, audacity, audaciousness, boldness, daring, mettle, manhood, pluck, nerve, "spunk."

Courageous, *a.* Fearless, undismayed, staunch, mettlesome, gallant, daring, valorous, chivalrous, valiant, bold, heroic, intrepid, dauntless, resolute, hardy, "nervy," "game," plucky, stout, lion-hearted, with a bold front. See BRAVE.

Courier, *n.* Messenger, express, runner.

Course, *n.* 1. Race, career, circuit, run.

2. Route, way, track, road.

3. Direction, bearing, point of compass, line of progress, path, track, tenor.

4. Round, beat, orbit, ambit.

5. Progress, process, sequence.

6. Regularity, order, succession, turn.

7. Deportment, conduct, behavior, line of conduct, manner of proceeding.

8. Series, system, methodical arrangement.

——, *v. t.* Pursue, hunt, chase, run after, give chase to.

——, *v. i.* Run, move swiftly.

Courser, *n.* Racer, race-horse, swift steed.

Court, *n.* 1. Royal household, princely retinue.

2. Judicial tribunal, court of justice, bar.

3. Courtyard, inclosed area. quadrangle, *patio.*

4. Solicitation(s), addresses, civilities, flattering attention, respects, homage.

——, *v. t.* 1. Flatter, coddle, try to please, endeavor to ingratiate one's self with, fawn upon, pay court to.

2. Woo, pay one's addresses to, make suit to, make up to, make love to.

3. Seek, solicit, strive to gain.

4. Invite, solicit, woo.

Courteous, *a.* Polite, civil, affable, urbane, complaisant, gracious, courtly, ceremonious, debonair, respectful, obliging, well-bred.

Courtesan, *n.* Prostitute, whore, harlot, strumpet, punk, wench, drag, trull, quean, rig, wanton, frail sister, Cyprian, night-walker, street-walker, lewd woman, woman of ill-fame, public woman, demi-rep, *fille de joie,* Messalina, Delilah, *grisette,* member of the *demi-monde.*

Courtesy, *n.* Politeness, courteousness, civility, urbanity, complaisance, affability, good-breeding, elegance of manners.

Courtly, *a.* Polished, elegant, polite. See COURTEOUS.

Courtship, *n.* Wooing.

Courtyard, *n.* Court, quadrangle, inclosed area.

Cove, *n.* Inlet, bight, small bay.

Covenant, *n.* Agreement, bargain, contract, compact, stipulation, arrangement, treaty, convention, concordat, pact.

Cover, *v. t.* 1. Overspread, overlay.

2. Conceal, hide, secrete, cloak, veil, curtain, screen, shroud, mask, disguise.

3. Shield, shelter, protect, guard, defend.

4. Clothe, invest, envelop, sheathe, case, jacket, fold up, inwrap, wrap up.

5. Comprehend, embrace, include, comprise, contain, embody.

COVER, *n.* 1. Covering, tegument, integument, capsule, top, case.

2. Screen, veil, disguise, cloak.

3. Shelter, protection, guard, defence, shield, safeguard.

4. Underwood, underbrush, shrubbery, undergrowth, thicket, woods.

5. Plate, dish.

Covercle, *n.* Lid, small cover.

Covering, *n.* Cover, tegument, integument, capsule, top, case, coating, crust, overlay, sheathing.

Coverlet, } *n.* Counterpane.
Coverlid, }

Covert, *n.* 1. Thicket, shade, shrubbery, underwood.

2. Shelter, refuge, asylum, harbor, sanctuary, retreat, defence, hiding-place.

Covert, *a.* Hidden, concealed, secret, disguised, clandestine, underhand, sly, insidious, stealthy.

Covet, *v. t.* 1. Desire, long for, aim after, aspire to.

2. Desire inordinately, long for enviously, lust after, hanker after.

Covetous, *a.* Enviously desirous, inordinately desirous, avaricious.

Covetousness, *n.* Avarice, cupidity, inordinate desire *or* greed, greed of gain.

Covey, *n.* 1. Brood.

2. Flock.

3. Set, company, party, bevy.

Covinous, *a.* (*Law.*) Fraudulent, deceitful, dishonest, deceptive, collusive.

COW, *n.* Heifer, bovine.

Cow, *v. t.* Overawe, intimidate, frighten, daunt, abash, discourage, dishearten, break, subdue by fear.

Coward, *n.* Dastard, poltroon, caitiff, craven, recreant, milksop, "wheyface."

Cowardice, *n.* Pusillanimity, poltroonery, timidity, fear, cowardliness, the white feather.

Cowardly, *a.* Pusillanimous, dastardly, craven, fearful, timorous, timid, coward, recreant, base, faint-hearted, chicken-hearted, white-livered, showing the white feather.

Cower, *v. i.* Crouch, cringe, fawn, stoop, squat, bend the knee.

Coxcomb, *n.* Beau, fop, dandy, popinjay, exquisite, jackanapes, *petit-maître*, man of dress; vain, showy fellow.

Coy, *a.* Modest, diffident, shy, shrinking, timid, bashful, reserved, distant, demure.

Cozen, *v. t.* Cheat, trick, defraud, deceive, swindle, chouse, dupe, gull, overreach, circumvent, beguile, victimize, take in, impose upon.

Cozenage, *n.* Fraud, deceit, artifice, trickery, deception, imposition, imposture, duplicity, guile, double dealing.

Cozy, *a.* 1. Snug, comfortable, easy.

2. [*Eng.*] Chatty, talkative, social, conversable.

Crabbed, *a.* 1. Sour, tart, rough, acrid.

2. Morose, surly, testy, touchy, cross, growling, snarling, snappish, cantankerous, waspish, petulant, peevish, churlish, harsh, acrimonious, caustic, captious, censorious, splenetic, out of sorts, ill-tempered.

3. Difficult, perplexing, trying, unmanageable, tough, intractable, hard to deal with.

Crabbedness, *n.* 1. Sourness, roughness, tartness, acridity, acridness.

2. Asperity, acerbity, moroseness,

sullenness, moodiness, churlishness, harshness, ill-temper, acrimoniousness.

3. Difficulty, perplexity, intractability.

CRACK, *n.* 1. Break, cleft, breach, chink, fissure, fracture, crevice, cranny, opening, rift, rent, split.

2. Report, clap, pop, burst, explosion.

3. Snap (*of a whip*).

——, *v. t.* 1. Break (*partially*).

2. Split, chop, cleave, rend asunder.

3. Snap (*as a whip*).

4. Craze, drive insane, madden.

——, *v. i.* 1. Break, split, burst, chap, open in chinks.

2. [With *of.*] Brag, bluster, vapor, vaunt, boast, gasconade, crow.

——, *a.* (*Colloq.*) Excellent, capital, tip-top, first-rate, first-class.

Cracked, *a.* 1. Broken, crackled, split.

2. Crazed, crazy, crack-brained, insane, demented, deranged, flighty, with a bee in the bonnet, with a bee in the head.

Crackle, *v. i.* Decrepitate, crepitate, snap.

Craft, *n.* 1. Skill, ability, talent, power, cleverness, dexterity, tact, aptitude, aptness, expertness, readiness.

2. Artifice, artfulness, shrewdness, guile, deceit, deceitfulness, deception, subtlety, cunning, craftiness.

3. Art, handicraft, trade, employment, business, vocation, calling, avocation.

4. Vessel.

Craftsman, *n.* Artisan, mechanic, artificer, workman, hand operative, handicraftsman.

Crafty, *a.* Cunning, artful, deceitful, sly, arch, subtle, shrewd, wily, intriguing, tricky, crooked, diplomatic, Machiavelian.

Crag, *n.* 1. Rough, steep rock.

2. Neck, throat.

Craggy, *a.* Cragged, rugged, rough, jagged, broken, uneven, scraggy.

Cram, *v. t.* 1. Stuff, gorge, glut, fill full, fill to repletion.

2. Crowd, press, compress.

3. Prepare for examination, grind, coach.

——, *v. i.* Eat to satiety, eat greedily, stuff, gorge *or* glut one's self, gluttonize.

Cramp, *n.* 1. Spasm, crick, convulsion.

2. (*Rare.*) Check, restriction, restraint, obstruction.

——, *v. t.* 1. Affect with spasms, convulse.

2. Restrain, obstruct, hinder, check, confine.

3. Fasten with a cramp, confine *or* hold with a cramp *or* cramp-iron.

4. Stretch *or* shape with a cramp, fashion with a boot-cramp.

Cranium, *n.* Skull, brain-pan.

Crank, *n.* 1. Turning-handle.

2. Bend, turn, winding, involution, twist, quirk.

——, *a.* 1. Easy to be overset, unsteady.

2. Shaky, crazy, loose, disjointed.

——, *v. i.* Bend, wind, turn, twist, wind in and out, crankle, crinkle.

Cranny, *n.* Cleft, crack, fissure, chink, crevice, rift, gap, break, breach, interstice, opening.

Crapulous, *a.* (*Rare.*) Crapulent, drunken, drunk, inebriated, intoxicated, tipsy, surfeited with drink.

Crash, *v. t.* and *v. i.* Shatter, shiver, smash, dash in pieces, splinter.

——, *n.* Shattering sound, splintering uproar, rending, shivering noise.

Crass, *a.* Gross, coarse, thick, unabated, unrefined, raw.

Crate, *n.* Hamper.

Cravat, *n.* Neckcloth, neckerchief, necktie.

Crave, *v. t.* 1. Entreat, beseech, beg, solicit, implore, supplicate.

2. Desire, long for, hunger for, wish for, yearn for, hanker after.

Craven, *n.* Dastard, coward, poltroon, recreant, milksop.

Craving, *n.* Longing, hungering, yearning, hankering, strong desire.

Craw, *n.* Crop, first stomach (*of a bird*).

Crawl, *v. i.* Creep.

Crayon, *n.* 1. Pencil, chalk.

2. Crayon-drawing, pastel.

Craze, *v. t.* 1. Make crazy, make insane, madden, drive wild, derange.

2. Impair, weaken, confuse, throw into disorder, disarrange.

Crazy, *a.* 1. Shattered, broken, tottering, rickety, shaky, crank, worn out, out of order.

2. Insane, distracted, mad, lunatic, demented, deranged, delirious, crackbrained, cracked, crazed, out of one's head, out of one's senses, out of one's wits.

Cream, *n.* Choice part, best part.

Create, *v. t.* 1. Originate, procreate, bring into being, call into existence.

2. Produce, cause, form, fashion, design, invent, occasion.

3. Make, appoint, constitute.

Creation, *n.* 1. Invention, origination, formation, production.

2. Universe, cosmos.

3. Appointment, constitution, nomination, establishment.

Creator, *n.* 1. Originator, maker, author, fashioner, designer, inventor.

2. The First Cause, the Maker, the Supreme Original. See God.

Creature, *n.* 1. Being (*animate* or *inanimate*), created being.

2. Animal, living being.

3. Man, person.

4. Dependant, retainer, vassal, parasite, minion, hanger-on.

5. Wretch, miscreant, piece of baseness.

Credence, *n.* Belief, acceptance, credit, trust, faith, confidence, reliance.

Credentials, *n. pl.* Testimonials, vouchers, certificates, passport.

Credibility, *n.* Trustworthiness, credibleness.

Credible, *a.* Trustworthy, reliable, to be believed, worthy of belief, not improbable.

Credibleness, *n.* Trustworthiness, credibility.

CREDIT, *n.* 1. Belief, trust, faith, confidence, credence, reliance.

2. Reputableness, esteem, regard, good repute, good reputation, high character.

3. Influence (*of a good name*), power.

4. Merit, honor, proof of desert.

5. Trust (*in future payment*), loan.

6. Money due, securities, evidence of debt (*on the part of others*).

——, *v. t.* 1. Believe, give faith to, put faith in, rely upon, confide in, doubt not, make no doubt of, take upon credit.

2. Place to the credit of, carry to the credit of one's account, enter upon the credit side.

3. Trust (*for future payment*), loan (*on trust* or *security*).

Creditable, *a.* Reputable, honorable, estimable.

Credulity, *n.* Ease in believing, readiness to believe (*on slight evidence*), credulousness.

Credulous, *a.* Easily convinced, too ready to believe, over-trustful, lax in seeking evidence, easily duped.

Creed, *n.* Belief, tenets, dogmas, doctrines, system of opinions, summary of belief, *Credo.*

Creek, *n.* 1. Inlet, cove, bight, small bay.

2. Rivulet, small river.

Creep, *v. i.* 1. Crawl.

2. Steal, glide stealthily, come unnoticed.

3. Fawn, cringe, grovel, play the sycophant.

Creeping, *a.* 1. Crawling.

2. Fawning, sycophantic.

3. (*Bot.*) Growing on the ground *or* on supports, trailing, running.

Crenate, *a.* Notched, indented, scalloped.

Crepitate, *v. i.* Crackle, snap, decrepitate.

Crescent, *n.* 1. New moon, moon in her first quarter.

2. Figure of the new moon, lune, lunule, demilune, half-moon.

3. [With *The* prefixed.] Turkish power, Ottoman Empire, Sublime Porte; Mohammedanism, Islamism, Islam.

——, *a.* Growing, enlarging, increasing.

Crescent-shaped, *a.* (*Bot.*) Lunate, lunated, lunular.

Crest, *n.* 1. Tuft, plume, comb, topknot.

2. Top, crown, summit, ridge, highest part.

3. Armorial bearings, device.

Crested, *a.* 1. With a crest, tufted.

2. (*Bot.*) Cristate.

Crestfallen, *a.* Discouraged, disheartened, dispirited, depressed, dejected, desponding, chap-fallen, melancholy, sad, downhearted, downcast, cast down, low-spirited, in low spirits.

Crevasse, *n.* [Fr.] Crevice, gap, opening, break, rent, chasm.

Crevice, *n.* Fissure, chink, rift, gap, cleft, crack, cranny, interstice.

Crew, *n.* 1. Ship's company.

2. Company, gang, band, set, horde, party, throng, mob, crowd.

Crib, *n.* 1. Rack, manger, feeding-place.

2. Bin, bunker.

3. Child's bed.

4. Theft, piece of plunder, plagiarism.

——, *v. t.* 1. Enclose (*as in a crib*), cage, encage, confine, imprison, shut up.

2. Pilfer, purloin.

Crick, *n.* Spasm, cramp, convulsion.

CRIME, *n.* 1. Felony, aggravated misdemeanor, gross offence (*against law*) *such as* arson, rape, robbery, embezzlement, murder, etc.

2. Sin, transgression, iniquity, wickedness, unrighteousness, wrong, delinquency (*of a violent* or *high-handed nature*).

Criminal, *a.* 1. Grossly contrary to law, illegal, felonious, tending to crime, stained by crime.

2. Culpable, guilty, wicked, iniquitous, flagitious.

——, *n.* Culprit, delinquent, offender, transgressor, trespasser, malefactor, convict, felon.

Criminality, *n.* Guiltiness, guilt, culpability.

Criminate, *v. t.* 1. Accuse, charge, arraign, impeach, allege to be guilty.

2. Involve in crime, implicate in guilt, show guilty.

Crimination, *n.* Accusation, impeachment, arraignment, charge.

Crimp, *v. t.* 1. Curl, crisp.

2. Plait, form into ridges.

Cringe, *v. i.* Crouch, fawn, truckle, sneak, stoop, bend the knee.

Cringing, *a.* Crouching, fawning, servile, abject, sneaking, obsequious.

Crinkle, *v. i.* 1. Crankle, run in and out, wind, bend.

2. Wrinkle, curl, be corrugated.

——, *v. t.* Wrinkle, corrugate, curl.

Cripple, *n.* Lame man, lame woman.

——, *v. t.* 1. Lame, make lame.

2. Disable, weaken, impair, break down.

Crisis, *n.* 1. Acme, height, decisive turn, turning point, critical juncture.

2. Exigency, emergency, juncture, conjuncture, pass, strait, rub, pinch, push, critical situation.

Crisp, } *a.* 1. Brittle, friable.
Crispy, } 2. Curled, frizzled.

Crisp, *v. t.* Twist, curl.

Criterion, *n.* Standard, test, touchstone, measure, rule, canon.

Critic, *n.* 1. Reviewer, censor, connoisseur, judge (*of artistic merit*).

2. Censurer, caviler, carper.

Critical, *a.* 1. Exact, nice, accurate.

2. Censorious, carping, caviling, captious, exacting, nasute.

3. Determining, decisive, crucial, turning, important.

4. Dangerous, exigent, hazardous, imminent, momentous, dubious, precarious, ticklish.

Criticise, *v. t.* Examine and estimate (*as works of àrt* or *of literature*), remark upon (*with reference to merits and defects*), pass judgment upon, judge, appraise, evaluate.

Criticism, *n.* Critique, strictures, animadversion, appreciation, evaluation, review, critical remarks.

Critique, *n.* Criticism, review, critical examination, critical remarks, critical notice.

Croak, *v. i.* 1. Talk croakingly, talk hoarsely, mumble and groan.

2. Forebode, cry things down, be depreciatory, take a gloomy view of things.

Croaker, *n.* Decrier, depreciator, one that takes a gloomy view, alarmist, foreboder.

Crock, *n.* 1. Earthen jar, pot, piece of crockery.

2. Low seat, stool.

3. Soot, smut.

Crockery, *n.* Earthen-ware.

Crone, *n.* Old woman (*in contempt*), beldam, hag.

Crony, *n.* (*Colloq.*) Associate, intimate friend, bosom friend, "pal."

Crook, *n.* 1. Bend, flexure, curvature, turn.

2. Bent staff, shepherd's crook, bishop's crook or staff, crosier.

3. Trick, artifice, machination.

Crook, *v. t.* Bend, curve, incurvate, bow, inflect, make crooked.

——, *v. i.* Bend, curve, become crooked, wind, turn.

Crooked, *a.* 1. Bent, angular, curved, bowed, winding, zigzag.

2. Distorted, twisted, wry, awry, askew, aslant, deformed, disfigured.

3. Dishonest, unfair, dishonorable, knavish, unscrupulous, deceitful, devious, tricky, insidious, crafty, intriguing, diplomatic, Machiavelian.

Croon, *v. t.* Hum, sing softly, sing in a low tone.

Crop, *n.* 1. Harvest.

2. Craw, first stomach (*of a bird*).

——, *v. t.* 1. Lop, clip, cut off.

2. Gather, pluck, pick.

3. Browse, nibble, feed upon.

Cross, *n.* 1. Gibbet (*made of pieces of wood placed transversely*), crucifix, rood.

2. [With *The* prefixed.] Gospel, Christianity.

3. Trial, vexation, trouble, affliction, misfortune.

4. Intermixture (*of species*), hybrid, cross-breeding.

——, *a.* 1. Transverse, lying athwart.

2. Fretful, peevish, petulant, pettish, snappish, waspish, touchy, testy, crusty, churlish, crabbed, captious, ill-natured, morose, sulky, sullen, spleeny, surly, cynical, snarling, sour, ill-tempered, out of humor, "grouchy."

——, *v. t.* 1. Put across, put athwart.

2. Mark with a line *or* lines across.

3. Traverse, pass over, intersect.

4. Thwart, hinder, obstruct, interfere with.

5. Intermix, interbreed.

Cross-examine, *v. t.* Cross-question.

Cross-grained, *a.* Stubborn, obdurate, untractable, perverse, wayward, headstrong, refractory.

Crossing, *n.* Intersection, traversing, overpass, underpass.

Cross-question, *v. t.* Cross-examine.

Crosswise, *adv.* Across, transversely, over.

Crotch, *n.* Fork, angle, corner.

Crotchet, *n.* Whim, freak, quirk, vagary, whimsey, fancy, caprice, maggot in the brain.

Crotchety, *a.* Whimsical, fantastic, fantastical, odd, queer, fanciful, capricious, humorsome, wayward, fitful, freakish.

Crouch, *v. i.* 1. Crouch, squat, lie flat, stoop low, lie close to the ground.

2. Cower, cringe, fawn, truckle.

Croup, *n.* Rump (*especially of a horse*), buttocks, crupper.

Crow, *v. i.* Boast, brag, vaunt, bluster, swagger, vapor, triumph, gasconade, chuckle, exult.

Crowd, *n.* 1. Throng, multitude, concourse, press, "jam," host, herd, horde.

2. Rabble, mob, populace, vulgar herd, rout, pack, lower classes, lower orders, common people, *ignobile vulgus*, *profanum vulgus.*

Crowd, *v. t.* 1. Fill by compression, fill to excess.

2. Compress, cram, press, press together, jam, pack.

3. Throng about, press upon.

——, *v. i.* 1. Swarm, flock together, collect, congregate, herd, huddle, swarm, be numerous, come thick.

2. Press forward, make one's way, elbow one's way.

Crown, *n.* 1. Diadem.

2. Royalty, kingly power, sovereignty.

3. Coronet, coronal, garland, chaplet, wreath, laurel, bays.

4. Dignity, honor, reward, recompense, honorary distinction.

5. Top, summit, crest.

——, *v. t.* 1. Put a crown upon, invest with a crown.

2. Adorn, dignify, honor.

3. Recompense, reward, requite.

4. Perfect, complete, finish, consummate.

Crowning, *a.* Perfecting, finishing, consummating, completing, supremely dignifying.

Crucial, *a.* 1. Transverse, intersecting.

2. Severe, searching, trying, decisive, critical.

Cruciform, *a.* Cross-shaped, cruciate.

Crucify, *v. t.* 1. Put to death upon the cross.

2. Torture, sacrifice, immolate, annihilate, exterminate.

3. Subdue (*as the passions, by Christian principles*), overcome, mortify.

Crude, *a.* 1. Raw, uncooked, undressed, in a raw state, unworked.

2. Immature, unripe, harsh, rough.

3. Coarse, unrefined, crass.

4. Unpremeditated, indigested, immature, unpolished, rude, uncouth, awkward.

Crudeness, *n.* Rawness, crudity, coarseness, immaturity, awkwardness.

Crudity, *n.* Rawness. See CRUDENESS.

CRUEL, *a.* 1. Unmerciful, inhuman, merciless, unfeeling, uncompassionate, fell, dire, ruthless, barbarous, pitiless, relentless, unrelenting, inexorable, savage, ferocious, brutal, sanguinary, truculent, blood-thirsty, hard-hearted.

2. Severe, hard, sharp, bitter, cold, unfeeling.

Cruelty, *n.* Inhumanity, barbarity, ruthlessness, brutality, brutishness, ferocity, savageness, truculence, blood-thirstiness.

Cruet, *n.* Vial, cruse, caster.

Cruise, *v. i.* Rove over the sea, sail about.

——, *n.* Roving voyage.

Crumble, *v. t.* Crush, break to pieces, disintegrate, reduce to fragments.

——, *v. i.* 1. Fall to pieces, break into pieces, become disintegrated.

2. Perish, fall into decay.

Crumple, *v. t.* Wrinkle, rumple.

Cruse, *n.* Vial, cruet, caster.

CRUSH, *v. t.* [*The noun is Basic Eng.*]

1. Compress, squeeze, bruise, squash, contuse.

2. Break in pieces, crumble, disintegrate, comminute, bray, mash.

3. Demolish, break down, shatter, raze.

4. Overpower, overcome, overwhelm, subdue, quell, conquer.

Crust, *n.* Incrustation, hard coating.

Crusty, *a.* Touchy, testy, pettish, waspish, snappish, peevish, fretful, petulant, churlish, crabbed, froward, surly, morose, cynical, snarling, ill-tempered. See CROSS.

Cry, *v. i.* 1. Exclaim, clamor, call, make an outcry, cry out.

2. Weep, sob, shed tears, snivel, wail, whimper, "blubber."

3. Vociferate, shout, hoot, yell, roar, bawl, squall, scream, screech, squawk, squeal.

——, *v. t.* Proclaim, publish, make public, make proclamation of, blazon, blaze abroad.

CRY, *n.* 1. Exclamation, ejaculation, outcry, clamor, acclamation.

2. Plaint, lament, lamentation, crying, weeping.

3. Scream, shriek, screech, howl, yell, roar, bawl.

Cry down. Decry, depreciate, condemn.

Cry out. Exclaim, clamor.

Cry out against. Blame, censure, condemn, complain of, denounce.

Crypt, *n.* Vault, tomb, catacomb.

Cry up. Extol, commend, praise, laud.

Cub, *n.* 1. Whelp, young beast (*especially a young bear*).

2. [*In contempt.*] Child, young boy *or* young girl, brat.

Cube, *n.* Regular hexahedron, die.

Cucking-stool, *n.* Castigatory, trebuchet, tumbrel, ducking-stool.

Cuddle, *v. i.* Snuggle, nestle, squat, lie close, lie snug, move close together.

——, *v. t.* Hug, embrace, fondle, fold warmly up.

Cuddy, *n.* Dolt, clown, stupid fellow.

Cudgel, *n.* Club, bludgeon, bastinado, shillalah.

——, *v. t.* Cane, drub, thrash, baste, beat with a cudgel. See BEAT.

Cue, *n.* 1. Hint, suggestion, intimation, catchword, wink, nod.

2. Rod (*in billiards*).

Cuff, *n.* Blow, stroke, box, slap.

——, *v. t.* Beat, strike, buffet, box, slap.

Cuirass, *n.* Breastplate.

Cuisine, *n.* [Fr.] 1. Kitchen, cooking department.

2. Cookery, style of cooking.

Cul-de-sac, *n.* [Fr.] Blind alley, pocket, impasse.

Culinary, *a.* Cooking, kitchen.

Cull, *v. t.* 1. Select, elect, choose, pick, single out, fix upon, pitch upon, pick out.

2. Gather, pluck, collect, pick up.

Culmination, *n.* Acme, topmost point, zenith, climax.

Culpability, *n.* Blameworthiness, remissness, guilt, culpableness, blame, sinfulness, criminality.

Culpable, *a.* Blamable, censurable, reprehensible, transgressive, faulty, blameworthy, wrong.

Culprit, *n.* Criminal, malefactor, delinquent, felon.

Cult, *n.* 1. Homage, worship.

2. System *or* mode of worship, ceremonial, religious ceremonial, ritual.

Cultivate, *v. t.* 1. Till, prepare for crops, raise crops from, improve by husbandry, work.

2. Improve, refine, elevate, civilize, meliorate, make better, train, discipline, develop.

3. Study, investigate, pursue, search into.

4. Foster, cherish, promote, nourish, patronize.

Cultivation, *n.* 1. Tillage, tilth, farming, agriculture, husbandry, culture.

2. Improvement, refinement, elevation, civilization, culture.

3. Study, pursuit, investigation.

4. Fostering, cherishing, nourishing, promotion, patronage.

Culture, *n.* 1. Agriculture, tillage.

2. Improvement, refinement, cultivation, civilization.

Cumber, *v. t.* 1. Overload, oppress, clog, hamper, obstruct, encumber.

2. Distract, trouble, embarrass, perplex, plague, harass, worry, torment.

Cumbersome, *a.* 1. Burdensome, embarrassing, troublesome, vexatious, cumbrous.

2. Unwieldy, unmanageable, clumsy, awkward, inconvenient.

Cumulative, *a.* Continually increasing, successively gaining in force.

Cuneiform, *a.* Cuneate, wedge-shaped.

Cunning, *a.* 1. Crafty, artful, sly, astute, subtle, wily, shrewd, sharp, designing, intriguing, deceitful, tricky, crooked, diplomatic, Machiavelian.

2. Skilfully wrought, ingenious, curious.

3. [*Archaic* or *poetical*.] Skilled, dexterous, skilful.

——, *n.* 1. Craft, art, shrewdness, subtlety, artifice.

2. Craftiness, craft, artifice, deceit, deception, subtlety, intrigue, chicane, chicanery.

CUP, *n.* 1. Chalice, beaker, goblet, bowl, mug.

2. Draught, potion, cupful.

Cupboard, *n.* Buffet, china-closet, closet.

Cupidity, *n.* 1. Longing, avidity, hankering, greed, lust, strong desire.

2. Avarice, covetousness, inordinate desire of wealth.

Cups, *n. pl.* Orgies, revels, bacchanals, carousal, wassail, compotation, drinking-bout.

Curative, *a.* Remedial, sanatory, healing, restorative, medicinal.

Curator, *n.* Guardian, custodian, superintendent, keeper.

Curb, *n.* 1. Restraint, hindrance, bridle. See CHECK, 1.

2. Curb-stone, edge-stone.

3. Breast-wall, retaining-wall.

——, *v. t.* Check, restrain, control, repress, bridle, put under restraint, keep under, hold in check.

Curb-stone, *n.* Curb, edge-stone.

Curd, *n.* Caseine, coagulated milk, coagulum, clabber.

——, *v. t.* 1. Coagulate, convert into curds.

2. Thicken, coagulate, stiffen, chill, congeal.

——, *v. i.* 1. Coagulate, turn to curds.

2. Thicken, coagulate, stiffen, chill, congeal.

Cure, *n.* 1. Remedy, antidote, restorative, reparative, corrective, help, specific.

2. Healing, restoration.

3. Remedial treatment, method of treatment, therapy.

4. Spiritual charge *or* treatment, curacy.

——, *v. t.* 1. Remedy, heal, sanitate, restore.

2. Preserve (*from putrefaction*), prepare for preservation, as by drying, smoking, pickling, kippering.

Curiosity, *n.* 1. Inquisitiveness, inquiringness.

2. Phenomenon, wonder, marvel, rarity, curio, sight, spectacle.

Curious, *a.* 1. Inquisitive, scrutinizing, prying, peering.

2. Rare, singular, strange, unusual, unique, extraordinary, queer, out of the way.

3. Elegant, neat, nice, finished, skilful, cunning, well-wrought.

Curl, *n.* 1. Ringlet, curlicue, lovelock.

2. Sinuosity, winding, undulation, flexure, wave, waving.

——, *v. t.* 1. Crisp, turn in ringlets.

2. Writhe, wind, twist, coil.

3. Raise in waves.

——, *v. i.* Be bent into curls *or* waves, ripple, buckle, wind, twist, turn, writhe.

Curmudgeon, *n.* Miser, niggard, churl, hunks, skinflint, scrimp, lickpenny, screw, mean fellow, sordid wretch.

Currency, *n.* 1. Publicity, general reception.

2. Circulation, transmission from hand to hand.

3. Money; aggregate of coin, bills and notes; circulating medium.

Current, *a.* 1. Common, general, popular, rife, generally received, in every one's mouth.

2. Circulating (*as money*), passing from hand to hand.

3. Present, prevalent, existing, instant, now passing.

CURRENT, *n.* 1. Stream, moving volume (*of fluid*).

2. Tide, running water, race, undertow.

3. Course, progression.

Currently, *adv.* Generally, commonly, publicly, popularly.

Curry, *v. t.* 1. Dress (*tanned leather*).

2. Comb, clean with a comb *or* curry-comb.

3. Beat, drub, thrash, cudgel.

Curse, *v. t.* 1. Execrate, anathematize, "damn," denounce, invoke *or* imprecate evil upon, imprecate, maledict.

2. Blast, blight, doom, destroy, bring a curse upon.

3. Injure, vex, harass, torment, torture, scourge, plague, afflict, annoy.

——, *v. i.* Utter curses, blaspheme.

——, *n.* 1. Malediction, anathema, execration, imprecation, fulmination, denunciation, ban, malison.

2. Scourge, plague, torment, affliction,

trouble, vexation, annoyance, bitter pill, thorn in the side.

3. Sentence, condemnation, condemning sentence, ban, penalty.

Cursed, *a.* 1. Accursed, blighted, banned, curse-laden.

2. Detestable, hateful, abominable, execrable, villanous.

3. Scourging, plaguing, tormenting, annoying, troublesome, vexatious, "confounded," "plaguy."

Cursory, *a.* Hasty, slight, superficial, careless, desultory, transient, passing, brief.

Curt, *a.* 1. Short, brief, concise, terse, laconic.

2. Short and dry, crusty, snappish, short and rude, tart.

Curtail, *v. t.* 1. Shorten, abridge, retrench, lop, cut short.

2. Diminish, lessen, decrease.

Curtailment, *n.* Abbreviation, abridgment, contraction, shortening, reduction, retrenchment, cutting off *or* down.

CURTAIN, *n.* Hanging fabric, screen, drop, veil, arras, portière, lambrequin, shade.

Curvature, *n.* 1. Bending, bend, flexure, camber, crook, curvity, curve, incurvation, arcuation.

2. Rate of curvature *or* inflection.

CURVE, *n.* Bend. See CURVATURE, 1.

——, *v. t.* and *v. i.* Bend, crook, inflect, turn, wind.

Curvet, *v. i.* 1. Leap, bound, vault.

2. Caper, frisk.

——, *n.* 1. Leap, bound.

2. Caper, frolic, prank.

CUSHION, *n.* Pillow, pad, bolster, hassock, woolsack.

Cusp, *n.* Point, angle, horn.

Cuspidate, } *a.* (*Bot.*) Pointed, acute,
Cuspidated, } sharp, acuminate, acuminated.

Custodian, *n.* Guardian, keeper, curator, warden, sacristan, superintendent.

Custody, *n.* 1. Keeping, care, watch, guardianship, protection, safe-keeping.

2. Confinement, imprisonment, prison, durance, duress.

Custom, *n.* 1. Habit (*of a majority*), usage, fashion, practice, rule, consuetude, wont. See HABIT.

2. Form, formality, observance.

3. Patronage.

4. Tax, impost, duty, tribute, toll.

Customary, *a.* Usual, common, wonted, habitual, accustomed, conventional, consuetudinary, nomic, prescriptive.

Customer, *n.* Purchaser, buyer, patron.

Cut, *v. t.* 1. Divide *or* sever (*by an edged tool*), chop, make an incision in, wound

(*with a cutting instrument*), incise, **gash**, chop, cleave, lance, slit, slice.

2. Sculpture, carve, chisel.

3. Cross, intersect.

4. Wound, hurt, touch, move, pierce.

5. (*Colloq.*) Slight (*by not recognizing*), ignore.

CUT, *n.* 1. Gash, incision, nick, **slit**, groove.

2. Channel, passage.

3. Slice, piece.

4. Sarcasm, fling, taunt, cutting remark.

5. Fashion, style, form, shape.

Cut capers. Frolic, be merry, be frolicsome, play pranks, cut didos.

Cut down. 1. Fell.

2. Diminish, lessen, abridge, abbreviate, curtail, retrench.

Cuticle, *n.* Epidermis, scarf-skin.

Cut out. 1. Remove (*by cutting*), excise.

2. Shape, form, fashion, contrive, prepare, lay out, plan.

3. Outdo, excel, surpass, take precedence of. See BEAT.

4. Debar, hinder, prevent.

Cutpurse, *n.* Pickpocket, thief, robber.

Cut short. 1. Bring to a sudden close, end abruptly.

2. Check suddenly, hinder from proceeding.

3. Abridge, diminish.

Cut-throat, *n.* Murderer, assassin, ruffian, bravo.

Cutting, *a.* 1. Sharp, keen.

2. Severe, sarcastic, satirical, wounding.

Cycle, *n.* Period, circle of time, revolution of time, round of years.

Cyclopædia, *n.* Encyclopædia.

Cyclopean, *a.* Gigantic, colossal, vast, enormous, immense, Herculean.

Cynic, *n.* 1. Follower of Diogenes.

2. Misanthrope, man-hater.

Cynical, *a.* 1. Carping, censorious, satirical, sarcastic, captious, snarling, snappish, waspish, pettish, petulant, fretful, peevish, touchy, testy, crusty, churlish, crabbed, cross, morose, surly, ill-tempered, ill-natured.

2. Contemptuous, derisive, scornful, bitterly unbelieving, pessimistic, misanthropic.

Cynosure, *n.* 1. Lesser Bear, Ursa Minor.

2. Point *or* centre of attraction.

Cyprian, *n.* Prostitute, harlot, whore, drab, strumpet, night-walker, lewd woman, woman of the town, woman of ill-fame. See COURTESAN.

Cyst, *n.* Pouch, sac.

D

Dab, *v. t.*   1. Strike, slap, box.
   2. Pat, strike gently.
——, *n.*   1. Blow, stroke, pat.
   2. Lump, pat, lumpy mass.
   3. (*Colloq.*) Adept, expert, proficient, master hand, capital hand, nice hand, good hand, "dabster."

Dabble, *v. t.*   Wet, spatter, sprinkle, moisten, dip, soak.
——, *v. i.*   1. Play in water, splash about, puddle.
   2. Work superficially, make slight efforts, potter, smatter, trifle.

Dabbler, *n.*   Sciolist, quack, superficial trifler, potterer, dilettante.

Dabster, *n.*   (*Colloq.*) Expert, adept, dab.

Dædalian, *a.*   Intricate, maze-like, mazy, dædal.

Daft, *a.*   [Scotch.]   1. Stupid, silly, foolish, delirious, insane, absurd.
   2. Playful, frolicsome, mirthful, merry, sportive.

Dagger, *n.*   Poniard, dirk, stiletto.

Daggle, *v. t.*   Draggle, bemire, befoul, soil, dirty.

Daily, *a.*   Diurnal, quotidian.

Dainty, *a.*   1. Delicious, savory, nice, delicate, tender, palatable, luscious, toothsome.
   2. Elegant, exquisite, choice, delicate, beautiful, neat, fine.
   3. Fastidious, squeamish, scrupulous, over-nice.
——, *n.*   Delicacy, tidbit, titbit, nice bit, choice morsel, delicate morsel.

Dale, *n.*   Vale, valley, bottom, dell, glen, dingle.

Dalliance, *n.*   Caressing, fondling, endearments, billing and cooing.

Dally, *v. i.*   1. Trifle, dawdle, lose time, waste time, idle away time, fritter away time.
   2. Fondle, toy, interchange caresses.

DAMAGE, *n.*   Injury, harm, hurt, detriment, mischief, loss.
——, *v. t.*   Injure, impair, hurt, harm, mar.

Damages, *n. pl.*   Indemnity, satisfaction, fine, forfeiture.

Dame, *n.*   Mistress, matron, lady, madam.

Damn, *v. t.*   1. Condemn, judge to be guilty.
   2. (*Theol.*) Doom to perdition, doom to eternal punishment, punish eternally.
   3. (*Metaphorical.*) Condemn, doom, put down, ruin, kill.

Damnable, *a.*   Odious, detestable, execrable, hateful, abominable, outrageous, atrocious, cursed, accursed.

Damp, *n.*   1. Moisture, vapor, fog, dampness, dank.
   2. Noxious exhalation, choke-damp *or* fire-damp.
   3. Depression, dejection, chill.
——, *a.*   Moist, humid, dank, wet.
——, *v. t.*   1. Moisten, dampen.
   2. Check, repress, restrain, moderate, allay, abate.
   3. Chill, cool, deaden, depress, deject.

Dampen, *v. t.*   Moisten, damp.

Damper, *n.*   1. Check, hindrance, obstacle, impediment, lion in the way.
   2. Discouragement, depression, depressing influence, damp, wet blanket, cold water.

Damsel, *n.*   Maiden, maid, girl, lass, lassie, miss, young lady.

Dance, *n.*   Measured movement, figured and rhythmic motion, waltz, cotillion, etc.
——, *v. i.*   1. Step rhythmically, move to music, take part in a dance, waltz, pirouette, etc.
   2. Frisk, caper, hop about.
——, *v. t.*   Dandle, toss up and down, bob.

Dandle, *v. t.*   1. Dance, toss up and down.
   2. Fondle, caress, pet, amuse with trifles, play with.

Dandy, *n.*   Beau, fox, coxcomb, "dude," exquisite, popinjay, macaroni, jackanapes, jack-a-dandy, man milliner, vain fellow, *cicisbeo*.

Dandyism, *n.*   Foppishness, foppery, man millinery.

DANGER, *n.*   Peril, hazard, risk, jeopardy, venture.

Dangerous, *a.*   Perilous, hazardous, unsafe, critical, ticklish, risky.

Dangle, *v. i.*   1. Swing, hang loose, hang pendulous.
   2. Fawn, hang about, be obsequious.
——, *v. t.*   Swing, make oscillate, pendulate, wave pendulously.

Dank, *a.*   Moist, damp, humid, wet.

Dapper, *a.*   1. Active, lively, brisk, agile, nimble, spry, smart, quick, alert, ready.
   2. Spruce, nice, neat, trim, pretty.

Dapple, *a.*   Variegated, spotted, dappled.
——, *v. t.*   Variegate, spot, diversify.

Dare, *v. i.*   Venture, presume, make bold, have courage, be bold enough, be not afraid.
——, *v. t.*   Brave, defy, challenge.

Dare-devil, *n.*   Desperado, rash adventurer, reckless *or* desperate fellow.
——, *a.*   Reckless, rash, inconsiderate.

Daring, *a.*   Bold, adventurous, fearless, brave, intrepid, valorous, valiant, courageous, gallant, chivalrous, doughty, heroic, undaunted, dauntless.

Daring, *n.* Boldness, intrepidity, valor. See BRAVERY, COURAGE.

DARK, *a.* 1. Unilluminated, unenlightened, dusky, caliginous, shadowy, rayless, sunless, darksome, lurid, murky, cloudy, shady, umbrageous, atramentous, tenebrous, inky, overcast, black, ebon, swart, Cimmerian, pitchy.

2. Mysterious, obscure, opaque, unillumined, incomprehensible, unintelligible, enigmatical, mystic, mystical, recondite, occult, transcendental, abstruse, cabalistic.

3. Gloomy, disheartening, discouraging, cheerless, dismal, funereal.

4. Untaught, ignorant, unlettered, rude, darkened, benighted.

5. Wicked, atrocious, infamous, foul, nefarious, flagitious, horrible, damnable, vile, infernal.

——, *n.* 1. Darkness, obscurity, want of light, murkiness, dusk.

2. Concealment, secrecy, privacy.

3. Ignorance, blindness, want of knowledge.

Darken, *v. t.* 1. Obscure, eclipse, cloud, dim, shade, shadow, make dark, make dim.

2. Gloom, make gloomy, sadden, depress, damp, chill.

3. Benight, make ignorant, stultify, stupefy.

4. Perplex, obscure, make intricate.

5. Sully, stain, dull, dim, defile.

——, *v. i.* Grow dark.

Darkling, *a.* In the dark, obscure, mysterious, mystic, hidden, concealed.

Darkness, *n.* 1. Obscurity, dimness, dark, want of light. See DARK, *a.* 1.

2. Ignorance, blindness, want of knowledge.

3. Gloom, despondency, cheerlessness, joylessness.

Darling, *n.* Favorite, idol, pet, dear, love, sweetheart, dear one.

——, *a.* Favorite, beloved, dear, precious, much loved.

Dart, *v. t.* 1. Hurl, throw, launch, jaculate, let fly.

2. Emit, shoot, send off.

——, *v. i.* Rush, fly swiftly, spring, "scoot," dartle.

Dash, *v. t.* 1. Strike violently, hurl forcibly.

2. Disappoint, frustrate, thwart, ruin, destroy, shatter, spoil.

3. Surprise, confound, abash, put to shame.

——, *v. i.* Rush, dart, fly swiftly.

——, *n.* 1. Stroke, blow.

2. Rush, onset, sudden advance.

3. Infusion, tinge, tincture, sprinkling, spice, touch, smack, little, small quantity.

4. Spirit, vigor, energy, verve, *élan.*

5. Flourish, show, ostentatious display.

Dashing, *a.* 1. Rushing, precipitate, impetuous, headlong.

2. Spirited, showy, brilliant, gay.

Dastard, *n.* Coward, poltroon, craven, recreant, milksop.

——, *a.* Cowardly, pusillanimous, craven, recreant, coward, cowering, base, dastardly.

Dastardly, *a.* Cowardly. See DASTARD.

Data, *n. pl.* Facts, premises, given conditions.

Date, *n.* Time, epoch, era, age.

——, *v. t.* Fix the date of, note the time of, affix a date to.

——, *v. i.* Begin, be reckoned, be dated.

Daub, *v. t.* Smear, besmear, plaster, cover, bedaub, begrime, soil, sully, defile, deface.

——, *n.* 1. Coarse painting.

2. Smear, smirch, smeary mass.

Dauby, *a.* Adhesive, viscous, viscid, glutinous, smeary, sticky.

DAUGHTER, *n.* (*Basic Eng.*) Stepdaughter, daughter-in-law.

Daunt, *v. t.* Check (*by alarm*), thwart, deter *or* stop from one's purpose, frighten off, intimidate, discourage, crush the courage of, dismay, appall, cow, tame, subdue.

Dauntless, *a.* Indomitable, unconquerable, unaffrighted, undaunted, undismayed, not to be daunted *or* dismayed, fearless, intrepid, bold, brave, daring, courageous, gallant, valiant, valorous, doughty, chivalrous, heroic.

Dawdle, *v. i.* Trifle, dally, fiddle, potter, quiddle, waste time, idle away time, fritter away time, fool away time.

Dawdler, *n.* Idler, trifler, lounger, laggard, drone, sluggard, slow-back, inefficient person.

Dawn, *v. i.* 1. Break, begin to be light, grow light.

2. Appear, open, break, begin to appear.

——, *n.* Daybreak, cockcrowing, dayspring, dawning, daypeep, peep of day, prime of day, first blush of morning, break of day.

Dawning, *n.* 1. See DAWN, *n.*

2. Beginning, first appearance.

DAY, *n.* 1. Daytime (*between sunrise and sunset*).

2. Sunshine, daylight, sunlight, light of day.

3. Lifetime, time, epoch, age, generation.

4. Appointed time, set time, promised time.

Daybreak, *n.* Dawn, dawning, cockcrowing, dayspring, daypeep, break of day, peep of day.

Day-dream, *n.* Dream, conceit, idle fancy, visionary scheme, castle in the air, castle in Spain.

Daylight, *n.* Sunlight, sunshine, day, light of day, light of heaven.

Daze, *v. t.* 1. Dazzle, blind.

2. Bewilder, confuse, confound, perplex, stupefy, stun.

Dazzle, *v. t.* 1. Daze, blind (*by excess of light*).

2. Astonish, surprise, overpower, confound (*by splendor* or *brilliancy*).

——, *n.* 1. Brightness, brilliancy, splendor, dazzling light.

2. Meretricious brilliancy *or* display, false splendor, surface show.

DEAD, *a.* 1. Lifeless, breathless, inanimate, deceased, defunct, departed, gone, gone to one's last home, gathered to one's fathers.

2. Dull, frigid, cold, torpid, inert, unfeeling, callous, obtuse, indifferent, lukewarm.

3. Vapid, tasteless, insipid, flat, stagnant.

4. Unemployed, useless, unprofitable.

——, *n.* Depth, midst, darkest *or* coldest *or* gloomiest period.

Deaden, *v. t.* 1. Weaken, impair, abate, restrain, retard, dull, damp, dampen, muffle, mute, smother.

2. Blunt, benumb, paralyze, obtund, hebetate, make insensible.

Dead-lock, *n.* Complete standstill, insoluble difference.

Deadly, *a.* 1. Mortal, fatal, destructive, deleterious, noxious, murderous, lethal.

2. Implacable, rancorous, sanguinary, mortal.

Deaf, *a.* Without hearing, hard of hearing.

Deafen, *v. t.* 1. Make deaf, deprive of hearing.

2. Stun, confuse with clamor.

Deal, *n.* Quantity, degree, extent, lot.

——, *v. t.* Distribute, give, bestow, dispense, apportion, allot, divide, share, deal out, dole out, mete out.

——, *v. i.* Traffic, trade, do business, have commerce.

Dealer, *n.* Trader, trafficker, merchant, vendor, -monger (*in compounds,* as balladmonger).

Deal in. 1. Have to do with, be engaged in, practise.

2. Trade *or* traffic in, buy and sell.

Dealing, *n.* 1. Conduct, behavior, action.

2. Commerce, intercourse, business, trade, traffic.

DEAR, *a.* 1. Costly, expensive, high-priced, at a high price, of great price.

2. Precious, beloved, darling, much loved, highly esteemed *or* valued.

Dearth, *n.* 1. Scarcity, insufficiency, deficiency, short supply.

2. Need, want, lack, famine, short commons.

DEATH, *n.* Decease, demise, dying, dissolution, departure, exit, end of life, King of terrors, debt of nature.

Death-like, *a.* Cadaverous, pale, wan, ghastly.

Debacle, *n.* 1. Breakdown, collapse, cataclysm.

2. Rout, wild flight, stampede.

Debar, *v. t.* Exclude, prohibit, prevent, hinder, restrain, withhold, shut out.

Debark, *v. i.* Land, disembark, go on shore, come to land, leave ship.

Debase, *v. t.* 1. Lower, depress, reduce, deteriorate, impair, vitiate, injure, pervert, alloy.

2. Degrade, abase, disgrace, dishonor, humble, humiliate, shame, mortify, bring low, take down.

3. Contaminate, taint, defile, pollute, foul, befoul, corrupt, soil.

Debasement, *n.* 1. Deterioration, vitiation, adulteration, perversion.

2. Abasement, degradation, humiliation, depravation, corruption, pollution, contamination, defilement.

Debatable, *a.* Disputable, open to discussion.

Debate, *n.* 1. Disputation, controversy, discussion.

2. Altercation, contest, contention, dispute, logomachy, strife of words, war of words.

——, *v. t.* 1. Discuss, argue, dispute, contest, canvass.

2. Battle for, contest, combat for, contend for, contest by arms.

——, *v. i.* Argue, contend, wrangle, dispute, deliberate, hold an argument.

Debauch, *v. t.* 1. Corrupt, vitiate, deprave, pollute.

2. Seduce, corrupt (to lewdness), deflower, rob of virginity.

——, *n.* 1. Debauchery, excess, intemperance, dissipation, dissoluteness, licentiousness, lewdness, lust *or* gluttony.

2. Potation, compotation, revels, revelry, orgies, bacchanals, saturnalia,

carousal, drinking-bout, drunken frolic, spree.

3. Orgy, indulgence in lust, wantoning, excesses, bestial indulgence.

Debauchee, *n.* Libertine, rake, voluptuary, profligate, man of pleasure, *roué*.

Debauchery, *n.* 1. Excesses, dissipation, dissoluteness.

2. Licentiousness, lewdness. See DEBAUCH, *n.*

Debilitate, *v. t.* Weaken, enervate, enfeeble, exhaust, prostrate, relax, render weak, make languid.

Debility, *n.* Weakness, feebleness, languor, prostration, exhaustion, enervation, imbecility, infirmity, frailty, loss of strength.

Debonair, *a.* 1. Courteous, affable, polite, refined, civil, urbane, complaisant, obliging, gracious, easy, kind, well-bred.

2. Light-hearted, buoyant, vivacious, sparkling, sprightly, cheery, bright, lightsome.

3. Elegant, graceful, lithe, easy, of fine bearing.

Débris, *n.* [Fr.] Rubbish, fragments, ruins, remains, *detritus*.

DEBT, *n.* 1. Due, obligation, liability, debit, arrears.

2. Trespass, offence, transgression, sin, fault, shortcoming, misdoing.

Debut, *n.* [Fr.] First appearance, coming-out.

Decadence, } *n.* Decay, decline, fall, declension, degeneracy, caducity.
Decadency, }

Decamp, *v. i.* 1. Break up camp, march away, march off, move off.

2. Flee, fly, escape, hasten away, run away, go away, make off, pack off, steal away.

Decant, *v. t.* Pour off.

Decapitate, *v. t.* Behead, decollate, guillotine, deprive of the head, bring to the scaffold, bring to the block.

Decapitation, *n.* Beheading, decollation.

Decay, *v. i.* 1. Decline, fail, deteriorate, disintegrate, wither, waste, perish, be impaired, waste away, fall into ruin.

2. Rot, putrefy, decompose, be spoiled.

——, *n.* Decline, decadence, declension, disintegration, dilapidation, ruin, decrepitude, falling off, deterioration, degeneracy, caducity.

Decease, *n.* Demise, dying. See DEATH.

——, *v. i.* Depart. See DIE.

Deceased, *a.* Dead, defunct, departed, gone, lost, late.

Deceit, *n.* Deception, fraud, imposition, imposture, finesse, artifice, duplicity, guile, trickery, chicanery, cozenage,

cheating, double-dealing, crooked ways, dark ways, underhandedness, deceitfulness.

Deceitful, *a.* 1. Deceptive, delusive, illusive, illusory, fallacious, misleading, counterfeit, hollow, insidious.

2. Full of deceit, dissembling, false, fraudulent, designing, cunning, underhanded, circumventive, evasive, "dodgy," insincere, tricky, wily, guileful, double, double-faced, double-hearted, hypocritical.

Deceive, *v. t.* Delude, cheat, defraud, dupe, gull, cozen, fool, befool, trick, circumvent, overreach, chouse, beguile, hoodwink, hoax, humbug, outwit, impose upon, make a fool of, play a trick upon, pull wool over one's eyes.

Deceiver, *n.* Impostor, cheat, humbug, charlatan, sharper, trickster, rogue, knave, pretender.

Decency, *n.* 1. Propriety, decorum, proper formality.

2. Modesty, delicacy, purity.

Decent, *a.* 1. Proper, becoming, fit, befitting, suitable, decorous, seemly, comely.

2. Modest, delicate, pure.

3. (*Colloq.*) Tolerable, passable, moderate, respectable.

Deception, *n.* 1. Imposture, imposition. See DECEIT.

2. Cheat, ruse, wile, stratagem, chouse. See TRICK.

Deceptive, *a.* Deceitful, deceiving, disingenuous, delusive, illusive, illusory, misleading, fallacious, false.

Decide, *v. t.* Settle, conclude, determine, fix upon, close, terminate, end.

——, *v. i.* Determine, conclude, resolve, come to a conclusion, make a decision, make up one's mind.

Decided, *a.* 1. Determined, unwavering, unhesitating, resolute.

2. Unequivocal, categorical, positive, absolute.

3. Unquestionable, undeniable, indisputable, unmistakable, certain, clear, beyond all question, beyond a doubt, past dispute.

Deciduous, *a.* (*Bot.*) Non-perennial, temporary, caducous.

Decipher, *v. t.* 1. Unravel, unfold, interpret, reveal, explain, expound.

2. Read, make out.

DECISION, *n.* 1. Conclusion, judgment, determination, settlement.

2. Adjudication, award, pronouncement, decree, sentence.

3. Resolution, firmness.

Decisive, *a.* Conclusive, determinative, final.

Deck, *v. t.* 1. Adorn, embellish, decorate, ornament, array, beautify.

2. Dress, clothe, apparel, robe.

3. Cover with a deck, cover, cover in.

Declaim, *v. i.* 1. Harangue, speak (*rhetorically*), mouth, rant, "spout."

2. Recite a speech, practise speaking.

Declamation, *n.* 1. Declaiming, haranguing, mouthing, ranting, "spouting."

2. Harangue, set speech.

Declamatory, *a.* 1. In the style of declamation.

2. Rhetorical, grandiloquent, inflated, bombastic, swelling, pompous, turgid, pretentious, high-flown, high-sounding, fustian.

Declaration, *n.* 1. Affirmation, assertion, asseveration, averment, protestation, avowal.

2. Proclamation, publication, public *or* official announcement.

Declaratory, *a.* 1. Expressive, affirmative, enunciative, enunciatory, assertive, declarative.

2. Explanatory, expository, declarative.

Declare, *v. t.* Affirm, assert, aver, asseverate, state, proclaim, publish, promulgate, advertise, blazon, bruit, announce, utter, make known.

——, *v. i.* Make a declaration, come out, pronounce, proclaim one's self.

Declension, *n.* 1. Decline, deterioration, degeneracy, decay, diminution, falling off.

2. (*Gram.*) Inflection, variation; mode of inflection.

3. Refusal, declination, declinature, non-acceptance.

Declination, *n.* 1. Bending, inclination.

2. Deterioration. See DECLENSION, 1.

3. Deviation, departure, oblique movement.

4. Declinature. See DECLENSION, 3.

Decline, *v. i.* 1. Lean downward, incline, slope.

2. Decay, sink, droop, languish, pine, fail, flag, become feeble.

3. Deteriorate, degenerate, depreciate, be impaired.

4. Decrease, lessen, diminish, wane, fade, ebb, dwindle, lapse, fall away.

——, *v. t.* 1. Refuse, reject, avoid.

2. (*Gram.*) Inflect, vary.

——, *n.* 1. Deterioration, degeneracy, decay, decadence, wane, diminution, falling off, declension, declination.

2. Consumption, phthisis, marasmus, atrophy, gradual wasting, progressive emaciation.

Declivity, *n.* Slope (*downward*), descent.

Declivous, *a.* Sloping, descending.

Decompose, *v. t.* Decompound, disintegrate, analyze, resolve, resolve into its elements.

——, *v. i.* Decay, putrefy, rot, become corrupt, fall into decay, go to pieces, be resolved into its elements.

Decomposition, *n.* 1. Analysis, resolution, disintegration, break-up.

2. Decay, corruption, putrescence, disintegration, crumbling, caries, dissolution, rotting, falling to pieces.

Decorate, *v. t.* Adorn, deck, ornament, embellish, beautify, enrich, garnish.

Decoration, *n.* 1. Adorning, decking, ornamenting, ornamentation, embellishing, embellishment, beautifying, enriching, enrichment, garnishing.

2. Ornament, embellishment, adornment, enrichment.

Decorous, *a.* Decent, becoming, suitable, proper, befitting, seemly, comely, fit.

Decorum, *n.* Decency, propriety, seemliness, appropriate behavior, dignified behavior, dignity, sedateness.

Decoy, *v. t.* Allure, lure, entice, inveigle, seduce, tempt, entrap, ensnare.

——, *n.* Lure, allurement, enticement.

Decrease, *v. i.* Diminish (*gradually*), lessen, wane, decline, ebb, subside, dwindle, contract, abate, grow less.

——, *v. t.* Diminish, lessen, retrench, curtail, reduce, lower, make less.

——, *n.* Diminution, lessening, decrement, reduction, wane *or* waning, declension, decline, ebb, ebbing, subsidence, contraction, abatement.

Decree, *v. t.* Order, ordain, appoint, enjoin, command, determine, adjudge, decide, enact.

——, *n.* Edict, enactment, regulation, law, command, order, mandate, fiat, ordinance, statute.

Decrement, *n.* Decrease, diminution, lessening, waste, loss.

Decrepit, *a.* Superannuated, effete, shattered, broken down with age, infirm through age.

Decrepitate, *v. i.* Crackle, snap, crepitate.

Decrepitude, *n.* Infirmity of age, decline of life.

Decry, *v. t.* Disparage, depreciate, discredit, condemn, traduce, cry down, run down, bring into disrepute, bring discredit on.

Decuple, *a.* Tenfold.

——, *v. t.* Increase tenfold, multiply by ten, make ten times as great.

Dedicate, *v. t.* 1. Devote, hallow, sanctify, consecrate, set apart (*to God* or *the purposes of religion*).

2. Devote, consecrate, give earnestly *or* wholly, apply completely *or* devotedly.

3. Address (*as a literary work*), inscribe.

Dedication, *n.* 1. Consecration, devotion.

2. Address, inscription.

Deduce, *v. t.* Derive, conclude, infer, draw as an implication.

Deducible, *a.* Inferrible, derivable.

Deduct, *v. t.* Subtract, withdraw, remove, take away, take out.

Deduction, *n.* 1. Subtraction, withdrawal, removal, taking out *or* away.

2. Abatement, allowance, defalcation, offtake, reduction, discount, rebate, reprise.

3. Inference, conclusion, consequence, corollary.

Deed, *n.* 1. Act, action, performance, exploit, "gest," "derring-do," achievement, feat.

2. Reality, fact, truth.

3. (*Law.*) Indenture, charter.

Deem, *v. t.* Think, regard, consider, hold, believe, suppose, imagine, judge, count, account, look upon.

——, *v. i.* Think, believe, suppose, opine, fancy, be of opinion.

DEEP, *a.* 1. Down-reaching, reaching far down, profound, abysmal, of great depth.

2. Mysterious, intricate, knotty, difficult, abstruse, hard (*to comprehend*), unfathomable, profound.

3. Sagacious, penetrating, intelligent, discerning, shrewd, astute.

4. Absorbed, engrossed, rapt up.

5. Grave, low, bass, not high, not sharp.

6. Great, thorough, entire, heartfelt.

——, *n.* 1. Sea, ocean, main, abyss of waters.

2. Depth, profound, abyss, deepest part *or* place, recess, bottom.

3. Mystery, enigma, profound riddle.

4. Stillness, silence, stillest part, inmost part, midst.

Deepen, *v. t.* 1. Make deeper, increase the depth of.

2. Make darker, make more intense, darken, intensify.

3. Reduce to a lower tone, make more grave, lower.

4. Make more impressive *or* efficient, intensify, strengthen, increase, heighten, make more vivid.

——, *v. i.* Grow deeper, become deeper, increase, heighten, become intenser *or* more decided.

Deeply, *adv.* 1. Profoundly, deep, to *or* at a great depth, far down.

2. Thoroughly, entirely, completely, profoundly.

3. Greatly, very much, in a high degree, profoundly.

Deface, *v. t.* Disfigure, deform, mar, mutilate, blotch, spoil, injure, soil, tarnish.

Defacement, *n.* Disfigurement, injury.

De facto. [L.] 1. In fact, really, actually, as a matter of fact.

2. Real, actual.

Defalcate, *v. t.* [*Applied especially to public accounts, estimates, etc.*] Lop, lop off, cut off, deduct a part of, retrench, curtail, reduce, abate, deduct from.

Defalcation, *n.* 1. Diminution, abatement, reduction, deduction, discount.

2. Deficiency, deficit, default, shortage, short-coming, falling short.

3. Fraudulent shortage (*in accounts*), defaulting, breach of trust, embezzlement.

Defamation, *n.* Slander, calumny, detraction, obloquy, aspersion, abuse, backbiting, scandal, false accusation.

Defamatory, *a.* Slanderous, calumnious, libellous, abusive, false and injurious.

Defame, *v. t.* Asperse, slander, malign, calumniate, traduce, vilify, revile, libel, blacken, smirch, abuse blemish, run down, speak ill of.

Default, *n.* 1. Omission, neglect, failure.

2. Want, lack, destitution, defect, deficiency.

——, *v. i.* Fail to keep one's engagement *or* contract, break one's trust, be guilty of defaulting *or* defalcation.

Defaulter, *n.* Delinquent (*in failing to appear in court,* or *in accounting for money intrusted*), embezzler.

Defeat, *n.* 1. Overthrow, downfall, rout, discomfiture, repulse.

2. Frustration, bafflement, checkmate.

——, *v. t.* 1. Conquer, overthrow, overcome, vanquish, repulse, beat, discomfit, rout, checkmate.

2. Frustrate, baffle, foil, balk, block, thwart, disconcert, disappoint.

Defecate, *v. i.* 1. Clarify, clear, purify, refine.

2. Go to stool, ease one's self, evacuate the bowels, void excrement.

Defect, *n.* 1. Deficiency, lack, want, destitution, default.

2. Imperfection, blemish, flaw.

3. Fault, failing, foible.

Defection, *n.* 1. Desertion, abandonment of allegiance, revolt.

2. Apostasy, backsliding.

Defective, *a.* 1. Deficient, insufficient, inadequate, incomplete.

2. Imperfect, faulty, marred.

Defend, *v. t.*   1. Guard, shield, secure from danger, secure from attack, rally to. See PROTECT.

2. Vindicate, assert, maintain, uphold, justify, espouse, plead.

Defender, *n.*   1. Asserter, pleader, maintainer, upholder.

2. Champion, vindicator, protector.

Defense, *n.*   1. Defending, protection, guarding, maintaining, maintenance, holding.

2. Protection, guard, buckler, shield, bulwark, fortification, tower of strength.

3. Vindication, justification, apology, plea, excuse.

Defenseless, *a.*   Unprotected, exposed, weak, helpless, unshielded, unguarded, unarmed.

Defer, *v. t.*   Postpone, delay, adjourn, table, procrastinate, put off, stave off, let lie over.

Deference, *n.*   1. Respect, regard, esteem, honor, reverence, veneration, homage, obeisance.

2. Complaisance, consideration.

3. Obedience, submission.

Deferential, *a.*   Respectful, reverential.

Defer to.   Respect, value, yield to, pay respect to, think much of, think highly of, pay deference to, accord superiority to.

Defiance, *n.*   1. Daring, challenge, invitation to combat *or* contest (*of any kind*).

2. Contempt, opposition, spite, despite.

Defiant, *a.*   1. Resistant, contumacious, recalcitrant.

2. Bold, daring, courageous.

Deficiency, *n.*   1. Want, lack, default, insufficiency, scantiness, shortness, meagreness, dearth, scarcity, shortage, deficit.

2. Failing, failure, frailty, defect, infirmity, imperfection, foible, fault, error, weakness, weak side, blind side.

Deficient, *a.*   Defective, insufficient, scant, imperfect, incomplete, inadequate, unsatisfactory.

Deficit, *n.*   [L.] Shortage. See DEFICIENCY.

Defile, *v. t.*   1. Soil, dirty, stain, tarnish, make foul *or* filthy.

2. Sully, taint, pollute, corrupt, vitiate, debase, contaminate, poison.

3. Debauch, corrupt, seduce, deflower, rob of virginity.

Defilement, *n.*   Pollution, contamination, taint, uncleanness, abomination, foulness.

Definable, *a.*   Determinable, that may be defined.

Define, *v. t.*   Limit, delimit, demarcate, bound, circumscribe, set bounds to, fix the limits of.

Definite, *a.*   1. Determinate, determined, defined, precisely bounded.

2. Precise, exact, determinate, certain, unequivocal, explicit.

Definition, *n.*   1. Explanation (*of the meaning*), exact meaning.

2. Description (*by a statement of characteristic properties*).

3. Defining, exact statement of the meaning.

Definitive, *a.*   1. Determinate, positive, express, explicit, categorical, unconditional.

2. Final, conclusive, decisive.

Deflect, *v. i.*   Deviate, diverge, swerve, turn aside, bend, waver.

——, *v. t.*   Bend, turn aside, bend down, press down.

Deflection, *n.*   Deviation, bending, divergence.

Deflower, *v. t.*   1. Debauch, defile, constuprate, corrupt (*to lewdness*), seduce, rob of virginity.

2. Rob of its first bloom, spoil of its primal beauty, deprive of its freshness.

Deform, *v. t.*   Disfigure, distort, deface, mar, injure, spoil, make unsightly, make ugly.

Deformity, *n.*   Distortion, malformation, misproportion, misshapenness, crookedness, ugliness, inelegance, disfigurement, monstrosity, want of symmetry.

Defraud, *v. t.*   Cheat, cozen, trick, dupe, gull, deceive, overreach, circumvent, delude, hoodwink, chouse, beguile, impose upon, swindle.

Defray, *v. t.*   Pay, discharge, settle, bear.

Deft, *a.*   Dexterous, skilful, clever, apt, adroit, ready, expert, "dab," neat-handed.

Defunct, *a.*   1. Dead, deceased, departed, gone.

2. Inoperative, abrogated, cancelled, annulled, dead.

Defy, *v. t.*   1. Challenge, dare, bid defiance to, hurl defiance at, call to combat.

2. Brave, disregard, slight, scorn, spurn, despise, contemn, flout, treat with contempt, trample on, set at nought, snap the fingers at, set at defiance.

Degeneracy, *n.*   1. Deterioration, debasement, abasement, depravation, degeneration, degenerateness, declension, caducity, degradation, decline, decrease, falling off, growing worse.

2. Inferiority, meanness, poorness, low estate *or* state.

Degenerate, *v. i.*   Deteriorate, decline, decay, sink, retrograde, become worse, grow worse, fall off, run down, become enfeebled *or* impaired *or* perverted.

Degenerate, *a.* Inferior, mean, base, corrupt, fallen, degenerated, decayed, in decadence.

Degradation, *n.* 1. Dishonor, disgrace, ignominy, humiliation, deposition.

2. Deterioration, abasement, debasement, degeneracy, degeneration, decadence, corruption, caducity, decline, vitiation, perversion.

Degrade, *v. t.* 1. Disgrace, dishonor, discredit, abase, break, cashier, humiliate, humble, depose, unfrock, reduce to inferior rank.

2. Lower, sink, deteriorate, impair, injure, debase, vitiate, pervert, alloy.

DEGREE, *n.* 1. Step, stage, point arrived at.

2. Class, rank, order, grade, quality, station, standing.

3. Measure, extent.

4. Remove (*in the line of descent*).

5. Division (*as on a scale*), interval, space.

Dehiscent, *a.* Opening, gaping.

Deification, *n.* Apotheosis, deifying.

Deify, *v. t.* 1. Raise to the rank of a deity, place among the gods, apotheosize.

2. Idolize, cultivate idolatrously, make a god of, make into an object of worship, praise *or* revere as a deity.

3. Make godlike, exalt, elevate, ennoble.

Deign, *v. i.* Condescend, vouchsafe, think fit, see fit.

Deist, *n.* Unbeliever in the miraculous origin of Christianity, believer in God but not in Providence *or* revelation, freethinker.

Deity, *n.* 1. Divinity, Godhead, the Divine Nature.

2. God *or* goddess, demiurge, divine being, Providence.

Deject, *v. t.* Dishearten, dispirit, discourage, depress, sadden, make despondent, make sad.

Dejected, *a.* Disheartened, dispirited, discouraged, depressed, down-hearted, downcast, despondent, doleful, cast down, chapfallen, crestfallen, down in the mouth, blue, gloomy, hipped, dumpish, in the dumps.

Dejection, *n.* Depression, despondency, sadness, melancholy, gloom, dumps, blues, lowness of spirits, low spirits.

Delay, *v. t.* 1. Defer, postpone, procrastinate, put off, stave off, let lie over.

2. Detain, arrest, check, hinder, retard, stop, stay, impede.

——, *v. i.* Linger, loiter, tarry, stop, procrastinate.

——, *n.* 1. Procrastination, postponement, deferring, the Fabian policy, masterly inactivity.

2. Lingering, tarrying, stay, stop, dallying, dawdling.

3. Detention, hindrance, retardation, impediment, stoppage.

Delectable, *a.* Pleasing, pleasant, delightful, agreeable, gratifying.

Delectation, *n.* Delight, joy, gladness, rapture, transport, ravishment, ecstasy, great pleasure.

Delegate, *v. t.* 1. Depute, commission, "deputize," appoint as agent, send on an embassy.

2. Intrust, commit.

——, *n.* Deputy, commissioner, representative.

Delegation, *n.* 1. Delegating, intrusting, committal.

2. Deputies, delegates, body of delegates *or* representatives.

Delete, *v. t.* Erase, efface, expunge, cancel, obliterate, remove, dele, blot out.

Deleterious, *a.* 1. Destructive, deadly, poisonous, noxious, lethal.

2. Injurious, pernicious, hurtful, harmful, unwholesome.

Deliberate, *v. i.* Reflect, ponder, consider, think, cogitate, ruminate, muse, meditate, take counsel with one's self.

——, *a.* 1. Wary, cautious, careful, circumspect, considerate, thoughtful.

2. Well considered, well advised.

3. Purposed, done on purpose, intentional, premeditated, aforethought, studied, done in cold blood.

4. Slow, unhurried, leisurely.

Deliberation, *n.* 1. Consideration, meditation, cogitation, thought, reflection, circumspection, wariness, caution, thoughtfulness.

2. Purpose, conscious determination, distinct intention, cold blood, malice prepense.

3. Consultation, discussion.

Delicacy, *n.* 1. Pleasantness, agreeableness, deliciousness, daintiness, savoriness, relish.

2. Dainty, tidbit, titbit, *bonne-bouche.*

3. Fineness, softness, smoothness, tenderness, lightness, nicety, niceness, elegance.

4. Slightness, slenderness, weakness, frailty, fragility, tenderness.

5. Carefulness, scrupulousness, fastidiousness, daintiness, discrimination, tact, finesse, sensitivity, nicety, subtlety.

6. Refinement, purity, sensibility, fine feeling.

DELICATE, *a.* 1. Pleasant, pleasing, delicious, agreeable, savory, palatable.

2. Fine, nice, elegant, exquisite.

3. Slight, slender, weak, frail, tender, sensitive.

4. Discriminating, careful, scrupulous, fastidious, dainty, of nice perception.

5. Refined, pure.

Delicious, *a.* 1. Luscious, savory, palatable, delicate, dainty, nice.

2. Pleasant, grateful, agreeable, charming, delightful, exquisite.

Delight, *n.* Joy, gladness, delectation, satisfaction, charm, gratification, rapture, transport, ravishment, ecstasy, great pleasure.

——, *v. t.* Enrapture, transport, ravish, enchant, charm, gratify, rejoice, please highly.

——, *v. i.* Take delight, have great pleasure, rejoice.

Delightful, *a.* Charming, enchanting, ravishing, very agreeable, highly pleasing, rapturous, enrapturing, transporting.

Delineate, *v. t.* 1. Design, sketch, figure, draw, trace, represent by outlines.

2. Describe, portray, depict, picture, set forth.

Delineation, *n.* 1. Sketch, design, outline, draught, drawing, figure.

2. Description, account, portrayal.

Delinquency, *n.* Fault, misdeed, misdemeanor, transgression, offence, crime, failure in duty.

Delinquent, *a.* Failing in duty, offending, negligent.

——, *n.* Offender, culprit, criminal, wrongdoer, misdoer, miscreant, malefactor, transgressor.

Deliquesce, *v. i.* Melt (gradually), liquefy.

Deliquescent, *a.* 1. Liquefying, tending to melt or become liquid.

2. Vanishing, tending to disappear or go to waste.

Delirious, *a.* Insane (*as in fevers*), mad, deranged, demented, wandering, lightheaded, crazy, raving, frantic, frenzied.

Delirium, *n.* Wandering (*as in fevers*), incoherence, hallucination, derangement, insanity, frenzy, raving, madness, alienation of mind.

Deliver, *v. t.* 1. Liberate, release, free, emancipate, set free, set at liberty.

2. Rescue, save, extricate, redeem.

3. Commit, transfer, give, impart, hand over, pass over, make over.

4. Yield, cede, grant, surrender, relinquish, resign, give up.

5. Pronounce, utter, emit, speak, declare, promulgate.

6. Discharge, deal, give forth.

Deliverance, *n.* 1. Release, liberation, emancipation, redemption, escape.

2. Extrication, rescue, acquittance.

Delivery, *n.* 1. Surrender, conveyance, giving up.

2. Giving, handing over, transmission, transferal, commitment, intrusting, passing over, rendering.

3. Utterance, enunciation, pronunciation, speech, elocution.

4. Childbirth, parturition, labor, travail, lying-in, confinement.

Dell, *n.* Dale, dingle, valley, ravine, glen.

Delude, *v. t.* Deceive, beguile, mislead, cheat, cozen, chouse, gull, dupe, circumvent, overreach, trick, impose upon, lead astray, lead into error.

Deluge, *n.* Flood, overflow, inundation, cataclysm.

——, *v. t.* Submerge, inundate, overflow, drown, overwhelm.

Delusion, *n.* 1. Trick, imposition, imposture, cheat, fraud, artifice, wile, snare, ruse, dodge, fetch, clap-trap.

2. Illusion, deception, fallacy, error, hallucination, mockery, phantasm, false show.

Delusive, *a.* Fallacious, deceitful, deceptive, deceiving, illusive, illusory.

Demagogue, *n.* Ringleader of the populace, unscrupulous agitator.

Demand, *v. t.* 1. Claim, require, exact, challenge, call for, ask for.

2. Necessitate, require, rightfully claim, make necessary.

——, *v. i.* Ask, inquire, make inquiry.

——, *n.* 1. Claim, requisition, requirement, draft, exaction.

2. Want, call, desire to obtain.

3. Question, inquiry, interrogation.

Demarcation, *n.* Division, separation, distinction, limit, bound, boundary.

Demeanor, *n.* Behavior, carriage, deportment, conduct, manner, bearing, air, mien.

Demented, *a.* Idiotic, foolish, infatuated, insane, lunatic, crazy, crack-brained, daft, deranged.

Dementia, *n.* [L.] (*Med.*) Idiocy, insanity, lunacy.

Demerit, *n.* Fault, delinquency, ill-desert.

Demi-monde, *n.* [Fr.] Kept-mistresses (*collectively*), the courtesan class.

Demise, *n.* 1. Conveyance, alienation, transfer, transferrence, making over.

2. Death (*of a ruler* or *a distinguished person*), decease.

——, *v. t.* 1. Alienate, transfer, consign, devolve, convey, make over, deliver over.

2. Bequeath, devise, will, grant by will.

Demiurgic, *a.* Creative, formative.

Democracy, *n.* 1. Government by the people.

2. Republic, representative government.

3. [*U. S.*] Democrats, democratic party.

Democratic, } *a.* 1. Popular, of the
Democratical, } people.

2. Representative, republican.

Demolish, *v. t.* Destroy, overthrow, raze, level, ruin, dash to pieces, break to pieces, pulverize.

Demolition, *n.* Overthrow, destruction, ruin.

Demon, *n.* 1. Devil, fiend, evil spirit, goblin, troll.

2. Spirit, genius, guardian spirit, tutelary deity.

Demoniac, } *a.* Diabolical, devilish,
Demoniacal, } fiendish, hellish, infernal.

Demonstrable, *a.* Provable, capable of being proved, capable of absolute proof *or* demonstration.

Demonstrate, *v. t.* Prove, establish, show, make evident, make certain, show beyond the possibility of doubt.

Demonstration, *n.* 1. Proof, rigorous *or* absolute establishment.

2. Manifestation, show, exhibition, display.

Demonstrative, *a.* 1. Conclusive, apodictic, absolute, certain, producing demonstration, probative.

2. Energetically expressive, free in expression (*of feeling*), unreserved, effusive, prone to display of feeling.

Demoralization, *n.* 1. Corruption of morals, depravity, want of principle.

2. (*Mil.*) Loss of morale, destruction of discipline.

Demoralize, *v. t.* 1. Corrupt, deprave, vitiate, deprive of moral principle.

2. (*Mil.*) Deprive of courage *or* confidence, break down the morale *or* discipline of.

Demulcent, *a.* Mild, soothing, lenitive, emollient, sedative.

Demur, *v. i.* 1. Hesitate, pause, stop, waver, be in doubt, stop to consider.

2. Object, raise objections, scruple, state scruples, take exceptions.

Demure, *a.* 1. Affectedly modest, prudish, over-modest, putting on shyness *or* coyness.

2. Sober, sedate, grave, modest, coy, downcast.

Demurrer, *n.* (*Law.*) Objection, issue on matter of law.

Den, *n.* 1. Cavern, cave.

2. [*Often in bad sense, implying squalor, misery,* or *vice.*] Haunt, retreat, resort, place of resort.

Dendriform, *a.* Arborescent, arboriform, dendritic, dendroid, branching.

Denial, *n.* 1. Contradiction, negation, controverting.

2. Disavowal, disclaimer, abjuration, disowning.

3. Refusal (*to grant a request*), rejection, disallowance.

Denizen, *n.* 1. (*Eng. law.*) Naturalized citizen, adopted citizen.

2. Inhabitant, dweller, resident.

Denominate, *v. t.* Name, designate, entitle, style, call, dub, christen, phrase.

Denomination, *n.* 1. Name, title, style, designation, appellation.

2. Class, kind, sort.

3. Sect, school, persuasion.

Denote, *v. t.* Signify, mean, imply, connote, betoken, indicate, typify, note, mark, designate, point out.

Dénouement, *n.* [Fr.] 1. Catastrophe (*of a drama* or *a novel*), unravelling of the plot.

2. Issue, upshot, conclusion, termination, *finale,* consummation, winding up, finishing stroke, final event.

Denounce, *v. t.* 1. Threaten, menace.

2. Brand, stigmatize, arraign, upbraid, censure.

3. Inform against, accuse, lay information *or* charges against.

De novo. [L.] Anew, newly, afresh, again, over again.

Dense, *a.* Close, compact, condensed, compressed, thick.

Density, *n.* Closeness, compactness.

Dent, *n.* Indentation, dint, nick, notch.

——, *v. t.* Indent, make a dent upon.

Dentate, } *a.* Toothed, notched, serrate,
Dentated, } serrated, jagged.

Denude, *v. t.* Strip, divest, make bare, make naked.

Denunciation, *n.* 1. Menace, threat.

2. Arraignment, severe censure, fulmination, invective.

3. Exposure, informing against.

Denunciatory, *a.* Condemnatory, stigmatizing, upbraiding.

Deny, *v. t.* 1. Contradict, gainsay, declare to be untrue, traverse.

2. Renounce, abjure, disown, disavow, disclaim, abnegate, refuse to acknowledge.

3. Withhold, refuse to grant, disallow.

Deodorize, *v. t.* Disinfect, deprive of odor.

Depart, *v. i.* 1. Disappear, vanish, go away, withdraw.

2. Go, start, set out, be off, take leave, bid adieu, bid farewell, make one's exit, take one's self off.

3. Die, decease, leave the world.

Depart from. 1. Leave, quit, go away from.

2. Abandon, forsake, desert, give up, cease to adhere to.

3. Deviate from, vary from.

Department, *n.* 1. Part, portion, division (*especially a territorial division*), province, district.

2. Province, function, office, bureau, station, sphere of duty.

3. Province, branch, division *or* subdivision (*of a subject or notion*).

Departure, *n.* 1. Withdrawal, exit, going, leaving, parting, recession, retirement, removal.

2. Abandonment (*of*), forsaking (*of*).

3. Deviation, variation, declension, declining, declination.

4. Death, decease, demise, exit.

Depend, *v. i.* 1. Hang, be pendent.

2. Hinge (*fig.*), hang, turn, be conditioned.

Dependent, *n.* 1. Vassal, minion, retainer, henchman, client, hanger-on.

2. Consequence, corollary, attendant circumstance, concomitant.

Dependence, *n.* 1. Connection, concatenation, interdependence.

2. Reliance, trust, confidence.

3. Stay, staff, support, prop, buttress, supporter.

4. Subordination, subjection, conditioned existence, contingency, need (*of*).

Dependency, *n.* 1. Adjunct, appurtenance.

2. Colony, province, subject territory.

DEPENDENT, *a.* 1. Hanging, pendent.

2. Conditioned, contingent, unable to exist without, at the disposal of, sustained by.

Depend on. 1. Rely upon, rest upon, confide in, trust to, count upon, reckon upon, build upon, depend upon.

2. Be conditioned *or* dependent on, be contingent upon, require, demand, imply, presuppose.

Depict, *v. t.* 1. Paint, sketch, portray, delineate, limn, pencil.

2. Describe, set forth, portray, delineate, render, represent.

Deplete, *v. t.* Exhaust, drain, reduce, empty, evacuate.

Depletion, *n.* Exhausting, exhaustion, reducing, reduction, draining, emptying, evacuation.

Deplorable, *a.* Lamentable, pitiable, sad, calamitous, grievous, miserable, mournful, wretched, distressing, melancholy, to be deplored.

Deplore, *v. t.* Mourn, bewail, lament, bemoan, grieve for, sorrow over.

Deploy, *v. t.* (*Mil.*) Open, unfold, extend, expand, display.

——, *v. i.* (*Mil.*) Open, display.

Depopulate, *v. t.* Dispeople, unpeople, deprive of inhabitants.

Deportment, *n.* Demeanor, behavior, carriage, port, conduct, bearing, manner, mien, air, breeding.

Deport one's self. Behave, act, conduct one's self, demean one's self, acquit *or* quit one's self, bear one's self, comport one's self.

Depose, *v. t.* Dethrone, dismiss, oust, cashier, displace, break, degrade, reduce.

——, *v. i.* Testify, declare, bear witness, depone (*Old Eng. and Scotch*).

Deposit, *v. t.* 1. Drop, let fall, throw down, dump, precipitate.

2. Lay, lay down, put, place, put down.

3. Lodge, put, store, hoard, save, lay up, lay by.

4. Intrust, commit, put for safe keeping.

——, *n.* 1. Precipitate, sediment, diluvium, silt, settlings.

2. Security, pledge, pawn, stake.

Depositary, *n.* Trustee, guardian, fiduciary.

Deposition, *n.* (*Law.*) 1. Testimony (*in writing, signed and sworn to before a magistrate, after cross-examination*), evidence, affidavit.

2. Dethroning, dismission, displacement, removal.

Depository, *n.* Storehouse, depot, place of deposit, deposit.

Depot, *n.* Depository, storehouse, warehouse, magazine.

Depravation, *n.* 1. Vitiation, corruption, deterioration, abasement, debasement, impairing, injury.

2. Depravity, degeneracy, degeneration, deterioration, debasement, impairment, impaired condition.

Deprave, *v. t.* Vitiate, corrupt, contaminate, pollute, demoralize, make bad.

Depraved, *p.* and *a.* Corrupted, corrupt, degenerate, vicious, perverted, wicked, profligate, dissolute, reprobate, graceless, abandoned, shameless, hardened, lost.

Depravity, *n.* 1. Degeneracy, depraved *or* depressed state, low condition, depravation, corruption.

2. Corruptness, corruption, wickedness, viciousness, demoralization, vice, immorality, perversion, license, iniquity.

Deprecate, *v. t.* View with regret, wish not to have occur, regard with regretful disfavor.

Depreciate, *v. t.* 1. Underrate, undervalue, lessen the price of, diminish the value of.

2. Disparage, decry, traduce, malign, belittle, degrade, censure, find fault with.

——, *v. i.* Fall in price, fall in value, become of less worth, decline, fall off, fall, "slump," lose value.

Depreciation, *n.* 1. Fall in price, diminution of value, decline in value, fall, decline.

2. Detraction, disparagement, derogation, belittling, traducing, maligning, censure.

Depreciative, *a.* Derogatory, depreciatory, disparaging.

Depredation, *n.* Spoliation, rapine, robbery, theft, pillage, plunder, pilfering.

Depredator, *n.* Plunderer, robber, thief, spoiler, brigand, freebooter, pirate, corsair, buccaneer, marauder.

Depress, *v. t.* 1. Lower, detrude, drop, sink, bow, reduce, press down, let down, let fall, cast down, bring down.

2. Degrade, humble, disgrace, humiliate, debase, abase, abash, bring low, take down.

3. Discourage, dishearten, dispirit, deject, damp, dampen, chill, sadden, make sad, make despondent.

4. Make dull (*as trade*), lower, deaden.

Depression, *n.* 1. (*Rare*) Abasement, degradation.

2. Hollow, hollowness, cavity, concavity, indentation, dent, dint, dimple, excavation, pit.

3. Dejection, dejectedness, dispiritedness, cheerlessness, disheartenment, disconsolateness, downheartedness, hypochondria, sadness, despondency, melancholy, dolefulness, dole, gloom, gloominess, dumps, blues, lowness of spirits, low spirits, depression of spirits, vapors.

4. Lowness, dulness, inactivity, stagnation.

Deprivation, *n.* Loss, privation, bereavement, dispossession, stripping, spoliation.

Deprive, *v. t.* Dispossess, divest, denude, strip, rob. See BEREAVE.

Depth, *n.* 1. Deepness, profundity, drop.

2. Extent, measure.

3. Middle, central part, midst (*of winter, etc.*), stillest part, stillness, silence (*of night*).

4. Discernment, sagacity, shrewdness, penetration, astuteness, perspicacity, profoundness, profundity.

Deputation, *n.* 1. Delegation, commission.

2. Deputies, delegates, body of delegates, delegation, commissioners, envoys, legation, embassy.

Depute, *v. t.* Delegate, commission, send out, appoint as agent.

Deputy, *n.* Delegate, representative, substitute, proxy, envoy, legate, vicegerent, agent, factor.

Derange, *v. t.* 1. Disorder, confuse, unsettle, disarrange, displace, turn topsy-turvy, put out of place.

2. Disturb, discompose, disconcert, perturb, ruffle, upset.

3. Make *or* render insane, craze, madden, unbalance, unhinge.

Derangement, *n.* 1. Disorder, confusion, disarrangement.

2. Disturbance, discomposure, perturbation.

3. Insanity, lunacy, madness, mania, delirium, mental aberration, mental alienation, dementia.

Derelict, *a.* 1. (*Law.*) Forsaken, relinquished, abandoned, left.

2. Unfaithful, faithless, delinquent, negligent, guiltily neglectful.

——, *n.* (*Law.*) 1. Abandoned property.

2. Tract of land (*fit for cultivation*) left dry by the retirement of the sea.

Dereliction, *n.* 1. Abandonment, renunciation, desertion, relinquishment.

2. Faithlessness, failure in duty, delinquency, neglect, negligence.

Deride, *v. t.* Ridicule (*contemptuously* or *maliciously*), mock, scout, satirize, lampoon, jeer, taunt, chaff, scoff at, jeer at, laugh at, make fun of, make sport of, make game of, turn to ridicule, hold up to ridicule, make a butt of, make merry with, poke fun at. See RIDICULE.

Derision, *n.* Ridicule, mockery, scorn, contempt.

Derisive, } *a.* Scoffing, mocking, ridiculing, **Derisory,** } scornful, contemptuous, contumelious.

Derivable, *a.* 1. Obtainable, to be derived.

2. Deducible, that may be inferred (*from premises*).

3. Traceable (*to a root*).

Derivation, *n.* 1. Descent, genealogy, extraction.

2. Etymology.

3. Deriving, obtaining, getting, drawing, deducing.

4. Source (*in*), origination (*from*), foundation (*in*).

Derivative, *a.* Derived, derivate.

Derive, *v. t.* 1. Draw, receive, obtain, get.

2. Deduce, trace.

Derogate from. Disparage, detract from, take something from, be derogatory of or to, lessen, diminish, compromise, be hostile to.

Derogation, *n.* Detraction, disparagement, depreciation.

Derogatory, *a.* Detracting, dishonoring, depreciative, disparaging, belittling.

Descant, *n.* 1. Melody (*with variations*), tune; esp. (*Mus.*) soprano, treble, highest part in a score.

2. Commentary, animadversion, remarks, series of comments.

3. Discourse, discussion, disputation.

——, *v. i.* Expatiate, enlarge, dilate, discourse, make remarks, treat copiously, animadvert freely.

Descend, *v. i.* 1. Fall, sink, drop, pitch, go down, come down.

2. Dismount, alight, get down.

3. Go, pass, proceed, be transferred *or* transmitted *or* handed down, devolve (*upon*).

4. Originate, be derived, issue, take rise.

Descendants, *n. pl.* Progeny, posterity, offspring, issue.

Descending, *p. a.* Descendant, downgoing, declivitous.

Descent, *n.* 1. Fall, coming down, drop, downrush.

2. Going down, descending, journey *or* voyage down.

3. Declivity, decline, dip, pitch, slope.

4. Extraction, derivation, parentage, lineage, pedigree, ancestry, genealogy.

5. Attack, assault, incursion, foray, raid, hostile invasion.

Describe, *v. t.* 1. Delineate, trace, draw, sketch, limn, mark out.

2. Represent (*by words*), portray, depict, detail, explain, recount, narrate, relate, give an account of, set forth.

3. Characterize, specify the peculiarities of, set forth the character of.

Description, *n.* 1. Delineation, tracing.

2. Representation, portrayal, depiction, explanation, account, relation, recital, report, narration, narrative.

3. Sort, kind, class, species.

Descry, *v. t.* 1. Discover, discern, espy, perceive, see, behold, get sight of, get a glimpse of.

2. Detect, recognize, find out, spy out.

Desecrate, *v. t.* Profane, pollute, defile, violate, treat sacrilegiously, pervert to unholy uses.

Desecration, *n.* Profanation, pollution, perversion to unholy uses, sacrilege, violation.

Desert, *a.* Uninhabited, desolate, forsaken, wild, waste, barren, untilled.

——, *n.* Wilderness, waste, solitude, deserted region.

——, *n.* (*Pron.* desert'.) Deserving, due, merit *or* demerit.

——, *v. t.* 1. Forsake, leave, quit, abandon, renounce, leave in the lurch, turn one's back upon.

2. Leave unlawfully, run away from, bolt.

——, *v. i.* Abandon one's post, run away from military service.

Deserted, *a.* Forsaken, abandoned, relinquished, given up, cast off, lonely, lone.

Deserter, *n.* 1. Forsaker, abandoner, quitter, "ratter," runaway.

2. Backslider, renegade, recreant, apostate, revolter, turncoat.

3. Delinquent soldier, renegade from military service.

Desertion, *n.* 1. Abandonment, relinquishment, dereliction, recreancy.

2. Abandonment of one's post of duty.

Deserve, *v. t.* Merit, be worthy of, be entitled to.

Deserving, *a.* Meritorious, meedful.

Desiccate, *v. t.* Dry, exsiccate, dry up, make dry.

Desiccative, *a.* Drying.

Desiderate, *v. t.* Desire, want, miss, lack, feel the want of.

Desideratum, *n.* [L. *pl. Desiderata.*] Object of desire, thing wanted, want generally felt.

Design, *v. t.* 1. Project, plan, devise, contrive, invent, scheme, concoct, brew.

2. Purpose, intend, mean, propose to one's self, have in view.

3. Draw, delineate, sketch, describe, trace out.

DESIGN, *n.* 1. Intention, intent, purpose, project, plan, device, scheme, proposal, aim, intent, meaning, purport, drift, scope, object, mark.

2. Sketch, drawing, outline, delineation, plan, draught.

3. Contrivance, invention, artifice, inventiveness, adaptation of means to ends.

Designate, *v. t.* 1. Specify, particularize, stipulate, distinguish, indicate, denote, show, point out, mark out, select.

2. Characterize, describe, define.

3. Denominate, name, entitle, style, call, term, christen, dub.

4. Appoint, assign, allot.

Designation, *n.* 1. Indication, specification, pointing out, particularization, selection.

2. Kind, class, description.

3. Name, appellation, title, style, denomination. See EPITHET.

Designedly, *adv.* Purposely, intentionally, on purpose, deliberately.

Designing, *a.* Crafty, insidious, deceitful, artful, intriguing, sly, wily, astute, subtle, cunning, arch, trickish, tricky, treacherous, crooked, diplomatic, Machiavelian.

Desirable, *a.* Eligible, enviable, to be desired.

DESIRE, *n.* 1. Wish, will, aspiration.

2. Longing, craving, hankering, avidity, eagerness, itch, hunger, inclination, proclivity, impulse, drawing, appetency, appetite, yearning.

3. Sexual love, love, passion, lust, burning.

——, *v. t.* 1. Wish, crave, covet, desiderate, want, fancy, wish for, long for, hanker after, lust after, yearn for, aspire after.

2. Solicit, request, ask.

Desirous, *a.* Eager, longing, solicitous, desiring, wishful, avid.

Desist, *v. i.* Cease, stop, pause, forbear, stay, leave off, break off, give over.

Desolate, *a.* 1. Uninhabited, unfrequented, bleak, lonely, solitary, desert, forsaken, wild, waste, barren.

2. Lonely, lonesome, solitary, companionless.

3. Ruined, destroyed, devastated, ravaged, laid waste, desolated.

4. Comfortless, cheerless, dreary, miserable, wretched, forlorn.

——, *v. t.* Ravage, devastate, depopulate, ruin, destroy, despoil, sack, lay waste.

Desolation, *n.* 1. Ruin, devastation, ravage, havoc, destruction.

2. Desolateness, loneliness, solitude, solitariness, barrenness, wildness, bleakness, dreariness.

3. Gloom, gloominess, sadness, unhappiness, wretchedness, misery.

Despair, *n.* Desperation, despondency, loss of hope, complete *or* utter hopelessness.

——, *v. i.* Despond, lose all hope, give up all expectation, be without any hope.

Despatch, *v. t.* [Written also *Dispatch.*] 1. Send away (*in haste*).

2. Kill, slay, slaughter, assassinate, put to death, send out of the world.

3. Hasten, expedite, accelerate, forward, speed, quicken, finish, conclude, wind up, push *or* urge forward, press *or* urge on, make short work of.

——, *n.* 1. Despatching, sending, dismissal on an errand.

2. Speed, haste, expedition, diligence, due diligence.

3. Transaction, carrying on, conduct, completion, doing, transacting.

4. Message (*expeditiously sent*), communication, missive, instruction, report.

Desperado, *n.* Dare-devil, apache, gangster, marauder, tough, thug, desperate fellow, reckless man, ruffian.

Desperate, *a.* 1. Despairing, hopeless, desponding, despondent, without hope.

2. Wretched, forlorn, beyond hope, irretrievable, past cure, hopeless, despaired of, lost beyond recovery.

3. Extreme, prompted by despair, heroic, done as a last resort *or* in defiance of consequences.

4. Rash, reckless, precipitate, headlong, frantic, despairing.

5. (*Colloq.*) Great, extreme, prodigious, monstrous, supreme.

Desperation, *n.* 1. Despair, hopelessness.

2. Rage, fury, defiance of consequences, reckless fury.

Despicable, *a.* Contemptible, base, mean, abject, vile, worthless, low, paltry, pitiful.

Despise, *v. t.* Contemn, scorn, spurn, disdain, misprize, scout, slight, disregard, hold in contempt, look down upon.

Despite, *n.* 1. Malevolence, malignity, malice, spite.

2. Defiance, contempt, contemptuous opposition, contumacy.

——, *prep.* Notwithstanding, in spite of, in the face of, in the teeth of.

Despoil, *v. t.* 1. Strip, denude, divest, deprive, bereave.

2. Rob, plunder, pillage, ravage, devastate, rifle, fleece.

Despond, *v. i.* Despair, be cast down, be disheartened, lose hope, lose courage, be despondent, give up, abandon hope. See DESPAIR.

Despondency, *n.* Dejection, discouragement, depression, sadness, gloom, blues, vapors, blue devils, lowness of spirits. See MELANCHOLY, *n.*

Despondent, *a.* Dispirited, disheartened, discouraged, dejected, depressed, lowspirited, in low spirits. See MELANCHOLY, *a.*

Despot, *n.* 1. Autocrat, dictator, absolute sovereign, absolute ruler.

2. Tyrant, oppressor, arbitrary *or* wilful ruler.

Despotic, } *a.* 1. Absolute, imperious,
Despotical, } autocratic.

2. Tyrannical, tyrannous, arbitrary, oppressive.

Despotism, *n.* 1. Autocracy, absolutism, dictatorship, absolute power.

2. Tyranny, arbitrary *or* capricious rule, oppression.

3. Overpowering control, overweening influence.

Desquamation, *n.* (*Med.*) Exfoliation, scaling.

Destination, *n.* 1. Fate, lot, doom, fortune, foreordainment, star, destiny.

2. Purpose, design, end, object, aim, scope, drift.

3. Goal, harbor, haven, bourne, landing-place, resting-place, journey's end, terminus.

Destine, *v. t.* 1. Appoint, ordain, allot, devote, consecrate.

2. Intend, design, predetermine.

3. Doom, decree, foreordain, predestine.

Destiny, *n.* 1. Lot, doom, fortune, fate, star, destination.

2. Fate, necessity, decrees of fate, wheel of fortune.

Destitute, *a.* Indigent, needy, poor, penniless, necessitous, distressed, reduced, pinched, short of money, out of money, out of cash, out of pocket, in need, in want, moneyless.

Destitution, *n.* Indigence, want, need, poverty, penury, privation.

Destroy, *v. t.* 1. Demolish, overturn, overthrow, subvert, raze, ruin, throw down, pull down, dismantle, break up, sap the foundations of.

2. Annihilate, quench, dissolve, efface, take away, put an end to, bring to nought, nullify.

3. Waste, ravage, desolate, devastate, devour, lay waste, make desolate, swallow up, ravage with fire and sword.

4. Extirpate, eradicate, uproot, kill, slay, extinguish, carry off, root out, grub up, pluck up by the roots, cut up root and branch, strike at the root of, give a death-blow to, scatter to the winds.

DESTRUCTION, *n.* 1. Demolition, subversion, overthrow, ruin, havoc, shipwreck.

2. Desolation, devastation, holocaust, ravage.

3. Eradication, extirpation, extinction, annihilation, ruin.

4. Death, slaughter, murder, massacre.

Destructive, *a.* 1. Ruinous, pernicious, deleterious, baleful, mischievous, fatal, deadly.

2. [With *of*.] Extirpative, eradicative, exterminative, annihilatory.

Desuetude, *n.* Disuse, discontinuance, non-observance, obsoleteness *or* obsolescence.

Desultory, *a.* Immethodical, unconnected, unsystematic, irregular, fitful, capricious, rambling, wandering, roving, discursive, cursory, slight, by fits and starts.

Detach, *v. t.* 1. Separate, disjoin, disengage, unfix, disconnect, disunite, sever, dissever, part, divide.

2. Detail, send away, appoint to a special service.

Detail, *v. t.* 1. Relate, recount, narrate, rehearse, delineate, portray, depict, enumerate, particularize, describe, set forth.

2. Detach, send away, appoint to a special service.

DETAIL, *n.* 1. Account, narration, narrative, relation, recital.

2. Detachment, sending off, appointment to special service.

3. Individual part, item, particular, particularity.

Details, *n. pl.* Particulars, minutiæ, distinct parts, minor circumstances.

Detain, *v. t.* 1. Restrain, stay, check, delay, hold, retain, stop, keep back.

2. Confine, hold *or* keep in custody.

Detect, *v. t.* Discover, expose, descry, ascertain, find, find out, bring to light, lay open.

Detection, *n.* Discovery, finding out, exposure.

Deter, *v. t.* Restrain, hinder, discourage, prevent, hold back, withhold (*by fear*).

Deteriorate, *v. t.* Impair, degrade, debase, vitiate, make worse.

——, *v. i.* Degenerate, decline, depreciate, become impaired, grow worse, worsen.

Deterioration, *n.* 1. Debasement, degradation, depravation, vitiation, perversion.

2. Degeneration, degeneracy, decadence, decay, caducity, decline, impairment.

Determinable, *a.* Definable, fixable, capable of decision, that may be determined.

Determinate, *a.* 1. Determined, definite, fixed, limited, settled, established, explicit, positive, express, absolute, certain.

2. Decisive, conclusive, definitive, decided.

Determination, *n.* 1. Determining, settling, fixing, ascertainment, settlement, deciding, decision.

2. Decision, resolution, conclusion, judgment, purpose, resolve, result.

3. Direction, tendency, leaning.

4. Resoluteness, resolution, fixity of purpose, firmness, constancy, "grit," persistence, stamina.

5. (*Log.*) Definition, qualification, limitation, adding of determinants *or* predicates.

Determine, *v. t.* 1. Settle, decide, adjust, conclude, end, fix.

2. Ascertain, certify, verify, find out, make out, fix upon.

3. Influence, lead, induce, incline, turn, give direction to.

4. Resolve, decide, set one's purpose on.

5. (*Log.*) Define, condition, limit, give marks *or* qualifications *or* predicates.

6. Necessitate, compel, subject to unyielding conditions.

Determine, *v. i.* Conclude, decide, resolve.

Detest, *v. t.* Hate (*extremely*), abominate, abhor, loathe, execrate, nauseate, shrink from, recoil from.

Detestable, *a.* 1. Execrable, abominable, odious, hateful, cursed, accursed, abhorred, damnable.

2. Loathsome, disgusting, sickening, repulsive, offensive, nauseating.

Detestation, *n.* 1. Hatred, abhorrence, abomination, detesting.

2. Loathing, disgust, antipathy.

Dethrone, *v. t.* Depose, drive from the throne, drive out of power.

Detonate, *v. i.* Explode with a loud report, detonize.

——, *v. t.* Detonize, cause to explode *or* burst with a loud report.

Detour, *n.* Circuitous route, indirect way, roundabout way.

Detract, *v. t.* Depreciate, disparage, etc. See under 1, in next entry.

Detract from. 1. Depreciate, disparage, decry, asperse, abuse, calumniate, vilify, traduce, defame, derogate from.

2. Subtract from, lessen, diminish, depreciate, deteriorate, lower, derogate from.

Detraction, *n.* Depreciation, slander, aspersion, abuse, calumny, defamation, disparagement, derogation, censure.

Detractor, *n.* Slanderer, defamer, calumniator, vilifier, depreciator, asperser.

Detriment, *n.* Loss, damage, injury, cost, disadvantage, mischief, prejudice, evil, harm, hurt.

Detrimental, *a.* Injurious, hurtful, harmful, deleterious, mischievous, pernicious, prejudicial.

Deuce, *n.* 1. Two, two-spot (*said of cards or dice*).

2. (*Colloq.*) Devil.

Devastate, *v. t.* Ravage, pillage, plunder, harry, sack, spoil, despoil, destroy, desolate, strip, lay waste.

Devastation, *n.* 1. Ravaging, pillaging, etc. See the verb.

2. Ravage, desolation, destruction, havoc, ruin, waste, pillage, rapine.

Develop, *v. t.* 1. Unfold, evolve, disclose, exhibit, unravel, disentangle, explicate, make known, lay open.

2. Cause to grow, mature, ripen, bring to maturity, bring out.

3. (*Alg.*) Expand, perform the operations indicated in.

——, *v. i.* Unfold, open, grow, be developed, evolve, advance to maturity, advance in successive *or* continuous gradation.

DEVELOPMENT, *n.* 1. Unfolding, disclosure, exhibition, unravelling, disentanglement.

2. Growth, increase, progress to maturity.

3. Evolution, progressive growth, progression in a continuously ascending gradation.

4. Expansion, explication, elaboration.

Deviate, *v. i.* 1. Digress, diverge, deflect, veer, tack, wheel, sheer off, slew, turn aside, alter one's course, wheel about.

2. Err, stray, swerve, wander, go astray, go out of one's way, lose one's way.

3. Differ, vary, diverge.

——, *v. t.* Turn aside, cause to deviate.

Deviation, *n.* 1. Divergence, departure, depression, divarication, turning, aberration.

2. Difference, variation, variance, change, alteration.

Device, *n.* 1. Contrivance, invention, "contraption," "gadget"; scheme, design, plan, project, expedient, shift, resort, resource.

2. Artifice, stratagem, wile, ruse, manœuvre, trick, fraud, evasion.

3. Design, fanciful conception, piece of fancy.

4. Emblem, symbol, type, sign, emblazoned bearing.

5. Motto, emblematic legend, legend.

Devil, *n.* 1. Satan, Lucifer, Belial, Apollyon, Arch-fiend, Arch-enemy, Deuce, the Evil One, the Old Serpent, Old Harry, Old Nick, the Prince of Darkness, the Foul Fiend, the Enemy, the Adversary. See APOLLYON.

2. Demon, evil spirit, goblin.

Devilish, *a.* 1. Diabolical, satanic, infernal, demon, demonic, demoniac, fiendish, hellish.

2. Atrocious, malignant, malign, malicious, malevolent, wicked, cruel, barbarous; *and all under* 1, *taken figuratively.*

Devilry, *n.* 1. Mischief, diablery, *diablerie*, devilment, wanton rollicking.

2. Wickedness, devilishness, satanic evil, fiendishness.

Devious, *a.* 1. Deviating, erratic, wandering, roundabout, out of the common way.

2. Crooked, mazy, circuitous, labyrinthine, obscure, confusing.

3. Crooked, disingenuous, misleading, treacherous.

Devise, *v. t.* 1. Contrive, invent, imagine, plan, scheme, project, brew, concert, concoct, excogitate, compass.

2. Bequeath, demise, leave, give by will.

——, *n.* Bequest, legacy.

Devoid, *a.* Vacant, empty, bare, destitute, void.

Devolve, *v. t.* Alienate, transfer, demise, consign, convey, deliver over, make over.

——, *v. i.* Fall (*by succession* or *by inheritance*), pass, be transferred, be handed over.

Devote, *v. t.* 1. Appropriate (*by vow*), consecrate, dedicate, destine, set apart.

2. Addict, apply, resign, give up.

3. Doom, give over, consign.

Devoted, *a.* 1. Attached, loving, affectionate.

2. Ardent, zealous, earnest, assiduous.

Devotee, *n.* Bigot, fanatic, zealot, enthusiast.

Devotion, *n.* 1. Consecration, dedication.

2. Piety, religion, devoutness, religiousness, devotedness, holiness, sanctity, saintliness, godliness.

3. [*Usually in pl.*] Worship, adoration, prayer, devoutness.

4. Attachment, affection, love.

5. Ardor, earnestness, eagerness, zeal, devotedness.

Devotional, *a.* Devout, religious, pious, saintly, godly.

Devour, *v. t.* 1. Gorge, engorge, raven, eat greedily *or* ravenously, swallow eagerly, gulp down, "wolf."

2. Destroy, consume, annihilate, waste, spend, expend, swallow up, destroy swiftly *or* rapidly.

Devout, *a.* 1. Religious, pious, holy, saintly, devotional, godly, saint-like, heavenly-minded.

2. Sincere, earnest, serious, grave, solemn.

Dexterity, *n.* Skill, skilfulness, adroitness, expertness, readiness, facility, aptness, aptitude, address, quickness, cleverness, knack, ability, tact, art.

Dexterous, *a.* Skilful, adroit, expert, adept, handy, apt, nimble-fingered, deft, ready, quick, clever, able, facile.

Diabolic, } *a.* Fiendish, infernal, satanic,
Diabolical, } impious, atrocious, wicked. See DEVILISH.

Diagram, *n.* Figure, graph, delineation, tabular sketch.

Dialect, *n.* 1. Provincialism, idiom; lingo, patter, jargon, patois.

2. Language, tongue, speech, form of speech, phraseology, parlance.

Dialectic, } *a.* 1. Logical.
Dialectical, }

2. Negative, critical, exposing limits, exposing inadequacy.

3. Idiomatic, provincial.

Dialectician, *n.* Logician, reasoner.

Dialectics, *n.* 1. Application of logical principles, applied logic.

2. Logic, science of the laws of thought, science of reasoning.

Dialing, *n.* Gnomon, gnomonics.

Dialogue, *n.* Colloquy, conference, conversation.

Diameter, *n.* Distance through the centre (*as of a circle*), central chord.

Diaphanous, *a.* Transparent, translucent, pellucid, clear.

Diaphragm, *n.* Midriff.

Diarrhœa, *n.* (*Med.*) Relax, flux, purging, looseness of the bowels.

Diary, *n.* Journal, register, chronicle.

Diatribe, *n.* 1. Disputation, dissertation, disquisition.

2. Invective, philippic, abusive harangue, reviling, tirade.

Dictate, *v. t.* Prescribe, direct, ordain, enjoin, command, order, bid, require, decree.

——, *n.* 1. Injunction, command, bidding, order, decree.

2. Precept, maxim, rule.

Dictation, *n.* Prescription, direction, order.

Dictator, *n.* Despot, autocrat, absolute ruler.

Dictatorial, *a.* 1. Absolute, unlimited, unrestricted.

2. Imperious, authoritative, overbearing, peremptory, domineering, dictatory.

Dictatorship, *n.* Despotism, absolutism, arbitrary power, absolute power, iron rule.

Diction, *n.* 1. Style, phraseology, language, expression, mode *or* manner of expression, turn of expression, form of expression.

2. Choice of words, words employed, vocabulary.

Dictionary, *n.* 1. Lexicon, vocabulary, glossary, thesaurus, word-book.

2. Encyclopædia, cyclopædia, alphabetical summary (*in any department of knowledge*).

Dictum, *n.* (L. *pl. Dicta.*) 1. Saying, assertion, affirmation.

2. (*Law.*) (*a*) Extra-judicial opinion; (*b*) award, arbitrament, decision (*of an arbitrator*).

Didactic, ⎫ *a.* Preceptive, instructive, in-
Didactical, ⎰ tended for teaching.

Didactics, *n. pl.* Science and art of teaching, pædeutics, pedagogy.

Diddle, *v. i.* Trifle, dawdle, waste time.

Die, *v. i.* 1. Expire, decease, demise,
"pass on," depart, leave the world, draw
the last breath, give up the ghost, pay
the debt of nature, shuffle off this mortal
coil, go the way of all flesh, be numbered with the dead, cross the Styx.

2. Wither, perish, decay, decline, fade,
fade out, lose life.

3. Cease, vanish, disappear, come to
nothing, come to an end, be lost, be heard
of no more.

4. Sink, faint, fall.

5. Gradually cease, become fainter
and fainter, subside, gradually disappear.

——, *n.* 1. Cube (*for gaming*); *pl.*
"bones."

2. Stamp.

Diet, *n.* 1. Food, provision, victuals,
aliment, nutriment, nourishment, subsistence, provision, fare, viands, regimen,
cheer, rations, commons.

2. Assembly, convention, council, convocation, congress, parliament.

——, *v. i.* 1. Eat sparingly, eat by rule,
regulate the diet.

2. Feed, eat, take nourishment, nourish one's self.

Differ, *v. i.* 1. Vary, deviate, diverge, be
unlike.

2. Disagree, dissent, be of a different
opinion, think differently.

3. Wrangle, dispute, quarrel, contend,
bicker, be at variance.

Difference, *n.* 1. Dissimilarity, unlikeness, nuance (*French*), variation, diversity, heterogeneity, disparity, dissimilitude, divergence, departure, inconformity, deviation, contrariety, contrast, disagreement, opposition, antitheticalness.

2. Disagreement, variance, alienation,
misunderstanding, dissension, disaccord,
irreconcilability, disharmony, jarring,
breach, rupture, schism, contest, contention, quarrel, dispute, debate, controversy, altercation, bickering, embroilment, wrangle, strife, falling out.

3. Distinction, discrimination.

DIFFERENT, *a.* 1. Distinct, separate,
other, non-identical, not the same.

2. Unlike, dissimilar, various, diverse,
contrary, contrasted, contradistinct,
variant, deviating, divergent, disagreeing,
incongruous, incompatible, discrepant.

3. Various, heterogeneous, divers,
many, manifold, sundry.

Differential, *a.* Discriminating.

Difficult, *a.* 1. Hard, arduous, Herculean,
"tough," "stiff," exacting, up-hill, beset
with difficulty.

2. Obscure, hard to be understood,
intricate, knotty, abstruse, perplexing.

3. Austere, rigid, unyielding, unaccommodating, uncompliant, *difficile*,
hard to manage *or* persuade.

4. Fastidious, dainty, squeamish, hard
to please.

Difficulty, *n.* 1. Arduousness, laborious-
ness.

2. Obstacle, impediment, bar, obstruction, barrier, hindrance, thwart,
perplexity, exigency, crux, knot, trouble,
trial, dilemma, embarrassment, emergency, pinch, predicament, fix, pickle,
stand, dead-set, set fast, dead-lock, dead-
stand, stand-still, horns of a dilemma, uphill work, peck of troubles, hard row to
hoe, hard nut to crack.

3. Objection, cavil, obstacle to belief.

4. Embroilment, complication, controversy, embarrassment, imbroglio, misunderstanding, difference.

Diffidence, *n.* 1. Distrust, doubt, hesitation, hesitancy, reluctance.

2. Bashfulness, timidity, sheepishness,
shyness, extreme modesty, distrust of
one's self, lack *or* want of self-reliance.

Diffident, *a.* 1. Distrustful, doubtful, hesitating, reluctant.

2. Bashful, timid, sheepish, over-
modest, shy, distrustful of one's self.

Diffuse, *v. t.* Disperse, scatter, disseminate,
spread, circulate, propagate, distribute,
pour out, strew, send abroad, spread
abroad.

——, *a.* (*Pron.* diffūs'.) 1. Prolix, copious,
rambling, loose, verbose, wordy, long-
winded, long-spun, spun out.

2. (*Med.*) Spreading, ill-defined,
vaguely defined.

Diffusion, *n.* Dispersion, spread, extension,
propagation, circulation, distribution,
dissemination, strewing.

Diffusive, *a.* 1. Expansive, wide-reaching,
permeating.

2. Spreading in every direction, dis-
seminative, dispersive, distributive, dis-
tributory.

Dig, *v. t.* Excavate, delve, scoop, hollow
out, grub, channel, quarry.

——, *v. i.* Delve, work with a spade, hoe,
etc., grub.

——, *n.* Punch, poke, thrust.

Digest, *n.* 1. Pandect.

2. Code, system.

3. Abridgment, abstract, compend,
compendium, epitome, summary, synop-

sis, conspectus, breviary, brief, sum and substance.

Digest, *v. t.* 1. (*Pron.* digest'.) Methodize, systematize, arrange, codify, classify, dispose, reduce to order.

2. Concoct, convert into chyme.

3. Study, ponder, consider, contemplate, reflect upon, think on, meditate upon, con over, revolve in the mind.

4. Appropriate completely (*in the mind*), make one's own, assimilate, master.

5. (*Chem.*) Soften by a gentle heat, macerate, steep, soak.

DIGESTION, *n.* 1. Conversion of food into chyme, eupepsy.

2. Methodizing, digesting, classifying.

3. (*Chem.*) Macerating, maceration, steeping.

Digit, *n.* 1. Finger.

2. Numerical symbol (*in the Arabic notation*).

3. Finger's breadth, three fourths of an inch.

Dignified, *a.* Stately, noble, majestic, courtly, august, grave, imposing, decorous.

Dignify, *v. t.* 1. Advance, promote, elevate, exalt, ennoble, prefer to office.

2. Honor, grace, adorn, exalt, ennoble, give lustre to, add dignity to.

Dignity, *n.* 1. Rank, elevation, standing, station, place, greatness, eminence, exaltation, glory, honor, reputableness, respectability.

2. Stateliness, grandeur, majesty, nobleness, lofty bearing *or* conduct, elevation of aspect *or* deportment, dignified behavior, decorum.

3. Honor, preferment, high station *or* office.

4. Magistrate, dignitary, person in office.

5. Height, elevation, importance, worth.

Digress, *v. i.* Wander, deviate *or* diverge *or* turn aside from one's main topic.

Digression, *n.* 1. Deviation *or* divergence *or* departure from the main topic.

2. Episode, incidental passage, excursus.

Dilapidate, *v. t.* Waste, ruin, destroy, pull down, throw down, suffer to go to ruin.

Dilapidated, *a.* Decayed, ruined, run-down, decadent, wasted, in ruins.

Dilapidation, *n.* Ruin, decay, disrepair, downfall.

Dilatation, *n.* Expansion, expanding, distension, enlargement, spreading, amplification, swelling, dilation.

Dilate, *v. t.* Expand, tend, enlarge, inflate, widen, distend, swell.

——, *v. i.* 1. Expand, widen, be distended.

2. Expatiate, descant, enlarge, dwell, be diffuse, be prolix, launch out, branch out, spin a long yarn.

Dilation, *n.* Dilatation, expansion, expanding, swelling, bloating, distension, enlargement, amplification, spreading.

Dilatory, *a.* Slow, tardy, lingering, loitering, sluggish, laggard, lagging, behindhand, backward, procrastinating.

Dilemma, *n.* Quandary, strait, difficult choice, puzzling alternative, awkward *or* bad predicament.

Dilettante, *n.* [It.] 1. Amateur, trifling *or* desultory cultivator.

2. Pretender to taste (*in the fine arts*).

Diligence, *n.* Assiduity (*in some specific pursuit*), assiduousness, activity, sedulousness, constancy, perseverance, steady application (*to some pursuit that one likes*). See INDUSTRY.

Diligent, *a.* Assiduous, sedulous, industrious, active, busy, persevering, notable, hard-working, studious, at work, diligently employed, busily engaged, up and stirring, busy as a bee.

Dillydally, *v. i.* Loiter, linger, delay, lag, saunter, trifle, dally, dawdle, idle away time.

Dilute, *v. t.* 1. Thin (*with water* or *other liquid*), make more liquid, make thinner.

2. Attenuate, reduce, weaken, thin, make thin, make weak.

——, *a.* Thin, diluted, attenuated, weak, "wishy-washy."

Dim, *a.* 1. Dusky, dark, obscure, mysterious, indistinct, ill-defined, indefinite, shadowy, cloudy, faint.

2. Dull, obtuse, slow to see, slow of understanding *or* perception.

3. Darkened, obscured, clouded, faint, confused, shorn of its beams.

4. Tarnished, blurred, sullied, dulled, dull.

——, *v. t.* Darken, obscure, cloud, sully, tarnish, dull.

Dimension, *n.* Extent, extension, measure (*in one direction*).

Dimensions, *n. pl.* 1. Size, magnitude, bulk, volume, bigness, capacity, amplitude, greatness, largeness, mass, massiveness.

2. Measurements, linear dimensions; length, breadth, and thickness.

Diminish, *v. t.* Lessen, decrease, abate, reduce, contract, make smaller, belittle.

——, *v. i.* Decrease, dwindle, taper off, lessen, abate, subside, melt, narrow, shrink, shrivel, contract, grow *or* become less, be reduced, become smaller.

Diminution, *n.* Decrease, lessening, curtailment, abridgment, decrement, diminishing, shrinkage, attenuation, decrescendo, reduction, abatement, contraction.

Diminutive, *a.* Little, small, dwarfish, tiny, puny, pygmy, pygmean, contracted, minute, of small size.

Din, *n.* Noise, uproar, racket, bruit, clamor, clangor, clash, crash, crashing, clatter, hubbub, hullabaloo, hurly-burly, uproar.

Dingy, *a.* 1. Dun, dusky, brown.

2. Soiled, sullied, smirched, dimmed, dulled, faded.

Dint, *n.* 1. Stroke, blow.

2. Dent, indentation, nick, notch.

3. Force, power. [Only in the phrase *By dint of.*]

Diocese, *n.* Bishopric, see, jurisdiction, charge (*of a bishop*), episcopate.

Dip, *v. t.* 1. Immerse, plunge, douse, souse, duck.

2. Take out (*with a ladle, cup, etc.*), ladle, bail.

3. Baptize by immersion.

——, *v. i.* 1. Thrust a ladle (*cup, etc., into a liquid*).

2. Incline, tend downward.

3. Engage cursorily, enter slightly.

4. Dive, plunge, duck, pitch, immerse one's self.

Diplomacy, *n.* 1. Art of negotiating, negotiation, international business.

2. Artful management, tact, indirection, politic approach.

Diplomatist, *n.* Negotiator, diplomat, envoy, legate, minister, expert in international affairs.

Dipper, *n.* 1. Plunger, ladler, etc. See verb.

2. Immersionist, dunker, tunker, tumbler.

3. Charles' Wain, Great Bear, Ursa Major, Cleaver.

4. Water-craw, water-pyet, water-crake, water-ouzel (*Cinclus aquaticus*).

Dire, *a.* Dreadful, dismal, fearful, direful, shocking, terrible, horrid, horrible, awful, terrific, tremendous, portentous, gloomy, woful, disastrous, calamitous, destructive, cruel, inexorable, implacable.

DIRECT, *a.* 1. Straight, in a right line, not crooked; immediate.

2. Plain, express, categorical, unambiguous, not equivocal.

3. Open, sincere, ingenuous, frank, outspoken.

——, *v. t.* 1. Aim, point, level, cast, turn.

2. Regulate, dispose, manage, conduct, control, govern, rule, guide.

3. Order, command, bid, instruct, prescribe to, give directions to.

4. Show, point, guide, lead, put upon the right track.

5. Address, superscribe.

DIRECTION, *n.* 1. Aim.

2. Tendency, line of motion.

3. Course, bearing, point of compass, quarter.

4. Management, oversight, superintendence, government, control, conduct.

5. Guidance, lead.

6. Order, command, prescription.

7. Address, superscription.

Directly, *adv.* 1. In a straight line, in a straight course.

2. Expressly, absolutely, unambiguously, openly, without circumlocution.

3. Immediately, quickly, promptly, speedily, soon, presently, forthwith, instantly, *instanter*, in a short time, without delay.

Director, *n.* 1. Superintendent, manager, boss.

2. Guide, counsellor, adviser, instructor, mentor, monitor.

Direful, *a.* Dreadful, fearful, horrible, terrible, shocking, horrid, terrific, awful, tremendous. See DIRE.

Dirge, *n.* Elegy, funeral song, mournful song, monody, threnody, requiem, burial hymn, coronach.

Dirt, *n.* Filth, foul matter, muck, grime.

DIRTY, *a.* 1. Unclean, foul, filthy, nasty, soiled, begrimed, defiled.

2. Clouded, cloudy, dark, sullied, dull.

3. Mean, base, vile, low, groveling, sneaking, pitiful, paltry, beggarly, scurvy, shabby, despicable, contemptible.

4. [*Said of weather.*] Foul, rainy, sloppy, muddy, sleety, uncomfortable, disagreeable, nasty.

——, *v. t.* Foul, befoul, soil, defile, draggle, sully, pollute.

Disability, *n.* Disqualification, disablement, unfitness, inability, incapacity, incompetence, impotence, incapability.

Disable, *v. t.* 1. Weaken, enfeeble, cripple, hamstring, paralyze, unman, deprive of strength.

2. Disqualify, incapacitate, disenable, unfit, make incapable.

Disabuse, *v. t.* Undeceive, set right.

Disadvantage, *n.* 1. Unfavorableness, disadvantageousness, inconvenience.

2. Injury, loss, damage, detriment, disservice, hindrance, prejudice, hurt, drawback, harm.

Disadvantageous, *a.* 1. Unfavorable, ineligible, inconvenient.

2. Injurious, prejudicial, hurtful, detrimental, deleterious.

Disaffect, *v. t.* Alienate, estrange, make unfriendly.

Disaffected, *a.* Alienated, estranged, dissatisfied, disloyal.

Disaffection, *n.* Alienation, estrangement, breach, disagreement, dissatisfaction, disloyalty, ill-will.

Disagree, *v. i.* 1. Differ, vary, diverge, be unlike.

2. Dissent, be of different opinions, differ in opinion.

3. Quarrel, wrangle, dispute, bicker, clash, fall out.

4. Be unsuitable, be unfit, be unsuited.

Disagreeable, *a.* Unpleasant, unpleasing, displeasing, distasteful, offensive, "nasty."

Disagreement, *n.* 1. Difference, dissimilarity, unlikeness, dissimilitude, diversity, discrepancy, incongruity, divergence, deviation.

2. Dissent, difference of opinion, disaccord.

3. Discord, disunion, disunity, conflict, contention, variance, misunderstanding, dissension, jarring, clashing, strife, quarrel, dispute, wrangle, bickering.

Disallow, *v. t.* 1. Prohibit, forbid, refuse permission to.

2. Reject, disapprove, set aside, refuse *or* decline to sanction.

3. Disavow, disclaim, disown, deny.

Disannul, *v. t.* Nullify, cancel, rescind, quash, vacate, annul, abolish, abrogate, void, invalidate, render void, set aside, do away.

Disappear, *v. i.* 1. Vanish, recede from view, be lost to view, pass out of sight.

2. Cease, cease to be, dissolve.

Disappoint, *v. t.* Balk, frustrate, foil, defeat, thwart, baffle, disconcert, bring to nought, foil of one's expectations.

Disappointment, *n.* 1. Frustration, foiling, baffling, unfulfilment.

2. Frustration of hopes, sense of frustration, feeling of thwarted expectation.

Disapprobation, *n.* Disapproval, censure, condemnation, displeasure, dislike.

Disapproval, *n.* Disapprobation, censure, condemnation, non-approval.

Disapprove, *v. t.* 1. Condemn, censure, deprecate, dislike, regard as wrong.

2. Reject, disallow, refuse *or* decline to sanction.

Disarm, *v. t.* 1. Deprive of arms *or* weapons.

2. Disable, incapacitate, render powerless, harmless, *or* innocuous.

——, *v. i.* Lay down arms, reduce the military establishment, dismiss *or* disband troops, reduce forces to a peace footing.

Disarrange, *v. t.* Disorder, unsettle, derange, dislocate, dishevel, rumple, tumble, jumble, disturb, put out of order, throw into disorder, confuse, throw into confusion.

Disarray, *n.* Confusion, disorder; dishabille.

Disaster, *n.* Mishap, misfortune, reverse, mischance, misadventure, adversity, calamity, catastrophe, blow, stroke, casualty, ruin.

Disastrous, *a.* 1. Calamitous, unfortunate, unlucky, hapless, adverse, ruinous, destructive, untoward, unprosperous, ill-fated, ill-starred.

2. Foreboding, threatening, gloomy, dismal, portentous, portending disaster.

Disavow, *v. t.* Disclaim, disown, deny, disallow.

Disband, *v. t.* Break up, dismiss from (*military*) service, disperse, send home.

——, *v. i.* Separate, disperse, scatter, break up, retire from military service.

Disbelief, *n.* 1. Doubt, unbelief, nonconviction, agnosticism, rejection, lack of conviction.

2. Distrust, want of confidence, lack of trust.

Disbelieve, *v. t.* Discredit, not believe, refuse to credit, hold *or* consider not to be true.

Disbeliever, *n.* [With *in* or *of*.] Unbeliever, doubter, questioner, denier, non-adherent, opponent.

Disburden, *v. t.* Disencumber, unburden, unload, ease, rid, free, relieve, disburthen.

Disburse, *v. t.* Spend, expend, lay out, pay out.

Disbursement, *n.* Expenditure, paying out, laying out, spending.

Discard, *v. t.* 1. Reject, throw *or* thrust aside, abandon, throw away, cast away, lay aside, cast off.

2. Dismiss, discharge, cashier, break, cast off, turn away.

Discern, *v. t.* 1. Discriminate, distinguish, note the distinctions of.

2. Perceive, see, discover, descry, behold, espy.

——, *v. i.* Discriminate, judge, make distinction.

Discernible, *a.* Perceptible, discoverable, detectible, to be discerned *or* descried.

Discerning, *a.* Discriminating, discriminative, sagacious, perspicacious, judicious, acute, astute, sharp, piercing, clear-sighted, keen-sighted, eagle-eyed, hawk-eyed, Argus-eyed.

Discernment, *n.* 1. Discrimination, sagacity, shrewdness, sharpness, brightness, astuteness, acuteness, cleverness, perspicacity, ingenuity, penetration, insight, judgment, intelligence, acumen, mother wit, quick parts.

2. Discerning, perception, notice, espial, discovery, descrying, beholding.

Discharge, *v. t.* 1. Unload, disburden, unburden, relieve of a load.

2. Emit, expel, excrete, eject, void, throw off, project, send out, give forth.

3. Set off, fire off, let fly, give vent to, shoot, fire.

4. Pay, liquidate, cash.

5. Release, absolve, exonerate, acquit, clear, relieve, liberate, free, set free.

6. Dismiss, discard, cashier, "sack," turn away, send away.

7. Remove, destroy, put away, clear from.

8. Perform, execute, fulfil, observe, acquit one's self of.

9. (*Law.*) Cancel, rescind, annul, nullify, invalidate, make void.

——, *n.* 1. Unloading, disburdening.

2. Emission, ejection, expulsion, dismissal, displacement, excretion, vent, evacuation, voiding.

3. Firing, explosion, blast, burst, firing off.

4. Observance, performance, fulfilment, execution.

5. Payment, settlement, liquidation, annulment, satisfaction, clearance.

6. Release, liberation, exemption.

7. Acquittal, exoneration, absolution.

8. Flow, flux, excretion.

Disciple, *n.* 1. Scholar, pupil, learner, student.

2. Follower, adherent, supporter.

Disciplinarian, *n.* Enforcer of discipline, martinet.

Discipline, *n.* 1. Training, drilling, drill, exercise, diligent practice.

2. Control, regulation, government, good order, subjection.

3. Branch of knowledge, elements of culture.

4. Punishment, chastisement, correction.

5. Rule of practice, regulations.

——, *v. t.* 1. Instruct, train, breed, educate, teach, drill, exercise, form, bring up.

2. Regulate, control, govern, school, bring under subjection.

3. Punish, chastise, correct.

Disclaim, *v. t.* 1. Disown, disavow, deny any knowledge of.

2. Renounce, reject, repudiate, cast off.

Disclaimer, *n.* 1. Disavowal, abjuration, disowning, repudiation.

2. (*Law.*) Renunciation (*of a claim or a title*), relinquishment.

Disclose, *v. t.* 1. Uncover, expose, exhibit, manifest, bring to view, bring to light.

2. Reveal, divulge, show, unfold, unveil, tell, publish, bare, "blab," utter, betray, communicate, lay open, make known.

Disclosure, *n.* Revelation, exposure, *exposé*, betrayal, uncovering, discovery.

Discolor, *v. t.* Stain, tarnish, tinge, change the color of.

Discomfit, *v. t.* 1. Defeat, overthrow, rout, overcome, overpower, conquer, vanquish, subdue, beat, checkmate, put to flight, put down, get the upper hand of, scatter in flight.

2. Foil, disconcert, abash, confound, upset, baffle, balk, frustrate one's plans, perplex.

Discomfiture, *n.* Rout, defeat, overthrow, ruin. See DISCOMFIT.

Discomfort, *n.* Uneasiness, disquiet, inquietude, *malaise*, distress, trouble, annoyance.

Discommode, *v. t.* Disturb, annoy, molest, trouble, disquiet, incommode, inconvenience, put to inconvenience.

Discompose, *v. t.* 1. Disorder, derange, disarrange, embroil, jumble, unsettle, confuse, disturb, throw into disorder *or* confusion.

2. Displease, disquiet, ruffle, agitate, upset, harass, worry, annoy, plague, trouble, vex, fret, nettle, irritate, provoke, chafe.

3. Disconcert, perplex, bewilder, fluster, embarrass, abash, put out.

Discomposure, *n.* 1. Derangement, confusion.

2. Agitation, disquiet, uneasiness, excitement, flurry, vexation, worry, perturbation, annoyance.

Disconcert, *v. t.* 1. Frustrate, defeat, balk, baffle, upset, thwart, contravene, interrupt, undo.

2. Discompose, confuse, demoralize, "faze," perplex, bewilder, embarrass, disturb, abash, put out, unbalance, throw off one's balance.

Disconnect, *v. t.* Disjoin, separate, disengage, dissociate, uncouple, unlink, disunite, sever. Compare DETACH.

Disconnection, *n.* Disjunction, disassociation, disunion, separation, isolation, severance.

Disconsolate, *a.* Inconsolable, desolate, forlorn, heart-broken, broken-hearted, comfortless, cheerless, sorrowful, woeful, melancholy, sad.

Discontent, *n.* Dissatisfaction, uneasiness, heartburn, inquietude, restlessness, discontentment.

Discontinuance, *n.* Cessation, intermission, suspension, interruption, disruption, stoppage, stop, breaking off.

Discontinue, *v. t.* Intermit, stop, cease, interrupt, quit, break off, leave off, desist from, put an end to.

Discontinuous, *a.* Interrupted, broken, intermittent, discrete.

Discord, *n.* 1. Disagreement, contention, strife, quarreling, dissension, variance, opposition, wrangling, difference, rupture, falling out.

2. Dissonance, discordance, harshness, jangle, cacophony, jarring, want of harmony.

Discordance, *n.* 1. Disagreement, inconsistency, incongruity, opposition, conflict, repugnance.

2. Discord, dissonance.

Discordant, *a.* 1. Disagreeing, incongruous, inconsistent, contradictory, contrary, opposite, repugnant, at variance.

2. Dissonant, harsh, jarring, jangling, inharmonious, cacophonous.

Discount, *n.* Allowance, deduction, reduction, drawback, abatement, rebate.

Discountenance, *v. t.* 1. (*Rare.*) Abash, put to shame, put out of countenance.

2. Discourage, disfavor, check, frown upon, show disapprobation of.

Discourage, *v. t.* 1. Dishearten, dispirit, daunt, depress, deject.

2. Dissuade, deter, keep back.

3. Disfavor, discountenance, throw cold water upon, put a damper on, cover with a wet blanket.

Discouragement, *n.* 1. Disheartening.

2. Dissuasion, dehortation, counter influence.

3. Embarrassment, hindrance, deterrent, obstacle, impediment, damper, wet blanket, cold water.

Discourse, *n.* 1. Dissertation, treatise, disquisition, homily, sermon, preachment, descant, address.

2. Conversation, talk, converse, colloquy, oral communication, verbal intercourse.

——, *v. i.* 1. Speak, expatiate, hold forth, sermonize, lucubrate, deliver a discourse.

2. Talk, converse, parley, confer, advise, hold a conversation, hold a parley *or* conference, talk together. Cf. Discuss.

3. Reason, make inferences, draw conclusions.

——, *v. t.* Utter, emit, give forth, pour forth.

Discourteous, *a.* Uncivil, impolite, uncourtly, uncomplaisant, ungentlemanly, disrespectful, inurbane, unmannerly, uncourteous, brusque, abrupt, rude, ill-bred, ill-mannered.

Discourtesy, *n.* Incivility, impoliteness, rudeness, abruptness, brusqueness, inurbanity, ill-breeding.

Discover, *v. t.* 1. Reveal, communicate, tell, disclose, exhibit, show, manifest, make manifest, impart, make known, lay open, lay bare, expose to view.

2. Ascertain, detect, uncover, unearth, find out.

3. Descry, discern, espy, see, behold, get sight of, get a glimpse of.

DISCOVERY, *n.* 1. Disclosure, revelation, making known.

2. Finding, finding out, detection, discernment, espial, unearthing, first sight, ascertainment.

Discredit, *n.* 1. Doubt, question, loss of credit *or* credence.

2. Disrepute, dishonor, disgrace, reproach, scandal, opprobrium, obloquy, odium, ignominy, ill repute.

——, *v. t.* 1. Disbelieve, give no credit to, place no confidence in, refuse credence to, question, doubt.

2. Disgrace, dishonor, bring reproach upon, make disreputable, blow upon, disparage, depreciate, destroy confidence in, bring into disfavor, make distasteful, deprive of credit.

Discreditable, *a.* Disgraceful, disreputable, dishonorable, unworthy, derogatory, scandalous, infamous, ignominious, inglorious.

Discreet, *a.* Prudent, cautious, judicious, wise, circumspect, considerate, heedful, wary.

Discrepancy, *n.* Difference, incongruity, disagreement, contrariety, inconsistency, variance, divergence, discordance.

Discrepant, *a.* Differing, disagreeing, incongruous, inconsistent, contrary, discordant, jarring, clashing, conflicting.

Discrete, *a.* 1. Separate, distinct, disjunct, discontinuous.

2. Disjunctive, discretive.

Discretion, *n.* 1. Prudence (*in things immediately before us*), judgment, caution, wariness, carefulness, circumspection, considerateness, judiciousness. See Prudence.

2. Sound judgment, good sense, discrimination, mature judgment, maturity, responsibility.

3. Will, pleasure, choice, liberty of judgment.

Discretionary, *a.* Optional.

Discriminate, *v. t.* Distinguish, mark the difference between, tell one from the other.

——, *v. i.* Distinguish, make a distinction, note differences, judge nicely *or* accurately, be discriminating.

Discrimination, *n.* 1. Distinction, difference.

2. Discernment, penetration, acuteness, acumen, judgment, sagacity, insight.

Discriminative, *a.* Discriminating, distinguishing, characterizing, characteristic, distinctive.

Discursive, *a.* 1. Reasoning, argumentative, capable of reasoning.

2. Traversing a field of particulars, derived through particulars, passing from many to one, from manifoldness to unity.

3. Roving, wandering, rambling, cursory, digressive, excursive, desultory, taking a wide range.

Discus, *n.* Quoit, disk.

Discuss, *v. t.* Debate, sift, canvass, ventilate, agitate, argue, reason about, consider, deliberate (upon).

DISCUSSION, *n.* 1. Debating, ventilation, agitation, canvassing.

2. Debate, disputation, controversy, parley.

Disdain, *v. t.* Despise, contemn, scout, scorn, spurn, look down upon, hold in contempt, consider beneath notice.

——, *n.* Scorn, contempt, contumely, haughtiness, superciliousness, arrogance, *hauteur.*

Disdainful, *a.* Scornful, contemptuous, supercilious, contumelious, haughty, cavalier.

DISEASE, *n.* Disorder, distemper, malady, complaint, ail, ailment, sickness, illness, indisposition, infirmity.

Diseased, *a.* Disordered, distempered, unsound, unwell, sickly, sick.

Disembark, *v. t.* Land, put on shore, send ashore, debark.

——, *v. i.* Land, go on shore, debark.

Disembarrass, *v. t.* Disengage, extricate, release, disburden, disencumber, disentangle, ease, rid, free, clear, set free.

Disembodied, *a.* Unbodied, incorporeal, disincarnate, immaterial, spiritual, bodiless, divested of the body.

Disembogue, *v. t.* Discharge (*at the mouth, as a river*), empty, pour out, give vent to.

——, *v. i.* Issue, flow out (*at the mouth, as a river*), discharge itself, be discharged.

Disembowel, *v. t.* Eviscerate, embowel, take out the bowels of, "gut."

Disembroil, *v. t.* Disentangle, free from perplexity, extricate from confusion.

Disenable, *v. t.* Disqualify, disable, unfit, incapacitate, make incapable.

Disenchant, *v. t.* Free from enchantment, deliver from illusions, remove the spell from.

Disencumber, *v. t.* Disburden, disengage, disembarrass, release, ease, rid, set free.

Disengage, *v. t.* 1. Release, extricate, liberate, clear, disentangle, disembroil, disembarrass, disencumber, loose, unloose, free, set free.

2. Separate, detach, divide, disjoin, disunite, dissociate.

3. Withdraw, wean, draw off.

Disengaged, *a.* Unengaged, unoccupied, at leisure, not busy.

Disengagement, *n.* 1. Detachment, separation.

2. Liberation, release, extrication, disentanglement.

3. Leisure, freedom from business.

Disennoble, *v. t.* Degrade, disgrace, make ignoble, deprive of rank *or* dignity, strip of title.

Disentangle, *v. t.* 1. Unravel, untwist, unfold, loosen, separate, straighten out.

2. Extricate, disengage, disembroil, liberate, clear, loose, unloose, disconnect, detach, free, set free.

Disenthrall, *v. t.* Liberate, enfranchise, free, release from bondage, rescue from slavery *or* oppression.

Disestablish, *v. t.* 1. (*Rare.*) Abolish, overthrow, annul, discontinue, abrogate, set aside, do away.

2. Deprive of public support, strip of State authority, abolish as a State institution.

Disestablishment, *n.* 1. (*Rare.*) Abolition, annulment, discontinuance, abrogation, overthrow, subversion, destruction, annihilation, extinction.

2. Deprivation of public support, stripping of State authority, abolition as a State institution.

Disfavor, *n.* 1. Disregard, disesteem, dislike, disrespect, little *or* slight esteem, low regard, slight displeasure, unfavorable regard, disapproval.

2. Unacceptableness, (*state of*) disapproval *or* low regard, discredit, disrepute, disgrace, uninfluential position.

3. Unkindness, disobliging act, ill turn, disservice, act of ill-will.

Disfigure, *v. t.* Deform, deface, mar, injure, blemish, spoil, make ugly, make unsightly.

Disfigurement, *n.* 1. Defacement, injury, deforming, marring, blemishing, spoiling.

2. Deformity, blemish, injury.

Disfurnish, *v. t.* Unfurnish, strip, divest, dismantle, disgarnish.

Disgorge, *v. t.* 1. Vomit, spew, cast up, throw up.

2. Eject, discharge, throw out.

3. Relinquish, surrender, yield, give up, give back.

Disgrace, *n.* 1. Disfavor, disesteem, degradation.

2. Dishonor, discredit, disrepute, disesteem, shame, reproach, disparagement, ignominy, infamy, opprobrium, obloquy, odium, scandal, blot on one's escutcheon.

——, *v. t.* 1. Put out of favor, dismiss from favor, humiliate, humble, degrade, strip of rank *or* honors.

2. Dishonor, discredit, degrade, debase, tarnish, stain, sully, taint, bring shame, reproach, dishonor, *or* a stain upon.

Disgraceful, *a.* Shameful, ignominious, scandalous, dishonorable, discreditable, disreputable, infamous, opprobrious, that deserves reproach, odium, *or* obloquy.

Disguise, *v. t.* Conceal (*by dress* or *outward appearance*), cloak, veil, shroud, muffle, mask, hide, dissemble.

——, *n.* 1. Mask, cover, concealment, veil, counterfeit dress.

2. False appearance, counterfeit show, veneer, cloak, masquerade, blind, pretence, pretext.

Disguised, *a.* Cloaked, masked, veiled, in disguise, incognito.

DISGUST, *n.* 1. Nausea, disrelish, distaste, loathing.

2. Dislike, repugnance, aversion, antipathy, abomination, detestation, revulsion, abhorrence.

——, *v. t.* 1. Sicken, affect with nausea, turn one's stomach, go against one's stomach.

2. Displease, offend, be repellent, repulsive, repugnant, hateful, detestable, *or* abhorrent to.

Disgusting, *a.* 1. Nauseous, nauseating, loathsome, sickening.

2. Repulsive, loathsome, loathly, revolting, offensive, odious, hateful, foul, abominable, repugnant, abhorrent, detestable, distasteful.

Dish, *n.* 1. Vessel, plate, bowl, saucer, etc.

2. Viand, article of food.

——, *v. t.* 1. Put in a dish, put into dishes, serve.

2. (*Colloq.*) Do for, put *hors de combat*, balk, upset, thwart, shelve, lay up, render helpless.

Dishabille, *n.* *Déshabillé,* undress, loose dress.

Dishearten, *v. t.* Dispirit, discourage, deject, depress.

Dished, *a.* (*Colloq.*) Frustrated, balked, foiled, baffled, upset, disconcerted, disappointed.

Disheveled, *a.* Disordered (*as the hair*), "mussed," tousled, tumbled, unkempt, hanging loose *or* negligently, at loose ends.

Dishonest, *a.* Faithless, knavish, false, unfair, disingenuous, fraudulent, deceitful, treacherous, crooked, slippery, unscrupulous, perfidious, false-hearted, without probity, destitute of integrity.

Dishonesty, *n.* Improbity, faithlessness, knavery, treachery, falsehood, deceitfulness, perfidiousness, fraud, fraudulency, fraudulence, trickery.

Dishonor, *n.* Disgrace, discredit, disrepute, disparagement, reproach, degradation, shame, ignominy, obloquy, infamy, opprobrium, odium, scandal, abasement.

——, *v. t.* 1. Disgrace, discredit, degrade, abase, bring shame *or* reproach upon, defame, stain the character of.

2. Debauch, deflower, corrupt.

Dishonorable, *a.* 1. Disreputable, discreditable, disgraceful, shameful, scandalous, infamous, ignominious.

2. Base, devoid of honor, shameless, false, false-hearted.

Disinclination, *n.* Indisposition, reluctance, repugnance, aversion, unwillingness.

Disinclined, *a.* Unwilling, indisposed, reluctant, grudging, averse.

Disinfect, *v. t.* Deodorize, fumigate, purify, asepticize, sterilize, cleanse *or* free from infection.

Disingenuous, *a.* Insincere, uncandid, artful, deceitful, double-minded, hollow, dishonest.

Disintegrate, *v. t.* Crumble, decompose, dissolve, reduce to fragments, break to pieces.

Disinter, *v. t.* Exhume, unbury, disentomb, disinhume, dig up.

Disinterested, *a.* Unbiassed, unselfish, liberal, high-minded, impartial, fair, candid.

Disjoin, *v. t.* Disunite, separate, divide, part, sunder, sever, dissever, detach, dissociate.

Disjoint, *v. t.* 1. Dislocate, luxate, put out of joint.

2. Unloose, disconnect, disjoin, separate at the joints *or* original divisions.

3. Break up, disarrange, derange, throw into confusion.

Disjointed, *a.* Disconnected, loose, incoherent, desultory.

Disjunction, *n.* Separation, disconnection, disassociation, disunion, isolation, severance, parting.

Disjunctive, *a.* Disjoining, discretive, alternative.

Disk, *n.* 1. Quoit, discus.
2. Face (*of the sun, moon, etc.*)
3. Circular plate, flat circular surface, paten, roundel.

Dislike, *n.* Disinclination, aversion, disfavor, distaste, disrelish, antipathy, repugnance, displeasure, disgust.

——, *v. t.* Disrelish, feel aversion to, be disinclined *or* averse *or* reluctant, disapprove, hold in disfavor.

Dislimb, *v. t.* Dismember, mutilate.

Dislocate, *v. t.* 1. Displace, disarrange, disturb, put out of place *or* out of order.
2. Disjoint, luxate, disarticulate, slip, put out of joint.

Dislocation, *n.* 1. Derangement, displacement.
2. Luxation, disjointing.

Dislodge, *v. t.* Displace, dispel, dismount, expel, oust, eject, remove, force out, push out, get out.

Disloyal, *a.* Unfaithful, undutiful, disaffected, faithless, false, treacherous, perfidious, untrue, false to one's allegiance.

Disloyalty, *n.* Unfaithfulness, undutifulness, faithlessness, treachery, perfidy, want of loyalty, lack of fidelity, dereliction of allegiance.

Dismal, *a.* 1. Cheerless, gloomy, dark, dull, dreary, lonesome.
2. Melancholy, depressed, in low spirits, "blue," mournful, sad, doleful, dolorous, sombre, lugubrious, funereal.

Dismantle, *v. t.* Unrig, strip of covering, deprive of apparatus, furniture, rigging, equipments, armament, *or* defences.

Dismay, *v. t.* Terrify, frighten, appall, affright, daunt, scare, alarm, intimidate, paralyze with fear.

——, *n.* Terror, fright, affright, fear, alarm, horror, consternation.

Dismember, *v. t.* 1. Mutilate, dislimb, disjoint.
2. Divide, separate, sever, pull apart, break up, dilacerate, rend asunder.

Dismiss, *v. t.* 1. Send away, give leave to go, permit to go.
2. Discharge, discard, cashier, turn off, turn out, remove from office, turn adrift, send packing, send about one's business.

Dismissal, *n.* 1. Permission to go, leave to depart, release, discharge, dismission, liberation, manumission.

2. Discharge, removal from office, dismissal.

Dismount, *v. t.* 1. Unhorse.
2. Displace, throw out of position, dislodge.

——, *v. i.* Alight (*from a horse*), descend, get down.

Disobedience, *n.* 1. Infraction *or* violation (*of a command*), refusal to obey, mutiny, recalcitrance, insubordination, recusance, disobeying.
2. Undutifulness, neglect of duty, unruliness, frowardness, indiscipline, contumacy.

Disobedient, *a.* Unsubmissive, uncomplying, non-compliant, rebellious, refractory, obstinate, undutiful, unruly, froward.

Disobey, *v. t.* 1. Refuse to obey, break *or* disregard the command of, refuse submission to, defy.
2. Transgress, violate, infringe, disregard, ignore, set at nought *or* defiance, go counter to.

Disoblige, *v. t.* Displease, offend.

Disobliging, *a.* Unaccommodating, unkind, unamiable, unfriendly, ill-natured.

Disorder, *n.* 1. Confusion, derangement, disarrangement, disarray, disorganization, irregularity, jumble, litter, topsy-turvy, "mess," want of order.
2. Tumult, disturbance, commotion, riot.
3. Turbulence, tumultuousness, riotousness.
4. Distemper, complaint, malady, sickness, illness, disease, ail, ailment, indisposition.

——, *v. t.* 1. Derange, disarrange, disturb, discompose, confuse, unsettle, disorganize, upset, throw into confusion, turn topsy-turvy, put out of place.
2. Impair the functions of, produce disease in.

Disorderly, *a.* 1. Immethodical, irregular, confused, out of order, in bad order, untidy, chaotic, "messy."
2. Lawless, rebellious, turbulent, unmanageable, ungovernable, unruly, tumultuous, riotous.

Disorganization, *n.* 1. Disorganizing, deranging, etc. See the verb.
2. Disorder, derangement, demoralization, confusion, chaos.

Disorganize, *v. t.* Disorder, derange, disarrange, upset, confuse, unsettle, demoralize, disturb, discompose, put out of order, throw into disorder.

Disown, *v. t.* 1. Disclaim, disavow, repudiate, renounce, reject, cast off, refuse to acknowledge.
2. Deny, disallow, refuse to admit.

Disparage, *v. t.* 1. Depreciate, decry, belittle, undervalue, underrate, underestimate, underpraise, run down, detract from, derogate from.

2. Asperse, reproach, traduce, defame, vilify, slur, reflect upon, inveigh against, speak ill of.

Disparagement, *n.* 1. Depreciation, derogation, detraction, undervaluing, underrating.

2. Lessening, diminution, detraction, derogation, impairment, injury, worsening, prejudice, harm.

3. Reproach, aspersion, reflection, defamation, calumny, traduction, vilification.

4. Reproach, indignity, dishonor, disgrace, blackening, dispraise.

Disparity, *n.* 1. Inequality, difference, disproportion.

2. Dissimilitude, unlikeness.

Dispart, *v. t.* Sunder, disunite, separate, divide, sever, dissever, burst, rend, rive, cleave, split, break asunder.

Dispassion, *n.* 1. Calmness, calm, dispassionateness, collectedness, freedom from agitation, unruffled state.

2. Apathy, insensibility, impassibility, coldness, dulness, torpor, indifference, unconcern, want of feeling.

Dispassionate, *a.* 1. Unimpassioned, imperturbable, inexcitable, unexcited, composed, collected, temperate, undisturbed, unruffled, quiet, calm, cool, staid, serene, sober.

2. Impartial, unbiased, fair, candid, disinterested.

Dispatch, *n.* and *v. t.* See DESPATCH.

Dispel, *v. t.* Disperse (*completely*), scatter, dissipate, banish, drive away.

Dispensable, *a.* 1. Distributable, apportionable.

2. To be spared *or* dispensed with, unnecessary, needless, superfluous, removable.

Dispensation, *n.* 1. Dispensing, distributing, distribution, apportioning, apportionment, allotment.

2. Administration, stewardship.

3. Scheme, plan, system, economy.

Dispensatory, *n.* Pharmacopœia.

Dispense, *v. t.* 1. Distribute, apportion, allot, deal out.

2. Administer, apply, execute, carry out.

3. Exempt, release, relieve, excuse, absolve.

Dispenser, *n.* Distributer, divider.

Dispense with. 1. Do without, spare.

2. Disregard, neglect, set aside, suspend the use of, omit.

Disperse, *v. t.* 1. Scatter, separate, dissipate, dispel, dissolve, drive to different parts, scatter to the winds.

2. Diffuse, disseminate, spread, scatter abroad, sow broadcast.

——, *v. i.* 1. Scatter, separate, be scattered, go different ways.

2. Break up *or* away, vanish, disappear, be dispelled, be dissipated.

Dispersion, *n.* Scattering.

Dispirit, *v. t.* Dishearten, depress, deject, discourage.

Dispirited, *a.* Dejected, disheartened, depressed, discouraged, down-hearted, downcast, despondent, cast down, crestfallen, chapfallen, down in the mouth.

Displace, *v. t.* 1. Move, dislocate, misplace, mislay, put out of place, change the place of.

2. Remove, dislodge, take out *or* away.

3. Depose, unseat, oust, dismiss, discharge, cashier, remove, eject from office.

Display, *v. t.* 1. Expand, unfold, extend, open, spread.

2. Exhibit, show, bring into view, hold up to view, make manifest.

3. Parade, flaunt, show off.

——, *n.* 1. Exhibition, manifestation, show.

2. Parade, pomp, pageant, ostentation, flourish.

Displease, *v. t.* 1. Offend, dissatisfy, disgust, "disgruntle," disoblige, give offence to.

2. Provoke, irritate, annoy, vex, chagrin, affront, pique, chafe, fret, anger, nettle, make angry.

Displeasure, *n.* 1. Dissatisfaction, disaffection, dislike, distaste, disapprobation, disapproval.

2. Anger, indignation, vexation, resentment, wrath.

3. Offence, injury.

Disport, *n.* (*Poetical.*) Play, amusement, diversion, pastime, sport, merriment.

——, *v. i.* Play, gambol, frisk, frolic, sport, make merry, wanton, caper.

——, *v. t.* Amuse, divert, entertain, cheer, solace, beguile, relax.

Disposal, *n.* 1. Arrangement, disposition.

2. Management, control, government, regulation, disposure, direction, ordering, conduct.

3. Dispensation, distribution, bestowment.

Dispose, *v. t.* 1. Arrange, distribute, range, rank, group, marshal, set, place, place in order.

2. Adjust, regulate, settle, determine, set right.

3. Incline, lead, move, induce, bias, predispose.

Dispose, *v. i.* 1. Control, regulate, rule, settle, decide.

2. Bargain, compound, make terms, arrange, have an understanding.

Disposed, *a.* Inclined, tending, ready, apt, prone.

Dispose of. 1. Sell, transfer, convey, alienate, part with, put out of one's possession, get rid of.

2. Determine the condition of, arrange for.

3. Remove, put away, get rid of.

4. Employ, use, put to use, do with.

Disposer, *n.* 1. Bestower, giver, distributer, donor, dispenser.

2. Regulator, director, governor, manager, controller.

Disposition, *n.* 1. Disposing, arranging, arrangement, placing, location, grouping.

2. Management, regulation, control, direction, ordering, adjustment, disposure, disposal.

3. Tendency, proneness, inclination, proclivity, propensity, predisposition, bent, bias, aptitude.

4. Temper, temperament, nature, native character, constitution, native impulses, humor, turn.

5. Willingness, inclination.

6. Dispensation, distribution, bestowment, bestowal.

Dispossess, *v. t.* 1. Deprive, divest, expropriate, strip.

2. Dislodge, eject, oust, drive out.

3. (*Law.*) Disseize, oust.

Dispossession, *n.* 1. Deprivation, expropriation.

2. (*Law.*) Ouster, disseizin.

Dispraise, *n.* 1. Blame, censure.

2. Reproach, dishonor, disgrace, disparagement, discredit, shame, opprobrium.

Disproof, *n.* Confutation, refutation, rebuttal.

Disproportion, *n.* 1. Want of symmetry, asymmetry, ill *or* bad proportions.

2. Disparity, inequality, unsuitableness, inadequacy, insufficiency.

3. Incommensurateness.

Disproportionate, *a.* 1. Unsymmetrical, ill-proportioned, out of proportion, disparate.

2. [With *to*.] Out of proportion, lacking proportion, incommensurate (with), improperly proportioned, unsuitable, lacking proper adjustment *or* adaptation, ill-adapted.

Disprove, *v. t.* Confute, refute, rebut, show to be false.

Disputable, *a.* Controvertible, debatable, doubtful, questionable, open to discussion.

Disputant, *n.* Controversialist, arguer, contender, debater, disputer.

Disputation, *n.* Debate, dispute, controversy, argumentation, verbal contest.

Disputatious, *a.* Cavilling, captious, contentious, bickering, dissentious, quarrelsome, polemical.

Dispute, *v. i.* 1. Debate, argue, altercate, contend in argument, question, litigate.

2. Bicker, wrangle, quarrel, brawl, spar, spat, jangle, squabble, tiff, fall out, have words, have an altercation.

——, *v. t.* 1. Debate, discuss, agitate, ventilate, argue, reason about.

2. Controvert, impugn, challenge, deny, contradict, call in question, oppose by argument.

3. Contest, struggle for, make resistance on.

——, *n.* 1. Debate, disputation, discussion, controversy.

2. Altercation, dissension, bickering, wrangle, squabble, spat, tiff, verbal contest, verbal quarrel, war of words.

Disputer, *n.* See DISPUTANT.

Disqualification, *n.* Incapacitation, disability, want of qualification.

Disqualify, *v. t.* 1. Unfit, disable, incapacitate (*naturally*).

2. Disenable, prohibit, preclude, incapacitate (*legally*).

Disquiet, *n.* Uneasiness, restlessness, disturbance, anxiety, vexation, trouble, disquietude, inquietude, unrest.

——, *v. t.* Trouble, agitate, excite, annoy, vex, disturb, fret, worry, harass, plague, bother, molest, pester, incommode.

Disquietude, *n.* Uneasiness. See DISQUIET.

Disquisition, *n.* Dissertation, treatise, discourse, essay, formal inquiry.

Disregard, *n.* 1. Neglect, slight, pretermit, contempt, ignoring, wilful oversight.

2. Disesteem, disfavor, indifference.

——, *v. t.* Neglect, slight, overlook, ignore, contemn, disobey, pay no attention to, pay no heed to, take no notice of, turn a deaf ear to.

Disrelish, *n.* 1. Dislike, distaste, want of relish.

2. Insipidity, insipidness, flatness, bad taste, nauseousness.

3. Aversion, antipathy, repugnance, disgust.

——, *v. t.* Dislike, loathe, have an aversion to.

Disreputable, *a.* 1. Discreditable, dishonorable, disgraceful, shameful, scandalous, infamous, opprobrious, derogatory.

2. Of bad reputation (*deservedly*), low, mean, vulgar, base, of bad character.

Disrepute, *n.* Discredit, dishonor, disgrace, degradation, derogation, abasement, odium, ill repute.

Disrespect, *n.* 1. Disesteem, irreverence, slight, neglect, disregard.

2. Incivility, discourtesy, rudeness.

Disrespectful, *a.* 1. Irreverent, slighting, contemptuous.

2. Uncivil, impolite, impertinent, discourteous, uncourteous, rude.

Disrobe, *v. t.* Divest, strip, undress, uncover, unclothe.

Disruption, *n.* Breach, rent, rupture, burst, breaking *or* tearing asunder, schism, scission, fission.

Dissatisfaction, *n.* 1. Discontent, uneasiness, inquietude. See DISQUIET.

2. Displeasure, dislike, disapprobation, disapproval.

Dissatisfied, *a.* Discontented, uneasy, displeased.

Dissect, *v. t.* 1. Anatomize, cut in pieces.

2. Analyze, scrutinize, sift, examine, investigate, explore, lay open.

Dissection, *n.* 1. Anatomy.

2. Scrutiny, analysis, examination, investigation, sifting.

Dissemble, *v. t.* Conceal, hide, disguise, cloak, cover.

——, *v. i.* Conceal one's real purposes, disguise the feelings *or* character, dissimulate, pretend, feign, counterfeit.

Dissembler, *n.* Disguiser of one's feelings, motives, *or* character (*as the case may be*).

Disseminate, *v. t.* Spread, propagate, diffuse, scatter, disperse, circulate, promulgate, spread abroad.

Dissemination, *n.* Diffusion, dispersion, propagation, scattering, spreading, promulgation.

Dissension, *n.* Discord, contention, strife, variance, disagreement, difference, quarrel, breach of friendship.

Dissent, *v. i.* 1. Withhold assent, refuse *or* decline to agree, disagree (*in an opinion*).

2. Refuse to conform (*to the Church of England*), be a non-conformist.

——, *n.* 1. Disagreement, difference of opinion.

2. Non-conformity, refusal to conform (*to the Church of England*), recusancy.

Dissenter, *n.* Non-conformist, sectary, dissident, "come-outer."

Dissentient, *a.* Disagreeing, dissenting, not acquiescent, dissident, factious.

Dissertation, *n.* Disquisition, treatise, discourse, essay.

Disservice, *n.* Injury, harm, mischief, hurt, disadvantage, disfavor, ill-turn.

Dissever, *v. t.* Disjoin, disunite, separate, part, sunder, dispart, divide, rend, sever, dissociate, disconnect.

Dissidence, *n.* Dissent, disagreement, non-conformity, sectarianism, principles of non-conformance.

Dissident, *n.* Dissenter, non-conformist, sectary.

Dissimilar, *a.* Unlike, different, heterogeneous, diverse, divergent, various.

Dissimilarity, *n.* Unlikeness, dissimilitude, diversity, disparity, variation, divergence.

Dissimulation, *n.* Concealment, dissembling, deceit, duplicity, double-dealing, false pretence.

Dissipate, *v. t.* 1. Disperse, dispel, scatter, drive away.

2. Waste, squander, lavish, consume, spend lavishly, throw away.

——, *v. i.* 1. Vanish, disappear, scatter, disperse.

2. Live dissolutely, be dissolute, practise debauchery, indulge in dissipation.

3. Live idly and luxuriously, enervate one's self, be an idler and spendthrift.

Dissipation, *n.* 1. Dispersion, scattering, vanishing.

2. Waste, squandering, lavish expenditure.

3. Dissoluteness, debauchery, profligacy, excess, crapulence, loose living.

Dissociate, *v. t.* Disjoin, disunite, separate, sever, dissever, divide, part, sunder, detach, disconnect.

Dissociation, *n.* Disunion, separation, severance, severing, dividing, disjoining, dissevering, parting, sundering, detachment, disconnection.

Dissoluble, *a.* 1. Dissolvable, capable of liquefaction.

2. Separable, capable of being sundered *or* disunited, temporary.

Dissolute, *a.* Loose, licentious, lax, debauched, wanton, lewd, corrupt, profligate, rakish, depraved, dissipated, reprobate, abandoned, vicious, graceless, shameless, wild.

Dissolution, *n.* 1. Liquefaction, melting, solution.

2. Decomposition, putrefaction.

3. Death, disease, extinction of life.

4. Destruction, overthrow, ruin.

5. Termination, breaking up.

Dissolve, *v. t.* 1. Liquefy, melt.

2. Disunite, sever, separate, divide, loose, disorganize, break apart.

3. Destroy, ruin.

4. Terminate, bring to an end, put an end to, break up.

——, *v. i.* 1. Melt, liquefy, be melted.

2. Vanish, disappear, fade, melt away, be dissipated, scatter.

3. Perish, crumble, disintegrate, decompose, be destroyed.

Dissonance, *n.* 1. Discord, discordance, harshness, jarring, want of harmony, cacophony.

2. Disagreement, inconsistency, incongruity, discrepancy.

Dissonant, *a.* 1. Discordant, unharmonious, harsh, grating, jangling, jarring, out of tune.

2. Disagreeing, incongruous, inconsistent, contradictory, discrepant.

Dissuade, *v. i.* 1. Urge *or* exhort against, attempt to divert, urge not to.

2. Turn from a purpose, divert by persuasion, render averse, persuade not to.

Dissuasion, *n.* Dehortation, dissuasive advice.

Dissuasive, *a.* Dissuading, dehortatory, tending to dissuade.

DISTANCE, *n.* 1. Remoteness, farness, degree of removal.

2. Remote region, distant quarter.

3. Interval, space, space intervening, interspace, remove.

4. Reserve, coldness, stiffness, offishness, aloofness, distant behavior, frigidity.

——, *v. t.* Outdo, surpass, excel, outstrip, leave behind.

Distant, *a.* 1. Remote, far, far-away.

2. Reserved, frigid, cold, cool, stiff, uncordial.

3. Slight, faint, indirect, indistinct, obscure.

Distaste, *n.* 1. Disrelish, disgust.

2. Aversion, disinclination, dislike, repugnance, displeasure, dissatisfaction.

Distasteful, *a.* 1. Nauseous, nauseating, unpalatable, unsavory, loathsome, disgusting.

2. Disagreeable, offensive, unpleasant, unpleasing, repugnant, repulsive.

Distemper, *n.* 1. Disease, malady, complaint, disorder, ail, ailment, illness, indisposition, sickness.

2. Tempera, size-mixed color.

Distempered, *a.* 1. Diseased, disordered, out of order.

2. Immoderate, intemperate, inordinate, unregulated.

Distend, *v. t.* Expand, dilate, inflate, bloat, enlarge, swell, stretch, swell out.

Distension, *n.* Dilation, dilatation, enlargement, swelling, expansion, stretching.

Distill, *v. i.* Drop, drip, trickle, dribble, fall in drops.

——, *v. t.* 1. Drop, let fall in drops.

2. Separate by evaporation, extract by heat.

3. Extract spirit from.

Distinct, *a.* 1. Separate, different, discrete, disjunct.

2. Definite, defined, clear, plain, unmistakable, unconfused, well-defined.

Distinction, *n.* 1. Discrimination, notice of difference, distinguishing, discernment.

2. Difference, point of difference, characteristic difference.

3. Repute, reputation, celebrity, note, name, fame, renown, account, credit, respectability, eminence, superiority.

Distinctive, *a.* Distinguishing, differentiating, discriminative, characteristic.

Distinctness, *n.* 1. Difference, separateness.

2. Clearness, precision, perspicuity, explicitness, lucidness, lucidity.

Distinguish, *v. t.* 1. Characterize, mark, indicate by a mark, mark out.

2. Discriminate, discern, differentiate, single out, perceive, tell.

3. Separate, divide, demarcate.

4. Signalize, make famous, make celebrated, make known, bring into notice.

——, *v. i.* Make distinction, show the difference.

Distinguishable, *a.* 1. Separable, divisible.

2. To be distinguished, to be recognized as distinct.

Distinguished, *a.* 1. Illustrious, famous, noted, eminent, celebrated.

2. Conspicuous, marked, extraordinary, superior, laureate, transcendent, shining.

Distort, *v. t.* 1. Twist, deform, contort, warp, gnarl, screw, wrest.

2. Pervert, misrepresent, falsify, wrest, strain the sense of.

Distortion, *n.* 1. Twist, wryness, deformity, deformation.

2. Perversion, misrepresentation, falsification, wresting.

Distract, *v. t.* 1. Divert, draw away, turn aside.

2. Perplex, confuse, discompose, harass, disturb, disconcert, bewilder, confound, mystify, embarrass.

Distracted, *a.* Deranged, insane, mad, frantic, furious, raving, wild, crazed, beside one's self.

Distraction, *n.* 1. Confusion, perplexity, embarrassment, bewilderment, abstraction, mystification.

2. Disturbance, discord, tumult, disorder, division, perturbation, commotion, turmoil, agitation.

3. Derangement, madness, raving,

frenzy, insanity, alienation, aberration, incoherence, wandering, delirium, mania, lunacy, hallucination, loss of reason.

Distress, *n.* 1. Affliction, calamity, disaster, misery, misfortune, adversity, hardship, trial, tribulation, trouble, perplexity.

2. Anguish, agony, suffering, sorrow, dolor, grief.

3. Pain, anguish, agony, torment, torture, gripe, griping, gnawing.

4. Privation, destitution, poverty, indigence, want, straits.

——, *v. t.* 1. Afflict, perplex, pain, trouble, harry, rack, annoy, grieve, make unhappy, make miserable.

2. (*Law.*) Take, seize, distrain.

Distribute, *v. t.* 1. Apportion, assign, allot, dispense, mete, divide, share, dole (out), parcel out, deal out, portion out, partition, prorate.

2. Classify, class, arrange, assort, dispose.

DISTRIBUTION, *n.* 1. Apportionment, allotment, assignment, dole, partition, division, dispensation, dispensing.

2. Arrangement, disposal, disposition, grouping.

District, *n.* Region, tract, territory, circuit, department, ward, neighborhood, section, province, quarter.

Distrust, *v. t.* Doubt, suspect, lack confidence in, mistrust, disbelieve in.

——, *n.* Suspicion, misgiving, doubt, mistrust, want of confidence.

Distrustful, *a.* Suspicious, doubting, dubious (about), apt to distrust.

Disturb, *v. t.* 1. Agitate, shake, stir.

2. Disarrange, derange, disorder, confuse, upset, unsettle, throw into confusion, put into disorder.

3. Molest, annoy, disquiet, distract, "fuss," disconcert, perturb, discompose, vex, ruffle, worry, plague, trouble, incommode.

4. Interrupt, impede, hinder.

Disturbance, *n.* 1. Agitation, derangement, unsettlement, commotion, disorder, confusion, convulsion, perturbation.

2. Perturbation, excitement, discomposure, distraction, "fuss," annoyance, agitation.

3. Interruption, hindrance, molestation.

4. Tumult, excitement, commotion. fracas, "row-de-dow," "ruction," hubbub, turmoil, disorder, riot, *émeute,* rising, uproar.

Disunion, *n.* 1. Separation, disjunction, division, severance, disconnection.

2. Schism, breach, rupture, feud.

Disunite, *v. t.* 1. Disjoin, dissociate, separate, sever, dissever, part, divide, detach, rend, sunder.

2. Set at variance, alienate, put discord between, estrange.

——, *v. i.* Part, separate, fall asunder, be separated.

Disuse, *n.* 1. Failure to use, non-employment, ceasing to use, abandonment.

2. Desuetude, discontinuance, neglect, non-observance, disusage.

Ditch, *n.* Trench, channel, drain, fosse, moat.

Ditty, *n.* Song, lay.

Diurnal, *a.* Daily, quotidian.

Divagation, *n.* Wandering, rambling, roaming, straying, deviation, digression.

Divan, *n.* Sofa, long seat.

Divaricate, *v. i.* Diverge. part. fork, separate into two, open wide, branch off, spread asunder.

Divarication, *n.* Divergence, forking, separation, spreading.

Dive, *v. i.* 1. Plunge, make *or* take a plunge, take a header.

2. Penetrate, go deep, plunge, explore, sound, fathom.

Diverge, *v. i.* 1. Radiate, divide, separate, go asunder, tend from one point in different directions.

2. Divaricate, separate, branch off, fork.

3. Differ, vary, deviate, disagree.

Divergence, *n.* 1. Radiation.

2. Divarication, forking, separation.

3. Difference, variation, variance, disagreement, deviation.

Divergent, *a.* 1. Radiating.

2. Divaricating, separating, parting.

3. Disagreeing, dissimilar, differing, variant, diverse.

Divers, *a.* Various, several, sundry, numerous, many, manifold, different.

Diverse, *a.* Different, differing, unlike, varying, multifarious, heterogeneous, multiform, variant, dissimilar, disagreeing, divergent.

Diversify, *v. t.* 1. Vary, variate, make different, give variety to.

2. Dapple, spot, streak, stripe, variegate.

Diversion, *n.* 1. Turning aside, diverting, deflection.

2. Amusement, recreation, pastime, sport, play, entertainment, relaxation, beguilement, solace, distraction, divertissement.

Diversity, *n.* 1. Difference, dissimilitude, dissimilarity, unlikeness, variation, divergence.

2. Variety, multiformity, manifoldness, multifariousness, heterogeneity.

Divert, *v. t.* 1. Turn aside, draw away.

2. Call off, distract, draw away, disturb.

3. Amuse, entertain, recreate, beguile, solace, exhilarate, refresh.

Divest, *v. t.* 1. Strip, undress, unclothe, disrobe.

2. Deprive, strip, dispossess.

Divide, *v. t.* 1. Sever, dissever, split, rend, dismember, sunder, part, separate, cleave, disunite.

2. Make hostile, make discordant, set at variance, disunite, alienate, estrange.

3. Distribute, allot, apportion, assign, share, mete, dispense, dole, deal out, parcel out, portion out.

4. Partition, demarcate, compart.

——, *v. i.* Part, separate, cleave, open, diverge, go asunder, divaricate, fork, be divided, be separated.

Dividend, *n.* 1. Number to be divided.

2. Share, division, profits divided.

Divider, *n.* 1. Distributer, dealer.

2. Separator.

Divination, *n.* 1. Divining, foretelling, soothsaying, augury, hieromancy, hieroscopy, magic, incantation.

2. Presage, prediction, prophecy.

Divine, *a.* 1. Godlike, superhuman, deiform.

2. Sacred, holy, spiritual, heavenly, celestial, angelic, seraphic.

3. Rapturous, supreme, transcendent, exalted, exalting.

——, *n.* Minister, priest, clergyman, pastor, parson, ecclesiastic, churchman.

——, *v. t.* 1. Predict, foretell, presage, prognosticate, vaticinate, prophesy.

2. Conjecture, surmise, guess.

——, *v. i.* 1. Vaticinate, prophesy, play the prophet, utter presages.

2. Conjecture, guess, fancy, surmise, suspect, think, believe.

Diviner, *n.* 1. Conjurer, magician, sorcerer, seer, soothsayer.

2. Conjecturer, guesser.

Divinity, *n.* 1. Deity, Godhead, divine nature, divine essence.

2. Theology, science of divine things.

3. Divine being, deity, god *or* goddess.

Divisible, *a.* Separable.

DIVISION, *n.* 1. Separation, disjunction, severance, splitting apart, segmentation, scissure, disconnection, dismemberment.

2. Portion, section, class, head, category, compartment, separate part, segment, parcel.

3. Partition, demarcation, districting.

4. Apportionment, allotment, distribution.

5. Difference, disagreement, variance,

breach, rupture, disunion, discord, feud, alienation, estrangement.

Divorce, *n.* Separation (*of husband and wife*), dissolution of the marriage bond.

——, *v. t.* 1. Dissolve the marriage of, put out of wedlock, put away, unmarry.

2. Separate, part, sever, sunder, disunite.

Divulge, *v. t.* Disclose, communicate, discover, reveal, impart, tell, make known, make public, publish, spread abroad.

Dizzy, *a.* 1. Giddy, vertiginous.

2. Thoughtless, heedless, careless, giddy.

DO, *v. t.* 1. Perform, effect, execute, commit, accomplish, achieve, bring about, work out, carry into effect.

2. Complete, finish, conclude, end, settle, terminate.

3. Transact, carry on, conduct.

4. Practise, observe, perform, carry into practice.

5. Produce, make, work.

6. Translate, render.

7. Prepare, cook.

8. Hoax, cheat, swindle, chouse, cozen.

——, *v. i.* 1. Act (*well* or *ill*), behave.

2. Fare.

3. Answer, answer the purpose, be enough, be sufficient.

Docile, *a.* Teachable, tractable, easily taught, pliant, yielding, tame.

Docility, *n.* Teachableness, readiness to learn, tractableness, pliableness, pliancy, gentleness.

Dock, *v. t.* 1. Curtail, clip, cut short, truncate.

2. Shorten, lessen, deduct from.

Doctor, *n.* 1. Adept, savant, learned man.

2. Physician, medical practitioner, healer, leech.

Doctrinaire, *n.* [Fr.] Theorist, ideologist, unpractical thinker, preacher of abstractions.

Doctrine, *n.* Dogma, tenet, opinion, precept, teaching, principle.

Document, *n.* Paper, writing (*official*), certificate, instrument.

Dodge, *v. i.* 1. Start aside, shift place suddenly, duck.

2. (*Colloq.*) Shuffle, evade, equivocate, quibble, prevaricate, use artifice, play fast and loose, be evasive.

——, *v. t.* Evade (*by starting* or *ducking*).

——, *n.* 1. Starting aside.

2. (*Colloq.*) Evasion, artifice, trick, subterfuge, quibble, cavil.

Doer, *n.* Actor, operator, performer, perpetrator, agent, executor.

Doff, *v. t.* Put off, lay aside, cast, remove.

DOG, *n.* Canine, cur, pup, whelp.

Dog days, *n. pl.* Canicular days.

Dogged, *a.* 1. See DOGGISH.

2. Stubborn, obstinate, wilful, mulish, inflexible, tenacious, pertinacious, unyielding, headstrong, intractable, perversely resolute.

Doggish, *a.* Snarling, snappish, growling, churlish, surly, sullen, sour, morose, dogged.

Dogma, *n.* Doctrine, tenet, opinion, principle, article of faith.

Dogmatic, } *a.* 1. Authoritative, formal,
Dogmatical, } categorical, settled.

2. Positive, confident, peremptory, magisterial, oracular, dictatorial.

3. Doctrinal, setting forth doctrines, expounding dogma.

Dogmatism, *n.* Positiveness of opinion, arrogance of assertion.

Dogmatize, *v. i.* Assert positively, speak with an air of authority, express one's self arrogantly.

Doings, *n. pl.* Deeds, actions, acts, transactions, ongoings.

Dole, *n.* 1. Apportionment, allotment, distribution.

2. Part, share, portion.

3. Gift, gratuity, donation, pittance, alms.

4. Grief, sorrow, distress, woe, affliction.

Doleful, *a.* 1. Sorrowful, rueful, woful, piteous, melancholy, lugubrious, sad.

2. Dismal, gloomy, cheerless, dark, dreary, dolorous, dolesome.

Dole out. Distribute, divide, apportion, allot, assign, share, deal, deal out.

Dolesome, *a.* See DOLEFUL.

Do-little, *n.* [*U. S.*] Idler, sluggard, drone, laggard, lounger, trifler, dawdler, doodle, do-nought (donnat, donnot, *Scotch*), do-nothing, good-for-nothing.

Doll, *n.* Puppet (*for a child*), baby.

Dolorous, *a.* 1. Dismal, gloomy, cheerless, dark, dolesome.

2. Sorrowful, sad, piteous, rueful, woful, lugubrious, mournful, doleful, dolesome.

Dolt, *n.* Simpleton, fool. See DUNCE.

Doltish, *a.* Stupid, stolid, dull, foolish, blockish, simple, witless, thick-skulled, beetle-headed, beef-brained, beef-witted, thick-headed, heavy-headed.

Domain, *n.* 1. Sway, authority, dominion, province, empery.

2. Dominion, empire, territory, realm.

3. Estate, lands, landed estate.

4. Province, department, region, realm, branch.

Dome, *n.* 1. Cupola, tholus, spherical vaulted roof.

2. (*Poetical.*) Building, fabric, house.

Domestic, *a.* 1. Home, family, household, pertaining to home *or* the family.

2. Fond of home, domesticated.

3. Intestine, internal, home (*in opposition to foreign*).

——, *n.* Servant, house-servant, maid, familiar.

Domesticate, *v. t.* 1. Make domestic, accustom to keep at home.

2. [*Animals.*] Tame, attach to the house.

3. [*Plants.*] Accustom to the garden, reduce to cultivation, cultivate.

4. Familiarize, naturalize, adopt, make at home, assimilate.

Domicile, *n.* Habitation, dwelling, residence, abode, home, mansion, place of abode, place of residence.

Dominant, *a.* Prevailing, ruling, chief, predominant, predominating, pre-eminent, preponderant, paramount, ascendant, in the ascendant.

Dominate, *v. t.* 1. Rule, sway, control, reign over, keep in subjection, keep down.

2. Overlook, overtop, surmount, command (*visually* or *defensively*).

——, *v. i.* (*Rare.*) Prevail, predominate, have sway, be in the ascendant.

Domination, *n.* Sway, ascendancy, rule, dominion, supremacy, command, government, mastery.

Domineer, *v. i.* 1. [With *over.*] Tyrannize, rule masterfully *or* tyrannously, lord it, "boss," play the autocrat *or* dictator, be overbearing.

2. Hector, bully, bluster, swagger, swell, play the bully, lay down the law, ride a high horse, carry it with a high hand.

Dominican, *n.* Predicant, jacobin, black friar, preaching friar, *frère prêcheur.*

Dominie, *n.* 1. [*Scotch.*] Pedagogue, schoolmaster, teacher, instructor.

2. [*U. S. Colloq.*] Minister, pastor.

Dominion, *n.* 1. Sway, command, rule, government, supremacy, domination, mastery, ascendancy, control, sovereignty, sovereign authority, domain, jurisdiction.

2. Territory, region, country, realm.

Don, *v. t.* Put on, slip on, dress in.

Donation, *n.* Gift, grant, largess, gratuity, benefaction, boon, present, offering, contribution, subscription, donative, dole.

Done, *p.* 1. Performed, executed, accomplished, achieved, effected.

2. Completed, finished, concluded, ended, terminated.

3. Transacted, carried on.

4. Translated, rendered. See Do.

Done for. (*Colloq.*) Spoiled, ruined, wound up, shelved, *hors de combat*, dished, damned.

Donkey, *n.* 1. Ass, mule.

2. Simpleton, fool. See DUNCE.

Donor, *n.* Giver, bestower; (*law*) donator.

Doom, *v. t.* 1. Condemn, sentence, pronounce sentence on.

2. Destine, appoint, decree.

——, *n.* 1. Sentence, judgment, condemnation, judicial decree.

2. Fate, destiny, lot, ill fate, ruin.

Doomsday, *n.* Day of judgment, the crack of doom.

DOOR, *n.* 1. Entrance, doorway, portal.

2. Passage, avenue, way, means of access, means of approach.

Doorkeeper, *n.* Porter, *concierge*, janitor, janitress.

Dormant, *a.* 1. Sleeping, comatose, quiescent, at rest, lethargic.

2. Latent, unexerted, suspended, inert, inactive, in abeyance.

Dormer, *n.* Luthern, dormer-window.

Dormer-window, *n.* Dormer, luthern.

Dormitory, *n.* 1. Chamber, bedroom, sleeping room, place to sleep in.

2. Building containing sleeping apartments.

Dorsal, *a.* On the back, tergal.

Dose, *n.* 1. Prescribed portion (*of medicine*), potion, drench, draught.

2. Disagreeable lot *or* fate *or* portion, bitter pill.

3. Sufficient quantity, quantity, portion, *quantum*.

——, *v. t.* Administer a dose to, give doses to.

Dot, *n.* Point, period, spot, speck.

——, *v. t.* 1. Mark with dots, stipple, speckle.

2. Variegate, diversify.

Dotage, *n.* Imbecility, senility, second childhood.

Dotard, *n.* Driveller, imbecile, doting old man.

Dote, *v. i.* 1. Drivel, be imbecile, be foolish, be in one's dotage *or* second childhood.

2. Be over-fond, be foolishly fond.

Double, *a.* 1. Coupled, in pairs, paired, geminate, binary.

2. Twice as much.

3. Twofold, duplex, dual.

4. Deceitful, dishonest, knavish, false, perfidious, hollow, insincere, double-dealing, double-faced, double-tongued, full of duplicity.

——, *adv.* Twice, doubly, twofold.

——, *v. t.* 1. Fold, plait.

2. Duplicate, geminate, multiply by two, make twice as much.

——, *v. i.* 1. Increase twofold, be doubled.

2. Return upon the same track.

——, *n.* 1. Twice as much.

2. Doubling, plait, fold.

3. Returning upon one's track (*to elude pursuit*).

4. Trick, stratagem, ruse, shift, artifice, wile, manœuvre.

5. Counterpart.

Double-dealer, *n.* Deceiver, cheat, trickster, tricker.

Double-dealing, *n.* Deceit, duplicity, dissimulation, artifice, deception, fraud, dishonesty, trickery, Machiavelism.

Double-entendre, *n.* [Fr.] Pun, *équivoque*, quirk, quibble, *calembour*, play upon words, equivocation, paronomasia.

Double-faced, *a.* Hypocritical, deceitful, knavish, dishonest, false, perfidious, double.

Double-minded, *a.* Unsettled, undetermined, undecided, changeable, fickle, vacillating, wavering.

Doublet, *n.* 1. Body-garment, jacket, jerkin.

2. One of a pair.

Doublets, *n. pl.* Pair, couple, two, twins.

Doubling, *n.* 1. Fold, plait.

2. Artifice, trick, shift, stratagem.

Doubly, *adv.* Twice, double, twofold.

Doubt, *v. i.* Hesitate, waver, be doubtful, be in suspense, withhold judgment, dubitate, be undetermined, entertain doubts, be in a state of uncertainty, not know what to think.

——, *v. t.* 1. Question, query, hesitate to believe, consider questionable, have doubts about.

2. Distrust, suspect, not confide in.

DOUBT, *n.* 1. Indecision, hesitation, hesitancy, dubiousness, dubiety, question, irresolution, uncertainty, incertitude, vacillation, suspense.

2. Suspicion, skepticism, distrust, mistrust, misgiving.

Doubtful, *a.* 1. Wavering, undecided, hesitating, dubious, skeptical, undetermined, in suspense.

2. Ambiguous, dubious, equivocal, obscure, enigmatical, problematical.

3. [*Of events, state of affairs, etc.*] Indeterminate, undecided, uncertain, questionable.

Doughface, *n.* [*U. S.*] Pliable politician, nose of wax.

Doughfaced, *a.* [*U. S.*] Pliable, weak, pusillanimous, easily influenced, without any backbone.

Doughty, *a.* Brave, courageous, bold, fearless, dauntless, valiant, valorous, gallant, intrepid, adventurous, chivalrous, heroic.

Douse, *v. t.* 1. Plunge, immerse, submerge, dip, souse, put under water (or *other liquid*).

2. (*Naut.*) Strike *or* lower quickly *or* in haste, slacken suddenly.

Dove-cot, *n.* [Written also *Dove-cote.*] Columbary, pigeon-house.

Dowdy, *a.* [*Said of women.*] Slovenly (*in dress*), slatternly, ill-dressed, vulgar-looking, awkward.

Dowel, *n.* Pin, tenon, peg, pinion.

Dower, *n.* 1. Endowment, gift.

2. Dowry.

3. (*Law.*) Widow's portion (*of real estate*).

Do without. Dispense with, forgo.

DOWN, *prep.* 1. From the top to the bottom of.

2. Along the course of.

——, *adv.* 1. Downward, in a descending course, netherwards, earthward, from a high to a low position.

2. On the ground, the floor, etc., prostrate.

3. Into disrepute, into disgrace, into disfavor *or* disuse.

4. Low, humbled, in distress, in adversity.

Downcast, *a.* Sad, dejected, dispirited, disheartened, despondent, discouraged, depressed, cast down, down-hearted, crestfallen, chapfallen.

Downfall, *n.* Ruin, destruction, fall.

Downright, *a.* 1. Plain, simple, sheer, explicit, clear, undisguised, unequivocal, positive, absolute, categorical.

2. Honest, sincere, artless, ingenuous, frank, open, above-board, direct, straightforward, unceremonious, blunt.

Downward, } *adv.* Down, in a descend-
Downwards, } ing course.

Downy, *a.* Lanate, lanated, lanuginous.

Dowry, *n.* Dower, dot.

Doxy, *n.* 1. Mistress, paramour.

2. Prostitute, strumpet, harlot, whore, drab, street-walker, Cyprian, night-walker, loose wench. See Courtesan.

Doze, *v. i.* Slumber, drowse, nap, sleep lightly, be half asleep, be drowsy.

——, *n.* Light sleep, drowse, nap, light slumber.

Dozy, *a.* Sleepy, drowsy, heavy, sluggish.

Drab, *n.* 1. Strumpet, prostitute, trull. See Courtesan.

2. Slut, draggle-tail, trollop, slattern, dowdy, slovenly woman.

——, *a.* and *n.* Dun, dull brown, brownish-yellow.

Drabble, *v. t.* [*Archaic and provincial.*] Draggle, trail, daggle, befoul, bemire.

Draff, *n.* Refuse, lees, dregs, sediment, scum, rubbish, stuff, waste *or* worthless matter.

Draft, *n.* 1. Drawing, selection; conscription.

2. Bill of exchange, check.

3. [Written also *Draught.*] Outline, delineation, rough sketch, rough copy.

——, *v. t.* 1. Detach, select.

2. (*Mil.*) Conscript, impress, commandeer.

3. Make an outline of, make a draft of, make a rough sketch of.

Drag, *v. t.* Draw, pull, haul, tug, draw heavily and slowly.

——, *v. i.* 1. Trail, be drawn along.

2. Linger, move slowly, make slow progress.

Draggle, *v. t.* Trail, daggle, befoul, bemire, drabble.

Draggle-tail, *n.* Slut, drab, sloven, slattern, dowdy, slovenly woman.

Dragoon, *n.* Horse-soldier, cavalier, equestrian, mounted soldier, *chasseur.*

——, *v. t.* Compel, force, drive, persecute, harass, harry.

Drain, *v. t.* 1. Draw off, tap, "milk," sluice.

2. Empty, exhaust.

3. Make dry, clear of water *or* moisture.

——, *v. i.* 1. Flow off.

2. Become dry.

DRAIN, *n.* Sewer, channel, culvert, trench, ditch, water-course.

Drama, *n.* 1. Dramatic composition, play, theatrical piece, spectacle.

2. Dramatic literature.

3. Historic *or* cosmical pageant (*series of events invested with dramatic unity*).

4. The stage, dramatic representation, histrionic art.

Dramatis personæ. [L.] Characters (of the play), interlocutors (in the drama), personages of the drama.

Drape, *v. t.* Cover with drapery, arrange with hangings *or* decorative folds.

Drapery, *n.* 1. Hangings, tapestry.

2. Clothing, hanging garments (*especially in statuary and painting*).

Drastic, *a.* Powerful, active, efficacious.

Draught, *n.* 1. Drawing, pulling.

2. Potion, drink, cup, dose, drench.

3. [Written also *Draft.*] Sketch, outline, delineation, design, rough sketch, rough copy.

Draughts, *n. pl.* Checkers.

Draw, *v. t.* 1. Pull, drag, haul, hale, tow, tug, pull along.

2. Attract, bring toward, pull toward.

3. Suck, drain, siphon, suck dry.

4. Inhale, inspire, breathe in, take into the lungs.

5. Extract, take out, draw out, force out, extort.

6. Induce, move, lead, allure, entice, engage, persuade, influence.

7. Extend, protract, stretch, lengthen out.

8. Delineate, sketch, depict, trace, trace out, describe (*as a line*).

9. Deduce, derive, infer.

10. Compose, write, prepare, draw up, draft, formulate.

——, *v. i.* 1. Pull. Cf. *v. t.* 1, above.

2. Move, come, go, proceed.

3. Sketch, practise drawing *or* the art of delineation.

4. Produce inflammation, vesicate, blister.

5. Request payment by draft, make a draft.

Draw back. Retire, withdraw, retreat.

Drawback, *n.* 1. Disadvantage, detriment, fault, imperfection, deficiency, defect.

2. Discount, deduction, reduction, rebate, abatement, allowance.

DRAWER, *n.* (*Basic Eng.*) Sliding tray in a chest.

Drawing, *n.* 1. Pulling, traction, attracting, draining, inhaling, etc. See DRAW.

2. Delineation, sketch, picture, plan, outline, draught.

Draw near, } Approach, come near.
Draw nigh, }

Draw up. 1. Raise, lift, elevate, pull up, haul up.

2. Compose, write, prepare, frame, draw, draft.

3. Array, marshal, form in order, set in line, set in order of battle.

4. Come to a halt *or* stop, halt, stop.

Dread, *n.* 1. Fear, apprehension, terror.

2. Awe, veneration.

——, *a.* 1. Frightful, terrible, horrible, dreadful.

2. Venerable, awful.

——, *v. t.* See FEAR.

Dreadful, *a.* 1. Terrible, horrible, horrid, direful, dire, fearful, frightful, terrific, awful, awesome, tremendous, formidable.

2. Venerable, awful.

Dream, *n.* 1. Sleeping vision.

2. Reverie, fancy, fantasy, conceit, illusion, delusion, vagary, idle fancy, day-dream, castle in the air, *château en Espagne.*

——, *v. i.* 1. Have visions in sleep.

2. Think, imagine, fancy, have a notion.

3. Give rein to the fancy *or* imagination, indulge in reverie, build castles in the air.

Dreamer, *n.* Visionary, enthusiast, castle-builder.

Dreamland, *n.* Fairyland, land of dreams, realms of fairy, realm of fancy and imagination, region of reverie, cloudland.

Drear, *a.* Gloomy. See DREARY, 1.

Dreary, *a.* 1. Gloomy, dismal, dark, drear, lonely, solitary, lonesome, cheerless, comfortless, chilling, depressing.

2. Monotonous, dull, tiresome, uninteresting.

Dreggy, *a.* Muddy, turbid, dirty, feculent, foul.

Dregs, *n. pl.* 1. Sediment, lees, grounds, offscourings, feculence.

2. Dross, scum, refuse, draff.

Drench, *v. t.* 1. Saturate, soak, douse, souse, steep, imbrue, wet through and through.

2. Physic, purge.

Drenching, *n.* Soaking, wetting, ducking.

Dress, *v. t.* 1. Align, make straight.

2. Adjust, arrange, dispose, set *or* put in order.

3. Prepare, fit, make suitable *or* fit, get ready, make ready.

4. Clothe, array, attire, apparel, accoutre, robe, rig, trick out.

5. Adorn, deck, decorate, embellish, trim, set out, set off.

——, *v. i.* Get *or* put on one's clothes, make one's toilet, attire one's self, busk (*Scot.*).

DRESS, *n.* 1. Clothes, clothing, raiment, garments, garb, guise, habit, toilet, apparel, attire, habiliment, vesture, suit, costume.

2. Array, fine clothes, rich garments, elegant attire, bedizenment, bravery.

3. (Lady's) gown, frock.

Dressing, *n.* 1. Preparing, putting in order.

2. Manure, fertilizer, compost.

3. Force-meat, stuffing.

Dressy, *a.* (*Colloq.*) Showy, flashy, gaudy, fond of dress.

Drib, *v. t.* 1. Crop, lop, cut off, lop off (*little by little*).

2. Purloin, appropriate in driblets, cabbage, crib.

3. Entice, allure, decoy, coax, wheedle.

Dribble, *v. i.* Drip, trickle, fall in drops.

Driblet, *n.* Fragment, small portion.

Drier, *n.* Desiccative.

Drift, *n.* 1. Course, bearing, direction.

2. Aim, purpose, intention, intent, proposal, design, scope, tendency, object, mark.

3. (*Geol.*) Diluvium, diluvial formations, deposit, detritus.

4. (*Mining.*) Passage (*under ground, between shafts*), gallery, tunnel.

5. Sweep, rush, current, sweeping pressure, driving impulse.

6. Heap, heaped pile, driven mass, drifted pile.

Drift, *v. i.* 1. Float, be wafted, be borne *or* carried by the current *or* aimlessly.

2. Accumulate in heaps, be driven into heaps.

Drill, *n.* 1. Borer, boring-tool.

2. Training, discipline, methodical exercise.

3. Furrow, channel, trench (*for planting*).

——, *v. t.* 1. Pierce, perforate, bore.

2. Exercise in tactics, train in martial exercises.

3. Instruct, exercise, teach, train.

Drink, *v. i.* 1. Take a drink, imbibe, sip, "swill," "guzzle."

2. Tipple, tope, be a drunkard, be a toper, be intemperate (*in the use of spirituous liquors*), take a drop too much.

——, *v. t.* 1. Swallow, quaff.

2. Imbibe, absorb, swallow up, suck in.

DRINK, *n.* 1. Beverage, potion, potation, draft.

2. [*Referring to the amount.*] Sip, "nip," bumper, "bracer."

Drinkable, *a.* Potable, that may be drunk, fit to drink, suitable for drinking.

Drinking, *a.* Tippling, toping, intemperate, bibulous.

——, *n.* Tippling, potation, compotation, cups (*fig.*).

Drinking-bout, *n.* Carouse, carousal, revel, revelry, jollification, bacchanals, saturnalia, debauch, compotation, wassail, orgies, "spree."

Drink to. Pledge, toast, drink in honor of, drink the health of.

Drip, *v. i.* Trickle, fall in drops, dribble.

Drive, *v. t.* 1. Impel, push forward, propel, thrust, shoot, hurl, send.

2. Actuate, urge, press, incite.

3. Force, coerce, compel, constrain, oblige.

4. Guide (*by reins*), manage as to direction.

——, *v. i.* 1. Be forced along, be impelled, move helplessly, drift, scud.

2. Rush, press with violence, go furiously.

3. Go driving, take a drive, go by carriage.

4. Aim, intend.

——, *n.* 1. Airing, ride.

2. Carriage-road, driving-course.

Drive at. Intend, purpose, aim at, tend to, be after, endeavor after.

Drive away. Expel, disperse, scatter, dispel, drive off.

Drive back. Repel, repulse.

Drivel, *v. i.* 1. Slaver, slobber, drool.

2. Dote, be imbecile, be foolish.

——, *n.* 1. Slaver, driveling, "drool."

2. Nonsense, balderdash, stuff, foolish talk, twaddle, twattle, imbecile prating. See PRATE.

Driveler, *n.* 1. Slaverer, drooler.

2. Dotard, idiot, simpleton, fool, imbecile, twattler, senseless gabbler.

Driveling, *n.* 1. Slaver, "drool."

2. Foolishness, folly, idiocy.

Drive off. Expel, drive away.

Drive out. Expel, reject, eject, cast out, turn out.

DRIVING, *n.* Coercing, urging; directing.

Drizzle, *v. i.* Rain (*in small drops*), mizzle.

Droll, *n.* 1. Jester (*by profession*), buffoon, harlequin, mountebank, punch, punchinello, clown, zany, scaramouch, fool, jack-pudding, merry-andrew, pickle-herring.

2. Farce, comic show.

——, *a.* 1. Comic, comical, funny, ludicrous, farcical, laughable, ridiculous.

2. Odd, queer, facetious, waggish, amusing, diverting.

Drollery, *n.* Pleasantry, fun, facetiousness, waggishness, waggery, buffoonery, comicality.

Drone, *n.* 1. Idler, sluggard, lounger, idle fellow, lazy fellow, do-nothing, good-for-nothing.

2. Humming, humming noise.

——, *v. i.* 1. Lounge, dawdle, idle, waste time in trifles, live in idleness.

2. Make a dull humming sound, hum.

Dronish, *a.* Idle, lazy, indolent, sluggish, slow, inactive, drony.

Drool, *v. i.* [*U. S. and parts of England.*] Slaver, drivel, drop saliva.

Droop, *v. t.* Let droop, let sink *or* fall, let bend down, dangle, make hang.

——, *v. i.* 1. Sink *or* hang down, drop, bend downward, loll, sag, slouch.

2. Wilt, wither, fade.

3. Languish, weaken, faint, sink, fail, flag, decline, grow weak, be dispirited.

DROP, *n.* 1. Globule, droplet, bead, gutta.

2. Ear-ring, pendant.

3. Small quantity, very little, least bit.

DROP, *v. t.* 1. Distil, send down *or* let fall in drops, shed.

2. Lower, sink, depress, dump, let down, let fall, let go.

3. Leave, quit, forsake, desert, relinquish, abandon, forswear, give up, give over, omit.

4. Discontinue, intermit, remit, cease, desist from, break off, leave off, lay aside.

——, *v. i.* 1. Distil, fall in drops, drip, bleed.

2. Fall suddenly, precipitate.

3. Cease, come to an end, come to nothing.

Dross, *n.* 1. Scum, recrement, scoria, slag, cinder.

2. Refuse, waste matter.

Drought, *n.* Dryness (*of weather*), aridity, drouth, want of rain.

Drove, *n.* 1. Herd, flock.

2. Crowd, collection, herd (*of people in motion*).

Drown, *v. t.* 1. Suffocate in water.

2. Overflow, inundate, deluge, overwhelm, flood.

3. Overcome, overpower.

Drowse, *v. i.* Slumber, doze, nap, be half asleep.

Drowsy, *a.* 1. Sleepy, dozy.

2. Lethargic, comatose, stupid.

3. Soporific, lulling.

Drub, *v. t.* Beat, thrash, cudgel, cane, flog, pound, thump, etc. See BEAT.

Drubbing, *n.* Beating, flogging, thrashing, cudgelling, caning, pounding, flagellation.

Drudge, *v. i.* Slave, toil, plod, "fag," grub, grind, work hard, do heavy menial service.

——, *n.* Slave, menial, scullion, hack, fag, grind, hard-worker, toiler.

Drudgery, *n.* Hard *or* toilsome work, ignoble toil, mean labor, hackwork.

Drug, *n.* Medicine, physic, remedy.

——, *v. t.* 1. Medicate, dose.

2. Deaden with narcotics *or* anæsthetics, deaden, dull, stupefy, "dope."

3. Dose to excess, stuff with drugs.

4. Surfeit, disgust.

Drunkard, *n.* Toper, tippler, sot, inebriate, dipsomaniac, carouser, reveller, bacchanal, bacchanalian.

Drunken, *a.* 1. Intoxicated, drunk, inebriated, "boozy."

2. Sottish, given to intoxication *or* drink.

3. Drenched, saturated, soaked.

DRY, *a.* 1. Dried, unmoistened, juiceless, sapless, desiccated.

2. Arid, parched, droughty.

3. Thirsty, craving drink.

4. Uninteresting, barren, dull, jejune, tame, vapid, insipid, pointless, tiresome, tedious, unembellished, plain.

5. Sarcastic, severe, sly, keen, sharp.

——, *v. t.* Desiccate, exsiccate, parch, dehydrate, free from moisture, make dry.

——, *v. i.* Become dry, lose moisture.

Dryad, *n.* Wood-nymph.

Dualism, *n.* 1. Parseeism, Zoroastrianism, Mazdeism, Manicheism, doctrine of two supreme principles (*good and evil*).

2. (*Met.*) Natural realism, doctrine of two primal realities (*mind and matter*).

Dub, *v. t.* Name, style, term, denominate, designate, call, entitle, christen.

Dubiety, *n.* See DOUBT, *n.*

Dubious, *a.* 1. Doubtful, undecided, hesitant, uncertain, wavering, fluctuating, unsettled.

2. Uncertain, doubtful, equivocal, ambiguous, not plain, not clear.

Duck, *v. t.* Immerse, plunge, souse, dip.

——, *v. i.* 1. Dive, plunge, dip, immerse one's self.

2. Bow, cringe, dodge (*downward*), bob.

Ducking-stool, *n.* Trebuchet, tumbrel, castigatory, cucking-stool.

Duct, *n.* Conduit, channel, canal, pipe, tube.

Ductile, *a.* 1. Tractable, compliant, docile, yielding, facile.

2. Pliant, flexible, easily bent.

3. Extensible, capable of being drawn out, tensile.

Ductility, *n.* 1. Tractableness, docility, compliancy, flexibility, yielding disposition.

2. Extensibility.

Dudgeon, *n.* Anger, resentment, indignation, ire, malice, ill-will.

Duds, *n. pl.* (*Colloq.*) 1. Old clothes, tattered garments.

2. Effects, things, clothes, traps.

Due, *a.* 1. Owed, to be paid.

2. Proper, fit, suitable, appropriate, becoming, befitting.

3. Owing, to be ascribed.

——, *n.* 1. Debt, what is due, charge.

2. Right, just title, lawful claim, desert.

Duel, *n.* Affair of honor, combat.

Due to. 1. Owing to, occasioned by, to be ascribed to.

2. Belonging of right to, fit for, befitting, suited to, appropriate to.

Dug, *n.* Teat (*of a beast*), nipple, pap, udder (*rarely*).

Dulcet, *a.* 1. Sweet, luscious, honeyed, delightful to the taste, delicious.

2. Melodious, harmonious, sweet, delightful to the ear.

3. Pleasing, agreeable, pleasant, delightful, charming, sweet.

Dull, *a.* 1. Stupid, stolid, doltish, blockish, brutish, unintelligent, blunt-witted, obtuse.

2. Apathetic, insensible, unimpassioned, passionless, dead, callous, unfeeling, unresponsive, phlegmatic.

3. Inert, inactive, lifeless, inanimate, heavy, languid, sluggish, slow, torpid.

4. Blunt, obtuse, dulled.

5. Gloomy, sad, dismal, cheerless, dreary, somber.

6. Dim, obscure, lacklustre, lustreless, tarnished, matt, opaque.

7. Tedious, wearisome, tiresome, irksome, insipid, flat, uninteresting, prosy, dry, jejune.

——, *v. t.* 1. Blunt, make blunt.

2. Stupefy, benumb, deaden, paralyze, besot, obtund, hebetate, make *or* render insensible, heavy, *or* lethargic, render callous, make obtuse.

3. Depress, dishearten, dampen, discourage, dispirit, deject, make dumpish, make sad, gloomy, *or* dejected.

4. Quiet, allay, moderate, assuage, mitigate, alleviate, soften.

5. Sully, tarnish, dim, deaden.

Dullard, *n.* Simpleton. See DUNCE.

Duly, *adv.* 1. Properly, fitly, befittingly, rightly, decorously, in a suitable manner.

2. Regularly, in course, at the proper time.

Dumb, *a.* 1. Unable to speak, incapable of speech, inarticulate, voiceless.

2. Mute, speechless, silent.

Dumb-show, *n.* Pantomime.

Dumfound, ⎫ *v. t.* (*Colloq.*) Confuse,
Dumfounder, ⎭ confound, pose, nonplus, strike dumb, astound, amaze.

Dummy, *n.* Mute, dumb person.

Dumpish, *a.* Sad, dejected, dispirited, despondent, moping. See MELANCHOLY, *a.*

Dumps, *n. pl.* Dejection, depression, sadness, despondency, blues, blue devils. See MELANCHOLY, *n.*

Dumpy, *a.* Short and thick (*in person*), squat.

Dun, *a.* Dull brown, yellowish-brown, drab.

——, *v. t.* Press (*for a debt*), importune, urge.

Dunce, *n.* Simpleton, fool, dolt, ignoramus, witling, blockhead, block, numskull, dullard, thickhead, dunderhead, dunderpate, clodpoll, clodpate, beetle-head, bull-head, addle-head, chuckle-head, jolt-head, lackbrain, moon-calf, lackwit, halfwit, oaf, changeling, booby, noodle, spooney, "nincompoop," ninny, ninnyhammer, gaby, flat, driveller, noddy, natural, innocent, lout, stick, ass, jackass, donkey, goose, loon, calf, noncompos.

Dung, *n.* Excrement, ordure, fæces.

Dungeon, *n.* Prison (*especially one underground and dark*), keep, donjon-keep.

Dupe, *n.* Gull, cully, credulous person, victim of fraud.

——, *v. t.* Cheat, deceive, delude, trick, circumvent, overreach, beguile, cully, chouse, cozen, gull, impose upon, victimize.

Duplicate, *a.* Double, twofold.

——, *n.* Copy, transcript, counterpart, replica, facsimile.

Duplicity, *n.* Dissimulation, chicanery, guile, deceit, deception, hypocrisy, circumvention, artifice, Machiavelism, double-dealing, falseness, fraud, perfidy, dishonesty.

Durability, *n.* Durableness, lasting quality.

Durable, *a.* Permanent, firm, lasting, abiding, persisting, continuing, constant, stable.

Durableness, *n.* Permanence, durability, lasting quality.

Duration, *n.* 1. Continuance (*in time*), continuation, lasting period.

2. Time, extension in time.

Duress, *n.* Constraint, restraint, captivity, confinement, imprisonment, durance.

During, *prep.* For the time of, for the period of; pending.

Dusk, *n.* 1. Twilight, approach of night *or* darkness, edge of darkness, nightfall.

2. Dark color, approach to blackness, duskiness.

Dusky, *a.* 1. Obscure, murky, dim, shadowy, cloudy, shady, overcast, somewhat dark.

2. Dark, dark-colored, swarthy, tawny.

DUST, *n.* Powdery dirt, ash.

Dutiful, *a.* 1. Obedient, submissive, duteous.

2. Reverential, respectful, deferential.

Duty, *n.* 1. What one ought to do, what one is morally bound to do, obligation, responsibility, devoir.

2. Service, business, function, office.

3. Tax, impost, toll, custom, excise.

Dwarf, *n.* Pygmy, hop o' my thumb, bantam, midget, "runt," manikin.

——, *v. t.* Stunt, hinder from growth.

Dwarfish, *a.* Stunted, dwarfed, undersized, diminutive, small, little, tiny, Lilliputian, pygmean, pygmy.

Dwell, *v. i.* Inhabit, reside, live, stay, sojourn, tenant, lodge, tarry, abide, be settled, have a habitation.

Dweller, *n.* Inhabitant, inhabiter, resident, citizen, denizen.

Dwelling, *n.* Habitation, abode, residence, establishment, cot, dugout, hutch, mansion, lodging, quarters, domicile, home, place of residence, place of abode, dwelling-place, house.

Dwell on. } 1. Hang upon fondly, be
Dwell upon. } absorbed with, be deeply interested in.

2. Continue long upon, occupy a long time with.

Dwindle, *v. i.* 1. Diminish, decrease, lessen, shrink, grow less, grow little.

2. Sink, degenerate, decline, decay, fall away, fall off.

——, *v. t.* Diminish, decrease, lessen, make less.

Dye, *n.* Color, hue, tint, tinge, stain, cast, shade.

——, *v. t.* Color, tinge, stain.

Dying, *a.* 1. Expiring.

2. Mortal, perishable.

——, *n.* Death, decease, demise, dissolution, departure, exit, end of life.

Dynasty, *n.* 1. Government, sovereignty, dominion, empire.

2. Race of rulers, family of sovereigns, succession.

Dyspepsia, *n.* (*Med.*) Indigestion, difficulty of digestion.

E

Each, *a.* 1. One and the other (*of two*), both, either (*archaic and poetical*).

2. Every one (*of several*).

Eager, *a.* 1. Longing, yearning, greedy, anxious, avid, agog, fain, impatient, keen, desirous.

2. Ardent, zealous, enthusiastic, vehement, impetuous, forward, earnest, animated, fervent, fervid, glowing, hot, sanguine.

Eagle-eyed, *a.* Sharp-sighted, discerning, lynx-eyed, etc.

EAR, *n.* 1. Organ of hearing, "lug."

2. Musical perception, sense of hearing.

3. Regard, heed, attention, hearing.

4. Spike (*of grain*), head.

EARLY, *a.* 1. Timely, seasonable, in season.

2. Forward, premature.

3. Matutinal, dawning.

Early, *adv.* 1. Soon, betimes, seasonably, in good season, in good time.

2. At dawn, at daybreak.

Earn, *v. t.* 1. Gain, get, acquire, win, obtain, procure.

2. Merit, deserve, be entitled to.

Earnest, *a.* 1. Ardent, zealous, eager, fervent, impassioned, fervid, glowing, animated, importunate, warm, hearty, cordial.

2. Intent, steady, fixed.

3. Sincere, true, truthful.

4. Serious, important, momentous, weighty.

——, *n.* 1. Seriousness, reality, truth, good faith.

2. Pledge, promise, foretaste, first-fruits.

3. (*Law.*) Earnest-money, handsel, payment.

Earnings, *n. pl.* Income, proceeds, profits, gettings. See WAGES.

EARTH, *n.* 1. World, globe, planet, terrestrial ball, terraqueous orb.

2. Soil, ground, land, clod, turf, sod, glebe, clay, loam, dirt, humus.

3. World, mankind.

4. This world, nature, natural order, temporal things, transitory state.

Earth-born, *a.* 1. Terrigenous, human, worldly.

2. Of low birth, of mean extraction, meanly born.

3. Earthly, low, mean, base, abject, grovelling, earth-bred, unspiritual, merely temporal.

Earth-bred, *a.* Low, base, vile, abject, grovelling, earth-born, earth-fed.

Earthly, *a.* 1. Terrestrial.

2. Sensual, sordid, worldly, low, grovelling, vile, base, gross, earthly-minded, earth-born, earth-fed, earth-bred, carnal, unspiritual.

3. Natural, merely natural *or* physical, bodily, temporal, carnal, merely temporal, non-spiritual, material, mundane, secular.

4. On earth, in the world, possible, conceivable.

Earthy, *a.* 1. Terrene, clayey, earthlike.

2. Earthly, terrestrial.

3. Gross, coarse, unrefined, material.

Ease, *n.* 1. Rest, repose, quiescence, leisure.

2. Quiet, quietude, quietness, tranquillity, peace, content, contentment, satisfaction, relief.

3. Facility, easiness, readiness.

4. Freedom, flexibility, lightness, naturalness, unconstraint, unconcern, liberty.

5. Comfort, elbowroom.

——, *v. t.* 1. Relieve, disburden, disencumber, free from pain *or* anxiety, pacify, quiet, still, give rest *or* repose *or* relief.

2. Alleviate, allay, assuage, appease, mitigate, soothe, abate, diminish.

3. [With *of.*] Relieve (*from* or *of*), disburthen.

4. Release (from pressure), loosen, give more room.

5. Facilitate, favor.

EAST, *n.* Orient.

Eastern, *a.* Oriental, orient, easterly, eastward.

Easy, *a.* 1. Light, not difficult, not burdensome.

2. Quiet, tranquil, untroubled, comfortable, contented, satisfied, at rest, at ease, without anxiety, painless, effortless, careless.

3. Yielding, complying, compliant, pliant, facile, submissive, accommodating, complaisant, tractable, indolent, manageable.

4. Unconstrained, graceful, informal, natural.

5. Natural, flowing, unaffected, smooth, ready.

6. Gentle, moderate, lenient, mild.

7. Not straitened (*pecuniarily*), comfortable, affluent, unembarrassed, unconcerned, loose.

Eat, *v. t.* 1. Chew and swallow, ingest, consume, devour, mandicate, engorge, ravage.

2. Corrode, erode, consume, demolish.

——, *v. i.* 1. Feed, take food, dine, sup, breakfast, etc.

2. Act corrosively.

Eatable, *a.* Esculent, edible.

Eavesdrop, *v. i.* Listen stealthily.

Ebb, *n.* 1. Regression, regress, retrocession, retrogression, reflux, refluence, return.

2. Decline, decay, deterioration, degeneration, degeneracy, caducity, wane, waning.

3. Decrease, diminution, abatement, decrement.

——, *v. i.* 1. Recede, retire, flow back.

2. Decline, decrease, decay, wane, sink, fall away.

Ebon, *a.* 1. Dark, black, inky.

2. Made of ebony.

Ebullience, *n.* 1. Effervescence, ebullition, boiling over.

2. Bursting forth, overflow, burst, rush, bursting vigor, over-enthusiasm.

Ebullition, *n.* 1. Boiling.

2. Effervescence, fermentation.

3. Burst, outburst, bursting forth, outbreak, fit, paroxysm.

Eccentric, *a.* 1. Decentered, parabolic.

2. With different centers, non-concentric.

3. Irregular, abnormal, anomalous, peculiar, uncommon, unnatural, singular, strange, wayward, odd, aberrant, erratic, whimsical, cranky, outlandish, fantastic.

——, *n.* "Crank," curiosity, original, "guy."

Eccentricity, *n.* 1. Deviation from circularity, ellipticity, oblateness, flatness, flattening.

2. Distance from center to focus.

3. Irregularity, peculiarity, oddness, oddity, singularity, waywardness, strangeness, aberration.

Ecclesiastic, } *a.* Of the Church, belong-
Ecclesiastical, } ing *or* relating to the Church, churchly, religious, non-secular.

Ecclesiastic, *n.* Priest, clergyman, churchman, minister, parson, pastor, divine, person in holy orders *or* in orders, "religious."

Echo, *n.* 1. Reverberation, reflected sound, repercussion of sound.

2. Assenting repetition, slavish imitation.

——, *v. i.* Resound, reverberate, reply, ring.

——, *v. t.* Reverberate, re-echo, repeat, sound loudly, sound faintly.

Eclat, *n.* Brilliancy, splendor, show, pomp, lustre, effect, striking effect, glory.

Eclectic, *a.* Selecting, selective.

Eclipse, *n.* 1. Obscuration, darkening, dimming, clouding, veiling, hiding, shrouding, disappearance, concealment, vanishing, occultation.

2. Extinguishment, extinction, obliteration, blotting out, destruction, annihilation.

——, *v. t.* 1. Darken, obscure, dim, cloud, veil, shroud, hide, hide from view.

2. Throw into the shade, utterly surpass, put out of competition.

3. Extinguish, blot out, put out, annihilate, annul.

Eclogue, *n.* Bucolic, idyl, pastoral, pastoral poem.

Economic, } *a.* 1. Household, house-
Economical, } keeping, relating to house keeping *or* the household, housewifely.

2. Relating to economics, concerning public economy.

3. Saving, sparing, provident, thrifty, frugal, "scrimpy," free from lavishness *or* waste, parsimonious, cheap.

Economics, *n.* 1. Science of wealth, method of developing public wealth, plutology, public economy, political economy.

2. Household management, household economy, housewifery.

Economize, *v. t.* Save, husband, manage frugally, use prudently, expend with frugality *or* without waste.

——, *v. i.* Retrench, be frugal, be prudent, husband one's resources, avoid waste.

Economy, *n.* 1. Frugality, thrift, thriftiness, husbandry, good housewifery, saving, providence, parsimony, skimping, retrenchment.

2. Arrangement, regulation, management, administration, system, plan.

3. Dispensation, established order.

Ecstasy, *n.* 1. Trance, frenzy, madness, paroxysm.

2. Transport, rapture, ravishment, delight, excessive joy, supreme delight, gladness, rhapsody.

Ecstatic, *a.* Ravished, transported, rapturous, enraptured, beatific.

Eddy, *n.* 1. Counter-current.

2. Whirlpool, vortex, swirl.

EDGE, *n.* 1. Cutting side (*of a blade*).

2. Border, rim, hem, brim, margin, verge, brink, bound, bordure, lip, fringe, crest; beginning *or* end, opening *or* close (*as the case may be*).

3. Keenness, sharpness, intensity, interest, animation, zest.

4. Power to wound, sharpness, sting, acrimony, bitterness, gall.

——, *v. t.* 1. Sharpen.

2. Fringe, border, rim.

3. Move sideways, move little by little, hitch up, hitch along.

——, *v. i.* Move sideways, move little by little, hitch along, sidle.

Edging, *n.* Fringe, border, trimming, frill.

Edible, *a.* Eatable, esculent.

Edict, *n.* Command, order, decree, rescript, mandate, ordinance, proclamation, ban, bull, constitution, decision, notice, manifesto.

Edifice, *n.* Building, fabric, structure.

Edify, *v. t.* Upbuild (morally), nurture in religion, instruct, improve, teach.

Edit, *v. t.* 1. Revise and correct, prepare for the press, annotate and emend, arrange, redact, bring out.

2. Conduct (*a journal, etc.*), manage.

Edition, *n.* Issue (*of a literary work*), impression, number.

Educate, *v. t.* Train, discipline, teach, instruct, indoctrinate, school, nurture, breed, bring up, develop the faculties of, form the mind and character of, cultivate.

Educated, *a.* Lettered, literate, cultured.

EDUCATION, *n.* Training, teaching, tuition, schooling, instruction, pedagogics, discipline, cultivation, nurture, breeding, development, culture.

Educe, *v. t.* Extract, draw out, bring out, elicit, evolve.

Efface, *v. t.* Obliterate, erase, expunge, blot, cancel, rub out, wipe out, scratch out, rub off, blot out, strike out, remove, excise, delete, sponge.

EFFECT, *n.* 1. Consequence, result, issue, event, fruit, outcome.

2. Force, validity, weight, power, efficiency.

3. Purport, import, drift, tenor, meaning, general intent.

——, *v. t.* 1. Cause, produce, create.

2. Accomplish, achieve, execute, perform, do, consummate, complete, realize, carry, compass, bring about, bring to pass, carry out, work out, work, force, contrive, negotiate, conclude.

Effective, *a.* 1. Competent, adequate, sufficient, effectual.

2. Powerful, forcible, energetic, potent, cogent, efficacious.

3. Operative, active, efficient.

Effects, *n. pl.* Goods, furniture, movables, personal estate.

Effectual, *a.* 1. Operative, successful.

2. Efficacious, effective, active, efficient, of adequate power.

Effectuate, *v. t.* Accomplish, secure, achieve, effect, execute, carry out, bring to pass.

Effeminacy, *n.* [*Said of men.*] Weakness, softness, timidity, unmanly delicacy, womanishness, femininity.

Effeminate, *a.* [*Said of men.*] Womanish, feminine, timorous, unmanly.

Effervesce, *v. i.* 1. Froth, foam, bubble, ferment.

2. Be lively, gay, hilarious, etc.

Effete, *a.* 1. Barren, unprolific, unfruitful, fruitless, addle.

2. Decayed, spent, exhausted, wasted, worn out.

Efficacious, *a.* Effectual, effective, powerful, active, operative, efficient, energetic, of adequate power.

Efficacy, *n.* Potency, competency, power, strength, force, efficiency, effectiveness, energy, vigor, virtue.

Efficient, *a.* 1. Operative, active, efficacious, effective, effectual, potent.

2. Able, energetic, skilful, ready.

Effigy, *n*. Image, figure, statue, representation, likeness, portrait.

Effloresce, *v. i.* 1. Bloom, flower, burst into bloom, break into flower.

2. Break into florid ornament, become florid.

3. (*Chem.*) Grow pulverulent (*on the surface*), acquire a bloom *or* down, crust.

Efflorescence, *n*. Flowering, bloom, blossoming.

Effluence, *n*. Emanation, efflux, outflow.

Effluvium, *n*. Exhalation, vapor, noxious exhalation.

Efflux, *n*. 1. Flow, effusion.

2. Emanation, effluence.

Effort, *n*. Endeavor, attempt, trial, essay, exertion, struggle, strain, strife, spurt, trouble, application, pains, stretch.

Effrontery, *n*. Assurance, impudence, audacity, hardihood, presumption, shamelessness, sauciness, "brass," brazen boldness.

Effulgence, *n*. Brilliancy, lustre, splendor, brightness, radiance, refulgence.

Effulgent, *a*. Brilliant, shining, lustrous, splendid, resplendent, bright, radiant, refulgent, dazzling, blazing, flaming, glowing, burning, beaming.

Effuse, *v. t.* Shed, spill, pour out *or* forth.

——, *v. i.* Issue, emanate, come forth, spread forth.

Effusion, *n*. 1. Outpouring, efflux, gush.

2. Shedding, spilling, waste, effuse.

3. Utterance, expression of thought *or* sentiment, desultory composition *or* effort (*literary*).

Effusive, *a*. 1. Lavish, generous, largely *or* freely outpouring, effuse, demonstrative, gushing, exuberant.

2. Poured abroad, spread widely, diffused.

EGG, *n*. Ovum.

——, *v. t.* 1. [With *on*.] Urge, incite, instigate, push, stimulate, encourage.

2. [With *into*.] Provoke, harass, harry.

Egg-shaped, *a*. Ovate.

Ego, *n*. [L.] (*Psychol.*) Subject, conscious subject, self, me; id, superego.

Egoism, *n*. 1. (*Met.*) Subjective *or* sceptical *or* negative idealism, solipsism (*limitation of certainty to the self*), individualism.

2. Egotism, selfishness, extravagant love of self.

Egotism, *n*. 1. Self-importance, self-conceit, self-esteem, self-assertion, self-admiration, self-praise, self-commendation, "bumptiousness."

2. Selfishness, passionate *or* extravagant self-love, egoism.

Egotistic, } *a*. Conceited, vain, opinion-
Egotistical, } ated, self-centered, self-loving, self-important, self-conceited, self-admiring, self-asserting, "bumptious."

Egregious, *a*. [*Usually in a bad sense.*] Extraordinary, remarkable, enormous, monstrous, outrageous, great, huge, prodigious, tremendous, flagrant, gross.

Egress, *n*. Passage out, power to go out; way out, exit, outlet; departure, emergence.

Either, *a*. and *pron*. 1. One or the other (*of two*).

2. [*Archaic or poetical.*] Each (*of two*), both, one and the other.

Ejaculate, *v. t.* Utter in an exclamation, utter briefly and suddenly, blurt.

——, *v. i.* Cry *or* exclaim passionately *or* hurriedly.

Ejaculation, *n*. Exclamation, brief and sudden utterance, *ecphonesis*.

Eject, *v. t.* 1. Emit, discharge, void, evacuate, vomit, spew, puke, belch, spit, spout, spurt, disgorge, throw out, cast up.

2. Expel, oust, dismiss, discharge, cashier, turn out, thrust out, put out, eliminate, dispossess, "bounce," evict, "fire."

3. Reject, banish, throw aside, cast away, throw overboard.

Ejection, *n*. Expulsion, dismission, discharge, emission, extrusion, banishment, thrusting out, turning out.

Eke out, *v. t.* Add to, supply the deficiency of, stretch out, make out, make out with difficulty, increase, enlarge.

Elaborate, *v. t.* 1. Bestow labor upon, work out, develop, devise.

2. Improve, refine, mature, ripen, prepare thoroughly, work out with (great) care.

——, *a*. 1. Labored, studied, operose, complicated, detailed, "dressy."

2. Minutely and intricately wrought.

Elaboration, *n*. 1. Labor, painstaking development.

2. Ripening, maturing, working out.

Elapse, *v. i.* Pass, lapse, glide away, slip away, pass away.

ELASTIC, *a*. 1. Springy, rebounding, resilient, recoiling.

2. Recuperative, buoyant.

Elasticity, *n*. 1. Springiness, resiliency, tendency to rebound, buoyancy.

2. Tendency to recover, power to endure strain *or* depression.

Elate, *v. t.* Cheer, exhilarate, elevate, animate, enliven, exalt, please, gladden, excite, flush, puff up, make proud, inflate.

Elated, *a*. Flushed (*with success*), elate, excited, exultant, exhilarated, puffed up, in high spirits.

Elation, *n.* Exultation, elevation, exaltation, pride, high spirits, excitement, enlivenment, flush, joy.

Elbow, *n.* Angle, bend, turn, flexure, joining.

——, *v. t.* Push, crowd, jostle, hustle, shoulder, nudge, force.

——, *v. i.* Jostle, hustle, shoulder, crowd, push, push one's way.

Elbow-room, *n.* Scope, swing, range, sweep, opportunity, liberty of action, a fair field, room enough.

Elder, *a.* 1. Older, senior, earlier born.

2. Senior, ranking, previously appointed *or* commissioned.

3. Earlier, more ancient, ancient, olden.

——, *n.* 1. Senior, superior in age; ancestor.

2. Old man, aged man, venerable man.

3. Presbyter, ruling elder.

Elderly, *a.* Somewhat old, "oldish," somewhat advanced in life.

Eldership, *n.* 1. Seniority.

2. Elder's office.

3. Order of elders, body of elders.

Eldest, *a.* Oldest.

Elect, *v. t.* Choose, select, cull, pick, prefer, single out, fix upon, pitch upon, pick out, make choice of, predestinate.

——, *a.* 1. Chosen, selected, picked, choice.

2. Elected, appointed (*but not installed in office*).

3. (*Theol.*) Redeemed, predestinated to salvation, saved, chosen to salvation.

Election, *n.* 1. Selection, preference, choice.

2. Appointment by vote.

3. Choice, alternative, liberty, freedom, free-will, power to choose.

4. (*Theol.*) Predestination.

Electioneer, *v. i.* Canvass.

Elective, *a.* 1. Chosen by election, determined by suffrage, dependent on suffrage, constituent.

2. Concerning suffrage, of suffrage, electoral.

3. Selective, mutually attractive, optative, optional.

Elector, *n.* Voter, constituent, chooser.

ELECTRIC, *a.* 1. Charged with electricity, voltaic.

2. Marked by electricity, relating to electricity.

3. Full of fire *or* spirit, inspiriting, inspiring, stimulating.

4. Lightning-like, swift and flashing, instantaneous and thrilling, rousing, thrilling, stirring, exciting.

Electrify, *v. t.* 1. Render electric, charge with electricity, galvanize.

2. Rouse, thrill, excite, stir, enchant, startle.

Elegance, *n.* 1. Grace, beauty, symmetry, propriety.

2. Refinement, polish, politeness, gentility, courtliness, daintiness, nicety.

Elegant, *a.* 1. Graceful, beautiful, handsome, fine, symmetrical, classical, tasteful, chaste, neat, dainty, trim, well-made, well-proportioned, in good taste.

2. Polished, refined, accomplished, cultivated, polite, genteel, courtly, fashionable, Chesterfieldian.

Elegiac, *a.* Mournful, plaintive, sorrowful, dirgelike.

Elegy, *n.* 1. Dirge, lament, epicedium, mournful song, funeral song.

2. Serious, meditative, *or* melancholy poem.

Element, *n.* 1. Simple body, uncompounded body, ultimate part.

2. Constituent, component, ingredient, constituent principle, component part, factor, germ.

3. Proper state, proper sphere, natural medium, vital air.

4. [In *pl.*] Rudiments, first steps *or* principles, outlines, essential parts, principle.

Elementary, *a.* 1. Simple, uncompounded, primordial.

2. Rudimentary, rudimental, primary, component, fundamental, basic.

Elephantine, *a.* 1. Huge, immense, gigantic, colossal, Cyclopean, Herculean, enormous, heavy.

2. Clumsy, unwieldy.

Elevate, *v. t.* 1. Raise, lift, lift up, hoist, erect.

2. Exalt, promote, advance, aggrandize.

3. Improve, dignify, ennoble, refine, exalt, greaten.

Elevated, *a.* High, lofty, grand, sublime, grandiose, dignified.

Elevation, *n.* 1. Raising, elevating.

2. Exaltation, aggrandizement, promotion.

3. Dignity, refinement, improvement, ennobling.

4. Hill, elevated place, height, rise.

5. Height, altitude, eminence.

Elf, *n.* 1. Fairy, fay, sprite, imp, urchin, diminutive spirit, puck, pixy, pygmy.

2. Dwarf, gnome.

Elfish, *a.* Elf-like, mischievous, elvish, weird.

Elicit, *v. t.* 1. Draw out, bring out, educe, evoke, extract, fetch, wrest, wring, extort, "pump," call forth, succeed in obtaining.

2. Bring to light, educe, deduce.

Elide, *v. t.* Cut off (*a syllable*), strike out, nullify, curtail.

Eligible, *a.* 1. Desirable, preferable, worthy of choice, fit to be chosen.

2. Legally qualified (*for election*).

Eliminate, *v. t.* Exclude, remove, expel, reject, eradicate, erase, thrust out, drive out, get clear of, get rid of.

Élite, *n.* [Fr.] Flower (*of a society*), best part, select body, chosen, best.

Elixir, *n.* 1. Cordial.

2. (*Med.*) Compound tincture; refined spirit, quintessence.

Ellipse, *n.* 1. Closed conic (section).

2. Oval, oval figure, flattened circle, rounded oblong.

Ellipsis, *n.* Omission, gap, hiatus, lacuna.

Elliptic,
Elliptical, } *a.* 1. Oval, oblong rounded.

2. Relating *or* belonging to the ellipse, like an ellipse.

3. Defective, incomplete, containing omissions.

Elocution, *n.* 1. Speech, faculty of speech, power of expression.

2. Utterance, delivery, manner of speaking, oral expression.

3. Art of delivery, art of oral expression, reading art, declamatory art, oratory.

Elongate, *v. t.* Lengthen, stretch, extend, draw out, lengthen out.

Elope, *v. i.* Abscond (*as a woman with a paramour*), run away, run off.

Eloquence, *n.* 1. Oratory, art of speaking well (*in public*).

2. Graceful and vigorous utterance, fit words in fit places, appropriate expression.

3. Impassioned utterance, flowing and impassioned speech, speech full of appropriate feeling.

Eloquent, *a.* 1. Persuasive, impressive.

2. Graceful and vigorous.

3. Impassioned, flowing and full of feeling, fluent and powerful, Ciceronian.

Else, *a.* or *pron.* Other, beside *or* besides, different.

——, *adv.* or *conj.* Otherwise, differently; besides.

Elucidate, *v. t.* Explain, illustrate, unfold, make clear, make plain, clarify, illuminate, interpret, demonstrate.

Elucidation, *n.* 1. Clearing up, elucidating, explanation, explaining, illustration, illustrating, unfolding.

2. Explanation, illustration, exposition, comment, annotation, commentary, gloss, scholium.

Elucidative, *a.* Explanatory.

Elude, *v. t.* 1. Escape, evade, avoid, shun,

get away from, steal away from, slip from, slip away from.

2. Baffle, frustrate, foil, balk, thwart, disconcert, disappoint, escape (*notice* or *inquiry*).

Elusive, *a.* 1. Evasive. See ELUSORY.

2. Equivocating, shuffling, equivocatory.

Elusory, *a.* Evasive, elusive, delusive, deceptive, fraudulent, fallacious, deceitful, illusory.

Elvish, *a.* Elf-like, mischievous, elfish.

Elysian, *a.* Charming, delightful, ravishing, enchanting, blissful, heavenly, celestial, exceedingly happy.

Emaciate, *v. t.* Make lean *or* thin *or* spare, reduce in flesh, cause to waste away.

Emaciated, *a.* Lean, thin, lank, attenuated, wasted, gaunt, skinny, meagre, worn to a shadow.

Emaciation, *n.* Leanness, lankness, meagreness, wasting away, pining away, tabes, tabefaction.

Emanate, *v. i.* 1. Flow forth.

2. Issue, arise, spring, flow, proceed, emerge, come, radiate, go out.

Emanation, *n.* 1. Flowing out, issuing, issuance, arising, springing, flowing, emerging, emergence.

2. Efflux, effluence, issue, effluvium; aura.

Emancipate, *v. t.* Enfranchise, manumit, liberate, disenthrall, release, unfetter, unshackle, unchain, free, set free, set at liberty.

Emancipation, *n.* Enfranchisement, manumission, liberation, release, deliverance.

Emasculate, *v. t.* 1. Castrate, geld, glib, deprive of virility.

2. Weaken, enervate, debilitate, unman, effeminize, emolliate, deprive of native vigor.

Embalm, *v. t.* 1. Preserve from decay (*by aromatics* or *antiseptics*).

2. Preserve, enshrine, cherish, keep unimpaired.

3. Scent, perfume, make fragrant *or* balmy, fill with balm.

Embargo, *n.* Prohibition, prohibitory restriction, ban, restraint, hindrance, stoppage, impediment.

Embark, *v. i.* 1. Go on shipboard, go on board, go aboard, take ship.

2. Engage, enlist, enter upon, take the first step, go into.

Embarrass, *v. t.* 1. Perplex, entangle, beset, make intricate, make difficult.

2. Harass, distress, trouble, vex, annoy, plague, hamper, clog, involve, bother.

3. Confuse, confound, nonplus, pose, dumfound, discomfort, disconcert, discomfit, abash, shame, mortify.

Embassy, *n.* 1. Commission, mission, ambassadorial office *or* function.

2. Legation, ambassadors.

3. Ambassadorial residence, legation.

Embattle, *v. t.* 1. Array (*in order of battle*), set in battle (*array*), put in line.

2. Make battlements in, fit *or* adorn with battlements.

Embed, *v. t.* Bed, inlay.

Embellish, *v. t.* Decorate, deck, bedeck, ornament, adorn, beautify, set out, set off, enrich, emblazon.

Embers, *n. pl.* Cinders, live coals, smouldering remains (*of the fire*).

Embezzle, *v. t.* Appropriate to one's own use (*what is intrusted*), misappropriate, purloin, steal, defalcate, peculate.

Embitter, *v. t.* 1. Make bitter *or* more bitter.

2. Aggravate, exacerbate, envenom.

3. Exasperate, anger, make hostile, madden, enrage.

Emblazon, *v. t.* 1. Blazon, emblaze, adorn with ensigns armorial, depict.

2. Deck (*with showy ornaments*), decorate, adorn, embellish, emblaze, set off, set out, show off, display.

Emblazonry, *n.* 1. Heraldry, blazonry.

2. Heraldic ornaments.

Emblem, *n.* Type, symbol, sign, representation, token, badge, mark, device, cognizance, allusive figure.

Emblematic, } *a.* Typical, figurative,
Emblematical, } representative, symbolical, allusive.

Embodiment, *n.* Bodily presentation, material representation, realization, incorporation, image, incarnation, personification.

Embody, *v. t.* 1. Invest with a body, make corporeal, form into a body, incarnate, personify.

2. Incorporate, concentrate, compact, integrate, combine, collect into a whole, draw into one mass.

3. Comprehend, include, embrace, comprise, contain.

Embolden, *v. t.* Encourage, animate, inspirit, hearten, nerve, reassure, make bold.

Embolism, *n.* 1. Intercalation, interpolation (*of time*).

2. Time *or* period intercalated.

3. (*Med.*) Obstruction, stoppage, occlusion.

Embosom, *v. t.* Enfold, nurse, foster, cherish, enwrap, surround, envelop, hide, conceal, bury.

Emboss, *v. t.* 1. Adorn with raised work, ornament in relief.

2. Cover with bosses *or* protuberances *or* relief.

Embowel, *v. t.* 1. Eviscerate, disembowel, gut, take out the bowels *or* entrails of, free from the viscera.

2. Embed, bury, hide, conceal.

Embrace, *v. t.* 1. Clasp in the arms, hug, press to the bosom, fold to the heart.

2. Welcome, seize, accept, lay hold on, accept eagerly.

3. Comprehend, hold, enfold, include, cover, contain, comprise, enclose, encompass, encircle, embody, take in.

——, *n.* Hug, clasp, fold.

Embroider, *v. t.* Adorn with needle-work. work, decorate, embellish.

Embroidery, *n.* Variegated needle-work.

Embroil, *v. t.* 1. Entangle, ensnarl, implicate, commingle, involve.

2. Disturb, perplex, confuse, distract, trouble, disorder, discompose, throw into disorder.

Embryo, *n.* 1. Germ, rudiment.

2. Rudimentary state, first stage, beginning.

——, *a.* Rudimentary, incipient, undeveloped.

Emend, *v. t.* Improve the text of, subject to textual criticism, supply with improved readings, correct, amend, rectify.

Emerge, *v. i.* 1. Rise (*out of a fluid*), come up.

2. Issue, emanate, escape, come forth.

3. Appear, become visible, rise into view, outcrop, arise.

Emergency, *n.* Exigency, urgency, necessity, crisis, pinch, pass, push, strait, difficulty, extremity, pressing necessity; juncture, conjuncture, crisis, pass, turn of events.

Emigrate, *v. i.* Migrate, remove (*from one country to settle in another*), depart.

Emigration, *n.* 1. Migration, removal, exodus.

2. Body of emigrants.

Eminence, *n.* 1. Prominence, projection, protuberance; elevation, hill, elevated ground, high point.

2. Exaltation, celebrity, distinction, prominence, conspicuousness, loftiness, note, renown, repute, reputation, fame, high rank *or* position, great station, celebrity, preferment.

3. Supreme, degree, superiority, marked degree.

Eminent, *a.* 1. High, lofty, elevated.

2. Distinguished, conspicuous, celebrated, prominent, illustrious, exalted,

famous, renowned, remarkable, of great repute.

Emissary, *n.* Messenger, spy, scout, secret agent.

Emission, *n.* 1. Emitting, sending out, throwing out, discharge, projection, radiation, emanation, expression.

2. Issue, issuing, issuance, putting into circulation.

Emit, *v. t.* Eject, discharge, exhale, breathe, breathe out, send forth, throw out, give out, emanate, shoot, spurt, dart, squirt, jet, shed, gush, throw, hurl, outpour.

Emolliate, *v. t.* Soften, effeminate, emasculate, make effeminate.

Emollient, *a.* Softening, relaxing, soothing.

——, *n.* Softener, application to allay soreness.

Emolument, *n.* 1. Gain, lucre, pay, compensation, remuneration, profits, wages, salary, stipend, income, hire, pecuniary profit.

2. Advantage, profit, benefit, perquisites.

Emotion, *n.* Feeling, passion, excitement (*of sensibility*), mental agitation, sentiment.

Emphasis, *n.* 1. Stress (*on certain words*), force of utterance, accent.

2. Impressiveness, significance, weight.

Emphatic, *a.* Expressive, significant, strong, impressive, intensive, positive, earnest, forcible, energetic, decided, unequivocal, distinct.

Empire, *n.* 1. Sovereignty, supremacy, dominion, domain, absolute authority, supreme dominion, imperial power.

2. Rule, sway, command, control, government.

Empiric, } *a.* 1. Experimental, experien-
Empirical, } tial, from experience (*as distinguished from inference* or *reasoning*), based on evidence of the senses (*in opposition to the creations of reason*).

2. Tentative, provisional, hypothetical, experimental, that feels its way, awaiting verification.

3. Charlatanic, quackish.

Empiricism, *n.* 1. Dependence on experience, reliance on the evidence of sense alone.

2. (*Philos.*) Empirical philosophy, sensationalism, sensualism, theory of the sole validity of sense.

3. Quackery, charlatanism, charlatanry.

Employ, *v. t.* 1. Busy, engage, engross, exercise, occupy, devote.

2. Use, apply, make use of.

3. Enlist in one's service, give employment to, hire.

Employe, *n.* [Fr.] Agent, clerk, servant, hand, workman, employee.

Employment, *n.* 1. Business, occupation, work, engagement, pursuit, vocation, avocation, calling, profession, trade, craft, employ.

2. Service, agency, office, employ.

3. Employing, use, application.

4. Busy state, being busied, occupation, engrossment.

Emporium, *n.* Mart, market; place of trade; shop, store.

Empower, *v. t.* 1. Authorize, commission, warrant, qualify, give authority to.

2. Enable, make able.

Empty, *a.* 1. Void, vacant, unoccupied, hollow, vacuous, blank.

2. [With *of.*] Devoid, destitute, depleted, hungry.

3. Unfurnished, unsupplied, unfilled.

4. Unsubstantial, unsatisfying, unsatisfactory, useless, vain.

5. Desolate, waste, deserted, clear, unloaded, exhausted, free, unburdened.

6. Senseless, silly, weak, frivolous, inane, foolish, trivial, stupid.

——, *v. t.* 1. Exhaust, drain, evacuate, deplete.

2. Discharge, disembogue, pour out, void.

——, *v. i.* Flow, disembogue, embogue, discharge, fall, flow out, be discharged.

Empyreal, *a.* Ethereal, aerial, airy, highly refined, sublimed, sublimated.

Empyrean, *n.* Highest heaven.

Emulate, *v. t.* Rival, vie with, compete with, strive to equal *or* to excel.

Emulation, *n.* 1. Rivalry, competition, vying, desire to excel, desire of superiority.

2. Envy, jealousy, contention, envious strife.

Emulous, *a.* 1. Competing, rivalling.

2. Very desirous *or* eager to excel *or* equal.

3. Contentious, envious, jealous.

4. [With *of.*] Very desirous, eager.

Enable, *v. t.* Empower, qualify, capacitate.

Enact, *v. t.* Ordain, decree, establish by law, make, pass into a law, give legislative sanction to.

Enactment, *n.* Law, act, decree, edict, ordinance.

Enamour, *v. t.* Charm, captivate, fascinate, bewitch, inflame with love.

Encamp, *v. i.* Camp, pitch one's camp, pitch camp, pitch one's tent, form a camp.

Encampment, *n.* Camp.

Enchain, *v. t.* 1. Bind, shackle, manacle, restrain, confine, enslave, hold in chains, hold in bondage.

2. Hold, rivet, fix, hold fast.

Enchant, *v. t.* 1. Practise sorcery upon, cast a spell on, throw under a spell, bind by incantations, fascinate, bewitch, charm, delude, beguile.

2. Charm, captivate, fascinate, bewitch, enamour, win, catch, lead captive.

3. Delight, enrapture, rapture, ravish, beatify, transport, fill with bliss.

Enchanting, *a.* Charming, captivating, fascinating, bewitching, delightful, rapturous, enrapturing, blissful, ravishing, Circean.

Enchantment, *n.* 1. Incantation, conjuration, necromancy, magic, sorcery, witchery, spell, charm.

2. Delight, fascination, rapture, ravishment, transport, bliss.

Enchantress, *n.* 1. Sorceress, witch.

2. Charmer, *inamorata*, fair enslaver.

Enchase, *v. t.* 1. Enclose (*as a gem in gold*), incase, infix, set, encircle.

2. Chase, emboss, ornament, engrave, inlay.

Encircle, *v. t.* 1. Surround, encompass, environ, gird, belt, engird, enclose, span, ring, twine, enring.

2. Embrace, fold, clasp, enfold.

Enclose, *v. t.* [Written also *Inclose.*] 1. Encircle, surround, encompass, imbosom, circumscribe, shut in, fence in.

2. Cover, envelop, wrap.

Enclosure, *n.* [Written also *Inclosure.*]
1. Being enclosed.
2. Thing enclosed.
3. Circle, compass, space enclosed.
4. Yard, compound.

Encomiast, *n.* Eulogist, panegyrist, praiser, extoller.

Encomiastic, } *a.* Panegyrical, eulogistic,
Encomiastical, } laudatory, commendatory.

Encomium, *n.* Praise, eulogy, eulogium, laudation, commendation, panegyric, good word.

Encompass, *v. t.* 1. Surround, environ, compass, gird, engird, belt, encircle, enclose.

2. Invest, beset, besiege, surround, hem in, include, wall in, lay siege to.

Encore, *v. t.* Call back, recall.

——, *adv.* [Fr.] Again, once more.

Encounter, *n.* Meeting, rencounter, clash, collision; attack, onset, assault; conflict, combat, fight, contest, dispute, battle, engagement, action, skirmish, brush, affair.

——, *v. t.* 1. Meet (*suddenly*), meet face to face; confront, face; meet with, fall upon, come upon.

2. Attack, engage with, contend against, join battle with, cope with, compete with, struggle with, strive with, fight with.

——, *v. i.* Clash, skirmish, rencounter, fight, come into collision.

Encourage, *v. t.* 1. Embolden, inspirit, animate, enhearten, hearten, stimulate, cheer, incite, instigate, assure, reassure, comfort, console, buoy up, strengthen, fortify, "chirrup," urge on.

2. Support, favor, countenance, further, advance, promote, foster, aid, help, abet, patronize, help forward, approve.

Encroach, *v. i.* 1. Trespass, usurp, invade, intrude, infringe, trench, make inroad, make invasion.

2. Creep, advance stealthily, overtake unawares.

Encumber, *v. t.* 1. Load, clog, oppress, impede, hinder, obstruct, overload, burden, hamper.

2. Embarrass, perplex, entangle, involve, complicate.

Encumbrance, *n.* [Written also *Incumbrance.*] 1. Load, clog, impediment, hindrance, hampering, dead-weight, drag.

2. Debt, claim, liability, lien.

Encyclical, *n.* Circular letter (*especially of the Pope*).

Encyclopedia, *n.* Cyclopedia.

Encyclopedic, *a.* That embraces the whole circle of learning, all-embracing, comprehensive, exhaustive, encyclopedian.

Encysted, *a.* Enclosed in a cyst *or* sac, bagged, capsuled.

END, *n.* 1. Extremity, extreme point, tip.

2. Close, cessation, period, expiration, *finale*, finish, ending, stoppage, wind-up, denouement, finis, last, fall of the curtain; conclusion, completion, consummation.

3. Destruction, catastrophe, annihilation, dissolution.

4. Termination, bound, limit, terminus.

5. Final state, ultimate condition.

6. Result, event, consequence, sequel, upshot, (final) issue, settlement.

7. Fragment, scrap, remnant, stub, tail, tag.

8. Aim, purpose, object, design, objective, goal, intent, intention.

——, *v. t.* 1. Terminate, conclude, finish, close, stop, discontinue, dissolve, abolish, drop, put an end to, bring to an end, make an end of, cut short, wind up.

2. De.t.by, kill, put to death, annihilate.

——, v. i. 1. Conclude, terminate, cease, be finished, come to an end, come to a close, wind up.

2. Close, conclude a discourse, cease speaking.

Endanger, v. t. Hazard, risk, peril, imperil, jeopardize, commit, compromise, expose to danger, put at hazard.

Endear, v. t. Attach, make dear, secure the affection of, bind by ties of affection.

Endearment, n. 1. Fondness, tenderness, attachment, love, tender affection, close tie, fond attachment.

2. Caress, blandishment, fondling.

Endeavor, n. Effort, attempt, essay, trial, struggle, exertion, conatus, *nisus*, aim.

——, v. i. Try, attempt, essay, labor, strive, seek, struggle, study, aim, make an effort, make an attempt.

Endless, a. 1. Interminable, indeterminable, illimitable, unlimited, boundless, limitless, immeasurable, infinite.

2. Eternal, everlasting, perpetual, unending, dateless, never-ending, without end.

3. Uninterrupted, incessant, ceaseless, unceasing, perpetual, continual, continuous, eternal, constant, unbroken.

4. Immortal, undying, deathless, everliving, ever-enduring, never-dying, imperishable, eternal.

Endorse, v. t. [Written also *Indorse.*] 1. Superscribe, write on the back of.

2. (*Com.*) Guarantee (*by superscription*), become surety for, become responsible for.

3. Sanction, warrant, confirm, ratify, guarantee, vouch for.

Endow, v. t. 1. Furnish with a dowry, settle a dower upon.

2. Furnish with a fund, supply with means, finance, supply.

3. Enrich, endue, indue, clothe, invest, gift.

Endowment, n. 1. Gift, grant, bequest, boon, largess, bounty, present.

2. Property, fund, revenue, foundation.

3. Talent, faculty, quality, power, ability, capacity, capability, aptitude, parts, genius, qualification, gift.

Endue, v. t. [Written also *Indue.*] Supply, invest, clothe, endow, enrich.

Endurance, n. 1. Bearing, suffering, sufferance, abiding, tolerance, toleration.

2. Patience, fortitude, resignation, constancy, backbone, bottom, "sand," "guts," forbearance.

3. Continuance, continuation, lastingness, permanence, persistence, vitality.

Endure, v. t. 1. Bear, sustain, support, bear up under.

2. Suffer, undergo, experience, go through, weather.

3. Brook, tolerate, abide, submit to, put up with, bear with, take patiently *or* easily, abide, withstand, stomach, swallow, pocket, permit.

——, v. i. 1. Remain, continue, persist, last, abide, be permanent, be durable, wear.

2. Bear, suffer, submit, resign one's self, be patient, "take it," take it easily *or* quietly, not fret about it.

Enemy, n. 1. Foe, adversary.

2. Opponent, antagonist, foeman.

3. [With *The* prefixed.] See DEVIL.

Energetic, a. Vigorous, active, forcible, powerful, strong, effective, efficacious, potent, mettlesome, hearty, strenuous, forceful, emphatic, enterprising.

Energize, v. t. Give energy to, give force to, animate, excite to action.

Energy, n. 1. Force, power, might, efficacy, potency, efficiency, strength, activity, intensity, "go," mettle, dash, impetus, verve, drive, "vim."

2. Spirit, spiritedness, animation, life, vigor, manliness, zeal, animal spirits.

3. (*Mech.*) Capacity of work, mechanical value.

Enervate, v. t. Unnerve, weaken, enfeeble, devitalize, soften, effeminate, effeminize, emasculate, debilitate, paralyze, break, deprive of force *or* strength, render feeble.

Enfeeble, v. t. Weaken, unnerve. See ENERVATE.

Enforce, v. t. 1. Give force to, urge with energy, set forth strongly, impress on the mind, emphasize.

2. Compel obedience to, execute, sanction, have executed *or* obeyed.

3. Constrain, compel, oblige, force, require.

Enfranchise, v. t. 1. Admit as a free man, endow with a franchise.

2. Free, emancipate, manumit, release, set free, make free, restore to liberty.

Engage, v. t. 1. Pledge, commit, promise, bind, obligate, put under pledge.

2. Plight, affiance, betroth, promise *or* pledge in marriage.

3. Enlist, induce to serve, hire, book, retain, brief, employ.

4. Gain, win, attach, attract, allure, entertain, draw, fix, arrest, gain over.

5. Occupy, employ, busy, engross.

6. Attack, encounter, fight with, join battle with.

Engage, v. i.   1. Fight, combat, contend, struggle, contest, join battle, interlock.

2. Embark, enlist, take the first step.

3. Promise, agree, stipulate, bargain, undertake, warrant.

Engagement, n.   1. Promise, stipulation, assurance, contract, pledge, obligation, appointment.

2. Plighting, betrothal, betrothment, affiancing.

3. Employment, occupation, business, calling, vocation, avocation, enterprise.

4. Battle, conflict, combat, contest, action, fight, encounter, rencounter.

Engaging, a.   Attractive, winning, captivating, charming, taking, pleasing.

Engender, v. t.   1. Generate, beget, bear, propagate, procreate, breed.

2. Produce, cause, occasion, give rise to, call forth, incite.

ENGINE, n.   1. Machine, invention.

2. Implement, instrument, weapon, agent, means, device, method.

Engird, v. t.   Surround, environ, gird, begird, encircle, encompass.

Engorge, v. t.   1. Gorge, devour, swallow up, swallow greedily, gulp down.

2. (*Med.*) Fill to excess, stuff, glut, obstruct.

Engrave, v. t.   1. Incise, etch, hatch, cut, chisel, carve, sculpture, grave.

2. Imprint, infix, grave, impress deeply.

Engraving, n.   Cutting, carving, chiselling, incision.

Engross, v. t.   1. Absorb, engage, occupy, take up.

2. Monopolize, buy up, forestall.

3. Copy in large hand, write out fair.

Engrossment, n.   Absorption, monopoly, forestalling.

Engulf, v. t.   Absorb, swallow up.

Enhance, v. t.   Raise (*as price*), advance, elevate, heighten, swell; increase, intensify, augment, aggravate.

Enhearten, v. t.   Encourage, embolden, animate, hearten, inspirit, cheer, incite, stimulate, assure, reassure, comfort, console, buoy up.

Enigma, n.   Riddle, conundrum, puzzle, dark saying, obscure question.

Enigmatic, } a.   Obscure, mysterious,
Enigmatical, }   dark, occult, recondite, ambiguous, hidden, unintelligible, incomprehensible, puzzling, perplexing.

Enjoin, v. t.   1. Urge *or* admonish *or* advise with authority *or* authoritatively.

2. Order, direct, bid, command, require, prescribe to.

3. (*Law.*) Prohibit, restrain, put an injunction on.

Enjoy, v. t.   1. Take pleasure in, take delight in, derive pleasure from, like, relish, fancy.

2. Have fruition of, have the advantage *or* blessing of, profit from.

Enjoyment, n.   1. Pleasure, gratification, delight, happiness.

2. Fruition, satisfactory *or* advantageous *or* beneficent possession.

Enkindle, v. t.   1. Inflame, ignite, kindle, set on fire.

2. Incite, excite, rouse, stimulate, instigate, provoke, stir up, set on.

Enlarge, v. t.   1. Increase, augment, extend, widen, broaden, dilate, distend, expand, magnify, amplify, make larger, make greater.

2. Greaten, engreaten, aggrandize, ennoble, expand, give larger scope to, make more comprehensive.

——, v. i.   1. Expatiate, dilate, descant, speak at length, launch out.

2. Increase, swell, grow, extend, expand, grow larger.

Enlargement, n.   1. Expansion, dilatation, dilation, extension, augmentation, increase.

2. Expatiation, copious discourse, extended remark.

Enlighten, v. t.   1. Illuminate, illume, illumine, irradiate, make light.

2. Instruct, inform, teach, educate, civilize, make intelligent, render more intelligent.

Enlightened, a.   Instructed, informed, educated, intelligent, refined, highly civilized, freed from ignorance.

Enlightenment, n.   Instruction, illumination, culture, education, learning.

Enlist, v. t.   1. Enroll, levy, recruit, register, record, list.

2. Engage, induce to serve, secure the assistance of.

——, v. i.   1. List, enroll one's self.

2. Embark, engage, pledge one's assistance.

3. Take service in the army *or* navy, enroll one's self in the army *or* navy.

Enliven, v. t.   1. Quicken, animate, reanimate, wake, rouse, invigorate, give life to, fire.

2. Inspire, inspirit, exhilarate, cheer, delight, gladden, brighten, elate, rouse.

Enmity, n.   Animosity, hatred, hate, hostility, aversion, malignity, malice, malevolence, rancor, bitterness, ill-will.

Ennoble, v. t.   1. Raise to nobility, raise to the peerage.

2. Exalt, dignify, elevate, glorify, raise, aggrandize, enlarge, engreaten, greaten.

Ennui, *n.* [Fr.] Listlessness (*for want of occupation*), languor, boredom, tedium, lassitude, wearisomeness, tiresomeness, irksomeness.

Enormity, *n.* 1. Atrociousness, depravity, atrocity, flagitiousness, heinousness, nefariousness, outrageousness, wickedness.

2. Atrocious crime, flagitious villany.

Enormous, *a.* 1. (*Rare.*) Inordinate, irregular, abnormal, exceptional.

2. Huge, monstrous, immense, vast, gigantic, tremendous, colossal, prodigious, Cyclopean, Herculean, titanic, elephantine, vefy large.

Enough, *n.* Sufficiency, plenty, *quantum sufficit.*

ENOUGH, *a.* Sufficient, plenty, adequate, ample.

——, *adv.* Sufficiently, satisfactorily, to satisfaction.

Enquire, *v. t.* [Written also and usually *Inquire.*] Ask, ask about.

——, *v. i.* [Or *Inquire.*] 1. Ask, question, seek information (*by questioning*), make inquiry.

2. Make investigation, make examination.

Enrage, *v. t.* Irritate, exasperate, incense, madden, infuriate, provoke, inflame, chafe, anger, make furious, excite to rage.

Enrapture, *v. t.* Enchant, entrance, enravish, transport, beatify, delight surpassingly.

Enravishment, *n.* Rapture, ecstasy, transport, thrill, ravishment.

Enrich, *v. t.* 1. Endow, make rich, make wealthy.

2. Adorn, decorate, deck, ornament, embellish.

Enrichment, *n.* 1. Enriching. See the verb.

2. Adornment, decoration, ornament, ornamentation, embellishment.

Enrobe, *v. t.* Dress, clothe, invest, attire, array, apparel, robe.

Enroll, *v. t.* 1. Enlist, list, register, catalogue, engross.

2. Record, chronicle.

Ensconce, *v. t.* Shelter, cover, shield, secure, screen, hide, conceal, settle snugly, protect, harbor.

Ensemble, *n.* [Fr.] The whole, all the parts taken together, effect, total effect, general impression.

Enshrine, *v. t.* 1. Enclose in a shrine, inshrine.

2. Preserve (*as something sacred*), embalm, treasure, cherish, keep unimpaired.

Ensign, *n.* 1. Banner, standard colors, streamer, flag, national flag, pennon, gonfalon, eagle.

2. Symbol, sign, signal.

3. Badge, distinctive mark, mark of distinction, hatchment.

4. Standard bearer, commissioned officer (navy).

Enslave, *v. t.* 1. Reduce to bondage, enthrall, make a slave of.

2. Overpower, master, overmaster, subjugate, dominate; captivate.

Ensnare, *v. t.* 1. Entrap, catch.

2. Inveigle, allure, seduce.

3. Entangle, embarrass, encumber.

Ensue, *v. i.* 1. Follow, succeed, come after.

2. Issue, arise, spring, flow, come, result, proceed, be derived.

Ensure, *v. t.* [Written also *Insure.*] Make secure, render certain, make sure.

Entail, *v. t.* 1. Transfer (*by inalienable title*), settle inalienably, make incapable of conveyance.

2. Transmit (*by necessity*), fix unalterably, devolve as a necessary consequence, involve inevitably.

Entangle, *v. t.* 1. Ensnare, entrap, catch.

2. Confuse (*by twisting* or *crossing*), intertwine, intertwist, interweave, tangle, knot, mat, ravel, enmesh.

3. Perplex, bewilder, puzzle, nonplus, involve, embarrass, encumber, ensnare.

Entanglement, *n.* 1. Intricacy, involution, complication.

2. Perplexity, embarrassment, confusion, bewilderment.

Enter, *v. t.* 1. Go into, come into, board, pierce, penetrate, invade, trespass.

2. Record, register, enroll, inscribe, note, set down, chronicle, jot down, take down.

3. Insert, set in.

4. Begin, commence, commence upon, start.

5. Engage in, enlist in, embark in, join, become a member of.

6. (*Law.*) Take possession of, take up.

——, *v. i.* 1. Come in, go in, pass in; come upon the stage.

2. Embark, enlist, be initiated.

Enter into. 1. Penetrate, pierce, perforate, consider in detail.

2. Form a part of, be a component *or* constituent in.

3. Share, participate in, partake of.

4. Sympathize with.

Enterprise, *n.* 1. Undertaking, project, adventure, venture, scheme, attempt, effort, essay, endeavor, cause.

2. Energy, activity, adventurousness, "push," "go-ahead," initiative, willingness to make ventures.

Enterprising, *a.* 1. Adventurous, venturesome, venturous, dashing, daring, audacious, bold.

2. Active, prompt, alert, stirring, adventurous, smart, energetic, efficient, spirited, zealous, strenuous, eager, on the alert, in earnest, willing to make ventures, prompt to undertake difficulties.

Entertain, *v. t.* 1. Lodge, treat hospitably, show hospitality to, receive as a guest, "treat," regale, fête, receive.

2. Hold, cherish, harbor, shelter.

3. Take into consideration, consider, admit.

4. Divert, amuse, please.

Entertainer, *n.* Host; amuser (professional).

Entertainment, *n.* 1. Hospitable treatment.

2. Feast, banquet, treat, festival, collation, reception.

3. Amusement, diversion, recreation, pastime, sport.

Enter upon. Begin, commence, take the first steps in.

Enthrall, *v. t.* 1. Enslave, reduce to servitude, put under restraint, make a thrall *or* slave *or* bondsman of.

2. Enslave, overpower, overmaster, enchain, put in bondage (*morally*).

3. Captivate, charm, hold spell-bound.

Enthralment, *n.* Enslavement, servitude, slavery, bondage, vassalage, serfdom, thraldom, captivity.

Enthrone, *v. t.* 1. Invest with sovereign power, seat upon the throne.

2. Exalt, elevate, raise to superiority.

Enthusiasm, *n.* 1. Ecstasy (*from a belief of being inspired*), fanaticism, religious frenzy, exaltation of soul.

2. Ardor, zeal, warmth, earnestness, passion, devotion, eagerness, fervor.

3. Heat of imagination, mental excitement.

Enthusiast, *n.* 1. Fanatic, devotee, bigot, zealot, religious madman.

2. Zealot, visionary, dreamer, castle-builder.

Enthusiastic,
Enthusiastical, } *a.* 1. Fanatical, bigoted.

2. Visionary, extravagant.

3. Ardent, earnest, vehement, zealous, fervent, fervid, burning, flaming, glowing, passionate, impassioned.

Entice, *v. t.* Allure (*to evil*), lure, attract, decoy, wile, bait, seduce, tempt, coax, inveigle, wheedle, cajole, persuade, lead astray.

Entire, *a.* 1. Whole, complete, perfect, integrated, undivided, unbroken, undiminished, unimpaired.

2. Full, complete, plenary, thorough, unalloyed; mere, sheer, pure, unmixed, unmingled, unmitigated, unalloyed.

Entirety, *n.* Whole, sum total, entire amount, undiminished quantity.

Entitle, *v. t.* 1. Name, designate, denominate, style, call, dub, christen. See TITLE.

2. Give a claim to, give a right to, qualify for, empower, enable, fit for.

Entity, *n.* Being, existence, essence.

Entomb, *v. t.* Bury, inhume, inter.

Entombment, *n.* Burial, interment, inhumation, sepulture.

Entrails, *n. pl.* Intestines, bowels, viscera, inwards, guts.

Entrance, *n.* 1. Ingress, access, approach, incoming, avenue.

2. Entry, inlet, mouth, avenue, adit, passage, door, gate, portal, aperture, doorway, vestibule, hallway, lobby, stile.

3. Beginning, commencement, initiation, introduction, debut.

4. Admission, entrée.

——, *v. t.* Charm, enchant, enrapture, delight, transport, ravish, throw into ecstasies, surpassingly delight.

Entrap, *v. t.* 1. Ensnare, catch.

2. Inveigle, seduce, allure, entice.

3. Entangle, involve, perplex, embarrass, stagger, pose, nonplus, catch in difficulties, involve in contradictions.

Entreat, *v. t.* Beg, crave, beseech, implore, supplicate, solicit, pray, importune, petition, enjoin, appeal to, prefer a prayer to. See ADJURE.

Entreaty, *n.* Supplication, prayer, petition, suit, solicitation, appeal, importunity. See ADJURATION.

Entrée, *n.* [Fr.] 1. Admittance, admission, free access.

2. Made dish, side dish, *entremet*.

Entry, *n.* 1. Ingress, entrance, access, approach.

2. Passage (*into a house*), avenue, inlet, hall.

3. Record, note, minute, memorandum, registration, posting.

4. First attempt, beginning, debut.

Entwine, *v. t.* [Written also *Intwine*.] 1. Twine, twist together.

2. Encircle, surround, embrace, wind about, wind around.

Enumerate, *v. t.* Reckon, compute, count, number, tell, cite, recount, numerate, call over, detail, relate in detail, mention one by one, specify, recapitulate, sum up, rehearse.

Enunciate, *v. t.* 1. Declare, speak, proclaim, publish, express, relate, promulgate, state, propound, announce, enounce.

2. Utter, pronounce, articulate.

Enunciate, *v. i.* Articulate, speak, utter articulate sounds.

Enunciation, *n.* 1. Declaration, utterance, expression, announcement.

2. Elocution, articulation, manner of utterance.

Enunciative, *a.* Declarative, expressive, declaratory, enunciatory.

Envelop, *v. t.* 1. Enfold, inwrap, wrap, fold, pack, wrap up, put a wrapper about.

2. Surround, encircle, involve, encompass, enfold, enshroud, fold, cover, hide.

Envelope, *n.* [Fr.] Wrapper, covering, case, capsule, skin, integument, shroud, vesture, veil, wrap.

Envenom, *v. t.* 1. Poison, taint with venom.

2. Embitter, taint with malice, fill with hate, render malignant.

3. Enrage, exasperate, incense, provoke, irritate, madden, aggravate, inflame, make furious.

Enviable, *a.* Desirable, to be envied.

Envious, *a.* 1. Jealous, disposed to envy.

2. Grudging.

Environ, *v. t.* 1. Surround, encompass, encircle, envelop, gird, begird, engird, belt, enclose.

2. Invest, besiege, beset, encompass.

Environment, *n.* Surroundings, influences, atmosphere.

Environs, *n. pl.* Neighborhood, vicinity, vicinage.

Envoy, *n.* Minister, ambassador, legate, plenipotentiary.

Envy, *v. t.* 1. Hate (*for excellence* or *success*), view with jealousy, feel ill-will toward.

2. Grudge, begrudge.

3. Be discontented at, repine at (*another's prosperity*).

4. Long for, earnestly desire, desire eagerly and emulously, emulate, covet.

——, *n.* 1. Hate (*on account of excellence* or *success*), hatred, jealousy, spite, enviousness, ill-will, malice.

2. Grudging, grudge.

3. Object of envy, person to be envied.

Ephemeral, *a.* Short-lived, transitory, transient, diurnal, fleeting, flitting, evanescent, fugitive, fugacious, occasional, momentary, brief.

Epic, *a.* Narrative, heroic, Homeric.

——, *n.* Narrative poem, epic poem, heroic poem.

Epicure, *n.* 1. Gourmand, *gourmet*, refined glutton, dainty feeder, high liver, gustatory sensualist, voluptuary of the palate.

2. Voluptuary, sensualist, Sybarite, Epicurean, free liver, man of pleasure.

Epicurean, *n.* 1. See EPICURE, 2.

2. Adherent of Epicurus, hedonist, eudæmonist.

Epicureanism, *n.* Doctrines of Epicurus, Epicurism, hedonism, eudæmonism.

Epicurism, *n.* 1. Sensuality, luxury, luxurious living, free living, Sybaritism.

2. Doctrines of Epicurus, Epicureanism, hedonism, eudæmonism.

Epidemic, *a.* General, prevailing, prevalent, pandemic.

Epidermis, *n.* 1. Cuticle, scarf-skin.

2. (*Bot.*) Exterior coating.

Epigrammatic, } *a.* Concise, laconic, terse,
Epigrammatical, } pointed, antithetic, poignant, piquant, sharp, pungent.

Epiphany, *n.* 1. Manifestation, appearance (*especially that of Christ by the star which guided the Magi to Bethlehem*).

2. (*Eccl.*) Festival of the Epiphany, 6th of January.

Episcopacy, *n.* Episcopalianism, prelacy, government by bishops, episcopal rank.

Episcopal, *a.* Episcopalian, pontifical, prelatical.

Episcopalian, *n.* Churchman, believer in episcopacy *or* prelacy, Anglican.

Episcopate, *n.* 1. Bishopric, office of a bishop, term of bishop's office, dignity of a bishop.

2. Body of bishops.

Episode, *n.* 1. Digression, incidental narrative.

2. Incidental event.

Epistle, *n.* Letter, note, written communication, missive.

Epitaph, *n.* Inscription (*on a tomb* or *monument*), brief commemorative writing.

Epithalamium, *n.* Nuptial song, marriage poem.

Epithet, *n.* Name, appellation, designation, title, qualifying word *or* term, descriptive term, predicate.

Epitome, *n.* Abridgment, abstract, compend, compendium, conspectus, syllabus, brief, breviary, condensation, summary, synopsis, digest, sum and substance.

Epitomize, *v. t.* Abridge, abstract, summarize, abbreviate, shorten, condense, reduce, contract, make an abstract of.

Epoch, *n.* Period, date, era, age, point *or* period of time (*remarkable for some event*).

Equable, *a.* Even, uniform, equal, steady, regular, even-tempered, always the same, calm, unruffled, serene, tranquil.

Equableness, *n.* Evenness, equability, serenity, unruffled character.

EQUAL, *a.* 1. Like, alike, tantamount, equivalent; "quits," of the same extent, measure, degree, rank, *or* value, identical in quantity *or* value, coördinate.

2. Uniform, even, regular, equable, level.

3. Impartial, unbiassed, equitable, fair, just, even-handed.

4. Proportionate, commensurate, co-extensive, parallel, corresponding.

5. Adequate, competent, fit, sufficient, of sufficient strength *or* ability.

——, *n.* Peer, compeer, fellow, match.

——, *v. t.* 1. Equalize, make equal, make alike, equate, coördinate.

2. Rival, rise to the same level with.

3. Be adequate to, be sufficient for, be equal to, be commensurate with.

Equality, *n.* 1. Likeness, identity in quantity, identical value.

2. Uniformity, evenness.

3. Sameness of rank, co-equality.

Equanimity, *n.* Evenness of mind *or* temper, regularity, composure, steadiness of disposition, calmness, serenity, self-possession, peace, unruffled temper, undisturbed feeling.

Equate, *v. t.* 1. Make equal, set equal to (each other).

2. Average, reduce to an average, equalize.

Equestrian, *n.* 1. Horseman, rider.

2. Knight, cavalier, chevalier, horse-soldier.

Equilibrate, *v. t.* Keep in balance, maintain in equipoise, balance, poise.

Equilibrist, *n.* Rope-walker, balancer, funambulist. See ACROBAT.

Equilibrium, *n.* Equipoise, even balance, equality of weight, equality of pressure, neutralization of forces.

Equip, *v. t.* 1. Furnish, provide, arm, fit out, supply with outfits *or* apparatus, appoint, "rig."

2. Dress, accoutre, array, dress out.

Equipage, *n.* 1. Apparatus, equipment, furniture, baggage, effects, bag and baggage.

2. Carriage, vehicle, "turnout."

3. Train, retinue, attendance, procession, suite.

Equipment, *n.* Accoutrement, furniture, apparatus, "rigging," gear, outfit.

Equipoise, *n.* Equilibrium, even balance, equality of weight.

Equitable, *a.* 1. Upright, just, honest, impartial, unbiassed, unprejudiced, even-handed.

2. Reasonable, fair, impartial, just, right, proper.

Equity, *n.* 1. Justice, right.

2. Justice, rectitude, uprightness, righteousness, impartiality, fairness, reasonableness, fair play.

3. (*Law.*) Theoretical *or* ideal justice, justice (*as distinguished from con-*formity *to mere enactments* or *statutes*), spirit of law (*as against its mere letter*).

4. (*Law.*) Equitable claim.

Equivalence, ⎫ *n.* Essential *or* substantial
Equivalency, ⎬ equality, parity, parity of
value, equality in result, amounting to the same thing.

Equivalent, *a.* 1. Equal, commensurate, tantamount, equipollent.

2. Synonymous, interchangeable, equipollent, of the same meaning, of like import.

Equivocal, *a.* 1. Ambiguous, of doubtful meaning, to be taken in a double sense.

2. Uncertain, doubtful, dubious, puzzling, perplexing, problematic, enigmatic, indeterminate.

Equivocate, *v. i.* Quibble, shuffle, dodge, fence, palter, evade the truth, use equivocal expressions, mislead by double meanings (*for the sake of deception*), prevaricate.

Equivocation, *n.* 1. Quibbling, prevarication, evasion, shuffling, paltering, ambiguity of speech.

2. Quibble, equivoque, double meaning, *double-entendre.*

Era, *n.* 1. Series *or* succession of years (*marked by any administration* or *dispensation*).

2. Epoch, period, date, age, period of time.

Eradicate, *v. t.* 1. Extirpate, uproot, root out, pull up by the roots.

2. Destroy, exterminate, annihilate.

Erase, *v. t.* Efface, obliterate, expunge, cancel, delete, blot, scratch out, scrape out, rub out, blot out, rase (*obsolescent*).

Erasure, *n.* Obliteration, effacing, expunging, cancellation, cancelling, scratching out, rasure (*obsolescent*).

Ere, *adv.* and *prep.* (*Poetical.*) Before, sooner than, prior to.

Erect, *v. t.* 1. Set up, place upright, set upright.

2. Raise, build, construct, rear.

3. Institute, found, form, plant, establish, create.

——, *a.* 1. Upright, standing, unrecumbent, uplifted.

2. Elevated, turned upward, straight, vertical, perpendicular.

3. Bold, undaunted, undismayed, unterrified, firm, unshaken.

Erelong, *adv.* Soon, before long.

Eremite, *n.* (*Poetical.*) Hermit, anchoret, anchorite, solitary, *solitaire*, recluse.

Ergo, *adv.* [L.] Therefore, consequently, hence.

Erode, *v. t.* Consume, destroy, canker, corrode, eat away, fret, rub.

Erosion, *n.* Corrosion, eating away.

Erosive, *a.* Corrosive, corroding, caustic, acrid, virulent, eating, catheretic.

Erotic, *a.* Amatory, amorous, Anacreontic.

Err, *v. i.* 1. Deviate (*from the right way*), stray, wander, ramble, rove.

2. Mistake, blunder, misjudge, make a mistake, be at fault, labor under a mistake.

3. Sin, lapse, nod, stumble, fall, trip, trespass, offend, go astray, do amiss, commit a fault.

Errand, *n.* Message, mandate, mission, business, trip, purpose, commission.

Errant, *a.* Wandering, roving, rambling, stray, adventurous.

Errata, *n. pl.* [L.] Errors (*in printing*), mistakes, misprints.

Erratic, *a.* 1. Wandering, roving, rambling, nomadic.

2. Moving, planetary.

3. Irregular, eccentric, abnormal, odd, queer, strange, capricious, deviating.

Erratum, *n.* [L.] 1. Corrigendum, correction.

2. Misprint, error, mistake.

Erring, *a.* Sinful, fallible, peccable, liable to err.

Erroneous, *a.* False, incorrect, inexact, inaccurate, wrong, untrue, mistaken.

ERROR, *n.* 1. Mistake, blunder, misapprehension, oversight, inaccuracy, fallacy.

2. Sin, fault, offence, trespass, transgression, obliquity, misstep, delinquency, iniquity, misdoing, misdeed, shortcoming, wrong-doing.

Erudite, *a.* Learned, lettered, well-read, polished, instructed, scholarly, deeply read.

Erudition, *n.* Knowledge (*gained by reading and study*), learning, lore, scholarship, literary learning, historical and archæological lore.

Erupt, *v. i.* Burst forth, give vent to eruptions, belch, vomit, eruct, be in eruption.

——, *v. t.* Hurl forth, eject, cast forth violently.

Eruption, *n.* 1. Explosion, outburst, outbreak.

2. Sally, sudden excursion.

3. (*Med.*) Rash.

Escalade, *v. t.* Scale.

——, *n.* Assault with ladders.

Escapade, *n.* 1. Vagary, prank, frolic, freak, mad prank.

2. Impropriety, indiscretion, act of folly.

Escape, *v. t.* 1. Avoid, shun, evade, elude, flee from, get out of the way of.

2. Pass unobserved.

——, *v. i.* 1. Get away, make *or* effect one's escape, get free, get into safety, get away safely, get off *or* through without harm.

2. Flee, fly, abscond, decamp, make off, steal away, hasten away, slink away, run away, break loose, break away, gain one's freedom, whip off, take one's self off, beat a retreat, take to one's heels, cut and run, take French leave, be among the missing.

3. Slip, pass, go by, slip through the fingers, be passed over, be omitted, leak out.

4. Pass out, off, *or* away, be emitted.

——, *n.* 1. Flight.

2. Release (*from threatened danger*).

3. Passing, passage, running *or* passing out *or* off.

4. Leakage.

Escheat, *v. i.* (*Law.*) Be forfeited back, revert.

Eschew, *v. t.* Avoid, shun, flee from, keep away from, keep clear of, steer clear of, keep out of the way of, be shy of, have nothing to do with.

Escort, *n.* 1. Convoy, guard, body guard, conduct, attendant, companion, gallant, cavalier, squire.

2. Protection, safeguard, safe-conduct.

3. Attendance, company.

——, *v. t.* (*Pron.* escort'.) 1. Convoy (*by land*), guard, protect.

2. Attend (*as a guard of honor*), conduct.

3. Attend (*in courtesy*), accompany, wait upon.

Esculent, *a.* Eatable, edible.

Escutcheon, *n.* Shield, scutcheon, ensign armorial.

Esophagus, *n.* [Written also Œsophagus.] Gullet.

Esoteric, *a.* Private, secret, recondite, inner, inmost, known to the initiated.

Especial, *a.* Particular, special, chief, distinguished, uncommon, peculiar, unusual, marked.

Espial, *n.* Notice, observation, discovery.

Espouse, *v. t.* 1. Betroth, promise in marriage, plight.

2. [*Said of a bridegroom.*] Marry, wed.

3. Adopt, defend, embrace, maintain, support, take up.

Esprit de corps. [Fr.] Group feeling, mutual interest in one another (*as between members of the same society* or *of the same profession*), morale, sense of union.

Espy, *v. t.* Discern, descry, perceive, spy, discover, catch a glimpse of, catch sight of.

Esquire, *n.* Squire, armiger; gentleman, landed proprietor, escort, attendant.

Essay, *v. t.* Attempt, try, endeavor.

——, *n.* (*Pron.* es'say.) 1. Attempt, trial, effort, struggle, aim.

2. Dissertation, disquisition, brief discourse, article, paper.

Essence, *n.* 1. Nature, substance, quintessence, essential part, central nature, inmost nature *or* substance, inwardness, endeavor, vital element *or* part, principle, necessary constituent.

2. Extract, volatile part, rectified portion, immaterial being.

3. Odor, perfume, scent.

4. Being, existence, entity, nature.

Essential, *a.* 1. Vital, necessary, requisite, indispensable, highly important, inward, fundamental, intrinsic.

2. Volatile, diffusible, pure, highly rectified.

3. (*Med.*) Idiopathic.

——, *n.* [*Usually in pl.*] 1. Indispensable element, life, secret, absolute requisite.

2. Rudiment, first principle, first step, outline.

Establish, *v. t.* 1. Fix, settle, set, secure, make stable *or* steadfast.

2. Enact, decree, ordain.

3. Institute, originate, plant, pitch, found, erect, raise, build, constitute, organize, form.

4. Place, ground, secure, plant, set up, install, root, ensconce.

5. Confirm, ratify, sanction, approve.

6. Prove, substantiate, verify, make good.

Establishment, *n.* 1. Establishing. See the verb, in all its senses.

2. Institution, organization for work (*of any kind*) *or* business.

3. Domestic arrangements, household *ménage.*

4. Allowance, stipend, income, subsistence, salary.

Estate, *n.* 1. State, condition.

2. Rank, position (*in life* or *society*), social standing; order, division.

3. Property, effects, possessions, fortune.

4. (*Law.*) Interest (*in any species of permanent property*).

Esteem, *v. t.* 1. Estimate, appreciate, value, rate, reckon, set a value on.

2. Admire, like, prize, value, appreciate (highly), honor, revere, reverence, venerate, worship, respect, think well of, think highly of, set a high value on.

3. Regard, consider, deem, think, account, believe, hold, suppose, imagine, fancy, look upon as

——, *n.* 1. Estimation, estimate, appreciation, consideration, valuation, reckoning, account, opinion, judgment.

2. Respect, reverence, honor, credit, high regard, favorable opinion.

Esthetics, *n.* [Written also *Æsthetics.*] Philosophy of the fine arts, theory *or* philosophy of taste, science of the beautiful.

Estimable, *a.* 1. Appreciable, calculable, computable, capable of being estimated.

2. Worthy, respectable, good, excellent, meritorious, admirable, precious, valuable, creditable, deserving, worthy of regard, deserving of respect *or* esteem.

Estimate, *v. t.* 1. Value, appraise, rate, prize, esteem, appreciate, set a value on, set a price on.

2. Compute, reckon, count, calculate, gauge, judge.

——, *n.* 1. Valuation, estimation.

2. Calculation, computation.

Estimation, *n.* 1. Valuation, appraisement, appreciation, estimate.

2. Judgment, opinion, estimate, esteem.

3. Respect, honor, regard, esteem, reverence, favorable opinion.

Estop, *v. t.* (*Law.*) Bar, stop, impede, preclude, stop the progress of.

Estrange, *v. t.* 1. Withdraw, withhold, keep away.

2. Divert, alienate, apply to a foreign purpose.

3. Disaffect, alienate, make unfriendly, make disaffected, destroy one's affections, turn away.

Estuary, *n.* Frith, firth, fiord, inlet, creek, arm of the sea.

Et cætera. [L.] And others, and the rest, and so forth, and so on.

Etch, *v. t.* 1. Engrave (*by corrosion of an acid*), corrode, eat out.

2. Delineate for etching, draw with the etching-needle.

Eternal, *a.* 1. Self-existent, self-originated, absolute, necessary, inevitable, self-active, without beginning *or* end, superior to time *or* cause.

2. Endless, everlasting, never-ending, unending, interminable, ever-enduring, perpetual, sempiternal, ceaseless, unceasing, incessant, perennial, abiding, abiding forever.

3. Imperishable, undying, indestructible, incorruptible, deathless, never-dying, immortal.

4. Immutable, unchangeable.

5. Incessant, unbroken, uninterrupted, ceaseless, persistent, continual, continuous.

Eternally, *adv.* 1. In eternal wise. See the adjective under 1, 3, 4, 5.

2. Endlessly, interminably, perpetually, ceaselessly, continually, everlastingly, always, ever, aye, evermore, for everlasting, forever, for aye, forever and ever, world without end, time without end, to the end of time, till doomsday.

Eternity, *n.* 1. Eternal quality. See ETERNAL, in its various senses.

2. The eternal world, supramundane being, the supersensible order.

3. Endless duration, infinite duration, perpetuity, everlastingness, timelessness.

Ethereal, *a.* 1. Airy, aerial, empyreal; celestial, heavenly.

2. Light, volatile, subtile, tenuous, attenuated, sublimated.

3. Subtilized, subtile, light, airy, aerial, refined, delicate, fragile, flimsy, spirit-like, fairy.

Etherealize, *v. t.* Subtilize, make ethereal, spiritualize.

Etherealness, *n.* Airiness, rarity, subtilty, subtileness, delicacy, tenuity, attenuation, fairy-like delicacy, ethereality.

Ethical, *a.* Moral.

Ethics, *n.* Morals, moral philosophy, science of duty, ethical science, moral principles *or* quality *or* practice.

Ethnology, *n.* Science of races (*treating of the mental as well as of the physical differences of the races of mankind*).

Etiolate, *v. t.* Bleach, blanch, whiten, make *or* render white.

Etiolated, *a.* Whitened (*by exclusion from light*), blanched, bleached.

Etiquette, *n.* Prescribed form (*of behavior, as that set down on a card* or *ticket on the occasion of ceremonies at court*), fashionable ceremony, ceremonial code, forms of good-breeding, conventional decorum, manners.

Etymology, *n.* 1. Science of etymons, science of primitive (linguistic) roots.

2. Derivation of words.

Etymon, *n.* Root, radical, radix, primitive word.

Eucharist, *n.* Communion, mass, viaticum, consecrated elements, sacrament, Lord's Supper, Christian sacrament.

Eulogist, *n.* Encomiast, panegyrist, lauder, laureate, praiser, extoller.

Eulogistic, *a.* Encomiastic, panegyrical, commendatory, laudatory.

Eulogize, *v. t.* Extol, laud, applaud. See PRAISE, *v.*

Eulogy, *n.* 1. Eulogistic speech *or* discourse, eulogium, panegyric, *éloge.*

2. Praise, laudation, encomium, panegyric, applause, commendation.

Euphemism, *n.* 1. Softened expression (*to avoid offending by harshness,* or *by indelicacy*), substitution of inoffensive for unpleasant word.

2. Over-delicacy of speech, affected refinement of language, euphuism.

Euphonious, *a.* Euphonic, smooth, mellifluous, clear, silvery, musical, sweettoned, sweetly flowing, free from harshness, mellow, melodious, harmonious.

Euphony, *n.* Agreeable sound (*in language*), smoothness, ease of utterance.

Euphuism, *n.* 1. Purism, finical style, fastidious delicacy (*in the use of language*), affected elegance.

2. High-flown diction, pompous style, extravagantly ornate diction.

Evacuant, *a.* (*Med.*) Purgative, cathartic, emetic, abstergent, cleansing.

——, *n.* Cathartic, purgative, purgative medicine.

Evacuate, *v. t.* 1. Empty, make empty.

2. Eject, expel, excrete, void, discharge, throw out, purge, empty, clear out, clean out.

3. Quit (*as a house* or *a country*), leave, relinquish, forsake, desert, abandon, withdraw from.

Evacuation, *n.* 1. Emptying.

2. Discharge, ejection, excretion.

3. Quitting, withdrawal, retirement, retreat.

Evade, *v. t.* 1. Elude, escape, escape from, steal away from, get away from (*by artifice*).

2. Avoid, shun, dodge, "funk," decline.

3. Baffle, foil, elude.

——, *v. i.* Equivocate, shuffle, fence, quibble, dodge, prevaricate, palter.

Evanesce, *v. i.* Vanish, disappear, be dissipated, be seen no more.

Evanescence, *n.* 1. Evanishing, vanishing, evanishment, disappearance, being dissipated, gradual disappearance.

2. Transitoriness, transientness, speedy passage, short continuance, fleeting nature.

Evanescent, *a.* Vanishing, fleeting, transitory, transient, passing, flitting, fugitive, flying, ephemeral, short-lived.

Evangel, *n.* (*Poetical.*) 1. Gospel, glad tidings.

2. The gospel, Christian revelation, plan of salvation.

3. [*pl.*] The Gospels, New Testament.

Evangelical, *a.* 1. According to the gospel, consonant with the Gospels, founded on the New Testament.

2. Contained in the Gospels *or* the New Testament.

3. Earnest for the teachings of the Gospels, sound in the gospel, adhering to the letter of the gospel.

4. Devout, fervent, deeply pious, edifying.

5. Pietist, Protestant who emphasizes sin, atonement, and regeneration, salvation through atonement of Christ.

Evangelist, *n.* 1. Writer of one of the Gospels.

2. Missionary, revivalist.

Evangelize, *v. t.* Preach the gospel to, instruct in the gospel, convert to Christianity.

Evaporate, *v. i.* 1. Fly off in vapor, turn to vapor, volatilize, distill.

2. Disappear, be dissipated, vanish, evanesce.

——, *v. t.* 1. Vaporize, convert into vapor, disperse in vapor.

2. Exhale, emit in vapor.

Evasion, *n.* 1. Evading. See EVADE.

2. Shift, subterfuge, deceit, equivocation, prevarication, quibble, tergiversation, shuffling, sophistical excuse, disingenuous escape, "bluffing," "funking."

Evasive, *a.* Equivocating, shuffling, sophistical, elusive, elusory, shifty.

Eve, *n.* Day *or* night before *or* preceding.

Eve,
Even, } *n.* (*Poetical.*) See EVENING.

EVEN, *a.* 1. Smooth, level, plane, flat.

2. Uniform, equable, equal, calm, steady, regular, unruffled.

3. On a level, on the same level, flush.

4. Fair, just, equitable, impartial, straightforward, direct.

——, *adv.* 1. Exactly, verily, just.

2. At the very time.

3. Likewise, in like manner, not only so, but also.

4. So much as.

Even-handed, *a.* Impartial, fair, equitable, just.

Evening, *n.* Eve, even, eventide, nightfall, dusk, twilight, close of the day, fall of day, decline of day, sunset.

Evening star. Vesper, Hesper, Hesperus, Venus.

EVENT, *n.* 1. Occurrence, incident, fact, circumstance.

2. Adventure, affair, marked occurrence.

3. Result, issue, consequence, conclusion, termination, end, sequel, outcome.

Eventful, *a.* Full of incidents, stirring, memorable, signal, momentous, important, critical, remarkable.

Eventual, *a.* 1. Final, ultimate, last.

2. Contingent, conditional, possible.

Eventuate, *v. i.* 1. Issue, terminate, close, end, result.

2. Result, come about, come to pass, happen, occur, take place, fall out.

EVER, *adv.* 1. At any time.

2. Always, evermore, perpetually, continually, eternally, aye, for aye, forever, at all times, to the end of time, through all ages, till doomsday.

Ever and anon. Often, every now and then, at short intervals.

Everlasting, *a.* 1. Endless, unending, everduring, constant, perpetual, incessant, ceaseless, continual, uninterrupted, interminable, unceasing, never-ceasing, unintermitting, never-ending, eternal.

2. Imperishable, undying, never-dying, ever-living, deathless, immortal.

Ever-living, *a.* Eternal, immortal, undying, deathless, never-dying, everlasting.

Evermore, *adv.* Always, forever, ever, constantly, perpetually, continually, aye, for aye, at all times, to the end of time, through all ages, eternally, world without end.

EVERY, *a.* Each (*of several*), all.

Every-day, *a.* Common, customary, usual, routine, wonted, accustomed, habitual, commonplace.

Everywhere, *adv.* Throughout, in every place, in all places, in every part *or* quarter, from pole to pole.

Evict, *v. t.* (*Law.*) Dispossess, eject, thrust out.

Eviction, *n.* (*Law.*) Dispossession, deprivation.

Evidence, *n.* Testimony, proof, ground of belief, attestation, token, voucher, trace.

——, *v. t.* Prove, show, manifest, evince, make manifest, make clear, vouch, testify.

Evident, *a.* Plain, clear, manifest, indubitable, apparent, obvious, palpable, patent, unmistakable, open, conspicuous, distinct, bald, downright, overt.

Evidential, *a.* Indicative, evidentiary, evincive, demonstrative.

Evil, *a.* 1. Bad, ill.

2. Wicked, sinful, vicious, corrupt, perverse, wrong, base, vile, nefarious, malicious, malign, malevolent, bad.

3. Mischievous, hurtful, harmful, injurious, pernicious, destructive, baneful, baleful, noxious, deleterious, bad.

4. Unhappy, unfortunate, adverse, unpropitious, disastrous, calamitous, woful, bad.

——, *n.* 1. Calamity, ill, woe, misery, pain, suffering, sorrow, misfortune, disaster, reverse.

2. Wickedness, sin, depravity, malignity, wicked disposition, corruption, wrong, viciousness, baseness, badness.

3. Wrong, injury, mischief, harm, ill, curse, bale, blast, canker, bane.

Evil-doer, *n.* Sinner, criminal, malefactor, culprit, offender, delinquent, wrong-doer.

Evil one. Devil, Satan, Lucifer, Belial, Apollyon, Arch-fiend, the Tempter, the Wicked One, the Old Serpent, the Prince of Darkness, the Foul Fiend, the Enemy. See APOLLYON.

Evince, *v. t.* 1. Prove, show, evidence, manifest, establish, make evident, make clear.

2. Exhibit, indicate, manifest, show, display, disclose, bring to view.

Eviscerate, *v. t.* Disembowel, embowel, paunch, gut, take out the bowels of.

Evoke, *v. t.* 1. Summon, call forth, call up, summon forth.

2. Excite, arouse, elicit, call out, rouse, provoke.

Evolution, *n.* 1. Evolving, unfolding, expansion, evolvement, development.

2. Descent by continuous differentiation, development, doctrine of development, ascent from simplicity to complexity.

3. Movement, marching, figure.

Evolve, *v. t.* Unroll, unfold, expand, open, educe, exhibit, develop.

Exacerbate, *v. t.* 1. Irritate, exasperate, provoke, embitter, inflame, excite, infuriate, enrage.

2. Aggravate, heighten, increase.

Exacerbation, *n.* See EXASPERATION, AGGRAVATION.

Exact, *a.* 1. Strict, rigid, rigorous, severe, scrupulous.

2. Precise, without the least error, diametric (opposite), express, true, faultless.

3. Accurate, correct, close, literal, faithful, definite, undeviating.

4. Accurate, critical, nice, delicate, fine, sensitive.

5. Methodical, regular, precise, careful, punctilious, punctual, orderly.

——, *v. t.* 1. Extort, require authoritatively, mulct, "squeeze," elicit.

2. Ask, take, requisition, compel, claim, demand, enforce.

Exacting, *a.* Critical, difficult; extortionary, exactive, rigid.

Exactness, *n.* 1. Accuracy, correctness, faultlessness, precision, nicety, faithfulness, fidelity, rigor, exactitude.

2. Strictness, regularity, method, scrupulosity, rigidness, precision, scrupulousness, carefulness.

Exaggerate, *v. t.* Overstate, magnify, enlarge, overcharge, strain, stretch, overstrain, overcolor, depict extravagantly, color too highly, romance.

Exaggeration, *n.* Hyperbole, overstatement, stretching, extravagant statement, high coloring.

Exalt, *v. t.* 1. Raise, elevate, erect, lift up, heighten, raise high *or* on high *or* aloft, make lofty.

2. Ennoble, dignify, aggrandize, elevate.

3. Praise (*highly*), extol, magnify, glorify, bless.

Exalted, *a.* Elevated, elated, high, lofty, highflown; magnificent, lordly, proud.

Exaltation, *n.* Elevation, dignity, loftiness, nobility, grandeur.

Examination, *n.* 1. Inspection, observation.

2. Inquiry, search, research, exploration, perusal, survey, scrutiny, investigation, inquisition.

3. Trial by questions (*in order to elicit truth or to test qualifications*), test, review, probation, catechism.

Examine, *v. t.* 1. Inspect, observe.

2. Scrutinize, investigate, study, consider, canvass, test, inquire into, search into, look into, inquire about.

3. Interrogate (*in order to elicit truth or to test qualifications*), catechise, put questions to.

EXAMPLE, *n.* 1. Pattern, copy, model, archetype, sample, sampler, specimen, piece, representative, standard, prototype.

2. Precedent.

3. Instance, illustration, exemplification, case in point, warning.

Exanimate, *a.* 1. Lifeless, dead, defunct, inanimate.

2. Inanimate, torpid, inert, sluggish, spiritless.

Exasperate, *v. t.* 1. Irritate, provoke, chafe, vex, nettle, incense, anger, affront, offend, enrage, make angry.

2. Exacerbate, aggravate, inflame, render more violent.

Exasperation, *n.* 1. Irritation, provocation, exacerbation.

2. Wrath, anger, rage, ire, fury, violent passion.

3. Aggravation, exacerbation, increase, heightening, worsening.

Ex cathedra, *a.* [L.] 1. Authoritative, formal, official, from the bench, from high authority.

2. Dogmatic, magisterial, dictatorial.

——, *adv.* [L.] 1. Authoritatively, formally, officially, from the bench.

2. Dogmatically, magisterially, dictatorially.

Excavate, *v. t.* Hollow, hollow out, dig, burrow, delve, expose by digging, scoop out, dig out, cut out.

Excavation, *n.* 1. Excavating. See the verb.

2. Cutting, cavity, hollow, cut, hole, burrow, pit, trench.

Exceed, *v. t.* 1. Transcend, surpass, cap, overstep, go beyond.

2. Excel, outdo, outstrip, outvie, pass, surpass, out-Herod, be superior to.

Exceedingly, *adv.* Very, highly, greatly, extremely, vastly, superlatively, surpassingly, beyond measure, to a great *or* unusual degree.

Excel, *v. t.* 1. Surpass, outdo, outvie, outrival, outstrip, beat, be superior to, cast in the shade, throw into the shade, eclipse.

2. Exceed, transcend, cap, go beyond, surpass.

——, *v. i.* Win eminence, gain *or* have excellence, surpass others, attain superiority, win *or* acquire distinction, be superior, be eminent, bear the palm, bear the bell, take precedence.

Excellence, *n.* 1. Superiority, eminence, distinction, pre-eminence, transcendence.

2. Good quality, fineness, goodness, purity, superior quality, superiority, perfection.

3. Valuable point *or* property *or* characteristic, advantage, good point.

4. Worth, goodness, uprightness, probity, virtue, purity.

Excellent, *a.* 1. Superior, eminent, first-rate, "tip-top," "crack," choice, transcendent, sterling, prime, admirable, of the best, of the first water, of the first grade, of the best quality, of the highest order, extremely good.

2. Virtuous, worthy, estimable, admirable, thoroughly good, highly deserving, worthy of great praise.

Except, *v. t.* Exclude, reject, omit, leave out.

——, *prep.* Excepting, excluding, save, leaving out, with the exception of.

——, *conj.* Unless, unless it be that, if it be not that.

Exception, *n.* 1. Exclusion, omission, leaving out, non-inclusion.

2. Objection; irritated objection, affront, offence.

3. Instance to be excepted, unusual case, anomalous case, anomaly, deviation from the rule.

Exceptional, *a.* Irregular, unusual, special, superior, rare, uncommon, unnatural,

peculiar, anomalous, abnormal, aberrant, exceptive.

Excerpt, *n.* Extract, quotation, citation, selected passage.

——, *v. t.* Extract, select, cite, quote, take.

Excess, *n.* 1. Superfluity, redundance, superabundance, fulsomeness, plethora, surfeit, oversupply, glut, redundancy, disproportion, undue amount.

2. Surplus, overplus, remainder.

3. Intemperance, immoderation, over-indulgence, dissoluteness, dissolute behavior *or* living, unrestraint, dissipation, debauchery.

4. Extravagance, immoderation, over-doing.

Excesses, *n. pl.* 1. Debauchery, orgies, revels, drunkenness, saturnalia.

2. Rages, furies, cruelties, brutalities, enormities.

Excessive, *a.* 1. Superabundant, disproportionate, undue, too great, superfluous, exuberant.

2. Extravagant, inordinate, enormous, outrageous, unreasonable, very great.

3. Immoderate, intemperate, extreme.

4. Vehement, violent.

Exchange, *v. t.* 1. Barter, commute, substitute, shuffle, trade (*off* or *away*), swap, truck, change.

2. Interchange, bandy, give and take reciprocally.

EXCHANGE, *n.* 1. Barter, traffic, dealing, trade, change, substitution, shuffle, commutation.

2. Interchange, reciprocity.

3. Bourse, market, bazaar, fair.

Excise, *n.* Inland duty, tax upon home products, internal tax *or* impost *or* revenue.

——, *v. t.* Cut off, remove, efface.

Excision, *n.* Extirpation, eradication, destruction, extermination, cutting out *or* off *or* up.

Excitability, *n.* Sensibility, sensitiveness, etc. See the adjective.

Excitable, *a.* 1. Sensitive, nervous, susceptible, impressible.

2. Irascible, irritable, passionate, choleric, hot-headed, hasty, hot-tempered, quick-tempered.

Excite, *v. t.* 1. Arouse, rouse, awaken, move, evoke, provoke, call forth, stimulate, incite, animate, impel, prompt, spur, instigate, kindle, inflame, brew, stir up.

2. Raise, create, evoke, elicit, give rise to, put in motion.

3. Disturb, agitate, discompose, irritate, provoke.

Excitement, *n.*   1. Excitation, exciting. See the verb, under 1 and 2.

2. Incitement, motive, stimulus.

3. Agitation, perturbation, commotion, disturbance, tension, activity, bustle, ferment, stir, flutter, sensation.

4. Irritation, warmth, heat, violence, choler, passion.

Exclaim, *v. i.*   Vociferate, shout, call, ejaculate, cry out, call aloud.

Exclamation, *n.*   Vociferation, outcry, ejaculation, clamor.

Exclude, *v. t.*   1. Bar, debar, blackball, ostracize, preclude, reject, shut out.

2. Prohibit, restrain, hinder, prevent, withhold.

3. Except, omit, not include.

4. Expel, eject, extrude, thrust out, eliminate.

Exclusive, *a.*   1. Excluding, debarring.

2. Illiberal, selfish, narrow, uncharitable, narrow-minded.

3. Fastidious (*in social relations*), invidiously choice, cliquish, clannish, snobbish, aristocratic.

4. Sole, only, special.

Excogitate, *v. t.*   Think out, make up, invent, contrive, imagine, create.

Excommunicate, *v. t.*   Dismiss *or* expel (*from the Church*), unchurch, denounce, proscribe, anathematize, curse, expel from fellowship, exscind.

Excoriate, *v. t.*   Flay, skin, gall, scar, scarify, score, gouge out, abrade, strip the skin from.

Excrement, *n.*   1. Excretion, excreted matter.

2. Dung, fæces, ordure, dejections, alvine discharges, stool, excreta.

Excrescence, *n.*   1. Wart, tumor, outgrowth, lump, fungus, morbid protuberance *or* growth.

2. Superfluity, useless outgrowth, deforming attachment *or* appendage.

Excrete, *v. t.*   Separate, discharge, eject, eliminate, throw off.

Excretion, *n.*   1. Separation, discharge.

2. Excrement, excreted matter.

Excretory, *a.*   Excretive.

Excruciate, *v. t.*   Torture, torment, rack, agonize.

Excruciating, *a.*   Torturing, tormenting, agonizing, very painful.

Excruciation, *n.*   Torture, torment, agony, anguish.

Exculpate, *v. t.*   Absolve, exonerate, acquit, clear, vindicate, set right.

Exculpation, *n.*   Exoneration, vindication, clearing.

Exculpatory, *a.*   Excusatory, vindicative, vindicatory, exonerative.

Excursion, *n.*   1. Journey, tour, trip, expedition, voyage, pleasure trip; sally, ramble, jaunt; walk, drive, ride, etc.

2. Digression, episode.

Excursive, *a.*   Rambling, wandering, roving, roaming, devious, erratic.

Excursus, *n.*   [L.] Dissertation, disquisition, discussion (*entered by way of appendix*).

Excusable, *a.*   Pardonable, venial, allowable, defensible.

Excusatory, *a.*   Apologetic; vindicative, vindicatory, exculpatory, exonerative.

Excuse, *v. t.*   1. Pardon, forgive, acquit, absolve, remit, exculpate, exonerate.

2. Extenuate, justify, form *or* constitute an apology *or* excuse for, condone.

3. Exempt, release, free, let off.

4. Overlook, regard indulgently, treat as venial.

——, *n.*   (*Pron.* excūs'.) 1. Apology, plea, justification, defense, extenuation, absolution.

2. Pretext, pretence, color, guise, disguise, semblance, makeshift, subterfuge, evasion, false show.

Execrable, *a.*   1. Detestable, hateful, odious, abhorrent, damnable, cursed, accursed, abominable, villanous.

2. Offensive, disgusting, obnoxious, nauseous, nauseating, sickening, repulsive, revolting, loathsome, vile.

3. Bad, wretched.

Execrate, *v. t.*   1. Curse, imprecate ill upon, call down curses on.

2. Abominate, detest, hate, abhor.

Execration, *n.*   1. Curse, malediction, ban, anathema, imprecation of evil.

2. Detestation, abhorrence, abomination, horror, loathing.

3. Thing detested, abominated, *or* abhorred, curse, horror.

Execute, *v. t.*   1. Accomplish, effect, effectuate, perform, do, consummate, finish, complete, achieve, carry out, carry through, carry into effect, work out, perpetrate.

2. Put to death (*in pursuance of a judicial sentence*).

3. (*Law.*) Sign, seal, and deliver (*as a deed*), give effect to, make valid; administer, enforce.

Execution, *n.*   Performance, operation, accomplishment, achievement, completion, consummation.

Executioner, *n.*   Killer, headsman, hangman.

Executive, *a.*   Executory, charged with execution *or* carrying into effect; skillful in execution *or* administration.

Executive, *n.* 1. Chief magistrate, administrative head, head of government, head of affairs, head of the nation.

2. Administration, administrative body, body charged with administration *or* the execution of the laws.

Executory, *a.* 1. Executive.

2. (*Law.*) To be executed.

Exegesis, *n.* Interpretation, exposition, explanation, critical explanation.

Exegetic, } *a.* Explanatory, expository,
Exegetical, } hermeneutical, explicative, explicatory, interpretative.

Exegetics, *n.* Exegesis, science of interpretation, hermeneutics.

Exemplar, *n.* Pattern, model, copy, example, prototype, archetype.

Exemplary, *a.* 1. Worthy of imitation, fit for a pattern.

2. Pattern-like, closely adherent to the pattern, faithful, close, exact, assiduous, scrupulous, punctual, punctilious, rigid, rigorous.

3. Remarkably good, excellent, highly virtuous, correct, estimable, commendable, worthy, deserving of approval.

4. Monitory, warning, admonitory, condign.

Exemplify, *v. t.* 1. Illustrate, show by example, embody.

2. (*Law.*) Make a certified copy of.

Exempt, *v. t.* Relieve, release, free, let off, grant immunity to, excuse, except, exonerate (*of an obligation* or *burden*).

——, *a.* Exempted, free, liberated, released, not liable, possessed of immunity.

Exemption, *n.* Immunity, privilege, release, exception, freedom from liability.

Exercise, *n.* 1. Practice, custom, usage; use, appliance, application, performance, operation, working, play, plying, employment.

2. Exertion, labor, work, toil, effort, action, activity.

3. Training, schooling, discipline, drill, drilling.

4. Lesson, task, study, theme, test-lesson, examples for practice, praxis.

——, *v. t.* 1. Exert (*constantly*), employ, busy, apply, use, put in action, set to work.

2. Exert, wield, effect, produce, carry into effect.

3. Discipline, train, drill, school, break in, habituate to practice.

4. Practise, pursue, carry on, use, prosecute.

5. Task, try, test, put to the test.

6. Try, afflict, burden, annoy, trouble, pain, agitate, make anxious, render uneasy.

Exert, *v. t.* Use, put forth, emit, bring into operation, set to work, put into vigorous action. See EXERCISE, 1 and 2.

Exertion, *n.* 1. Exerting, exercise, use. See the verb.

2. Effort, endeavor, struggle, attempt, trial, strain, stretch.

Exert one's self. Labor, toil, strive, try, endeavor, work, take pains, bestir one's self, fall to work, work with a will, leave no stone unturned, do one's best, make effort, make great efforts.

Exfoliate, *v.i.* Scale off, shell off, peel off, shed, desquamate, fall off in scales.

Exfoliation, *n.* (*Med.*) Desquamation.

Exhalation, *n.* 1. Evaporation, emission of vapor.

2. Vapor, fume, effluvium, steam, reek, smoke, fog.

Exhale, *v. t.* Emit, evaporate, breathe, emanate, emit in vapor, throw off in effluvia, reek.

——, *v. i.* Fly off, pass off, be evaporated, expire, puff, blow, exsufflate, be exhaled.

Exhaust, *v. t.* 1. Drain, empty, draw.

2. Expend, spend, waste, squander, consume, impoverish, use up, wear out, destroy, lavish, dissipate, fritter away, run through (with).

3. Prostrate, cripple, weaken, enervate, deplete, overtire, debilitate, disable, deprive of strength, wear out.

4. Develop completely, discuss thoroughly.

——, *n.* Vent, opening, valve, escape.

Exhibit, *v. t.* 1. Show, display, present to view, offer for inspection; manifest, express, indicate, disclose, evince, reveal, expose, make known, bring to notice, bring into view, point out, set forth.

2. (*Law.*) Offer, present, propose.

Exhibition, *n.* 1. Display, show, manifestation.

2. Exposition, laying open to public view.

3. (*Eng. Universities.*) Allowance, pension, benefaction.

Exhilarate, *v. t.* Cheer, enliven, inspirit, inspire, animate, stimulate, elate, gladden, make merry, make glad *or* joyous.

Exhilaration, *n.* 1. Cheering, enlivening, animating, etc. See the verb.

2. Animation, gayety, hilarity, glee, cheer, gladness, joyousness, cheerfulness, good-humor, good spirits, high spirits.

Exhort, *v. t.* Urge, incite, stimulate, persuade, advise, caution, warn; encourage (*to do well*).

——, *v. i.* Give exhortation, offer advice, preach.

Exhortation, *n.* 1. Advice, counsel.

2. Persuasive discourse.

Exhortative, *a.* Exhortatory, hortatory.

Exhume, *v. t.* Disinter, unbury, disentomb, disinhume.

Exigence, } *n.* 1. Demand, urgency, ne-
Exigency, } cessity, need, want, requirement.

2. Emergency, crisis, strait, juncture, conjuncture, quandary, difficulty, extremity, pressure, pass, pinch, nonplus, critical situation, pressing necessity.

Exigent, *a.* Urgent, pressing, critical.

Exiguity, *n.* Smallness, slenderness, fineness, exility, attenuation, exiguousness.

Exiguous, *a.* Small, diminutive, tiny, slender, scanty, meagre, slim, attenuated, fine.

Exile, *n.* 1. Banishment, ostracism, proscription, expulsion *or* separation (*from one's country*), expatriation.

2. Banished person, isolated person, outcast.

——, *v. t.* Banish, expatriate, ostracize, proscribe, expel (*from one's country*).

Exist, *v. i.* 1. Be, subsist, have being.

2. Live, breathe, have life, be alive.

3. Continue, remain, endure, last, abide.

EXISTENCE, *n.* 1. Being, existing, subsisting, subsistence.

2. Entity, being, essence, creature, thing.

3. Life, animation.

4. Continuance, duration.

Exit, *n.* 1. Departure, withdrawal, going off *or* away (*especially from the stage*).

2. Decease, death, demise, end.

3. Egress, passage out, way out, outlet.

Exodus, *n.* Departure (*from a country*), great emigration.

Exonerate, *v. t.* 1. Exculpate, absolve, acquit, clear, justify, vindicate.

2. Release, absolve, discharge, exempt, except, free, let off.

Exoneration, *n.* 1. Exculpation, acquittal, clearance, justification, vindication.

2. Release, absolution, discharge, exemption, exception, liberation, letting off.

Exorable, *a.* To be moved by entreaty, yielding to prayer, gracious, merciful.

Exorbitance, } *n.* Extravagance, exces-
Exorbitancy, } siveness, enormity, excess.

Exorbitant, *a.* Extravagant, inordinate, excessive, enormous, unreasonable, greedy.

Exorcise, *v. t.* 1. Drive away (*by conjurations*), cast out.

2. Deliver from malignant spirits, purify from evil influence.

3. Address *or* conjure (spirits).

Exorcism, *n.* 1. Exorcising. See the verb.

2. Spell, charm, incantation, exorcising formula.

Exordium, *n.* [L. *pl. Exordia; Eng. pl. Exordiums.*] Introduction, opening, preamble, preface, proem, prelude, prologue.

Exoteric, *a.* Public, open, external, superficial, addressed to the public, for the multitude, *ad populum.*

Exotic, *a.* Foreign, extraneous, not indigenous, not native, derived from abroad.

Expand, *v. t.* 1. Spread, open, unfold, evolve, develop, unfurl, lay open, spread out.

2. Dilate, distend, swell, fill out, blow up.

3. Extend, stretch, enlarge, increase, diffuse.

——, *v. i.* 1. Open, be unfolded, develop, widen, be spread out.

2. Dilate, enlarge, be distended, increase in bulk.

Expanse, *n.* Extent, expansion, stretch, area, spread, field, expanded surface.

EXPANSION, *n.* 1. Expanding, spreading, opening.

2. Dilation, diastole, distension, swelling.

3. Enlargement, increase, diffusion, development.

4. Extent, expanse, stretch.

Expansive, *a.* 1. Expanding, dilating, tending to expand *or* be expanded, to dilate *or* be dilated.

2. Diffusive, pervasive, wide.

3. Wide-reaching, comprehensive, elastic, extensible, generous, effusive, wide-embracing, far-reaching, wide-extending.

Ex parte. [L.] One-sided, partisan, one-sidedly, with partisan bias.

Expatiate, *v. i.* 1. Rove at large, range at will, take a wide survey.

2. Dilate, enlarge, descant, be copious, launch out.

Expatriate, *v. t.* Banish, exile, ostracize, proscribe, expel (*from one's country*).

Expect, *v. t.* 1. Await, wait for.

2. Anticipate, look for, contemplate, look forward to, count upon, reckon upon, calculate upon, hope for, rely upon.

Expectancy, *n.* 1. Expectation, expectance.

2. (*Law.*) Abeyance, prospect.

Expectant, *a.* Waiting, looking for, looking forward to.

Expectation, *n.* 1. Anticipation, prospect, expectance, expectancy.

2. Reliance, confidence, assurance, presumption.

Expectorate, *v. t.* Hawk up, cough up, eject from the trachea, spit, raise.

Expedience, **Expediency,** *n.* 1. Fitness, propriety, suitableness, advisability, desirableness (*to* or *for a given end*), policy; opportunism.

2. Advantage, profit, utility.

3. Advantageousness, profitableness, usefulness, utility, judiciousness.

Expedient, *a.* 1. Fit, proper, suitable, advisable, politic, desirable (*in view of an end proposed*).

2. Advantageous, profitable, useful, for one's advantage, for one's interest.

——, *n.* Shift, resource, resort, contrivance, device, "dodge," "stopgap," makeshift, means.

Expedite, *v. t.* Hasten, accelerate, despatch, speed, hurry, quicken, precipitate, forward, facilitate, help forward, advance, press forward, urge forward, press on, urge on.

Expedition, *n.* 1. Haste, speed, despatch, celerity, quickness, promptness, alacrity, alertness.

2. Enterprise, undertaking.

3. March *or* voyage, hostile undertaking, campaign, quest, journey, excursion.

Expeditious, *a.* 1. Speedy, quick, swift, rapid.

2. Prompt, swift, punctual, diligent, nimble, alert.

Expel, *v. t.* 1. Eject, dislodge, drive out, excrete, egest, eliminate, force away, thrust out *or* forth.

2. Eject, void, evacuate, discharge.

3. Remove (*by penalty*), exclude permanently, oust, discharge, "fire," "bounce," relegate, exscind.

4. Banish, exile, expatriate, ostracize, excommunicate, unchurch, disown, proscribe.

Expend, *v. t.* 1. Disburse, spend, lay out.

2. Use, employ, exert, consume.

3. Exhaust, consume, waste, scatter, dissipate.

Expenditure, *n.* 1. Disbursement, spending, outlay, outlaying, laying out.

2. Expense, cost, charge, outlay.

Expense, *n.* Cost, charge, expenditure, outlay.

Expensive, *a.* 1. Dear, costly, high-priced, of great price, requiring great outlay.

2. Lavish, extravagant, wasteful.

EXPERIENCE, *n.* 1. Actual observation, actual trial, actual feeling, actual presentation.

2. Continued *or* repeated observation, long practice, thorough acquaintance with facts, knowledge gained from observation, experimental knowledge, practical wisdom, skill.

——, *v. t.* 1. Feel, know, be the subject of, have in one's own perceptions *or* sensations *or* feelings, actually observe, have before one's own senses, prove by trial, try, have practical acquaintance with.

2. Undergo, be the subject of, encounter, meet.

3. Endure, suffer, be subjected to.

Experienced, *a.* Practised, instructed, accomplished, thoroughbred, versed, qualified, able, skillful, knowing, trained, old, wise, veteran, expert.

Experiment, *n.* 1. Trial, test, examination, assay, proof, touchstone, ordeal.

2. Organized observation, prearranged investigation, exact trial, use of experiments, experimentation.

——, *v. i.* Make experiment, make trial.

Experimental, *a.* 1. Empiric, empirical, experiential, from experience, tried, tested, verified, ascertained, founded on fact, supported by experiment *or* observation.

2. Inwardly felt, actually undergone, really had *or* experienced.

3. Tentative, in the way of experiment, trial, that feels its way, empirical, awaiting verification.

Expert, *a.* Adroit, dexterous, ready, prompt, quick, apt, clever, able, skilful, "crack," proficient.

EXPERT, *n.* Adept, "dabster," "crack," "shark," specialist, experienced person, person specially versed (*in a given subject*), skilled hand, connoisseur, master, master-hand.

Expiate, *v. t.* Atone for, redeem, do penance for, make satisfaction *or* reparation for.

Expiation, *n.* 1. Atonement, satisfaction, reparation.

2. Expiatory offering, penitential act.

Expiration, *n.* 1. Emission of breath, exhalation.

2. Death, decease, demise, exit, departure.

3. Termination, cessation, close, end, conclusion.

Expire, *v. t.* Breathe out, emit from the lungs, expel, exhale.

——, *v. i.* 1. Decease, draw the last breath. See DIE.

2. End, terminate, cease, conclude, stop, come to an end.

Explain, *v. t.* 1. Interpret, elucidate, expound, illustrate, unfold, clear up, make plain, solve, resolve, unfold, demonstrate, unravel, throw light upon.

2. Account for, give the reasons for, make intelligible, solve, warrant, justify, reduce to law *or* to ascertained principles, trace to causes.

——, *v. i.* Make an explanation.

Explainable, *a.* Explicable, accountable, understandable, that may be explained.

Explanation, *n.* Interpretation, elucidation, illustration, exposition, description, explication, exegesis.

2. Solution, account, warrant, justification, deduction, key, secret.

Explanatory, *a.* 1. Illustrative, elucidative, expository, serving to explain.

Expletive, *a.* Superfluous, redundant.

——, *n.* Expletive word *or* syllable, oath.

Explicable, *a.* Explainable, to be accounted for *or* made intelligible.

Explication, *n.* Interpretation, explanation, exposition, illustration.

Explicit, *a.* Express, clear, plain, positive, definite, determinate, categorical, unambiguous, unreserved.

Explode, *v. t.* 1. Discharge, burst, displode, detonate.

2. Discard, repudiate, scout, scorn, contemn, cry down, treat with contempt, bring into disrepute.

——, *v. i.* Burst, displode, detonate, be discharged.

Exploit, *n.* Act (*especially an heroic act*), deed, feat, achievement.

——, *v. t.* Utilize, put to use *or* service, work up, "milk," "work."

Exploration, *n.* Examination, scrutiny, inquiry, search, prospecting, probe, research, inquisition.

Explore, *v. t.* 1. Examine, scrutinize, investigate, search into, inquire into, pry into, plumb, fathom, prospect.

2. Examine (*countries*) geographically, travel through observingly.

Explosion, *n.* Burst, bursting, detonation, fulmination, blast, clap, pop, crack, sudden discharge.

Exponent, *n.* Index, indication, representative, type, example, specimen, symbol, illustration.

Export, *v. t.* Send out (*merchandise from one country to another*), carry out, send abroad, ship.

——, *n.* (*Pron.* ex'port.) Commodity exported.

Expose, *v. t.* 1. Uncover, bare, make bare.

2. Disclose, unearth, detect, descry, lay open, show up, bring to light.

3. Unmask, denounce, show up, strip of disguises *or* concealments, show in one's real light.

4. Subject, make liable.

5. Endanger, jeopardize, venture, risk, put in danger, put in peril.

6. Exhibit, set in view, put in a conspicuous place.

Exposé, *n.* [Fr.] 1. Exposition, formal statement, exhibit, manifesto.

2. Exposure, divulgement, revelation, denouncement, deprecated publication.

Exposition, *n.* 1. Exposure, disclosing, laying open.

2. Explanation, interpretation, elucidation, exegesis, explication.

3. Exhibition, show, display.

Expositor, *n.* Expounder, explainer, interpreter.

Expository, *a.* Explanatory, illustrative, exegetical, elucidative.

Expostulate, *v. i.* [Followed by *with*.] Remonstrate, reason earnestly and dissuasively.

Expostulation, *n.* Remonstrance, protest.

Exposure, *n.* 1. Exposing. See EXPOSÉ, in all senses.

2. Position (*with reference to the points of the compass*), aspect, prospect, outlook, frontage, front.

Expound, *v. t.* 1. Give an account of, rehearse, state fully, reproduce, present, unfold, develop.

2. Explain, interpret, elucidate, clear up, lay open, make plain.

Express, *v. t.* 1. Squeeze out, press out.

2. Utter, speak, declare, assert, state, emit, manifest, enunciate, vent, air, voice, signify, set forth, give vent to, give utterance to.

3. Represent, indicate, show, signify, exhibit, symbolize, present, betoken, mean, equal, denote, intimate.

4. Send by express, send express, hasten.

——, *a.* 1. Explicit, clear, plain, definite, positive, determinate, categorical, unambiguous, clearly stated, outspoken.

2. Exact, accurate, close, faithful, true, precise.

3. Special, particular.

4. Swift, rapid, fast.

——, *n.* 1. Special messenger *or* courier.

2. Message, despatch.

3. Speedy conveyance, rapid transmission.

Expression, *n.* 1. Utterance, declaration, assertion, statement, emission, communication, voicing.

2. Phrase, locution, word, saying, term, form of words, mode of speech.

3. Look, cast of countenance, play of features.

4. General tone, pervading effect, pervasive feeling.

5. Lively representation, effective exhibition.

6. Modulation, suitable feeling and execution.

Expressive, *a.* 1. [With *of*.] Significant, meaningful, indicative.

2. Emphatic, strong, forcible, energetic, lively, demonstrative, eloquent, vivid.

3. Appropriate, sympathetic, well-modulated.

Express one's self. 1. Speak *or* write, deliver one's self, make known one's opinions, sentiments, *or* feelings.

2. Speak one's mind, say one's say.

3. Say, state, declare.

Expulsion, *n.* 1. Expelling, driving out, discharge, eviction, ousting; elimination, excretion, evacuation.

2. Ejection, extrusion, banishment, deportation, relegation, transportation, expatriation, rustication.

3. Permanent exclusion, separation from membership, excision, ostracism, excommunication.

Expunge, *v. t.* Erase, efface, obliterate, delete, blot out, strike out, rub out, wipe out, cancel, destroy.

Expurgate, *v. t.* Purify, purge, cleanse, free from objectionable matter; bowdlerize, emasculate.

Exquisite, *a.* 1. Nice, exact, accurate, discriminating, delicate, refined, fastidious, keenly appreciative.

2. Select, choice, excellent, rare, valuable, precious.

3. Consummate, complete, perfect, matchless.

4. Acute, intense, poignant, keen.

—, *n.* Dandy, fop, coxcomb, beau, popinjay, jackanapes, jack-a-dandy, man milliner, man of dress, vain fellow.

Exsiccate, *v. t.* Dry, desiccate, make dry, dry up.

Extant, *a.* Existing, undestroyed, in being, in existence, not lost, present, visible.

Extemporaneous, *a.* Unpremeditated, offhand, spontaneous, impromptu, unprepared, extemporary, extempore, improvised.

Extempore, *adv.* [L.] Suddenly, without premeditation, without preparation, offhand, on the spur of the moment.

—, *a.* [L.] See EXTEMPORANEOUS.

Extemporize, *v. i.* Speak extempore, improvise, speak without notes, speak without premeditation, make an off-hand speech *or* address.

Extend, *v. t.* 1. Stretch out, reach out, reach forth, run.

2. Prolong, continue, lengthen out, elongate, widen, protract.

3. Expand, dilate, enlarge, distend, augment, increase, fill out.

4. Diffuse, spread abroad.

5. Offer, yield, give, impart.

—, *v. i.* Stretch, reach, spread, range, lie.

Extensible, *a.* Extendible, extensile, protractile, ductile, elastic.

Extension, *n.* 1. Extendedness.

2. Expansion, dilatation, dilation, enlargement, increase, augmentation.

Extensive, *a.* Wide, large, broad, comprehensive, capacious, extended, expanded, wide-spread, far-reaching.

Extent, *n.* 1. Expansion, expanse, amplitude.

2. Bulk, size, magnitude, volume, amount, degree, content.

3. Length, reach, stretch, compass, measure, proportions.

4. Field, latitude, range, scope, area.

5. Breadth, width, height, depth.

Extenuate, *v. t.* 1. Lessen, diminish, reduce in size *or* bulk, make thin.

2. Palliate, mitigate, qualify, excuse, apologize for.

Extenuation, *n.* 1. Diminution, abatement, mitigation.

2. Palliation, excuse, apology.

Exterior, *a.* 1. Outward, external, outer, outlying, outside, superficial, surface.

2. Extrinsic, foreign, from without.

—, *n.* 1. Outside, outer part, outer surface.

2. (Outward) appearance.

Exterminate, *v. t.* 1. Extirpate, eradicate, uproot, annihilate, destroy, abolish, root out, put an end to.

2. (*Math.*) Eliminate.

External, *a.* 1. Outward, outer, exterior, outside, superficial.

2. Extrinsic, foreign, from without.

3. Visible, apparent.

Externals, *n. pl.* Outside, outward parts, things as seen, visible forms.

Extinct, *a.* 1. Extinguished, quenched, put out.

2. Ended, terminated, closed, vanished, dead, lapsed, brought to an end, no longer existing.

Extinction, *n.* 1. Extinguishment, death.

2. Destruction, annihilation, extirpation, extermination, excision, abolition, abolishment.

Extinguish, *v. t.* 1. Quench, put out, choke, quell, douse, suppress, stifle, smother, suffocate.

2. Destroy, suppress, put down, subdue; nullify.

3. Obscure, eclipse.

Extirpate, *v. t.* Eradicate, uproot, exterminate, deracinate, annihilate, destroy, abolish, root out, weed out.

Extol, *v. t.* 1. Praise, laud, magnify, exalt, celebrate, glorify.

2. Eulogize, panegyrize, applaud, be laudatory of, glorify, commend highly.

Extort, *v. t.* Exact, wrest, wring, wrench, force, elicit, extract, squeeze, wring from by intimidation *or* terrorism.

Extortion, *n.* 1. Exaction, illegal compulsion, tribute, blackmail, oppression, rapacity, over-charge.

2. (*Colloq.*) Exorbitance, exorbitant charge.

Extortionate, *a.* 1. Oppressive, exacting, severe, "blood-sucking," hard, harsh.

2. Exorbitant, unreasonable.

Extra, *a.* 1. Additional, supplementary, accessory, spare, supplemental.

2. Unusual, extraordinary, extreme.

Extract, *v. t.* 1. Draw out, pull out, take out, extort, remove, withdraw.

2. Derive (*by chemical process*), distill, squeeze.

3. Select (*from a literary work*), cite, quote.

4. (*Math.*) Determine *or* find (*a root*).

——, *n.* 1. Quotation, citation, selection, excerpt, passage quoted.

2. (*Chem.*) Essence, distillation, juice, inspissated infusion *or* decoction.

Extraction, *n.* 1. Drawing out, pulling out, elicitation, derivation, distillation, essence.

2. Lineage, descent, birth, origin, genealogy, parentage.

3. (*Math.*) Determination (*of a root*).

Extradite, *v. t.* Deliver, surrender, send to a foreign nation *or* state (*on demand for trial*).

Extraneous, *a.* 1. Foreign, extrinsic.

2. Non-pertinent, not germane, unessential, superfluous.

Extraordinary, *a.* Remarkable, unusual, special, uncommon, singular, signal, egregious, rare, prodigious, phenomenal, distinguished, amazing, monstrous, abnormal, extra, out of the way, unheard of, more than common.

Extravagance, *n.* 1. Excess, exorbitance, enormity, unreasonableness, preposterousness.

2. Irregularity, wildness, folly, excess, absurdity.

3. Prodigality, profusion, profuseness, lavishness, superabundance; hyperbolism, waste, lavish expenditure.

Extravagant, *a.* 1. Excessive, inordinate, exorbitant, unreasonable, preposterous.

2. Irregular, wild, foolish, absurd.

3. Wasteful, lavish, profuse, prodigal, spendthrift.

Extreme, *a.* 1. Outermost, utmost, farthest, uttermost, most distant, most remote.

2. Greatest, highest, of the highest degree, of the rarest kind.

3. Last, final, ultimate.

4. Extravagant, immoderate, excessive, unreasonable, drastic, intense, egregious, outrageous, radical.

——, *n.* 1. End, extremity, limit, terminal point.

2. Highest degree, acme, climax, pink, height.

3. Danger, distress.

Extremity, *n.* 1. End, termination, limb (*chiefly in pl.*), verge, edge, border, extreme.

2. Utmost point, highest degree; last resource.

3. Utmost distress, greatest difficulty.

Extricate, *v. t.* Disengage, disentangle, clear, disembarrass, relieve, liberate, deliver, free, set free.

Extrinsic, ⎫ *a.* External, outward, extra-
Extrinsical, ⎬ neous, foreign, applied from
     ⎭ without.

Extrude, *v. t.* Expel, eject, push out, force out, thrust out.

Exuberance, *n.* 1. Luxuriance, copiousness, abundance, plenitude, flood.

2. Superabundance, superfluity, redundance, redundancy, excess, overgrowth, rankness, over-luxuriance, over-abundance, wantonness, overflow, lavishness, profusion.

Exuberant, *a.* 1. Luxuriant, copious, abundant, abounding, prolific, rich, fertile, flowing.

2. Over-abundant, superabundant, superabounding, redundant, excessive, rank, over-luxuriant, profuse, lavish, overflowing, wanton.

Exudation, *n.* Excretion, secretion, sweating, oozing.

Exude, *v. t.* Excrete, secrete, sweat, discharge (*by pores*), throw out.

——, *v. i.* Ooze, be excreted, be secreted, percolate, infiltrate, come out through the pores, come out in drops *or* beads.

Exult, *v. i.* Triumph, rejoice (*for success or victory*), vaunt, jubilate, gloat, glory, leap for joy, be in transport, rejoice excessively, rejoice tauntingly.

Exultant, *a.* Exulting, triumphing, joyous, jubilant, transported, elated.

Exultation, *n.* Joy (*for success or victory*), transport, elation, delight, triumph.

EYE, *n.* 1. Organ of sight, organ of vision, "peeper," "lamp."

2. Sight, view, vision, look, estimate, judgment.

3. Watch, notice, vigilance, observation, inspection.

4. Perforation, aperture, peep-hole, eyelet, eyelet-hole.

5. Bud, shoot.

Extreme, *v. t.* Watch, observe, view, look on, ogle, fix the eye on, keep in view, have an eye on.

Eyelet, *n.* Perforation, aperture, eye, eye-let-hole.

Eyesight, *n.* 1. Vision, sense of seeing.

2. View, observation, inspection.

Eyrie, *n.* Nest (*of a bird of prey*), secure retreat.

F

Fabian, *a.* Dilatory, inactive, procrastinating, delaying.

Fable, *n.* 1. Story (*fictitious*), tale, parable, apologue, allegory, myth, legend.

2. Fiction, falsehood, lie, untruth, forgery, invention, fabrication, figment, coinage of the brain.

——, *v. i.* Tell fables, make fables, fabricate tales, write fiction.

——, *v. t.* Feign, invent, fabricate.

Fabric, *n.* 1. Building, structure, edifice, pile.

2. Texture, conformation, make, workmanship.

3. Cloth, textile, stuff, tissue, web, material.

Fabricate, *v. t.* 1. Frame, construct, build.

2. Manufacture, make, devise, compose, fashion.

3. Invent, feign, forge, coin.

Fabrication, *n.* 1. Construction.

2. Manufacture.

3. Invention, fiction, forgery, falsehood, figment, coinage of the brain, fable.

Fabulous, *a.* Invented, feigned, fictitious, romancing, legendary, mythical, apocryphal, marvellous, unreal, fabricated, coined.

Façade, *n.* [Fr.] Front (*of a building*), face, elevation, front view.

FACE, *n.* 1. Surface, external part, cover, facet, finished side.

2. Front, front part, escarpment, breast.

3. Visage, countenance, features, physiognomy, "phiz," "mug"; grimace.

4. Look, appearance, semblance, external aspect, expression.

5. Confidence, assurance, boldness, impudence, audacity, effrontery, "brass."

——, *v. t.* 1. Confront, meet in front, meet face to face.

2. Front, oppose, "buck," brave, beard, defy, dare, stand opposite to, stand over against.

3. Put a face *or* surface on, polish, dress, smooth, level.

4. Cover, put a facing on, incrust, veneer.

5. Put face upward.

——, *v. i.* Front, turn the face.

Facet, *n.* Small face *or* surface, cut, lozenge.

Facetious, *a.* 1. Witty, jocular, jocose, humorous, waggish, funny, comical, pleasant, droll.

2. Gay, merry, sportive, sprightly, lively, entertaining.

Face to face. 1. Confronting one another.

2. Close, side by side, cheek by jowl. in close proximity, *tête à tête, vis-à-vis.*

3. Immediately, without anything interposing.

Facile, *a.* 1. Easy.

2. Mild, courteous, affable, complaisant, approachable, conversable.

3. Pliant, pliable, flexible, ductile, yielding, fluent, tractable, manageable, compliant, easily persuaded.

4. Dexterous, ready, skilful.

Facilitate, *v. t.* Make easy, render less difficult.

Facility, *n.* 1. Easiness (*in doing anything*), ease.

2. Readiness, dexterity, expertness, quickness, knack, ability.

3. Pliancy, ductility, flexibility.

4. Means, resource, appliance, convenience, advantage.

Fac-simile, *n.* Exact copy, reproduction, duplicate.

FACT, *n.* 1. Incident, event, occurrence, circumstance, act, deed, performance, thing done.

2. Reality, actuality, certainty, real existence, truth.

Faction, *n.* 1. Combination (*against a government*), cabal, junto, clique, party, side, division.

2. Tumult, turbulence, turbulency, disorder, sedition, seditiousness, refractoriness, recalcitration, discord, dissension, disagreement.

Factious, *a.* 1. Turbulent, seditious, refractory, recalcitrant, rebellious, given to faction.

2. Full of faction, proceeding from faction, seditious, rebellious.

Factitious, *a.* Artificial, made by art, not natural; false.

Factor, *n.* 1. Agent, substitute, consignee, middleman, go-between, broker, commission merchant; steward, bailiff.

2. (*Math.*) Divisor, element of a product.

3. Constituent, constitutive element, determining element *or* circumstance *or* influence.

——, *v. t.* Resolve into factors, find the factors of.

Factory, *n.* Manufactory, mill, manufacturing establishment, workshop, works.

Factotum, *n.* Doer of all work, jack-at-all-trades, handy man.

Faculty, *n.* 1. Power, capability, ability, capacity, endowment, property, quality, sense, wits; reason.

2. Skill, skilfulness, ability, ableness, power, capacity, dexterity, adroitness, expertness, address, ingenuity, competency, efficiency, cleverness, aptitude, aptness, knack, turn, quickness, readiness, facility, talent, forte.

3. Department, profession, body (*of a learned profession, especially medicine*).

4. Body of professors, officers of instruction (*in a university* or *college*).

5. (*Law.*) Privilege, license, right, power, authority, prerogative.

Fade, *v. i.* 1. Vanish, disappear, evanesce, faint, die, pass away, be seen no more.

2. Decline, droop, languish, decay, wither.

3. Lose color, lose lustre, grow dim, blanch, pale, bleach; dissolve, disperse.

Fadge, *v. i.* 1. Suit, fit, agree, harmonize, be suitable.

2. Agree, maintain concord, harmonize, live in amity.

3. Succeed, hit.

Fæces, *n.* 1. Sediment, dregs, lees, settlings.

2. Excrement, dung, ordure, dejections, alvine discharges.

Fag, *v. i.* 1. Droop, sink, flag, grow weary, become fatigued, be tired.

2. Drudge, toil, work to weariness.

3. Be a fag, play the fag, do menial service.

——, *v. t.* 1. Make a fag of, compel to serve *or* drudge.

2. Tire, weary, fatigue, jade, use up, tire out, exhaust.

——, *n.* [*Especially applied in England to a schoolboy who does menial service for another.*] Drudge, menial, slave.

Fagged, *a.* Wearied, tired, fatigued, exhausted, jaded, used up, beat out.

Fagot, *n.* [Written also *Faggot.*] Bundle of sticks, fascine (*fort.*).

Fail, *v. i.* 1. Fall short, come short, be insufficient, be lacking, err, "flunk," be deficient, be wanting.

2. Decline, sink, decay, wane, fade, break, collapse, sicken, give out.

3. Cease, disappear, become extinct, be wanting.

4. Miss, miscarry, "fizzle," be unsuccessful, be frustrated, end in smoke, come to nothing, fall stillborn, flash in the pan, miss fire, miss stays, fall to the ground.

5. Omit, neglect.

6. Break, become insolvent, become bankrupt, suspend payment, "smash," "swamp."

——, *v. t.* Disappoint, be wanting to, not be sufficient for, not answer the expectation of.

Failing, *n.* 1. Decline, decay.

2. Miscarriage, failure.

3. Fault, foible, frailty, shortcoming, imperfection, deficiency, defect, weakness, infirmity, weak side, blind side.

4. Lapse, error, slip.

5. Bankruptcy, insolvency, becoming bankrupt *or* insolvent.

Failure, *n.* 1. Deficiency, defectiveness, delinquency, shortcoming.

2. Omission, neglect, fail, non-performance, slip, negligence, non-observance.

3. Miscarriage, botch, abortion, ill success, collapse, "fizzle," fiasco, muff, breakdown, flash in the pan, labor for one's pains, losing game, wild-goose chase, sleeveless errand.

4. Insolvency, bankruptcy, suspension of payment, failing, becoming bankrupt *or* insolvent, break, "smash," "crash."

5. Decay, decline, declension, loss.

Fain, *a.* Glad, pleased, rejoiced, well-pleased, eager, inclined, anxious.

——, *adv.* Gladly, joyfully, with pleasure, with joy, eagerly, willingly.

Faint, *v. i.* 1. Swoon, faint away.

2. Languish, fail, fade, grow weak, decline, fail in vigor, lose strength.

3. Be disheartened, be discouraged, be dejected, be depressed, lose courage, be dispirited, be down-hearted, sink into dejection.

——, *a.* 1. Swooning, fainting away.

2. Weak, feeble, drooping, exhausted, listless, sickly, languid.

3. Small, little, slight, inconsiderable, soft, gentle, thin.

4. Dim, dull, slight, indistinct, scarce perceptible, almost imperceptible.

5. Fearful, timid, timorous, cowardly, dastardly, faint-hearted.

6. Dejected, depressed, dispirited, disheartened, discouraged.

Faint-hearted, a. Timid, timorous, fearful, cowardly, dastardly, faint.

Fair, a. 1. Spotless, unspotted, untarnished, unblemished, unstained.

2. White, light, blond, lily.

3. Handsome, comely, beautiful, shapely.

4. Pleasant, clear, cloudless, unclouded.

5. Favorable, prosperous.

6. Promising, hopeful, propitious.

7. Open, distinct, plain, clear, unobstructed, unencumbered.

8. Frank, honest, candid, ingenuous, just, open, honorable, upright, impartial, unbiassed.

9. Reasonable, proper, equitable, just.

10. Tolerable, passable, pretty good, more than middling, above mediocrity, fairish, "so-so," moderate, indifferent, respectable, reasonable, decent, ordinary, average.

Fair-minded, a. Candid, just, equitable, impartial, unbiassed.

Fair play. Justice, equity, fairness, equitable treatment or action.

Fair-spoken, a. 1. Civil, courteous, bland, complaisant, gracious.

2. Plausible, smooth, bland, oily, unctuous.

Fairy, n. Fay, elf, pigwidgeon, demon, spirit, sprite, brownie, nix.

Faith, n. 1. Belief (that prompts to action), credence, credit, trust, assurance, confidence, dependence, reliance.

2. Creed, persuasion, tenets, dogmas, doctrines, religion, system of religion.

3. Fidelity, faithfulness, truthfulness, truth, constancy, loyalty.

4. Engagement, promise, word of honor.

Faithful, a. 1. True, loyal, devoted, constant, steadfast, staunch.

2. Trusty, trustworthy, reliable, honest, upright.

3. Truthful, trustworthy, reliable, worthy of credit, worthy of belief, to be relied on, to be depended upon.

4. Exact, strict, conscientious, accurate, close, nice.

——, n. Belonging to "the Faith," esp. Mohammedan (with the).

Faithless, a. 1. Unbelieving.

2. Perfidious, treacherous, dishonest, inconstant, fickle, variable, mutable, wavering, fluctuating, vacillating, unsteady, mercurial, shifting, false, disloyal, untruthful, truthless.

Falcate, a. (Bot.) Hooked, sickle-shaped.

Falchion, n. Scimeter.

Fall, v. i. 1. Drop, depend, descend, sink, drop down, topple, collapse, tumble, be lowered, be depressed.

2. Decrease, decline, abate, subside, ebb, be diminished, depreciate, become less, die away.

3. Sin, err, transgress, lapse, trip, trespass, commit a fault, do amiss, go astray, stumble.

4. Die, perish, come to destruction.

5. Happen, befall, come, pass, occur, chance.

6. Become (sick, asleep, in love, etc.), get.

7. Pass, come, be transferred.

FALL, n. 1. Descent, dropping, downfall, downcome, flop, plop, collapse, tumble, falling.

2. Cataract, cascade, waterfall.

3. Destruction, death, ruin, overthrow, surrender, downfall.

4. Degradation, loss of eminence, "comedown."

5. Apostasy, loss of innocence, lapse, declension, slip, going astray, failure.

6. Diminution, decrease, decline, ebb, sinking, subsidence; depreciation.

7. Sinking (of the voice), cadence, close.

8. Declivity, slope, inclination.

Fallacious, a. 1. Deceptive, delusive, deceiving, absurd, erroneous, illusive, illusory, misleading, disappointing, false.

2. Sophistical, worthless, paralogistic.

Fallacy, n. 1. Illusion, aberration, deception, deceit, delusion, "bubble," mistake, error, misconception, misapprehension.

2. Sophism, paralogism, non sequitur, sophistry, deceitful or worthless argument.

Fall away. 1. Pine, grow lean, be emaciated, lose flesh.

2. Backslide, apostatize, fall off.

3. Defect, revolt, become disloyal or disaffected, forsake the cause of.

Fall back. 1. Recede, retreat, give way, retire, yield.

2. [With on or upon.] Rally, retreat, retire.

Fallibility, n. Frailty, imperfection, uncertainty, liability to error.

Fallible, a. Frail, imperfect, weak, ignorant, uncertain, erring, liable to error or mistake.

Fall in. 1. (*Mil.*) Come into line, form into ranks.

2. Concur, consent, agree, assent, acquiesce, go with the stream, go with the current.

Falling-star, *n.* Shooting-star, meteor.

Fall in with. 1. Meet, encounter.

2. Comply with, assent to, come into.

Fall off. 1. Drop, be detached, drop off.

2. Withdraw, separate.

3. Decline, wane, dwindle, decay, fade, fail, wither.

4. Backslide, apostatize, fall away.

5. Revolt, defect, become disaffected *or* disloyal, fall away.

Fall on. 1. Drop on, descend upon.

2. Attack, assault, assail, rush upon, fall upon.

Fall out. 1. Disagree, wrangle. See QUARREL.

2. Happen, befall, chance, occur, come about, come to pass, take place.

Fallow, *a.* 1. Pale red *or* pale yellow.

2. Untilled, unsowed, left uncultivated, neglected.

3. Inert, inactive, dormant.

Fall short. Fail, be deficient.

Fall to. Begin, set about, apply one's self to.

FALSE, *a.* 1. Untrue, unveracious, mendacious, truthless, lying, contrary to truth.

2. Dishonest, perfidious, treacherous, disloyal, unfaithful, faithless, disingenuous, dishonorable, double-tongued, double-faced, false-hearted.

3. Fictitious, forged, made-up, untrustworthy, unreliable.

4. Counterfeit, spurious, forged, not genuine, pseudo, bastard, supposititious, hollow, bogus, pretended, artificial, factitious, feigned, hypocritical, make-believe, sham.

5. Incorrect, improper, erroneous, wrong, unfounded; not in tune, off pitch.

6. Fallacious, deceptive, deceiving, deceitful, delusive, misleading, disappointing.

False-hearted, *a.* Perfidious, treacherous, faithless, false, double, double-tongued, double-faced, dishonorable, disloyal.

Falsehood, *n.* 1. Falsity, want of truth, inconformity to fact *or* truth.

2. Untruth, lie, fabrication, fiction, false assertion, fib.

3. Imposture, counterfeit, cheat, treachery.

Falsetto, *n.* Head voice, artificial voice, high-pitched voice.

Falsify, *v. t.* 1. Belie, misrepresent, alter, "fake," "cook up," doctor, adulterate, counterfeit, misstate, garble, represent falsely.

2. Disprove, prove to be false, show unsound.

3. Violate, break by falsehood.

——, *v. i.* Lie, tell lies *or* falsehoods, violate the truth.

Falsity, *n.* Falsehood, untruthfulness, untruth.

Falter, *v. i.* 1. Hesitate (*in speech*), stammer, halt, quaver, lisp, "hem-and-haw," stutter.

2. Fail, waver, tremble, totter, stumble, stagger.

3. Hesitate, waver, dodder, give way, show weakness, be undecided.

Fame, *n.* 1. Rumor, report, bruit, hearsay.

2. Reputation, repute, celebrity, glory, illustriousness, luster, "kudos," eminence, greatness, notoriety, renown, honor, credit.

Familiar, *a.* 1. Conversant, well acquainted, aware, well versed.

2. Intimate, close, near, domestic, homely, friendly, amicable, fraternal, cordial, on a friendly footing, on friendly terms.

3. Friendly, social, sociable, accessible, affable, kindly, courteous, civil, companionable, conversable.

4. Unceremonious, unconstrained, free, easy, informal, free and easy.

5. Too free, lacking in proper reserve, deficient in proper respect.

6. Well-known, common, frequent.

——, *n.* 1. Intimate, intimate friend, bosom friend, boon companion, close acquaintance, near associate.

2. Familiar spirit, demon *or* evil spirit at call.

Familiarity, *n.* 1. Acquaintance, familiar knowledge, etc.

2. Intimacy, fellowship, friendship, etc.

3. Friendliness, sociability, etc.

4. Informality, freedom, etc.

5. Over-freedom, disrespect, etc.

6. General recognition, etc. See FAMILIAR.

Familiarize, *v. t.* Accustom, habituate, inure, use, train.

FAMILY, *n.* 1. Household, parents and children, brood, "people."

2. Lineage, race, tribe, clan, kindred, house, stock, strain, blood, breed, dynasty, line of ancestors.

3. Subdivision of an order, group of genera, kind, class.

Famine, *n.* Dearth, scarcity, starvation.

Famish, *v. t.* 1. Starve, kill *or* destroy with hunger.

2. Distress with hunger, pinch, exhaust by hunger.

Famish, *v. i.* 1. Starve, die of hunger, perish for want of food.

2. Be distressed by hunger, suffer extreme hunger, pine for food.

Famous, *a.* Celebrated, renowned, distinguished, illustrious, eminent, remarkable, famed, noted, notable, great, fabled, heroic, immortal; notorious, far-famed.

Fan, *v. t.* 1. Use a fan upon, cool *or* refresh with a fan.

2. Agitate, move,, beat gently, winnow.

3. Blow *or* breathe upon, cool, refresh.

4. Excite, stimulate, increase, rouse, fire.

Fanatic, *n.* Enthusiast, visionary, zealot, bigot.

Fanatic, } *a.* Enthusiastic, visionary,
Fanatical, } wild, mad, frenzied, rabid.

Fanaticism, *n.* Irrational enthusiasm, rabid zeal.

Fanciful, *a.* 1. Visionary, imaginative, whimsical, capricious; crotchety.

2. Chimerical, imaginary, ideal, fantastical, wild.

Fancy, *n.* 1. Imagination (*as exercised in sportive or whimsical moods*).

2. Pleasing conceit, happy conception, striking thought, ideal image, bright stroke.

3. Notion, idea, thought, conception, conceit, impression, apprehension, image.

4. Liking, fondness, inclination, *penchant*, approval, judgment. taste.

5. Caprice, humor, whim, crotchet, quirk, freak, vagary, whimsey, maggot, fantasy, odd fancy.

6. Phantasm, hallucination, delusion, megrim, reverie, vision, chimera, daydream, apparition.

——, *v. i.* Imagine, think, suppose, apprehend, conjecture, believe, take it.

——, *v. t.* 1. Conceive, imagine, form a conception of, figure to one's self.

2. Like, be pleased with, have a fancy for, approve of.

——, *a.* 1. Imaginative, of the fancy, fancied.

2. Ornamental (*rather than useful*), elegant, fine, nice.

3. Fanciful, extravagant, beyond all real worth.

Fane, *n.* (*Poetical.*) Temple, church, shrine, sanctuary.

Fanfare, *n.* [Fr.] Flourish of trumpets.

Fanfaron, *n.* 1. Bully, hector, blusterer, swaggerer, vaporer, braggadocio.

2. Empty boaster, vain pretender, blatherskite.

Fanfaronade, *n.* 1. Bluster, swaggering, boasting, bragging, bullying, hectoring, gasconade, braggadocio.

2. Empty boasting, vain pretence, ostentation, flourish, bombast, rodomontade.

Fang, *n.* 1. Tusk, pointed tooth.

2. Claw, talon, nail.

Fantasia, *n.* (*Mus.*) Fantastical air, capricious composition, *capriccio.*

Fantastic, } *a.* 1. Imaginary, fanciful,
Fantastical, } chimerical, visionary, unreal, romantic, merely ideal.

2. Whimsical, capricious, odd, queer, quaint, grotesque, strange, wild, bizarre.

Far, *a.* 1. Remote, distant, long, protracted.

2. Farther, remoter, more distant.

3. Estranged, alienated, hostile.

FAR, *adv.* 1. To a great distance, widely, remotely.

2. Almost, well-nigh, in great part.

3. Very much, in a great degree, greatly.

Farce, *n.* 1. Burlesque, caricature, travesty, parody, after-piece, low comedy, ludicrous representation.

2. Mere show, ridiculous pageantry, empty parade, utter sham, mockery.

3. Stuffing, forcemeat.

Farcical, *a.* Droll, ludicrous, ridiculous, absurd.

Fardel, *n.* 1. Bundle, pack, burden, load.

2. Trouble, annoyance, ill, burden.

Fare, *v. i.* 1. Go, pass, travel, journey.

2. Be situated (*with respect to what may befall one*), be treated, prosper, prove, happen, turn out; be in any state, go through any experience.

3. Feed, be entertained.

——, *n.* 1. Charge (*for conveyance of a person*), passage-money, price of a ticket.

2. Victuals, commons, provisions, food, table, board.

3. Condition, experience, fortune, luck, outcome.

Farewell, *adv.* or *interj.* Adieu, good-by.

——, *n.* 1. Adieu, valediction, leave-taking.

2. Leave, departure, *congé*, parting, valedictory, last look, last glance.

Far-fetched, *a.* Recondite, abstruse, forced, strained, catachrestic, studiously sought.

Farinaceous, *a.* Yielding farina *or* flour; (consisting) of meal *or* flour, starchy; mealy, like meal.

FARM, *n.* Landed estate.

——, *v. t.* 1. Let out (*land, revenues, etc.*).

2. Take on lease (*land, revenues, etc.*).

3. Cultivate (*land*), till.

Farm, *v. i.* Till the soil, carry on a farm, do farmer's work, practise husbandry.

Farmer, *n.* 1. Agriculturist, husbandman, cultivator *or* tiller of the soil.

2. Collector, tax-gatherer; lessee of taxes, customs, etc.

Farming, *n.* Agriculture, husbandry.

Farrago, *n.* Medley, mixture, jumble, hodge-podge, hotch-potch, salmagundi, gallimaufry, olla-podrida, potpourri.

Farrier, *n.* 1. Shoer of horses, horseshoer, blacksmith.

2. Horse-doctor, horse-leech, veterinary surgeon.

Far-sighted, *a.* 1. Long-sighted.

2. Of great foresight, far-seeing, penetrating to remote consequences.

Farther, *adv.* 1. Beyond, further, more remotely, to *or* at a greater distance, past.

2. Moreover, besides, furthermore.

——, *a.* 1. Further, more remote, remoter, ulterior, at a greater distance, more distant.

2. Additional.

Farthest, *a.* Furthest, remotest, most remote, ultimate, most distant.

Farthingale, *n.* Crinoline, hoop, hoop-skirt.

Fascinate, *v. t.* 1. Stupefy, bewitch, transfix, overpower, affect *or* bind with a spell, spell-bind.

2. Charm, enchant, bewitch, enrapture, entrance, captivate, absorb, catch, delight, enamour.

Fascination, *n.* Enchantment, spell, charm, absorption, witchery, witchcraft, magic, sorcery.

Fash, *v. t.* [*Scotch.*] Vex, tease, plague, harass, torment, perplex, trouble, worry.

——, *n.* [*Scotch.*] Trouble, care, anxiety, vexation.

Fashion, *n.* 1. Form, figure, shape, make, cut, cast, stamp, mould, pattern, model, appearance, conformation, configuration.

2. Way, manner, method, sort.

3. Custom (*particularly as respects dress*), mode, style, usage, conventionality, conventionalism, general practice; fad, vogue, "the rage."

4. Gentility, formal breeding.

5. People of fashion, the *beau monde;* high life.

——, *v. t.* 1. Form, shape, mould, pattern, design, make, create, contrive, forge, give figure to.

2. Adapt, accommodate, fit, suit, adjust.

Fashionable, *a.* 1. According to (prevailing) fashion, in fashion, in vogue, *à la mode,* modish, stylish, "all the go," the rage.

2. Following fashion, addicted to fashion, who set fashion, of fashion, who affect elegance.

3. Customary, usual, prevailing, current, in vogue.

Fast, *v. i.* Abstain from food, forbear eating, go without food, go hungry.

——, *n.* 1. Fasting, abstinence from food.

2. Fast-day, day of fasting, banyan day.

——, *a.* 1. Fastened, fixed, close, tight, immovable, firm, tenacious.

2. Constant, steadfast, stanch; permanent, faithful, resolute, unswerving, unwavering.

3. Fortified, strong, impregnable.

4. Sound, deep, profound.

5. Swift, quick, fleet, rapid.

6. Dissipated, dissolute, wild, giddy, reckless, thoughtless, thriftless, extravagant.

——, *adv.* 1. Firmly, tightly, immovably.

2. Swiftly, quickly, rapidly.

3. Extravagantly, prodigally, recklessly, wildly.

Fasten, *v. t.* 1. Secure, bind, tie, attach, fix, catch, lock, gird, bolt, chain, pin, lace, strap, cleat, tether, etc., make fast, belay (*naut.*), bend (*naut.*).

2. Join, connect, attach, hold, unite, hold together.

——, *v. i.* Be fixed, fix one's self, cling, cleave, catch hold.

Fastidious, *a.* Squeamish, difficult, queasy, particular, delicate, exquisite, precise, critical, dainty, finicking, "niminy-piminy," "prunes-and-prisms," precious over-nice, over-delicate, hard to please.

Fasting, *n.* Fast, abstinence from food.

Fastness, *n.* Fort, fortress, stronghold, castle, fortified place.

FAT, *a.* 1. Oleaginous, unctuous, adipose, oily, greasy, fatty.

2. Plump, fleshy, corpulent, obese, portly, gross, paunchy, pudgy, pursy.

3. Coarse, heavy, dull, sluggish, stupid, fat-witted.

4. Rich, profitable, lucrative.

5. Fertile, fruitful, productive, rich.

Fatal, *a.* 1. Deadly, mortal, lethal.

2. Calamitous, destructive, ruinous, mischievous, baneful, baleful, pernicious, most harmful.

Fatalism, *n.* Necessarianism, necessitarianism, submission to fate.

Fatality, *n.* 1. Destiny, fate, inevitable necessity.

2. Mortality.

3. Calamity, disaster.

Fate, *n.* 1. Destiny, destination, fatality, inevitable necessity.

2. Doom, lot, die, cup, experience, portion, fortune, weird, predetermined event.

3. Death, destruction, ruin.

4. Final event, ultimate fortune.

Fated, *a.* Doomed, destined, appointed, foredoomed, predestined, predestinated, preordained, predetermined.

Fateful, *a.* Momentous, portentous, ominous.

Fates, *n. pl.* (*Mythol.*) Destinies, Parcæ, three sisters (*Clotho, Lachesis, Atropos*).

Fat-headed, *a.* Dull, thick-witted. See STUPID.

FATHER, *n.* 1. Male parent, sire, "governor," "dad," "papa," "pater."

2. Ancestor, forefather, progenitor.

3. Creator, maker, originator, author, inventor.

——, *v. t.* 1. Beget, engender.

2. Adopt, become a (*moral*) father to.

3. Assume the authorship of, become responsible for, acknowledge.

Fatherhood, *n.* Fathership, paternity.

Fatherland, *n.* Mother country, native land, one's country.

Fatherly, *a.* Paternal, tender, kind, benign, protecting.

Fathom, *n.* Six feet, two yards.

——, *v. t.* 1. Sound, try the depth of, measure by a sounding-line.

2. Divine, penetrate, reach, understand, comprehend.

Fathomless, *a.* Bottomless, abysmal, profound, immeasurable, deep; impenetrable, incomprehensible, obscure.

Fatigue, *n.* 1. Weariness, lassitude, tiredness, exhaustion.

2. Labor, toil, hardship.

——, *v. t.* Tire, weary, exhaust, jade, fag.

Fatten, *v. t.* 1. Make fat.

2. Fertilize, make fertile.

——, *v. i.* Grow fat, batten.

Fatty, *a.* Unctuous, oleaginous, oily, fat, adipose, greasy.

Fatuity, *n.* 1. Foolishness, imbecility, idiocy, feebleness of intellect, want of understanding.

2. Folly, madness, inane absurdity, infatuation.

Fatuous, *a.* 1. Foolish, stupid, witless, driveling, idiotic.

2. Infatuated, mad, senseless, absurdly foolish.

3. Illusory, deceptive (*like the "ignis fatuus"*).

Fat-witted, *a.* Dull, heavy, fat. See STUPID.

Fault, *n.* 1. Defect, blemish, flaw, imperfection, spot, shortcoming, infirmity, offence, negligence, foible, failing, weakness, frailty, obliquity, moral defect.

2. Misdeed, misdemeanor, offence, trespass, vice, wrong, delinquency, transgression, error, peccadillo, lapse, slip, indiscretion.

3. Mistake (*of judgment*), error, lapse, slip; culpability, blame.

Fault-finder, *n.* Censurer, objector, complainer, murmurer, repiner.

Faultless, *a.* 1. Perfect, without blemish, without fault, free from defect.

2. Innocent, guiltless, blameless, stainless, sinless, immaculate, spotless.

Faulty, *a.* 1. Bad, defective, imperfect.

2. Blamable, culpable, censurable, reprehensible, blameworthy, worthy of censure.

Faun, *n.* Sylvan, woodland deity.

Faux pas. [Fr.] Mistake, blunder, indiscretion, false step.

Faveolate, *a.* (*Bot.*) Alveolate, cellular, favose, favaginous, honeycombed.

Favillous, *a.* Ashy, ashen, cinereous, cineritious, like ashes.

Favor, *v. t.* 1. Countenance, befriend, encourage, patronize.

2. Approve, be in favor of, regard with favor.

3. Facilitate, ease, make easier, be favorable *or* propitious to.

4. Support, aid, help, assist, oblige.

5. Humor, indulge, spare, ease, palliate, extenuate, represent favorably *or* in a favorable light.

——, *n.* 1. Kindness, friendliness, countenance, esteem, benignity, approval, grace, kind regard, good-will, propitious aspect.

2. Benefit, kindness, act of grace, good deed, benefaction, boon, dispensation, kind act, friendly turn.

3. Patronage, championship, support, popularity.

4. Gift, present, token of good-will, love-token.

5. Decoration, knot, rosette, bunch of ribbons, badge.

6. Leave, permission, pardon, goodwill.

7. Advantage, protection, cover, indulgence.

8. (*Law.*) Bias, partiality, prejudice.

Favorable, *a.* 1. Friendly, kind, willing, well disposed, propitious, auspicious.

2. Conducive, contributing, propitious.

3. Advantageous, beneficial, benign, auspicious, fair, helpful, good, convenient, suitable, adapted, fit.

Favorite, *a.* 1. Dear, darling, beloved.

2. Preferred, pet, especially liked, choice; probable winner.

Favoritism, *n.* Partiality.

Favose, *a.* (*Bot.*) Alveolate, cellular, faveolate, favaginous, honeycombed.

Fawn, *v. i.* Crouch, cringe, bow, stoop, kneel, creep, dangle, fall on one's knees, curry favor, toady, truckle, play the sycophant.

Fawning, *n.* Sycophancy, servility, obsequiousness, cringing, mean flattery.

Fawn upon. 1. Cringe to, crouch to, truckle to.

2. Flatter, wheedle, cajole, blandish, pay court to.

Fay, *n.* Fairy, elf.

——, *v. t.* (*Shipbuilding.*) Fit, joint, join closely.

——, *v. i.* Fit, lie close, make a good joint.

Fealty, *n.* 1. Allegiance, homage, loyalty (*to a feudal lord*).

2. Fidelity, loyalty, faithfulness, honor, good faith, devotion.

FEAR, *n.* 1. Alarm, dread, phobia, apprehension, fright, "funk," scare, affright, terror, horror, dismay, consternation, panic.

2. Tremor, trembling, trepidation, perturbation, flutter, disquietude, palpitation, quaking, quivering.

3. Anxiety, solicitude, concern, apprehension, misdoubt, misgiving, qualm.

4. Veneration, reverence, awe, dread, reverential regard.

——, *v. t.* 1. Dread, apprehend, be afraid of.

2. Apprehend, be solicitous, anxious, *or* concerned about.

3. Reverence, revere, venerate, stand in awe of, have a reverential regard for.

——, *v. i.* Be afraid, alarmed, frightened, *or* scared, have apprehensions, live in terror, stand aghast.

Fearful, *a.* 1. Afraid, apprehensive, haunted with fear.

2. Timid, timorous, nervous, faint-hearted, chicken-hearted, white-livered, cowardly, pusillanimous, showing the white feather, easily frightened.

3. Terrible, dreadful, frightful, dire, direful, shocking, horrible.

4. Awful, to be reverenced *or* revered.

Fearless, *a.* Dauntless, unterrified, courageous, daring, bold, intrepid, brave, valorous, valiant, gallant.

Feasibility, *n.* Practicability, feasibleness.

Feasible, *a.* Practicable, possible, suitable.

Feast, *n.* 1. Banquet, treat, entertainment, carousal, regale, sumptuous repast, symposium.

2. Festival, holiday, *fête*, day of feasting, festive celebration, joyful anniversary, day of rejoicing, festal day.

3. Enjoyment, delight.

——, *v. i.* Eat (*plentifully*), be entertained, fare sumptuously.

——, *v. t.* 1. Entertain sumptuously, feed luxuriously.

2. Delight, gratify, rejoice, gladden.

Feat, *n.* 1. Act, deed, exploit, achievement, accomplishment.

2. Trick, act of dexterity, "stunt."

FEATHER, *n.* 1. Plume.

2. Kind, nature, species.

Feathery, *a.* Plumose.

Featly, *a.* Nimbly, dexterously, adroitly, skilfully.

Feature, *n.* 1. Lineament, cast of the face, turn of expression.

2. Fashion, make, conformation, aspect, appearance.

3. Outline, prominent part.

4. Characteristic, trait, point, item, mark.

Feaze, *v. t.* Untwist (*as the end of a rope*), ravel, ravel out, unravel.

Fecund, *a.* Fruitful, prolific, fertile, rich, impregnated, productive.

Fecundate, *v. t.* 1. Make prolific, make fruitful, enrich.

2. Impregnate, cause to germinate, cover with pollen *or* germinal fluid, fertilize.

Fecundation, *n.* 1. Enriching, rendering fertile *or* prolific.

2. Impregnation, fertilization.

Fecundity, *n.* Fruitfulness, fertility, productiveness, prolific character *or* quality.

Federal, *a.* 1. Treaty, founded on *or* relating to treaty, pertaining to alliance.

2. Confederate, federated, united.

Federation, *n.* 1. Uniting, federating, federation, confederation, leaguing, union, allying, alliance, forming *or* formation into a confederacy.

2. League, alliance, coalition, union, confederation, confederacy, federacy, combination, co-partnership, federal union, federal compact.

Fee, *n.* 1. Pay (*for professional service*), compensation, remuneration, honorarium, charge, toll, "tip."

2. Feud, fief, fee-simple, absolute title *or* possession, unconditional tenure, benefice.

——, *v. t.* Pay, reward, recompense, give a fee to.

FEEBLE, *a.* 1. Weak, not strong.

2. Debilitated, anemic, enervated, sickly, infirm, languishing, languid, declining, drooping, frail.

3. Faint, imperfect, dim, indistinct, without vigor, lacking intensity *or* vividness *or* force.

Feed, *v. t.* 1. Give food to, furnish with provisions, supply with nourishment.

2. Supply, contribute to, provide for.

3. Nourish, cherish, sustain.

4. Supply with material, fuel.

——, *v. i.* 1. Eat, take food, take nourishment.

2. Subsist, sustain life, fare.

——, *n.* 1. Food (*for beasts*), provender, fodder.

2. Feeding mechanism, feeder.

Feel, *v. i.* 1. Perceive (*by the touch*), have feeling.

2. Be perceived (*by the touch*).

3. Be moved (*in the affections*), be excited, be stirred, be warmed, be wrought up, be impressed.

4. Have the impression, have the consciousness of being, be conscious of being (*sorry, grieved, hurt,* or *the like*).

——, *v. t.* 1. Touch, handle, feel of, sound, probe.

2. Experience, suffer *or* enjoy, have the sense of.

3. Be affected by, be moved by.

4. Sound, try, prove, put to the test.

Feeling, *a.* 1. Affecting, moving, touching, melting, pathetic.

2. Sensitive, tender, sympathetic.

FEELING, *n.* 1. Sense of touch.

2. Sensation, perception by touch, sentience.

3. Sensibility, emotion, sentiment, passion, soul, heart-strings, sympathy, affection, impression.

4. Tenderness, susceptibility, sensibility, sentiment, fine feeling, delicate sentiment.

5. Attitude, opinion, impression.

Feign, *v. t.* 1. Invent, imagine, devise, fabricate, forge.

2. Counterfeit, simulate, sham, affect, assume, pretend to, put on, make a show of.

Feint, *n.* 1. Pretence, blind, artifice, trick, expedient, stratagem, make-believe, false appearance.

2. (*Mil.*) Mock attack, pretended movement.

Felicitate, *v. t.* 1. Congratulate, wish joy to, rejoice with.

2. (*Rarer.*) Delight, bless, beatify, fill with happiness.

Felicitation, *n.* Congratulation, wish for happiness.

Felicitous, *a.* 1. Fit, appropriate, apt, pertinent, inspired, happily expressed, opportune, seasonable, well-timed, happy, skilful, ingenious.

2. Prosperous, successful, fortunate, lucky, auspicious, propitious.

Felicity, *n.* 1. Bliss, blissfulness, blessedness, happiness, gladness.

2. Aptness, aptitude, propriety, fitness, readiness, grace, suitableness, appropriateness, felicitousness.

3. Success, (good) luck, (good) fortune.

Fell, *a.* Cruel, inhuman, barbarous, ruthless, relentless, unrelenting, implacable, pitiless, malignant, malign, malicious, savage, ferocious, fierce, sanguinary, bloody, blood-thirsty, Vandalic; deadly, destructive.

——, *v. t.* 1. Prostrate, level, hurl down, knock down, lay prostrate, bring to the ground.

2. Cut down, hew down, lay low.

Fellow, *n.* 1. Companion, associate, comrade.

2. Equal, peer, compeer.

3. Mate, counterpart, match, one of a pair.

4. [*Eng.*] Member (*of a college, participating in its instruction and sharing its revenues*), don.

5. Person, "customer," "cove," etc., individual.

Fellowship, *n.* 1. Brotherhood, companionship, comradeship, familiarity, intimacy, close acquaintance.

2. Partnership, participation, joint interest, membership.

3. Converse, intercourse, communion.

4. [With *good.*] Sociability, sociableness, affability, kindliness, good company, jolly companionship.

Felon, *n.* 1. Culprit, criminal, malefactor, convict, outlaw.

2. Whitlow, inflammation of finger *or* toe.

Felonious, *a.* 1. Malignant, malign, malicious, villanous, nefarious, infamous, heinous, atrocious, cruel, felon.

2. Perfidious, traitorous, base, disloyal.

3. (*Law.*) Deliberately criminal, criminal, with malice prepense.

Felony, *n.* Crime (*punishable by death* or *by imprisonment*), high crime, heinous crime, gross offence.

FEMALE, *a.* 1. Breeding, bearing, conceiving, offspring-bearing, child-bearing.

2. Pistillate, pistil-bearing, fertile.

3. Feminine, delicate, soft, weak, gentle, womanly, womanlike, ladylike, etc.

Feminine, *a.* 1. Soft, tender, delicate, female. See WOMANLY.

2. Effeminate, unmanly, weak.

Feminity, } *n.* 1. Female quality, feminineness, muliebrity, feminality, womanhood, womanliness.
Femininity, }

2. Effeminacy, effeminateness, womanishness, softness, weakness, unmanliness, want of masculine force.

Fen, *n.* Marsh, swamp, bog, moor, morass, quagmire.

Fence, *n.* 1. Protecting enclosure, — wall, hedge, post-and-rail framing, wire-guard, palings, barrier, palisade, stockade, hoarding, etc. (*as the case may be*).

2. Shield, guard, security, protection, defence.

3. Fencing, art of self-defence, swordsmanship, sword-play.

4. Defensive argument, skill in refutation.

5. Receiver (*of stolen goods*).

——, *v. t.* 1. Enclose with a fence.

2. Guard, fortify, defend.

——, *v. i.* 1. Practise fencing, use the sword.

2. Shuffle, evade, equivocate, prevaricate, hedge; guard, parry.

Fencing, *n.* Manual defence (*with small swords* or *foils*), art of self-defence, swordsmanship, fence.

Fend off. (*Naut.*) Keep off, ward off, keep from collision.

Fenny, *a.* Marshy, swampy, boggy, fennish.

Ferine, *a.* Wild (*as lions, tigers, etc.*), untamed, ferocious, savage, fierce, ravenous, rapacious.

Ferment, *n.* 1. Yeast, leaven, barm.

2. Fermentation, fungic transformation.

3. Agitation, commotion, tumult, heat, glow, fever, state of excitement.

——, *v. t.* 1. Set in fermentation, set fermenting, produce fermentation in, transform by means of a ferment.

2. Excite, agitate, heat.

——, *v. i.* 1. "Work," be in a ferment, undergo fermentation, be fermented.

2. Be excited, be agitated, be on fire.

Ferocious, *a.* 1. Untamed (*like a wild beast*), savage, fierce, wild, ravenous, rapacious, ferine.

2. Barbarous, cruel, inhuman, brutal, fell, violent, truculent, remorseless, ruthless, relentless, merciless, pitiless, sanguinary, bloody, bloodthirsty, murderous, Vandalic.

Ferocity, *n.* 1. Savageness, fierceness, ferociousness, wildness, rapacity.

2. Barbarity, cruelty, inhumanity.

Ferret out. Search out.

FERTILE, *a.* 1. Prolific, fecund, breeding, bearing.

2. Fruitful, productive, rich, plenteous, luxuriant, exuberant, teeming.

3. (*Bot.*) Fruit-bearing, pistillate, female.

Fertility, *n.* 1. Fecundity, fertileness.

2. Fruitfulness, productiveness, plenteousness, exuberance, luxuriance, abundance, richness.

Fertilize, *v. t.* 1. Enrich, make fertile, make fruitful.

2. Fecundate, impregnate, supply with pollen *or* semen.

Fervent, *a.* 1. Hot, glowing, burning, melting, seething.

2. Ardent, fiery, earnest, eager, zealous, warm, glowing, animated, vehement, passionate, intense, fierce, impassioned, fervid.

Fervid, *a.* 1. Hot, burning, boiling, seething, fiery, fervent.

2. Ardent, earnest, glowing. See FERVENT, 2.

Fervor, *n.* 1. Heat, warmth.

2. Ardor, intensity, zeal, earnestness, eagerness, fervency.

Festal, *a.* Convivial. See FESTIVE.

Fester, *v. i.* 1. Rankle, corrupt, suppurate, ulcerate; putrefy, rot.

2. Become malignant, grow virulent *or* violent, rankle.

——, *n.* 1. Pustule, sore, abscess, imposthume, gathering.

2. Festering, rankling.

Festival, *n.* Feast, carnival, gala day, jubilee, holiday, festive celebration, (joyful) anniversary, day of rejoicing, *fête*.

Festive, *a.* Convivial, jovial, joyous, gay, merry, jolly, uproarious, carnival, mirthful, festal.

Festivity, *n.* Conviviality, gayety, joyousness, jollity, joyfulness, merry-making, social joy.

Festoon, *n.* Hanging garland, looped garland.

——, *v. t.* 1. Loop, loop up, wreathe, form into festoons.

2. Decorate with festoons, hang with looped garlands.

Fetch, *v. t.* 1. Bring (*when one goes for the purpose of bringing*), go and bring, elicit, get.

2. Perform, make, effect, bring to accomplishment, achieve.

3. (*Naut.*) Reach, attain, arrive at, come to, get to.

——, *n.* Trick, artifice, ruse, stratagem, dodge, sharp practice.

Fetch a compass. Make a circuit.

Fête, *v. t.* Feast, honor with an entertainment.

Fetich, *n.* 1. Object of superstition *or* superstitious awe; charm, medicine, talisman.

2. Object of unreasoning devotion.

Fetichism, *n.* 1. Fetich-worship.

2. Superstitious regard, unreasoning devotion.

Fetid, *a.* Stinking, offensive, noisome, mephitic, foul, rank, rancid, malodorous, strong-smelling, rank-smelling.

Fetor, *a.* Stench, stink, foul odor, offensive odor, strong smell.

Fetter, *n.* Shackle (*for the feet*), chain, bond, clog, hamper.

——, *v. t.* 1. Shackle (*the feet*), clog, trammel, hamper, put fetters on.

2. Chain, bind, tie, confine, restrain, hamper, trammel, encumber.

Feud, *n.* 1. Quarrel, broil, contention, clashing, fray, affray, contest, strife, dissension, jarring, rupture, bickering, falling out.

2. Blood-feud, hereditary enmity, vendetta, clan-quarrel, family-feud.

3. Fee, fief.

Feudalism, *n.* Feudal system.

Fever, *n.* 1. Febrile affection, febrile disease.

2. Heat, flush, agitation, excitement, ferment, fire, ardor, desire.

Few, *a.* Not many, small in number, hardly any, scarcely any.

Fewness, *n.* Paucity, small number, scarcity, sparsity.

Fey, *a.* [*Scotch.*] Doomed (*unwittingly*), death-doomed, death-smitten, impelled to foretoken one's own doom, death, *or* destruction, possessed by fatal propensities.

Fiasco, *n.* [It.] Failure, fizzle, abortive attempt, ignominious failure.

Fiat, *n.* Decree, order, ordinance, command.

Fib, *n.* (*Colloq. and euphemistic.*) Lie, falsehood, intentional untruth.

Fibre, *n.* Filament, thread, staple, pile, strand.

Fibril, *n.* Small fibre, slender thread.

Fibrous, *a.* Filamentous, stringy.

Fickle, *a.* Wavering, inconstant, faithless, unsteady, unstable, variable, vacillating, veering, shifting, mutable, volatile, mercurial, changeable, fitful, irresolute, unsettled, capricious, like a weather-cock.

FICTION, *n.* 1. Invention, fancy, fantasy, imagination.

2. Novel, romance, work of fiction, feigned story.

3. Fabrication, figment, invention, fable, falsehood, lie, forgery.

Fictitious, *a.* 1. Feigned, invented, imaginary, assumed, fabulous, fanciful, unreal, purely ideal, mythical.

2. False, counterfeit, spurious, supposititious, "dummy," artificial.

Fiddle, *n.* Violin.

——, *v. i.* 1. Play on a fiddle.

2. Trifle, dawdle, lose time, waste time, idle away time, fritter away time, fool away time.

Fiddle-de-dee, *interj.* Nonsense, stuff, fudge, moonshine.

Fiddle-faddle, *n.* (*Colloq.*) Nonsense, trifling, frivolity, stuff, twaddle, twattle, prate, gabble, gibberish, gibble-gabble.

Fiddling, *a.* Trifling, frivolous, trivial, idle. See FIDDLE-FADDLE.

Fidelity, *n.* 1. Faithfulness, devotedness, devotion, truth, .true-heartedness, loyalty, fealty, constancy, dutifulness, adherence to duty, observance of good faith.

2. Accuracy, closeness, exactness, faithfulness, precision.

Fidget, *v. i.* 1. Move nervously about, twitch, hitch, hitch about.

2. Fret, chafe, worry, be uneasy, be restive, be impatient, worry one's self.

——, *n.* Uneasiness, restlessness, impatience, fidgetiness.

Fiduciary, *n.* Trustee, depositary.

——, *a.* 1. Confident, undoubting, trustful, firm, steadfast, unwavering, fiducial.

2. Trusty, trustworthy, reliable.

3. Held in trust, in the nature of a trust, confidential.

Fief, *n.* Fee, feud, feudal estate.

FIELD, *n.* 1. Tract of land (*for tillage* or *for pasture*), clearing, glebe, meadow, open country; land used for special crops, etc., *or* sports.

2. Battle-field, field of battle; scene of military operations, theatre of war.

3. Surface, expanse, range, scope, extent, sphere of activity; opportunity, room.

4. Province, department, domain, region, realm.

Fiend, *n.* 1. Demon, devil, infernal spirit, malignant supernatural being, hellhound.

2. Supremely malignant person, demon, devil, monster, utterly malicious being, atrocious being, monster of cruelty *or* malice.

3. Hopeless addict; enthusiast, "fan."

Fiendish, *a.* Diabolical, devilish, demoniac, hellish, infernal, malignant, malign, malicious, malevolent, implacable, atrocious, cruel, delighting in cruelty.

Fierce, *a.* 1. Savage, ferocious, ravenous, furious, cruel, infuriate, barbarous, fell.

2. Violent, vehement, impetuous, turbulent, truculent, murderous, tigerish, etc., tearing, uncurbed, untamed, fiery, passionate.

Fiery, *a.* 1. Igneous, of fire.

2. Hot, heated, fervid, fervent, glowing, lurid, flaming.

3. Ardent, impetuous, vehement, fierce, passionate, impassioned, fervent, fervid, glowing, inflamed, flaming.

Fight, *v. i.* 1. Combat, war, battle, contend (*in arms*), draw the sword, take up arms, go to war.

2. Do battle, ply one's weapons, contend, struggle, strive.

3. Come to blows, engage in fisticuffs, fall to blows *or* loggerheads, scuffle, box, brawl, spar, bicker, skirmish.

4. Contend, contest, struggle, strive, dispute, oppose, wrestle, make resistance, act in opposition.

——, *v. t.* 1. War against, combat against, contend against, join battle with, break a lance with, encounter, engage, come to close quarters with.

2. Carry through (*by fighting*), win, gain, sustain, maintain.

3. Wage, carry on, conduct.

4. Manœuvre, manage (*in battle*), handle, carry through the fight.

FIGHT, *n.* 1. Combat, battle, conflict, contest, struggle, engagement, encounter, action, affair, quarrel, brush, fray, affray, *mêlée.*

2. Affray, fray, personal encounter, turn at fisticuffs.

3. Broil, riot, *mêlée,* affray, "row," brawl.

4. Fighting temper, spirit, resistance, disposition to struggle, pugnacity, pluck.

Fighter, *n.* Combatant, warrior. See CHAMPION.

Fighting, *n.* Contention, strife, quarrel, warfare, warring.

Figment, *n.* Invention, fiction, fabrication, fable.

Figurative, *a.* 1. Typical, representative, symbolic, emblematical.

2. Tropical, metaphorical.

3. Flowery, florid, ornate.

Figure, *n.* 1. Form, shape, conformation, configuration, outline.

2. Image, likeness, effigy, representation (*in sculpture, carving, etc.*).

3. Appearance (*as respects action or conduct*); distinguished appearance.

4. Design (*on cloth, paper, etc.*), pattern; diagram, drawing.

5. (*Rhet.*) Metaphor, trope, image, metaphorical term *or* expression.

6. (*Theol.*) Type, emblem, symbol.

7. (*Arith.*) Digit, number, numeral, character.

8. Evolution (*dance*).

——, *v. t.* 1. Adorn (*with figures*), diversify, ornament, variegate.

2. Represent, symbolize, signify, typify, depict, delineate, be typical of, shadow forth.

3. Imagine, image, conceive, picture, represent, have an idea of.

4. Make a drawing of, make a representation of.

5. Calculate, compute, cipher.

——, *v. i.* 1. Appear, act, perform, take *or* sustain the part of.

2. Make a figure, make a distinguished appearance, be distinguished, be conspicuous.

3. Show off, cut a dash, make a great show, cut a figure.

Figure up. (*Colloq.*) 1. Add, sum up, find the amount of.

2. Calculate, reckon, compute.

Filament, *n.* Fibre, thread, strand, hair, gossamer; tendril, cirrus, fibril.

Filamentous, *a.* 1. Filiform, thread-shaped, fibrillous.

2. Consisting of filaments, fibrous.

Filch, *v. t.* Pilfer, purloin, steal, crib, "snitch."

File, *n.* 1. Toothed *or* threaded tool, rasp.

2. (*Mil.*) Row (*of soldiers ranged one behind another*), line.

3. Bundle of papers, roll, list.

——, *v. t.* 1. Rasp, rub down with a file, smooth *or* finish with a file.

2. Place on file, record, pigeonhole.

3. Smooth, polish.

——, *v. i.* March in a file.

Filibuster, *n.* 1. Pirate, freebooter, buccaneer, sea-robber, sea-rover; lawless adventurer.

2. Obstructionist.

Filiform, *a.* Filamentous, thread-shaped, long and slender.

Fill, *v. t.* 1. Make full, fill up, inject with; pervade, occupy, occupy completely.

2. Dilate, expand, stretch, trim, distend.

3. Store, supply, furnish, replenish, stock.

4. Satisfy, content, sate, glut, satiate, cloy, stuff, cram, pack, line, congest, crowd, saturate, suffuse, pall.

5. Occupy (*as a place of trust*), hold, fulfil, perform the duties of, officiate in, execute, discharge, do.

Fillet, *n.* Band, bandage, snood.

Film, *n.* 1. Pellicle, thin skin *or* coating, membrane, nebula, veil, scum, gauze, cloud.

2. Thread, fine thread, cobweb thread.

Filter, *v. t.* Strain, filtrate, pass through a strainer *or* filter.

——, *v. i.* Percolate, transude, exude, ooze.

——, *n.* Strainer.

Filth, *n.* 1. Dirt, nastiness, foul matter, ordure.

2. Grossness, foulness, corruption, pollution, impurity, nastiness, defilement, uncleanness, vileness, obscenity, indecency; squalor.

Filthy, *a.* 1. Dirty, nasty, foul, defiled, unclean, squalid.

2. Impure, gross, corrupt, unclean, foul.

Filtration, *n.* Filtering, straining.

Final, *a.* 1. Last, latest, ultimate, eventual, terminal, extreme.

2. Decisive, conclusive, definitive, irrevocable.

Finale, *n.* [It.] End, termination, conclusion, closing part (*primarily and strictly, of an opera* or *a concert*).

Finality, *n.* 1. Completeness, conclusiveness, terminality, definitiveness, final character.

2. Final settlement, final arrangement, consummation.

Finance, *n.* 1. Monetary theory, science *or* art of monetary relations, theory of revenue *or* fiscal relations.

2. *Revenue, money, money matters.

Finances, *n. pl.* 1. Revenues, public funds, public resources, treasury, fiscal resources.

2. (*Colloq.*) Income, money matters, resources, property, affairs (*of a private person*).

Financial, *a.* Monetary, pecuniary, fiscal.

Find, *v. t.* 1. Discover, fall upon, light upon, meet with, fall in with.

2. Obtain, get, procure, gain, arrive at, attain to; regain the use of.

3. Observe, remark, notice, perceive, ascertain, discover (*by experiment*).

4. Detect, catch.

5. Supply, furnish, contribute, provide.

——, *v. i.* (*Law.*) Declare a verdict, determine an issue, decide.

——, *n.* Discovery.

Find fault. Complain, grumble.

Find fault with. Blame, censure, criticise, reprove.

Find out. 1. Discover, detect, bring to light.

2. Ascertain, decipher, solve, unriddle, make out, get at.

Fine, *a.* 1. Minute, small, little, comminuted.

2. Slender, delicate, capillary.

3. Light, of delicate material, of fine texture, choice.

4. Keen, sharp, exact.

5. Thin, subtile, tenuous, attenuated.

6. Exquisite, nice, refined, fastidious, sensitive, subtle.

7. Excellent, superior, very good, "nifty," "bully," "dandy," etc., superb.

8. Beautiful, handsome, splendid, elegant, magnificent.

9. Clear, pure, unadulterated.

——, *n.* Mulct, amercement, forfeit, forfeiture, pecuniary penalty.

——, *v. t.* 1. Defecate, purify, refine.

2. Amerce, mulct, impose a fine upon, punish by a fine.

Finery, *n.* Gewgaws, trinkets, ornaments, decorations, trimmings, fine things, showy dress, frippery, tinsel trappings.

Finesse, *n.* Artifice, strategy, stratagems, ruses, manœuvring, wiles, cunning, craft, subtle contrivance.

——, *v. i.* Use stratagem, practise tricks, employ artifice, manœuvre.

FINGER, *n.* Digit, pointer.

——, *v. t.* Handle, touch, purloin.

Finical, *a.* Fastidious, squeamish, dainty, trim, spruce, dapper, foppish, jaunty, over-particular, over-nice, affectedly elegant.

Finish, *v. t.* 1. Accomplish, complete, consummate, fulfil, execute, perform, achieve, do, get done.

2. Perfect, polish, elaborate, make perfect.

3. End, terminate, close, conclude, bring to an end, put an end to.

——, *n.* 1. Polish, elaboration, perfection, elegance.

2. Polishing, last *or* final touch *or* touches; surface.

3. End, close, termination, wind-up, death.

Finished, *a.* 1. Completed, complete, perfect.

2. Polished, perfected, elegant, rounded, highly wrought.

3. Experienced, practised, qualified, accomplished, thorough-bred, able, proficient.

Finite, *a.* Bounded, limited, contracted, terminable, conditioned, definable.

FIRE, *n.* 1. Combustion, intense heat.

2. Conflagration, blaze.

3. Firing, discharge of fire-arms, discharges.

4. Heat, ardor, fever, inflammation, fervor, impetuosity, violence, force, passion, fervency, intensity, animation, spirit, vigor, enthusiasm.

5. (*Poetical.*) Light, lustre, radiance, splendor.

6. Vivacity, inspiration, imagination, imaginativeness, force of sentiment.

7. Torture, trouble, affliction, persecution, bitter trial.

——, *v. t.* 1. Kindle, set on fire, ignite.

2. Animate, excite, inspirit, invigorate, kindle, enliven, rouse, inflame, stir up.

3. Discharge, fire off, eject, expel, hurl.

Fire-arm, *n.* Gun, pistol, musket, rifle, etc., explosive weapon.

Firebrand, *n.* 1. Brand.

2. Incendiary, agitator.

Fire-eater, *n.* Blusterer, swaggerer, vaporer, quarrelsome brawler, mock hero.

Fireside, *n.* 1. Hearth, chimney-corner, place near the fire.

2. Home, domestic life.

Firing, *n.* 1. Kindling, setting on fire.

2. Discharge (*of guns*), firing off, volley, fusillade.

Firm, *a.* 1. Compact, compressed, solid, dense, hard, not soft, not fluid.

2. Fixed, fast, rooted, established, rigid, settled, coherent, consistent, confirmed, stable, secure, immovable, inflexible.

3. Steady, stable, steadfast, unshaken, resolute, stanch, constant, determined.

4. Strong, robust, sinewy, sturdy, stout, stanch, loyal.

——, *n.* Concern, house, company, partnership, association, corporation, commercial house.

Firmament, *n.* Sky, the heavens, the welkin.

Firmness, *n.* 1. Solidity, compactness, hardness.

2. Stability, strength.

3. Constancy, steadfastness, steadiness.

FIRST, *a.* 1. Foremost, leading, prime, chief, highest, principal, capital.

2. Earliest, eldest, original; maiden.

3. Primary, elementary, rudimentary.

4. Primitive, primeval, pristine, primal, aboriginal.

——, *adv.* In the first place, at the outset, in the beginning, first and foremost, formerly, before anything else.

First-rate, *a.* Excellent, prime, superior, of the first class, of the highest order, of the best sort, of the highest grade, "first-class."

Fiscal, *a.* Financial.

FISH, *v. i.* [*The noun is Basic Eng.*]

1. Angle, bob, try to catch fish.

2. [With *for.*] Angle, seek by indirection, endeavor to call out, hint after, seek by artifice.

——, *v. t.* 1. Angle, try to take in.

2. Grapple, catch, draw up.

3. Rake, drag, search by dragging *or* raking.

Fisherman, *n.* Fisher, angler, piscator.

Fish for. Angle for, try to get (*by artifice*), hint at indirectly.

Fissure, *n.* Cleft, crevice, chink, crack, cranny, break, breach, gap, interstice, opening, chasm, rift, fracture.

Fist, *n.* Clenched hand.

Fisticuffs, *n.* Blows, encounter with the fists, personal encounter, fist fight.

Fistular, } *a.* Hollow, pipe-like, tubular,
Fistulous, } fistulose.

Fit, *n.* 1. Paroxysm, spasm, qualm, spell, convulsion, "turn," sudden *or* violent attack, stroke of disease.

2. Humor, whim, fancy, temporary affection; tantrum, pet, passing mood.

3. Interval, turn, period, spell.

——, *a.* 1. Qualified, competent, capacitated, fitted; trained, in trim.

2. Suitable, appropriate, apt, apposite, meet, consonant, adequate, pertinent, seemly, becoming, fitting, befitting, proper, convenient, good.

——, *v. t.* 1. Suit, adapt, adjust, make suitable.

2. Become, be adapted to, be suitable for, be becoming to.

3. Accommodate, provide, qualify, equip, prepare, get ready.

——, *v. i.* 1. Be proper, be becoming.

2. Be suited, be adapted.

Fitful, *a.* 1. Variable, irregular, spasmodic, intermittent, convulsive, impulsive, unstable, fickle, whimsical, fanciful, capricious, fantastic, humorsome, odd.

2. Eventful, checkered, full of vicissitude.

Fitfully, *adv.* 1. Irregularly, capriciously, in a fitful manner.

2. At intervals, by fits, by starts, by turns, intermittently, flickeringly.

Fitness, *n.* 1. Suitableness, adaptation, aptness, aptitude, appropriateness, pertinence, propriety.

2. Qualification, preparation.

Fit out. Equip, furnish, supply with necessaries.

Fit up. Prepare, make ready.

Fix, *v. t.* 1. Set, place, establish, plant, fasten, make firm *or* stable; adjust, put to rights, repair.

2. Attach, tie, bind, lock, stay, clinch, connect, fasten, make fast.

3. Determine, define, limit, appoint, settle, decide, seal.

4. Direct steadily, rivet, fasten.

5. Solidify, consolidate, harden.

——, *v. i.* 1. Rest, remain, abide, settle, become permanent.

2. Solidify, congeal, stiffen, grow firm, cease to be fluid *or* volatile, harden.

Fix, *n.* Predicament, dilemma, plight, "pickle."

Fixation, *n.* 1. Fixing.

2. Fixedness, fixity, fixure, firmness, stability.

3. Fixed idea.

FIXED, *a.* Fastened, firm, settled.

Fix on. } Settle on, determine upon, de-
Fix upon. } cide upon, select, choose.

Fizzle, *v. i.* 1. Hiss, burn hissingly and then go out, make a hissing noise, fizz.

2. (*Colloq.*) Fail, make a failure of it, fizzle out.

——, *n.* (*Colloq.*) Failure, fiasco, abortive attempt.

Flabbergast, *v. t.* (*Colloq. and humorous.*) Confound, confuse, abash, astonish, disconcert, nonplus, dumfound, take aback, throw off one's balance.

Flabby, *a.* Soft, yielding, inelastic, limp, weak, feeble. See FLACCID.

Flaccid, *a.* Soft, limber, limp, flabby, yielding, lax, drooping, relaxed, inelastic, hanging loose, pendulous, baggy.

Flaccidity, } *n.* Limberness, softness,
Flaccidness, } laxity, limpness, relaxed condition, flabbiness, looseness.

Flag, *v. i.* 1. Hang loose, droop.

2. Languish, droop, faint, decline, pine, sink, lag, fail, succumb, become weak, grow languid, lose vigor, become dejected; pall, grow stale, become vapid, lose interest.

FLAG, *n.* 1. Flag-stone, flat paving stone.

2. Banner, streamer, colors, standard, pennon, pennant, ensign, gonfalon.

Flagellate, *v. t.* Whip, scourge, castigate, flog, thrash, beat, cudgel, drub.

Flagitious, *a.* Atrocious, heinous, villanous, infamous, scandalous, nefarious, flagrant, profligate, corrupt, abandoned, enormously wicked.

Flagrant, *a.* 1. Flaming, glowing, burning, raging.

2. Notorious, crying, glaring, enormous, monstrous, outrageous, shameful, wicked, nefarious, wanton, flagitious.

Flag-stone, *n.* Flag, flat paving stone.

Flake, *n.* Scale, lamina, layer.

——, *v. i.* Scale, scale off, come off in flakes, desquamate.

Flambeau, *n.* Torch.

Flamboyant, *a.* Bright, ornate, gorgeous, rococo.

FLAME, *n.* 1. Blaze, burning vapor, light, flare.

2. Ardor, fervor, fervency, warmth, enthusiasm.

——, *v. i.* 1. Blaze.

2. Glow, burn, warm, be fervid *or* fervent, thrill, be enthusiastic.

Flaming, *a.* 1. Blazing.

2. Violent, vehement, exciting, intense, lambent, glowing, burning, bursting.

Flank, *n.* Side.

——, *v. t.* 1. (*Mil.*) Attack on the side, approach on the side, turn the flank of.

2. Border (upon), stand at the side of, lie along, shut in at the side.

——, *v. i.* 1. [With *upon*.] Border, touch, lie, have the side.

2. Be posted on the side.

Flap, *n.* 1. Hanging fold, lap, lappet, fly, tab, apron.

2. Flapping, swinging, pendulous motion, flutter, flop, flapping stroke, slap.

——, *v. t.* Wave about, shake, beat, vibrate, flutter.

——, *v. i.* Wave, vibrate, move in folds, flutter noisily.

Flare, *v. i.* 1. Waver, flicker, flutter, stream broadly sideways, blaze unsteadily.

2. Glare, dazzle, shine forth suddenly, flame, blaze.

3. Widen, widen out, spread outward, flue, splay.

——, *n.* Glare, unsteady light, brief blaze.

Flare up. Fly into a passion, get angry, fire up, lose one's temper, boil over with rage.

Flash, *n.* 1. Momentary blaze, sudden burst of light, gleam, glare; glisten, shimmer, glance, spark, sparkle, glint.

2. Instant, moment, glimpse, glimmer, twinkling, twinkling of an eye.

3. Slang (*of thieves and gypsies*), argot, cant language.

——, *v. i.* 1. Emit a sudden light, glisten, shimmer, glance, sparkle, scintillate, twinkle.

2. Break (forth) suddenly.

Flashy, *a.* 1. Showy, ostentatious, loud, flaunting, gawdy, tawdry, pretentious, tinsel, glittering but superficial.

2. Insipid, tasteless, mawkish, flat, vapid, stale.

FLAT, *a.* 1. Level, horizontal, champaign (*said of an extent of land*).

2. Even, plane, smooth, unbroken, without prominences.

3. Low, prostrate, level with the ground, overthrown, laid low.

4. Dull, lifeless, spiritless, unanimated, frigid, uniform, monotonous, jejune, tame, prosaic, uninteresting, pointless.

5. Vapid, tasteless, insipid, stale, dead, flashy, mawkish.

6. Peremptory, absolute, positive, direct, clear, downright.

FLAT, *n.* 1. Shoal, shallow, strand, bar, sandbank.

2. Plain, lowland, level piece of country, champaign.

3. Floor, story, apartment.

Flat-iron, *n.* Sad-iron, smoothing iron.

Flatten, *v. t.* Make flat (*in all the senses of the adjective; which see*).

——, *v. i.* Become flat (*in all the senses of the adjective; which see*).

Flatter, *v. t.* 1. Compliment, gratify by praise.

2. Cajole, wheedle, blandish, humor, coax, gloze, "butter," "blarney," court, coddle, pay court to, fawn upon, curry favor with, try to win by adulation, make much of.

3. Encourage by plausible representations, inspire with false hopes.

Flatterer, *n.* Sycophant, fawner, parasite, wheedler, toady, flunky, spaniel, lickspittle, pick-thank, toad-eater.

Flattery, *n.* 1. Pretended compliment, insincere commendation, false praise.

2. Obsequiousness, sycophancy, servility, cajolery, fawning, adulation, blandishment, blarney.

Flatulence, } *n.* Windiness (*in the bowels*).
Flatulency, }

Flatulent, *a.* Windy, gassy.

Flaunt, *v. i.* Flutter, make a show, make a parade, cut a dash, be ostentatious.

——, *v. t.* 1. Brandish, wave ostentatiously, brazenly, insolently, *or* boldly.

2. Display with effrontery, toss, flourish, disport, vaunt, boast.

Flaunting, *a.* Ostentatious, showy, flashy, garish, tawdry, gaudy.

Flavor, *n.* 1. Taste, savor, relish, zest, smack, gust, gusto; admixture, seasoning, lacing.

2. Subtle quality, essence, spirit, soul, aroma.

Flaw, *n.* 1. Break, crack, breach, cleft, fissure, gap, rift, fracture, rent.

2. Blemish, spot, speck, fleck, fault, defect, imperfection.

Flay, *v. t.* Skin, excoriate, strip the skin from; criticise severely.

Fleck, *v. t.* Spot, streak, dapple, speckle, variegate.

Flecked, *a.* Spotted, streaked, striped, dappled, mottled, variegated, piebald.

Flee, *v. i.* Fly, run, decamp, escape, abscond, "skedaddle," hasten away, run away, make off, turn tail, cut and run; vanish.

Fleece, *v. t.* 1. Clip, shear, deprive of fleece.

2. Strip, rob, plunder, despoil, rifle, steal from, cheat, "pluck," "bleed."

3. Cover fleecily, shroud softly, wrap in misty clouds, fold in snow.

Fleecy, *a.* Woolly; fleece-like.

Fleer, *n. and v. i.* Gibe, scoff, mock, jeer.

Fleet, *n.* Flotilla, squadron, navy, armada, escadrille.

——, *a.* Swift, rapid, quick, nimble, fast of foot.

Fleeting, *a.* Transitory, caducous, transient, ephemeral, temporary, passing, evanescent, fugitive, flitting, flying, brief, short-lived, here to-day and gone to-morrow.

Fleetness, *n.* Swiftness, quickness, rapidity, celerity, velocity, speed, nimbleness.

Flesh, *n.* 1. Muscle and fat (*of animal bodies*).

2. Meat, animal food.

3. Body (*as opposed to spirit*), flesh and blood, natural man (*as opposed to the spiritual*).

4. Carnality, sensual appetites, bodily desires.

5. Kindred, stock, race, flesh-and-blood.

6. Mankind, man, the world.

Fleshiness, *n.* Fatness, plumpness, corpulence, corpulency, *embonpoint*, obesity.

Fleshly, *a.* 1. Human, of flesh.

2. Carnal, sensual, lustful, lascivious, lecherous.

Fleshy, *a.* Fat, plump, corpulent, obese.

Flexibility, *n.* 1. Pliancy, pliability, flexibleness, limberness, litheness, suppleness.

2. Compliance, yielding disposition, ductility, complaisance, pliancy, affability, tractableness, easy temper.

Flexible, *a.* 1. Pliable, pliant, limber, lithe, supple, easily bent, flexile, willowy.

2. Tractable, pliant, pliable, yielding, complaisant, compliant, affable, gentle, ductile, docile, responsive to change.

Flexuous, *a.* Winding, bending, tortuous, sinuous, wavy, sinuate, crooked, serpentine.

Flexure, *n.* 1. Bending, curving, incurvating, incurvation.

2. Bend, crook, turn, fold, winding, incurvation, curvature.

3. Curvature, mode of bending, rate of incurvation.

Flibbertigibbet, *n.* Imp, sprite, demon, malignant spirit, little devil.

Flicker, *v. i.* 1. Flutter.

2. Fluctuate, waver, float, flutter, flare.

FLIGHT, *n.* 1. Flying, soaring, mounting, volitation.

2. Fleeing, hasty departure, flying, stampede, rout; exodus, hegira.

3. Volley, shower.

4. Stairs, steps from one landing to next.

Flighty, *a.* Giddy, wild, volatile, mercurial, frivolous, capricious, fickle, whimsical, deranged, unbalanced, light-headed, without ballast.

Flimsy, *a.* 1. Slight, thin, unsubstantial, of frail texture.

2. Weak, feeble, trivial, frivolous, foolish, trifling, light, puerile, shallow, superficial, trashy.

3. Sleazy, slimsy, jerry-built.

Flinch, *v. i.* Shrink, withdraw, retreat, swerve, wince, draw back, hold back.

Flinders, *n. pl.* Splinters, fragments.

Fling, *v. t.* Throw, cast, hurl, toss, dart, emit, pitch, heave, flirt, chuck, shy.

——, *v. i.* 1. Flounce, wince, fly into violent motions.

2. Start *or* rush angrily, flounce.

Flippancy, *n.* 1. Volubility, fluency.

2. Pertness, inconsiderate glibness, unscrupulous smartness, superficial assurance.

Flippant, *a.* 1. Voluble, fluent, glib, talkative, nimble of speech, of ready utterance.

2. Pert, impertinent, malapert, forward, bold, inconsiderately glib, unscrupulously pert, frivolous, trifling.

Flirt, *v. t.* 1. Throw (*with a jerk*), toss, fling, pitch, hurl, chuck, shy.

2. Twirl, flutter, whirl, whisk.

——, *v. i.* Coquet, philander, dally, wanton, make love, make a show of love, affect to be in love, play at courtship.

——, *n.* 1. Coquette, jilt, philanderer.

2. Jerk, sudden fling.

Flirtation, *n.* Coquetry, affectation of love, dalliance, philandering.

Flit, *v. i.* Fly rapidly, dart along; flutter, flicker, hover; hasten, depart.

Flitting, *a.* Fleeting, evanescent, transient, transitory, passing, fugitive, ephemeral.

Float, *v. i.* Swim, waft, be buoyed up, ride, drift, hang, glide, sail, soar.

——, *v. t.* Buoy up, bear up, keep afloat, bear on the surface, support, launch, waft; get support for, start.

FLOAT, *n.* 1. Raft, floating mass.

2. Buoy.

3. Float-board.

4. Pageant.

Flock, *n.* 1. Collection (*of sheep, etc.*), company, multitude, group; troupe, bevy, herd, pack, drove, swarm, team, etc.

2. Congregation.

3. Lock of wool, tuft.

4. Cotton and woollen refuse.

——, *v. i.* Congregate, herd, gather in crowds, swarm.

Flog, *v. t.* Beat, lash, whip, thrash, drub, scourge, flagellate, castigate, chastise.

Flood, *n.* 1. Inundation, deluge, overflow, freshet, tide.

2. Great flow, rush, downrush, multitude, overflow, outburst, spate, downpour, bore, eagre.

3. Abundance, excess.

——, *v. t.* Overflow, inundate, deluge, flow.

Flood-gate, *n.* Sluice-gate.

Floor, *v. t.* 1. Cover with a floor, put a floor on, deck, pave.

2. Overthrow, prostrate, bring to the floor, knock down.

3. Prevail over (*in argument*), pose, nonplus, get the better of.

FLOOR, *n.* 1. Bottom, flooring, pavement, stage, deck; story.

2. Main part of room (*as distinguished from gallery, platform*).

Flora, *n.* Plants (*of a country*), vegetation, vegetable life.

Floret, *n.* Floweret, little flower.

Florid, *a.* 1. (*Poetical.*) Flowery.

2. Rubicund, flushed, of a bright red color, red-faced.

3. Ornate, rhetorical, figurative, highly embellished, rococo, luxuriant.

Flotsam, *n.* Floating wreckage.

Flounce, *v. i.* 1. Fling, wince, fly into violent motions (*as an animal in a passion*). See FLING, *v. i.*

2. Toss about. See FLOUNDER.

——, *n.* 1. Jerk, spring.

2. Frill (*on a gown, etc.*), furbelow, ruffle.

Flounder, *v. i.* Struggle (*as an animal in the mire*), toss, tumble, wallow, flounce, toss about, plunge, blunder, flop.

Flourish, *v. i.* 1. Thrive, grow.

2. Prosper, succeed, be successful, go on well.

3. Boast, brag, vaunt, vapor, gasconade, bluster, make a show, be ostentatious, show off, cut a dash, make a flourish.

4. Attain one's prime, be at the height of one's powers, be in vigor, exercise one's full powers.

——, *v. t.* Brandish, wave, swing, flaunt.

——, *n.* 1. Ostentation, parade, show, display, dash.

2. Bombast, grandiloquence, altiloquence, fustian, flowery speech, high-sounding words.

3. Fanciful strokes (*of a pen, etc.*).

4. Brandishing, waving, shake.

5. Fanfare, blast, tantivy.

Flout, *v. t.* Insult, mock, jeer, gibe, fleer, deride, taunt, chaff, scoff at, sneer at, treat with contempt.

Flout, *v. i.* Sneer, jeer, gibe, scoff, fleer, fling, be contemptuous.

——, *n.* Insult, mocking, mockery, mock, sneer, jeer, gibe, fling, scoffing, scoff, taunt.

Flow, *v. i.* 1. Stream, run, pour, roll on, sweep along.

2. Melt, liquefy, be molten, deliquesce.

3. Issue, emanate, proceed, come, grow, arise, well up, follow, spring, result, be derived.

4. Glide, move along easily *or* smoothly.

5. Wave, float, undulate, waver, hang loosely.

6. Abound, be full, be copious, run.

——, *n.* 1. Stream, current, flux, flood, trickle, gush, rush, discharge.

2. Abundance, copiousness.

FLOWER, *n.* 1. Blossom, bloom.

2. Best part, finest part, essence, *élite.*

3. Prime, early vigor.

——, *v. i.* Blossom, bloom, be in flower, effloresce, put forth flowers; develop.

Floweret, *n.* Floret, little flower.

Flowery, *a.* 1. Bloomy, full of flowers, florid.

2. Ornate, figurative, florid.

Flowing, *a.* 1. Running.

2. Fluent, copious, abundant, smooth.

Fluctuate, *v. i.* 1. Oscillate, undulate, wave, swing, vibrate, be unsteady, rise and fall, roll hither and thither, move to and fro, move up and down.

2. Vary, change, rise and fall.

3. Waver, vacillate, be irresolute *or* inconstant *or* unsettled.

Fluctuation, *n.* 1. Oscillation, undulation, rolling, unsteadiness, rising and falling.

2. Variation, change, shifting, rise and fall.

3. Wavering, inconstancy, vacillation, hesitation.

Flue, *n.* 1. Smoke-vent.

2. Heat-pipe, heating-tube (*in a boiler*), chimney, duct.

3. Flew, fluff, nap, soft down, downy fur, flossy hair.

Fluency, *n.* 1. Smoothness, flowing quality, liquidness.

2. Copiousness, affluence, readiness of speech, ready utterance, command of language, facility of expression, "gift of the gab."

Fluent, *a.* 1. Flowing, gliding, liquid, current.

2. Smooth.

3. Copious, affluent, ready (*in speech*), facile, easy, voluble, glib, talkative.

Fluff, *n.* Nap, down, flue, flew, downy fur, flossy hair, lint.

Fluffy, *a.* Nappy, downy, flossy.

Flugelman, *n.* File-leader, leader, director, fugleman.

Fluid, *a.* Liquid and gaseous, liquid *or* gaseous (*as the case may be*), running, fluent.

——, *n.* Liquid, liquor; gas, vapor.

Fluke, *n.* 1. Anchor-flake, grappling-flap.

2. Lucky stroke, stroke of luck (*primarily, at billiards*).

Flume, *n.* Chute, race, mill-race, channel; ravine *or* gorge made by mountain stream.

Flummery, *n.* 1. Sowens, sowins *or* sowans, porridge (*made of the dust of oatmeal*).

2. Trash, frivolity, chaff, moonshine, trifling, froth, frippery, empty nonsense.

3. Flattery, adulation, blandishment, blarney, empty compliment.

Flunkey, *n.* [Written also *Flunky.*] 1. Lackey, livery-servant.

2. Mean fellow, mean-spirited person, obsequious person, toady, snob, tuft-hunter.

Flurry, *n.* 1. Flaw, squall, gust of wind.

2. Agitation, hurry, bustle, confusion, excitement, commotion, perturbation, disturbance, flutter, ruffle, hurry-skurry.

——, *v. t.* Excite, agitate, confuse, disconcert, disturb, perturb, fluster, hurry.

Flush, *v. i.* 1. Flow *or* rush suddenly, spread suddenly, start forth.

2. Glow, redden, mantle.

——, *v. t.* 1. Redden, color, cause to glow.

2. Animate, elevate, elate, excite, erect, make proud.

3. Drench, flood, cleanse by flooding, wash out.

——, *a.* 1. Glowing, bright, fresh, vigorous.

2. Prolific, exuberant, fecund, fertile, prodigal, lavish, abundant, well-supplied.

3. Level, even, plane, flat.

——, *n.* 1. Redness, ruddiness, rosiness, glow, bloom, blush.

2. Sudden impulse, thrill, shock.

Fluster, *v. t.* 1. Excite, heat, flush.

2. Hurry, agitate, perturb, disturb, flurry, ruffle.

3. Confuse, disconcert, discompose, confound, throw off one's balance.

——, *n.* 1. Heat, glow.

2. Agitation. See FLURRY.

Fluted, *a.* Grooved (*as a column*), channelled.

Flutist, *n.* Flute-player, flautist, piper, fifer.

Flutter, *v. i.* 1. Hover, flap the wings quickly.

2. Flap, move rapidly, flirt, flit.

3. Tremble, palpitate, beat *or* move tremulously.

4. Fluctuate, waver, oscillate, vacillate, be fickle, be inconstant, be unsteady, be in doubt *or* uncertainty.

Flutter, *n.*   1. Agitation, tremor, quick motion.

2. Confusion, hurry, commotion, agitation, twitter, tremble, excitement, perturbation, flurry, fluster, hurry-skurry.

Flux, *n.*   1. Flow, flowing.

2. Mutation, change, transition, shifting.

3. Diarrhœa, dysentery, looseness, lax state (*of the bowels*).

4. Fusion, melting.

5. Fusing mixture, fusing agent, solvent, menstruum.

Fly, *v. i.*   1. Soar, mount, hover, take wing, aviate.

2. Flutter, flap, float, wave, undulate, vibrate, sail, soar, play.

3. Burst, explode, be scattered, break in pieces, be broken to pieces.

4. Flee, run away, decamp, abscond, depart, vanish, make off, pack off, slip away, steal away, slink away.

5. Pass, elapse, slip, glide, flit, roll on, flow on.

——, *v. t.*   1. Flee from, shun, avoid, flee.

2. Let fly, set flying, cause to fly *or* float.

FLY, *n.*   1. Winged insect, dipteron.

2. Hackney-coach, cab, light vehicle.

3. Stage gallery, scene-shifting gallery.

4. Lap, flap.

Fly at.   Assail, attack, assault, rush upon, spring upon.

Foal, *n.*   Colt, filly.

Foam, *n.*   Froth, spume, spray, scum, cream, head, suds.

Foamy, *a.*   Frothy, spumy, spumous.

Focus, *n.*   Point of concentration, point of convergence, converging-point, focal point, center, nucleus.

Fodder, *n.*   Forage, food (*for cattle*), provender, feed.

Foe, *n.*   Enemy, adversary, opponent, antagonist, foeman.

Fog, *n.*   Haze, mist, vapor.

Foggy, *a.*   1. Misty, hazy, dimmed.

2. Confused, dazed, bewildered, muddled, muddy.

Fogy, *n.*   [Written also *Fogey*.] Dull fellow, one behind the times, conservative (*in an ill sense*), old fogy, fogram *or* fogrum.

Foible, *n.*   Frailty, weakness, failing, defect, infirmity, imperfection, fault, weak point.

Foil, *v. t.*   Defeat, frustrate, balk, baffle, thwart, check, circumvent, disappoint, checkmate.

——, *n.*   1. Film, flake, lamina (*of metal*).

2. Contrast, background, set-off.

3. Blunted rapier.

Foist, *v. t.*   Impose, thrust (*surreptitiously* or *wrongfully*), palm off, insert *or* interpolate surreptitiously.

FOLD, *n.*   1. Pen (*for sheep*), cot *or* cote, enclosure.

2. Flock (of sheep).

3. Plait, double, doubling, folding, gather, plicature.

——, *v. t.*   1. Double, lay in folds, lap.

2. Wrap, inwrap, envelop, infold, embrace, clasp.

Folding, *n.*   Plait, double, fold.

Foliaceous, *a.*   1. (*Bot.*) Leafy, foliate.

2. (*Min.*) Lamellar, lamellate, lamellated, laminate(d), scaly, flaky, foliated, schistose.

Foliage, *n.*   Leaves, clusters of leaves, leafage.

Foliate, *a.*   (*Bot.*) Leafy, foliaceous.

Foliated, *a.*   (*Min.*) Lamellar, lamellate, lamellated, laminate(d), foliaceous, schistose.

Folk, *n.*   Kindred, people, nation.

Folk-lore, *n.*   Popular superstitions, customs, wisdom; study of traditional customs, beliefs, etc.

Follow, *v. t.*   1. Come *or* go after *or* behind, go in the rear *or* in the wake of, tread in the steps of, tread on the heels of, heel.

2. Succeed, come next, tread close upon.

3. Pursue, chase, run after, go after, tag after, dog, hound, trail.

4. Attend, accompany, go along with, keep company with.

5. Obey, heed, observe, be guided by, conform to, yield to.

6. Seek, cherish, cultivate, strive for.

7. Practise, pursue, attend to, make the object of pursuit.

8. Imitate, copy, pattern after, copy after, take as an example, adopt.

——, *v. i.*   1. Come *or* go after.

2. Succeed, come next.

3. Ensue, result, arise, proceed, flow, come, spring, issue, be inferred *or* inferrible, be deduced *or* deducible.

Follower, *n.*   1. Pursuer.

2. Attendant, retainer, supporter, dependant, companion, associate, acolyte.

3. Adherent, disciple, pupil, partisan, admirer.

4. Imitator, copier.

Following, *n.*   Clientele, adherents, retinue, train.

Follow up. 1. Examine, scrutinize, investigate, sift, inquire into, look into, pursue closely.

2. [With *by* or *with*.] Accompany, cause to be followed by, strengthen by further action.

3. Persist in, pursue persistently, keep at.

Folly, *n.* 1. Foolishness, imbecility, fatuity, levity, shallowness, dulness, doltishness.

2. Absurdity, foolishness, extravagance, unwisdom, imprudence, nonsense, inanity, ineptitude, senselessness, fatuity, indiscretion.

3. Act of folly, foolish act, indiscretion, blunder, *faux pas*.

Foment, *v. t.* 1. Stupe, bathe with warm lotions, apply warm lotions to, embrocate.

2. Excite, instigate, stimulate, brew, stir up, encourage, abet, promote, foster.

Fomentation, *n.* 1. Stupe *or* stupa, local bathing (*with warm lotions*), embrocation.

2. Instigation, excitement, brewing, stirring up, abetting, promoting, encouragement.

Fond, *a.* 1. Foolish, silly, weak, empty, vain, absurd, senseless, baseless.

2. Doting, over-affectionate, amorous, foolishly loving, excessively tender.

Fondle, *v. t.* 1. Caress, coddle, cosset, blandish, pet.

2. Pet, treat with fondness, indulge, spoil, make much of, make a pet of.

Fondness, *n.* 1. Folly, silliness, delusion, weakness, absurdity.

2. Foolish love, childish affection, excessive tenderness, doting.

3. Liking, partiality, predilection, preference, propensity, warm love, strong affection.

4. Relish, liking, appetite, taste.

Fond of. 1. [With *be*.] Have appetite *or* relish for, relish, like, like very much.

2. Taken with, attached to, much pleased with, delighted with.

Font, *n.* 1. Baptismal vessel.

2. Fount, assortment of types.

3. Fount, spring, source.

FOOD, *n.* 1. Aliment, nutriment, nutrition, sustenance, bread, nourishment, meat, provisions, victuals, viands, diet, regimen, rations, board, fare, cheer, commons, pabulum, subsistence.

2. [For *cattle*, etc.] Feed, fodder, forage, provender.

Fool, *n.* 1. Idiot, natural, half-wit.

2. Dolt, witling, driveller, idiot, imbecile, "nit-wit," "sap," simpleton, ninny, nincompoop, blockhead. See DUNCE.

3. Buffoon, harlequin, droll, punch, antic, jester, zany, clown, merry-andrew, scaramouch.

4. Dupe, butt.

——, *v. i.* Trifle, toy, play, jest, play the fool, play the monkey, act like a fool.

——, *v. t.* Deceive, cheat, trick, dupe, gull, delude, circumvent, cozen, overreach, beguile, hoodwink, impose upon.

Foolery, *n.* 1. Absurdity, nonsense, folly, foolishness.

2. Buffoonery, tomfoolery, mummery, foolish conduct.

Foolhardy, *a.* Rash, venturous, adventurous, incautious, venturesome, reckless, desperate, hot-headed, hare-brained, headlong, precipitate.

FOOLISH, *a.* 1. Senseless, idiotic, silly, weak, fatuous, inane, vain, inept, daft, simple, irrational, insensate, shallow, brainless, witless, thick-skulled, buffle-headed.

2. Unwise, unreasonable, absurd, ridiculous, nonsensical, ill-judged, preposterous, indiscreet, imprudent.

3. Idle, trivial, trifling, vain, childish, puerile, contemptible.

Foolishness, *n.* 1. Folly, silliness, imbecility, stupidity, fatuity, shallowness, dulness, doltishness.

2. Absurdity, extravagance, nonsense, imprudence, indiscretion.

3. Puerility, childishness, triviality.

FOOT, *n.* 1. Lower extremity, paw *or* hoof (*in brutes*).

2. Base, bottom, lower part.

3. (*Mil.*) Infantry, foot-soldiers.

——, *v. t.* 1. Add up (*figures*), sum up.

2. Pay, stand, settle, discharge (*a bill of expenses*).

Footboy, *n.* Menial, liveried attendant, footman, runner, lackey, page.

Footfall, *n.* Footstep, tread, tramp, step, sound of one's step.

Foothold, *n.* Footing, place to stand on.

Footing, *n.* 1. Foothold, purchase.

2. Basis, foundation, groundwork.

3. Rank, standing, grade, state, status, condition.

4. Settlement, establishment, stable position.

Footman, *n.* 1. Foot-soldier, infantry soldier, infantryman.

2. Runner, footboy, liveried servant, man in waiting, menial, lackey.

Footpad, *n.* Highwayman, brigand, robber, freebooter, bandit.

Footpath, *n.* Footway, path, trail.

Footprint, *n.* Footmark, footstep, footfall, track, trace.

Footstalk, *n.* Petiole, leaf-stalk.

Footstep, *n.* 1. Footprint, footmark, track, trace.

2. Footfall, step, tread, sound of one's step.

3. Token, mark, sign, trace, vestige.

Fop, *n.* Coxcomb, dandy, "dude," exquisite, beau, jack-a-dandy, macaroni, popinjay, "swell," man milliner.

Foppery, *n.* Coxcombry, dandyism, foppishness, vanity in dress.

Foppish, *a.* Dandyish, coxcomical, dandified, vain of dress.

FOR, *prep.* 1. Because of, by reason of.

2. On account of, for the sake of.

3. In the place of, instead of.

4. Concerning, with respect to, with regard to.

5. Conducive to, beneficial to.

6. During, during the term of.

7. In spite of, notwithstanding, despite.

8. In favor of, on the side of.

9. In quest of, with a view to.

——, *conj.* Because, since, on this account that.

Forage, *n.* 1. Food (*for horses and cattle*), fodder, provender.

2. Foraging, foraging expedition.

——, *v. i.* 1. Wander in search of forage, take forage.

2. Ravage, feed on forage, subsist by foraging.

Foramen, *n.* (*Anat.* and *Bot.*) Hole, orifice, perforation, opening.

Foraminated, *a.* Perforated, foraminous, with an opening *or* orifice.

Forasmuch as. Since, whereas, inasmuch as, because that, in consideration that, seeing that.

Foray, *n.* Inroad, irruption, raid, descent, piratical invasion, hostile incursion, predatory incursion.

Forbear, *v. i.* 1. Stop, pause, cease, desist, stay, hold, break off, leave off, give over.

2. Abstain, refrain, do without, hold back.

3. Be tolerant, endure, be patient.

——, *v. t.* 1. Shun, decline, avoid.

2. Omit, withhold, abstain from.

3. Spare, tolerate, endure, put up with, be patient with, treat with indulgence.

Forbearance, *n.* Forbearing, shunning, abstinence, avoidance, self-restraint; patience, lenity, indulgence, long-suffering, command of temper.

Forbid, *v. t.* Prohibit, inhibit, interdict, enjoin; ban, taboo, proscribe, veto, embargo.

Forbidding, *a.* Repellent, repulsive, unpleasant, abhorrent, odious, disagreeable, offensive.

FORCE, *n.* 1. Strength (*regarded as active*), power, might, energy, vigor, head, "vim"; emphasis, stress, pith.

2. Efficacy, efficiency, potency, validity, cogency, virtue, agency.

3. Violence, vehemence, compulsion, coercion, constraint, enforcement.

4. [*Most frequently in pl.*] Army, array, soldiery, troop, posse, legion, host, squadron, phalanx, battalion, etc.

——, *v. t.* 1. Compel, coerce, constrain, oblige, necessitate.

2. Impel, drive, urge, press.

3. Ravish, violate, constuprate, commit a rape on.

Forced, *a.* 1. Compelled, constrained, enforced, compulsory.

2. Strained, unnatural, artificial, catachrestic, far-fetched, studiously sought.

Forcible, *a.* 1. Powerful, strong, mighty, weighty, potent, impressive, irresistible, cogent, all-powerful.

2. Violent, impetuous, vehement, unrestrained.

3. Compulsory, coerced, coercive.

4. Energetic, vigorous, convincing, telling, effective, efficacious.

Forcibly, *adv.* 1. Powerfully, mightily.

2. Violently, compulsorily, coercively, by force, perforce, by compulsion *or* coercion, at the point of the sword, *vi et armis*.

3. Energetically, vigorously, effectively, with might and main.

Ford, *n.* 1. Wading-place, shallow crossing.

2. (*Poetical.*) Stream, current, flood.

——, *v. t.* Wade through (*a river*), cross on foot, cross by wading.

Fore, *a.* 1. Anterior, preceding, prior, antecedent, previous, foregoing, former, forward, first.

2. Front, anterior, face.

3. Advanced, leading, head, foremost, first, front.

Forebear, *n.* Forefather, ancestor.

Forebode, *v. t.* 1. Foretell, predict, signify, presage, portend, augur, betoken, foreshadow, foreshow, prognosticate, prefigure, be ominous of, threaten.

2. Foreknow, be prescient of, have foreknowledge of, have prescience of, have premonition of, surmise, have presentiment of, divine.

Foreboding, *n.* Prognostication, premonition, presentiment, presage, omen, augury.

Forecast, *v. t.* 1. Foresee, anticipate, look forward to, provide against, predict, calculate *or* estimate beforehand.

2. Contrive, plan, project, devise, scheme.

Forecast, *n*. 1. Foresight, prevision, prophecy, forethought, anticipation, provident regard to the future.

2. Contrivance, scheming, planning.

Foreclose, *v. t.* 1. Preclude, prevent, stop, debar, hinder, shut out.

2. (*Law.*) Deprive of the power of redeeming (*a mortgage*).

Foredoom, *v. t.* Predestine, foreordain, preordain, doom beforehand.

Forefather, *n.* Progenitor, ancestor, father, foregoer.

Forefend, *v. t.* Avert, prevent, hinder, forbid, ward off, keep off.

Forego, *v. t.* Relinquish, resign, renounce, surrender, cede, yield, abandon, give up, part with, let go.

Foregoer, *n.* 1. Precursor, forerunner, herald, harbinger, avant-courier.

2. Ancestor, forefather, progenitor, father.

Foregoing, *a.* Preceding, previous, antecedent, prior, former, fore, anterior.

Foregone, *a.* 1. Predetermined, decided before hand.

2. Bygone, past, previous, former.

Forehanded, *a.* Beforehand, provident, thrifty, in comfortable circumstances (*as respects property*), well off, well to do.

Forehead, *n.* Front, brow.

Foreign, *a.* 1. Alien, external, exterior, outward, strange, exotic, from abroad, outlandish, unnative; remote, distant.

2. Extraneous, extrinsic, exterior, outside, unnatural, unrelated, inappropriate, adventitious, irrelevant.

Foreigner, *n.* Alien, stranger, outsider, barbarian.

Foreknowledge, *n.* Foresight, prescience, prognostication, previous knowledge.

Foreland, *n.* Promontory, cape, headland, point of land.

Foreman, *n.* 1. Presiding officer (*of a jury*).

2. Overseer, superintendent, boss, chief workman, master workman.

Foremost, *a.* First, most advanced, front, leading.

Forensic, *a.* 1. Juridical, judicial, proper to courts.

2. Disputative, proper *or* belonging to debate *or* discussion, argumentative, rhetorical.

Foreordain, *v. t.* Predestinate, predetermine, appoint, preordain, foredoom.

Forerunner, *n.* 1. Precursor, harbinger, herald, predecessor, foregoer, avant-courier.

2. Prelude, prognostic, sign, omen, premonition, precursor.

Foresee, *v. t.* Foreknow, forecast, anticipate, prognosticate, see beforehand, have prescience of, be prescient of.

Foreshadow, *v. t.* Prefigure, presage, forebode, prognosticate, presignify, indicate *or* suggest beforehand, foretell dimly.

Foresight, *n.* 1. Foreknowledge, prescience, prevision.

2. Forecast, forethought, precaution, prudence, providence, anticipation.

Forest, *n.* Wood (*of large extent*), woods, woodland, grove.

Forestall, *v. t.* 1. Shut off, preclude, prevent, hinder (*by prior influences*).

2. Anticipate, foretaste, antedate, take in advance.

3. Engross, monopolize, regrate, "get ahead of," get exclusive possession of (*in order to enhance prices*).

Foretaste, *v. t.* Anticipate. See FORESTALL, 2.

——, *n.* Anticipation, antepast, prelibation, forestalling, taste beforehand.

Foretell, *v. t.* 1. Predict, prophesy.

2. Prognosticate, foreshow, foreshadow, presignify, betoken, portend, augur, bode, forebode, forecast, presage.

Forethought, *n.* Foresight, forecast, anticipation, precaution, prudence, providence.

Forever, *adv.* Always, perpetually, eternally, everlastingly, endlessly, ever, evermore, constantly, continually, unceasingly, aye, for aye, at all times, to the end of time, for good and all, world *or* time without end, through endless ages, to eternity.

Forewarn, *v. t.* Caution *or* admonish *or* advise *or* warn beforehand, premonish.

Forfeit, *n.* Fine, mulct, amercement, penalty, forfeiture.

——, *v. t.* Lose (*by some offence, by neglect,* or *by breach of condition*), alienate.

Forfeiture, *n.* 1. Loss (*by some offence, etc.*), amercement, confiscation.

2. Fine, mulct, amercement, penalty, forfeit.

Forge, *n.* Smithy (*for heavy work*), iron-works; furnace (*to make iron more malleable*), shingling-mill.

——, *v. t.* 1. Beat (*metal*), hammer out, form (*by heating and hammering*), fabricate, frame.

2. Devise, invent, frame, coin.

3. Falsify, counterfeit, fabricate, feign.

Forger, *n.* Maker, contriver; counterfeiter, falsifier.

Forgery, *n.* 1. Counterfeiting, falsification.

2. Counterfeit, "fake."

Forget, *v. t.* 1. Lose the remembrance of, let slip from the mind.

2. Overlook, think no more of, consign to oblivion.

3. Slight, neglect, cease to care for.

Forgetful, *a.* 1. Apt to forget.

2. Negligent, inattentive, neglectful, careless, oblivious, unmindful, heedless, mindless.

Forgetfulness, *n.* 1. Aptness to forget, failure of memory.

2. Forgottenness. See OBLIVION.

3. Negligence, inattention, carelessness, heedlessness.

Forget one's self. Lose self-control, commit an indiscretion.

Forgive, *v. t.* Pardon (*especially for a small offence*), absolve, excuse, acquit.

Forgiveness, *n.* Pardon, absolution, remission, amnesty, reprieve.

Forgiving, *a.* Clearing, acquitting, releasing, pardoning, absolutory, absolvatory, excusing, placable.

Forgotten, *a.* Gone from one's mind, out of one's recollection; buried in oblivion, sunk in oblivion, unremembered, lost.

FORK, *n.* Branch, branching, division, crotch, divarication.

——, *v. i.* Branch, divide, divaricate.

Forked, *a.* Furcate, furcated, divaricated, branching.

Forlorn, *a.* 1. Deserted, abandoned, forsaken, helpless, friendless, solitary, lost.

2. Wretched, miserable, pitiable, destitute, hopeless, lamentable, abject, dejected, desolate, helpless, comfortless, disconsolate, woe-begone.

FORM, *n.* 1. Shape (*with especial reference to structure*), figure, configuration, conformation, pattern, outline, build, format, contour, body, mould, fashion, cast, cut, *tournure.*

2. Mode, method, formula, formulary, ritual, established practice.

3. Manner, system, sort, kind, order, class, type, model.

4. Regularity, order, arrangement, shapeliness.

5. Ceremony, formality, ceremonial, ritual, rite, observance, ordinance, punctilio, conventionality, etiquette, conventional rule.

6. Bench, long seat (*without a back*); class, rank of students.

7. (*Met.*) Arrangement, organization, combination, law of combination, principle of arrangement *or* synthesis, *a priori* principle.

——, *v. t.* 1. Fashion, shape, mould, model.

2. Make, create, produce, conceive, fabricate, construct, build.

3. Contrive, devise, invent, frame.

4. Constitute, compose, make up, develop, organize.

5. Arrange, dispose, combine.

Formal, *a.* 1. Express, explicit, positive, strict, official, in due form, according to established form, conventional; regular, methodical, set, fixed, rigid, stiff; ceremonious, ritual, precise, punctilious, starch, starched, prim, affectedly exact.

2. Constitutive, essential.

3. External, as mere form, merely formal, outward, perfunctory.

4. (*Met.*) Organic, formative, primordial, innate, *a priori.*

Formality, *n.* 1. Custom, established mode, settled method, rule of proceeding.

2. Ceremony, ceremonial, rite, ritual, conventionality, etiquette, punctilio, mere form.

Formation, *n.* 1. Creation, production, genesis.

2. Composition, constitution, making up.

3. Arrangement, combination, disposal, disposition.

Formative, *a.* 1. Plastic, creative, shaping, determinative.

2. (*Gram.*) Derivative, non-radical, inflectional.

Former, *a.* 1. Previous, prior, earlier, anterior, antecedent, preceding, foregoing.

2. Quondam, *ci-devant,* late, old-time; past, gone by, bygone, foregone, previous, whilom.

3. First named, first mentioned.

Formerly, *adv.* Heretofore, anciently, aforetime, of old, in times past, in days of yore, long ago, in past ages.

Formidable, *a.* Fearful, dreadful, terrible, menacing, redoubtable, frightful, terrific, horrible, tremendous; difficult, dangerous, etc.

Formless, *a.* Shapeless, amorphous, chaotic.

Formula, *n.* Form, rule, model, formulary, recipe, prescription.

Formulary, *n.* 1. Book of forms.

2. Form, model, rule, formula.

3. Ritual, ceremonial.

Fornicate, *a.* (*Bot.*) Arched, vaulted.

Forsake, *v. t.* 1. Leave, quit, desert, abandon, cast off.

2. Abandon, renounce, forswear, surrender, forego, relinquish, drop, give up, give over.

Forsooth, *adv.* [*Usually ironical.*] Certainly, truly, really, indeed, to be sure, in truth, in fact, of a truth, in good truth.

Forswear, *v. t.* 1. Renounce (*upon oath*), reject, leave, quit, desert, forsake, abandon, drop.

2. Deny, abjure, perjure, recant, retract, renounce.

Forswear one's self. Perjure one's self, take a false oath, swear falsely, bear false witness, break one's oath, break one's word, break one's faith, play false.

Fort, n. Fortification, fortress, stronghold, defense, bulwark, castle, citadel, fastness, fortified place.

Forte, n. Peculiar talent, special gift, chief excellence, strong point, that in which one excels.

Forth, adv. 1. Onward, forward, ahead.

2. Out, away, abroad, from retirement, from confinement.

Forthwith, adv. Immediately, directly, instantly, *instanter*, without delay.

Fortification, n. 1. Military architecture.

2. Fort, stronghold, castle, citadel, bulwark, defense, fastness, rampart, redoubt, breastwork, earthwork, tower, keep, fortified place. See FORTRESS.

Fortify, v. t. 1. Protect by fortifications, surround with fortifications.

2. Brace, strengthen, entrench, stiffen, reinforce, encourage, add strength to.

3. Strengthen, confirm, corroborate.

Fortitude, n. Endurance (*with courage*), bravery, firmness, resolution, patience, strength of mind, passive courage.

Fortnight, n. Two weeks.

Fortress, n. Fortification, fort, stronghold, castle, citadel, fastness, bulwark, fortified place (*of great magnitude*). See FORTIFICATION.

Fortuitous, a. Accidental, casual, contingent, incidental, chance, happening by chance.

Fortuity, n. Accidentalness, casualness, chance, contingency.

Fortunate, a. 1. Successful, prosperous, favored, happy. See LUCKY.

2. Propitious, auspicious, favorable, advantageous, lucky, happy.

Fortune, n. 1. Chance, accident, luck, hap, fortuity, casualty.

2. Estate, substance, property, possessions; wealth, riches, opulence, affluence, prosperity, felicity.

3. Destiny, fate, destination, doom, lot, star, future condition.

4. Event, issue, result; success, favorable issue.

Forum, n. Tribunal, court, court of justice, popular assembly place.

FORWARD, } adv. Onward, in advance,
Forwards, } ahead.

Forward, a. 1. Onward, progressive, advancing.

2. Front, fore, anterior, head, at the fore part, near the fore part.

3. Ready, prompt, willing, eager, earnest, zealous.

4. Bold, confident, presumptuous, presuming, impertinent, pert, flippant, brazen, assuming, brazen-faced, "brassy," "fresh."

5. Early, premature, precocious.

——, v. t. 1. Advance, promote, further, foster, support, aid, favor, encourage, help on, help forward.

2. Quicken, hasten, accelerate, expedite, speed, despatch, hurry.

3. Transmit, ship, send on, send forward.

Fosse, n. (*Fort.*) Ditch, moat, graff, canal.

Fossil, n. Petrifaction; petrified remains; fogy.

Foster, v. t. 1. Nurse, nourish, feed, support, mother, cosset, sustain.

2. Rear, breed, bring up, rear up, cherish, encourage, favor, patronize, promote, aid, stimulate, foment, further, advance, help on, help forward, harbor, cultivate.

Foul, a. 1. Impure, nasty, squalid, dirty, polluted, filthy, unclean, soiled, tarnished, stained, sullied, rank, fetid, putrid.

2. Disgusting, loathsome, hateful, odious, offensive, noisome.

3. Unfair, dishonorable, underhanded, sinister.

4. Base, scandalous, infamous, vile, wicked, dark, abominable, detestable, disgraceful, shameful, scurvy.

5. Obscene, vulgar, coarse, low.

6. Abusive, insulting, scurrilous, foul-mouthed, foul-spoken.

7. Stormy, rainy, cloudy, rough, wet.

8. Turbid, thick, muddy, feculent.

9. Entangled, tangled, in collision.

Foul play. 1. Injustice, unfairness, dishonesty, wrong, guile, secret misdoing, perfidy, treachery.

2. Outrage, violence, crime, treacherous violence, perfidious crime.

Foul-mouthed, a. Abusive, insulting, insolent, blackguard, scurrilous, foul, foul-spoken, obscene, filthy, profane, indecent, blasphemous.

Found, v. t. 1. Base, set, fix, place, ground, rest, lay the foundation of.

2. Build, construct, erect, raise.

3. Establish, institute, originate, set up, plant, colonize.

4. Cast, mould, form in a mould.

Foundation, n. 1. Basis, base, groundwork, support, substructure, ground, bed, footing, bottom.

2. Establishment, settlement; endowment.

Founder, *n.* 1. Originator, institutor, author, father, organizer, builder, establisher, planter.

2. Caster (*of metals*), moulder.

——, *v. i.* 1. Sink (*as a ship by filling with water*), go to the bottom, swamp, welter.

2. Fail, miscarry, collapse.

3. Trip, stumble, fall.

Foundling, *n.* Abandoned infant, orphan.

Fountain, *n.* 1. Spring, well, fount.

2. Jet, upwelling.

3. Source, original, origin, cause, first principle, fountain-head.

Fountain-head, *n.* Source, original, origin, cause, fountain, first principle.

Fourfold, *a.* Quadruple.

——, *n.* Four times as many, four times as much.

Four-handed, *a.* Quadrumanous.

Foursquare, *a.* Quadrangular; honest, downright, open.

FOWL, *n.* 1. Bird, winged animal.

2. Poultry, barn-door fowl, domestic fowl, etc.

Foxy, *a.* Artful, wily, cunning, crafty, sly, subtle.

Fracas, *n.* Uproar, tumult, disturbance, outbreak, noisy quarrel, "row," brawl.

Fraction, *n.* Part, portion, fragment, section, piece, bit, scrap.

Fractious, *a.* Cross, captious, petulant, touchy, perverse, testy, peevish, fretful, splenetic, pettish, snappish, waspish, irritable.

Fracture, *n.* 1. Breaking, rupture.

2. Break, crack, breach, cleft, fissure, rift, flaw, rent, opening.

Fragile, *a.* 1. Brittle, frangible, easily broken.

2. Frail, weak, feeble. See INFIRM.

Fragility, *n.* 1. Brittleness, frangibleness.

2. Frailty, weakness, feebleness.

Fragment, *n.* Remnant, scrap, chip, fraction, detached part, part broken off.

Fragmentary, *a.* Fractional, broken, incomplete, disconnected, scattered.

Fragrance, } *n.* Perfume, aroma, redolence,
Fragrancy, } smell, bouquet, balminess, incense, pleasing scent, grateful odor, sweetness of smell.

Fragrant, *a.* Aromatic, spicy, redolent, balmy, sweet, ambrosial, redolent, odoriferous, odorous, perfumed, sweet-smelling, sweet-scented.

Frail, *a.* 1. Fragile, frangible, brittle, slight, delicate, easily broken (*across*).

2. Weak, feeble, fragile. See INFIRM.

3. Liable to err, easily led astray, of infirm virtue.

Frailty, *n.* 1. Weakness, feebleness, infirmity, frailness.

2. Fault, foible, defect, imperfection, failing, weak point, weak side, blind side.

3. Liability to err, proneness to error, want of moral strength.

Frame, *v. t.* 1. Construct, build, put together, erect; form, compose, make, constitute.

2. Invent, devise, plan, contrive; fabricate, forge.

FRAME, *n.* 1. Skeleton, framing, framework, carcass.

2. Form, structure, fabric, system, scheme, constitution.

3. Condition, state, temper, humor, mood, state of mind *or* feeling.

Framer, *n.* Former, maker, author, creator, constructer.

Framework, *n.* Skeleton, frame, framing, carcass.

Franchise, *n.* 1. Right, privilege; voting-power.

2. Immunity, exemption.

Frangible, *a.* Brittle, fragile, easily broken, breakable.

Frank, *a.* Open, ingenuous, free, sincere, candid, artless, frank-hearted, unreserved, outspoken, plainspoken, direct, point-blank, unequivocal, naïve, guileless, genuine, straightforward, without disguise.

Frankincense, *n.* Olibanum, incense.

Frantic, *a.* Furious, raving, raging, mad, distracted, wild, infuriate, frenzied, phrenetic, transported, crazy, distraught, rabid.

Fraternal, *a.* Brotherly.

Fraternity, *n.* 1. Association, society, company, club, circle, brotherhood, sodality, league, clan, united body.

2. Brotherhood, brotherly relation, brotherliness.

Fraternize, *v. i.* Sympathize, harmonize, consort, coalesce, concur, associate (*as brothers*), make common cause.

Fraud, *n.* Deceit, deception, duplicity, imposition, imposture, guile, craft, trick, cheat, artifice, stratagem, wile, humbug, hoax, sham.

Fraudulent, *a.* Dishonest, knavish, treacherous, deceitful, deceptive, false, crafty, wily, tricky, trickish.

Fraught, *a.* Filled, stored, freighted, laden, weighted, burdened, charged, abounding, pregnant, big.

Fray, *n.* 1. Combat, battle, fight.

2. Broil, quarrel, riot, contention. See AFFRAY.

——, *v. t.* Rub, wear, fret, chafe; ravel, shred.

Freak, *n.* 1. Whim, whimsey, caprice, fancy, humor, crotchet, maggot, vagary, quirk.

2. Gambol, antic, caper.

3. Abnormality, monstrosity, abortion.

Freakish, *a.* Whimsical, capricious, odd, queer, humorsome, erratic, fanciful, full of vagaries.

FREE, *a.* 1. Independent, unrestrained, at liberty, loose, unconfined, bondless, untrammelled, unimpeded, unattached, unentangled.

2. Released, delivered, emancipated, liberated, manumitted, ransomed, free-born; self-governing, autonomous.

3. Exempt, clear, immune, privileged.

4. Allowed, permitted, open.

5. Unobstructed, unimpeded, unrestricted, open; devoid, empty.

6. Frank, ingenuous, candid, artless, sincere, unreserved, frank-hearted, affable.

7. Generous, liberal, bountiful, hospitable, charitable, munificent, free-hearted, open-handed, not parsimonious.

8. Prodigal, lavish, immoderate.

9. Ready, eager, prompt, willing.

10. Gratuitous, without charge, available, spontaneous, willing.

11. Loose, lax, careless.

12. Unconstrained, easy, informal, familiar; bold, over-familiar.

——, *v. t.* 1. Liberate, emancipate, manumit, release, disinthrall, enfranchise, deliver, set free, set at liberty, rescue, redeem, ransom, save, enlarge, discharge.

2. Rid, clear, disengage, extricate, disencumber; unbind, unchain, etc.

3. Exempt, privilege, immunize.

Freebooter, *n.* 1. Robber, plunderer, pillager, despoiler, highwayman, footpad, brigand, bandit, gangster, marauder.

2. Pirate, buccaneer, rover.

Freedom, *n.* 1. Independence, exemption from restraint, emancipation, liberation, release. See LIBERTY.

2. Scope, range, play, swing, elbow-room, margin, wide berth, free play, full play, full swing.

3. Franchise, immunity, privilege.

4. Familiarity, license, laxity, looseness.

Free-hearted, *a.* Liberal, generous, bounteous, bountiful, open-handed.

Free play. Freedom, range, scope, full play, swing, full swing.

Free-spoken, *a.* Frank, unreserved.

Free-thinker, *n.* Sceptic, unbeliever, infidel. See DEIST.

Free-will, *n.* 1. Unrestrained will, power of choice.

2. Spontaneity, voluntariness.

Freeze, *v. i.* 1. Be congealed, be frozen.

2. Be chilled.

——, *v. t.* 1. Congeal, solidify by cold, glaciate, turn to ice, harden.

2. Chill, benumb.

Freight, *v. t.* Load, lade, charge, burden *or* burthen.

——, *n.* 1. Cargo, lading, load, burden.

2. Freightage, freight money, charge for freight.

Frenzy, *n.* Madness, rage, fury, distraction, raving, insanity, lunacy, derangement, mania, delirium, aberration, transport

FREQUENT, *a.* 1. Oft-repeated, iterative, of frequent occurrence.

2. Common, usual, every-day, familiar, habitual, customary, persistent, of common occurrence.

3. Incessant, constant, continual, thick-coming.

——, *v. t.* Haunt, visit often, resort to frequently, attend much *or* regularly.

Frequently, *adv.* 1. Often, repeatedly, many times, at short intervals, not rarely, not seldom.

2. Commonly, as a common thing *or* matter.

Fresh, *a.* 1. New, recent, novel.

2. New, renewed, *de novo*, revived.

3. Blooming, flourishing, unfaded, unwithered, green, unfaded, unobliterated, unwilted, well-preserved, in good condition, unimpaired, undecayed.

4. Of recent make, not stale *or* sour, sweet.

5. Rosy, blooming, ruddy, fair, delicate, fresh-colored.

6. Florid, healthy, well, hearty, vigorous, hardy, strong.

7. Vigorous, energetic, active, unwearied, unexhausted, unfatigued, not blown, unworn.

8. Vivid, lively, keen, unabated, undecayed, not dulled, unimpaired.

9. Just received, just arrived; additional, further.

10. Unsmoked, undried, uncured; unsalted, free from salt.

11. Pure and cool, sweet, refreshing, invigorating, bracing, health-giving.

12. Brisk, strong, stiff (*of wind*).

13. Raw, uncultivated, unpractised, untrained, unused, unskilled, inexperienced.

Freshen, *v. t.* 1. Make fresher *or* less salt.

2. Freshen up, reinvigorate, refresh, revive, quicken.

Freshen, *v. i.* 1. Grow fresh, revive.

2. Grow brisk (*said of the wind*), rise.

Freshman, *n.* 1. Novice, tyro, beginner, learner.

2. Student of the first year (*in colleges*), student of the lowest class.

Fret, *v. t.* 1. Rub, chafe, wear (*by friction*), abrade, fray, gall, wear away.

2. Vex, tease, irritate, gall, ruffle, provoke, agitate, nettle, affront, make angry; annoy, worry, weary, harass, wear.

3. Ripple, ruffle, agitate, roughen.

4. Wear, wear away, gnaw into, corrode, cover with depressions.

5. Variegate, diversify, ornament with raised *or* depressed work.

——, *v. i.* Chafe, fume, rage, "stew," worry, be vexed, be irritated, be chafed, be peevish, be fretful, be angry.

——, *n.* 1. Agitation, irritation, vexation, fretfulness, fretting, peevishness.

2. Herpes, tetter, ringworm.

3. Fretwork, intertwined linear ornament, square raised ornament, key ornament.

4. Ridge, raised line, whelk, wale.

Fretful, *a.* Peevish, petulant, touchy, testy, snappish, waspish, pettish, splenetic, spleeny, captious, irritable, ill-humored, ill-tempered.

Friable, *a.* Crumbling, pulverable, easily crumbled.

Fribble, *a.* Trifling, frivolous, silly, fribbling, frippery.

——, *v. i.* Trifle, cavil feebly, play the fribbler.

Friction, *n.* 1. Attrition, abrasion, confrication, rubbing.

2. Rubbing *or* rolling resistance, resistance from roughness.

3. Dissension, disagreement, wrangling, clash of temperament *or* opinion.

FRIEND, *n.* 1. Confidant, intimate, dear companion, loved *or* loving associate, bosom friend.

2. Ally, associate, *confrère*, adherent of the same cause, fellow-partisan, fellow-adherent.

3. Favorer, encourager, well-wisher, patron, advocate, adherent, defender, supporter, good genius.

4. Quaker.

Friendly, *a.* 1. Kind, kindly, amiable, benevolent, well-disposed, kindly disposed, kind-hearted, affectionate.

2. Mutually kind, well-affected toward each other, of mutual regard, on good terms, on friendly terms, on a friendly, familiar *or* intimate footing.

3. Amicable, fraternal, neighborly, cordial.

4. Peaceable, disposed to peace, unhostile, not inimical.

5. Favorable, propitious, salutary, advantageous, favoring, auspicious.

Friendship, *n.* 1. Attachment, affection, fondness, love, deep regard.

2. Intimacy, intimate relation, close fellowship, close tie.

3. Friendliness, amity, amicableness, fellowship, kindly association, fraternization, cordiality, friendly regard, good-fellowship, harmony, mutual regard *or* good feeling.

4. Favor, kindness, aid, help, assistance, good-will.

Fright, *n.* 1. Alarm, affright, terror, dismay, scare, "funk," horror, consternation, panic.

2. Frightful object, thing of terror, scarecrow.

Frighten, *v. t.* Alarm, affright, terrify, dismay, appall, intimidate, scare, shock with sudden fear, stampede.

Frightful, *a.* 1. Terrible, terrific, fearful, alarming, dread, dreadful, direful, dire, horrid, horrible, awful, shocking.

2. Hideous, ghastly, grim, grisly, grewsome *or* gruesome.

Frigid, *a.* 1. Cold, cool, gelid, of a low temperature.

2. Dull, uninteresting, uninterested, unanimated, lifeless, cold, destitute of enthusiasm, without fervor, spiritless, tame.

3. Forbidding, formal, prim, stiff, rigid, distant, repellent, repelling, repulsive, chilling, freezing.

Frigidity, *n.* 1. Coldness, coolness, chilliness, frigidness, gelidity, gelidness, low temperature.

2. Dulness, frigidness, lifelessness, want of animation.

3. Frigidness, formality, primness, stiffness, rigidity, repelling manner, forbidding manner, chilliness, chill.

Frill, *n.* Ruffle, edging, gathering, frilling, ruche, ruching, furbelow; affectation, mannerism.

Fringed, *a.* Bordered, edged, fimbriated.

Frippery, *n.* 1. Old clothes, cast-off dresses.

2. Trumpery, second-hand finery.

3. Trifling, trifles, stuff, nonsense, fribbling. See FLUMMERY.

Frisk, *v. i.* Leap, skip, hop, jump, frolic, romp, caper, gambol, dance.

Frisky, *a.* Gay, lively, playful, sportive, frolicsome, coltish, full of frolic.

Frith, *n.* 1. Strait.

2. Estuary, inlet, firth, fiord, creek, arm of the sea.

Fritter, *n.* 1. Pancake, fried cake, batter cake.

2. Fragment, piece, shred, bit, scrap, splinter, flinder (*Scotch*).

Fritter, *v. t.* 1. Slice, cut into small pieces.

2. Break into fragments, break to pieces, shiver, shatter.

3. (With *away*) Waste bit by bit, pare off, reduce to nothing; misuse (*time*), waste, dawdle away, idle away, fool away, trifle.

Frivolity, *n.* Levity, puerility, trifling, triviality, frivolousness, folly, fribbling, frippery, flummery.

Frivolous, *a.* Trifling, trivial, worthless, light, empty, giddy, silly, flighty, flippant, petty, flimsy, idle, puerile, childish, trashy, foolish.

Frizzle, *v. t.* Curl, crisp, frieze, frizz.

Frolic, *n.* 1. Gambol, escapade, lark, skylark, trick, romp, wild prank, flight of levity, "spree."

2. Fun, pleasantry, drollery, play, sport.

——, *v. i.* Be merry, be frolicsome, play pranks, cut capers, caper, gambol, frisk.

Frolicsome, *a.* Sportive, playful, gamesome, gay, lively, frisky, coltish, full of frolic, frolic.

FROM, *prep.* (*Basic Eng.*)

From hand to mouth. Precariously, as want requires, by a bare subsistence, as chance provides, without any margin, by spending the wages of to-day for to-day's necessities.

FRONT, *n.* 1. Forehead, brow, face.

2. Effrontery, "face," impudence, assurance, brass.

3. Van, vanguard, fore-rank, front rank, head, breast.

4. Forepart, forward part, anterior, face; obverse.

5. Façade, front elevation, frontage.

——, *v. t.* 1. Face, stand over against, stand opposite to.

2. Confront, encounter, oppose, meet face to face.

3. Fit with a front, face, make a front to *or* for.

——, *a.* 1. Forward, anterior.

2. Frontal, foremost, headmost.

——, *v. i.* Face, be *or* stand opposite.

Frontal, *n.* Frontlet, brow-band, fillet.

Frontier, *n.* 1. Confine, border, boundary, marches, limits, coast (*archaic*).

2. [*In pl.*] Back *or* remote districts, backwoods.

Frontlet, *n.* See FRONTAL.

Frost, *n.* 1. Rime, hoar-frost, frozen dew, white-frost.

2. Cold manner, reserve, frigidity, iciness, indifference, coldness, stiffness, want of cordiality, unsociability.

——, *v. t.* 1. Ice, cover with frosting.

2. Whiten, sprinkle with white, sprinkle with gray hairs.

3. Frost-bite, injure by frost *or* cold, nip.

Frost-bite, *v. t.* Bite with frost, frost, nip, wither, blight, shrivel, injure by frost *or* cold.

Frosting, *n.* Icing, concreted sugar (*for coating cake*).

Frosty, *a.* 1. Cold, icy, wintry, stinging, chilly, chill.

2. Cold, frigid, unloving, unimpassioned, indifferent, cold-hearted, unaffectionate, uncordial.

3. Cold, spiritless, unanimated, lifeless, dull-hearted.

4. White, gray-haired, frosted, hoary.

Froth, *n.* 1. Spume, foam.

2. Triviality, nonsense, empty show, mere words, balderdash, trash, flummery, "bosh."

——, *v. i.* Foam, effervesce, gush, emit foam, show violent anger.

Frothy, *a.* 1. Foamy, spumy.

2. Trifling, light, empty, trivial, vain, frivolous, unsubstantial.

Froward, *a.* Fractious, perverse, contumacious, obstinate, stubborn, refractory, untoward, unyielding, ungovernable, disobedient, wayward, peevish, petulant, cross, captious.

Frown, *v. i.* Scowl, look stern, lower, glower.

Frowzy, *a.* [Written also *Frowsy.*]

1. Fetid, rank, noisome, stinking, offensive, musty, stale, rancid, ill-scented, strong-smelling.

2. Rough and tangled (*as the hair*).

3. Disordered, disorderly, slovenly, slatternly, dowdy.

Fructify, *v. t.* Fertilize, make fruitful, fecundate, impregnate.

——, *v. i.* Be fruitful, bear fruit, bring forth fruit, bear, be productive.

Frugal, *a.* Provident, economical, saving, abstemious, temperate, sparing, choice, chary, careful, thrifty, unwasteful.

Frugality, *n.* Economy, thrift, thriftiness, good husbandry.

FRUIT, *n.* 1. Produce (*of the earth for the supply of man and animals*), production, harvest, crop.

2. Product, result, consequence, effect, good, profit, advantage, outcome.

3. Offspring, issue, young.

Fruitful, *a.* 1. Productive, abounding in fruit.

2. Prolific, fertile, fecund.

3. Plentiful, plenteous, abundant, rich, teeming, exuberant.

Fruition, *n.* 1. Enjoyment (*in the possession or the use of anything*).

2. Fulfilment.

Fruitless, *a.* 1. Unfruitful, unproductive, barren, sterile, unprolific, unfertile, infecund, acarpous.

2. Useless, unavailing, bootless, profitless, ineffectual, unprofitable, barren, vain, idle, futile, abortive, without avail.

Frumpish, ⎫ *a.* Cross, cross-tempered,
Frumpy, ⎭ grumpy, cross-grained, snappish, irritable; dowdy, shabby, slatternly.

Frustrate, *v. t.* Defeat, disappoint, balk, foil, baffle, disconcert, circumvent, check, thwart, disappoint, bring to nought; outwit, check, cross, hinder.

——, *a.* Vain, useless, ineffectual, frustrated, null, void, of no effect.

Frustration, *n.* Disappointment, defeat, balking, foiling, baffling, circumvention, check, thwarting, bringing to nought.

Fry, *v. t.* Cook in the frying-pan, cook in boiling fat, frizzle, fricassee.

——, *v. i.* 1. Be frying, be cooking in fat.

2. Simmer, stew, ferment (*with excessive heat*).

——, *n.* 1. Fried dish.

2. Agitation, "stew," (mental) ferment.

3. Small fishes, swarm of little fishes, small fry, crowd or swarm (*of insignificant objects*).

Fuddle, *v. t.* Intoxicate, inebriate, muddle, confuse, make drunk, stupefy with drink.

Fuddled, *a.* Drunk, intoxicated, inebriated, muddled, befuddled, corned, tipsy, crapulous, groggy, boozy, tight, high, slewed, muzzy, nappy, mellow, in liquor, half seas over, in one's cups, the worse for liquor.

Fudge, *n.* Nonsense, stuff, moonshine, bosh, twaddle. See BALDERDASH.

Fuel, *n.* Firing, combustible matter, combustibles, material for burning, firing material.

Fugacious, *a.* Transitory, transient, evanescent, fleeting. See FUGITIVE.

Fugitive, *a.* 1. Fleeing, flying, escaping.

2. Transitory, transient, evanescent, fleeting, uncertain, unstable, volatile, flying, fugacious, flitting, passing, momentary, short, brief, temporary, temporal, ephemeral, short-lived.

——, *n.* Runaway, deserter, refugee.

Fugleman, *n.* See FLUGELMAN.

Fulcrum, *n.* Support (*of a lever*), prop.

Fulfil, *v. t.* [Written also *Fulfill.*] 1. Accomplish, effectuate, realize, effect, execute, bring to pass, complete, consummate, bring to completion, perfect, bring to perfection, carry out *or* to its intention.

2. Observe, obey, perform, do, discharge, keep, adhere to, comply with, be faithful to.

3. Meet, satisfy, answer, comply with, fill, fill out.

Fulfilment, *n.* [Written also *Fulfillment.*] 1. Accomplishment, realization, execution, completion, consummation.

2. Performance, discharge.

3. Satisfaction, answering, meeting, filling.

Fulgurate, *v. i.* Flash, lighten.

Fuliginous, *a.* 1. Sooty, smoky, fumy.

2. Dusky, dark.

FULL, *a.* 1. Filled, replete, brimful, flush.

2. Abounding, replete, well stocked *or* provided.

3. Loose, flowing, baggy, voluminous.

4. Satiated, sated, glutted, cloyed, swollen, chock-full, crammed, packed, stuffed, overflowing, gorged; saturated, soaked.

5. Complete, entire, perfect, adequate, mature.

6. Abundant, plentiful, copious, plenteous, sufficient, ample.

7. Loud, deep, strong, clear, distinct, rounded.

8. Comprehensive, capacious, broad, large, plump, extensive.

9. Exhaustive, detailed, circumstantial.

——, *n.* Entire extent, full measure, utmost, farthest *or* extreme limit.

——, *adv.* 1. Quite, to the same degree.

2. Completely, fully.

3. Exactly, precisely, directly.

——, *v. t.* Thicken and cleanse (*cloth*); gather, make full, pucker.

Full-grown, *a.* Mature, ripe, adult, complete.

Fullness, *n.* 1. Plenitude, copiousness, abundance, profusion, affluence, plenty.

2. Repletion, satiety, sating, glut.

3. Completeness, completion, perfection, entireness.

4. Strength, loudness, clearness, resonance.

5. Enlargement, swelling, distention, dilatation, dilation; plumpness, rotundity, roundness.

Fully, *adv.* Completely, entirely, abundantly, to the same degree, plentifully, copiously, amply, sufficiently, largely, full, to the full.

Fulminate, *v. i.* 1. Explode, detonate.

2. Utter denunciations, thunder, pour out threats, hurl denunciations, curse.

Fulminate, *v. t.* 1. Utter with a menace, proclaim with denunciation, hurl, thunder, fulmine.

2. Explode, burst, rend asunder.

Fulmination, *n.* 1. Fulminating, hurling (*of threats, etc.*), threatening, denunciation, denouncing.

2. Denunciation, threat, threatening, anathema, ban, curse, malediction.

3. Explosion, detonation.

Fulsome, *a.* 1. Gross, excessive, offensively extravagant, offensive, nauseous.

2. Nauseous, nauseating, offensive, disgusting, repulsive.

3. (*Rare*) Ribald, coarse, gross, tending to obscenity, lustful, questionable.

Fulvous, *a.* Yellow, tawny, fulvid, yellowish-brown, dull yellow.

Fumble, *v. i.* 1. Feel about (*awkwardly or childishly*).

2. Grope, grope about, stumble, bungle, mismanage, make awkward attempts, search to no purpose.

3. Mumble, stammer, stutter, stumble in speech.

Fume, *n.* 1. Smoke, vapor, steam, exhalation, smell, effluvium, reek.

2. Passion, rage, pet, fry, fret, storm, agitation, "stew."

——, *v. i.* 1. Smoke, reek, emit vapor, throw off vapor, give out exhalations.

2. Rage, rave, fret, bluster, storm, chafe, flare up.

Fumigate, *v. t.* Smoke, expose to smoke *or* vapor, cleanse by smoke *or* vapor, disinfect; perfume.

Fumy, *a.* Smoky, fuliginous, vaporous, full of smoke *or* vapor.

Fun, *n.* Pleasantry, drollery, sport, merriment, humor, waggishness, pranks, jollity, frolic, gayety, diversion.

Function, *n.* 1. Performance, execution, discharge, exercise.

2. Office, duty, capacity, activity, business, employment, occupation, part, province.

3. Ceremony, elaborate social occasion.

4. (*Math.*) Dependent, derivative, value derived.

Functionary, *n.* Office-holder, incumbent of an office.

Fund, *n.* 1. Stock, capital, accumulation, reserve, endowment; store, supply; foundation, permanent fund.

2. [*In pl., with The.*] National debt, national obligations, government bonds, consols, public funds; money, means, resources.

Fundament, *n.* Bottom, seat, buttocks, rump (*humorous or contemptuous*).

Fundamental, *a.* Essential, primary, indispensable, radical, constitutional, organic, most important, principal, basic, basal, underlying, bottom, cardinal, elementary.

——, *n.* Leading principle, basis, grounding, element, essential part, essential principle.

Funeral, *n.* Obsequies, exequies, burial, interment, burial rites, funeral solemnities, funeral rites.

Funereal, *a.* Mournful, sad, woful, lugubrious, melancholy, sepulchral, dark, sombre, gloomy, dismal, suitable to a funeral.

Fungosity, *n.* Excrescence, fungous quality.

Fungous, *a.* 1. Excrescent, fungus-like, spongy.

2. Sudden and transient, ephemeral, mushroom, trashy, upstart.

Fungus, *n.* Spongy excrescence, morbid growth.

Funicle, *n.* Fibre, filament, stalk, small cord, small ligature.

Funk, *n.* 1. Stink, stench, fetor, bad odor, offensive smell.

2. (*Colloq.*) Fear, fright, shrinking panic.

——, *v. i.* (*Colloq.*) Shrink back, be in fear, be frightened, quail, blench.

Funnel, *n.* 1. Tunnel, channel.

2. Stove-pipe, smoke-pipe, smokestack.

Funny, *a.* 1. Comical, droll, farcical, ludicrous, facetious, sportive, humorous, laughable, diverting, amusing.

2. Odd, strange, queer, curious.

Furbelow, *n.* Flounce, frill, fussy trimming, finery.

Furbish, *v. t.* Burnish, polish, renovate, renew, rub *or* scour bright.

Furcated, *a.* Forked, fork-shaped, branching, divaricated, furcular.

Furcular, *a.* Forked, fork-like, forking, furcate, furcated, fork-shaped, branching, divaricated.

Furfuraceous, *a.* 1. Scurfy, branny, scaly, scabby, lentiginous.

2. Made of bran, bran, branny, full of bran, furfurous.

Furious, *a.* 1. Raging, frantic, infuriated, fuming, frenzied, mad, violent, wild, fierce, excessively angry.

2. Vehement, impetuous, fierce, tempestuous, stormy, boisterous, tumultuous, turbulent.

Furl, *v. t.* Fold up, wrap up, roll up, fold, stow, take in, haul in.

Furlough, *n.* Leave of absence, vacation, sabbatical leave.

Furnish, *v. t.* 1. Provide, supply, endow, appoint.

2. Equip, fit, fit up, fit out, fill *or* supply with furniture.

3. Give, bestow, present, contribute, afford, produce, yield.

FURNITURE, *n.* 1. Movables, house-fittings, household goods.

2. Appendages, apparatus, appliances, fittings, furnishings, equipment.

Furor, } *n.* Fury, rage, madness, mania, **Furore,** } fad, excitement, craze, vogue.

Furrow, *n.* Trench (*made by a plough*), channel, groove, hollow, fluting, chamfer, depression, track, rut, cut, wrinkle, seam, line.

——, *v. t.* 1. Make furrows in, plough in furrows.

2. Hollow, cut in furrows, groove, channel, corrugate, cleave, cut, flute, chamfer.

3. Wrinkle, seam, pucker.

Furrowed, *a.* 1. Sulcate.

2. Grooved, wrinkled, etc. See the verb.

Further, *a.* 1. Farther, more remote, more distant.

2. Farther on, to a greater distance *or* length, more in advance, farther.

3. Additional, farther.

——, *adv.* 1. Farther, more remotely, more in advance, to a greater distance (*from the starting point*), farther on.

2. Farther, moreover, besides, further-more, also.

——, *v. t.* Promote, forward, encourage, aid, strengthen.

Furtherance, *n.* Promotion, advancement, aid, helping forward.

Furthermore, *adv.* Moreover, besides, and then too, also.

Furthest, *a.* 1. Farthest, remotest, most remote, most distant.

2. Longest, greatest, farthest reaching.

Furtive, *a.* Stolen, stealthy, surreptitious, clandestine, secret, sly, sneaking, skulk-ing.

Fury, *n.* 1. Rage, frenzy, madness, furor, fit, storm of anger.

2. Impetuosity, vehemence, fierceness, violence, turbulence, headlong rush.

3. Goddess of Vengeance, avenging deity.

4. Vixen, virago, hag, shrew, terma-gant, beldam.

Fuse, *v. t.* 1. Melt, liquefy (*by heat*), smelt.

2. Amalgamate, blend, commingle, in-termingle, intermix, make homogeneous, unite.

——, *v. i.* 1. Melt, be fused.

2. Blend, intermingle, coalesce, amal-gamate, merge.

——, *n.* Match, igniting tube, firing ma-terial.

Fusiform, *a.* Spindle-shaped, tapering.

Fusion, *n.* 1. Liquefaction (*by heat*), melt-ing.

2. Amalgamation, blending, commin-gling, union, commixture, intermingling, intermixture, making homogeneous; coa-lition, merging.

Fuss, *n.* Ado, bustle, fidget, hurry, worry, flurry, disturbance, commotion, pother, bustle, fluster, fret, stir, excitement, agita-tion, to-do, much ado about nothing.

——, *v. i.* 1. Bustle, be in a fidget, make much ado about trifles *or* about nothing, be in a stew *or* pucker (*colloq.*).

2. Fume, fret, worry.

Fussy, *a.* Bustling, fidgety, busy about trifles, making needless ado, making a great ado, overnice, overdetailed *or* elabo-rate.

Fustian, *n.* 1. Bombast, rant, rhodomon-tade, claptrap, inflated style, swelling *or* pompous phraseology.

2. Stuff, nonsense, trash, twaddle, inanity, etc. See BALDERDASH.

3. Coarse cotton cloth.

Fusty, *a.* Musty, mouldy, rank, ill-smell-ing, malodorous.

Futile, *a.* 1. Trifling, frivolous, trivial.

2. Worthless, valueless, useless, profit-less, fruitless, bootless, vain, idle, unprof-itable, unavailing, ineffectual, of no *or* none effect, to no purpose.

Futility, *n.* 1. Triviality, frivolousness.

2. Uselessness, worthlessness, vanity, bootlessness, fruitlessness.

Future, *n.* Futurity, time to come, coming time, subsequent time, by-and-by, here-after; coming events, events to come, what is yet to be, what may occur here-after.

FUTURE, *a.* Coming, prospective, to come, yet to be, that will be, hereafter.

Futurity, *n.* The future.

G

Gab, *n.* (*Colloq.*) 1. Mouth.

2. Prate, prattle, gabble, idle talk. See PRATE, *n.*

Gabble, *n.* Prate, prattle, chatter, babble, clack, jabber, gossip, palaver, gab, idle talk, small talk.

Gabbler, *n.* Prater, prattler, babbler, chatterer, rattle-head, tattler, gossip.

Gad, *v. i.* 1. Rove about idly, ramble without definite purpose.

2. Go unrestrainedly, wag, run loose.

Gadabout, *n.* 1. Rover, idler, rambler, vagrant, loafer.

2. Gossip, tattler, talebearer.

Gaffer, *n.* 1. Goodman.

2. Old rustic, old fellow.

3. Foreman (*of navvies*), overseer.

Gag, *v. t.* Silence, stifle, muzzle, muffle, choke, throttle.

——, *v. i.* Retch, keck (*rare*).

Gage, *n.* 1. Pawn, pledge, security, surety.

2. Challenge, defiance, gauntlet, glove.

——, *v. t.* Pawn, impawn, pledge, give as security.

Gain, *n.* 1. Profits, gainings, increase, addition, accretion, winnings, gettings, excess of earnings over outlay.

2. Emolument, lucre, acquisition, money-making.

3. Profit, advantage, benefit, good, blessing.

——, *v. t.* 1. Get (*by effort*), acquire, obtain, procure, achieve, secure, carry, win, earn, reap, get possession of.

2. Conciliate, persuade, enlist, get the goodwill of, prevail upon, bring over, win over, gain over.

3. Reach, attain, arrive at, win to, win.

4. Get more, get a profit, profit, net, clear.

Gainful, *a.* 1. Advantageous, profitable, beneficial.

2. Lucrative, remunerative, productive, paying.

Gain ground. Increase, advance, progress, make progress.

Gain over. Gain, enlist, persuade, conciliate, win over, bring over, prevail upon.

Gainsay, *v. t.* Contradict, deny, controvert, forbid, dispute.

Gait, *n.* Carriage, walk, manner of walking, pace, step, stride.

Gala-day, *n.* Holiday, day of festivity, day of rejoicing.

Galaxy, *n.* Milky way; cosmic system.

Gale, *n.* 1. (*Poetical.*) Wind, breeze, current of air.

2. Strong wind, violent wind, hard blow, storm, tempest, hurricane.

Gall, *n.* 1. Bitterness, rancor, acerbity, spite, malice, maliciousness, malignity.

2. (*Colloq.*) Impudence, effrontery.

——, *v. t.* 1. Chafe, fret, excoriate, hurt by rubbing.

2. Provoke, vex, irritate, tease, exasperate, incense, affront, harass, annoy, plague, sting.

Gallant, *a.* 1. Gay, showy, fine, splendid, magnificent, well-dressed.

2. Courageous, brave, valiant, intrepid, valorous, heroic, chivalrous, fearless, bold, daring, high-spirited.

3. Magnanimous, noble, chivalrous, high-minded, fine, lofty, honorable.

4. Attentive to ladies, polite, courteous.

——, *n.* 1. Beau, spark, blade.

2. Suitor, wooer, lover.

Gallantry, *n.* 1. Bravery, courage, courageousness, valor, intrepidity, prowess, heroism, boldness, fearlessness, chivalry, contempt of danger.

2. Courtesy, politeness, polite attention (*to ladies*).

Galleon, *n.* Argosy, carrack.

Gallery, *n.* 1. Corridor, passage.

2. Hanging platform, balcony, loft, veranda.

Galley, *n.* 1. Oared ship.

2. Cook-room (*of a ship*), caboose.

Gallimaufry, *n.* 1. Olio, ragout, hash.

2. Medley, farrago, jumble, miscellany, salmagundi, olio, olla-podrida, hotch-potch, hodge-podge, confused mixture.

Gallop, *v. i.* 1. Go at a gallop, ride at a gallop.

2. Hurry, rush, fly, speed, scamper, run.

Galvanize, *v. t.* 1. Affect with galvanism, treat with galvanism, charge with voltaic electricity.

2. Stimulate by galvanism, bring to a mock vitality, excite, electrify.

Gamble, *v. i.* Game, play for money, practise gaming, play for stakes, dice, wager, plunge, hazard, practise gambling.

Gambler, *n.* 1. Gamester, player, plunger, dicer, player for stakes.

2. Professional gambler, blackleg, cheating gamester, card-sharper.

Gambol, *v. i.* Frisk, frolic, romp, caper, cut capers, leap, hop, *or* skip (*in sport*).

Gambrel-roof, *n.* Curb-roof, mansard-roof.

Game, *n.* 1. Sport, play, amusement, pastime, diversion; contest.

2. Plan, scheme, stratagem, bit of strategy, enterprise, project, adventure, undertaking, measure.

3. Quarry, prey.

——, *a.* 1. Courageous, brave, resolute, unflinching, fearless, valorous, dauntless, intrepid, gallant, heroic; ready, "in the running."

2. Made of game, of game.

3. (*Colloq.*) Disabled, lame.

——, *v. i.* Gamble, play for money *or* stakes, practise gaming *or* gambling, be addicted to play.

Gamesome, *a.* Gay, sportive, vivacious, sprightly, merry, frolicsome, playful, lively, frisky, full of frolic.

Gamin, *n.* [Fr.] Idle boy, blackguard boy, street Arab, hoodlum, young rough, "mucker."

Gammer, *n.* Goody, goodwoman, goodwife.

Gammon, *n.* 1. Imposition, hoax, humbug; nonsense, "bosh."

2. Smoked ham, ham of bacon.

——, *v. t.* Deceive, cheat, humbug, hoax, chouse, trick, dupe, gull, cozen, overreach, outwit, bamboozle, circumvent, delude, beguile, mislead, inveigle, impose upon.

Gamut, *n.* Scale, compass.

Gamy, *a.* High, almost tainted, high-flavored.

Gang, *n.* Company, crew, band, horde, party, set, clique, coterie, cabal.

Gangrene, *n.* Mortification.

——, *v. i.* Mortify, be mortified, lose vitality.

Gangway, *n.* Passage-way, passage, gang-plank, aisle.

Gaol, *n.* [Written also and usually *Jail.*] Prison.

Gap, *n.* Cleft, crevice, opening, chink, cranny, chasm, pass, ravine, crack, interstice, breach, rift, break, hiatus, vacancy, space, interval, lacuna.

Gape, *v. i.* 1. Yawn.

2. Open, dehisce, yawn, be opened, be separated.

Garb, *n.* Dress, clothes, habit, apparel, garments, vesture, raiment, attire, habiliment, costume.

Garbage, *n.* Refuse (*of flesh*), offal.

Garble, *v. t.* Mutilate (*a quotation*), falsify, pervert, corrupt, misrepresent, misquote.

GARDEN, *n.* Tract for flowers *or* horticulture.

Gargantuan, *a.* Brobdingnagian, huge beyond belief, incredibly big, prodigious, enormous, tremendous.

Gargoyle, *n.* Spout, projecting conductor, waterspout; grotesque carving.

Garish, *a.* Flaunting, bright, dazzling, staring, glaring, showy, gaudy, tawdry, flashy.

Garland, *n.* Wreath, chaplet, crown, coronal, festoon, bays.

GARMENT, *n.* Vestment, article of clothing. [*pl.*] Clothes, clothing, dress, habit. See GARB.

Garner, *n.* Granary, storehouse.

——, *v. t.* Gather (*for preservation*), store, accumulate, hoard, deposit, save, husband, reserve, collect, garner up, treasure up, lay in, lay up, lay by, set by.

Garnish, *v. t.* Adorn, decorate, embellish, deck, bedeck, beautify, grace, ornament, prank, trim, set off, set out, trick out.

Garniture, *n.* Embellishments, decorations, trimming, ornaments, adornments, furniture, ornamental appendages, setting off.

Garret, *n.* Attic, loft, cock-loft, upper story, "sky parlor."

Garrulity, *n.* Loquacity, loquaciousness, babble, babbling, talkativeness, prattle, prate.

Garrulous, *a.* Loquacious, talkative, prating, prattling, babbling.

Gas, *n.* Aeriform fluid, elastic fluid; fume, damp, vapor.

Gasconade, *n.* Boast, brag, vaunt, bravado, vaporing, fanfaronade, bluster, swagger.

Gash, *v. t.* Cut deeply, score, slash, slit, make a deep incision *or* deep incisions in.

——, *n.* Deep cut, gaping wound.

Gasp, *v. i.* Pant, puff, blow, labor for breath, choke, breathe convulsively; exclaim.

Gassy, *a.* 1. Gas-like, gaseous.

2. (*Colloq.*) Inflated, bombastic, pompous, boastful.

Gastric, *a.* Of the stomach.

Gastronomy, *n.* 1. Art of cookery.

2. Epicurism, pleasures of the table.

Gather, *v. t.* 1. Collect, muster, assemble, group, rally, cluster, convene, mobilize, congregate, bring together, draw together; accumulate, amass, hoard, garner, garner up, heap up, gather up; lump, huddle.

2. Pluck, crop, pick, cull, reap, glean, rake, shock, stack, bunch.

3. Gain, win, acquire, get.

4. Infer, deduce, conclude, draw the inference, derive.

5. Fold, fold up *or* together, draw together.

6. Plait, pucker, shirr, full.

——, *v. i.* 1. Muster, congregate, assemble, collect, come together.

2. Collect, increase, thicken, be condensed, suppurate, come to a head.

Gathering, *n.* 1. Acquisition, collecting, procuring, earning, gain.

2. Assemblage, assembly, company, meeting, collection, concourse, congregation, muster.

3. Abscess, sore, ulcer, fester, imposthume, pustule, suppuration, suppurating tumor.

Gaucherie, *n.* [Fr.] Uncouthness, awkwardness, tactlessness, blundering, bungling, lack of social polish.

Gaudy, *a.* Flaunting, garish, tawdry, glittering, gimcrack, brummagem, cheap, spurious, sham; tinsel, over-decorated, flashy, showy, ostentatious, "loud."

Gauge, *v. t.* 1. Measure (*a cask, etc.*), find the contents of, ascertain the capacity of.

2. Measure (*as to ability*), estimate; adjust.

——, *n.* 1. Measure, standard, means of estimating.

2. Measure, measuring instrument, carpenter's gauge.

Gaunt, *a.* Lean, thin, lank, emaciated, meagre, slender, spare, attenuated.

Gavel, *n.* Mallet (*of a presiding officer*), hammer.

Gawk, *n.* Clown, boor, booby, awkward simpleton, lout, bumpkin, gawky.

Gawky, *a.* Awkward, ungainly, clownish, boorish, rustic, clumsy, raw, green, uncouth, loutish.

Gay, *a.* 1. Showy, bright, fine, brilliant, dashing.

2. Gaudy, flaunting, flashy, garish, tawdry, glittering, tinsel, "loud."

3. Merry, lively, cheerful, gleeful, jovial, mirthful, festive, jaunty, frivolous, sprightly, blithe, blithesome, airy, sportive, frolicsome, gladsome, jolly, vivacious, hilarious, light-hearted.

Gayety, *n.* [Written also *Gaiety*.] 1. Show, showiness, gaudiness, finery, glitter, brilliancy, tinsel, garishness, flashiness.

2. Liveliness, cheerfulness, joyousness, joviality, sprightliness, mirth, blithesomeness, merriment, glee, hilarity, jollity, vivacity, animation, good-humor, high spirits.

Gaze, *v. i.* Look intently, look long, look fixedly, stare, pore, keep one's look fixed, look long and earnestly.

Gazette, *n.* 1. Newspaper, journal.

2. Official newspaper *or* journal.

——, *v. t.* Publish officially, officially announce.

Gear, *n.* 1. Array, dress, apparel, clothing, garb.

2. Accoutrements, harness, array, armor, appointments; appliances, appurtenances, equipments, accessories, subsidiaries; goods, movables.

3. Harness, trappings, accoutrements, tackle, draught-gear.

4. Mechanism, machinery, apparatus, mechanical appliances; gearing, toothed wheels, series of cogwheels.

5. Rigging, tackle.

Geld, *v. t.* Castrate, emasculate, glib, deprive of virility.

Gelidity, *n.* Extreme cold, chill, chilliness, frigidity.

Gem, *n.* 1. Jewel, precious stone; work of art, great treasure.

2. (*Bot.*) Bud, germ.

Geminate, *a.* (*Bot.*) Doubled, twin, in pairs, binate.

Gemination, *n.* 1. (*Zoöl.*) Reproduction by buds.

2. (*Bot.*) Budding, germination, leaving out.

Gender, *n.* 1. Sex.

2. (*Gram.*) Inflection for sex, form relative to sex.

Genealogy, *n.* 1. Pedigree, list of ancestors, family tree, lineage; history of descent.

2. Descent, derivation.

GENERAL, *a.* 1. Universal, of the whole (*genus, class, etc.*), generic, not partial, not special, not particular; widespread, broad, collective, popular.

2. Ecumenical, catholic.

3. Common, usual, ordinary, current.

4. Vague, indefinite, ill-defined, inexact, inaccurate.

——, *n.* 1. Whole, total.

2. (*Mil.*) Commander-in-chief, generalissimo, captain-general.

3. (*Mil.*) General officer (*brigadier, major-general, lieutenant-general*).

Generality, *n.* 1. Universality, generic extent.

2. Bulk, mass, greater part, main body, common run.

3. Vague phrase *or* statement.

Generally, *adv.* 1. Commonly, usually, in general, in the usual course of things, as the world goes, in most cases, extensively, universally.

2. In the main, without particularizing, without details, on the whole.

Generate, *v. t.* 1. Beget, procreate, engender, breed, propagate, reproduce, spawn.

2. Produce, form, make, beget, engender, breed, cause, bring about, bring into existence.

Generation, *n.* 1. Procreation, engendering.

2. Production, formation.

3. Progeny, offspring, succession of descendants.

4. Family, stock, race, breed.

Generosity, *n.* 1. Nobleness, disinterestedness, magnanimity, high-mindedness.

2. Liberality, bounty, bounteousness, bountifulness, charity, munificence.

Generous, *a.* 1. Noble, magnanimous, honorable, high-minded.

2. Liberal, bountiful, beneficent, munificent, charitable, open-handed, free-hearted; abundant, rich, ample.

Genial, *a.* 1. Fostering, cheering, enlivening, inspiriting, encouraging.

2. Cordial, hearty; kindly; cheerful, pleasant, merry, mirthful, jovial.

Genitals, *n. pl.* Sexual organs, private parts, organs of generation, pudenda.

Genius, *n.* 1. Bent, turn, aptitude, aptness, capacity, faculty, endowment, talent, gift, flair.

2. Invention, ingenuity, intellect, sagacity, brains, parts, wit, mother-wit, inspiration, creative power, power of invention.

3. Adept, proficient, master, master-hand, man of genius.

4. Nature, character, disposition, natural disposition, peculiar constitution, characteristic quality.

5. Spirit, tutelary deity, guardian spirit, guardian angel; djinn.

Genteel, *a.* 1. Refined, polite, courteous, polished, civil, well-bred, gentlemanly *or* lady-like.

2. Fashionable, stylish, elegant, graceful (*in dress, style of living, etc.*).

Gentile, *n.* Non-Jew, uncircumcised, Aryan, pagan.

Gentility, *n.* Politeness, courtesy, urbanity, good-breeding, good behavior, refinement of manners.

Gentle, *a.* 1. Mild, bland, moderate, kind, tender, compassionate, indulgent, meek, soft, humane, clement, lenient, merciful, of a sweet disposition, gentle-hearted, tender-hearted, amiable.

2. Tame, docile, peaceable, quiet, tractable, pacific, dove-like.

3. Light, moderate, soft, bland, zephyr-like, mild; gradual, easy, slight.

4. High-born, noble, well-born, of good family.

5. Refined, cultivated, well-bred, polished, courteous, chivalrous.

Gentlefolk, } *n. pl.* People of good family
Gentlefolks, } and good breeding, lords and ladies, ladies and gentlemen.

Gentleman, *n.* 1. [*Eng.*] Man of good family (*above the rank of yeoman*), aristocrat, "gent."

2. Man of good breeding, well-mannered man, refined *or* polished man, man of delicacy and honor.

Gentlemanly, } *a.* Polite, courteous, civil,
Gentlemanlike, } refined, cultivated, honorable, delicate, urbane, genteel, well-bred.

Gentry, *n.* [*Eng.*] Middle class, people of good position (*between the nobility and the vulgar*).

Genuine, *a.* 1. Pure, uncorrupt, unalloyed, unadulterated, true, real, veritable, authentic, right, proper, Simon-pure, honest, "true-blue," what it purports to be.

2. Native, unaffected, sincere, frank.

Genus, *n.* 1. Group (*subordinate to a class, tribe*, or *order*), assemblage of species, class, order, kind, sort.

2. (*Log.*) Relative, universal, kind *or* sort *or* class to which particulars belong.

Geoponics, *n. pl.* Agriculture, husbandry, culture of the soil, tillage, rural economy.

Germ, *n.* 1. Embryo, ovum (*in animals*), ovule (*in plants*), seed, seed-bud, young bud; microörganism, microbe, bacterium.

2. Origin, source, first principle, originating *or* originative principle, beginning, rudiment.

German, *a.* 1. Born of the same father and mother, full.

2. Born of brothers *or* sisters *or* of brothers and sisters.

3. Cognate, pertinent, relevant, appropriate, closely allied. See GERMANE.

Germane, *a.* 1. Related, akin, allied, cognate.

2. Relevant, pertinent, apposite, appropriate, suitable, fitting, to the purpose, to the point.

Germinate, *v. i.* Sprout, shoot, vegetate, bud, push, pullulate, put forth, burst forth, spring up, begin to vegetate, grow, burgeon, generate.

Gestation, *n.* Pregnancy.

Gestic, *a.* Related to bodily motion, terpsichorean.

Gesticulate, *v. i.* Make gestures, gesture, motion, signal.

Gesture, *n.* Action (*accompanying oral utterance*), gesticulation, gesturing, motion, signal, sign.

——, *v. i.* Gesticulate, make gestures.

GET, *v. t.* 1. Procure, obtain, acquire, receive, gain, win, earn, achieve, realize, secure, come by.

2. Master, finish, prepare.

3. Learn, memorize, commit to memory, get by heart.

4. Beget, generate, engender, procreate, breed.

5. Procure to be, cause to be, have.

6. Persuade, induce, dispose, influence, prevail upon.

GET, *v. i.* 1. Become, fall, go.

2. Arrive, reach, win.

Get ahead. Proceed, progress, advance, get on, get forward, get along.

Get at. 1. Discover, determine, ascertain, find out.

2. Reach, make way to, get hold of.

Get away from. Quit, leave, disengage one's self from.

Get back. 1. Return, come back.

2. Obtain again, get possession of again.

3. Obtain in return.

Get behind. 1. Lag, fall behind *or* below, fall in the rear.

2. Take a position behind, get in the rear of.

Get by heart. Memorize, learn, learn by heart *or* by rote, commit to memory.

Get down. Descend, come down, alight.

Get forward. Proceed, progress, advance, get along, get ahead, get on.

Get into. 1. Mount, climb into.

2. Be admitted into.

3. Penetrate, get inside of.

Get off. 1. Escape, get clear, get free, be acquitted.

2. Depart, go away.

3. Alight from, descend from, dismount, disembark.

Get on, *v. t.* Put on, draw on, don.

——, *v. i.* Proceed, progress, advance, get along, get ahead, get forward.

Get out. 1. Come out.

2. Be extricated.

3. "Clear out," begone, avaunt, away with you, be off, get you gone.

Get over. 1. Climb over.

2. Surmount, conquer, overcome.

3. Recover from.

Get rid of. 1. Dispose of, shift off, cast off.

2. Be freed from, be relieved from, get clear of, get quit of.

Get the hang of. Understand, comprehend, get acquainted with, get accustomed to, get used to, become familiar with, see into, know all about.

Get the start of. Be ahead of, have the advantage of, take the lead of, outstrip, get at a disadvantage.

Get through. 1. Pass through, go through.

2. Accomplish, finish, complete, do.

Getting, *n.* Acquisition, acquirement.

Get together. (*Trans.*) 1. Collect, assemble, muster, convene.

2. Collect, accumulate, amass, pile up, heap up.

3. Combine, make up, contrive, conjoin. put together.

——. (*Intrans.*) Meet, convene, assemble, congregate, come together.

Get up, *v. t.* Prepare, make ready.

——, *v. i.* Arise, rise; ascend, climb.

Gewgaw, *n.* Bawble, trifle, trinket, toy, kickshaw, knick-knack, gimcrack, plaything, gaud, worthless piece of finery.

Ghastly, *a.* 1. Pale, pallid, wan, cadaverous, death-like, ghostly, deathly, corpse-like, lurid.

2. Dismal, hideous, grim, grisly, terrible, dreadful, gruesome, fearful, horrible, frightful, shocking.

Ghost, *n.* 1. Spirit, soul.

2. Apparition, spectre, sprite, phantom, shade, revenant, "spook," departed spirit.

Ghostly, *a.* 1. Spiritual, of the soul.

2. Spectral, phantom-like, ghost-like, "spooky," shadowy.

Giant, *n.* Monster, Cyclops, colossus, Hercules, huge man.

Gibberish, *n.* Jargon, gabble, jabber, gibble-gabble, balderdash, nonsense, prate, prating, drivel, idle talk, empty babble, empty sound.

Gibbet, *n.* Gallows, hangman's tree.

Gibbous, *a.* 1. Convex, protuberant, swelling, rounded.

2. Humped, hunched, hump-backed, crook-backed.

Gibe, *v. i.* Sneer, scoff, jeer, fleer, flout.

——, *v. t.* Flout, taunt, deride, ridicule, jeer, fleer, twit, scoff at, sneer at, jeer at.

——, *n.* Sneer, etc. See the verbs.

Giddy, *a.* 1. Vertiginous, dizzy.

2. Changeable, fickle, inconstant, unsteady, mutable, unstable, vacillating, irresolute; careless, heedless, thoughtless, wild, frivolous, reckless, headlong, flighty, hare-brained, giddy-brained, light-headed.

Gift, *n.* 1. Donation, present, benefaction, boon, favor, gratuity, "tip," grant, offering, bonus, premium, prize, contribution, subscription, largess, subsidy, allowance, endowment, bounty, bequest, legacy, dower, honorarium.

2. Talent, power, faculty, capability, capacity, bent, aptitude, ability, endowment, genius, turn, *forte.*

Gifted, *a.* Talented, able, ingenious, sagacious, inventive, intelligent.

Gigantic, *a.* Huge, vast, enormous, colossal, immense, prodigious, Cyclopean, Herculean, giant, very large.

Giggle, *n.* Titter, silly laugh, snicker, snigger.

Gild, *v. t.* 1. Coat with gold-leaf, overlay with gold.

2. Adorn, brighten, illuminate, make lustrous, embellish, make bright.

Gimcrack, *n.* Trifle, toy, knicknack, knack, jiggumbob.

Gin, *n.* (*Archaic.*) Trap, snare, net, toils, noose, springe.

Gingerly, *adv.* Cautiously, tenderly, carefully, timidly; daintily, fastidiously.

Gird, *v. t.* 1. Girdle, bind round, bind with a girdle, belt.

2. Surround, encircle, encompass, enclose, environ, engird, begird.

3. Brace, support.

——, *v. i.* Gibe, sneer, make scornful jests, utter sarcasms.

Girder, *n.* 1. Main beam.

2. Sneerer, giber, sarcastic derider.

Girdle, *n.* Band (*for the waist*), belt, cincture, surcingle, cestus.

——, *v. t.* 1. Gird, bind round.

2. Environ, encompass, surround, enclose, embrace, girt, shut in.

Girdled, *a.* Girded, cinctured, belted.

GIRL, *n.* 1. Lass, lassie, damsel, miss, maiden, maid, virgin.

2. Servant, domestic (*female*).

Girth, *n.* 1. Belly-band, girdle, cinch.

2. Circumference; distance around.

Gist, *n.* Essence, pith, marrow, core, substance, basis, ground, main point.

GIVE, *v. t.* 1. Bestow (*voluntarily and without compensation*), accord, present, bequeath, devise, entrust. See CONFER.

2. Furnish, supply, afford, spare, accommodate with; donate, contribute, proffer.

3. Impart, communicate.

4. Pay, exchange; requite, deliver, hand over.

5. Permit, allow, vouchsafe, deign. See GRANT.

6. Utter, pronounce, emit, render.

7. Produce, yield, show as a product.

8. Cause, occasion.

9. Devote, apply, addict, give up, surrender.

——, *v. i.* 1. Yield (*to pressure*), give way, sink, bend; yield, recede, retire, give way, retreat.

2. Lead, open, afford entrance, look out, afford a view.

Give away. Transfer (*without an equivalent*), make over gratis, part with gratuitously.

Give back. Return, restore.

Give chase. Pursue, follow on.

Give ear. Listen, hear, hearken, attend.

Give in. (*Trans.*) 1. Hand in, pass in.

2. Abate, deduct, discount.

——. (*Intrans.*) Yield, surrender, give up, cry quits, cry quarter.

Give over. 1. Leave, quit, abandon, cease from.

2. Consider hopeless, consider lost, give up.

Give out. (*Trans.*) 1. Emit, send forth.

2. Proclaim, announce, report, publish.

——. (*Intrans.*) 1. Fail, come short.

2. Be exhausted, spend one's strength.

Give place. 1. Withdraw, retire, recede, retreat, give way, make room.

2. Yield precedence.

Giver, *n.* Donor, bestower, disposer, donator (*law*).

Give up, *v. t.* 1. Resign, relinquish, yield, surrender.

2. Abandon, forsake, leave, quit, cease from, give over.

3. Consider hopeless, consider lost, give over.

——, *v. i.* Yield, surrender, give in, cry quits, cry quarter.

Give way. 1. Withdraw, recede, retire, retreat, make room.

2. Fail, break, be broken.

Glabrous, *a.* Smooth, hairless, destitute of pubescence.

Glacial, *a.* 1. Icy, frozen, consisting of ice, icy-looking.

2. Of glaciers, pertaining to glaciers.

Glaciate, *v.* Freeze, congeal, turn into ice.

Glacier, *n.* Ice-torrent, ice-stream.

Glad, *a.* 1. Pleased, delighted, gratified, rejoiced, happy, well contented.

2. Cheerful, joyous, joyful, gladsome, happy, blithe, merry, elate, elated, jocund, playful, light-hearted, light, animated, cheery.

3. Cheering, animating, gratifying, pleasing, exhilarating, bright, gladdening, joyous, joyful.

Gladden, *v. t.* Delight, cheer, gratify, rejoice, bless, exhilarate, glad, make glad, please highly, make joyous *or* happy, fill with joy *or* pleasure, render light-hearted.

——, *v. i.* Become glad, grow happy *or* joyous, smile, beam, light up, grow light, brighten, grow bright.

Gladiate, *a.* (*Bot.*) Sword-shaped, ensiform.

Gladiator, *n.* Sword-player, swordsman, prize-fighter (*in ancient Rome*).

Gladness, *n.* Joy, joyfulness, joyousness, happiness, gratification, delight, pleasure.

Gladsome, *a.* Pleased, delighted, cheerful, joyful, joyous, glad, gay, blithe, blithesome, gleeful, jovial, jolly, merry, lively, jocund, airy, vivacious, sprightly, sportive, frolicsome, light-hearted.

Glamour, *n.* 1. Witchery (*as making things seem to be what they are not*), magic, enchantment, charm, spell.

2. Fantastic light, imaginary glory, bewitchment, glow, enthusiasm, fascination, attraction, captivation.

Glance, *n.* 1. Glitter, gleam.

2. Glimpse, transitory view, rapid look.

——, *v. i.* 1. Glitter, gleam, shine, flash, coruscate, scintillate, glisten, glister.

2. Flit, dart, appear and disappear.

3. Dart aside, fly off obliquely, ricochet.

4. Snatch a glance, snatch a momentary look, look hurriedly.

5. Make passing allusion, reflect upon, hint at, intimate.

Glare, *v. i.* 1. Flare, flame, dazzle, glitter, glisten, gleam, sparkle.

2. Glower, look fierce, look black.

——, *n.* 1. Glitter, flare, dazzling light, bright, glassy surface.

2. Fierce look, glower.

Glaring, *a.* 1. Dazzling, glittering.

2. Barefaced, notorious, conspicuous, open, manifest, extreme.

GLASS, *n.* Crystal, glazing.

Glasses, *n. pl.* Spectacles, eye-glasses, binoculars, etc.

Glassy, *a.* 1. Vitreous.

2. Hyaline, crystal, crystalline, transparent, shining, lucent, gleaming, brilliant.

3. Dull, glazed.

Glaucous, *a.* Sea-green.

Glaze, *v. t.* Calender, polish, gloss, burnish, furbish, give a glossy surface to.

——, *v. i.* Become glassy, grow dim, grow filmy, become lusterless.

——, *n.* Glazing, enamel, coat, varnish, polish, finish; luster.

Glazing, *n.* 1. Setting glass.

2. Glaze, enamel.

Gleam, *n.* 1. Ray, beam, glance, glow, flash, glimmer, glimmering.

2. Luster, brightness, splendor, gleaming, flash, flashing, coruscation, glitter, glittering.

——, *v. i.* Glimmer, shine, glitter, sparkle, coruscate, flash, beam, glance.

Glean, *v. t.* 1. Gather (*after reapers*).

2. Collect, cull, pick up, harvest, get.

Glebe, *n.* 1. Soil, clod, sod, turf, ground, earth.

2. Parish land, church demesne; field.

Glee, *n.* 1. Merriment, mirth, gayety, joviality, joy, jollity, exhilaration, liveliness, sportiveness, jocularity, hilarity.

2. Light song, song of interwoven melodies.

Gleeful, *a.* Glad, merry, joyous, light, light-hearted, gay, happy, jocund, elate.

Glen, *n.* Valley, vale, dale, dell, dingle.

Glib, *a.* 1. Smooth, slippery.

2. Voluble, fluent, facile, ready, talkative, nimble of speech, ready in speech, of a ready tongue; flippantly smooth.

Glide, *v. i.* 1. Slip, slide, move smoothly, glissade, sail, float, skate, skim.

2. Flow, lapse, run, roll on.

——, *n.* Lapse, slip, gliding, sliding, continuous motion.

Glimmer, *v. i.* Shine (*faintly*), gleam, glitter, flash, flicker, twinkle.

——, *n.* 1. Gleam (*of faint, unsteady light*), ray, beam, glimmering.

2. Glimpse, glance, transitory view, faint view.

Glimpse, *n.* Glance, glimmering, transitory view, flash, sight, rapid look, momentary perception, glint (*Scotch*).

Glint, *n.* Glance. See GLIMPSE.

Glisten, *v. i.* Sparkle, glitter, shine fitfully, flash.

Glitter, *v. i.* Glisten, glister, sparkle, gleam, flash, flare, glare, glance, scintillate, coruscate.

——, *n.* Sparkle, glister, luster, brilliancy, splendor, brightness, shine, radiance, gleam, scintillation, coruscation, beam, beaming.

Gloaming, *n.* Twilight, dusk, fall of evening, eventide, nightfall.

Gloat, *v. i.* Stare, gaze, gaze earnestly, look intently, gaze passionately, gaze with passionate satisfaction; exult, rejoice, triumph.

Globate, *a.* Globular, globose, spherical, round, spheroidal, globe-shaped.

Globe, *n.* 1. Sphere, ball, orb.

2. Earth, terraqueous globe, terrestrial ball.

Globose, *a.* Spherical, globular, globate, globated, round, globe-shaped.

Globular, *a.* Spherical, globate, globated, globose, globulous, round, globe-shaped.

Globule, *n.* Spherule, little globe, small round particle, drop, bead.

Gloom, *n.* 1. Obscurity, darkness, dimness, shade, shadow, gloominess, cloud.

2. Sadness, dejection, depression, despondency, melancholy, heaviness of mind, low spirits, cheerlessness.

Gloomy, *a.* 1. Obscure, dark, dim, dusky.

2. Dismal, cheerless, lowering, lurid.

3. Sad, dejected, depressed, dispirited, disheartened, despondent, desponding, melancholy, downcast, crestfallen, chapfallen, down-hearted, glum, heavy of heart; sullen, morose.

4. Depressing, dispiriting, saddening, sad, disheartening, melancholy, heavy, dark.

Glorify, v. t. 1. Extol, exalt, magnify, bless, honor greatly, praise highly, give glory to.

2. Brighten, make bright, add luster to, make illustrious, elevate, exalt, ennoble, adorn, surround with a halo.

Glorious, a. 1. Illustrious, renowned, celebrated, famous, famed, eminent, preeminent, distinguished, conspicuous.

2. Resplendent, splendid, bright, brilliant, radiant.

3. Noble, exalted, lofty, high, excellent, consummate, supreme.

Glory, n. 1. Honor, renown, fame, celebrity, illustriousness, eminence, distinction, praise.

2. Splendor, luster, brightness, brilliancy, resplendence, effulgence, pride.

3. Gloriousness, exaltation, nobleness, grandeur, exceeding greatness *or* excellence, supreme nobility.

4. State, pomp, parade, magnificence, dignity; height of prosperity.

5. Heavenly bliss, celestial happiness.

6. Boast, occasion of pride, matter for pride.

7. (*Painting.*) Halo, aureola.

——, v. i. Exult, vaunt, boast, take pride, triumph, be proud, pride one's self, plume one's self, pique one's self, pat one's self on the back.

Gloss, n. 1. Comment, note, explanation, interpretation, scholium, annotation, commentary.

2. Pretext, pretence, specious plea.

3. Luster, polish, shining surface, sheen, veneer, varnish.

——, v. i. Comment, make notes, make explanatory remarks.

——, v. t. Varnish, make lustrous; disguise, veil, smooth over, extenuate, palliate, color, apologize for, gloss over.

Glossarist, n. Scholiast, commentator, annotator.

Glossary, n. Dictionary (*of obscure, antiquated,* or *local words*), list of glosses, dialectical vocabulary.

Glossology, n. Glottology, linguistics, comparative philology, comparative grammar, science of language.

Gloss over. Disguise, varnish, color, palliate, endeavor to excuse, extenuate, make plausible.

Glossy, a. Smooth and shining, sheeny.

GLOVE, n. Gauntlet, mitten, handwear.

Glow, v. i. 1. Be incandescent, radiate; shine brightly.

2. Burn, be hot; be ardent, be warm, warm, feel intensely; blush, flush.

——, n. 1. Incandescence, white heat, luminosity, burning, blaze, brilliance; brightness, bright color, reddening.

2. Ardor, warmth, vehemence, impetuosity, flush, bloom, fervency, fervor, enthusiasm.

Glower, v. i. Stare (*in anger*), glare, look black, lower, scowl, look fierce.

Glose, v. i. Explain, expound, comment, gloss, make glosses.

——, v. t. Gloss over, put a specious face upon, extenuate, palliate, cover up, color, smooth over.

——, n. Specious show, gloss, plausible covering.

Glue, v. t. Cement (*as with glue*), fix, stick.

Gluey, a. Viscous, viscid. See GLUTINOUS.

Glum, a. Sullen, moody, sulky, morose, depressed, sour, crabbed, crusty, grum, glowering, frowning, surly, spleeny, cross-grained.

Glut, v. t. 1. Cloy, satiate, sate, surfeit, pall.

2. Gorge, stuff, cram, overfeed, fill full, fill to repletion, obstruct.

——, n. 1. Repletion.

2. Superabundance, over-abundance, overplus, surplus, redundancy, superfluity, over-stock.

Glutinous, a. Gluey, viscous, viscid, sticky, gummy, adhesive, tenacious, clammy.

Glutton, n. Gormandizer, gourmand, gobbler, gorger, pig, greedy-gut, voracious eater, excessive eater, belly-slave, lurcher; sensualist.

Gluttonish, } a. Voracious, gormandizing,
Gluttonous, } edacious, greedy, swinish, given to excess in eating.

Gluttony, n. Voracity, edacity, excess in eating, worship of the palate, belly-worship.

Gnarl, } v. i. Growl, snarl, murmur, grum-
Gnarr, } ble.

Gnarl, n. Protuberance, knot, contortion, snag, gnarled lump.

Gnarled, a. Knotty, knotted, twisted, contorted, snaggy, cross-grained, gnarly, full of knots.

Gnash, v. t. Strike together (*the teeth*), grind.

Gnaw, v. t. 1. Bite, nibble, champ, crunch, nibble at, keep biting.

2. Corrode, eat away, wear away, consume, erode.

GO, v. i. 1. Move, pass, proceed, advance, repair; hie, pass from point to point, make progress, go on; operate, act.

2. Walk, go on foot, wend, extravagate; travel, journey, fare.

3. Depart, set out, go away, disappear.

4. Reach, extend, range, elapse, run, lead.

5. Contribute, concur, tend, avail, have effect, be of use, be of service.

6. Fare, eventuate, turn out.

7. Be considered, be reckoned, be esteemed; be habitually, be expressed or phrased.

8. Be about, be on the point.

GO, *v. t.* Accept, approve, endure, tolerate, bear, swallow; afford, wager, bet, risk.

——, *n.* 1. Doings, case, business, action, circumstance, state of facts; turn, chance.

2. Fashion, mode, vogue, custom, fad.

3. Endurance, power, stamina, energy; "go-ahead."

——, *interj.* Begone, avaunt, aroynt, get you gone, be off, go along, off with you, get along with you, go your way, go about your business.

Go about. 1. Endeavor, attempt, undertake, set one's self about.

2. (*Naut.*) Tack, change the course.

Goad, *n.* Prick, point.

——, *v. t.* 1. Prick with a goad.

2. Harass, worry, sting, annoy, irritate, badger.

3. Incite, stimulate, instigate, urge, impel, spur, arouse, stir up, set on.

Go ahead. Proceed, advance, go on, push on, press forward.

Goal, *n.* Post (*set to bound a race*), mark, home, mete, limit, bound; object, end, design, destination, aim, height of one's ambition.

GOAT, *n.* Billy-goat, nanny-goat, kid.

Goatish, *a.* 1. Goatlike, like a goat.

2. Lecherous, lustful, lascivious, salacious, lubric, lubricous.

Gobble, *v. t.* Swallow (*greedily*), bolt, gulp.

Gobbler, *n.* 1. Gormandizer, gourmand. See GLUTTON.

2. (*Colloq.*) Turkey-cock.

Go between. Mediate, interpose.

Go-between, *n.* Agent, broker, factor, dealer, procurer; intermediary, middleman.

Go beyond. Transgress, overstep, transcend, exceed, surpass.

Goblin, *n.* Hobgoblin, spectre, sprite, demon, bogy, etc., frightful apparition, evil spirit.

Go by, *n.* (*Colloq.*) Passing by, neglect to notice, avoidance, disregard, ignoring.

God, *n.* 1. Jehovah, Lord, Providence, Heaven, the Creator, the Maker, the Deity, the Godhead, the Infinite, the Eternal, the Omnipotent, the Father, the Trinity, the Supreme Being, the First Cause, the Author of all things, God the Father, Sovereign of the Universe, the Eternal and Infinite Spirit, the Most High, the Supreme Goodness.

2. Deity, divinity, superhuman being, divine being.

3. Idol, worshipped image.

Goddess, *n.* Female divinity; the adored one, inamorata.

Godhead, *n.* 1. Deity, divinity, godship.

2. [With *The* prefixed.] The Deity. See GOD, 1.

Godless, *a.* 1. Irreligious, impious, profane, wicked, ungodly.

2. Atheistical, given to atheism.

Godlike, *a.* Divine, heavenly, supernal, celestial, preëminently good.

Godly, *a.* Pious, holy, righteous, religious, devout, saintly, saint-like, heavenly-minded, God-fearing.

Godsend, *n.* Windfall, unexpected gift, good luck, piece of good fortune, piece of good luck, stroke of fortune.

Godship, *n.* Deity, divinity, godhead.

Go for. 1. Pass for, be taken for, pass current for.

2. Favor, support, be in favor of, go in for.

Goggle, *v. i.* Roll the eyes, squint, stare.

——, *n.* Stare, owlish look, strained look.

Go halves. (*Colloq.*) Share equally.

Go hard with. Be disastrous to, have serious consequences for.

Go in for. Favor, support. See GO FOR.

Goings on. (*Colloq.*) Proceedings, conduct.

Go it. Bear it, accept it, tolerate it, endure it.

GOLD, *n.* Aurum (*chem.*), gilding, gilt.

Golden, *a.* 1. Of gold, aureate; bright, shining, splendid, resplendent, brilliant; yellow, of a gold color.

2. Excellent, precious, of great value.

3. Auspicious, favorable, opportune, propitious.

4. Delightful, glorious, happy, blest, halcyon.

Gonfalon, } *n.* Ensign, standard, banner,
Gonfanon, }   flag, pennon.

GOOD, *a.* 1. Advantageous, beneficial, useful, favorable, profitable, serviceable.

2. Suitable, fit, proper, convenient, satisfactory, adequate, appropriate, becoming, well adapted.

3. Virtuous, upright, honest, reliable, dutiful, religious, pious, righteous, worthy, well-behaved, decorous.

4. Excellent, valuable, precious, sterling, capital, admirable; healthy, sound, valid, genuine, sincere.

5. Kind, benevolent, humane, friendly, favorable, gracious, merciful, obliging, well-disposed.

6. Unblemished, unimpeached, untarnished, unsullied, immaculate, fair, honorable.

7. Companionable, social, genial, lively, cheerful.

8. Able, skilful, ready, expert, dexterous, well qualified.

9. Competent (*pecuniarily*), of established credit.

10. Pleasant, agreeable, gratifying, cheering.

GOOD, *n.* 1. Benefit, behoof, advantage, profit, gain, favor, utility.

2. Welfare, weal, prosperity, interest.

3. Righteousness, virtue, excellence, worth, moral qualities.

Good-breeding, *n.* Politeness, civility, courtesy, urbanity, affability, polish, good manners.

Good-by, } *n.* or *interj.* Farewell, adieu.
Good-bye, }

Good fortune. Prosperity, success, good luck.

Good graces. Friendship, favor.

Good heed. Great care, due caution.

Good-humor, *n.* Cheerfulness, cheer, joyousness, good spirits, flow of spirits.

Good-humored, *a.* Cheerful, buoyant, of a placid temper.

Good luck. Prosperity, success, good fortune.

Goodly, *a.* 1. Beautiful, graceful, comely, good-looking.

2. Pleasant, happy, agreeable, desirable.

3. Considerable, pretty large.

Good-nature, *n.* Kindliness, amiability, good-will, good feeling, kind-heartedness, fellow-feeling.

Goodness, *n.* 1. Excellence, value, worth.

2. Righteousness, virtue, integrity, uprightness, probity, honesty, principle.

3. Kindness, benevolence, good-will, benignity, beneficence, humaneness, humanity.

Good offices. Mediation, intervention, assistance, aid, help.

Good opinion. Approbation, esteem, regard, favorable opinion.

Goods, *n. pl.* 1. Movables, effects, chattels, furniture.

2. Commodities, wares, merchandise, stock.

Goodwife, *n.* 1. Goodwoman, goody, gammer.

2. Wife, housewife, mistress of the house.

Good-will, *n.* 1. Benevolence, kindness. See GOOD-NATURE.

2. Earnestness, heartiness, ardor, zeal.

3. (*Law.*) Custom (*of an established place of business*), patronage, public favor.

Goody, *n.* Gammer. See GOODWIFE.

Goody-goody, *a.* Righteous, pious, moral, affectedly good.

Go off. 1. Depart, go away, be off, go to a distance.

2. Explode, be discharged.

3. Sell, be sold, be taken.

4. Die, decease, depart this life.

Go on. 1. Proceed, advance, go ahead, move forward.

2. Progress, make progress, get along.

3. Continue, persist, persevere, keep on, hold out.

Goose, *n.* 1. Tailor's smoothing iron.

2. Simpleton, fool. See DUNCE.

Go out. 1. Issue, go forth.

2. Go abroad, go out of doors.

3. Expire, become extinct, be extinguished, be quenched, be put out.

Go over. 1. Read (*cursorily*), peruse, run over.

2. Examine, review.

3. Study, revolve, think over.

4. Pass over, change sides.

Gore, *n.* 1. Blood, clotted blood.

2. Gusset, triangular piece (*of cloth, etc.*).

——, *v. t.* Stab, pierce, horn.

Gorge, *n.* 1. Ravine, defile, notch, deep and narrow pass.

2. Throat, gullet, œsophagus.

——, *v. t.* 1. Swallow, devour, eat heartily, bolt.

2. Glut, satiate, cram, stuff, fill full, surfeit, fill to repletion.

——, *v. i.* Feed *or* eat greedily, stuff one's self.

Gorgeous, *a.* Showy, splendid, shining, glittering, bright, brilliant, dazzling, resplendent, magnificent, fine, rich, superb.

Gorgon, *n.* Spectre, hobgoblin, ogre, fright, poker, bugaboo, hydra, frightful object; ugly *or* terrible woman.

——, *a.* Gorgon-like, terrible, frightful, terrific, horrible, petrifying, paralyzing.

Gormand, *n.* [Written usually *Gourmand*, which see.] Gormandizer. See GLUTTON.

Gormandize, *v. i.* Gorge, stuff, eat greedily, feed ravenously *or* excessively.

Gory, *a.* Bloody, ensanguined, sanguinary.

Gospel, *n.* 1. [With *The* prefixed.] Christianity, revelation by Christ, Christian religion, divine revelation.

2. Doctrine, creed, principle of action.

Gossamer, *n.* Floating spider's web, filmy cobweb.

Gossamery, *a.* Light, flimsy, unsubstantial, cobwebby.

Gossip, *n.* 1. Tattler, babbler, chatterer, gadabout, idle talker, busybody, talebearer, quidnunc, "granny"; boon companion.

2. Chat, chit-chat, tattle, prate, prattle, cackle, groundless rumor, clack, small talk, idle personal talk.

Gossip, *v. i.* Chat, tattle, prate, prattle, gabble, clack, cackle, talk idly.

Gothic, *a.* Rude, barbaric, barbarous.

——, *n.* Gothic language.

Go through. 1. Execute, accomplish, finish, carry out.

2. Bear, endure, undergo, suffer.

Gourmand, *n.* 1. Glutton, gormandizer, belly-god, belly-slave, greedy-gut, high liver, excessive eater.

2. Epicure, cultivator of the palate, connoisseur of cookery, *gourmet.*

Gourmet, *n.* [Fr.] Epicure, refined feeder, cultivator of the palate, connoisseur of the cooking art.

Gouty, *a.* Podagric, podagrical, arthritic, swollen.

Govern, *v. t.* 1. Conduct, manage, supervise, regulate, have the direction of, have the charge of, administer the laws of.

2. Direct, guide, steer.

3. Control, restrain, curb, bridle, rule, sway, command.

——, *v. i.* Rule, have control, exercise authority, hold the reins, bear sway, have the charge.

Governable, *a.* Controllable, manageable.

Governess, *n.* Gouvernante, instructress, tutoress, woman teacher in private household.

GOVERNMENT, *n.* 1. Rule, management, autonomy, regulation, conduct; direction, guidance, rulership; control, command, restraint, sway, discipline, dominion.

2. Polity, commonwealth, state, form of sovereignty, body politic; administration, body of executive officers, ruling power, powers that be.

Governor, *n.* 1. Ruler, director, manager, comptroller, superintendent, overseer, head, master.

2. Executive, chief magistrate.

3. Tutor, instructor, guardian.

4. (*Mech.*) Regulator.

Grab, *v. t.* Snatch, clutch, seize violently, capture, take unscrupulously, grip suddenly.

Grace, *n.* 1. Favor, kindness, condescension, benignity, love, good-will.

2. Divine goodness *or* favor, divine influence, God's love.

3. Piety, devotion, devoutness, holiness, religion, sanctity, love; virtue, efficacy.

4. Pardon, forgiveness, mercy, reprieve.

5. Elegance, polish, refinement, accomplishment; attractiveness, charm, propriety.

6. Beauty, symmetry, comeliness, gracefulness, ease.

7. Short prayer (*over food at table*), petition, blessing, thanks.

8. (*Mus.*) Embellishment (*appoggiatura, shake, trill, turn*).

——, *v. t.* 1. Adorn, decorate, beautify, embellish, deck.

2. Dignify, honor.

Graceful, *a.* 1. Elegant, comely, becoming, easy, beautiful, full of grace.

2. Easy, natural, unlabored, flowing, rounded; appropriate.

3. Happy, felicitous, tactful.

Graceless, *a.* Depraved, degenerate, corrupt, profligate, reprobate, dissolute, abandoned, lost, shameless, obdurate, hardened, incorrigible, irreclaimable.

Gracious, *a.* 1. Benevolent, benignant, benign, good-natured, favorable, kind, friendly, merciful, condescending, compassionate, tender, lenient, mild, gentle.

2. Affable, familiar, courteous, civil, polite, easy.

Gradation, *n.* Regular progress (*step by step*), series, gradual advance, regular progression, succession, successive degrees.

Grade, *n.* 1. Rank, degree, step, stage, brand, intensity.

2. Gradient, rate of ascent *or* of descent (*as on a railroad*), slope.

Gradient, *n.* Grade, rate of ascent *or* of descent.

Gradual, *a.* 1. Regular (*step by step*), gradational, progressive.

2. Slow, approximative, by degrees, gentle.

Gradually, *adv.* 1. Regularly, in due succession, progressively.

2. By degrees, step by step, little by little, by little and little, a little at a time, slowly, by slow degrees.

Graduate, *v. t.* 1. Mark with degrees, divide into regular intervals.

2. Adjust, adapt, proportion, regulate.

3. Confer a degree upon, honor with a degree, invest with a degree.

——, *v. i.* Take a degree, receive a diploma.

——, *n.* Laureate, recipient *or* bearer of a degree, alumnus *or* alumna.

Graff, *n.* Ditch, moat, fosse.

Graft, *n.* 1. Shoot (*inserted in another tree*), scion, slip, sprout.

2. (*Colloq.*) Illegal gain, unjust acquisition.

——, *v. t.* Ingraft, inoculate.

GRAIN, *n.* 1. Seed, kernel, matured ovule.

2. Corn (*wheat, rye, oats, barley, maize, etc.*), cereals, cereal products, grist.

3. Particle, atom, bit, scrap, jot, whit, mite, ace, iota, tittle, scintilla, trace, spark, shadow, glimmer.

4. Fibre, texture; temper, disposition, humor.

5. Dye, tint, color, stain, tinge, hue, shade, tincture.

Gramineous, } *a.* Grassy.
Graminaceous, }

Graminivorous, *a.* Grass-eating, phytophagous.

Grammar, *n.* 1. Accidence, laws *or* rules of a language, forms of a language, correct mode of writing and speaking a language.

2. Propriety of speech, right use of language, art of speaking *or* writing correctly.

3. Treatise on grammar, manual *or* handbook of grammar, grammatical textbook.

Grammarian, *n.* Adept in grammar, grammatist, writer on grammar, grammatical author.

Granary, *n.* Garner, corn-house, storehouse, grange.

Grand, *a.* 1. Stately, lordly, princely, august, majestic, exalted, elevated, dignified, eminent, illustrious, great, high in power, of great dignity.

2. Magnificent, splendid, superb, glorious, fine, noble, sublime, lofty, Miltonic.

3. Principal, chief, superior, main, leading, pre-eminent.

Grandee, *n.* Nobleman, noble, lord.

Grandeur, *n.* 1. Greatness, vastness, immensity, loftiness, elevation, imposing character, impressiveness.

2. Majesty, loftiness, stateliness, state, dignity, glory, nobility, eminence, pomp, magnificence, augustness, splendor.

Grandfather, *n.* Grandsire, grandpapa, grandparent; forefather.

Grandiloquence, *n.* Bombast, fustian, turgidity, lofty language, high-sounding words, lofty style of speech, high-flown language, altiloquence.

Grandiloquent, *a.* Bombastic, turgid, tumid, swelling, inflated, stilted, pompous, declamatory, rhetorical, high-sounding, high-flown, altiloquent.

Grange, *n.* 1. Farm, farm-house, farming establishment.

2. Farmers' association, agricultural society.

Grant, *v. t.* 1. Admit, allow, concede, cede, indulge, accord, agree to, yield.

2. Give (*in answer to a request*), bestow, confer, vouchsafe, deign.

3. (*Law.*) Convey (*by deed*), transfer, make conveyance of.

——, *n.* 1. Gift, boon, donation, benefaction, indulgence, allowance, bestowal, bounty, largess, present, concession.

2. (*Law.*) Conveyance, cession.

Granulate, *v. t.* Form into grains, reduce to grains.

——, *v. i.* Be formed into grains, become granular, roughen.

Granule, *n.* Little grain, small particle.

Graphic, *a.* Vivid, lively, picturesque, descriptive, pictorial, figural, diagrammatic, well-drawn, well-delineated, striking, telling.

Grapple, *v. t.* Seize, gripe *or* grip, grasp, catch, tackle, clasp, clutch, lay hold of.

Grapple with. Struggle with, engage with, close with, contend with (*in close fight*).

Grasp, *v. t.* Clasp, gripe *or* grip, seize, clinch, clutch, catch, grapple, lay hold of, comprehend, understand.

——, *n.* 1. Clasp, gripe *or* grip.

2. Hold, possession.

3. Reach, power of seizing *or* of comprehending, compass, scope.

Grasping, *a.* Avaricious, covetous, rapacious, greedy, exacting, sordid, with an itching palm.

GRASS, *n.* (*Basic Eng.*)

Grassy, *a.* 1. Gramineous, graminaceous, grass-like; green.

2. Grass-covered, grass-grown, full of grass.

Grate, *v. t.* 1. Rub, scrape, abrade.

2. Rasp, comminute, reduce to particles by rubbing.

——, *v. i.* 1. Jar, grind, rasp, creak, etc.

2. Be irritating, be disagreeable, be offensive.

——, *n.* 1. Grating, bars, lattice-work, screen.

2. Fire-bed, receptacle for fuel, basket.

Grateful, *a.* 1. Thankful, obliged, indebted, beholden, under obligation.

2. Agreeable, pleasing, pleasant, gratifying, acceptable, satisfying, satisfactory, delightful, welcome, charming.

3. Delicious, palatable, savory, nice, luscious, cordial, refreshing, invigorating.

4. Soothing, comforting, alleviating.

Gratification, *n.* 1. Gratifying, pleasing, satisfying, satisfaction, indulgence, indulging.

2. Delight, satisfaction, enjoyment, pleasure, fruition.

3. Reward, recompense.

Gratify, *v. t.* 1. Please, delight, give pleasure to, make glad, gladden.

2. Indulge, satisfy, humor, fulfil, grant.

Gratifying, *a.* Pleasing, agreeable, welcome, delightful, grateful.

Grating, *a.* Harsh, irritating, displeasing, disagreeable, offensive.

——, *n.* Partition, grate.

Gratis, *adv.* [L.] Gratuitously, freely, for nothing, without compensation *or* recompense.

Gratitude, *n.* Thankfulness, feeling of obligation, sense of obligation, thankful good-will, grateful love.

Gratuitous, *a.* 1. Voluntary, free, spontaneous, of one's own accord.

2. Free, without recompense, without compensation, unrecompensed, without any equivalent.

3. Unwarranted, unfounded, groundless, without proof, baseless, uncalled for, not necessitated, wanton.

Gratuity, *n.* Present, gift, donation, benefaction, bounty, largess, grant, free gift, charity.

Gratulation, *n.* Congratulation, felicitation, gratification, thanks.

Gravamen, *n.* (*Law.*) Burden (*of a charge*), substance, essential point.

Grave, *v. t.* 1. Engrave, imprint, infix, impress deeply.

2. Carve, form by cutting.

——, *n.* Pit (*for a dead body*), sepulchre, burial place, sepulture, mausoleum, tomb, ossuary, charnel-house, narrow house, long home.

——, *a.* 1. Important, weighty, serious, momentous, cogent, of great consequence.

2. Sober, serious, sedate, thoughtful, staid, dignified, slow, sage, solemn.

3. Plain, sober, quiet, subdued, dull, somber.

4. (*Mus.*) Deep, not acute, low in pitch.

Grave clothes, *n. pl.* Shroud, winding sheet, cerements.

Gravel, *n.* Sand, grit, small pebbles, shingle; ballast.

——, *v. t.* 1. Cover with gravel.

2. Puzzle, embarrass, perplex, bewilder, stagger, pose, nonplus, put out.

Graveyard, *n.* Cemetery, necropolis, mortuary, churchyard, burial-ground, burying-ground, God's Acre.

Gravitate, *v. i.* Tend by gravity, descend, tend, incline.

Gravitation, *n.* Gravity, centripetal force, attraction of gravitation.

Gravity, *n.* 1. Heaviness, weight.

2. Gravitation, centripetal force, attraction of gravitation.

3. Sobriety, seriousness, sedateness, thoughtfulness, demureness.

4. Importance, moment, momentousness, weightiness, seriousness.

GRAY, *a.* [Written also *Grey.*] 1. Hoary, black and white, ashen, ash colored, grizzled, pearly, leaden, cloudy, drab.

2. Gray-haired, gray-headed, silver-haired.

Graze, *v. i.* 1. Eat grass, feed upon grass.

2. Touch in passing, rub slightly together.

——, *v. t.* 1. Feed with grass, pasture.

2. Feed upon, eat grass from, browse.

3. Shave, scrape, skim, touch lightly (*in passing over*), rub, brush, scratch, glance.

Grease, *n.* Unctuous matter (*lard, tallow, etc.*), fatty *or* oily substance.

——, *v. t.* 1. Smear with grease, lubricate.

2. Bribe, give a *douceur* to, corrupt with gifts.

Greasy, *a.* Unctuous, fat, fatty, oily, adipose, sebaceous, oleaginous; smooth, slippery.

GREAT, *a.* 1. Large, big, vast, huge, bulky, ample, immense, gigantic, Herculean, Cyclopean, enormous, pregnant.

2. Much, excessive, high, pronounced, decided.

3. Numerous, countless.

4. Considerable, important, weighty; chief, principal, main, leading, grand, superior, pre-eminent.

5. Distinguished, eminent, prominent, exalted, elevated, excellent, noted, illustrious, celebrated, famous, famed, renowned, far-famed.

6. Grand, august, dignified, noble, majestic, sublime, elevated, lofty, exalted.

7. Magnanimous, generous, chivalrous, high-minded.

8. Sumptuous, rich, magnificent, fine.

——, *n.* [With *The* prefixed.] Great persons, persons of rank, people of distinction.

Great-bellied, *a.* Abdominous, large-bellied, big-bellied, pot-bellied, tun-bellied, gor-bellied, paunchy, pursy.

Greatness, *n.* 1. Largeness, magnitude, size, bulk, dimensions.

2. High degree.

3. Distinction, eminence, elevation, fame, importance, renown.

4. Dignity, augustness, majesty, sublimity, grandeur, loftiness, exaltation, nobility, nobleness.

5. Magnanimity, generosity, nobleness, disinterestedness, chivalrous spirit.

Greed, *n.* Eagerness, longing. See GREEDINESS.

Greediness, *n.* 1. Voracity, ravenousness, omnivorousness, gluttony, excessive hunger.

2. Eagerness, longing, greed, avidity, covetousness, insatiableness, intense desire.

3. Grasping, graspingness, avarice, rapacity, cupidity, selfishness.

Greedy, *a.* 1. Voracious, ravenous, gluttonous, edacious, devouring, rapacious, insatiable, insatiate.

2. Eager, very desirous.

3. Grasping, avaricious, rapacious, selfish.

Greek, *a.* 1. Of Greece, Grecian, Hellenic.

2. Grecian, classic, classical, after the Greek, in the manner of Greece.

GREEN, *a.* 1. Verdant, virid, emerald, olive, aquamarine, greenish.

2. Flourishing, blooming, fresh, undecayed.

3. New, recent, fresh.

4. Unripe, not fully grown, unfledged, immature.

5. Inexperienced, unskilful, inexpert, ignorant, young, untrained, crude, callow, raw, verdant.

6. Unseasoned, not dry, raw.

——, *n.* 1. Color mixed of blue and yellow.

2. Lawn, grass-plot, grassy plain, common, greensward, verdure.

Greenhorn, *n.* (*Colloq.*) Novice, inexperienced youth, raw hand, tyro.

Greenhouse, *n.* Conservatory.

Greenness, *n.* 1. Verdancy, viridity; verdure, greenery.

2. Vigor, freshness.

3. Unripeness, immaturity.

Greet, *v. t.* 1. Salute, welcome, hail, address, receive, accost.

2. Compliment, send greeting to.

Greeting, *n.* 1. Salutation, welcome, salute.

2. Compliment, expression of goodwill.

Grewsome, *a.* Frightful, ugly, terrible, awesome, grisly, grim.

Grief, *n.* 1. Sorrow, regret, affliction, distress, suffering, tribulation, woe, dole, sadness, bitterness, anguish, misery, agony, heartache, heartbreak, heavy heart, bleeding heart, broken heart.

2. Trial, grievance, cause of sorrow, sorrow, affliction, distress, woe.

3. Mishap, disaster, failure.

Grievance, *n.* 1. Hardship, wrong, injury, complaint, burden, oppression.

2. Grief, trial, cause of sorrow, sorrow, affliction, distress, woe.

Grieve, *v. t.* Afflict, pain, hurt, distress, sadden, discomfort, aggrieve, oppress, agonize, wound the feelings of, make sorrowful.

——, *v. i.* Sorrow, mourn, lament, suffer, bewail, feel regret, be sad, be heavyhearted, be in pain of mind, be anguished.

Grievous, *a.* 1. Distressing, afflictive, afflicting, sorrowful, heavy, burdensome, oppressive, painful, sad, deplorable, lamentable, hard to bear.

2. Hurtful, injurious, baneful, noxious, troublesome, mischievous, detrimental, destructive, calamitous.

3. Atrocious, heinous, flagitious, outrageous, intense, severe, intolerable, dreadful, gross, iniquitous, flagrant, aggravated.

Grill, *n.* Gridiron, broiler, grating; grill-room.

——, *v. t.* Broil, cook on a grill *or* gridiron; torment, inquisition.

Grim, *a.* 1. Fierce, ferocious, ruthless, cruel, stern, unyielding, relentless, harsh, savage.

2. Frightful, horrible, hideous, grisly, fearful, appalling, dire, horrid, terrific, dreadful, of forbidding look.

Grimace, *n.* Distortion of countenance, wry face, contemptuous face; smirk, affected face, affected contortion of countenance, mow, mop, mouth.

Grime, *n.* Dirt, foulness, smut.

——, *v. t.* Begrime, sully, soil, befoul, defile, ingrain with filth.

Grimy, *a.* Foul, begrimed, defiled, dirty, filthy, full of grime.

Grind, *v. t.* 1. Triturate, pulverize, bruise, bray, crush, crunch, grate, grit, comminute by attrition.

2. Sharpen (*by rubbing*), whet.

3. Oppress, harass, persecute, plague, trouble, afflict, be hard upon.

——, *n.* Hard job, drudgery; a drudge, hard student.

GRIP, *n.* Grasp, clutch, clasp, gripe, hold, control, domination.

——, *v. t.* Grasp, clutch, seize, seize hold of, catch, catch hold of, hold firmly, seize forcibly, impress deeply, hold fast.

Gripe, *v. t.* 1. Seize, clutch, grasp, clasp, snatch, lay hold of, grip.

2. Press, compress, squeeze, pinch, hold fast, grip.

3. Pain, distress, pinch, straighten, give pain to (*especially in the bowels*).

——, *n.* 1. Grasp, clutch, hold, seizure, grip.

2. Affliction, distress, griping, pinching.

Gripes, *n. pl.* Colic, griping, pain in the bowels.

Grisly, *a.* Frightful, horrible, horrid, terrific, hideous, appalling, dreadful, grim, gray.

Gristle, *n.* Cartilage.

Grit, *n.* 1. Bran.

2. Sand, gravel, small pebbles, dirt.

3. Gritstone, gritrock.

4. Firmness, decision, courage, "nerve."

——, *v. t.* Grate, grind, gnash.

Grizzled, *a.* Grayish, grizzly, gray.

Grizzly, *a.* Grayish, grizzled, somewhat gray, a little gray.

Groan, *v. i.* Moan; complain; creak.

Groats, *n. pl.* Grits, hulled oats *or* hulled wheat.

Grocery, *n.* 1. [*Eng.*] Groceries.

2. [*U. S.*] Grocer's shop.

Grog-shop, *n.* Dram-shop, drinking-house.

Groom, *n.* 1. Waiter, servant, valet, equerry; stable-servant, hostler.

2. Bridegroom.

Groove, *n.* Furrow, channel, rut, rabbet, cut, scoring; routine.

Grope, *v. i.* Feel one's way (*as in the dark*), pick one's way move blindly, move stumblingly, search.

Gross, *a.* 1. Large, big, bulky, great, burly, fat.

2. Dense, thick, dull, stupid.

3. Coarse, rough, rude, unrefined, unseemly, unbecoming, crass; indelicate, sensual, impure, vulgar, low, obscene, earthy, carnal, beastly, licentious, broad.

4. Enormous, flagrant, shameful, outrageous, brutal, grievous, aggravated; palpable, plain, obvious, manifest, glaring.

5. Whole, total, entire, aggregate.

——, *n.* 1. Whole, total, aggregate, bulk, gross amount, sum total.

2. Twelve dozen.

Grossness, *n.* 1. Greatness, bulkiness, bigness.

2. Density, thickness.

3. Coarseness, rudeness, vulgarity, want of refinement, ill-breeding.

4. Indelicacy, impurity, coarseness, licentiousness, sensuality, brutality, bestiality, carnality.

Grotesque, *a.* 1. Fantastic, fanciful, odd, whimsical, extravagant, unnatural, incongruous, wild, strange, bizarre.

2. Ludicrous, absurd, antic, burlesque, ridiculous.

——, *n.* 1. Capricious arabesque, whimsical arabesque.

2. Whimsical, fantastic, odd, extravagant, *or* bizarre figure.

Grotto, *n.* Grot, cave, cavern.

Grouchy, *a.* Sulky, sullen, surly, morose, moody, crabbed, spleeny, glum, cross, out of humor.

Ground, *n.* 1. Soil, earth, clod, turf, sod, loam, mould, surface of land, area, distance.

2. Region, territory, country, land, domain.

3. Estate, acres, field, real property, landed estate.

4. Foundation, support, base, basis, groundwork.

5. Motive, consideration, reason, cause, inducement, account, excuse, gist, opinion.

——, *v. t.* 1. Place on the ground; fell.

2. Found, establish, base, fix, set.

3. Train in rudiments, make thorough in the elements, teach.

——, *v. i.* Run aground, get aground.

Groundless, *a.* Baseless, unfounded, causeless, uncalled for, idle, unsought, unsolicited, unjustifiable, unwarranted, unauthorized, false, gratuitous.

Grounds, *n. pl.* 1. Lees, dregs, sediment, grouts, deposit, precipitate, settlings.

2. Reasons, considerations, arguments, supports, accounts.

3. Yard, premises, campus, lawns, gardens.

Groundwork, *n.* 1. Base, basis, substratum, background, foundation, support, bottom, ground.

2. Source, origin, first principle, basis.

GROUP, *n.* Cluster, collection, assemblage, combination, body, aggregation.

——, *v. t.* Arrange, dispose, assign places to, form into groups.

Grouty, *a.* (*Colloq.*) See GROUCHY.

Grove, *n.* Wood, woodland, thicket, copse. See FOREST.

Grovel, *v. i.* 1. Creep, crawl, sneak, fawn, cringe, lie low, lie prone.

2. Behave abjectly, be mean, be low, tend downward, tend to the base and mean.

Grovelling, *a.* 1. Creeping, crouching, squat.

2. Low, mean, base, vile, abject, servile, slavish, cringing, fawning, beggarly, sneaking, earth-born, undignified, unworthy, without elevation.

Grow, *v. i.* 1. Enlarge, increase, expand, swell, extend, be augmented, become (*by degrees*) greater *or* larger.

2. Vegetate, sprout, germinate, shoot, bourgeon, pullulate, put forth, shoot up, spring up, develop, arise.

3. Advance, improve, wax, extend, swell, thrive, make progress, make improvement.

4. Become, wax, come to be, get to be.

5. Adhere, become attached, get fastened.

Grow, *v. t.* Raise, produce, cultivate.

Growing, *a.* Increasing, enlarging, expanding, extending, augmenting.

Growl, *v. i.* Snarl, gnarl, grumble, murmur, complain.

GROWTH, *n.* 1. Increase, expansion, development, growing, extension.

2. Vegetation, sprouting, germination, formation, shooting, bourgeoning, pullulation, putting out; excrescence.

3. Produce, product, production, cultivation.

4. Advancement, advance, progress, development, improvement.

5. Adulthood, maturity.

Grub, *v. t.* Dig, eradicate, dig up, root up, clear, root out, grub up.

———, *v. i.* Dig, be meanly employed, drudge; eat (*colloq.*).

———, *n.* Caterpillar, larva, maggot; drudge, plodder.

Grudge, *v. t.* 1. Grant with reluctance, give unwillingly.

2. Envy, begrudge, repine at, see with discontent.

———, *v. i.* 1. Be reluctant, be unwilling.

2. Repine, murmur, grieve, complain.

3. Be envious, feel envy, cherish illwill.

———, *n.* Hatred (*secretly and persistently entertained*), pique, spite, malice, rancor, resentment, malevolence, ill-will, inveterate dislike, sullen malice, secret hate, concealed enmity.

Gruff, *a.* Rough, churlish, rude, uncivil, uncourteous, ungracious, impolite, bluff, blunt, surly, harsh, brusque, grumpy; hoarse.

Grumble, *v. i.* 1. Complain, murmur, repine, croak, find fault.

2. Growl, snarl, gnarl.

3. Rumble, roar.

Grumbler, *n.* Murmurer, complainer, croaker, censurer, fault-finder, growler.

Grumbling, *n.* Complaint, murmuring, repining, fault-finding.

Grumous, *a.* Clotted, concreted, thick.

Grumpy, *a.* Sullen, grum, sour, surly. See GROUCHY.

Guarantee, *n.* [Written preferably *Guaranty*.] Surety, security, warrant, assurance.

———, *v. t.* (*Law.*) Warrant, insure, assure, secure, vouch for, guaranty, become surety for, be responsible for, answer for.

Guarantor, *n.* (*Law.*) Warrantor, voucher, underwriter, insurer.

Guaranty, *n.* Warrant, security, surety, assurance.

Guard, *v. t.* 1. Protect, defend, shield, shelter, safeguard, watch, keep in safety, attend for protection.

2. Provide against objections, secure against attack, make with caution.

———, *v. i.* Watch, take care, be cautious, beware, be vigilant; patrol.

———, *n.* 1. Defence, protection, shield, security, bulwark, rampart, ægis, palladium, safeguard, custody.

2. Sentinel, sentry, watch, watchman, keeper, guardian, warden, patrol.

3. Convoy, escort, conduct, body of defenders.

4. Circumspection, care, watchfulness, caution, attention, heed.

5. Conductor (*of a coach* or *of a railway train*).

Guarded, *a.* Cautious, wary, circumspect, protected, watchful, careful.

Guardian, *n.* 1. Warden, keeper, custodian, protector, defender, preserver.

2. Guardian angel, tutelary saint, good genius, attendant spirit.

———, *a.* Protecting, tutelary.

Guardsman, *n.* Watchman, sentinel, sentry, guard.

Guerdon, *n.* (*Poetical.*) Recompense, remuneration, requital, reward.

Guess, *v. t.* 1. Conjecture, divine, surmise, suspect, mistrust, judge at random, judge with uncertainty.

2. Find out, solve, penetrate, fathom (*by conjecture*).

3. Suppose, think, believe, fancy, imagine, take it, dare say, venture to say.

———, *v. i.* Conjecture, divine, surmise, suspect, theorize, imagine, mistrust.

———, *n.* Conjecture, surmise, supposition, "shot," divination.

Guest, *n.* Visitor, visitant, person entertained.

Guffaw, *n.* Laugh (*boisterous* or *loud*), horse-laugh.

Guidance, *n.* Direction, leadership, lead, pilotage, steering, escort, conduct, government.

Guide, *v. t.* 1. Lead, conduct, pilot, escort.

2. Direct, rule, govern, manage, regulate, control, steer, preside over, have charge of, take the direction of.

GUIDE, *n.* 1. Director, conductor, pilot, cicerone.

2. Mentor, monitor, adviser, counsellor, instructor.

3. Clew, key, thread, index, directory.

4. Guide-book, itinerary; landmark, guide-post.

Guild, *n.* Fraternity, association, society, company, corporation, corporate body, joint concern (*of craftsmen* or *tradesmen having like vocations*).

Guile, *n.* Cunning, craft, subtlety, artfulness, artifice, duplicity, deceit, deception, trickery, fraud, wiles, wiliness.

Guileful, *a.* Crafty, wily, artful, cunning, deceitful, dishonest, insincere, double, fraudulent, tricky.

Guileless, *a.* Artless, honest, sincere, undesigning, unsophisticated, frank, pure, truthful, candid, ingenuous, open, straightforward, single-minded, openhearted, simple-hearted, simple-minded.

Guilt, *n.* 1. Criminality, guiltiness, culpability, blame.
2. Wrong, iniquity, wickedness, offensiveness, ill-desert.

Guiltless, *a.* Innocent, sinless, spotless, unspotted, unpolluted, immaculate, unsullied, untarnished, blameless.

Guilty, *a.* 1. Criminal, culpable, wicked, wrong.
2. Found in guilt, having violated law, actually transgressing, actually offending.

Guise, *n.* 1. Appearance, aspect, garb, dress, costume, form, shape, figure, fashion, manner, mode.
2. (*Poetical.*) Air, mien, demeanor, behavior.
3. Practice, habit, custom, manner, mode; pretense, disguise.

Gulch, *n.* Ravine (*made by running water*), gully, gorge.

Gulf, *n.* 1. Large bay.
2. Abyss, chasm, opening; wide separation.
3. Whirlpool, swallowing eddy, engulfing sea.

Gull, *v. t.* Deceive, cheat, dupe, trick, chouse, cozen, overreach, circumvent, beguile, impose upon.
——, *n.* 1. Cheat, trick, deception, imposition, fraud.
2. Dupe, cat's paw.

Gullet, *n.* Œsophagus, gorge, neck, throat.

Gullible, *a.* Credulous, easily duped, unsuspicious, confiding, overtrustful.

Gully, *n.* Gulch, ravine.

Gulp, *v. t.* Swallow greedily, bolt.

Gumption, *n.* (*Colloq.*) Shrewdness, sagacity, discernment, skill, cleverness, ability, penetration, capacity, power, commonsense.

GUN, *n.* Fire-arm, cannon.

Gurgle, *v. i.* Ripple, purl, murmur, "guggle," bubble.

Gush, *v. i.* 1. Spout out, burst forth, rush forth (*as a liquid*), flow out suddenly, spurt.
2. Sentimentalize, be over-effusive, emotionalize, be carried away by feeling.
——, *n.* 1. Rush (*as of a liquid*), sudden efflux *or* outflow.
2. Effusive sentiment, sentimentalism, silly sentiment.

Gushing, *a.* 1. Rushing, issuing violently, flowing copiously.
2. Sentimental, demonstrative, effusive, exuberantly affectionate.

Gust, *n.* 1. Blast, squall.
2. Burst, outburst, fit, paroxysm.

Gustable, *a.* Relishable, savory, pleasant to the taste, sapid.

Gusto, *n.* Relish, zest, liking, gust, pleasure, enjoyment.

Gusty, *a.* Stormy, tempestuous, windy, squally, unsteady, puffy, blustering.

Gut, *n.* 1. Intestine.
2. Strait, narrow pass.
——, *v. t.* Eviscerate, disembowel, embowel, paunch, take out the bowels of, destroy.

Guts, *n. pl.* Viscera, intestines, entrails, bowels, inwards.

Gutter, *n.* Channel, conduit, kennel.

Guttural, *a.* 1. Of the throat, formed in the throat.
2. Gruff, hoarse, deep, hoarse and low, throaty, thick.

Guy, *n.* 1. Stay, shore.
2. Fright, dowdy, scarecrow, eccentric.

Guzzle, *v. i.* Drink (*greedily* or *much*), carouse, tipple, tope.
——, *v. t.* Drink (*greedily* or *much*), quaff, swill, "swig."

Gymnast, *n.* Athlete, adept at gymnastics *or* athletics.

Gymnastics, *n. pl.* Athletic exercises, athletics, calisthenics.

Gypsy, *n.* 1. Fortune-telling nomad.
2. Gypsy language, Romany, chib, Romanes.

Gyrate, *v. i.* Rotate, revolve, whirl, spin, turn round, wheel round, move in a circle.

Gyration, *n.* Rotation, whirling, revolution, spinning, circular motion.

Gyves, *n. pl.* Fetters, shackles, chains.

H

Habiliment, *n.* Dress, garment, clothes, apparel, attire, raiment, vesture, garb, habit, costume, vestment.

Habit, *n.* 1. Condition (*of the body*), constitution, temperament.

2. Custom (*of an individual*), usage, wont, rule, consuetude, addiction, practice, habitude, way, manner, second nature.

3. Dress, garb, costume. See HABILIMENT.

——, *v. t.* Dress, clothe, array, attire, accoutre.

Habitable, *a.* Inhabitable.

Habitat, *n.* Natural locality (*of a plant* or *an animal*), area of distribution.

Habitation, *n.* Abode, dwelling, lodging, domicile, home, quarters, headquarters, dwelling-place, place of abode, place of residence.

Habitual, *a.* Usual, customary, accustomed, wonted, common, regular, routine, ordinary, familiar, every-day, settled, confirmed, inveterate.

Habituate, *v. t.* Accustom, familiarize, inure, use, train, harden.

Habitude, *n.* Custom, usage, practice, wont. See HABIT.

Habitué, *n.* [Fr.] Frequenter.

Hack, *v. t.* Cut (*clumsily*), hew, chop, mangle, hackle, haggle.

——, *n.* 1. Notch, cut.

2. Hired horse, worn-out horse.

3. Drudge, over-worked man, penny-liner.

——, *a.* Hired, mercenary, hireling, hackney.

Hackle, *v. t.* 1. Cut (*clumsily*), hew, chop, hack, haggle, mangle.

2. Hatchel; dress (*flax*).

Hackney, *a.* Common, hired, hack.

Hackneyed, *a.* 1. Worn out, much used.

2. Common, banal, commonplace, threadbare, trite, stale.

Hades, *n.* Grave, invisible world, underworld, hell, world below, Pluto's realms, region of the dead.

Haft, *n.* Handle (*of an instrument*), hilt, stock.

Hag, *n.* Fury, beldam, she-monster, Jezebel, witch, harridan, crone, virago, vixen, ugly old woman.

Haggard, *a.* 1. Wild, wayward, intractable, unruly, refractory, untamed, not domesticated.

2. Gaunt, lean, meagre, spare, worn, wasted, rawboned.

Haggle, *v. i.* Higgle, chaffer, cavil, dispute, stickle, be tedious in a bargain.

——, *v. t.* 1. Cut (*clumsily*), hew, chop, hack, hackle.

2. Worry, tease, harass, badger, annoy, fret, bait.

Hail, *v. t.* 1. Salute, greet, welcome, call in honor.

2. Call, call to, hallo, accost, signal, speak.

Hail-fellow, *a.* Intimate, associate, companion, familiar, hearty.

HAIR, *n.* Pile, fur, down.

Halcyon, *a.* Placid, calm, quiet, still, peaceful, tranquil, undisturbed, unruffled, serene, palmy, happy, golden, halcyonian.

Hale, *a.* Healthy, sound, strong, hearty, hardy, vigorous, robust, well, in good health.

Half, *n.* Moiety.

Half-note, *n.* (*Mus.*) Minim.

Half-wit, *n.* Blockhead, simpleton, moron. See DUNCE.

Half-witted, *a.* Dull, stupid, stolid, doltish, foolish, soft, silly, shallow, sappy, weak-headed, feeble-minded, shallow-brained, dull-witted, thick-skulled.

Hall, *n.* 1. Large room, chamber.

2. Entry (*of a house*), entrance, vestibule, hallway, lobby; passage, corridor.

3. Manor-house; public building.

4. Public room, assembly room, lecture room, auditorium.

Hallelujah, *interj.* Hosanna, praise ye Jehovah.

Halloo, *v. i.* Shout, call, cry out.

——, *n.* Holla, shout, call.

Hallow, *v. t.* 1. Consecrate, sanctify, dedicate, devote, make holy, invest with solemnity.

2. Reverence, honor, respect, venerate, observe with reverence, pay homage to, render honor to.

Hallowed, *a.* Holy, sacred, blessed.

Hallucination, *n.* 1. Error, blunder, mistake, fallacy.

2. Illusion, delusion, self-deception, phantasm, aberration, wandering of the mind.

Halo, *n.* 1. Ring (*of light*).

2. (*Painting.*) Glory, aureole, aura, nimbus.

Halt, *v. i.* 1. Stop, hold, stand (still), stop short, pull up, come to a stop.

2. Limp, hobble, walk lamely.

——, *a.* Lame, crippled, disabled.

——, *n.* 1. Stop, stand, standstill.

2. Limp, limping gait.

Halve, *v. t.* Divide into two equal parts, cut in two, bisect.

Hamlet, *n.* Small village.

HAMMER, *v. t.* [*The noun is Basic Eng.*]

1. Forge, shape with the hammer, beat out, shape by beating.

2. Contrive, excogitate, invent, work out.

Hammer and tongs. (*Colloq.*) Strenuously, vigorously, earnestly, zealously, resolutely, energetically, with all one's might, with might and main, tooth and nail, through thick and thin, through fire and water, *pugnis et calcibus.*

Hamper, *n.* 1. Crate, packing basket.

2. Fetter, shackle, clog-chain, hindrance, encumbrance, embarrassment.

——, *v. t.* Shackle, fetter, entangle, clog, encumber, restrain, hinder, impede, embarrass, restrict, confine, bind, trammel, curb, tie.

Hamstring, *v. t.* Hough; cripple, disable.

HAND, *n.* 1. Palm and fingers; palm, four inches (*in estimating the height of a horse*), hand-breadth.

2. Side (*right* or *left*), direction, part.

3. Skill, ability, talent, faculty, dexterity.

4. Mode of procedure, course, management; turn, inning.

5. Agency, intervention, participation, share.

6. (*Usually pl.*) Possession, control, power.

7. Laborer, workman, operative, artisan, artificer, craftsman, employee.

8. Index, pointer, indicator.

9. Chirography, handwriting, style of penmanship.

——, *v. t.* 1. Give (*with the hand*), transmit, deliver, present, pass by hand.

2. Lead, conduct, guide.

Hand and glove. Very intimate.

Handbook, *n.* Manual, guidebook.

Handcuff, *n.* Manacle, hand-fetter.

Hand down. Transmit in succession.

Handful, *n.* Maniple, fistful, small quantity, manageable amount.

Handicap, *n.* Hampering, encumbrance, hindrance, disadvantage.

Handicraft, *n.* Manual occupation, trade.

Handicraftsman, *n.* Artisan, mechanic, artificer, workman, hand, craftsman.

Hand in hand. Conjointly, unitedly, in union.

Handiwork, *n.* Work, workmanship, manufacture, hand.

Handle, *v. t.* 1. Touch, feel, feel of, take in the hand, take hold of; "paw," finger, manhandle.

2. Manage, use, wield, manipulate; direct, deal with.

3. Treat, discuss, discourse on, treat of.

——, *n.* Haft, stock, helve, etc.

Handmaiden, *n.* Maid-servant, female servant.

Handsel, *n.* [Written also *Hansel.*] Earnest, first receipts, first-fruits, first gift, beginning of fortune, gift with promise.

Hands off. Forbear, desist, keep off, don't touch it, let it alone.

Handsome, *a.* 1. Comely, well-formed, well-proportioned, stately, fine-looking.

2. Graceful, easy, becoming, appropriate, suitable.

3. Generous, liberal, disinterested, noble, gracious, magnanimous.

4. Ample, sufficient, plentiful, large.

Handwriting, *n.* Hand, chirography, script, calligraphy, style of penmanship.

Handy, *a.* 1. Dexterous, adroit, ready, expert, skilful, skilled, clever.

2. Convenient, near, at hand, close at hand.

Hang, *v. t.* 1. Suspend; attach (*so as to swing*).

2. Execute (*by the halter*), hang by the neck, gibbet, truss.

3. Incline (*the head*), decline, drop, droop, bend down, let droop.

4. Drape, adorn with hangings.

——, *v. i.* 1. Depend, dangle, be suspended, impend, swing.

2. Incline, droop, tend downward, trail.

3. Depend, rely, be dependent.

4. Rest, cling, stick, loiter.

5. Be held in fixed attention.

6. Hover, float, play.

Hang back. Demur, hesitate, be backward, tarry, be reluctant.

Hang-dog, *a.* Sneaking, base, low, blackguard, ashamed, villainous, scurvy.

Hanger-on, *n.* Parasite, dependant, minion, vassal; client.

Hang fire. Be long *or* slow in discharging (*said of a gun*).

HANGING, *n.* [*The adjective is Basic Eng.*]

1. Suspension.

2. Death by the halter, death on the gallows.

Hangings, *n. pl.* Drapery, tapestry.

Hang on. 1. Continue, last, be protracted.

2. Stick, cling, keep hold, hold fast, hold on, stick to.

3. Stay, rest, reside, continue, remain.

4. Attend admiringly, regard with passionate admiration.

Hang out. Display.

Hanker after. Covet, long for, desire ardently, have a strong desire for, lust after.

Hankering, *n.* Longing, craving, strong desire, burning want.

Hap, *n.* Chance, fortune, accident, haphazard, luck, casual event.

Haphazard, *a.* Chance, random, aimless, without order or purpose.

Hapless, *a.* Luckless, unlucky, unfortunate, unhappy, wretched, miserable, ill-starred, ill-fated.

Haply, *adv.* Perhaps, perchance, possibly, peradventure (*archaic*), by chance, by accident, maybe, it may be, as luck may have it, as it may turn up, as it may happen.

Happen, *v. i.* Chance, occur, befall, betide, come, take place, turn up, fall out, come to pass.

Happily, *adv.* 1. Luckily, fortunately, by good fortune, as luck would have it.

2. Successfully, prosperously, fortunately, agreeably, delightfully, in a happy manner.

3. Gracefully, dexterously, skilfully, aptly, felicitously.

Happiness, *n.* 1. Joy, delight, pleasure, gayety, light-heartedness, merriment, cheerfulness, brightness.

2. Felicity, bliss, beatitude, blessedness, enjoyment; welfare, well-being, prosperity.

HAPPY, *a.* 1. Joyous, joyful, light-hearted, contented, gay, merry, cheerful, blissful, blessed, blest.

2. Pleased, gratified, delighted, rejoiced, glad, gladdened, charmed.

3. Lucky, fortunate, prosperous, successful, favored by fortune.

4. Ready, apt, skilful, adroit, dexterous, expert, able.

5. Seasonable, opportune, befitting, pertinent, felicitous, well-timed.

6. Auspicious, propitious, favorable, bright.

Harangue, *n.* 1. Speech, public address, popular oration, formal address.

2. Declamatory speech, noisy ranting speech, bombastic performance, tirade, screed.

—, *v. i.* 1. Speak to a large assembly, make a formal address.

2. Declaim, spout, make a declamatory speech, indulge in a tirade.

—, *v. t.* Address, make a declamatory speech to.

Harass, *v. t.* 1. Fatigue, tire, weary, fag, jade, exhaust, tire out.

2. Vex, plague, worry, distress, trouble, molest, badger, heckle, gall, tease, tantalize, disturb, harry, annoy, torment,

keep in alarm, keep assaulting, drive from pillar to post.

Harbinger, *n.* Forerunner, precursor, herald.

HARBOR, *n.* 1. Asylum, refuge, shelter, cover, sanctuary, retreat, resting-place, place of shelter.

2. Port, haven, harbor, destination.

—, *v. t.* 1. Shelter, lodge, protect.

2. Entertain, cherish, indulge, foster.

3. (*Law.*) Secrete, receive clandestinely.

HARD, *a.* 1. Firm, solid, compact, impenetrable, indurated, stubborn, adamantine, resistant, stony, flinty, marble, implastic, sclerotic, unyielding, rigid.

2. Difficult, perplexing, puzzling, knotty, intricate.

3. Laborious, arduous, exacting, toilsome, fatiguing, wearying.

4. Unfeeling, unkind, insensible, unsusceptible, rigorous, exacting, severe, untender, austere, unfeeling, unsympathetic, unyielding, inflexible; callous, obdurate, hard-hearted, incorrigible, reprobate.

5. Grievous, distressing, calamitous, painful, disagreeable, unpleasant.

6. Harsh, rough, sour, acid; alcoholic.

7. Excessive, intemperate.

—, *adv.* 1. Close, near.

2. Laboriously, diligently, earnestly, incessantly, energetically.

3. With difficulty, not easily.

4. Distressfully, painfully, severely, rigorously.

5. Vehemently, forcibly, violently.

Harden, *v. t.* 1. Indurate, make hard, toughen, temper, case-harden, make callous.

2. Habituate, inure, season, accustom, form, train, discipline.

3. Strengthen, fortify, steel, nerve, brace, stiffen.

4. Sear, make callous, render insensible *or* unimpressible, make unfeeling.

5. Make obdurate, confirm in wickedness.

—, *v. i.* Grow or become hard, indurate.

Hardened, *a.* 1. Indurated, made hard, annealed, tempered, case-hardened.

2. Confirmed, inured, accustomed, habituated, seasoned, trained; deadened, seared, steeled, unfeeling, benumbed, callous, insensible; depraved, reprobate, obdurate, impenitent, lost, abandoned, incorrigible, irreclaimable.

Hard-favored,) *a.* Ugly, ill-favored,
Hard-featured,) homely, ill-looking, hard-visaged, of coarse features.

Hard-headed, *a.* Shrewd, sagacious, intelligent and firm, not to be imposed upon, of strong sense, cool, collected, well-balanced.

Hard-hearted, *a.* Cruel, unfeeling, merciless, unmerciful, uncompassionate, unpitying, ruthless, fell, pitiless, relentless, unrelenting, inexorable, implacable.

Hardihood, *n.* 1. Firmness, fortitude, resolution, pluck, mettle, manhood, courage, bravery, stoutness, intrepidity, boldness, audacity, determination, resolution, decision.

2. Effrontery, audacity, assurance, brass, impudence.

Hardly, *adv.* 1. Scarcely, barely, but just.

2. Severely, rigorously, unkindly, cruelly, harshly, roughly.

Hardness, *n.* 1. Firmness, solidity, compactness, impenetrability.

2. Difficulty, perplexity, perplexing character *or* nature.

3. Severity, rigor, cruelty.

4. Hardship, suffering, tribulation, trial.

Hardship, *n.* 1. Toil, fatigue, weariness.

2. Grievance, suffering, trial, affliction, calamity, misfortune, trouble, burden, hardness; privation, injury.

Hard-visaged, *a.* See HARD-FAVORED.

Hardy, *a.* 1. Bold, intrepid, resolute, brave, daring, valiant, heroic, manly, courageous, stout-hearted.

2. Strong, robust, firm, stout, lusty, rigorous, enduring, inured, sturdy, tough, rugged, healthy, hearty, hale, sound.

Hare-brained, *a.* Rash, reckless, headlong, heedless, careless, wild, unsteady, giddy, volatile, changeable, flighty, harum-scarum.

Harem, *n.* Seraglio.

Hark, *interj.* Hear, listen, give ear, attend, hearken.

Harlequin, *n.* Buffoon, jester, droll, merry-andrew, punch, clown, zany, scaramouch, fool, antic.

Harlequinade, *n.* Masking, mummery, masquerade, buffoonery, foolery, tomfoolery.

Harlot, *n.* Whore, prostitute, courtesan, street walker. See STRUMPET.

Harm, *n.* 1. Injury, hurt, detriment, mischief, ill, injury, misfortune, damage, prejudice, disadvantage.

2. Evil, wrong, criminality, wickedness.

——, *v. t.* 1. Injure, hurt, damage, do harm to, scathe.

2. Maltreat, molest, abuse, ill-use, ill-treat, desecrate.

Harmful, *a.* Injurious, detrimental, mischievous, pernicious, deleterious, noxious, baneful, prejudicial, disadvantageous, hurtful.

Harmless, *a.* 1. Innoxious, innocuous, not hurtful, innocent.

2. Inoffensive, unoffending, innocent, safe.

Harmonic, *a.* 1. Harmonious, concordant, consonant.

2. Melodious, tuneful, musical.

3. Pertaining to harmony, relating to music, musical.

Harmonious, *a.* 1. Concordant, harmonic, consonant.

2. Melodious, tuneful, musical, dulcet, smooth, euphonious, mellifluous.

3. Correspondent, consistent, conformable, congruent, orderly, symmetrical.

4. Friendly, amicable, cordial, brotherly, agreeable, fraternal, neighborly.

Harmonize, *v. t.* 1. Make harmonious, unite, adapt, attune, reconcile, adjust to each other.

2. (*Mus.*) Set accompanying parts to.

——, *v. i.* Accord, agree, correspond, tune, blend, sympathize, chime, comport, tally, square, conform with, be in unison, be harmonious.

HARMONY, *n.* 1. Concord (*especially of sounds or tones*), accord, accordance, consonance, order, concordance, unison, agreement, chime.

2. Adaptation, correspondence, consistency, smoothness, congruity, congruence, fitness, suitableness.

3. Peace, amity, friendship, kind feeling, good understanding.

Harness, *n.* Tackling, tackle, gear, equipment; accoutrements, armor, array, mail; mounting (*of a loom*).

——, *v. t.* Tackle, put in harness, hitch.

Harp, *v. i.* 1. Play on the harp, strike the lyre.

2. Dwell (*tediously*), iterate.

Harpy, *n.* 1. (*Mythol.*) Defiling monster, — half bird, half woman.

2. Extortioner, sharper, plunderer, (*particularly female*).

Harrow, *v. t.* 1. Draw a harrow over, till with a harrow.

2. Lacerate, tear, rend, wound, torment, torture, harass.

Harry, *v. t.* 1. Pillage, plunder, rob, raid, ravage.

2. Worry, annoy, molest, plague, torment, trouble, tease, vex, harass, fret, gall, chafe, incommode, disturb, harrow.

Harsh, *a.* 1. Rough.

2. Sour, acid, astringent, acrid, tart, crabbed, hard, biting, sharp, caustic, corrosive.

3. Grating, discordant, jarring, cacophonous, unmelodious, metallic, strident, stridulous, raucous.

4. Crabbed, morose, stern, severe, austere, hard, cruel, acrimonious, ill-tempered, ill-natured, sour, unkind, unfeeling.

5. Rude, uncivil, bluff, blunt, gruff, ungracious, churlish, bearish, brutal.

Harshness, *n.* 1. Roughness, raucity, stridor.

2. Austerity, rigor, severity, sternness, crabbedness,, moroseness, churlishness, ill-temper, asperity, ill-nature, hardness, unkindness, acerbity.

3. Rudeness, incivility, bluntness, bluffness, ungraciousness, churlishness, gruffness.

Harum-scarum, *a.* (*Colloq.*) Volatile, rash, reckless, precipitate, wild. See HARE-BRAINED.

Harvest, *n.* 1. Ingathering, harvesting, harvest-time.

2. Produce, crops, yield.

3. Effect, product, result, consequence, issue, outcome.

——, *v. t.* Gather in, reap, glean.

Hash, *v. t.* Mince, chop, mangle.

——, *n.* Minced meat, hashed meat, hash-meat.

Hastate, *a.* (*Bot.*) Spear-shaped.

Haste, *n.* 1. Despatch, promptitude, quickness, nimbleness, alacrity, velocity, rapidity, expedition, celerity, speed.

2. Hurry, precipitance, precipitation, vehemence, rush, press, rashness, impetuosity, hustle, flurry.

——, *v. i.* Hasten, be quick, make haste.

Hasten, *v. i.* Haste, hurry, move quickly, move speedily, be quick, be in a hurry, make haste, mend one's pace, lose no time, wing one's way, crowd sail, clap spurs to one's horse.

——, *v. t.* Expedite, despatch, speed, accelerate, quicken, precipitate, press on, urge on, urge forward, push forward, bring speedily.

Hasty, *a.* 1. Quick, swift, rapid, fleet, speedy, fast, brisk.

2. Cursory, slight, hurried, rapid, superficial, passing.

3. Rash, precipitate, headlong, reckless; helter-skelter, pell-mell.

4. Passionate, irritable, touchy, testy, pettish, waspish, petulant, peevish, fretful, fiery, choleric, abrupt, irascible, excitable, hot-headed, peppery.

HAT, *n.* 1. Head-cover.

2. Cardinal's office, dignity of a cardinal.

Hatch, *v. t.* 1. Breed (*from eggs*).

2. Concoct, devise, plan, contrive, plot, design, scheme, project, brew, lay out, excogitate, think out.

3. Inlay, engrave.

——, *n.* 1. Brood.

2. Hatchway; hatchway-grating, door, wicket; sluice-gate.

Hatchet, *n.* Small axe.

Hatchment, *n.* Escutcheon, emblazoning.

Hate, *v. t.* 1. Bear malice to, owe a grudge to, keep a grudge against, be hostile to, dislike intensely, bear deadly malice to.

2. Abhor, abominate, loathe, nauseate, shrink from, recoil from, execrate, abominate. See DETEST.

HATE, *n.* Hatred, detestation, animosity, enmity, hostility, antipathy. See HATRED.

Hateful, *a.* 1. Malignant, malevolent, malign, malicious, spiteful, rancorous.

2. Abominable, detestable, execrable, odious, abhorrent, horrid, shocking, damnable, accursed.

3. Loathsome, disgusting, nauseous, offensive, repellent, foul, repulsive, obnoxious, revolting, vile, abhorrent, repugnant.

Hatred, *n.* 1. Hate, enmity, hostility, rancor, malevolence, malignity, odium, animosity, ill-will.

2. Abhorrence, detestation, abomination, aversion, execration, horror, loathing, disgust, antipathy, repugnance.

Haughtiness, *n.* Arrogance. See HAUTEUR.

Haughty, *a.* Arrogant, disdainful, supercilious, lordly, "hoity-toity," assuming, proud, lofty, contemptuous.

Haul, *v. t.* Drag, draw, pull, tug, tow, lug, trail, take in tow.

Haunch, *n.* Hip, quarter.

Haunt, *v. t.* 1. Frequent, resort to.

2. Hang upon, importune, follow importunately.

3. Inhabit, hover about, frequent (*as a spectre* or *ghost*), obsess.

——, *n.* Retreat, resort, den, frequented place.

Hauteur, *n.* [Fr.] Haughtiness, arrogance, loftiness, disdain, contempt, contemptuousness, superciliousness, pride, self-importance.

HAVE, *v. t.* 1. Hold (*whether one's own or not*), be in actual possession of; possess, own, be in possession of; exercise, keep, cherish; experience, enjoy.

2. Obtain, acquire, receive, get, gain.

3. Be obliged, be under the necessity, be compelled.

4. Accept (*as husband* or *as wife*), take.

Have a finger in. Have a share in, be concerned in, have a hand in.

Have a hand in. Be concerned in, have a share in, have a finger in.

Have an eye to. Pay particular attention to, have especial regard to, not overlook, not lose sight of, aim at.

Have at heart. Be deeply interested in, be specially anxious about.

Have done with. Have no further concern with, be through with, have ceased to be concerned with, give up, give over, abandon, let alone.

Have in hand. Be engaged upon.

Haven, *n.* Harbor, port; shelter, asylum, place of safety.

Havoc, *n.* Ravage, devastation, destruction, desolation, waste, ruin; carnage, slaughter, destruction of life.

Haw, *v. i.* Hesitate (*in speaking*), stammer, stutter, falter, hem and haw.

Hawk, *v. t.* Cry, sell by outcry, carry about for sale, peddle.

Hawk-eyed, *a.*   1. Sharp-sighted, quick-sighted, keen-eyed, eagle-eyed, lynx-eyed, Argus-eyed.

2. Discerning, penetrating, astute, sagacious, keen.

Haycock, *n.* Hayrick, haystack.

Hazard, *n.* Chance, stake, casualty, accident, contingency, fortuitous event; danger, peril, risk, jeopardy, venture.

——, *v. t.*   1. Venture, adventure, risk.

2. Jeopard, peril, imperil, endanger, put in danger, put at hazard.

Hazardous, *a.* Dangerous, perilous, unsafe, fraught with danger, full of risk, risky.

Haze, *n.* Fog, mist; obscurity, dimness, cloud, fume, miasma, pall.

Hazel, *a.* Light brown.

Hazy, *a.* Foggy, misty; confused, uncertain, indistinct, vague.

HE, *pron.* (*Basic Eng.*)

HEAD, *n.*   1. Seat of the brain, head-piece, "noddle."

2. Top, summit, upper part, acme; fore part, front part, front, chief position; first place, place of honor.

3. Commencement, beginning, rise, source, origin.

4. Chief part, principal part.

5. Chief, chieftain, leader, principal, commander, master, director, superintendent, superior.

6. Understanding, intellect, mind, thought.

7. Topic, subject; class, division, section, department, category.

——, *a.*   1. Chief, principal, highest, first, leading, main, grand.

2. (*Naut.*) Adverse (*said of the wind*), contrary.

——, *v. t.*   1. Lead, direct, command, govern, guide, control, rule.

2. (*With "off."*) Get in front of (*in order to stop*), intercept.

——, *v. i.* Tend, be pointed, be directed, aim, be aimed.

Head and ears. Completely, entirely, wholly.

Head-dress, *n.* Coiffure, head covering, head ornament.

Head-foremost, *adv.*   1. With the head first, heels over head.

2. Rashly, hastily, precipitately, headlong, headfirst, heels over head.

Headiness, *n.*   1. Rashness, hurry, precipitation.

2. Obstinacy, stubbornness.

Heading, *n.* Title.

Headland, *n.* Promontory, cape, foreland, cliff, bluff, escarpment.

Headless, *a.*   1. Acephalous; beheaded; leaderless, undirected.

2. Imprudent, senseless, rash, obstinate, stubborn, heady. See HEAD-STRONG.

Headlong, *a.*   1. Rash, inconsiderate, hasty, heady, reckless, thoughtless, impulsive, perilous, dangerous, ruinous, precipitate.

2. Rushing precipitately, wildly tumbling.

3. Steep, precipitous, sheer.

——, *adv.*   1. Rashly, hastily, precipitately, head-foremost, thoughtlessly, without deliberation.

2. Hastily, hurriedly, without pause, without respite.

3. At a rush, hurriedly, full tilt, helter-skelter, pell-mell, hurry-skurry.

4. Prone, head-foremost, heels over head, on one's head, sheer downward.

Head-master, *n.* Principal (*of a school*).

Head off. Intercept, head, get before, prevent, stop.

Head-piece, *n.*   1. Helmet, helm, morion, casque, armor for the head.

2. Head, brain, seat of understanding, understanding.

Headsman, *n.* Executioner.

Headstone, *n.* Corner-stone; gravestone.

Headstrong, *a.* Stubborn, obstinate, dogged, violent, ungovernable, unruly, intractable, heady, headless, self-willed, cross-grained, cantankerous, froward, wayward.

Heady, *a.*   1. Rash, impetuous, hasty, precipitate, inconsiderate, reckless, thoughtless, impulsive; violent, impetuous, rushing, headlong.

2. Inflaming, intoxicating, exciting, strong, highly spirituous, apt to affect the head.

Heal, *v. t.* 1. Cure, remedy, amend, repair, restore, make sound *or* whole.

2. Reconcile, compose, soothe, settle, harmonize, make up.

——, *v. i.* Be cured, become sound, get well.

Healing, *a.* 1. Sanative, curative, restoring, restorative.

2. Mild, composing, lenitive, assuasive, gentle, soothing, assuaging, comforting.

Health, *n.* Soundness, freedom from disease, healthfulness, tone, sanity, hale condition.

Healthful, *a.* 1. Full of health, healthy, sound, hale, hearty, in the enjoyment of health, marked by health, coming of health.

2. Wholesome, salubrious, salutary, beneficial, invigorating, bracing, nutritious, nourishing, health-giving, healthy.

HEALTHY, *a.* 1. Sound, hale, hearty, lusty, vigorous, strong, of good health, of a sound constitution.

2. Well, in good health, in a sound condition, in good case.

3. Wholesome, salubrious, salutary, healthful, hygienic, bracing, invigorating, health-giving.

Heap, *n.* 1. Pile, mass, collection, accumulation, cumulus, huddle, mound, stack.

2. Great quantity, large amount, lot, abundance.

——, *v. t.* 1. Pile, lay in a heap, throw into a heap.

2. Amass, accumulate, heap up, overfill.

Hear, *v. t.* 1. Perceive by the ear.

2. Give audience to, listen to, attend to, hearken to, accede to.

3. Regard, heed, give heed to.

4. Try, examine judicially.

——, *v. i.* 1. Enjoy the sense of hearing, exercise the sense of hearing, have hearing.

2. Listen, hearken, attend, give ear.

3. Be told, be informed, have an account, learn.

HEARING, *n.* 1. Sense of hearing.

2. Audition (*tech.*), auscultation (*med.*).

3. Audience, opportunity to be heard, interview, trial, judicial examination.

Hearken, *v. i.* 1. Listen, hear.

2. Attend, give heed, pay regard.

Hearsay, *n.* Rumor, report, fame, bruit, common talk, town talk.

HEART, *n.* 1. Seat of life, center of circulation, organ of circulation; bosom, breast.

2. Center, interior, core, kernel, essence, inner part, vital part, meaning.

3. Disposition, mind, will, inclination, purpose, intent, affection, passion.

4. Courage, spirit, firmness, fortitude, resolution.

5. Love, affections, feeling, emotion, emotional nature, ardor, seat of affection *or* love, seat of feeling *or* passion.

6. Conscience, moral nature, sense of good and ill, moral feeling, seat of character, character, seat of moral life.

Heartache, *n.* Grief, sorrow, distress, anguish, affliction, woe, bitterness, dole, heartbreak, broken heart, heavy heart, bleeding heart.

Heart-broken, *a.* Disconsolate, inconsolable, woe-begone, forlorn, miserable, wretched, desolate, cheerless, comfortless, broken-hearted, in despair.

Heart-burning, *n.* Grudge, envy, resentment, spleen, gall, rankling, animosity, secret enmity, sense of wrong, suppressed anger, feeling of injury.

Hearten, *v. t.* Encourage, embolden, animate, inspirit, enhearten, heart, cheer, incite, stimulate, assure, reassure, comfort, console, buoy up.

Heartfelt, *a.* Deep, profound, hearty, sincere, cordial, deep-felt, home-felt.

Hearth, *n.* Hearthstone, fireplace, bottom of fireplace, forge; fireside, home, hearthstone, domestic circle.

Heartily, *adv.* Sincerely, cordially, from the heart, with all the heart; vigorously, earnestly, eagerly, ardently, warmly, zealously, with ardor, with zeal, with resolution, with good appetite, freely, largely, abundantly, completely.

Heartless, *a.* 1. Unfeeling, cruel, pitiless, unsympathetic, merciless, hard, harsh, brutal, cold.

2. Spiritless, timid, timorous, uncourageous, destitute of spirit *or* courage.

3. Without a heart, robbed of one's heart, stripped of one's affections.

Heart-rending, *a.* Heart-breaking, anguishing, deeply afflicting, most distressing, piteous, affecting, crushing.

Heart-shaped, *a.* Cordate.

Hearty, *a.* 1. Earnest, warm, cordial, sincere, true, deep, profound, deep-felt, heartfelt, unfeigned.

2. Zealous, active, earnest, warm, vigorous, energetic, animated.

3. Healthy, hale, sound, strong, well, robust, in good health.

4. Abundant, full, heavy.

5. Nourishing, rich, nutritious, full of nutriment.

HEAT, *n.* 1. Caloric, caloricity, warmth; torridity, degree of temperature.

2. Excitement, flush, vehemence, impetuosity, violence, passion, fever.

3. Ardor, glow, fervency, intensity, earnestness, fervor, zeal.

4. Exasperation, rage, fierceness, frenzy.

——, *v. t.* 1. Make hot.

2. Excite, flush, make feverish, inflame; warm, animate, rouse, stir, stimulate.

Heath, *n.* Field covered with heather, heathery field, moor, waste land; shrubby field *or* plain.

Heathen, *n.* Gentile, pagan, infidel, idolater.

Heathenish, *a.* 1. Heathen, pagan, Gentile, unconverted.

2. Barbarous, savage, cruel, inhuman.

Heating, *a.* 1. Calorific, heat-producing, warming.

2. Stimulating, exciting. See HEADY.

Heave, *v. t.* 1. Lift, hoist, raise, elevate, raise up.

2. Breathe, force from the breast, raise, exhale, utter with effort.

3. Throw, toss, hurl, send, fling, cast.

——, *v. i.* 1. Pant.

2. Swell, dilate, expand, rise.

3. Retch, keck, try to vomit.

4. Struggle, strive, make an effort.

Heaven, *n.* 1. Firmament, sky, welkin, empyrean, celestial sphere, starry heaven, vault of heaven, canopy of heaven.

2. Paradise, Zion, Elysium, bliss, abodes of bliss, the Eternal Rest, our eternal home, our Father's house, Abraham's bosom, the Divine abode, God's dwelling-place, the house not built with hands, the New Jerusalem, the city of our God, the abode of saints, abode of the blessed.

3. See GOD.

4. Exalted state, state of bliss, great felicity, supreme happiness, ecstasy, transport, rapture, transcendent delight, Paradise, Elysium.

Heavenly, *a.* 1. Celestial, ethereal, empyreal, of the firmament, of the visible heavens.

2. Divine, angelic, seraphic, cherubic, elysian, god-like, celestial, blest, saintly, sainted, holy, beatified, beatific, glorified.

3. Enrapturing, ravishing, rapturous, enravishing, ecstatic, transporting, delightful, celestial, divine, angelic, seraphic, blissful, glorious, golden, beatific.

Heaviness, *n.* 1. Gravity, weight, ponderousness, heft.

2. Oppressiveness, grievousness, severity.

3. Languor, dulness, stupidity, sluggishness.

4. Dejection, depression, sadness, melancholy, despondency, gloom, low spirits, depression of spirits.

Heavy, *a.* 1. Weighty (*with reference to one's strength*), ponderous, hard *or* difficult to lift, "hefty," massive; gravid, grave, onerous.

2. Oppressive, grievous, severe, burdensome, cumbersome, afflictive; serious.

3. Dull, sluggish, inert, inactive, dilatory, stupid, torpid, indolent, slow, lifeless, sleepy, inanimate.

4. Dejected, depressed, sorrowful, sad, gloomy, melancholy, despondent, disconsolate, crushed, cast down, downcast, down-hearted, low-spirited, crestfallen, chapfallen, in low spirits, sobered.

5. Onerous, difficult, laborious, hard.

6. Tedious, tiresome, wearisome, weary.

7. Loaded, burdened, encumbered, weighed down.

8. Miry, muddy, cloggy, clayey; clammy (*as bread*), ill-raised, soggy, hard to digest, burdensome, oppressive.

9. Stormy, tempestuous, violent, severe, strong, energetic, boisterous; loud, deep, roaring.

10. Dense, dark, gloomy, lowering, cloudy, overcast.

Hebdomadal, *a.* 1. Weekly, occurring every week *or* seven days.

2. By sevens, in groups of seven.

Hectic, *a.* 1. Habitual (*as the fever attending consumption*), constitutional.

2. Feverish, hot, heated, fevered, flushed.

Hector, *n.* Bully, blusterer, swaggerer, noisy fellow.

——, *v. t.* Bully, threaten, menace; vex, tease, annoy, fret, harry, harass, worry, irritate, provoke.

Hedge, *n.* Fence (*of bushes or shrubs*), hedge-fence, hedgerow, barrier, limit.

——, *v. t.* 1. Enclose with a hedge.

2. Obstruct, hinder, encumber, hem in, surround.

3. Fortify, guard, protect.

——, *v. i.* Hide, skulk, disappear, take refuge in a hiding-place, evade, dodge, proceed stealthily, temporize.

Hedonism, *n.* Eudæmonism, utilitarianism, theory of pleasure *or* happiness as the supreme good, Epicureanism, Benthamism.

Hedonist, *n.* Utilitarian, moralist, eudæmonist, Epicurean, Benthamite.

Heed, *v. t.* Regard, mind, notice, mark, observe, consider, attend to, give heed to, pay attention to, take notice of, hearken to, listen to, obey.

——, *n.* Regard, notice, care, attention, caution, consideration, mindfulness, carefulness, heedfulness, watchfulness, wariness, vigilance, circumspection, observation.

Heedful, *a.* Observant, observing, mindful, regardful, watchful, cautious, careful, wary, circumspect, attentive, provident.

Heedless, *a.* Unobserving, unobservant, inattentive, careless, thoughtless, negligent, neglectful, unmindful, regardless, inconsiderate, unwatchful, reckless, precipitate, rash, headlong, headless.

Heedlessness, *n.* Carelessness, thoughtlessness, inattention, inadvertence, neglect, oversight, recklessness, rashness, precipitancy, negligence, inconsiderateness.

Heel, *n.* 1. Back of the foot *or* stocking *or* shoe.

2. Foot, bottom, lower end.

3. Fag end, remnant, remainder, leavings, crust.

——, *v. t.* 1. Put a heel on, fit with a heel.

2. Arm with spurs, fit gaffs upon.

3. Perform with the heels, dance.

——, *v. i.* (*Naut.*) Incline, lean; follow.

Heft, *n.* Handle, haft, helve; weight, bulk.

Hegemony, *n.* Leadership, headship, ascendancy, authority, predominating influence, predominance, preponderance, rule.

Hegira, *n.* 1. Flight of Mahomet (*September* 13, 622).

2. Exodus, departure, going out.

Height, *n.* 1. Elevation, altitude, tallness.

2. Eminence, summit, apex, acme, head, top, meridian, zenith, climax, pinnacle, culminating point.

3. Hill, mountain, high ground, high land, eminence.

4. Utmost degree.

5. Elevation, high point, lofty position, altitude.

6. Eminence, exaltation, dignity, perfection, grandeur, loftiness, lofty position *or* character.

Heighten, *v. t.* 1. Elevate, raise, make higher *or* more lofty.

2. Exalt, greaten, magnify, ennoble.

3. Increase, enhance, augment, improve, strengthen.

4. Intensify, aggravate.

Heinous, *a.* Flagrant, flagitious, atrocious, odious, hateful, infamous, villainous, ne-farious, crying, very wicked, enormous, aggravated, excessive, monstrous.

Heir, *n.* 1. Inheritor, heiress, possessor by descent.

2. Offspring, child, product.

Helical, *a.* Spiral, winding, cochleary, cochleated, screw-shaped.

Helix, *n.* 1. Coil, circumvolution, spiral line.

2. Snail-shell.

Hell, *n.* 1. Gehenna, limbo, abyss, Tartarus, Sheol, Pandemonium, Tophet, Hades, Avernus, Erebus, place of torment, bottomless pit, everlasting fire, infernal regions, shades below, realms of Pluto, the lower world, underworld, inferno, abode of the damned.

2. Misery, moral agony, unassuaged remorse, inward torment, stings of conscience, spiritual agony, sense of curse.

Hellenic, *a.* Grecian, Greek.

Hellish, *a.* 1. Of hell.

2. Infernal, diabolical, fiendish, devilish, Satanic, demoniacal, fiend-like, atrocious, detestable, abominable, execrable, nefarious, curst, accursed, damnable, damned, monstrous.

Helm, *n.* 1. Helmet, morion, head-piece, casque, armor for the head.

2. Steering apparatus, rudder, tiller, the wheel.

3. Direction, control, command, rule, reins, post of command.

Helmet, *n.* Helm, morion, casque, head-piece, armor for the head.

Helot, *n.* 1. Spartan slave *or* serf.

2. Slave (*in general*), bondsman, serf, bond-slave.

Help, *v. t.* 1. Relieve, succor, save.

2. Assist, serve, support, aid, second, back, abet, co-operate with, take part with, wait upon, sustain.

3. Remedy, cure, heal, restore, better, improve, alleviate, ameliorate.

4. Prevent, hinder, withstand, resist, repress, control.

5. Avoid, forbear, refrain from.

——, *v. i.* Lend aid, contribute assistance, give a lift.

HELP, *n.* 1. Assistance, aid, succor, support.

2. Remedy, relief.

3. Helper, assistant, servant.

Helper, *n.* Assistant, ally, auxiliary, coadjutor, aider, abettor, colleague, partner, helpmate, help-fellow.

Helpful, *a.* 1. Useful, beneficial, convenient, assistant, contributory, aidful, favorable, auxiliary, serviceable, advantageous, profitable.

2. Ready to help, kind, benevolent,

full of help, inclined to aid others, co-operative.

Helpless, *a.* 1. Weak, feeble, powerless, impotent, imbecile, disabled, infirm, prostrate, resourceless.

2. Exposed, defenceless, unprotected, abandoned.

3. Irremediable, beyond help, remediless, irreparable, irretrievable, desperate.

Helpmate, ⎫ *n.* 1. Wife, consort, partner,
Helpmeet, ⎭ companion.

2. Partner, helper, associate, aider, help-fellow, companion, assistant.

Help on. Forward, further, promote, advance.

Helter-skelter, *adv.* Pell-mell, irregularly, disorderly, in disorder, in confusion, precipitately, with precipitancy, at a rush, headlong, hurry-skurry, pell-mell, head-foremost, heels over head.

Helve, *n.* Handle (*of an ax* or *a hatchet*), haft, heft.

Hem, *n.* Border, edge, margin.

——, *v. t.* Border, edge, skirt; sew.

——, *v. i.* Cough slightly, hesitate, "haw."

Hem in. Enclose, confine, environ, surround, beset, shut in, hedge in.

Hemisphere, *n.* Half-globe, half-sphere.

Hen, *n.* 1. Female bird.

2. Female of the domestic fowl, "biddy," pullet, Partlet.

Hence, *adv.* 1. From this place, from here, away.

2. From this time, henceforth, henceforward, from this time forth *or* forward.

3. Therefore, from this cause, for this reason, as a consequence.

4. From this source.

Henceforth, *adv.* Henceforward, from this time forward, hence.

Henchman, *n.* Retainer, follower, supporter, servant, attendant.

Herald, *n.* 1. Proclaimer, publisher, crier, announcer.

2. Forerunner, precursor, harbinger.

Heraldry, *n.* Blazonry, emblazonry, the heraldic art, the herald's art; heraldic pomp.

Herbage, *n.* Herbs, grass, pasture, plants, vegetation of the fields, herbal vegetation.

Herbal, *a.* Pertaining *or* relating to herbs, herbaceous.

——, *n.* Herbarium, herbary, hortus siccus; a book describing herbs.

Herbalist, *n.* 1. Expert in herbs *or* plants, collector of herbs, plant-collector, botanist.

2. Dealer in medicinal plants.

Herbarium, *n.* Herbal, hortus siccus.

Herculean, *a.* 1. Strong, mighty, powerful, puissant, vigorous, sturdy, athletic,

brawny, muscular, sinewy, stalwart, able-bodied.

2. Difficult, hard, perilous, dangerous, toilsome, troublesome, laborious.

3. Large, great, gigantic, strapping, huge, colossal, Cyclopean.

Herd, *n.* 1. Drove (*of the larger animals*).

2. Crowd, rabble, multitude, populace, vulgar herd (*ignobile vulgus*).

3. Herder, shepherd, herdsman.

——, *v. i.* Associate (*as beasts*), keep company.

——, *v. t.* Drive, tend, gather, lead.

HERE, *adv.* 1. In this place.

2. In the present state, in the present life, now.

3. Hither, to this place.

Hereafter, *adv.* 1. In time to come, in some future time, henceforth.

2. In a future state.

——, *n.* Future state, world *or* life beyond the grave.

Hereby, *adv.* By this, close by, by this means.

Hereditable, *a.* Inheritable.

Hereditary, *a.* Ancestral, patrimonial, by inheritance; inherited, transmitted (*from ancestors*).

Herein, *adv.* 1. In this, inside of this.

2. In this, in this respect *or* regard.

3. In here, inside this place.

Heresy, *n.* Heterodoxy, error, unsound doctrine; recusancy, dissent.

Heretic, *n.* Sectary, schismatic, separatist; unbeliever, recusant, dissenter.

Heretical, *a.* Heterodox, schismatic, schismatical, sectarian.

Heretofore, *adv.* Formerly, hitherto, before the present time.

Hereupon, *adv.* Upon this, on this.

Herewith, *adv.* With this.

Heritage, *n.* Inheritance, portion, patrimony, legacy, estate.

Hermaphrodite, ⎫ *a.* 1. Androgynous, par-
Hermaphroditic, ⎭ taking of both sexes, bisexual.

2. Hybrid, mongrel.

Hermetic, ⎫ *a.* 1. Air-tight, impervious
Hermetical, ⎭ to air.

2. Secret, mysterious, mystic, mystical, occult, magical, symbolical, emblematic, cabalistic, containing doctrines clothed *or* concealed in symbols.

Hermit, *n.* Anchorite, anchoret, recluse, solitary, solitaire, eremite (*poetical*); ascetic.

Hero, *n.* 1. Brave man; lion, warrior.

2. Principal character, protagonist.

3. (*Mythol.*) Demigod, man of superhuman achievements.

Heroic, *a.* 1. Brave, valiant, courageous, intrepid, bold, daring, gallant, fearless, dauntless, noble, magnanimous, illustrious.

2. Epic.

3. Violent, extreme, desperate, extravagant.

——, *n. pl.* Bombast, extravagance of expression.

Heroine, *n.* 1. Intrepid woman, supremely courageous woman.

2. Principal female character.

Heroism, *n.* Bravery, valor, courage, gallantry, prowess, daring, intrepidity, fearlessness, fortitude, boldness, endurance, great-heartedness.

Hesitancy, *n.* 1. Hesitation, indecision, halting, reluctance, holding back.

2. Indecision, doubt, uncertainty, suspense, vacillation.

Hesitate, *v. i.* 1. Pause, delay, demur, doubt, scruple, stickle, boggle, "shilly-shally," waver, vacillate, be undetermined, stop to consider, be in doubt, be in suspense, be doubtful.

2. Falter, stammer, have an impediment in speech.

Hesitation, *n.* 1. See HESITANCY.

2. Faltering, stammering, stuttering, difficulty of utterance.

Hesperian, *a.* (*Poetical.*) Western, occidental.

Heteroclite, *a.* Irregular, anomalous, abnormal.

Heterodox, *a.* Heretical, unorthodox, contrary to the accepted standards, schismatic, recusant; uncanonical, apocryphal.

Heterogeneous, *a.* Unlike, dissimilar, different, diverse, unhomogeneous, miscellaneous, mixed, indiscriminate, opposed, contrary, contrasted.

Hew, *v. t.* 1. Cut, chop, hack, fell.

2. Smooth (*with an axe*), fashion, form.

Hexahedron, *n.* Cube, six-sided figure.

Heyday, *n.* Frolic, play, exultation; height, prime, zenith; flush, acme.

Hiatus, *n.* Opening, gap, break, interval, chasm, blank, rift, lacuna.

Hibernate, *v. i.* 1. Winter, pass the winter.

2. Lie torpid in winter.

Hibernian, *a.* Irish.

Hibernicism, } *n.* Irishism, Irish idiom,
Hibernianism, } Irish bull.

Hidden, *a.* 1. Concealed, secret, latent, occult, covered, covert, cloaked, masked, enshrouded, veiled, undiscovered, suppressed, blind, private, clandestine, close.

2. Abstruse, recondite, mysterious, mystic, mystical, dark, obscure, cabalistic, occult, inward, oracular, esoteric, cryptic, hermetic.

Hide, *v. t.* 1. Secrete, conceal, cover, bury, keep out of sight, suppress, withhold.

2. Shelter, cloak, screen, veil, mask, disguise, hoard, gloze, eclipse, suppress.

——, *v. i.* Lie hid, lie concealed, be concealed, conceal one's self, lie in ambush, keep one's self out of sight, be withdrawn from view.

——, *n.* Skin (*of the larger animals*), coat, pelt.

Hideous, *a.* Frightful, dreadful, appalling, ugly, abominable, revolting, terrible, horrible, horrid, ghastly, grisly, grim, shocking.

Hie, *v. i.* (*Poetical and often with the reciprocal pronoun.*) Hasten, go in haste, go.

Hierarchy, *n.* 1. Ecclesiastical government, ecclesiastical establishment.

2. Body of ecclesiastical dignitaries.

3. Scale of succession in ecclesiastical rank; system of gradation (*generally*), order *or* succession of dignities.

Hieratic, *a.* Sacerdotal, priestly, sacred, consecrated, devoted to sacred uses.

Hieroglyph, *n.* Symbol, sign, pictorial word symbol *or* sound symbol.

Hieroglyphic, *a.* Emblematical, symbolical.

Hierophant, *n.* Priest, expounder of religious mysteries.

Higgle, *v. i.* 1. Peddle, hawk.

2. Haggle, bargain, negotiate, chaffer, stickle for advantage.

Higgledy-piggledy, *adv.* (*Colloq.*) Confusedly, disorderly, pell-mell, in disorder, helter-skelter, topsy-turvy, at sixes and sevens.

HIGH, *a.* 1. Lofty, elevated, tall, high-reaching, towering, soaring, heaven-kissing, of great altitude.

2. Eminent, prominent, pre-eminent, distinguished, superior; elevated, exalted, noble, dignified, lofty, great, admirable.

3. Proud, haughty, arrogant, supercilious, lordly, lofty.

4. Violent, strong, boisterous, turbulent, tumultuous.

5. Dear, of great price, "fancy," "stiff," costly.

6. Acute, sharp, shrill, piercing, high-toned, high-pitched.

——, *adv.* 1. Aloft, on high, to a great height.

2. Profoundly, powerfully.

3. Eminently, loftily.

4. Richly, luxuriously.

High-flavored, *a.* Pungent, piquant, high-seasoned.

High-flown, *a.* 1. Elevated, presumptuous, swollen, proud, lofty.

2. Extravagant, lofty, high-colored, overdrawn, overstrained.

3. Turgid, swollen, inflated, bombastic, pretentious, pompous, strained.

High-handed, *a.* Overbearing, oppressive, arbitrary, violent, despotic, wilful, self-willed, domineering.

Highland, *n.* Mountainous region.

Highlander, *n.* Mountaineer, hillsman.

Highly, *adv.* Extremely, exceedingly, very much, in a great degree, in a high degree. See HIGH, in its various senses.

High-mettled, *a.* 1. Fiery, spirited.

2. Ardent, high-spirited, proud, quick, fiery, intense, excitable. See HIGH-STRUNG, 2.

High-minded, *a.* 1. Proud, arrogant, haughty, lofty.

2. Noble, honorable, elevated, lofty, great-minded, magnanimous, high-toned, spiritual, firm in principle.

High-priced, *a.* Costly, dear, high.

High-school, *n.* Academy, seminary, (*in Germany*) gymnasium.

High-seasoned, *a.* Pungent, piquant, high-flavored, highly spiced.

High-spirited, *a.* 1. Spirited, bold, daring, fiery, high-mettled.

2. Proud, high-strung, ardent.

High-strung, *a.* 1. Of great tension, excitable, nervous, strung to a high pitch, in a state of high tension.

2. Proud, high-spirited, sensitive, quick to honor.

High-toned, *a.* 1. Acute, sharp, shrill, high.

2. Noble, lofty, honorable. •See HIGH-MINDED, 2.

3. Aristocratic, stylish, fashionable.

Highway, *n.* High-road, public road, main road.

Highwayman, *n.* Robber, footpad, bandit, brigand, freebooter, marauder, outlaw, highway robber.

Hilarious, *a.* Gay, jovial, jolly, joyful, merry, noisy, boisterous, mirthful, in high spirits, exhilarated.

Hilarity, *n.* Gayety, mirth, merriment, jollity, joviality, joyousness, exhilaration, cheerfulness, glee, high spirits.

Hill, *n.* Eminence (*less than a mountain*), mount, ascent, rise, hillock, rising ground, elevation.

Hillock, *n.* Knoll, mound, small hill, slight elevation.

Hilt, *n.* Handle (*of a weapon*).

Hind, *a.* Back, hinder, posterior, rear, rearward, hindmost.

——, *n.* 1. Female deer (*of the stag* or *red deer*).

2. Peasant, swain, boor, lout, rustic, clod-poll, bumpkin, clown, ploughman, bog-trotter, clodhopper, countryman; farm servant.

Hinder, *a.* Hind, back, posterior, rear.

——, *v. t.* Prevent (*temporarily*), impede, obstruct, stop, interrupt, retard, delay, bar, restrain, check, thwart, oppose, embarrass, encumber, clog.

Hindmost, *a.* Last.

Hindrance, *n.* Impediment, obstacle, stop, obstruction, interruption, check, restraint, encumbrance.

Hinge, *v. i.* Turn, depend, hang, be dependent.

Hint, *v. t.* Suggest, intimate, insinuate, imply, allude to, refer to, hint at, glance at, just mention, give an inkling of.

——, *n.* Intimation, suggestion, insinuation, allusion, slight mention, trace.

Hip, *n.* Haunch, thigh.

Hire, *v. t.* 1. Rent, secure (*temporarily*) for pay.

2. Employ, engage, charter, lease, take into service, take into one's employ.

3. Bribe, buy up, obtain one's services by corruption.

——, *n.* Wages, stipend, allowance, salary, pay, reward, compensation, rent, bribe, remuneration.

Hireling, *n.* Mercenary, hired soldier, myrmidon; hired servant.

Hirsute, *a.* 1. Hairy, shaggy, bristled, bristly.

2. Coarse, rough, rude, uncouth, boorish, unmannerly, rustic, ill-bred, loutish.

Hispid, *a.* Bristly, rough, shaggy.

Hiss, *n.* Sibilation, hissing, fizzle, sizzle.

——, *v. i.* 1. Sibilate.

2. Whiz, shrill, whistle, whir.

——, *v. t.* Condemn by hisses, scout, ridicule, damn.

Historian, *n.* Chronicler, annalist, writer of history.

HISTORY, *n.* Account, narration, narrative, relation, record, recital, story, chronicle, annals, memoirs, biography, genealogy, etc.

Histrionic, *a.* 1. Theatric, theatrical.

2. Acting, actor's.

Hit, *v. t.* 1. Strike, strike against, knock, discomfit, hurt.

2. Attain, reach, gain, win, secure.

3. Suit, fit, accord with, be conformable to, be suitable to.

——, *v. i.* 1. Clash, collide, come in contact, strike together.

2. Succeed, be successful, be crowned with success, come off successful, carry the point, gain the point.

——, *n.* 1. Stroke, blow, collision.

2. Chance, venture, fortune, hazard, good stroke; lucky venture.

3. Happy remark, apt expression.

Hitch, *v. i.* 1. Catch, get stopped, stick, get impeded.

2. Go by jerks.

——, *v. t.* Fasten, tie, attach, connect, unite.

——, *n.* 1. Catch, impediment, obstacle, hindrance, check, interruption.

2. Jerk, jerking motion.

3. (*Naut.*) Knot, noose.

Hither, *adv.* To this place, here.

Hitherto, *adv.* Yet, till now, to this time, up to this time, until this time, thus far, before this.

Hitherward, *adv.* This way, toward this place.

Hit off. Imitate, personate, mimic, take off.

Hit upon. Find, discover, find out, fall upon, light upon, chance upon.

Hive, *n.* 1. Habitation of bees, bee-hive, apiary; busy place.

2. Swarm of bees, swarm.

——, *v. t.* 1. Put into a hive.

2. Store, collect, gather. See HOARD.

Hoar, *a.* Hoary, white, gray; old, ancient.

Hoard, *v. t.* Store (*secretly*), deposit, save, garner, husband, hive, accumulate, amass, treasure up, lay in, lay by, set by, lay up, lay away, hide away.

Hoar-frost, *n.* White frost, frozen dew.

Hoarse, *a.* 1. Husky, raucous.

2. Rough, grating, harsh, low, guttural.

Hoarseness, *n.* 1. Huskiness, raucity.

2. Roughness, harshness, grating character.

Hoary, *a.* Hoar, white, gray; old, ancient, venerable.

Hoax, *n.* Deception (*for sport*), cheat, fraud, imposition, imposture, canard, practical joke, humbug, "sell," trick.

Hobble, *v. i.* Limp, halt, hop, walk lamely.

——, *v. t.* Fetter, hopple, shackle.

——, *n.* 1. Limp, halt; fetter, shackle, clog.

2. Perplexity, embarrassment, difficulty, strait, pickle.

Hobby, *n.* 1. Nag, pacing horse, garran.

2. Hobby-horse, wooden horse.

3. Favorite object, favorite pursuit, pet topic, fad, avocation.

Hobgoblin, *n.* Goblin, spectre, sprite, bogy, bugbear, frightful apparition; mischievous sprite, Robin Goodfellow, Puck.

Hobnail, *n.* 1. Heavy nail, large-headed nail.

2. Clown, lout, bumpkin, churl, clodhopper, rustic.

Hobnob, *adv.* At random, take or not.

——, *v. i.* Play pot companion, clink glasses, be jolly companions, associate intimately.

Hocus-pocus, *n.* 1. Juggler, trickster, impostor, cheater, swindler, sharper.

2. Cheat, juggle, trick, deception, imposition, imposture, delusion, deceit, artifice, circumvention, chouse, piece of *finesse.*

Hodge-podge, *n.* Medley, farrago, jumble, stew, mixture, miscellany, salmagundi, hotch-potch, gallimaufry, olio, olla-podrida.

Hoe-cake, *n.* [*U. S.*] Johnny-cake.

Hog, *n.* Swine, porker, grunter; beast, pig, glutton.

Hoggish, *a.* 1. Swinish, brutish, filthy.

2. Greedy, grasping, selfish, mean, sordid.

Hog-sty, *n.* Hog-pen, pig-sty, pig-pen.

Hoist, *v. t.* Raise, lift, elevate, heave, raise up, rear.

——, *n.* Lift, heave.

Hold, *v. t.* 1. Grasp, clutch, clinch, gripe *or* grip, clasp, seize.

2. Possess, retain, have, occupy, keep.

3. Restrain, confine, detain, imprison, shut in, control, bind, shut up, hem in.

4. Bind, fasten, unite, connect, fix, lock.

5. Stop, stay, arrest, suspend, withhold, check.

6. Maintain, support, continue, sustain, manage, prosecute, keep up, carry on.

7. Embrace, entertain, cherish, take as true.

8. Think, regard, consider, believe, judge, entertain, esteem, count, account, reckon, deem.

9. Contain, admit, take in, have a capacity for, receive, accommodate, stow, carry.

10. Assemble, convene, call together, conduct.

——, *v. i.* 1. Be firm, be fast, continue unbroken, not break, not give way.

2. Continue, remain, persist, last, endure.

3. Adhere, cohere, cling, stick, cleave, remain attached.

4. Think, believe, be of opinion.

5. Stand, be true, prove good, hold true, be valid.

——, *n.* 1. Grasp, gripe *or* grip, clasp, retention, anchor, bite, purchase, embrace, foothold, control, possession.

2. Support, stay, prop.

3. Footing, vantage-ground; claim.

4. Fort, castle, fortress, fortification, stronghold, fortified place.

5. Storage, below decks, cargo space.

Hold forth. 1. *v. t.* Offer, propose, exhibit, hold out.

2. *v. i.* Harangue, preach, speak in public.

Hold good. Stand, be valid, be true, be applicable, hold.

Hold in. 1. *v. t.* Check, restrain, repress, rein in.

2. *v. i.* Restrain one's self.

Hold on. 1. *v. t.* Continue, maintain, keep up, push forward.

2. *v. i.* Cling, stick, hold fast, keep hold of.

3. *v. i.* Continue, remain, endure, last.

4. Persevere, persist, be steady, be steadfast, be constant, go on, keep on, keep one's course, keep *or* maintain one's ground, stick to it, not give it up, stand fast, stand firm.

Hold out. 1. *v. t.* Offer, propose, hold forth.

2. *v. i.* Last, endure, continue.

3. *v. i.* Not yield, not be subdued, persist, stand firm, keep one's ground, maintain one's purpose.

Hold together. 1. Remain united, keep together.

2. Be consistent, hang together.

Hold up. 1. Clear up, cease raining.

2. Keep up, bear up, endure, support one's self, keep one's courage.

Holdup, *n.* Assault, robbery.

HOLE, *n.* 1. Perforation, aperture, opening.

2. Cavity, cave, cavern, hollow, concavity, void, hollow, depression, eye, pore, bore, chasm, abyss, gulf, excavation, pit.

3. Lair, den, cover, retreat, burrow (*of an animal*).

4. Hovel, kennel, den, mean habitation, cell, chamber.

Holiday, *n.* 1. Festival, anniversary, celebration, fête-day, fête.

2. Day of amusement; playtime, vacation.

Holiness, *n.* 1. Sanctity, piety, purity, devotion, devoutness, godliness, religiousness, saintliness, sinlessness, consecration, heavenly-mindedness.

2. Divineness, sacredness, sanctity.

Hollow, *a.* 1. Vacant, empty, void, cavernous, concave, depressed, sunken.

2. Insincere, treacherous, false, faithless, unfeeling, hypocritical, pharisaical, deceitful, false-hearted, hollow-hearted.

3. Deep, low, rumbling, sepulchral, muffled, reverberating.

HOLLOW, *n.* 1. Depression, low spot, low place, basin, bowl.

2. Cavity, concavity, depression, excavation, pit, hole, cave, cavern, dent, dint, dimple.

3. Groove, channel, canal, cup, pocket, dimple, dip, sag.

——, *v. t.* Excavate, scoop, dig out.

Holocaust, *n.* 1. Burnt-offering (*wholly consumed*).

2. Vast slaughter, immolation, wholesale destruction.

Holy, *a.* 1. Sacred, consecrated, hallowed, sanctified, blessed, devoted, set apart.

2. Righteous, saintly, devout, spiritual, sinless, saintlike, religious, godly, pious, pure, heavenly-minded, profoundly good, spiritually perfect.

Holy Ghost. Paraclete, Comforter, Holy Spirit, the Spirit of God, the Sanctifier, Spirit of Truth, third Person in the Trinity.

Holy Writ. Bible, Scriptures, Sacred Scriptures, Holy Scriptures, Old and New Testaments.

Homage, *n.* 1. Fealty, allegiance, loyalty, fidelity, devotion.

2. Reverence, obeisance, respect, deference, court, duty, service, honor.

3. Worship, adoration, devotion.

Home, *n.* 1. Domicile, dwelling, residence, abode, place of abode, abiding-place, native land; habitat, seat, quarters.

2. Fireside, hearth, hearthstone, household, family, family circle, domestic circle.

3. Goal, destination, asylum.

——, *adv.* 1. To one's home.

2. Close, closely, pointedly.

——, *a.* 1. Domestic, family, home-born *or* home-made.

2. Internal, within the country, interior, inland.

3. Close, pointed, direct, severe, poignant, effective, intimate, penetrating, home-reaching, that goes to the core, that is felt.

Home-bred, *a.* 1. Native, natural, home-born.

2. Domestic, not foreign.

3. Unpolished, uncultivated, unrefined, uncouth, rude, plain, homely.

Homelike, *a.* Domestic, intimate, simple, plain, unpretending, cozy, friendly.

Homeliness, *n.* Plainness, uncomeliness.

Homely, *a.* 1. Domestic, homelike.

2. Plain, coarse, uncomely, homespun, inelegant.

3. Plain, plain-looking, of plain features, uncomely, rather ugly.

Home-made, *a.* Homespun, of domestic manufacture.

Homesickness, *n.* 1. Longing for home, pining for friends and kindred.

2. (*Med.*) Nostalgia, sickness from loss of home and kindred.

Homespun, *a.* 1. Home-made, of domestic manufacture.

2. Plain, coarse, homely, rude, inelegant, rustic, unpolished.

Homeward, } *adv.* Toward home.
Homewards, }

Homicide, *n.* 1. Killing of a human being, murder, manslaughter.

2. Manslayer, murderer.

Homiletic, *a.* 1. Of homilies *or* sermons, relating to sermons.

2. Hortatory, persuasive.

Homiletics, *n.* Art of preaching *or* sermonizing, art of making homilies.

Homily, *n.* Sermon, discourse.

Homogeneous, *a.* Uniform, of uniform structure, of one kind throughout, of the same nature throughout, all alike, the same.

Homologous, *a.* 1. Of the same ratio, of the same proportion, in the same relation, similar, corresponding.

2. Of the same type, corresponding in structure.

Homophonous, *a.* Unisonous, of the same sound, of like pitch.

Hone, *n.* Oilstone, fine whetstone.

——, *v. t.* Whet, sharpen on a hone, put a fine edge upon.

Honest, *a.* 1. Honorable, fair, straightforward, equitable, open, free from fraud, faithful to contract, according to agreement, just as represented.

2. Upright, virtuous, conscientious, just, true, square, sound, uncorrupted, equitable, fair, faithful, reliable, trusty, trustworthy, observant of obligations, that stands by one's word, as good as one's word.

3. Genuine, free from shams, thorough, faithful, unadulterated.

4. Decent, honorable, reputable, respectable, creditable, suitable, proper.

5. (*Archaic.*) Decent, chaste, virtuous, faithful.

6. Sincere, candid, frank, unreserved, direct, open, ingenuous.

Honesty, *n.* 1. Integrity, probity, uprightness, fairness, justice, equity, trustiness, trustworthiness, fidelity, faithfulness, honor, freedom from fraud.

2. Truthfulness, truth, veracity, observance of one's word.

3. Genuineness, thoroughness, faithfulness.

4. (*Archaic.*) Honor, chastity, virtue, fidelity, morality.

5. Sincerity, candor, frankness, ingenuousness, truth, truthfulness, openness, unreserve, plain dealing.

Honey-combed, *a.* 1. Alveolate, cellular.

2. Perforated in every direction, eaten through in every part.

Honeyed, *a.* Sweet, dulcet.

Honor, *n.* 1. Veneration, reverence, respect, esteem, homage, deference, civility.

2. Dignity, distinction, elevation, high rank, nobleness, distinguished position.

3. Dignity of mien, noble bearing, majesty, majestic appearance, exalted looks.

4. Reputation, repute, fame, consideration, esteem, credit, glory, good name.

5. Integrity, probity, honesty, magnanimity, uprightness, high-mindedness, nobleness of mind, manly virtue.

6. Virtue, chastity, purity, womanly honor.

7. Nice sense of right *or* justice, high feeling of obligation, sense of honor.

8. Ornament, boast, glory, pride, credit.

——, *v. t.* 1. Dignify, exalt, glorify, grace, raise to distinction.

2. Reverence, revere, venerate, respect, pay respect to, pay deference to, render honor to, decorate, compliment.

3. Reverence, adore, revere, worship, hallow the name of, do the will of.

4. Commemorate, celebrate, observe, keep.

5. (*Com.*) Accept and pay (*a draft*), credit.

Honorable, *a.* 1. Illustrious, famous, elevated, noble, great, of high rank.

2. Upright, just, honest, fair, trustworthy, trusty, true, conscientious, virtuous, worshipful, admirable, magnanimous, high-minded, as good as one's word.

3. Reputable, creditable, estimable, esteemed, respected, right, proper, equitable.

Honors, *n. pl.* 1. Dignities, titles, privileges.

2. Adornments, decorations, beauties, glories.

3. Civilities, formal acts of respect, tokens of respect.

4. Academic distinctions, scholarly rank.

Hood, *n.* 1. Cowl, head cover, padded bonnet, coif, capuche.

2. Cover, protection, shelter; concealment, cloak, blind.

——, *v. t.* 1. Cover with a hood, put a hood on.

2. Cover (*in any way*), shelter, protect.

3. Hide, cover, conceal, shade, blind.

Hooded, *a.* (*Bot.*) Cucullate, hood-shaped.

Hoodoo, *n.* Black magic, voodoo, sorcery, "jinx."

Hoodwink, *v. t.* 1. Blind, blindfold.

2. Cover, hide, conceal, cloak.

3. Deceive, cheat, delude, dupe, gull, cozen, fool, befool, trick, circumvent, overreach, chouse, impose upon, make a fool of, play a trick upon, pull wool over one's eyes.

HOOK, *n.* 1. Catch, clasp, hasp, bent holder, curved catch.

2. Snare, trap.

3. Sickle, reaping-hook, reaper, cutter, grass-hook.

——, *v. t.* 1. Catch *or* fasten with a hook, take with a hook.

2. Catch, snare, ensnare, entrap.

3. Bend, curve, make into a hook, make hook-shaped.

4. Fit *or* furnish with hooks, apply hooks to.

Hooked, *a.* Bent, curved, curvated, crooked, aduncous, unciform, hamate, hamiform.

HOOP, *n.* 1. Ring, circlet, band.

2. Farthingale, crinoline, hoop-skirt, hoop-petticoat.

——, *v. t.* 1. Bind, fasten with hoops, put hoops upon *or* around.

2. Clasp, enclose, encircle, surround.

Hoop-skirt, *n.* Hoop, farthingale, crinoline, hoop-petticoat.

Hoot, *v. i.* 1. Shout *or* cry out *or* yell in contempt, jeer, boo.

2. Cry like an owl.

——, *v. t.* Execrate, denounce, hiss, boo, cry down, cry out against, hoot at.

——, *n.* Shout *or* cry *or* outcry *or* yell of contempt.

Hop, *v. i.* 1. Spring *or* leap on one leg *or* foot.

2. Leap, bound, jump, skip, spring, caper, frisk, frisk about; dance, trip.

3. Limp, halt, hobble, walk lame.

——, *n.* Leap, bound, jump, spring, skip, caper; dance.

Hope, *n.* 1. Trust, confidence, faith, reliance, sanguineness.

2. Expectancy, trustful longing, anticipation, waiting under the possibility of fulfilment, sense of possible fulfilment.

3. Possibility of good, chance of the desired end, room for expectation, chance of a favorable result.

4. Object of trust *or* reliance, ground of confidence, dependence.

——, *v. t.* 1. Await (*something agreeable*), hope for, trustingly long for.

2. Anticipate, desire expectantly.

——, *v. i.* Trust, wait in trustful longing, indulge *or* entertain a hope, be in hopes, live in hopes, look on the bright side, flatter one's self.

Hopeful, *a.* 1. Expectant, anticipatory; sanguine, fond, optimistic, confident.

2. Roseate, rosy.

Hopeless, *a.* 1. Despairing, desperate, depressed, abject, despondent, forlorn, disconsolate, downcast, crushed.

2. Remediless, irremediable, incurable, abandoned, past cure, helpless, past help.

3. Impossible, impracticable.

Hop-o'-my-thumb, *n.* Dwarf, pygmy.

Hopple, *v. t.* Fetter (*an animal*), hobble.

Horde, *n.* 1. Gang (*not living in fixed habitations*), troop, crew, clan, tribal group, migratory company *or* throng.

2. [*Usually in pl.*] Multitude, throng, crowd, pack, vast number, great crowd.

Horizontal, *a.* Level, parallel to the horizon, flat, plane.

HORN, *n.* 1. Bony excrescence *or* projection, antler.

2. Trumpet, wind-instrument.

3. Drinking-cup, beaker; cornucopia.

4. (*Bot.*) Spur, spike.

5. Cusp, curved extremity, prong, wing (*of a battle line*).

——, *v. t.* Gore, pierce.

Horn of plenty. Cornucopia.

Horny, *a.* Corneous, hard and rough, callous; spiny.

Horologe, *n.* Time-piece (*of any kind*).

Horoscope, *n.* Ascendant, star-scheme at one's birth.

Horrid, *a.* 1. Frightful, terrible, terrific, horrible, bristling, rough, alarming, portentous, formidable, appalling, dire, horrifying, horrific, harrowing, dreadful, fearful, awful, hideous.

2. (*Colloq.*) Shocking, offensive, disgusting, revolting, repulsive, odious, disagreeable, unpleasant, vile, abominable.

Horrific, *a.* Frightful.

Horrify, *v. t.* Frighten, terrify, fill with horror, shock, strike with terror, make one's blood run cold.

Horror, *n.* 1. Fright, affright, alarm, fear, dread, awe, terror, dismay, consternation, panic.

2. Abomination, abhorrence, detestation, aversion, disgust, loathing, hatred, antipathy.

3. (*Med.*) Shuddering, horripilation.

Horrors, *n. pl.* [With *The* prefixed.] Delirium tremens, *mania a potu*.

Hors de combat. [Fr.] Disabled, out of condition to fight.

HORSE, *n.* 1. Steed, charger, courser, stallion, gelding, mare, filly, colt, pony, sheltie or shelty, palfrey, pad, nag, barb, cob, etc., "dobbin," "mount."

2. Cavalry, horsemen.

3. Stand, frame, support, buck, saw-horse, clotheshorse.

Horse-laugh, *n.* Guffaw, cachinnation, boisterous laugh.

Horse-leech, *n.* 1. Horse-doctor, veteri-narian, veterinary surgeon.

2. Leech; sucker.

Horseman, *n.* 1. Rider, cavalier, eques-trian.

2. Cavalryman, horse-soldier, mounted man, mounted soldier, dragoon, *chas-seur*.

Hortatory, *a.* Homiletic, inciting, exhort-ing, advisory, full of exhortation *or* urgency.

Horticulture, *n.* Gardening.

Hosanna, *interj.* Hallelujah, alleluia praise ye Jehovah.

Hose, *n.* 1. Stockings.

2. Tubing, flexible pipe.

3. [*Archaic.*] Trousers, breeches.

Hospitable, *a.* 1. Kind *or* attentive to strangers, given to bounty *or* entertain-ing.

2. Generous, liberal, bountiful, open, kind, unconstrained, unreserved, largely receptive, cordial, large-minded.

HOSPITAL, *n.* Infirmary, sanitarium.

Hospitality, *n.* 1. Hospitableness, kind-ness to strangers, generosity in entertain-ment.

2. Openness (*of mind*), liberality, wel-come to new *or* various views.

Host, *n.* 1. Entertainer.

2. Landlord, innkeeper.

3. Army, legion, armed force, array.

4. Multitude, horde, throng, vast as-semblage.

Hostile, *a.* 1. Inimical, unfriendly, war-like.

2. Adverse, opposite, contrary, repug-nant, at variance, opposed, opposing.

Hostilities, *n. pl.* Warfare, hostile, un-friendly, *or* inimical actions, acts of war. See WAR.

Hostility, *n.* 1. Enmity, animosity, an-tagonism, hatred, unfriendliness, ill-will.

2. Opposition, repugnance, contrari-ety, variance.

Hostler, *n.* Groom, stable-servant, stable-boy.

Hot, *a.* 1. Burning, fiery, scalding; very warm, torrid, parching, roasting; incan-descent, candent, flaming, boiling, of high temperature, heated.

2. Very warm, oppressive, heated, sweltering, of high temperature (*said of weather*).

3. Irascible, excitable, impetuous, pas-sionate, angry, impatient, urgent, lustful, hasty, choleric, furious, touchy, violent.

4. Ardent, vehement, fervent, eager, glowing, animated, fervid, violent, pas-sionate.

5. Pungent, piquant, sharp, acrid, biting, stinging, peppery, high-flavored, high-seasoned.

Hotch-potch, *n.* Medley, farrago, jumble, stew, miscellany, gallimaufry, salma-gundi, olio, hodge-podge, confused mix-ture, *olla podrida*.

Hotel, *n.* Inn, tavern, public-house, house of entertainment, *cabaret*.

Hot-headed, *a.* Violent, rash, precipitate, reckless, impetuous, vehement, furious, passionate, headlong, heady, headstrong, inconsiderate, hot-brained.

Hotspur, *n.* Madcap, blood, wild fellow, hot-brained fellow, rash man, excitable fellow, man of touchy temper.

Hough, *v. t.* Hamstring.

Hound, *v. t.* 1. Incite, urge, spur, set on, drive, urge on, spur on.

2. Hunt, pursue, chase.

3. Hunt hard, pursue cruelly, harass, bait, harry, drive to bay.

HOUR, *n.* Sixty minutes, twenty-fourth part of a day; time of day.

Houri, *n.* Nymph of Paradise; beauty, fascinator.

Hourly, *adv.* 1. Every hour.

2. Frequently, continually, constantly.

HOUSE, *n.* 1. Habitation, abode, dwell-ing, mansion, residence, domicile, dwell-ing-place, home.

2. Building, edifice.

3. Family, household.

4. Lineage, race, kindred, tribe.

5. Legislative body, assembly.

6. Firm, partnership, company, con-cern, commercial establishment.

7. Hotel, inn, tavern, place of enter-tainment, public-house.

——, *v. t.* Shelter, protect, harbor, put under cover (*of a roof*), furnish with a house, procure a house *or* home for.

House-breaking, *n.* Burglary.

Household, *n.* Family, house.

Householder, *n.* Occupier of a house, head of a family.

Housewife, *n.* Mistress of a family, good-woman; huswife, female economist, thrifty woman.

Housing, *n.* 1. Horse-cloth, saddle-cloth, trappings.

2. Covering, protection (*from the weather*), shelter.

Hovel, *n.* Shed, hut, cot, cabin, mean habitation, hole, den.

Hover, *v. i.* 1. Flutter.

2. Hang about, hang over.

3. Vacillate; waver.

HOW, *adv.* 1. In what manner, in what way, by what mode, by what means, whereby.

2. To what extent, to what degree.

3. For what cause, for what reason.

4. In what state, in what condition, in what plight, with what meaning, by what name.

However, *adv.* Howsoever, in whatever manner, in whatever degree.

——, *conj.* Yet, still, nevertheless, but, though, notwithstanding.

Howl, *n.* Cry (*as of a dog*), yell, ululation.

——, *v. i.* Cry (*as a dog*), bawl, yowl, yell; wail, lament.

Howsoever, *adv.* However, in whatever manner, in whatever degree.

Hoyden, *a.* Rustic, rude, inelegant, uncouth, ungenteel, hoydenish, rough, ill-taught, ill-behaved, bad-mannered, tomboyish, romping.

——, *n.* Tomboy, romp, rude bold girl.

Hubbub, *n.* Uproar, clamor, din, racket, outcry, confusion, disorder, hullabaloo, tumult, disturbance, riot.

Huckster, *n.* Retailer, hawker, pedler, hucksterer; mercenary person.

Huddle, *v. t.* 1. Throw together in confusion, throw in a heap, crowd confusedly.

2. Hurry away, push away in a heap.

——, *v. i.* Crowd, press together in confusion.

——, *n.* Crowd, tumult, disorder, confusion, jumble, disturbance.

Hue, *n.* Color, tint, tinge, shade, cast, tone, complexion.

Hue and cry. Shouting, clamor, outcry.

Huff, *n.* Miff, pet, tiff, rage, passion, fume, fit of anger, angry mood, quarrel.

Huffish, ⎫ *a.* 1. Angry, petulant, pettish,
Huffy, ⎭ irritable, easily offended.

2. Blustering, arrogant, insolent, hectoring.

Hug, *v. t.* 1. Embrace, clasp, fold in the arms, fold to the breast *or* heart.

2. Retain, cherish, nurse in the mind, hold fast, cling to, keep hold of.

3. (*Naut.*) Go near, keep close to.

Huge, *a.* Vast, bulky, enormous, immense, stupendous, gigantic, colossal, elephantine, Herculean, Cyclopean, very great, very large.

Hugger-mugger, *a.* (*Contemptuous.*) 1. Secret, clandestine, sly.

2. Mean, unfair, base, contemptible.

3. Confused, disorderly, slovenly.

Hulk, *n.* Hull (*of an old vessel*), broken and dismasted vessel.

Hull, *n.* 1. Husk, outer covering, shell, rind.

2. Body of a vessel.

——, *v. t.* Peel, strip the hull from, husk, shuck, shell.

Hullabaloo, *n.* Racket, din, clamor, uproar, hubbub, outcry, vociferation, disturbance, confusion, noisy sport.

Hum, *v. i.* Buzz, make a buzzing sound, murmur, drone.

——, *v. t.* Sing (*in a low voice*), croon.

Human, *a.* 1. Man's, of man, belonging to man; proper to man.

2. Common to mankind, mortal.

3. Like a man, like a human being, full of fellow-feeling, humane, sympathetic.

Humane, *a.* 1. Kind, benevolent, benignant, obliging, accommodating, tender, sympathetic, charitable, compassionate, clement, merciful, lenient, gentle, kind-hearted, tender-hearted, good-hearted.

2. Elevating, refining, cultivating, humanizing, spiritual, rational.

Humanist, *n.* Student of polite literature, devotee of culture.

Humanities, *n. pl.* [With *The* prefixed.] Belles-lettres, polite literature.

Humanity, *n.* 1. Human nature.

2. Mankind, the human race.

3. Kindness, benevolence, benignity, philanthropy, tenderness, sympathy, charity, humaneness, kind-heartedness, fellow-feeling, good nature, milk of human kindness.

4. Human spirit, spirit *or* essence of man, reason, rationality, culture, spirit of truth and beauty.

Humanize, *v. t.* 1. Soften, make humane.

2. Civilize, cultivate, refine, polish, improve, enlighten, educate, reclaim from barbarism, fill with sensibility to justice, truth, and beauty.

Humble, *a.* 1. Meek, modest, unassuming, unpretending, unobtrusive, lowly, submissive, unambitious, free from pride, without arrogance.

2. Low, small, poor, unpretending, undistinguished, meek, obscure, mean, plain.

——, *v. t.* 1. Humiliate, shame, mortify, degrade, crush, break, subdue, abash, abase, make ashamed, bring down, put down, take down, put out of countenance.

2. Make humble, make lowly, render meek *or* modest *or* unpretending, free from pride.

Humbug, *n.* (*Colloq.*) 1. Imposition, imposture, fetch, deception, fraud, trick, cheat, gammon, dodge, gouge, blind, feint, chouse, hoax.

2. Charlatanry, charlatanism, quackery, mummery, cant, hypocrisy.

3. Impostor, charlatan, quack, cheat.

Humbug, *v. t.* (*Colloq.*) Deceive, cheat, cozen, swindle, trick, hoax, befool, chouse, impose upon.

Humdrum, *a.* Dull, prosy, dronish, stupid, monotonous, tedious, wearisome, tiresome, dry, dreary.

Humid, *a.* Wet, moist, damp, dank.

Humiliate, *v. t.* Mortify, shame, abash, abase, put to shame, put down. See HUMBLE, 1.

Humiliation, *n.* Humbling, abasement, mortification, degradation, crushing, putting to shame, dishonoring.

Humility, *n.* Humbleness, meekness, submissiveness, lowliness, self-abasement, lowliness of mind, freedom from pride *or* arrogance, freedom from self-righteousness.

Hummock, *n.* 1. Hillock, knoll, knob of soil.

2. Ridge, pile, hump, knob, protuberance (*in a field of ice*).

HUMOR, *n.* 1. Moisture, vapor, fluid (*of animal bodies*).

2. Temper, disposition, bent, bias, vein, propensity, predilection, turn of mind.

3. Mood, temper, state of feeling, frame of mind.

4. Fancy, whim, caprice, freak, vagary, crotchet, whimsey, maggot, wrinkle.

5. Pleasantry, facetiousness, fun, jocoseness, jocularity, kindly wit, comic *or* ludicrous feeling *or* tone.

——, *v. t.* 1. Indulge, gratify, give way to, comply with the wishes of.

2. Favor, suit the nature of, meet the requirements of.

Humorist, *n.* Wag, wit, droll fellow, joker, jester, funny fellow.

Humorous, *a.* Facetious, jocular, jocose, droll, funny, sportive, comical, comic, ludicrous, witty, pleasant.

Humorsome, *a.* 1. Petulant, peevish, snappish, moody, waspish, crusty, captious, perverse, wayward, cross-grained.

2. Capricious, whimsical, fanciful, fitful, fantastic, odd.

Humpback, *n.* 1. Crooked back, crook-back.

2. Hunchback, crook-back.

Hunch, *n.* 1. Hump, protuberance, knob, bunch, lump.

2. Punch, push, shove, nudge.

3. (*Colloq.*) Lump, hunk, large piece, thick slice.

4. Intuition, premonition.

——, *v. t.* Punch, push, shove, jostle, nudge, arch.

Hunchback, *n.* Humpback, crook-back.

Hundred, *n.* Century; division of land.

Hunger, *v. i.* 1. Feel hunger, feel hungry, be hungry, crave food, want nourishment; famish, starve.

2. Long, hanker, feel longing desire, desire eagerly, pine.

Hungry, *a.* 1. Craving (*food*), of keen appetite, sharp-set, in want of food, starving, voracious, famishing (*by hyperbole*), ravenous, edacious, insatiate.

2. Longing, in painful desire, eagerly desirous, avid, greedy.

3. Poor, barren, unfertile, unproductive.

Hunk, *n.* Lump, hunch, large piece, thick slice, chunk.

Hunks, *n.* Miser, niggard, curmudgeon, codger, lickpenny, skinflint, scrimp, screw, muckworm, sordid wretch, mean fellow.

Hunt, *v. t.* Chase, pursue, stalk, trail, trap, hound; look for; seek, follow, drive.

——, *v. i.* 1. Follow the chase; shoot, poach.

2. Search, seek.

——, *n.* Chase, pursuit, hunting, field-sport.

Hunter, *n.* 1. Huntsman.

2. Hound, hunting-dog; hunting-horse, hunting-nag, horse for the chase.

Huntsman, *n.* Hunter; manager of chase.

Hurl, *v. t.* 1. Throw, fling, cast, pitch, send, project, dart, sling, throw violently, send whirling, send whizzing.

2. Utter violently, fulminate, thunder.

Hurly-burly, *n.* (*Colloq.*) Hurl, hurly, turmoil, uproar, tumult, commotion, confusion, bustle, disturbance.

Hurrah, *interj.* Huzza.

Hurricane, *n.* Tornado, cyclone, typhoon; violent gale, wild storm.

Hurried, *a.* 1. Driven (*by work*), over head and ears, pressed for time.

2. Hasty, cursory, slight, superficial.

Hurry, *v. t.* 1. Drive, precipitate.

2. Hasten, expedite, speed, despatch, quicken, urge *or* push forward, urge *or* press on.

——, *v. i.* 1. Act precipitately, be in a flutter, be in a flurry.

2. Haste, hasten, move quickly, scurry, be in haste, be quick, be in a hurry, make haste, mend one's pace, move with celerity, lose no time, lose not a moment.

——, *n.* 1. Precipitation, flurry, flutter, agitation, confusion, bustle, perturbation, hurry-skurry.

2. Haste, despatch, celerity, quickness, promptitude, expedition.

Hurry-skurry, *n.* (*Colloq.*) Flutter, flurry, agitation, confusion, hurry, fluttering haste.

——, *adv.* Confusedly, pell-mell, helter-skelter, headlong, with a huddling rush, heels over head.

Hurt, *v. t.* 1. Injure, harm, damage, mar, impair, do harm to, inflict injury upon.

2. Pain, wound, give pain to.

3. Grieve, afflict, pain, wound, offend, wound the feelings of, give (*mental*) pain to.

——, *n.* 1. Harm, injury, damage, detriment, mischief, disadvantage.

2. Wound, bruise; ache, pain, suffering.

Hurtful, *a.* Injurious, detrimental, mischievous, pernicious, deleterious, unwholesome, noxious, baneful, prejudicial, disadvantageous, harmful, baleful.

Husband, *n.* Spouse, married man.

——, *v. t.* Save, economize, spend frugally, manage with frugality.

Husbandman, *n.* Agriculturist, farmer, tiller of the ground, cultivator of the soil.

Husbandry, *n.* 1. Agriculture, farming, tillage, geoponics, cultivation of the soil.

2. Frugality, thrift, domestic economy, management of domestic affairs.

Hush, *v. t.* 1. Still, silence, quiet, repress the cries *or* clamor of.

2. Appease, assuage, still, calm, quiet, allay, console.

——, *interj.* Silence, whist, be still, keep quiet, make no noise.

——, *n.* Stillness, silence, quiet.

Hush up. Suppress, conceal, cover over, hide, keep secret, keep private.

Husk, *n.* Rind, bark, hull, glume, outer covering; worthless shell.

——, *v. t.* Strip off the husk from (*as from Indian-corn*).

Husky, *a.* 1. Dry, shrivelled.

2. Hoarse, rough, raucous, harsh, guttural.

3. Powerful, strong.

Hussar, *n.* Light-armed dragoon, light-cavalryman.

Hussy, *n.* Jade, quean, base woman, sorry wench, minx, pert girl.

Hustle, *v. t.* Push, jostle, justle, elbow, crowd; hasten, hurry; force onward.

Hut, *n.* Cot, cabin, shed, hovel, poor cottage, mean dwelling.

Hutch, *n.* 1. Chest, coffer, bin.

2. Trap (*as for rabbits*), coop; hut, shed.

Hyaline, *a.* Glassy, crystalline, transparent.

Hybrid, *n.* Mongrel, mule, cross, half-breed.

——, *a.* Mongrel, cross-bred, mixed.

Hydra, *n.* 1. (*Mythol.*) Many-headed monster.

2. Gorgon, frightful object, raw head and bloody bones; persistent evil.

Hydrant, *n.* Discharge-pipe (*from the main of an aqueduct*), water-plug.

Hydropathist, *n.* 1. Water-doctor, expert in hydropathy.

2. Believer in hydropathy, practiser of water-cure.

Hydropathy, *n.* Water-cure.

Hydrous, *a.* Watery.

Hygiene, *n.* Hygienics, science of health, sanitary science.

Hymen, *n.* 1. (*Mythol.*) God of marriage; marriage.

2. (*Anat.*) Virginal membrane, maidenhead.

Hymeneal, *a.* Nuptial, connubial, matrimonial, bridal, conjugal, conjugial.

Hymn, *n.* Song (*of praise*), devotional song, spiritual song, sacred song, sacred lyric, psalm, canticle, paean.

Hyperbaton, *n.* (*Rhet.*) Inversion, transposition of words.

Hyperbole, *n.* (*Rhet.*) Exaggeration, excessive statement.

Hyperborean, *a.* 1. Most northern, far north.

2. Very cold, boreal, wintry, hiemal, brumal, frosty, icy, frigid.

Hypercritical, *a.* Over-critical, captiously critical.

Hypnotic, *a.* Soporific, somniferous; mesmeric.

——, *n.* Narcotic, soporific, opiate.

Hypnotism, *n.* Sleepiness, lethargy; mesmerism.

Hypochondria, *n.* (*Med.*) Melancholy, spleen, vapors, depression, dejection, hypochondriasis, low spirits.

Hypochondriac, *n.* Seek-sorrow, self-tormentor, victim of melancholy *or* hypochondria.

Hypochondriacal, } *a.* Melancholy, sple-
Hypochondriac, } netic, dispirited, dejected, depressed, hipped.

Hypocrisy, *n.* 1. Pharisaism, formalism, sanctimoniousness, cant, pietism, assumed piety.

2. Dissimulation, deceit, deception, imposture, pretence, false profession.

Hypocrite, *n.* 1. Pharisee, formalist, canter.

2. Dissembler, deceiver, impostor, pretender, cheat.

Hypocritical, *a.* 1. Pharisaical, canting, sanctimonious.

2. Dissembling, insincere, false, hollow, deceitful, faithless.

Hypostasis, *n.* 1. Substance, subsistence.

2. Person, personality.

3. Principle, element.

Hypothecate, *v. t.* Pledge (*as ship, freight, cargo, etc., without delivery*), mortgage.

Hypothesis, *n.* Supposition, theory, assumption, conjecture, unproved theory.

Hypothetical, *a.* Conditional, that involves an hypothesis, conjectural.

Hysteria, *n.* (*Med.*) Hysterics; loss of emotional control, morbid excitement.

Hysterical, *a.* 1. Spasmodic, convulsive.

2. Affected with hysterics.

I

I, *pron.* Ego.

Iambic, *n.* Iambus; iambic verse.

Ibidem, *adv.* [L.] In the same place.

ICE, *n.* 1. Frozen water, crystal.

2. Concreted sugar, icing, frosting.

3. Ice-cream.

——, *v. t.* 1. Freeze, congeal, convert into ice.

2. Coat *or* cover with ice, ice over.

3. Coat *or* cover with icing, frost.

4. Chill, make icy.

Ichor, *n.* 1. (*Mythol.*) Blood of the gods.

2. Serous humor, watery fluid.

Ichorous, *a.* Serous, watery, thin.

Icing, *n.* Frosting, concreted sugar (*for coating cake*).

Iconoclast, *n.* Image-breaker, attacker of cherished beliefs, radical.

Icy, *a.* 1. Glacial.

2. Cold, chilling, frosty, intensely cold.

3. Frigid, indifferent, distant, unemotional, cold-hearted.

IDEA, *n.* 1. [*In the Platonic philosophy.*] Archetype (*conceived of as existing from eternity*), pattern, model, exemplar, form, essence (*common to many individual things and represented by a general term*), creative *or* self-active ideal.

2. [*In the Kantian philosophy.*] Supreme principle of pure reason, regulative first principle, highest unitary principle of thought. [*There are three such, — the Self, the Cosmic Force, and God.*]

3. [*In the Hegelian philosophy.*] Supreme principle, the Absolute, the Self-existent, as the unity of subject and object, God.

4. Universal concept, conception, notion, general *or* universal conception.

5. Object of thought, image in the mind, mental representation of an object, image in reflection, memory, *or* imagination; fiction, fantasy, imagination.

6. Impression, apprehension, thought, fancy, conceit.

7. Opinion, belief, supposition, judgment, sentiment.

8. Guiding conception, organizing conception, formative notion, regulative principle.

Ideal, *a.* 1. Intellectual, mental.

2. Imaginary, unreal, fanciful, fantastic, fancied, illusory, chimerical, visionary, shadowy.

3. Complete, perfect, consummate, filling our utmost conceptions.

4. Impractical, Utopian.

——, *n.* Imaginary standard, ideal model of perfection.

Idealism, *n.* Idealistic philosophy, theory that matter is the phenomenon of mind, theory that mind alone is absolute; romanticism.

Ideality, *n.* Imagination, conception, invention, fancy.

Idem. [L.] The same, ditto.

Identical, *a.* Same, selfsame, very same, one and the same, exactly the same, not different; equivalent, tantamount.

Identify, *v. t.* 1. Prove to be identical, prove to be the same, ascertain to be the same; recognize.

2. Make identical, regard as one, consider the same, take for identical.

Identity, *n.* Sameness.

Ideology, *n.* 1. Science of ideas, theory of the origin of ideas, doctrine of the evolution of ideas.

2. Sensationalism, sensualism, empiricism, sensuous theory of the origin of ideas, doctrine that all ideas are evolved from elementary sensations; visionary speculation.

Idiocy, *n.* 1. Condition of an idiot, imbecility, native irrationality, congenital imbecility.

2. Foolishness, imbecility, fatuity,

feebleness of intellect, want of understanding.

Idiom, *n.* 1. Language peculiar to people, district, community; expression peculiar to itself in grammatical construction.

2. Genius (*of a language*), characteristic quality.

3. Dialect.

Idiomatic, *a.* Peculiar (*as respects any mode of expression*).

Idiosyncrasy, *n.* Peculiarity (*of constitution*), idiocrasy, peculiar temperament; eccentricity.

Idiot, *n.* Fool, natural, natural fool, congenital imbecile, imbecile; simpleton, blockhead, dunce, booby.

Idiotic, *a.* 1. Marked by idiocy, imbecile, born imbecile.

2. Pertaining to idiots, characteristic of idiots.

3. Foolish, sottish, fatuous; irrational.

Idle, *a.* 1. Unemployed, unoccupied, unbusied, inactive.

2. Indolent, lazy, slothful, sluggish, inert.

3. Vacant, unused, leisure.

4. Useless, ineffectual, bootless, fruitless, groundless, unavailing, vain, futile, abortive.

5. Trifling, trivial, unimportant, frivolous, trashy, foolish, unprofitable.

Idler, *n.* Drone, sluggard, laggard, lounger, dawdler, trifler, doodle, slowback, inefficient person.

Idol, *n.* 1. Pagan deity, false god; image, simulacrum, "Mumbo-Jumbo."

2. Falsity, illusion, delusion, deluding assumption; pretender, sham.

3. Favorite, pet, darling, beloved.

Idolater, *n.* 1. Worshipper of idols, pagan, heathen.

2. Adorer, great admirer.

Idolatry, *n.* 1. Worship of idols.

2. Excessive love, extravagant fondness, excessive veneration.

Idolize, *v. t.* 1. Deify, make an idol of; canonize.

2. Adore, reverence *or* love excessively, be extravagantly fond of; honor, venerate, love.

Idyl, *n.* [Written also *Idyll.*] Bucolic, eclogue, pastoral, pastoral poem; short poem (*highly wrought*).

IF, *conj.* 1. Suppose that, admitting that, allowing that, granting that, grant that, provided, though, in case that, on the supposition that.

2. Whether, whether or not.

Igneous, *a.* 1. Fiery.

2. Molten, produced under the action of fire.

Ignis fatuus. [L.] Jack-a-lantern, Will-o'-the-wisp; misleading influence.

Ignite, *v. t.* Kindle, set fire to, set on fire, light, inflame.

——, *v. i.* Kindle, take fire, catch fire.

Ignoble, *a.* 1. Plebeian, vulgar, untitled, base-born, low-born, mean, low, rustic, peasant, hedge-born.

2. Worthless, insignificant, mean, contemptible, degraded, vile; dishonorable, disgraceful, base, unworthy, infamous, low.

Ignominious, *a.* 1. Dishonorable, disgraceful, discreditable, shameful, infamous, scandalous, disreputable, opprobrious, full of ignominy.

2. Deserving ignominy, despicable, contemptible, base, infamous.

Ignominy, *n.* Dishonor, disgrace, discredit, disrepute, shame, infamy, obloquy, contempt, opprobrium, odium, scandal, abasement.

Ignoramus, *n.* Sciolist, smatterer, novice, "duffer," greenhorn, simpleton, numskull, know-nothing. See DUNCE.

Ignorance, *n.* Illiteracy, nescience, darkness, benightedness, rusticity; unawareness, blindness, want of knowledge.

Ignorant, *a.* Unlearned, uninstructed, uninformed, uneducated, untaught, unenlightened, unread, untutored, nescient, blind, illiterate, unlettered, unaware, unconversant, unwitting.

Ignore, *v. t.* Regard as unknown, shut one's eyes to, leave out of view, not recognize, not take into account, wilfully disregard, neglect, pass over, skip, utterly overlook.

ILL, *a.* 1. Bad, evil, unfortunate, unfavorable, faulty, harmful; wicked, wrong, iniquitous, unjust, naughty.

2. Sick, diseased, ailing, disordered, very unwell, indisposed, out of health, seriously indisposed.

3. Cross, crabbed, surly, peevish, malicious, unkind, malevolent, hateful.

4. Ugly, ill-favored.

——, *n.* 1. Wickedness, depravity, evil.

2. Misfortune, calamity, misery, harm, pain, evil, affliction.

——, *adv.* 1. Badly, not well.

2. With difficulty, not easily.

Ill-advised, *a.* Injudicious, unwise, imprudent, foolish, ill-judged.

Illative, *a.* Inferential, deductive.

Ill-bred, *a.* Impolite, uncivil, uncourteous, discourteous, uncourtly, unpolished, uncouth, rude, ill-behaved, ill-mannered, badly brought up.

Illegal, *a.* Unlawful, illicit, unlicensed, unauthorized, illegitimate, contraband, prohibited.

Illegible, *a.* Unreadable, impossible to be read, undecipherable, indecipherable.

Illegitimate, *a.* 1. Unlawfully begotten, born out of wedlock, bastard, natural, misbegotten.

2. Spurious, not genuine.

3. Unauthorized, unlawful, illicit, improper.

Ill-fated, *a.* Luckless, unlucky, unfortunate, ill-starred.

Ill-favored, *a.* Ugly, homely, plain, ill-looking; offensive, unpleasant.

Ill-humor, *n.* Fretfulness, peevishness, petulance, testiness, ill-temper.

Illiberal, *a.* 1. Parsimonious, stingy, miserly, narrow, niggardly, penurious, ungenerous, sordid, covetous, mean, selfish, close, close-fisted.

2. Uncharitable, narrow, narrow-minded, bigoted; vulgar, ungentlemanly.

Illicit, *a.* 1. Unlawful, illegal, illegitimate, unauthorized, unlegalized, unlicensed.

2. Improper, forbidden, wrong, guilty, criminal.

Illimitable, *a.* Boundless, infinite, unbounded, endless, immeasurable, immense, vast.

Illiteracy, *n.* Ignorance, want of learning, want of literary culture.

Illiterate, *a.* Uninstructed (*in books*), unlettered, unlearned, untaught, ignorant; unable to read and write.

Ill-judged, *a.* See ILL-ADVISED.

Ill-mannered, *a.* Impolite, uncivil, uncourteous, discourteous, uncourtly, unpolished, uncouth, rude, ill-behaved, ill-bred.

Ill-natured, *a.* 1. Malevolent, unkind, disobliging, unfriendly, unamiable, hateful.

2. Morose, sullen, sulky, cross, churlish, spiteful, crabbed, sour, perverse, wayward, crusty, petulant, cross-grained, ill-tempered, acrimonious, bitter.

Illness, *n.* Disease, sickness, indisposition, ailing, malady, ailment, complaint, disorder, distemper.

Illogical, *a.* Inconclusive, inconsequent, invalid, absurd, unreasonable, fallacious, incorrect, unsound, inconsistent.

Ill-proportioned, *a.* Misshapen, misproportioned, shapeless, ill-shaped, ill-made, awkward.

Ill-starred, *a.* Unlucky, luckless, unfortunate, ill-fated, unhappy.

Ill-temper, *n.* Moroseness, sullenness, sulkiness, crabbedness, crossness, perverseness, bad temper, ill-nature, "grouchiness."

Ill-timed, *a.* Unseasonable, untimely, inopportune, inapposite, irrelevant, out of place.

Ill-treat, *v. t.* Maltreat, injure, abuse, illuse, abuse, misuse, mishandle.

Illuminate, *v. t.* 1. Light, illumine, illume, brighten, supply with light.

2. Adorn with lights (*as a building*), light up.

3. Adorn with colored letters, ornament, emblaze.

4. Enlighten, illumine, make wise, instruct, inspire, give insight.

Illumine, *v. t.* 1. Light, illuminate, illume, supply with light.

2. Enlighten. See ILLUMINATE, 4.

Illusion, *n.* Delusion, hallucination, deception, error, fallacy, mockery, fantasy, phantasm, chimera, false show.

Illusive, } *a.* Deceptive, deceitful, delu-
Illusory, } sive, fallacious, tantalizing, mock, make believe, Barmecide, sham, unsatisfying, visionary, unsubstantial, unreal.

Illustrate, *v. t.* 1. Elucidate, explain, exemplify, make clear, make plain, throw light upon.

2. Adorn with pictures.

Illustration, *n.* 1. Elucidation, explanation, exemplification.

2. Illustrative picture.

Illustrative, *a.* Explanatory, elucidative.

Illustrious, *a.* 1. Glorious, splendid, brilliant, bright, radiant.

2. Famous, famed, noted, distinguished, renowned, celebrated, conspicuous, eminent, signal, remarkable.

Ill-will, *n.* Malevolence, unkindness, malice, dislike, hostility, malignity, venom, animosity, enmity, hate, hatred, rancor, uncharitableness, ill-nature, envy, grudge, spleen, spite.

Image, *n.* 1. Statue.

2. Idol, object of worship.

3. Likeness, effigy, figure, similitude, imago, simulacrum, shape, statue, form, symbol, resemblance, picture, representation of an object (*real* or *fancied*); reflection, embodiment, counterpart; conception, idea.

4. Trope, figurative expression.

——, *v. t.* 1. Form an image of.

2. Fancy, picture. See IMAGINE.

Imagery, *n.* 1. Phantasm, phantom, vision, dream, fanciful forms.

2. Tropes, figures of speech, figurative language.

Imaginable, *a.* Conceivable.

Imaginary, *a.* 1. Visionary, ideal, fancied, invented, fictitious, fantastic, fanciful, chimerical, dreamy, unreal, illusory, illusive, shadowy, wild, Quixotic, Utopian.

2. Hypothetical, supposed, assumed, conceivable.

Imagination, *n.* 1. Conception (*with the recombining of ideas so as to form a new creation*), invention, creative power, fancy, fantasy; faculty of original conception, power to mould the manifold of experience into new unities.

2. Imaging power, vision of the past as present *or* of the possible as actual, reproductive perception, anticipative perception.

3. Mental image, idea, conception, notion.

4. Contrivance, scheme, device, plot.

5. Illusion, arbitrary notion *or* supposition, fanciful opinion, fancy.

Imaginative, *a.* Inventive, creative, plastic, fanciful, visionary, dreamy, poetical, esemplastic.

Imagine, *v. t.* 1. Conceive, image, fancy, picture, dream, pretend, picture to one's self, figure to one's self.

2. Devise, contrive, project, frame, invent, mould, create.

3. Suppose, assume, take for hypothesis, make the hypothesis.

4. Think, believe, suppose, apprehend, deem, guess, assume, opine.

——, *v. i.* Suppose, think, opine, believe, deem, assume, fancy, dream, take it into one's head, have a notion.

Imbecile, *a.* Foolish, witless, cretinous, feeble-minded, driveling, idiotic, fatuous, inane.

——, *n.* 1. Dotard, feeble person, driveler.

2. Idiot, natural, congenital imbecile, moon-calf, fool, half-wit, cretin.

Imbecility, *n.* 1. Weakness, feebleness, debility, infirmity, helplessness.

2. Foolishness, childishness, idiocy, fatuity, stupidity.

Imbibe, *v. t.* 1. Absorb, drink, assimilate, take in, suck in, suck up, swallow up.

2. Receive, gather, acquire, gain, get, pick up.

Imbricated, *a.* Overlapping.

Imbroglio, *n.* [It.] 1. Intricate plot.

2. Complication, complexity, entanglement, embarrassing situation, complicated misunderstanding.

Imbrue, *v. t.* Wet, moisten, steep, soak, drench, stain.

Imbrute, *v. t.* Brutify, brutalize, degrade utterly.

Imbue, *v. t.* 1. Tinge, dye, stain, tint, tincture, color.

2. Tincture deeply, pervade, infuse, steep, saturate, bathe, impregnate, inoculate, permeate.

Imitate, *v. t.* 1. Copy, follow, pattern after, reproduce, mirror, counterfeit, emulate, echo, follow, forge, duplicate.

2. Mimic, ape, mock, personate, impersonate, take off.

3. Parody, travesty, burlesque, turn into burlesque.

Imitation, *n.* 1. Copying, imitating, mimicking, aping, parrotry.

2. Copy, resemblance, likeness, duplicate.

3. Mimicry, mocking.

4. Parody, travesty, burlesque.

Imitative, *a.* 1. Imitating, copying, mimetic, simulating.

2. Mimicking, aping, apish.

Imitator, *n.* Copyist.

Immaculate, *a.* 1. Spotless, unspotted, stainless, unsullied, unsoiled, untainted, unblemished, untarnished, undefiled, clean, pure.

2. Innocent, guiltless, sinless, faultless, pure, saintly, stainless, holy, untainted by sin.

Immanent, *a.* 1. Intrinsic, inherent, internal, indwelling.

2. (*Met.*) Empirical, remaining within the bounds of experience, belonging to the world of sense.

Immaterial, *a.* 1. Incorporeal, bodiless, unbodied, unsubstantial, impalpable, metaphysical, extramundane, aerie, ethereal, mental, unfleshly, spiritual, supersensible.

2. Unimportant, insignificant, unessential, non-essential, of no importance, of no consequence.

Immature, *n.* 1. Unripe, crude, green, raw, unformed, unprepared, rudimental, imperfect, undeveloped, unfinished; youthful.

2. Premature, hasty, untimely, unseasonable, out of season.

Immeasurable, *a.* Illimitable, limitless, boundless, unbounded, measureless, immense, infinite.

Immediate, *a.* 1. Proximate, close, near, next.

2. Direct, without other agency, unmediated; intuitive; primary.

3. Instantaneous, instant, present, prompt.

Immediately, *adv.* 1. Closely, proximately.

2. Directly, without any intervention.

3. Instantly, forthwith, just now, without delay, this moment, directly, *instanter*, presto.

Immemorial, *a.* Beyond memory, that cannot be remembered, olden, ancient, hoary, reaching back beyond tradition.

Immense, *a.* 1. Illimitable, boundless, unbounded, unlimited, interminable, measureless, infinite.

2. Vast, enormous, prodigious, stupendous, huge, gigantic, colossal, Cyclopean, Herculean, very great, large, tremendous, elephantine, titanic, monstrous, mountainous.

Immensity, *n.* 1. Infinity, infinitude, boundlessness, illimitableness.

2. Vastness, hugeness.

3. Infinite extension, boundless space, space.

Immerse, *v. t.* 1. Dip, plunge, immerge, bathe, submerge, overwhelm, sink, douse, souse, duck; baptize.

2. Involve, engage, absorb, sink.

Immersion, *n.* 1. Dipping, plunging, immersing.

2. Engagement, absorption.

3. (*Astron.*) Disappearance, occultation.

4. Baptism by dipping *or* immersion.

Imminent, *a.* 1. Impending, overhanging, threatening, near at hand.

2. Threatening harm, perilous, dangerous, alarming.

Immitigable, *a.* Not to be mitigated, that cannot be mitigated, unappeasable, that cannot be allayed *or* assuaged.

Immobile, *a.* 1. Fixed, motionless, stationary, steadfast, static, quiescent, stable, inflexible, immovable.

2. Rigid, stiff, expressionless, without play of features, dull, stolid, impassive.

Immobility, *n.* 1. Unmovableness, immovableness, immovability, fixity, fixedness, movelessness, steadfastness, stability.

2. Inflexibility, rigidity, stiffness, lack of expression, lack of play in features, dulness, stolidity.

Immoderate, *a.* Inordinate, excessive, extreme, unreasonable, extravagant, exorbitant, intemperate.

Immodest, *a.* 1. Indelicate, indecorous, shameless, gross, coarse, lewd; impure, obscene, indecent, smutty, unchaste, filthy, broad.

2. Bold, forward, brazen, impudent, indecent, destitute of proper reserve.

Immodesty, *n.* 1. Indelicacy, indecorum, grossness, coarseness, shamelessness, impudicity.

2. Boldness, forwardness, brass, impudence, want of proper reserve, impudicity.

3. Impurity, obscenity, lewdness, unchastity, smuttiness, indecency, impudicity.

Immolate, *v. t.* Sacrifice, offer up, offer in sacrifice, kill as a victim.

Immoral, *a.* 1. [*Said of actions.*] Wrong, unethical, anti-social, wicked, vicious, sinful, corrupt, loose.

2. [*Said of persons.*] Bad, wicked, unprincipled, depraved, loose in behavior, profligate, dissolute, vicious.

3. [*Said of habitual conduct.*] Loose, depraved, unprincipled, dissolute, licentious, abandoned, indecent.

Immorality, *n.* 1. Wickedness, vice, sin, sinfulness, depravity, corruption, corruptness, impurity, demoralization, criminality, profligacy, want of principle.

2. Immoral action, sin, vice, wrong, anti-social act.

Immortal, *a.* 1. Undying, deathless, everliving, imperishable, incorruptible, unfading, indestructible, indissoluble, never-dying.

2. Eternal, everlasting, endless, perpetual, continuing, perdurable, ceaseless, never-ending, sempiternal.

3. [*By hyperbole.*] Lasting, enduring, permanent, abiding, lasting through all time *or* as long as the world endures.

Immortality, *n.* 1. Exemption from death, unending life, deathlessness, indestructibility, incorruptibility, incorruption.

2. Perpetuity, unlimited existence, endless life, eternal continuance.

3. Perpetual fame, exemption from oblivion.

Immortalize, *v. t.* 1. Exempt from death, make immortal.

2. Perpetuate, make everlasting.

3. Perpetuate in memory, exempt from oblivion, make forever famous.

Immovable, *a.* 1. Fixed, firm, stable, immobile, stationary, not to be moved.

2. Steadfast, unshaken, unalterable, unyielding, impassive, unchangeable.

Immunity, *n.* 1. Freedom, exemption, release, exoneration.

2. Privilege, prerogative, right, liberty, charter, franchise.

Immure, *v. t.* Confine, shut up, wall up, entomb; imprison, incarcerate.

Immutable, *a.* Unchangeable, invariable, unalterable, undeviating, inflexible, constant, permanent, stable, fixed.

Imp, *n.* Sprite, elf, hobgoblin, flibbertigibbet, little demon *or* devil, malignant spirit; mischievous child.

Impact, *n.* 1. Impulse, shock, impression, stroke; brunt, touch.

2. Collision, impinging, contact, striking.

——, *v. t.* Pack together, pack close, wedge, press close together, drive firmly together.

Impair, *v. t.* 1. Deteriorate, injure, vitiate, damage, spoil, mar, ruin, blemish, deface, make worse, harm.

2. Lessen, diminish decrease, make less. reduce; weaken, enfeeble, enervate.

Impale, *v. t.* 1. Thrust upon a stake, kill by impaling, transfix.

2. Fence, surround with palings, enclose with palisades.

Impalpable, *a.* 1. Intangible, very fine, delicate, attenuated, not palpable, not to be felt, not perceptible by the touch.

2. Imperceptible, shadowy, indistinct, inapprehensible, unsubstantial, incorporeal.

Impart, *v. t.* 1. Give, grant, bestow. See CONFER.

2. Communicate, share, divulge, disclose, reveal, tell, make known.

Impartial, *a.* Unbiassed, unprejudiced, unwarped, candid, dispassionate, disinterested, equitable, just, fair, honorable, even-handed, equal.

Impassable, *a.* Impervious, impermeable, impenetrable, pathless.

Impassibility, *n.* 1. Insensibility, indifference, insusceptibility to pain *or* grief.

2. See IMPASSIVITY, 2.

Impassible, *a.* 1. Insensible, indifferent, insusceptible, incapable of suffering.

2. See IMPASSIVE, 2.

Impassioned, *a.* Passionate, vehement, impetuous, glowing, intense, excited, animated, fervid, fervent, zealous, warm, ardent.

Impassive, *a.* 1. Not showing emotion, calm, passionless.

2. See IMPASSIBLE, 1.

Impassivity, *n.* 1. Calmness, passionlessness.

2. See IMPASSIBILITY, 1.

Impatience, *n.* 1. Disquietude, restlessness, uneasiness.

2. Vehemence, impetuosity, haste, eagerness, precipitation.

3. Lack of forbearance, want of patience, irritability, irritableness, heat, violence of temper.

Impatient, *a.* 1. Unquiet, uneasy, restless.

2. Hasty, precipitate, vehement, impetuous, eager.

3. Without forbearance, intolerant, irritable, hot, violent, vehement, testy, fretful, peevish, choleric.

Impeach, *v. t.* 1. Arraign, accuse, indict.

2. Arraign for malfeasance in office, accuse of maladministration.

3. Discredit, asperse, call in question, censure, impute fault to, denounce, disparage, criminate, impair, lessen.

Impeccable, *a.* Sinless, faultless, immaculate, stainless, incapable of wrong.

Impede, *v. t.* Hinder, obstruct, stop, clog, check, retard, delay, interrupt, thwart, restrain, block, encumber.

Impediment, *n.* Hindrance, obstruction, obstacle, check, bar, difficulty, stumbling-block, encumbrance.

Impel, *v. t.* 1. Drive, push, urge, send, put in motion, press on, urge forward.

2. Induce, move, persuade, influence, instigate, incite, actuate, stimulate, set on, stir up, constrain, compel.

Impend, *v. i.* 1. Threaten, hang over, be imminent, be in store, stare one in the face.

2. Be near, draw near, approach, be at hand.

Impending, *a.* Impendent, threatening, imminent, near at hand.

Impenetrable, *a.* 1. Not to be penetrated, impermeable, impervious, inaccessible, not to be pierced.

2. Dull, obtuse, senseless, insensible, indifferent, impassive, unsympathetic, stolid, cold; dense, proof.

3. Unfathomable, reticent, that keeps his own counsel, not to be found out.

Impenitent, *a.* Uncontrite, unrepentant, obdurate, hardened, seared, recusant, relentless, incorrigible, irreclaimable, unconverted.

Imperative, *a.* 1. Commanding, authoritative, peremptory, urgent. See IMPERIOUS.

2. Binding, obligatory.

Imperceptible, *a.* 1. Invisible, undiscernible, indistinguishable, inaudible, not to be perceived.

2. Fine, minute, very small, impalpable, inappreciable; gradual.

Imperfect, *a.* 1. Incomplete, deficient, poor, crude, abortive, garbled, not entire.

2. Defective, faulty, out of order, impaired.

Imperfection, *n.* 1. Defectiveness, faultiness, deficiency, incompleteness, want of perfection.

2. Defect, lack, fault, blemish, stain, flaw, taint.

3. Weakness, frailty, liability to err, limitation, foible, failing, vice.

Imperial, *a.* 1. Belonging *or* relating to an empire.

2. Kingly, regal, royal, sovereign.

3. Majestic, grand, exalted, magnificent, august, noble, great, regal, royal, kingly *or* queenly, supreme, sovereign, consummate.

Imperious, *a.* Dictatorial, magisterial, domineering, tyrannical, despotic, overbearing, lordly, haughty, arrogant; imperative, urgent, compelling.

Imperishable, *a.* Indestructible, everlasting, unfading, eternal, perennial, immortal, never-ending, incorruptible.

Impermeable, *a.* Impervious, impenetrable, impassable.

Impersonate, *v. t.* 1. Personate, take *or* act the part of, act, enact, imitate, ape, mimic, mock, take off.

2. Incarnate, personify, embody, typify, invest with personality.

Impersonation, *n.* 1. Incarnation, personification, bodily manifestation, investment with personality.

2. Impersonating, personating, enacting, representation, imitation, mimicking.

Impertinence, *n.* 1. Irrelevance, irrelevancy; unfitness, impropriety.

2. Rudeness, intrusiveness, impudence, insolence, incivility, sauciness, forwardness, boldness, presumption, effrontery, pertness, assurance, face, front, brass, brazen face.

3. Impertinent action, piece of impertinence, piece of rudeness, etc.

Impertinent, *a.* 1. Irrelevant, inapposite, inapplicable, not to the point, not pertaining to the matter in hand, non-pertinent.

2. Intrusive, meddling, officious, insolent, rude, impudent, saucy, forward, pert, bold, malapert, unmannerly.

Imperturbability, *n.* Calmness, etc. See the adjective following.

Imperturbable, *a.* Calm, cool, composed, serene, unmoved, undisturbed, tranquil, unruffled, collected, placid, inexcitable, sedate, not to be disturbed.

Impervious, *a.* Impermeable, impenetrable, impassable.

Impetuosity, *n.* Vehemence, etc. See the adjective following.

Impetuous, *a.* Vehement, violent, furious, fierce, ardent, fiery, passionate, precipitate, hasty, hot, hot-headed, brash, over-zealous, headlong, break-neck.

Impetus, *n.* Momentum, force, propulsive force, energy.

Impiety, *n.* 1. Irreverence, ungodliness, irreligion, profanity.

2. Ungodliness, wickedness, unrighteousness, sin, sinfulness, iniquity, unholiness.

3. Act of impiety, sin, iniquity.

4. Unfilial character, lack of filial devotion.

Impinge, *v. i.* Strike, hit, fall against, strike against, dash against, clash upon, collide with; encroach, infringe.

Impious, *a.* Irreverent, ungodly, irreligious, blasphemous, wicked, sinful, unrighteous, unholy, iniquitous, profane.

Implacability, *n.* Vindictiveness, etc. See the adjective following.

Implacable, *a.* Vindictive, inexorable, unforgiving, unrelenting, relentless, rancorous, unappeasable, unpropitiating, merciless, pitiless, deadly.

Implant, *v. t.* 1. Ingraft, infix, set, put, place, insert, introduce.

2. Instil, infuse, inculcate.

Implement, *n.* Instrument, tool, utensil.

Implicate, *v. t.* 1. Infold, entangle.

2. Involve, entangle, make participator, bring into connection with.

3. Prove to be concerned *or* participant in, show to be privy to *or* an abettor of.

Implication, *n.* 1. Involution, involvement, entanglement.

2. Tacit inference, suggested meaning, connotation, intimation, hint, innuendo.

Implicit, *a.* 1. Implied, inferred, understood, tacit.

2. Unreserved, unhesitating, firm, unquestioning, undoubting, steadfast, unshaken.

Implicitly, *adv.* 1. Impliedly, virtually, tacitly, by inference, by implication.

2. Unreservedly, with unshaken confidence, without hesitation.

Implore, *v. t.* Entreat, supplicate, beseech, ask, crave, adjure, pray, pray to; solicit, beg, petition for.

Imply, *v. t.* Involve (*as a consequence*), include (*by implication*), import, signify, mean; connote, presuppose; insinuate.

Impolicy, *n.* Imprudence, indiscretion, folly, bad policy, ill-judgment, inexpediency.

Impolite, *a.* Uncivil, uncourteous, discourteous, ill-bred, unmannerly, disrespectful, ungentle, ungracious, unpolished, rude, ungentlemanly, rough, boorish, savage, bearish, unrefined.

Impolitic, *a.* Imprudent, injudicious, indiscreet, unwise, ill-advised, ill-judged, inexpedient.

Import, *v. t.* 1. Bring into (*a country from abroad*), introduce.

2. Imply, denote, purport, signify, betoken, mean.

3. Concern, be of importance to, be of consequence to, be of interest to.

——, *n.* 1. Signification, meaning, purport, matter, interpretation, sense, drift, gist, spirit, bearing, tenor, intention.

2. Importance, consequence, weight, moment, significance.

Importance, *n.* 1. Consequence, weight, weightiness, moment, momentousness, significance, import, concern.

2. Self-importance, consequence, pomposity.

IMPORTANT, *a.* 1. Weighty, momentous, grave, notable, considerable, ponderous, valuable, serious, material, significant, of importance, of moment, of great weight; urgent, importunate.

2. Influential, prominent, of influence, esteemed, substantial, of high standing *or* station.

3. Self-important, consequential, pompous.

Importation, *n.* 1. Importing.

2. Import, merchandise imported.

Importunate, *a.* Urgent, pertinacious, pressing, persistent, teasing, busy, earnestly solicitous; troublesome.

Importune, *v. t.* Press (*by entreaty*), urge (*by repeated requests*), beset, entreat, dun, ask urgently, ply, solicit earnestly.

Importunity, *n.* Entreaty, urgency, insistence, pressing solicitation, persistent entreaty.

Impose, *v. t.* 1. Put, lay, set, place.

2. Prescribe, enjoin, appoint, dictate, force, charge, tax, inflict, obtrude.

3. Palm, pass off.

Impose on. Deceive, cheat, chouse, trick, befool, hoax, dupe, delude, circumvent, victimize, play upon, put upon.

Imposing, *a.* Grand, stately, august, majestic, dignified, magnificent, grandiose, stately, lofty, exalted, impressive, noble, commanding.

Imposition, *n.* 1. Imposing, putting, placing, laying.

2. Constraint, oppression, burden, charge, injunction, levy, tax.

3. Deception, fraud, trickery, artifice, cheating. See IMPOSTURE.

Impossibility, *n.* See the adjective following.

Impossible, *a.* 1. Impracticable, unfeasible, unattainable, unachievable, out of the question, hopeless.

2. Inconceivable, unthinkable, that cannot be, incapable of occurring *or* of being so, absurd, self-contradictory.

Impost, *n.* Tax, duty, custom, excise, toll, tribute, rate.

Imposthume, *n.* Abscess, gathering, ulcer, fester, sore, pustule.

Impostor, *n.* Deceiver, pretender, cheat, rogue, humbug, trickster, tricker, knave, hypocrite, Pharisee, quack, charlatan, mountebank, double-dealer, counterfeiter.

Imposture, *n.* Cheat, trick, deception, imposition, hoax, fraud, delusion, artifice, ruse, dodge, wile, deceit, stratagem, chouse, crafty device.

Impotence, *n.* 1. Inability, disability, incapacity, incapability, incompetence, powerlessness, helplessness, inefficiency, inefficacy, weakness, feebleness, infirmity, frailty.

2. Lack of procreative power.

Impotent, *a.* 1. Powerless, unable, incapable, incompetent, disabled, incapacitated, weak, feeble, nerveless, infirm, frail, inefficient.

2. Unable to procreate, incapable of begetting offspring, barren, sterile.

Impound, *v. t.* 1. Put into a pound.

2. Confine, encage, imprison, shut up, coop up.

Impoverish, *v. t.* 1. Beggar, pauperize, ruin, make poor, bring to want, reduce to poverty, reduce to indigence.

2. Exhaust the fertility of, make sterile, render barren *or* unfertile, deplete, drain.

Impracticability, *n.* Impossibility, infeasibility, impracticableness.

Impracticable, *a.* 1. Impossible, unfeasible, not practicable.

2. Hard to deal with, hard to get along with, obstinate, recalcitrant, unmanageable, untractable, stubborn, thorny.

3. Impassable (*as a road*).

Imprecate, *v. t.* Invoke (*a curse* or *some evil*), call down; curse, maledict, execrate, anathematize.

Imprecation, *n.* Invocation (*of evil*); curse, malediction, execration, denunciation, anathema.

Imprecatory, *a.* Maledictory, execrating, cursing, conveying curses.

Impregnable, *a.* Unassailable, inexpugnable, not to be taken by assault, not to be stormed, secure from capture, tenable against all odds; invulnerable, invincible, unconquerable, immovable, not to be shaken, irrefragable.

Impregnate, *v. t.* 1. Fecundate, fructify; fertilize, make prolific, make pregnant, get with child, get with young, cause to conceive.

2. Imbue, infuse, saturate, fill, tincture, permeate, imbrue, pervade, soak, dye, tinge.

Impregnation, *n.* See the adjective preceding.

Impress, *v. t.* 1. Stamp, print, imprint, mark by pressure.

2. Affect, strike, move.

3. Inculcate, fix deeply.

4. Press, force into public service, levy, enlist, draft, requisition.

——, *n.* 1. Print, imprint, stamp, impression, mark, seal.

2. Device (*as upon a seal*), motto, cognizance, symbol, emblem; characteristic, mark of distinction.

Impressibility, *n.* 1. Susceptibility to impression.

2. Sensitiveness, sensibility, susceptibility.

Impressible, *a.* 1. Susceptible of impression, impressionable, capable of an imprint, that can be indented.

2. Sensitive, susceptible, easily affected, movable, tender, soft, plastic.

Impression, *n.* 1. Printing, imprinting, edition, stamping.

2. Mark, stamp, impress, brand.

3. Sensation, influence, effect.

4. Notion, opinion, idea, fancy, indistinct recollection.

Impressive, *a.* Affecting, touching, moving, effective, speaking, telling, splendid, emphatic, solemn, stirring, powerful, striking, overpowering.

Imprimis, *adv.* [L.] In the first place, first of all, first in order, first.

Imprint, *v. t.* 1. Print, stamp, mark by pressure.

2. Impress, inculcate, fix deeply.

Imprison, *v. t.* Incarcerate, immure, confine, jail, commit, shut up, put in duress *or* durance, place in confinement.

Imprisonment, *n.* Incarceration, confinement, commitment, restraint, constraint, duress, durance.

Improbability, *n.* Unlikelihood.

Improbable, *a.* Unlikely, not probable, unplausible.

Improbity, *n.* Dishonesty, unfairness, knavery, faithlessness, bad faith, fraud, fraudulence, want of probity, lack of integrity.

Impromptu, *a.* Extempore, unpremeditated, off-hand, improvised.

Improper, *a.* 1. Unsuitable, unsuited, unfit, unfitting, irregular, immodest, unapt, inapposite, inappropriate, unadapted, not proper.

2. Unseemly, unbecoming, indelicate, indecent, indecorous.

3. Inaccurate, incorrect, erroneous, wrong.

Impropriety, *n.* 1. Unsuitableness, unfitness, inappositeness, inappropriateness.

2. Unseemliness, indecorum, indecorousness.

3. Inaccuracy, incorrectness.

Improve, *v. t.* 1. Amend, mend, better, meliorate, ameliorate, make better, rectify, correct, edify.

2. Use, make use of, turn to account, avail one's self of.

3. Make a good use of, turn to good account, cultivate, raise the value of, employ advantageously, make productive.

——, *v. i.* 1. Mend, gain, become better, get better, get on, gain ground, pick up.

2. Make progress, take a step forward.

3. (*Com.*) Increase, rise, be enhanced.

Improvement, *n.* 1. Improving, amending, meliorating, melioration, ameliorating, amelioration, bettering.

2. Amendment, melioration, amelioration, betterment, progress, proficiency, advancement.

3. Good use, beneficial employment.

Improve on. Make better, make improvement in, bring nearer to perfection.

Improvidence, *n.* Thriftlessness, unthrift, unthriftiness, imprudence, want of forethought, carelessness of the future, neglect of preparation.

Improvident, *a.* Thriftless, unthrifty, imprudent, heedless, shiftless, prodigal, wasteful, without forecast, without foresight, careless of the future.

Improvisation, *n.* 1. Improvising, extemporizing.

2. Impromptu.

Improvise, *v. t. and v. i.* Improvisate, compose *or* poetize extempore; invent *or* provide offhand.

Imprudence, *n.* 1. Indiscretion, rashness, inconsiderateness, incaution, incautiousness, carelessness, heedlessness.

2. Improvidence (*which see*).

Imprudent, *a.* 1. Indiscreet, inconsiderate, incautious, injudicious, unadvised, ill-advised, ill-judged, rash, careless, heedless.

2. Improvident (*which see*).

Impudence, *n.* Insolence, assurance, presumption, forwardness, audacity, boldness, shamelessness, effrontery, rudeness, impertinence, sauciness, pertness, flippancy, brass, "cheek," "cheekiness," "nerve," "gall," "lip," "jaw," brashness, bumptiousness, front, face.

Impudent, *a.* Insolent, insulting, presumptuous, bold, shameless, impertinent, rude, saucy, pert, flippant, "cool," brazen, forward, bold-faced, brazen-faced.

Impugn, *v. t.* Attack (*by words* or *arguments*), assail, oppose, resist, contradict, gainsay, call in question.

IMPULSE, *n.* 1. Thrust, push, impetus, impelling force, momentum.

2. Passion, instinct, appetite, inclination, proclivity.

3. Incitement, instigation, influence, sudden feeling *or* motive.

Impulsive, *a.* 1. Impelling, moving, propulsive.

2. Passionate, rash, quick, hot, hasty, heedless, careless, mad-cap.

Impunity, *n.* 1. Exemption from punishment.

2. Exemption from injury, immunity.

Impure, *a.* 1. Foul, unclean, dirty, filthy, feculent, defiled, polluted.

2. Unchaste, unclean, lewd, loose, gross, licentious, immoral, coarse, indelicate, immodest, smutty, obscene, indecent, ribald, bawdy.

3. Mixed, adulterated, corrupt, dreggy, admixed with foreign matter *or* elements.

Impurity, *n.* 1. Foulness, uncleanness, feculence, defilement, pollution.

2. Unchastity, lewdness, looseness, grossness, coarseness, indelicacy, immodesty, impudicity, smuttiness, obscenity, "smut," indecency, ribaldry.

3. Admixture with foreign matter, adulterated condition.

Imputable, *a.* Attributable, referrible *or* referable, chargeable, traceable, owing, to be imputed, to be charged, to be attributed.

Imputation, *n.* 1. Imputing, attributing, charging.

2. Charge, accusation, censure, reproach, blame.

Impute, *v. t.* Ascribe (*especially to some evil cause*), attribute, refer, charge, consider as due, imply, insinuate.

IN, *prep.* Within.

Inability, *n.* 1. Want of ability (*to*), lack of power, being unable.

2. Incapacity, incapability, impotence, incompetence, incompetency, inefficiency, want of power, want of capacity.

3. Disability, disqualification.

In a box. In a perplexity, in a difficulty, in a dilemma, in an embarrassing position, in an awkward predicament, in a bad fix.

Inaccessible, *a.* 1. Unapproachable, not to be reached.

2. Unattainable.

Inaccuracy, *n.* 1. Incorrectness, impropriety, erroneousness, inexactness.

2. Mistake, error, blunder.

Inaccurate, *a.* Incorrect, inexact, erroneous, improper.

Inactive, *a.* 1. Inert, destitute of activity, without inherent energy.

2. Inert, inoperative, not in action, not in force, idle, quiet, quiescent, dormant, peaceful.

3. Inert, lazy, indolent, idle, slothful, supine, "do-nothing," torpid, sluggish, dronish, lumpish, passive, drowsy, sleepy, inanimate, lifeless, dull, stagnant, Fabian, dilatory.

Inactivity, *n.* Inaction, inertness, laziness, indolence, idleness, sloth, supineness, torpor, torpidity, sluggishness, dilatoriness, Fabian policy.

Inadequacy, *n.* 1. Insufficiency, inadequateness.

2. Incompleteness, defectiveness, imperfection.

Inadequate, *a.* 1. Insufficient, unequal, disproportionate.

2 Incomplete, defective, imperfect.

Inadmissible, *a.* Not to be admitted, not to be allowed.

Inadvertence, *n.* 1. Inattention, inconsiderateness, carelessness, thoughtlessness, heedlessness, negligence.

2. Oversight, slip, blunder, error from inattention.

Inadvertent, *a.* Inattentive, thoughtless, careless, heedless, inconsiderate, unobservant, negligent.

Inadvertently, *adv.* 1. Thoughtlessly, inconsiderately, carelessly, heedlessly, negligently, in an unguarded moment.

2. By inattention, without thinking, without intention, unintentionally, by accident, by a slip.

Inalienable, *a.* Not to be alienated, not transferable, indeprivable, untransferable, unforfeitable.

Inane, *a.* 1. Empty, void.

2. Vain, frivolous, trifling, puerile, worthless, foolish, senseless, silly, empty.

Inanimate, *a.* 1. Destitute of life, inorganic, mineral.

2. Deprived of life, dead, breathless, extinct.

3. Lifeless, dead, inert, soulless, spiritless, dull.

Inanition, *n.* 1. Emptiness, vacuity, inanity.

2. Exhaustion from hunger, innutrition.

Inanity, *n.* 1. Emptiness, vacuity, inanition, foolishness.

2. Vanity, frivolousness, puerility, folly, worthlessness.

Inapplicable, *a.* Unfit, unsuitable, irrelevant, inapt. See INAPPOSITE.

Inapposite, *a.* 1. Irrelevant, inapplicable, impertinent, non-pertinent, out of place, not to the purpose *or* point.

2. Unfit, unsuitable, inappropriate, out of keeping, out of place.

Inappreciable, *a.* Not appreciable, not to be appreciated, imperceptible, impalpable, trifling, very little, very small.

Inappropriate, *a.* Unfit, unsuited, unsuitable, unadapted, unbecoming, inapposite, out of character, out of keeping, out of place, in bad taste.

Inapt, *a.* 1. Unfit, unsuitable, unapt. See INAPPOSITE.

2. Unapt, dull, slow, stupid, stolid, clumsy, awkward, not ready.

Inaptitude, } *n.* Unfitness, unsuitableness,
Inaptness, } inappropriateness, inapplicability, awkwardness.

Inarticulate, *a.* 1. Indistinct, blurred,
thick.

2. Dumb, mute.

3. (*Zoöl.*) Inarticulated, not jointed.

Inartificial, *a.* 1. Natural, not made by
art.

2. Artless, ingenuous, guileless, sincere, simple, simple-minded, single-
minded, naïve, direct.

Inasmuch as. Since, seeing that, considering that.

Inattention, *n.* 1. Want of attention, wandering of attention, wandering of mind.

2. Inadvertence, heedlessness, thoughtlessness, inconsiderateness, carelessness,
neglect, unobservance, unmindfu'ness,
slip, inapplication, absent-mindedness,
disregard, remissness.

Inattentive, *a.* 1. Lacking in attention,
wandering, not attentive.

2. Unobservant, unobserving, unmindful, inadvertent, heedless, thoughtless,
regardless, careless, negligent, remiss,
unwatchful, inconsiderate, absent, absent-minded, caught napping.

Inaudible, *a.* 1. Not audible, not to be
heard, too low to be heard, faint, indistinct, muffled.

2. Still, silent, mute, noiseless.

Inaugurate, *v. t.* 1. Install, invest with an
office, introduce into an office, induct
into office.

2. Celebrate the institution of, introduce with fitting ceremonies.

3. Commence, begin, set in action, set
going, institute, initiate, originate.

Inauguration, *n.* 1. Investiture, installation, ceremony of induction *or* of consecration.

2. Ceremony of institution, ceremony
of initiation.

3. Commencement, beginning, institution, initiation, origination, formal opening.

Inauspicious, *a.* Unpropitious, unfavorable, unlucky, unfortunate, untoward,
unpromising, ill-starred, ominous, ill-
omened.

Inborn, *a.* Innate, inherent, inbred, natural, instinctive, congenital, ingrained, in
the grain, bred in the bone, implanted by
nature.

In brief. Concisely, briefly, in short, in a
few words.

Incage, *v. t.* [Written also *Encage*.] 1. Put
into a cage.

2. Confine, impound, imprison, shut
up, coop up.

Incalculable, *a.* Not to be calculated, not
to be reckoned, beyond calculation, enormous, inestimable, unknown, sumless,
untold, incalculable, countless, very
great, immense, innumerable, beyond
computation.

Incalescence, *n.* Calefaction, warmth, incipient heat.

Incandescence, *n.* White heat, glowing
whiteness.

Incandescent, *a.* White-hot, glowing white.

Incantation, *n.* Conjuration, sorcery,
charm, spell, enchantment, magic, necromancy, witchery, witchcraft.

Incapability, *n.* Incapacity, inability, disability, incompetence.

Incapable of. 1. Without capacity for, unable to, incompetent for, not capable of,
disqualified for.

2. Not susceptible of, not admitting of.

3. Not base enough for, too good *or*
great for, utterly above.

Incapacious, *a.* Narrow, scant, of small
capacity, not ample, not capacious; incapable, deficient.

Incapacitate, *v. t.* 1. Disable, make incapable.

2. Disqualify, unfit, make unfit.

Incapacity, *n.* 1. Inability, incapability,
disability, incompetency.

2. Disqualification, unfitness.

Incarcerate, *v. t.* Imprison, put in prison,
place in confinement, put in duress, place
in durance, immure, hem in, confine,
commit, send to jail.

Incarnate, *a.* Clothed with flesh, embodied
in flesh, personified.

——, *v. t.* Embody, clothe with flesh, give
concrete form to.

Incarnation, *n.* 1. Incarnating.

2. Hypostatic union.

3. Impersonation, personification, exemplification, bodily manifestation.

Incautious, *a.* 1. Unwary, indiscreet, uncircumspect, imprudent, impolitic.

2. Inconsiderate, thoughtless, careless,
heedless, negligent, neglectful, headlong,
reckless, rash.

Incendiary, *a.* Inflammatory, seditious,
factious, dissentious.

——, *n.* 1. Burner of buildings.

2. Firebrand, political agitator.

Incense, *v. t.* Enrage, exasperate, inflame,
enkindle, irritate, provoke, anger, chafe,
heat, excite, madden, make angry.

——, *n.* 1. Perfume (*exhaled by a burning
substance*), fragrance.

2. Admiration, applause, laudation,
adulation.

Incentive, *n.* Incitement, inducement,
stimulus, mainspring, instigation, provo-

cation, impulse, spur, provocative, goad, motive, cause, encouragement.

Inception, *n.* Beginning, commencement, initiation, inauguration.

Inceptive, *a.* Inchoative, that denotes a beginning.

Incertitude, *n.* Uncertainty, doubtfulness, doubt, indecision, ambiguity.

Incessant, *a.* Ceaseless, unceasing, uninterrupted, unremitting, continual, perpetual, constant, eternal (*colloq.*), everlasting (*colloq.*).

Inchoate, *a.* Beginning, commencing, incipient, initial.

Inchoative, *a.* Inceptive, that denotes a beginning.

Incident, *a.* 1. Happening, liable to happen.

2. Belonging, pertaining, appertaining, accessory, relating, natural, naturally liable to befall.

3. (*Optics.*) Falling, impinging.

——, *n.* Event, occurrence, circumstance.

Incidental, *a.* 1. Accidental, casual, fortuitous, subordinate, contingent.

2. Occasional, adventitious, extraneous, non-essential.

Incinerate, *v. t.* Burn to ashes, reduce to ashes, cremate.

Incipient, *a.* Beginning, commencing, inchoate.

Incised, *a.* 1. Cut, gashed.

2. Cut, carved, graved, engraved, graven.

Incision, *n.* Cut, gash; penetration.

Incisive, *a.* 1. Cutting.

2. Sharp, acute, sarcastic, satirical, severe, biting.

3. Sharp-cut, clear, distinct, trenchant, penetrating, acute, going straight to the heart of the matter.

Incisor, *n.* Cutting tooth.

Incite, *v. t.* Rouse (*to action*), arouse, animate, actuate, instigate, hound, drive, prod, push, "sick on," egg on, foment, provoke, stimulate, impel, prompt, urge, encourage, spur, goad, excite, set on, spur on, stir up, work up.

Incitement, *n.* Inducement, stimulus, impulse, spur, provocative, incentive, motive, encouragement, goad.

Incivility, *n.* Discourtesy, discourteousness, disrespect, impudence, rudeness, impoliteness, uncourteousness, uncourtliness, inurbanity, unmannerliness, disrespect, ill-breeding, ill manners; act of rudeness, discourtesy, piece of ill-breeding, slight.

Inclemency, *n.* 1. Severity, rigor, harshness, boisterousness, storminess, tempestuousness, roughness.

2. Want of clemency, harshness, unmercifulness, severity.

Inclement, *a.* 1. Severe, rigorous, harsh, boisterous, stormy, rough, not mild.

2. Unmerciful, harsh, severe, cruel, destitute of clemency.

Inclination, *n.* 1. Inclining, leaning, slope, slant.

2. Trending, verging, oblique direction.

3. Disposition, predilection, predisposition, mind set, twist, turn, bent, bias, proneness, proclivity, tendency, leaning, aptitude, propensity, *penchant*.

4. Desire, wish, partiality, fondness, liking, taste, predilection.

5. Obeisance, nod, bow.

Incline, *v. i.* 1. Lean, slope, slant.

2. Trend, verge, tend obliquely, nod, bend forward.

3. Be disposed, have a disposition, have a desire, feel a propensity.

4. Tend, go naturally, tend by nature, have a propensity, proclivity, leaning, bent, bias, *or* predisposition.

——, *v. t.* 1. Give a direction toward.

2. Dispose, predispose, turn, bias.

3. Bend, bow.

Inclose, *v. t.* [Written also *Enclose.*] Encircle, surround, encompass, imbosom, circumscribe, include, pen, coop, incase, corral, hedge, box, shut in, fence in, cover, envelop, wrap.

Include, *v. t.* 1. (*Rare.*) Hold, contain.

2. Comprise, comprehend, contain, embrace, involve, incorporate, cover, embody, take in.

Inclusive, *a.* 1. Inclosing, encircling.

2. Including both, both being included.

Inclusive of. Comprehending, embracing, taking in, including.

Incogitable, *a.* Unthinkable, unintelligible, inconceivable, incapable of being made coherent.

Incognito, *a. and adv.* [It.] Unknown (*in one's true character*), disguised, in disguise, in an assumed character.

——, *n.* 1. Disguised person, person under an assumed name.

2. Concealment, disguise, state of concealment.

Incognizable, *a.* Indistinguishable, unnoticeable, unobservable, incognoscible.

Incoherence, } *n.* 1. Looseness (*of parts*),
Incoherency, } want of cohesion.

2. Incongruity, inconsistency, inconsequence, want of connection, want of agreement.

Incoherent, *a.* 1. Loose, detached, nonadhesive, non-cohesive.

2. Incongruous, inconsistent, inconsequential, unco-ordinated, without connection, disconnected.

3. Unintelligible, irrational, illogical, confused, wild, rambling.

Incombustible, *a.* Not to be burned, that will not burn, indestructible by fire, fireproof.

Income, *n.* Revenue, profits, gains, return, receipts, perquisite, emolument.

Incommensurable, *a.* Without a common measure.

Incommensurate, *a.* 1. Disproportionate.
2. Inadequate, insufficient, unequal.

Incommode, *v. t.* Disturb, annoy, trouble, molest, disquiet, vex, discommode, inconvenience, put to inconvenience.

Incommodious, *a.* 1. Inconvenient, cumbersome, cumbrous, unhandy, awkward, unwieldy, unsuitable, not affording convenience, unmanageable.
2. Disadvantageous, troublesome, annoying, vexatious, harassing, irritating, provoking.

Incommunicable, *a.* Not to be communicated, that cannot be communicated *or* imparted.

Incommunicative, *a.* Reserved, unsociable, exclusive, unsocial.

Incomparable, *a.* Transcendent, peerless, matchless, unrivalled, unequalled, unparalleled, inimitable, surpassing.

Incompatibility, *n.* Inconsistency, incongruity, unsuitableness, want of agreement, want of adaptation, contrariety, contradictoriness, irreconcilable opposition.

Incompatible, *a.* Inconsistent, incongruous, inharmonious, unsuitable, unadapted, contradictory, irreconcilable, incapable of agreement *or* coexistence.

Incompetence, } *n.* 1. Incapacity, inability.
Incompetency, } ity.
2. Insufficiency, inadequacy.
3. Disqualification, unfitness.

Incompetent, *a.* 1. Unable, incapable, not competent.
2. Insufficient, inadequate.
3. Disqualified, incapacitated, unfit, unfitted.

Incomplete, *a.* 1. Defective, deficient, imperfect, partial, short of.
2. Unfinished, uncompleted, unaccomplished, inexhaustive, unexecuted, not completed, left undone.

Incomprehensibility, *n.* Inconceivableness, etc. See the adjective following.

Incomprehensible, *a.* 1. Inconceivable, unimaginable, not to be comprehended, past finding out, unfathomable, inexhaustible.

2. Inconceivable, unthinkable, incogitable, unintelligible, incapable of being made coherent.

Incompressible, *a.* Not to be compressed, not compressible.

Incomputable, *a.* Not to be computed, that cannot be computed, incalculable, past calculation, beyond estimate, enormous, immense, prodigious, innumerable.

Inconceivable, *a.* Unimaginable, unthinkable, incredible, unbelievable. See INCOMPREHENSIBLE.

Inconclusive, *a.* Unconvincing, indecisive, not conclusive.

Incongruity, *n.* Unsuitableness, inconsistency, unfitness, inappropriateness, discrepancy, incompatibility, incoherence, absurdity, contrariety, contradiction, contradictoriness.

Incongruous, *a.* Inconsistent, unfit, inappropriate, inharmonious, disagreeing, incompatible, incoherent, discrepant, absurd, unsuitable, contrary, contradictory; grotesque.

Inconsequent, *a.* Inconclusive, illogical, inconsistent, disconnected, loose, desultory, inconsecutive, fragmentary, irrelevant.

Inconsiderable, *a.* Unimportant, insignificant, small, slight, trivial, trifling, petty, immaterial, of no consequence, of no moment.

Inconsiderate, *a.* 1. Unthoughtful, uncharitable, intolerant, lacking in calmness and candor.
2. Thoughtless, careless, heedless, inattentive, indifferent, inadvertent, negligent, imprudent, indiscreet, rash, hasty, giddy, headlong, hare-brained, giddy-brained, light-headed.

Inconsistency, *n.* 1. Incongruity, incompatibility, unsuitableness, incoherence.
2. Contrariety, contradiction.
3. Unsteadiness, vacillation, changeableness, inconstancy, lack of steadfast and consistent character, lack of stability, instability.

Inconsistent, *a.* 1. Incongruous, incompatible, illogical, inconsonant, different, inconsequent, unsuitable, incoherent, irreconcilable, discrepant.
2. Contrary, contradictory.
3. Unstable, unsteady, changeable, variable, fickle, vacillating. See INCONSTANT.

Inconsolable, *a.* Disconsolate, woe-begone, comfortless, heart-broken, brokenhearted, forlorn, crushed, hopeless.

Inconstancy, *n.* Changeableness, etc. See the adjective following.

Inconstant, *a.* [*Said of persons.*] 1. Changeable, mutable, variable, varying, fluctuating, faithless, unsettled, fickle, capricious, vacillating, wavering, unsteady, volatile, mercurial, like a weathercock.

2. [*Said of things.*] Unstable, mutable, variable, unsettled, uncertain.

Incontestable, *a.* Indisputable, incontrovertible, unquestionable, undeniable, indubitable, irrefragable, certain, not to be disputed, beyond all question, beyond a doubt, past dispute.

Incontinence, *n.* 1. Non-retention, inability to retain.

2. Lewdness, lasciviousness, indulgence of lust.

Incontinent, *a.* Lewd, lustful, lascivious, unchaste, licentious, unrestrained, uncontrolled.

Incontrovertible, *a.* Indisputable, undeniable, unquestionable. See INCONTESTABLE.

Inconvenience, *n.* 1. Annoyance, vexation, molestation, disturbance, trouble, disadvantage.

2. Awkwardness, cumbersomeness, unwieldiness, incommodiousness.

3. Unfitness, unsuitableness, unseasonableness.

Inconvenient, *a.* Troublesome, annoying, vexatious, disadvantageous, uncomfortable; cumbersome, cumbrous, unwieldy, awkward, unmanageable, unhandy, disadvantageous, incommodious; unfit, unsuitable, unseasonable, inopportune, untimely.

Inconvertibility, *n.* Unchangeableness.

Inconvertible, *a.* Unchangeable, not transmutable, not convertible.

Incorporate, *v. t.* 1. Unite, combine, mix, blend, merge, consolidate, form into one body.

2. Form into a corporation, form into a body politic.

3. Incarnate, embody.

——, *a.* 1. Incorporeal, immaterial, supernatural, spiritual.

2. Non-corporate, not incorporated.

3. Intimately united, consolidated, blended, merged.

Incorporation, *n.* 1. Combination, union, blending, mixture, intimate union, consolidation.

2. Association (*as a body politic*).

Incorporeal, *a.* Immaterial, spiritual, bodiless, unsubstantial, impalpable, supernatural, incorporate.

Incorrect, *a.* 1. Inexact, inaccurate, erroneous, false, untrue, wrong.

2. Ungrammatical, faulty, unsound; improper, unbecoming.

Incorrectness, *n.* 1. Inaccuracy, inexactness, error, mistake.

2. (*Rhet.*) Barbarism, solecism, impropriety.

Incorrigible, *a.* 1. Irremediable, remediless, irreparable, irretrievable, irreversible, irremediable, irrecoverable, helpless, hopeless, incurable, past cure, past mending, beyond help.

2. Obdurate, hardened, lost, abandoned, shameless, graceless, recreant, irreclaimable, reprobate.

Incorruptibility, *n.* 1. Imperishableness, incorruptibleness, incorruption, indestructibility, immortality, deathlessness, perpetuity of being.

2. Superiority to corruption, unpurchasableness, inflexible honesty, incorruptible integrity.

Incorruptible, *a.* 1. Imperishable, incapable of decay, indestructible, immortal, undying, deathless, everlasting.

2. Of inflexible honesty, not to be bribed.

Increase, *v. i.* 1. Grow, augment, enlarge, wax, accrue, mount, intensify, extend, advance, greaten, be augmented, become greater *or* larger.

2. Multiply, be fruitful.

——, *v. t.* 1. Augment, enlarge, greaten, make greater, make larger.

2. Enhance, raise, advance, heighten, add to, reinforce.

3. Extend, prolong.

4. Aggravate, intensify.

INCREASE, *n.* 1. Augmentation, enlargement, extension, expansion, growth, addition, accession, development, multiplication, crescendo, swelling, accumulation, heightening, intensification, increment, accretion.

2. Product, produce, gain, profit.

3. Offspring, issue, progeny, descendants.

Incredible, *a.* Inadmissible, beyond belief, unbelievable; absurd, nonsensical.

Incredulity, *n.* Incredulousness, distrust, scepticism, unbelief, doubt, indisposition to believe.

Incredulous, *a.* Unbelieving, sceptical, disposed to doubt, indisposed to believe.

Increment, *n.* Augmentation, addition, increase, enlargement.

Incriminate, *v. t.* Accuse, impeach, charge, inculpate, blame, criminate, involve in guilt, make out guilty.

Incrust, *v. t.* Cover with a crust, coat over.

Incubate, *v. i.* Brood, develop, hatch, sit.

Incubus, *n.* 1. Demon of nightmare, nightmare-fiend.

2. Encumbrance, clog, impediment, oppression, load, burden, hindrance, drag weight, dead weight.

Inculcate, *v. t.* Impress, enforce, instil, infuse, teach, inspire, infix, ingraft, implant.

Inculpable, *a.* Unblamable, irreprehensible, irreprovable, irreproachable, blameless, faultless, sinless, innocent.

Inculpate, *v. t.* Accuse, charge, impeach, criminate, incriminate, blame, censure, impute guilt to, involve in guilt.

Inculpatory, *a.* Incriminating, criminatory, tending to criminate *or* inculpate, implicating, tending to establish guilt, involving in guilt.

Incumbent, *a.* 1. Obligatory, binding, devolving, devolved, laid.

2. Leaning, reclining, bearing down, pressing down, resting, weighing down, prone.

——, *n.* Holder, occupant (*of a benefice or office*).

Incumbrance, *n.* [Written also *Encumbrance.*] 1. Load, burden, clog, impediment, incubus, hindrance, dead weight, drag weight.

2. Debt, claim, liability.

Incur, *v. t.* 1. Contract, become liable to *or* for, become subject to.

2. Bring on, run, gain, acquire.

Incurable, *a.* 1. Immedicable, irremediable, cureless, remediless, hopeless, irrecoverable, past cure, beyond recovery, beyond medical skill.

2. Irremediable, irretrievable, remediless, irreparable, hopeless, helpless, past mending, not to be got rid of, incorrigible.

Incurious, *a.* Uninquisitive, inattentive, unobservant, careless, heedless, indifferent, uninterested, destitute of curiosity.

Incursion, *n.* Inroad, irruption, foray, raid, descent, partial invasion.

Incursive, *a.* Hostile, aggressive, raiding, invasive, predatory.

Incurvate, *v. t.* Bend, bow, crook, curve, make crooked.

——, *a.* (*Bot.*) Hooked, curved, bowed, crooked, aduncous, arcuate.

Indebted, *a.* 1. Owing, in debt.

2. Obliged, beholden, under obligation.

Indecency, *n.* 1. Indecorum, impropriety, unseemliness, offensiveness, outrageousness.

2. Indelicacy, coarseness, grossness, immodesty, impurity, obscenity, foulness, filthiness, vileness.

Indecent, *a.* 1. Indecorous, improper, unbecoming, unseemly, offensive, outrageous, bold.

2. Indelicate, coarse, gross, immodest, impure, obscene, filthy, nasty, dirty, shameless, "smutty," pornographic, salacious, unchaste, lewd.

Indecipherable, *a.* 1. Illegible, unreadable, undecipherable.

2. Impossible to make out, inexplicable, unintelligible, undiscoverable, hopelessly obscure, incapable of interpretation, undecipherable.

Indecision, *n.* Irresolution, vacillation, hesitation, unsteadiness, inconstancy, changeableness, fickleness.

Indecisive, *a.* 1. Inconclusive, not decisive.

2. Unsettled, wavering, vacillating, irresolute, hesitating, undecided, dubious.

Indeclinable, *a.* Undeclinable, uninflected, without declension, without case-endings.

Indecorous, *a.* Unbecoming, improper, unseemly, gross, rude, coarse, indecent, uncivil, impolite, violating good manners, ill-bred.

Indecorum, *n.* 1. Indecorousness, indecency, impropriety, grossness, rudeness, incivility, impoliteness, violation of propriety, ill-breeding, ill manners, want of decorum, impropriety of behavior.

2. Act of indecorum, breach of decorum, breach of propriety, violation of propriety, unseemly act, *faux pas.*

Indeed, *adv.* 1. Truly, really, veritably, verily, actually, positively, absolutely, certainly, in fact, in truth, in reality.

2. Strictly, strictly speaking, to tell the truth, in point of fact, in fact, in fine, as a matter of fact.

——, *interj.* Really, is it so, you don't say so, who'd have thought it, is it possible, Heaven save the mark.

Indefatigable, *a.* Unwearied, untiring, tireless, unflagging, persevering, persistent, sedulous, assiduous, unremitting, never-tiring.

Indefeasible, *a.* Irreversible, unalterable, inalienable, irrevocable, immutable, that cannot be defeated *or* thwarted, that cannot be abrogated, that cannot be made void.

Indefensible, *a.* 1. Untenable, defenseless.

2. Inexcusable, unjustifiable, unwarrantable, insupportable, censurable, unpardonable, faulty, wrong.

Indefinite, *a.* 1. Indeterminate, undefined, indefinable, indecisive, undetermined, indistinct, confused.

2. Vague, obscure, doubtful, uncertain, equivocal, unsettled, unfixed, loose, general, inexplicit, nondescript, inexact.

Indelible, *a.* Ineffaceable, ingrained, not to be blotted out, fixed, fast, permanent.

Indelicacy, *n.* 1. Want of delicacy, lack of refined feeling, rudeness, intrusiveness, want of regard for the delicacy of others.

2. Indecorum, unseemliness, impropriety, offensiveness, coarseness, grossness, vulgarity.

3. Immodesty, indecency, lewdness, unchastity (of expression), foulness, obscenity, coarseness, grossness, vulgarity.

Indelicate, a. 1. Wanting in delicacy, lacking in refined feeling, rude, intrusive, deficient in regard for the delicacy of others, deficient in proper reserve.

2. Indecorous, unbecoming, unseemly, coarse, broad, gross, rude.

3. Immodest, indecent, unchaste or lewd (in expression), coarse, gross, broad, vulgar, foul, obscene.

Indemnification, n. Indemnifying, etc. See the verb following.

Indemnify, v. t. 1. Secure (against loss, injury, or penalty), save harmless, guarantee.

2. Compensate (for loss or injury), remunerate, reimburse, requite, make good, make restitution to, pay.

Indent, v. t. 1. Notch, jag, make notches in, serrate, pink, scallop, bruise, make dents or bruises in.

2. Indenture, bind, bind by indenture.

3. (Printing.) Set in, begin farther in.

Indentation, n. Notch, jag, dent, bruise, depression.

Indenture, n. 1. Written contract, document, instrument, legal instrument.

2. Indented state, indentation.

——, v. t. Indent, bind by indenture.

Independence, n. 1. Freedom, liberty, self-direction, exemption from arbitrary control.

2. Non-dependence, distinctness, separation, unconditioned state.

3. Competence (of income), easy circumstances, ease.

Independent, a. 1. Free, self-directing, autonomous, uncoerced, unrestricted, unrestrained, absolute, voluntary, exempt from arbitrary control.

2. [Said of persons.] Unconstrained, unconventional, self-reliant.

Indescribable, a. Inexpressible, ineffable, nameless, unutterable, that cannot be described, that beggars description.

Indestructible, a. Imperishable, incorruptible, undecaying, abiding, enduring, fadeless, endless, everlasting.

Indeterminate, a. Indefinite, unfixed, undetermined, uncertain, not settled, not precise.

Index, n. [L. pl. Indices, Eng. pl. Indexes.]
1. Pointer, hand, director; forefinger.
2. Exponent.

India-rubber, n. Caoutchouc, gum-elastic, rubber.

Indicate, v. t. 1. Show, denote, betoken, mark, evince, tell, register, manifest, exhibit, designate, signify, point out, shadow forth, foreshadow, presage, prefigure, be the sign of.

2. Show, point out, designate, specify, particularize.

3. Suggest, imply, hint, intimate, sketch briefly.

Indication, n. 1. Indicating. See preceding verb.

2. Sign, mark, token, note, index, symptom, manifestation, hint, suggestion.

Indicative, a. 1. Significant, suggestive, symptomatic, to be taken as a sign.

2. (Gram.) Affirmative, declarative.

Indict, v. t. (Law.) Accuse (formally, by finding of grand jury), present, charge with offense.

Indictable, a. Liable to indictment, open to prosecution.

Indictment, n. 1. (Law.) Indicting, presentment.

2. Accusation, charge, arraignment, crimination, impeachment.

Indifference, n. 1. Neutrality, impartiality, disinterestedness, freedom from bias or prejudice.

2. Unconcernedness, unconcern, apathy, coolness, coldness, carelessness, negligence, heedlessness, inattention, want of interest.

3. Triviality, unimportance, insignificance.

Indifferent, a. 1. Neutral, impartial, disinterested, unbiassed.

2. Unconcerned, unmoved, apathetic, cool, frigid, lukewarm, nonchalant, insouciant, easy-going, stoical, listless, distant, incurious, perfunctory, dull, insensible, cold, inattentive, dead, heedless, regardless, unmindful, uninterested.

3. Equal, all one, just the same, all one, the same thing; passable, tolerable, middling, ordinary, medium, moderate, fair; so-so, mediocre, neither bad nor good, rather poor; unimportant, immaterial.

Indigence, n. Poverty, penury, destitution, want, need, necessity, privation, distress, pauper state, pauperism.

Indigenous, a. Native, aboriginal, inborn, inherent, home-grown, not exotic.

Indigent, a. Poor, destitute, needy, necessitous, pinched, reduced, penniless, moneyless, insolvent, distressed, short of money, out of money, out of cash, out of pocket, in need, in want.

Indigested, *a.* 1. Unconcocted, undigested, not digested.

2. Crude, ill-judged, ill-advised, ill-considered.

3. Disorderly, confused, ill-arranged, immethodical, unmethodized, in confusion, in disorder.

Indigestible, *a.* That cannot be digested, innutritious.

Indigestion, *n.* Dyspepsia, dyspepsy, difficulty of digestion, difficult digestion.

Indignant, *a.* Angry, incensed, provoked, irate, exasperated, wrathful, wroth, ireful, roused (*with the sense of wrong and injustice*).

Indignation, *n.* Anger, wrath, ire, resentment, displeasure, fury, rage, choler, exasperation (*at wrong and injustice*).

Indignity, *n.* Insult, affront, outrage, slight, disrespect, dishonor, contumely, obloquy, opprobrium, reproach, abuse.

Indirect, *a.* 1. Circuitous, tortuous, roundabout, devious, oblique, sidelong, circumlocutory, collateral, not directly to the point.

2. Unfair, dishonest, dishonorable, deceitful.

3. Mediate, secondary, subordinate, remote.

Indiscernible, *a.* Undiscernible, imperceptible, invisible, undiscoverable, indistinguishable, not to be discerned.

Indiscipline, *n.* Lack of discipline, lax discipline, laxity, insubordination.

Indiscreet, *a.* Imprudent, injudicious, unwise, inconsiderate, foolish, rash, incautious, reckless, hasty, heedless, headlong.

Indiscretion, *n.* 1. Imprudence, inconsiderateness, rashness, folly.

2. Mistake, misstep, blunder, indiscreet act, act of indiscretion, *faux pas,* lapse.

3. Slip from virtue, false step, decline from chastity, imprudence, act of folly, misstep, *faux pas.*

Indiscriminate, *a.* 1. Undiscriminating, indiscriminative, undistinguishing.

2. Confused, mixed, mingled, undistinguishable, promiscuous, heterogeneous, miscellaneous.

Indispensable, *a.* Necessary, essential, requisite, needful, needed, not to be dispensed with.

Indispose, *v. t.* Disincline, render averse, make unfit, make unfavorable, render reluctant.

Indisposed, *a.* 1. Disinclined, unwilling, unfriendly, reluctant, averse, loath, backward, not disposed.

2. Ill, unwell, ailing, sick, out of health, out of sorts.

Indisposition, *n.* 1. Disinclination, unwillingness, reluctance, dislike, aversion, backwardness.

2. Illness, sickness, ailment, poor health.

Indisputable, *a.* Incontestable, incontrovertible, unquestionable, undeniable, indubitable, irrefragable, evident, obvious, certain, beyond all question, beyond a doubt, past dispute.

Indissoluble, *a.* 1. Inseparable, never to be sundered, impossible to be sundered *or* broken.

2. Indissolvable, that cannot be dissolved, that cannot be liquefied.

3. Indestructible, incorruptible, indiscerptible, imperishable, lasting, abiding, stable, firm, enduring, not to be broken.

Indistinct, *a.* 1. Undefined, ill-defined, inarticulate, indefinite, undistinguishable, confused, imperfectly distinguished.

2. Obscure, dim, vague, faint, nebulous, misty, shadowy, hazy, dull, blurred.

3. Ambiguous, uncertain, doubtful.

Indistinguishable, *a.* 1. Undistinguishable, that cannot be distinguished *or* discriminated.

2. Imperceptible, unobservable, unnoticeable, not to be made out, indiscernible.

3. Confused, indistinct, chaotic, vague, obscure, dim.

Indite, *v. t.* Compose, write, pen.

Individual, *a.* 1. Particular, special, separate, marked, single, one, unique.

2. Peculiar to one alone, one's own, peculiar, singular, proper, personal.

3. Full of character, positive, decided, definite, self-guided, unconventional, independent, unique, *sui generis.*

——, *n.* 1. Person, personage, character, being, somebody, some one.

2. Unit, single instance, particular one *or* object.

3. Person (*in the high* or *emphatic sense*),[1] person full of character, self-directed being, self-determined being.

Individuality, *n.* 1. Personality, definiteness, identity, distinct existence.

2. Decision of character, self-direction, originality, unique quality, self-engendered character, singularity, self-determination.

Individualize, *v. t.* 1. Particularize, singularize, consider individually, specify, name with precision.

2. Make individual, invest with fulness of character, render unique *or* original, render self-directing *or* self-determined, individuate.

Indivisible, *a.* 1. Inseparable, that cannot be divided *or* separated into parts.

2. Inseparable, indissoluble, unpartible, that cannot be sundered, not to be broken *or* dissolved.

3. (*Math.*) Incommensurable, destitute of common divisor *or* measure.

Indocile, *a.* Unteachable, intractable, stubborn, inapt, perverse, unruly, headstrong, refractory, obstinate, dogged, mulish, unmanageable, ungovernable, cantankerous, contumacious, froward.

Indocility, *n.* Unteachableness, etc. See INDOCILE, preceding.

Indoctrinate, *v. t.* Teach, instruct, initiate, imbue, give instruction to, ground, ground in doctrine *or* in the doctrines of.

Indoctrination, *n.* Instruction, initiation, grounding, telling people what to think.

Indolence, *n.* Laziness, slothfulness, sloth, inertness, idleness, sluggishness.

Indolent, *a.* 1. Lazy, slothful, inert, sluggish, otiose, easy, easy-going, inactive, listless, supine, lumpish, habitually idle.

2. Slowly operative, slow, sluggish, inactive, inert, acting slowly.

Indomitable, *a.* Unyielding, unconquerable, invincible, not to be subdued.

Indorse, *v. t.* [Written also *Endorse.*] 1. Superscribe, write on the back of, countersign.

2. Sanction, support, approve, confirm, ratify, visé, vouch for.

Indubitable, *a.* Unquestionable, indisputable, incontestable, undeniable, incontrovertible, evident, irrefragable, sure, certain, beyond all question, beyond a doubt, past dispute.

Induce, *v. t.* 1. Influence, impel, move, prompt, draw, bring, drive, entice, allure, actuate, instigate, persuade, urge, incite, spur, act upon, set on, weigh with, prevail on, prevail upon.

2. Cause, produce, lead, occasion, motivate, effect, bring on.

Inducement, *n.* 1. Inducing. See the verb.

2. Motive, reason, cause, consideration, incitement, incentive, stimulus, spur, influence, impulse.

Induct, *v. t.* Introduce (*into office*), install, initiate, inaugurate.

Induction, *n.* 1. Introduction (*into office*), installation, inauguration, institution.

2. Conclusion (*from many facts*), inference, generalization, tentative inference, inductive method, Baconian method.

3. (*Phys.*) Influence of proximity.

Indue, *v. t.* Supply, invest, clothe, endue, assume, endow.

Indulge, *v. t.* 1. Gratify, satisfy, license, yield to, give free scope to, give a loose rein to, give way to, give one's self up to.

2. Humor excessively *or* to excess, yield to the wishes of, pamper, humor, favor, coddle, cosset, pet, spoil, allow to follow one's appetites *or* caprices.

3. Allow, permit, suffer, harbor, foster, cherish.

——, *v. i.* Indulge one's self, revel, wallow.

Indulgence, *n.* 1. Gratification, humoring, pampering, etc.

2. Favor, liberality, lenity, lenience, kindness, tenderness.

3. (*Theol.*) Remission, absolution (*from canonical penance*).

Indulgent, *a.* Lenient, mild, clement, tolerant, gentle, favoring, humoring, easy, pampering, forbearing, kind, tender, not severe.

Indurate, *v. t.* 1. Harden, render hard, strengthen, inure, make hard.

2. Make obdurate, make unfeeling, sear.

Induration, *n.* 1. Hardening.

2. Obduracy, hardness of heart.

Industrious, *a.* 1. Diligent, assiduous, laborious, operose, sedulous, notable, hard-working, diligently employed, busily engaged, up and stirring, busy as a bee, brisk as a bee.

2. Busy, brisk, persistent, persevering, sedulous.

INDUSTRY, *n.* 1. Assiduity, assiduousness, activity, diligence, habitual devotion to labor, application.

2. Persistence, perseverance, sedulousness, assiduity, busy vigor.

3. Labor, toil, effort; labors, efforts, endeavors, results.

4. Industrial art, form of productive effort.

Inebriate, *v. t.* Intoxicate, make drunk, stupefy with drink.

Inebriety, *n.* Drunkenness, inebriation, intoxication.

Ineffable, *a.* Unspeakable, unutterable, inexpressible, indescribable, that cannot be spoken, beyond expression.

Ineffaceable, *a.* Indelible, ingrained, indestructible, inexpungeable, inerasable.

In effect. In fact, in truth, really, in reality.

Ineffectual, *a.* 1. Inefficacious, ineffective, unavailing, inadequate, useless, abortive, bootless, to no purpose, without effect, vain, fruitless, futile.

2. Powerless, weak, impotent, feeble, inefficient.

Inefficacy, *n.* Ineffectualness, inefficiency.

Inefficient, *a.* Ineffective, lacking in efficiency, ineffectual, inefficacious, incapable, weak, feeble.

Inelastic, *a.* Flabby, flaccid, inductile, inflexible, irresilient.

Inelegant, *a.* 1. Ungraceful, graceless, awkward, ungainly, uncouth, homely, clumsy, rude, coarse, without taste.

2. Unpolished, uncourtly, unrefined, ungraceful, rough, homespun, uncouth, ungainly, awkward.

3. Plain, homely, awkward-looking.

4. Stiff, constrained, harsh, crude, bald, cramped, abrupt.

Ineligible, *a.* 1. Not eligible, unqualified, disqualified (*for office*).

2. Inexpedient, unadvisable, objectionable, undesirable.

Inept, *a.* 1. Improper, unfit, unsuitable, inappropriate, inapposite, unapt, awkward.

2. Useless, worthless, void, null.

3. Foolish, silly, nonsensical, senseless, stupid, pointless.

Ineptitude, *n.* 1. Unfitness, unsuitableness, inaptitude, inappropriateness, impropriety, inappositeness.

2. Uselessness, worthlessness, emptiness, nullity.

3. Folly, foolishness, nonsense, silliness, senselessness, stupidity, pointlessness.

Inequality, *n.* 1. Disparity, difference, diversity; unevenness, imparity, irregularity, roughness.

2. Unfairness, injustice, inequitable character, disproportion.

3. Inadequacy, insufficiency, incompetency.

Inequitable, *a.* Unjust, unfair, destitute of equity.

Inert, *a.* 1. Inactive, lifeless, passive, motionless, quiescent, comatose, dead.

2. Dull, indolent, torpid, sluggish, slothful, lethargic, apathetic, phlegmatic, lazy, idle, supine, lumpish, dronish.

Inertia, *n.* 1. Passivity, passiveness, inertness, lack of activity.

2. Inertness, sluggishness, indisposition to move, lethargy, apathy.

3. (*Phys.*) *Vis inertiæ,* tendency to continuance (*whether of rest or of motion*), resistance to change.

Inestimable, *a.* Invaluable, priceless, incalculable, that cannot be estimated, above all price, precious, extremely valuable.

Inevitable, *a.* Unavoidable, necessary, not to be escaped, that must be suffered.

Inexact, *a.* Incorrect, inaccurate, without precision; loose, crude, careless.

Inexcusable, *a.* Unpardonable, indefensible, unjustifiable, irremissible, incapable of excuse, unallowable.

Inexhaustible, *a.* 1. Exhaustless, unfailing, boundless, unlimited, that cannot be exhausted.

2. Indefatigable.

Inexorable, *a.* 1. Unrelenting, relentless, implacable, pitiless, merciless, unmerciful, uncompassionate, hard, cruel.

2. Unyielding, inflexible (*to supplication*), unbending, immovable (*by prayers*), firm, steadfast, sternly just, severe.

Inexpedient, *a.* Unadvisable, disadvantageous, unwise, unprofitable, injudicious, imprudent, indiscreet, ill-judged, impolitic, inopportune.

Inexperience, *n.* Rawness, greenness, ignorance, want of experience.

Inexperienced, *a.* Unpractised, untrained, untried, unacquainted, uninitiated, unschooled, raw, callow, young, unversed, unconversant; undisciplined, unskilled, green, strange, without experience.

Inexpert, *a.* Unskilful, unskilled, awkward, clumsy, unhandy, inapt, bungling, maladroit, without dexterity.

Inexpiable, *a.* 1. Unpardonable, irremissible, unatonable, not to be atoned for, that admits of no satisfaction.

2. Implacable, unappeasable, inexorable, not to be appeased, irreconcilable.

Inexplicable, *a.* Unaccountable, unintelligible, incomprehensible, inscrutable, mysterious, strange, enigmatical, not to be explained.

Inexpressible, *a.* 1. Unutterable, unspeakable, indescribable, ineffable.

2. Surpassing, boundless, infinite.

Inexpressive, *a.* Unexpressive, characterless, blank, dull.

Inexpugnable, *a.* 1. Impregnable, unassailable, not to be taken by assault, not to be stormed, secure from capture, tenable against all odds.

2. Unconquerable, invincible, not to be subdued.

3. Incontrovertible, irrefragable, impregnable, unassailable, unanswerable.

Inextinguishable, *a.* Unquenchable, that cannot be extinguished.

In extremis. [L.] In one's last moments, at the point of death, in the very act of death, moribund.

Inextricable, *a.* Intricate, perplexed, entangled, unsolvable, that cannnot be disentangled, not to be unravelled.

In fact. 1. Really, truly, in truth, in reality, indeed.

2. As a matter of fact. in point of fact, indeed, to tell the truth.

3. Actually, as a mere fact, *de facto.*

Infallibility, *n.* 1. Infallibleness, exemption from liability to err, incapability of error, absolute perfection of judgment.

2. Certainty.

Infallible, *a.* 1. Unerring, not liable to err, perfect in judgment, incapable of error.

2. Certain, sure, unfailing, not liable to fail, oracular, indubitable.

Infamous, *a.* Disreputable, of ill repute, ill spoken of; disgraceful, dishonorable, shameful, shameless, odious, detestable, scandalous, outrageous, ignominious, base, vile, nefarious, villainous, discreditable, abominable, heinous, atrocious, wicked, dark, damnable.

Infamy, *n.* 1. Dishonor, disgrace, discredit, disrepute, shame, ignominy, obloquy, opprobrium, odium, scandal, abasement.

2. Disgracefulness, dishonorableness, shamefulness, odiousness, detestableness, scandalousness, wickedness, atrocity, villainy.

Infancy, *n.* 1. Babyhood, first part of life, early childhood.

2. Beginning, commencement, first age, early period of existence.

3. (*Law.*) Minority, nonage, pupilage, childhood.

Infant, *n.* 1. Babe, baby, nursling, papoose, suckling, chit, brat, bantling, little child, little one, bairn, "tot."

2. (*Law.*) Minor.

Infanticide, *n.* Child-murder.

Infantile, } *a.* 1. Childish, young, tender,
Infantine, } newborn.

2. Childish, babyish, weak.

3. Childlike, babylike.

Infantry, *n.* Foot-soldiers, foot, rifles.

Infatuate, *v. t.* 1. Befool, besot, stultify, delude, make foolish, deprive of reason, deprive of sound judgment *or* commonsense.

2. Prepossess extravagantly, carry beside one's self, absorb in an uncontrollable passion, captivate.

Infatuation, *n.* Folly, foolishness, stupefaction, besottedness, arrant folly, passionate absorption, senseless prepossession.

Infeasible, *a.* Impracticable, unfeasible, that cannot be accomplished, not to be done.

Infect, *v. t.* 1. Taint with disease, affect with contagious matter.

2. Pollute, contaminate, vitiate, poison, defile, corrupt.

Infection, *n.* 1. Contagion.

2. Contamination, taint, bane, pest, poison, pollution, vitiation, defilement, corruption, affection.

3. (*Med.*) Contagium, virus.

Infectious, *a.* 1. Contagious, pestilential, pestiferous, catching, communicable.

2. Contaminating, corrupting, vitiating, poisoning, defiling, polluting, demoralizing.

3. Sympathetic, "catching."

Infecund, *a.* Unfruitful, infertile, unproductive, unprolific, sterile, barren.

Infecundity, *n.* Unfruitfulness.

Infelicitous, *a.* 1. Unhappy, wretched, miserable, unfortunate, calamitous.

2. Unfavorable, unpropitious, inauspicious.

3. Inappropriate, unhappy, ill-chosen, unfitting, in bad taste, not well expressed.

Infelicity, *n.* Unhappiness. See the adjective.

Infer, *v. t.* Deduce, conclude, collect, gather, draw, derive, reason, glean, guess, presume, consider probable.

Inference, *n.* 1. Conclusion, deduction, implication, consequence, corollary.

2. Process of reasoning, process of inference, guess, conclusion, presumption.

3. Generalization, induction, illation.

Inferior, *a.* 1. Lower, nether.

2. Subordinate, secondary, junior, minor.

3. Poor, indifferent, bad, mean, base, paltry, shabby, humble, deficient, imperfect, second-rate, mediocre.

4. Poorer, less good, less valuable, of lower quality *or* grade.

Inferiority, *n.* 1. Lower state *or* condition.

2. Subordination, juniority, subjection.

3. Mediocrity, poor quality.

4. Deficiency, imperfection, shortcoming, inadequacy, lower quality, lower worth.

Infernal, *a.* 1. Hellish, Tartarean, Stygian, underworld, of hell.

2. Diabolical, devilish, demoniacal, fiendish, fiendlike, satanic, atrocious, nefarious, dark, damnable, accursed, abominable; malicious.

Inferrible, *a.* [Written also *Inferable.*] Deducible, to be inferred *or* concluded.

Infertility, *n.* Unfruitfulness, unproductiveness, barrenness, sterility, infecundity.

Infest, *v. t.* 1. Throng, overrun, beset, take complete possession of, swarm in.

2. Disturb, annoy, vex, tease, harass, plague, torment, trouble, molest, worry.

Infidel, *n.* 1. Unbeliever, atheist, heretic, heathen, sceptic, agnostic, disbeliever in God, denier of religious obligation.

2. (*Historical sense.*) Mahometan, Turk, defiler of the Holy Sepulchre.

3. (*Historical sense.*) Freethinker, denier of miracles and miraculous revelation, denier of revealed religion, deist.

Infidelity, *n.* 1. Unbelief, disbelief, scepticism.

2. Faithlessness (*in the marriage relation*), adultery, unfaithfulness.

3. Faithlessness (*generally*), bad faith, treachery, disloyalty.

Infiltrate, *v. i.* Soak (*into a porous substance*), pervade, be absorbed, pass by filtration.

Infinite, *a.* 1. Unbounded, boundless, endless, measureless, perfect, unlimited, illimitable, limitless, immeasurable, inexhaustible, interminable.

2. Immense, enormous, vast, stupendous, very great, very large.

3. Unconditioned, absolute, self-determined, self-existent, eternal.

Infinitesimal, *a.* Infinitely small.

——, *n.* Infinitely small quantity, quantity converging to zero, infinitely diminishing quantity, quantity whose limit is zero, vanishing fluxion.

Infinitude, *n.* 1. Boundlessness, infinity, endlessness, interminateness, immensity, vastness.

2. Innumerable quantity.

3. Infinite number, boundless multitude.

Infinity, *n.* 1. See INFINITUDE.

2. Unlimited degree, infiniteness.

3. Absoluteness, self-determination, self-existence, eternity.

Infirm, *a.* 1. Weak, feeble, enfeebled, frail, ailing, weakened, debilitated.

2. Irresolute, vacillating, wavering, faltering.

3. Insecure, unstable, unsound, precarious.

Infirmity, *n.* 1. Weakness, feebleness, debility, ailment, frailness, frailty.

2. Foible, fault, failing, defect, weakness.

Infix, *v. t.* 1. Fasten, plant, set, fix.

2. Implant, ingraft, instil, inculcate, infuse.

Inflame, *v. t.* 1. Excite, stimulate, enkindle, heat, intensify, incite, fire, rouse, arouse, animate, inspirit, set on, work up, stir up.

2. Exasperate, irritate, nettle, provoke, anger, enrage, incense, madden, infuriate.

Inflammability, *n.* Inflammableness, combustibility, combustibleness.

Inflammable, *a.* 1. Combustible, ignitible.

2. Excitable.

Inflammation, *n.* 1. Burning, conflagration, setting on fire.

2. Excitement, anger, animosity, turbulence, heat, violence, rage.

Inflammatory, *a.* 1. Inflaming, fiery.

2. Incendiary, seditious, dissentious.

Inflate, *v. t.* 1. Swell (*by blowing*), distend, sufflate, expand, bloat, blow up.

2. Puff up, make conceited, elate.

3. Enlarge, increase.

Inflated, *a.* 1. Distended (*with air*), swollen, bloated, puffed up.

2. Tumid, turgid, bombastic, grandiloquent, overblown, pompous, altiloquent, magniloquent, stilted, declamatory, rhetorical, high-flown.

Inflation, *n.* 1. Swelling (*by air*), distension, sufflation, bloatedness, expansion, blowing up.

2. Conceit, conceitedness, self-conceit, self-sufficiency, self-complacency, self-importance, bombast, vain-gloriousness, vain-glory.

3. Increase, enlargement.

4. (*Com.*) Over-enlargement (*of currency*), over-issue.

Inflect, *v. t.* 1. Bend, bow, curve, turn from a direct line.

2. (*Gram.*) Decline (*a noun or an adjective*), conjugate (*a verb*), vary the terminations of.

Inflection, *n.* 1. Bending, curvature, bend, curvity, flexure, crook.

2. (*Gram.*) Variation (*in declension or in conjugation*), accidence; declension, conjugation, and comparison.

3. (*Music and Speech.*) Modulation (*of the voice*).

Inflexibility, *n.* 1. Stiffness, inflexibleness, rigidity.

2. Pertinacity, doggedness, stubbornness, obstinacy.

3. Firmness, resolution, perseverance, tenacity of purpose.

Inflexible, *a.* 1. Stiff, rigid, rigorous, unbending.

2. Pertinacious, dogged, stubborn, obstinate, unyielding, refractory, headstrong, wilful, cantankerous, intractable, heady, obdurate, cross-grained.

3. Firm, resolute, steadfast, immovable, unbending, persevering.

4. Inexorable, unyielding, immovable by entreaties.

Inflict, *v. t.* Impose, lay on, bring.

Infliction, *n.* 1. Inflicting, imposition.

2. Punishment, judgment.

Inflorescence, *n.* 1. Flowering, blossoming, blooming.

2. Mode of flowering.

Influence, *n.* 1. Authority, sway, control, mastery, rule, ascendancy, potency, predominance, ascendency, power of impelling *or* directing controlling power, directing agency, "pull," impulse.

2. Reputation, credit, weight of character.

3. Influx, inflow, inflowing.

4. Mystic power, unseen *or* mysterious agency, magnetism, spell.

——, *v. t.* 1. Control, sway, bias, lead, direct, modify, affect.

2. Move, induce, impel, instigate, persuade, actuate, incite, rouse, arouse, work upon, prevail upon.

Influential, *a.* 1. Potent, powerful, controlling, strong, effective, effectual.

2. Of influence, of authority, substantial, weighty, momentous.

Influx, *n.* Introduction, flowing in.

Infold, *v. t.* [Sometimes written *Enfold*.] 1. Inwrap, enclose, wrap, fold, envelop.

2. Clasp, embrace.

Inform, *v. t.* 1. Animate, inspire, quicken, give form to.

2. Acquaint, apprise, advise, tell, notify, teach, enlighten, instruct, "flag," warn, "tip," make known to, mention to, give notice to, signify to, send word to, write word to.

Informal, *a.* 1. Irregular, out of the usual course, not according to the prescribed form.

2. Unconventional, unceremonious, unofficial.

3. Simple, natural, familiar, easy.

Informality, *n.* 1. Irregularity, want of conformity to (the) prescribed rule.

2. Absence of ceremony, unconventionality, unceremoniousness.

3. Simplicity, naturalness, ease, familiarity.

Informant, *n.* 1. Informer, notifier, adviser, relator, intelligencer, newsmonger, advertiser.

2. Accuser, complainant, informer.

Information, *n.* 1. Intelligence, notice, advice; enlightenment, instruction, "tip," advertisement, advice, word, message, warning.

2. Knowledge, knowledge of facts.

3. (*Law.*) Accusation, complaint, denunciation.

Informer, *n.* 1. Informant.

2. Accuser, complainant, informant.

Infraction, *n.* Breaking, breach, infringement, encroachment, violation, transgression, disobedience, non-observance.

Infrangible, *a.* That cannot be broken, unbreakable, inseparable; not to be violated, that may not be infringed.

Infrequency, *n.* Uncommonness, rarity, rareness.

Infrequent, *a.* Uncommon, rare, unfrequent, unusual, seldom occurring; sparse, scarce, rare, scant, occasional, sporadic.

Infringe, *v. t.* Break, violate, transgress, disobey, break through, trench upon, set at nought, encroach upon, trespass, intrude.

Infringement, *n.* Breaking, breach, infraction, violation, transgression, disobedience, non-observance.

Infringe upon. Invade, trespass upon, encroach upon, intrude upon.

Infundibular, *a.* Funnel-shaped, infundibuliform.

Infuriated, *a.* Enraged, raging, incensed, angry, maddened, furious, wild with anger.

Infuse, *v. i.* 1. Instil, ingraft, implant, inspire, breathe into, introduce, inculcate, insinuate.

2. Introduce, diffuse, shed.

3. Steep (*in liquor*), macerate.

Infusion, *n.* 1. Introduction, inculcation, instillation.

2. Infusing, steeping, macerating.

3. Steeped liquor.

Infusoria, *n. pl.* Animalcules, animalcula.

Ingathering, *n.* Harvest.

In general. 1. Generally, in the main, for the most part, in most cases, with few exceptions.

2. Generally, upon the whole, speaking generally, to sum up, in a general way, to speak summarily.

Ingenious, *a.* 1. Inventive, gifted, able, sagacious, clever, bright, ready.

2. That shows invention, exhibiting ingenuity, artful, clever, fertile, adroit, shrewd, witty.

Ingenuity, *n.* Inventiveness, ingeniousness, acuteness, skill, readiness, ability, capableness, capacity, faculty, aptitude, aptness, cleverness, knack, turn, gift, genius.

Ingenuous, *a.* Artless, frank, open, candid, generous, plain, sincere, guileless, honest, downright, unreserved, straightforward, truthful, simple-minded, single-minded, open-hearted, transparent, childlike, naïve.

Ingenuousness, *n.* Artlessness, frankness, candor, sincerity, honesty, truthfulness, openness, guilelessness, single-mindedness, open-heartedness, childlikeness, naïveté.

Inglorious, *a.* 1. Obscure, mean, lowly, humble, unknown, undistinguished, nameless, unmarked, unnoted, unhonored.

2. Shameful, disgraceful, humiliating, discreditable, scandalous, ignominious.

Ingloriousness, *n.* 1. Obscurity, meanness, humbleness, lowliness, namelessness, want of fame, lack of distinction.

2. Abasement, discredit, disrepute, dishonor, disgrace, ignominy, ignominiousness, obloquy, shame, infamy, opprobrium, odium, humiliation.

Ingraft, *v. t.* 1. Graft.

2. Infix, implant, instil, infuse, inculcate.

Ingrain, *v. t.* Dye in the grain; imbue, impregnate.

Ingratiate, *v. t.* Insinuate.

Ingratitude, *n.* Unthankfulness, thanklessness, ungratefulness.

Ingredient, *n.* Element, constituent, component, component part.

Ingress, *n.* Entrance, entry, introgression; power of entrance, entrée.

Ingulf, *v. t.* [Written also *Engulf.*] Absorb, plunge, swallow up, overwhelm, whelm.

Inhabit, *v. t.* Occupy, people, dwell in, live in, reside in.

——, *v. i.* Dwell, reside, sojourn, live, abide.

Inhabitable, *a.* Habitable, livable.

Inhabitant, *n.* Dweller, inhabiter, resident, denizen, citizen.

Inhalation, *n.* Inspiration, inhaling, breath; sniff, snuff; something inhaled.

Inhale, *v. t.* Inspire, inbreathe, breathe in, draw into the lungs.

Inharmonious, *a.* Discordant, unmusical, inharmonic, unharmonious, out of tune.

Inhere, *v. i.* 1. Stick, stick fast, be fixed, cleave (to).

2. Exist (*as a part*), be fixed (*as a quality*), abide, lie, reside, belong, pertain, be immanent.

Inherent, *a.* 1. Sticking fast, adhering.

2. Innate, native, natural, inborn, inbred, proper, indwelling, intrinsic, immanent, ingrained, essential, inseparable.

Inherit, *v. t.* Get from ancestors, receive by inheritance, come into possession of as an heir.

Inheritance, *n.* 1. Inheriting.

2. Heritage, patrimony, legacy.

Inheritor, *n.* Heir, parcener (*Law*).

Inhibit, *v. t.* 1. Restrain, hinder, check, repress, obstruct, bar, debar, prevent, stop.

2. Prohibit, forbid, interdict.

Inhibition, *n.* 1. Restraint, hindrance, impediment, obstacle, obstruction, check.

2. Prohibition, interdiction, interdict, prevention, disallowance, embargo.

Inhospitable, *a.* 1. Unfriendly (*to strangers*), cool, forbidding, unkind, not hospitable; barren, wild.

2. Ungenerous, narrow, illiberal, unreceptive, intolerant, bigoted, prejudiced.

Inhospitality, *n.* Want of hospitality (which see).

Inhuman, *a.* Barbarous, brutal, savage, cruel, ruthless, pitiless, remorseless, merciless, fell, ferocious, unfeeling; nonhuman.

Inhumanity, *n.* 1. Barbarity, brutality, savageness, cruelty, ferocity.

2. Hard-heartedness, hardness of heart, unkindness.

Inhume, *v. t.* Bury, inter, entomb, deposit in the earth.

Inimical, *a.* 1. Hostile, unfriendly, antagonistic.

2. Adverse, unfavorable, opposed, contrary, repugnant, hurtful, harmful, noxious, pernicious.

Inimitable, *a.* Unparalleled, unequalled, unexampled, incomparable, unrivalled, unmatched, unparagoned, matchless, peerless, beyond compare.

Iniquitous, *a.* Unjust, unrighteous, unfair, criminal, atrocious, inequitable, wrong, wicked, sinful, nefarious, heinous, flagitious.

Iniquity, *n.* 1. Injustice, unrighteousness, wickedness, sin, sinfulness.

2. Sin, crime, misdeed, wicked act, offence.

Initial, *a.* 1. First, at the beginning, at the head.

2. Incipient, commencing, beginning, initiatory, introductory, opening, original; elementary, rudimentary, inchoate, in the first stages.

Initiate, *v. t.* 1. Introduce, give entrance to.

2. Indoctrinate, instruct, teach, prime, ground.

3. Begin, commence, open, inaugurate, enter upon.

Initiation, *n.* 1. Introduction, admission, entrance.

2. Instruction, indoctrination.

3. Beginning, inauguration, commencement, opening.

Initiative, *n.* 1. Beginning, first step.

2. Power to begin, power to originate, energy, enterprise.

Initiatory, *a.* Initiative, inceptive.

Inject, *v. t.* Throw in, dart in, introduce, intromit, interject, force in.

Injudicious, *a.* Unwise, indiscreet, imprudent, inconsiderate, foolish, rash, incautious, hasty, ill-judged, ill-advised.

Injunction, *n.* Command, order, precept, mandate, bidding, admonition.

Injure, *v. t.* 1. Maltreat, wrong, abuse, outrage, do wrong to, do an ill office to, treat unjustly; insult, affront, dishonor.

2. Harm, hurt, damage, spoil, impair, mar, wound, sully, disfigure, do harm to.

Injurious, *a.* 1. Wrongful, iniquitous, unjust, inequitable.

2. Hurtful, detrimental, prejudicial, pernicious, deleterious, noxious, deadly, baneful, mischievous, damaging, disadvantageous, destructive, ruinous, fatal, evil.

3. Contumelious, detractory, libellous, slanderous.

Injury, *n.* 1. Wrong, injustice, evil, ill.

2. Hurt, damage, harm, detriment, mischief, impairment, loss, prejudice.

Injustice, *n.* 1. Unfairness, unjust *or* inequitable nature *or* character.

2. Wrong, grievance, piece of injustice, injury, hardship.

INK, *n.* (*Basic Eng.*)

Inkhorn, *n.* Inkstand, inkbottle.

Inkling, *n.* Hint, intimation, whisper, suggestion.

Inky, *a.* Black, atramentous, murky.

Inlaid, *a.* Decorated with inlaying *or* inlaid work, set in.

Inland, *a.* 1. Interior, internal.

2. Domestic, not foreign, home, up-country, hinterland.

Inlay, *v. t.* Decorate with inserted material, hatch, tessellate.

Inlet, *n.* 1. Entrance, passage, place of ingress.

2. Bay, bight, cove, creek, arm.

Inmate, *n.* Occupant, dweller, denizen, intern, guest.

Inmost, *a.* Innermost, deepest, most inward.

Inn, *n.* Tavern, hotel, cabaret, public-house, hostel, hostelry, "pub," house of entertainment.

Innate, *a.* Inborn, inbred, native, natural, congenital, indigenous, instinctive, constitutional, inherited, inherent, organic.

Inner, *a.* Interior, internal.

Innermost, *a.* Inmost, deepest, most inward.

Innkeeper, *n.* Innholder, host, landlord, tavernkeeper.

Innocence, *n.* 1. Harmlessness, inoffensiveness, innocuousness, innoxiousness.

2. Guiltlessness, sinlessness, blamelessness, chastity, guilelessness, purity, simplicity, stainlessness.

Innocent, *a.* 1. Harmless, inoffensive, innocuous, innoxious; lawful, legitimate, permitted.

2. Guiltless, sinless, faultless, blameless, immaculate, spotless, pure, clean, clear, upright, unfallen.

3. Artless, guileless, simple, ingenuous, ignorant.

Innovate, *v. i.* Introduce novelties, make changes, make innovations.

Innovation, *n.* 1. Change, introduction of novelty.

2. Novelty, radically new measure, violent departure from established precedent.

Innuendo, *n.* Insinuation, remote intimation, indirect allusion, oblique hint, sly suggestion.

Innumerable, *a.* Numberless, countless, not to be counted, that cannot be numbered.

Inoculate, *v. t.* Vaccinate, infect.

Inoffensive, *a.* Harmless, unoffending, innocuous, unobjectionable, innoxious, innocent.

Inoperative, *a.* 1. Inactive, inefficacious, ineffectual, of no effect.

2. Out of force, not in force.

Inopportune, *a.* Unseasonable, untimely, ill-timed, not opportune.

Inordinate, *a.* Immoderate, extravagant, intemperate, excessive.

Inorganic, *a.* Unorganized, inanimate; mineral.

Inosculate, *v. i.* (*Bot. and Anat.*) Anastomose, unite at the ends (*as veins* or *arteries*), blend.

——, *v. t.* Unite by apposition *or* contact.

Inquest, *n.* 1. Inquisition, judicial inquiry (*especially by a coroner*), investigation, quest, search into facts.

2. Jury (*particularly a coroner's jury*).

Inquietude, *n.* Uneasiness, disquiet, disquietude, disturbance, restlessness, anxiety.

Inquire, *v. i.* [Written also *Enquire.*] 1. Ask, question, seek information (*by questioning*), make inquiry.

2. Make investigation, make examination.

——, *v. t.* [Written also *Enquire.*] Ask about, make inquiry about, ask, interrogate, query, catechize, interpellate.

Inquiry, *n.* 1. Interrogation, question, query, interrogatory, "quiz."

2. Investigation, examination, research, scrutiny, study, exploration.

Inquisition, *n.* Inquest, judicial inquiry, search, investigation, examination.

Inquisitive, *a.* 1. Curious, inquiring, scrutinizing, given to research, fond of investigation.

2. Curious, prying, intrusively curious, meddlesome.

Inroad, *n.* Irruption, foray, incursion, raid, encroachment, partial invasion, predatory incursion.

Insalubrious, *a.* Unhealthy, unwholesome, unhealthful, noxious, unfavorable to health.

Insane, *a.* Deranged, crazy, crazed, lunatic, mad, distracted, demented, delirious, out of one's mind, out of one's head, out of one's senses, out of one's wits, unsound.

Insanity, *n.* Derangement, lunacy, craziness, dementia, mania, madness, delirium, aberration of mind, alienation of mind, loss of reason.

Insatiable, *a.* 1. Insatiate, unappeasable, not to be satisfied, that cannot be sated.
2. Greedy, voracious, rapacious.

Inscribe, *v. t.* Write, engrave, emblaze, indorse, letter, mark, enroll, imprint, impress; address (*as a literary work*), dedicate.

Inscrutable, *a.* Undiscoverable, unsearchable, impenetrable, incomprehensible, inexplicable, unfathomable, hidden, mysterious, past comprehension, above comprehension, not to be understood.

Inscrutableness, *n.* Inscrutability, impenetrability, incomprehensibility, incomprehensibleness, unfathomableness, mysteriousness, mystery, inexplicability, unsearchableness.

INSECT, *n.* Bug, arthropod.

Insecure, *a.* 1. Uncertain, not sure, risky, not confident.
2. Unsafe, unprotected, ill-protected, exposed, exposed to risk *or* danger, in danger.
3. Dangerous, hazardous, perilous.
4. Unstable, infirm, weak, shaking, tottering, "wobbly."

Insecurity, *n.* See the adjective preceding.

Insensate, *a.* 1. Dull, torpid, indifferent, insensible.
2. Stupid, senseless, foolish, destitute of sense, unwise, brutal.
3. Inanimate, insentient, unconscious, insensible, unperceiving, non-percipient, destitute of sensation *or* perception.

Insensibility, *n.* 1. Torpor, lethargy, dulness, insentience, want of sensibility.
2. Apathy, indifference, insusceptibility, unfeelingness.
3. Dulness, stupidity.
4. Unconsciousness, suspension of consciousness, coma, stupor, anæsthesia.

Insensible, *a.* 1. Imperceptible, imperceivable, not discoverable.
2. Insensate, dull, stupid, torpid, obtuse, unconscious, blunted, deaf, sluggish, numb, stolid, brutish, senseless, without sensibility; unfeeling, apathetic, phlegmatic, insentient, insensitive, indifferent, callous, impassive, unsusceptible, unimpressible.

Insensibly, *adv.* Imperceptibly.

Insentient, *a.* Inert, senseless, non-sentient. See INSENSATE, 3.

Inseparable, *a.* 1. Indivisible, not to be separated.
2. Indissoluble, not to be severed *or* sundered, inseverable.
3. Extremely intimate, constantly together, always in each other's company.

Insert, *v. t.* Set in, place in, put in, introduce, infix, inject, interpolate, parenthesize, intercalate, inweave.

Inside, *n.* Interior, interior part, inner part; nature.
——, *a.* Interior, internal, inner, intimate.
——, *prep.* Within, inside of, in the interior of.

Insidious, *a.* 1. Artful, sly, wily, guileful, arch, crafty, cunning, subtle, intriguing, designing, deceitful, treacherous, crooked, trickish, tricky, foxy, snaky, diplomatic, Machiavelian.
2. Secret, deceptive, that creeps upon one unawares, delusively gradual.

Insight, *n.* 1. Deep view, thorough knowledge, discerning look, intelligent grasp.
2. Discernment, penetration, perspicuity, intuition, penetrating vision *or* judgment, spontaneous understanding, quick perception.

Insignia, *n. pl.* [L.] Badges of office, marks of distinction *or* authority.

Insignificance, *n.* Unimportance, paltriness, triviality, emptiness, nothingness.

Insignificant, *a.* 1. Without meaning, meaningless, not significant.
2. Unimportant, paltry, petty, empty, trivial, small, inconsiderable, inferior, sorry, contemptible, trifling, immaterial, unessential, of little consequence, of little account, of no moment.

Insincere, *a.* False, faithless, truthless, untrue, disingenuous, uncandid, dishonest, hollow, empty, hypocritical, pharisaical, double-tongued, deceitful, double-faced, dissimulating, dissembling.

Insincerity, *n.* Duplicity, hypocrisy, dissimulation, deceitfulness, disingenuousness, dishonesty, falseness, faithlessness, bad faith.

Insinuate, *v. t.* 1. Introduce gently, infuse, instill.
2. Ingratiate, push artfully.
3. Instill (*artfully*), infuse, inculcate.
4. Hint, suggest, intimate, hint *or* suggest remotely (*something unfavorable* or *discreditable*).

Insinuation, *n.* See the verb preceding.

Insipid, *a.* 1. Tasteless, gustless, savorless, vapid, mawkish, stale, flat.
2. Spiritless, lifeless, heavy, stupid, dull, dead, tame, prosaic, prosy, uninteresting, pointless, flat, jejune, monotonous, unentertaining.

Insipidity, } *n.* 1. Tastelessness, vapid-
Insipidness, } ness, mawkishness, unsavoriness, staleness, flatness, lack of zest.

2. Dulness, lifelessness, stupidity, tameness, prosiness, heaviness, lack of interest, uninteresting character.

Insist, *v. i.* Urge, demand persistently; maintain persistently.

Insistence, *n.* Urging, urgency, importunity, solicitousness, persistent urgency.

Insnare, *v. t.* [Written also *Ensnare.*]
1. Entrap, catch.

2. Inveigle, allure, seduce.

3. Entangle, embarrass, perplex, confound, bewilder.

Insolence, *n.* 1. Insulting rudeness, overbearing contempt, haughty disrespect, contumely.

2. Impertinence, impudence, sauciness, pertness, malapertness.

3. Contumacy, frowardness, impudent disrespect, insulting disobedience *or* insubordination.

Insolent, *a.* 1. Rude, abusive, overbearing, domineering, contemptuous, insulting, contumelious, supercilious.

2. Impertinent, impudent, saucy, "cheeky," pert, malapert.

3. Insultingly disobedient *or* insubordinate, impudently *or* outrageously disrespectful (*to superiors*), froward, contumacious.

Insoluble, *a.* 1. That cannot be dissolved *or* melted *or* liquefied, indissoluble, indissolvable, irreducible.

2. Insolvable, inexplicable, that cannot be solved, not to be explained.

Insolubleness, *n.* Insolubility. See preceding adjective.

Insolvable, *a.* Inexplicable, that cannot be solved, not to be explained.

Insolvent, *a.* Bankrupt, broken, failed, ruined.

Insomnia, *n.* [L.] (*Med.*) Wakefulness, sleeplessness, indisposition to sleep, inability to sleep.

Inspect, *v. t.* 1. Examine, scrutinize, investigate, look into, pry into.

2. Superintend, supervise, oversee.

Inspection, *n.* 1. Examination, scrutiny, investigation.

2. Superintendence, supervision, oversight.

Inspector, *n.* 1. Examiner, censor, critic, visitor.

2. Superintendent, supervisor, overseer, boss.

Inspiration, *n.* 1. Inhalation, breathing in.

2. Afflatus, supernatural influence, inflatus, fire.

3. Divine influence *or* afflatus, theopneusty.

4. Inspired state *or* character, frenzy.

5. Elevation, inspiriting, elevating influence.

6. Exaltation, lofty mood, enthusiasm, enthusiastic impulse, elevating sentiment.

7. Supreme *or* extraordinary insight, genius.

Inspire, *v. i.* Inhale air, draw in the breath.

——, *v. t.* 1. Inhale, breathe in.

2. Breathe into, fill with the breath.

3. Infuse, instil.

4. Animate, inspirit, enliven, cheer, arouse, stir.

5. Affect by supernatural influence, fill with supernatural knowledge, endow with superhuman insight.

6. Endow with extraordinary insight, fill *or* endow with genius.

7. Elevate, exalt, stimulate to aspiration, fill with enthusiasm.

8. Animate, imbue, inform, quicken, enliven, fill.

Inspirit, *v. t.* Animate, invigorate, enliven, encourage, enhearten, hearten, embolden, cheer, comfort, stimulate, incite, quicken, rouse, arouse, fire, give new life to.

Inspissate, *v. t.* Thicken, make thick.

——, *a.* Thick, inspissated.

Instable, *a.* [Written preferably *Unstable.*]
1. Unsettled, insecure, liable to fall, not stable, not permanent, not firm, tottering.

2. Mutable, variable, changeable, wavering, weak, liable to change.

3. Inconstant, fickle, changeable, volatile, mercurial.

Install, *v. t.* Inaugurate, induct, introduce into office; place, set up, establish.

Installation, *n.* Inauguration, investiture, instalment, ceremony of induction.

Instalment, *n.* [Written also *Installment.*]
1. See INSTALLATION.

2. Successive portion, partial payment, portion, earnest.

Instance, *n.* 1. Solicitation, request, prompting, instigation, incitement, impulse, motive.

2. Urgency, urgent solicitation, importunity, persistent pressure.

3. Example, exemplification, illustration, case, occasion.

——, *v. t.* Mention (*as an instance*), bring forward as an example, cite, specify, adduce.

Instant, *a.* 1. Pressing, urgent, importunate, earnest.

2. Immediate, quick, instantaneous.

3. Current, present, now passing.

Instant, *n.* 1. Moment, second, twinkling, flash, trice, "jiffy," twinkling of an eye, smallest conceivable point of time.

2. Time, particular time, hour, moment.

Instantaneous, *a.* Immediate, quick, instant, sudden, abrupt, in a flash.

Instantaneously, } *adv.* Immediately, forth-
Instantly, } with, presto, in a trice, *instanter*, on the instant, right away, on the moment, on the spur of the moment, in less than no time, quick as thought, quick as lightning.

Instauration, *n.* Restoration, renewal, reestablishment, reinstatement, renovation, reconstruction, redintegration, reconstitution, rehabilitation.

Instead, *adv.* In lieu, in the room, in (the) place, rather.

Instigate, *v. t.* [*In a bad sense.*] Incite, prompt, tempt, impel, move, urge, provoke, stimulate, rouse, actuate, persuade, influence, encourage, set on, prevail upon, agitate, stir up, spur on.

Instigation, *n.* Incitement, urgency, encouragement, prompting, influence, solicitation, instance.

Instil, *v. t.* [Written also *Instill.*] 1. Infuse, drop in, impart gradually, insinuate.

2. Inculcate, impress, enforce, implant, ingraft.

Instillation, *n.* Infusion, insinuation, gentle introduction.

Instinct, *n.* Natural impulse, blind impulse, native tendency, innate *or* inborn proclivity.

——, *a.* Alive, quick, animated, informed, imbued, charged, alert.

Instinctive, *a.* Natural, spontaneous, innate, intuitive, automatic, inherent, involuntary, prompted by instinct; impulsive, unreflecting, not deliberate.

Institute, *v. t.* 1. Establish, found, originate, appoint, settle, fix, set up.

2. Enact, ordain, establish, pass.

3. Begin, commence, set in operation, inaugurate, set going, set on foot.

4. Invest with a sacred office, invest with the care of souls.

——, *n.* 1. Doctrine, dogma, precept, maxim, principle, tenet.

2. Scientific body, literary *or* philosophical society.

3. School, academy, gymnasium, seminary, place of education, institution of learning, institution.

Institution, *n.* 1. Establishing, founding, foundation, enactment, etc. See INSTITUTE, *v. t.*, 1 and 2.

2. Establishment, organized society.

3. Investiture.

4. Custom, law, established practice.

5. Institute, school, academy, seminary, gymnasium, college, university, place of education.

Instruct, *v. t.* 1. Teach, inform, enlighten, indoctrinate, exercise, train, school, educate, discipline.

2. Direct, command, order, enjoin, bid, apprise, prescribe to.

Instruction, *n.* 1. Teaching, information, education, indoctrination, training, schooling, discipline, tuition, nurture, breeding.

2. Advice, counsel, precept.

3. Direction, order, command, mandate.

Instructor, *n.* Teacher, tutor, preceptor, master, school-master, educator.

INSTRUMENT, *n.* 1. Tool, implement, utensil, device, appliance, apparatus, contrivance; musical instrument.

2. Medium, agent, means.

3. Writing, document, charter, deed, indenture.

Instrumental, *a.* Conducive, subservient, serviceable, helping, helpful, assisting, contributory, contributive, auxiliary, ancillary, subsidiary, ministerial, ministrant.

Instrumentality, *n.* Agency, intermediary; mediation, means, intervention.

Insubordinate, *a.* Disobedient, unruly, mutinous, riotous, seditious, disorderly, turbulent, ungovernable, refractory.

Insubordination, *n.* 1. Disobedience, revolt, insurrection, mutiny, riotousness, sedition.

2. Indiscipline, lax discipline, laxity.

Insufferable, *a.* 1. Intolerable, insupportable, unbearable, unendurable, that cannot be borne *or* endured.

2. Outrageous, disgusting, detestable, abominable, execrable.

Insufficiency, *n.* Inadequateness, inadequacy, incompetence, deficiency, lack, shortage, paucity, defectiveness, dearth.

Insufficient, *a.* 1. Inadequate, incompetent, scanty, incommensurate, deficient.

2. Unsuited, unfitted, incapable, unqualified, incompetent.

Insular, *a.* 1. Surrounded by water, with the characteristics of an island.

2. Of islands, belonging to islands, characteristic of islands.

3. Narrow, contracted, prejudiced, petty, illiberal, limited, restricted; isolated, remote.

Insulate, *v. t.* Detach, isolate, separate, disconnect, disunite, disengage, separate by non-conductors.

Insulation, *n.* Isolation, separation, disconnection, disengagement.

Insulator, *n.* (*Phys.*) Non-conductor.

Insult, *n.* Affront, offence, indignity, outrage, insolence, abuse, contumely, "sauce," "cheek."

——, *v. t.* Affront, offend, abuse, treat with insolence, offer an indignity to, show *or* display insolence toward, commit an indignity upon.

Insulting, *a.* Insolent, abusive, vituperative, arrogant, grossly abusive, contumelious.

Insuperable, *a.* Insurmountable, impassable, too great to be overcome, that cannot be got over.

Insupportable, *a.* Intolerable, unbearable, unendurable, insufferable.

Insuppressible, *a.* 1. Uncontrollable, irrepressible, not to be kept down, that cannot be held in check.

2. Impossible to conceal *or* suppress, that cannot be covered up.

INSURANCE, *n.* Assurance, security against loss.

Insure, *v. t.* [Written also *Ensure*.]
1. Make secure, make sure *or* certain.

2. Assure, secure against loss, agree to indemnify for loss, guarantee.

——, *v. i.* Underwrite, furnish insurance.

Insurgent, *a.* Rebellious, seditious, revolting, revolutionary, insubordinate, disobedient, mutinous.

——, *n.* Rebel, revolter, mutineer.

Insurmountable, *a.* See INSUPERABLE.

Insurrection, *n.* Rebellion, revolt, sedition, insurgence, mutiny, rising, uprising.

Insurrectionary, *a.* Rebellious, seditious, mutinous, insubordinate.

Insusceptible, *a.* 1. Insensible, unimpressible, insusceptive, not susceptible.

2. Incapable, incapable of receiving, not admitting, that does not admit.

Intact, *a.* 1. Untouched, uninjured, unhurt, unimpaired, unharmed, scathless.

2. Undiminished, unbroken, whole, integral, complete, sound, entire, unaffected by injury, without a fracture.

Intangible, *a.* 1. Impalpable, that cannot be touched, that cannot be felt.

2. Impalpable, imperceptible, intactile, indefinite, shadowy, insubstantial, vague, dim; aërial, spiritous, phantom.

Intangibleness, *n.* Intangibility. See preceding adjective.

Integer, *n.* Whole number.

Integral, *a.* Whole, entire, total, component, integrant, necessary for completeness, complete, entire.

Integrity, *n.* 1. Wholeness, entireness, entirety, completeness; soundness, purity.

2. Rectitude, uprightness, probity, honesty, virtue, goodness, principle, moral soundness.

Integument, *n.* Covering, envelope, tegument, skin, coat.

Intellect, *n.* Understanding, reason, mind, sense, intelligence, brains, thinking principle, reasoning faculty, rational faculty, discursive faculty, intellectual powers, cognitive faculty.

Intellection, *n.* 1. Apprehension, cognition, cognizance, knowing.

2. Thinking, comprehending, comprehension, understanding.

Intellectual, *a.* 1. Mental, of the intellect, of the understanding, pertaining *or* relating to the intellect.

2. Of intellect, marked by intellect, of marked intellect, full of intellect *or* intelligence, thoughtful, imaginative.

Intelligence, *n.* 1. Information, knowledge, acquired knowledge.

2. News, tidings, advice, notice, notification, instruction.

3. Spirit, spiritual being, intellect, mentality, "brains," sense.

4. Penetration, acumen, quickness, insight, imagination, sagacity, shrewdness, wits, brightness, quick understanding, discernment, clear apprehension.

Intelligent, *a.* 1. Instructed, enlightened, well-informed.

2. Astute, acute, quick, alert, knowing, sensible, understanding, sagacious, shrewd, "brainy," clever, bright, apt, discerning, clear-sighted, keen-sighted, quick-sighted, sharp-sighted, sharp-witted, keen-eyed, long-headed, clear-headed.

Intelligibility, *n.* Comprehensibility, intelligibleness, clarity, perspicuity.

Intelligible, *a.* Clear, plain, distinct, obvious, manifest, patent, evident, lucid, transparent, perspicuous, comprehensible, that may be understood.

Intemperance, *n.* 1. Excess (*in any action* or *in any indulgence*), want of moderation, immoderation, excessiveness, unrestraint.

2. Habitual excess in drinking intoxicating liquors.

Intemperate, *a.* 1. [*Said of things.*] Excessive, inordinate, immoderate, uncontrolled, unrestrained, unbridled, extravagant, extreme.

2. [*Said of persons.*] Wanting in moderation, inconsiderate, extreme, extravagant; self-indulgent, luxurious.

3. Given to excess in drinking intoxicating liquors.

Intend, *v. t.* Mean, design, purpose, determine, meditate, contemplate, propose to one's self, have in view, think of, aim at, drive at.

Intendant, *n.* Superintendent, overseer, supervisor, inspector.

Intense, *a.* 1. Close, strict, intent, severe, strained, stretched.

2. Extreme, very great, of high *or* great degree, acute, exquisite, grievous, poignant, deep.

3. Forcible, energetic, vigorous, powerful, strong, violent, sharp, potent, keen.

4. Ardent, vehement, earnest, passionate.

Intensify, *v. t.* Strengthen, deepen, quicken, heighten, enhance, concentrate, whet, aggravate, make intense, make more intense.

Intensity, *n.* 1. Intenseness, closeness, strictness, severity.

2. Excess, vehemence, extremity, violence, high degree, extreme degree.

3. Vigor, strength, power, activity, force, energy.

4. Ardor, earnestness, vehemence.

Intensive, *a.* 1. Intensifying, emphatic, serving to add force.

2. Capable of intensification.

Intent, *a.* 1. Eager, earnest, close, closely fixed, attentive.

2. Bent, resolutely bent, set.

——, *n.* Design, purpose, intention, aim, end, meaning, drift, purport, import, plan, object, scope, mark, purview.

Intention, *n.* Design, purpose. See INTENT.

Intentional, *a.* Designed, intended, premeditated, purposed, predetermined, contemplated, preconcerted, studied, deliberate, wilful, voluntary.

Inter, *v. t.* Bury (*with funeral rites*), inhume, entomb, inurn, commit to the earth.

Intercalate, *v. t.* Interpolate, insert.

Intercede, *v. i.* 1. Mediate, arbitrate, interpose.

2. Plead, make intercession.

Intercept, *v. t.* 1. Stop on the way, seize on the passage.

2. Interrupt, obstruct, cut off.

Intercession, *n.* 1. Mediation, interposition, intervention.

2. Pleading, supplication, entreaty, prayer.

Intercessor, *n.* Mediator, interceder.

Interchange, *v. t.* Exchange, alternate, vary, change reciprocally, give and take mutually.

——, *n.* 1. Exchange, barter, "swap"; reciprocity, reciprocation, *quid pro quo.*

2. Alternation, alternate succession.

Interchangeableness, *n.* Interchangeability.

Interchangeably, *adv.* Alternately, by interchange, by reciprocation.

Intercourse, *n.* Communication, commerce, dealings, "truck," correspondence, fellowship, converse, communion, connection, mutual exchange.

Interdependence, *n.* Mutual *or* reciprocal dependence.

Interdict, *v. t.* Forbid, prohibit, inhibit, proscribe.

——, *n.* 1. Prohibition, interdiction, decree.

2. (*Eccles.*) Ban, suspension of religious privileges.

Interdiction, *n.* 1. Interdicting.

2. Prohibition, interdict, ban.

Interest, *v. t.* 1. Concern, affect, touch, be of importance to.

2. Engage, enlist, attract, grip, absorb, excite, occupy, hold.

INTEREST, *n.* 1. Good, benefit, profit, weal, advantage.

2. Share, portion, part, participation, stake.

3. Concern, regard, sympathy, pleased attention.

4. Premium (*for the use of money*), business advantage, discount, profit (*from money loaned*).

Interested, *a.* 1. Partial, biassed, prejudiced; involved, concerned.

2. Selfish, self-seeking.

3. Attentive, occupied, held attentive.

Interesting, *a.* Engaging, attractive, pleasing, entertaining.

Interfere, *v. i.* 1. Intermeddle, meddle, interpose, put in one's oar.

2. Clash, conflict, be opposed, come into collision.

Interference, *n.* 1. Intermeddling, interposition, interposal.

2. Clashing, opposition, interfering, collision.

Interim, *n.* Interval, intermediate time, meantime.

Interior, *a.* 1. Internal, inner, inward, insight, inmost.

2. Inland, remote (*from the shore or the frontier*), up-country.

3. Home, domestic (*opposed to foreign or external*).

——, *n.* Inside, inner part, interior part; inland.

Interjacent, *a.* Intervening, intermediate, interposed, parenthetical.

Interject, *v. t.* Insert, put between, inject, interpose, comment, throw in between.

Interjection, *n.* 1. Exclamation.

2. Exclamatory particle.

Interlace, *v. t.* Intertwine, interweave, inweave, unite, bind, intwine, twine together, complicate, knit, twist, plait, intersperse, mix.

Interlard, *v. t.* Mix, intersperse, intertwine, interminate, diversify, vary.

Interline, *v. t.* 1. Write between the lines of, insert.

　2. Write in alternate lines.

Interlineal, *a.* Interlined, interlinear.

Interlink, ⎫ *v. t.* Interchain, join closely to-
Interlock, ⎭ gether, connect, interrelate.

Interlocution, *n.* Dialogue, colloquy, conference, interchange of speech.

Interlocutor, *n.* Speaker (*in a dialogue*), respondent, companion in conversation.

Interloper, *n.* Meddler, intruder.

Intermeddle, *v. i.* Interfere, meddle, interpose, take part officiously.

Intermediary, *n.* Mediator, go-between.

Intermediate, *a.* Intervening, interposed, interjacent, median, middle, mean, transitional.

Interment, *n.* Burial, inhumation, entombment, sepulture.

Interminable, *a.* 1. Illimitable, unlimited, immeasurable, boundless, unbounded, limitless, endless, infinite.

　2. Wearisomely protracted, tediously long, long-drawn, that seems as if it would never end.

Intermingle, *v. t.* and *v. i.* Blend, mingle, commingle, intermix, commix, mix, mix together.

Intermission, *n.* Remission, suspension, cessation, lull, interval, suspense, stoppage, stop, interruption, pause, rest, respite.

Intermit, *v. t.* 1. Suspend, interrupt, stop for a while *or* for a time.

　2. Discontinue, cease, stop, leave off, give over.

——, *v. i.* Cease, abate, subside, be suspended, be interrupted, cease for a time.

Intermittent, *a.* Intermitting, remittent, discontinuous, broken, spasmodic, fitful, capricious, periodic, recurrent, flickering.

Intermix, *v. t.* and *v. i.* See INTERMINGLE.

Internal, *a.* 1. Interior, inner, inward, inside.

　2. Spiritual, incorporeal, mental, in the mind *or* heart.

　3. [*Said of meaning or sense.*] Inner, interior, under, hidden, deeper, higher, spiritual, secret, metaphorical, emblematic, symbolical.

　4. Intrinsic, real, genuine, true, inherent.

　5. Domestic, home, interior (*as opposed to foreign*), inside, inland.

International, *a.* Between nations, common to nations.

Internecine, *a.* Mortal, deadly, exterminating, exterminatory, mutually destructive, interneciary, internecinal, internecive.

Interpellate, *v. t.* Question, interrogate, question imperatively and officially.

Interpellation, *n.* 1. Interruption (*of one who is speaking*).

　2. Intercession, interposition.

　3. Official questioning *or* interrogation (*of a minister by the legislative body*).

Interplay, *n.* Reciprocal action, interaction.

Interpolate, *v. t.* 1. Insert, foist in, add, interpose.

　2. (*Math.*) Introduce, intercalate (*terms to complete a series*).

Interpose, *v. t.* 1. Intrude, thrust in.

　2. Put in, insert, set *or* place between, interject, sandwich.

　3. Offer (*or* bring in *or* to bear) by way of mediation.

——, *v. i.* 1. Mediate, intercede, arbitrate, intervene.

　2. Interfere, intermeddle, tamper, interrupt.

Interposition, *n.* Mediation, intervention, interpellation, intercession.

Interpret, *v. t.* 1. Explain, expound, decipher, decode, solve, unravel, elucidate, unfold, define, make out, make clear, explain the meaning of.

　2. Construe, translate, render.

Interpretation, *n.* 1. Explanation, explication, exposition, elucidation.

　2. Rendering, rendition, translation, version, construction.

　3. Meaning, sense, signification.

Interpreter, *n.* Expounder, expositor.

Interrogate, *v. t.* Question, catechise, examine, ask, inquire of, put questions to, interpellate.

Interrogation, *n.* 1. Interrogating, questioning, catechising, examining, examination, interpellation.

　2. Question, inquiry, interrogatory, query.

Interrogative, *a.* Interrogatory, questioning.

Interrupt, *v. t.* 1. Disturb, stop, break, hinder, intercept, obstruct, pretermit, check, cause to delay, cause to cease, interfere with, break in upon, hinder from proceeding.

　2. Separate, divide, break, disconnect, disunite, disjoin, sunder, dissever, sever, cut, dissolve.

　3. Intermit, suspend, discontinue, break off, leave off, cease for a time.

Interruption, *n.* 1. Hindrance, stop, stoppage, obstruction, obstacle, impediment.

2. Intermission, pause, suspension, cessation, discontinuance.

3. Separation, division, breaking, break, disconnection, disconnecting, disuniting, disunion, disjunction, sundering, severance, dissolution.

Intersect, *v. t.* Cross, cut, decussate, interrupt, divide.

——, *v. i.* Cross each other, cut each other.

Intersection, *n.* Crossing.

Interspace, *n.* Interval, interlude, interstice.

Intersperse, *v. t.* Scatter *or* set here and there, intermingle, sprinkle; interlard, mix, diversify by mixture.

Interstice, *n.* Interval, interspace, intervening space, space between; chink, crevice.

Interstitial, *a.* Intervening, intermediate.

Intertexture, *n.* 1. Interweaving, intertwining.

2. Interwoven condition, intertwined state.

3. Interwoven mass.

Intertwine, *v. t.* Interweave, interlace, intwine, inweave, twine together.

——, *v. i.* Interlace, be intertwined, be interlaced, be twined together, be mutually woven together.

Intertwist, *v. t.* Twist *or* twine together. See INTERTWINE.

Interval, *n.* 1. Interstice, space between, distance, skip, intermediate space.

2. Season, spell, period, term, space of time, pause, recess, interregnum, interlude, interim, intermediate time, intervening time *or* period.

Intervene, *v. i.* 1. Interfere, come between, mediate.

2. Happen (*in the meantime*), occur, befall.

3. Be intermediate *or* interjacent, come between, interpose.

Intervening, *a.* 1. Intermediate, interjacent.

2. Interstitial.

Intervention, *n.* 1. Interposition, interference.

2. Mediation, agency.

Interview, *n.* 1. Meeting.

2. Conference, parley, consultation.

Interweave, *v. t.* 1. Intertwine, interlace, inweave, weave together.

2. Mix, mingle, intermix, intermingle.

Intestine, *a.* Internal, interior, domestic.

Intestines, *n. pl.* Entrails, bowels, viscera, inwards, insides, guts.

Intimacy, *n.* 1. Familiarity, fellowship, friendship, close acquaintance.

2. Intimate character, nearness, closeness.

Intimate, *a.* 1. Near, close.

2. Familiar, friendly, hand and glove, hail fellow well met.

3. Close, bosom, very dear, confidential, homelike, special, "chummy."

4. Inward, internal, interior, from within, deep-seated, innermost, intrinsic.

——, *n.* Confidant, crony, familiar friend, associate, "chum," intimate acquaintance, bosom friend.

——, *v. t.* Suggest, hint, insinuate, indicate, allude to, make allusion to, give an inkling of, glance at, remind of, put in mind of.

Intimately, *adv.* 1. Closely, nearly.

2. Familiarly, closely, confidentially.

3. Thoroughly, familiarly, through and through, to the core, to the bottom.

Intimation, *n.* Hint, suggestion, allusion, insinuation, innuendo.

Intimidate, *v. t.* Frighten, affright, alarm, scare, subdue, terrorize, bullyrag, browbeat, cow, overawe, abash, bully, daunt, dismay, terrify, appall, put in fear, fright (*poetical*).

Intimidation, *n.* 1. Intimidating.

2. Fear, terror, terrorism, reign of terror.

Intolerable, *a.* Insufferable, insupportable, unbearable, unendurable, not to be tolerated *or* borne.

Intolerance, *n.* 1. Bigotry, narrowness, proscriptive *or* persecuting spirit, want of toleration, want of forbearance.

2. Non-endurance, inability to bear, rejection, impatience.

Intolerant, *a.* 1. Overbearing, supercilious, dictatorial, imperious, impatient.

2. Narrow, bigoted, proscriptive.

Intonation, *n.* Tone, cadence, modulation of voice; musical recitation.

In toto. [L.] Entirely, wholly.

Intoxicate, *v. t.* Inebriate, fuddle, muddle, make drunk, make tipsy.

Intoxicated, *a.* Inebriated, drunk, tipsy, drunken, "boozy," "tight," "stewed," fuddled, muddled, disguised, maudlin, mellow, in liquor, in one's cups, half-seas-over, three sheets in the wind.

Intoxication, *n.* 1. Inebriation, ebriety, inebriety, drunkenness.

2. Infatuation, great excitement, great exhilaration.

Intractability, *n.* Stubbornness, obstinacy, perverseness, intractableness. See following adjective.

Intractable, *a.* Stubborn, obstinate, perverse, tough, uncontrollable, stubborn, contrary, restive, refractory, dogged, headstrong, unmanageable, ungovernable, indocile, obdurate, cross-grained, wilful, inflexible, unyielding, contumacious, cantankerous, froward, unruly, pig-headed, mulish.

Intrench, *v. t.*   1. Furrow, make furrows in.

2. Fortify with intrenchments, circumvallate.

3. Encroach, infringe, trench, trespass.

Intrenchment, *n.*   1. Intrenching.

2. Fortification (*by trenches and parapet*), earthwork.

3. Defence, protection, shelter.

4. Encroachment, inroad, invasion (*of rights*).

Intrench on. Invade, trespass upon, encroach upon, trench upon, intrench upon.

Intrepid, *a.* Bold, fearless, dauntless, undaunted, undismayed, unterrified, unappalled, unawed, brave, courageous, valorous, valiant, heroic, gallant, daring, doughty.

Intrepidity, *n.* Boldness, fearlessness, dauntlessness, bravery, courage, valor, prowess, gallantry, spirit, heroism, daring, contempt of danger.

Intricacy, *n.* Perplexity, complexity, complication, entanglement, involution, obscurity, difficulty, intricateness.

Intricate, *a.* Entangled, complicated, involved, perplexed, obscure, mazy, difficult.

Intrigue, *n.*   1. Plot, conspiracy, cabal, deception, scheme, wire-pulling, Machiavelianism, machination, stratagem, manœuvre, wile, finesse, ruse.

2. Amour, love affair, *liaison*, illicit intimacy.

3. Gallantry, libertinism.

——, *v. i.*   1. Manœuvre, form plots.

2. Carry on an amour *or* amours.

Intriguing, *a.* Cunning, crafty, artful, sly, wily, subtle, insidious, designing, arch, deceitful, tortuous, trickish, tricky, crooked, diplomatic, politic, foxy, snaky, Machiavelian.

Intrinsic, *a.* 1. Inherent, internal, inward, inborn, inbred, native, natural, ingrained, not extrinsic.

2. Real, genuine, true, essential.

Intrinsically, *adv.*   1. Naturally, inherently, in the nature of things, in the nature of the case, in the grain.

2. Really, truly, essentially.

Introduce, *v. t.*   1. Conduct, lead in, bring in, insert, inject, import, induct, usher in.

2. Present, make acquainted.

3. Bring into notice, bring before the public, usher in, bring into use.

4. Begin, commence, be the first to take up, start, inaugurate, initiate, broach, institute.

Introduction, *n.*   1. Introducing, ushering in.

2. Presentation.

3. Preface, prelude, proem, exordium, preliminary part.

Introductory, *a.* Prefatory, preliminary, precursory, proemial.

Introspection, *n.* Looking within, introversion, self-contemplation.

Intrude, *v. i.*   1. Obtrude, force one's self, thrust one's self, enter where one is not welcome, impose, interlope.

2. Encroach, trench, infringe, trespass.

——, *v. t.* Obtrude, force in, thrust in, interlope, encroach, interfere, press in, foist in, worm in.

Intruder, *n.* Interloper, intermeddler, meddler, stranger.

Intrusion, *n.*   1. Intruding, obtrusion.

2. Encroachment, infringement.

Intrusive, *a.* Obtrusive, trespassing.

Intrust, *v. t.* Confide, commit, consign, give in trust, deliver in trust.

Intuition, *n.*   1. Immediate perception (*by the intellect*), insight, instinctive knowledge, direct cognition, apprehension at first sight.

2. Divination, clairvoyance, presentiment.

Intuitive, *a.*   1. Apprehended immediately, perceived at once (*without reasoning*), instinctive, natural, intuitional.

2. Immediate, full, clear, distinct.

Intumesce, *v. i.* Swell, expand, dilate, bubble up, become tumid.

Intumescence, *n.* Swelling, tumefaction, turgescence, inturgescence.

Intwine, *v. t.* Inweave, interweave, intertwine, interlace, twine together.

Inundate, *v. t.*   1. Flood, deluge, submerge, overflow, overwhelm, drown.

2. Fill to superfluity, flood, deluge, glut.

Inundation, *n.*   1. Inundating. See the verb.

2. Flood, deluge, overflow, cataclysm.

Inurbane, *a.* Unpolished, uncourtly, uncourteous, uncomplaisant, uncouth.

Inure, *v. t.* Habituate, accustom, use, familiarize, train, harden, toughen, discipline.

Inurn, *v. t.* Bury, inter, entomb, inhume, lay in the grave, consign to the grave, consign to earth.

Inutile, *a.* Useless, unprofitable, unavailing, inoperative, bootless, ineffectual.

Invade, *v. t.*   1. March into, enter in force, enter with an army, attack.

2. Infringe, violate, encroach upon, trench upon.

Invalid (*in-val'id*), *a.* 1. Weak, of no weight, of no force.

2. (*Law.*) Void, null, of no legal force, null and void.

3. Unsound, unfounded, baseless, untrue, fallacious, that does not hold (good).

—— (*in'val-id*), *a.* Weak, feeble, infirm, sick, ailing, sickly, weakly, frail, valetudinary; suitable to an invalid.

—— (*in'val-id*), *n.* Valetudinarian, feeble person, infirm person, sick person.

Invalidate, *v. t.* Nullify, annul, cancel, unmake, undo, vitiate, abrogate, quash, repeal, reverse, overthrow, make void, render of no effect.

Invalidism, *n.* Feebleness, infirmity, illness, sickness, valetudinarianism, chronic ill-health.

Invalidity, *n.* Unsoundness, lack of validity, nullity, baselessness, fallaciousness, fallacy, falsity.

Invaluable, *a.* Inestimable, priceless, very precious, above all value, above all price. See INESTIMABLE.

Invariable, *a.* 1. Unchangeable, immutable, unalterable, changeless.

2. Constant, unchanging, uniform, changeless, unvarying.

Invariableness, *n.* 1. Unchangeableness, immutability, invariability, changelessness.

2. Constancy, uniformity, changelessness, unvarying character.

Invasion, *n.* 1. Attack, assault, aggression, inroad, incursion, irruption, foray, raid.

2. Encroachment, infringement, violation, intrusion.

3. Invading. See the verb.

Invective, *n.* 1. Abuse, contumely, reproach, denunciation, censure, railing, vituperation, sarcastic attack, rhetorical assault.

2. Satire, sarcasm, pasquinade, philippic, diatribe, fling.

——, *a.* 1. Abusive, reproachful, censorious, captious, railing, scolding, harsh, denunciatory.

2. Satirical, sarcastic, assailing.

Inveigh. Censure, reproach, condemn, blame, denounce, declaim against, rail at, exclaim against, vituperate.

Inveigle, *v. t.* Entice, decoy, beguile, entrap, cajole, ensnare, lure.

Invent, *v. t.* 1. Contrive (*what did not before exist*), devise, be the first to contrive *or* devise.

2. Originate, create, frame, imagine, excogitate, conceive, concoct, design.

3. Fabricate, forge, coin, spin.

INVENTION, *n.* 1. Inventing, origination, creation, discovery.

2. Contrivance, device, design.

3. Ingenuity, power of inventing.

4. Fabrication, forgery, fiction, coinage.

Inventive, *a.* Ingenious, creative, quick at contrivance, fertile in expedients.

Inventor, *n.* Contriver, originator, creator, father, author.

Inventory, *n.* List (*as of the goods of a merchant* or *of a deceased person*), roll, schedule, record, account, register. See CATALOGUE.

Inverse, *a.* Inverted (*as respects order* or *relation*), reversed, indirect, opposite.

Inversion, *n.* 1. Inverting, reversing, placing in contrary order, transposition, transposal.

2. Inverting, upsetting, turning upside down.

3. (*Rhet.*) Hyperbaton, transposition of words.

Invert, *v. t.* 1. Turn upside down, upset, capsize, overturn.

2. Reverse, place in contrary order, transpose, turn about.

Invertebrate, *a.* 1. (*Zoöl.*) Without vertebræ, destitute of a backbone, invertebral.

2. Spineless, lacking in resolution.

Invest, *v. t.* 1. Clothe, dress, array.

2. Endow (*as with authority* or *power*), endue, confer.

3. Put at interest (*as money*).

4. (*Mil.*) Enclose, surround, beset, besiege, lay siege to.

Investigable, *a.* That may be investigated, capable of investigation, that admits of investigation.

Investigate, *v. t.* Examine, scrutinize, canvass, study, sift, consider, overhaul, explore, probe, scrutate, question, dissect, look into, search out, search into, inquire into, follow up.

Investigation, *n.* Examination, study, scrutiny, search, overhauling, inquiry, research, exploration, inquisition, sifting.

Investiture, *n.* Installation, induction, ordination, habilitation.

Investment, *n.* 1. Investing. See INVEST.

2. Vestment, dress, robe, garments, habiliments, clothes.

3. Money invested.

4. (*Mil.*) Siege, beleaguerment.

Inveteracy, *n.* Inveterateness, obstinacy, chronic state.

Inveterate, *a.* Obstinate, besetting, chronic, deep-seated, long established, habituated, habitual, accustomed, ingrained, confirmed, hardened.

Invidious, *a.* Offensive, hateful, odious, likely to excite ill-will.

Invigorate, *v. t.* Strengthen, fortify, animate, refresh, vivify, stimulate, quicken, energize, give vigor to, give life and energy to.

Invincible, *a.* 1. Unconquerable, indomitable, unyielding, unsubduable, incapable of subjugation.

2. Unconquerable, insuperable, irrepressible, ineradicable, incapable of eradication *or* suppression.

3. Insuperable, insurmountable, too great to be overcome.

Inviolable, *a.* Sacred, inviolate, stainless, holy, hallowed, sacramental, sacrosanct.

Inviolate, *a.* 1. Unbroken, unviolated.

2. Unhurt, uninjured, unprofaned, unpolluted, unblemished, undefiled, pure, unstained, stainless.

3. Sacred, inviolable.

Invisibility, *n.* Invisibleness, indistinctness, obscurity, imperceptibility.

Invisible, *a.* Imperceptible, unseen, undiscernable, unapparent, indistinguishable, that cannot be seen, incapable of being seen.

Invitation, *n.* Solicitation, bidding, call, challenge, summons.

Invite, *v. t.* 1. Solicit, bid, summon, call, ask, request, challenge.

2. Allure, attract, entice, lead, draw on, persuade, prevail upon.

Inviting, *a.* 1. Alluring, attractive, winning, engaging, captivating, pleasing, fascinating, bewitching.

2. Prepossessing, promising.

Invocation, *n.* Supplication, prayer, petition, summoning, conjuration, orison.

In vogue. Fashionable, modish, in fashion, having a run, the rage.

Invoice, *n.* List (*of articles of merchandise shipped* or *sold*), inventory, bill, schedule.

——, *v. t.* List, bill.

Invoke, *v. t.* Implore, supplicate, pray, entreat, summon, beg, beseech, importune, solicit, conjure, adjure, call upon, pray to, appeal to, prefer a request to.

Involuntary, *a.* 1. Instinctive, automatic, blind, spontaneous, mechanical, reflex, unintentional, independent of volition.

2. Unwilling, reluctant, compulsory, against one's will.

Involution, *n.* 1. Complication, intricacy, complexity, entanglement.

2. Inwrapping, infolding, infolded state, degeneration.

3. (*Math.*) Raising to a power.

4. (*Med.*) Resorption.

Involve, *v. t.* 1. Envelop, inwrap, wrap, cover, surround.

2. Include (*as a consequence*), imply, comprise, embrace, contain, lead to.

3. Entangle, implicate, inculpate, incriminate, embarrass.

4. Complicate, make intricate.

5. Join, conjoin, connect, unite, mingle, blend.

6. Twine, intwine, intertwine, interweave, interlace, inweave, intertwist, twist together.

Invulnerability, *n.* Invulnerableness.

Invulnerable, *a.* 1. Incapable of being wounded, secure from injury, that cannot be wounded.

2. Unassailable, irrefragable, invincible, incontrovertible.

Inward, *a.* Interior, internal, inner, incoming; mental, spiritual, hidden, essential; secret, private.

Inward, ⎫ *adv.* Within, inwardly, toward
Inwards, ⎭ the inside.

Inwards, *n. pl.* Entrails, bowels, viscera, intestines, insides, guts.

Inweave, *v. t.* Intwine, interweave, intertwine, interlace, weave together.

Inwrap, *v. t.* Infold, involve, cover, envelop, wrap, wrap up, absorb, engross.

Iota, *n.* Jot, whit, tittle, bit, grain, particle, atom, scrap, mite, scintilla, spark, glimmer, shadow, trace.

Ipse dixit. [L.] Mere assertion.

Irascibility, *n.* Irritability, irascibleness. See following adjective.

Irascible, *a.* Irritable, touchy, testy, waspish, cranky, quick, snappish, splenetic, petulant, choleric, hot-blooded, impatient, nettlesome, "huffish," peevish, pettish, peppery, hot, hasty, like tinder, like touchwood.

Irate, *a.* Angry, provoked, piqued, irritated, incensed, ireful, in a passion.

Ire, *n.* (*Poetical.*) Wrath, anger, rage, fury, choler, indignation, resentment, passion, exasperation.

Ireful, *a.* Angry, raging, furious, passionate, irate, incensed.

Iridescent, *a.* Rainbow-like, irisated, nacreous, opalescent, prismatic, pavonine.

Iris, *n.* 1. Rainbow.

2. (*Bot.*) Flower-de-luce, fleur-de-lis.

3. Diaphragm of the eye.

Irishism, *n.* Hibernicism, Hibernianism, Irish idiom.

Irksome, *a.* Wearisome (*in consequence of being distasteful*), tiresome, wearying, weary, devoid of interest, tedious, humdrum, burdensome, monotonous, annoying.

IRON, *a.* [*The noun is Basic Eng.*] Ferrous, ferric.

Ironical, *a.* Mocking, full of irony, sarcastic, expressing irony.

Irons, *n. pl.* Fetters, shackles, manacles, chains, hampers, gyves.

Irony, *n.* Mockery (*saying one thing and meaning the opposite*), sarcasm.

Irradiate, *v. t.* Illuminate, illumine, illume, brighten, light up, make bright, shine upon, throw light upon, cast luster upon, adorn with light.

Irrational, *a.* 1. Brutish, brute, void of reason, without reason.

2. Unreasoning, unthinking, unreasonable; absurd, preposterous, foolish, silly, unwise, injudicious, extravagant.

3. Demented, alienated (*in mind*), crazy, brainless, insane, idiotic, fantastic, lunatic, aberrant.

4. (*Math.*) Surd.

Irrationality, *n.* 1. Brutishness, want of reason.

2. Absurdity, folly, foolishness, unreasonableness.

Irreclaimable, *a.* 1. Irrecoverable, hopeless, irreparable, past cure, past hope, remediless, irretrievable, irreversible, incurable, past mending.

2. Obdurate, hardened, impenitent, incorrigible, lost, abandoned, profligate, graceless, shameless, recreant, unrepentant, reprobate.

Irreconcilable, *a.* 1. Unappeasable, inexorable, implacable, inexpiable.

2. Inconsistent, incompatible, incongruous.

Irrecoverable, *a.* 1. Irretrievable, lost forever, never to be regained.

2. Irreparable, remediless, irremediable, not to be repaired, that cannot be restored, not to be remedied.

3. Incurable, immedicable, remediless, irremedicable, hopeless, past cure, past hope, past mending.

Irrefragable, *a.* Indisputable, incontestable, irrefutable, incontrovertible, invincible, unassailable, inexpugnable, impregnable, irresistible, unanswerable, undeniable.

Irrefutable, *a.* See IRREFRAGABLE.

Irregular, *a.* 1. Anomalous, abnormal, heteromorphous, ragged, anomalistic, unusual, unconformable, aberrant, exceptional, eccentric, erratic, devious, tortuous, crooked.

2. Uncertain, unpunctual, capricious, desultory, fitful, variable, changeable, unsettled, spasmodic.

3. Immethodical, disordered, disorderly, improper, uncanonical, unparliamentary, unsystematic, desultory.

4. Unsymmetrical, asymmetric, uneven.

5. Disorderly, dissolute, loose, immoral, wild.

Irregularity, *n.* 1. Aberration, abnormity, abnormality, anomaly, anomalousness singularity.

2. Uncertainty, capriciousness, variableness, changeableness.

3. Want of method, lack of order.

4. Lack of symmetry, asymmetry.

5. Immorality, laxity, looseness, disorderliness, dissoluteness, wildness.

Irrelevancy, *a.* Inapplicability, impertinency, non-pertinency.

Irrelevant, *a.* Inapplicable, impertinent, unrelated, extraneous, inconsequent, inapposite, inappropriate, foreign, illogical, unessential, aside from the point, beside the mark, travelling out of the record.

Irreligion, *n.* Impiety, ungodliness, godlessness, atheism.

Irreligious, *a.* 1. Ungodly, undevout.

2. Profane, impious, wicked, irreverent, ribald, blasphemous, disrespectful.

Irremediable, *a.* 1. Irreparable, irrecoverable, remediless, beyond correction, beyond redress, past mending.

2. Incurable, remediless, immedicable, irremedicable, hopeless, irrecoverable, beyond cure.

Irremissible, *a.* Unpardonable, inexpiable, unatonable, not to be forgiven, obligatory, binding.

Irreparable, *a.* Irremediable, remediless, irrecoverable, irretrievable, not to be repaired.

Irreprehensible, *a.* Irreproachable, irreprovable, unblamable, blameless, faultless, inculpable, innocent, undeserving of blame or censure.

Irrepressible, *a.* Uncontrollable, insuppressible, unsmotherable, unquenchable, not to be repressed.

Irreproachable, *a.* See IRREPREHENSIBLE.

Irresistible, *a.* 1. Overpowering, overwhelming, incapable of being successfully resisted, that carries all before it.

2. Irrefragable (*which see*).

Irresolute, *a.* Undetermined, undecided, spineless, changeable, inconstant, unstable, fickle, mutable, uncertain, wavering, vacillating, unsettled, unsteady, hesitating, hesitant, faltering, infirm of purpose.

Irrespective, *a.* Regardless, without regard, independent.

Irresponsible, *a.* Unaccountable, not answerable; untrustworthy.

Irretrievable, *a.* 1. Irrecoverable, lost forever, never to be regained.

2. Irreparable, irremediable, remediless, incurable, beyond reparation, beyond repair.

Irreverence, *n.* 1. Impiety, profaneness, profanity, blasphemy, want of reverence.

2. Disrespect, disesteem, slight, want of respect.

Irreverent, *a.* 1. Impious, profane, blasphemous, irreligious.

2. Disrespectful, slighting.

Irreversible, *a.* 1. Unchangeable, unalterable, irrevocable, irrepealable.

2. Immutable, invariable, changeless.

Irrevocable, *a.* 1. Unchangeable, unalterable. See IRREVERSIBLE, 1.

2. Incapable of recall *or* revocation.

Irrigate, *v. t.* Water, moisten, wet, wash.

Irrigation, *n.* Watering.

Irritability, *n.* 1. Irascibility, fretfulness, testiness, peevishness, petulance, excitability, snappishness.

2. Susceptibility (*to the influence of a stimulus*).

3. Excitability, high susceptibility.

Irritable, *a.* 1. Irascible, fretful, testy, touchy, peevish, pettish, waspish, snappish, choleric, splenetic, captious, petulant, excitable, hot, hasty, peppery, passionate, fiery.

2. Susceptible (*to the influence of a stimulus*), responsive.

3. Excitable, highly susceptible.

Irritate, *v. t.* 1. Provoke, nettle, chafe, incense, exasperate, enrage, anger, fret, offend, vex, annoy, "rile," nag, rasp, ruffle, "jar," exacerbate; tease, gall.

2. (*Med.*) Inflame (*by friction*), excite, stimulate.

Irritation, *n.* 1. Irritating.

2. Exasperation, provocation, wrath, ire, anger, exacerbation, passion, excitement, indignation, resentment.

3. (*Med.*) Inflammation (*by friction*), itch, burn, etc., excitation, stimulation.

Irruption, *n.* 1. Bursting in, breaking in.

2. Incursion, inroad, foray, raid, partial invasion.

Islam, *n.* 1. Islamism, Mahometanism *or* Mohammedanism.

2. The Mahometans, the Moslems, the Musselmans.

ISLAND, *n.* Isle, islet, reef, atoll.

Isochronal, *a.* Isochronous, uniform in time, performed in equal times, of equal duration (*as the vibrations of a pendulum*).

Isolate, *v. t.* Separate, dissociate, detach, insulate, quarantine, segregate, place by itself, set apart.

Isolated, *a.* Detached, separate, solitary, single.

Isolation, *n.* 1. Separation, disconnection, quarantine, insulation, segregation, detachment.

2. Loneliness, solitariness, solitude.

Israelite, *n.* Jew, Hebrew.

Israelitic, } *a.* Jewish, Hebrew.
Israelitish, }

Issue, *n.* 1. Egress, exit, outlet, way out, vent, passage out; escape, sally, sortie.

2. Delivering, delivery, sending out, issuance, emergence, debouchment, emigration, emission, discharge; stream, flux, outpouring, outflow.

3. Edition, copy, number.

4. Event, consequence, end, termination, conclusion, consummation, result, effect, outcome, upshot, *dénouement*, *finale*, final *or* ultimate result, final event, finishing stroke, winding up.

5. Offspring, progeny, children, posterity, lineal descendants.

6. (*Med.*) Fontanel, artificial ulcer.

7. Antagonism, contest, controversy, controversial *or* antagonistic stand.

——, *v. t.* 1. Deliver, send out, put forth, emit, discharge.

2. Distribute, give out; publish, utter.

3. Put into circulation.

——, *v. i.* 1. Flow, flow out *or* forth, spring, spout, spurt, run, well, gush, come out, rush out.

2. Proceed, flow, emanate, arise, spring, originate, follow, ensue, come, take rise, be the effect, be derived, go forth, grow out, depart, debouch, appear, emerge, come out.

3. End, terminate, result, eventuate.

Italicism, *n.* Italian idiom, Italianism.

Italicize, *v. t.* Print in Italics, distinguished by Italics; underline; emphasize.

Italics, *n. pl.* Italic letters.

Itch, *n.* 1. Itching.

2. (*Med.*) Psora.

3. Teasing desire, uneasy hankering, importunate craving, burning.

——, *v. i.* 1. Tingle, feel itchy, have an itching sensation.

2. Feel an itching, have an itching sensation.

Itching, *n.* 1. Itch.

2. Craving, longing, teasing desire, uneasy hankering, importunate craving, burning.

Item, *adv.* [L.] Also, in like manner, as an additional article.

——, *n.* Article, particular, detail, entry, separate paragraph.

Iterate, *v. t.* Repeat, reiterate.

Itinerant, *a.* Travelling, wandering, roving, peripatetic, roaming, nomadic, going from place to place, unsettled.

Itinerary, *n.* Guide, guidebook; route, circuit.

J

Jabber, *v. i.* Prate, chatter, prattle, gabble, talk rapidly, talk idly.

Jack-a-lantern, *n.* Jack-with-a-lantern, Will-o'-the-wisp, Will-with-the-wisp, *ignis fatuus.*

Jackanapes, *n.* [Written also *Jackanape.*]
1. Monkey. See APE.
2. Beau, fop, dandy; puppy, coxcomb, impertinent fellow.

Jackass, *n.* 1. Male ass, donkey.
2. Blockhead, simpleton, dunce, dolt.

Jack-of-all-trades, *n.* Factotum, doer of all work, handy man.

Jacket, *n.* Jerkin, short coat, doublet, sack; outer covering, casing.

Jacobin, *n.* 1. Dominican, predicant, blackfriar, preaching friar, *frère prêcheur.*
2. Member of the Jacobin Club (*radical body in the French Revolution of* 1789).
3. Anarchist, red republican, turbulent demagogue, plotter, violent radical.

Jacobinic,
Jacobinical, } *a.* Turbulent, revolutionary.

Jacobite, *n.* 1. Adherent of the Stuarts *or* (*especially*) of James II.
2. Monophysite, Eutychian.

Jaculate, *v. t.* Dart, throw, launch, hurl, let fly.

Jade, *n.* 1. Hack, tired horse, worthless horse.
2. Hussy, quean, base woman, sorry wench.
3. Jade-stone, tremolite, nephritic stone, nephrite.
——, *v. t.* Tire, weary, fatigue, fag, exhaust, dull, tire out.

Jag, *n.* 1. Notch, denticulation, protuberant point.
2. (*Colloq.*) Spree.

Jagged, *a.* Notched, serrated, indented, denticulated, cleft, divided, uneven, ragged (*on the edges*).

Jahweh, *n.* JEHOVAH. See GOD.

Jail, *n.* [Written also, but not commonly, *Gaol.*] Prison, penitentiary, bridewell, workhouse, lockup, house of correction.

Jakes, *n.* (*Archaic.*) Privy, necessary, latrine, water-closet.

Jam, *v. t.* Press, crowd, squeeze tight, crush, block, wedge in, bruise.
——, *n.* 1. Conserve (*boiled in mass*), thick preserve.
2. Pressure (*from a crowd*), crowding.
3. Crowd, throng, pack, press, mass of people (*crowded together*), block, crush.

Jamb, *n.* Side-piece (*of a fireplace, a door, a window, etc.*).

Jangle, *v. i.* 1. Wrangle, squabble, bicker, chatter, gossip, talk idly, quarrel, dispute, spar, spat, jar, tiff, have words, have an altercation.
2. Clash and clang, sound harshly *or* discordantly.
——, *n.* 1. Discord, discordant sound.
2. Wrangling, jangling.

Jangled, *a.* Discordant, inharmonious, out of tune.

Jangling, *n.* Wrangling, bickering, quarrelling, altercation, jangle, jar.

Janitor, *n.* Porter, doorkeeper, *concierge*, caretaker, custodian.

Japan, *v. t.* Varnish, lacquer.

Japanese, *a.* Of Japan.
——, *n.* 1. Native of Japan.
2. Language of Japan, Japanese language.

Jar, *v. i.* 1. Vibrate harshly, grate, shake; clash, interfere.
2. Wrangle, contend, quarrel, bicker, spat, spar, jangle, squabble, tiff, have words, have an altercation.
——, *v. t.* Shake, agitate, jolt, jounce.
——, *n.* 1. Shake, agitation, jolt.
2. Crock, can, cruse, ewer.

Jargon, *n.* 1. Gabble, gibberish, rigmarole, nonsense, unintelligible talk.
2. Slang, cant, argot, "shop," lingo.
3. Confusion, disorder, jumble, chaos, disarray.

Jarring, *a.* 1. Discordant, harsh.
2. Wrangling, disagreeing, at variance.
3. Conflicting, incompatible, inconsistent.
——, *n.* 1. Clashing, collision.
2. Shaking, agitation, jar.
3. Quarrel, dispute, altercation, bickering, wrangling.

Jaundiced, *a.* 1. Bilious.
2. Biassed, prejudiced, envious; colored by prejudice.

Jaunt, *n.* Ramble, excursion, trip, tour, stroll, short journey.

Jaunty, *a.* Airy, showy, finical, fluttering, bedizened, garish, gay, fine; unconcerned, sprightly.

Jaw, *n.* 1. Maxillary bone, jaw-bone.
2. (*Low.*) Vituperation, abusive talk.
3. Wall (*of a pass*), enclosing crag, throat.

Jaws, *n. pl.* 1. Chaps, mouth.
2. Walls, enclosing walls *or* crags, craggy opening, throat.

Jaw-tooth, *n.* Grinder, molar.

Jealous, *a.* 1. Envious (*especially at being supplanted in the affections of another*), enviously suspicious, resentful at preference, distrustful, suspicious in love.

2. Anxious, apprehensive, solicitous, zealous, intolerant.

3. Watchful, suspiciously vigilant.

Jealousy, *n.* 1. Suspicion, envy, envious suspicion (*especially in matters of love*).

2. Watchfulness, vigilance, suspicious vigilance.

Jeer, *v. i.* Sneer, scoff, flout, mock, gibe, fleer, jape, "hit," taunt, jest, "hoot," ridicule, rail.

——, *v. t.* Flout, taunt, deride, ridicule, mock, gibe, scoff, spurn, despise, contemn, chaff at, sneer at, jeer at, rail at, gibe at, crook the finger at.

——, *n.* Sneer, scoff, taunt, gibe, biting jest, fling, quip, sarcasm, flout.

Jehovah, *n.* See GOD.

Jejune, *a.* Barren, meagre, sterile, dry, bare, insipid, lean, uninteresting.

JELLY, *n.* Aspic, gelatin.

Jeopard, *v. t.* Hazard, imperil, peril, endanger, jeopardize, risk, put in jeopardy, put at hazard, put at risk.

Jeopardize, *v. t.* [*Recent.*] Hazard, endanger. See JEOPARD.

Jeopardy, *n.* Hazard, danger, peril, risk, venture.

Jeremiad, *n.* Tale of woe, lamentation, lament, dolorous tirade.

Jerk, *v. t.* Yerk, twitch, pull suddenly, flip, "yank," hitch, tweak, pluck.

Jerkin, *n.* Jacket, short coat.

Jest, *v. i.* Joke, crack a joke, perpetrate a joke, "jolly," quiz, banter.

——, *n.* 1. Joke, quip, quirk, crank, witticism, sally, *jeu d'esprit*, gag, pleasantry.

2. Raillery, fun, sport, prank.

Jester, *n.* 1. Joker, wag, humorist.

2. Buffoon, harlequin, zany, droll, fool, clown, punch, punchinello, scaramouch, merry-andrew, jack-pudding, pickle-herring.

Jesuitical, *a.* 1. Of the Jesuits.

2. [*A sense introduced by partisans hostile to the Jesuits.*] Crafty, cunning, wily, deceitful, designing, sophistical, double, double-faced, full of chicane, Machiavelian.

Jetty, *n.* Mole.

Jeu d'esprit. [Fr.] Joke, jest, quirk, quip, crank, sally, witticism, *mot.*

Jew, *n.* Hebrew, Israelite.

JEWEL, *n.* Gem, brilliant, precious stone, treasure.

Jewelry, *n.* Jewels, bijouterie, trinkets.

Jewish, *a.* Hebrew, Judaic, Judaical, Israelitish.

Jewry, *n.* Judea, Israel, ghetto.

Jezebel, *n.* Fury, Gorgon, brazen woman, virago, she-monster, abandoned woman, painted woman.

Jiffy, *n.* (*Colloq.*) Instant, moment, second, twinkling, trice, flash, twinkling of an eye.

Jilt, *n.* Coquette, flirt, light-o'-love.

——, *v. t.* Trick *or* deceive (*by playing the jilt*), desert, cast off.

Jingle, *v. i.* Tinkle, clink, chink, jangle.

——, *n.* Tinkling, jingling, jingling sound, tintinnabulation; catchy repetition in verse.

Job, *n.* Piece of work, work, chore, stint; business, affair; situation, employment.

——, *v. i.* Do job-work, work at jobs; sublet work, buy and sell.

Jockey, *n.* 1. Horse-jockey, dealer in horses.

2. Cheat, swindler, sharper, rogue, trickster, knave, impostor, blackleg, shark.

——, *v. t.* Cheat, trick, deceive, gull, dupe, over-reach, cozen, chouse, outwit, bamboozle, circumvent, delude, hoodwink, beguile, mislead, inveigle, gammon, impose upon, "humbug."

Jocose, *a.* Jocular, facetious, humorous, witty, jesting, waggish, droll, funny, comical, sportive, merry.

Jocular, *a.* See JOCOSE.

Jocularity, *n.* Jocoseness, facetiousness, waggishness, waggery, drollery, sportiveness, merriment, pleasantry, mirth, fun.

Jocund, *a.* Joyous, joyful, merry, frolicsome, cheerful, blithe, blithesome, sportive, jolly, playful, airy, lively, gay, debonair.

Jocundity, *n.* Joyousness, joyfulness, cheerfulness, hilarity, sprightliness, exhilaration, liveliness, vivacity, sportfulness, frolicsomeness, blithesomeness, jocularity, gayety, merriment, mirth, good-humor, high spirits, high glee.

Jog, *v. t.* Push (*gently*), jostle, nudge, notify by a push, remind, notify, warn.

——, *v. i.* Trot slowly, trudge.

——, *n.* 1. Push, slight shake, reminder.

2. Notch, denticulation, jag.

Joggle, *v. t.* Shake (*by hitting*), jostle.

Jog-trot, *n.* Slow pace, slow trot.

Johnny-cake, *n.* Hoe-cake, corn-cake.

JOIN, *v. t.* [*The noun is Basic Eng.*]

1. Add, annex, attach, append.

2. Connect, couple, combine, conjoin, link, yoke, dovetail, miter, cement, unite, unite together, join together; marry, unite in matrimony, wed, "splice."

3. Adjoin, be adjacent to, connect with, open into, be connected with.

4. Unite with, associate one's self with, affiliate with, go into, take part in *or* with, take one's place in, meet, come to meet.

——, *v. i.* Associate, confederate, unite, assemble, consolidate, merge, amalgamate, be united, league.

Joint, *n.* 1. Juncture, union, junction, connection, mortise, hinge, splice.

2. Seam, commissure.

3. (*Anat.*) Articulation.

4. (*Bot.*) Knot.

5. (*Bot.*) Internode, space between two joints.

——, *a.* United, combined, concerted, conjoint, concurrent.

——, *v. t.* 1. (*Carpentry.*) Join, unite, fit together.

2. Disjoint, divide (*at the joints*), cut up (*as meat*).

Jointed, *a.* Articulated, with joints.

Jointly, *adv.* Unitedly, together, conjointly, in conjunction.

Joke, *n.* Jest, quip, quirk, crank, witticism, sally, *jeu d'esprit*; laughing stock.

——, *v. i.* Jest, crack a joke, banter, "josh," rally, perpetrate a joke.

Joker, *n.* Jester, wag, humorist; extra card in the pack.

Jollification, *n.* (*Colloq.*) Conviviality, revelry, festivity, carouse, carousal, revel, compotation, potation, wassail, merry frolic, jolly time, merry-making, drinking-bout, "spree."

Jollity, *n.* Merriment, gayety, mirth, fun, frolic, festivity, joviality, hilarity.

Jolly, *a.* 1. Merry, joyous, joyful, gay, jovial, airy, mirthful, jocund, playful, frolicsome, sportive, gamesome, funny, facetious, jocular, waggish, sprightly, lively, blithe, blithesome, cheery, cheerful.

2. Plump, stout, lusty, bouncing, portly, chubby, in good case.

Jolt, *v. i.* Be shaken (*as a wagon by passing over rough ground*).

——, *v. t.* Shake, shock.

——, *n.* Shaking, jolting, jar, jounce.

Jolthead, *n.* Simpleton, fool. See DUNCE.

Jostle, *v. t.* 1. Collide, strike against, hit against.

2. Shake (*by hitting*), joggle, shove, elbow, shoulder, hustle.

Jot, *n.* Iota, tittle, whit, bit, grain, particle, atom, scrap, mite, ace, corpuscle, scintilla

Jot down, *v. t.* Record, state, note, chronicle, register, set down, take down, note down, make a note of, make a memorandum of.

Jotting, *n.* Memorandum, note.

Journal, *n.* 1. Diary, daily register, day-book, log.

2. Newspaper, magazine, periodical, gazette.

Journalize, *v. t.* Record, register, note, chronicle, set down, jot down.

JOURNEY, *n.* Travel (*by land*), tour, excursion, trip, expedition, jaunt, peregrination, voyage, pilgrimage, passage.

——, *v. i.* 1. Travel, ramble, roam, rove, take a tour, make a tour, take a trip, make an excursion.

2. Travel, go, proceed, fare.

Journeyman, *n.* 1. Day-laborer.

2. Hired mechanic.

Joust, *n.* Tilt.

——, *v. i.* 1. Tilt.

2. [Written also *Just.*] Jostle, push, jar.

Jove, *n.* (*Mythol.*) Jupiter.

Jovial, *a.* Merry, joyous, gay, airy, mirthful, convivial, jolly, festive. See JOYFUL.

Joviality, *n.* Merriment, gayety, mirth, fun, frolic, jollity, hilarity.

Joy, *n.* 1. Gladness, delight, glee, exultation, pleasure, ecstasy, rapture, ravishment, transport, beatitude, beatification.

2. Happiness, felicity, bliss.

3. Cause of gladness, delight, happiness, merriment, festivity, hilarity.

——, *v. i.* Exult, rejoice, be glad, be delighted, be joyful.

Joyful, *a.* Glad, joyous, merry, buoyant, happy, jocund, blithe, blithesome, jolly, jovial, delighted, elate, elated.

Joyous, *a.* Glad. See JOYFUL.

Jubilant, *a.* Rejoicing, exulting, exultant, triumphing, triumphant, shouting with joy.

Jubilee, *n.* Season of rejoicing, anniversary, festival.

Judaic,
Judaical, } *a.* Jewish, Hebrew, Israelitish.

Judaism, *n.* Religion of the Jews, Jewish religion.

JUDGE, *n.* 1. Justice, bencher, arbiter, arbitrator, umpire, referee, magistrate, adjudicator, justiciar, moderator.

2. Critic, connoisseur.

——, *v. i.* Decide, determine, conclude, pronounce, decree, pass an opinion, pass judgment, get at the truth, sit in judgment.

——, *v. t.* 1. Try, doom, condemn, pass sentence upon, adjudicate, arbitrate, umpire, sentence.

2. Consider, regard, think, esteem, reckon, account, deem, believe, hold, suppose, imagine, decide, apprehend, measure, think, guess.

3. Appreciate, estimate, form an opinion about.

Judgment, *n.* 1. Discernment, understanding, discretion, judiciousness, wit, circumspection, sensibility, intelligence, discrimination, taste, sagacity, penetration, wisdom, brains, prudence, ballast, depth, sense, mother-wit, quick parts, common-sense, good sense.

2. Determination, decision, conclusion, consideration, estimation, thought, opinion, notion, estimate.

3. (*Law.*) Sentence, award, decree, adjudication, doom, arbitration, condemnation, censure.

4. (*Log.*) Sentence, proposition.

Judgment-day, *n.* Day of judgment, the last day, doomsday, *Dies Iræ.*

Judgment-seat, *n.* Tribunal, court, bar, bench, throne of God. .

Judicature, *n.* 1. Administration of justice.

2. Jurisdiction.

Judicial, *a.* Juridical, forensic, legal, judiciary, judicatory, juristic.

Judiciary, *n.* Body of judges, courts, judicial department, department of justice.

Judicious, *a.* Sensible, wise, prudent, discreet, discriminating, critical, cautious, considerate, rational, reasonable, enlightened, sagacious, provident, sober, sound, staid, solid, cool, politic, well-considered, well-chosen.

Jug, *n.* Pitcher, ewer, cruse, vessel; (*colloq.*) prison, gaol.

Juggle, *v. i.* 1. Conjure, play tricks, practise jugglery, practise legerdemain.

2. Practise artifice, practise imposture, cheat.

Juggler, *n.* Prestidigitator, sleight-of-hand man; deceiver, cheat.

Jugglery, *n.* 1. Legerdemain, prestidigitation, sleight of hand, conjury.

2. Trickery, imposture, deceit.

Juice, *n.* 1. Sap.

2. Fluid part, fluid, extract, liquid.

Juiceless, *a.* 1. Sapless.

2. Dry, arid.

Juicy, *a.* Succulent, moist, watery, sappy, lush, full of juice.

Jumble, *v. t.* Mix confusedly, throw together in disorder, confuse, mix up, huddle.

——, *n.* Disorder, confusion, hodge-podge, hotch-potch, gallimaufry, olio, olla-podrida, confused mass, disorderly mixture.

Jump, *v. t.* Jump over, leap over, skip over, pass by a leap, vault, clear.

——, *v. i.* Leap, spring, bound, skip, hop, bounce, vault, caper.

JUMP, *n.* Leap, spring, bound, hop, vault, caper.

Junction, *n.* 1. Joining, union, combination, seam, connection, linking, coupling, hook-up.

2. Juncture, joint, conjunction, place of meeting.

Juncture, *n.* 1. Joint, junction, union.

2. Conjuncture, crisis, exigency, emergency, contingency, pass, predicament, pinch, quandary, strait.

Jungle, *n.* Thicket (*of brushwood, shrubs, and woods*), brake.

Junior, *a.* Younger.

Junket, *n.* 1. Sweetmeat, delicacy, pudding.

2. Feast, entertainment.

——, *v. i.* Feast, banquet, indulge in feasting.

——, *v. t.* Feast, entertain, regale.

Junto, *n.* Cabal, faction, combination (*against a government*), party, coterie, clique, set, gang, league, confederacy, secret council.

Juridical, *a.* Judicial, forensic, legal.

Jurisconsult, *n.* Jurist, civilian, counsellor, lawyer.

Jurisdiction, *n.* Judicature, extent of authority, legal power, authority; sphere, range, compass, reach, circuit, control, province.

Jurist, *n.* Civilian, jurisconsult, lawyer, counsellor.

Juror, *n.* Juryman.

Just, *a.* 1. Equitable, right, rightful, lawful, well-founded, legitimate, reasonable.

2. Fair, fair-minded, candid, even-handed, impartial.

3. Honest, upright, righteous, blameless, pure, "white," "square," conscientious, uncorrupt, virtuous, honorable, good, straightforward.

4. Exact, true, proper, accurate, correct, normal, regular.

5. Deserved, merited, condign, suitable, due.

6. Appropriate, fit, suitable, happy.

——, *adv.* Exactly, precisely, neither more nor less, almost; a moment ago; barely, by a little; simply, very, quite.

Justice, *n.* 1. Equity, equitableness, right, justness, fairness, impartiality, fair play, honesty, lawfulness, accuracy.

2. Judge, justiciary, justiciar.

Justifiable, *a.* Defensible, warrantable, vindicable, right, fit, proper.

Justification, *n.* 1. Vindication, defence, warrant, reason, excuse, exculpation, exoneration.

2. (*Theol.*) Absolution, remission of sin.

Justify, *v. t.* 1. Vindicate, warrant, defend, support, approve, maintain, exculpate, excuse, exonerate, set right.

2. (*Theol.*) Absolve, acquit, free from sin, excuse, clear from guilt.

3. (*Printing.*) Adjust.

Justness, *n.* 1. Justice, equity, equitableness, fairness, right.

2. Propriety, fitness, suitableness.

3. Exactness, accuracy, precision.

Jut, *v. i.* Project, protrude, stand out, jut out.

Juvenile, *a.* 1. Young, youthful, childish, puerile, immature.

2. Suited to youth, intended for youth.

Juxtaposition, *n.* Proximity, contiguity, contact, adjacency.

K

Keen, *a.* 1. Eager, zealous, ardent, earnest, intense, vivid, fervid, vehement.

2. Sharp, acute, with a fine edge.

3. Piercing, penetrating, cutting.

4. Severe, bitter, poignant, acrimonious, pungent, caustic, sarcastic, biting.

5. Shrewd, discerning, quick, sagacious, intelligent, astute, keen-sighted, keen-eyed, clear-sighted, sharp-sighted, long-headed.

Keen-eyed, *a.* Keen, keen-sighted, sharp-sighted.

Keenness, *n.* 1. Ardor, vehemence, eagerness, earnestness, fervor, zest.

2. Sharpness, acuteness.

3. Severity, rigor, sternness.

4. Causticity, acrimony, asperity, bitterness, pungency.

5. Poignancy, acuteness, bitterness.

6. Shrewdness, sagacity, astuteness.

Keen-sighted, *a.* Keen, sharp-sighted, keen-eyed.

KEEP, *v. t.* 1. Retain, detain, hold, hold fast, possess.

2. Preserve, maintain, continue.

3. Restrain, withhold, reserve, detain, confine.

4. Guard, protect, preserve, take care of, tend, attend.

5. Fulfil, observe, adhere to, be faithful to, be true to, stand by.

6. Celebrate, honor, solemnize, commemorate, observe, perform, do honor to.

7. Sustain, support, maintain.

8. Preserve, store, store up, lay away, save, husband.

——, *v. i.* 1. Continue, remain, persist.

2. Stay, abide, lodge, dwell.

3. Endure, last.

——, *n.* Stronghold, donjon; maintenance, support.

Keep an eye on. Watch, mark, observe.

Keep dark. Keep one's own counsel, seal the lips, not breathe a syllable about it, keep the matter to one's self, be silent, be secret.

Keeper, *n.* Curator, custodian, conservator, warden, warder, watchman.

Keeping, *n.* 1. Care, custody, charge, guard, guardianship; possession.

2. Support, maintenance, feed.

3. Harmony, conformity, congruity, consistency, agreement.

Keepsake, *n.* Memento, souvenir, token.

Ken, *n.* View, cognizance, sight, field of vision, field of knowledge.

Kennel, *n.* 1. Dog-house.

2. Pack of hounds.

3. Hole (*of a wild animal*), haunt; gutter.

——, *v. i.* Dwell (*as a dog*), lodge, harbor, take shelter.

KETTLE, *n.* Cauldron; tea-kettle.

KEY, *n.* 1. Lock opener.

2. Clew, guide, explanation, solution, elucidation, *clavis*, translation, "pony," "crib."

3. (*Mus.*) Tonic, key-note, fundamental note, first note of the scale.

4. Wedge, clamp; lever.

Key-note, *n.* Tonic. See KEY, 3.

KICK, *v. t.* [*The noun is Basic Eng.*] Calcitrate, punt, spurn.

Kick the beam. Be outweighed, be overbalanced.

Kick up a dust. (*Colloq.*) Make a commotion, create an excitement, make a stir.

Kid, *n.* 1. Young goat.

2. (*Colloq.*) Child.

Kidnap, *v. t.* Abduct (*any human being*), carry off, steal away, run off with.

Kill, *v. t.* Slay, slaughter, murder, despatch, massacre, smite down, do to death, put to death, deprive of life, make away with, give one his quietus. See ASSASSINATE.

Kilt, *n.* Fillibeg.

Kin, *n.* 1. Relationship (*by blood* or *by marriage*), consanguinity.

2. Relations, relatives, kindred, kinsfolk, siblings, connections.

——, *a.* Related, allied, kindred, akin, cognate, of the same nature, of the same kind, of the same family.

KIND, *a.* Benevolent, beneficent, benignant, humane, gracious, friendly, brotherly, kindly, complaisant, bland, generous, obliging, bounteous, accommodating, compassionate, mild, benign, clement, good, good-natured, amiable, charitable, gentle, lenient, indulgent, forbearing, tender, sympathetic, tender-hearted, kind-hearted.

——, *n.* 1. Race, genus, family, breed, species, set, class, type, genre, caste.

2. Sort, nature, character, manner, description, style, denomination, brand, form, make, stamp, "stripe," strain, persuasion, color, character.

Kind-hearted, *a.* Tender-hearted. See KIND.

Kindle, *v. t.* 1. Light, ignite, enkindle, inflame, set fire to, set on fire.

2. Excite, rouse, awaken, provoke, incite, stimulate, animate, whet, stir up, foment.

3. Exasperate, excite, provoke, enrage.

——, *v. i.* 1. Take fire, catch.

2. Get excited, grow warm, fly into a passion.

3. Fire, glow, warm, thrill, stir, start, quicken, become impassioned.

Kindliness, *n.* 1. Benignity, kindness, benevolence, humanity, charity, sympathy, compassion, amiability, kind-heartedness, good-nature, good feeling, fellow-feeling.

2. Mildness, softness, gentleness.

Kindly, *a.* 1. Natural, homogeneal, congenial, kindred, proper, appropriate.

2. Sympathetic, benevolent, gracious, well-disposed, friendly, considerate, humane. See KIND.

——, *adv.* Affectionately, with good-will, in kindness.

Kindness, *n.* 1. Benevolence, beneficence, benignity, humanity, generosity, philanthropy, charity, kindliness, sympathy, tenderness, mildness, grace, goodness, amiability, fellow-feeling, clemency, good feeling.

2. Kind act, good turn, kind office, favor, charity, benefaction.

Kindred, *n.* 1. Relationship, affinity, consanguinity, flesh.

2. Relations, relatives, kin, kinsfolk, kinsmen, family, "folks," kith and kin.

——, *a.* Related, cognate, allied, kin, akin, connected, of the same kind, of the same nature, of the same family; congenial, sympathetic.

King, *n.* Sovereign, monarch.

Kingdom, *n.* 1. Sovereignty, empire, dominion, supremacy, sovereign power, rule, monarchy, supreme power.

2. Dominion(s), realm(s).

3. Tract, region.

4. Division, department, realm, domain, province.

Kingly, *a.* 1. Royal, regal, monarchical, kinglike, sovereign, imperial.

2. Noble, august, imposing, splendid, magnificent, grand, majestic, regal, imperial, royal, glorious.

Kingship, *n.* Royalty, monarchy, sovereignty.

Kink, *n.* 1. Twist, knot, curl, loop, entanglement; cramp, crick.

2. Whim, crotchet, wrinkle.

Kinsfolk, *n.* Relations, relatives, kin, kindred, kinsmen, kith and kin.

Kiss, *v. t.* 1. Salute, greet with a kiss.

2. Caress with the lips, press one's lips upon, osculate, "peck," "smack."

KISS, *n.* 1. Salute.

2. Caress (*with the lips*), osculation.

Kit, *n.* Outfit, working implements, set.

Kleptomania, *n.* Klopemania, propensity to steal, mania for stealing.

Knack, *n.* 1. See KNICKNACK.

2. Dexterity, adroitness, dextrousness, skill, ability, skilfulness, facility, aptness, aptitude, quickness, readiness, address, expertness.

Knarl, *n.* Knot, knob, snag.

Knave, *n.* 1. Villain, rascal, scoundrel, rogue, miscreant, cheat, caitiff, swindler, sharper, trickster, scamp, scapegrace.

2. Jack (*of cards*).

Knavery, *n.* Villainy, rascality, fraud, knavishness, dishonesty, criminality, trickery, scoundrelism.

Knavish, *a.* Dishonest, unprincipled, villainous, rascally, scoundrelly, fraudulent, trickish, tricky, roguish.

KNEE, *n.* (*Basic Eng.*)

Kneepan, *n.* Patella.

Knell, *n.* Death-bell, passing-bell, signal of doom *or* death.

——, *v. i.* Knoll, sound warningly, sound with doom, ring, toll.

Knick-knack, *n.* Toy, trifle, plaything, gimcrack, gewgaw, bawble, knack, jiggumbob (*comic*).

KNIFE, *n.* Jackknife, lance, cutting instrument.

Knight, *n.* 1. Cavalier, chevalier, horseman.

2. Partisan, champion.

3. Lover, gallant.

Knight-errantry, *n.* Chivalry, knighthood; quixotic act.

Knighthood, *n.* Chivalry, knight-errantry.

Knit, *v. t.* Join, unite, connect, weave, interlace.

Knob, *n.* 1. Protuberance, boss, bunch, hunch, lump, stud.

2. Handle (*of a door*).

Knock, *n.* 1. Rap (*as at a door*), clap, stroke.

2. Blow, slap, cuff, buffet, box.

——, *v. i.* Rap (*as at a door*), rattle.

——, *v. t.* Beat, strike, hit, bump, slap.

Knock down. Fell, prostrate.

Knock off. (*Colloq.*) Stop, quit.

Knoll, *n.* Hillock, mound.

KNOT, *n.* 1. Entanglement, complication.

2. Tie, connection, bond of union.

3. Joint, node, knag.

4. Tuft, bunch, rosette.

5. Group, band, clique, gang, crew, squad, cluster, set, pack.

6. Nautical mile.

——, *v. t.* Entangle, tie, complicate, kink, weave, gnarl.

Knotty, *a.* 1. Knotted, gnarled, full of knots, knaggy, knurly, hard, rough, rugged.

2. Intricate, difficult, perplexing, embarrassing, hard, troublesome, involved, complex.

Know, *v. t.* 1. Perceive, apprehend, cognize, see, comprehend, understand, discern, be aware of, be assured of, be sure *or* certain of, see through, make out.

2. Recognize.

3. Be acquainted with, have an acquaintance with, be familiar with, "wot of."

4. Distinguish, discriminate.

——, *v. i.* 1. Have knowledge, cognize, exercise cognition.

2. Be informed, be made aware.

3. Be sure, feel certain.

Knowing, *a.* 1. Intelligent, skilful, competent, qualified, experienced, accomplished, proficient, well-informed.

2. Conscious, intelligent, percipient, thinking, cognizant, aware, sensible.

3. Expressive, significant, cunning.

KNOWLEDGE, *n.* 1. Apprehension, comprehension, perception, understanding, discernment, judgment, wit.

2. Learning, erudition, scholarship, enlightenment, lore, acquirements, attainments, information, mastery, command, cunning, skill, science, acquaintance, familiarity.

3. Cognizance, cognition, notice, information, ken, consciousness, recognition, prescience.

Knuckle, *v. i.* Yield (*obsequiously*), submit, cringe, stoop, crouch, give up, "knuckle under."

Knurly, *a.* Knotty, knotted, gnarled.

L

Labor, *n.* 1. Toil, work, exertion, effort, pains, industry, drudgery.

2. Travail, parturition, childbirth, delivery.

——, *v. i.* 1. Toil, strive, drudge, work, exert one's self, take pains.

2. Suffer, be afflicted, be distressed.

3. Travail, be in travail, be in labor.

Labored, *a.* Overwrought, forced, stiff, heavy, smelling of the lamp.

Laborer, *n.* Workman, operative, artisan, artificer, craftsman, "hand," mechanic.

Laborious, *a.* 1. Industrious, sedulous, assiduous, toiling, hard-working, painstaking. See DILIGENT.

2. Difficult, arduous, onerous, toilsome, tiresome, wearisome, fatiguing, irksome, hard, Herculean.

Labyrinth, *n.* Maze, perplexity, intricacy.

Labyrinthian, *a.* Mazy, confused, perplexed, intricate, involved, many-winding, labyrinthal, labyrinthine.

Labyrinthic, } *a.* Labyrinthiform, laby-
Labyrinthical, } rinthine.

Lacerate, *v. t.* 1. Tear, sever, mangle, rend, lancinate, laniate, claw, tear asunder, tear to pieces.

2. Harrow, wound, torture, rend.

Lack, *v. t.* Want, need, be in want of, be in need of, be destitute of, be without.

——, *v. i.* 1. Be in want.

2. Be wanting.

——, *n.* Need, deficiency, destitution, want, scantiness, insufficiency, scarcity, dearth, default, defectiveness, shortness, shortcoming, deficit.

Lackadaisical, *a.* Sentimental, Wertherish, die-away, languishing, affectedly pensive, "lackadaisy."

Lackaday, *interj.* Alas, well-a-day, alack, woe's the day.

Lackey, *n.* Footman, footboy, flunky, valet.

——, *v. t.* Attend (*as a servant*), wait on, dance attendance on.

Laconic, *a.* Short, brief, concise, succinct, compact, sententious, terse, pithy.

Lacquer, *v. t.* Varnish (*with lacquer*), japan.

Lactescence, *n.* 1. Milkiness, milky color.

2. (*Bot.*) Bleeding, effusion of sap.

Lad, *n.* Boy, stripling, youngster, youth, schoolboy, younker, young man.

Lade, *v. t.* 1. Load, freight.

2. Dip, bale.

Lading, *n.* Freight, cargo, load, burden.

Lady, *n.* 1. Mistress, matron.

2. Woman of rank, woman of distinction.

3. Woman of refinement, well-bred woman.

4. Wife, spouse.

Ladylike, *a.* Genteel, courtly, refined, well-bred.

Lady-love, *n.* Sweetheart, flame, mistress.

Lag, *v. i.* Loiter, linger, saunter, fall behind, move slowly, delay.

Laggard, *n.* Loiterer, lingerer, idler, saunterer, lagger.

Lagoon, *n.* Lake (*shallow and communicating with the sea*), bayou, sound.

Laic,
Laical, } *a.* Lay, secular.

Lair, *n.* Couch (*of a beast*), resting-place, den, burrow, form.

Laity, *n.* Laymen, body of the people, the people (*as distinguished from the clergy*).

Lambent, *a.* 1. Playing about (*like the tongue in licking*), touching lightly, gliding over, licking.

2. Gleaming, flickering, twinkling.

Lame, *a.* 1. Crippled, halt, hobbling, limping.

2. Insufficient, unsatisfactory, weak, feeble, poor.

——, *v. t.* Cripple, make lame, disable, hobble.

Lamella, *n.* [L.] Scale, lamina, layer, coat, flake, coating, thin plate.

Lamellar, *a.* Lamellate, lamellated, laminar, laminated, foliated, foliaceous, scaly, flaky, schistose.

Lament, *v. i.* Mourn, grieve, weep, sorrow, wail, moan, complain.

——, *v. t.* 1. Bewail, deplore, bemoan, mourn, sorrow over *or* for.

2. Regret, deplore.

——, *n.* 1. Wailing, moaning, moan, lamentation, plaint, complaint.

2. Dirge, elegy, epicedium, mournful song, funeral song.

Lamentable, *a.* 1. Deplorable, grievous, to be lamented, woeful, doleful, melancholy.

2. Pitiful, contemptible, miserable, poor, low.

Lamentation, *n.* Wailing, moaning, moan, plaint, complaint, lament, ululation, hubbuboo.

Laminated, *a.* See LAMELLAR.

Lampoon, *n.* Pasquinade, satire, squib.

——, *v. t.* Satirize, ridicule, lash.

Lance, *n.* Spear, javelin.

——, *v. t.* 1. Hurl, throw, launch, dart, send, fling, toss, pitch, jaculate, let fly.

2. Pierce, cut with a lancet.

Lance-shaped, *a.* Lanciform, lanceolate, lanceolated.

Lancinate, *v. t.* Tear, rend, sever, mangle, lacerate, laniate, claw, tear to pieces.

Lancinating, *a.* Piercing, darting, cutting.

LAND, *n.* 1. Ground, soil, earth.

2. Country, district, tract, region, weald, reservation.

——, *v. t.* Disembark, debark, put on shore, set on shore.

——, *v. i.* Disembark, debark, go on shore, come to land.

Landing, *n.* 1. Coming to land, disembarking, debarking.

2. Landing-place.

Landlord, *n.* 1. Owner, proprietor.

2. Host, inn-keeper.

Landscape, *n.* View, prospect, scene, rural scene.

Lane, *n.* Alley, narrow street, narrow passage *or* way.

LANGUAGE, *n.* 1. Speech, tongue, dialect, vernacular.

2. Speech, power *or* faculty of speech, utterance.

3. Style, expression, phraseology, diction, idiom, parlance, slang, form of expression.

4. Expression, utterance, voice.

Languid, *a.* 1. Faint, exhausted, drooping, pining, languishing, flagging, weak, feeble.

2. Dull, torpid, listless, spiritless, heartless, lukewarm, heavy, inactive, slow, sluggish.

Languidness, *n.* 1. Languor, faintness, feebleness, lassitude.

2. Dullness, listlessness, heaviness, heartlessness.

Languish, *v. i.* 1. Droop, pine, faint, fade, wither, decline, fail, sink, sicken, become feeble, pine away, waste away.

2. Look tender, have the air of a lover.

Languishment, *n.* 1. Feebleness, decline, weakness, drooping, pining, withering, wasting.

2. Look of tenderness.

Languor, *n.* 1. Feebleness, debility, languidness, faintness, languishment.

2. Dullness, torpidness, listlessness, heartlessness, heaviness, *ennui.*

Lank, *a.* Lean, thin, meagre, attenuated, slim, slender, starveling, skinny, scraggy, gaunt, emaciated.

Lap, *v. t.* 1. Fold, turn over, lay over.

2. Wrap, cover, twist round.

3. Lick, lick up, take up with the tongue.

——, *v. i.* Be folded over, be laid over, reach over.

Lapidary, *n.* Lapidist, stoneworker.

Lapidescence, *n.* Lapidification, petrifaction.

Lapse, *n.* 1. Flow, gliding, flowing, smooth course.

2. Fall, decline, declension, falling off.

3. Slip, fault, error, shortcoming, misstep, indiscretion.

——, *v. i.* 1. Slip, glide, slide, sink, pass slowly.

2. Fail in duty, commit a fault, fall from innocence.

3. (*Law.*) Become void.

Larboard, *n.* (*Naut.*) Port, left-hand side.

Larceny, *n.* Theft, stealing, pilfering, robbery, thievery.

Lard, *v. t.* 1. Grease.

2. Dress with bacon.

3. Intermix, interlay, interlard.

Large, *a.* 1. Big, great, bulky, huge, immense, elephantine, colossal, heroic, vast, of great size.

2. Extensive, expanded, spacious, broad, wide.

3. Abundant, plentiful, ample, full, copious, liberal.

4. Capacious, comprehensive.

5. Comprehensive, broad, wide, liberal, generous.

Large-bellied, *a.* Abdominous, big-bellied, pot-bellied, paunchy.

Largess, *n.* Bounty, present, donation, gift, endowment, grant, bequest.

Lariat, *n.* Lasso.

Larva, *n.* Caterpillar, grub, worm, slug.

Lascivious, *a.* Lustful, lecherous, libidinous, lickerish, salacious, concupiscent, lubric, lubricous, lewd, prurient, wanton, loose, unchaste, incontinent, sensual, goatish.

Lash, *n.* 1. Thong (*of a whip*), scourge, whip.

2. Stroke, stripe.

——, *v. t.* 1. Scourge, whip, flog, castigate, chastise, swinge, beat, "beat up," flagellate.

2. Beat, beat against.

3. Bind, tie, tie together.

4. See ABUSE.

Lass, *n.* Girl, damsel, maiden, lassie, miss.

Lassitude, *n.* Weariness, exhaustion, fatigue, prostration, languor, languidness.

Lasso, *n.* Lariat.

LAST, *a.* 1. Latest.

2. Hindmost, hindermost.

3. Final, ultimate.

4. Highest, greatest, utmost, extreme.

——, *adv.* 1. The last time.

2. After all the rest.

3. Finally, in conclusion.

——, *v. i.* 1. Endure, remain, continue.

2. Hold out, be unexhausted, be unconsumed.

Lasting, *a.* Enduring, permanent, abiding, durable, perdurable, perennial, fixed, stable, of long continuance.

Lastly, *adv.* Finally, in fine, at last, at length, in the end, in conclusion.

LATE, *a.* 1. Slow, tardy, behindhand, overdue, long delayed.

2. Far advanced.

3. Recently deceased.

4. Recent.

——, *adv.* 1. Tardily, after the proper time, at the eleventh hour, a day after the fair.

2. Recently, lately, not long ago, sometime, sometime since.

Lately, *adv.* Recently, latterly, late, of late, not long ago.

LATENT, *a.* Concealed, hidden, secret, occult, veiled, unseen, abeyant.

Lather, *n.* Foam (*of soap and water*), froth.

Latitude, *n.* 1. Extent, range, scope, amplitude, compass.

2. Freedom, liberty, indulgence, free play.

3. Laxity, loose interpretation, indefinite meaning.

4. (*Geog.*) Angular distance from the equator.

5. (*Astron.*) Angular distance from the ecliptic.

Latitudinarian, *a.* Liberal to an extreme (*in opinion*), over-liberal, loose, lax, freethinking, over-tolerant.

Latter, *a.* 1. Last mentioned (*of two*).

2. Recent, modern.

Latterly, *adv.* Lately, recently, of late.

Lattice, *n.* Trellis, lattice-work, grating, espalier.

Laud, *v. t.* Praise, extol, celebrate, magnify.

Laudable, *a.* Commendable, praiseworthy.

Laudation, *n.* Praise, commendation, eulogy, compliment, encomium.

Laudatory, *a.* 1. Commendatory, panegyrical, praiseful, eulogistic, complimentary, encomiastic, adulatory, flattering.

2. Lavish *or* extravagant of praise.

LAUGH, *n.* Laughter, cachinnation. See the verb.

——, *v. i.* Cachinnate, giggle, guffaw, snicker, chuckle, "chortle," cackle, titter, snigger.

Laughable, *a.* Comical, droll, funny, ludicrous, farcical, ridiculous.

Laugh at. Ridicule, deride, mock, scoff, scoff at, sneer at, laugh to scorn, make fun of, poke fun at.

Laughing, *a.* Merry, mirthful, gay, gleeful.

Laughing-stock, *n.* Butt (*of jests*), object of ridicule.

Launch, *v. t.* 1. Throw, hurl, cast, dart, lance.

2. Slide from the stocks (*as a ship*).

——, *v. i.* Enlarge, expatiate, descant, dilate, launch out.

Laundress, *n.* Washerwoman.

Lave, *v. t.* Wash, bathe.

Lavish, *a.* Profuse, prodigal, thriftless, unthrifty, wasteful, extravagant, too free, over-liberal.

——, *v. t.* 1. Waste, squander, dissipate, spend lavishly.

2. Bestow prodigally, pour out.

LAW, *n.* 1. Rule (*prescribed by authority*), regulation, statute, enactment, decree, ordinance, edict, order, canon, expressed command.

2. Formula, principle, form.

3. Code, body of rules.

4. Jurisprudence, science of laws, legal science.

5. [With *The* prefixed.] Mosaic code *or* dispensation, the old covenant.

6. Suit, process, litigation.

7. Controlling idea, governing principle, principle, determining rule (*of the invariable sequence of events or forms*).

Lawful, *a.* 1. Legal, legalized, legitimate, constitutional, constituted.

2. Allowable, permissible, warrantable.

3. Rightful, just, proper, valid.

Lawfulness, *n.* 1. Legality, conformity to law.

2. Allowableness, permissibleness, permissibility.

Lawgiver, *n.* Legislator, lawmaker.

Lawsuit, *n.* Action, suit in law.

Lawyer, *n.* Counsellor, counsel, advocate, attorney, attorney-at-law, solicitor, barrister, limb of the law, pettifogger.

Lax, *a.* 1. Loose, slack, relaxed.

2. Soft, flabby, drooping, relaxed.

3. Remiss, negligent, neglectful.

4. Licentious, dissolute, loose.

Laxative, *a.* Loosening, aperient, deobstruent, purgative.

Laxity, *n.* 1. Looseness, slackness, laxness, latitude.

2. Remissness, negligence.

3. Dissoluteness, licentiousness.

Lay, *v. t.* 1. Put, place, lay down, deposit.

2. Impose, assess.

3. Impute, charge, ascribe.

4. Spread (*on a surface*).

——, *a.* Laic, laical, non-professional, popular.

Lay aside. 1. Reject, discard, put away, put off, lay on the shelf.

2. Put by, store, lay by.

Lay by. Reserve, keep, retain, husband, reserve for future use.

Lay down. 1. Resign, give up, offer up, sacrifice.

2. Leave, quit, relinquish.

3. Advance, propound, assert, allege, enunciate.

Layer, *n.* 1. Stratum, bed, lay, seam.

2. Course (*as of bricks*).

Lay hold of. Seize, catch, grasp, clutch.

Lay open. 1. Open, lance, cut open.

2. Expose, reveal, exhibit, disclose, unveil, divulge, publish, show, make known.

Lay out. 1. Spend, expend, disburse.

2. Plan, dispose, arrange.

3. Display, show, exhibit.

4. Prepare for burial.

Lay up. 1. Store, provide, treasure up, lay in.

2. Confine to the bed *or* the house.

Lay waste. Desolate, destroy, ruin.

Lazaretto, *n.* Hospital, infirmary, pesthouse, lazar-house.

Lazy, *a.* 1. Slothful, sluggish, sluggard, indolent, idle, inert, inactive, supine, torpid, slack, dronish, lumpish.

2. Sluggish, slow, creeping.

Lea, *n.* Meadow, mead, grass land, sward land, lay.

Lead, *v. t.* 1. Guide (*by the hand or something connected with the hand*).

2. Conduct, direct, escort, go before as guide.

3. Head, be at the head of, precede, front.

4. Surpass, excel, have the lead of, take the lead of, outstrip, be in advance of.

5. Allure, entice, induce, persuade, draw, prevail on.

——, *v. i.* 1. Show the way (*by going before*).

2. Be the commander (*as of troops*).

3. Conduce, contribute, tend, serve.

LEAD, *n.* 1. Guidance, direction, leadership.

2. Precedence.

Leader, *n.* 1. Guide, director, conductor, corypheus, choregus.

2. Chief, chieftain, commander, captain, head.

3. Superior, victor, dominator, corypheus, cock of the walk, ruler of the roost, first fiddle.

Leadership, *n.* 1. Guidance, direction, lead, conduct.

2. Primacy, supremacy, predominance, domination, hegemony, headship.

Leading, *a.* 1. Governing, ruling.

2. Chief, principal, capital, most important.

LEAF, *n.* Blade.

League, *n.* Alliance, confederation, confederacy, combination, coalition, union.

——, *v. i.* Unite, combine, confederate, band, form a league, form an alliance.

Leagued, *a.* United, combined, allied, confederated, confederate, banded.

Leak, *n.* 1. Fissure (*letting a liquid in* or *out*), chink, crevice, hole.

2. Leaking, leakage, percolation.

——, *v. t.* 1. Percolate, leak in *or* out, ooze, pass slowly.

2. Let in (*water* or *other liquid*), take water, etc.

Lean, *v. i.* 1. Incline (*from a perpendicular*), slope.

2. Recline, bear, rest, repose.

3. Tend, have a tendency.

4. Repose, rely, depend, confide, trust.

——, *v. t.* Rest, incline for support, lay.

——, *a.* 1. Thin, poor, gaunt, emaciated, meagre, lank, skinny, fallen away.

2. Barren, jejune, meagre, tame, prosy, dull.

3. Scanty, slender, pitiful, inadequate, not full *or* abundant, not plentiful, not ample, not enough.

4. Free from fat, destitute of fat.

5. Barren, bare, unfertile, unproductive.

LEANING, *n.* Bent, inclination, bias, propensity, proneness. See TENDENCY.

Lean-to, *n.* Penthouse, shed.

Leap, *v. i.* 1. Jump, bound, spring, vault.

2. Hop, frisk, gambol, caper.

——, *v. t.* Jump over, bound across.

——, *n.* 1. Jump, spring, bound, vault.

2. Hop, frisk, frisking, caper, gambol.

Leap-year, *n.* Bissextile.

Learn, *v. t.* 1. Get a knowledge of, acquire skill in, make one's self acquainted with, make one's self master of.

2. Be informed of, hear, hear of.

——, *v. i.* 1. Get learning, acquire knowledge, gain experience, acquire information, acquire.

2. Be informed, hear.

Learn by heart. Memorize, commit to memory, get by heart, learn *or* get by rote.

Learned, *a.* 1. Erudite, lettered, deep-read.

2. [With *in*.] Knowing, skilled, expert, experienced, well-informed.

Learning, *n.* 1. Acquisition of knowledge.

2. Erudition, scholarship, acquirements, attainments, lore, large knowledge, wide information, acquired knowledge.

Lease, *v. t.* Let (*for a term of years*).

Leash, *n.* Thong *or* string (*for holding a dog* or *a hawk*).

——, *v. t.* Tie, tie together.

Least, *a.* Smallest, minutest.

LEATHER, *n.* Cordovan, shagreen, chamois, etc.

Leathery, *a.* Tough, coriaceous.

Leave, *n.* 1. Permission, liberty, allowance, sufferance, license.

2. Withdrawal, retirement, departure.

3. Farewell, adieu, congé.

——, *v. t.* 1. Quit, vacate, abandon, withdraw from, depart from, go away from, retire from, get away from.

2. Abandon, forsake, desert, relinquish, renounce, put aside, lay aside, give up, give over.

3. Let alone, let be, suffer to remain undisturbed, forbear to meddle with.

4. Commit, consign, refer.

5. Stop, forbear, cease from, desist from, refrain from, leave off, break off, make an end of.

6. Permit, allow, let, give leave, give permission.

7. Bequeath, demise, devise, will, give by will.

8. Leave behind one, leave at one's death, leave remaining after death.

——, *v. i.* Desist, stop, cease, forbear, leave off.

Leaven, *n.* 1. Yeast, ferment, barm, fermenting substance.

2. Pervading influence.

——, *v. t.* 1. Produce *or* excite fermentation in, ferment, raise, lighten.

2. Imbue, pervade, permeate, tinge, color, inspire, elevate, lift.

3. Imbue, infect, vitiate, taint.

Leaves, *n. pl.* Foliage.

Leavings, *n. pl.* Remains, remnants, relics, fragments, scraps, pieces, refuse, odds and ends.

Lecherous, *a.* Lewd, lascivious, libidinous, lustful, carnal, salacious, lickerish, con-

cupiscent, lubric, lubricous, wanton, unchaste, incontinent.

Lechery, *n.* Lewdness, lasciviousness, concupiscence, lust, salacity, salaciousness,
lubricity, carnal desire, brutal appetite.

Lecture, *n.* 1. Discourse, prelection.

2. Censure, lesson, lecturing, reprimand, reproof, scolding.

——, *v. t.* 1. Deliver a lecture to.

2. Reprove, reprimand, scold, chide,
rate, sermonize.

Ledge, *n.* 1. Shelf.

2. Ridge of rocks.

Lee, *a.* To leeward (*opposed to weather*).

——, *n.* Leeward, lee-side, side sheltered
from the wind.

Leer, *v. i.* Look askance (*in contempt*).

Lees, *n. pl.* Dregs, sediment, settlings,
precipitate, dunder.

Leeward, *n.* Lee, lee-side.

LEFT, *a.* Larboard (*naut.*), leftward,
sinistral.

LEG, *n.* Lower limb, prop.

Legacy, *n.* Bequest, devise, gift by will.

Legal, *a.* Lawful, legitimate, legalized,
authorized *or* sanctioned (*by law*), according to law.

Legality, *n.* Lawfulness, conformity to law.

Legalize, *v. t.* 1. Authorize, permit by law.

2. Sanction, legitimate, legitimize,
make legal, confirm by law.

Legate, *n.* 1. Envoy, deputy, delegate.
See AMBASSADOR.

2. Papal ambassador, pope's legate,
cardinal legate. See *nuncio.*

Legation, *n.* Embassy, deputation, body
of diplomatists.

Legend, *n.* 1. Fable, myth, fiction, doubtful narrative, fictitious story.

2. Motto (*round a coin or a medal*).

Legendary, *a.* Fabulous, fictitious, mythical.

Legible, *a.* 1. Readable, plain, fair, de-
cipherable.

2. Manifest, apparent, recognizable,
discoverable.

Legion, *n.* 1. Army, host, military force,
body of troops.

2. Multitude, host, army, great number, horde.

Legislate, *v. i.* Make laws, enact laws.

——, *v. t.* Enact, ordain, create *or* annul
by law *or* legislation, speak into *or* out
of (*being or existence*).

Legislative, *a.* Law-making.

Legislator, *n.* Lawgiver, lawmaker.

Legislature, *n.* Legislative body, parliament, senate, etc.

Legitimacy, *n.* 1. Legality, lawfulness,
accordance with law.

2. Genuineness.

Legitimate, *a.* 1. Legal, lawful, in accordance with law.

2. Born in wedlock, lawfully begotten.

3. Genuine.

4. Valid, logical, warranted, warrantable, correct.

Legitimate, } *v. t.* Legalize, make legiti-
Legitimize, } mate.

Leisure, *n.* 1. Spare hours, spare time,
time to spare.

2. Convenience, ease.

3. Freedom from business, ease.

LEMON, *n.* (*Basic Eng.*) The yellow
acid fruit.

Lend, *v. t.* 1. Loan, accommodate with.

2. Give, grant, afford, furnish, bestow, confer, impart.

Lend a hand. Render assistance, put one's
shoulder to the wheel, hold out a helping
hand, give one a lift, give one a turn, do
one a favor, help a lame dog over a stile.

Length, *n.* 1. Extent, longitudinal dimensions.

2. Long duration, duration, continuance.

3. Detail, amplification, fulness.

Lengthen, *v. t.* 1. Elongate, extend (*in
space*), stretch, draw out, produce, prolong.

2. Protract, continue, prolong, extend
(*in time*), spin out.

——, *v. i.* Become longer, grow longer, increase in length.

Lengthways, } *adv.* Longitudinally, end-
Lengthwise, } ways.

Lengthy, *a.* Long, lengthened, prolonged,
prolix, protracted.

Lenience, } *n.* Clemency, mildness, lenity,
Leniency, } mercy, tenderness, gentleness, forbearance.

Lenient, *a.* 1. Softening, assuasive, soothing, mitigating, mitigative, lenitive.

2. Mild, gentle, clement, merciful,
tender, forbearing, long-suffering, indulgent, humoring, tolerant, easy.

Lenitive, *a.* Soothing, assuasive, emollient,
lenient, mitigative, balmy, sedative, demulcent.

——, *n.* Palliative, emollient, lenient, opiate, anodyne, soothing medicine.

Lenity, *n.* Mildness, clemency, gentleness,
tenderness, mercy, kindness, forbearance,
lenience, leniency.

Lens-shaped, *a.* Lentiform, lenticular.

Lenten, *a.* 1. Of Lent, belonging to Lent,
used in Lent, in Lent.

2. Sparing, meagre, abstemious, spare,
light, lean, slender.

Leonine, *a.* 1. Lion-like.

2. Characteristic of a lion, belonging
to a lion *or* lions.

Leprous, *a.* 1. Infected with leprosy.

2. (*Bot.*) Scaly, lepidote, lepidoted.

3. Corrupt, foul, vile, defiling, infectious, poisonous, polluting.

Lesion, *n.* (*Med.*) Injury, hurt, disorder, derangement, morbid change.

Less, *a.* Smaller, inferior.

——, *adv.* Not so much, in a less degree.

——, *n.* Not so much, smaller quantity, less amount.

Lessen, *v. t.* 1. Diminish, decrease, reduce, abate, abridge, make less.

2. Lower, degrade.

——, *v. i.* Decrease, diminish, abate, dwindle, shrink, be reduced.

Lessening, *n.* Diminution, decrement, decrease, reduction, abatement.

Lesser, *a.* Less, smaller, inferior.

Lesser Bear. [With *The* prefixed.] Little Bear, Ursa Minor.

Lesson, *n.* 1. Exercise (*of a learner*), task.

2. Instruction, precept.

3. Reproof, rebuke, lecture, censure, lecturing, scolding, chiding.

Lest, *conj.* That not, for fear that.

LET, *v. t.* 1. Allow, permit, suffer, give leave to, give permission to.

2. Lease, put to hire.

——, *n.* Hindrance, impediment, obstacle, obstruction.

Let alone. Leave, let be, suffer to remain undisturbed, forbear to meddle with.

Let down. Lower, depress.

Let go. Release, loose, set free, let loose, let slip, cast off, let out.

Lethal, *a.* Deadly, mortal, fatal.

Lethargic, } *a.* Drowsy, dull, torpid,
Lethargical, } heavy, stupid, stupefied, comatose, morbidly sleepy.

Lethargy, *n.* Stupor, torpor, coma, stupefaction, hypnotism, stupidity, morbid drowsiness.

Let loose. Release, liberate, let free, free from restraint, let out, let go set at liberty.

Let off. 1. Discharge, explode.

2. Excuse, exonerate, exempt.

Let out. 1. Release, liberate, set free, let loose, free from restraint, set at liberty.

2. Extend, loosen.

3. Blab, disclose, divulge, reveal.

LETTER, *n.* 1. Alphabetic character.

2. Epistle, note, missive.

3. Literal meaning, literal sense, verbal expression.

Lettered, *a.* Learned, literary, bookish, well-read, deep-read, book-learned.

Letters, *n. pl.* 1. Literature, learning, culture, erudition.

2. Correspondence.

Levee, *n.* 1. Time of rising.

2. [*U. S.*] Ceremonious party, reception, entertainment, *soirée.*

3. [*U. S.*] Embankment (*along a river to prevent inundation*).

Level, *a.* 1. Horizontal.

2. Even, flat, plain.

3. Flush, on a level, of the same height.

4. Of the same rank, condition, etc., on a par.

——, *v. t.* 1. Make horizontal, flatten.

2. Bring to the same level, make equal.

3. Raze, demolish, destroy.

4. Aim, direct, point, take aim.

LEVEL, *n.* 1. Horizontal surface, horizontal line.

2. State of equality, equal elevation.

Leverage, *n.* Purchase (*obtained by the lever*).

Levigate, *v. t.* Pulverize, comminute, triturate, grind, bruise, bray, reduce to powder.

Levity, *n.* 1. Lightness, want of weight.

2. Frivolity, flightiness, giddiness, volatility, want of seriousness.

Levy, *v. t.* 1. Raise, muster, call together.

2. Collect, gather.

Lewd, *a.* 1. [*Archaic.*] Vile, despicable, loose, profligate, wicked.

2. Lustful. See LIBIDINOUS.

Lexicon, *n.* Dictionary, glossary, vocabulary, word-book.

Liability, *n.* 1. Responsibility, accountableness, accountability, bounden duty.

2. Exposedness.

Liabilities, *n. pl.* (*Com.*) Debts, obligations.

Liable, *a.* 1. Answerable, responsible, accountable, amenable.

2. Exposed, subject, obnoxious.

Liaison, *n.* [Fr.] 1. Amour, intrigue, illicit intimacy, criminal intimacy.

2. (*Rare.*) Connection, union, bond of union, relation.

Libel, *n.* 1. Malicious publication, defamation, defamatory writing.

2. (*Law.*) Charge, statement of complaint.

——, *v. t.* 1. Lampoon, defame (*by some publication*).

2. (*Law.*) Proceed against by a libel, bring a charge against.

Libellous, *a.* [Written also *Libelous.*] Defamatory, malicious.

Liberal, *a.* 1. Generous, bountiful, free, beneficent, munificent, princely, charitable, open-hearted, free-hearted, unselfish, disinterested.

2. Enlarged, catholic, tolerant, unbigoted, broad-minded, high-minded, magnanimous, honorable, chivalrous.

3. Large, full, unstinted, abundant, bounteous, ample, plentiful.

4. Refined, liberalizing, refining, befitting a freeman, humanizing.

Liberal, *n.* Liberalist, advocate of liberal principles, Latitudinarian.

Liberality, *n.* 1. Generosity, bounty, beneficence, munificence, disinterestedness, bountifulness, charity.

2. Present, gift, benefaction.

3. Catholicity, toleration, magnanimity, candor, impartiality, largeness of mind, large-mindedness, freedom from narrowness, freedom from bigotry.

Liberalize, *v. t.* 1. Enlarge, make liberal, free from prejudice, broaden.

2. Make liberal, refine, elevate, cultivate.

Liberate, *v. t.* Release, free, emancipate, manumit, disinthrall, ransom, discharge, deliver, set free, set at liberty, let go, let loose, let out.

Liberties, *n. pl.* 1. Limits (*of a prison, etc.*).

2. Unwarrantable freedom.

3. Immunities, franchises, privileges.

Libertine, *n.* Rake, debauchee, profligate, *roué,* lecher, dissolute man, man of pleasure.

——, *a.* Licentious, dissolute, depraved, corrupt.

Liberty, *n.* 1. Freedom (*after previous restraint*), liberation from foreign restraint, independence, self-direction, self-government.

2. Privilege, immunity, franchise.

3. Leave, permission, license.

Libidinous, *a.* Lascivious, lustful, carnal, lecherous, lickerish, lewd, salacious, concupiscent wanton, loose, unchaste, incontinent, lubric, lubrical, lubricous, sensual, impure.

LIBRARY, *n.* (*Basic Eng.*) Place shelved for books.

Librate, *v. t.* Balance, poise, hold in equipoise.

Libratory, *a.* Balancing.

License, *n.* 1. Permission, privilege, leave, right, authorization.

2. Permit, warrant, imprimatur, dispensation, certificate, charter.

3. Laxity, excessive liberty, exorbitant freedom, disorder, anarchy, lawlessness.

——, *v. t.* Permit, allow, grant authority to, give a permit *or* warrant to.

Licentious, *a.* 1. Unrestrained, riotous, uncurbed, wanton, uncontrolled, unruly, ungovernable, disorderly.

2. Dissolute, debauched, profligate, rakish, libertine, loose, lax.

3. Sensual, unchaste, immoral, impure, libertine, lascivious, lewd, libidinous, lecherous, lustful.

Lick, *v. t.* 1. Pass the tongue over.

2. Lap, take up with the tongue.

——, *n.* 1. Taste.

2. Blow, slap, stroke.

3. Salt-lick, saline, salt-spring.

Lickerish, *a.* 1. Hankering (*to lick* or *taste*), craving, longing.

2. Lecherous. See LIBIDINOUS.

3. Dainty, nice, fastidious.

4. Dainty, tempting, appetizing.

Lickspittle, *n.* Abject parasite, mean flatterer, lick-platter, lick-trencher.

Lid, *n.* 1. Cover, covercle, top.

2. Eyelid.

Lie, *n.* 1. Falsehood, malicious *or* deliberate falsification, intentional untruth, misrepresentation, *suggestio falsi, suppressio veri,* fib, equivocation, prevarication.

2. Delusion, illusion, fleeting show.

——, *v. i.* 1. Falsify, fib, tell a lie, equivocate, prevaricate, romance.

2. Recline, lie, couch, lie down, be prostrate, be recumbent.

3. Be placed, be laid.

4. Be, rest, remain.

5. Be situated, be located.

Lief, *adv.* Willingly, gladly, freely.

Liege, *n.* Superior, sovereign, liege lord.

Lieu, *n.* [Fr.] Place, room, stead.

Life, *n.* 1. Vitality, the vital spark, the breath of life, the breath of one's nostrils.

2. Time from birth to death, period of life, lifetime.

3. Animated existence, living beings.

4. Mode *or* course of living, manner of life, course, career.

5. Conduct, deportment, behavior.

6. Animation, vigor, spirit, vivacity, alertness, briskness, sprightliness, activity, energy.

7. Biography, memoir.

8. Real person, living form.

9. Society, social manners, human affairs, course of things.

Lifeless, *a.* 1. Dead, defunct, extinct, inanimate.

2. Torpid, sluggish, pulseless, inert, dull, tame, spiritless, passive.

Lift, *v. t.* Raise, elevate, lift up.

LIFT, *n.* 1. Lifting, raising.

2. (*Colloq.*) Aid, assistance, help.

3. Elevator.

Ligament, *n.* Band, ligature.

Ligature, *n.* 1. Band, bandage, ligament, tie.

2. Binding, tying.

LIGHT, *n.* 1. Daybreak, sunrise, dawn, daylight, break of day, peep of day.

2. Radiance, effulgence, luminosity, phosphorescence.

3. Candle, lamp, taper.

4. Instruction, knowledge, information, comprehension, insight.

5. Illustration, explanation, elucidation.

6. Window, pane (*of glass*), etc.

LIGHT, *a.* 1. Buoyant, of little weight.

2. See EASY.

3. Porous, spongy, well leavened (*said of bread*).

4. Loose, sandy (*said of soil*).

5. Unencumbered, unburdened, free from impediments.

6. Slight, trifling, small, inconsiderable, moderate, unimportant.

7. Gossamery, flimsy, unsubstantial, airy, ethereal, feathery, weightless.

8. Frivolous, fickle, unsteady, volatile, unsettled.

9. Gay, airy, buoyant, light-hearted.

10. Bright, clear, not dark.

——, *v. t.* 1. Kindle, ignite, set fire to, set on fire, apply the match to.

2. Illumine, give light to, guide by light; illuminate, lighten, illume, irradiate, brighten.

Lighten, *v. i.* 1. Flash (*said of lightning*).

2. Grow lighter, brighten, clear off.

——, *v. t.* 1. Illuminate, irradiate, illume, light.

2. Enlighten, fill with knowledge *or* wisdom, illumine.

3. [With *forth.*] Flash, flash forth, emit.

4. Ease, make lighter, make easier.

Light-fingered, *a.* Thievish.

Light-headed, *a.* 1. Dizzy, vertiginous, giddy.

2. Delirious, wandering.

3. Giddy, heedless, light, thoughtless, rattlebrained, frivolous, volatile, indiscreet.

Light-hearted, *a.* Gladsome, cheerful, joyful, joyous, gay, merry, glad, blithe, blithesome, gleeful, jovial, jolly, jocund, frolicsome, lightsome.

Lighthouse, *n.* Pharos.

Lightning-rod, *n.* Paratonnerre.

Light on. 1. Happen upon, fall upon by chance, happen to find, light upon, strike upon.

2. Alight on.

Ligneous, *a.* Woody.

LIKE, *a.* 1. Similar, resembling, analogous, allied, parallel, cognate, of a piece.

2. Equal, same.

3. Likely, probable.

——, *n.* 1. Equal, peer.

2. Preference, partiality, liking.

——, *adv.* 1. In the manner of, in the same manner as.

2. Likely, probably.

——, *v. t.* 1. Approve, be pleased with, take pleasure in, find to one's mind, taste, *or* fancy.

2. Relish, enjoy, be fond of.

3. Esteem, fancy, have a regard for, take a liking to, take to, take a fancy to.

——, *v. i.* Choose, prefer, elect, wish, list, think fit, be pleased.

Likelihood, *n.* Probability, verisimilitude.

Likely, *a.* 1. Probable, credible.

2. In a fair way, to be expected.

3. Pleasing, agreeable, likable, that may be liked.

4. Suitable, well-adapted, well-suited, convenient.

Liken, *v. t.* Compare, show the resemblance of.

Likeness, *n.* 1. Resemblance, similarity, similitude, semblance, form, external appearance.

2. Copy, facsimile, counterpart, image, representation, portrait, effigy.

Likewise, *adv.* Also, too, besides, moreover, furthermore, in addition, to boot, in like manner.

Liking, *n.* 1. Fondness, partiality, desire, wish.

2. Inclination, disposition, tendency, turn, leaning, bias, bent, propensity, proclivity, proneness, predisposition, appetency, *penchant.*

Lilliputian, *a.* Pygmean, little, small, tiny, puny, dwarfish, diminutive.

Limb, *n.* 1. Member, extremity.

2. Branch, bough.

Limber, *a.* Supple, pliable, pliant, flexible, lithe.

Limbo, *n.* 1. Limbus, place of spirits, place of the departed (*awaiting final judgment*).

2. Hell, infernal regions, shades below.

LIMIT, *n.* 1. Bound, frontier, boundary, confine, terminus, term, bourn, termination, precinct, march.

2. Restriction, restraint, obstruction, check, hindrance.

——, *v. t.* 1. Bound, circumscribe, define, set bounds to, fix the limits of.

2. Restrain, restrict, condition.

Limitation, *n.* Restriction, restraint.

Limp, *a.* Limber, flaccid, flexile, slack, relaxed.

——, *v. t.* Halt, hitch, hobble, walk lame.

——, *n.* Halt, limping gait.

Limpid, *a.* Clear, lucid, pure, bright, transparent, pellucid, crystal, crystalline, translucent.

Limpidity, *n.* Clearness, brightness, purity, transparency, limpidness.

Lin, *n.* 1. Pool, pond.

2. [*Scotch.*] Cataract, waterfall.

Linden, *n.* Lime-tree, lime.

LINE, *n.* 1. Streak, stripe, extended mark.

   2. Thread, cord, string, rope, cable.

   3. Row, rank.

   4. Lineage, race, family, ancestry.

   5. Course, method.

   6. Occupation, employment, calling, business, pursuit.

Lineage, *n.* Progeny, race, family, house, genealogy, descent, line, birth, breed, extraction.

Lineal, *a.* 1. In a direct line (*from an ancestor*).

   2. Linear, in the direction of a line.

Lineament, *n.* Outline (*particularly of the face*), feature, trait, line.

Linear, *a.* Lineal, in the direction of a line.

LINEN, *n.* Cloth of flax, flaxen fabric, linen cloth, lingerie.

Linger, *v. i.* Loiter, delay, tarry, lag, saunter, be slow, wait long, remain long.

Lingering, *a.* 1. Delaying, loitering.

   2. Protracted, prolonged.

Linguiform, *a.* (*Bot.*) Tongue-shaped, lingulate.

Linguist, *n.* Adept in languages, linguistic scholar, philologist, polyglot.

Linguistics, *n.* Glossology, glottology, science of language, linguistic science.

Liniment, *n.* Embrocation, soft ointment.

Link, *n.* Connective, copula, vinculum, bond, juncture, coupler.

——, *v. t.* Connect, conjoin, join, unite, bind, tie, fasten, fasten together.

Lion, *n.* See CELEBRITY.

Lion-hearted, *a.* Brave, courageous, daring, intrepid, dauntless, bold, valiant.

Lion-like, *a.* Leonine.

LIP, *n.* Edge *or* border (*of the mouth, etc.*), labium.

Liquefaction, *n.* Melting, dissolving, thawing, fusion, dissolution.

Liquefy, *v. t.* Melt, dissolve, fuse, make liquid.

——, *v. i.* Melt, dissolve, be fused, become liquid.

Liqueur, *n.* [Fr.] Cordial, aromatized spirit; *specif.*, benedictine, chartreuse, curaçao, etc.

Liquid, *a.* 1. Fluid, liquiform.

   2. Mellifluous, dulcet, soft, clear, flowing, melting.

LIQUID, *n.* Fluid, liquor, liquid substance.

Liquidate, *v. t.* Settle, adjust, pay, extinguish, pay off, clear off.

Liquidation, *n.* Settlement, discharge, adjustment, payment.

Liquor, *n.* 1. Liquid, fluid, liquid substance.

   2. Spirituous *or* alcoholic liquid, spirituous liquor, alcoholic drink, strong drink.

LIST, *n.* 1. Register, roll, catalogue, inventory, schedule, invoice.

   2. Border, bound, limit.

   3. Strip (*of cloth, on the edge*), selvage, border, edge.

   4. (*Arch.*) Fillet, annulet, listel.

——, *v. i.* Wish, choose, desire, prefer, like, please, elect, think fit, think best, think proper.

Listen, *v. i.* Hearken, hark, hear, attend, eavesdrop, give ear, lend an ear, incline an ear, prick up the ears, be all ear.

Listless, *a.* Inattentive, indifferent, heedless, careless, thoughtless.

Lists, *n. pl.* Arena, palæstra, race-course.

Literal, *a.* 1. As regards letters, by letter.

   2. According to the exact meaning, following the exact words, strict, exact, *verbatim*.

   3. Following the exact words.

Literally, *adv.* 1. Really, actually.

   2. Exactly, precisely, rigorously, strictly.

Literary, *a.* 1. Of literature *or* learning.

   2. Learned, lettered, bookish, well-read, book-learned, literate, instructed, erudite, scholarly.

Literate, *a.* Learned, lettered.

Literature, *n.* 1. Learning, erudition, letters, lore.

   2. The humanities, the Muses, belles-lettres, polite literature.

   3. Literary productions, literary works.

Lithe, *a.* Limber, flexible, flexile, pliable, pliant, supple.

Lithesome, *a.* Pliant, limber, nimble, lissome, lithe.

Litigate, *v. t.* Contest in law, defend in a lawsuit.

——, *v. i.* Dispute in law, carry on a lawsuit.

Litigation, *n.* Lawsuit, suit at law, judicial contest.

Litigious, *a.* 1. Contentious, disputatious, quarrelsome.

   2. Disputable, controvertible.

Litter, *n.* 1. Vehicle with a bed (*borne by hand*), sedan, palanquin.

   2. Bedding of straw, hay, etc.

   3. Shreds, fragments, waste matter, scattered rubbish.

   4. Confusion, disorder.

   5. See OFFSPRING.

——, *v. t.* 1. Cover with straw, hay, etc., for bedding.

   2. Cover with things negligently scattered, strew, scatter, disorder, derange.

   3. Give birth to (*said of quadrupeds*), bring forth, bear.

LITTLE, *a.* 1. Small (*in size* or *extent*), minute, diminutive, tiny.

2. Small (*in quantity* or *amount*); brief, short.

3. Small (*in dignity, power,* or *importance*), inconsiderable, insignificant, unimportant, petty, slight, trivial, slender, feeble, moderate, scanty, weak, small (*in force* or *efficiency*).

4. Mean, selfish, narrow, paltry, contemptible, niggard, illiberal, small (*in generosity*).

——, *n.* 1. Small quantity, jot, modicum, pinch, handful, pittance, trifle, whit.

2. Miniature, small scale, small degree.

——, *adv.* Slightly, in a small degree, in some degree, not much.

Liturgy, *n.* Ritual, formulary of public worship, *agenda.*

Live, *v. i.* 1. Exist, have being, have life, be alive, be animated.

2. Remain, continue, endure, be permanent, last, survive.

3. Dwell, abide, reside.

4. Feed, subsist, fare, be nourished, be supported (with *on*).

5. Subsist, acquire a livelihood (with *on* or *by*).

——, *v. t.* 1. Lead, pass, continue.

2. Practise, put in practice.

——, *a.* 1. Living, alive, animate, quick.

2. Ignited, burning, hot.

3. Vivid, bright, lively, glowing, brilliant.

4. Earnest, active, wide-awake, glowing, animated.

Livelihood, *n.* Maintenance, support, sustenance, subsistence, living.

Liveliness, *n.* 1. Sprightliness, vivacity, animation, spirit, briskness, activity.

2. Activity, effervescence.

Livelong, *a.* Lasting, durable, long-enduring.

Lively, *a.* 1. Active, agile, nimble, supple, brisk, alert, quick, stirring, smart, vigorous, vivacious, energetic.

2. Animated, spirited, sprightly, vivacious, airy, gay, blithe, blithesome, gleeful, jocund, buoyant, joyous, frolicsome, buxom, jolly.

3. Vivid, bright, brilliant, fresh, glowing, strong, clear.

4. Vigorous, forcible, strong, energetic, keen, nervous, glowing, sparkling, racy, piquant, impassioned.

Live-stock, *n.* Stock, domestic animals (*on a farm*).

Livid, *a.* Discolored (*as flesh by a bruise*), black and blue, lead-colored, gray-blue.

LIVING, *a.* 1. Existing, live, alive, quick, breathing, organic.

2. Quickening, active, lively.

——, *n.* 1. Livelihood, maintenance, support, subsistence, keeping, estate.

2. Benefice, ecclesiastical living.

Lo, *interj.* Look, see, behold, observe.

Load, *n.* 1. Burden, weight, pack, freightage.

2. Lading, cargo, freight.

3. Encumbrance, pressure, clog, incubus, drag weight, dead weight, oppression.

——, *v. t.* 1. Freight, lade, put *or* lay a load upon.

2. Encumber, oppress, burden, weigh down, cumber.

3. Charge (*as a gun*).

4. See ADULTERATE.

Loader, *n.* Lumper.

Loadstar, *n.* [Written also *Lodestar.*] Pole-star, cynosure, the north star, guiding-star.

Loadstone, *n.* [Written also *Lodestone.*] Magnet, natural magnet.

Loaf, *v. i.* Lounge, be idle, idle away one's time.

Loafer, *n.* Idler, lounger, vagabond, idle wanderer, vagrant, "bum."

Loam, *n.* Mould, soil.

Loan, *v. t.* Lend.

Loath, *a.* [Written also *Loth.*] Reluctant, backward, unwilling, averse, disinclined, indisposed.

Loathe, *v. t.* 1. Feel disgust at, feel nausea at.

2. Abhor, detest, hate, abominate, feel disgust at, shrink from, recoil from.

Loathing, *n.* Abhorrence, aversion, disgust, detestation, abomination, hatred, antipathy.

Loathsome, *a.* 1. Disgusting, sickening, nauseous, nauseating, repulsive, offensive, revolting, palling.

2. Hateful, detestable, odious, shocking, abominable, abhorrent, execrable.

Local, *a.* Topical, limited, provincial, regional, sectional, territorial.

Locale, *n.* Place, spot, location, locality.

Locality, *n.* Position, situation, place, location.

Locate, *v. t.* Place, set, establish, fix, settle.

——, *v. i.* Reside, be placed, place one's self, settle.

Location, *n.* 1. Situation, place, locality.

2. Locating, establishing, marking out the limits *or* boundaries.

Loch, *n.* [*Scotch.*] 1. Lake, pond, mere.

2. Creek, inlet, bay.

LOCK, *n.* 1. Fastening, bolt, padlock.

2. Grapple, hug, embrace.

3. Tuft, tress, ringlet.

LOCK, *v. t.* 1. Fasten (*with a lock*), close fast, bolt, padlock.

2. Confine (*by locking*), shut up, lock up.

3. Stop, clog, impede, fasten.

4. Seal, close, press together.

5. Join, unite, clasp.

6. Enclose, encircle, embrace, clasp.

Lock up. 1. Clasp, fasten, lock, close fast.

2. Confine, shut up, restrain.

Locution, *n.* Discourse, phrase, mode of speech.

Lode, *n.* [Written also *Load.*] Metallic vein, mineral vein.

Lodge, *n.* 1. Hut, cottage, cot, small house.

2. Den, lair, haunt, cave.

——, *v. t.* 1. Place, put, deposit, set, lay.

2. Plant, infix, fix, settle, place, throw in.

3. Harbor, quarter, cover, provide lodging for, accommodate.

4. Lay flat, beat down.

——, *v. i.* 1. Settle, be deposited, be fixed.

2. Inhabit (*for a season*), dwell, live, reside, abide, rest.

3. Sojourn, tarry, rest, stop, stay, remain, abide, take up one's quarters, pitch one's tent, put up, take lodgings, have lodgings.

Lodgement, *n.* 1. Accumulation, collection.

2. Repository, room, lodging-place.

Lodging, *n.* 1. Place of rest, apartment for sleeping.

2. Habitation (*for a season*), abode, residence, dwelling, quarters, dwelling-place, place of residence.

3. Harbor, cover, refuge, shelter.

Loftiness, *n.* 1. Height, elevation, altitude.

2. Pride, haughtiness, vanity, arrogance.

3. Sublimity, dignity, grandeur.

Lofty, *a.* 1. High, elevated, tall, towering.

2. Proud, haughty, arrogant.

3. Sublime, exalted, elevated.

4. Stately, dignified, imposing, majestic.

Loggerhead, *n.* Simpleton, dunce, blockhead, dolt, thick-skull.

Logic, *n.* Dialectics, reasoning.

Logical, *a.* 1. Dialectical, coherent, consistent, sound, close, valid.

2. Discriminating, skilled in reasoning, versed in logic.

Logomachy, *n.* Dispute, controversy, argumentative debate, altercation, bickering, wrangling, war of words, words.

Loins, *n. pl.* Reins, lumbar region.

Loiter, *v. i.* Lag, linger, delay, tarry, saunter, dillydally, move slowly, be dilatory.

Loiterer, *n.* Lingerer, idler, laggard.

Loitering, *a.* Dilatory, lingering.

Loll, *v. i.* 1. Lounge, recline, lean, sprawl, lie at ease.

2. Hang out, hang extended.

Lollipop, *n.* Sugar-plum, sweetmeat.

Lone, *a.* 1. Solitary, secluded, lonely, unfrequented, deserted, uninhabited, unoccupied, lonesome, retired.

2. Single, solitary, isolated, lonely, alone.

Loneliness, *n.* 1. Solitariness, seclusion, solitude, retirement, isolation.

2. Forlornness, desolateness, dreariness.

Lonely, *a.* 1. Apart, retired, solitary, secluded, isolated, sequestered, remote, dreary, lonesome.

2. Lone, alone, solitary, unaccompanied, companionless.

3. Desolate, dreary, forsaken, deserted, forlorn.

LONG, *a.* 1. Lengthy, drawn out, protracted, prolonged, extended.

2. Long-winded, spun out, long-spun, tedious, prolix, diffuse.

3. Slow, dilatory, slack, lingering, tardy.

——, *adv.* 1. To a great extent.

2. A long time, for a long time.

Long for. Crave, hanker for, hanker after, lust after, pine for, have a longing for, yearn for, aspire after, desire earnestly.

Long-headed, *a.* Sagacious, discerning, intelligent, acute, shrewd, clear-sighted, keen-sighted, far-seeing, perspicacious.

Longing, *n.* Craving, yearning, earnest desire, eager desire, aspiration, hankering, hunger, pining.

Longitudinally, *adv.* Lengthwise, from end to end.

Long-suffering, *a.* Forbearing, patient, enduring.

——, *n.* Forbearance, clemency, patient endurance (*of injuries*).

Long-winded, *a.* 1. Long-breathed.

2. Protracted, prolonged, spun out.

3. Tedious, wearisome.

Look, *v. i.* 1. Direct the eye. See SEE.

2. Turn the thoughts, apply the mind, consider, examine, contemplate.

3. Expect, await, anticipate.

4. Mind, consider, take care, take heed, watch.

5. Front, face, be turned, be directed.

6. Appear, seem.

Look, *interj.* See, lo, behold, take notice, observe.

LOOK, *n.* 1. Gaze, glance, peep, peer.

2. Appearance, aspect, complexion.

3. Mien, manner, air, aspect.

Look after. 1. Attend to, take care of, see to.

2. Seek, search for, look for.

Look down upon. Despise, contemn, spurn, regard with contempt.

Look for. 1. Expect, await.

2. Search, seek, look after.

Look into. Investigate, examine, study, consider, inspect closely, observe narrowly.

Look on. 1. Be a spectator.

2. Regard, esteem.

3. Consider, view, conceive of, think.

Look out, *v. t.* Search for, look up.

——, *v. i.* Be on the watch, be on one's guard, beware, be circumspect.

Look over. Examine, cast the eye over, scrutinize.

Look through. Penetrate, solve.

Look up. Search for, look out.

Look up to. Respect, honor, defer to, think much of, think highly of.

Loon, *n.* Simpleton, fool, dunce, blockhead, loggerhead.

Loop, *n.* 1. Noose, bight.

2. Link, crook, bend, turn.

3. Loophole, aperture.

Loophole, *n.* 1. Opening (*in the wall of a fortification*), aperture, loop, crenelation.

2. Plea, pretext, pretence, excuse, way for evasion, way of escape, loop.

Loose, *v. t.* 1. Unfasten, untie, unbind, unlash, unloose, undo, unlock, free, liberate, set free.

2. Relax, loosen, slacken.

3. Detach, disconnect, disengage.

LOOSE, *a.* 1. Unbound, untied, unsewed, unconfined, unfastened.

2. Free, unattached, disengaged.

3. Slack, relaxed.

4. Prolix, rambling, diffusive, unconnected, diffuse.

5. Vague, indefinite, indistinct, indeterminate, ill-defined.

6. Lax, careless, slack, negligent, heedless.

7. Immoral, dissolute, unchaste, wanton, licentious.

Loosen, *v. t.* 1. Slacken, relax, make loose, make less tight.

2. Release, unloose, loose, let loose, free.

3. Make lax (*as the bowels*), relax.

Looseness, *n.* 1. Slackness, easiness.

2. Laxity, levity.

3. Irregularity.

4. Lewdness, unchastity, wantonness, wickedness.

5. Diarrhœa, flux, laxity.

Loot, *n.* Booty, plunder, spoil.

——, *v. t.* Plunder, ransack, rifle.

Lop, *v. t.* 1. Cut, cut off, obtruncate.

2. Dock, crop, curtail, prune, cut short.

3. Sever, dissever, detach, cut off.

Lopper, *v. t.* Curdle, coagulate, spoil, sour, clot.

Loquacious, *a.* 1. Talkative, garrulous, voluble.

2. Speaking, noisy, talking.

3. Blabbing, babbling, tattling, telltale.

Loquacity, *n.* Talkativeness, garrulity, gift of gab, loquaciousness, chattering, volubility, multiloquence.

Lord, *n.* 1. Master, ruler, governor, sovereign, king, monarch, superior, prince, liege, seignior.

2. Noble, nobleman, peer.

3. Husband, spouse.

4. Christ, the Saviour, the Master. See GOD.

Lordly, *a.* 1. Dignified, majestic, grand, noble, lofty.

2. Proud, haughty, domineering, imperious, overbearing, insolent, tyrannical, despotic, arrogant.

3. Large, liberal, noble.

Lordship, *n.* 1. Authority, dominion, rule, sway, command, control, government, direction, domination, empire, sovereignty.

2. Manor, seigniory, domain.

Lord's-supper, *n.* Eucharist, communion, sacrament, Christian sacrament.

Lore, *n.* 1. Learning, erudition, knowledge.

2. Instruction, counsel, admonition, teaching, doctrine, lesson, wisdom, advice.

Lorn, *a.* (*Poetical.*) Lost, undone, forsaken, deserted, lone, bereft, lonely.

Lose, *v. t.* 1. Be deprived of, fail to keep, let slip, let slip through the fingers.

2. Forfeit, fail to win, fail to obtain.

3. Deprive, dispossess of.

4. Displace, dislodge, displant.

5. Miss, wander from.

——, *v. i.* 1. Forfeit, fail to win, be defeated.

2. Succumb, decline, fail, suffer by comparison, yield.

Lose ground. 1. Fall behind.

2. Decline, lose credit.

Lose heart. Despair, be discouraged, give up hope.

LOSS, *n.* 1. Privation, deprivation, forfeiture.

2. Forfeiture, failure to win.

3. Destruction, overthrow, damage, detriment, ruin, defeat, injury, casualty, damage, disadvantage.

4. Waste, squandering.

Lost, *a.* 1. Missing, not to be found, astray.

2. Forfeited, missed, unredeemed.

3. Misspent, wasted, squandered, dissipated, thrown away.

4. Bewildered, confused, perplexed, puzzled, distracted.

5. Abstracted, preoccupied, absent, absent-minded, dreamy, napping.

6. Depraved, corrupt, abandoned, profligate, dissolute, reprobate, graceless, shameless, obdurate, hardened, incorrigible, irreclaimable.

7. Ruined, destroyed.

Lot, *n.* 1. Destiny, doom, allotment, apportionment, fate.

2. Chance, hazard, fortune, hap, haphazard, accident, fate.

3. Portion, parcel, division, part.

Loth, *a.* Unwilling, averse, disliking, disinclined, reluctant.

Lothario, *n.* Libertine, seducer, deceiver.

Lotion, *n.* Wash.

LOUD, *a.* 1. Resounding, high-sounding, noisy, sonorous.

2. Deafening, stunning, stentorian.

3. Clamorous, vociferous, boisterous, noisy, obstreperous, tumultuous, turbulent, uproarious.

4. Vehement, emphatic, positive, emphatical, impressive.

5. (*Colloq.*) Flashy, showy.

Loudly, *adv.* 1. Loud, noisily.

2. Clamorously, vehemently.

3. (*Colloq.*) Ostentatiously, showily.

Loudness, *n.* 1. Clamor, clamorousness, turbulence, uproar.

2. (*Colloq.*) Ostentation, flashiness, showiness.

Lounge, *v. i.* 1. Recline, loll.

2. Loll, dawdle, live lazily, loaf, idle.

Lout, *n.* Bumpkin, clown, boor, lubber, clumsy fellow, awkward fellow, booby, clodhopper.

Loutish, *a.* Clownish, rude, boorish, awkward, lubberly.

Lovable, *a.* Amiable, sweet, winning.

Love, *v. t.* 1. Have affection for, regard with affection, delight in, be fond of.

2. Have a passionate affection for, be in love with, be enamoured of.

3. Like, be pleased with.

——, *v. i.* Delight, take pleasure.

LOVE, *n.* 1. Affection, affectionate regard, friendship, kindness, tenderness, fondness, delight.

2. Attachment, passionate affection, the tender passion, amour.

3. Liking, fondness, inclination, devotion, strong attachment.

4. Cupid, Eros; Venus, Aphrodite.

5. Good-will, benevolence, charity.

Love-letter, *n.* *Billet-doux.*

Loveliness, *n.* 1. Amiableness.

2. Beauty, beautifulness.

Lovely, *a.* 1. Beautiful, pleasing, delightful, charming, enchanting, winning, sweet, delectable.

2. Amiable, admirable.

Lover, *n.* Admirer, "leman," paramour, sweetheart, "inamorato."

Loving, *a.* Affectionate, fond, kind.

Loving-cup, *n.* Grace-cup.

Loving-kindness, *n.* Mercy, favor, tenderness, tender regard.

LOW, *a.* 1. Depressed, basal, profound.

2. Grave, gentle, subdued, soft.

3. Humble, mean, plebeian, vulgar.

4. Abject, degraded, servile, slavish, menial, mean, base, ignoble, grovelling, vile, base-minded, low-minded, shabby, scurvy, dirty.

5. Dishonorable, disreputable, derogatory, unhandsome, unbecoming, disgraceful, unmanly, ungentlemanly, undignified.

6. Weak, exhausted, reduced, feeble.

7. Plain, simple, frugal, spare, poor.

8. Submissive, humble, reverent, lowly.

9. Dejected, depressed, dispirited, cast down.

——, *v. i.* Bellow, moo.

Low-bred, *a.* Vulgar, unrefined, coarse.

Lower, *v. t.* 1. Depress, drop, sink, let down, bring down, take down.

2. Degrade, debase, disgrace, humble, humiliate, reduce.

3. Lessen, diminish, reduce, decrease.

——, *v. i.* Fall, sink, diminish, decrease, grow less, subside.

—— (*pron.* lou'er), *v. i.* 1. Grow dark, be clouded, appear gloomy, appear stormy.

2. Frown, glower, look sullen, look black.

Lowering, *a.* Cloudy, clouded, overcast, lurid, murky, threatening, lowery, dark.

Lowermost, *a.* Lowest.

Lowing, *n.* Low, moo, bellowing, cry of cattle.

Lowliness, *n.* 1. Humility, humbleness, meekness, self-abasement, submissiveness.

2. Lowness, meanness of condition.

Lowly, *a.* 1. Modest, unpretending, meek, humble, mild.

2. Mean, low in rank or station.

Low-minded, *a.* Base-minded, base, mean, servile, vile, grovelling, slavish, abject, low.

Low-spirited, *a.* Dispirited, dejected, depressed, disheartened, discouraged, downhearted, desponding, cast down.

Low spirits. Dejection, dejectedness, depression, despondency, hypochondria, melancholy, hypochondriasis.

Loyal, *a.* Faithful, true, devoted, constant.

Loyalty, *n.* Allegiance, fealty, fidelity, faithfulness, constancy.

Lozenge, *n.* Rhomb, rhombus, oblique-angled parallelogram (*with equal sides*), diamond.

Lubber, *n.* Clown, boor, lout, clumsy fellow, awkward fellow.

Lubberly, *a.* Clumsy, awkward, clownish, bungling.

Lubric,   } *a.* See LUBRICOUS.
Lubrical, }

Lubricate, *v. t.* Smooth, make slippery, oil, grease.

Lubricity, *n.* 1. Smoothness, slipperiness.

  2. Instability, uncertainty, unsteadiness, slipperiness.

  3. Lasciviousness, lewdness, lechery, incontinency, licentiousness.

Lubricous, *a.* 1. Smooth, slippery, lubric.

  2. Wavering, unstable, uncertain, lubric.

  3. Lascivious, lewd, wanton, licentious, impure, salacious, unchaste, incontinent, lecherous, lustful, libidinous.

Lucent, *a.* Shining, bright, resplendent, brilliant, glittering, beaming, luminous, effulgent.

Lucid, *a.* 1. Shining, radiant, bright, beaming, resplendent, brilliant, luminous.

  2. Clear, transparent, pure, pellucid, limpid, diaphanous, crystalline, luculent.

  3. Distinct, intelligible, perspicuous, plain, clear, rational, luculent.

  4. Sane, sober, sound (*in mind*), reasonable.

Lucidity, *n.* 1. Brightness, clearness, transparency, lucidness.

  2. Intelligibility, clearness, perspicuity, transparency, plainness, lucidness.

Lucifer, *n.* 1. Venus, Phosphorus, the morning star.

  2. Satan, Belial, Apollyon, Devil, Arch-fiend, the Tempter, the Evil One, the Man of Sin, the Wicked One, the Old Serpent, the Prince of Darkness, the Foul Fiend, the Enemy, the Author of Evil.

Luck, *n.* 1. Chance, fortune, hazard, hap, haphazard, fate, accident, casualty.

  2. Success, good fortune.

Luckily, *adv.* Fortunately, by good luck, as good luck would have it.

Luckless, *a.* Unfortunate, unlucky, unprosperous, unsuccessful, ill-fated, ill-starred, unpropitious, unhappy.

Lucky, *a.* 1. Fortunate (*in an unexpected way*), happy, blessed, favored, successful.

  2. Prosperous, auspicious, propitious, favorable, fortunate.

Lucrative, *a.* Profitable, remunerative, gainful, paying.

Lucre, *n.* Gain, profit, emolument, pelf, riches, wealth, mammon, greed.

Ludicrous, *a.* Laughable, comical, comic, odd, ridiculous, droll, funny, farcical, absurd, sportive, burlesque.

Lug, *v. t.* Pull, tug, haul, drag.

Luggage, *n.* 1. Baggage, bag and baggage.

  2. Effects, things, stuff, " traps."

Lugubrious, *a.* Mournful, sorrowful, doleful, sad, gloomy, melancholy, complaining.

Lukewarm, *a.* 1. Tepid, blood-warm, slightly warm, thermal.

  2. Indifferent, unconcerned, listless, cold, torpid, dull.

Lull, *v. t.* Compose, quiet, calm, still, hush, tranquillize, put to rest.

——, *v. i.* Subside, cease, abate, decrease, diminish, become calm.

——, *n.* Calm, calmness, temporary quiet, cessation.

Lullaby, *n.* Cradle-song.

Lumber, *n.* Trash, trumpery, rubbish, refuse.

——, *v. t.* 1. Heap in disorder.

  2. Fill with trumpery, choke, crowd, obstruct, encumber.

——, *v. i.* 1. Trudge, move heavily.

  2. Rumble.

  3. [*U. S.*] Cut timber, prepare logs for lumber.

Lumbering, *a.* 1. Trudging, moving slowly.

  2. Cumbrous, cumbersome, clumsy, awkward, unwieldy, ponderous.

Luminous, *a.* 1. Shining, radiant, resplendent, effulgent, refulgent, incandescent.

  2. Bright, brilliant, clear.

  3. Lucid, clear, perspicuous, luculent, plain.

LUMP, *n.* Shapeless mass, chunk, hunk.

——, *v. t.* Throw into an aggregate, take in the gross.

Lumpish, *a.* 1. Heavy, gross, bulky.

  2. Dull, heavy, stupid, gross, inactive.

Lunacy, *n.* Insanity, madness, mania, derangement, craziness, mental aberration, crack.

Lunatic, *a.* Insane, mad, deranged, crazy.

——, *n.* Madman, maniac, insane person, crack.

Lunatic asylum. Madhouse, bedlam, insane asylum, insane hospital, hospital for the insane.

Lunch, *n.* Luncheon, slight repast, tiffin.

Lunge, *n.* Pass, thrust, allonge, longe.

Lupine, *a.* Wolfish, ravenous.

Lurch, *v. t.* 1. Rob, deprive of, outstrip in acquiring.

2. Steal, appropriate, take privily, filch, purloin, pilfer.

3. Deceive, disappoint, leave in the lurch, defeat, evade.

——, *v. i.* 1. Lurk, skulk, lie close, lie in ambush.

2. Shift, play tricks, contrive, dodge.

3. (*Naut.*) Roll suddenly.

Lure, *n.* Enticement, bait, attraction, allurement, decoy, temptation.

——, *v. t.* Entice, allure, attract, decoy, tempt, seduce, inveigle.

Lurid, *a.* Gloomy, murky, ghastly, dismal, pale, lowering.

Lurk, *v. i.* 1. Lie hid, lie concealed, lie in wait, lurch.

2. Skulk, keep out of sight, keep out of the way.

Luscious, *a.* 1. Delicious, savory, palatable, grateful, pleasing, delightful.

2. Honeyed, excessively sweet, cloying, sugary.

3. Unctuous, fulsome, rank, nauseous.

Lush, *a.* Juicy, succulent, watery, sappy, moist, full of juice, fresh, luxuriant.

Lust, *n.* 1. Cupidity, inordinate desire, longing desire, eagerness to possess.

2. Concupiscence, carnality, lechery, salaciousness, salacity, lubricity, wantonness, lasciviousness, carnal desire, brutal appetite.

Lust after. 1. Long for, desire eagerly *or* inordinately.

2. Have carnal desire for.

Luster, *n.* 1. Brightness, brilliancy, sheen, sparkle, splendor, gleam, radiance, refulgence, resplendence, glitter.

2. Distinction, repute, renown, eminence, celebrity, glory, honor, *éclat*.

Lustful, *a.* Concupiscent, libidinous, lubric,

lubricous, salacious, lecherous, lascivious, lickerish, carnal, licentious.

Lustily, *adv.* Vigorously, strongly.

Lustration, *n.* 1. Purification, cleansing, washing.

2. Religious purification, ceremony of cleansing, lustrum.

Lustrous, *a.* Bright, shining, beaming, luminous, glossy, sheeny, radiant, brilliant.

Lusty, *a.* 1. Stout, vigorous, robust, healthful, lively, strong, sturdy.

2. Bulky, large, corpulent, fat, burly, stout.

Luxuriance, } *n.* Exuberance, superabun-
Luxuriancy, } dance, profusion, rank growth.

Luxuriant, *a.* Exuberant, profuse, superabundant, plentiful, plenteous.

Luxuriate, *v. i.* 1. Flourish, grow luxuriantly.

2. Revel, wanton, live luxuriously, live in clover.

3. Delight, indulge to excess, revel.

Luxurious, *a.* Voluptuous, epicurean, effeminate, sensual, intemperate, self-indulgent, sybaritic.

Luxuriously, *adv.* Voluptuously, in luxury, in clover, on velvet, on a bed of roses, in the lap of luxury.

Luxury, *n.* 1. Voluptuousness, luxuriousness, sensuality, epicurism, effeminacy, sensuality, animalism.

2. Pleasure, gratification, enjoyment, delight.

3. Dainty, treat, delicacy.

Lydian, *a.* Soft, effeminate, voluptuous.

Lying, *a.* 1. False, mendacious, equivocating, untruthful, untrue.

2. Recumbent.

——, *n.* Falsehood, fabling, mendacity, equivocation.

Lymphatic, *a.* 1. Enthusiastic, frantic, raving, mad, insane, wild.

2. Pertaining to lymph.

Lyn, *n.* Waterfall, lin, cascade.

Lynx-eyed, *a.* Sharp-sighted, eagle-eyed, hawk-eyed, keen-eyed, Argus-eyed.

Lyric, *a.* Melic, tuneful, melodious.

M

Macaroni, *n.* 1. Italian paste, Genoese paste.

2. Medley, extravaganza.

3. Droll, fool, jester, merry-andrew, scaramouch.

4. Beau, exquisite, fop, popinjay, dandy, coxcomb, jackanapes, jack-a-dandy, man milliner, man of dress, vain fellow.

Mace, *n.* Truncheon, staff, *bâton*.

Macerate, *v. t.* 1. Make lean, wear away.

2. Harass, mortify, subject to hardships, torture.

3. Soften (*by steeping*), steep, soak, digest.

Maceration, *n.* 1. Mortification.

2. Softening, steeping, soaking.

Machiavelian, *a.* Artful, designing, insidious, sly, shrewd, astute, subtle, diplomatic, arch, intriguing, cunning, crafty, wily, crooked, tricky, deceitful.

Machiavelianism, *n.* Duplicity, chicane, guile, chicanery, trickery, cunning, circumvention, deceit, deception, artifice, dissimulation, double-dealing, hocus-pocus, shifting, quibbling, stratagem, roguery, craft, subtlety, insidiousness.

Machinate, *v. t.* Plan, contrive, form, plot, scheme, devise.

Machination, *n.* Plot, complot, conspiracy, intrigue, cabal, stratagem, trick, design, contrivance, artifice, scheme.

MACHINE, *n.* 1. Engine, instrument of force.

2. Tool, instrument, puppet.

3. Organization, system.

Machinery, *n.* Enginery, mechanism.

Maculate, *v. t.* Spot, stain, blur, blotch.

——, *a.* 1. Spotted, blotted, maculose, blurred, blotched.

2. Defiled, impure, corrupt, unclean.

Mad, *a.* 1. Insane, crazy, crazed, distracted, lunatic, delirious, deranged, demented, maniac, maniacal.

2. Furious, enraged, raging.

3. Angry, exasperated, provoked, incensed, enraged, wrathful, furious.

4. Infatuated, distracted, wild.

5. Frenzied, frantic, raving, distracted.

Madcap, *n.* Hotspur, blood, hot-headed person.

Madden, *v. t.* Irritate, provoke, enrage, infuriate, craze, exasperate, inflame, make mad, drive mad, turn one's head, lash into fury, make one's blood boil.

Madhouse, *n.* Bedlam, lunatic hospital, lunatic asylum, hospital for the insane.

Madman, *n.* Lunatic, maniac, bedlamite, insane person, crazy person.

Madness, *n.* 1. Insanity, derangement, craziness, lunacy, distraction, mental aberration, mania.

2. Frenzy, fury, rage, delirium, franticness.

Maelstrom, *n.* Whirlpool.

Magazine, *n.* 1. Warehouse, storehouse, receptacle, depository, repository, *entrepôt*, *dépôt*.

2. Periodical pamphlet.

Maggot, *n.* 1. Grub, worm.

2. Caprice, whim, crotchet, quirk, freak, vagary, humor, fancy, whimsey.

Maggoty, *a.* 1. Fly-blown, full of maggots.

2. Whimsical, crotchety, capricious, fantastic, fantastical, odd, strange, fanciful, freakish.

Magic, *n.* 1. Sorcery, necromancy, thaumaturgy, Magianism, conjury, voodoo, enchantment, the black art, witchcraft.

2. Witchery, enchantment, charm, fascination.

Magic, } *a.* Necromantic, thaumaturgic, **Magical,** } occult.

Magician, *n.* Sorcerer, enchanter, necromancer, wizard, conjurer, *magus*, shaman.

Magister, *n.* Master, sir, doctor.

Magisterial, *a.* Domineering, lordly, imperious, proud, arrogant, lofty, authoritative, despotic, dictatorial, consequential, pompous, dogmatical, haughty.

Magistrate, *n.* Officer (*in civil service*); judge, prefect, consul, etc.

Magnanimity, *n.* Generosity, disinterestedness, high-mindedness, forbearance, greatness *or* nobleness of mind, elevation of soul, chivalrous spirit.

Magnanimous, *a.* 1. Brave, dauntless, heroic, illustrious.

2. Noble, elevated, lofty, generous, disinterested, chivalrous, liberal, unselfish, high-minded, great-souled, exalted, honorable.

Magnate, *n.* Noble, nobleman, grandee, man of rank, distinguished person.

Magnet, *n.* Loadstone.

Magnetic, *a.* Attractive.

Magnetize, *v. t.* Attract, move, influence.

Magnificence, *n.* Grandeur, splendor, pomp, grand appearance, *éclat*.

Magnificent, *a.* 1. Grand (*in appearance*), splendid, superb, majestic, sublime, noble.

2. Pompous, imposing, stately, showy, gorgeous, superb.

Magnify, *v. t.* 1. Enlarge, augment, amplify, make great, increase the size of (*to the eye*).

2. Extol, exalt, elevate, celebrate, glorify, bless, laud, praise.

3. Exaggerate.

Magniloquence, *n.* Bombast, grandiloquence, turgidity, inflation, fustian, flourish, pompous language.

Magniloquent, *a.* Grandiloquent, tumid, bombastic, inflated, swelling, declamatory, turgid, pompous, stilted, high-flowing, high-flown.

Magnitude, *n.* 1. Size, bulk, volume, extent, bigness, dimension, mass.

2. Greatness, importance, consequence.

3. Grandeur, sublimity, loftiness.

Mahometan, *n.* Mohammedan, Mussulman, Moslem, Muslim.

Mahometanism, *n.* Mohammedanism, Islam.

Maid, *n.* 1. Girl, lass, lassie, virgin, maiden, damsel.

2. Maid-servant, female servant.

Maiden, *a.* 1. Of maids, of virgins, unmarried.

2. Pure, chaste, undefiled, virgin, unpolluted.

3. Fresh, new, unused.

Maidenhood, *n.* 1. Virginity, virgin purity, maidhood.

2. Freshness, newness.

Maidenly, *a.* Modest, gentle, reserved, maidenlike.

Maid-servant, *n.* Maid, female servant, handmaid, "biddy."

Mail, *n.* 1. Armor, defensive covering.

2. Post, conveyance for mailed matter.

3. Mailed matter.

——, *v. t.* Put in the mail, put in the post-office, send by post, post.

Maim, *v. t.* Cripple, mutilate, disable, obtruncate, mangle, mar.

——, *n.* 1. [Written also *Maihem* and *Mayhem.*] Crippling, mutilation, disfigurement.

2. Injury, mischief, harm, hurt.

Main, *a.* 1. Chief, principal, leading, cardinal, capital.

2. Important, essential, necessary, requisite, indispensable, vital.

3. Mighty, vast, huge, enormous.

4. Sheer, pure, directly applied.

5. Absolute, mere, direct, entire.

——, *n.* 1. Ocean, great sea, high sea.

2. Continent, mainland.

3. Main conduit, main pipe, main duct, main channel.

4. Force, power, strength, might, violent effort.

5. The gross, the bulk, the greater part, majority.

Mainland, *n.* Continent.

Mainly, *adv.* 1. Chiefly, principally, in the main.

2. Greatly, mightily, largely, absolutely, entirely.

Main-stay, *n.* Principal support, chief reliance, main dependence.

Maintain, *v. t.* 1. Sustain, support, preserve, uphold, keep.

2. Hold, keep, keep possession of.

3. Defend, vindicate, justify.

4. Continue, keep up, carry on.

5. Provide food for, supply with means of living, support, keep up.

6. Assert, allege, declare.

——, *v. i.* Affirm, aver, allege, declare, hold, say, contend, hold the opinion.

Maintenance, *n.* 1. Support, vindication, justification, defence, preservation, sustenance.

2. Sustenance, food, victuals, provisions, bread, livelihood, subsistence.

Majestic, *a.* 1. August, imposing, dignified, noble, princely, stately, imperial, royal, regal, lofty, pompous.

2. Splendid, grand, sublime, magnificent.

3. Elevated, lofty, stately, exalted.

Majesty, *n.* 1. Grandeur, dignity, stateliness, loftiness.

2. Dignity, elevation, loftiness.

Major, *a.* Greater.

Major-domo, *n.* Steward.

Majority, *n.* 1. Greater number, more than half, preponderance, bulk, mass.

2. Manhood, full age, adulthood.

MAKE, *v. t.* 1. Create, bring into being.

2. Frame, fashion, mould, shape, form, figure.

3. Fabricate, construct, produce, effect, be productive of, cause.

4. Constitute, cause to be, cause to become.

5. Perform, do, execute, practise.

6. Secure, gain, acquire, get, raise.

7. Compel, constrain, force, require, cause, occasion.

8. Constitute, compose, form, make up.

9. Serve, answer for, form, do the part of, become.

10. (*Naut.*) Reach, attain, arrive at.

——, *v. i.* 1. Do, act, be active, interfere.

2. Proceed, go, travel, journey, tend, move.

3. Contribute, conduce, operate, have effect, tend, be of advantage, favor.

——, *n.* Structure, construction, shape, form, constitution, build.

Make believe. Pretend, feign, appear, seem, act as if, make as if.

——, *n.* Sham, feint, pretence, pretext, counterfeit.

——, *a.* Unreal, sham, pretended, counterfeited, mock, clap-trap.

Make for. 1. Move toward, go toward, strike for.

2. Favor, tend to the advantage of.

Make good. 1. Defend, maintain, vindicate, justify, stand by.

2. Fulfil, accomplish.

3. Establish, verify, confirm, prove, substantiate.

4. Compensate for, make compensation for, supply by an equivalent, make up for.

Make known. Publish, declare, bring to light, proclaim.

Make merry. Feast, be jovial, be joyful.

Make much of. Cherish, foster, fondle, pet, coddle, treat with fondness.

Make of. 1. Understand, interpret.
2. Effect *or* produce from.
3. Consider, account, esteem.

Make off with. 1. Take away, carry off.
2. Steal, pilfer, filch, purloin, cabbage.

Make out, *v. t.* 1. Discover, ascertain, learn, determine, interpret, decipher, get a clear understanding of.
2. Prove, establish, evince.
3. Prepare, draw up.
4. Provide, furnish, supply, find.

——, *v. i.* Succeed, be able at last, make a shift.

Make over. Transfer, convey, alienate.

Maker, *n.* 1. Creator, God.
2. Manufacturer, former, builder, constructor.
3. Author, writer, composer.
4. (*Law.*) Signer of a promissory note.

Makeshift, *n.* Substitute, temporary expedient.

Make sport of. Mock, ridicule, deride, scout, scoff at, jeer at, laugh at.

Make sure of. 1. Secure, make certain.
2. Consider as certain.

Make up, *v. t.* 1. Collect, get together.
2. Constitute, form, compose.
3. Reconcile, settle, adjust, compose.
4. Compensate, make good, make up for.
5. Supply, furnish, provide.
6. Determine, bring to a conclusion.

Make up with. Settle differences, become friends.

Make way. 1. Advance, proceed.
2. Clear a way, open a passage.

Making, *n.* 1. Workmanship, construction, fabrication, formation.
2. Composition, structure, form, make.
3. Material.

Maladministration, *n.* Misrule, misgovernment, malversation.

Maladroit, *a.* Awkward, clumsy, unskilful, unskilled, bungling, unhandy, inapt, inexpert.

Malady, *n.* Disease, distemper, disorder, complaint, ail, ailment, sickness, illness, indisposition.

Malapert, *a.* Saucy, impudent, rude, forward, flippant, bold, impertinent, impudent, insolent, cavalier, quick.

Malaria, *n.* Miasma, miasm, noxious exhalation, bad air.

Malarious, *a.* Insalubrious, miasmatic, unhealthy, unwholesome, malarial.

Malcontent, *a.* Discontented, dissatisfied, unsatisfied, uneasy, insurgent.

——, *n.* Agitator, irreconcilable.

MALE, *a.* Masculine, he, man.

——, *n.* Male animal, he, tom- (*in compounds*).

Malediction, *n.* Curse, cursing, denunciation, malison, execration, imprecation, anathema, ban.

Malefactor, *n.* Culprit, felon, convict, criminal, outlaw, evil-doer.

Maleficent, *a.* Harmful, mischievous, injurious, evil-doing.

Malevolence, *n.* Spitefulness. See MALICE.

Malevolent, *a.* See MALICIOUS.

Malformation, *n.* Deformity.

Malice, *n.* Malevolence, maliciousness, malignity, rancor, venom, hate, spite, ill-will, enmity, bitterness, grudge, pique.

Malicious, *a.* Malevolent, malignant, spiteful, ill-disposed, ill-natured, evil-minded, mischievous, resentful, bitter, rancorous, envious, invidious.

Malign, *a.* 1. Malicious, malevolent, malignant, ill-disposed.
2. Injurious, pernicious, unfavorable, baneful, very bad, unpropitious.

——, *v. t.* Revile, slander, abuse, calumniate, asperse, defame, blacken, traduce, scandalize, disparage, vilify.

Malignance, } *n.* 1. Malice, malignity,
Malignancy, } bitter enmity, extreme malevolence.
2. Unfavorableness, unpropitiousness.
3. See MALIGNITY, 2.

Malignant, *a.* 1. Malign, malicious, malevolent, bitter, rancorous, spiteful, resentful, envious, virulently inimical.
2. Unpropitious, unfavorable, ill-boding.
3. Extremely heinous, virulent, pernicious.
4. (*Med.*) Dangerous, fatal, virulent.

Maligner, *n.* Vilifier, slanderer, traducer, calumniator, backbiter, libeller, defamer.

Malignity, *n.* 1. Malice, malevolence, maliciousness, malignancy, hatred, animosity, ill-will, rancor, spite.
2. Virulence, fatality, malignancy, deadliness, destructiveness.
3. Heinousness, enormity, evilness.

Mall, *n. & v. t.* See MAUL.

——, *n.* 1. Public walk, shaded walk.
2. Court, pleading-house.

Mallet, *n.* Wooden hammer.

Malpractice, *n.* Misconduct, misbehavior, misdoing, dereliction, malversation.

Maltreat, *v. t.* Abuse, ill-treat, ill-use, injure.

Maltreatment, *n.* Abuse, ill treatment, bad treatment, ill usage.

Malversation, *n.* Misconduct (*in office*), fraudulent conduct (*as embezzlement, etc.*).

Mammon, *n.* Riches, wealth.

Mammonist, *n.* Worldling, mammonite.

Mammoth, *a.* Gigantic, very large, huge, colossal, immense.

MAN, *n.* 1. Person, individual, body, somebody, one, personage, soul, living soul, some one, human being.
   2. Mankind, the human race, humanity.
   3. Vassal, liege, subject, servant, attendant, dependant.
   4. Husband, married man.
   5. Workman, employee.
—, *v. t.* 1. Furnish with men, supply with hands, garrison.
   2. Strengthen, fortify, re-enforce.

Manacle, *n.* Shackle (*for the hands*), handcuff, hand-fetter.
—, *v. t.* 1. Handcuff, shackle.
   2. Shackle, fetter, tie, restrain, confine, bind.

Manage, *n.* Horsemanship, *manège*, equestrian art.
—, *v. t.* 1. Conduct, direct, regulate, superintend, supervise, administer, carry on, operate, guide, treat, handle, order, transact.
   2. Rule (*with address* or *artifice*), control, govern, guide.
   3. Wield, handle, have under command, manipulate, control.
   4. Husband, treat sparingly, economize, save, contrive.
—, *v. i.* Manœuvre, concert measures, contrive ways, direct affairs, pull the wires *or* strings, administer.

Manageable, *a.* Tractable, governable, docile, controllable, tamable.

Management, *n.* 1. Conduct, control, direction, charge, administration, government, guidance, disposal, economy, treatment, superintendence, care, surveillance, managery.
   2. Contrivance, prudent conduct, cunning practice, skill, address, skilful treatment.
   3. Negotiation, transactions, dealing.

MANAGER, *n.* 1. Director, superintendent, overseer, supervisor, comptroller, governor, conductor, impresario.
   2. Economist, good economist.

Managing, *a.* 1. Intriguing.
   2. Economical, frugal, thrifty, prudent, provident.

Mandate, *n.* Command, order, injunction, precept, charge, requirement, commission, edict.

Mandatory, *a.* Preceptive, directory.

Man-eater, *n.* Cannibal, anthropophagi (*pl.*).

Manes, *n. pl.* 1. Lares, benevolent infernal deities.
   2. Ghosts, shades, souls of the departed, spirits, spectres, *lemures*.

Manful, *a.* Courageous, bold, brave, stout, strong, vigorous, daring, heroic, intrepid, undaunted, manly, honorable, noble.

Mangily, *adv.* Meanly, basely, scurvily, scabbily, foully, vilely.

Mangle, *v. t.* 1. Lacerate, hack, tear (*in cutting*), mutilate.
   2. Mutilate, mar, destroy, spoil, maim.
   3. Polish, smooth, calender, press with a mangle.

Mangy, *a.* Scabby, infected with mange.

Man-hater, *n.* Misanthrope, misanthropist.

Manhood, *n.* 1. Virility.
   2. Courage, bravery, hardihood, firmness, resolution, fortitude, manliness, manfulness.
   3. Humanity, human nature.
   4. Man's estate, maturity, adulthood.

Mania, *n.* 1. Madness, insanity, violent derangement, lunacy, aberration, delirium, frenzy, *dementia*.
   2. Vehement desire.

Maniac, *n.* Madman, lunatic, bedlamite, insane person, crack.

Maniac, } *a.* Mad, insane, raving, deranged, demented.
Maniacal, }

Manifest, *a.* Apparent, open, obvious, plain, evident, patent, clear, palpable, visible, unmistakable, glaring, conspicuous, distinct, indubitable.
—, *v. t.* Show, exhibit, reveal, declare, display, disclose, prove, evince, evidence, discover, express, set forth, bring to light, expose to view, hold up to view, make known.

Manifesto, *n.* Declaration (*of a sovereign* or *a government*), manifest, public protestation.

Manifold, *a.* 1. Numerous, multiplied, multitudinous, various, many.
   2. Various, diverse, multifarious.

Maniple, *n.* 1. Handful, small band, company (*of Roman soldiers*).
   2. Fanon, stole, kind of scarf.

Manipulate, *v. t. and v. i.* Work *or* operate with the hands, handle.

Man-killer, *n.* Murderer, man-slayer, homicide.

Mankind, *n.* 1. Man, the human race, humankind.
   2. Men, the lords of creation.

Manliness, *n.* Bravery, courage, intrepidity, heroism, firmness, resolution, nobleness, dignity, boldness.

Manly, *a.* Brave, courageous, intrepid, stout, bold, firm, undaunted, vigorous, strong, daring, heroic, noble, manful, dignified.

Manner, *n.* 1. Method, mode, fashion, form, way, style.

2. Custom, habit, practice.

3. Degree, measure, extent.

4. [*sing. and pl.*] Sort, kind, sorts, kinds.

5. Behavior, carriage, deportment, air, mien, look, aspect, appearance, demeanor.

6. Mannerism, characteristic style, distinctive peculiarity.

7. Conduct, morals, habits, behavior.

8. Civility, ceremonious behavior, respectful deportment.

Mannerism, *n.* 1. Sameness of manner, uniformity, self-repetition.

2. Peculiarity, affectation.

Mannerly, *a.* Courteous, civil, polite, urbane, complaisant, refined, well-bred, respectful, ceremonious, well-behaved.

Manners, *n. pl.* 1. Morals, habits, conduct.

2. Behavior, deportment, etiquette, bearing, breeding, air, carriage.

Mannish, *a.* Bold, masculine.

Manœuvre, *n.* 1. Evolution, movement.

2. Scheme, plan, plot, stratagem, artifice, trick, finesse, artful management, adroit procedure, intrigue, *ruse.*

——, *v. i.* 1. Perform evolutions.

2. Contrive, plan, plot, manage, pull the wires *or* strings, scheme, intrigue, finesse.

Manœuvrer, *n.* Tactician, adroit manager, strategist.

Man-of-war, *n.* Ship of war, armed ship, battleship, dreadnaught.

Manor-house, *n.* Hall, manor-seat, mansion, mansion-house.

Manse, *n.* [*Scotch.*] Parsonage, parsonage-house.

Mansion, *n.* 1. Dwelling, seat, residence, habitation, dwelling-house, mansion-house, abode.

2. Manor-house (*which see*).

Manslaughter, *n.* Murder, homicide.

Man-slayer, *n.* Murderer, homicide, man-killer.

Mantilla, *n.* 1. Hood, head-covering, kind of veil.

2. Small mantle, light cloak.

Mantle, *n.* 1. Cloak, toga, chasuble.

2. Cover, covering.

3. Mantel-piece, mantel-shelf.

——, *v. t.* Cloak, overspread, cover, disguise, obscure.

——, *v. i.* 1. Expand, spread, be expanded.

2. Effervesce, bubble, foam, **sparkle,** froth, cream.

Manual, *a.* Of the hand, by the hand.

——, *n.* Hand-book, enchiridion.

Manufactory, *n.* Factory.

Manufacture, *n.* Production, fabrication, making.

Manumission, *n.* Emancipation, enfranchisement, liberation, deliverance, release, act of freeing a slave from bondage.

Manumit, *v. t.* Free, liberate, **release,** emancipate, enfranchise, set free.

Manure, *v. t.* Fertilize, enrich.

——, *n.* Fertilizer, compost, muck, guano, dressing, fertilizing mixture.

Manuscript, *n.* Copy, written document, writing, typescript.

Many, *a.* Numerous, manifold, various, multifold, multitudinous, multiplied, divers, frequent, sundry.

——, *n.* Multitude, people, many persons, many people, crowd, numerous company.

Many-sided, *a.* Polyhedral, multilateral.

MAP, *n.* Chart, diagram, plot.

Map, *v. t.* Delineate, draw, picture.

Mar, *v. t.* 1. Injure, spoil, ruin, hurt, damage, harm, impair.

2. Deface, deform, disfigure, spoil, maim.

Maraud, *v. i.* Rove for plunder.

——, *n.* Marauding, ravage, plunder, spoliation.

Marauder, *n.* Plunderer, ravager, pillager, robber, desperado, freebooter, brigand, outlaw, bandit, rover, reiver, filibuster.

March, *v. i.* 1. Walk (*by regular steps, as soldiers*), move forward.

2. Walk in a steady manner, step, go.

——, *n.* 1. Military movement, passage of soldiers, file, deploy, countermarch.

2. Stately walk, deliberate walk.

3. Progression, advance, advancement, progress, progressive development, movement.

4. Military tune.

Marches, *n. pl.* Borders, limits, frontiers, confines, precincts, boundaries.

Mare, *n.* Female horse, filly.

Margin, *n.* Border, edge, rim, brim, verge, brink, confine, limit, skirt.

Marine, *a.* 1. Oceanic, pelagic, pelagian, salt-water, sea.

2. Maritime, naval, nautical.

——, *n.* 1. Navy, shipping.

2. Soldier (*of a ship of war*), sea-soldier.

3. (*Painting.*) Sea-piece, sea-scape.

Mariner, *n.* Seaman, sailor, seafarer, sea-faring man, tar.

Marital, *a.* Of a husband, incident to a husband, matrimonial, connubial, conjugal.

Maritime, *a.* 1. Marine, naval, nautical.
2. Near the sea, bordering on the sea.

MARK, *n.* 1. Sign, token, symbol, trace, line, impress, impression, stamp, brand, character, print, characteristic.
2. Indication, evidence, proof, symptom, token, characteristic, trace, vestige, track.
3. Badge, sign.
4. Trace, track, vestige, footprint.
5. Object (*aimed at*), bull's-eye, target, butt.
6. Eminence, consequence, distinction, importance, pre-eminence, eminent position.
——, *v. t.* 1. Distinguish by a mark, put a mark upon, label, earmark.
2. Stamp, brand, designate, characterize, denote, single out, point out, indicate, betoken, imprint, impress, stigmatize.
3. Notice, note, observe, remark, take notice of, regard, heed, evince.
——, *v. i.* Observe, note, remark, take notice.

Marked, *a.* Notable, remarkable, noted, prominent, conspicuous, eminent, distinguished.

MARKET, *n.* 1. Mart, emporium, place of traffic, exchange, fair, *entrepôt*; market-house, market-place, bazaar.
2. Sale, opportunity to sell.
3. Price, cost, worth, valuation, rate, charge.
——, *v. t.* Vend, sell, traffic in, offer for sale, dispose of.

Marketable, *a.* 1. Salable, vendible, merchantable.
2. Current in market, current.

Marriage, *n.* 1. Nuptials, wedding, espousals, spousals, nuptial rites.
2. Matrimony, wedlock.
3. Union.

MARRIED, *a.* Conjugal, connubial, matrimonial.

Marrow, *n.* 1. Medulla, pith.
2. Essence, quintessence, best part, essential part.

Marry, *v. t.* 1. Join in marriage, unite in marriage.
2. Wed, espouse, take for husband *or* wife, lead to the altar, bestow one's hand upon.
3. Give in marriage, dispose of in wedlock.
4. Unite, join, make one.
——, *interj.* Indeed, forsooth, in truth.

Marsh, *n.* Fen, bog, quagmire, mire, morass, swamp, slough.

Marshal, *n.* 1. Chief officer of arms, commander-in-chief.

2. Conductor, director, regulator, master of ceremonies.
3. Harbinger, pursuivant, herald.
——, *v. t.* 1. Arrange, range, rank, dispose, array, draw up, set in order.
2. Lead, guide, prepare the way, herald.

Marshy, *a.* Boggy, fenny, paludal, palustrine, miry, morassy, swampy, "squashy," wet.

Mart, *n.* Market, emporium, *entrepôt*, place of traffic.

Martial, *a.* 1. Suited to war.
2. Warlike, brave, given to war.
3. Military.

Martinet, *n.* Precisian, formalist, strict *or* severe disciplinarian.

Martyr, *v. t.* 1. Sacrifice on account of faith.
2. Persecute, afflict, torment, torture, agonize, destroy.

Marvel, *n.* 1. Wonder, prodigy, miracle.
2. Wonder, admiration, astonishment, amazement, surprise.
——, *v. i.* Wonder, be surprised, be astonished.

Marvellous, *a.* 1. Wondrous, wonderful, amazing, stupendous, astonishing, miraculous, very extraordinary, most strange, prodigious.
2. Incredible, improbable, surpassing credit, surprising.

Marvellously, *adv.* Exceedingly, wonderfully, strangely.

Masculine, *a.* 1. Male, of the male sex.
2. Manly, virile, manlike, bold, hardy, manful.
3. Strong, robust, powerful.
4. Coarse, bold, forward, mannish.

Mash, *v. t.* Bruise, crush, beat, mix, knead, compound.

Mask, *n.* 1. Cover (*for the face*), visor.
2. Cloak, screen, blind, disguise, veil.
3. Subterfuge, evasion, trick, shift, pretence, pretext, plea, *ruse*.
4. Masquerade.
5. Revel, piece of mummery, bustle.
——, *v. t.* 1. Put a mask on.
2. Disguise, conceal, hide, cloak, veil, screen, shroud, cover.

Masker, *n.* Mummer, domino, person in disguise, masquerader.

Mason, *n.* 1. Builder in stone *or* brick.
2. Free-mason.

Masquerade, *n.* 1. Mask, revel, piece of mummery.
2. Disguise, mask, veil, cover.

Mass, *n.* 1. Lump, cake, clot.
2. Heap, assemblage, combination, congeries.
3. Size, magnitude, bulk, dimension.

4. Whole, aggregate, sum total, totality, body.

Mass, *n.* Communion service (*in the Roman Catholic Church*), celebration of the Lord's Supper, Eucharistic rite.

Massacre, *v. t.* Butcher (*human beings*), murder, kill, slay, slaughter.

——, *n.* Butchery, slaughter, carnage, pogrom.

Massive, } *a.* Bulky, heavy, weighty, ponderous, huge, immense.
Massy, }

Mast, *n.* Nuts, pannage, pawns, pawnage.

Master, *n.* 1. Ruler, director, governor, manager, superintendent, overseer, lord.

    2. Commander, captain.

    3. Teacher, instructor, tutor, preceptor, schoolmaster, pedagogue.

    4. Owner, proprietor, holder, possessor.

    5. Proficient, adept, master-hand.

    6. Employer.

    7. Chief, principal, head, leader.

——, *v. t.* 1. Overpower, overcome, conquer, subdue, subjugate, vanquish.

    2. Acquire, learn thoroughly, make one's self master of, become an adept in.

——, *a.* Main, chief, leading, principal, cardinal, prime, especial, great, grand, most important.

Master-hand, *n.* Adept, proficient, dab, expert, good hand, capital hand, nice hand.

Masterly, *a.* 1. Skilful, clever, dexterous, expert, adroit, excellent, finished.

    2. Imperious, domineering, arbitrary, despotical.

Master-mind, *n.* Master-spirit.

Master-piece, *n.* 1. Paragon, masterstroke, master-work, capital performance, principal performance, *chef-d'œuvre.*

    2. Chief excellence, forte, chief talent, strong side.

Mastership, *n.* 1. Headship.

    2. Dominion, rule, sway, mastery, supreme power.

    3. Superiority, supremacy, pre-eminence, mastery.

    4. Skill, cleverness, ability, talent.

Mastery, *n.* 1. Dominion, rule, sway, command, mastership, supreme power, supremacy.

    2. Superiority, pre-eminence, ascendency, supremacy, victory, conquest, leadership, headship, upper hand.

    3. Victory in war.

    4. Acquirement, attainment, acquisition.

    5. Skill, dexterity, great proficiency, cleverness, ability.

Masticate, *v. t.* Chew, eat, manducate.

Mastication, *n.* Chewing, manducation.

Masturbation, *n.* Onanism, self-pollution, secret vice, self-abuse, mastupration.

Mat, *v. t.* Interweave, entangle, twist together.

MATCH, *n.* 1. Equal, mate, companion, tally.

    2. Competition, trial, contest.

    3. Union, marriage.

——, *v. t.* 1. Rival, equal.

    2. Adapt, suit, fit, proportion, make equal, make harmonize.

    3. Marry, give in marriage, mate.

    4. Join, combine, couple, sort.

    5. Pit, oppose.

——, *v. i.* 1. Be married, mate.

    2. Suit, correspond, tally, be proportionate.

Matchable, *a.* 1. Equal, suitable, comparable.

    2. Correspondent, of like kind.

Matchless, *a.* Unrivalled, unparalleled, unequalled, peerless, incomparable, exquisite, inimitable, excellent, unmatched, consummate.

Mate, *n.* 1. Associate, companion, consort, fellow, compeer, intimate.

    2. Equal, match, suitable companion.

    3. Assistant, subordinate.

——, *v. t.* 1. Match, marry.

    2. Equal, vie with, cope with, compete with.

    3. Stupefy, confound, crush, appall, subdue, enervate.

MATERIAL, *a.* 1. Physical, corporeal, bodily.

    2. Essential, important, momentous, vital, weighty.

Material, *n.* Matter, substance, stuff.

Materially, *adv.* 1. Substantially, in substance, not in form merely.

    2. Importantly, essentially, vitally.

Maternal, *a.* Motherly, motherlike.

Maternity, *n.* Motherhood.

Mathematical, *a.* 1. Pertaining to mathematics.

    2. Precise, accurate, strict, rigid.

Matin, *a.* Morning.

Matins, *n. pl.* Morning prayers, morning service.

Matrimonial, *a.* Connubial, nuptial, hymeneal, conjugal, sponsal, spousal, marital.

Matrimony, *n.* Marriage, wedlock, nuptial state.

Matrix, *n.* 1. [Also written *Matrice.*] Womb.

    2. Mould (*especially one in which printers' letters are cast, and one in which coin is cast*).

Matron, *n.* 1. Wife, married woman, dame.

2. Elderly woman, dowager.

3. Head nurse, female head.

Matronize, *v. t.* 1. Render matronly.

2. Chaperon, act as mother to.

Matron-like, } *a.* 1. Elderly, matronal,
Matronly, } motherly.

2. Grave, sedate, matronal.

Matter, *n.* 1. Substance, body; content, sense (*as vs. form*).

2. Trouble, cause of distress, difficulty.

3. Indefinite amount, quantity, *or* portion.

4. Stuff, material, raw material.

5. Topic, subject, question, subject-matter, matter in hand.

6. Affair, business, concern, thing, event, course of things.

7. Importance, consequence, import, moment, significance.

8. Pus, purulence, purulent matter.

——, *v. i.* 1. Signify, import, be of importance, be of consequence, weigh.

2. Maturate, suppurate.

Matter-of-fact, *n.* Fact, reality, actuality.

——, *a.* 1. Ordinary, commonplace.

2. Practical, sensible, plain, prosaic, prosy, sober, unimaginative, dry, literal, unsentimental.

Mattock, *n.* Grub-axe, grubbing-hoe.

Maturate, *v. i.* 1. Ripen, mature.

2. Suppurate, matter.

Maturation, *n.* 1. Ripening, maturing.

2. Ripeness.

3. Suppuration.

Mature, *a.* 1. Perfected by time, complete, perfect, ripe, full-grown.

2. Prepared, ready, well-considered, well-digested, completed, ripe.

——, *v. t.* 1. Ripen.

2. Perfect, bring to perfection, bring to maturity, advance toward perfection.

——, *v. i.* 1. Become ripe.

2. Become due.

Maturely, *adv.* 1. Ripely, completely.

2. Carefully, cautiously.

Maturity, *n.* 1. Completion, ripeness, perfection, matureness.

2. Time of being due (*said of a promissory note, etc.*).

Matutinal, *a.* Morning, early.

Maudlin, *a.* 1. Intoxicated, inebriated, fuddled, muddled, disguised, tipsy, mellow, drunk, stupid, in liquor.

2. Silly, weak, over-emotional, sickly sentimental.

Maugre, *prep.* Notwithstanding, in spite of, in defiance of.

Maul, *n.* [Written also *Mall*.] Beetle, heavy mallet.

——, *v. t.* 1. Beat, bruise, wound, disfigure.

2. Injure grossly, abuse, deform, do much harm to.

Maunder, *v. i.* 1. Mutter (*as a beggar*), grumble, murmur.

2. Talk incoherently, drivel, wander.

Maunderer, *n.* Grumbler, murmurer, driveller.

Mausoleum, *n.* Sepulchral monument.

Maw, *n.* 1. Stomach (*of animals*).

2. Craw, crop, first stomach (*of a bird*).

Mawkish, *a.* Insipid, flat, vapid, tasteless, stale, sickly, nauseous, disgusting.

Maxim, *n.* Proverb, saying, saw, adage, aphorism, apothegm, dictum, by-word, sententious precept, axiom.

Maximize, *v. t.* Magnify, maximate, increase.

Maximum, *a.* Greatest, highest point, limit.

MAY, *v.* (*Basic Eng.*)

Maybe, *adv.* Perhaps, possibly, haply, it may be, as luck may have it.

Mayhap, *adv.* Perchance, perhaps, it may be, probably, it may happen, peradventure.

Maze, *n.* 1. Labyrinth, meander, intricacy, winding course.

2. Intricacy, perplexity, bewilderment, embarrassment, uncertainty, mizmaze.

——, *v. t.* Bewilder, amaze, confuse, perplex, confound.

Mazy, *a.* Labyrinthian, confused, winding, intricate, confusing, perplexing, embarrassing.

Meadow, *n.* Mead, lea, grass land, sward land.

Meagre, *a.* 1. Lean, thin, emaciated, spare, poor, lank, gaunt, skinny.

2. Barren, poor, sterile, unproductive.

3. Tame, feeble, jejune, vapid, bald, barren, dull, prosing, prosy, poor, mean, insignificant, small, scanty.

Meagreness, *n.* 1. Leanness, thinness, spareness.

2. Poorness, barrenness, sterility.

3. Scantiness, barrenness, smallness.

MEAL, *n.* 1. Repast, collation.

2. Flour, grain in powder, "grits."

Mealy, *a.* Farinaceous.

Mean, *a.* 1. Middle, medium, average, moderate.

2. Intermediate, intervening, coming between.

3. Ignoble, plebeian, low, ordinary, common, vulgar, coarse, humble.

4. Base, abject, grovelling, vile, contemptible, despicable, servile, beggarly, sneaking, dirty, scurvy, shabby, sorry, disingenuous, unfair, rascally, pitiful, base-minded, caitiff, low-minded, dishonorable, spiritless.

5. Sordid, penurious, miserly, stingy, niggardly, illiberal, ungenerous, unhandsome, selfish, narrow, mercenary, narrow-minded, parsimonious.

6. Small, little, paltry, insignificant, diminutive, petty, poor, wretched, contemptible, despicable.

Mean, *n.* 1. Medium, mediocrity, moderation, measure, middle state, middle course.

2. Average.

3. Instrument, method, mode, way, means, agency, instrumentality, measure.

——, *v. t.* 1. Intend, contemplate, purpose, design.

2. Signify, indicate, imply, denote, connote, purport, import, express, symbolize.

——, *v. i.* Intend, purpose, design.

Meander, *n.* 1. Labyrinth, maze, winding course, perplexity, intricacy.

2. Indirect course.

——, *v. i.* Wind, be tortuous, run in a serpentine course, turn, flow round.

Meandering, *a.* Winding, serpentine, tortuous, anfractuous, flexuous, meandrian, meandrous.

Meaning, *n.* 1. Intention, intent, purpose, design, aim, object.

2. Signification, sense, connotation, denotation, drift, acceptation, explanation, interpretation, import, purport, significance, force.

Meaningly, *adv.* Significantly.

Meanly, *adv.* Dishonorably, unworthily, depreciatingly, disrespectfully.

Meanness, *n.* 1. Humbleness, lowness.

2. Smallness, littleness, scantiness, slenderness, lowness, poverty, meagreness, poorness, rudeness.

3. Abjectness, vileness, baseness, contemptibleness, despicableness.

4. Illiberality, ungenerousness, sordidness, penuriousness, niggardliness.

Means, *n. sing* and *pl.* 1. Instrument, method, mode, way.

2. Resource, appliance, expedient, shift, step, measure.

3. Revenue, income, resources, the wherewithal, ways and means, substance, estate, property.

Mean-spirited, *a.* Base, low, beggarly, vile, grovelling, pitiful, despicable, abject, low-minded, base-minded, cowardly, timid.

Meantime, } *adv.* In the mean time, in
Meanwhile, } the interim.

Measurable, *a.* 1. Mensurable.

2. Moderate, temperate.

MEASURE, *n.* 1. Standard (*of measurement*), meter, rule, gauge.

2. Extent, degree, limit, determined length.

3. Allotment, share, due proportion.

4. Moderation, just degree.

5. Means to an end, step.

——, *v. t.* 1. Mete.

2. Estimate, appraise, judge of, appreciate, value, gauge.

3. Adjust, proportion, gauge.

4. Distribute, allot, apportion, mete out.

Measured, *a.* 1. Uniform, steady, equal, moderate, regular, moderated.

2. Limited, restricted.

Measureless, *a.* Immeasurable, unlimited, immense, boundless, limitless, endless, unbounded, vast, infinite.

Measurement, *n.* 1. Mensuration.

2. Bulk, size, area *or* content, quantity.

MEAT, *n.* 1. Food, aliment, nutriment, sustenance, nourishment, provision, victuals, viands, diet, regimen, cheer, subsistence, rations, feed, fare.

2. Flesh (*for food*), flesh-meat.

Meat-pie, *n.* 1. Mince-pie.

2. Pasty, meat pudding.

Mechanic, *n.* Artisan, artificer, craftsman, handicraftsman, operative, workman, hand.

Mechanical, *a.* Involuntary, blind, automatic.

Mechanism, *n.* Machinery, mechanical construction, apparatus, works.

Meddle, *v. i.* Interfere, intermeddle, interpose.

Meddler, *n.* Intermeddler, busybody.

Meddlesome, } *a.* Interfering, intermed-
Meddling, } dling, pragmatical, officious, intrusive.

Mediæval, *a.* [Written also *Medieval.*] Middle-age.

Medial, *a.* Mean, average.

Median, *a.* Middle.

Mediate, *a.* 1. Middle.

2. Interposed, intervening.

——, *v. i.* Interpose, intercede, arbitrate.

Mediation, *n.* 1. Intercession.

2. Interposition, intervention, arbitration, mediate agency.

Mediator, *n.* 1. Intercessor, advocate, propitiator, interceder, arbitrator, umpire.

2. Christ, Jesus, the Messiah.

Mediatory, *a.* Intermediary, mediative, intercessive.

MEDICAL, *a.* 1. Of medicine, of the healing art.

2. See MEDICINAL.

Medicament, *n.* Remedy, medicine, healing application.

Medicate, *v. t.* 1. Tincture *or* impregnate with something medicinal.

2. Heal, cure, treat with medicine.

Medicinal, *a.* Healing, curative, medical, medicative, sanatory, therapeutic, therapeutical.

Medicine, *n.* 1. Drug, physic, medicament, remedy, remedial agent.

2. Healing art, therapy, "leech-craft."

Mediocre, *a.* Indifferent, ordinary, commonplace, middling, mean, medium, average.

Mediocrity, *n.* 1. Inferiority, moderate degree, middle state.

2. Average, average standard, medial standard.

3. Moderation, temperance.

Meditate, *v. t.* 1. Plan, contrive, devise, scheme, concoct, intend, purpose, design.

2. Contemplate, study, chew, ruminate, think on, reflect upon, revolve in the mind, turn over in the mind, dwell intently upon, chew the cud upon.

——, *v. i.* Muse, ponder, think, cogitate, ruminate, study, contemplate, reflect, rack, beat *or* cudgel one's brains, collect one's thoughts, advise with one's pillow.

Meditation, *n.* Contemplation, reflection, study, musing, pondering, deep thought, close attention.

Mediterranean, *a.* 1. Midland.

2. Inland, mediterraneous.

Medium, *a.* Middle, mean, middling, mediocre.

——, *n.* 1. Intervening substance, pervading substance.

2. Means, instrumentality, agency, intermediary.

3. Mean average, mean proportion, mean.

Medley, *n.* Mixture, miscellany, jumble, farrago, hotch-potch, hodge-podge, salmagundi, gallimaufry, mish-mash, potpourri, olio, *mélange*, confused mass.

Meed, *n.* 1. Reward, recompense, remuneration, award, guerdon, premium, prize.

2. Gift, present.

Meek, *a.* Humble, lowly, submissive, yielding, pacific, unassuming, mild, soft, gentle, modest.

Meekness, *n.* Mildness, gentleness, humbleness, humility, lowliness, modesty, submission, submissiveness.

Meet, *a.* Fit, proper, fitting, befitting, suitable, suited, adapted, appropriate, qualified, convenient.

——, *v. t.* 1. Come together, intersect, transect, cross.

2. Confront, encounter, come up to face to face, engage.

3. Find, meet with, light on, fall upon, fall in with, happen upon, get, gain, receive.

4. Fulfil, comply with, satisfy, gratify, answer.

——, *v. i.* 1. Come together, come face to face, join each other.

2. Encounter one another, collide, join battle.

3. Unite, join, converge.

4. Assemble, congregate, muster, collect, convene, forgather, come together, meet together, rally.

MEETING, *n.* 1. Interview, encounter.

2. Assembly, assemblage, congregation, concourse, gathering, company, collection of people, convention, conference, auditory.

3. Conflux, joining, confluence, intersection, junction, union.

4. Duel, hostile encounter, collision.

Meeting-house, *n.* Church, temple, house of worship, house of God.

Meet with. 1. Find, meet, light on, fall upon, fall in with, happen upon, come to.

2. Suffer, be subjected to, be exposed to, encounter.

3. Join, unite in company.

Melancholic, *a.* 1. Dejected, depressed, hypochondriac, dispirited, melancholy.

2. Sombre, gloomy, unhappy, mournful, dismal.

Melancholy, *n.* Dejection, depression, gloominess, sadness, gloom, despondency, hypochondria, blues, blue devils, dismals, dumps, vapors, low spirits, depression of spirits.

——, *a.* 1. Dejected, dispirited, depressed, sad, sorrowful, unhappy, disconsolate, doleful, dismal, lugubrious, moody, gloomy, hypochondriac, dumpish, mopish, glum, down-cast, desponding, downhearted, low-spirited, cast down, in the dumps, down in the mouth, out of sorts, lackadaisical, atrabilious, blue, hippish.

2. Calamitous, afflictive, unfortunate, unlucky.

3. Grave, gloomy, sombre, dark, quiet, sad.

Mélange, *n.* [Fr.] Mixture, medley, farrago, jumble, hodge-podge, hotch-potch, salmagundi, olio, mingle-mangle, potpourri, gallimaufry, mish-mash, olla-podrida.

Mêlée, *n.* [Fr.] Fight (*of combatants confusedly mixed*), affray, contest, fray, broil, brawl, scuffle, mellay, hand-to hand conflict.

Meliorate, *v. t.* Improve, better, mend, amend, emend, ameliorate, make better.

Melioration, *n.* Improvement, amendment, emendation, amelioration, betterment.

Mellifluence, *n.* Smoothness, softness, mellowness, sweetness, sweet flow.

Mellifluent, } *a.* Smooth, soft, mellow,
Mellifluous, } euphonious, euphonic, sweet, silver-toned, sweetly flowing, dulcet, silvery.

Mellow, *a.* 1. Ripe, mature.

2. Soft, mellifluous, smooth, silver-toned, sweetly flowing, rich, dulcet, silvery.

3. Soft, rich, delicate.

4. Softened, matured, good-humored, genial, jovial.

5. Soft, loamy, unctuous, rich, mellowy.

6. Perfected, well prepared.

7. Tipsy, fuddled, disguised, intoxicated, half seas over.

——, *v. t.* 1. Ripen, mature.

2. Soften, tone down, smooth down, mature, improve.

3. Soften, pulverize.

4. Perfect, bring to perfection.

Melodious, *a.* Musical, tuneful, sweet, dulcet, euphonious, mellifluous, ariose, harmonious.

Melody, *n.* 1. Pleasing succession of sounds (as distinguished from *harmony* or the *concord* of sounds), sweetness of sound, music.

2. Song, descant, tune.

3. Air, tune, theme, plainsong.

Melt, *v. t.* 1. Liquefy (*by heat*), fuse, dissolve, thaw.

2. Soften, make gentle, make susceptible, mollify, subdue, relax.

3. Dissipate, waste away.

——, *v. i.* 1. Dissolve, become liquid, lose substance.

2. Be softened, be made gentle, become tender.

3. Blend, shade, pass.

4. Be weakened, be broken, be subdued.

Melting, *a.* 1. Dissolving, softening.

2. Affecting.

——, *n.* 1. Fusion.

2. Inteneration.

Member, *n.* 1. Limb.

2. Part, portion, constituent, component, subordinate part.

3. Head, clause, branch.

Membership, *n.* 1. Being a member.

2. Society, association, members, body of members, community.

Memento, *n.* Memorial, remembrancer, souvenir.

Memoir, *n.* 1. Personal narrative, familiar biography.

2. Record, register, journal, written account.

Memorable, *a.* Signal, notable, remarkable, extraordinary, illustrious, celebrated, distinguished, famous, great.

Memorandum, *n.* Note, minute.

Memorial, *n.* 1. Monument, commemorative record, memento.

2. Memorandum, record, remembrancer.

——, *a.* Commemorative.

Memorize, *v. t.* 1. Learn, learn by heart, commit to memory.

2. Cause to be remembered, hand down to memory by records, record.

MEMORY, *n.* 1. Recollection, remembrance, reminiscence.

2 Memorial, commemorative record, monumental record.

3. Fame, renown, reputation, celebrity.

Menace, *v. t.* Threaten, intimidate, alarm.

——, *n.* Threat, threatening.

Ménage, *n.* [Fr.] 1. Household.

2. Housekeeping, household management.

Mend, *v. t.* 1. Repair, refit, retouch, patch up, touch up, restore.

2. Improve, ameliorate, meliorate, correct, rectify, reform, amend, emend, make better.

3. Help, advance, further, improve.

4. Increase, add to, augment, make greater.

——, *v. i.* Improve, amend, become better.

Mendacious, *a.* False, lying, deceitful.

Mendacity, *n.* 1. Disposition to lie, habit of lying, falsehood, habitual lying, duplicity, deceit, untruthfulness, deception.

2. Falsehood, lie, untruth.

Mendicancy, *n.* Beggary, mendicity.

Mendicant, *n.* Beggar.

Menial, *a.* Servile, low, mean, base.

——, *n.* Servant, domestic, waiter, attendant, lackey, underling, flunky, understrapper, valet, footman, slave, serf, bondsman.

Menses, *n. pl.* Catamenia, monthly courses, menstrual discharges, menstrual flux.

Menstrual, *a.* 1. Monthly.

2. Catamenial.

Menstruum, *n.* Solvent, medium.

Mensurable, *a.* Measurable.

Mensuration, *n.* 1. Measuring, measurement.

2. Surveying, survey.

Mental, *a.* Intellectual, ideal, subjective, psychic, immaterial.

Mention, *n.* Cursory reference *or* allusion, citation, designation, notice, noting.

Mention, *v. t.* Declare, name, tell, state, communicate, impart, report, disclose, divulge, cite, speak of, make known, make mention of, allude to, refer to.

Mentor, *n.* Counsellor, adviser, monitor, guide, instructor.

Mephitic, } *a.* Fetid, foul, noisome, nox-
Mephitical, } ious, poisonous, pestilential, baleful.

Mercantile, *a.* Commercial, trading.

Mercenary, *a.* 1. Hired, purchased, paid, hireling, venal.

　2. Sordid, avaricious.

——, *n.* Hireling, Hessian, myrmidon.

Merchandise, *n.* Commodities, goods, wares.

Merchant, *n.* Trader (*particularly a whole-sale trader*), tradesman, dealer.

Merchantable, *a.* Marketable, salable, vendible.

Merchantman, *n.* Trading vessel, merchant-ship.

Merciful, *a.* 1. Clement, lenient, pitiful, forgiving, gracious, compassionate.

　2. Kind, tender, benignant, mild, gentle, tender-hearted, humane.

Merciless, *a.* Pitiless, cruel, unfeeling, unmerciful, uncompassionate, inexorable, unrelenting, relentless, fell, hard-hearted, severe, barbarous, savage, unsparing.

Mercurial, *a.* 1. Sprightly, active, spirited, quick, lively, prompt, nimble.

　2. Light-hearted, gay, lively, cheerful.

　3. Flighty, fickle, changeable, inconstant, volatile, mobile.

Mercy, *n.* 1. Clemency, lenity, lenience, leniency, compassion, pity, tenderness, kindness, mildness, gentleness, benevolence.

　2. Blessing, providential favor, grace.

　3. Discretion, disposal.

　4. Pardon, forgiveness.

Mere, *a.* 1. Bare, naked, plain, bald, sole, simple, nothing else but.

　2. Absolute, entire, unmixed, pure, sheer.

——, *n.* Pool, lake, pond.

Merely, *adv.* 1. Simply, purely, only, solely, barely.

　2. Purely, absolutely, utterly, entirely.

Meretricious, *a.* Deceitful (*by false show*), spurious, false, sham, make-believe, tawdry, showy, gaudy, brummagem.

Merge, *v. t.* Immerse, immerge, submerge, sink, bury, lose, involve.

——, *v. i.* Be lost, be swallowed up, be sunk.

Meridian, *n.* 1. Noon, noontide, mid-day, twelve o'clock.

　2. Summit, culmination, zenith, apex, acme, climax.

Meridional, *a.* 1. Southern, southerly.

　2. Mid-day.

Merit, *n.* 1. Desert, worth, worthiness, excellence, credit, goodness.

　2. [*pl.*] Claim, right.

——, *v. t.* 1. Deserve, have a right to, be entitled to, earn.

　2. Deserve, incur.

——, *v. i.* Profit, gain value, receive benefit, acquire desert.

Meritorious, *a.* Deserving, worthy, good, excellent, commendable.

Merriment, *n.* Mirth, jollity, gayety, hilarity, joviality, sportiveness, jocularity, liveliness, frolic, noisy sport, laughter.

Merry, *a.* 1. Pleasant, agreeable, exhilarating, delightful, brisk, lively, stirring.

　2. Mirthful, jovial, gleeful, gay, hilarious, sportive, jocund, joyous, facetious, lively, jolly, buxom, frolicsome, blithe, blithesome, airy, gladsome, vivacious, wanton, light-hearted, cheerful, comical, droll, sprightly.

Merry-andrew, *n.* Buffoon, zany, harlequin, scaramouch, fool, mountebank, jester, droll, jack-pudding, pickle-herring.

Merry-making, *n.* Festival, festivity, conviviality, frolic, jollification, "highjinks," merry bout.

MESH, *n.* Interstice (*of a net*), network.

——, *v. t.* Ensnare, entangle, snare.

Meshy, *a.* Reticulated, netted.

Mess, *n.* 1. Set (*who eat together*), company.

　2. Medley, mixture, miscellany, mass, farrago, hotch-potch, hodge-podge, jumble, salmagundi, mish-mash, olio, confused mass, *mélange*.

　3. Muddle, predicament, plight, confusion, perplexity, "pickle."

Message, *n.* Communication, despatch, intimation, notice, word, letter, telegram, etc.

Messenger, *n.* 1. Emissary, envoy, nuncio, express, courier, mercury, carrier, intelligencer.

　2. Harbinger, forerunner, herald, precursor.

METAL, *n.* Bullion, ore.

Metamorphic, *a.* Changeable, variable, mutable.

Metamorphose, *v. t.* Transform, transmute, transfigure, change the form of.

Metamorphosis, *n.* Transformation, transmutation, transfiguration, change of form, metaphysis.

Metaphoric, } *a.* Figurative, tropical,
Metaphorical, } allegorical, parabolic.

Metaphysics, *n.* Ontology, science of being, science of existence, philosophy, epistemology.

Mete, *v. t.* Measure.

——, *n.* Measure, bound, limit, term, boundary, terminus, butt.

Meteor, *n.* Aerolite, shooting-star, falling star.

Meteorolite, *n.* Aerolite, cloud stone, meteoric stone, meteorite.

Method, *n.* 1. Way (*viewed theoretically*), mode, manner, process, procedure, course, means, rule, *modus operandi.*

2. Arrangement, system, scheme, plan, classification, orderly disposition.

Methodic, } *a.* Orderly, systematical,
Methodical, } regular, systematic, exact, formal.

Methodize, *v. t.* Regulate, arrange, put in order, systematize.

Metre, *n.* Measure (*of verse*), rhythmical arrangement (*of syllables*), poetical measure, rhythm, verse.

Metrical, *a.* Measured.

Metropolis, *n.* Chief city, capital.

Metropolitan, *n.* Archbishop, primate.

Mettle, *n.* 1. Stuff, material, constitution, element.

2. Disposition, character, temper, spirit.

3. Spirit, nerve, vigor, ardor, pluck, hardihood, courage, fire, sprightliness, life.

Mettlesome, *a.* Spirited, ardent, fiery, lively, gay, brisk, sprightly, courageous, high-spirited.

Mew, *v. t.* 1. Confine, encase, coop, imprison, shut up, enclose.

2. Shed (*feathers*), moult, cast, change.

Mewl, *v. i.* Cry, squall, bawl.

Mezzo, *a.* (In *music.*) Middle, mean, medium.

Miasm, } *n.* Malaria, noxious exhalation,
Miasma, } bad air, floating effluvia, infection.

Microscopic, } *a.* Minute.
Microscopical, }

Mid, *a.* Middle, intervening.

Mid-day, *n.* Noon, noontide, meridian, high noon.

Middle, *a.* 1. Mean, medial, halfway, central, between the extremes.

2. Intermediate, intervening.

MIDDLE, *n.* 1. Midst, center, central part.

2. Mean, something intermediate.

Middle-age, *a.* Mediæval.

Middleman, *n.* Agent, broker, factor, intermediary, go-between.

Middle classes. *Bourgeoisie.*

Middling, *a.* Ordinary, average, moderate, passable, tolerable, mediocre, medium.

Midland, *a.* Mediterranean.

Midst, *n.* Middle, thick, heart.

Midsummer, *n.* Summer solstice.

Midwife, *n.* Accoucheuse.

Midwifery, *n.* Obstetrics, tocology.

Mien, *n.* Air, look, aspect, manner, port, carriage, demeanor, appearance, bearing, countenance, deportment.

Miff, *n.* (*Colloq.*) Pique, slight resentment.

——, *v. t.* (*Colloq.*) Affront, displease, offend slightly.

Might, *n.* Power, strength, puissance, force, main, potency, efficacy, ability, efficiency.

Mightily, *adv.* 1. Vigorously, vehemently, earnestly, powerfully, forcibly.

2. (*Colloq.*) Greatly, very much.

Mightiness, *n.* 1. Power, greatness.

2. Highness, excellency.

Mighty, *a.* 1. Strong, powerful, potent, robust, vigorous, sturdy, puissant, courageous, valiant, valorous, bold, able.

2. Vast, enormous, immense, huge, stupendous, monstrous, very great.

3. Forcible, efficacious, effective.

4. Important, momentous, very great.

——, *adv.* (*Colloq.*) Very, in a great degree.

Migratory, *a.* Nomadic, wandering, roving, unsettled.

Milch, *a.* Milk-giving (*applied only to beasts*).

Mild, *a.* 1. Tender, kind, gentle, merciful, clement, compassionate, indulgent, pacific.

2. Soft, gentle, bland, pleasant, suave.

3. Placid, calm, tranquil, soft, gentle, pleasant, kind.

4. Lenitive, assuasive, mollifying, soothing, emollient, demulcent.

Mildew, *n.* Blight, blast, mould, must, mustiness, smut, rust.

Militancy, *n.* Warfare, militarism.

Militant, *a.* Fighting, contending, combating.

MILITARY, *a.* 1. Martial.

2. Soldierly, soldier-like.

3. Warlike.

——, *n.* Soldiery, army, body of soldiers, soldiers, militia.

Militia, *n.* Trainband.

Milkiness, *n.* 1. Lactescence.

2. Mildness, softness.

Milk-livered, *a.* Cowardly, timorous, white-livered.

Milkmaid, *n.* Dairymaid.

Milksop, *n.* Mollycoddle, effeminate man.

MILK, *n.* (*Basic Eng.*) Beestings, buttermilk, skim, cream.

Milky, *a.* 1. Resembling milk, milk-like, lacteal, lacteous.

2. Soft, mild, gentle.

Milky-way, *n.* Galaxy.

Mill, *n.* Manufactory, factory.

——, *v. t.* Grind, comminute, pulverize, powder, levigate.

Millennium, *n.* Chiliad.

Miller, *n.* Moth.

Milliary, *n.* Mile-stone.

Million, *n.* [*With the definite article.*] The multitude, the public, the masses, the great body of the people.

Millionnaire, *n.* Nabob, Crœsus, Dives, person of great wealth.

Mime, *n.* Mimic.

Mimetic,
Mimetical, } *a.* Imitative, mimic.

Mimic, } *a.* Imitative, mimetic, mimeti-
Mimical, } cal.

2. Imitated.

Mimic, *v. t.* Ape, imitate, mock, counterfeit.

——, *n.* Mime.

Minacious, *a.* Threatening, menacing, minatory.

Minaret, *n.* Turret (*of a Mahometan mosque*).

Minatory, *a.* Threatening, menacing, minacious, frowning, lowering.

Mince, *v. t.* 1. Hash, cut into small pieces, chop fine.

2. Extenuate, palliate, be mealy-mouthed about, be reserved in speaking of.

——, *v. i.* Affect delicacy.

Mincing, *a.* Affected, over-nice.

MIND, *n.* 1. Soul, spirit, inner man.

2. Intellect, understanding, reason, sense, brains, thinking principle, intellectual powers, common-sense, intellectual faculties.

3. Inclination, disposition, will, wish, liking, desire, intention, purpose, choice, intent, affection.

4. Belief, opinion, thought, sentiment, reflection, contemplation, consideration, judgment.

5. Memory, remembrance, recollection.

——, *v. t.* 1. Notice, note, heed, regard, mark, attend to, take notice of, pay attention to, give heed to, fix the mind on.

2. Obey, be obedient to, attend to, regard with submission, observe.

3. (*Poetical.*) Remind, put in mind.

——, *v. i.* Mean, design, incline, intend, be inclined, be disposed.

Mindful of. Regardful of, heedful of, observant of, attentive to, thoughtful of.

Mindless, *a.* 1. Destitute of mind.

2. Stupid, unthinking, dull, heavy, senseless, sluggish, insensible.

3. Regardless, careless, heedless, forgetful, neglectful, negligent.

MINE, *n.* Colliery, pit, shaft.

——, *v. t.* 1. Sap, undermine.

2. Ruin, destroy (*secretly*).

Mineral, *n.* Inorganic body.

Mingle, *v. t.* 1. Mix, intermix, commingle, intermingle, compound, blend, combine, join, commix.

2. Confound, confuse, jumble.

3. Contaminate, alloy.

Miniature, *a.* Little, small, diminutive, tiny, bantam.

Minikin, *a.* Small, little, diminutive, wee, tiny, pygmy, pygmean, Liliputian, dwarfish.

Minimum, *n.* Least quantity, least part.

Mining, *a.* 1. Burrowing.

2. Insidious, subtle.

Minion, *n.* Favorite (*in an ill sense*), creature, dependant, parasite, hanger-on.

Minister, *n.* 1. Servant, subordinate, agent, underling, assistant.

2. Administrator (*of executive authority*), executive officer (*of a sovereign or of a government*), official.

3. Ambassador, envoy, plenipotentiary, delegate.

4. Clergyman, cleric, preacher, divine, priest, parson, ecclesiastic, churchman, pastor, rector, chaplain, curate, vicar.

——, *v. t.* Furnish, afford, supply, administer, give.

——, *v. i.* 1. Serve, perform service, do service, officiate, attend, administer.

2. Aid, help, assist, succor, give assistance to, supply with what is needed, contribute.

Ministerial, *a.* 1. Attendant, subservient, subsidiary, conducive, assistant.

2. Executive, ambassadorial, official.

3. Sacerdotal, ecclesiastical, priestly, official, clerical, pastoral.

Ministration, *n.* 1. Agency, instrumentality.

2. Service, ecclesiastical function.

Ministry, *n.* 1. Service, instrumentality, agency, aid, interposition, ministration, intervention.

2. Cabinet, council, administration, body of ministers.

Minor, *a.* 1. Less, smaller.

2. Inferior, subordinate.

3. Inconsiderable, petty, unimportant, small.

Minor,
Minorite, } *n.* Franciscan (friar).

Minority, *n.* Nonage, pupilage.

Minster, *n.* Cathedral church.

Minstrel, *n.* Musician, singer, bard, gleeman, *jongleur.*

Minstrelsy, *n.* Music, melody, harmony, song.

Mint, *v. t.* 1. Coin, stamp (*as money*).

2. Invent, forge, fabricate, fashion, produce.

Minus, *a.* Less, lacking, wanting.

Minute, *a.* 1. Little, slender, diminutive, fine, very small, tiny.

2. Circumstantial, particular, critical, precise, exact, detailed.

MINUTE, *n.* 1. Sixtieth part of an hour, sixty seconds.

2. Sixtieth part of a degree.

3. Note, memorandum.

——, *v. t.* Note, take a note of, jot down.

Minutiæ, *n. pl.* [L.] Minute particulars, minor details.

Minx, *n.* Hussy, jade, quean, baggage, pert girl, wanton girl.

Miracle, *n.* Marvel, wonder, prodigy.

Miraculous, *a.* 1. Supernatural, thaumaturgical.

2. Wonderful, extraordinary, passing strange, very strange, unaccountable, incredible.

Mire, *n.* Mud, ooze, slime.

Mirk, *n.* Darkness, gloom.

Mirky, *a.* Dark, gloomy. See MURKY.

Mirror, *n.* 1. Reflector, looking-glass.

2. Speculum.

3. Pattern, model, exemplar, example, prototype, archetype, paragon.

——, *v. t.* Reflect.

Mirth, *n.* Merriment, hilarity, jollity, joviality, gayety, merry-making, sport, fun, joyousness, gladness, frolic, glee, festivity, laughter.

Mirthful, *a.* 1. Merry, jovial, gay, lively, festive, joyful, joyous, cheery, hilarious, cheerful, jocund, vivacious, jolly, playful, sportive, frolicsome.

2. Funny, comic, droll, merry, jocose, jocular, humorous, sportive, witty, facetious, waggish, ludicrous.

Miry, *a.* Muddy, slimy.

Misadventure, *n.* Mischance, mishap, misfortune, reverse, ill luck, disaster, calamity, infelicity, cross.

Misanthrope, *n.* Man-hater, cynic, misanthropist.

Misapply, *v. t.* Misemploy, abuse, pervert, make an ill use of, misuse, misimprove.

Misapprehend, *v. t.* Misunderstand, misconceive, mistake.

Misbehaved, *a.* Ill-bred, rude, unmannerly, impolite, uncivil.

Misbehavior, *n.* Misconduct, miscarriage, ill conduct, ill behavior.

Miscalculate, *v. t.* Misreckon, miscast, miscompute, miscount, misestimate.

Miscall, *v. t.* Misname, misterm.

Miscarriage, *n.* 1. Failure, mishap, mischance, defeat, non-success.

2. Misconduct, misbehavior, ill conduct, ill behavior.

3. (*Med.*) Untimely birth, premature birth.

Miscarry, *v. i.* Fail, abort, go wrong, be unsuccessful, be defeated.

Miscellaneous, *a.* Diversified, various, promiscuous, mixed, mingled, heterogeneous, stromatic.

Miscellany, *n.* Mixture, medley, diversity, variety, olio, farrago, salmagundi, hodgepodge, hotch-potch, mish-mash, jumble, gallimaufry, miscellaneous collection, *mélange*.

Mischance, *n.* Misfortune, mishap, ill luck, misadventure, calamity, ill fortune, infelicity, disaster.

Mischief, *n.* 1. Evil, ill, harm, injury, damage, hurt, detriment, disadvantage, prejudice.

2. Trouble, misfortune, ill consequence, evil.

3. Wrong-doing, deviltry.

Mischievous, *a.* 1. Hurtful, injurious, detrimental, pernicious, destructive, noxious, harmful.

2. Vicious, wicked, sinful, malicious.

3. Troublesome, vexatious, annoying, naughty, impish.

Misconceit, *n.* Misconception, misapprehension, misunderstanding, mistake.

Misconceive, *v. t.* Misapprehend, misunderstand, misjudge, mistake.

Misconduct, *n.* 1. Misbehavior, ill conduct, bad conduct.

2. Mismanagement, ill management.

——, *v. t.* (*Pron.* misconduct') Mismanage (*which see*).

Misconstrue, *v. t.* 1. Mistranslate, misrender.

2. Misinterpret, misapprehend, misjudge, misunderstand.

Miscreant, *n.* Villain, scoundrel, knave, rascal, rogue, scamp, vile wretch, caitiff.

Misdeed, *n.* Transgression, trespass, offence, delinquency, misdemeanor, fault, misdoing, crime, evil deed.

Misdemeanor, *n.* Transgression, trespass, fault, misdeed, ill behavior, misconduct, misbehavior, offence.

Misdoer, *n.* Offender, criminal, malefactor.

Misdoing, *n.* Offence, misdeed, fault.

Misdoubt, *n.* 1. Suspicion.

2. Irresolution, hesitation.

Misemploy, *v. t.* Misuse, misapply, pervert, abuse, make an ill use of.

Misemployment, *n.* Misuse, abuse, misapplication.

Miser, *n.* Niggard, curmudgeon, hunks, skinflint, lickpenny, churl, sordid wretch, money-grubber, screw, scrimp, pinch-fist.

Miserable, *a.* 1. Unhappy (*as respects the condition of the mind*), wretched, distressed, afflicted, comfortless, disconsolate, forlorn, broken-hearted, heart-broken.

2. Wretched, pitiable, calamitous, unfortunate, unlucky, ill-starred, unhappy, hapless.

3. Worthless, valueless, very poor (*in quality*).

4. Low, mean, abject, despicable, contemptible, worthless.

Miserly, *a.* Covetous, avaricious, niggardly, sordid, stingy, parsimonious, penurious, close, mean, close-fisted.

Misery, *n.* 1. Distress, wretchedness, woe, tribulation, desolation, sorrow, grief, affliction, heartache, heavy heart, bleeding heart, broken heart, great unhappiness, suffering, anguish, torment.

2. Distress, suffering, wretchedness, agony, torture, torment, anguish.

3. Calamity, misfortune, disaster, evil.

Misfortune, *n.* Disaster, calamity, casualty, infliction, reverse, affliction, visitation, trial, blow, stroke, adversity, distress, hardship, trouble, ill luck, ill fortune, mishap, mischance, misadventure, ill, harm, scourge.

Misgiving, *n.* Doubt, distrust, suspicion, want of confidence, hesitation.

Misgoverned, *a.* 1. Ill-governed, anarchic.

2. Rude, unrestrained, rough, lawless, ungoverned.

Misgovernment, *n.* 1. Maladministration, misgovernment, misrule.

2. Irregularity, loose conduct, licentiousness, disorder.

Misguide, *v. t.* Mislead, misdirect.

Mishap, *n.* Misfortune, mischance, misadventure, calamity, ill luck, accident, disaster.

Misinterpret, *v. t.* Misconstrue, explain wrongly, put a wrong construction on, put a false construction on, give a false coloring to.

Misjudge, *v. t.* Mistake, misapprehend, misunderstand, misconceive.

Mislay, *v. t.* Misplace; lose.

Mislead, *v. t.* Delude, deceive, guide astray, misguide.

Mislike, *v. t.* Dislike, disapprove of.

——, *n.* Dislike, disapprobation, aversion.

Mismanage, *v. t.* Misconduct, misrule, mishandle, botch, fumble, manage ill, make a mess of, make sad work of.

Misname, *v. t.* Miscall, misterm.

Misnomer, *n.* 1. (*Law.*) Misnaming, mistaking of the true name (*of a person*).

2. Wrong name, inapplicable title, misapplied term.

Misogynist, *n.* Woman-hater.

Misprision, *n.* 1. Mistake, misconception, misunderstanding.

2. (*Law.*) Neglect, negligence, contempt.

3. Neglect, oversight, mistake.

Misprize, *v. t.* Undervalue, underrate, underestimate, slight, hold cheap.

Misrender, *v. t.* Misconstrue, mistranslate.

Misrepresent, *v. t.* Misstate, falsify, belie, caricature.

Misrepresentation, *n.* Misstatement, falsification.

Misrule, *n.* 1. Mismanagement, misgovernment, maladministration.

2. Disorder, anarchy, confusion, tumult, riot.

Miss, *v. t.* 1. Fail to hit, fail to reach, muff, fail of hitting, fail of reaching; lose, fail of finding, overlook.

2. Forego, pass by, leave out, go without, omit, dispense with.

3. Feel the want of, feel the loss of, require, want, desiderate.

——, *v. i.* 1. Fail to hit, fall short, miss one's aim, fly wide.

2. Fail, miscarry, not succeed, come to nothing, end in smoke.

3. Fail, mistake, err, trip, slip, fall.

——, *n.* 1. Blunder, slip, trip, oversight, failure, fault, mistake, error, omission.

2. Loss, want, felt absence.

——, *n.* 1. Girl, lass, maiden, damsel, maid, young lady.

2. Spinster, unmarried woman, maiden, maid.

Missal, *n.* Mass-book, prayer-book, service-book.

Misshapen, *a.* Ill-shaped, ill-formed, deformed, ugly, misproportioned, ungainly, misformed.

Missile, *n.* Projectile — bullet, etc.

——, *a.* Missive, to be thrown.

Missing, *a.* Lost, wanting, absent.

Mission, *n.* 1. Commission, legation.

2. Charge, business, errand, office, duty, commission, trust.

3. Delegation, embassy, deputation, legation.

——, *v. t.* Commission, despatch, send forth.

Missionary, *n.* Evangelist, colporteur.

Missive, *n.* Letter, message, communication.

Misspend, *v. t.* Squander, misuse, waste, fool away, fritter away, muddle away, spend foolishly.

Misstate, *v. t.* Misrepresent, falsify, garble, state wrongly.

Misstatement, *n.* Misrepresentation, falsification, wrong statement.

Misstep, *n.* Wrong step, false step.

MIST, *n.* 1. Fog, haze, cloud.

2. Obscurity, bewilderment, perplexity, haze.

——, *v. t.* Cloud, cover with mist.

——, *v. i.* Mizzle, drizzle.

Mistake, *v. t.* 1. Misapprehend, misunderstand, misconceive, misjudge.

2. Take (*one for another*), confound.

3. Mischoose, take in error.

——, *v. i.* Err, make a mistake, be at fault, be wide of the mark, be on the wrong scent.

——, *n.* 1. Misapprehension, misunderstanding, misconception, mistaking.

2. Blunder, error, slip, fault, trip, oversight, "break."

Mistaken, *a.* 1. Erroneous, incorrect, wrong.

2. Wrong, in error.

Misterm, *v. t.* Miscall, misname, mistitle.

Mistily, *adv.* Darkly, obscurely, cloudily.

Mistiness, *n.* Obscurity, fog, cloudiness.

Mistranslate, *v. t.* Misconstrue, misrender, misinterpret.

Mistreat, *v. t.* Maltreat, abuse, misuse, ill-treat.

Mistreatment, *n.* Wrong, abuse, maltreatment.

Mistress, *n.* 1. Female head, female sovereign, governess.

2. Instructress, female teacher, dame, governess.

3. Sweetheart, flame.

4. Concubine, paramour.

5. Goodwife, matron, madam.

Mistrust, *n.* Distrust, suspicion, doubt, misgiving, want of confidence.

——, *v. t.* 1. Distrust, doubt, suspect, be suspicious of.

2. Fear, apprehend, suspect, surmise.

Mistrustful, *a.* Distrustful, suspicious, doubting.

Misty, *a.* Obscure, dim, clouded.

Misunderstand, *v. t.* Misapprehend, misconceive, mistake, misconstrue.

Misunderstanding, *n.* 1. Misapprehension, misconception, error.

2. Difference, disagreement, dissension, quarrel, difficulty.

Misuse, *v. t.* 1. Misemploy, misapply, desecrate, profane, pervert, put to a wrong use.

2. Abuse, maltreat, ill-treat, ill-use.

3. Waste, squander, fool away, fritter away, muddle away, spend foolishly.

——, *n.* 1. Abuse, perversion, prostitution, profanation.

2. Abuse, ill-treatment, misusage, ill-usage, ill-use.

3. Misapplication, erroneous use, solecism.

Mite, *n.* Particle, atom, monad, corpuscle, molecule.

Mitigate, *v. t.* 1. Moderate, alleviate, assuage, abate, lessen, palliate.

2. Appease, soothe, soften, mollify, pacify, quiet, still, calm, quell, allay.

3. Moderate, temper, attemper.

4. Diminish, lessen, abate.

Mitigation, *n.* Alleviation, moderation, relief, abatement, diminution.

Mitigative, *a.* Lenitive, lenient, soothing, mollifying, assuaging, assuasive, emollient, mild.

Mix, *v. t.* 1. Mingle, commingle, commix, interlard, interfuse, unite, combine, blend, alloy, amalgamate, compound, incorporate.

2. Join, associate, unite with.

——, *v. i.* 1. Be mixed, be blended, coalesce.

2. Be joined, mingle, be associated with.

MIXED, *a.* 1. Mingled, blended, joined, associated.

2. Promiscuous, of various kinds, heterogeneous.

Mixture, *n.* 1. Union, association, admixture, intermixture.

2. Compound, medley, hash, commixture, jumble, olio, farrago, salmagundi, hotch-potch, gallimaufry, hodge-podge, olla-podrida, *mélange*.

3. Miscellany, variety, diversity.

Mizzle, *v. i.* Rain (*in small drops*), drizzle, mist.

Mnemonic, *a.* 1. Of the memory.

2. For the help of the memory, to assist the memory.

Moan, *v. t.* (*Poetical.*) Lament, deplore, mourn, bemoan, bewail, weep for, grieve for.

——, *v. i.* Grieve, mourn, make lamentation.

Moat, *n.* Ditch, fosse, graff.

Mob, *n.* 1. Tumultuous rabble, rude multitude, lawless crowd.

2. Populace, riff-raff, lower orders, vulgar herd, scum of society, dregs of the people, ragtag-and-bobtail, *canaille*.

Mobbish, *a.* Tumultuous, mean, vulgar.

Mobile, *a.* 1. Movable.

2. Expressive, sensitive.

3. Changeable, fickle, inconstant, volatile, variable.

Mobility, *n.* 1. Susceptibility of motion.

2. Aptitude to motion, activity, nimbleness.

3. Changeableness, fickleness, inconstancy, mutability, volatility.

Mob-law, *n.* Lynch-law, club-law.

Mock, *v. t.* 1. Ape, mimic, imitate, counterfeit, take off.

2. Deride, ridicule, gibe, jeer, taunt, flout, insult, scout, chaff, laugh at, make game of, make fun of, treat with contempt, treat with scorn, make a butt of.

3. Illude, deceive, disappoint, balk, cheat, dupe, fool, tantalize, delude, defeat, mislead, elude.

4. Defy, set at nought.

——, *a.* False, counterfeit, pretended, feigned, assumed, sham, spurious, claptrap, make-believe.

Mocker, *n.* 1. Scoffer, scorner, derider, railer, despiser, jeerer.

2. Deceiver, impostor, cheat.

Mockery, *n.* 1. Ridicule, derision, scorn, jeering, contemptuous mimicry.

2. Sport, subject of ridicule.

3. Show, imitation, counterfeit.

4. Vain effort, fruitless labor.

Mock-sun, *n.* Parhelion, sundog.

Mode, *n.* 1. Way (*viewed practically*), method, manner, style, fashion.

2. Fashion, custom, prevailing style.

3. Modification, quality, affection, accident, degree, gradation, variety.

Model, *n.* 1. Pattern, prototype, archetype, mould, protoplast, original, type, design.

2. Pattern, example, dummy, mould.

3. Standard, gauge.

4. Image, copy, facsimile, imitation, representation.

——, *v. t.* Shape, mould, form, plan, fashion, design.

Moderate, *a.* 1. Temperate, sparing, frugal.

2. Mediocre, limited.

3. Reasonable, judicious, deliberate, cool, mild, calm, steady.

4. Temperate, mild, gentle.

——, *v. t.* 1. Assuage, soothe, allay, mitigate, soften, mollify, appease, quiet, quell, still, pacify, repress, subdue, abate, reduce, lessen, dull, blunt.

2. Temper, qualify, attemper, diminish, slacken.

3. Control, regulate, govern, repress.

Moderation, *n.* 1. Temperance, frugality, sobriety, forbearance, restraint.

2. Calmness, coolness, deliberateness, sedateness, mildness, equanimity, composure.

Moderator, *n.* Chairman, president, presiding officer, regulator, conductor, manager.

Modern, *a.* Recent, late, new, novel, fresh, present, up-to-date.

Modest, *a.* 1. Unpretending, unobtrusive, unassuming, retiring, unostentatious.

2. Chaste, pure, virtuous.

3. Moderate, decent, becoming, proper.

Modesty, *n.* 1. Unobtrusiveness, retiring disposition, freedom from presumption.

2. Chastity, purity, decency.

3. Moderation, decency, propriety.

Modicum, *n.* Little, trifle, small quantity.

Modification, *n.* 1. Alteration, variation, qualification, change.

2. Form, mode, state, manner.

Modify, *v. t.* 1. Shape, alter, change, vary, give a new form to.

2. Moderate, qualify, soften, lower.

Modish, *a.* 1. Fashionable, stylish.

2. Conventional, ceremonious.

Modulate, *v. t.* 1. Attune, harmonize, tune.

2. Inflect (*as the voice*), vary in tune and accentuation.

3. Proportion, adjust, adapt.

Modus operandi. [L.] Process, way, method, mode of operation, way of doing, manner of operating.

Mohammedan, *n.* Mahometan, Mussulman, Moslem, Saracen.

Mohammedanism, *n.* Mahometanism, Islam.

Moiety, *n.* 1. Half.

2. Portion, share, part.

Moil, *v. t.* 1. Daub, spot, soil, defile, splash, bespatter, stain.

2. Fatigue, weary, tire.

——, *v. i.* Labor, toil, drudge.

Moist, *a.* Damp, humid, dank, wet, muggy.

Moisten, *v. t.* Dampen, damp.

Moisture, *n.* Dampness, humidity, wetness.

Molar, *n.* Grinder, grinding-tooth, molar tooth, double tooth, mill-tooth.

Mole, *n.* Jetty, pier, breakwater, mound, dike.

Molecular, *a.* Corpuscular.

Molecule, *n.* Particle, monad.

Mole-eyed, *a.* Blind, purblind, myopic, short-sighted, near-sighted.

Molest, *v. t.* Disturb, trouble, annoy, vex, tease, incommode, discommode, inconvenience, harass, worry, plague, bore, torment, bother, pester, harry, badger, irritate, fret, chafe, hector, gull, disturb, disquiet, oppress.

Mollify, *v. t.* 1. Soften, make soft.

2. Appease, pacify, compose, soothe, tranquillize, calm, quiet.

3. Assuage, mitigate, moderate, ease, allay, abate, temper, attemper, relieve, lessen, dull, blunt.

4. Qualify, tone down, moderate.

Moment, *n.* 1. Instant, second, trice, flash, jiffy, wink, twinkling, eyewink, point of time.

2. Importance, consequence, weight, significance, value, import, force, consideration, avail, signification, gravity.

3. Momentum, impulsive power, impetus, force.

4. Element, factor, constituent, essential circumstance, deciding point.

Momentarily, *adv.* Momently, every moment.

Momentary, *a.* Instantaneous.

Momentous, *a.* Important, weighty, significant, grave, serious, of importance, of great consequence.

Momentum, *n.* [L.] 1. Impetus, moment.

2. Constituent, essential element, moment.

Monachism, *n.* Monkery, monasticism, monastic life.

Monad, *n.* 1. Atom, molecule, ultimate particle, indivisible particle.

2. (*Zoöl.*) Minute animalcule.

Monarch, *n.* 1. Autocrat, despot.

2. Sovereign, king, emperor, potentate, prince, ruler, chief, dictator.

——, *a.* Supreme, ruling, sovereign, monarchal, pre-eminent.

Monarchic, ⎫ *a.* Kingly, royal, regal,
Monarchical, ⎭ imperial, sovereign.

Monarchy, *n.* 1. Kingdom, empire.

2. Kingship, empire, rule.

Monastery, *n.* Convent, cloister, abbey, priory, nunnery, lamasery.

Monastic, ⎫ *a.* 1. Monkish, monachal,
Monastical, ⎭ conventual, cenobitic, cenobitical.

2. Secluded, recluse.

Monasticism, *n.* Monastic life, monachism.

Monde, *n.* [Fr.] 1. World.

2. Society, people of the world.

Monetary, *a.* Pecuniary, financial, fiscal.

MONEY, *n.* 1. Coin (or *its representative*), cash, circulating medium, standard of value, currency, specie.

2. Wealth, riches.

Money-chest, *n.* Coffer, safe, strong-box.

Moneyed, *a.* [Written also *Monied.*] Rich, wealthy, affluent, opulent, well off, well to do.

Moneymaking, *a.* Lucrative, profitable, gainful.

Monger, *n.* (*Rare except in composition.*) Dealer, trader, trafficker.

Mongrel, *a.* Hybrid.

Monition, *n.* 1. Warning, admonition, counsel.

2. Information, indication, advice, hint, notice, intimation.

Monitor, *n.* 1. Adviser, counsellor, mentor, admonisher, warner.

2. Overseer (*in a school*).

Monitory, *a.* Warning, admonishing.

Monkery, *n.* Monachism, monasticism.

MONKEY, *n.* Simian, ape.

Monocracy, *n.* Autocracy, monarchy.

Monologue, *n.* Soliloquy.

Monomania, *n.* Hallucination, illusion, delusion, self-deception, partial insanity, insanity on one subject.

Monopolize, *v. t.* Forestall, engross, engross the whole of.

Monopoly, *n.* Exclusive possession.

Monotone, *n.* Sameness *or* uniformity of tone, drone, sing-song, monotony.

Monotonous, *a.* Uniform, unvaried.

Monotony, *n.* Uniformity, sameness, tedium, want of variety.

Monster, *n.* 1. Prodigy, enormity, marvel, wonder.

2. Prodigy, monstrosity, moon-calf, unnatural production.

3. Ruffian, wretch, miscreant, villain, demon, brute, fiend.

Monstrosity, *n.* 1. Monstrousness.

2. Prodigy, monster.

Monstrous, *a.* 1. Unnatural, preternatural, abnormal, prodigious.

2. Huge, enormous, immense, vast, colossal, stupendous, extraordinary, prodigious.

3. Wonderful, marvellous, strange, prodigious.

4. Shocking, horrible, frightful, hateful, hideous, dreadful, terrible.

MONTH, *n.* (*Basic Eng.*) Twelfth division of the year.

Monument, *n.* 1. Memorial, testimonial, remembrancer, record.

2. Tomb, gravestone, cenotaph.

Monumental, *a.* 1. Of a monument.

2. Memorial, commemorative.

Mood, *n.* Temper, humor, disposition, vein, frame of mind.

Moody, *a.* 1. Humorsome, capricious, variable.

2. Angry, petulant, irritable, irascible, passionate, snappish, pettish, sour, crusty, crabbed, waspish, captious, snarling, peevish, testy, fretful, ill-tempered, out of humor, out of temper.

3. Sullen, perverse, wayward, sulky, humorsome, glum, grum, glowering, morose, spleeny, frowning, stubborn, dogged, intractable, cross-grained.

4. Gloomy, melancholy, sad, pensive, abstracted, saturnine.

MOON, *n.* 1. Satellite, secondary planet, Luna, Cynthia.

2. Month, lunation.

Moon-calf, *n.* 1. Monster, deformed creature.

2. Blockhead, simpleton, fool, dunce, dolt.

Moonish, *a.* Variable, fickle, flighty, changeable, inconstant.

Moonlight, *n.* Moonshine, moonbeams.

Moon-shaped, *a.* Crescent-shaped.

Moonshine, *n.* 1. Moonlight.

2. Nonsense, trash, stuff, twaddle, fudge, flummery, balderdash, pretence, fiction, empty show, fustian, vanity.

Moonstricken, } *a.* Lunatic, simple, fool-
Moonstruck, } ish, idiotic, hazy, silly, bewildered.

Moor, *n.* 1. Heath, extensive waste.

2. Blackamoor, negro, colored person.

——, *v. t.* Secure, berth, fasten, fix firmly.

Moorish, *a.* Moresque, arabesque.

Moory, *a.* Moorish, marshy, fenny, boggy, watery.

Moot, *v. t.* Debate, discuss, dispute, argue, agitate.

Mooted, } *a.* Debatable, disputable, dis-
Moot, } puted, unsettled, in question.

Mop-board, *n.* Skirting, wash-board, skirting-board, surbase.

Mope, *v. i.* 1. Be sad, be gloomy, be dejected, look downcast, look blue, wear a long face.

2. Be dull, be listless, be stupid, take no interest in anything, be spiritless, be gloomy.

Mope-eyed, *a.* Short-sighted, purblind, myopic, mopsical.

Mopish, *a.* 1. Sad, gloomy, downcast, dejected, depressed, desponding, downhearted, chap-fallen, melancholy, dumpish, glum, hipped, blue, cast down, in the dumps, with a long face, down in the mouth, out of sorts.

2. Dull, spiritless, listless, inattentive, stupid.

Moral, *a.* 1. Accountable, bound by duty, bound to do what is right.

2. Virtuous, good, ethical, just, upright, honest, honorable.

3. Mental, intellectual, abstract, ideal.

——, *n.* Intent, meaning, significance.

Morality, *n.* 1. Morals, ethics, moral philosophy.

2. Virtue, goodness, honesty, integrity, honor.

Morals, *n. pl.* 1. Morality, ethics, moral philosophy.

2. Conduct, behavior, habits, manners, course of life.

Morass, *n.* Marsh, fen, bog, quagmire, swamp, slough.

Morbid, *a.* Diseased, sickly, unsound, sick, unhealthy, tainted, vitiated, corrupted.

Morbific, *a.* Noxious, deleterious, unwholesome, unhealthy, pestilential, poisonous, baneful.

Mordacious, *a.* 1. Biting, pungent, stinging, cutting, sharp, mordant, acrid, mordicant.

2. Poignant, caustic, sarcastic, satirical, severe, scathing.

Mordant, *a.* Biting, mordacious, keen, caustic, sarcastic, severe, satirical, nipping.

More, *a.* 1. Greater degree of, greater amount of.

2. In greater numbers.

3. Added, additional, other, besides.

——, *adv.* Again, further, besides, in addition, to a greater degree.

——, *n.* 1. Greater degree, greater quantity.

2. Else, other thing.

Moreover, *conj.* and *adv.* Besides, further, also, likewise, too, furthermore, more than that, over and above that.

Moresque, *a.* Moorish, arabesque, morisco.

Morgue, *n.* Dead-house.

Moribund, *a.* Dying, at the point of death, on one's death-bed, at death's door, with one foot in the grave, at the last gasp.

Morion, *n.* Helmet, helm, head-piece, burganet.

Mormon, *n.* Mormonite, Latter-day Saint.

MORNING, *n.* 1. Dawn, daybreak, aurora, sunrise, morn, morningtide, break of day, peep of day, prime of day, first blush of the morning.

2. Forenoon, early part of the day.

Morning star. Lucifer, Phosphorus, Phosphor, Venus.

Morose, *a.* Crabbed, sullen, churlish, sour, sulky, perverse, wayward, spleeny, spleenish, splenetic, humorsome, dogged, gloomy, moody, cross-grained, severe, austere, gruff, crusty, surly, ill-humored, ill-natured.

Moroseness, *n.* Crabbedness, sullenness, moodiness, churlishness, sourness, sulkiness, sulks, spleen, ill-temper.

Morsel, *n.* 1. Bite, mouthful, bit of food, tidbit.

2. Fragment, bit, little piece, *morceau*.

Mortal, *a.* 1. Deathbound, destined to die.

2. Deadly, fatal, destructive, mortiferous.

3. Final, death-bringing.

4. Human, of man.

——, *n.* Man, human being, earthling.

Mortality, *n.* 1. Subjection to death, necessity of dying, mortalness.

2. Death, destruction.

3. Frequency of death, number of deaths, actual death of numbers.

Mortally, *adv.* 1. In the manner of a mortal.

2. Irrecoverably, fatally, deadly.

Mortar, *n.* 1. Piece of ordnance for throwing bombs, mortar-piece.

2. Cement.

Mortgage, *n.* and *v. t.* Pledge (*for the payment of a debt*).

Mortification, *n.* 1. (*Med.*) Gangrene, sphacelus, necrosis.

2. Discontent, dissatisfaction, displeasure, vexation, chagrin, disappointment, humiliation, trouble, shame.

3. Humiliation, self-abasement, self-denial.

Mortify, *v. t.* 1. Gangrene.

2. Disappoint, dissatisfy, displease, vex, harass, plague, worry, disquiet, chagrin, annoy, trouble, humble, depress.

3. Humiliate, humble, shame, confound, abase, abash, put down, restrain, subdue.

——, *v. i.* Gangrene, lose vitality, corrupt, putrefy, fester.

Mortuary, *n.* 1. Cemetery, graveyard, church-yard, burial-place, necropolis, burial-ground, city of the dead.

2. Dead-house, morgue.

Mosaic, } *a.* Inlaid, tessellated.
Mosaical, }

Moslem, *n.* Mahometan, Mohammedan, Mussulman.

Most, *a.* 1. Greatest in quantity.

2. Greatest in number, most numerous.

——, *adv.* In the greatest degree, mostly, chiefly, principally.

——, *n.* 1. Greatest part, greatest number.

2. Utmost.

Mostly, *adv.* Mainly, chiefly, for the most part, for the greatest part.

Mote, *n.* Spot, speck, mite, particle, atom, corpuscle.

Moth, *n.* (*Ent.*) Miller.

MOTHER, *n.* 1. Female parent, mamma, mater.

2. Dam (*applied to a beast*).

3. Generatrix, origin, spring, source.

4. Chief, head.

——, *a.* 1. Native, natural.

2. Originating.

Motherly, *a.* Maternal, affectionate, kind, tender, parental.

Mother-wit, *n.* Native wit, common-sense.

Mothery, *a.* Concreted, slimy, dreggy, feculent.

MOTION, *n.* 1. [Opposed to *Rest.*] Movement, stir, drift, flux, passage, change of place.

2. Port, gait, air, appropriate motion.

3. Impulse, prompting, suggestion, mental act.

4. Proposition (*especially one made in a deliberative body*), proposal.

Motionless, *a.* Still, quiescent, stationary, immobile, fixed, unmoved, at rest, at a stand, stock still, standing still.

Motive, *n.* 1. Inducement, incentive, impulse, incitement, stimulus, spur, prompting, influence, reason, ground, consideration, cause, occasion, prime mover, why and wherefore.

2. (*Mus.*) Theme, subject, melody, *motif.*

Motley, *a.* 1. Variegated, dappled, party-colored, mottled.

2. Heterogeneous, diversified, mingled, composite, mixed.

Mottled, *a.* Variegated, spotted, motley, speckled, dappled, piebald, of various colors.

Mould, *n.* 1. Loam.

2. Material, composing substance, matter.

3. Mustiness, mildew, mouldiness, mucor, blight, smut.

4. Matrix, matrice, pattern.

5. Form, shape, cast, fashion, character.

——, *v. t.* Form, shape, fashion, model.

Moulder, *v. i.* Crumble, perish, decay, turn to dust, fall into decay, fall to pieces, waste away.

Mouldy, *a.* Musty, mildewed, fusty, decaying.

Moult, *v. i.* Shed feathers, hair, etc., mew, mue.

——, *v. t.* Shed (*feathers, hair, etc.*), mew.

Mound, *n.* 1. Hillock, knoll, hill, barrow, tumulus.

2. Rampart, bulwark, defence.

Mount, *n.* [*Poetic.*] Mountain, high hill.

——, *v. i.* 1. Rise, ascend, arise, uprise, soar, go up, rise on high.

2. Tower, rise, be built up.

3. Get on horseback.

4. Amount, attain in value, count up.

——, *v. t.* 1. Ascend, climb, scale, escalade, get upon.

2. Put or raise (*upon something*).

3. Embellish, cover with ornaments.

4. (*Mil.*) Carry, be furnished with.

5. Prepare, make ready.

6. Get upon, bestride.

MOUNTAIN, *n.* Mount, high hill, vast eminence.

Mountainous, *a.* 1. Full of mountains, hilly.

2. Huge, enormous, tremendous, bulky.

Mountebank, *n.* Pretender, charlatan, empiric quack, quack doctor.

Mourn, *v. i.* Grieve, lament, sorrow, be sorrowful, wail.

Mourn, *v. t.* Deplore, lament, bewail, bemoan, grieve for, sorrow over.

Mournful, *a.* 1. Sad, distressing, afflicting, afflictive, grievous, calamitous, lamentable, melancholy, deplorable, woful.

2. Sad, melancholy, lugubrious, doleful, sorrowful, heavy, heavy-hearted, tearful.

Mourning, *n.* 1. Lamentation, sorrow, grief.

2. Weeds, symbol of sorrow.

Mouse, *v. i.* 1. Catch mice.

2. Peer, search, pry about, look closely.

MOUTH, *n.* 1. Chaps, jaws, cavity between the jaws.

2. Aperture (*in a vessel for receiving or discharging anything*), opening, orifice.

3. Entrance (*as of a cave or a river*), inlet.

4. Oracle, mouthpiece, speaker, spokesman.

5. Grimace, wry face, mow.

——, *v. i.* Vociferate, rant, declaim.

Mouth-piece, *n.* 1. Piece (*in a wind instrument*) for the mouth.

2. Speaker (*in behalf of several persons*), spokesman, mouth.

Movable, *a.* 1. Portable.

2. Changeable, mobile.

Movables, *n. pl.* Goods, wares, effects, furniture, chattels, movable property.

Move, *v. t.* 1. Impel, dislodge, shift, start, put in motion, stir, propel, drive.

2. Incite, instigate, rouse, actuate.

3. Influence, persuade, induce, prevail upon, act upon, determine, prompt, incline.

4. Affect, touch, impress, stir, trouble.

5. Stir up, excite, rouse, awaken, irritate, incense, agitate.

6. Propose (*in a deliberative body*), bring forward, recommend, suggest, offer for consideration.

——, *v. i.* 1. Stir, budge, change place *or* posture.

2. Go, proceed, walk, march.

3. Act, live, have power of motion.

4. Remove, change residence.

MOVE, *n.* 1. Movement, motion, change of place.

2. Proceeding, action taken.

Movement, *n.* 1. Motion, move, change, passage.

2. Motion, emotion, mental action.

3. (*Referring to concerted action*) Drive, crusade.

4. (*Mus.*) (*a*) Rhythm, method of progression, *tempo*; (*b*) strain, part.

Moving, *a.* 1. Impelling, instigating, influencing, persuading.

2. Affecting, touching, pathetic, impressive.

MUCH, *a.* Abundant, plenteous, considerable, a great deal of, a great quantity *or* amount of.

——, *adv.* 1. Greatly, to a great degree.

2. Often, long, frequently, earnestly, a great deal.

3. Nearly, almost, about the same.

——, *n.* Great quantity, great deal, "heaps," "lot."

Mucilaginous, *a.* Slimy, gummy, ropy, mucous, glutinous, viscid.

Muckiness, *n.* Filthiness, nastiness.

Muckworm, *n.* See MISER.

Mucky, *a.* Filthy, nasty, dirty.

Mucous, *a.* Slimy, ropy, mucilaginous, gummy, glutinous, viscid, muculent, pituitous.

Mud, *n.* Mire, dirt, muck, slime.

Muddily, *adv.* 1. Turbidly.

2. Obscurely, cloudily, confusedly.

Muddiness, *n.* 1. Turbidness, foulness, feculence.

2. Obscurity, cloudiness, dulness.

Muddle, *v. t.* 1. Make muddy, make turbid.

2. Stupefy, fuddle, inebriate, confuse, make half drunk, make tipsy.

3. Make a mess of, muff, mull, spoil.

Muddled, *a.* 1. Fuddled, tipsy, disguised, mused, potulent, mellow, in liquor, half seas over, the worse for liquor, half drunk.

2. Stupefied, clouded, confused.

Muddy, *a.* 1. Miry.

2. Turbid, foul, impure, dirty, slimy, soiled.

3. Confused, dull, stupid, heavy, muddy-headed, muddy-brained, bothered.

4. Obscure, confused, incoherent, vague.

Muff, *v. t.* Muddle, mull, fumble, bungle.

Muffle, *v. t.* 1. Wrap, cover, shroud, envelop.

2. Blindfold.

3. Wrap up, cover, conceal, involve, disguise.

Muffled, *a.* 1. Wrapped up, concealed.

2. Dulled, deadened, suppressed.

Muggy, *a.* 1. Wet, damp, moist, mouldy.

2. Close, warm, oppressive (*said of the weather*), uncomfortable.

Mulct, *n.* Fine, amercement, forfeit, forfeiture, pecuniary penalty.

——, *v. t.* Fine, amerce, impose a fine upon.

Mule, *n.* Hybrid, mongrel, hinny.

Muleteer, *n.* Mule-driver.

Mulish, *a.* Stubborn, obstinate, headstrong, cross-grained, intractable.

Mulishness, *n.* Stubbornness, doggedness, obstinacy.

Multifarious, *a.* Multiform, manifold, various, divers, diversified, different, of many sorts, of various kinds, of all sorts and kinds.

Multifold, *a.* Manifold, numerous, diversified.

Multiform, *a.* 1. Many-shaped, diversified, of many shapes, of many forms.

2. Manifold, multifarious, multifold, multiple, multiplex.

Multiloquence, *n.* Loquacity, garrulity, talkativeness.

Multiplicity, *n.* Multitude, great number.

Multiplied, *a.* Numerous, many.

Multiply, *v. t.* Increase (*in number*), make more, make many.

——, *v. i.* 1. Increase, grow in number.

2. Increase, extend, spread.

Multitude, *n.* 1. Great number, numerousness.

2. Host, legion, a great many.

3. Throng, concourse, army, swarm, a great number, a great many, assembly, assemblage, collection, crowd.

4. The multitude, rabble, herd, pack, ruck, the populace, the vulgar, mass, commonalty.

Mum, *a.* Silent, mute, speechless, dumb.

Mumble, *v. i.* Mutter, speak inarticulately, muffle.

Mumbler, *n.* Mutterer.

Mummer, *n.* Masker, buffoon.

Mummery, *n.* 1. Masking, masquerade, sport, diversion, buffoonery, harlequinade, foolery, tomfoolery.

2. Empty show, solemn mockery, vain ceremony.

Mumpish, *a.* Sullen, morose, moody, spleeny, spleenish, dull, heavy, sour, sulky.

Munch, *v. t.* Chew audibly, masticate with sound, chew eagerly, mump, nibble.

Mundane, *a.* Earthly, terrene, terrestrial, terraqueous, worldly, sublunary, under the sun, secular, temporal.

Municipal, *a.* Civic, civil.

Munificence, *n.* Liberality, generosity, bountifulness, bounty, beneficence, bounteousness.

Munificent, *a.* Liberal, bountiful, generous, bounteous, beneficent, princely, free, free-hearted.

Muniment, *n.* 1. Fortification, stronghold, citadel, fortress, fort.

2. Support, defence.

3. (*Law.*) Record, title-deed.

Munition, *n.* Ammunition, military stores, provision.

Murder, *n.* Homicide (*with malice*), assassination, manslaughter.

——, *v. t.* 1. Kill (*with malice*), assassinate, massacre, put to death.

2. Kill cruelly, slay.

3. Destroy, put an end to.

4. Abuse, violate grossly, mar, spoil.

Murderer, *n.* Slaughterer, assassin, slayer, killer, butcher, cut-throat, blood-shedder, man-slayer.

Murderous, *a.* Sanguinary, bloody, cruel, savage, fell, bloodthirsty, blood-guilty.

Murky, *a.* Dark, gloomy, obscure, dim, cloudy, clouded, dusky, lurid, overcast, lowering.

Murmur, *n.* 1. Whisper; low, continuous sound, hum, undertone.

2. Complaint, plaint, whimper, grumble, mutter.

——, *v. i.* 1. Make a low, continued sound.

2. Complain, repine, croak, grumble, mutter.

Murmurer, *n.* Censurer, complainer, repiner, objector, fault-finder, grumbler.

Murrain, *n.* Cattle-plague, epizoötic disease, murr.

MUSCLE, *n.* Thew.

Muscular, *a.* 1. Musculous, sinewy.

2. Brawny, sinewy, strong, stalwart, vigorous, powerful, sturdy, lusty, athletic, Herculean, able-bodied, stout.

Muse, *n.* Revery, abstraction, musing, deep thought, brown study, absence of mind.

——, *v. i.* 1. Ponder, meditate, contemplate, reflect, cogitate, deliberate, ruminate, think, brood.

2. Be absent-minded, be in a revery, be in a brown study, dream.

——, *v. t.* (*Poetical.*) Consider, ponder, meditate on, think on.

Muses, *n. pl.* [With *The* prefixed.] The tuneful Nine, the tuneful quire (*Calliope, Clio, Erato, Euterpe, Melpomene, Polyhymnia, Terpsichore, Thalia, Urania*).

Mushroom, *n.* Upstart, parvenu.

——, *a.* Ephemeral, short-lived, transitory, transient.

MUSIC, *n.* Melody, harmony, symphony, minstrelsy.

Musical, *a.* 1. Melodious, harmonious, tuneful, canorous, symphonious, dulcet, sweet-sounding.

2. Melodious, harmonious.

Musing, *a.* Meditative, preoccupied, absent-minded.

——, *n.* Revery, abstraction, muse, meditation, reflection, contemplation, brown study, deep thought, absent-mindedness.

Muss, *n.* Scramble, confused struggle, disorder, state of confusion.

Mussulman, *n.* Mahometan, Mohammedan, Moslem, Muslim.

Must, *v. i.* Be obliged to, be required to, be bound to, be necessitated to, be under the necessity of.

——, *n.* 1. Grape-juice (*unfermented*), new wine.

2. Mould, fust, mustiness, mouldiness, fustiness, sourness.

Muster, *v. t.* Assemble, collect, gather, marshal, congregate, convene, bring together, call together, get together, muster up.

——, *v. i.* Be assembled, meet together, rally.

——, *n.* Gathering, assemblage, collected show, collection.

Musty, *a.* 1. Mouldy, fusty, sour, fetid, rank, foul, spoiled, stale, frowzy.

2. Stale, old, hackneyed, trite, threadbare.

3. Vapid, ill-flavored, stale, insipid.

4. Dull, heavy, spiritless, rusty.

Mutability, *n.* 1. Changeableness, mutableness, variableness.

2. Instability, fickleness, vacillation, inconstancy.

Mutable, *a.* 1. Changeable, alterable, variable.

2. Inconstant, unsettled, vacillating, fickle, unstable, changeable, unsteady, wavering, variable, irresolute, changeful, mutatory.

Mutation, *n.* 1. Change, alteration, variation.

2. Change.

Mute, *a.* 1. Dumb, obmutescent, unable to speak, incapable of speech.

2. Silent, speechless, still.

Mutilate, *v. t.* 1. Disfigure, maim, cripple, hamstring.

2. Mangle, injure, dismember.

Mutinous, *a.* 1. Turbulent, contumacious, refractory, unruly, insubordinate, riotous, rebellious.

2. Seditious, insurgent, insurrectionary.

Mutiny, *v. i.* Rebel, revolt, resist authority.

——, *n.* Sedition, revolt, rebellion, insurrection, riot, rising, uprising.

Mutter, *v. i.* Grumble, murmur, mumble, muffle.

——, *v. t.* Utter indistinctly, murmur.

——, *n.* Murmur, indistinct utterance.

Mutual, *a.* Reciprocal, interchanged, correlative, reciprocally given and received, common, interchangeable.

Muzzle, *n.* 1. Snout.

2. Mouth, nozzle.

Myopic, *a.* Near-sighted, short-sighted, dim-sighted, purblind, mope-eyed.

Myopy, *n.* Near-sightedness, myopia, mouse-sight.

Myriad, *a.* Innumerable, multitudinous, manifold, uncounted.

Mysterious, *a.* Unknown, enigmatical, obscure, hidden, occult, inscrutable, recondite, secret, unintelligible, mystic, mystical, dark, cabalistic, abstruse, incomprehensible, sphinxlike.

Mystery, *n.* 1. Secret, enigma, riddle.

2. Trade, art, calling, occupation, business.

Mystic,) *a.* 1. Mysterious, hidden, enigmatical, obscure, occult, recondite, inscrutable, abstruse, dark, transcendental.
Mystical,)

2. Allegorical, emblematical, cabalistic, symbolical.

Mysticism, *n.* Enthusiasm, quietism, cabala, Orphism, doctrine of the Mystics.

Mystify, *v. t.* Perplex, puzzle, bewilder, embarrass, pose, befog, obfuscate.

Myth, *n.* 1. Fable, legend, tradition.

2. Fable, invention, allegory, parable, fiction, fabulous story.

3. Falsehood, lie, untruth.

Mythic,) *a.* Fabulous, fabled, imaginary, mythological, fictitious, fanciful.
Mythical,)

Mythological, *a.* Fabulous, mythical.

N

Nab, *v. t.* (*Colloq.*) Seize (*suddenly*), catch, clutch, grasp, snatch, lay hands on, lay hold on, take possession of.

Nabob, *n.* 1. Indian deputy, viceroy, *or* governor.

2. Millionnaire, Crœsus, Dives, very rich man, man of great wealth, man of fortune.

Nacreous, *a.* Pearly, iridescent, irisated, opalescent, pavonine, polychromatic, pearlaceous.

Nag, *n.* Horse (*especially a small horse*), pony.

——, *v. t.* Torment, worry, pester, hector, harass.

Naiad, *n.* (*Mythol.*) Water-nymph.

NAIL, *n.* Claw, talon.

Naive, *a.* [Fr.] Artless, unaffected, ingenuous, natural, plain, simple, unsophisticated, candid.

Naiveté, *n.* [Fr.] Artlessness, ingenuousness, naturalness, simplicity, native candor, unaffected plainness.

Naked, *a.* 1. Nude, uncovered, bare.

2. Denuded, unclothed, unclad, undressed, *in puris naturalibus.*

3. Exposed, defenceless, unarmed, unprotected, unguarded, open.

4. Manifest, unconcealed, evident, open, plain, stark, undisguised.

5. Simple, mere, sheer, bare.

6. Unprovided, unfurnished, destitute, unaided, bare.

7. Plain, unvarnished, uncolored, unexaggerated.

Namby-pamby, *a.* Finical, affectedly fine, silly, weakly sentimental, insipid, vapid.

NAME, *n.* 1. Appellation, title, cognomen, nickname, surname, sobriquet, epithet, denomination, designation, descriptive term.

2. Reputation, repute, credit, character.

3. Note, distinction, fame, renown, celebrity, eminence, honor, praise.

——, *v. t.* 1. Denominate, entitle, style, term, call, dub, phrase, christen, give an appellation to.

2. Mention, speak of, call by name.

3. Nominate, designate, specify, indicate.

Nameless, *a.* 1. Without a name.

2. Obscure, undistinguished, unknown.

3. Inexpressible.

Namely, *adv.* Particularly, that is, that is to say, to wit, to particularize, *videlicet.*

Nap, *v. i.* Doze, slumber, drowse, take a short sleep.

——, *n.* Doze, slumber, short sleep, *siesta.*

Narcotic, *a.* Stupefying, stupefactive.

——, *n.* Stupefacient, anodyne, anæsthetic, "dope," opiate, sleeping draught, sedative.

Narrate, *v. t.* Relate, recite, recount, rehearse, tell, chronicle, detail, describe, give an account of.

Narration, *n.* 1. Recital, description, rehearsal, relation, account, statement.

2. Story, history, narrative, tale, chronicle, account.

Narrative, *n.* Narration, relation, tale, account, recital, rehearsal, description, story, history, chronicle.

Narrator, *n.* Relater, historian, *raconteur.*

NARROW, *a.* 1. Contracted, circumscribed, limited, confined, straitened, cramped, pinched, scanty, incapacious.

2. Ungenerous, bigoted, hidebound, illiberal.

3. Close, near.

——, *v. t.* Contract, straiten, cramp, restrict, limit, confine.

Narrow-minded, *a.* Illiberal, bigoted, prejudiced, warped, biassed, partial, narrowsouled, mean-spirited, of narrow *or* contracted views.

Narrows, *n. pl.* Strait, sound, narrow passage.

Nascent, *a.* Incipient, opening, initial, dawning, evolving, inchoative, initiatory, rudimental, beginning, commencing, at the start.

Nastiness, *n.* 1. Filth, filthiness, dirtiness, foulness, impurity, uncleanness, pollution, defilement, squalor.

2. Obscenity, smuttiness, smut, pornography, indecency, ribaldry, grossness.

Nasty, *a.* 1. Filthy, foul, unclean, impure, dirty, polluted, defiled, loathsome, squalid.

2. Obscene, smutty, gross, indelicate, lewd, indecent, ribald, loose.

3. Nauseous, sickening, disgusting, offensive, repulsive, odious, disagreeable.

4. Disagreeable, annoying, troublesome, aggravating, pestering, pesky.

Natal, *a.* Native, of birth, natalitious.

NATION, *n.* 1. State, commonwealth, realm, nationality.

2. People, community, population, race, stock.

National, *a.* Public, general.

Nationality, *n.* 1. State, nation, commonwealth.

2. Race, people, nation, stock.

Native, *a.* 1. Indigenous, autochthonous, home-grown, home-spun, domestic.

2. Original, genuine, intrinsic, real, unartificial, natural.

3. Natural, inherent, innate, inborn, natal, inbred, congenital, indigenous.

——, *n.* Original inhabitant, "aborigine," "autochthon."

Nativity, *n.* Birth.

Natty, *a.* (*Colloq.*) Neat, spruce, tidy, nice, fine, jaunty, trig, trim, finical, foppish, dandyish.

NATURAL, *a.* 1. Original, indigenous, native (*which see*).

2. Essential, characteristic, native.

3. Regular, normal, legitimate, in the course of nature, consistent with nature, conformable to nature.

4. Unaffected, real, genuine, simple, ingenuous, artless, spontaneous.

5. Illegitimate, bastard.

——, *n.* Fool, simpleton, idiot.

Natural child. Bastard, love-child, illegitimate child.

Naturalize, *v. t.* 1. Make natural, familiarize, make easy.

2. Adopt as a citizen, adopt as native.

3. Acclimatize, adapt, accustom, domesticate, habituate.

4. Adapt, make one's own.

Nature, *n.* 1. World, creation, universe, system of created things, aggregate of phenomena, world of matter and of mind, sum of causes and effects.

2. Character, essence, constitution, quality, sum of attributes.

3. Kind, sort, species, quality, character.

4. Temper, disposition, humor, mood, grain.

5. Mind, intelligence, intelligent being, intellect.

6. Active principle of the universe, soul of the Universe, God, Creator, Author.

7. Regular course of things, usual *or* established order of events, normal association.

8. What is natural, conformity with nature, natural condition, accordance with truth *or* reality.

Naught, *n.* Nothing, nought.

——, *a.* 1. Worthless, bad, of no value.

2. Naughty, vile, base.

Naughtiness, *n.* Perverseness, frowardness, mischievousness, misbehavior.

Naughty, *a.* 1. Bad, corrupt, worthless, good for nothing.

2. Perverse, froward, mischievous, bad.

Nausea, *n.* 1. Seasickness, queasiness.

2. Qualm, sickness of the stomach, inclination to vomit, squeamishness, loathing.

3. Disgust, loathing, repugnance, aversion, strong dislike.

Nauseate, *v. i.* Feel nausea, feel disgust, grow qualmish.

——, *v. t.* 1. Sicken, disgust, revolt, make sick, turn one's stomach, make one's gorge rise.

2. Loathe, abhor, detest, abominate, feel nausea *or* disgust at, shrink from, recoil from, reject with disgust.

Nauseous, *a.* Disgusting, loathsome, disgustful, nauseating, sickening, revolting, repulsive, distasteful, offensive.

Nautical, *a.* Maritime, marine, naval.

Naval, *a.* Nautical, marine, maritime.

Navicular, *a.* (*Anat. and Bot.*) Boat-shaped, cymbiform.

Navigate, *v. i.* Sail, cruise, course, go in a vessel, plough the waves, plough the deep.

——, *v. t.* 1. Sail over, sail on, pass in a vessel.

2. Steer, direct (*in sailing*), guide the course of.

Navigator, *n.* Navigating officer.

Navy, *n.* 1. Ships, vessels, shipping, fleet of ships.

2. Ships of war, naval establishment.

Nay, *adv.* No, not so.

Neap, *a.* Low (*applied to tides*).

Near, *a.* 1. Nigh, close, neighboring, adjacent, contiguous, proximate, adjoining, bordering upon, approximate to, close upon, close by, hard upon, close at hand.

2. Imminent, impending, forthcoming, approaching, threatening, at hand, about to happen, going to happen.

3. Intimate, dear, familiar, closely allied, related by blood, closely attached.

4. Direct, short, straight, immediate, close.

5. Close, literal, accurate.

6. Close, narrow, niggardly, parsimonious, close-fisted.

——, *adv.* Nearly, closely, within a little of, almost, well-nigh.

——, *prep.* Nigh, close to, close by, not far from.

——, *v. t.* and *v. i.* Approach, come nearer, draw near.

Nearly, *adv.* 1. Approximately, not remotely.

2. Almost, well-nigh, within a little.

3. Closely, intimately, pressingly.

4. Stingily, meanly, parsimoniously, penuriously.

Nearness, *n.* 1. Closeness, adjacency, neighborhood, proximity.

2. Propinquity, consanguinity.

3. Intimacy, familiarity.

4. Parsimony, penuriousness, closeness.

Near-sighted, *a.* Short-sighted, myopic, purblind.

Neat, *a.* 1. Clean, cleanly, unsoiled, orderly, trim, tidy, "swept and garnished."

2. Nice, spruce, trim, smart.

3. Chaste, simple, pure.

4. Pure, unadulterated, unmixed, excellent.

5. Exact, finished, adroit, clever.

6. Nice, dainty.

Neat-cattle, *n.* Bovine animals (*bulls, oxen, cows, calves, heifers, steers*), beeves.

Neatly, *adv.* 1. Cleanly, in a neat manner, tidily.

2. Nicely, handsomely.

3. Elegantly, nicely, quietly.

Neatness, *n.* 1. Cleanness, cleanliness, tidiness.

2. Nicety, spruceness, trimness, orderliness.

3. Chasteness, simplicity, purity.

Nebulosity, *n.* Cloudiness, haziness, mistiness, nebulousness.

Nebulous, *a.* 1. Cloudy, hazy, misty.

2. Nebular.

NECESSARY, *a.* 1. Inevitable, unavoidable, that must be.

2. Requisite, essential, indispensable, needful, that cannot be spared.

3. Involuntary, compulsory, compelled.

——, *n.* 1. Requisite, requirement, necessity, essential, indispensable thing, *sine qua non.*

2. Privy, jakes, water-closet, backhouse.

Necessitate, *v. t.* 1. Compel, force, oblige, constrain, impel.

2. Make necessary, render unavoidable.

Necessitous, *a.* 1. Needy, indigent, poor, penniless, moneyless, destitute, distressed, pinched, reduced, in need, in want, short of money, out of money, out of pocket, out of cash.

2. Narrow, destitute, pinching.

Necessity, *n.* 1. Unavoidableness, inevitableness.

2. Compulsion, fatality, fate, destiny, irresistible force, overruling power.

3. Indispensableness, indispensability, need.

4. Need, needfulness, urgency, exigency, pressing want.

5. Requirement, requisite, essential, necessary, indispensable thing, *sine qua non.*

6. Indigence, poverty, need, want.

NECK, *n.* (*Basic Eng.*)

Necktie, *n.* Cravat, neck-cloth, neckerchief.

Necrology, *n.* Obituary, register of deaths.

Necromancer, *n.* Sorcerer, conjurer, enchanter, juggler, charmer, diviner, wizard, magician, exorcist, seer, soothsayer.

Necromancy, *n.* Sorcery, magic, divination, enchantment, conjuration, black art, magical art.

Necropolis, *n.* Cemetery, churchyard, graveyard, mortuary, burial-ground, burial-place, city of the dead.

NEED, *n.* 1. Necessity, want, exigency, urgency, emergency, strait, extremity.

2. Indigence, poverty, penury, destitution, distress, neediness, privation.

——, *v. t.* Want, require, demand, lack, be in want of, stand in want of.

Needful, *a.* 1. Needy, necessitous, distressful.

2. Necessary, requisite, essential, indispensable.

NEEDLE, *n.* Bodkin, darner, straw, sharp.

Needle-shaped, *a.* Aciform, acicular, aciculate.

Needless, *a.* Unnecessary, useless, superfluous.

Needlewoman, *n.* Seamstress, sempstress.

Needle-work, *n.* Embroidery, "stitchery."

Needs, *adv.* Necessarily, indispensably, of necessity.

Needy, *a.* Indigent, destitute, poor, necessitous.

Nefarious, *a.* Abominable, atrocious, detestable, execrable, iniquitous, scandalous, wicked, infamous, villainous, heinous, flagitious, very wicked, horrible, dreadful, vile.

Negation, *n.* Denial, disavowal, disclaimer.

Neglect, *v. t.* 1. Omit, leave out, pass over.

2. Disregard, slight, contemn, overlook, pay no heed to, pay no regard to, leave out of view, leave on one side, not care a straw for, disesteem, despise.

——, *n.* 1. Omission (*of a particular act of duty*), failure, default, remissness, carelessness, heedlessness, inattention.

2. Slight, disregard, disrespect.

3. Negligence, indifference.

4. Neglectedness, state of being disregarded.

Neglectful, *a.* Heedless, careless, lax, negligent, thoughtless, inattentive, remiss, slack.

Negligée, *n.* [Fr.] Undress, dishabille, *déshabillé.*

Negligence, *n.* 1. Neglect carelessness, thoughtlessness, remissness, heedlessness, disregard, inattention, slackness, laches, inadvertency, indifference.

2. Shortcoming, fault, omission, defect, inadvertence.

Negligent, *a.* Careless (*habitually*), thoughtless, heedless, remiss, regardless, inattentive, neglectful, indifferent.

Negotiate, *v. i.* Treat, bargain.

——, *v. t.* 1. Treat for, arrange for, procure.

2. Pass, put into circulation, sell.

Negotiation, *n.* 1. Transaction.

2. Trading, business.

Negro, *n.* African, black man, blackamoor, "darkey," "nigger" (*contemptuous*).

Neigh, *v. i.* Whinny.

Neighborhood, *n.* 1. Vicinity, vicinage.

2. District, locality, environs.

3. Nearness, propinquity.

Neighboring, *a.* Near, adjacent, contiguous.

Neighborly, *a.* 1. Friendly, kind, civil.

2. Social, obliging, attentive, friendly.

Neither, *pron.* and *a.* Not either, nor one nor the other.

Neologism, *n.* New word *or* phrase, neonism; neology.

Neology, *n.* 1. Neologism, use of new words *or* phrases.

2. (*Theol.*) Rationalism, rationalistic interpretation.

Neophyte, *n.* 1. Convert, proselyte.

2. Novice, catechumen.

3. Beginner, tyro, pupil, novice.

Neoteric, *a.* New, modern, recent.

Nereid, *n.* Sea-nymph.

NERVE, *n.* 1. Strength, power, force, vigor, might.

2. Courage, pluck, fortitude, firmness, resolution, hardihood, manhood, self-command, steadiness, endurance, coolness.

——, *v. t.* Strengthen, invigorate, fortify, brace, energize.

Nerveless, *a.* Weak, flabby, flaccid.

Nervous, *a.* 1. Sinewy, strong, vigorous, robust, forcible, powerful, wellstrung, nervy.

2. Timid, timorous, easily agitated, weak, weakly, irritable, fearful.

3. Vigorous, forcible, powerful, forceful, strong, spirited.

Nervousness, *n.* 1. Strength, force, power, vigor, forcibleness.

2. Timidity, timorousness, trepidation, tremor, flutter, nervous agitation, weakness.

Nervy, *a.* Nervous, strong, sinewy, vigorous.

Ness, *n.* Naze, promontory, headland.

Nestle, *v. i.* Snuggle, cuddle, snug, harbor, lodge, lie close, nuzzle.

Net, *n.* Snare, gin, trammel, trap, toil.

——, *a.* 1. Clear, without deductions.

2. Pure, unadulterated.

——, *v. t.* Clear, get *or* gain over and above expenses.

Nether, *a.* Lower.

Nettle, *v. t.* Fret, chafe, ruffle, irritate, vex, tease, harass, provoke, incense, exasperate, sting.

Network, *n.* Netting, mesh, reticulated *or* decussated work, interlacement.

Neutral, *a.* 1. Indifferent, impartial, neuter, of neither party, taking no part with either side.

2. Indifferent, mediocre, colorless.

Neutralize, *v. t.* 1. Counterbalance, counterpoise, offset, render neutral, render inert, destroy the effect of, render of no effect.

2. Invalidate, cancel, render inoperative.

Never, *adv.* 1. At no time, not at any time, not ever.

2. In no degree, not at all, none.

Nevertheless, *adv.* However, notwithstanding, not at all the less, yet.

NEW, *a.* 1. Novel, fresh, of recent origin, newly come.

2. Recent, modern, of the present day, up-to-date, new-fangled.

3. Just discovered, recently made known, strange, unheard-of.

4. Unaccustomed, unused.

5. Repaired, renovated, reinvigorated.

6. Starting anew, commencing, renovated.

New-fangled, *a.* New-made, new-fashioned.

NEWS, *n.* Tidings, intelligence, information, advice, word, report, recent accounts.

Newsmonger, *n.* Quidnunc, gossip, talebearer, mumble-news.

Newspaper, *n.* Gazette, journal.

Next, *a.* Nearest; near to, bordering on, close to, allied to.

Nib, *n.* 1. Bill, beak, neb.

2. Point (*of a pen*).

Nibble, *v. t.* and *v. i.* 1. Gnaw, bite (*by nips*).

2. Carp, cavil, find fault.

Nice, *a.* 1. Exact, accurate, precise, exquisite, delicate, correct, critical, definite, strict, rigorous.

2. Fastidious, dainty, squeamish, punctilious, finical, difficult, over-scrupulous, exacting, hard to please, very particular.

3. Discerning, discriminating, particular, scrupulous, precise.

4. Neat, tidy, trim.

5. Subtile, fine, refined, minute.

6. Delicate, dainty, luscious, soft, tender, savory, delicious, palatable.

7. (*Colloq.*) Pleasant, agreeable, delightful, good.

Nicely, *adv.* 1. Fastidiously, critically, curiously.

2. Discriminatingly, keenly.

3. Accurately, exactly, delicately, daintily.

4. Agreeably, becomingly, pleasantly.

5. Well, cleverly, dexterously, deftly, neatly.

Niceness, *n.* 1. Exactness, accuracy, precision, nicety.

2. Scrupulousness, fastidiousness, delicacy, daintiness, squeamishness, particularity.

Nicety, *n.* 1. Accuracy, exactness, precision, truth, niceness.

2. Fastidiousness, daintiness, squeamishness.

3. Subtilty, nice point, minute distinction, discrimination.

Niche, *n.* Nook, recess.

Nick, *n.* 1. Critical point (*of time*), critical moment, fortunate conjuncture.

2. Notch, dent, dint, indentation, incision, score.

——, *v. t.* Notch.

Nickname, *n.* *Sobriquet*, by-name.

Niggard, *n.* Miser, curmudgeon, churl, hunks, lickpenny, skinflint, scrimp, screw, mean fellow, sordid wretch.

——, *a.* Parsimonious, miserly, covetous, sparing, stinted, niggardly.

Niggardliness, *n.* Parsimony, stinginess, avarice, meanness, covetousness.

Niggardly, *a.* 1. Parsimonious, skinflint, stingy, avaricious, miserly, penurious, sordid, mean, illiberal, mercenary, niggard, close, close-fisted.

2. Saving, sparing, chary.

Nigh, *a.* 1. Near, adjacent, adjoining, contiguous, close by, close, close at hand, bordering upon, approximate to, hard by.

2. Near, present, proximate.

——, *adv.* 1. Near.

2. Almost, nearly.

——, *prep.* Near, close to, close by, not far from.

NIGHT, *n.* Night-time, darkness, obscurity.

Night-fall, *n.* Evening, dusk, close of the day, sundown.

Nightly, *a.* Nocturnal.

Nightmare, *n.* Incubus.

Night-walker, *n.* Somnambulist, sleep-walker, noctambulist.

Nihilism, } *n.* Nothingness, nothing, non-
Nihility, } existence, nonentity, nullity.

Nimble, *a.* Agile, lively, brisk, active, quick, spry, alert, sprightly, swift, light-footed, tripping, speedy.

Nimbleness, *n.* Briskness, agility, spryness, alertness, activity, sprightliness, celerity, speed, swiftness.

Nincompoop, *n.* See NINNY.

Ninepins, *n. pl.* Skittles.

Ninny, *n.* [A contr. for *Nincompoop*.] Simpleton, fool, blockhead, dunce.

Nip, *v. t.* 1. Pinch, compress, squeeze, gripe.

2. Clip, cut off, sever.

3. Blast, destroy, ruin, frost.

4. Benumb, chill.

5. Bite, vex.

——, *n.* 1. Pinch, bite.

2. Dram, sip, drink, small draught.

Nipper, *n.* Fore tooth (*of a horse*).

Nippers, *n. pl.* Pincers, tweezers.

Nipple, *n.* Teat, dug, pap, mamilla.

Nix, } *n.* Water-spirit.
Nixie, }

NO, *adv.* 1. Nay, not so.

2. Not at all, in no degree.

——, *a.* None, not any, not one.

Nob, *n.* Head (*in burlesque*).

Nobility, *n.* 1. Grandeur, greatness, dignity, nobleness, elevation, superiority, worthiness, loftiness of character, eminence, moral excellence.

2. Noble birth, patrician dignity, gentility, eminence by rank.

3. Aristocracy, peerage, patriciate, patrician class, *noblesse*.

Noble, *a.* 1. Great, dignified, superior, elevated, worthy, exalted, illustrious, magnanimous, honorable, eminent.

2. Choice, excellent.

3. High-born, aristocratic, patrician, gentle.

4. Grand, stately, lordly, splendid, magnificent.

——, *n.* Nobleman, peer, grandee, lord, one of the nobility, aristocrat.

Nobleness, *n.* 1. Greatness, dignity, magnanimity, elevation, superiority, worthiness, nobility, loftiness of character, moral excellence.

2. Rank, distinction by birth, station.

3. Stateliness, grandeur, magnificence.

Noblesse, *n.* [Fr.] Aristocracy, nobility.

Nobly, *adv.* 1. Heroically, magnanimously, honorably.

2. Splendidly, magnificently, grandly.

Nobody, *n.* 1. No one, no person, not any one, not anybody.

2. Unimportant person, insignificant person, cipher, nonentity.

Nocturnal, *a.* Nightly.

Nod, *v. t.* and *v. i.* Bow.

——, *n.* Bow, beck, nutation.

Node, *n.* Knot, knob, protuberance, swelling, lump, prominence, process, excrescence, nodule, nodosity.

NOISE, *n.* 1. Sound.

2. Clamor, din, blare, clatter, uproar, outcry, tumult, ado, vociferation, hubbub, hullabaloo, pandemonium, racket, fuss.

3. Talk, stir, conversation, discussion.

Noiseless, *a.* Silent, inaudible, quiet.

Noisome, *a.* 1. Noxious, injurious, hurtful, unwholesome, insalubrious, unhealthy, pernicious, mischievous, detrimental, destructive, deleterious, baneful, poisonous, pestilential.

2. Offensive, fetid, disgusting.

Noisy, *a.* 1. Clamorous, boisterous, vociferous, blatant, brawling, blustering, uproarious, tumultuous, riotous, loud.

2. Full of noise, clamorous, boisterous, tumultuous.

Nomad, } *n.* Wanderer, one of a nomadic
Nomade, } people.

Nomadic, *a.* Wandering, migratory, pastoral, vagrant.

Nomenclature, n. Terminology.

Nominal, a. Titular, only in name, nuncupative, nuncupatory.

Nominate, v. t. Name for an office, propose as a candidate, designate for appointment or election.

Nonage, n. Minority, pupilage, legal immaturity.

Nonchalance, n. [Fr.] Carelessness, indifference, unconcern, coolness.

Nonchalant, a. [Fr.] Unconcerned, indifferent, careless, cool, apathetic.

Nondescript, a. Abnormal, amorphous, odd, unclassifiable, indescribable.

None, pron. sing. and pl. 1. Not one.

　2. Not any, not a part, not the least portion.

Nonentity, n. 1. Inexistence, non-existence.

　2. Nothingness, insignificance, futility.

　3. Nobody, cipher.

Non-essential, a. Adventitious, incidental, accidental, extraneous, extrinsic.

Nonesuch, n. Nonpareil, paragon, pattern, model, acme of perfection, pink of perfection, beau idéal.

Nonpareil, a. Peerless, unequalled, unparalleled.

Nonplus, n. Puzzle, perplexity, poser, quandary.

　——, v. t. Puzzle, confound, confuse, disconcert, floor, gravel, perplex, pose, put to a stand.

Nonsense, n. 1. Folly, absurdity, stuff, trash, trumpery, moonshine, twaddle, drivel, "claptrap," "bosh," "gammon," balderdash, fudge, inanity, platitude.

　2. Trifles, flummery, things of no consequence or importance.

Nonsensical, a. Absurd, foolish, silly, senseless, insensate, stupid, ill-judged, unreasonable, irrational, preposterous, unmeaning, frivolous, trifling.

Nook, n. Corner, recess, niche, retired place.

Noon, n. Mid-day, twelve o'clock, meridian, noonday, noontide.

Noose, n. Hitch, running knot.

Norm, n. 1. Rule, pattern, model, standard, norma.

　2. Type.

Norma, n. 1. Rule, principle, norm.

　2. Pattern, gauge, templet, model.

NORMAL, a. 1. Regular, analogical, ordinary, natural, legitimate, usual, according to rule.

　2. Perpendicular, vertical, erect.

NORTH, a. Northerly, northern, boreal, arctic, septentrional.

North star. Polestar, loadstar.

NOSE, n. Proboscis, snout, nasal organ; nozzle.

Nosegay, n. Bouquet, posy.

Nostalgia, n. (Med.) Homesickness, nostalgy.

Nostrum, n. Quack medicine, patent medicine, arcanum.

NOT, adv. (Basic Eng.)

Notability, n. 1. Notableness, remarkableness.

　2. Notable person, person of note, celebrity.

Notable, a. 1. Remarkable, memorable, extraordinary, signal, distinguished, noted, worthy of notice.

　2. Conspicuous, manifest, observable, plain, prominent, noticeable.

　3. Notorious, well-known.

Notary, n. Notary public.

Notch, n. Nick, indentation, dent, dint, incision.

　——, v. t. Nick, cut notches in, indent.

NOTE, n. 1. Memorandum, minute, record.

　2. Comment, annotation, scholium, remark.

　3. Catalogue, reckoning, account, bill, list of items.

　4. Official communication, diplomatic communication, report.

　5. Billet, short letter or epistle.

　6. Notice, heed, observation, regard, consideration.

　7. Distinction, reputation, celebrity, fame, repute, renown, credit, account, consequence, respectability, notedness, eminence.

　8. Bill, bank-note, promissory note, note of hand, paper-money.

　9. Voice, tune, song, strain.

　——, v. t. 1. Notice, remark, observe, mark, regard, heed, attend to, take notice of, pay attention to.

　2. Record, register, make a note of, make a memorandum of, make a minute of, set down in writing, jot down.

　3. Designate, denote.

　4. Annotate, furnish with notes.

Note-book, n. Memorandum-book, journal, commonplace book, diary, logbook.

Noted, a. Distinguished, celebrated, remarkable, notable, notorious, famous, famed, renowned, conspicuous, eminent, illustrious, well-known.

Noteworthy, a. Remarkable, extraordinary, unusual, rare, memorable, worthy of note, noticeable.

Nothing, n. 1. No thing, no quantity, no part, no degree.

　2. Non-existence, nihility, inexistence, nihilism, nonentity, nothingness, nullity.

3. Trifle, bagatelle, small matter, thing of no importance, matter of no consequence.

4. Cipher, zero, nought.

Nothing, *adv.* Not at all, in no degree.

Nothingness, *n.* 1. Nihility, nihilism, non-existence, nonentity.

2. Nothing, nought, worthless thing.

Notice, *n.* 1. Note, heed, observation, perception, regard, cognizance.

2. Information, notification, advice, news, intelligence, announcement, mention.

3. Intimation, premonition, warning, intelligence, communication.

4. Instruction, direction, order.

5. Attention, civility, consideration, respect.

6. Comments, remarks, critical review.

——, *v. t.* 1. Perceive, see, become aware of, heed, regard, reck, mark, note, observe, remark, mind, take cognizance of.

2. Remark upon, mention, comment on.

3. Treat with attention, be civil to.

Noticeable, *a.* Observable, perceptible, striking, worthy of notice, noteworthy.

Notification, *n.* Information, notice, advice, intelligence, announcement.

Notify, *v. t.* 1. Declare, promulgate, publish, announce, advertise, make known.

2. Inform, apprise, acquaint, make known to, give notice to, signify to.

Notion, *n.* 1. Conception, concept, universal idea, general *or* universal conception.

2. Opinion, sentiment, apprehension, judgment, belief, view, impression, estimation, conceit, conviction, expectation.

Notional, *a.* 1. Ideal, abstract.

2. Imaginary, fantastical, visionary, ideal, chimerical.

3. Whimsical, capricious, fanciful, crotchety, freakish.

Notoriety, *n.* 1. Publicity.

2. Repute (*generally in a bad sense*), reputation, celebrity, fame, name, note, vogue, figure.

Notorious, *a.* 1. Open, overt, patent, manifest, obvious, apparent, evident, well-known, egregious, notable.

2. Conspicuous (*generally in a bad sense*), flagrant, noted, celebrated, famous, famed, distinguished, remarkable, renowned.

Notwithstanding, *prep.* Despite, in spite of.

——, *conj.* Nevertheless, yet, however, for all that, despite, in spite of.

Nought, *n.* Nothing, naught.

Noun, *n.* Substantive.

Nourish, *v. t.* 1. Nurture, nurse, feed, tend, supply with food *or* nutriment, furnish sustenance to.

2. Support, maintain, provide for.

3. Train, educate, instruct, breed, bring up.

4. Cherish, encourage, foster, promote, succor, foment.

Nourishing, *a.* Nutritious, nutritive, strengthening, invigorating, healthful, wholesome.

Nourishment, *n.* 1. Nutrition, nourishing.

2. Food, aliment, diet, sustenance, nutriment, nutrition.

Novel, *a.* New, strange, unusual, modern, recent, neoteric, fresh, uncommon, rare.

——, *n.* Tale, romance, story, fiction, fictitious narrative.

Novice, *n.* 1. Convert, proselyte.

2. Probationer, novitiate, neophyte, initiate.

3. Tyro, beginner, learner, apprentice.

Novitiate, *n.* 1. Apprenticeship.

2. Probation, noviceship.

3. Novice, probationer.

NOW, *adv.* 1. At this time, at once, at this moment, at present.

2. After this, things being so.

3. Since, it being so that.

Nowadays, *adv.* In these days, in this age, in the present age, now.

Noway,   } *adv.* Not at all, in no degree, in
Noways, } no manner, nowise.

Noxious, *a.* 1. Injurious, hurtful, baneful, pernicious, detrimental, unwholesome, mischievous, insalubrious, deleterious, noisome, pestiferous, pestilent, deadly, destructive, poisonous.

2. Unfavorable, injurious, pernicious, baneful, harmful, corrupting.

Nozzle, *n.* Nose, snout.

Nucleus, *n.* Kernel, core, center.

Nude, *a.* Bare, uncovered, undressed, unclothed, naked, exposed, denuded, stark naked, in a state of nature, *in puris naturalibus.*

Nudge, *v. t.* Push gently, jog, poke.

——, *n.* Gentle push, jog, poke.

Nudity, *n.* Nakedness.

Nugatory, *a.* 1. Trifling, futile, vain, insignificant, trivial, frivolous, worthless.

2. Inoperative, ineffectual, inefficacious, unavailing, useless, bootless, null, to no purpose.

Nugget, *n.* Lump, mass.

Nuisance, *n.* Annoyance, plague, bane, infliction, pest, bore.

Null, *a.* 1. Void, invalid, useless, nugatory, of no efficacy, of no account, ineffectual.

2. Characterless, expressionless.

Nullify, *v. t.* Annul, invalidate, cancel, abrogate, negate, repeal, make void, make of no effect, abolish, revoke.

Nullity, *n.* 1. Non-existence, nonentity, nihility, nothingness, insignificance.

2. Nothing, nonentity.

3. Invalidity, inefficacy.

Numb, *a.* Torpid, benumbed, paralyzed, deadened, dulled, insensible.

——, *v. t.* Benumb, stupefy, deaden, make torpid.

Number, *v. t.* 1. Count, enumerate, tell, reckon, calculate, compute, numerate, call over, tell off, run over, sum up.

2. Reckon, account.

3. Amount to, reach the number of, contain, include, consist of.

NUMBER, *n.* 1. Figure, numeral, digit, *numero*.

2. Multitude, numerousness.

3. Collection of units, sum, total, aggregate.

Numberless, *a.* Innumerable, countless, infinite.

Numbers, *n. pl.* Verse, poetry, metrical composition.

Numbness, *n.* Torpor, insensibility, deadness, paralysis, torpidity, palsy.

Numeral, *n.* Figure, number, digit.

Numerate, *v. t.* Reckon, enumerate, count, number, call over, tell off.

Numerous, *a.* Large (*in number*), made up of many.

Numskull, *n.* Blockhead, simpleton, dunce, dolt, dullard, fool.

Nuncio, *n.* 1. Messenger, intelligencer.

2. Ambassador (*of the Pope*), legate.

Nuncupative, *a.* 1. (*Law.*) Oral.

2. Normal, nuncupatory.

Nunnery, *n.* Convent, cloister, abbey, monastery.

Nuptial, *a.* Bridal, hymeneal.

Nuptials, *n. pl.* Marriage, wedding, bridal, espousals, nuptial festival, marriage ceremony.

Nurse, *v. t.* 1. Nourish, nurture, supply with nourishment.

2. Suckle, feed at the breast, give suck to, nourish at the breast.

3. Cherish, foster, encourage, succor, promote, foment, feed, pamper.

4. Tend in sickness, care for, take care of, attend upon.

5. Manage, economize.

6. Caress, fondle, dandle.

7. Rear, nurture, bring up.

Nursling, *n.* Infant, babe, baby, suckling, child, fondling, nurse-child.

Nurture, *n.* 1. Nourishment, food, diet.

2. Training, education, instruction, discipline, tuition, schooling, breeding.

3. Nursing, nourishing, tender care, attention.

——, *v. t.* 1. Feed, nourish, nurse, tend.

2. Train, educate, instruct, school, rear, breed, discipline, bring up train up.

NUT, *n.* (*Basic Eng.*) Kernel.

Nutriment, *n.* 1. Aliment, nourishment, nutrition, food, sustenance, subsistence.

2. Pabulum.

Nutrition, *n.* 1. Nourishing, feeding.

2. Food, nutriment.

Nutritious, } *a.* Nourishing, strengthening,
Nutritive, } wholesome, nutrimental, alimental, nutrient.

Nymph, *n.* Dryad, naiad. *In poetry:* damsel, maiden, maid, lass, girl.

O

Oaf, *n.* 1. Changeling (*when a foolish child is left in place of another*).

2. Fool, simpleton, dolt, idiot, blockhead, dunce.

Oaky, *a.* Hard, firm, strong.

Oath, *n.* 1. Solemn affirmation, imprecatory pledge, vow, sworn statement *or* promise *or* pledge.

2. Imprecation, blasphemy, curse, expletive, malediction.

Obduracy, *n.* 1. Contumacy, stubbornness, doggedness, hardness of heart, obstinacy.

2. Impenitence, depravity.

Obdurate, *a.* 1. Hard, harsh, rugged, rough.

2. Hardened, obstinate, firm, callous, unfeeling, stubborn, unyielding, dogged, pig-headed, inflexible, inexorable, cantankerous, hard-hearted, unbending, unsusceptible, insensible.

3. Depraved, graceless, shameless, reprobate, lost, impenitent, irreclaimable, incorrigible.

Obedience, *n.* 1. Compliance, biddableness, submission, subservience.

2. Dutifulness, duty, reverence, respect.

Obedient, *a.* Compliant, submissive, deferential, dutiful, duteous, respectful, yielding compliance, observant, regardful, subservient.

Obeisance, *n.* Salutation, reverence, bow, courtesy.

Obelisk, *n.* Column, pillar, quadrangular pillar.

Obese, *a.* Fat, fleshy, corpulent, stout, plump, portly, gross.

Obesity, *n.* Fleshiness, fatness, corpulence, corpulency, plumpness, *embonpoint*, obeseness.

Obey, *v. t.* Mind, heed, comply with.

Obfuscate, *v. t.* 1. Darken, cloud, obscure.

2. Bewilder, confuse, muddle.

Obit, *n.* 1. Funeral rite, obsequies.

2. Death, decease.

Obituary, *n.* Necrology.

Object, *n.* 1. Thing, reality, particular, phenomenon, percept, thing perceived, external reality.

2. Mark, aim, target, butt; goal, end, destination; recipient, correlate, *or* complement (*of a conscious subject*).

3. End, aim, intent, intention, purpose, design, motive, use, view, drift, goal, final cause.

——, *v. i.* Disapprove, demur, "boggle," protest, take exception.

Objection, *n.* Exception, difficulty, doubt, protest, remonstrance, scruple.

Objective, *a.* 1. Belonging to *or* characterizing the object (*as distinguished from the subject*).

2. Outward, external, actual, positive, factual, unconditional, universal, nonsubjective.

3. Absorbed in objects, non-introversive, free from introversion, wholly occupied with the object *or* fact, that tells things as they are, that does not color facts, that paints things in their own light, extroitive (*rare*).

4. (*Mil.*) Destined, aimed at, of chief aim, of ultimate strategy.

Objectless, *a.* Aimless, purposeless, wandering, vague, desultory.

Objurate, *v. t.* Chide, reprove, reprehend.

Objurgation, *n.* Reproof, reprehension, rebuke.

Objurgatory, *a.* Culpatory, reprehensory, reproving, rebuking.

Oblation, *n.* Offering, sacrifice.

Obligate, *v. t.* Bind, oblige, bring under obligation.

Obligation, *n.* 1. Responsibility, accountableness, bond of duty, compulsion, incumbency.

2. Engagement, contract, agreement, stipulation, bond, covenant.

3. Debt, liability, indebtedness.

Obligato, *a.* (*Mus.*) [Written also *Obbligato.*] Required, necessary, indispensable.

Obligatory, *a.* Binding, coercive.

Oblige, *v. t.* 1. Compel, force, coerce, constrain, necessitate, bind.

2. Serve, accommodate, please, favor, benefit, convenience, gratify, do a service for, do a favor to.

3. Obligate, bind, bring *or* lay under obligation.

Obliging, *a.* Complaisant, kind, considerate, accommodating.

Oblique, *a.* 1. Inclined, aslant, slanting, sidelong.

2. Indirect, obscure.

Obliterate, *v. t.* 1. Efface, erase, expunge, cancel, rub out, rub off, blot out, scratch out, wipe out, strike out.

2. Wear out, destroy.

Obliteration, *n.* Effacement, erasure, extinction, blotting out.

Oblivion, *n.* Forgetfulness (Oblivion *refers especially to the thing forgotten*).

Oblivious, *a.* Forgetful, mindless, heedless, careless, negligent, neglectful.

Obloquy, *n.* Reproach, detraction, odium, censure, blame, calumny, contumely, slander, defamation, backbiting, traducing, aspersion, reviling.

Obnoxious, *a.* 1. Reprehensible, censurable, blameworthy, faulty.

2. Hateful, unpleasing, odious, offensive, repulsive, repellent.

Oboe, *n.* Hautboy.

Obscene, *a.* 1. Indecent, indelicate, immodest, impure, ribald, gross, coarse, broad, unchaste, lewd, loose, smutty, pornographic, offensive, shameless, filthy.

2. Dirty, filthy, foul, offensive, disgusting.

Obscenity, *n.* 1. Indecency, indelicacy, immodesty, unchastity, lewdness, obsceneness.

2. Ribaldry, lewdness, smuttiness, indelicacy.

Obscure, *a.* 1. Dark, gloomy, rayless, darksome, unilluminated, unenlightened, dusky, sombre, sombrous, lurid, shadowy, murky, dim.

2. Unintelligible, incomprehensible, indistinct, indefinite, vague, doubtful, enigmatical, mysterious, mystic, mystical, recondite, abstruse, cabalistic, transcendental, high, intricate, involved, difficult, blind.

3. Retired, remote, secluded.

4. Unknown, undistinguished, nameless, unnoted, unnoticed, renownless, unhonored, humble, inglorious.

Obscure, *v. t.* 1. Darken, cloud, becloud, befog, obnubilate, eclipse, dim, shade, obfuscate.

2. Hide, disguise, keep in the dark, conceal, cover.

Obscurity, *n.* 1. Darkness, dimness, gloom, gloominess, shade, obscuration, cloud, obfuscation, opacity.

2. Unintelligibleness, darkness of meaning.

3. Humbleness, namelessness.

4. Seclusion, retirement, privacy.

Obsequies, *n. pl.* Exequies, funeral rites, funeral solemnities, obit.

Obsequious, *a.* Fawning, sycophantic, deferential, flattering, cringing, servile, slavish, supple, subservient, truckling, meanly submissive.

Obsequiousness, *n.* Fawning, cringing, servility, slavishness, suppleness, sycophancy, mean compliance.

Observable, *a.* Noticeable, remarkable, marked, striking, noteworthy.

Observance, *n.* 1. Performance, fulfilment, discharge, acquittal.

2. Form, ceremony, ceremonial, rite, solemnization.

3. Practice, custom, usage, fashion.

4. Attention, service, respect.

Observant, *a.* 1. Mindful, regardful, heedful, attentive, watchful.

2. Obedient, attentive to.

OBSERVATION, *n.* 1. Notice, attention, observance.

2. Remark, note, annotation.

3. Knowledge, experience, note.

4. Remark, comment.

Observe, *v. t.* 1. Notice, remark, note, watch, eye, mark, take note of, pay attention to.

2. See, behold, notice, perceive, detect, discover.

3. Utter, express, remark, mention, say.

4. Fulfil, obey, follow, comply with, conform to, adhere to, be faithful to.

5. Celebrate, regard, keep, solemnize.

——, *v. i.* 1. Take notice, attend.

2. Make a remark, comment.

Observer, *n.* 1. Beholder, spectator, bystander, on-looker, looker-on.

2. Regarder, keeper.

3. Student, examiner, watcher.

Obsessed, *a.* Fixated, "hipped."

Obsolete, *a.* Antiquated, disused, neglected, unfashionable, old-fashioned, out of date, obsolescent, fallen into desuetude, ancient, antique, archaic, past, *passé.*

Obstacle, *n.* Hindrance, obstruction, impediment, difficulty, check, barrier, snag, stumbling-block.

Obstetrician, *n.* Midwife, *accoucheur.*

Obstetrics, *n. pl.* Midwifery, tocology.

Obstinacy, *n.* 1. Stubbornness, doggedness, headiness, wilfulness, perversity, contumacy, obduracy, inflexibility, intractability, pertinacity, persistency, firmness, resoluteness, setness.

2. Fixedness, immovability, stubbornness, tenacity, tenaciousness.

Obstinate, *a.* 1. Stubborn, dogged, contumacious, unyielding, inflexible, perverse, mulish, opinionated, opinionative, wilful, heady, headstrong, refractory, unruly, cross-grained, intractable, obdurate, persistent, self-willed, immovable, firm, resolute, pertinacious.

2. Unyielding, immovable, stubborn, tenacious.

Obstreperous, *a.* Loud, noisy, clamorous, turbulent, tumultuous, boisterous, uproarious.

Obstruct, *v. t.* 1. Close, bar, stop, choke, clog, glut, jam, blockade, barricade, block up, dam up, obturate.

2. Hinder, impede, oppose, stop, prevent.

3. Retard, interrupt, check, embarrass, arrest.

Obstruction, *n.* 1. Hindrance, obstacle, impediment, barrier, check, difficulty, bar.

2. Check, hindrance, embarrassment, clog, interruption, obturation.

Obtain, *v. t.* Procure, get, acquire, achieve, gain, win, earn, secure, get possession of, attain.

——, *v. i.* Hold good, subsist, continue in use, be received, become prevalent, be established.

Obtest, *v. t.* 1. Beseech, implore, conjure, supplicate, beg, invoke, entreat, pray, solicit, importune, conjure, adjure.

2. Beg for, supplicate.

Obtrude, *v. t.* Intrude, thrust in, press in, foist in, worm in, interfere.

Obtrusive, *a.* Intrusive, forward, officious, inclined to obtrude.

Obtuse, *a.* 1. Blunt.

2. Dull, stupid, stolid, doltish, blockish, stockish, heavy, slow, unintelligent, unintellectual, dull-witted, blunt-witted.

Obtuseness, *n.* 1. Bluntness.

2. Dulness, stupidity, stolidity, doltishness, obtusion, obtusity.

Obviate, *v. t.* Preclude, prevent, turn aside, remove, provide against.

Obvious, *a.* 1. Open, exposed, liable, subject.

2. Plain, evident, manifest, clear, palpable, visible, patent, apparent, unmistakable, perceptible, distinct, self-evident.

Occasion, *n.* 1. Occurrence, incident, casualty, event.

2. Opportunity, convenience, juncture, conjuncture, opening, suitable time, favorable time, nick of time, golden opportunity.

3. Necessity, need, exigency, requirement, want.

4. Cause (*incidental*), ground, reason.

5. Motive, reason, inducement, influence.

6. Circumstances, juncture, exigency.

——, *v. t.* 1. Cause, produce, originate, breed, create, bring about, give rise to, give occasion to, bring to pass, be the cause of.

2. Induce, influence, persuade, move.

Occasional, *a.* 1. Incidental, accidental, casual, irregular.

2. Causative, causing.

Occasionally, *adv.* Sometimes, casually, at times, now and then.

Occasive, *a.* Falling, setting, descending, western.

Occident, *n.* West.

Occidental, *a.* Western.

Occult, *a.* Hidden, secret, unrevealed, invisible, unknown, undiscovered, undetected, mysterious, mystic, mystical, recondite, cabalistic, latent, abstruse, veiled, shrouded.

Occupancy, *n.* Possession (*for the time*), tenure, holding, use, occupation, enjoyment.

Occupant, *n.* Possessor (*for the time*), occupier, holder, tenant.

Occupation, *n.* 1. Possession, holding tenure, use, occupancy.

2. Business, engagement, employment.

3. Employment, business, calling, vocation, avocation, profession, pursuit, trade, craft, walk of life.

Occupy, *v. t.* 1. Possess (*for the time*), keep, hold, have possession of.

2. Cover, fill, take up, possess, inhabit, garrison, tenant.

3. Employ, use.

4. Follow, pursue, be engaged with.

5. Employ, busy, engage.

Occur, *v. i.* 1. Appear, arise, offer, come into view, present itself, be met with, meet the eye, be found.

2. Come to one's mind, come into one's head, flash on the mind, present itself, appear.

3. Befall, happen, fall out, take place, come about, come to pass, eventuate, supervene.

Occurrence, *n.* Incident, event, happening, accident, casualty, adventure, affair, transaction, proceeding.

Ocean, *n.* 1. Sea, main, deep, great deep, great sea, high sea.

2. Immense expanse, infinity.

Oceanic, *a.* Marine, pelagic, Neptunian.

Octagon, *n.* Eight-sided figure.

Octagonal, *a.* Eight-sided, eight-angled.

Octuple, *a.* Eightfold.

Odd, *a.* 1. Unmatched, single (*of a pair or set*).

2. Supernumerary, redundant, left over (*from a specified number*), additional, remaining.

3. Incidental, casual, fragmentary.

4. Unsuitable, inappropriate, queer.

5. Singular, unusual, extraordinary, queer, uncouth, quaint, strange, uncommon, eccentric, erratic, irregular, fantastic, whimsical, peculiar, unique, comical, droll, grotesque, extravagant, out of the way, *bizarre, outré.*

Oddity, *n.* Singularity, strangeness, queerness.

Odds, *n. sing.* and *pl.* 1. Difference, disparity, inequality.

2. Probability.

3. Advantage, superiority, supremacy.

Odds and ends. Fragments, remnants, scraps, refuse.

Odious, *a.* 1. Hateful, detestable, execrable, abominable, shocking.

2. Hated, obnoxious, unpopular.

3. Disagreeable, offensive, disgusting, repulsive, loathsome, forbidding.

Odium, *n.* 1. Hatred, hate, dislike, enmity, abhorrence, detestation, antipathy.

2. Odiousness, repulsiveness.

3. Obloquy, opprobrium, reproach.

Odor, *n.* Scent (*good* or *bad*), smell, perfume, fragrance, redolence.

Odoriferous, } *a.* Fragrant, perfumed,
Odorous, } balmy, aromatic, sweet-smelling, sweet-scented, odorant, redolent.

Œsophagus, *n.* Gullet, throat.

OF, *prep.* (*Basic Eng.*)

OFF, *prep.* 1. Not on, not upon.

2. Against, opposite, opposite to, distant from, along, facing.

——, *a.* 1. Most distant, on the farther side.

2. Right side, right hand.

——, *adv.* 1. Away.

2. From, away.

3. Over, done.

Offal, *n.* 1. Garbage.

2. Waste, refuse, rubbish.

Offence, *n.* 1. Attack, assault, aggression, onset (*in the expression "weapons of offence"*).

2. Displeasure, anger, indignation, wrath, pique, "miff," umbrage, resentment.

3. Injury, injustice, affront, wrong, insult, indignity, outrage.

4. Trespass, transgression, misdeed, delinquency, misdemeanor, crime, sin, fault.

Offend, *v. t.* 1. Affront, displease, vex, chafe, annoy, irritate, provoke, nettle, mortify, fret, gall, give offence to, make angry.

2. Shock, wound, pain, annoy, molest.

——, *v. i.* 1. Give offence.

2. Transgress, sin, do wrong, commit offence, stumble, err, fall.

3. Take offence, be scandalized.

Offender, *n.* 1. Transgressor, culprit, trespasser, delinquent.

2. Convict, felon, criminal, malefactor.

Offensive, *a.* 1. Aggressive, assailant, attacking, invading.

2. Disgusting, nauseating, nauseous, sickening, loathsome, repulsive.

3. Disagreeable, unpleasant, unpalatable, displeasing, revolting, shocking, abominable, detestable, hateful, execrable, obnoxious, repugnant.

4. Irritating, disagreeable, unpleasant, impertinent, rude, saucy, opprobrious, insolent, insulting, abusive.

Offer, *v. t.* 1. Present, tender, proffer.

2. Exhibit, proffer, put forward.

3. Furnish, propose, propound, show, give.

——, *v. i.* 1. Occur, present itself, be at hand.

2. Volunteer, propose, make an offer.

3. Make an attempt, venture, dare, essay, endeavor.

OFFER, *n.* 1. Proposal, proposition, proffer, tender, overture.

2. Bid.

3. Attempt, endeavor, essay.

Offering, *n.* Sacrifice, oblation.

Off-hand, *a.* Unpremeditated, unstudied, extempore, free and easy, *impromptu.*

——, *adv.* Extempore, at the moment, on the spur of the moment, without premeditation *or* study, readily, with ease, *impromptu.*

OFFICE, *n.* 1. Work, service, duty, customary duty, function.

2. Station (*conferred by authority*), post, situation, place, position, berth.

3. Charge, trust, business, employment, duty, service, function, capacity.

4. Place of business, room, bureau.

5. Service, act of worship, formulary of devotion.

Officer, *n.* Official, functionary, office holder.

Official, *a.* Authoritative, by authority.

Officiate, *v. i.* Act, serve, perform.

Officious, *a.* Meddlesome, interfering, intermeddling, obtrusive, busy, pragmatical, meddling, pushing forward.

Offscouring, *n.* Refuse, sweepings, dirt, scum, dross, recrement, rubbish, offscum.

Offset, *n.* 1. Sprout, shoot, slip, branch, offshoot, twig, scion.

2. Counterpoise, counterbalance, set-off, equivalent.

Offshoot, *n.* Shoot, branch, offset.

Offspring, *n.* 1. Issue, progeny, children, brood, litter, descendants, posterity, "seed" (*Biblical*).

2. Child, scion, cadet.

Often, *adv.* Frequently, repeatedly, many times, oftentimes, ofttimes (*poetical*).

Ogee, *n.* (*Arch.*) Cymatium, cyma.

Ogle, *n.* Side glance, leer, fond look.

Ogre, *n.* Monster, spectre, goblin, hobgoblin, bugbear, frightful object.

OIL, *n.* (*Basic Eng.*)

Oil-skin, *n.* Waterproof cloth, dreadnaught.

Oily, *a.* 1. Unctuous, greasy, oleaginous, sebaceous, fatty, fat, oleose, oleous.

2. Unctuous, smooth, glib, lubricous, oleaginous, supple-chapped, plausible.

3. Supple, compliant, subservient.

Ointment, *n.* Unguent, nard, balm, salve, pomade, pomatum.

OLD, *a.* 1. Aged, elderly, of advanced age, advanced in years.

2. Ancient, antique, antiquated, old-fashioned, obsolete, archaic, olden.

3. Of long date, not new.

4. Going to decay, worn out, senile, decayed.

5. Ancient, pristine, primitive, original.

6. Former, pre-existing, preceding.

Olden, *a.* Ancient, old.

Old-fashioned, *a.* Antiquated, antique, ancient, old, archaic, out of fashion, out of date, fusty, "fogeyish."

Old-time, *a.* Former, quondam, late, in former times.

Old-womanish, *a.* Anile, aged, doting, imbecile, decrepit, superannuated.

Old-world, *a.* Antiquated, old-fashioned.

Oleaginous, *a.* Oily, unctuous, greasy, sebaceous, adipose, fatty, fat.

Olfactory, *a.* Smelling.

Olive, *a.* Olive-green, brownish-green, olivaceous, olivaster, olive-colored, brownish, tawny.

Omen, *n.* Prognostic, presage, augury, foreboding, portent, auspice, sign.

Ominous, *a.* Portentous, monitory, premonitory, inauspicious, unpropitious.

Omission, *n.* Failure, neglect, default, oversight.

Omit, *v. t.* 1. Leave out, drop, skip.
2. Neglect, miss, overlook, let slip, let go, pass by, disregard, pretermit.

Omnipotence, *n.* 1. Almighty power.
2. God, the Omnipotent.

Omnipotent, *a.* Almighty, all-powerful.

Omnipresent, *a.* Ubiquitous, universally present, ubiquitary.

Omniscient, *a.* Infinitely wise, all-wise, all-knowing, all-seeing.

Omnivorous, *a.* All-devouring, pantophagous.

ON, *prep.* Upon.
——, *adv.* 1. Forward, onward.
2. Forward, in succession.
3. In continuance, without interruption, without ceasing.
4. Steady, adhering.
5. Attached, put on, upon the body.

Once, *adv.* 1. One time.
2. Formerly.

On-coming, *a.* Approaching, nearing, impending.

One, *a.* 1. Single, individual.
2. The same, common, single in kind.
3. United, undivided, integrated.
4. Some, any.
——, *n.* 1. Unit.
2. Individual, person, human being.

Oneness, *n.* Individuality, unity, singleness.

Onerous, *a.* Burdensome, oppressive, heavy, weighty, hard, difficult.

One-sided, *a.* 1. Unilateral.
2. Partial, unjust, unfair, prejudiced.

On fire. Burning, aflame.

On hand. In possession, in store.

On high. Aloft, above, overhead.

On-looker, *n.* Spectator, beholder, observer, by-stander, looker-on.

ONLY, *a.* Sole, solitary, alone, single.
——, *adv.* 1. Merely, barely, simply, and nothing else.
2. Solely, no other than.
3. Singly, without more.
——, *conj.* But, excepting that.

Onset, } *n.* Attack, assault, charge,
Onslaught, } storm, storming, first brunt.

Onward, } *adv.* Forward, in advance, on,
Onwards, } ahead.

Onward, *a.* 1. Advancing.
2. Forward, advanced, improved.
3. Conducting.

Ooze, *n.* Mire, slime, mud.
——, *v. i.* Percolate, filter, transude, exude, strain, drain, leak.
——, *v. t.* Drip, drop, shed, distil.

Oozy, *a.* Miry, slimy, muddy.

Opacity, *n.* 1. Opaqueness, want of transparency.
2. Darkness, obscurity.

Opalescence, *n.* Iridescence, lustre.

Opalescent, *a.* Iridescent, irisated, polychromatic, nacreous.

Opaque, *a.* Not transparent, nontranslucent, obscure, clouded, turbid.

Opaqueness, *n.* Opacity, want of transparency.

Open, *v. t.* 1. Unclose, lay open, make open, render free of access.
2. Spread, expand.
3. Begin, commence, enter upon, initiate.
4. Show, bring to knowledge.
5. Reveal, disclose, exhibit.
6. Make liberal, liberalize.
——, *v. i.* 1. Part, be unclosed, be parted, be sundered, be severed.
2. Begin, commence.

OPEN, *a.* 1. Unclosed, uncovered, agape, ajar.
2. Expanded, extended, unclosed, spread, wide.
3. Frank, unreserved, candid, ingenuous, undisguised, undesigning, artless, undissembling, sincere, guileless, fair, honest, single-minded, above-board, open-hearted, hearty, cordial.
4. Liberal, generous, munificent, bountiful, open-handed, free, bounteous.
5. Exposed, unprotected, undefended.
6. Clear, unobstructed.
7. Unenclosed, accessible, public, unrestricted, free to all.
8. Mild, moderate.
9. Plain, evident, apparent, laid bare, obvious, patent.
10. Undetermined, to be debated, debatable.

Open-eyed, *a.* Watchful, vigilant, alert.

Open-handed, *a.* Generous, liberal, munificent, bountiful, open.

Open-hearted, *a.* Candid, frank, artless, guileless, open, sincere, ingenuous, honest, generous.

Opening, *a.* First, commencing, introductory, initiatory.
——, *n.* 1. Aperture, hole, orifice, perforation, breach, chasm, cleft, gap, gulf, fissure, interspace, interstice, loophole, rent, rift, flaw.
2. Beginning, commencement, dawn, first appearance.
3. Opportunity, chance, vacancy.

Openly, *adv.* 1. Publicly.
2. Candidly, frankly, plainly.

Open-mouthed, *a.* 1. Gaping, agape.
2. Greedy, ravenous.

Openness, *n.* Unreservedness, plainness, frankness, candor, honesty, ingenuousness.

Opera glass, *n.* Lorgnette.

Operate, *v. i.* [Followed by *on* or *upon*.] Act, work, have effect, have influence.

——, *v. t.* 1. Produce, effect, cause, occasion.

2. Work, manipulate, run, make go.

OPERATION, *n.* 1. Performance, procedure, process, proceeding, manipulation.

2. Movement, motion, manœuvre, action.

Operative, *a.* 1. Acting, active, in action, in operation, in effect.

2. Effective, efficient, effectual, efficacious, serviceable, vigorous.

——, *n.* Laborer, artisan, laboring man, workman.

Operator, *n.* 1. Doer, actor, performer, agent, executor.

2. Manipulator.

Operose, *a.* 1. Laborious, toilsome, hard, onerous, burdensome, difficult.

2. Wearisome, tedious, irksome.

Opiate, *n.* Anodyne, narcotic, sedative.

——, *a.* Soporiferous, somniferous, narcotic, anodynous, sedative.

Opine, *v. i.* Think, judge, believe, suppose, conceive, apprehend, fancy, presume, take it, be of opinion, have an opinion, ween.

OPINION, *n.* 1. Judgment, notion, view, idea, conception, impression, sentiment.

2. Belief, persuasion, tenet.

3. Estimation, favorable judgment, esteem.

Opinionated, *a.* Conceited, dogmatical, opinionative, stiff *or* stubborn in opinion, opinioned, cocksure.

Opponent, *n.* Antagonist, adversary, rival, competitor, enemy, foe, adverse party, counteragent, opposer, opposite.

——, *a.* 1. Opposing, antagonistic, adverse, repugnant, contrary.

2. Opposite.

Opportune, *a.* Seasonable, convenient, timely, fit, suitable, favorable, propitious, auspicious, fortunate, lucky, well-timed, felicitous, appropriate.

Opportunely, *adv.* Seasonably, in the nick of time, all in good time, in the fulness of time, apropos.

Opportunity, *n.* Chance; fit, suitable, *or* favorable time; good chance, fitting occasion, nick of time, occasion, time, turn.

Oppose, *v. t.* 1. Resist, withstand, counteract, contravene, thwart, obstruct, oppugn, combat, strive against, set one's face against, make a stand against.

2. Check, withstand, prevent, obstruct.

3. Set against, put in opposition, confront, counterpose.

Opposed, *a.* 1. Opposite, opponent.

2. Antagonistic, hostile, inimical, adverse, opposite.

Opposing, *a.* Conflicting, counteracting, antagonistic, adverse, opposite, hostile, inimical.

OPPOSITE, *a.* 1. Facing, over against, fronting.

2. Contrary, diverse, unlike, incompatible, inconsistent, irreconcilable.

3. Adverse, opposed, opposing, antagonistic, hostile, inimical, repugnant.

Opposition, *n.* 1. Contrariety, repugnance, antagonism, oppugnancy, antinomy, inconsistency.

2. Counteraction, counterinfluence, hostility, resistance.

3. Obstacle, obstruction, hindrance.

Oppress, *v. t.* 1. Load, burden, weigh heavily upon, bear hard upon.

2. Overburden, crush, overwhelm, overpower, tyrannize over, subdue.

Oppression, *n.* 1. Hardship, misery, suffering, calamity.

2. Tyranny, severity, cruelty, injustice, persecution.

3. Depression, lassitude, heaviness, dulness.

Oppressive, *a.* 1. Burdensome, severe.

2. Heavy, overwhelming, overpowering.

3. Tyrannical, cruel, severe, hard, rigorous, inhuman, grinding, galling.

4. Close, uncomfortable.

Oppressor, *n.* Tyrant, taskmaster.

Opprobrious, *a.* 1. Reproachful, scurrilous, abusive, vituperative, insolent, condemnatory, damnatory, scandalous, contemptuous, offensive, insulting.

2. Infamous, despised, shameful, dishonorable, disgraceful, disreputable, hateful.

Opprobrium, *n.* 1. Scurrility, abusive language, contemptuous reproaches, contumely.

2. Reproach, disgrace, infamy, ignominy, obloquy, odium.

Oppugn, *v. t.* Assail, attack, combat, resist, oppose, thwart, contravene, withstand, strive against.

Optic, } *a.* Visual.
Optical, }

Option, *n.* Choice, election, preference, discretion, selection.

Optional, *a.* Discretional, elective, voluntary, non-obligatory.

Opulence, *n.* Wealth, affluence, riches, fortune, independence, easy circumstances, ample means, opulency.

Opulent, *a.* Wealthy, rich, affluent, flush, moneyed, well off.

OR, *conj.* (*Basic Eng.*)

Oracle, *n.* 1. Divine communication.

2. (*Greek History.*) Deity *or* god (*from whom divine communications come*).

3. Sage, prophet, Solomon.

Oracular, *a.* 1. Prophetic, portentous, ominous.

2. Authoritative, magisterial, positive, dogmatical.

3. Sage, wise, grave.

4. Obscure, ambiguous, dark, blind, equivocal.

Oral, *a.* Spoken, verbal, nuncupative, parole, vocal.

Orally, *adv.* By word of mouth, in words, vocally, verbally (*a confused use*), *viva voce.*

ORANGE, *n.* Henna, ocher, old gold.

Oration, *n.* Discourse, address, speech, harangue, declamation.

Orator, *n.* Public speaker, eloquent speaker, "spellbinder."

Oratorical, *a.* Rhetorical, eloquent.

Oratory, *n.* 1. Eloquence, art of speaking well (*in public*), rhetoric, elocution.

2. Eloquence, eloquent language, exercise of eloquence.

Orb, *n.* 1. Globe, sphere, ball.

2. Circle, orbit, circuit, ring.

3. Wheel, disk, circle.

Orbicular, *a.* 1. Spherical, globular, globated, globous, globose, round, orbed, orbic.

2. Circular, orbed, round.

Orbit, *n.* Orb, circular path (*of a celestial body*), circuit, ambit.

Ordain, *v. t.* 1. Appoint, call, elect, consecrate, destine, set apart.

2. Establish, institute, constitute, regulate.

3. Decree, enact, order, prescribe, enjoin.

Ordeal, *n.* Trial, test, touchstone, proof, assay, experiment, scrutiny, probation.

ORDER, *n.* 1. Method, regularity, symmetry, regular arrangement, disposition.

2. Fit condition, proper state.

3. Regulation, rule, canon, prescription, law, standing rule.

4. Regular government, public tranquillity, peace, quiet, discipline.

5. Mandate, precept, injunction, command, direction, instruction.

6. Rank, class, grade, degree, kind.

7. (*Bot.*) Family, tribe.

8. (*Zoöl.*) Sub-class, subordinate class.

9. Fraternity, society, brotherhood, community, class.

10. Commission, direction.

11. Succession, sequence.

Order, *v. t.* 1. Regulate, arrange, systematize, adjust, methodize.

2. Manage, conduct, carry on.

3. Command, instruct, direct, bid, require, give an order to.

Orderly, *a.* 1. Regular, methodical, systematic.

2. Peaceable, quiet, well-behaved.

3. Well-regulated, well conducted.

4. Ship-shape, tidy, neat.

Orders, *n. pl.* Holy orders, office of the Christian ministry, the sacred profession, ecclesiastical office.

Ordinance, *n.* 1. Decree, edict, law, enactment, statute, rule, regulation, command, prescript, order, appointment.

2. Rite, ceremony, observance, sacrament.

Ordinarily, *adv.* 1. Commonly, usually, generally, as a rule.

2. Customarily, habitually.

Ordinary, *a.* 1. Customary, settled, established, wonted, every-day, regular, normal, accustomed.

2. Common, usual, frequent, habitual.

3. Mean, inferior, commonplace, indifferent, undistinguished, second-rate, mediocre, medium, average.

4. Plain, homely, commonplace.

——, *n.* 1. Eating-house (*where a meal is offered at a settled price*).

2. Public table, *table d'hôte.*

Ordination, *n.* 1. Consecration, induction, institution.

2. Tendency, foreordination.

Ordnance, *n.* Cannon, great guns, artillery.

Ordure, *n.* Dung, excrement, fæces.

Organ, *n.* 1. Instrument, means.

2. Medium, instrument, means of communication.

3. Voice, vocal organs.

Organic, *a.* 1. Radical, fundamental, constitutional, vital.

2. Organized, systematized.

Organism, *n.* 1. Organic structure.

2. Organization, organized being, organized existence.

ORGANIZATION, *n.* 1. Construction, constitution, systematization.

2. Organism, organized being, organized existence, organic structure.

Organize, *v. t.* 1. Constitute (*by assignment of parts*), dispose *or* arrange in parts (*for special functions*), construct, form, make, shape, frame, adjust.

2. Arrange, co-ordinate, correlate, establish, systematize.

Orgies, *n. pl.* Revels, bacchanals, saturnalia, carousal, revelry, wassail, debauch drunken bout.

Orient, *n.* 1. East.

    2. Morning land, Asia, East.

Oriental, *a.* 1. Eastern, orient.

    2. Precious, valuable, perfect.

Orifice, *n.* Hole, aperture, perforation, pore, vent, mouth.

Origin, *n.* 1. Source, rise, spring, fountain, fountain-head, beginning, commencement, derivation, root, foundation, birth, cradle, original, starting-point.

    2. Cause, occasion, derivation, root, foundation, fountain, spring.

Original, *a.* 1. Primitive, aboriginal, primeval, primary, primordial, pristine, first.

    2. Untranslated.

    3. Inventive, creative.

——, *n.* 1. Source, spring, origin, cause, commencement.

    2. Archetype, model, pattern, type, prototype, protoplast, exemplar, first copy.

    3. (*Colloq.*) Oddity, eccentric person.

Originate, *v. t.* Create, bring into existence, be the author of, be the cause of, give rise to, cause to be.

——, *v. i.* Arise, rise, begin, spring, proceed, emanate, flow, take its rise.

Originator, *n.* Inventor, author, maker, creator, father, former, first cause.

Orison, *n.* (*Poetical.*) Prayer, supplication, petition, solicitation.

ORNAMENT, *n.* Embellishment, decoration, adornment, ornamentation, garnish, bedizenment.

——, *v. t.* Decorate, adorn, embellish, beautify, garnish, bedeck, bedizen, grace, emblazon, deck, trick out.

Ornamental, *a.* Embellishing, serving for ornament.

Ornate, *a.* Ornamented, embellished, decorated, bedecked, adorned, rich-wrought, highly wrought, florid, figured.

Orotund, *a.* Round, rich, full, sonorous, mellow, musical, clear, ringing.

Orrery, *n.* Planetarium.

Orthodox, *a.* Sound (*in religious opinions*), of the true faith, in accord with the standard formulation.

Orthodoxy, *n.* True faith, soundness of doctrine.

Orthogonal, *a.* Rectangular, right-angled, perpendicular.

Orthography, *n.* Spelling.

Orts, *n. pl.* Fragments, scraps, refuse, odds and ends.

Oscillate, *v. i.* 1. Swing, vibrate, sway, move to and fro, move backward and forward.

    2. Vary, fluctuate.

Oscillation, *n.* Vibration, swinging.

Oscillatory, *a.* Vibratory, swinging, oscillating, vibrating, oscillative.

Oscitancy, *n.* 1. Gaping, yawning, oscitation.

    2. Sleepiness, drowsiness, dulness.

Oscitate, *v. i.* Gape, yawn.

Osculant, *a.* 1. Kissing, osculatory, osculating.

    2. (*Ent.*) Embracing, adhering.

Osculate, *v. t.* 1. Kiss.

    2. (*Geom.*) Touch.

Osier, *n.* 1. Willow, water-willow.

    2. Wicker, withe, willow twig.

Osseous, *a.* Bony.

Ossuary, *n.* Charnel-house, depository for bones.

Ostensible, *a.* 1. Shown, declared, avowed, assigned, manifest, apparent, exhibited, presented, visible.

    2. Specious, plausible, colorable, pretended, professed.

Ostentation, *n.* 1. Display, show, parade, pomp, flourish, dash, pomposity, pompousness, pageantry, high pretension, vaunting.

    2. Semblance, appearance, show.

Ostentatious, *a.* 1. Boastful, vain, showy, dashing, flaunting, pompous, vain-glorious, fond of display, pretentious.

    2. Showy, gaudy.

Ostentatiously, *adv.* Showily, pompously, boastfully, with a flourish of trumpets, with beat of drum.

Ostracism, *n.* Banishment, expulsion, exclusion, excommunication, separation.

Ostracize, *v. t.* Banish, exile, put under the ban.

OTHER, *a.* Another, additional, not the same.

Otherwise, *adv.* 1. Differently, not so.

    2. In other respects.

——, *conj.* Else, but for this.

Otiose, *a.* Idle, unemployed, indolent.

Oust, *v. t.* Eject, expel, dislodge, turn out, dispossess, evict.

OUT, *a.* 1. On the outside, without.

    2. Abroad, not at home, gone out.

    3. Revealed, public, disclosed.

    4. Lacking, wanting, deficient in.

    5. Extinguished.

Out and out. 1. (*Colloq.*) Completely, thoroughly, utterly, wholly.

    2. (*Colloq.*) Complete, thorough, consummate, unqualified, thorough-paced, extreme, absolute, perfect.

Outbalance, *v. t.* Overweigh, overbalance, overpoise, outweigh.

Outbreak, *n.* 1. Eruption, explosion, outburst, ebullition.

    2. Riot, row, fray, affray, broil, conflict, breach of the peace, commotion.

    3. Manifestation, flare-up.

Outcast, *n.* 1. Exile, expatriate.

2. Reprobate, castaway, vagabond, Pariah, abandoned wretch.

Outcome, *n.* Issue, result, consequence, upshot, event.

Outcrop, *n.* (*Geol.*) 1. Basseting, cropping out.

2. Basset, basset-edge, crop.

Outcry, *n.* 1. Cry, scream, screech, yell.

2. Clamor, bruit, vociferation, noise, hue and cry, tumult.

Outdo, *v. t.* Excel, surpass, exceed, beat, outstrip, outvie, outgo, go beyond, be superior to.

Outdoor, *a.* Exterior, open-air, out-of-door, extraforaneous.

Outdoors, *adv.* Abroad, out-of-doors, in the open air, out of the house.

Outer, *a.* Exterior, external.

Outface, *v. t.* Brave, look out of countenance, stare down.

Outfit, *n.* Equipment.

Outflow, *n.* Efflux, effusion, flow, outpouring.

Outgo, *v. t.* 1. Outstrip, go beyond.

2. Surpass, excel, exceed, outdo, outvie, beat, be superior to.

——, *n.* Expenditure, outlay, outgoing.

Outgrowth, *n.* Offshoot, result.

Outing, *n.* Excursion, airing.

Outlandish, *a.* 1. Foreign, strange, exotic, alien, from abroad.

2. Barbarous, strange, uncouth, queer, *bizarre.*

Outlaw, *n.* Robber, bandit, brigand, freebooter, highwayman, marauder, proscript.

——, *v. t.* Proscribe.

Outlay, *n.* Expenditure, outgo, disbursement.

Outlet, *n.* Exit, egress, vent, loophole.

Outline, *n.* 1. Contour, profile.

2. Outline drawing, sketch, plan, draft, delineation, drawing, rough draft.

Outlive, *v. t.* Survive, live longer than.

Outlook, *n.* 1. Watch.

2. Prospect, view, sight.

3. Watch-tower, lookout.

Outlying, *a.* 1. Remote, distant.

2. Exterior, frontier, bounding.

Outmost, *a.* Remotest, farthest, outermost.

Out of. 1. From.

2. By means of, in consequence of, induced by.

3. Abroad, not within.

Out of date. Antiquated, antique, archaic, obsolete, old-fashioned, outmoded, out of fashion, gone by, fallen into desuetude.

Out-of-doors, *adv.* Abroad, outdoors, in the open air, out of the house.

Out of humor. Irritated, ruffled, vexed, angry, sullen, peevish, out of temper, out of tune.

Out of sorts. Ill, unwell, ailing, sick, indisposed, laid up.

Out-of-the-way, *a.* 1. Remote, secluded, unfrequented.

2. Uncommon, unusual, singular, strange, rare.

Out of tune. 1. Harsh, discordant, inharmonious, not in tune.

2. Irritated, ruffled, out of humor.

Outpouring, *n.* Effusion, efflux, outflow.

Outrage, *n.* Insult, affront, indignity, abuse, offence.

——, *v. t.* Insult, abuse, maltreat, offend, shock, injure.

Outrageous, *a.* 1. Furious, violent, turbulent, abusive, raging, wild, mad, frantic, infuriate, frenzied.

2. Atrocious, flagrant, heinous, villainous, enormous, monstrous, nefarious.

3. Excessive, exorbitant, enormous, extravagant, unwarrantable.

Outré, *a.* [Fr.] Extravagant, excessive, exorbitant, immoderate, inordinate, overstrained.

Outright, *adv.* 1. Immediately, instantly, at once, without delay.

2. Completely, utterly, entirely, wholly, altogether.

Outrival, *v. t.* Surpass, excel.

Outrun, *v. t.* See OUTSTRIP.

Outset, *n.* Beginning, commencement, opening, starting-point, start, entrance.

Outshine, *v. t.* Eclipse, surpass, overshadow, throw into shadow.

Outside, *n.* 1. Exterior, surface, superficies, external part, externality.

2. Utmost, farthest limit.

——, *a.* Exterior, external, outward, outer, on the surface, superficial.

Outskirt, *n.* Suburb, border, precinct, purlieu, outpost.

Outspoken, *a.* Plain, plain-spoken, blunt, frank, candid, unreserved.

Outspread, *a.* Extended, expanded, outstretched, unfolded.

Outstanding, *a.* Unsettled, unpaid, owing, due, uncollected, ungathered.

Outstep, *v. t.* Exceed, overstep, transgress.

Outstretch, *v. t.* Extend, expand, outspread.

Outstrip, *v. t.* 1. Outgo, outrun, outdistance, go beyond, outspeed, outride, outwing, etc.

2. Excel, surpass, exceed, outvie, outdo, beat.

Outward, *a.* 1. External, exterior, outer, outside.

2. External, visible, showing, appearing, apparent, superficial.

3. Adventitious, extrinsic, extraneous.

4. Carnal, fleshly, corporeal.

Outweigh, *v. t.* Overbalance, overpoise, overweigh.

Outwit, *v. t.* 1. Outgeneral, out-manœuvre, baffle, steal a march upon.

2. Overreach, cheat, dupe, deceive, circumvent, swindle, defraud, victimize, cozen, gull, diddle, take in, impose upon.

Oval, *a.* Elliptical.

Ovate, *a.* Egg-shaped.

Ovation, *n.* Triumph.

OVEN, *n.* Baking-chamber, kiln.

OVER, *prep.* 1. Above.

2. Across, athwart, from one side of to the other.

3. Throughout, through, through the whole extent of.

4. More than, upward of.

5. Covering, immersing.

——, *adv.* 1. Above the top.

2. Across, athwart, transversely, from one side to the other.

3. From one to another, from hand to hand.

4. Besides, to boot, in addition, into the bargain, in excess.

5. Throughout, completely, from beginning to end.

6. Past, by.

7. Excessively, extremely, very, too.

——, *a.* 1. Covering, outer, upper.

2. Superior.

Over-abundant, *a.* Exuberant, plenteous, copious, full, rank, plentiful, ample, replete, liberal, lavish.

Overawe, *v. t.* Awe, intimidate, cow, frighten, affright, daunt, browbeat.

Overbalance, *v. t.* 1. Outweigh, overweigh, surpass, preponderate in.

2. Overpoise, lose balance.

Overbear, *v. t.* Overpower, overwhelm, subdue, overthrow, prostrate, repress, subdue.

Overbearing, *a.* 1. Overpowering, oppressive, repressing.

2. Imperious, domineering, dictatorial, supercilious, lordly, haughty, arrogant, overweening, "toplofty," dogmatical.

Over-bold, *a.* Forward, impudent, pert, officious, presuming.

Overcast, *v. t.* 1. Cloud, darken, obscure, eclipse.

2. Cover, overspread.

Overcharge, *v. t.* 1. Burden, oppress, surcharge, overload, overburden.

2. Crowd, overfill.

3. Exaggerate, overstate, overstrain, overlay with ornament.

Overcoat, *n.* Greatcoat, topcoat, ulster.

Overcome, *v. t.* 1. Subdue, conquer, vanquish, subjugate, overthrow, overwhelm, overturn, overbear, overpower, overmaster, defeat, crush, beat, rout, discomfit, choke, get the better of, get the upper hand of, prostrate.

2. Surmount, rise above.

——, *v. i.* Prevail, conquer, gain the victory.

Over-confident, *a.* Rash, brash, venturesome, presumptuous, overweening, headlong, precipitate, hot-headed, incautious, imprudent.

Overdo, *v. t.* 1. Do to excess.

2. Overact, exaggerate.

3. Surpass, exceed.

4. Fatigue, overtax.

Overestimate, *v. t.* Overvalue, overprize, overrate, make too much of.

Overfill, *v. t.* Surcharge.

Overflow, *v. t.* 1. Inundate, flow over.

2. Deluge, flood, overwhelm, cover, overspread, overrun.

——, *v. i.* Overrun, run over.

——, *n.* 1. Inundation, flooding.

2. Superabundance, exuberance, luxuriance, profusion, excess, surplus, overflowing, superflux, copiousness, redundancy.

Overflowing, *a.* Abundant, copious, exuberant.

Over-full, *a.* Surcharged, overcharged, overloaded, surfeited, plethoric.

Overhaul, *v. t.* 1. Overtake, come up with, gain upon.

2. Examine, look into.

Overhead, *adv.* Above, aloft.

Overjoyed, *a.* Transported, enraptured, in raptures, in ecstasies, in a transport.

Overlay, *v. t.* 1. Cover, spread over.

2. Smother, overlie, oppress.

3. Overwhelm, oppress with weight, crush, overpower.

4. Cloud, overcast, hide, obscure.

5. Span, over-span, cover.

Overload, *v. t.* Surcharge, overburden, overlade.

Overlook, *v. t.* 1. View from above.

2. Rise above, look down upon, over-top.

3. Inspect, superintend, supervise, oversee, have charge of.

4. Disregard, neglect, miss, slight, pass by, be inattentive to, not notice, not think of.

5. Excuse, forgive, pardon, pass over, forgive and forget.

Overnight, *adv.* 1. Last night, yesterday night.

2. During the night, all night.

Overpower, *v. t.* Subdue, conquer, overwhelm, overcome, overturn, overbear, overmaster, defeat, rout, crush, beat, vanquish, subjugate, discomfit, get the better of, get the upper hand of, overmatch.

Overpowering, *a.* Irresistible, overwhelming, subduing.

Overrate, *v. t.* Overestimate, overvalue, overprize, make too much of.

Overreach, *v. t.* Deceive, cheat, dupe, outwit, circumvent, defraud, swindle, cozen, gull, trick, victimize, diddle, take in, impose upon.

Override, *v. t.* 1. Pass, ride beyond, outride.

2. Outweigh, surpass, be superior to, take precedence of, supersede.

3. Ride over, overbear, trample down.

Over-righteous, *a.* Sanctimonious, pharisaical.

Overrule, *v. t.* 1. Control, govern, sway, have control of.

2. Annul, cancel, revoke, rescind, repeal, nullify, recall, reject, repudiate, supersede, set aside.

Overruling, *a.* Controlling, governing, directing, prevailing, predominant.

Overrun, *v. t.* 1. Run over, spread over, grow over.

2. Ravage, devastate, despoil, lay waste, harass, subdue, oppress.

——, *v. i.* Overflow, run over.

Oversee, *v. t.* Superintend, supervise, overlook, inspect, have charge of, have the direction of.

Overseer, *n.* Superintendent, inspector, supervisor, director, overman, foreman.

Overset, *v. t.* 1. Overturn, upset, capsize, turn topsy-turvy.

2. Subvert, overthrow, destroy.

Overshadow, *v. t.* 1. Overshade, overcloud.

2. Tower above, dominate.

Overshoe, *n.* Galosh, "rubber," arctic.

Oversight, *n.* 1. Superintendence, control, direction, management, supervision, inspection, charge, care, surveillance.

2. Error, blunder, mistake, slip, trip, lapse, miss, inadvertency, inattention, neglect, omission, fault.

Overspent, *a.* Wearied, exhausted, forspent, over-tired.

Overspread, *v. t.* Cover, spread over, overmantle, overstrew.

Overstate, *v. t.* Exaggerate, overcharge, overdo.

Overt, *a.* Open, manifest, public, patent, notorious, glaring, apparent, unconcealed.

Overtake, *v. t.* Catch, come up with, overhaul.

Overthrow, *v. t.* 1. Overturn, upset, overset, subvert, throw down.

2. Demolish, destroy, level, throw down.

3. Vanquish, conquer, defeat, worst, overcome, master, overpower, overbear, overwhelm, subjugate, crush, discomfit, beat, rout, foil.

——, *n.* 1. Fall, downfall; subversion, prostration.

2. Destruction, demolition, ruin, shipwreck.

3. Defeat, discomfiture, rout, dispersion.

Overtop, *v. t.* 1. Rise above, surpass in height.

2. Excel, transcend, surpass, exceed.

3. Obscure, make less important, eclipse.

Overture, *n.* Proposal, offer, proposition.

Overvalue, *v. t.* Overrate, overprize, overestimate, make too much of.

Overweening, *a.* Conceited, haughty, proud, arrogant, opinionated, egotistical, consequential, supercilious, vain, vainglorious, puffed up.

Overwhelm, *v. t.* 1. Overflow, spread over and cover, swallow up, whelm, submerge, swamp, drown.

2. Overbear, overpower, overcome, subdue, vanquish, conquer, defeat.

Overwrought, *a.* 1. Overdone, elaborated too much.

2. Over-excited, excessively stirred.

Oviform, *a.* Egg-shaped, ovoid, ovoidal.

Owe, *v. t.* 1. Be indebted to, be bound to pay.

2. Be obliged to ascribe to, be obliged for, have to attribute to.

3. Be due, be owing.

Owing, *a.* 1. Due.

2. Attributable, ascribable, traceable, resulting from, due, consequential.

3. Imputable, attributable.

Own, *v. t.* 1. Possess, hold, have, be in possession of, have a title to.

2. Acknowledge, confess, avow.

3. Admit, allow, concede, confess, acknowledge.

OWNER, *n.* Proprietor, possessor, holder.

Oxidize, *v. t.* Oxidate, calcine, convert into an oxide.

Oxygenize, *v. t.* Oxygenate.

Oxygon, *n.* Acute-angled triangle.

Oxygonal, *a.* Acute-angled.

P

Pabulum, *n.* Food, aliment, nutriment.

Pace, *n.* 1. Step.

   2. Gait, walk, manner of walking.

   3. Amble (*of a horse*), pacing.

   4. Rate, degree of progress.

——, *v. i.* 1. Walk (*with measured steps*), step, move, go.

   2. Hasten, hurry, make haste.

   3. Go at an ambling gait, rack, single-foot.

Pacific, *a.* 1. Conciliatory, appeasing, propitiatory, mollifying, placating, peace-making, irenic.

   2. Peaceful, peaceable, tranquil, gentle, calm, smooth, quiet, unruffled.

Pacification, *n.* Tranquillization, reconciliation, reconcilement, accommodation, appeasement.

Pacify, *v. t.* 1. Conciliate, appease, give peace to, restore harmony to, tranquillize.

   2. Tranquillize, assuage, calm, still, quiet, lull, smooth, compose, moderate, hush, quell, lay, allay, soften, soothe, mollify, appease.

Pack, *n.* 1. Bundle, package, budget, parcel, packet, bale.

   2. Burden, load.

   3. Collection, assemblage, assortment, set.

   4. Gang, crew, set, knot, band, clan, company, bevy, lot, squad.

——, *v. t.* Compress (*into a bundle*), crowd, put together (*in close order*), stow, compact.

Package, *n.* Bundle, budget, parcel, pack, packet, bale.

Pact, *n.* Compact, contract, agreement, league, bond, alliance, bargain, covenant, stipulation, convention, concordant.

Pad, *n.* 1. Horse (*for the saddle*), saddle-horse, easy-paced horse, padnag.

   2. Cushion, bolster.

   3. Blotter, tablet.

Pæan, *n.* [Written also *Pean*.] Triumphal song, hymn, jubilation, peanism.

Pagan, *n.* [Anciently written *Paynim*.] Heathen, gentile, idolater.

——, *a.* Heathenish, heathen, idolatrous, paganic, paganical, irreligious.

PAGE, *n.* Boy-servant (*attending a royal or noble personage or a legislature*), serving-boy, "buttons," bellboy; attendant.

Pageant, *n.* Spectacle, show, display, parade, float.

Pageantry, *n.* Show, display, parade, pomp, state, splendor, magnificence, flourish, showing off.

PAIN, *n.* 1. Suffering, distress, discomfort, ache, pang, hurt, smart, lancination, sting, gripe, soreness, torment, torture, anguish, agony, throe, twinge.

   2. Uneasiness, disquietude, anxiety, solicitude, care, grief, sorrow, bitterness, affliction, woe, heartache, chagrin, vexation, anguish, dolor, trouble, distress, unhappiness, misery, wretchedness.

——, *v. t.* 1. Torment, torture, rack, agonize, sting, bite, distress, hurt.

   2. Disquiet, trouble, afflict, grieve, aggrieve, displease, annoy, plague, bore, harass, vex, worry, tease, chafe, fret, incommode, distress.

——, *v. i.* Twinge, shoot, rankle, smart, sting, etc.

Painful, *a.* 1. Tormenting, torturing, agonizing, racking, distressing, distressful, excruciating, sharp.

   2. Grievous, afflicting, afflictive, distressing, disquieting, troublesome, displeasing, provoking, annoying, vexatious, unpleasant, disagreeable, dolorous, baleful.

   3. Toilsome, arduous, difficult, hard, severe, careful, sore.

Painfully, *adv.* 1. With pain.

   2. Laboriously, with toil, industriously, sedulously.

Pains, *n.* 1. Labor, care, trouble, toilsome effort, task.

   2. Travail, childbirth, labor.

Painstaking, *a.* Laborious, sedulous, diligent, industrious, careful, plodding, assiduous, strenuous, hard-working, persevering, sparing no pains.

Paint, *v. t.* 1. Represent (*by colors*).

   2. Color (*with a pigment*), coat with paint, smear.

   3. Depict, delineate, describe, sketch, portray, limn, pencil, set forth, image, picture, draw.

   4. Embellish, deck, adorn, beautify, ornament.

PAINT, *n.* Pigment, coloring matter, cosmetic.

Painting, *n.* 1. Coloring.

   2. Picture (*in colors*).

Pair, *n.* 1. Two (*of the same kind* or *suited to each other*).

   2. Couple, brace, span, yoke.

——, *v. t.* and *v. i.* 1. Couple, mate, match, marry.

   2. Suit, fit.

Palace, *n.* Stately mansion.

Paladin, *n.* Knight-errant, champion, hero.

Palatable, *a.* Savory, agreeable, enjoyable, gustable, flavorous, tasteful, tasty, relishable, toothsome, appetizing, acceptable, pleasing, pleasant, delicious, nice, luscious, delicate.

Palate, *n.* 1. Roof of the mouth.

2. Taste, relish.

Palatial, *a.* Stately, magnificent, splendid, imposing, grand.

Palaver, *n.* 1. Twaddle, chatter, balderdash, rigmarole, gibberish, stuff, trash, fudge, wish-wash, flummery, senseless prate, frothy discourse, idle talk; cajolery, beguiling talk.

2. Talk, conversation, conference, colloquy.

Pale, *a.* 1. White, pallid, wan, ashy, whitish, blanched, bloodless, waxy, sickly, colorless.

2. Dim, obscure, spectral, blank.

——, *n.* 1. Picket, stake.

2. Enclosure, circuit.

3. District, region, territory.

4. Confine, limit, boundary, fence.

Palfrey, *n.* Saddle-horse, riding-horse.

Paling, *n.* 1. Fence (*made of pales*), palisade, stockade.

2. Limit, enclosure.

Pall, *n.* 1. Cloak, mantle, outer garment, fine cloth; pallium, archbishop's scarf; gloomy covering, cloud.

2. [Written also *Pawl.*] Detent, click.

——, *v. t.* 1. Make vapid *or* insipid.

2. Satiate, cloy, surfeit, sate, glut, gorge, fill to repletion.

3. Dispirit, depress, discourage, dishearten, deject.

4. Cloak, cover, shroud, invest, overspread, drape.

——, *v. i.* Become insipid, grow tasteless, become vapid.

Palladium, *n.* Bulwark, safeguard, security.

Palliate, *v. t.* 1. Extenuate, excuse, gloss, apologize for, lessen, cover, cloak, hide, conceal.

2. Allay, ease, soothe, mitigate, moderate, assuage, alleviate, soften, abate, mollify, lessen, diminish, relieve, dull, blunt, quiet, still, quell.

Palliative, *n.* Lenitive, emollient.

Pallid, *a.* Wan, pale, whitish, ashy, colorless, cadaverous.

Pallor, *n.* Paleness, wanness, pallidness, pallidity, ghastliness, bloodlessness, blanching, etiolation.

Palm, *n.* 1. Token of victory, prize, crown, laurel, bays, trophies.

2. Hand-breadth, hand.

——, *v. t.* 1. Conceal in the palm (*as a juggler*).

2. Impose (*by fraud*), obtrude, pass off, foist.

3. Handle, touch.

Palmer, *n.* 1. Pilgrim (*returned from the Holy Land*), crusader, wandering religious votary.

2. Cozener, cheat, trickster (*at cards or dice*).

Palmistry, *n.* Chiromancy.

Palmy, *a.* 1. Palm-producing, palmiferous.

2. Prosperous, fortunate, flourishing, victorious, glorious, thriving, happy, joyous, halcyon, golden, Saturnian, worthy of the palm.

Palpable, *a.* 1. Tangible, tactile, material, corporeal.

2. Manifest, obvious, plain, evident, glaring, unmistakable, gross, easily seen, very perceptible, intelligible, patent.

Palpitate, *v. i.* 1. Pulsate, throb, flutter, beat rapidly, go pit-a-pat.

2. Tremble, quiver, shiver.

Palpitation, *n.* Throbbing, fluttering, beating, pulsation, throb. Cf. AGITATION.

Palsy, *n.* Paralysis.

——, *v. t.* Paralyze, benumb, deaden.

Palter, *v. i.* Equivocate, shuffle, dodge, haggle, traffic, shift, quibble, evade, prevaricate, trifle.

Paltry, *a.* 1. Small, little, diminutive, inconsiderable, insignificant, unimportant, petty, miserable, wretched, sorry, slight, slender, feeble, trifling, trivial, of no consequence, of no importance.

2. Base, vile, abject, grovelling, low, mean, scurvy, cheap, pitiable, rubbishy, trashy, beggarly, pitiful, despicable, contemptible, worthless, shabby, shuffling, shifty.

Paludal, *a.* Marshy, boggy, fenny, swampy.

Pamper, *v. t.* 1. Feed to excess, feed luxuriantly.

2. Indulge (*unduly*), coddle, cocker, gratify, humor, spoil, fondle.

Pamphlet, *n.* *Brochure*, booklet.

Panacea, *n.* Catholicon, cure-all, panpharmacon, universal medicine, universal remedy.

Pancake, *n.* Fritter, flapjack, griddlecake.

Pandemonium, *n.* Hell; wild uproar.

Pander, *n.* [Formerly written *Pandar.*] Procurer, pimp, male bawd, go-between.

Pander to. Subserve, cater to.

Panegyric, *n.* 1. Eulogy, eulogium, encomium, tribute of praise.

2. Praise, laudation, commendation.

Panegyric, ⎫ *a.* Encomiastic, encomiasti-
Panegyrical, ⎭   cal, eulogistic, eulogistical, commendatory, laudatory.

Panel, *n.* 1. (*Law.*) Array, body of jurors, list.

2. Partition, medallion, wainscot, section.

Pang, *n.* Pain (*sharp and sudden*), throe, twinge, gripe, distress.

Panic, *n.* Fright, affright, alarm, terror, consternation, sudden fear, "jitters."

Panic-stricken, *a.* Dismayed, terrified, horrified, appalled, frightened, horror-struck.

Panoply, *n.* Armor (*complete*), suit of armor; full array, outfit.

Panorama, *n.* Periscope, bird's eye view, complete view.

Pant, *v. i.* 1. Puff, gasp, blow, breathe hard, lose breath.

2. Throb, heave, palpitate, pulsate.

3. Languish, gasp.

4. Long, yearn, hunger, thirst, sigh, desire.

Pantaloons, *n. pl.* Trousers, pants.

Pantomime, *n.* Dumb show, mute action, gesture; mimic actor.

Pantry, *n.* Buttery, larder, spence.

Pap, *n.* 1. Nipple, teat, dug, *papilla.*

2. Food (*made soft for infants and weaklings*), nutriment, nourishment.

Papacy, *n.* 1. Popedom, pontificate.

2. Popes, line of popes, popes collectively.

Papal, *a.* Pontifical, apostolic, papistical, popish.

PAPER, *n.* 1. Document, writing, written instrument, certificate, deed.

2. Newspaper, journal.

3. Dissertation, essay, article, composition.

4. (*Com.*) Notes, bank-notes, drafts, bills of exchange, negotiable paper.

Papism, *n.* Popery. Cf. PAPACY, PAPISTRY.

Papist, *n.* Roman Catholic, Romanist.

Papistic,) *a.* Popish, papal, Roman
Papistical,) Catholic.

Papistry, *n.* Popery, papism, Roman Catholic religion.

Par, *n.* Equality, equivalence, balance, equal footing, level.

Parable, *n.* Fable, apologue, story, allegory.

Parabolic,) *a.* 1. Figurative, allegorical,
Parabolical,) expressed by a parable *or* similitude.

2. Parabola-shaped.

Paraclete, *n.* Comforter, consoler, intercessor, Holy Spirit, Spirit of Truth, Holy Ghost.

Parade, *n.* 1. Ostentation, display, ceremony, show, pompous exhibition, flaunting, pomp.

2. Pageant, spectacle, pompous procession, show.

3. Military display, review, array.

4. Drill-ground.

5. Public walk, promenade, mall.

——, *v. t.* Display, flaunt, show off.

——, *v. i.* Make a show, show off.

Paradigm, *n.* Example, model, pattern.

Paradise, *n.* Eden, the garden of Eden; Elysium, place of bliss, Heaven, abode of the blest.

Paradox, *n.* Absurdity (*as appears at first sight, yet not so in fact*), seeming contradiction, self-contradiction.

Paradoxical, *a.* Absurd (*to appearance, yet conformable to fact*), incredible, puzzling, inconceivable, contradictory.

Paragon, *n.* Model, pattern, masterpiece, nonpareil, flower, queen, none-such, pink, *beau idéal.*

Paragraph, *n.* 1. Passage, clause, section of a discourse, sentence.

2. Item (*as in a newspaper*), remark, short notice.

PARALLEL, *a.* 1. Equidistant throughout (*as lines*).

2. In conformity, in harmony, in accordance, abreast, concurrent.

3. Like, similar, analogous, resembling, allied, equal, correspondent.

——, *n.* 1. Resemblance, similarity, likeness, conformity.

2. Comparison.

3. Counterpart, analogue, correlative.

Paralogism,) *n.* Sophistry (*unintentional*),
Paralogy,) false reasoning.

Paralysis, *n.* Palsy.

Paralyze, *v. t.* Palsy, benumb, deaden, unnerve, freeze, lethargize.

Paramount, *a.* Supreme, superior, preeminent, principal, chief, dominant.

Paramour, *n.* 1. Illicit lover, leman.

2. Concubine, mistress.

Parapet, *n.* (*Fort.*) Breastwork (*on a rampart*), battlement; breast wall (*as on a bridge*), wall, railing.

Paraphernalia, *n. pl.* Appendages, ornaments, trappings, equipment, equipage, appurtenances, accoutrements.

Paraphrase, *n.* 1. Explanation (*by amplifying*), exposition.

2. Free translation, free wording, rewording, "rehash."

3. Metrical translation.

Paraphrastic,) *a.* Explanatory (*by am-*
Paraphrastical,) *plification*), free, diffuse.

Parasite, *n.* Sycophant, flatterer, toady, fawner, wheedler, flunky, spaniel, pickthank, toad-eater, time-server, hanger-on, trencher-friend; bloodsucker, leech, etc.

Parasitical, *a.* Sycophantic, fawning, flattering, wheedling, servile, slavish, meanly submissive.

Parasol, *n.* Sunshade.

Parboil, *v. t.* Coddle, boil slightly, overheat.

Parcæ, *n. pl.* Fates, sisters three.

PARCEL, *n.* 1. Bundle, package, packet, budget.

2. Set, lot, batch, collection, group, indefinite number.

3. (*Law.*) Piece, part, portion, tract, plot, division, patch.

——, *v. t.* Divide, distribute, apportion, deal out, allot.

Parch, *v. t.* 1. Burn (*slightly*), scorch.

2. Dry, shrivel, dry up.

Pardon, *v. t.* 1. Remit, overlook, pass over, forgive, condone.

2. Forgive (*especially for a grave offence*), absolve, excuse, acquit, discharge, release, clear.

——, *n.* Forgiveness (*especially of a grave offence after conviction, and granted to a specified person*), remission (*of a penalty incurred*), absolution, grace, mercy.

Pardonable, *a.* Excusable, venial.

Pare, *v. t.* 1. Peel (*by the use of a knife*).

2. Clip, cut, shave off, slice, "skive."

3. Diminish (*gradually*), lessen, reduce.

Parent, *n.* 1. Father *or* mother.

2. Author, cause, source, producer.

Parentage, *n.* Extraction, birth, descent, lineage, pedigree, stock, origin, family, ancestry; parenthood.

Parental, *a.* Tender, cherishing; fatherly, motherly, paternal, maternal.

Parget, *v. t.* Plaster, cover with plaster, whitewash, roughcast.

Pariah, *n.* Outcast, wretch, miserable person, member of a low caste.

Parish, *n.* District, subdivision, church territory *or* membership.

Parity, *n.* Equality, equivalence, likeness, sameness, analogy, close correspondence.

Parlance, *n.* Conversation, discourse, talk, phrase, language, diction.

Parley, *v. i.* Talk, converse, discourse, discuss, hold a conference (*especially with an enemy*), confer, treat.

——, *n.* Conference (*especially between enemies*), talk, discourse, conversation, discussion, oral treaty.

Parliament, *n.* House of Lords and House of Commons (*of Great Britain and Ireland*), British legislature; assembly.

Parlor, *n.* Sitting-room, living-room, drawing-room.

Parochial, *a.* Parish, pertaining to a parish, parishional; petty, narrow, provincial.

Parody, *n.* Travesty, burlesque, caricature, ludicrous imitation.

Parole, *n.* 1. (*Law.*) Word of mouth, oral declaration.

2. (*Mil.*) Word of honor, word of promise, plighted faith.

Paroxysm, *n.* (*Med.*) Exacerbation (*of a disease, periodically*), fit, convulsion, outburst, seizure, sudden attack, spasm, throe.

Parricide, *n.* Patricide *or* matricide, father-killer, mother-killer.

Parry, *v. t.* 1. Ward off, turn aside, prevent, avert.

2. Shift off, avoid, evade.

Parsimonious, *a.* Stingy, close, avaricious, mercenary, sordid, shabby, grudging, niggardly, miserly, mean, penurious, grasping, covetous, close-fisted, sordid, very saving, excessively frugal, "near," illiberal, hard-fisted, sparing, "scrimping."

Parsimony, *n.* Stinginess, niggardliness, penuriousness, avarice, covetousness, cupidity, meanness, closeness, miserliness, frugality, economy, illiberality, savingness, "cheese-paring."

Parson, *n.* Parish priest, rector, incumbent, minister, priest, clergyman, pastor, ecclesiastic, churchman, divine.

Parsonage, *n.* 1. Rectory; parson's mansion, parsonage house.

2. Parson's dues, benefice, living.

PART, *n.* 1. Piece, parcel, section, segment, fragment; scrap, crumb; moiety, remnant, portion, section, division, subdivision.

2. Member, organ, constituent, element, component, ingredient.

3. Share, portion, lot.

4. Concern, interest, participation.

5. Allotment, lot, dividend, apportionment.

6. Business, charge, duty, office, function, work.

7. Side, party, interest, concern, faction.

8. Character, *rôle*, cue, lines.

9. Portion, passage, clause, paragraph.

——, *v. t.* 1. Divide, sever, dissever, sunder, dismember, subdivide, break, break in pieces, tear asunder.

2. Disunite, separate, disjoin, disconnect, separate, detach, dissociate.

3. Hold apart, keep apart, stand between, intervene betwixt.

4. Apportion, allot, share, distribute, parcel out, deal out, divide, mete, dole out.

5. Secrete, secern.

——, *v. i.* 1. Be parted, be divided, become separated, divide.

2. Give up, quit, lose, let go hold.

3. Quit each other, take leave, bid farewell.

4. Share, have a share.

5. Break, be broken, be torn asunder.

6. Depart, go away, set out.

Partake, *v. i.* Participate, share, have a share of, take a part of, have a part of, participate in.

——, *v. t.* Share, partake of, participate in, have a part of, take a part of.

Partaker, *n.* Participator, sharer, communicant, participant.

Parterre, *n.* [Fr.] Pit. *parquet*, orchestra; ornamental garden.

Partial, *a.* 1. Incomplete, imperfect, limited, fractional, component.

2. Biassed, prejudiced, prepossessed, warped, interested, unfair, unjust, one-sided, influenced.

3. Fond, favorably disposed; indulgent.

Partiality, *n.* 1. Unfairness, injustice, favoritism, bias, onesidedness.

2. Fondness, predilection, preference, liking, fancy, inclination, leaning, bent.

Partially, *adv.* 1. Unfairly, unjustly.

2. Partly, imperfectly, in part.

Partible, *a.* Separable, divisible.

Participant, *a.* Sharing, partaking.

——, *n.* Participator, sharer.

Participate, *v. t.* and *v. i.* Partake, share, have a part in, take a part in.

Particle, *n.* Bit, atom, molecule, corpuscle, mote, snip, morsel, rap, drop, granule, shred, nip, glimmer, spark, fleck, crumb, driblet, electron, ion, jot, iota, tittle, whit, grain, scrap, mite, scintilla, ace, speck.

Particular, *a.* 1. Especial, special, specific.

2. Individual, single, separate, distinct, special, respective.

3. Peculiar, characteristic, distinctive.

4. Personal, private, individual, own, peculiar, intimate.

5. Notable, noteworthy, special.

6. Minute, circumstantial, precise, exact, definite, narrow, detailed.

7. Exact, precise, nice, scrupulous, fastidious, dainty, close, conscientious, critical, careful, strict, finical.

8. Peculiar, odd, singular, strange, notable, uncommon, marked.

——, *n.* Instance, circumstance, detail, item, particularity, special point, feature, respect, regard.

Particularity, *n.* 1. Exactness, preciseness, precision.

2. Singleness, individuality.

3. Detail, item, particular, special point, minute circumstance.

4. Peculiarity, singularity, characteristic.

Particularize, *v. t.* Specify, mention in detail, itemize, detail, set forth minutely.

——, *v. i.* Be particular, descend to particulars, mention particulars.

Particularly, *adv.* 1. Especially, specially, specifically.

2. Separately, singly, distinctly, individually, severally.

Parting, *a.* 1. Dividing, separating, breaking.

2. Last, farewell, valedictory, final.

3. Departing, declining.

——, *n.* 1. Breaking, rupture, disruption, severing, tearing asunder.

2. Separation, detachment, division.

3. Leave-taking, farewell, departure; death.

Partisan, *n.* 1. Adherent, follower, supporter, disciple, champion, votary, party-man.

2. Truncheon, staff, *bâton;* halberd, pike; quarter-staff.

——, *a.* Factionary, biassed.

Partisanship, *n.* Championship.

Partition, *n.* 1. Division, separation.

2. Dividing wall, division wall, barrier, screen.

3. Distribution, apportionment, allotment.

——, *v. t.* 1. Apportion, share, distribute, divide into shares, parcel out.

2. Divide by partitions.

Partitive, *a.* (*Gram.*) Distributive, dividing.

Partly, *adv.* In part, in some measure, in some degree, partially, not wholly.

Partner, *n.* 1. Associate, colleague, partaker, copartner, sharer, participator, participant; dance-partner.

2. Member of a partnership, member of a firm, one of a firm *or* house, coadjutor, confederate, accomplice.

3. Spouse, companion, consort.

Partnership, *n.* 1. Union, connection, interest, participation.

2. Copartnership, company, association, society, firm, house.

Parts, *n. pl.* 1. Talents, faculties, powers, abilities, endowments, gifts, genius, qualities, accomplishments, intellect, mind, intelligence.

2. Quarters, regions, districts.

Parturition, *n.* Delivery, labor, travail, childbirth, bringing forth, birth.

Part with. Relinquish, resign, surrender, lose, give up.

Party, *n.* 1. Faction, set, junto, circle, ring, association, group, combination, league, confederacy, alliance, cabal, clique, coterie.

2. Body, company, detachment, troop, squad.

3. Company, assembly, gathering, social assemblage.

4. Participator, participant, partaker, sharer.

5. Litigant, plaintiff or defendant.

6. Person, individual, one, somebody, some one.

7. Cause, side, division, interest.

Party-colored, *a.* Variegated, piebald, pied, motley, many colored, many hued, divers-colored.

Parvenu, *n.* [Fr.] Upstart, mushroom, snob, pretentious fellow, pretender to gentility.

Paschal, *a.* Passover, Easter.

Pasquin, *v. t.* Lampoon, satirize, abuse by satire.

Pasquinade, *n.* Lampoon, satire.

Pass, *v. i.* 1. Go, move, proceed, go on, make a transit, devolve, fall.

2. Elapse, lapse, be spent, pass away, change, flit, glide, slip.

3. Vanish, disappear, cease, fade, die, be lost, expire.

4. Occur, happen, take place.

5. Circulate, be current, gain currency, be received.

6. Be enacted, be sanctioned by a majority of votes.

7. Be deemed, be considered, be held, be regarded.

8. Answer, do, do well enough.

9. Go unheeded, go unregarded, go unchallenged, pass inspection.

10. Make a thrust, make a pass, thrust.

11. Determine, pass judgment, decide.

——, *v. t.* 1. Allow to proceed, let go.

2. Go by.

3. Go over, go across.

4. Go through, go along.

5. Undergo, experience, live through, make trial of, suffer.

6. Spend (*as time*), live through, wile, beguile.

7. Omit, neglect, disregard, take no notice of.

8. Overstep, go beyond, overpass; exceed, surpass, excel, transcend, outstrip.

9. Be enacted by, be passed by; enact, ratify, sanction by a majority of votes.

10. Utter, deliver, pronounce.

11. Void, discharge, eject, excrete.

12. Finish, accomplish, end, achieve.

13. Send, transmit, deliver, transfer, make over.

Pass, *n.* 1. Passage, way, road, avenue, route, ford.

2. Defile, ravine, gorge, narrow passage.

3. Passport, ticket, permission to pass, license, authorization.

4. Conjuncture, state, condition, situation, state of things, plight.

5. Thrust, push, allonge, lunge, tilt, passado; trick, sleight of hand, transfer.

Passable, *a.* 1. Fit for travel.

2. Tolerable, middling, moderate, ordinary, allowable, admissible, so-so, mediocre, pretty good, capable of passing.

3. Current, receivable, acceptable.

Passage, *n.* 1. Passing, transit, going, progress.

2. Transit, journey, voyage; migration, evacuation.

3. Road, path, way, avenue, pass, course, thoroughfare, channel, route.

4. Access, entry, reception, currency.

5. Exploit, act, deed, event, feat, occurrence, incident.

6. Gallery, corridor, hall, entry, door, gate, etc.

7. Clause, sentence, paragraph, text.

8. Lapse, course, expiration; departure, death, decease.

9. Enactment, passing, sanction.

10. (*Mus.*) Phrase, portion of a tune; (*lit.*) section of writing, paragraph, part.

11. Fare.

12. Pass, encounter, contest, combat, skirmish, change, exchange, conflict, collision, brush, joust, tilt, affair.

Pass by. 1. Overlook, disregard, omit, take no notice of, pass over, neglect.

2. Overlook, excuse, forgive.

Passé, *a.* [Fr.] Past, worn, faded, out of use, obsolete, past the prime, out of date, antiquated.

Passenger, *n.* Traveller, wayfarer, voyager, itinerant, tourist, fare.

Passim, *adv.* [L.] Here and there, everywhere, throughout.

Passing, *a.* Transient, fleeting, momentary, going by, current.

——, *adv.* Surpassingly, wonderfully, exceedingly, excessively, very.

——, *prep.* Exceeding, beyond, over.

Passion, *n.* 1. Suffering (*specifically that of Christ by crucifixion*).

2. Emotion, ardor, fervor, zeal, rapture, transport, excitement, impulse, glow, strong feeling.

3. Zeal, ardor, vehement desire.

4. Love, affection, attachment, fondness, devotion, adoration.

5. Anger, resentment, wrath, indignation, fury, rage, vehemence, excitement.

Passionate, *a.* 1. Warm, ardent, earnest, intense, vehement, excited, animated, fiery, enthusiastic, fervent, glowing, burning, zealous, violent, furious, impetuous, impulsive, impassioned.

2. Irascible, excitable, choleric, hasty, impatient, touchy, hot, peppery, hot-tempered, angry, quick-tempered, hot-headed, fiery, violent.

Passionless, *a.* 1. Impassive, unsusceptible, unimpressible, apathetic, cold, phlegmatic, stoical, cold-blooded, without passion *or* feeling, self-contained.

2. Cool, calm, collected, unmoved, quiet, imperturbable, of a calm temper.

Passion Week. Holy Week, week before Easter.

Passive, *a.* 1. Quiet, quiescent, inert, inactive, receptive.

2. Unresisting, submissive, patient, non-resistant, stoical, apathetic, long-suffering, enduring, suffering.

Pass muster. Answer, do, pass, serve, do well enough.

Pass off. Palm, palm off, impose by trick, impose fraudulently.

Pass over. Overlook, disregard, omit, pass by.

Passport, *n.* 1. Pass, license, credentials.

2. Safeguard, safe-conduct.

Password, *n.* Watchword, countersign, secret parole.

PAST, *a.* 1. Spent, gone, ended, accomplished.

2. Gone by, bygone, ancient, former, outworn, obsolete.

——, *n.* Past time, bygone time, heretofore, history, yesterday; previous history.

——, *prep.* 1. Beyond, out of the reach of, by.

2. After (*in time*).

3. Beyond (*in position*), farther than.

4. Above, more than, exceeding.

——, *adv.* By, beyond.

PASTE, *n.* Gum, cement, adhesive.

Pastime, *n.* Amusement, entertainment, diversion, sport, play, recreation.

Pastor, *n.* 1. Shepherd.

2. Minister, clergyman, priest, parson, ecclesiastic, churchman, divine.

Pastoral, *a.* 1. Rural, rustic, of shepherds.

2. Bucolic.

3. Ministerial, of a pastor.

——, *n.* Bucolic, idyl, eclogue, pastoral poem.

Pastorate, *n.* Pastorship, living, parish, ministry, church; body of pastors.

Pasturage, *n.* Pasture, grazing land.

Pasture, *n.* 1. Herbage, herbs, pasturage, grass.

2. Grazing land, pasturage, pasture-ground, grassland, range.

——, *v. t.* Supply with pasturage, graze, turn out to pasture.

Pasty, *n.* Meat-pie.

——, *a.* Doughy, sticky, white.

Pat, *a.* (*Colloq.*) Fit, apt, pertinent, suitable, appropriate.

——, *adv.* (*Colloq.*) Seasonably, fitly, aptly, opportunely, conveniently, apropos.

——, *n.* 1. Rap, dab, tap, hit, light blow, caress.

2. Small lump, cake.

——, *v. t.* Rap, dab, tap, strike lightly, hit; caress.

Patch, *n.* 1. Piece, repair.

2. Tract, parcel, plot.

——, *v. t.* Repair, mend.

Pate, *n.* (*Jocose.*) Head, crown.

Patent, *a.* 1. Open, spreading, expanded.

2. Patented.

3. Open, apparent, evident, plain, obvious, manifest, clear, public, conspicuous, unconcealed, palpable, unmistakable, glaring, notorious, indisputable.

——, *n.* Right, privilege, copyright.

Paternal, *a.* 1. Fatherly.

2. Hereditary.

Paternity, *n.* 1. Fathership, fatherhood.

2. Origin, derivation, from a father, descent.

3. Origin, authorship.

Pater noster. [L.] 1. The Lord's prayer; formal prayer, charm.

2. Rosary.

Path, *n.* Track (*trodden*), footway, trail, beaten way, pathway; road, way, course, route, passage, avenue, access.

Pathetic, *a.* Affecting, touching, moving, melting, tender, plaintive.

Pathless, *a.* Untrodden, trackless.

Pathos, *n.* 1. Passion, warmth of feeling, tender emotion,

2. Pathetic quality, tender tone, patheticalness.

Pathway, *n.* Path, footway, track.

2. Way, course of life.

Patience, *n.* 1. Endurance (*without complaint*), fortitude, resignation, submission, sufferance, long-sufferance, long-suffering.

2. Quietness, calmness, composure.

3. Forbearance, leniency, indulgence, long-suffering.

4. Perseverance, persistence, indefatigableness, constancy, diligence, assiduity.

Patient, *a.* 1. Submissive, resigned, uncomplaining, unrepining, passive, long-suffering.

2. Quiet, calm, contented, composed.

3. Indulgent, lenient, long-suffering.

4. Persevering, persistent, diligent, assiduous, indefatigable, constant.

——, *n.* Invalid, sufferer, sick person; subject, case.

Patrician, *n.* Nobleman, aristocrat, "blue-blood," "blue-stocking."

——, *a.* Noble, senatorial, aristocratic, highborn, well-born.

Patricide, *n.* Parricide.

Patrimony, *n.* Inheritance, heritage, paternal *or* hereditary estate, hereditament.

Patriot, *n.* Lover of one's country.

Patriotism, *n.* Love of country, devotion to one's country, national spirit, *amor patriæ.*

Patron, *n.* Defender, advocate, protector, supporter, favorer, guardian, good genius, tutelary saint; regular customer.

Patronage, *n.* 1. Favor, countenance, support, assistance, influence, friendship, aid, protection, encouragement; condescending favor.

2. Custom, good-will (*of an established place of business*).

Patronize, *v. t.* Favor, countenance, support, aid, assist, help, befriend, make interest for, notice, defend, maintain.

Patronymic, *n.* Surname, family name, ancestral name, cognomen.

Pattern, *n.* 1. Exemplar, model, archetype, paradigm, plan, last, prototype, original.

2. Specimen, sample, example; paragon, mirror.

3. Figure, shape, design.

4. Figure, style, type.

——, *v. t.* Imitate, copy, follow.

Paucity, *n.* 1. Fewness, small number, rarity.

2. Smallness of quantity, poverty, exiguity, insufficiency.

Paunch, *n.* 1. Abdomen, belly.

2. First stomach (*of a ruminating animal*).

Pauper, *n.* Poor person (*depending on charity*), beggar.

Pauperism, *n.* Indigence, destitution, penury, beggary, extreme poverty, want, need.

Pause, *n.* 1. Stop, cessation, suspension, interruption, rest, halt, intermission, interval, remission, stoppage, stopping, break, cæsura.

2: Suspense, hesitation, uncertainty.

3. Break, paragraph (*in writing*).

4. Point, punctuation-mark.

——, *v. i.* 1. Stop, cease, desist, wait, delay, rest, breathe, stay, break off.

2. Stop, wait, forbear, delay, tarry, stay, intermit.

3. Hesitate, demur, deliberate, waver, hold back.

Pave the way. Prepare, make ready, get ready, make preparation, smooth the way, prepare a way, prepare a passage for, facilitate the introduction of.

Pavilion, *n.* 1. Tent, canopy, covering; building.

2. (*Anat.*) Auricle, ala, external ear.

Paw, *n.* 1. Foot (*of beasts with claws*).

2. Hand (*in contempt*).

Pawl, *n.* Click, detent, catch, ratchet.

Pawn, *n.* 1. Pledge (*of a chattel to secure a debt*), gage, security.

2. Chessman.

——, *v. t.* 1. Pledge, offer *or* give as security.

2. Stake, wager, hazard, lay, bet, risk.

Pay, *v. t.* 1. Discharge, settle, liquidate, defray, quit, foot, honor, meet, discount.

2. Compensate, recompense, requite, reimburse, remunerate, reward, make payment to, satisfy, discharge one's obligation to, indemnify.

3. Punish, take revenge upon, retort upon.

4. Give, render, offer.

——, *v. i.* 1. Make compensation.

2. Be profitable, be remunerative, make a good return, be a good investment, give a good interest.

——, *n.* Compensation, recompense, remuneration, reward, requital, wages, hire, stipend, perquisite, commission, reimbursement, salary, allowance, emolument.

Payable, *a.* Due; that may be paid.

Pay for. 1. Give an equivalent for, bear the expense of, be mulcted on account of, defray the cost.

2. Atone for, make amends for.

Paying, *a.* Remunerative, profitable, gainful.

PAYMENT, *n.* 1. Paying, discharge of a debt, liquidation, quittance, defrayal, discount, settlement.

2. Recompense, requital, reward, satisfaction, reimbursement, remuneration, compensation, fee.

3. Chastisement, punishment.

Pay off. 1. Pay and discharge (*as hired men*).

2. Punish, pay, take revenge upon, retort upon, retaliate, be quits, be even with, give a *quid pro quo.*

3. (*Naut.*) Fall off, fall to leeward, fall off from the wind.

Pay up. (*Colloq.*) Settle, pay arrears, settle an account, square accounts, quit scores, strike a balance, pay the bill, pay the piper, pay the fiddler.

PEACE, *n.* 1. Calm, repose, quiet, tranquillity, stillness, silence, calmness, quietness.

2. Amity, harmony, friendliness.

3. Public tranquillity, freedom from war, good order, quiet.

4. Tranquillity, calmness, quiet of conscience, equanimity, composure, placidity, quietude, imperturbability.

5. Harmony, concord, accord, truce, reconciliation, pacification.

Peaceable, *a.* 1. Peaceful, pacific, free from war.

2. Gentle, mild, amicable, friendly, disposed to peace, inoffensive.

3. Quiet, tranquil, placid, unmoved, undisturbed, serene, peaceful, still.

Peaceful, *a.* 1. Quiet, undisturbed.

2. Mild, gentle, kindly, friendly, pacific, amicable, concordant, harmonious, peaceable.

3. Calm, still, placid, tranquil, serene, composed.

Peace-maker, *n.* Mediator, intercessor, makepeace, arbitrator, pacificator.

Peace-offering, *n.* 1. Atonement, satisfaction, amends, reparation, atoning sacrifice.

2. Mediation, olive-branch, intercession.

Peak, *n.* 1. Point.

2. Top (*of a mountain*), summit, crest, crown, pinnacle, *pico*.

——, *v. i.* Grow thin *or* lean, become emaciated, dwindle.

Peaked, *a.* Pointed, picked, piked, thin.

Peal, *n.* Blast, burst, blare, clang, ringing; set of bells, series of changes.

——, *v. i.* Resound, echo, re-echo, boom, thunder, roar.

Pearl, *n.* 1. Margarite.

2. Jewel, gem, nacre; precious thing.

3. Drop, tear.

Pearly, *a.* 1. Abounding in pearls.

2. Clear, pure, translucent, limpid, pellucid, nacreous.

Peasant, *n.* Rustic, countryman, hind, swain, clown, laborer, boor.

Peasantry, *n.* 1. Laborers, peasants, rustics, hinds, lowest agricultural class.

2. Rusticity, coarseness.

Pebble, *n.* 1. Stone (*of small size*), pebble-stone.

2. (*In jewelry.*) Agate.

3. (*Among opticians.*) Colorless rock-crystal, quartz, pure silica.

Peccability, *n.* Frailty, infirmity, weakness, liability to sin.

Peccable, *a.* Frail, weak, imperfect, erring, sinning, liable to sin.

Peccadillo, *n.* Petty fault, slight offence, petty trespass, slight crime.

Peccant, *a.* 1. Sinning, erring, guilty, criminal.

2. Morbid, malignant, corrupting, corroding, bad, corrupt, unhealthy.

3. Wrong, incorrect, bad, defective, informal.

Peculate, *v. i.* Embezzle, appropriate criminally, steal, pilfer, rob, defraud.

Peculation, *n.* Embezzlement, pilfering, theft.

Peculiar, *a.* 1. That specially pertains, that belongs exclusively, one's own, appropriate, proper, individual, idiosyncratic.

2. Singular, characteristic, exceptional, rare, striking, unusual, uncommon, eccentric, odd, extraordinary, strange, queer.

3. Special, select, particular, individual, especial, specific.

Peculiarity, *n.* 1. Appropriateness, specialty, individuality, distinctiveness.

2. Individuality, idiocrasy, idiosyncrasy, characteristic, specialty, singularity, particularity.

Peculiarly, *adv.* 1. Especially, particularly, unusually.

2. Particularly, singly.

Pecuniary, *a.* Monetary, nummular, nummulary, nummary, financial.

Pedagogue, *n.* 1. Schoolmaster, teacher, instructor.

2. Pedant.

Pedant, *n.* 1. Schoolmaster, pedagogue.

2. Vain scholar, conceited scholar, ostentatious man of learning, precisian, bluestocking.

Pedantic, } *a.* Conceited, pragmatical,
Pedantical, } vain of knowledge, ostentatious of learning, over-learned, pedagogic, pedagogical, priggish, pompous, stilted.

Pedantry, *n.* Ostentation of learning, boastful display of knowledge, pedantism.

Peddle, *v. t.* Hawk, retail, vend, sell.

——, *v. i.* 1. Hawk, retail, vend.

2. Trifle, dawdle, potter.

Peddler, *n.* Travelling chapman, hawker, vender, costermonger, coster, huckster, packman, colporteur, petty dealer, travelling trader.

Pedestrian, *n.* 1. Foot-traveller, traveller afoot, walker, "hiker."

2. Foot-racer, professional walker.

Pedigree, *n.* Lineage, descent, ancestry, genealogy, stock, breed, family, race, house, line of ancestors, strain, line, extraction, recorded descent.

Peel, *v. t.* 1. Pare (*by cutting*), bark, flay, decorticate.

2. Strip off, remove by stripping, skin, hull.

——, *v. i.* Exfoliate, come off (*as skin or rind*), peel off, desquamate.

——, *n.* Rind, skin, bark, hull.

Peep, *v. i.* 1. Chirp (*as a chicken*), pule, cheep, cry, pip.

2. Begin to appear, issue, come forth, emerge.

3. Peer, look slyly, peek, glance slyly.

Peer, *n.* 1. Equal, mate, match, compeer.

2. Companion, associate, fellow, comrade, contemporary.

3. Nobleman, lord.

——, *v. i.* 1. (*Poetical.*) Appear, peep, come in sight.

2. Peep, pry, look closely *or* narrowly, peek.

Peerless, *a.* Unequalled, unmatched, unsurpassed, matchless, superlative, unique, without an equal, without a peer.

Peevish, *a.* 1. Fretful, petulant, querulous, irascible, irritable, waspish, snappish, pettish, captious, cross, crusty, snarling, testy, churlish, crabbed, acrimonious, spleeny, splenetic, ill-natured, ill-tempered; discontented, fretful, captious, complaining.

2. Self-willed, stubborn, obstinate, headstrong, froward.

3. Silly, childish, thoughtless, trifling.

Pelagian, ⎫ *a.* Oceanic, marine, of the
Pelagic, ⎭ ocean.

Pelf, *n.* Money, riches, lucre, mammon, gain, wealth (*contemptuous term*).

Pellicle, *n.* Film, thin skin, thin coating, crust.

Pell-mell, *adv.* Confusedly, irregularly, disorderly, in confusion, in disorder, helter-skelter, at sixes and sevens.

Pellucid, *a.* Clear, limpid, crystalline, bright, transparent, lucid, translucent, diaphanous.

Pelt, *n.* Skin (*of a beast with the hair on it*), hide, raw hide, undressed hide.

——, *v. t.* 1. Strike (*with something thrown*), beat, batter, assail with missiles, belabor, pepper, stone, bombard.

2. Throw, cast, hurl.

——, *v. i.* Hurry, rush.

Pen, *v. t.* 1. Write, compose, indite, commit to paper, inscribe.

2. Encage, coop, confine, enclose, impound, imprison, incarcerate, shut up, shut in, hem in, wall in, rail in.

PEN, *n.* 1. Enclosure, pinfold, pound, sty, hutch, crib, pit, stall, cage, coop, penfold, paddock, corral.

2. Quill, stylus; style of writing.

Penal, *a.* Punitive, disciplinary, castigatory, corrective.

Penalty, *n.* 1. Punishment, penal retribution, chastisement; fine, forfeiture, mulct, amercement.

2. Disadvantage, handicap.

Penance, *n.* Punishment (*self-inflicted or imposed by ecclesiastical authority*), mortification, maceration, humiliation, penalty.

Penates, *n.* Household gods.

Penchant, *n.* [Fr.] Inclination, bent, propensity, proneness, proclivity, disposition, tendency, turn, leaning, predisposition, liking, fondness, predilection, taste, bias, propension.

PENCIL, *n.* Brush (*made of hair or fine bristles*), crayon, marker, chalk.

——, *v. t.* 1. Paint, depict, delineate, portray, sketch, outline.

2. Mark *or* draw with a pencil.

Penciling, *n.* Sketch, outline.

Pencraft, *n.* 1. Penmanship, chirography, writing.

2. Authorship, composition.

Pendant, *n.* 1. Hanging appendage, bob; appendix, addition, flap, tag.

2. Ear-ring, ear drop.

3. (*Naut.*) Pennant, pennon.

4. Chandelier, gas-fixture, lustre.

——, *a.* 1. Hanging, pendulous, suspended, pensile, depending.

2. Overhanging, projecting, jutting over.

Pending, *a.* Depending, undecided, undetermined, unsettled, in suspense.

——, *prep.* During.

Pendulous, *a.* Hanging loosely, pendent.

Penetrable, *a.* 1. Permeable, pervious.

2. Susceptible, impressible.

Penetrate, *v. t.* 1. Pierce, perforate, bore, enter, cut, invade, burrow, percolate, pervade, soak.

2. Touch, make sensible, affect.

3. Discern, understand, comprehend, perceive.

——, *v. i.* 1. Pass, make way, enter.

2. See into, make way intellectually.

Penetrating, *a.* 1. Sharp, subtle, piercing, penetrative, permeating.

2. Discerning, intelligent, sagacious, sharp-witted, clear-sighted, acute, keen, quick, shrewd, keen-sighted.

Penetration, *n.* 1. Penetrating.

2. Insight.

3. Acuteness, discernment, sagacity, sagaciousness, shrewdness, astuteness, sharpness, perspicacity, insight, discrimination, acumen.

Penetrative, *a.* Piercing, sharp, subtle, sagacious, discerning, acute, penetrating, keen, permeating.

Penitence, *n.* Repentance, contrition, compunction, regret, remorse, sorrow, qualms.

Penitent, *a.* Repentant, contrite, remorseful, regretful, conscience-stricken, compunctious, sorry, sorrowful.

——, *n.* 1. Repentant.

2. Penitentiary, repentant, penance-doer.

Penitentiary, *n.* 1. Prison, jail, bridewell, workhouse, house of correction.

2. Penitent, repentant, penance-doer.

Penman, *n.* 1. Teacher of penmanship, writing-teacher, calligrapher, calligraphist.

2. Writer, scribe, chirographer, chirographist, quill-driver, penner.

3. Author, writer, composer.

Penmanship, *n.* 1. Calligraphy, pencraft, art of writing.

2. Chirography, writing, handwriting.

Pennant, *n.* (*Naut.*) Pendant, pennon, small flag. ·

Penniless, *a.* Moneyless, destitute, poor, necessitous, needy, indigent, distressed, pinched, reduced, poverty-stricken, impecunious, out of money, out of cash, out of pocket, in need, in want.

Pennon, *n.* Banner, streamer, standard, flag, colors, ensign; wing, pinion.

Pensile, *a.* Hanging, suspended, pendent, pendulous.

Pension, *n.* 1. Allowance (*from a government for past services*), annuity.

2. Boarding-house.

——, *v. t.* Retire, to pension off.

Pensive, *a.* 1. Thoughtful, meditative, reflective, dreamy, sober, contemplative.

2. Expressive of sadness, sad, serious, grave, mournful, melancholy, solemn, *triste.*

Pentagonal, *a.* Five-angled, five-cornered, five-sided, pentangular, pentagonous.

Pentecost, *n.* Whitsuntide, Whit-Sunday, pinxter.

Pent-house, *n.* Lean-to.

Penult, *n.* Penultima, penultimate, last syllable but one, penultimate syllable.

Penurious, *a.* 1. Niggard, scanty, insufficient, inadequate, meagre, ill-provided, poor, stinted.

2. Parsimonious, covetous, avaricious, illiberal, miserly, niggardly, sordid, mercenary, close, stingy, mean, close-fisted, hard-fisted, grasping, near.

Penury, *n.* Indigence, destitution, extreme poverty, want, need.

People, *n.* 1. Tribe, nation, race, clan, family, country, state.

2. Population, folk, persons, the public, the community, the bulk of mankind.

3. Commonalty, populace, commons, proletariat, democracy.

4. Rabble, mob, the vulgar, vulgar herd, lower classes, humbler classes, the multitude, the million, the many, *hoi polloi*, the crowd, the masses, *canaille.*

5. Persons, men, "folks."

——, *v. t.* Populate, settle.

Peppery, *a.* 1. Hot, pungent, high-seasoned, hot as pepper.

2. Hot-tempered, irritable, irascible, touchy, testy, waspish, snappish, snarling, churlish, choleric, petulant, excitable, passionate, hasty, quick, like tinder, like touch-wood.

Peptic, *a.* Dietetic.

Per, *prep.* [L.] By, for, through, by means of.

Peradventure, *adv.* (*Archaic.*) Perhaps, perchance, it may be, by chance, maybe, haply, mayhap, possibly.

——, *n.* Chance, doubt, question.

Perambulate, *v. t.* Go around, go about, traverse.

Perambulation, *n.* Round, circuit, tour.

Per annum. [L.] Annually, by the year, in each year.

Per capita. [L.] By heads, by polls, according to the number of persons.

Perceivable, *a.* Discernible, cognizable, perceptible, appreciable, sensible, distinguishable.

Perceive, *v. t.* 1. See, discover, note, notice, recognize, detect, spot, discriminate, remark, observe, descry, behold, discern, distinguish.

2. Feel, be sensible of, sense.

3. Understand, comprehend, know, appreciate.

Per cent. [L.] By the hundred.

Perceptible, *a.* Visible, discernible, apparent, cognizable, perceivable.

Perceptibly, *adv.* Evidently, notably, noticeably.

Perception, *n.* 1. Seeing, discernment, cognition, apprehension, recognition, perceiving.

2. Perceptivity, understanding, apprehension, comprehension, discernment, feeling, consciousness.

3. Sensation, sense, feeling.

Perch, *n.* 1. Pole, staff, rod.

2. Roost, rest, seat.

3. Elevated position, height.

4. (*Arch.*) Bracket, console.

——, *v. i.* Roost, sit on a perch, rest lightly, alight.

Perchance, *adv.* Perhaps, possibly, by chance, haply, maybe, it may be, as luck may have it, peradventure, mayhap.

Percolate, *v. i.* Filter, transude, ooze, exude, penetrate, strain, drain.

Percolation, *n.* Filtration, straining, exudation.

Percussion, *n.* 1. Collision, clash, shock, concussion, encounter, crash.

2. Vibratory shock.

Perdition, *n.* 1. Ruin, destruction, overthrow, wreck, downfall, utter loss, demolition.

2. Eternal death, future misery.

Peregrination, *n.* Travelling, travel, wandering, journey, roaming, tour.

Peremptory, *a.* 1. Decisive, express, authoritative, categorical, imperative, positive, absolute, commanding, imperious.

2. Resolute, determined, resolved.

3. Dogmatic, arbitrary, incontrovertible.

4. (*Law.*) Final, determinate.

Perennial, *a.* Lasting, enduring, permanent, constant, continual, uninterrupted, undying, unceasing, ceaseless, perpetual, imperishable, deathless, never-failing, unfailing, immortal.

Perfect, *a.* 1. Finished, completed.

2. Full, complete, entire, whole, utter.

3. Complete, consummate, excellent, capital, ideal, exquisite, faultless.

4. Skilled, disciplined, accomplished, expert, fully informed.

5. Pure, holy, blameless, faultless, without sin, immaculate, unblemished, spotless.

6. Sound, faultless.

——, *v. t.* (*Pron.* perfect'.) 1. Finish, complete, consummate, elaborate, make perfect, bring to perfection.

2. Accomplish, instruct fully, make skilful, make expert, finish.

Perfection, *n.* 1. Perfectness, maturity, completion, consummation, wholeness, excellence, finish, faultlessness, correctness.

2. Excellent quality, beauty, excellence.

Perfectly, *adv.* 1. Exquisitely, consummately.

2. Fully, entirely, totally, completely, altogether, thoroughly.

3. Exactly, accurately.

Perfidious, *a.* 1. Faithless, unfaithful, venal, treacherous, false, dishonest, disloyal, double-faced, traitorous, false-hearted, deceitful, untrustworthy.

2. Perjured, forsworn, faithless, false.

Perfidy, *n.* Perfidiousness, treachery, faithlessness, infidelity, traitorousness, treason, defection, disloyalty, breach of faith, foul play, Punic faith.

Perforate, *v. t.* Pierce, penetrate, bore, drill, riddle, trepan, pink, punch, prick, bore through, puncture.

Perforation, *n.* 1. Pertusion, piercing.

2. Hole, aperture, opening, orifice.

Perforce, *adv.* By force, by violence, violently, necessarily, of necessity, absolutely, by compulsion, forcibly.

Perform, *v. t.* 1. Do, execute, effect, accomplish, achieve, compass, consummate, bring about, bring to pass, work out, transact.

2. Observe, fulfil, meet, discharge, satisfy, complete, adhere to, be faithful to, comply with, act up to, execute.

3. Act, represent, play, sustain a part, support a character.

4. Play, execute.

Performance, *n.* 1. Accomplishment, execution, discharge, fulfilment, completion, doing, consummation, achievement.

2. Action, deed, act, achievement, exploit, feat, work.

3. Composition, literary work, production, work.

4. Acting, exhibition of character on the stage, entertainment, exhibition, play, representation, show.

5. Playing, execution.

Performer, *n.* 1. Doer, operator, executor, agent.

2. Actor, player, stage-player; musician.

Perfume, *n.* 1. Fragrance, balminess, aroma, redolence, incense, pleasing scent, grateful odor, sweetness of smell, *bouquet.*

2. Sweet-smelling substance.

——, *v. t.* Scent, impregnate *or* imbue with grateful odor.

Perfunctory, *a.* Indifferent, careless, slovenly, heedless, reckless, negligent, slight, mechanical, formal, unmindful, thoughtless.

Perhaps, *adv.* Perchance, possibly, haply, belike, by chance, maybe, it may be, as luck may have it, peradventure.

Pericarp, *n.* (*Bot.*) Capsule, pod, seed-vessel, ripened ovary.

Peril, *n.* Danger, hazard, jeopardy, risk.

——, *v. t.* Risk, endanger, imperil, jeopard, hazard, put in danger, expose to danger.

Perilous, *a.* Dangerous, hazardous, full of danger, fraught with danger, full of risk.

Period, *n.* 1. Cycle, circle of time, revolution of time, round of years.

2. Time, term, era, eon, span, spell, stage, season, epoch, age, date.

3. Duration, continuance.

4. End, limit, term, bound, termination, conclusion, determination.

5. (*Rhet.*) Sentence (*full* or *completed*), proposition, phrase, clause.

Periodic, } *a.* Recurring (*regularly*), sea-
Periodical, } sonal, cyclic, intermittent.

Periodical, *n.* Magazine, review, serial.

Periodically, *adv.* Regularly, statedly, at stated times, at regular times, at fixed periods.

Peripatetic, *a.* 1. Itinerant, walking about, wandering.

2. Aristotelian, of Aristotle.

Periphery, *n.* 1. Outside, surface, superficies.

2. Perimeter, outer boundary, circumference.

Periphrasis, *n.* [L.] Circumlocution, circuit of words, roundabout expression, periphrase, redundancy.

Periphrastic, } *a.* Circumlocutory, round-
Periphrastical, } about, indirect, going round.

Perish, *v. i.* 1. Decay, waste, wither, shrivel, moulder.

2. Pass away, be destroyed, be ruined, be lost, come to nought, go to destruction.

3. Die, expire, decease, cease to exist, lose life, pass away.

Perishable, *a.* 1. Destructible, decaying, decomposable, liable to decay.

2. Dying, mortal, frail.

Periwig, *n.* Wig, peruke, scratch, scratchwig.

Perjured, *a.* Forsworn, perfidious, false, treacherous, traitorous, lost to shame.

Perjury, *n.* False swearing.

Perk, *v. t.* Dress, prank, make trim, make smart.

——, *v. i.* 1. Be perk, be proud, be perky, be smart.

2. Peer, look narrowly, look sharply, scan.

——, *a.* Pert, trim, smart, brisk, airy, jaunty, spruce, vain, perky.

Perking, *a.* Sharp, inquisitive, keen.

Perk up. Cheer up, brighten up, bear up, take heart, cast away care.

Perky, *a.* Perk, trim, jaunty, airy, forward.

Permanence, } *n.* Duration, durability,
Permanency, } lastingness, continuance, fixedness, stability.

Permanent, *a.* Lasting, abiding, fixed, enduring, continuing, durable, perdurable, stable, standing, steadfast, unchangeable, unchanging, immutable, unmovable, unfading, perpetual, invariable, constant, persistent.

Permeable, *a.* Pervious, penetrable, pervadible.

Permissible, *a.* Allowable, admissible, sufferable, free, unprohibited, lawful, legal, legitimate, proper.

Permission, *n.* Leave, license, liberty, allowance, consent, permit, warrant, authorization, sufferance, toleration, dispensation, permittance.

Permissive, *a.* 1. Permitting, allowing, dispensatory, granting.

2. Granted, suffered.

Permit, *v. t.* 1. Allow, let, suffer, tolerate, endure, put up with.

2. Empower, authorize, warrant, give permission to, give leave to, give *carte-blanche* to, grant, admit, license, consent to.

——, *n.* (*Pron.* per'mit.) Leave, license, permission, liberty, passport, warrant.

Permutation, *n.* Exchange, mutual transference, change.

Pernicious, *a.* 1. Hurtful, harmful, deleterious, injurious, detrimental, baneful, baleful, prejudicial, noxious, noisome, mischievous, damaging, disadvantageous, destructive, ruinous, fatal, deadly, malign.

2. Malicious, wicked, evil-hearted, malignant, malign, mischievous, mischief-making, malevolent.

Perorate, *v. i.* Speechify, spout, harangue, declaim; sum up a speech.

Perpendicular, *a.* 1. Vertical, upright, erect, pointing to the zenith.

2. At right angles, making a right angle, normal; precipitous.

Perpetrate, *v. t.* Do (*as something base*), commit, perform, execute, be guilty of.

Perpetration, *n.* Commission (*as of a crime*), doing, performing, evil act.

Perpetual, *a.* Endless, unending, everlasting, eternal, ever-during, ceaseless, unceasing, continual, incessant, unintermitted, uninterrupted, constant, interminable, perennial, never-ceasing, never-failing, unfailing, enduring, permanent, sempiternal.

Perpetuate, *v. t.* Eternize, eternalize, immortalize, make perpetual, continue, cause to last.

Perpetuity, *n.* Eternity, endless duration, continued existence, uninterrupted existence, perennity, sempiternity, everlastingness.

Perplex, *v. t.* 1. Entangle, tangle, complicate, involve, snarl, make intricate, make difficult, encumber.

2. Embarrass, puzzle, distract, pose, bewilder, fog, nonplus, set, corner, beset, mystify, confuse, confound, pother.

3. Plague, vex, harass, tease, molest, trouble, annoy, disturb, worry, pester, embarrass, bother.

Perplexing, *a.* Troublesome, puzzling, embarrassing, bewildering, confusing, difficult, intricate.

Perplexity, *n.* 1. Intricacy, intricateness, complexity, obscurity, hardness, complication, involution, unintelligibility, entanglement.

2. Concern, care, anxiety, solicitude, trouble, embarrassment, distraction, doubt, confusion, bewilderment.

3. Embarrassment, difficulty, strait, hobble, puzzle, puzzlement, fog, pickle, critical situation, plight, predicament, dilemma, quandary, pass, pinch, scrape.

Per se. [L.] By itself, alone, apart.

Persecute, *v. t.* 1. Oppress, harass, afflict, molest, distress, worry, hunt down, run down, pursue malignantly, drive from pillar to post, injure persistently.

2. Harass, solicit, importune, annoy, tease, beset, worry, pester.

Perseverance, *n.* Steadiness, persistence, continuance, pertinacity, persistency, constancy, steadfastness, resolution, indefatigableness.

Persevere, *v. i.* Persist, be steady, continue, be steadfast, be constant, go on, keep on, hold on, keep one's course, keep one's ground, maintain one's ground, stick to it, not give it up, stand firm, stand fast, move heaven and earth, go through fire and water, go all lengths, stick at nothing.

Persiflage, *n.* [Fr.] Banter, raillery, ridicule, jeering, mockery, quizzing, joking, pleasantry, frivolous talk.

Persist, *v. i.* 1. Continue, remain, last, endure.

2. Persevere, be steadfast.

Persistent, *a.* 1. Persevering, constant, enduring, tenacious, fixed, immovable, persistive, persisting, steady.

2. Obstinate, contumacious, dogged, pertinacious, obdurate, pig-headed, stubborn, perverse.

PERSON, *n.* 1. Individual, one, somebody, some one.

2. Body, bodily substance, bodily form, human frame, living body.

3. Character, part, *rôle*.

4. Moral agent, living soul, self-conscious being.

5. Human being, human creature; fellow, chap, personage.

Personable, *a.* Graceful, good-looking, well-appearing, comely, seemly, well-favored.

Personage, *n.* 1. Individual, person, figure.

2. Person of rank, great person, illustrious person, bigwig, "big shot."

3. Exterior appearance, stature, air.

Personal, *a.* 1. Individual, private, special.

2. Corporal, exterior, physical, material, bodily.

Personality, *n.* 1. Individuality, distinct existence.

2. Personal criticism, remark, reflection, allusion, animadversion, stricture, *or* exception.

Personally, *adv.* 1. Individually, as to one's person.

2. In person, by bodily presence.

Personate, *v. t.* 1. Play, act, act the part of, take the part of, assume the character of, imitate, personify, represent, impersonate.

2. Disguise, mask.

3. Counterfeit, feign, simulate.

Personation, *n.* Representation, acting, simulation.

Personification, *n.* (*Rhet.*) 1. Prosopopœia.

2. Embodiment, impersonation.

Personify, *v. t.* Impersonate, ascribe personal qualities to, embody.

Perspective, *n.* Vista, prospect, view; mental view; proportion, sense of values.

Perspicacious, *a.* 1. Quick-sighted, sharp-sighted, keen-sighted.

2. Discerning, acute, keen, sagacious, shrewd, clear-sighted, keen-sighted, sharp-witted, keen-witted, long-headed, eagle-eyed, penetrating.

Perspicacity, *n.* 1. Quick-sightedness, acuteness of sight.

2. Perspicaciousness, acuteness, sharpness, shrewdness, discernment, penetration, sagacity, astuteness, insight, acumen.

Perspicuity, *n.* Clearness, lucidness, lucidity, transparency, plainness, intelligibility, perspicuousness, distinctness, explicitness.

Perspicuous, *a.* Clear, lucid, plain, transparent, intelligible, distinct, explicit, unequivocal, obvious.

Perspiration, *n.* Exudation, sweating; sweat.

Perspire, *v. i.* Sweat, exhale, swelter.

Persuade, *v. t.* 1. Induce, influence, lead, incite, impel, actuate, move, entice, allure, prevail upon, bring over, win over, bring round.

2. Advise, counsel, try to influence.

3. Convince, satisfy by proof *or* evidence.

4. Inculcate by argument, teach.

Persuasion, *n.* 1. Influence, inducement, incitement, suasion, bringing over.

2. Conviction, belief, opinion.

3. Conviction, creed, belief, doctrine, tenet, dogma, way of thinking, system of opinions; kind, sort.

Persuasive, *a.* Convincing, cogent, logical, valid, sound, weighty, inducing, inducive, persuasory, suasive.

Pert, *a.* 1. Lively, brisk, smart, dapper, nimble, sprightly, perk.

2. Saucy, forward, bold, impertinent, impudent, flippant, free, presuming, malapert, indecorously free.

Pertain to. 1. Belong to, appertain to, be the property of.

2. Behoove, befit, beseem, be incumbent on, be the duty of, devolve on.

3. Regard, concern, relate to, refer to, answer to, have relation to.

Pertinacious, *a.* 1. Constant, steady, firm, persevering, determined, resolute, steadfast, stanch.

2. Stubborn, obstinate, dogged, wilful, mulish, unyielding, intractable, headstrong, perverse, wayward, inflexible.

Pertinacity, *n.* 1. Resolution, determination, steadiness, constancy, inflexibility, firmness, perseverance, persistence, persistency, tenacity of purpose.

2. Stubbornness, obstinacy, wilfulness, doggedness, headiness, mulishness, persistence, persistency.

Pertinence, } *n.* Fitness, appropriateness,
Pertinency, } relation, relevancy, appositeness, suitableness, applicability, propriety, patness.

Pertinent, *a.* 1. Fit, appropriate, suitable, applicable, relevant, apposite, adapted, apt, apropos, germane, pat, proper, to the point, to the purpose.

2. Regarding, concerning, belonging, pertaining, appurtenant.

Pertness, *n.* 1. Briskness, smartness, sprightliness, liveliness.

2. Sauciness, forwardness, impertinence, impudence, flippancy.

Perturb, *v. t.* 1. Disquiet, trouble, agitate, distress, discompose, excite, worry, vex, disturb.

2. Disorder, confuse.

Perturbation, *n.* 1. Disturbance, disorder, confusion, commotion.

2. Agitation, trepidation, disquiet, uneasiness, excitement, discomposure, worry, vexation, restlessness, commotion.

Perturbed, *a.* Disturbed, disquieted, distressed, agitated, discomposed, excited, worried, vexed.

Peruke, *n.* Wig, periwig, scratch, *perruque.*

Perusal, *n.* Reading, scrutiny, inspection.

Peruse, *v. t.* 1. Read.

2. Observe, examine, scrutinize, consider, survey, inspect.

Pervade, *v. t.* Permeate, penetrate, pass through, overspread, fill, run through, be diffused through, be disseminated through, interfuse, imbue, impregnate, infiltrate, extend through, affect entirely; animate.

Perverse, *a.* 1. Distorted (*from the right*), bad, perverted, oblique.

2. Obstinate, stubborn, wilful, dogged, mulish, untractable, unyielding, headstrong, contrary, pertinacious, wayward, ungovernable, pervicacious.

3. Cross, petulant, peevish, waspish, captious, cross-grained, cantankerous, wrongheaded, "cussed," snappish, touchy, testy, crusty, churlish, crabbed, froward,

morose, surly, snarling, ill-tempered, ill-natured, spleeny, spiteful, wicked.

4. Untoward, vexatious, troublesome, inconvenient.

Perverseness, *n.* 1. Obstinacy, stubbornness, wilfulness, waywardness, perversity.

2. Petulance, peevishness, churlishness, moroseness, surliness, ill-temper, perversity.

Perversion, *n.* Impairment, injury, vitiation, corruption, debasement, prostitution, abasement.

Pervert, *v. t.* 1. Distort, stretch, falsify, wrest, wrench, twist, misuse, warp, torture, strain, misapply, mutilate, misconstrue, garble, misrepresent, misinterpret.

2. Entice, tempt, corrupt, lead away.

3. Convert, proselyte.

Pervious, *a.* Permeable, penetrable.

Pest, *n.* 1. Plague, pestilence, infection, fatal epidemic, infectious disease.

2. Bane, scourge, curse, infliction, nuisance, trouble, great annoyance, plague.

Pester, *v. t.* Disturb, annoy, harass, provoke, nettle, trouble, plague, vex, tease, hector, harry, molest, bother, worry, fret, gall, bore, incommode, disquiet, infest, torment, badger, chafe, irritate.

Pest-house, *n.* Lazar-house, hospital for contagious diseases, isolation hospital, lazaretto.

Pestiferous, *a.* 1. Pestilential, infectious, contagious, pest-bearing, infected, malignant, morbific.

2. Noxious, mischievous, venomous; vexatious, troublesome, malign, injurious, harmful, deadly, destructive.

Pestilence, *n.* Plague, pest, infectious disease, contagious disease, fatal epidemic.

Pestilent, *a.* 1. Pestilential, contagious, infectious, malignant.

2. Mischievous, noxious, poisonous, evil, injurious, malign, deadly.

3. Troublesome, mischievous, corrupt, annoying, pernicious, vexatious.

Pestilential, *a.* 1. Infectious, contagious, catching, malignant, poisonous, pestilent.

2. Pestiferous, pest-bearing.

3. Mischievous, destructive, ruinous, deadly, pernicious, morally destructive.

Pet, *n.* 1. Fondling, darling, favorite, dear, "duck," cosset.

2. Angry mood, fit of peevishness, "miff," huff, "peeve."

——, *a.* Favorite, especially liked, petted, cherished, fond, cosset, darling.

——, *v. t.* Fondle, indulge, caress, make much of.

Petition, *n.* Request, prayer, supplication, entreaty, suit, solicitation, application, appeal, address.

Petition, *v. t.* Entreat, pray, supplicate, solicit, crave, ask, beg, apply to, make application to, prefer a request to.

Petitioner, *n.* Supplicant, solicitor, applicant, suitor.

Petrify, *v. t.* 1. Change to stone, lapidify, fossilize, calcify, convert to stone.

2. Make callous, make obdurate, benumb, deaden.

3. Astonish, amaze, astound, dumfound, paralyze, confound, stupefy, take by surprise, strike dumb, stun.

Petroleum, *n.* Rock oil, mineral oil, mineral pitch, mineral tar, stone oil, Barbadoes tar, Seneca oil, gasoline, petrol.

Petticoat, *n.* 1. Skirt, woman's skirt, underskirt.

2. Woman, girl.

Pettifogger, *n.* Petty lawyer.

Pettifogging, *n.* Legal tricks, chicanery.

Pettish, *a.* Peevish, fretful, petulant, testy, irascible.

Petty, *a.* Little, small, trifling, trivial, frivolous, inconsiderable, unimportant, insignificant, mean, slight, diminutive, of small moment, of small account.

Petulance, *n.* Peevishness, fretfulness, testiness, waspishness, crustiness, pettishness, snappishness, irritability, ill-temper.

Petulant, *a.* Irascible, irritable, fretful, querulous, peevish, hasty, touchy, testy, crusty, pettish, waspish, choleric, snappish, snarling, cross, crabbed, captious, censorious, acrimonious, perverse, froward, ill-tempered, out of sorts, cavilling, ill-humored.

Pew, *n.* Slip, box, bench, seat.

Phantasm, *n.* 1. Vision (*fancied*), appearance, ghost, spectre, delusion, apparition, phantom, illusion.

2. Idea, notion, fancy.

Phantasmagoria, *n.* 1. Magic lantern, phantasmagory.

2. Illusive images, optical illusions, medley of illusions.

Phantasmal, *a.* Spectral, illusive, dreamy.

Phantom, *n.* Spectre, apparition, vision, phantasm, illusion, ghost, airy spirit, ghost.

Pharisaic, ⎫ *a.* Sanctimonious, hypocriti-
Pharisaical, ⎭ cal, formal, self-righteous.

Pharisaism, *n.* Hypocrisy, formalism, sanctimoniousness, cant, pietism, phariseeism, assumed piety, false piety, self-righteousness.

Pharmaceutist, *n.* Apothecary, pharmacopolist.

Pharmacist, *n.* Druggist.

Phase, *n.* Appearance (*as of the moon* or *a planet*), aspect, phasis, state, condition, guise.

Phenomenon, *n.* [*pl. Phenomena.*] 1. Appearance, manifestation, what is seen (*as distinguished from its essence* or *substance*), occurrence.

2. Prodigy, wonder, marvel, miracle.

Philander, *v. i.* Coquet, flirt, make love triflingly, make a show of love, affect to be in love, play at courtship, pretend admiration, dally.

Philanthropic, ⎫ *a.* Benevolent, kind, be-
Philanthropical, ⎭ nignant, gracious, humane, loving mankind.

Philanthropy, *n.* Humanity, altruism, humanitarianism, love of mankind, general benevolence, good-will to all men, large-heartedness, public-spiritedness; public charity, almsgiving.

Philippic, *n.* Invective, tirade.

Philistine, *n.* Commonplace person, prosaic man, practical man, utilitarian, mediocre person, narrow-minded man; vandal.

Philology, *n.* Study of language, grammatical learning, linguistic science, linguistics.

Philomel, *n.* Nightingale.

Philosopher, *n.* 1. Searcher after truth, student of first principles, seeker of wisdom.

2. Theorist, theorizer, man of abstractions, metaphysician, speculator.

Philosophic, ⎫ *a.* 1. Wise, rational, rea-
Philosophical, ⎭ sonable, sound.

2. Calm, cool, collected, composed, unruffled, sedate, serene, tranquil, imperturbable, stoical, Platonic, making the best of things.

Philosophy, *n.* 1. Science of causes *or* first principles, science of the absolute, the science of sciences.

2. Principles (*of any department of knowledge*), laws.

3. Hypothesis, theory, system, doctrine.

4. Stoicism, practical wisdom, equanimity.

Philter, *n.* Love potion, love charm, magic potion.

Phiz, *n.* (*Colloq.*) Face, visage, countenance, physiognomy, phiznomy.

Phlegm, *n.* 1. Mucus, excrementitious humor.

2. Apathy, insensibility, dulness, indifference, coolness, equanimity, coldness, sluggishness.

Phlegmatic, *a.* Apathetic, stoical, dull, sluggish, calm, inert, tame, cold, frigid, unfeeling, unsusceptible, impassible, impassive, indifferent, cold-blooded, heavy.

Phœbus, *n.* Apollo, Sol, sun, god of day, Helios.

Phœnix, *n.* Paragon, nonesuch, nonpareil; emblem of immortality.

Phonetics, *n.* Phonics, phonology.

Phosphorescent, *a.* Phosphoric, phosphorical, luminescent, luminous, without heat.

Phrase, *n.* 1. Expression (*forming part of a sentence*), brief expression.

2. Idiom, peculiar expression, turn of expression.

3. Style, diction, phraseology, manner of expression, mode of speech.

——, *v. t.* Call, name, style, term, denominate, describe, entitle, designate, christen, dub; divide into melodic phrases.

Phraseology, *n.* Diction, style, phrase, expression, language, manner of expression, mode of speech.

Phrenology, *n.* Craniology, craniognomy.

Phylactery, *n.* Charm, amulet, talisman, spell, phylecter.

Physic, *n.* 1. Medicine, medical art, science of medicine, art of healing.

2. Drug, medicine, remedy, medicament.

3. Cathartic, purge, purgative, drench, drastic, scourer.

——, *v. t.* 1. Purge, drench, scour.

2. Cure, heal, treat with remedies.

PHYSICAL, *a.* 1. Material, natural.

2. Pertaining to physics *or* natural philosophy, natural.

3. External, corporeal, bodily, sensible, tangible, substantial.

Physician, *n.* 1. Doctor, medical man, practitioner, consultant, surgeon.

2. Curer, healer.

Physicist, *n.* Natural philosopher.

Physics, *n.* 1. Science of nature.

2. Natural philosophy, science of energy, dynamics.

Physiognomy, *n.* Face, countenance, visage, configuration, cast of countenance.

Physique, *n.* Physical structure, organization, build, constitution.

Piano, *n.* Pianoforte.

Piazza, *n.* Porch, portico, veranda.

Picaroon, *n.* 1. Rogue, cheat, adventurer.

2. Pirate, corsair, buccaneer, freebooter, marauder, sea-robber, sea-rover, plunderer.

Piccolo, *n.* [It.] Octave flute.

Pick, *v. t.* 1. Peck, pierce, strike at.

2. Pluck, pull off, pick off, detach, pull, cut, gather.

3. Choose, select, cull, single out, pick out, fix upon, pitch upon; find occasion for.

4. Gather up, collect, acquire, get.

——, *v. i.* 1. Nibble, eat slowly.

2. Steal, pilfer.

——, *n.* 1. Pickaxe, tooth-pick, pike, spike.

2. Choice, right of selection, the best.

Picket, *n.* 1. Stake, pale, tether.

2. (*Mil.*) Sentinel (*on the outposts*), guard, detail, watchman, guardsman, sentry.

Picklings, *n. pl.* Refuse, leavings, remnants, remains, odds and ends; pilferings, perquisites.

Pickle, *n.* 1. Salt and water (*for preserving meat*), brine.

2. Vinegar (*for preserving meats* or *vegetables*).

3. (*Colloq.*) Sorry condition, sad plight, predicament, quandary.

Pick off. 1. Pluck, pick, pull off.

2. Kill, wound (*as a marksman*).

Pick out. Select, cull, choose, single out, fix.

Pictorial, *a.* 1. Illustrated.

2. Picturable, picturesque, graphic.

PICTURE, *n.* 1. Painting, drawing, engraving, print.

2. Image, resemblance, semblance, likeness, portrayal, delineation, portraiture, counterpart, copy, embodiment, representation, similitude.

3. Description, representation.

——, *v. t.* Paint, draw, represent, delineate, imagine, form an image of.

Picturesque, *a.* Beautiful, picture-like, scenic, graphic, charming, suggesting a picture.

Piddling, *a.* Trifling, trivial, frivolous, petty, paltry, unimportant, insignificant, immaterial, inconsiderable, worthless, of little value *or* consequence, of no moment.

Piebald, *a.* 1. Motley, mottled, variegated, pied, party-colored, divers-colored.

2. Diversified, mixed, heterogeneous, mongrel.

Piece, *n.* 1. Part, fragment, bit, scrap, hunk, chunk, shred, cut, slice, quantity, amount.

2. Portion.

3. Thing, single object, item.

4. Composition, writing, lucubration, article, literary production, work.

——, *v. t.* 1. Patch, repair, mend.

2. Enlarge, add to, increase, augment, complete.

3. Unite, join, cement.

Piecemeal, *adv.* 1. In pieces, in fragments.

2. Part by part, by pieces, by little and little, by degrees.

Piece-work, *n.* Job-work.

Pied, *a.* Variegated, spotted, party-colored, piebald.

Pierce, *v. t.* 1. Transfix, stab, impale, prick, pink, gore.

2. Penetrate, enter, force a way into.

3. Perforate, drill, bore, puncture.

4. Affect, move, touch, strike, thrill, excite, rouse.

Piercing, *a.*   1. Penetrating, perforating.

2. Sharp, keen, cutting, shrill, discerning, acute, thrilling.

Piety, *n.*   1. Filial reverence.

2. Godliness, religion, devotion, devoutness, holiness, sanctity, grace.

PIG, *n.*   1. Young hog, swine, porker.

2. Pork, swine-flesh.

3. (*Colloq.*)   Glutton.

4. Iron casting.

Piggery, *n.*   Pig-sty, hog-sty, pig-pen.

Piggish, *a.*   Swinish, hoggish, greedy, gluttonous, selfish, filthy.

Pig-headed, *a.*   Obstinate, stupidly obstinate, foolish.

Pigment, *n.*   Paint, color, coloring matter.

Pig-pen, *n.*   Piggery.

Pig-tail, *n.*   1. Tail of a pig.

2. Cue, queue.

3. Rope of tobacco.

Pike, *n.*   1. Spike, point; halberd, spoontoon.

2. Turnpike, toll-bar.

Piked, *a.*   Acuminated, pointed, sharp, spiked.

Pile, *v. t.*   1. Accumulate, amass.

2. Collect *or* gather into a heap, heap up, load up.

——, *n.*   1. Heap, mass, collection, accumulation.

2. Building, edifice, structure, fabric, erection.

3. Nap, woolly surface.

Pilfer, *v. t.*   Steal (*by petty theft*), filch, purloin.

——, *v. i.*   Steal, thieve, practise petty theft.

Pilfering, *n.*   Stealing, thieving, thievery, larceny, petty theft, petty larceny, pilfery.

Pilgrim, *n.*   1. Traveller (*especially on a religious errand*), wanderer, wayfarer, journeyer.

2. Crusader, palmer, devotee.

3. Sojourner, traveller.

Pilgrimage, *n.*   Journey (*especially to some hallowed place*), expedition, tour, excursion; journey of life, earthly sojourn.

Pillage, *n.*   1. Spoliation, depredation, destruction, devastation, plundering, rapine.

2. Plunder, booty, spoil, prey.

——, *v. t.*   Plunder, spoil, despoil, sack, strip, rifle.

Pillar, *n.*   1. Column, columnar mass, pier, shaft, post, stanchion, pilaster.

2. Prop, support, supporter, maintainer, upholder.

Pilot, *n.*   1. Steersman, helmsman.

2. Guide, director, conductor, qualified guide, aviator.

——, *v. t.*   Guide, direct, conduct, steer, have *or* take the direction of.

Pimp, *n.*   Procurer, pander, bawd.

Pimple, *n.*   Blotch, eruption, pustule, wheal, carbuncle.

PIN, *n.*   1. Peg, bolt, dowel, thole, skewer.

2. Straw (*as something of no value*), fig, button, rush, feather, farthing, brass farthing, trifle.

——, *v. t.*   1. Fasten with a pin.

2. Fasten, fix, make fast, hold, bind, secure.

3. Shut up, confine, pen, enclose.

Pinafore, *n.*   Apron.

Pinch, *v. t.*   1. Nip, squeeze, compress, gripe, cramp, contract.

2. Oppress, straiten, distress, afflict, famish, stint.

3. Frost, nip, injure with frost.

4. Press hard, try thoroughly.

5. (*Colloq.*)   Arrest, apprehend.

——, *v. i.*   1. Bear hard.

2. Spare, stint, be niggardly, be parsimonious, be frugal, economize.

——, *n.*   1. Nip, gripe.

2. Gripe, pang, throe.

3. Emergency, exigency, crisis, strait, difficulty, push, pressure, oppression, stress.

4. Crowbar, iron lever.

5. Small quantity.

Pinchbeck, *n.*   Brummagem, sham, alloy.

Pinched, *a.*   Distressed, straitened, reduced, indigent, destitute, needy, poor, necessitous, penniless, moneyless, in need, in want, out of money, out of cash, out of pocket; narrow, thin.

Pinchpenny, *n.*   Miser, niggard, hunks, curmudgeon, skinflint, screw, scrimp.

Pine, *v. i.*   Languish, droop, flag, waste, decay, waste away, wither.

Pinfold, *n.*   [Written also *Penfold*.]   Pound, pen.

Pinguid, *a.*   Fat, unctuous, greasy, adipose, oily, oleaginous.

Pinion, *n.*   1. Wing, pennon.

2. Feather, quill, plume, pen.

3. Fetter (*for the arms*).

——, *v. t.*   Restrain (*by binding the arms*), bind, fasten, shackle, fetter, chain, maim.

Pink, *n.*   1. Rose-color.

2. Paragon, model, perfection, *beau idéal*, extreme.

——, *v. t.*   1. Scallop, embroider.

2. Stab, pierce, wound, perforate.

Pinnacle, *n.*   1. Turret, minaret.

2. Top, summit, apex, acme, zenith, highest point, culminating point, utmost height, peak.

Pin one's faith upon. Believe, put confidence in, trust, rely upon, take at one's word.

Pious, *a.* 1. Filial.

2. Religious, godly, holy, devout, saintly, reverential, righteous.

Pip, *v. i.* Chirp (*as a chicken*), mewl, peep, pipe; break through the shell.

PIPE, *n.* 1. Wind instrument.

2. Tube, conduit, reed.

3. Tobacco-pipe, clay-pipe.

4. Windpipe, trachea, weasand, throttle.

5. Bird-call, whistle.

6. Butt, cask.

——, *v. i.* Play, sound, whistle, sound shrill, sing; equip with pipes.

Piping, *a.* 1. Whining, feeble, sickly, weak.

2. Simmering, boiling, hissing; whistling, singing, playing.

Piquant, *n.* 1. Pungent, biting, pricking, piercing, stinging, high-flavored, high-seasoned, sharp.

2. Racy, lively, sparkling, interesting, stimulating.

3. Sharp, tart, severe, cutting, pointed, pungent, strong, keen.

Pique, *n.* 1. Resentment (*slight*), grudge, umbrage, offence, wounded pride, stinging vexation, displeasure, irritation, spite.

2. Point, nicety, punctilio.

——, *v. t.* 1. Stimulate, incite, urge, instigate, spur, goad, set on, stir up.

2. Offend, displease, affront, provoke, incense, irritate, chafe, nettle, vex, fret, sting, wound, give offence to, give umbrage to, pain.

Piracy, *n.* 1. Robbery on the high seas, sea robbery.

2. Literary theft.

Pirate, *n.* Corsair, buccaneer, privateer, picaroon, marauder, freebooter, sea-robber, sea-rover, sea-dog, sea-wolf.

Piratic,
Piratical, } *a.* Robbing, predatory.

Piscatory, *a.* Angling, fishing.

Piston, *n.* Plunger.

Pit, *n.* 1. Cavity, hollow.

2. Indentation, dent, dint, depression, dimple.

3. Excavation, hole, cavity, hollow, well, crater.

4. Coal-mine, coal-pit.

5. Vat.

6. Gulf, abyss, chasm.

7. [With *The* prefixed.] Hell, Hades, pandemonium, bottomless pit.

8. [With *The* prefixed.] Grave, death.

9. Snare, trap, pitfall.

10. *Parquet, parterre,* auditorium, orchestra.

Pit against. Set to fight (*as cocks in a pit*), set in opposition, match for a contest, set together by the ears.

Pit-a-pat, *adv.* In a flutter, with throbs, with palpitation.

Pitch, *n.* 1. Degree of elevation.

2. Degree, measure, extent, range, rate, intensity, modulation.

3. Height, loftiness, highest rise.

4. Declivity, descent, slope, inclination, degree of slope, degree of inclination.

5. Throw, toss, cast, jerk, plunge.

——, *v. t.* 1. Throw, cast, fling, hurl, toss, plunge, heave, launch, send, dart, lance, jaculate.

2. Set (*as a tent*), fix, plant, place, station, erect, locate, settle, establish.

3. Set, fix (*as price*).

——, *v. i.* 1. Fall, plunge, fall headlong, reel, lurch.

2. Light, settle, rest.

3. Encamp.

4. (*Naut.*) Rise and fall, plunge.

Pitcher, *n.* Jug, jar, pot, ewer.

Pitch upon. Pitch on, choose, select, decide on, determine on, fix upon, fix choice.

Pitchy, *a.* Dark, black, dismal, rayless, sunless, Cimmerian, piceous.

Piteous, *a.* 1. Sorrowful, mournful, woful, doleful, rueful, affecting, distressing, grievous, pathetic, moving pity, exciting compassion.

2. Pitiable, deplorable, wretched, miserable, deserving pity, to be pitied, lamentable.

3. Compassionate, tender.

Pitfall, *n.* Trap, snare, gin, springe, ambush; source of temptation.

Pith, *n.* 1. (*Anat.*) Marrow, spinal cord.

2. Essence, quintessence, substance, core, kernel, gist, soul, chief part, essential part, vital part, heart, marrow.

3. Weight, moment, importance.

4. Force, strength, energy, vigor.

5. Energy, cogency, force, vigor, closeness of thought.

Pithy, *a.* 1. Forcible, powerful, energetic, cogent.

2. Terse, laconic, brief, concise, short, substantial, meaty, compact, pointed, sententious, full of meaning.

3. Porous, corky.

Pitiable, *a.* Deplorable, wretched, lamentable, woful, pathetic, miserable, piteous, deserving pity, to be pitied.

Pitiful, *a.* 1. Compassionate, tender, tender-hearted, sympathetic, kind, merciful, lenient, mild.

2. Miserable, pitiable, piteous, pathetic, wretched, deplorable, lamentable.

3. Mean, base, vile, low, paltry, sorry, abject, rascally, contemptible, despicable, insignificant, disreputable, worthless.

Pitiless, *a.* 1. Merciless, hard-hearted, unmerciful, unpitying, relentless, ruthless, implacable, inexorable, cruel, unfeeling, unsympathizing.

2. Unpitied.

Pittance, *n.* 1. Allowance (*out of pity* or *charity*), alms, dole, allotment, charity, gift.

2. Modicum, trifle, small portion, mite, driblet, insufficiency, small allowance.

Pity, *n.* 1. Compassion, commiseration, mercy, charity, grace, sympathy, fellow-feeling, fellow-suffering, humanity, clemency, leniency, condolence, bowels of compassion, melting mood, tender-heartedness, quarter.

2. Ground of pity, cause of grief, subject of pity.

——, *v. t.* Commiserate, compassionate, sympathize with, feel for, have pity *or* compassion for, feel sorry for, condole with.

Pivot, *v. i.* Turn, hinge, depend.

——, *n.* Turning-point, axis, axle, center, focus, joint, hinge.

Pivotal, *a.* Turning, hinging, depending, axial, central, determining.

Pixie, } *n.* Fairy, elf, sprite, fay, pig-
Pixy, } widgin.

Placability, *n.* Placableness, forgiving disposition.

Placable, *a.* Appeasable, reconcilable, forgiving, pacifiable.

Placard, *n.* Poster, bill, hand-bill, broadside, notice, advertisement.

——, *v. t.* 1. Advertise (*by placards*), publish, announce, blazon, make known, blaze abroad, spread abroad.

2. Post, expose to obloquy.

Placate, *v. t.* Conciliate, appease, pacify.

PLACE, *n.* 1. Area, courtyard, broad way, open space, square.

2. Situation, position, locality, location, part, region, quarter, locale, district, division, bounds, whereabouts, tract, scene, station, spot, site, premises.

3. Office, charge, function, employment, post, pitch, official station, occupation, calling, function.

4. Rank, stakes, standing, station, sphere, standing, grade, condition, occupation, calling; order of importance, precedence.

5. Mansion, residence, abode, dwelling, seat, building, habitation.

6. Town, village, city, etc.

7. Stronghold, fortified post, fort, fortress.

8. Portion, passage, part, paragraph.

9. Point, degree in order.

10. Room, ground, occasion, reason, opportunity.

11. Stead, lieu, room.

——, *v. t.* 1. Put, pose, set, station, situate, rest, stand, pitch, install, plant, lodge, lay, settle, deposit, commit, locate, seat, fix, establish, dispose, bestow, arrange; orient, orientate; locate, classify, class, identify, recognize, localize, allocate, order, arrange, organize.

2. Invest, put at interest, lend, lay out.

3. Appoint, set, induct, establish in office; berth, billet, "put up," assign, nominate, commission.

4. Attribute, ascribe, impute.

Placid, *a.* 1. Quiet, tranquil, undisturbed, unmoved, unruffled, calm, peaceful, serene, composed, collected, cool, gentle, equable, unexcitable.

2. Serene, mild, unruffled, halcyon.

Placidity, *n.* Calmness, quietness, serenity, composure, coolness, tranquillity, imperturbability, mildness, gentleness, peacefulness, placidness.

Placket, *n.* Fent, opening, slit.

Plagiarism, *n.* 1. Literary theft.

2. Stolen idea, thought, expression, *or* passage.

Plague, *n.* 1. Pestilence, pest, disease.

2. Affliction, annoyance, vexation, trouble, nuisance, curse, torment, thorn in one's side.

——, *v. t.* Annoy, tease, vex, worry, trouble, molest, torment, harass, harry, disturb, fret, gall, chafe, bore, incommode, bother, pester, badger, hector, irritate, disquiet, distress, afflict, tantalize, embarrass, perplex.

Plaguy, *a.* (*Colloq.*) Vexatious, troublesome, tormenting, annoying, wearisome.

Plain, *a.* 1. Even, level, smooth, flat, plane, dull, uniform; campestral, champaign.

2. Open, clear, unencumbered, uninterrupted.

3. Manifest, visible, obvious, clear, unmistakable, apparent, certain, palpable, conspicuous, notable, notorious, glaring, patent, open, evident, distinct.

4. Unequivocal, unambiguous, distinct, explicit, intelligible, perspicuous.

5. Homely, ugly, ill-looking, ill-favored.

6. Honest, sincere, candid, frank, open, downright, direct, unsophisticated, ingenuous, undesigning, straightforward, single-minded, open-hearted, aboveboard, unreserved, crude, blunt.

7. Artless, simple, unlearned, unsophisticated, natural, unaffected, homely,
common.

8. Mere, absolute, unmistakable.

9. Easy, direct, clear.

10. Simple, frugal, homely.

11. Unornamented, unfigured, unvarie-
gated, unadorned.

Plain, *n.* Plateau, level, lowland, prairie,
champaign, table-land, champaign country.

Plain-dealing, *n.* Honesty, sincerity, frankness, candor, ingenuousness, openness,
truthfulness, plainness, straightforwardness, bluntness.

Plainly, *adv.* 1. Honestly, sincerely, blunt-
ly, candidly, point-blank, in common
parlance.

2. Evidently, clearly, distinctly, unmistakably.

3. Soberly, quietly, simply.

Plain-spoken, *a.* Frank, candid, blunt,
open, free-spoken, plain of speech.

Plaint, *n.* 1. Lamentation, lament, moan,
wail, cry, complaint.

2. Complaint.

Plaintiff, *n.* Accuser, prosecutor.

Plaintive, *a.* Mournful, sorrowful, sad,
piteous, woful, rueful, grievous, dirgelike, melancholy.

Plait, *n.* 1. Fold, doubling, double, gather.

2. Braid.

——, *v. t.* 1. Fold, double.

2. Braid, plat, weave, interweave.

3. Mat, felt.

Plaited, *a.* 1. Folded, braided, interwoven.

2. Wrinkled, contracted, knitted.

Plan, *n.* 1. Draught, sketch, plot, drawing, map, diagram, chart, delineation,
"layout."

2. Scheme, project, system, method,
device, design, contrivance, proposal,
proposition, idea, conception, program,
arrangement, system, line; intrigue,
cabal, machination, conspiracy, "racket."

3. Method, process, way, custom.

——, *v. t.* 1. Delineate, figure, represent,
diagram, arrange, study, provide for,
concert, calculate, project, premeditate,
devise, mark out, chalk out, sketch
out.

2. Devise, contrive, scheme, project,
plot, manœuvre, conspire, machinate,
invent, design, concoct, digest, lay out,
block out, shape; prepare, hatch.

PLANE, *n.* 1. Paring tool.

2. Even surface, flat, level, stratum.

Plane, *a.* Level, flat, even, smooth,
plain.

Planetarium, *n.* Orrery.

PLANT, *n.* 1. Vegetable, organism, herb.

2. Equipment, factory, establishment,
"works."

3. Snare, trick, hoax, trap.

Plant, *v. t.* 1. Put in the ground (*as seed*),
sow.

2. Set in the ground (*as a shrub*), implant, bed.

3. Engender, breed.

4. Set, direct, point.

5. Settle, furnish inhabitants to.

6. Introduce, establish.

7. Fix, establish, settle, found, hide,
deposit.

——, *v. i.* Sow, scatter seed, put in seed.

Plaque, *n.* 1. Brooch, ornamental plate,
plate of a clasp.

2. Flat plate of metal, enamelled
plate.

Plash, *v. t.* Dash, spatter.

——, *v. i.* Splash, dabble in water.

——, *n.* 1. Dash, splash.

2. Puddle, pool, collection of standing
water, pond.

Plaster, *n.* Mortar, stucco, cement, parget.

——, *v. t.* 1. Parget, cover with plaster.

2. (*Colloq.*) Bedaub, smear, lay on
coarsely.

Plastic, *a.* 1. Formative.

2. Soft, pliable, easily moulded, ductile, pliant.

Plat, *n.* Plot, piece of ground, diagram,
map.

PLATE, *n.* 1. Lamina, layer, sheet, paten,
plaque, slab, tile; coat, coating, veneer.

2. Dish, platter, silverware.

Plateau, *n.* 1. Plain (*elevated*), table-land,
highland, platform.

2. Twisted silver-wire.

Platitude, *n.* 1. Insipidity, flatness, dulness, mawkishness.

2. Truism, trite remark, commonplace,
banality.

3. Twaddle, verbiage, palaver, trash,
chatter, stuff, fudge, nonsense, moonshine, flummery, wish-wash, balderdash,
jargon, senseless prate, frothy discourse,
idle talk.

Platonic, *a.* 1. Academic, of Plato.

2. Contemplative, speculative, philosophical, theoretical.

3. Passionless, impassible, unimpressible, cold, apathetic, cool, calm, serene.

Platter, *n.* Large dish, plate, charger,
trencher.

Plaudit, *n.* Applause, acclamation, clapping
of hands, acclaim, shout of approbation,
encomium, approbation.

Plausible, *a.* 1. Specious, colorable, seemingly fair, probable, reasonable, credible.

2. Fair-spoken, glib, using specious
arguments, smooth, suave, bland.

Play, *v. i.* 1. Sport, disport, frolic, skip, frisk, gambol, revel, romp, caper, make merry, make fun.

2. Trifle, toy, wanton, dally, idle, flirt.

3. Hover, flutter, sport, wave.

4. Game, gambler.

5. Act (*on the stage*), take a part, personate a character, represent, impersonate.

6. Perform, execute.

7. Act, operate, work freely, move.

8. Do, act, behave.

——, *v. t.* 1. Put in action, put in operation.

2. Perform, execute.

3. Put down, exhibit, use in playing, move.

4. Compete, engage in play.

5. Perform on, play on *or* upon.

6. Act (*on the stage*), enact, represent, exhibit, perform.

7. Personate, act the part of, take the part of.

8. Engage in, take part in.

9. Do, perform, execute.

PLAY, *n.* 1. Game.

2. Amusement, sport, frolic, gambols, jest, romp, prank, pastime.

3. Gaming, gambling.

4. Practice, use, manner of dealing.

5. Action, use, employment.

6. Dramatic composition, drama, comedy, tragedy, melodrama *or* farce.

7. Performance.

8. Motion, movement, action.

9. Liberty of action, scope, swing, elbow-room, range, latitude, sweep, freedom, opportunity.

Player, *n.* 1. Actor, play-actor, stage-player, mimic, imitator, mime.

2. Performer, operator, instrumentalist.

Playful, *a.* 1. Sportive, frolicsome, frisky, rollicking, kittenish, merry, mirthful, jolly, gamesome.

2. Sprightly, humorous, amusing, arch, lively, roguish, jolly, mirthful, vivacious.

Playhouse, *n.* Theatre, opera-house.

Playmate, *n.* Playfellow, comrade.

Play on. } 1. Mock, deride, delude, be-
Play upon. } fool, trifle with, make sport of.

2. Turn, quibble, give a fanciful turn to.

Plaything, *n.* Toy, bawble, trifle, sport, doll, bagatelle.

Play upon words. Punning, quibbling.

Play-writer, *n.* Dramatist, playwright, dramatic author, dramatic writer.

Plea, *n.* 1. (*Law.*) Allegation.

2. Suit, action, cause in court.

3. Defence, excuse, apology, justification, claim, appeal, vindication, argument, pleading; pretext, claim, ostensible reason.

4. Entreaty, prayer, call, cry, request, petition, intercession.

Plead, *v. i.* 1. (*Law.*) Make an allegation, carry on a suit.

2. Reason, argue, offer reasons, use arguments, appeal, answer.

3. Apologize, offer apology *or* justification, make defence.

——, *v. t.* 1. Allege, offer in excuse.

2. Argue, discuss, defend, maintain by arguments, reason, rejoin.

3. Entreat, beg, sue, petition, beseech, supplicate, implore, appeal.

Plead guilty. Confess guilt, acknowledge the charge, own the soft impeachment, cry *peccavi*, make a clean breast of it.

Pleasant, *a.* 1. Pleasing, agreeable, delightful, enjoyable, prepossessing, nice, seemly, gratifying, delectable, grateful, pleasurable, acceptable, welcome.

2. Cheerful, gay, lively, sprightly, vivacious, likable, gracious, merry, good-humored, enlivening, sportive.

3. Witty, facetious, humorous, jocose, jocular, sportive, amusing.

Pleasantry, *n.* 1. Gayety, merriment, sport, fun, frolic, jollity.

2. Facetiousness, jocularity, jocoseness, drollery, good-humor, waggery.

3. Lively *or* witty remark, witticism, joke, banter, badinage, persiflage, sally, sprightly saying, jest, quip, quirk, *bon mot.*

4. Raillery, wit, lively talk.

5. Trick, gambol, frolic, prank.

PLEASE, *v. t.* [*The noun is Basic Eng.*] 1. Gratify, delight, gladden, rejoice, pleasure, charm, elate, make glad, give joy to, take one's fancy, tickle one's fancy, do one's heart good.

2. Satisfy, content, oblige.

3. Seem good to, be one's will.

——, *v. i.* 1. Give pleasure, gain approbation.

2. Like, prefer, choose.

3. Condescend, comply, be pleased.

Pleasing, *a.* Agreeable, grateful, gratifying, acceptable, welcome, pleasant, delectable, pleasurable, charming, delightful.

PLEASURE, *n.* 1. Enjoyment, gratification, comfort, delight, joy, gladness, temporary happiness, pleasance, joyance, delectation, elation, cheer, relish, gusto, exhilaration, satisfaction, solace; treat, entertainment, diversion, refreshment, amusement, indulgence.

2. Sensuality, voluptuousness, luxury, animal gratification.

3. Will, choice, preference, purpose, wish, mind, desire.

4. Favor, kindness.

Plebeian, *a.* Ignoble, low, mean, base, vulgar, lowborn, obscure, common, popular.

Pledge, *n.* 1. Pawn, gage, deposit, collateral.

2. Guarantee, security, earnest.

3. Surety, hostage.

4. Health (*in drinking*).

——, *v. t.* 1. Pawn, impawn, plight, mortgage, hypothecate, put in pledge, deposit as security.

2. Gage, give as a guarantee.

3. Engage, bind, plight, promise, contract, affiance.

4. Toast, drink to, drink the health of, drink in honor of.

Plenary, *a.* Full, complete, entire, absolute.

Plenipotentiary, *n.* Ambassador, minister, envoy.

Plenitude, *n.* 1. Abundance, fulness, completeness, plenty.

2. Repletion, plethora, animal fulness.

Plentiful, *a.* 1. Abundant, ample, copious, full, enough, sufficient, plethoric, plenteous.

2. Fruitful, plenteous, exuberant, productive, luxuriant.

Plenty, *n.* 1. Fulness, sufficiency, plenitude, amplitude, enough, adequate supply.

2. Abundance, copiousness, luxuriance, exuberance, profusion, affluence, fertility, overflow.

Pleonasm, *n.* Redundancy, diffuseness, tautology, prolixity, redundant expression.

Pleonastic, *a.* Redundant, tautological, diffuse, verbose, circumlocutory, wordy, superfluous.

Plethora, *n.* 1. (*Med.*) Fulness (*of blood*), repletion, plenitude.

2. Superabundance, superfluity, redundance, redundancy, excess, surfeit, more than enough, enough and to spare.

Pliable, *a.* 1. Flexible, flexile, pliant, supple, limber, lithe, lithesome, easily bent.

2. Compliant, yielding, manageable, tractable, adaptable, easily persuaded, docile, obsequious, ductile, facile.

Pliancy, *n.* 1. Pliability. See *adj.* 1 above.

2. Docility, readiness to be influenced, ductility.

Plicature, *n.* Fold, doubling, double, plait, gather, plication.

Plight, *v. t.* Pledge, pawn, hypothecate, put in pledge, give as security.

——, *n.* 1. Pledge, pawn, gage, security, word ; betrothal, affiancing.

2. Condition, state, situation, case, predicament, category, dilemma, "scrape."

Plod, *v. i.* 1. Trudge, jog on lumber, travel slowly but steadily.

2. Toil, drudge, moil, hold on, keep on, persist, persevere, keep at it, work hard.

Plodding, *a.* Hard-working, patiently laborious, diligent, pedestrian, painstaking, industrious.

Plot, *n.* 1. Plat, piece of ground, patch, field.

2. Plan (*of a piece of land*), draught, sketch, skeleton, scenario, diagram, outline.

3. Scheme (*especially for a bad purpose*), stratagem, conspiracy, intrigue, cabal, machination, plan, project, combination.

4. Story, intrigue.

5. Contrivance, reach of thought, ability to plot.

——, *v. i.* Plan (*for some mischief*), conspire, scheme, contrive, lay a plan, form a plot, machinate.

——, *v. t.* Plan (*as something mischievous*), concoct, contrive, project, devise, frame, brew, hatch, compass.

Plotter, *n.* Contriver, conspirator, schemer.

PLOUGH, *v. t.* [*The noun is Basic Eng.*] Till.

Pluck, *v. t.* 1. Gather, pick, cull.

2. Pull (*quickly*), twitch, snatch, jerk, yerk, tug, tear.

3. Pull, draw.

4. Strip by plucking.

——, *n.* (*Colloq.*) Spirit, courage, resolution, bravery, daring, manhood, indomitableness, backbone, determination, energy, force, mettle, nerve, hardihood, heroism, valor, grit, force of character, strength of will.

Plucky, *a.* (*Colloq.*) Brave, spirited, courageous.

Plug, *n.* 1. Stopple, stopper, cork, wadding.

2. Chew, quid.

Plumage, *n.* Feathers, down.

Plumb, *a.* Perpendicular (*to the horizon*), vertical, upright.

Plumbing, *n.* Plumbery.

Plume, *n.* Feather, plumage, aigrette, quill, panache, crest, tuft.

Plumose, *a.* Feathery.

Plump, *a.* 1. Stout, portly, fat, bouncing, chubby, rotund, embonpoint, full-figured, corpulent, obese, fleshy, round, bonny, burly, in good case, buxom, sleek, well-rounded.

2. Tumid, swollen, distended, full.

3. Complete, full, downright, direct, unqualified, blunt, unreserved.

Plump, *adv.* Suddenly, heavily, directly.

Plunder, *v. t.* Pillage, spoil, despoil, rob, rifle, harry, devastate, loot, desolate, maraud, ransack, raid, ravage, spoliate, free boot, forage, sack, fleece, strip, lay waste.

——, *n.* 1. Robbery, rapine, ravin, sack, harrying, freebooting, devastation, marauding; stolen goods, booty, spoil, pillage, prey.

2. [*Southern and Western U. S.*] Baggage, luggage, goods, effects.

Plunge, *v. t.* Immerse, submerge, dip, souse, sink, thrust, douse, put under water (*or other liquid*).

——, *v. i.* Dive, pitch, thrust one's self, descend suddenly, gamble, swoop, drop, "take a header," cast one's self.

Plus, *adv.* [L.] More, in addition.

Plutonian, ⎫ *a.* Subterranean, dark, infer-
Plutonic, ⎭ nal.

Pluvial, *a.* Rainy, humid, pluvious.

Ply, *v. t.* 1. Employ, apply, keep busy, exert, work at, use, wield, manipulate.

2. Exercise, practise, put in practice.

3. Press hard, beset, assail briskly, lay on, assail, belabor.

4. Urge, solicit, importune.

5. Offer repeatedly, present urgently, urge upon, press upon.

——, *n.* 1. Fold, plait, twist, layer.

2. Bent, turn, direction, bias.

Pneumonic, *a.* Pulmonic, pulmonary.

Poach, *v. t.* 1. Cook slightly (*as eggs*).

2. Steal, filch, purloin, pilfer, plunder by stealth.

——, *v. i.* Steal game.

Pock, *n.* Pustule (*as of small-pox*).

POCKET, *n.* Pouch, cavity, hollow, receptacle, cul-de-sac.

——, *v. t.* (*Colloq.*) Endure (*as an affront*), suffer, bear, tolerate, put up with; appropriate, steal.

Pod, *n.* Legume, capsule, seed-vessel, hull, skin.

Podgy, *a.* Dumpy, fat, pudgy.

Podium, *n.* Stylobate, continuous pedestal.

Poem, *n.* Metrical composition, piece of poetry; ballad, lyric, ode, sonnet, etc.

Poesy, *n.* 1. Poet craft, poet skill.

2. Poetry, verse, metrical composition.

Poet, *n.* 1. Bard, author of poems, maker, versifier, poetaster, rhymer.

2. Imaginative thinker *or* writer.

Poetaster, *n.* Rhymester, petty poet, inferior poet.

Poetic, ⎫ *a.* 1. Metrical.
Poetical, ⎭ 2. Imaginative, idyllic.

Poetry, *n.* Verse, rhyme, poesy, poetics, song, metrical composition, numbers.

Poignancy, *n.* 1. Piquancy, pungency, acridity, sharpness.

2. Point, sharpness, keenness, asperity, causticity.

3. Bitterness, intensity, sharpness.

Poignant, *a.* 1. Sharp, severe, piercing, penetrating, intense, bitter.

2. Pungent, biting, acrid, piquant, sharp, pricking, stinging, mordacious.

3. Keen, pointed, caustic, irritating, bitter, satirical, sarcastic, severe, mordant.

POINT, *n.* 1. Sharp end, spike, pin, needle, stylus, prong, nib, tine, tip, apex.

2. Cape, headland, projection, promontory, naze.

3. Moment, instant, period, verge, eve.

4. Spot, place, station, stage, site.

5. Degree, grade, state, condition, rank.

6. Object, end, aim, purpose, design, limit, period, intent.

7. Punctilio, nicety, pique, trifling concern.

8. Question, position, thesis, theme, proposition, text, subject-matter, moot point, case, point at issue.

9. Respect, particular aspect, matter, single thing.

10. Characteristic, peculiarity, salient trait.

11. Mark (*as of punctuation*), character, stop.

12. Dot, speck, jot.

13. Sally, witticism, flash of wit, lively turn of thought, epigram, quip, quirk, *jeu d'esprit.*

14. Poignancy, sting.

——, *v. t.* 1. Sharpen, make pointed, acuminate.

2. Aim, level, direct.

3. Indicate, designate, show, point out, direct attention to.

4. Punctuate.

Point-blank, *adv.* Direct, plainly, explicitly, expressly.

Pointed, *a.* 1. Peaked, sharp, acuminated, picked.

2. Personal, distinct, marked, explicit.

3. Epigrammatic, keen, poignant.

Pointer, *n.* Index, hand, director, finger, tip.

Pointless, *a.* 1. Blunt, obtuse.

2. Dull, stupid, vapid, aimless, vague, flat.

Poise, *n.* 1. Weight, gravity.

2. Counterweight, counterpoise.

3. Regulating power, balance.

4. Balance, equilibrium, equipoise, carriage.

5. Self-possession, equanimity, composure.

Poise, *v. t.*   1. Balance, hold *or* place in equilibrium.

2. Weight.

POISON, *n.*   Venom, virus, bane, pest, taint, noxious influence, virulence, toxin, contagion.

Poison, *v. t.*   Infect, taint, contaminate, corrupt, canker, mar, impair, vitiate, envenom, pollute, intoxicate, defile; embitter.

Poisonous, *a.*   Venomous, noxious, baneful, pestilential, pestiferous.

Poke, *n.*   1. Thrust, push, shove, jog.

2. Pocket, pouch, bag, sack.

——, *v. t.*   Push, thrust, jab, punch, prod, nudge.

——, *v. i.*   1. Grope, feel one's way.

2. Mope, shut one's self up, confine one's self, dawdle, trifle, delay.

Poke fun at.   (*Colloq.*)   Jeer, ridicule, deride, flout, taunt, mock, scoff at, sneer at, jeer at, rail at, make a butt of.

Poky, *a.*   Confined, cramped, musty; slow, tedious.

Pole, *n.*   1. Extremity (*of an axis or a diameter*), terminal point; hub, pivot, axis.

2. Staff, rod, stick, mast, post.

3. Rod, perch.

4. Shaft, thill, pile.

5. Polander, native of Poland.

6. See POLESTAR.

7. Firmament, sky.

Polemic,) *a.*   1. Controversial, disputa-
Polemical,)   tive.

2. Disputatious, contentious.

Polemic,) *n.*   Disputant, controversialist.
Polemist,)

Polemics, *n. pl.*   Controversy (*especially on theological subjects*), disputation, contest.

Polestar, *n.*   1. North star, polar star, loadstar, Polaris.

2. Guide, cynosure, guiding star.

Policy, *n.*   1. Administration, management, government, rule, mode of management, course of action; plank, platform, plan, rôle.

2. Cunning, art, address, skill, prudence, expediency, shrewdness, worldly wisdom, stratagem, strategy, tactics, discretion.

3. Wisdom, wit, acumen, shrewdness, astuteness.

Polish, *v. t.*   1. Burnish, furbish, levigate, scour, rub up, brighten, make glossy, shine, smooth, glaze, buff.

2. Refine, civilize, make elegant.

POLISH, *n.*   1. Lustre, brightness, brilliance, brilliancy, splendor.

2. Grace, refinement, accomplishment, elegance.

Polished, *a.*   1. Burnished, made bright *or* glossy, lustrous, smooth, glossy, bright, shining.

2. Refined, accomplished, cultivated, elegant, polite.

3. Classic, classical, Attic, chaste, pure, refined, elegant, finished.

Polite, *a.*   Accomplished, genteel, cultivated, gentle, gentlemanly, chivalrous, gallant, suave, refined, courteous, civil, affable, complaisant, courtly, gracious, urbane, polished, well-behaved, well-mannered, mannerly, well-bred, elegant, obliging, attentive.

Politeness, *n.*   1. Courtesy, civility, good manners, courteousness, gentility, affability, complaisance, comity, amenity, suavity, decorum, good-breeding, obliging manner, refinement, urbanity, courtliness.

2. Refinement, elegance, finish.

Politic, *a.*   1. Civil, political, civic.

2. Wise, prudent, judicious, discreet, non-committal, sagacious, prudential, wary, provident, astute, long-headed.

3. Artful, cunning, shrewd, intriguing, sly, expedient, time-serving, wily, subtle, foxy, Machiavelian, ingenious, unscrupulous, crafty, skilful, diplomatic, strategic.

4. Well-devised, well-adapted.

POLITICAL, *a.*   Civil, civic, public, politic, national.

Politician, *n.*   1. Statesman, statist.

2. Partisan, dabbler in politics.

Politics, *n. pl.*   1. Political science, political economy, science of government.

2. Political affairs, party politics.

Polity, *n.*   Form of government, civil constitution.

Poll, *n.*   1. Head, skull, cranium.

2. Person, individual.

3. Catalogue of heads, catalogue of persons, list, voting list, register.

4. Club, cheven, pollard.

5. Election, ballot.

——, *v. t.*   1. Lop, clip, shear, cut closely, mow, crop.

2. Enumerate, enroll, list.

3. Register, give, deposit (*as a vote*).

Polliwog, *n.*   Tadpole.

Poll-tax, *n.*   Capitation tax, poll-money, poll-silver.

Pollute, *v. t.*   1. Defile, soil, taint, make foul, make unclean.

2. Corrupt, infect, contaminate, vitiate, demoralize, deprave, debase, poison, impair, taint, pervert, tarnish, stain.

3. Desecrate, profane.

4. Violate, debauch, dishonor, ravish, abuse, defile, deflower.

Pollution, *n.* 1. Defilement, contamination, foulness, taint, impurity, uncleanness, abomination, pollutedness, vitiation, corruption.

2. Violation, debauchment, ravishment.

Poltroon, *n.* Coward, dastard, craven, milksop, mean wretch, skulk, recreant, sneak.

Poltroonery, *n.* Cowardice, baseness, dastardy, dastardliness, cowardliness, want of spirit.

Polygamy, *n.* 1. Plurality of wives, polygyny.

2. Polyandry, plurality of husbands.

Pomade, *n.* Pomatum.

Pommel, *n.* [Written also *Pummel.*] Knob, ball, protuberant part.

——, *v. t.* [Written also *Pummel.*] Beat, bruise, thrash, flog, bang, maul, thwack, thump, drub, pound, belabor, trounce.

Pomp, *n.* Parade, display, show, splendor, magnificence, pageantry, pageant, flourish, state, style, pride, ostentation, pompousness, grandeur.

Pomposity, *n.* Boastfulness, boasting, pretension, ostentation, pompousness, parade.

Pompous, *a.* 1. Showy, ostentatious, stately, lofty, grand, majestic, magnificent, superb, splendid, august, magisterial, dignified, self-important, vainglorious.

2. Swelling, inflated, bombastic, turgid, pretentious, stilted, boastful, grandiloquent, high-flowing, high-sounding, high-flown, ostentatious, arrogant, tumid, grandiose, magniloquent, flaunting, puffy.

Pompousness, *n.* 1. Grandeur, magnificence, pageantry, splendor, state, pomp, dignity.

2. Pretension, boastfulness, ostentation, pomposity.

Ponder, *v. t.* Consider, weigh, contemplate, muse, study, meditate, think on, reflect upon, deliberate upon, revolve in the mind, examine.

——, *v. i.* Think, muse, reflect, cogitate, meditate, study, deliberate.

Ponderosity, *n.* Weight, gravity, heaviness, ponderousness.

Ponderous, *a.* 1. Heavy, weighty, massive, bulky; labored, dull, slow-moving.

2. Momentous, important, weighty.

3. Forcible, mighty.

Poniard, *n.* Dagger (*small*), dirk, stiletto.

Pontiff, *n.* 1. High-priest.

2. Pope, bishop of Rome, *Pontifex Maximus.*

Pontifical, *a.* Popish, papal.

Pontificate, *n.* Popedom, papacy.

——, *v. i.* Pronounce judgment, play the pontiff.

Pony, *n.* 1. Sheltie, small horse, Shetland.

2. "Crib," "trot."

Pooh, *interj.* Poh, pshaw, pish, pah.

Pool, *n.* 1. Pond (*small*), mere, lake, loch, tarn, reservoir.

2. Puddle, plash, collection of standing water.

——, *v. t.* Combine, merge, contribute.

POOR, *a.* 1. Indigent, needy, necessitous, pinched, straitened.

2. Penniless, moneyless, impecunious, destitute, distressed, poverty-stricken, seedy, reduced, insolvent, short of money, out of money, without a penny, out of pocket, out of cash, out at the elbows, out at the heels, in need, in want, "hard up," in distress, living from hand to mouth, not worth a farthing, not worth a sou, badly off.

3. Emaciated, lean, thin, meagre, lank, gaunt, spare, underfed, skinny, shrunk, fallen away.

4. Barren, sterile, unfruitful, unfertile, unproductive, fruitless, unprolific.

5. Trifling, trivial, slight, small, slender, flimsy, insufficient, inadequate, worthless, unimportant, of little use *or* worth, valueless, paltry, insignificant.

6. Unsound, infirm, feeble, delicate, weak, frail.

7. Shabby, seedy, worthless, valueless, inferior, not good, below par.

8. Contemptible, despicable, paltry, mean, humble, sorry, beggarly, pitiful, shabby, bad, low, inferior.

9. Feeble, languid, weak, bald, tame, jejune, vapid, cold, frigid, dull, prosing, prosy, prosaic, spiritless, barren, mean, meagre, dry.

10. Miserable, wretched, unfortunate, luckless, ill-fated, ill-starred, unlucky, unhappy, pitiable.

11. Meagre, insufficient, inadequate, scant, deficient, imperfect, small.

12. Faulty, unsatisfactory.

13. Thin, scanty.

14. Weak, feeble, poor, flimsy.

Poorhouse, *n.* Workhouse, almshouse.

Poorly, *a.* (*Colloq.*) Indisposed, ailing, not well, feeble, somewhat ill.

Pop, *n.* Report, clap, burst, explosion, detonation, crack.

——, *v. t.* Crack, explode.

Pope, *n.* Pontiff, bishop of Rome, *Pontifex Maximus,* high priest.

Popedom, *n.* 1. Papacy, pontificate.

2. Papal jurisdiction, apostolic see.

Popery, *n.* Papism, papistry, Roman Catholic religion.

Popinjay, *n.* Fop, coxcomb, dandy, exquisite, beau, macaroni, jackanapes, jack-a-dandy, man milliner, man of dress; vain, showy fellow, *petit-maître.*

Popish, *a.* Papistic, papistical, Roman Catholic.

Populace, *n.* Commonalty, the people, the crowd, the multitude, the many, the masses, the million, the vulgar herd, the common people, proletariat, the lower classes, the vulgar, the humbler classes, mob, rabble.

Popular, *a.* 1. Of the people, public, lay, plebeian.

2. Plain, familiar, easy, comprehensible.

3. Received (*by the people*), accepted, acceptable, pleasing, praised, admired, accredited, favorite, liked, approved.

4. Current, prevailing, prevalent, common, general, in vogue, in favor; cheap, inexpensive.

Popularity, *n.* 1. Favor (*of the people*), popular regard *or* acceptance, popularness.

2. Fame, repute, celebrity, vogue.

Populate, *v. t.* People.

Population, *n.* 1. Peopling.

2. Inhabitants, people, number of people, nation, race.

3. Populousness.

Populous, *a.* Crowded, thickly settled.

Porcelain, *n.* China, china ware.

Porch, *n.* 1. Portico, entrance-way, vestibule, stoop, Galilee, gallery, veranda, piazza, entrance.

2. [With *The* prefixed.] The Stoic philosophy, philosophy of Zeno, school of the Stoics.

Porcine, *a.* 1. Pertaining to swine.

2. Hog-like, swinish.

Pore, *n.* Orifice, spiracle, small opening.

——, *v. i.* Brood, dwell, look steadily, gaze, fix the attention, give one's mind, consider, read steadily, examine diligently.

Pork, *n.* Swine-flesh, pig-meat.

Porker, *n.* Hog, pig, sow, swine, porkling.

Porosity, *n.* Porousness.

Porous, *a.* Pervious, permeable, penetrable, percolable, pory, holey, open, honeycombed, perforated; sandy, light, loose.

Porpoise, *n.* 1. Sea-hog.

2. Monster, mammoth, behemoth, mountain, leviathan, Triton among the minnows.

Porridge, *n.* Broth, soup, pottage, gruel, pap, mush.

Port, *n.* 1. Harbor, haven, roadstead, anchorage, shelter.

2. Entrance, passage-way, gate door.

3. Embrasure, port-hole.

4. Larboard, left side.

5. Demeanor, behavior, bearing, air, presence, mien, carriage, deportment, appearance.

Portable, *a.* Movable, light, handy, convenient, portative, transmissible, easily transported, manageable.

Portal, *n.* Gate, gateway, entrance, passage-way, door, entry, entrance.

Portend, *v. t.* Presage, forebode, foretoken, betoken, foreshow, foreshadow, augur, prognosticate, threaten, indicate, bode, signify.

Portent, *n.* Omen (*of ill*), presage, prognostic, augury, sign, warning; wonder, marvel, phenomenon.

Portentous, *a.* 1. Ominous (*of ill*), premonitory, ill-boding, inauspicious, unpropitious, significant.

2. Monstrous, prodigious, wonderful, amazing, tremendous, stupendous, marvellous, extraordinary.

PORTER, *n.* 1. Carrier, bearer, "red cap."

2. Door-keeper, gate-keeper; warder, sentinel, guard, *concierge.*

Port-hole, *n.* Embrasure, port.

Portico, *n.* 1. Covered walk, colonnade, arcade.

2. Porch, vestibule, entrance-way.

Portière, *n.* Door-curtain.

Portion, *n.* 1. Part, piece, fragment, bit, scrap, section, morsel.

2. Share, allotment, division, parcel, lot, ration, measure, quantity, dividend, quota, contingent.

3. Fate, final state.

4. Dowry, wife's fortune.

5. Share, inheritance.

——, *v. t.* 1. Divide, allot, deal out, distribute, parcel.

2. Endow, supply with a portion.

Portly, *a.* 1. Stately, grand, majestic, magisterial, dignified, imposing.

2. Stout, plump, fleshy, round, in good case, corpulent, large, bulky, burly.

Portmanteau, *n.* Valise, travelling bag, Gladstone.

Portrait, *n.* Representation (*of a face* or *a person, drawn* or *painted*), description, likeness, portraiture, picture.

Portray, *v. t.* 1. Paint, delineate, depict, draw, act, sketch, represent.

2. Describe, set forth.

Portrayal, *n.* 1. Delineation, painting, representation, sketch.

2. Description, account.

Pose, *n.* Attitude (*formally assumed*), posture, artificial position.

——, *v. t.* Puzzle, stagger, embarrass, bewilder, perplex, mystify, nonplus, put out, put to a stand, confound, dumfound, place, set, arrange.

——, *v. i.* Attitudinize, affect.

Poser, *n.* 1. Puzzler, close examiner.

2. Riddle, enigma, mystery, knotty point.

POSITION, *n.* 1. Station, situation, spot, place, locality, post, site.

2. Relation.

3. Attitude, posture, bearing.

4. Proposition, principle, thesis, dictum, assertion, doctrine, predication, affirmation.

5. Place, standing, social rank, dignity, honor; caste, status.

6. State, condition, place, circumstances, phase.

7. Place, situation, post, berth, billet, incumbency, office, job.

Positive, *a.* 1. Express, direct, explicit, determinate, defined, precise, definite, clear, unequivocal, unmistakable, unqualified, categorical, expressed, laid down.

2. Real, actual, veritable, substantial, true, absolute, existing in fact.

3. Absolute, not relative.

4. Confident, sure, assured, certain, fully convinced.

5. Indisputable, decisive, incontrovertible, inescapable, indubitable.

6. Decisive, unconditional, imperative.

7. Dogmatic, stubborn, peremptory, obstinate, decided, emphatic, over-confident, tenacious, overbearing.

Positively, *adv.* 1. Expressly, explicitly, precisely, categorically, definitely, directly.

2. Actually, really, truly, in fact, in reality.

3. Absolutely.

4. Really, directly, inherently.

5. Certainly, surely, assuredly, confidently.

6. Certainly, indubitably, assuredly.

7. Peremptorily, dogmatically, arbitrarily.

Possess, *v. t.* 1. Own, have a title to, be seized of.

2. Have, hold, keep, occupy, control, command.

3. Put in possession.

4. Acquaint, inform, make known.

5. Seize, obtain, take possession of, affect, influence, obsess.

Possession, *n.* 1. Ownership, proprietorship; monopoly, corner.

2. Occupation, occupancy, control, tenure, seizin, tenancy, retention.

3. Thing possessed, property.

4. State of being possessed, fixed conviction, bedevilment, obsession, madness, lunacy.

Possessions, *n. pl.* Property, estate, effects, belongings, holdings, wealth, assets; dominions, colonies, territory.

Possibility, *n.* 1. Potentiality, potency; practicability, workability, feasibility.

2. Contingency; chance, hazard, "toss-up."

POSSIBLE, *a.* 1. Potential, in posse, contingent; conceivable, imaginable.

2. Practicable, feasible, likely, workable, within reach, accessible.

Possibly, *adv.* Perhaps, perchance, peradventure, mayhap, haply, maybe, it may be, as luck may have it.

Post, *n.* 1. Pillar, column, support, stake, picket, pier.

2. Station, position, seat; office, employment, place, situation, station, billet, quarter.

3. Messenger, intelligencer, mercury; postman, courier, letter-carrier, express, mail-carrier.

4. Mail.

5. Speed, haste, hurry, dispatch.

——, *v. t.* 1. Place, station, set, put, fix, establish.

2. Placard, advertise, announce, make known, blaze abroad, spread abroad, inform, publish.

3. Stigmatize (*by public notice*), vilify, brand, defame, disgrace.

4. Put in the ledger, carry to the ledger, record, enter, slate, register.

5. Mail, put in the mail, put in the post-office, drop, dispatch.

6. Hasten, speed, hurry.

Poster, *n.* Placard, bill, hand-bill, broadside, notice, *affiche*.

Posterior, *a.* 1. Subsequent, following, later, after, succeeding, ensuing, more recent, latter, post prandial.

2. Hind, hinder, back, rear, rump, buttocks.

Posterity, *n.* Descendants, offspring, progeny, seed, succeeding generations; breed, brood, issue, children, heirs, family.

Postfix, *n.* Affix, suffix.

Posthaste, *adv.* With speed, with expedition, fast, apace, swiftly, speedily, rapidly; rashly.

Posthumous, *a.* Post-obit, after death.

Postman, *n.* Courier, post, letter-carrier.

Post mortem. [L.] 1. After death, posthumous.

2. Autopsy, post-mortem examination, post-obit.

Postpone, *v. t.* Defer, delay, adjourn, retard, procrastinate, put off, stave off, let lie over, prorogue, shelve, table.

Post-prandial, *a.* After-dinner.

Postscript, *n.* Appendix, supplement, addition, afterthought.

Postulate, *n.* 1. Supposition, conjecture, hypothesis, assumption, theory, speculation, axiom, proposition, assumed truth, *postulatum.*

2. (*Geom.*) Self-evident problem.

——, *v. t.* 1. Assume, presuppose.

2. Solicit, entreat, supplicate, beseech.

Postulation, *n.* 1. Gratuitous assumption, supposition.

2. Supplication, intercession, solicitation, request.

3. Suit, cause.

Posture, *n.* 1. Position, attitude, pose.

2. State, condition, situation, phase.

3. Disposition, mood, condition, state, phase.

——, *v. i.* Pose, attitudinize.

Posy, *n.* 1. Nosegay, bouquet, bunch of flowers.

2. Inscription (*as on a ring*), legend, motto, verse.

POT, *n.* 1. Kettle, saucepan, pan, skillet.

2. Mug, cup, stoop, tankard, can.

3. Jar, jug, crock.

Potable, *a.* Drinkable, potulent, that may be drunk.

——, *n.* Beverage, drink.

Potation, *n.* 1. Drinking.

2. Dram, drink, potion, draught.

3. Drinking-bout, debauch, carouse, perpotation, tippling.

POTATO, *n.* (*Basic Eng.*) The edible tuber.

Pot-bellied, *a.* Large-bellied, great-bellied, big-bellied, tun-bellied, paunchy, abdominous.

Potency, *n.* 1. Power, might, efficacy, force, intensity, strength, energy, vigor, puissance.

2. Authority, influence, sway, control.

Potent, *a.* 1. Strong, forcible, forceful, powerful, intense, efficacious, physically strong.

2. Powerful, mighty, able, efficient, puissant, capable, strong.

3. Influential, efficacious, cogent, powerful.

Potentate, *n.* Monarch, sovereign, king, emperor, prince, ruler.

Potential, *a.* Possible, in posse, dormant, latent, hidden; dynamic.

Pother, *n.* Bustle, tumult, turmoil, flutter, fuss, rumpus, confusion, pudder, huddle,

turbulence, disturbance, hurly-burly, commotion.

——, *v. t.* Harass, perplex, puzzle, tease, embarrass, beset, confuse, confound, bewilder, pose.

Potion, *n.* Draught (*especially of medicine*), dose, drench, cup.

Pot-pourri, *n.* [Fr.] Medley, mixture, hotch-potch, hodge-podge, farrago, jumble, miscellany, salmagundi, gallimaufry, olio, mish-mash, confused mass, *mélange.*

Potter, *v. i.* Trifle, pudder, putter, fiddle, dawdle, fuss, busy one's self about trifles.

Pottery, *n.* Earthen ware, clay ware, ceramics.

Potulent, *a.* 1. Drinkable, potable.

2. Muddled, fuddled, boozy, mellow, muzzy, worse for liquor.

Pouch, *n.* Bag (*small*), sack.

Poultice, *n.* Cataplasm.

Poultry, *n.* Domestic fowls, fowls (*chickens, ducks, geese*).

Pounce, *n.* Claw, talon.

Pounce upon. Seize (*as with claws*), fall upon.

Pound, *v. t.* 1. Beat, strike, thump.

2. Bray, bruise, crush, pulverize, triturate, comminute, levigate.

3. Impound, confine in a pound, coop, enclose, shut up.

——, *n.* Pen, fold, inclosure.

Pour, *v. t.* 1. Let flow (*by decanting*).

2. Emit, let out, give vent to, send forth, lavish.

——, *v. i.* Flow, issue, stream, flood, cascade, shower, rain, emerge, flow out of.

Pourboire, *n.* Drink-money, *Trinkgeld,* tip, fee.

Pout, *v. i.* Look sullen (*by protruding the lips*), look black, show ill-temper, sulk.

Poverty, *n.* 1. Indigence, penury, want, destitution, need, necessity, privation, neediness, impecuniosity, difficulties, straits, narrow circumstances, wolf at the door, distress, straitened circumstances.

2. Beggary, mendicancy, pauperism, pennilessness.

3. Need, lack, want, deficiency, scantiness, dearth, sparingness, meagreness, jejuneness.

4. Paucity, exiguity, poorness, smallness; humbleness, lowliness; inferiority.

5. Barrenness, sterility, unproductiveness, unfruitfulness.

POWDER, *n.* 1. Dust, pulverized substance.

2. Gunpowder, explosive.

——, *v. t.* 1. Comminute, pulverize, levigate, triturate.

2. Sprinkle, bepowder, dust, dredge; pound, granulate, crumble.

Powdery, *a.* 1. Dusty, mealy, pulverulent.

2. Friable, crumbling.

POWER, *n.* 1. Ableness, efficacy, ability, potency, validity, capability, faculty, talent, efficiency, cogency, competency, might.

2. Force, energy, strength, ability, virtue.

3. Susceptibility, capacity.

4. Faculty, talent, endowment, gift.

5. Authority, carte blanche, warrant, proxy, authoritativeness, rule, prerogative, sovereignty, sway, control, pressure, predominance, ascendancy, omnipotence, domination, puissance, dominion, influence, command, government.

6. Sovereign, potentate, governor, ruler, monarch.

7. Divinity, angel (*good* or *bad*), spirit.

8. Host, army, troop.

Powerful, *a.* 1. Mighty, potent, puissant.

2. Vigorous, robust, sturdy, strong, able-bodied, muscular, sinewy, nervous, Herculean.

3. Of great power, commanding, able, over-powering, dominating, forcible, forceful.

4. Efficacious, effective, efficient, effectual, energetic, operative, influential, cogent, valid.

Practicability, *n.* 1. Feasibility, feasibleness, possibility, practicableness.

2. Fitness for use, being open to travel *or* passage, passability, passableness, openness to entrance.

Practicable, *a.* 1. Feasible, performable, possible, achievable, attainable.

2. Capable of use, usable, operative, capable of passage *or* entrance, passable, penetrable.

Practical, *a.* 1. Adapted to practice *or* use, pragmatical, hard-headed, matter-of-fact, not speculative, not theoretical, adjusted to facts, not visionary.

2. Experienced, versed, proficient, trained, qualified, practised, skilled, thoroughbred, able, *au fait*.

3. Workable, useful, virtual, effective.

Practically, *adv.* Actually, as a matter of fact, in fact, in effect, so far as results are concerned.

Practice, *n.* 1. Custom, habit, wont, manner, method, frequent repetition.

2. Use, usage, customary course, procedure.

3. Acting out, actual performance, doing, habitual doing.

4. Exercise (*as of a profession*), pursuit, application.

5. Exercise, drill, habitual performance (*for skill's sake*), constant exercise *or* use, drill, training.

6. Actions, acts, behavior, conduct, proceeding, dealing.

Practise, *v. t.* [Written also *Practice.*] 1. Do *or* perform repeatedly, exercise *or* drill one's self in, train, apply one's self to.

2. Exercise, apply, pursue, carry on, use.

3. Put into action *or* practice, carry out, do, prosecute, act, perform, perpetrate.

Practised, *a.* Experienced, instructed, versed, thoroughbred, trained, accomplished, proficient, able, skilled, qualified, practical, *au fait*.

Pragmatical, *a.* 1. Meddling, officious, meddlesome, impertinent, intermeddling, interfering, intrusive, obtrusive, overbusy.

2. Very matter-of-fact, absorbed in realism, hostile to ideals, fond of the material, obtuse to ideas, stolid, of the earth, earthy.

Praise, *n.* 1. Commendation, approval, acclaim, approbation. See APPLAUSE.

2. Eulogy, eulogium, encomium, laud, laudation, glorification, panegyric, tribute of praise.

3. Glorification, homage, worship, tribute of gratitude, exaltation, extolling, *Te Deum*, *Laus Deo*, *Gloria in Excelsis*, *Gloria*, hosanna, alleluia.

4. Fame, renown, celebrity, distinction, honor, glory.

5. Merit, desert, praiseworthiness, ground for praise.

——, *v. t.* 1. Commend, approve, approbate, acclaim, applaud.

2. Extol, eulogize, panegyrize, celebrate, laud, "puff," flatter, compliment.

3. Magnify, glorify, exalt, worship, adore, bless, do homage to, do honor to.

Praiseworthy, *a.* Commendable, laudable, good, meritorious, deserving of approbation.

Prank, *n.* Caper, frolic, antic, gambol, trick, escapade.

——, *v. t.* Bedizen, begaud, trick out.

——, *v. i.* Make ostentation, make a gaudy show.

Pranked out. Bedizened, jaunty, showy, ostentatious, finical, airy, garish, flashy.

Prankish, *a.* Sportive, playful, frolicsome, gamesome, antic, mischievous, full of play, full of fun.

Prate, *v. i.* Prattle, chatter, tattle, babble, gabble, palaver, jabber, be loquacious, be garrulous.

——, *v. t.* Tell (*foolishly*), babble, utter, prate about.

Prate, *n.* Prattle, gabble, chatter, twaddle, palaver, idle talk, childish talk, twattle, nonsense.

Prater, *n.* Chatterer, rattle-head, prattler, tattler, babbler, gabbler, palaverer.

Prattle, *v. i.* and *n.* See PRATE.

Pray, *v. t.* Ask (*earnestly*), request, entreat, solicit, importune, beseech, supplicate, implore, beg, petition, invoke, conjure, call upon. See ADJURE.

——, *v. i.* 1. [Usually with *for*.] Supplicate, entreat, petition, beg, implore, importune, prefer a petition *or* request, offer prayer.

2. Commune with God, address the Supreme Being, seek the throne of grace, approach the mercy seat.

Prayer, *n.* 1. Supplication, entreaty, solicitation, imploration, beseeching, suit, petition, request.

2. Communion with God, invocation of God, supplication of God, devotion(s), invocation, orison, litany, suffrage (*eccles.*), adoration, praise.

Prayerful, *a.* Given to prayer, of much converse with God, devout, devotional, religious, pious, lowly-minded, reverent.

Preach, *v. t.* 1. Proclaim (*as in a religious discourse*), declare, publish, pronounce, deliver.

2. Inculcate, teach, urge, press urgently.

——, *v. i.* 1. Deliver sermons, discourse on religious subjects, exhort.

2. Prate sanctimoniously, exhort over-righteously, moralize *ex cathedra*, lecture, sermonize, moralize.

Preamble, *n.* Introduction (*especially of a legislative act*), prelude, preface, introductory part, prologue.

Precarious, *a.* Uncertain, unsettled, unsteady, unstable, doubtful, dubious, equivocal, insecure, not to be depended upon, unreliable, hazardous, perilous, risky, riskful, unassured, critical.

Precatory, *a.* Suppliant, beseeching, supplicating, asking, imploring, praying, begging, entreating, of supplication, prayer *or* entreaty.

Precaution, *n.* 1. Forethought, foresight, timely care, prudence, providence, circumspection, wariness, care, caution, safeguard.

2. Premunition, prior measure, anticipation, preventive measure, provision.

Precautionary, *a.* Provident, preservative, preventive.

Precede, *v. t.* Go before (*in place or in time*), go ahead of, take the lead of, outrank, rank, be anterior to, antecede, antedate, forerun, come first, take preced-ence of, lead, introduce, herald, usher in, head.

Precedence, } *n.* 1. Priority (*in time*), an-
Precedency, } teriority, antecedence, superiority.

2. Preference, pre-eminence, the lead, supremacy, advantage.

Precedent, *n.* Authoritative example, original, prototype, standard, model, prior instance, antecedent, example, pattern, historic warrant, authority in past practice, custom, usage.

Preceding, *a.* Antecedent, precedent, anterior, introductory, prefatory, superior, preliminary, previous, prior, precursory, earlier, foregoing, above, above-mentioned, aforesaid, above-named, above-stated.

Precept, *n.* 1. Command, injunction, instruction, order, mandate, commandment, behest, bidding, charge, command, fiat, dictate, decree, edict, law, ordinance, ordination, regulation, canon.

2. Doctrine, principle, maxim, rule, direction, golden rule, teaching, unwritten law, rubric.

Preceptor, *n.* Teacher, tutor, instructor, master, schoolmaster. See PEDAGOGUE.

Precinct, *n.* 1. Limit, confine, bound, boundary, inclosure, terminus, term, list, border, frontier, march, purlieu, environs, neighborhood.

2. District, territorial division, area.

Precious, *a.* 1. Costly, of great price, priceless.

2. Very valuable, of great worth, of great value, inestimable, priceless.

3. Dear, beloved, darling, very estimable, highly esteemed *or* valued, cherished, treasured, prized, idolized, adored.

4. Fastidious, precisian, overrefined, overnice.

Precipice, *n.* Cliff, crag, steep, abrupt declivity, bluff, clift.

Precipitance, } *n.* 1. Haste, hurry, precip-
Precipitancy, } itation, rush, flurry.

2. Rashness, temerity, precipitation, recklessness, heedlessness, inconsiderateness, thoughtlessness. See RASHNESS.

Precipitate, *v. t.* 1. Throw *or* hurl headlong, cast down, fling downward.

2. Hasten, hurry, accelerate, speed, expedite, urge forward, quicken, despatch, forward, advance, further, bring on, cause to occur too soon, bring on sooner.

3. (*Chem.*) Throw down, cause to subside.

——, *a.* 1. Hasty, hurried, rash, headlong, reckless, indiscreet, over-hasty, rashly hasty, impetuous, hot-headed.

2. Violent, sudden, abrupt.

Precipitation, *n.* 1. Haste, hurry, flurry, precipitance, precipitancy.

2. Rashness, recklessness, thoughtlessness, heedlessness, inconsiderateness, temerity.

3. Condensation, rainfall, dewfall, etc.

Precipitous, *a.* 1. Steep, abrupt, sheer, perpendicular, uphill, cliffy, craggy.

2. Precipitate, headlong, rushing, sudden, sheer downward.

Precise, *a.* 1. Exact, correct, definite, strict, express, distinct, explicit, severe, well-defined, accurate, nice, pointed, unequivocal.

2. Scrupulous, strict, careful, exact (*in conduct*).

3. Formal, ceremonious, stiff, rigid, starch, unbending, starched, prim, punctilious, finical.

Precisian, *n.* Formalist, martinet, precisianist, stickler; prig, pedant.

Precision, *n.* Exactness, preciseness, accuracy, nicety, distinctness, exactitude, severe correctness, rigorous truth.

Preclude, *v. t.* Prevent, hinder, debar, restrain, check, prohibit, inhibit, stop, bar, shut out, obviate.

Precocious, *a.* Premature (*especially in mental development*), too forward, overforward, advanced.

Precocity, *n.* Prematureness (*of the mental faculties*), precociousness, unusually early development.

Preconception, *n.* Anticipatory notion, anticipation, conception previous to the fact, prejudiced view, prejudice, prejudgment.

Preconcert, *v. t.* Premeditate, predetermine, consider beforehand, agree to beforehand, prearrange, concoct, prepare.

Precursor, *n.* 1. Forerunner, predecessor, antecedent, cause.

2. Messenger, harbinger, herald, vancourier, avant-courier, pioneer, advanceguard; prognostic, sign, presage, omen.

Precursory, *a.* 1. Forerunning, preceding, precedent, antecedent, anterior, prior, previous, prevenient.

2. Prelusive, prelusory, introductory, prefatory, precursive, preliminary, proemial, preparatory, initiatory, premonitory, prognosticative.

Predacious, *a.* Rapacious, ravenous, greedy, voracious, living by prey.

Predatory, *a.* Plundering, pillaging, ravaging, rapacious, predacious, ravenous, greedy.

Predecessor, *n.* 1. Precursor (*in any office or position*), forerunner, antecedent, foregoer.

2. Ancestor, forefather, progenitor, elder.

Predestinate, *v. t.* Predetermine, foreordain, preordain, predestine, foredoom, appoint beforehand.

Predestination, *n.* Predetermination, foreordination, preordination, foreordainment, foredoom, necessity, fate.

Predestine, *v. t.* Predetermine. See PREDESTINATE.

Predetermined, *a.* Foregone, already settled, appointed, decided, destined.

Predicable, *a.* Affirmable, attributable, holding true *or* good.

Predicament, *n.* 1. Situation (*especially a bad situation*), condition, state, position, posture, attitude, plight, case.

2. (*Colloq.*) Pass, pinch, push, extremity, dilemma, quandary, corner, hole, impasse, scrape, fix, mess, exigency, emergency, conjuncture.

3. (*Log.*) Category, head of predication.

Predicant, *n.* Dominican, Jacobin, Blackfriar, preaching friar, *frère prêcheur*.

Predicate, *v. t.* Assert, maintain, aver, declare, state, say.

Predication, *n.* Assertion, declaration, averment, statement.

Predict, *v. t.* Foretell, prophesy, prognosticate, forecast, foresee, forewarn, forespeak, bode, foredoom, soothsay, read, shadow forth, signify, point to, presage, augur, betoken, foretoken, portend, divine, forebode. See VATICINATE.

Prediction, *n.* Prophecy, prognostication, augury, presage, foreboding, vaticination, divination, soothsaying, foretelling, fore-announcement.

Predictive, *a.* Prophetic, presaging, foretelling, soothsaying, fatidic, oracular, Sibylline, monitory, prescient, pregnant with, portending, betokening, foreshadowing.

Predilection, *n.* Prepossession (*in favor of*), prejudice, partiality, preference, inclination, bent, leaning, bias, predisposition, liking, fondness, love, desire.

Predispose, *v. t.* Incline, dispose, bias, fit, prepare, make ready.

Predisposition, *n.* 1. Inclination, disposition, willingness, propensity, proclivity, leaning, bent, bias, proneness, natural tendency, aptitude.

2. Prepossession. See PREDILECTION.

Predominance, } *n.* Supremacy, ascend-
Predominancy, } ancy, dominion, domination, dominance, rule, reign, prevalence, superiority, sovereignty, mastery, preponderance, prepollence, prepotency, controlling influence, sway, authority.

Predominant, *a.* Prevailing, prevalent, supreme, ascendant, overruling, dominant, sovereign, ruling, controlling, regnant.

Predominate, *v. i.* Prevail, dominate, rule, preponderate, be supreme, be sovereign, be in the ascendant.

Pre-eminence, *n.* Superiority, supremacy, precedence, priority of place, excellence, supreme excellence, commanding position.

Pre-eminent, *a.* Superior, supreme, excellent, chief, controlling, excelling, surpassing, peerless, unequalled, distinguished, conspicuous, renowned, transcendent, paramount, consummate, predominant.

Preface, *n.* Introduction, preamble, proem, foreword, prologue, induction, premise, prelude, prolegomena, exordium, preliminary, prelusion, prolusion. See PROLOGUE.

Prefatory, *a.* Introductory, preliminary, prelusive, prelusory, precursory, precursive, proemial, preparatory, initiative.

Prefer, *v. t.* 1. Offer, proffer, tender, present, address, bring forward, set forth.

2. Raise, elevate, promote, advance.

3. Choose, select, elect, adopt, pick, pick out, single out, fix upon, pitch upon, fancy, count more desirable.

Preferable, *a.* More eligible, more desirable, deserving of preference, worthier of choice, to be preferred, better.

Preferably, *adv.* Rather, by preference, by choice.

Preference, *n.* Choice, election, advancement, selection, liking, predilection, estimation, precedence, priority.

Preferment, *n.* Promotion, advancement, exaltation, elevation, dignity, benefice.

Prefigure, *v. t.* Foreshow, foretoken, betoken, foreshadow, portend, signify, indicate.

Pregnant, *a.* 1. With child, gravid, big, parturient, great with child, *enceinte.*

2. Fraught, replete, full, teeming with meaning, important, significant, weighty.

3. Fruitful, fertile, prolific, productive, potential, impregnating, generative, fecund, procreant.

Prejudge, *v. t.* Forejudge, prejudicate, presuppose, presume.

Prejudice, *n.* 1. Prejudgment, predilection, prepossession (*against*), bias, unfairness, preconception, partiality, intolerance.

2. Harm, mischief, hurt, detriment, loss, injury, damage, disadvantage, impairment.

——, *v. t.* 1. Bias, warp, incline, turn, prepossess unfavorably, influence against.

2. Injure, damage, hurt, impair, diminish.

Prejudiced, *a.* Biassed, bigoted, wedded to an opinion, unfair, partial, partisan, one-sided.

Prejudicial, *a.* Hurtful, mischievous, injurious, detrimental, deleterious, noxious, damaging, disadvantageous, unfavorable, inimical, hostile.

Prelacy, *n.* 1. Office of prelate, prelateship, prelature, episcopal office.

2. Episcopacy, prelatism, hierarchy, hierarchism, hierocracy.

Prelate, *n.* Archbishop, bishop, cardinal, patriarch, primate, pope, pontiff, ecclesiastic in authority.

Preliminary, *a.* Introductory, preparatory, prefatory, proemial, prelusive, prelusory, precursory, precursive, initiatory, previous, prior, precedent, antecedent.

——, *n.* Introduction, preparatory step, act *or* measure. See PRELUDE.

Prelude, *n.* Introduction, preparation, prelusion, overture, opening, voluntary; preliminary, preface, preamble, proem, exordium. See PROLOGUE.

Premature, *a.* 1. Precocious, too forward, too soon ripe.

2. Unseasonable, too early, untimely, precipitate, hasty, ill-considered, sooner than intended, unprepared, unripe, sooner than due, unmatured.

Prematurely, *adv.* Precociously, too early, too soon.

Premeditate, *v. t.* Precontrive, plan beforehand, deliberate, deliberately intend, predetermine, predesign, plan, plot, prearrange.

Premeditation, *n.* Forethought, previous deliberation, reflection *or* thought, predetermination, deliberate intent *or* intention, design, distinct purpose.

Premier, *n.* Prime minister.

Premise, *v. t.* Preface, lay down beforehand, state at the outset, set forth at the beginning, explain previously.

——, *v. i.* Begin, enter upon the subject, open, set out.

——, *n.* 1. Antecedent, proposition, ground, argument, support.

2. [*Only in pl.*] 1. Conditions, relations, data, testimony, facts rehearsed, circumstances.

2. Land, buildings, grounds, place.

Premium, *n.* 1. Reward, recompense, remuneration, meed, guerdon, encouragement, *douceur*, gift, payment, fee, bounty, prize, bonus.

2. Annual rate (*of insurance*), yearly payment.

3. Rate above par, amount over par, enhancement, appreciation.

Premonition, *n.* Caution, warning, indication, presentiment, foreboding, foreshadowing, forewarning, sign, omen, presage, portent.

Premonitory, *a.* Betokening, indicating, indicative, warning, portentous, threatening, minatory, ominous, cautionary, foretokening.

Preoccupation, *n.* 1. Prior occupation, previous occupation, earlier possession.

2. Prepossession, engrossment, absorption.

3. Abstraction, inattention, inadvertence, distraction, inadvertency, revery, musing, absence, muse, absence of mind, brown study.

Preoccupied, *a.* Inattentive, abstracted, absent, absorbed, engrossed, absentminded, lost, dreaming, musing, in a brown study, unobservant, inadvertent.

Preordain, *v. t.* Predetermine, pre-establish, foreordain, predestinate, predestine, foredoom, appoint beforehand.

Preparation, *n.* 1. Act of preparing, making ready, arrangement, plan, formation, evolution, development.

2. State of being prepared, preparedness, provision, adaptedness, case, condition, readiness.

3. Combination, confection, composition.

4. Qualification, fitting, training, education.

Preparatory, *a.* Introductory, preliminary, prefatory, previous, antecedent, inchoate, in embryo, brewing.

Prepare, *v. t.* 1. Fit, adapt, qualify, adjust.

2. Provide, procure, get ready, put in order, arrange, order, make, plan, concoct, fabricate, block out.

——, *v. i.* Get ready, put things in order, set one's house in order, make arrangements, make provision, take steps.

Preponderance, *n.* 1. Outweighing, preponderating.

2. Superiority of weight, influence *or* power, predominance, supremacy, control, prevalence, ascendency.

Preponderant, *a.* Outweighing, overbalancing, preponderating.

Preponderate, *v. i.* 1. Weigh the most, exceed in weight.

2. Prevail, be superior, have the superiority, predominate, exceed in influence *or* power, incline to one side.

Prepossess, *v. t.* 1. Preoccupy, have prior possession of.

2. Bias, prejudice, give previous inclination to, for *or* against.

Prepossessing, *a.* Attractive, alluring, engaging, inviting, winning, fascinating, taking, captivating, bewitching, winning *or* inviting favor, charming.

Prepossession, *n.* 1. Preoccupation, prior possession.

2. Bias, one-sidedness, bent, preconceived opinion, inclination, preconception, prejudgment, partiality, prejudice.

Preposterous, *a.* 1. Perverted, having the cart before the horse, reversed.

2. Absurd, unreasonable, extravagant, nonsensical, excessive, ridiculous, irrational, foolish, monstrous, exorbitant, perverted, wrong, improper, unfit.

Preposterousness, *n.* Absurdity, unreasonableness, irrationality, foolishness, folly, extravagance, inconsistency with nature *or* reason.

Prepuce, *n.* Foreskin.

Prerogative, *n.* Privilege, immunity, right, liberty, franchise, advantage, claim, birthright.

Presage, *v. t.* 1. Forebode, divine, foreknow, have a presentiment of.

2. Foretell, predict, prophesy, soothsay, bode, signify, portend, foreshow, indicate, betoken, foretoken, prognosticate, augur. See VATICINATE.

——, *n.* 1. Omen, sign, prognostic, augury, portent, token, boding, foreshowing, indication, foreboding, auspice.

2. Prophecy, prediction, foreboding, premonition, foreknowledge, presentiment.

Prescience, *n.* Foreknowledge, precognition, foresight, forecast, prevision.

Prescribe, *v. t.* Direct, order, appoint, command, ordain, dictate, enjoin, decree, institute, advocate, establish.

Prescript, *n.* Direction, decree, rule, ordinance, edict, law, precept, mandate.

Prescription, *n.* 1. Direction, prescript, dictation, appointing.

2. Custom, usage.

3. (*Med.*) Recipe, formula, receipt, remedy.

Presence, *n.* 1. Nearness, neighborhood, vicinity, attendance, company, occupancy, residence, inhabitancy, ubiquity, proximity, propinquity.

2. Personality.

3. Mien, air, appearance, carriage, port, demeanor.

4. Presence-chamber, state-room.

PRESENT, *a.* 1. At hand, not absent, near, not away.

2. Instant, current, existing, living, actual, immediate, not past nor future.

3. Quick in emergencies, ready, at hand, available.

4. Propitious, attentive, favorable.

5. Favorably attentive, not heedless, propitious.

Present, *n.* 1. Gift, donation, donative, benefaction, favor, offering, gratuity, largess, boon, grant, *douceur*.

2. Now, today, nonce, the times.

——, *v. t.* (*Pron.* present'.) 1. Introduce, make known, nominate.

2. Exhibit, offer, bring to notice, set forth.

3. Give, bestow, confer, grant.

4. Hand, put into one's hands, deliver, make over.

5. Proffer, offer openly, tender, advance, express, bring, prefer, "pop."

6. Point, level, aim.

Presentation, *n.* 1. Introduction.

2. Exhibition, representation, show, display, appearance, figure, semblance.

3. Bestowal, donation, giving, offering, gift.

Presentiment, *n.* Foreboding, foretaste, forethought, prescience, forecast, anticipation, apprehension.

Presently, *adv.* Directly, immediately, without delay, forthwith, soon, "eftsoons," shortly, pretty soon, by and by, in a short time.

Presentment, *n.* Appearance, representation.

Preservation, *n.* 1. Maintenance, conservation, cherishing, support, protection; curing.

2. Security, safety, salvation.

3. Integrity, soundness, keeping.

Preservative, *a.* Conservative, preservatory.

Preserve, *v. t.* 1. Keep, guard, protect, defend, rescue, secure, shield, save.

2. Maintain, uphold, sustain, guard, keep, support, keep up.

3. Conserve, keep sound, save from decay; husband, economize.

——, *n.* 1. Sweetmeat, confect, confection, compote, comfit, confit, confiture, jam, conserve, jelly, marmalade.

2. Enclosure (*for game*), warren.

Preserver, *n.* 1. Saviour, protector, keeper, defender, guardian, safeguard.

2. Preservative, means of preservation.

Preside, *v. i.* Direct, control, govern, manage, act as president.

Presignify, *v. t.* Prefigure, foreshow, preshow, foretoken, foreshadow, portend, augur, betoken.

Press, *v. t.* 1. Compress, squeeze, crowd, crush.

2. Squeeze out, express.

3. Make smooth, smooth, flatten, iron.

4. Embrace closely, hug, clasp.

5. Constrain, compel, force.

6. Enjoin, enforce, urge, inculcate, emphasize, stress.

——, *v. i.* 1. Bear heavily, exert pressure, push, bear down, crowd.

2. Hasten, hurry, push, rush.

3. Crowd, throng, force a way.

4. Approach unseasonably *or* importunately, solicit, entreat, importune.

5. Encroach.

——, *n.* 1. Machine for printing, printing-press, roller.

2. "Newspaperdom."

3. Literary publications.

4. Crowd, throng, multitude, crush.

5. Urgency, pressure, hurry.

6. Case, closet, wardrobe, bureau, repository.

Pressing, *a.* Urgent, importunate, constraining, persistent, critical, distressing.

Pressure, *n.* 1. Compressing, squeezing, crushing.

2. Influence, constraining force.

3. Urgency, exigency, press, hurry, stress, compulsion, persuasion.

4. Affliction, grievance, calamity, distress, straits, oppression, difficulty, embarrassment.

5. Impression, stamp, character impressed.

Prestidigitation, *n.* Legerdemain, sleight-of-hand, conjuration, juggling, prestigiation.

Presto, *adv.* Quickly, in haste, immediately, rapidly, suddenly.

Presumable, *a.* Probable, reasonable, likely, credible, that stands to reason.

Presume, *v. i.* 1. Suppose, conjecture, think, infer, deduce, expect, surmise, believe, assume, apprehend, anticipate.

2. Venture, make bold, take the liberty.

——, *v. t.* Consider, suppose, presuppose, take for granted.

Presumption, *n.* 1. Opinion, belief, supposition, conjecture, guess, anticipation, hypothesis, deduction, inference, conclusion, assumption, understanding, condition, concession.

2. Arrogance, forwardness, audacity, haughtiness, boldness, assurance, effrontery, brass, presumptuousness.

3. Probability, ground for believing.

Presumptive, *a.* Grounded on probable evidence, probable.

Presumptuous, *a.* 1. Arrogant, bold, forward, presuming, assuming, "cheeky," intrusive, "brash," insolent, audacious.

2. Rash, over-confident, foolhardy.

3. Irreverent.

Presuppose, *v. t.* Imply as antecedent, assume, presume, surmise, suppose, take for granted.

Pretense, *n.* 1. Show (*to conceal a thing to be done*), false appearance, seeming, semblance, mask, cloak, color, simulation, affectation, window dressing.

2. Subterfuge, excuse, pretext, fabrication, sham, evasion, makeshift.

3. Assumption, claim to notice.

4. Pretension, claim.

Pretend, *v. t.* 1. Feign, affect, simulate, dissemble, counterfeit, sham.

2. Lay claim to, claim, allege a title to.

——, *v. i.* 1. Make believe, make a show, lie, act, profess, feign, sham; imagine.

2. Strive after, lay claim to.

Pretension, *n.* Claim, ostentation, airs, affectation.

Pretentious, *a.* Assuming, presuming, affected, unnatural, conspicuous, showy, ostentatious, tawdry, conceited, vain, priggish.

Preternatural, *a.* Irregular (*as being aside from the ordinary course of nature, but not necessarily supernatural or miraculous*), abnormal, anomalous, unnatural, inexplicable, strange, extraordinary.

Preternaturally, *adv.* Exceedingly, unusually.

Pretext, *n.* 1. Show, appearance, affectation, semblance, guise, cloak, simulation, mask, color, veil, blind, pretense.

2. Vindication, excuse, justification, plea.

Pretty, *a.* 1. Pleasing without being striking, moderately beautiful, bonny, beautiful (*without dignity or grandeur*), comely, fair.

2. Pleasing, neat, elegant without grandeur.

3. Affectedly nice, foppish, affected, petty.

——, *adv.* Moderately, tolerably, considerably, fairly, in some degree.

Prevail, *v. i.* 1. Overcome, triumph.

2. Predominate, preponderate, succeed, have the superiority, gain the advantage, be in the ascendant, get the upper hand, reign, rule, carry the day, gain the day, win the palm, obtain, have effect, power *or* influence, have sway, have currency, be in vogue, be rife, exist, be.

Prevailing, *a.* 1. Effectual, dominant, predominant, efficacious, preponderating, persuading, controlling, ruling, overruling, influential, operative, successful.

2. Prevalent, most common, most general.

Prevail on. ⎫ Persuade (*by argument*), in-
Prevail upon. ⎬ fluence, induce, urge.

Prevail with. Persuade (*by appeal to the feelings*), influence, induce.

Prevalence, ⎫ *n.* 1. Superiority, success,
Prevalency, ⎬ currency, predominance, preponderance.

2. Influence, efficacy, power, force, strength, operation.

3. Universality, wide extension, general reception, general existence.

Prevalent, *a.* 1. Superior, predominant, successful, prevailing, efficacious.

2. Prevailing, predominant, most general, extensively existing.

Prevaricate, *v. i.* Quibble, shuffle, cavil, palter, dodge, evade the truth, equivocate, shift, tergiversate, pettifog, deviate.

Prevarication, *n.* Equivocation, cavil, quibbling, shuffling.

Prevenient, *a.* 1. Preliminary, prefatory, antecedent, initiatory, introductory, going before, preceding.

2. Preventing, preventive.

Prevent, *v. t.* Obstruct, stop, hinder, forestall, inhibit, prohibit, impede, deter, help, save, stop, restrain, check, thwart, intercept, preclude, interrupt, obviate, bar, debar.

Prevention, *n.* Obstruction, stoppage, hindrance, preclusion, prohibition, determent, restriction, interception, interruption.

Preventive, *a.* Deterrent, tending to prevent.

Previous, *a.* Antecedent, precedent, prior, former, preceding, anterior, foregoing, foregone.

Previously, *adv.* Before, antecedently, beforehand.

Prevision, *n.* Foresight, foreknowledge, prescience.

Prey, *n.* 1. Plunder, booty, spoil, pillage, rapine, prize, loot.

2. Ravin, food, victim, quarry, kill, game, victim.

3. Ravage, depredation.

Prey on or upon. 1. Plunder, pillage, rob, ravage, despoil.

2. Devour, feed upon.

3. Waste, corrode, waste gradually.

PRICE, *n.* 1. Value (*in money*), cost, expense, amount, outlay.

2. Estimation, worth, value, excellence, charge, rate, quotation, valuation, appraisal, figure.

3. Recompense, reward, compensation, guerdon, return.

Priceless, *a.* Invaluable, inestimable, without price.

Prick, *v. t.* 1. Pierce (*with a small hole*), stick, perforate, puncture.

2. Spur, goad, incite, impel, urge, drive.

3. Sting, wound, pain, hurt, cut.

——, *v. i.* Spur, ride, gallop, hasten, post.

——, *n.* 1. Goad, point.

2. Puncture, perforation, mark (*made by a point*), point.

3. Sharp, stinging pain; remorse, tormenting thought, thorn in the mind.

4. Puncture, wound, sting, prickle.

Prickle, *n.* Little prick, thorn, spine, bristle, barb, sting, needle; small, sharp-pointed projection.

Pride, *n.* 1. Self-esteem, self-exaltation, self-importance, egotism, "swank," "side," toploftiness, swagger, self-complacency, self-sufficiency, conceit, vanity.

2. Haughtiness, loftiness, lordliness, superciliousness, assumption, insolence, vain-glory, disdain, pomposity, arrogance, presumption, hauteur.

3. Elevation (*of character*), dignity, decorum, lofty self-respect, noble self-esteem.

4. Ornament, decoration, splendor, show, glory.

5. Boast, occasion of pride.

6. Splendid show, ostentation.

Pride one's self on. Boast, take pride in, rate highly, glory in, pique one's self on, plume one's self on.

Priest, *n.* Clergyman, divine, minister, pastor, hierophant, parson, ecclesiastic, churchman, presbyter.

Priestly, *a.* Sacerdotal, ministerial, hieratic, levitical, pontifical.

Prig, *n.* Puppy, coxcomb, conceited fellow, precisian, pedant.

Priggery, *n.* Pertness, conceit, coxcombry, priggism.

Priggish, *a.* Conceited, affected, precious, pedantic, affected, prim.

Prim, *a.* Formal, stiff, precise, starch, starched, prudish, strait-laced, affectedly nice, demure.

Primacy, *n.* 1. Excellency, supremacy, headship.

2. Primateship.

Prima facie. [L.] At first sight, on the first view.

Primal, *a.* First, original.

Primarily, *adv.* Originally, in the first place, in a primary manner.

Primary, *a.* 1. Primitive, aboriginal, original, prime, initial, primordial, primeval, pristine, first, earliest.

2. Chief, principal, main.

3. Elementary, preparatory.

4. Radical, original.

Primate, *n.* Archbishop, metropolitan.

Prime, *a.* 1. First, original, primitive, primal, initial, primeval, primordial, pristine, aboriginal.

2. Highest, chief, principal, main, leading.

3. Early, blooming.

4. First-rate, first-class, capital, excellent.

——, *n.* 1. Beginning, opening, first part, earliest stage, dawn, morning.

2. Youth, spring of life, spring-time, early days.

3. Perfection, flower, bloom, greatest beauty, health *or* strength, best days, heydey, May; zenith, height.

Prime minister. Premier.

Primeval, *a.* Original, primitive, primordial, pristine.

Primitive, *a.* 1. Original, primeval, primal, primordial, aboriginal, prehistoric, prime, primary, pristine, first.

2. Old-fashioned, antiquated, quaint, simple, unsophisticated, crude.

3. Original, primary, radical, underived.

4. Formal, solemn, prim, grave.

Primness, *n.* Stiffness, formality, prudery, affected niceness, preciseness.

Primogenial, *a.* First-born, first-made, original, primary, elemental, primitive.

Primordial, *a.* Original, first in order, elementary. See PRIMITIVE.

Primrose, *a.* Flowery, gay.

Prince, *n.* 1. Sovereign, ruler, monarch, potentate.

2. Sovereign's son (*especially the eldest son*); infant, dauphin, etc., heir apparent.

3. Chief, leader, potentate.

Princely, *a.* 1. Royal, regal, imperial.

2. August, grand, royal, titled, magnificent, superb, splendid, pompous, majestic, noble, munificent, liberal, generous, magnanimous.

3. Stately, dignified, high-minded, noble, lofty, elevated.

Princess, *n.* 1. Female ruler.

2. Sovereign's daughter, infanta, dauphiness, etc.

3. Prince's consort.

Principal, *a.* Chief, main, first, highest, leading, prime, foremost, pre-eminent, cardinal, most considerable, most important, great, capital, essential.

——, *n.* 1. Chief, head, leader, chief actor, chief party.

2. Master, head-master.

3. Capital sum (*placed at interest*), original sum; body, corpus.

Principally, *adv.* Chiefly, mainly, especially, particularly, above all.

Principia, *n. pl.* First principles, elements, fundamental beginnings.

Principle, *n.* 1. Origin, source, cause, original cause, spring, mainspring, fountain, groundwork, nature, prime mover, fountain-head.

2. Element, substratum, basis, constituent, fundamental *or* primordial substance.

3. Postulate, axiom, maxim, law, elementary proposition, fundamental truth, assumption.

4. Doctrine, tenet, dogma, theory, precept, maxim, opinion, rule of action, law of conduct.

5. Ground, motive, reason, conviction.

6. Integrity, uprightness, rectitude, probity, truth, justice, equity, honesty, virtue, righteousness, incorruptibility, goodness, trustworthiness, trustiness, worth, honor.

7. Faculty, power, endowment of the soul.

Prink, *v. t.* Deck, adorn, decorate.

——, *v. i.* Spruce, dress finically *or* ostentatiously, prank, primp.

Print, *v. t.* 1. Impress, imprint, engrave, strike off; issue, publish, bring out.

2. Make an impress *or* impression of.

3. Stamp, form by impression, brand.

PRINT, *n.* 1. Impression, impress, mark, stamp, indentation.

2. Mark, vestige, stamp, form, figure, brand.

Printing, *n.* Typography, presswork, composition.

Prior, *a.* Former, preceding, earlier, previous, superior, anterior, antecedent, precedent, foregoing, precursory.

Priority, *n.* Antecedence, anteriority, precedence, pre-existence, pre-eminence.

Priory, *n.* Convent, cloister, monastery, nunnery.

PRISON, *n.* Jail, gaol, penitentiary, "quod," "pen," bridewell, reformatory, workhouse, house of correction, "jug," cage; dungeon, keep, lock up.

Prisoner, *n.* Captive, convict, jailbird.

Pristine, *a.* Primitive, primary, original, ancient, old, former, primeval, primordial, first.

Privacy, *n.* 1. Secrecy, concealment.

2. Retreat, retirement, seclusion, solitude.

PRIVATE, *a.* 1. Secluded, retired, sequestered, solitary.

2. Individual, personal, unofficial, special, peculiar, particular, own.

3. Confidential, not to be disclosed *or* communicated, privy.

4. Secret, concealed, hidden, clandestine.

——, *n.* (*Mil.*) Common soldier, "doughboy," "Tommy," *poilu.*

Privation, *n.* 1. Deprivation, loss, bereavement, dispossession.

2. Destitution, want, need, necessity, distress, indigence.

3. Absence, negation.

4. Degradation.

Privilege, *n.* Prerogative, right, favor, charter, license, claim, advantage, franchise, liberty, immunity, exemption.

——, *v. t.* 1. Exempt, deliver, set apart.

2. Grant (*some particular exemption*), invest (*with some peculiar right*).

Privily, *adv.* Privately, secretly.

Privity, *n.* 1. Knowledge, cognizance, private concurrence, complicity.

2. Private matter, secret.

Privy, *a.* 1. Individual, special, private, personal, peculiar, particular.

2. Secret, clandestine.

3. Cognizant of, acquainted with, accessory.

4. Private, retired, sequestered.

——, *n.* Back-house, water-closet, latrine, toilet.

Prize, *n.* 1. Reward, premium, guerdon, meed; (*pl.*) honors; laurels, palm, trophy, medal, decoration, cup.

2. Capture, booty.

3. Privilege, gain, advantage.

——, *v. t.* 1. Estimate, rate, appraise.

2. Esteem, value highly, cherish, hold dear.

Pro and con. For and against.

Probability, *n.* 1. Likelihood, presumption, appearance of truth, fair chance, favorable chance, prospect.

2. Verisimilitude, likeliness, credibleness, appearance.

PROBABLE, *a.* Likely, presumable, credible, reasonable, to be expected, that stands to reason, apparent; on the cards.

Probably, *adv.* Apparently, to all appearance, in all probability, in likelihood, with appearance of truth, presumably, seemingly, most likely, *prima facie.*

Probation, *n.* 1. Novitiate.

2. Moral trial, ordeal, test, essay.

3. Examination, trial.

4. Proof.

Probationer, *n.* Novice, candidate.

Probe, *v. t.* Prove, test, verify, investigate, scrutinize, examine, search, sound, explore, sift, look into, fathom, measure.

Probity, *n.* Integrity, uprightness, honesty, faith, morality, loyalty, worth, rectitude, virtue, goodness, righteousness, trustworthiness, trustiness, principle, sincerity, truthfulness, truth, candor, veracity, honor, conscientiousness, justice, equity, fairness, incorruptibility, soundness, singleness of heart.

Problem, *n.* Question (*to be solved*), enigma, puzzle, riddle, moot point, point in dispute, point to be solved or settled, question at issue, vexed question; exercise, theorem, proposition.

Problematic, ⎫ *a.* Uncertain, doubtful,
Problematical, ⎭ dubious, questionable, disputable, enigmatical, puzzling, unsettled.

Proboscis, *n.* Snout, trunk, nose, neb.

Procedure, *n.* 1. Conduct, practice, course, process, management, operation, manner of proceeding, way, form, policy, custom, method.

2. Act, transaction, deed, action, performance, proceeding, measure, step.

Proceed, *v. i.* 1. Progress, advance, continue, go or pass on, move forward, make progress, get on, push on, go ahead, get ahead, make headway, get forward, get along, hold or keep one's course.

2. Arise, spring, come, issue, emanate, originate, flow, follow, result, ensue, accrue, come out, go forth, be derived, be caused, take rise, be owing, be due, be produced.

3. Act, conduct one's self, take steps, take measures, set to work, go about anything, act by method, promote a design.

Proceeding, *n.* Act, deed, transaction, action, process, move, measure, performance, step, procedure, course.

Proceeds, *n. pl.* Product, produce, effect, income, profit, issue, result, earnings, gain, balance, yield, receipts, returns, avails.

PROCESS, *n.* 1. Course, progress, advance continued movement, train.

2. Operation, procedure, proceeding, action, practice, way, performance, step, transaction, measure, conduct, management, series of measures, mode of operation, course, continuous experiment.

3. (*Law.*) Suit, trial, action, case.

4. (*Anat.*) Projection, protuberance, outgrowth.

Procession, *n.* Train, retinue, cavalcade, march, parade, file, *cortège.*

Proclaim, *v. t.* 1. Announce, publish, declare, promulgate, advertise, trumpet, broach, cry, herald, circulate, broadcast, make known, blaze abroad, spread abroad, noise abroad, bruit, give notice of, make proclamation of.

2. Outlaw (*by public denunciation*), proscribe, ban.

Proclaimer, *n.* Promulgator.

Proclamation, *n.* 1. Announcement, publication, promulgation, advertisement, declaration, blazon.

2. Edict, decree, ordinance, ban, manifesto.

Proclivity, *n.* 1. Inclination, tendency, proneness, propensity, bias, disposition, leaning, bent, predisposition, direction, determination, bearing, drift, turn.

2. Readiness, aptitude, facility.

Procrastinate, *v. t.* Defer, delay, postpone, adjourn, put off, prolong, protract, retard; omit, neglect.

——, *v. i.* Delay, lag, loiter, be dilatory.

Procrastination, *n.* Dilatoriness, postponement, protraction, putting off, delay, tardiness, slowness.

Procreant, *a.* Producing young, procreating.

Procreate, *v. t.* Generate, engender, beget, breed, propagate.

Procreation, *n.* Generation, begetting, production.

Procreator, *n.* Generator, father, sire, begetter.

Procumbent, *a.* Prone, lying down or on the face, prostrate, leaning forward, stooping.

Procurable, *a.* Obtainable, acquirable, compassable.

Procuration, *n.* 1. Agency, management.

2. Authority as an agent, authority to act for another; bawdry.

Procurator, *n.* (*Law.*) Agent, proxy, deputy, representative, proctor, attorney, solicitor.

Procure, *v. t.* 1. Get, acquire, obtain, gain.

2. Contrive, compass, cause, effect, bring about.

3. Attract, bring on, induce.

Procurer, *n.* Pimp, pander, bawd.

Prodigal, *a.* Wasteful, lavish, extravagant, profuse, thriftless, unthrifty, improvident, squandering, dissipated, generous, abundant.

——, *n.* Spendthrift, waster, squanderer.

Prodigality, *n.* Wastefulness, extravagance, excess, profusion, lavishness, unthriftiness, squandering, waste, profuse liberality.

Prodigious, *a.* 1. Marvellous, wonderful, portentous, amazing, astonishing, surprising, astounding, strange, startling, extraordinary, uncommon, wondrous, miraculous, very strange, unheard of.

2. Enormous, monstrous, huge, vast, immense.

Prodigy, *n.* 1. Marvel, portent, wonder, miracle, phenomenon, sign.

2. Monster, monstrosity, unnatural product, freak of nature, curiosity.

Produce, *v. t.* 1. Exhibit, show, bring forward, bring out, bring into view.

2. Generate, beget, engender, conceive, procreate, hatch, bring into being, bear, furnish, yield, bring forth, breed.

3. Cause, occasion, originate, make, create, effect, give rise to, bring about, achieve, accomplish.

4. Yield, bear, give, afford, render, make accrue, impart.

5. Extend, protract, prolong, draw out, lengthen.

6. Manufacture, make, fabricate, fashion.

PRODUCE, *n.* 1. See PRODUCT.

2. Agricultural products; truck gardening; goods, stock, merchandise.

Producer, *n.* 1. Farmer, husbandman, grocer, raiser, agriculturist.

2. Inventor, maker, originator, creator, prime mover.

Product, *n.* 1. Produce, yield, proceeds, returns, crops, harvest, fruits, production, outcome.

2. Result, effect, work, fruit, production, performance, issue, consequence.

Productile, *a.* Extensible, ductile.

Production, *n.* 1. Produce, product, fruit; creation, construction, making, fabrication, erection, performance; fruition, completion; propagation, growth, breeding, development, birth.

2. Work, opus, publication.

3. Prolongation, extension, lengthening, continuation.

Productive, *a.* 1. Fertile, prolific, fruitful, uberous, teeming, copious, plenteous, luxuriant.

2. Efficient, causative, producing, bringing into being, creative, life-giving, constructive, originative.

Proem, *n.* Preface, introduction, prelude, exordium, prolegomena, foreword, preliminary remarks.

Profanation, *n.* 1. Desecration, violation.

2. Misuse, abuse, pollution.

Profane, *a.* 1. Irreverent, irreligious, blasphemous, wicked, sacrilegious, impious, ungodly, godless.

2. Unhallowed, impure, polluted, unholy, unconsecrated, unsanctified.

3. Secular, not sacred, temporal, worldly.

——, *v. t.* 1. Desecrate, pollute, violate, defile.

2. Abuse, debase.

Profanity, *n.* 1. Irreverence, profaneness, blasphemy.

2. Profane language, blasphemy.

Profess, *v. t.* 1. Avow, acknowledge, own, confess, declare, affirm, avouch, aver, allege, state, proclaim.

2. Pretend, lay claim to, feign, affect.

——, *v. i.* Confess, declare openly.

Profession, *n.* 1. Declaration, avowal, assertion, claim, acknowledgment.

2. Declaration, representation, protestation, pretence, pretension, evasion.

3. Employment (*that requires a learned education*), calling, occupation, business, vocation, office, avocation.

Proffer, *v. t.* Tender, offer, volunteer.

——, *n.* Tender, offer, proposal.

Proficiency, } *n.* 1. Advancement, im-
Proficience, } provement, forwardness.

2. Skill, mastery.

Proficient, *a.* Skilled, skilful, expert, adept, dextrous, conversant, competent, well-versed, qualified, practised, masterly, trained, accomplished, able, thoroughbred, finished, good, at home, *au fait*.

——, *n.* Adept, expert, master, "dab," master-hand.

Profile, *n.* 1. Side face, side view, half face.

2. Outline, contour.

PROFIT, *n.* 1. Gain, produce, emolument, return, clearance, lucre, fruit, aid, earnings, avails.

2. Advantage, benefit, service, weal, utility, perquisite, "velvet," interest, accession of good, improvement, advancement, use.

——, *v. i.* 1. Improve, gain, advance, make improvement, gain advantage.

2. Bring good, be of use *or* advantage, serve, avail.

Profitable, *a.* 1. Gainful, advantageous, productive, beneficial, useful, desirable.

2. Lucrative, remunerative.

Profitableness, *n.* Gainfulness, usefulness, advantageousness.

Profitably, *adv.* Gainfully, usefully, advantageously.

Profitless, *a.* Useless, worthless, fruitless, bootless, unprofitable, valueless, of no use, void of profit.

Profligacy, *n.* Dissoluteness, depravity, shameless vice, shamelessness, reprobation, profligateness.

Profligate, *a.* Depraved, corrupt, immoral, vitiated, dissolute, dissipated, corrupted, very wicked, graceless, very vicious, shameless, abandoned, lost to virtue.

——, *n.* Debauchee, rake, libertine, man of pleasure, reprobate, *roué*.

Profound, *a.* 1. Deep, fathomless, abysmal; heavy, undisturbed.

2. Penetrating, sagacious, skilled, learned, erudite, intellectually deep.

3. Lively, vivid, strong, deep-felt, far-reaching, intense, heartfelt, touching.

4. Submissive (*of a bow, obeisance, etc.*), low-bending, very low.

5. Mysterious, occult, abstruse, obscure, subtle, recondite.

6. Thorough, complete.

Profound, *n.* 1. The deep, the abyss.

2. Sea, ocean.

Profundity, *n.* Depth, deepness, profoundness.

Profuse, *a.* 1. Lavish, prodigal, improvident, generous, abundant, extravagant, wasteful, too liberal, too bountiful.

2. Exuberant, over-abounding, in profusion, bountiful, redundant, excessive.

Profusion, *n.* 1. Lavishness, excess, superflux, prodigality, extravagance, waste, profuseness.

2. Abundance, exuberance, plenty.

Progenitor, *n.* Ancestor, forefather, forebear.

Progeny, *n.* Offspring, children, issue, descendants, race, breed, stock, lineage, young, scion, offshoot, posterity, family.

Prognostic, *a.* Foreshowing, foretokening, significant.

——, *n.* 1. Sign, token, presage, omen, symptom, indication, augury, foreboding, prognostication.

2. Foretelling, prediction, prophecy.

3. Symptom, indication.

Prognosticate, *v. t.* 1. Foretell, predict, prophesy.

2. Foreshadow, indicate, portend, augur, foreshow, foretoken, betoken, forebode, presage.

Prognostication, *n.* 1. Act of prognosticating, foreshowing, foretelling, foreknowledge, presage, prediction.

2. Augury, prediction, vaticination, prophecy, indication, foretoken, previous sign, portent, foreboding.

Program, *n.* Order of exercises, advertisement, notice, plan (*of public performance*); draft, prospectus, outline, syllabus.

Progress, *n.* 1. Advancement, advance, progression, movement forward; passage, course, ongoing, headway.

2. Growth, increase, improvement, reform, development.

3. Journey of state, circuit, procession.

——, *v. i.* 1. Advance, proceed.

2. Take head, make headway, work one's way, make one's way, make progress, proceed, continue onward, get ahead, go on, gain, forge ahead; mend, improve.

Progression, *n.* 1. Advancement, advance, progress, improvement, rise.

2. Course, passage, lapse *or* process of time.

3. Series, gradation, rate.

Progressive, *a.* 1. Advancing, proceeding, forward looking.

2. Improving, developing.

Progressiveness, *n.* Forward-looking, open-mindedness, pioneer spirit, liberality of opinion.

Prohibit, *v. t.* 1. Hinder, prevent, debar, preclude.

2. Forbid, inhibit, disallow, interdict.

Prohibition, *n.* Interdiction, interdict, inhibition, forbiddance, veto, ban, tabu, proscription, prevention, disallowance, embargo.

Prohibitive, } *a.* Restrictive, prohibiting, **Prohibitory,** } forbidding, out of reach.

Project, *v. t.* 1. Throw, cast, throw out, shoot forward, hurl, fling, propel, eject, shoot.

2. Scheme, devise, contrive, frame, intend, purpose, design, plan, plot, concoct, brew.

3. Delineate (*as a sphere upon a plane*), draw, exhibit.

——, *v. i.* Protrude, jut, bulge, jut out, stand out, be prominent, shoot forward.

——, *n.* (*Pron.* pro'ject.) Plan, scheme, contrivance, device, intention, design, proposal, purpose.

Projectile, *n.* Missile, bullet, shell.

Projection, *n.* 1. Propulsion, throwing, emission, ejection, delivery.

2. Planning, designing, contriving, scheming.

3. Prominence, protuberance, protrusion, extension, spur, salience, outshoot, jutty, bulge, process.

4. Plan, delineation, map.

Prolegomena, *n. pl.* Introduction, preface, prelude, prologue, preamble, proem, preliminary remarks.

Proletarian, *a.* Mean, vulgar, vile, plebeian.

Proletariat, *n.* Laboring class, the commonalty, the people, the masses, the lower classes.

Prolific, *a.* Fruitful, fertile, productive, generative, teeming.

Prolix, *a.* 1. Diffuse, wordy, verbose, circumlocutory, prosaic, loose, long, lengthy, lengthened out, full of detail, prolonged, protracted, long-spun, spun-out, long-winded, discursive, rambling, not concise.

2. Tiresome, tedious, wearisome.

Prolixity, *n.* Diffuseness, prolixness, verbosity, tedious length, minute detail.

Prolocutor, *n.* Speaker, spokesman, chairman.

Prologue, *n.* Introduction (*to a play*), preface, prelude, proem, preamble.

Prolong, *v. t.* 1. Lengthen, protract, continue, sustain, draw out, extend, lengthen in time.

2. Put off, postpone, defer.

Prolusion, *n.* 1. Prelude, introduction, preliminary.

2. Essay, trial.

Promenade, *n.* 1. Walk, stroll; dance.

2. Walk, sidewalk, place for walking.

——, *v. i.* Take a walk, saunter.

Prominence, *n.* 1. Protuberance, projection, bulge, process.

2. Conspicuousness, eminence, distinction, celebrity, fame.

Prominent, *a.* 1. Protuberant, convex, projecting, jutting, relieved, embossed, raised.

2. Conspicuous, eminent, celebrated, influential, distinguished, famous.

3. Distinctly manifest, conspicuous, important, salient, marked, principal, main.

Promiscuous, *a.* 1. Mixed, mingled, miscellaneous, indiscriminate, confused.

2. Indiscriminate, common.

Promise, *n.* 1. Word, engagement, assurance, agreement, undertaking, vow, oath, parole, contract, profession, pledge.

2. Ground *cr* basis of hope, earnest, pledge.

3. Bestowal, fulfilment, grant of what is promised.

——, *v. t.* 1. Pledge, engage, covenant, vow, swear, subscribe, underwrite.

2. Give expectation of, excite a hope of, assure, warrant, guarantee, attest.

3. Pledge, engage to bestow.

——, *v. i.* Engage, agree, stipulate, bargain, undertake, be sworn, pledge one's self, plight one's word, pass one's word, give assurance, make an agreement, tie one's self.

Promising, *a.* Encouraging, giving ground of hope, auspicious, likely, hopeful, encouraging, propitious.

Promissory note. Note of hand, promise to pay.

Promontory, *n.* Headland, foreland, high cape, jutland.

Promote, *v. t.* 1. Forward, advance, further, cultivate, encourage, help, assist, aid.

2. Elevate, exalt, raise, prefer, dignify, pass, graduate.

3. Excite, stir up.

Promotion, *n.* 1. Furtherance, encouragement, advancement.

2. Elevation, preferment.

Prompt, *a.* 1. Ready, quick, apt, alert, active.

2. Hasty, forward, quick.

3. Inclined, disposed, apt, prone, propense.

4. Early, timely, seasonable, punctual, immediate, instant.

——, *v. t.* 1. Incite, induce, stimulate, impel, incline, dispose, urge, set on, draw on, instigate, actuate.

2. Put in mind, give the cue to, assist (*a speaker*), remind.

3. Dictate, suggest, hint.

Promptness, *n.* Readiness, quickness, alacrity, alertness, promptitude, activity, quickness of decision.

Promulgate, *v. t.* Publish, announce, proclaim, declare, advertise, bruit, trumpet, make known, blaze abroad, spread abroad, noise abroad, give notice of, make promulgation of, divulge.

Prone, *a.* 1. Prostrate (*with the face downward*), recumbent, lying flat, horizontal.

2. Sloping, inclining, inclined, declivous.

3. Disposed, inclined, tending, bent, apt, predisposed, propense.

4. Bending forward, inclined, bowed.

5. Ready, eager, prompt.

6. Headlong, running downward *or* headlong.

Proneness, *n.* 1. Disposition, tendency, proclivity, inclination, bias, bent, propensity, aptness, turn, leaning, predisposition, ply.

2. Descent, declivity.

Pronounce, *v. t.* 1. Utter (*with proper accent and tone*), speak, enunciate, articulate, say, frame.

2. Declare, affirm, assert, announce, state.

3. Deliver (*as an oration*).

Pronunciamento, *n.* Proclamation, announcement, declaration, manifesto, pronouncement.

Pronunciation, *n.* 1. Utterance, enunciation, articulation.

2. Delivery.

Proof, *n.* 1. Test, trial, essay, ordeal, examination.

2. Demonstration, certification, attestation, verification, conclusiveness, corroboration, ratification, satisfactory evidence, confirmation, testimony.

3. Proof-sheet, trial impression.

——, *a.* Firm, steadfast, stable, fixed, impenetrable.

Prop, *v. t.* Support, sustain, uphold, hold up, truss, shore up.

——, *n.* 1. Support, stay, brace.

2. Buttress, strut, pin, shore, fulcrum, stay, brace.

Propaganda, *n.* Promotion, indoctrination, inculcation.

Propagate, *v. t.* 1. Multiply, increase, continue.

2. Spread, diffuse, disseminate, circulate, publish, transmit, extend, spread abroad, promulgate, promote.

3. Generate, beget, engender, procreate, breed, produce, bring into being, originate.

Propagation, *n.* 1. Multiplication, increase, continuance.

2. Dissemination, diffusion, extension, enlargement, circulation.

3. Generation, procreation, breeding, production.

Propel, *v. t.* Impel, drive forward, push forward, urge on, thrust, force.

Propeller, *n.* Screw, screw-steamer.

Propensity, *n.* Inclination, proneness, disposition, bent, aptitude, tendency, bias, proclivity, ply.

Proper, *a.* 1. Particular, peculiar, individual, inherent, natural, original, special, specific.

2. Fit, fitting, befitting, suitable, appropriate, pertinent, respectable, decent, decorous, demure, meet, seemly, convenient, adapted, becoming, right, legitimate.

3. Exact, accurate, precise, correct, just, fastidious, formal.

4. Real, actual, properly so called.

Properly, *adv.* 1. Fitly, suitably.

2. Strictly, in a strict sense.

PROPERTY, *n.* 1. Quality, attribute, peculiarity, trait, mark, virtue, disposition, characteristic.

2. Wealth, estate, goods, possessions, assets, belongings, circumstances, resources, effects, appurtenance, personalty, chattels, one's own, thing owned.

3. Ownership, exclusive right, tenure, possession, proprietorship.

4. Participation, right, interest, claim, title, copyright.

Prophecy, *n.* 1. Prediction, prognostication, forecast, presage, vaticination, foretelling, divination, augury, portent.

2. Preaching, exhortation, instruction.

Prophesy, *v. t.* Predict, foretell, prognosticate, divine, augur, premonish.

Prophet, *n.* Predicter, foreteller, seer, soothsayer, prognosticator, oracle, Sibyl.

Prophetic, *a.* Predictive, foretelling, predicting. fatidical.

Prophylactic, *a.* Preventive, protective, health-giving, preservative, synteretic.

Propinquity, *n.* 1. Nearness, proximity, vicinity, neighborhood, contiguity, adjacence.

2. Kindred, affinity, nearness of blood, relationship, consanguinity, connection.

Propitiate, *v. t.* Conciliate, appease, pacify, reconcile, gain the favor of, make propitious, satisfy, make favorable.

——, *v. i.* Atone, make propitiation, mediate, intercede.

Propitiation, *n.* 1. Conciliation, reconciliation, pacification.

2. Atonement, expiation, satisfaction, reparation, atoning sacrifice.

Propitiatory, *a.* Conciliatory, expiatory.

Propitious, *a.* 1. Gracious, benevolent, benign, kind, favorable, friendly, merciful, ready to bless.

2. Auspicious, lucky, happy, fortunate, encouraging, thriving, timely, favorable, well-disposed, opportune, prosperous, promising, in a fair way.

Proportion, *n.* 1. Arrangement, relation, adaptation (*of parts*).

2. Distribution, adjustment, symmetry, symmetrical relation, commensuration, dimension, comparative size.

3. Share, lot, part, portion, ratio, extent, quota.

——, *v. t.* 1. Adjust (*in proper relations*), regulate, graduate, put in proportion.

2. Form, shape with symmetry *or* suitableness.

Proportionable, *a.* 1. Proportional, corresponding.

2. Well-proportioned, symmetrical.

Proportional, *a.* Proportionate, proportionable, relative, symmetrical, corresponding.

Proportionally, *adv.* Proportionably, relatively, proportionately, in proportion, in due degree.

Proposal, *n.* Offer (*of something to be done*), statement, motion, recommendation, proffer, tender, suggestion, proposition, scheme, design, terms proposed, overture.

Propose, *v. t.* Offer (*for consideration*), proffer, state, propound, submit, pose, put, tender, present, suggest, recommend, move; offer marriage.

——, *v. i.* Intend, design, mean, purpose, have the intention, propose to one's self, declare a purpose.

Proposition, *n.* 1. Offer (*of something to be considered*), proffer, tender, overture, suggestion, project, undertaking, proposal.

2. Position, thesis, axiom, postulate, predication, theorem, statement, declaration, dictum, assertion, affirmation, doctrine.

3. (*Log.*) Period, complete sentence.

Propound, *v. t.* Exhibit, propose, lay before, set forth, suggest, offer.

Proprietor, *n.* Possessor, owner, proprietary, lord, master.

Propriety, *n.* 1. Fitness (*to a proper standard* or *rule*), appropriateness, suitableness, becomingness, rightness, aptness, seemliness, justness, correctness, accuracy, consonance, adaptation, reasonableness.

2. Decorum, demureness, decency, respectability, good behavior, proper formality, modesty, fastidiousness, conventionality.

Propulsive, *a.* Propelling, driving on, urging on, pushing, impulsive, projective, impellent, projectile, ballistic.

Pro rata. [L.] Proportionally, proportionably, proportionately, in proportion.

Prorogation, *n.* Adjournment, postponement, continuance.

Prorogue, *v. t.* Adjourn (*as Parliament*), postpone, continue.

Prosaic, } *a.* 1. Prosy, unpoetical.
Prosaical, } 2. Dull, flat, stupid, uninteresting, unimaginative, sober, unentertaining, tiresome, tedious, prolix, prosing, vapid, tame, humdrum, matter-of-fact, commonplace, pedestrian.

Proscribe, *v. t.* 1. Banish, exile, ostracize, expel, excommunicate, doom, outlaw.

2. Exclude, interdict, prohibit, forbid.

3. Denounce, censure, condemn, reject utterly, curse.

Proscription, *n.* 1. Banishment, exile, outlawry, ostracism, expulsion.

2. Exclusion, interdiction, prohibition, outlawry.

3. Denunciation, censure, condemnation.

PROSE, *a.* [*The noun is Basic Eng.*] Prosaic, matter-of-fact, unromantic, plain, pedestrian.

Prosecute, *v. t.* 1. Pursue, continue, follow out, exercise, carry out, carry on, persevere in, conduct.

2. Arraign, indict, take the law of, bring before a court, sue.

3. Sue, seek to obtain by legal process.

Prosecution, *n.* 1. Pursuit, undertaking.

2. Arraignment, bringing to trial.

3. Suit, legal process.

Prosecutor, *n.* Plaintiff, accuser.

Proselyte, *n.* Convert, catechumen, neophyte.

Prospect, *n.* 1. View, survey, display, sight, outlook, scene, field, landscape, show, spectacle, vision, vista, perspective.

2. Landscape, scenery, picture.

3. Expectation, anticipation, contemplation, calculation, expectance, foreseeing, promise, foresight, presumption, hope, trust.

4. Probability, likelihood.

——, *v. i.* (*Pron.* prospect'.) Explore.

Prospective, *a.* Future, coming, approaching, impending, foreseen, expected.

Prospectus, *n.* Plan (*of a literary work*), outline, syllabus, description, design, sketch, scheme, programme, announcement.

Prosper, *v. t.* Favor, befriend, aid, forward, help, make successful.

——, *v. i.* Flourish, thrive, succeed, make gain, go on well, be successful, get on, feather one's nest; bear fruit, batten, increase.

Prosperity, *n.* Success, thrift, welfare, happiness, felicity, well-being, weal, luck, good fortune, good luck, bed of roses, prosperousness, run of luck, palmy days, halcyon days, smiles of fortune, affluence, blessings; boom, heydey.

Prosperous, *a.* 1. Successful, thriving, flourishing, fortunate, lucky, happy, well off, well to do, blooming, rich, palmy, halcyon, golden.

2. Favorable, propitious, auspicious, good, golden, bright, fortunate, lucky, providential, rosy, promising, booming.

Prostitute, *v. t.* Misuse, abuse, misapply, pervert, make a bad use of.

——, *n.* See STRUMPET.

Prostitution, *n.* 1. Misuse, abuse, perversion, degradation, profanation.

2. Unlawful sexual intercourse (*on the part of a woman for hire*), harlotry.

Prostrate, *a.* Prostrated, prone, recumbent, supine, stretched out, flat, fallen; helpless, powerless.

——, *v. t.* 1. Overthrow, overturn, level, fell, demolish, destroy, ruin, throw down, lay flat.

2. Exhaust, reduce, overcome, depress, bring low.

Prostration, *n.* 1. Overthrow, destruction, demolition.

2. Exhaustion, depression, dejection.

Prosy, *a.* 1. Prosaic, unpoetical.

2. Dull, flat, stupid, uninteresting, jejune, unentertaining, tiresome, tedious.

Protean, *a.* Changeable, variable, multiform.

Protect, *v. t.* Defend (*by a covering*), guard, watch over, cover, shield; fortify, screen, shelter, house, preserve, secure, save, harbor; countenance, champion, patronize, foster.

Protection, *n.* 1. Shelter, defence, security, care, safety, refuge, guard, preservation.

2. Shield, ægis, buckler, palladium, bulwark, wall, hedge, safeguard.

3. Passport, safeguard.

4. Aid, championship, support, patronage.

Protective, *a.* Defensive, sheltering, shielding, affording protection.

Protector, *n.* Guardian, defender, champion, patron, warden, custodian.

Protest, *v. i.* Declare (*solemnly*), aver, affirm, assert, asseverate, avow, profess, attest, testify; remonstrate, object, demur, "kick," expostulate.

——, *v. t.* Declare (*solemnly*), assert, affirm, repudiate, asseverate.

——, *n.* Declaration (*made in a formal manner against something*), objection, "kick," expostulation.

Protestation, *n.* 1. Declaration, asseveration, affirmation, averment, avowal.

2. Declaration of dissent, statement, protest.

Prototype, *n.* Original, original pattern, model, precedent, paradigm, ideal, copy, type, exemplar, example, archetype, protoplast.

Protract, *v. t.* 1. Prolong, continue, extend, lengthen (*in time*), spin out.

2. Lengthen, prolong (*in space*).

3. Delay, put off, postpone, defer.

Protrude, *v. t.* 1. Shoot out, thrust forward, push forth.

2. Beetle, jut out, hang over.

——, *v. i.* Project, jut, bulge, jut out, extend, shoot, stand out.

Protuberance, *n.* Prominence, projection, roundness, swelling, bulge, process, excrescence, lump, hump, bump, elevation, bunch *or* knob.

Proud, *a.* 1. Conceited, over-weening, self-satisfied, vain, contented, self-conscious, egotistical, assuming.

2. Arrogant, haughty, imperious, supercilious, uppish, "high-hat," orgulous, presumptuous, lordly, lofty, vain-glorious, boastful, high-spirited, high-strung.

3. Grand, stately, noble, imposing, magnificent, splendid, ostentatious, lofty, exalted, dignified, lordly, majestic.

Prove, *v. t.* 1. Demonstrate, show, manifest, confirm, establish, evidence, evince, substantiate, sustain, ascertain, justify, verify, make good.

2. Try, test, examine, check, make trial of, assay, put to the test, experiment upon, submit to the test *or* proof.

3. Experience, suffer.

——, *v. i.* 1. Turn out, be found to be.

2. Essay, make trial.

3. Make certain.

Provender, *n.* Dry food (*as hay, corn, etc., for brutes*), fodder, forage.

Proverb, *n.* 1. Adage, maxim, saying, dictum, precept, saw, aphorism, apothegm, by-word.

2. By-word, expression of contempt.

Proverbial, *a.* Notorious, current, acknowledged, unquestioned.

Provide, *v. t.* 1. Prepare, procure, get ready, make ready, arrange, collect for use, lay in, lay by, procure, plan; gather, store, keep.

2. Supply, furnish, contribute, yield, produce, victual, provision, stock, feed, afford.

——, *v. i.* 1. Cater, furnish supplies, purvey.

2. Take measures, make provision, prepare, plan, arrange.

3. Stipulate, bargain, contract, engage, agree, condition, covenant.

Provided, *conj.* If, on condition, with the understanding, granted, supposing, on these terms, by stipulation, in case, in the event.

Providence, *n.* 1. Divine government, divine superintendence.

2. Prudence; foresight, caution, consideration.

3. Frugality, economy.

Provident, *a.* 1. Careful (*for the future*), prudent, discreet, cautious, forecasting, foreseeing, farseeing, forehanded, considerate.

2. Frugal, economical.

Province, *n.* 1. Territory, region, tract, domain, district, section, large extent.

2. Dependency, colony.

3. Business, employment, function, duty, charge, calling, office, part, post, capacity, department, sphere.

4. Division, department, jurisdiction.

Provincial, *a.* 1. Of a province, of provinces.

2. Appendant, annexed, outlying.

3. Rude, unpolished, unrefined, rustic, countrified, rural, bucolic; narrow, local, insular.

Provision, *n.* 1. Providing, anticipation.

2. Preparation, provident measures *or* steps, provident care, arrangement; readiness.

3. Stock, store, hoard, fund, supply, supplies, reserve, grist, resources, equipment.

4. Proviso, stipulation, clause, condition, previous agreement, prerequisite, reservation.

Provisional, *a.* Temporary, provisory, tentative, makeshift.

Provisionally, *adv.* Temporarily, for the present occasion, for the present exigency.

Provisions, *n. pl.* Food, victuals, provender, fare, eatables, viands, supplies.

Proviso, *n.* Condition, provision, clause, conditional stipulation.

Provisory, *a.* 1. Conditional, hypothetical, dependent, subject.

2. Temporary, provisional.

Provocation, *n.* 1. Incitement, stimulus, stimulant, incentive, provocative.

2. Affront, offence, indignity, insult.

3. Vexation, angering.

Provocative, *a.* Stimulating, exciting, inciting, provoking.

Provoke, *v. t.* 1. Excite, stimulate, arouse, rouse, awaken, incite, move, kindle, inflame, animate, instigate, impel, stir up, work up, induce.

2. Exasperate, incense, enrage, chafe, vex, annoy, nettle, aggravate, anger, irritate, exacerbate, pique, offend, affront, infuriate, give offence *or* umbrage to, put out, put out of humor, work into a passion, raise one's ire, make one's blood boil.

3. Cause, promote, occasion, instigate, evoke, elicit, call forth, produce.

Provoking, *a.* Irritating, vexing, vexatious, annoying, tormenting, aggravating, offensive.

Prow, *n.* Bow, beak.

Prowess, *n.* Bravery, valor, intrepidity, courage, gallantry, heroism, fearlessness, daring, courageous deeds, reputation for valor.

Prowl, *v. i.* Rove, roam, wander, ramble; slink, sneak.

Proximate, *a.* Next, nearest, immediate, closest, direct.

Proximity, *n.* 1. Nearness.

2. Nearness, contiguity, adjacency, vicinity, propinquity, vicinage, neighborhood.

Proxy, *n.* Substitute, agent, deputy, delegate, representative, *locum tenens,* attorney, commissioner, lieutenant.

Prudence, *n.* Discretion (*accompanied with forecast*), providence, forecast, sense, caution, carefulness, circumspection, considerateness, commonsense, judiciousness, judgment, wisdom (*applied to the ordinary affairs of life*), tact, policy, foresight.

Prudent, *a.* 1. Discreet, cautious, careful, heedful, politic, circumspect, wary, considerate, judicious, provident, foreseeing, wise, prudential.

2. Frugal, economical, thrifty, provident, sparing, saving.

Prudential, *a.* 1. Politic, prudent.

2. Discretionary, advisory.

Prudery, *n.* Coyness, demureness, stiffness, primness, prudishness, propriety, affected reserve, excessive nicety, preciousness.

Prudish, *a.* Coy, demure, reserved, over-modest, strait-laced, prim, affectedly modest *or* nice, very formal, precise.

Prune, *v. t.* 1. Lop, trim, clip, dock, thin, abbreviate.

2. Dress, trim, preen.

Prurient, *a.* Itching, longing, desiring, hankering, craving, lustful, covetous, lascivious.

Pry, *v. i.* Peer, peep, search, ferret, look closely *or* narrowly, scrutinize, examine, inspect, question, investigate, be inquisitive.

——, *v. t.* Force, lever, prize, pull open.

Prying, *a.* Curious, inquisitive, peering, peeping, scrutinizing.

Psalm, *n.* Sacred song, hymn.

Psalmody, *n.* Psalm-singing, psalmistry.

Psalter, *n.* Book of Psalms.

Pseudonym, *n.* False name, fictitious name, pen name, *nom de plume.*

Psyche, *n.* Soul, mind.

PUBLIC, *a.* 1. Of the whole, not private, national, political, civil, state, country-wide, common, general.

2. Open, notorious, published, known.

3. Common, general, popular.

——, *n.* [Preceded by *The.*] Persons, men, society, the people, the community, the world, general body of mankind.

Publican, *n.* 1. Tax-gatherer.

2. Inn-keeper, victualler.

Publication, *n.* 1. Promulgation, proclamation, announcement, disclosure, advertisement, report, divulgation, open declaration, blazon.

2. Literary production (*book, pamphlet, magazine, etc.*), issue, issuance, edition, printing.

Public-house, *n.* Inn, tavern, house of entertainment, hotel, ale-house, roadhouse, eating-house, victualling-house, restaurant.

Publicity, *n.* Notoriety, currency, publicness; spotlight, limelight, daylight; vent, outlet.

Publish, *v. t.* 1. Promulgate, proclaim, utter, blaze, blazon, announce, declare, disclose, divulge, reveal, advertise, bruit, impart, communicate, broach, make known, spread, spread abroad, blaze abroad, tell, ventilate, air, vent, diffuse, disseminate, make public, give out, "drag into the limelight," post, placard.

2. Issue (*as a book*), emit, send forth, bring out, put forth, print and offer for sale.

Puce, *a.* Dark-brown, reddish-brown, flea-colored.

Puck, *n.* Robin Good-fellow, Hobgoblin.

Pucker, *v. t.* Corrugate, furrow, cockle, wrinkle, contract, pinch, purse, shirr, crinkle, crease, gather into wrinkles *or* folds, gather.

Puddle, *n.* Pool (*of dirty water*), muddy plash.

Pudicity, *n.* Modesty, chastity.

Puerile, *a.* 1. Boyish, childish, juvenile, youthful.

2. Foolish, weak, petty, frivolous, trifling, trivial, idle, silly, simple, senseless, nonsensical.

Puerility, *n.* 1. Boyishness, childishness, youthfulness, juvenility.

2. Folly, foolishness, nonsense, weakness, silliness, insipidity.

Puff, *n.* Whiff, sudden gust; short, quick blast, breath, cloud.

——, *v. i.* 1. Blow in puffs.

2. Pant, breathe hard, gasp.

3. Brag, boast.

——, *v. t.* 1. Blow, inflate, swell.

2. Praise (*extravagantly*), compliment, flatter, laud, eulogize.

Puffed up. Conceited, proud, haughty, overweening, vain-glorious, vain.

Puffy, *a.* 1. Swelled, swollen, tumid, turgid, puffed out, distended.

2. Bombastic, inflated, extravagant, turgid, tumid, pompous.

Pugilism, *n.* Boxing, fisticuffs, fighting with the fist, prize-fighting.

Pugnacious, *a.* Quarrelsome, fighting, contentious, belligerent.

Puissant, *a.* Powerful, strong, mighty, forcible, potent.

Puke, *v. i.* 1. Vomit, spew.

2. Sicken, be disgusted.

——, *v. t.* Vomit, spew, cast up, throw up.

Pulchritude, *n.* Beauty, comeliness, grace, loveliness.

Pule, *v. i.* Whine, whimper, cry, snivel.

Puling, *a.* 1. Whining, whimpering.

2. Infantine, childish, trifling.

PULL, *n.* 1. Pluck, shake, twitch, tug, wrench.

2. Contest, struggle.

3. Magnetism, gravity, attraction.

4. (*Colloq.*) Power, influence, graft.

——, *v. t.* 1. Draw, haul, tug, drag, row, paddle, tow.

2. Pluck, gather, pick, extract, draw out.

3. Tear, rend, draw apart, detach, wrest.

——, *v. i.* Tug, give a pull.

Pull down. 1. Demolish, subvert, destroy.

2. Degrade, humble, bring down.

Pull in one's horns. (*Colloq.*) Repress one's ardor, restrain one's pride, cease boasting.

Pull up. 1. *v. t.* Draw up, haul up.

2. *v. t.* Extirpate, eradicate, destroy, pluck up, root out.

3. *v. i.* Stop, halt, draw the reins.

Pulmonary, *a.* Pulmonic, consumptive.

Pulp, *n.* Soft part, soft mass, pap, paste, jelly, mash, mush.

Pulpit, *n.* 1. Desk, sacred desk, rostrum, ambo, platform.

2. Preaching, public religious exercises; priesthood, ministry.

Pulpy, *a.* Soft, fleshy, succulent, pulpous.

Pulsate, *v. i.* Beat, throb, palpitate, thump, pant, vibrate.

Pulsation, *n.* Beating, beat, throbbing, throb, palpitation, pit-a-pat, ictus, accent.

Pulse, *n.* 1. Beating *or* throbbing of an artery, pulsation, throb.

2. Oscillation, vibration, pulsation, measured *or* regular beat.

3. Legumes, fruit of leguminous plants.

Pultaceous, *a.* Macerated, softened, pappy, nearly fluid.

Pulverize, *v. t.* Triturate, comminute, bruise, grind, bray, levigate, reduce to powder, pulverate.

Pulverulent, *a.* Dusty, powdery.

Pummel, *n.* [Written also and preferably *Pommel.*] Knob, protuberant part, ball.

——, *v. t.* Beat, strike, knock, hit, punch, whack, batter, belabor, bruise, thrash, flog, drub, bang, maul, thwack, thump, cudgel, baste.

PUMP, *v. t.* [*The noun is Basic Eng.*] 1. Cross-examine, interrogate, cross-question, draw out, catechize.

2. Pump up, inflate.

Pun, *n.* Quibble, clinch, calembourg, play upon words, witticism, conceit, paragram, paronomasia.

Punch, *v. t.* 1. Perforate, bore, pierce, puncture.

2. Push, poke, strike.

——, *n.* 1. Borer, puncheon.

2. Push, poke, blow, thrust.

3. Buffoon (*of a puppet-show*), clown, harlequin, punchinello, merry-andrew, mountebank, jester, droll, zany, scaramouch, fool, antic, pickle-herring, jack-pudding, mime.

Punctilio, *n.* Nicety (*of behavior*), nice point, form, point, pique.

Punctilious, *a.* Nice, exact, particular, careful, formal, precise, strict, scrupulous, over-scrupulous, conscientious, punctual, ceremonious.

Punctual, *a.* 1. Nice, exact, minutely correct, precise, punctilious.

2. Prompt, seasonable, timely, ready, early; regular.

Punctuality, *n.* 1. Nicety, scrupulosity, exactness.

2. Promptness, punctualness.

Punctuate, *v. t.*   Point, mark with points, separate into sentences, accentuate.

Puncture, *n.*   Small hole, wound, bite, sting.

——, *v. t.*   Prick, perforate, pierce.

Pungency, *n.*   1. Acridness, acrimony, acrimoniousness, tartness, causticity, poignancy, piquancy, sharpness.

2. Keenness, severity, satire, pointedness, smartness.

Pungent, *a.*   1. Smart, stinging, stimulating, pricking, sharp, biting, mordant, sour, acid, burning, caustic, racy, spicy, seasoned, salty, pyrotic, hot, peppery, piercing, penetrating, piquant, acrid.

2. Acute, keen, trenchant, cutting, acrimonious, severe, peevish, tart, waspish, distressing, irritating, poignant, smart, painful, satirical, pointed, piquant.

Punic, *a.*   1. Of the Carthaginians, Carthaginian.

2. Faithless, perfidious, treacherous, deceitful, untrustworthy, false, betraying, traitorous.

Punish, *v. t.*   1. Chastise, castigate, lash, chasten, correct, scourge, whip, flog, torture.

2. Discipline, correct, visit with pain *or* suffering, take vengeance on, inflict penalties upon, penalize, subject to penalty.

PUNISHMENT, *n.*   1. Chastisement, castigation, chastening, retribution, infliction, trial, scourging, correction, discipline.

2. Penalty, judgment, Nemesis.

Punitive, *a.*   Penal, corrective, disciplinary, retributive, castigatory.

Puny, *a.*   1. Weak, feeble, inferior.

2. Little, small, petty, insignificant, diminutive, undeveloped, undersized, tiny, dwarf, small, dwarfish, pygmy, pygmean, stunted, Liliputian.

Pup, *n.*   1. Puppy, whelp, young dog.

2. Young seal.

Pupa, *n.*   Chrysalis, aurelia.

Pupil, *n.*   Learner, scholar, disciple, student, tyro, beginner, novice, neophyte, catechumen.

Pupilage, *n.*   Nonage, minority, wardship, pupilarity, tutelage.

Puppet, *n.*   1. Marionette, image, manikin, lay-figure.

2. Tool, catspaw, pawn.

Puppy, *n.*   1. Pup, whelp, young dog.

2. Fop, coxcomb, prig, jackanapes, dandy.

Purblind, *a.*   Dim-sighted, near-sighted, short-sighted, myopic, mope-eyed; stupid, dull, obtuse.

Purchase, *v. t.*   1. Buy, bargain for, get by payment.

2. (*Rare*.) Obtain, acquire, procure, get, gain, invest in.

——, *n.*   1. Bargain, buying, acquirement, "buy."

2. Property, possession, acquisition, thing acquired.

3. Hold, advantage, power, force, leverage.

4. Tackle, lever, capstan.

Pure, *a.*   1. Clean, clear, unsullied, unstained, stainless, undefiled, spotless, unspotted, fair, immaculate, untainted, untarnished, unpolluted, unmixed, unadulterated, unalloyed, uncorrupted, unblemished.

2. Innocent, guiltless, guileless, true, virtuous, sincere, clean, white, chaste, continent, modest, virgin, upright, honest, incorrupt, holy.

3. Genuine, unadulterated, unmixed, real, true, perfect, simple, clear, single.

4. Mere, absolute, sheer.

5. Classic, classical, Attic.

Purely, *adv.*   1. Genuinely.

2. Innocently, chastely, guilelessly.

3. Merely, absolutely, entirely, completely, totally.

Purgation, *n.*   Clearing, cleansing, purification, evacuation, lustration, clarification, defecation, detersion.

Purgative, *a.*   Cathartic, abstergent, abstersive, cleansing, purifying, evacuant, detersive, detergent.

——, *n.*   (*Med*.) Purge, physic, cathartic, scourer, purgative medicine.

Purgatory, *a.*   Cleansing, expiatory.

——, *n.*   Limbo, hell, infernal regions, shades below.

Purge, *v. t.*   1. Cleanse, clear, purify, free from impurity.

2. Clarify, defecate, evacuate; physic, scour; deterge, wash away.

3. Absolve, pardon, shrive.

Purification, *n.*   1. Cleansing, purifying.

2. Defecation, clearing, clarification, depuration.

3. Lustration.

Purify, *v. t.*   1. Clear, clean, cleanse, purge, free from impurity, make pure, depurate, refine, wash, expurgate.

2. Defecate (*as liquors*), clarify, fine.

Purism, *n.*   Nicety (*in the use of words*), fastidiousness, squeamishness, daintiness, euphuism, affected elegance, finical style.

Puritanic, } *a.* Strict, rigid, ascetic, over-
Puritanical, }   scrupulous, prim, strait-laced, severe, prudish, precise in religious matters.

Purity, *n.*   1. Clearness, fineness.

2. Cleanness, clearness, immaculateness, faultlessness, correctness.

3. Innocence, virtue, guiltlessness, guilelessness, holiness, honesty, integrity, uprightness, piety, truth, simplicity.

4. Genuineness, excellence, integrity; homogeneity, simpleness.

5. Modesty, chastity, chasteness, continence, pudicity, virginity.

Purl, v. i. Murmur, ripple, gurgle, bubble.

Purlieus, n. pl. [*Used generally in a bad sense.*] Environs, precincts, suburbs, neighborhood, vicinage, borders, bounds, limits, outskirts, confines.

Purloin, v. t. Steal, rob, pilfer, thieve, filch, abstract, crib, cabbage.

Purport, n. Design, meaning, signification, import, significance, drift, current, tenor, bearing, scope, sense, tendency, gist, intent, spirit.

——, v. t. (*Pron.* purport'.) Intend, mean, signify, import, show, design.

PURPOSE, n. 1. Aim, intent, intention, design, resolve, resolution, object, end, drift, view, final cause.

2. Design, project, plan, intention.

3. Sense, meaning, purport.

4. End, effect, consequence.

——, v. t. Intend, design, mean, meditate, think of, have in mind, resolve upon, propose to one's self, harbor a design, contemplate, determine upon.

——, v. i. Intend, design, mean, have in mind, determine, resolve.

Purposely, adv. Intentionally, designedly, by design, on purpose, advisedly, wittingly, knowingly, deliberately.

Pursuance, n. Pursuit, prosecution, following out.

Pursue, v. t. 1. Follow, chase, hunt, track, dog, shadow, hound, go after, give chase to.

2. Continue, prosecute, conduct, keep up, push, carry on, persist in, engage in, follow up, maintain, stick to, practise, cultivate, go in for.

3. Seek, strive for, try to obtain.

4. Follow, proceed along, keep to, hold to, keep on.

5. Imitate, follow as an example.

6. Attend, accompany, follow close.

Pursuit, n. 1. Chase, race, hunt.

2. Pursuance, prosecution, following out, practice, conduct, cultivation.

3. Business, occupation, vocation, calling, employment, avocation, hobby, fad.

Pursuivant, n. 1. Follower, attendant.

2. State messenger.

Pursy, a. 1. Fat, corpulent, fleshy, plump, short, thick, pudgy, podgy.

2. Short-breathed, short-winded, thick-winded.

3. Rich, opulent.

Purulent, a. Feculent, suppurating, festering, corrupt.

Purvey, v. i. 1. Provide, furnish, cater, procure provisions, provide food, victual, find provision.

2. Procure, get, obtain.

Purveyance, n. Provisions, food, victuals provided, furnishing.

Purveyor, n. Provider, caterer, victualler.

Purview, n. Limit, sphere, scope, extent, reach, body, view, compass.

Pus, n. Purulence, matter, purulent matter, humor.

Puseyite, a. Tractarian, Tractite, Oxford school.

Push, v. t. 1. Thrust, impel (*by pressure*), hustle, jostle, justle, elbow, crowd, shove.

2. Urge, press forward, drive on, advance, propel.

3. Force, press, drive, embarrass by arguments.

4. Importune, tease, press with solicitation.

5. Prosecute, follow closely.

6. Impel, drive, urge.

——, v. i. 1. Thrust, make a thrust.

2. Endeavor, strive, try, exert one's self.

3. Bud, sprout, germinate, vegetate, grow, burst out, put forth, shoot forth.

PUSH, n. 1. Thrust, foin, pressure, shove; determination, perseverance.

2. Trial, test, exigence, exigency, extremity, emergency, pinch, strait.

3. Onset, attack, assault, charge, strong effort, endeavor.

Pusillanimity, n. Cowardice, cowardliness, timidity, poltroonery, recreancy, dastardliness, mean-spiritedness, pusillanimousness, effeminacy, faint-heartedness, fear.

Pusillanimous, a. Cowardly, timorous, timid, feeble, recreant, dastardly, effeminate, spiritless, weak, mean-spirited, little-souled, faint-hearted.

Pustule, n. Ulcer, fester, imposthume, gathering, pimple, blotch, blain, sore, abscess, aposteme.

PUT, v. t. 1. Place, set, lay, deposit, bring, impose, collocate, locate, place, repose, plant; cast, throw.

2. Impose, enjoin, levy, inflict.

3. Propose, offer, state, present, bring forward.

4. Oblige, compel, force, constrain, push to action.

5. Incite, urge, entice, induce.

6. Express, utter, state in language.

Put about. (*Naut.*) Tack, turn, change the course.

Putative, *a.* Reputed, supposed, commonly esteemed, deemed, reckoned, reported.

Put away. 1. Lay away, set aside, put aside.

2. Renounce, discard, reject, put off, expel.

3. Divorce.

Put by. 1. Lay by, lay aside.

2. Thrust aside, turn off.

Put down. 1. Deposit, lay down.

2. Repress, crush, baffle, overthrow, destroy, conquer.

3. Degrade, confute, humiliate, abash, shame, disconcert, humble, extinguish, suppress.

4. Confute, silence.

Put forth, *v. t.* 1. Exert, bring into play, bring into action, make manifest.

2. Extend, thrust out, reach, stretch out.

3. Emit, send out, throw out.

4. Publish, issue.

5. Propose, offer to notice.

——, *v. i.* 1. Leave port, put to sea.

2. Bud, shoot, germinate, push, vegetate, grow.

Put forward. Promote, advance.

Put in mind. Remind, call to remembrance.

Put in practice. Apply, exercise, make use of.

Put off, *v. t.* 1. Discard, renounce, reject, cast aside, lay aside, divest one's self of.

2. Defeat, frustrate, disappoint, turn aside, baffle.

3. Defer, delay, procrastinate, postpone, suspend.

4. Get rid of, dispose of, pass fraudulently.

——, *v. i.* Leave shore, put to sea, put forth, push from land.

Put on. 1. Invest with, clothe.

2. Assume, take on.

3. Impose, inflict.

Put out. 1. Eject, expel, drive out.

2. Extend, protrude, hold out, stretch forth.

3. Emit, send out, throw out, shoot out.

4. Extinguish.

5. Publish, issue, make public.

6. Dislocate, luxate.

7. Confuse, disconcert, interrupt.

8. Offend, displease, anger, provoke, vex, irritate.

Put over. 1. Place in command of, give authority over.

2. Defer, postpone, put off.

3. Refer, send.

4. Accomplish, perform successfully.

Putrefy, *v. t.* Corrupt, rot, render putrid.

——, *v. i.* Rot, decay, decompose, become rotten, become putrid.

Putrid, *a.* Decomposed, rotten, decayed, corrupt, putrefied, stinking.

Put the hand to. Apply, take hold, begin, undertake.

Put to death. Kill.

Put to it. Distress, perplex, puzzle, embarrass.

Put to rights. Adjust, regulate, set in order, set to rights.

Put to shame. Shame, abash, mortify, make ashamed, put to the blush, put out of countenance, put down.

Put up, *v. t.* 1. Store, pack away, preserve.

2. Expose, offer publicly.

3. Put away, lay away, set aside.

4. Hoard, save.

——, *v. i.* Lodge, stay, take lodgings. See STOP.

Put up with. Endure (*without complaint*), bear, tolerate, suffer, overlook, submit to, make the best of.

Puzzle, *v. t.* 1. Perplex, embarrass, bewilder, confound, stagger, pose, nonplus, confuse, mystify, gravel.

2. Make intricate, entangle, complicate.

——, *n.* 1. Riddle, enigma, conundrum, labyrinth, maze.

2. Perplexity, embarrassment, bewilderment, question, complication, mystification, dilemma, confusion, dark problem, difficulty, poser, knotty point, quandary, nonplus.

Pygmean, *a.* Dwarfish, dwarfed, diminutive, small, stunted, Liliputian, pygmy, little.

Pygmy, *n.* Dwarf, hop o' my thumb, atomy, Liliputian, midget.

Pyre, *n.* Funeral pile, heap.

Pyriform, *a.* Pear-shaped, obconical.

Pyrotechnics, *n.* Pyrotechny, fireworks.

Pyrotic, *a.* Caustic, burning.

Pyrrhonism, *n.* Scepticism, unbelief, incredulity.

Pyrrhonist, *n.* Sceptic, doubter.

Pyx, *n.* Box (*especially that in which the host is kept*), tabernacle, vessel, pyxis.

Q

Quack, *n.* Charlatan, empiric, mountebank, impostor, pretender, humbug.

——, *v. i.* Cackle, cry, squeak.

Quadrangular, *a.* Four-cornered.

Quadrate, *a. & n.* Square.

Quadrifoil,
Quadrifoliate, } *a.* Four-leaved.

Quadrilateral, *a.* Four-sided.

Quadruped, *n.* Four-footed animal.

Quadruple, *a.* Fourfold, quadruplicate, four-cycle.

Quaff, *v. t.* Drink (*copiously*), swallow in large draughts, "swig," drain.

Quaggy, *a.* Boggy, marshy, swampy, queachy.

Quagmire, *n.* Bog, fen, slough, morass, marsh, swamp.

Quail, *v. i.* Cower, shrink, flinch, faint, blench, droop, quake, tremble, be quelled, give way, lose courage, lose spirit, be cast down.

Quaint, *a.* 1. Odd, strange, queer, singular, antique, antiquated, old-fashioned, archaic, unusual, uncommon, extraordinary, unique, curious, droll, fanciful.

2. Far-fetched, affected, odd, whimsical, fantastic, out of the way.

Quake, *v. i.* 1. Shake, tremble, shudder, shiver, quiver.

2. Shake, tremble, vibrate, quiver, move.

——, *n.* Shake, trembling, shudder, tremulous agitation, earthquake.

Quaker, *n.* Friend.

Qualification, *n.* 1. Fitness, suitableness, capability, accomplishment, requisite capacity, ability, eligibility, competency, legal power.

2. Modification, limitation, restriction, coloring, proviso, stipulation, exception, condition.

3. Abatement, diminution, mitigation, allowance, grains of allowance, consideration, extenuating circumstances.

4. Adaptation, fitting, preparation.

Qualified, *a.* 1. Modified, limited.

2. Competent, fit, adapted, able, eligible, capable, fitted, accomplished.

Qualify, *v. t.* 1. Fit, adapt, capacitate, equip, prepare, empower, make fit, make suitable, entitle, make capable.

2. Modify, limit, restrict, restrain, narrow.

3. Soften, abate, diminish, mitigate, ease, assuage, moderate, temper, reduce.

4. Regulate, vary, temper, modulate, allow for, affect.

5. Dilute, modify.

QUALITY, *n.* 1. Property, attribute, nature, feature, singularity, affection, tinge, color, mark, flavor, timbre, characteristic, peculiarity, trait.

2. Disposition, humor, temper, mood, character, condition, characteristic.

3. Rank, condition, high descent, station, standing, status, stamp, calibre, class, brand, chop, grade, character, sort, kind, description, capacity.

4. [With *The* prefixed.] Nobility, gentry, aristocracy, persons of rank, *noblesse.*

5. Part, special character, assumed position.

Qualm, *n.* 1. Throe, pang, agony, sudden attack.

2. Sickness (*of the stomach*), nausea, queasiness.

3. Twinge (*of conscience*), scruple, uneasiness, compunction, remorse.

Quandary, *n.* Difficulty, perplexity, doubt, puzzle, plight, uncertainty, embarrassment, bewilderment, nonplus, strait, dilemma, pickle, predicament.

Quantity, *n.* 1. Size, greatness, extent, measure, content, number, portion, share.

2. Amount, aggregate, bulk, sum, quantum, volume, mass, lot, batch, store.

3. Length, duration.

Quarrel, *n.* 1. Brawl, feud, affray, fray, tumult, contention, altercation, tiff, miff, spat, misunderstanding, wrangle, contest, squabble, broil, jar, breach, row, clash, rupture, dispute, difference, disagreement, disturbance, fight, controversy, discord, embroglio, imbroilment, dissension, bickering, quarrelling, strife, breeze, falling out, variance.

2. Dispute, contest, open variance, breach of concord.

3. Objection, ill-will.

——, *v. i.* 1. Wrangle, scold, altercate, squabble, bicker, brawl, dispute, spar, jangle, spat, cavil, clash, fall out, have words, have an altercation, be at variance.

2. Scuffle, squabble, fight, strive.

3. Cavil, find fault, carp.

4. Disagree, clash, jar, be discordant, differ, contend.

Quarrelsome, *a.* Irascible, choleric, irritable, petulant, cross, contentious, disputatious, combative, dissentious, discordant, pugnacious, wranglesome, "cantankerous," ugly, fiery.

Quarry, *n.* 1. Stone-pit, stone-bed.

2. Prey (*especially that of the hunting falcon*), game, object of the chase.

Quarter, *n.* 1. Fourth part; three months, one fourth.

2. District, region, territory, locality, place, lodge, billet, abode; direction, place, point of compass.

3. Mercy (*granted by a combatant*), clemency, mildness.

4. Station, position, location, specific place.

5. Proper position, specific place, special location.

——, *v. t.* 1. Divide in four equal parts.

2. Divide, separate into parts, cut to pieces, carve.

3. Lodge, billet, furnish with quarters (*as soldiers*), locate, post, station.

4. Allot, share, deal out, furnish.

——, *v. i.* Lodge, abide, have lodgings, be stationed.

Quarter-note, *n.* Crotchet.

Quarters, *n. pl.* 1. Stations, posts, cantonments, billet.

2. Lodgings, dwelling, abode, habitation, shelter, entertainment, temporary residence.

Quash, *v. t.* 1. Crush, beat to pieces.

2. Crush, subdue, quell, repress, suppress, stop, extinguish, put down.

3. (*Law.*) Annul, nullify, overthrow, cancel, invalidate, abolish, make void, abate.

Quasi. [L.] Apparently, as if, as though, as it were, in a certain sense, to a certain extent, in a manner.

Quaternary, *a.* Four, fourfold, consisting of four.

Quaver, *v. i.* Tremble, shake, quiver, vibrate, shudder, oscillate, trill, falter.

——, *n.* (*Mus.*) 1. Shake.

2. Eighth-note, eighth of a semibreve, quarter of a minim, half of a crotchet.

Quay, *n.* Wharf, artificial bank, landing-place, dock, pier, levee.

Queachy, *a.* Shaking, yielding, trembling, moving.

Queasy, *a.* 1. Qualmish, sick (*at the stomach*), inclined to vomit, nauseated.

2. Fastidious, squeamish, difficult, over-nice, sensitive, scrupulous, delicate.

Queer, *a.* Odd, strange, singular, droll, whimsical, peculiar, quaint, curious, fantastic, unusual, uncommon, extraordinary, unique.

Quell, *v. t.* 1. Subdue, suppress, crush, put down, conquer, overcome, overpower.

2. Repress, restrain, check, smother, stifle, extinguish, quench, curb, bridle, lay, rein in.

3. Quiet, calm, still, compose, lull, hush, tranquillize, pacify, allay, reduce to peace, subdue.

4. Moderate, assuage, mitigate, allay, appease, alleviate, mollify, soften, dull, soothe, blunt, deaden.

Quench, *v. t.* 1. Extinguish, put out.

2. Destroy, still, stifle, repress, check, suppress, put an end to; sate, satiate, appease.

3. Allay, slake, cool, extinguish, dampen.

Quenchless, *a.* Inextinguishable, unquenchable, irrepressible.

Querist, *n.* Inquirer, interrogator, investigator, questioner.

Querulous, *a.* Complaining, murmuring, querimonious, petulant, peevish, cross, dissatisfied, touchy, irritable, discontented, fault-finding, bewailing, lamenting, plaintive, whining, mourning, fretful.

Query, *n.* Question, inquiry, interrogatory, problem, issue.

——, *v. i.* Make inquiry, ask questions.

——, *v. t.* 1. Question, inquire, ask.

2. Doubt, dispute, hesitate to believe, consider questionable.

Quest, *n.* 1. Search; journey, expedition.

2. Pursuit, suit.

3. Inquiry, examination.

4. Request, desire, prayer, solicitation, invitation, demand.

QUESTION, *n.* 1. Interrogation, examination, interpellation, inquiry, act of asking.

2. Interrogatory, query, inquiry.

3. Discussion, inquiry, debate, disquisition, issue, investigation, trial, examination.

4. Dispute, controversy, doubt, verbal contest.

5. Proposition, motion, topic, point, problem, puzzle, mystery, poser, theme of inquiry, subject of investigation.

6. Examination, investigation, trial, judicial *or* official inquiry.

——, *v. t.* 1. Interrogate, ask, catechise, sound out, seek out, "quiz," "pump," interpellate, examine, inquire of, put questions to.

2. Doubt, query, hesitate to believe, consider questionable, be uncertain of.

3. Dispute, call in question, challenge, take exception to.

Questionable, *a.* Doubtful, suspicious, uncertain, undecided, equivocal, problematical, disputable, controversial, "fishy," ambiguous, controvertible, debatable, liable to question.

Questioner, *n.* Inquirer, interrogator.

Quibble, *n.* 1. Evasion, cavil, subterfuge, pretence, subtlety, quirk, shift, shuffle, prevarication, equivocation, sophism, quiddity, trifling nicety.

2. Pun, clinch, calembourg, play upon words.

Quibble, *v. i.* 1. Cavil, shuffle, prevaricate, equivocate, practise evasion, evade the truth, trifle, shift.

2. Pun, play upon words.

Quibbling, *a.* Shuffling, evasive, prevaricating, disingenuous.

QUICK, *a.* 1. Active, nimble, agile, animated, sprightly, lively, smart, alert, brisk, prompt, ready.

2. Rapid, swift, speedy, fleet, fast, hasty, expeditious, hurried, flying.

3. Dexterous, adroit, skilful, expert, apt.

4. Acute, clever, sharp, shrewd, keen, intelligent, sagacious, discerning, sensitive.

5. Hasty, precipitate, sharp, unceremonious, choleric, passionate, testy, irritable, touchy, waspish, petulant, irascible, peppery, snappish.

6. Alive, living, live, animate.

Quicken, *v. t.* 1. Vivify, revive, resuscitate, energize, make alive, animate, give life to.

2. Revive, cheer, reinvigorate, refresh, enliven, whet.

3. Hasten, accelerate, speed, hurry, expedite, despatch.

4. Stimulate, sharpen, excite, incite, refresh, kindle, actuate.

——, *v. i.* Live, come alive, accelerate, work, take effect.

Quickly, *adv.* 1. Speedily, swiftly, rapidly, nimbly, readily, fast, quick, with haste, with celerity, post-haste, apace.

2. Soon, without delay, immediately, forthwith, in a short time.

Quickness, *n.* 1. Celerity, expedition, velocity, speed, speediness, fleetness, rapidity, swiftness, despatch, haste.

2. Activity, briskness, nimbleness, readiness, promptness, promptitude, alertness, agility, smartness, liveliness.

3. Dexterity, adroitness, expertness, dexterousness, aptness, aptitude, facility, knack.

4. Sharpness, penetration, keenness, acuteness, sagacity, shrewdness, perspicacity, acumen.

5. Sharpness, pungency, keenness.

Quick-witted, *a.* Witty, smart, nimble-witted, ready.

Quid, *n.* Cud.

Quiddity, *n.* 1. Essence, nature.

2. Quibble, cavil, evasion, sophism, subterfuge, prevarication, equivocation, trifling nicety, subtlety, quirk.

Quid pro quo. [L.] Equivalent, tit for tat.

Quiescence, *n.* 1. Rest, repose, quiet, quietude, stillness, calmness, calm, tranquillity, peace.

2. Suspense, intermission, remission, dormancy, abeyance.

3. Silence.

Quiescent, *a.* 1. Quiet, resting, still, motionless, at rest, at a stand, stock-still, standing still.

2. Quiet, still, placid, calm, unagitated, undisturbed, tranquil, serene, unruffled.

QUIET, *a.* 1. Still, quiescent, unmoved, motionless, hushed.

2. Tranquil, calm, peaceful, peaceable, silent, undemonstrative, modest, unobtrusive, gentle, mild, meek, contented.

3. Smooth, unruffled, unmolested, undisturbed, placid, tranquil.

4. Calm, patient, contented.

5. Retired, secluded.

——, *n.* 1. Rest, repose, stillness, calm, gentleness, relaxation, hush, calmness, quietude, quiescence, quietness.

2. Tranquillity, peace, security, ease, calm, calmness, silence, quietness, serenity, repose, freedom from disturbance *or* alarm.

3. Patience, calmness.

——, *v. t.* 1. Stop, suspend, still, arrest, interrupt, intermit, discontinue, put a stop to.

2. Tranquillize, calm, compose, lull, pacify, appease, soothe, sober, allay.

3. Still, silence, hush.

4. Moderate, allay, assuage, mitigate, mollify, alleviate, soften, dull, blunt.

Quietly, *adv.* 1. Peaceably, at rest, without disturbance, without agitation.

2. Calmly, patiently.

3. Silently, noiselessly.

Quietness, *n.* Tranquillity, stillness, calmness, peace, silence.

Quietus, *n.* Acquittance, final discharge, settlement.

Quill, *n.* Pen; shaft, feather, plume.

Quill-driver, *n.* 1. Writer, scribbler.

2. Clerk, scribe, secretary, amanuensis.

Quintessence, *n.* Essence, essential part, extract.

Quintuple, *a.* Fivefold.

Quip, *n.* Taunt, gibe, jeer, scoff, sneer, mock, flout, sally, quirk, crank, repartee. retort, sharp saying, caustic *or* cutting remark, biting jest, sarcasm, witticism.

Quirk, *n.* 1. Evasion, subterfuge, prevarication, shift, make-shift, loop-hole, quibble, pretense, pretext, excuse.

2. Taunt, gibe, jeer, sally, quip.

Quit, *v. t.* 1. Deliver, release, free, acquit, absolve, set free.

2. Free, relieve, clear, liberate, discharge from, deliver.

3. Acquit, conduct, behave (*used reflexively*).

4. Resign, give up, renounce, relinquish, surrender, stop.

5. Perform, carry through.

6. Pay, discharge, requite, repay.

7. Leave (*with the purpose of never returning*), withdraw from, go away from, retire from, depart from, get away from.

8. Abandon, desert, forsake, forswear, cast off.

Quit, *a.* Clear, free, absolved, released, acquitted, discharged.

QUITE, *adv.* 1. Completely, wholly, entirely, totally, perfectly, positively, exactly, precisely.

2. Very, considerably, in a great degree, to a great extent.

Quittance, *n.* 1. Discharge, acquittance, receipt.

2. Recompense, return, repayment, reward, requital.

Quiver, *v. i.* Quake, shake, tremble, play, be agitated, shudder, shiver, vibrate, oscillate, palpitate, flutter, flicker, twitch.

——, *n.* Trembling, tremulous motion, shake, shudder, shiver, etc.

Quixotic, *a.* Visionary, imaginary, wild, mad, fanciful, freakish, Utopian, chimerical, fantastic, fantastical, absurdly romantic.

Quiz, *n.* 1. Puzzle (*by way of sport*), enigma, riddle, knotty question, hoax, joke, jest.

2. Odd fellow, joker, jester, hoax.

——, *v. t.* 1. Puzzle (*for sport*), ridicule, banter, hoax, run upon, make fun of, make sport of.

2. Stare at (*in mockery*), peer at.

3. Examine, question.

Quondam, *a.* [L.] Former, late, old-time, in former times, past, *ci-devant*.

Quota, *n.* Portion, share, contingent, proportion, allotment, apportionment, quantity, proportional part.

Quotation, *n.* 1. Citation, extract, selection, excerpt, cutting, clipping, reference.

2. Rate, current price.

Quote, *v. t.* Cite, adduce, name, repeat, instance, illustrate, excerpt, extract, take.

R

Rabbi, *n.* Hebrew doctor, teacher, master.

Rabble, *n.* 1. Mob, rout, rabble-rout, horde, tumultuous crowd of vulgar people; confused, disorderly crowd.

2. Populace, commonalty, dregs of the people, scum of society, trash, lower classes, the masses, riff-raff, ignoble vulgar, vulgar herd, *canaille*.

3. Rhapsody, incoherent discourse, medley.

Rabid, *a.* 1. Furious, raging, mad, frantic.

2. Rampant, intolerant, excessively enthusiastic, fanatical.

Race, *n.* 1. Generation, lineage, stock, breed, strain, family, line, house, kindred.

2. Tribe, family, clan, people, nation, folk.

3. Progeny, descendants, offspring, children, breed, lineage, issue, stock.

4. Trial of speed, competition, course, career, run, contest, sprint, dash, heat; chase, pursuit.

5. Mill-race, head-race, current, channel.

6. Flavor, taste, strength, quality, smack (*of wine*).

——, *v. i.* 1. Run swiftly, hasten.

2. Contend in running.

——, *v. t.* Drive swiftly, run.

Race-course, *n.* Ring, racing ground, course, hippodrome.

Racer, *n.* 1. Runner, competitor, entrant.

2. Race-horse, courser, blood-horse, thorough-bred horse.

Rachitic, *a.* Rickety.

Racial, *a.* Ancestral, lineal, phyletic (*biol.*).

Rack, *n.* 1. Torture, torment, anguish, agony, pang, extreme pain.

2. Crib, manger.

3. Neck (*of mutton*), crag.

4. Mist, vapor, flying cloud, moisture, dampness.

5. Stand, frame.

——, *v. t.* 1. Torture, torment, distress, rend, agonize, excruciate, pain extremely.

2. Stretch, strain, force, wrest.

3. Harass (*by exaction*), exhaust, oppress.

Racket, *n.* 1. Uproar, clamor, hubbub, tumult, din, carouse, frolic, dissipation, clatter, fracas, noise, outcry, disturbance.

2. (*Colloq.*) Scheme, game, understanding, graft.

Racy, *a.* 1. That tastes of the soil (*as wine*), of a peculiar flavor, pungent, flavorous, fine-flavored, palatable, rich, piquant, strong.

2. Strong (*as peculiar qualities of thought* or *of expression*), vigorous, forcible, of a distinctive character, spirited, pungent, piquant, lively, stimulating.

Raddle, *v. t.* 1. Interweave, twist together.

2. Wrinkle.

Radiance, *n.* Brilliance, brilliancy, lustre, light, luminosity, emission, brightness, splendor, resplendence, effulgence, refulgence, glare, glitter, shine, glister.

Radiant, *a.* 1. Beaming, shining, brilliant, splendid, resplendent, effulgent, sparkling, lustrous, glittering, luminous, glorious.

2. Pleased, happy, ecstatic.

Radiate, *v. i.* 1. Shine, gleam, emit rays, beam, glitter.

2. Issue in rays, emanate in rays.

3. Emit heat, throw off heat, be radiant.

4. Diverge, branch out (*from a center*).

——, *v. t.* Emit (*heat* or *light*) in straight lines, shed, diffuse, spread.

Radiation, *n.* Irradiance, irradiation, emission of rays, beamy brightness, rays, emanation, shining.

Radical, *a.* 1. Original, fundamental, organic, constitutional, native, natural, innate, essential, ingrained, deep-seated.

2. Primitive, underived, uncompounded, simple, original.

3. Thorough, entire, complete, perfect, total, ultra, "leftist," rebellious, insurgent, extreme, thorough-going, fundamental.

——, *n.* 1. Radical reformer.

2. Primitive letter.

3. Root, radix, etymon, primitive word.

4. (*Chem.*) Base.

Radically, *adv.* 1. Fundamentally.

2. Primitively, essentially, originally.

Radicle, *n.* Rootlet.

Rag, *n.* 1. Shred, tatter, fragment, bit, patch, clout, cloth.

2. [*pl.*] Mean attire, mean dress.

Ragamuffin, *n.* Tatterdemalion, mean fellow, ragabash, wretch, paltry fellow.

Rag-baby, *n.* Moppet, mopsey.

Rage, *n.* 1. Fury, frenzy, wrath, vehemence, storm, rampage, excitement, passion, madness, raving, violent anger, furor.

2. Extreme eagerness, vehement desire.

3. (*Colloq.*) Fashion, vogue, mode, craze, mania, style.

——, *v. i.* 1. Rave, storm, fume, fret, chafe, foam, boil, bluster, be violent, be furious.

2. Ravage, prevail without restraint.

Ragged, *a.* 1. Tattered, torn, rent.

2. Dressed in rags, contemptible, shabby, poor, mean.

3. Uneven, jagged, rough.

4. Rough, rugged, shaggy.

5. Unmusical, dissonant, inharmonious, discordant.

Raging, *a.* Furious, enraged, infuriate, infuriated, incensed, very angry.

Raid, *n.* Invasion, inroad, foray, irruption, plunder, pillage, attack, hostile incursion (*especially of mounted men*).

——, *v. t.* Assault, plunder, invade, fall upon, pillage, forage.

Rail at. Censure, reproach, upbraid, abuse, scoff at, sneer at, scold at, inveigh against, exclaim against, declaim against.

Railing, *n.* 1. Vituperation, abuse, scolding, reviling, contumely, reproach, invective, aspersion, censure.

2. Banister, parapet, fence, barrier, bar, balustrade.

Raillery, *n.* Banter, irony, slight ridicule, pleasantry, chaff, good-humored satire, joke, satirical merriment, jesting language.

Railroad, *n.* Railway, tramway, tracks.

Raiment, *n.* Clothes, clothing, dress, attire, apparel, vesture, vestments, garments, habiliment, habit, garb, costume, array.

RAIN, *n.* Downpour, drizzle, mist, shower, sprinkle, cloudburst.

Rainbow, *n.* Iris.

Rain-gauge, *n.* Pluviometer, ombrometer, udometer.

Rainy, *a.* Showery, wet, moist, drizzly.

Raise, *v. t.* 1. Lift, uplift, set up, raise up, upraise, make upright, hoist, heave, boost, erect, rear, construct, build up, uprear, float.

2. Exalt, elevate, advance, promote, ennoble.

3. Enhance, heighten, increase, aggravate, advance, augment, amplify, enlarge, intensify, invigorate.

4. Excite, rouse, arouse, awake, stir up, call up, call forth, put in action, put in motion, cause to arise, give rise to, originate, produce, cause, effect; occasion, start, set going.

5. Collect, levy, obtain, get, bring together, assemble.

6. Grow, cause to grow, propagate, breed, cultivate; rear, bring up.

7. Make light *or* spongy (*as bread*), work, ferment, leaven.

8. Bring back to life, raise from the dead.

9. Utter, strike up, give utterance to.

Rake, *n.* Libertine, debauchee, man of pleasure, *roué.*

——, *v. t.* 1. Gather, collect, draw together, heap together, gather together, scrape together, comb, scratch, rake up, heap up, scrape over.

2. Scour, search closely, ransack.

3. Enfilade.

——, *v. i.* Search, grope, scrape, scratch in order to find.

Rakish, *a.* Lewd, debauched, dissolute, licentious, dissipated.

Rally, *v. t.* 1. Reunite, restore to order, gather, recover, concentrate, encourage, rouse, revive.

2. Banter, joke, ridicule, satirize, deride, mock, quiz, taunt, treat with raillery.

——, *v. i.* 1. Be restored to order, come into order, take courage.

2. Recover, recover strength, gain ground, get better, pick up.

3. Meet, convene, assemble, collect.

4. Jest, indulge in banter *or* raillery.

Ram, *v. t.* 1. Drive down, force down, beat.

2. Cram, stuff, force in, tamp, drive, crowd, dam, stop.

3. Butt, strike, run into.

Ramble, *v. i.* Rove, wander, stroll, range, roam, saunter, straggle, stray; digress, maunder.

——, *n.* Stroll, excursion, trip, tour, wandering, rambling, roving.

Rambling, *a.* Strolling, rambling, wandering, straggling, irregular; discursive.

Ramification, *n.* 1. Branching, forking, arborescence, radiation, divarication.

2. Branch, division, subdivision, offshoot, subordinate branch.

Ramify, *v. t.* Separate into branches.

——, *v. i.* Branch, divaricate, extend, shoot into branches.

Ramp, *n.* 1. Leap, spring, bound.

2. Incline, sloping passageway.

——, *v. i.* 1. Climb, creep up.

2. Spring, bound, leap, prance, gambol, frolic, sport, play, romp.

3. Spring violently, rage, bound wildly.

Rampancy, *n.* Exuberance, extravagance, excessive prevalence.

Rampant, *a.* 1. Rank, exuberant, luxuriant, wanton, excessive.

2. Vehement, impetuous, boisterous, raging, ungovernable, uncontrollable, headstrong, dominant, unbridled, violent, predominant.

Rampart, *n.* 1. Bulwark, defence, fence, security, guard, fortification, circumvallation, wall.

2. Mound, elevation, embankment.

Ramrod, *n.* Rammer, gun-stick.

Rancid, *a.* Rank, fetid, musty, fusty, strong-smelling, sour, tainted, foul, offensive, bad.

Rancor, *n.* Malignity, malice, malevolence, spite, venom, gall, grudge, ill-will, hate, hatred, enmity, animosity, vindictiveness, bitterness.

Rancorous, *a.* Malignant, malign, vindictive, hateful, malevolent, malicious, bitter, spiteful, virulent.

Random, *a.* Chance, casual, fortuitous, stray, accidental, haphazard, irregular, wandering.

RANGE, *n.* 1. Row, rank, line, tier, file; line of mountains.

2. Class, order, kind, sort.

3. Excursion, wandering, ramble, expedition, roving.

4. Scope, sweep, compass, extent, reach, bound, view, distance, amplitude, latitude, command, discursive power.

5. (*Mus.*) Compass, register.

——, *v. t.* 1. Class, rank, arrange, set in a row, dispose in order, align, classify.

2. Rove over, pass over, traverse.

3. Sail along, pass near.

——, *v. i.* 1. Rove, ramble, wander, stroll, stray, extend, cruise, roam, course, straggle, rove at large.

2. Consort, be classed, be ranked, rank.

3. Lie, run, bend, correspond in direction.

Rank, *a.* 1. Luxuriant, vigorous, exuberant, dense, overgrown, wild, over-abundant, high-growing, strong in growth.

2. Excessive, extravagant, rampant, very great, extreme, unmitigated, flagrant, violent, gross, sheer, utter.

3. Rancid, musty, fusty, fetid, offensive, foul, strong-smelling, strong-scented, frowzy.

4. Fertile, rich, productive.

5. Gross, coarse, foul, disgusting.

——, *n.* 1. Row, line, tier, range, order, file.

2. Class, order, division, series, group.

3. Degree, grade, quality, relative station, birth, quality, blood; caste, position, standing, stakes, sphere, estate.

4. Dignity, high degree, distinction, eminence, nobility.

Rank, *v. t.* 1. Class, arrange, range, classify.

2. Outrank, take precedence of, precede.

——, *v. i.* Be ranked, be classed, take rank, have rank.

Rank and file. Privates, common soldiers (*including corporals*).

Rankle, *v. i.* 1. Fester, be inflamed, ulcerate; pain.

2. Be embittered, become more bitter, grow more intense, be inflamed.

Rankling, *n.* 1. Festering.

2. Animosity, hatred, heart-burning.

Rankly, *adv.* 1. Luxuriantly, with vigorous growth.

2. Rancidly, with strong scent.

3. Coarsely, grossly.

Ransack, *v. t.* 1. Plunder, pillage, sack, ravage, rifle, strip.

2. Explore, rummage, search thoroughly, seek.

Ransom, *n.* 1. Price of redemption, expiation.

2. Release, liberation, redemption, deliverance.

——, *v. t.* 1. Redeem.

2. Rescue, liberate, deliver, redeem, free.

Rant, *v. i.* Spout, declaim (*boisterously*), rave (*in high-sounding phrases*), vociferate, mouth, tear a passion to tatters.

——, *n.* Fustian, bombast, rhodomontade, exaggeration, boisterous declamation.

Rap, *n.* Knock, stroke, pat, thump, thwack, slap, whack, cuff, smart blow.

——, *v. t.* Strike (*suddenly*), knock.

Rapacious, *a.* 1. Raptorial, preying, predacious.

2. Ravenous, greedy, plundering.

3. Avaricious, grasping, greedy.

Rapacity, *n.* 1. Ravenousness, rapaciousness, voraciousness, voracity, avidity, canine appetite.

2. Greed, ravenousness, exercise of plunder, extortion.

3. Avariciousness, greediness of gain.

Rape, *n.* Violation, defloration, constupration, devirgination, ravishment, defilement.

Rapid, *a.* 1. Swift, quick, fleet, fast.

2. Speedy, fast, hasty, quick.

3. Brisk, hasty, hurried, expeditious, quick, smart, lively, spanking.

Rapidity, *n.* 1. Swiftness, quickness, celerity, expeditiousness, velocity, rapidness, haste, speed, fleetness, agility.

2. Quickness, rapidness.

3. Haste, quickness.

Rapidly, *adv.* Swiftly, fast, quickly, expeditiously.

Rapier, *n.* Small sword.

Rapine, *n.* Plunder, pillage, spoliation, robbery, depredation.

Rapscallion, *n.* See RASCAL.

Rapt, *a.* 1. Enraptured, transported, ravished, ecstatic, entranced, charmed, delighted, enchanted, absorbed, engrossed, fascinated, spell-bound, inspired.

2. Abducted, ravished, kidnaped.

Raptorious, *a.* Preying, raptorial.

Rapture, *n.* 1. Transport, ecstasy, ravishment, beatitude, beatification, bliss, great happiness, enchantment, heavenly joy.

2. Delight, exultation, enthusiasm, rhapsody.

——, *v. i.* Ravish, transport, enrapture.

Rapturous, *a.* Ecstatic, ravishing, transporting.

Rara avis. [L.] 1. Rare bird.

2. Curiosity, rare thing, unusual thing, rarity, prodigy.

Rare, *a.* 1. Sparse, thinly scattered.

2. Thin, subtile.

3. Uncommon, infrequent, scarce, unfrequent, singular, extraordinary, strange, out of the way, unusual.

4. Choice, fine, excellent, exquisite, incomparable, inimitable.

5. Underdone, imperfectly cooked, nearly raw.

Rarefy, *v. t.* Make rarer, make less dense, make thin, make porous, thin, purify, refine, attenuate.

Rarely, *adv.* 1. Seldom, not often.

2. Finely, excellently.

Rareness, *n.* 1. Thinness, tenuity, rarity.

2. Uncommonness, infrequency, scarcity.

Rarity, *n.* 1. Thinness, tenuity, tenuousness, ethereality, rarefaction, attenuation, rareness.

2. Uncommonness, infrequency, unwontedness, sparseness, singularity, fewness, scarcity.

3. Uncommon thing, scarce thing.

Rascal, *n.* Knave, rogue, villain, scoundrel, blackguard, scalawag, vagabond, reprobate, scapegrace, caitiff, scamp, miscreant, mean wretch.

——, *a.* Mean, low, pitiful, paltry, base.

Rascality, *n.* Knavery, knavishness, wickedness, scoundrelism, roguery, blackguardism, reprobacy, baseness, villainy, dishonesty, trickery, chicane, chicanery, fraud, "skulduggery."

Rascally, *a.* 1. Wicked, villainous, bad, trickish, scoundrelly, knavish, reprobate, blackguardly, dishonest, vile, base.

2. Mean, base, sorry, pitiful, worthless.

Rase, *v. t.* 1. Erase, efface, cancel, expunge, obliterate, rub out, blot out

2. Level, overthrow, destroy, demolish, subvert, ruin, prostrate. See RAZE.

Rash, *a.* Reckless (*in action*), headlong, hasty, over-hasty, head-strong, precipitate, heedless, thoughtless, unadvised, imprudent, injudicious, inconsiderate, indiscreet, impulsive, careless, incautious, unwary, adventurous, venturesome, temerous, over-confident, over-venturesome, audacious, foolhardy, hot-headed, hot-brained, hare-brained, madcap, unbalanced, without ballast.

——, *n.* (*Med.*) Exanthem, exanthema, eruption, breaking out.

Rasher, *n.* Slice (*of pork* or *bacon*), collop.

Rashness, *n.* Recklessness (*in action*), precipitancy, precipitation, hastiness, venturesomeness, temerity, heedlessness, thoughtlessness, indiscretion, carelessness, inconsiderateness, inconsideration, foolhardiness.

Rasp, *n.* Coarse file.

——, *v. t.* Grate harshly upon, offend, scrape.

Rasure, *n.* Erasure, obliteration, scraping, shaving.

RAT, *n.* Rodent.

——, *v. i.* Desert one's party (*from interested motives*), bolt.

Ratable, *a.* 1. To be rated, estimated, reckoned, set at a certain value.

2. Proportional, *pro rata*, correspondent.

3. Liable to taxation.

Ratchet, *n.* Click, catch, detent, pawl, ratch.

RATE, *n.* 1. Standard, fixed measure.

2. Cost, price.

3. Worth, value, valuation, estimate, rank, class, degree.

4. Proportion, ratio, degree; relative speed.

5. Tax, assessment, impost, charge, duty.

——, *v. t.* 1. Estimate, value, appraise, set a value on, compute, reckon, class, tax.

2. Scold, chide, reprimand, berate, reprove, censure, blame, find fault with.

Rather, *adv.* 1. Preferably, in preference, more readily, more willingly, sooner, more.

2. Moderately, in some measure, in some degree, somewhat, tolerably, slightly, fairly.

3. Especially, the sooner, the more so, for better reason.

Ratification, *n.* Confirmation, substantiation, corroboration, establishment, approval, consent, sanction, indorsement.

Ratify, *v. t.* 1. Confirm, substantiate, seal, indorse, corroborate, establish, settle.

2. Approve, sanction, bind, consent to, make valid.

Ratio, *n.* Proportion, rate, fixed relation, quota, percentage, comparison.

Ratiocination, *n.* Reasoning, argumentation, deduction.

Ration, *n.* Portion (*of food* or *drink*), allowance, quota, share.

Rational, *a.* 1. Intellectual, endowed with reason, reasoning.

2. Reasonable, just, right, equitable, normal, natural, moderate, fair, fit, proper, agreeable to reason, according to reason.

3. Judicious, sagacious, enlightened, sensible, discreet, wise, intelligent.

4. Sane, sound, sober, in one's right mind, in one's sober senses.

Rationale, *n.* Reason, cause, theory, exposition, explanation, solution, the why and the wherefore, the reason why, theoretical explanation, theoretical solution.

Rationality, *n.* 1. Sanity, soundness of mind.

2. Reasonableness, rationalness.

Rattle, *n.* 1. Loud talk, empty talk, clamorous chiding.

2. Jabberer, prater.

——, *v. i.* 1. Clatter.

2. Jabber, talk noisily, chatter, prate, prattle, clack, babble.

——, *v. t.* 1. Stun, deafen, daze, confuse, drive (*with noise*).

2. Scold, chide, rail at.

Rattle-brained, *a.* Giddy, noisy, wild, rattle-headed, unsteady.

Rattle-pate, *n.* Chatterer, gabbler, prater.

Raucous, *a.* Hoarse, husky, rough, harsh.

Ravage, *v. t.* Ruin, spoil, waste, devastate, destroy, despoil, sack, ransack, desolate, pillage, harry, overrun, plunder, strip, lay waste, consume.

——, *n.* Ruin, waste, spoil, pillage, plunder, rapine, desolation, destruction, devastation, havoc, despoilment.

Rave, *v. i.* 1. Rage, be mad, be wild, fume, be furious, rant.

2. Be delirious, talk irrationally, wander, be mad.

Ravel, *v. t.* 1. Disentangle, untwist, unravel, unweave, take apart, unroll, undo, unwind.

2. Entangle, entwist, involve, make intricate, net, perplex.

Raven, *a.* Black, ebony, inky, sable.

——, *v. t.* Devour, eat with voracity, plunder.

——, *v. i.* [Written also *Ravin*.] Prey, be greedy, show rapacity.

Ravenous, *a.* Voracious, rapacious, devouring, gluttonous, omnivorous, ravening, greedy, insatiable, insatiate, ferocious.

Ravin, *n.* 1. Rapine, rapacity, rapaciousness.

2. Prey, plunder, food obtained by violence.

Ravine, *n.* Gorge, defile, deep pass, cleft, gap, cañon, mountain cleft, gulch, gully.

Raving, *n.* 1. Madness, frenzy, fury, rage, furious exclamation, delirium.

——, *a.* Furious, frenzied, frantic, distracted, deranged, raging, mad, infuriate, phrenetic, delirious.

Ravish, *v. t.* 1. Violate, deflower, constuprate, defile, abuse, debauch, force, outrage, commit rape upon.

2. Enchant, charm, captivate, delight, enrapture, transport, entrance, overjoy.

3. Strip, seize, snatch by force, abduct, kidnap.

Ravishment, *n.* 1. Rape, defloration, constupration, violation, defilement.

2. Rapture, ecstasy, transport, great delight, enravishment.

3. Abduction.

Raw, *a.* 1. Uncooked.

2. Inexperienced, unskilled, unskilful, unprepared, green in experience, unseasoned, fresh, unpractised, untried.

3. Immature, unripe, green, unfinished, crude.

4. Cold, bleak, chilly, damp, piercing, cutting, windswept, exposed.

5. Bare, sore, sensitive, galled, excoriated, chafed.

RAY, *n.* 1. Beam, gleam, shaft, emanation, sunbeam, moonbeam, radiance.

2. Perception, vision, sight, apprehension, notice, intellectual light, beam.

Rayless, *a.* Sunless, beamless, darksome, dark, blind, dismal, Cimmerian.

Rase, *v. t.* 1. Overthrow, demolish, subvert, fell, destroy, ruin, level.

2. Erase, efface, obliterate, rase.

3. Extirpate, destroy.

4. Graze, rase.

Reach, *v. t.* 1. Extend, stretch, stretch forth, hold forth.

2. Touch in extent, extend to.

3. Strike, hit, grasp.

4. Arrive at, come to, get to, get at, overtake, attain, make way to.

5. Get, obtain, attain to, gain, be advanced to, win.

——, *v. i.* Extend, be extended.

——, *n.* 1. Reaching, extension.

2. Capacity, capability, grasp, power of attainment.

3. Penetration, depth of thought.

4. Extent, extension, stretch, range, compass, scope, distance, space, span, spread, expanse.

5. Application, influence, result.

Reachable, *a.* Attainable, within reach.

React, *v. t.* Repeat, re-enact, perform again, act again.

——, *v. i.* 1. Recoil, rebound, fly back, spring back.

2. Act reciprocally.

REACTION, *n.* 1. Rebound, recoil, response, reflex, return, reversion, revulsion.

2. Reciprocal action, reverse action.

Reactionary, *a.* Conservative, revulsionary, tory, Bourbon.

Read, *v. t.* 1. Peruse, con, study.

2. Interpret, decipher, utter, deliver, unravel, explain, make out, understand.

3. Comprehend, understand, know fully, perceive, discern.

——, *v. i.* 1. Practise reading, be studious in books.

2. Be read, appear in reading.

——, *a.* Learned, versed in books.

Readable, *a.* 1. Legible, that may be read.

2. Worth reading, fit to be read.

Readily, *adv.* 1. Quickly, promptly, easily.

2. Willingly, cheerfully.

Readiness, *n.* 1. Promptness, promptitude, expedition, quickness, alertness, alacrity.

2. Dexterity, aptness, aptitude, expertness, facility, knack, easiness, skill, quickness.

3. Preparedness, ripeness, fit state, preparation.

4. Willingness, disposition, inclination, cheerfulness, ease, alacrity.

READING, *n.* 1. Perusal.

2. Study of books, lesson.

3. Version, interpretation, lection.

4. Lecture, prelection, public recital.

5. Delineation, representation, rendering.

READY, *a.* 1. Prepared, in readiness, fitted, ripe.

2. Prompt, quick, expeditious, speedy, alacritous, alert, punctual.

3. Apt, expert, dexterous, keen, prompt, nimble, unhesitating, facile, adroit, clever, quick, sharp, smart, skilful, handy, quick-witted.

4. Willing, disposed, inclined, free, eager, cheerful.

5. Near, handy, convenient, commodious, available, accessible, at hand.

6. Easy, opportune, facile, fluent, spontaneous, offhand, short.

Real, *a.* 1. Actual, veritable, substantial, substantive, absolute, positive, certain, actually being *or* existing.

2. True, genuine, authentic.

3. Intrinsic, internal, essential.

Reality, *n.* 1. Truth, verity, actuality, fact, actual existence, matter of fact.

2. Substantiality, being, substantialness, entity, existence.

Realize, *v. t.* 1. Effect, effectuate, accomplish, discharge, perfect, perform, bring into being *or* act, work out, bring to pass.

2. Make real, consider as real, bring home to one's self, feel strongly, understand, experience, apprehend, recognize.

3. Make certain, substantiate, externalize, objectify.

4. Earn, gain, acquire, get, net, make clear, produce, obtain, sell.

Really, *adv.* Actually, truly, absolutely, positively, certainly, verily, indeed, in fact, in reality, in truth, veritably.

Realm, *n.* 1. Kingdom.

2. Province, department, region, sphere, domain.

Realty, *n.* (*Law.*) Reality, immobility; real estate, property.

Ream, *n.* Twenty quires.

Reanimate, *v. t.* 1. Resuscitate, revive, bring to life, restore to life.

2. Reinvigorate, revive, enliven, cheer.

Reanimation, *n.* Reinvigoration, revival, resuscitation, quickening.

Reap, *v. t.* Cut with a sickle; gather, gain, get, obtain, receive, harvest, crop.

——, *v. i.* Gather the harvest.

Rear, *n.* 1. Hind part, background, setting, reverse.

2. Hind part (*particularly of an army*); posterior, tail, after part, stern, heel, rump; wake, train, trail, path.

——, *v. t.* 1. Raise, elevate, lift, raise up, hoist; build up, construct, erect.

2. Exalt, elevate, lift up.

3. Bring up, raise, educate, instruct, train, nurture, foster, cherish, nurse.

4. Raise, breed, grow.

5. Stir up, rouse.

Rearward, *n.* 1. Rearguard.

2. End, tail, latter part, train behind.

REASON, *n.* 1. Intellect, mind, sense, sanity, intelligence, understanding, rational faculty, conception, judgment, intuitional faculty, thinking principle, intellectual powers *or* faculties, discursive power *or* faculty.

2. Cause, ground, principle, motive, "wherefore," consideration, account, efficient cause, sake, occasion, basis, gist, excuse, pretense, explanation.

3. Design, purpose, end, object, aim, final cause.

4. Argument, reasoning, ratiocination, right judgment, chain of reasoning, process of reasoning.

5. Reasonableness, wisdom, common-sense, good sense, right *or* just view.

6. Right, justice, fairness, equity.

7. Theory, exposition, rationale.

——, *v. i.* 1. Draw conclusions, draw inferences, make deductions, ratiocinate, think, intellectualize, syllogize.

2. Argue, debate, dispute, chop logic, try conclusions, bandy words *or* arguments, hold *or* carry on an argument.

Reasonable, *a.* 1. Right, equitable, fair, suitable, just, rational, honest, fit, proper, according to reason, agreeable to reason, logical.

2. Judicious, sensible, wise, sagacious, enlightened, intelligent.

3. Tolerable, moderate, considerable, fair.

4. Rational, intellectual, endowed with reason, well-founded, credible, plausible.

5. Sane, sound, sober, rational.

6. Cheap, low-priced, inexpensive.

Reasonably, *adv.* 1. Moderately, tolerably, in a moderate degree.

2. Rationally, with reason.

Reasoning, *n.* Ratiocination, argumentation, dialectics, logic, induction, inference, debate, discussion, pros and cons, thinking, argument.

Reassume, *v. t.* Resume, take again.

Reassure, *v. t.* Hearten, enhearten, encourage, cheer, comfort, embolden, strengthen, inspirit, assure again, restore courage to.

Rebate, *v. t.* 1. Blunt, beat back.

2. Diminish, lessen, reduce, abate, bate, deduct.

3. Cut, pare, rabbet.

——, *n.* 1. Diminution, lessening.

2. (*Com.*) Discount, allowance, deduction, reduction, drawback, abatement, decrement, decrease.

Rebel, *n.* Insurgent, traitor, revolter.

——, *v. i.* Revolt, resist lawful authority, mutiny, strike.

Rebellion, *n.* Insurrection, sedition, revolt, defiance, mutiny, resistance, contumacy.

Rebellious, *a.* Insubordinate, intractable, disobedient, mutinous, refractory, contumacious, defiant, seditious.

Rebound, *v. i.* 1. Reverberate, recoil, react, kick, spring back, fly back, bound back, ricochet.

2. Reverberate, re-echo.

——, *n.* Resilience, repercussion, reaction, recoil, reverberation.

Rebuff, *n.* 1. Repulse, check, opposition, resistance, defeat, discouragement, "snub."

2. Refusal, rejection, repulse.

——, *v. t.* Repel, resist, reject, check, oppose, "snub," refuse, beat back.

Rebuild, *v. t.* Reconstruct, renew, reorganize, re-establish, restore.

Rebuke, *v. t.* Censure, reprove, reprehend, reprimand, chide, admonish, blame, upbraid, lecture, scold, scold at, find fault with, remonstrate with, silence.

——, *n.* 1. Censure, reprimand, remonstrance, expostulation, reproof, chiding, reproval, reprehension, blame, reproach.

2. Chastisement, punishment, affliction.

Rebut, *v. t.* 1. Repel, rebuff, drive back.

2. Repel (*by argument* or *by evidence*), retort, oppose, confute, refute, disprove, show the fallacy of.

Recalcitrant, *a.* Opposing, refractory, disobedient.

Recalcitrate, *v. t.* Oppose, kick against, be refractory.

Recalcitration, *n.* Opposition, repugnance, kicking back.

Recall, *v. t.* 1. Revoke, retract, recant, repeal, swallow, withdraw, unsay, abnegate, deny, repudiate, abjure, rescind, annul, overrule, cancel, nullify, countermand, set aside.

2. Recollect, remember, recall to mind, review, retrace, commemorate, revive.

3. Encore, applaud.

Recant, *v. t.* Retract, revoke, recall, annul, abjure, disown, disavow, unsay, renounce, objure, repudiate.

Recantation, *n.* Retraction, revocation, recall, abjuration.

Recapitulate, *v. t.* Repeat, reiterate, rehearse, restate, review, summarize, recite, run over, sum up, give a summary of.

Recapitulation, *n.* Summary, summing up, concise statement.

Recede, *v. i.* 1. Retire, withdraw, retreat, retrograde, move back, return, ebb, regress; slope backward.

2. Withdraw, desist.

RECEIPT, *n.* 1. Reception, acceptation, acceptance, receiving, taking.

2. Reception, admission.

3. Recipe, prescription, formulary.

4. (*Com.*) Acquittance, quittance, acknowledgment of payment.

Receive, *v. t.* 1. Take, accept, derive, obtain, come by, gain, pocket, acquire, get.

2. Admit, take in, shelter.

3. Entertain, welcome, greet.

4. Allow, permit, tolerate.

5. Believe, embrace, give credence to, credit, approve, adopt; understand, learn, follow.

6. Hold, contain, have capacity for, retain, accommodate, carry, include, admit.

7. Suffer, meet, encounter, experience, bear, sustain, endure, submit to.

Received, *a.* Accepted, current, admitted, believed.

Receiver, *n.* 1. Recipient, collector, teller, treasurer, legatee, trustee; fence; bankruptcy administrator.

2. Receptacle.

Recension, *n.* 1. Review, examination, enumeration.

2. Review, re-examination, revisal, editing.

Recent, *a.* 1. New, novel.

2. Late, fresh, newly come.

3. Latter, modern, young.

4. Retiring, late, deceased, foregoing, preceding.

Recently, *adv.* Lately, latterly, of late, newly, freshly, not long ago.

Receptacle, *n.* Depository, repository, receiver, vessel, container, bin, well, safe, box, case, basket, reservoir.

Reception, *n.* 1. Receiving, receipt, acceptance.

2. Welcome, entertainment, greeting.

3. Party, *soirée*, levee.

4. Admission, credence, acceptance, allowance.

5. Admission, admittance, entrance, entrée.

6. Belief, credence, admission, recognition.

Recess, *n.* 1. Retreat, nook, corner, niche, hollow, alcove, place of retirement.

2. Intermission, respite, remission of labor, interval, break, suspension of business, vacation.

3. Withdrawing, withdrawal, retreat, retirement, recession.

Recherche, *a.* [Fr.] Choice, select, uncommon, rare, exquisite, elegant.

Recipe, *n.* Receipt, prescription, formulary, formula.

Recipient, *n.* Receiver, beneficiary, pensioner, fence, assignee.

Reciprocal, *a.* 1. Mutual, commutual, correspondent, complementary, correlative.

2. Interchangeable; alternate.

Reciprocally, *a.* Mutually, interchangeably.

Reciprocate, *v. i.* Alternate, act interchangeably, return, requite, vary.

——, *v. t.* Interchange, exchange, requite.

Reciprocation, *n.* 1. Interchange, exchange, mutuality, correspondence, give-and-take, reciprocity.

2. Alternation.

Reciprocity, *n.* Interchange, reciprocation, correspondence, reciprocalness, exchange, mutuality.

Recital, *n.* 1. Repetition, rehearsal, recitation.

2. Narration, relation, description, telling, account, statement, explanation, detail.

3. Narrative, story, history.

4. Concert.

Recitation, *n.* Recital, rehearsal, repetition, saying, speech, declamation, account, mention; lesson.

Recite, *v. t.* 1. Repeat, rehearse, say by heart, repeat by note, declaim, deliver.

2. Narrate, relate, tell, describe, recount, mention.

3. Enumerate, tell over, recapitulate, detail, number, count.

Reckless, *a.* Careless, heedless, rash, thoughtless, temerous, negligent, indifferent, regardless, unconcerned, inattentive, remiss, mindless, inconsiderate, uncircumspect, headlong, breakneck, indiscreet, incautious, giddy, imprudent, improvident, volatile, wild, desperate, flighty, unsteady, giddy-brained, hare-brained, harum-scarum, wanton, devil-may-care, dare-devil, foolhardy, over-venturesome.

Reckon, *v. t.* 1. Count, number, compute, consider, guess, calculate, enumerate, cast, cast up.

2. Estimate, esteem, account, regard, repute, class, value.

——, *v. i.* Compute, calculate, estimate, cast account.

Reckoning, *n.* 1. Counting, computation, consideration, calculation.

2. Estimate.

3. Account, register, score, charge, bill.

4. Esteem, account, estimation.

5. Arrangement, settlement.

Reclaim, *v. t.* 1. Reform, amend.

2. Regain, recover, restore, reinstate, regenerate, redeem.

3. Correct, reduce to order, amend.

4. Tame, make gentle, civilize.

Reclaimable, *a.* 1. Recoverable, redeemable.

2. Reformable, amendable, corrigible, improvable.

Reclamation, *n.* Recovery, reform, regeneracy.

Recline, *v. t.* Lean.

——, *v. i.* 1. Lean.

2. Couch, lie, lie down, be recumbent.

3. Rest, repose, take one's ease.

Reclining, *a.* 1. Leaning, recumbent, lying.

2. Resting, reposing.

Recluse, *a.* Secluded, sequestered, retired, solitary, shut up.

——, *n.* Hermit, anchoret, solitary, solitaire, anchorite, eremite, ascetic.

Reclusion, *n.* Seclusion, retirement.

Recognition, *n.* 1. Recollection, identification, memory, remembrance.

2. Acknowledgment, avowal, confession, notice, appreciation, comprehension.

3. Allowance, concession.

Recognizance, *n.* 1. Recognition, acknowledgment, avowal.

2. Badge, token.

Recognize, *v. t.* 1. Know again, remember as formerly known, notice as already known, verify, identify; perceive, apprehend.

2. Acknowledge, admit, own, avow, confess, confess knowledge of.

3. Allow, concede, grant, acquiesce in.

4. Greet, salute.

Recoil, *v. i.* 1. Rebound, reverberate, react, spring back, fly back, bound back, kick, ricochet.

2. Retire, retreat, withdraw.

3. Shrink, falter, fail, flinch, blench, quail, draw back.

——, *n.* Resilience, rebound, reaction, repercussion, boomerang, kick, back-stroke, ricochet, elasticity, shrinking, revulsion.

Recoil from. Abhor, loathe, abominate, detest, feel disgust at, shrink from.

Recollect, *v. t.* Recall, remember, call up, call to mind, call to remembrance.

Recollection, *n.* 1. Remembrance, memory.

2. Reminiscence, memory.

Recommend, *v. t.* 1. Commend, praise, approve, endorse, sanction.

2. Make acceptable, attract favor to.

3. Commit, commend.

4. Advise, counsel, prescribe, suggest.

Recommendation, *n.* Commendation, praise, approval, approbation, good opinion, advocacy, counsel, testimonial, credential.

Recompense, *v. t.* 1. Reward, repay, requite, compensate, satisfy, remunerate.

2. Reimburse, indemnify, redress, make up for, make amends for.

3. Redeem, pay for.

——, *n.* 1. Reward, satisfaction, repayment, remuneration, compensation, indemnity, indemnification, amends, satisfaction.

2. Requital, retribution.

Reconcilable, *a.* 1. Appeasable, placable, forgiving.

2. Consistent.

Reconcile, *v. t.* 1. Conciliate, pacify, appease, placate, propitiate, restore to friendship, reunite.

2. Content, bring to acquiescence, resign, make contented.

3. Harmonize, regulate, make consistent, bring into harmony.

4. Settle, adjust, compose, heal, make up.

Reconciliation, *n.* 1. Pacification, accommodation, reconcilement, reunion, adjustment, settlement, restoration of harmony.

2. Agreement, congruity, consonance, harmony, concordance, consistency, congruency, correspondence.

3. Appeasement, propitiation, atonement, expiation.

Recondite, *a.* 1. Hidden, occult, dark, obscure, transcendental, mystic, mystical, secret, concealed.

2. Profound, deep, abstruse.

Reconnoissance, *n.* Preliminary survey, rough survey, examination.

Reconnoitre, *v. t.* Inspect, view, survey, inquire, search, scan, examine, spy out, look the ground over.

Reconstruct, *v. t.* Rebuild, re-establish, construct again, reform.

Reconstruction, *n.* Rebuilding, re-establishment, restoration, renovation, redintegration, reconstitution.

Record, *v. t.* Register, enroll, chronicle, enter, note, make an entry of, take down, make a memorandum of.

RECORD, *n.* 1. Register, account, note, chronicle, archive, annals, diary, report, roll, list, entry, minute, proceedings, score, file, docket, memorandum, memorial, enrolment, registry, memoir.

2. Vestige, trace, memorial, relic, footprint, track, mark, trail.

3. Memory, remembrance.

4. Attestation, testimony, witness.

5. History, personal history, achievement, career.

Recorder, *n.* Registrar, register, clerk, chronicler; marker, scorer.

Recount, *v. t.* Rehearse, relate, recite, narrate, enumerate, detail, describe, particularize, tell, mention, portray, report, give an account of, repeat.

Recourse, *n.* Resort, recurrence, application.

Recover, *v. t.* 1. Regain, recapture, reclaim, get back, win back.

2. Retrieve, repair, recruit, rally, make up for.

3. Heal, cure, restore, revive.

4. Rescue, save, salvage, redeem.

5. (*Law.*) Obtain by course of law, get by judgment.

——, *v. i.* 1. Rally, regain health, get well, recuperate, recruit, convalesce, be restored to health.

2. Be restored, be reinstated, regain the former state.

3. (*Law.*) Obtain judgment, succeed.

Recovery, *n.* 1. Regaining, recuperation, retrieval, repossession, recapture, redemption.

2. Recruiting, restoration, convalescence, cure.

Recreant, *a.* 1. Cowardly, dastardly, base, craven, pusillanimous, mean-spirited, faint-hearted, yielding.

2. Apostate, treacherous, false, unfaithful, faithless, untrue, backsliding.

——, *n.* 1. Coward, dastard.

2. Apostate, renegade, backslider.

Recreate, *v. t.* 1. Refresh, entertain, divert, amuse, cheer, enliven.

2. Delight, gratify, please.

3. Relieve, revive, reanimate, renew.

——, *v. i.* Unbend, take recreation, be diverted, be amused.

Recreation, *n.* 1. Amusement, diversion, entertainment, relaxation, sport, play, pastime, cheer.

2. Relief, refreshment.

Recreative, *a.* Refreshing, relieving, relaxing, diverting.

Recrement, *n.* Scoria, dross, spume, scum, refuse, dregs.

Recriminate, *v. i.* Return an accusation, retort a charge.

Recrimination, *n.* Counter-accusation, counter-charge, retort.

Recriminatory, *a.* Recriminating, retorting, accusing.

Recruit, *v. t.* 1. Repair, replenish, supply lack.

2. Refresh, revive, restore, renovate, renew, strengthen, recover, reinvigorate, regain, retrieve.

3. (*Mil.*) Reinforce, supply with new men, enlist.

——, *v. i.* 1. Raise new soldiers, get supplies of men, enlist troops.

2. Revive, recover, regain health, be restored to health, get well.

——, *n.* Supporter, helper, auxiliary, new member, "rookie."

Rectangular, *a.* Right-angled, square, orthogonal, normal.

Rectify, *v. t.* 1. Correct, redress, mend, amend, emend, better, improve, reform, adjust, regulate, straighten, set right, make right.

2. (*Chem.*) Refine, purify.

Rectilineal, } *a.* Right-lined, straight,
Rectilinear, } straight-lined.

Rectitude, *n.* 1. Right, uprightness, integrity, probity, honesty, justice, equity, virtue, goodness, righteousness, principle, conscientiousness, straightforwardness.

2. Correctness.

Rector, *n.* Pastor, clergyman, minister, director.

Rectory, *n.* Parsonage, rector's mansion, manse.

Recumbent, *a.* 1. Leaning, reclining, lying, prone, prostrate.

2. Reposing, inactive, listless, idle.

Recuperate, *v. t.* Recover, regain, get back.

Recuperation, *n.* Recovery, restoration, convalescence.

Recur, *v. i.* 1. Return, come back, come again, reappear, be repeated.

2. Run in the mind, run in one's head, return to the thought.

3. Resort, revert, have recourse, go for help.

Recurrence, } *n.* 1. Return, repetition, it-
Recurrency, } eration, frequency, reversion.

2. Resort, the having recourse.

Recurrent, } *a.* Returning (*at intervals*), re-
Recurring, } appearing, cyclic, renewed, intermittent, periodical.

Recurved, *a.* (*Bot.*) Curved outward, curved backward, recurvous, recurvate.

Recusancy, *n.* Nonconformity, dissent, heterodoxy, heresy.

Recusant, *n.* Dissenter, nonconformist, heretic, "come-outer."

Recusative, *a.* Refusing, denying, negative.

RED, *a.* 1. Carmine, crimson, magenta, pink.

2. Blushing, flushed, ruddy, rubicund.

Redden, *v. t.* Make red.

——, *v. i.* Blush, color, become red.

Reddition, *n.* 1. Restitution, restoration, rendition, surrender.

2. Explanation, representation.

Redeem, *v. t.* 1. Repurchase, buy back, regain, retrieve, reform.

2. Ransom, free, liberate, save, rescue.

3. Deliver, recover, rescue, save, reclaim, reinstate.

4. Compensate, recompense, make amends for, expiate, atone for.

5. Fulfil, keep, discharge, make good, perform.

6. Improve, employ well.

Redeemable, *a.* Recoverable, retrievable.

Redeemer, *n.* 1. Ransomer.

2. [With *The* prefixed.] Christ, Jesus, Immanuel, Emmanuel, the Saviour, the Messiah, the Anointed, the Word, the Son of Man, the Son of God, the Son of David, the Lamb of God, Shiloh, the Prince of Peace, the Bread of Life, the Lord, the Light of the World, the Good Shepherd.

Redemption, *n.* 1. Repurchase, retrieval, buying, compensation, recovery.

2. Ransom, release, liberation, deliverance, rescue, salvation.

3. Performance, discharge, fulfilment.

Redintegrate, *v. t.* Restore, renew, reconstitute, re-establish, reconstruct, renovate.

Red-letter, *a.* Fortunate, lucky, happy, memorable, auspicious.

Redolence, } *n.* Fragrance, aroma, odor,
Redolency, } perfume, sweet scent, grateful odor, savor.

Redolent, *a.* Fragrant, odoriferous, odorous, aromatic, balmy, scented, sweet-smelling.

Redouble, *v. t.* 1. Reduplicate, multiply, double again, reiterate.

2. Augment, increase.

——, *v. i.* Be repeated, become twice as much.

Redoubt, *n.* (*Fort.*) Outwork, temporary fieldwork, fortification.

Redoubtable, *a.* 1. Formidable, terrible (*to foes*), dreadful, awful.

2. Valiant, doughty.

Redound, *v. i.* Result, contribute, conduce, tend, accrue.

Redress, *v. t.* 1. Remedy, repair, set right, amend, correct, rectify, adjust, order.

2. Relieve, ease, compensate, make amends to.

——, *n.* Remedy, relief, amends, compensation, reparation, atonement, indemnification, rectification, righting, correction, satisfaction.

Reduce, *v. t.* 1. Bring, restore.

2. Render, form, mould, make, shape, model, remodel, convert into, resolve into, change into, bring into, bring to.

3. Diminish, contract, lessen, abate, decrease, abbreviate, minimize, thin, decimate, attenuate, abridge, curtail, shorten, cut short, cut down, make less.

4. Depress, debase, abase, degrade, lower, impair, weaken, dwarf.

5. Subdue, subject, conquer, subjugate, capture, overpower, overthrow, vanquish, master, bring into subjection.

6. Impoverish, ruin, bring to want, bring to poverty.

7. (*Math.*) Solve, resolve.

Reduction, *n.* 1. Conversion, resolution, transmutation.

2. Diminution, contraction, decrease, abridgment, lessening, retrenchment, abatement, decrement, curtailment, lowering.

3. Depression, detrusion, abasement, lowering.

4. Subjugation, conquest, subjection, mastery, subdual.

5. (*Math.*) Resolution, solution.

Redundance, ⎫ *n.* 1. Excess, superabun-
Redundancy, ⎭ dance, superfluity, exuberance.

2. Diffuseness.

Redundant, *a.* 1. Excessive, superabundant, inordinate, overmuch, replete, lavish, prodigal, fulsome, unnecessary, needless, useless, exuberant, superfluous, overflowing, plentiful, copious.

2. Diffuse, tautological, verbose, wordy, periphrastic, pleonastic.

Redundantly, *adv.* Superfluously, superabundantly, excessively.

Reduplicate, *v. t.* Redouble, repeat, multiply, double again.

Reduplication, *n.* Doubling, duplication, redoubling, repetition.

Re-echo, *v. t.* Reverberate, echo back, repeat.

——, *v. i.* Resound, echo back.

Reed, *n.* 1. Pastoral pipe, rustic pipe, musical instrument.

2. Arrow.

3. Rush, flag.

Reed-organ, *n.* Harmoneon, melodeon, seraphine.

Reef, *v. t.* Take in, shorten (*sail*).

——, *n.* Shoal, bar, ridge, ledge, key.

Reek, *n.* 1. Smoke, steam, exhalation, vapor, effluvium, fume, smell, mist.

2. Rick, stack.

——, *v. i.* Smoke, steam, exhale, emit vapor, smell.

Reeking, *a.* Smoking, steaming.

Reeky, *a.* 1. Smoky, foul, sooty, sweaty.

2. Tanned, black, dark.

Reel, *v. i.* •1. Totter, stagger, falter, vacillate, sway, be giddy, waver.

2. Whirl, spin.

Re-enforce, *v. t.* Strengthen, augment, fortify, give additional support to, enforce anew.

Re-establish, *v. t.* Restore, reinstate, replace, replant, refound, rehabilitate, reinstall, renew, renovate, establish again.

Refection, *n.* Luncheon, refreshment, simple repast, meal.

Refectory, *n.* Refreshment-room, eating-room.

Refer, *v. t.* 1. Direct, consign, commit, leave, relegate, submit, send, deliver over, give in charge.

2. Attribute, ascribe, impute, assign.

——, *v. i.* 1. Relate, point, belong, pertain, touch, concern, appertain, have reference, respect.

2. Appeal, have recourse, apply, consult.

3. Allude, advert, direct attention, make allusion, make reference, hint at, cite, quote.

Referable, *a.* Ascribable, attributable, assignable, imputable, to be referred.

Referee, *n.* Arbitrator, arbiter, judge, umpire.

Reference, *n.* 1. Respect, regard, relation, connection, concern.

2. Allusion, intimation, hint, ascription, citation; reference mark, relegation.

Refine, *v. t.* 1. Purify, clarify, fine, defecate, cleanse.

2. Cultivate, polish, make elegant, spiritualize, humanize, rarefy, improve, subtilize.

——, *v. i.* 1. Become pure, be clarified.

2. Improve, make improvement.

3. Be over-nice, affect nicety, split hairs, make useless distinctions.

Refined, *a.* 1. Purified, clarified.

2. Accomplished, cultivated, cultured, ladylike, gentlemanly, spiritual, polished, elegant, genteel, stylish, courtly, polite, civilized, well-bred, fine, finished.

3. Classic, classical, pure, chaste, Attic, delicate, nice, exquisite, elevated.

Refinement, *n.* 1. Clarification, purification, filtration, defecation, sublimation.

2. Improvement, betterment.

3. Elegance, polish, purity, delicacy, cultivation, civility, civilization, culture, politeness, finish, spirituality, elevation, gentility, good-breeding.

4. Subtilty, nicety, fineness, delicacy.

5. Subtilty, finesse, sophistry, artifice, nicety, hair-splitting.

Refit, *v. t.* Repair, fit anew, restore.

Reflect, *v. t.* Mirror, throw back, imitate, copy, reproduce.

——, *v. i.* 1. Think, cogitate, muse, meditate, deliberate, ponder, consider, contemplate, study, ruminate.

2. Bring reproach, cast reproach.

Reflection, *n.* 1. Reflecting.

2. Reflected image, echo, shadow.

3. Thought, meditation, cogitation, deliberation, contemplation, rumination, consideration, musing, thinking.

4. Thought, opinion, result of reflection, remark, idea.

5. Censure, reproach, criticism, blame, disparagement.

Reflective, *a.* 1. Reflecting, reflexive.

2. Thoughtful, musing, deliberating, pondering, cogitating, reasoning.

Reflector, *n.* Mirror, speculum.

Reflex, *a.* 1. Retroactive, introspective, reflective.

2. (*Bot.*) Reflected, bent back, reflexed.

Reflexive, *a.* Reflective.

Refluence, *n.* Reflux, ebb, regurgitation, return, flowing back.

Refluent, *a.* Ebbing, flowing back.

Reflux, *a.* Ebb, refluence, back-water.

Reform, *v. t.* 1. Correct, amend, mend, emend, ameliorate, meliorate, better, improve, rectify, redeem, regenerate, repair, restore, reclaim.

2. Remodel, form anew, reconstruct, reshape.

——, *v. i.* Amend, become better.

——, *n.* Reformation, amendment, reconstruction, rectification, correction, progress.

Reformation, *n.* Reform, amendment, correction, rectification, act of reforming.

Reformative, } *a.* Reforming.
Reformatory, }

Refract, *v. t.* Deflect (*rays*), deviate, turn from a straight course.

Refraction, *n.* Deflection (*of rays*), deviation, divergence, near-sightedness.

Refractive, *a.* Refracting, deflecting.

Refractory, *a.* Stubborn, obstinate, stiff, perverse, dogged, mulish, heady, headstrong, crossgrained, intractable, unyielding, contumacious, sullen, selfwilled, incoercible, disobedient, unruly, ungovernable, cantankerous, unmanageable, recalcitrant.

Refrain, *v. i.* Abstain, forbear, withhold, desist, hold one's self back.

——, *n.* Burden (*of a song*), chorus, undersong.

Refrangibility, *n.* Refrangibleness, breakableness.

Refresh, *v. t.* 1. Invigorate, reanimate, revive, brace, exhilarate, brisk, recruit, recreate, enliven, freshen, cheer, reinvigorate, give fresh vigor to; cool, air, slake, regale.

2. Repair, restore, renew, retouch, renovate, freshen up.

Refreshing, *a.* Reviving, invigorating, cooling, restful, reanimating, grateful, pleasant, comfortable.

Refreshment, *n.* 1. Relief, invigoration, new life, restoration.

2. Food, nourishment, bait.

3. Regalement, entertainment, repast.

Refrigerant, *n.* Refrigerative, cooling medicine.

Refrigerate, *v. t.* Cool, chill, make cool, freeze, reduce the heat of, refresh.

Refrigeration, *n.* Cooling, infrigidation, regelation, glaciation.

Refrigerative, *a.* Cooling, refrigeratory, refrigerant.

Refuge, *n.* 1. Shelter, safety, security, protection.

2. Asylum, retreat, sanctuary, stronghold, haven, covert, ark, home, hiding-place, harbor, place of safety, place of refuge, fastness, keep.

3. Resort, expedient, device, contrivance, shift.

Refulgence, } *n.* Brightness, brilliancy,
Refulgency, } splendor, resplendence, lustre, radiance, effulgence.

Refulgent, *a.* Bright, shining, brilliant, splendid, luminous, resplendent, lustrous, radiant, effulgent.

Refund, *v. t.* 1. Repay, reimburse, pay back, restore.

2. Return, repay, restore, give back.

Refusal, *n.* 1. Denial, negation, disclaimer, repudiation, rejection, declination, nonacceptance, noncompliance, regrets; disavowal, dissent, debarment.

2. Option, pre-emption, choice of accepting *or* declining.

Refuse, *v. t.* 1. Deny, decline.

2. Reject, repudiate, exclude, repel, rebuff, renege, revoke, "turn down," disallow, disavow, veto, forswear, renounce, decline.

——, *n.* (*Pron.* ref'use) Dross, scum, dregs, sediment, lees, lumber, sweepings, chaff, discard, rummage, junk, litter, leavings, draff, recrement, rubbish, trash, offscum, offscouring, scoria, slag, offal, garbage, waste matter.

Refutation, *n.* Confutation, disproof, refutal.

Refute, *v. t.* Confute, disprove, repel, defeat, silence, rebut, overthrow.

Regain, *v. t.* Recover, get back, gain anew, recapture, retrieve, reobtain, repossess.

Regal, *a.* Kingly, royal, imposing, noble, sovereign, imperial.

Regale, *v. t.* Entertain, refresh, gratify, delight.

——, *v. i.* Feast, fare sumptuously.

——, *n.* Banquet, feast, sumptuous repast.

Regalement, *n.* Refreshment, entertainment, gratification.

Regalia, *n. pl.* Ensigns of royalty, regal paraphernalia, insignia, emblems, decorations.

Regality, *n.* Royalty, sovereignty, kingship.

Regally, *adv.* Royally.

Regard, *v. t.* 1. Observe, notice, mark, remark, see, look, view, gaze, watch, behold, set eyes on, look at, look upon, turn one's eyes.

2. Heed, mind, attend to, respect, consider, pay attention to, give heed to, care for.

3. Esteem, value, respect, reverence, honor.

4. Consider, reckon, account, deem, think, believe, hold, suppose, imagine, treat, look upon, use, estimate.

5. Have reference to, relate to, respect.

——, *v. i.* Consider, reflect, care, bear in mind.

——, *n.* 1. Look, view, gaze.

2. Notice, consideration, attention, heed, observation, observance, care, concern.

3. Relation, reference, respect, account, view.

4. Esteem, affection, liking, respect, consideration, estimation, attachment, reverence, sympathy, interest, concern, love, deference, honor, value.

5. Repute, esteem, note, account, eminence, reputation.

6. Matter, point, particular, consideration, condition.

Regardful, *a.* Heedful, mindful, careful, watchful, attentive, observing, thoughtful, considerate, deferential.

Regardfully, *adv.* 1. Attentively, heedfully.

2. Respectfully.

Regarding, *p. a.* Touching, concerning, respecting, having regard to, in reference to, about.

Regardless, *a.* Heedless, unmindful, careless, negligent, indifferent, disregarding, unconcerned, neglectful, unobservant, mindless, inattentive.

Regards, *n. pl.* Commendations, compliments, respects, remembrances, good wishes.

Regency, *n.* Rule, authority, government.

Regenerate, *v. t.* 1. Reproduce, revive, renovate, generate anew.

2. (*Theol.*) Convert, change, renew.

——, *a.* 1. Reproduced.

2. Converted, regenerated, renewed in spirit, reformed, born again.

Regeneration, *n.* 1. Reproduction.

2. Conversion, new birth, transformation, revival.

Regent, *n.* Governor, ruler, director, commander, vicegerent.

Regicide, *n.* 1. Murderer of a king, king-killer.

2. Murder of a king.

Régime, *n.* [Fr.] Government, administration, rule, political system, form of government.

Regimen, *n.* 1. Dietetics, regulation of diet.

2. Diet, food, fare.

3. Hygiene, preservation of health.

Region, *n.* 1. Country, clime, territory, division, scene, latitude, climate, district, tract, province, quarter, locality, locale.

2. Portion, part, space, neighborhood, vicinity, area, place, terrain, spot, sphere.

Register, *n.* 1. Record (*as of deeds*, or of *births and deaths*), list, chronicle, roll, schedule, catalogue, archive, annals, entry, minute.

2. Registrar, clerk, keeper of a record, registrary.

3. Compass, range.

——, *v. t.* 1. Record, make a record of, enroll, enter on a list, chronicle, book.

2. Portray, show, delineate.

Registrar, *n.* Keeper of a record, register, official recorder.

Registration, *n.* Enrolment, registry.

Registry, *n.* Registering, enrolment, recording.

Regnancy, *n.* Rule, reign, predominance.

Regnant, *a.* 1. Reigning, regent.

2. Ruling, predominant, prevalent, controlling, predominating.

Regorge, *v. t.* 1. Devour, swallow eagerly.

2. Vomit, disgorge.

Regress, *n.* Return, retrocession, reflux, retrogression, refluence, ebb, retirement, passage back, retrogradation, regression.

Regressively, *adv.* Backward, by return.

REGRET, *n.* 1. Grief, sorrow, trouble, sorrowful longing, concern, lamentation, disappointment, rue.

2. Penitence, compunction, remorse, repining, repentance, contrition, self-condemnation, self-reproach.

——, *v. t.* 1. Lament, grieve at, be sorry for, deplore, bewail, sorrow for, repine.

2. Repent, repent of, mourn for, rue, bewail, bemoan.

REGULAR, *a.* 1. Normal, formal, according to rule, typical, natural, conventional, ordinary.

2. Stated, fixed, established, periodical, customary, habitual, usual, cyclic, recurring, seasonal, rhythmic, correct.

3. Steady, constant, uniform, even.

4. Orderly, methodical, systematic, just, uniform, unvarying, punctual.

5. Thorough, out-and-out, perfect, complete, genuine, indubitable.

6. Symmetrical, balanced, consistent.

Regularity, *n.* 1. Order, rule, method, system, uniformity, even tenor, regular course.

2. Punctuality, regular recurrence.

3. Steadiness, constancy.

Regulate, *v. t.* 1. Methodize, dispose, adjust, standardize, settle, time, arrange, order, systematize, reduce to method, adjust by rule, put in order, keep in order.

2. Direct, order, manage, govern, conduct, control, guide, rule.

Regulation, *n.* 1. Adjustment, disposition, disposure, disposal, ordering, arrangement, settlement, control, management.

2. Rule, order, law, precept.

Regurgitate, *v. i.* Flow back, be poured back.

Regurgitation, *n.* 1. Flowing back, reflux, refluence.

2. Reabsorption.

Rehabilitate, *v. t.* 1. Reinstate (*in a former right* or *privilege*), re-establish, restore, qualify again.

2. Re-establish, restore, renew, reinvigorate, repair, reinstate, redintegrate, renovate, reconstruct, reconstitute, restore to former vigor and splendor.

Rehabilitation, *n.* 1. Reinstatement (*in a former right* or *privilege*), restoration, re-establishment, reinvestiture.

2. Instauration, restoration to former power and splendor, renewal, renovation, redintegration, reconstitution, revivification, reinvigoration.

Rehearsal, *n.* 1. Repetition, recital, recitation; practise, drill.

2. Narration, narrative, statement, relation, mention, telling, recounting, account, story, history.

Rehearse, *v. t.* 1. Repeat, recite.

2. Narrate, relate, recount, describe, tell, tell over, enumerate, portray, delineate, depict, set forth, recapitulate, detail, give an account of.

——, *v. i.* Drill, practise, train.

Reign, *v. i.* 1. Rule, be king, exercise sovereign authority.

2. Prevail, be predominant.

3. Rule, govern, administer.

——, *n.* 1. Royalty, sovereignty, royal authority, supreme power, imperial sway.

2. Power, influence, rule, sway, prevalence, control.

3. Realm, empire, kingdom, dominions.

Reimburse, *v. t.* 1. Refund, repay, pay back, restore, make up anew.

2. Indemnify, requite, compensate.

Rein, *v. t.* Check, restrain, control, curb, bridle, guide, hold.

Reinforce, *v. t.* See RE-ENFORCE.

Reinstate, *v. t.* Re-establish, replace, re-install, place in a former state, rehabilitate, restore, reinvest with.

Reinstatement, *n.* Re-establishment, replacement, rehabilitation, restoration.

Reiterate, *v. t.* Repeat, repeat again, do again and again.

Reject, *v. t.* 1. Exclude, discard, eject, set aside, pass over, throw aside, cast off, lay aside, cast aside, cast away, put away, throw overboard, dismiss, cashier, pluck.

2. Decline, refuse, repudiate, scout, disbelieve, repel, rebuff, disallow, deny, veto, spurn, slight, despise, disapprove, renounce.

3. Refuse, jilt.

Rejoice, *v. t.* Gladden, exhilarate, cheer, gratify, please, delight, transport, enrapture, make glad, enliven.

——, *v. i.* Exult, triumph, glory, joy, delight, jubilate, congratulate oneself, make merry, be joyful, be gladdened, be exhilarated, be pleased, be delighted, take delight, gloat, crow, vaunt.

Rejoicing, *n.* Festivity, exultation, elation, triumph, joy, jubilee, jubilation, exultancy, delight, gladness, reveling, merrymaking, thanksgiving, pæan, cheering.

Rejoin, *v. i.* 1. Answer (*to a reply*); respond, retort, rebut.

2. Reunite, meet again.

Rejuvenate, *v. t.* Make young again, restore to youth, renew.

Rejuvenated, *a.* Renascent.

Relapse, *v. i.* Fall back, return to a former state (*especially a bad state*), backslide, regress, revert, weaken.

——, *n.* 1. Falling back, return to a former state (*especially a bad state*), lapse, backsliding, regress, throwback, reversion; apostasy.

2. Falling back, return to a former state, fall, deterioration.

Relate, *v. t.* 1. Tell, recount, rehearse, recite, narrate, report, mention, detail, describe, give an account of.

2. Connect, correlate, apply.

Related, *a.* 1. Connected, cognate, of the same nature, correlative, paronymous, *en rapport*.

2. Kindred, akin, kin, allied, of the same family, consanguineous, germane.

Relate to. Respect, regard, concern, refer to, appertain to, belong to, pertain to, bear on.

Relating, *p. a.* Respecting, pertaining, belonging, relative.

RELATION, *n.* 1. Recital, narration, narrative, account, statement, story, history, chronicle, tale, description, detail, report, rehearsal, mention, explanation.

2. Connection, relationship, dependency, apposition, relevance, pertinence, correlation, affinity, application, bearing.

3. Reference, respect, regard, concern.

4. Connection, relative position, alliance, nearness, propinquity, rapport.

5. Relationship, kindred, family tie, connection, kinship, affinity, consanguinity, kin, blood, cousinship.

6. Kinsman, relative, connection.

Relationship, *n.* 1. Connection, relation, dependence.

2. Kindred affinity, consanguinity, propinquity, kinship.

Relative, *a.* 1. Referring (*to something else*), not absolute, comparative, approximate.

2. Respecting, relating to, pertaining to, belonging to, connected with.

3. Particular, special, positive, definite, apposite, germane, correspondent, pertinent, relevant.

——, *n.* Relation, kinsman, connection.

Relatively, *adv.* With reference to something else, comparatively.

Relax, *v. t.* 1. Loosen, slacken, loose, unbrace, unstrain.

2. Weaken, enfeeble, debilitate, enervate, unbrace, prostrate, unstring.

3. Lessen, diminish, reduce, abate, remit, soften, mitigate.

4. Unbend, ease, divert, recreate, entertain, amuse.

——, *v. i.* 1. Become lax, unbend, soften.

2. Recreate, unbend, take recreation.

Relaxation, *n.* 1. Loosening, slackening, diastole, diminution, lessening, unbending, mitigation.

2. Rest, recreation, ease, diversion, amusement.

Relay, *n.* Supply, relief, recruitment, shift, squad, reinforcement.

Release, *v. t.* 1. Liberate, unloose, free, loose, disengage, discharge, deliver, exempt, extricate, set free, set at liberty, let loose, let out.

2. Quit, let go, give up, acquit, remit, discharge, relinquish.

——, *n.* 1. Liberation, deliverance, discharge, freedom.

2. Exemption, exoneration, excuse, dispensation, absolution.

3. Acquittance, clearance, receipt in full.

Relegate, *v. t.* 1. Transfer, remove, consign, assign, refer, remand, despatch.

2. Banish, expatriate, exile, transport, expel.

Relent, *v. i.* Soften (*in temper*), grow lenient *or* tender, abate severity *or* rigor,

yield, relax, comply, feel compassion, forbear.

Relentless, *a.* Unrelenting, unpitying, unforgiving, implacable, inexorable, impenitent, obdurate, unappeasable, cruel, vindictive, rancorous, merciless, unmerciful, uncompassionate, pitiless, hard, unyielding, ruthless, unfeeling, remorseless.

Relevant, *a.* Pertinent, applicable, fit, proper, relative, germane, apropos, apt, suitable, appropriate, apposite, to the purpose, to the point.

Reliability, *n.* Reliableness, trustworthiness.

Reliable, *a.* Trustworthy, trusty, unfailing, dependable, sure, certain, authentic, constant.

Reliance, *n.* 1. Dependence, trust, confidence, assurance, credence.

2. Hope, ground of trust, sure dependence.

Reliant, *a.* Confident, trusting, self-reliant.

Relics, *n. pl.* 1. Remains, remnants, scraps, fragments, leavings, remainder.

2. Corpse, dead body, remains.

3. Memorial, memento, remembrance, token, souvenir, keepsake.

Relict, *n.* Widow.

Relief, *n.* 1. Succor, help, assistance, aid, reinforcement, deliverance, support, alleviation, mitigation, palliation, amelioration, assuagement, easement, softening; rest, respite, ease, comfort.

2. Redress, indemnification, remedy.

3. Projection, prominence, protrusion, embossment.

4. Vividness, clearness, distinctness, perspective.

Relieve, *v. t.* 1. Succor, aid, help, assist, comfort, free, sustain, support.

2. Allay, mitigate, assuage, soothe, lessen, palliate, ease, remedy, cure, remove, alleviate, abate, lighten, diminish; "spell."

3. Redress, indemnify, right, repair.

4. Release, remedy, rescue, make amends for, free, disengage, release.

5. Put in relief, set off by contrast.

RELIGION, *n.* 1. Science of duty (*to God and our fellows*), science of obligation (*as creatures of God*), that which binds us to the practice of righteousness, theology, theism.

2. Sentiment of faith, reverence, and love towards God; godliness, devoutness, devotion, holiness, sanctity, piety, virtue, goodness, practical piety.

3. System of faith, system of worship.

Religious, *a.* 1. Devout, holy, godly, pious, spiritual, God-fearing, pietistic, other-worldly, prayerful, devotional.

2. Conscientious, scrupulous, exact, strict, rigid.

3. Divine, canonical, theological.

Religiously, *adv.* 1. Piously, devoutly.

2. Reverently.

3. Strictly, conscientiously, scrupulously, punctiliously, exactly.

Relinquish, *v. t.* 1. Leave, quit, vacate, resign, part with, throw away, forsake, desert, renounce, forswear, abandon, cast off, give over, withdraw from, go back on.

2. Surrender, cede, yield, resign, renounce, forbear, abdicate, forego, deliver up, give up, part with, lay down, lay aside, waive, give up claim to.

Relinquishment, *n.* 1. Abandonment, dereliction, desertion, abjuration.

2. Renunciation, surrender, cession, resignation, abandonment.

Relish, *n.* 1. Taste, flavor, savor.

2. Liking, fondness, taste, appreciation, zest, enjoyment, gratification, gusto, palate, appetite, predilection, partiality, inclination.

3. Quality, tinge, cast, touch, twang, manner, flavor, savor, sort, seasoning.

4. Appetizer, condiment.

5. Delight, power of pleasing.

6. Tincture.

——, *v. t.* 1. Like the taste *or* flavor of, taste with pleasure.

2. Like, enjoy, appreciate, be pleased with, take delight in, delight in, have a liking for.

Relucent, *a.* 1. Shining, luminous, lucent, bright, glittering, resplendent.

2. Bright, shining, eminent.

Reluctance, *n.* Repugnance, unwillingness, aversion, dislike, disinclination.

Reluctant, *a.* Unwilling, loath, averse, backward, disinclined, indisposed.

Rely, *v. i.* Depend, rest, count, confide, reckon, trust, lean, hope.

Remain, *v. i.* 1. Continue, endure, abide, stay, last.

2. Be left, be left behind, survive, exceed.

3. Stay, tarry, sojourn, dwell, abide, continue, wait, rest, halt, stop.

4. Continue, stay, keep.

Remainder, *n.* Remnant, residue, rest, remains, residuum, balance, excess, leavings, relics, surplus.

Remains, *n. pl.* 1. Relics, remnants, scraps, fragments, leavings, remainder, refuse, odds and ends, lees, dregs.

2. Dead body, corpse, fossils, ashes, bones.

Remand, *v. t.* Send back, order back, call back, consign.

Remark, *n.* 1. Notice, observation, heed, regard, consideration.

2. Comment, note, annotation, stricture, gloss.

3. Assertion, declaration, averment, statement, comment, utterance, saying.

——, *v. t.* 1. Note, notice, observe, heed, regard, take notice of, attend to, pay attention to.

2. Express, observe (*in words*), utter, say, state, mention.

——, *v. i.* Say, observe, state, comment.

Remarkable, *a.* Noticeable, observable, notable, memorable, important, extraordinary, uncommon, unusual, singular, strange, rare, wonderful, distinguished, famous, eminent, conspicuous, prominent, striking, noteworthy, peculiar.

Remarkably, *adv.* Extraordinarily, uncommonly, unusually, notably, conspicuously, singularly, surprisingly, markedly.

Remediable, *a.* Curable, medicable, retrievable, reparable, rectifiable, to be cured, to be remedied.

Remedial, *a.* Curing, healing, sanatory, sanative, reparative, curative, restorative, prophylactic, therapeutic, tonic, antidotal; corrective, amendatory, compensatory.

Remediless, *a.* 1. Incurable, irremediable, cureless, desperate, hopeless, past cure.

2. Irreparable, irretrievable, irreclaimable, irrecoverable, irreversible, hopeless, past mending, past hope.

3. Ineffectual, powerless, incapable.

Remedy, *n.* 1. Cure, antidote, antitoxin, specific, restorative, help, medicine, corrective, counteractive, panacea, nostrum.

2. Reparation, redress, restoration, restitution, counteraction.

3. Relief, aid, help, assistance.

——, *v. t.* 1. Cure, heal, help, relieve, palliate.

2. Repair, redress, restore, rectify, retrieve, amend, correct.

Remember, *v. t.* 1. Recall, recollect, call to mind, call up, call to remembrance, bethink, have at one's fingers' ends, know by heart.

2. Retain, bear in mind, keep in mind, bear in memory, preserve the memory of, treasure in the memory, tax the memory with.

Remembrance, *n.* 1. Reminiscence, recollection, retrospect, calling to mind, revival in the mind.

2. Memory.

3. Memento, memorial, remembrancer, token, reminder, keepsake, souvenir.

4. Thought, regard, consideration.

Remembrancer, *n.* Token, memorial, memento, remembrance, testimonial, monument, record, souvenir.

Remind, *v. t.* Suggest to, put in mind, jog the memory of, put in remembrance, prompt.

Reminiscence, *n.* Remembrance, recollection, retrospect, calling to mind, memory.

Remiss, *a.* 1. Slack, dilatory, slow, backward, indolent, behindhand, tardy, lax, languid.

2. Inattentive, negligent, careless, thoughtless, heedless, neglectful, lax, slothful, slack, slow, idle, shiftless, dilatory.

Remissible, *a.* Excusable, venial, pardonable.

Remission, *n.* 1. Relaxation, moderation, mitigation, lessening, abatement, diminution.

2. Release, relinquishment, discharge, cancellation.

3. Intermission, suspension, interruption, suspense, stop, stoppage, respite, pause, rest, abatement.

4. Forgiveness, absolution, pardon, indulgence, acquittal, discharge, exoneration, excuse.

5. Release, relinquishment, surrender, renunciation.

Remit, *v. t.* 1. Return, restore, replace, send back.

2. Relax, diminish, abate, bate.

3. Release.

4. Forgive, pardon, absolve, excuse, overlook, condone, pass over.

5. Resign, surrender, give up, deliver up, relinquish.

6. Refer, transmit, forward, send, consign.

——, *v. i.* Slacken, abate, lessen, diminish, decrease, grow less, intermit.

Remittal, *n.* 1. Surrender, giving up.

2. Remission, remittance.

Remnant, *n.* 1. Residue, remainder, remains, trace, rest.

2. Scrap, fragment, piece, little bit.

Remonstrance, *n.* Expostulation, protestation, protest, dissuasion, reproof.

Remonstrate, *v. i.* Protest, expostulate, make objections to, take exception.

Remorse, *n.* Penitence, compunction, contrition, qualm, repentance, sorrow, regret, self-reproach, reproach of conscience, stings of conscience, self-condemnation.

Remorseful, *a.* Compunctious, contrite, repentant, penitent, sorrowful.

Remorseless, *a.* Unpitying, pitiless, relentless, unrelenting, uncompassionate, cruel, ruthless, merciless, unmerciful, savage, implacable, inexorable.

Remote, *a.* 1. Far, distant, far off, out-of-the-way.

2. Alien, foreign, unallied, unconnected, unrelated, far-fetched, inappropriate.

3. Abstracted, separated.

4. Slight, inconsiderable.

5. Secluded, sequestered, removed, isolated.

Remoteness, *n.* 1. Distance.

2. Slightness, distance.

Remount, *v. t.* Reascend.

Removal, *n.* 1. Displacement, remove, dislodgment, transference, relegation, change of place, shift, abstraction, departure.

2. Withdrawal, elimination, extraction, taking away.

3. Destruction, suppression, abatement.

4. Dismission, ejection, deprivation of office, discharge, expulsion.

Remove, *v. t.* 1. Displace, dislodge, transfer, transport, transplant, carry, shift.

2. Withdraw, extract, abstract, take out.

3. Banish, destroy, abate, suppress, take away, put an end to, do away with, make a clean sweep of, raze.

4. Separate, withdraw, take away, carry off.

5. Dismiss, eject, oust, put out, turn out, expel, discharge, "fire," cashier, retire, depose.

——, *v. i.* Move, change place, depart.

——, *n.* 1. Change of place. See RE-MOVAL.

2. Interval, distance, separation, stage, step.

3. Step (*in a scale of gradation*).

Removed, *a.* Secluded, sequestered, remote, separate.

Remunerate, *v. t.* 1. Reward, requite, compensate, pay, recompense, satisfy, repay.

2. Reimburse, repay, pay, indemnify.

Remuneration, *n.* 1. Reward, requital, recompense, compensation, repayment, satisfaction.

2. Reparation, amends, recompense, restitution, compensation.

3. Reimbursement, indemnification, repayment, indemnity.

Remunerative, *a.* 1. Profitable, paying, gainful, lucrative, paying a good interest, bringing a good return.

2. Remuneratory, rewarding, requiting, reparative, compensatory, recompensing.

Renaissance, } *n.* Revival, revival of letters and arts, awakening,
Renascence, } rebirth.

Renascent, *a.* 1. Reappearing, reproduced.

2. Rejuvenated.

Rencounter, *n.* 1. Clash, shock, collision.

2. Encounter, conflict, combat, fight,
battle, contest, duel, engagement, action,
skirmish, brush, affair.

3. Meeting.

——, *v. i.* Encounter, clash, skirmish,
meet, fight, come into collision.

Rend, *v. t.* 1. Break, sever, dissever,
sunder, rive, rupture, shiver, cleave, split,
crack, snap, disrupt, dismember, divide,
destroy, burst, fracture, lacerate, dilacerate, tear, tear asunder, break asunder.

2. Tear away, part with violence.

Render, *v. t.* 1. Return, restore, pay back,
surrender.

2. Give, assign, present, deliver.

3. Furnish, contribute, supply, afford,
yield.

4. Make, cause to be.

5. Translate, construe, interpret, set
forth.

Rendering, *n.* 1. Translation, version,
construction, interpretation, rendition.

2. Interpretation, delineation, reproduction, representation, exhibition.

Rendezvous, *n.* 1. Place of meeting.

2. Meeting.

Rendition, *n.* 1. Return, restitution, surrender.

2. Translation, rendering, version.

3. Rendering, interpretation, delineation, reproduction, representation, exhibition.

Renegade, *n.* 1. Apostate, backslider,
renegado, recreant, turncoat.

2. Deserter, revolter, rebel, traitor.

3. Vagabond, worthless fellow.

Renew, *v. t.* 1. Renovate, restore, re-
establish, repair, refit, rebuild, revive, recreate, make new, resuscitate, refurbish,
replenish, rejuvenate, refresh.

2. Repeat, recommence, begin again,
resume, continue.

3. Repeat, iterate, reiterate.

4. Regenerate, transform.

Renewal, *n.* 1. Renovation, restoration,
renewing, revival, regeneration, recru-
descence, renascence, re-establishment,
repair.

2. Repetition, recommencement, recurrence, iteration, resumption, continuance.

Renitency, *n.* 1. Resistance (*of solid bodies
to pressure*), opposition, antagonism.

2. Reluctance, moral resistance, disinclination.

Renitent, *a.* Resisting (*pressure*), opposing,
counteracting, antagonistic, resistant,
recalcitrant.

Renounce, *v. t.* 1. Reject, repudiate, disclaim, disown, disavow, abjure, forswear,
recant, deny, decline, slight, abnegate,
neglect, cast off, trample on.

2. Relinquish, abandon, forego, resign, surrender, desert, forsake, leave,
quit, abdicate, drop, lay down, lay aside,
give up, cast off, give over, drop all idea
of.

Renouncement, *n.* See RENUNCIATION.

Renovate, *v. t.* 1. Renew, restore, reconstitute, refresh, repair, revamp, refurbish,
re-establish.

2. Reproduce, regenerate, revivify,
recreate, reanimate, revive, resuscitate.

Renovation, *n.* 1. Renewal, restoration,
reconstitution.

2. Revival, revivification, regeneration, reproduction, restoration, reconstitution, redintegration, rehabilitation.

Renown, *n.* Distinction, repute, name,
reputation, greatness, note, notoriety,
notability, figure, fame, celebrity, glory,
honor, eminence, luster.

Renowned, *a.* Distinguished, famous,
famed, notable, illustrious, celebrated,
eminent, noted, honored, far-famed, remarkable, wonderful.

Rent, *n.* 1. Break, breach, separation,
fissure, split, crack, crevice, rift, cleft, gap,
opening, flaw, rupture, disrupture, disruption, fracture, laceration, dilaceration,
divulsion, tear, solution of continuity.

2. Schism, separation.

3. Income, revenue (*from land* or *tenements*), rental, rent-roll.

——, *v. t.* 1. Lease, let, hire.

2. Hold by paying rent, lease, hire.

—— *v. i.* Be leased, be let.

Rental, *n.* Rent-roll, account of rents, rent.

Renter, *n.* Lessee, tenant.

Renumerate, *v. t.* Recount, count again.

Renunciation, *n.* 1. Rejection, repudiation, abnegation, abjuration, disowning,
disownment, disavowal, disavowment,
disclaimer, recantation, denial, renouncement; self-denial.

2. Surrender, cession, abandonment,
resignation, relinquishment.

Repair, *v. t.* 1. Mend, refit, retouch, vamp,
tinker, piece, patch, touch up, vamp up,
"doctor," patch up, renew, amend.

2. Retrieve, restore, make good, recruit, correct.

3. Redress, atone for, make amends
for.

——, *v. i.* Go, resort, betake one's self.

——, *n.* Restoration, reparation, renewal,
refitting, mending.

Reparable, *a.* Retrievable, restorable, recoverable, curable.

Reparation, *n.* 1. Restoration, renewal, repair.

2. Redress, indemnification, amends, atonement, restitution, compensation, satisfaction, correction, requital, recompense.

Reparative, *a.* Restoring, restorative, reviving, amendatory, corrective, remedial, amending.

——, *n.* Cure, remedy, medicine, restorative, corrective.

Repartee, *n.* Retort, smart *or* witty reply, rejoinder, banter.

Repast, *n.* 1. Food, victuals.

2. Meal, entertainment.

Repay, *v. t.* 1. Refund, reimburse, pay back, restore, return.

2. Remunerate, compensate, reward, recompense, require, satisfy.

3. Retaliate, revenge, avenge.

Repeal, *v. t.* Abrogate (*a law*), rescind, revoke, recall, reverse, annul, cancel, abolish, set aside, do away, make void.

——, *n.* Abrogation, revocation, rescission, rescinding, annulment, abolition.

Repeat, *v. t.* 1. Iterate, reiterate, do again, make again; duplicate, double.

2. Recite, rehearse, recapitulate, tell over, narrate, cite, quote, say over, relate.

3. Renew, reproduce, echo, re-echo.

Repeatedly, *adv.* Again and again.

Repel, *v. t.* 1. Repulse, drive, beat, *or* force back, disperse, scatter.

2. Resist, oppose, check, withstand, confront, ward off, parry, rebuff, strive against, make a stand against.

3. Reject, refuse, decline.

4. Sicken, revolt, disgust.

Repellent, *a.* Repulsive, repelling, uninviting, repugnant, forbidding, abhorrent, disgusting, revolting.

Repent, *v. t.* Rue, be sorry for, regret, remember with sorrow.

——, *v. i.* Regret, be sorry, be penitent, feel remorse, rue.

Repentance, *n.* Penitence, contrition, contriteness, compunction, remorse, regret, sorrow for wrong-doing, self-reproach, self-reproof, self-accusation, self-condemnation, stings of conscience.

Repentant, *a.* 1. Penitent, sorry, sorrowful, regretful, contrite, remorseful, rueful.

2. Penitential.

Repercussion, *n.* Reverberation, rebound, recoil.

Repercussive, *a.* 1. Rebounding, reverberating.

2. Driven back, reverberated.

Repertory, *n.* 1. Repository, depository.

2. Treasury, magazine, depot, museum, repository, storehouse, thesaurus.

Repetition, *n.* 1. Iteration, reiteration, reiterance, recapitulation, harping.

2. Tautology, pleonasm, redundancy, diffuseness, verbosity.

3. Recital, rehearsal, relation, narration, retailing.

4. Recurrence, renewal.

Repine, *v. i.* Complain, murmur, croak, fret, long, mope, pine, grumble, be discontented, be dissatisfied.

Replace, *v. t.* 1. Reinstate, re-establish, reset, put back.

2. Refund, repay, restore, pay back.

3. Take the place of, supply the want of, succeed, be a substitute for, displace, supersede, supplant.

Replenish, *v. t.* 1. Fill, stock, fill up, refill, renew, resupply.

2. Supply, furnish, provide, store, enrich.

Replete, *a.* Full, abounding, charged, exuberant, fraught, well-stocked, well-provided, completely full, filled again.

Repletion, *n.* 1. Satiety, glut, surfeit, exuberance, abundance, profusion, satiation, fulness.

2. (*Med.*) Plethora.

Replica, *n.* Autograph copy, duplicate, facsimile, reproduction.

Replication, *n.* 1. Answer, reply, response.

2. Rejoinder.

3. Repetition.

4. Copy, portrait.

Reply, *v. i.* Answer, respond, rejoin, echo.

——, *n.* Answer, response, replication, retort, repartee, rejoinder, acknowledgment.

Report, *v. t.* 1. Announce, annunciate, declare, communicate, set forth, make known, give an account of.

2. Relate, mention, bruit, advertise, publish, narrate, noise, broadcast, herald, tell, promulgate, give out, state, rumor, circulate publicly.

3. Take down (*in writing*), make minutes of, record.

4. Relate, tell, narrate, recite, describe, detail, state, make known.

——, *n.* 1. Account, announcement, statement, declaration, communication.

2. Relation, account, narration, detail, talk, news, advice, tidings, description, recital, narrative, story, tale.

3. Rumor, common fame, hearsay, gossip.

4. Explosion, noise, sound, detonation, clap, discharge, repercussion.

5. Repute, reputation, fame, public character.

6. Record, note, minute, account, bulletin, statement (*in writing*).

Repose, *v. t.* 1. Compose, rest, put to rest, lay down to rest, give repose to, settle, recline.

2. Place (*in confidence*), put, stake.

3. Lodge, reposit, deposit, lay up, store.

——, *v. i.* 1. Lie, rest.

2. Rest, sleep, slumber, recline, couch.

3. Lean (*in confidence*), confide, put confidence, rely.

——, *n.* 1. Rest, sleep, slumber, quiet, recumbency.

2. Relaxation, respite, breathing-time, inactivity, leisure.

3. Ease, quiet, quietness, quietude, stillness, peacefulness, tranquillity, peace, calm.

Reposit, *v. t.* Lodge, deposit, place, store, lay up, hoard.

Repository, *n.* Depository, repertory, reservatory, magazine, conservatory, storehouse, receptacle, storeroom, vault, museum, treasury, thesaurus, depot.

Reprehend, *v. t.* Reprove, chide, rebuke, reproach, upbraid, reprimand, accuse, censure, blame.

Reprehensible, *a.* Blamable, culpable, censurable, condemnable, uncommendable, reprovable, rebukable, deserving censure, blameworthy.

Reprehension, *n.* Reproof, blame, censure, reproach, reprimand, rebuke, admonition.

Represent, *v. t.* 1. Exhibit, show, express.

2. Delineate, depict, portray, set forth, picture, draw, limn, sketch, describe, exhibit, give an account of, show.

3. Personate, take the part of, act, impersonate, pose as, personify, mimic, stand for, portray by action.

4. Stand for, stand in the place of.

5. Delineate, portray, reproduce, depict, image, symbolize, typify, illustrate, exemplify.

Representation, *n.* 1. Exhibition, delineation, show.

2. Personation, impersonation, simulation.

3. Description, account, narration, relation, narrative, statement.

4. Likeness, semblance, image, portraiture, model, resemblance.

5. Acting for others, supplying another's place.

6. Body of delegates *or* deputies.

7. Spectacle, sight, public exhibition.

8. Remonstrance, expostulation.

Representative, *a.* 1. Figurative, typical, symbolical, illustrative.

2. Delegated, acting for others, representing, deputed.

REPRESENTATIVE, *n.* 1. Delegate, deputy, substitute, commissioner, legate, emissary, messenger, envoy, agent, proxy, *locum tenens,* lieutenant, vicegerent.

2. Example, sample.

Repress, *v. t.* 1. Suppress, subdue, crush, quell, choke, silence, dull, overpower, overcome, put down, smother.

2. Restrain, check, curb, bridle, control, chasten, chastize, rein in, sober down.

3. Calm, quiet, appease.

Reprieve, *v. t.* 1. Respite, delay the punishment of, give a respite to.

2. Relieve.

——, *n.* 1. Respite, suspension of punishment; interval of ease.

2. Pardon, remission.

Reprimand, *v. t.* Reprove, censure, rebuke, reprehend, reproach, chide, upbraid, blame, admonish, find fault with.

——, *n.* Reproof, reprehension, censure, rebuke, reproach, blame, admonition, reprobation, reproval.

Reprint, *n.* Reimpression, republication.

Reproach, *v. t.* 1. Censure, blame, reprove, rebuke, reprimand, reprehend, upbraid.

2. Revile, vilify, defame, asperse, condemn, abuse, speak ill of, accuse, discredit, disparage, traduce.

——, *n.* 1. Censure, reproof, disapprobation, disapproval, blame, invective, upbraiding, condemnation, reprobation, remonstrance, reprehension, expostulation, rebuke, reprimand, railing, contumely, reviling, abuse, vilification, scurrility, insolence, scorn, contempt.

2. Dishonor, disgrace, shame, disrepute, stigma, slur, obloquy, opprobrium, odium, scandal, ignominy, infamy, abasement, indignity, insult, discredit, scorn, offence.

Reproachable, *a.* Censurable, reprehensible, blamable.

Reproachful, *a.* 1. Opprobrious, scurrilous, abusive, railing, scolding, upbraiding, vituperative, condemnatory, censorious, reproving, damnatory, invective, contumelious, offensive, sarcastic, insulting, contemptuous, scornful, insolent.

2. Shameful, infamous, base, vile, disreputable, discreditable, dishonorable, disgraceful, scandalous.

Reprobate, *a.* Depraved, abandoned, profligate, corrupt, hardened, lost, graceless, base, shameless, wicked, vile, vitiated, irredeemable, cast-away.

——, *n.* Villain, castaway, outcast, rascal, sinner, scamp, scoundrel, miscreant, caitiff, vile wretch.

Reprobate, *v. t.* 1. Disapprove, reject, discard, condemn, censure, reprehend.

2. Disallow.

3. Disown, abandon.

Reprobation, *n.* Condemnation, censure, rejection.

Reproduce, *v. t.* 1. Generate, propagate, multiply.

2. Copy, imitate, represent, repeat, portray.

Reproduction, *n.* 1. Generation, propagation.

2. Copy, imitation, representation, portrayal, ectype, repetition.

Reproof, *n.* Censure, condemnation, rebuke, monition, criticism, reproach, objurgation, castigation, admonition, chiding, reprimand, reprehension, animadversion, blame, reproval, lecture, upbraiding, rating, correction, dressing down.

Reprovable, *a.* Censurable, blamable, blameworthy, reproachable, culpable, reprehensible, deserving censure, worthy of blame, rebukable.

Reproval, *n.* Reproof, admonition, chiding, reprehension.

Reprove, *v. t.* Censure, lecture, blame, inculpate, reprehend, condemn, reprimand, chide, criticize, reproach, objurgate, castigate, upbraid, rate, scold, correct, rebuke, admonish, find fault with, remonstrate with, expostulate with.

Reptile, *a.* 1. Creeping, crawling.

2. Grovelling, abject, mean, vile, low, vulgar; treacherous.

Republic, *n.* Commonwealth, democracy, state, popular government, representative government.

Repudiate, *v. t.* 1. Discard, reject, disclaim, renounce, cast off, abjure, disavow, nullify.

2. Divorce, put away.

3. Disown (*debts*), refuse to pay, refuse to acknowledge.

Repudiation, *n.* 1. Rejection.

2. Divorce, putting away.

3. Disavowal, disowning, disclaiming.

Repugnance, *n.* 1. Contrariety, contrariness, inconsistency, incompatibility, irreconcilableness, unsuitableness.

2. Opposition, resistance, struggle, contest.

3. Unwillingness, aversion, hatred, reluctance, repulsion, detestation, dislike, antipathy, antagonism, hostility.

Repugnant, *a.* 1. Inconsistent, irreconcilable, incompatible.

2. Opposed, opposing, opposite, contrary, hostile, adverse, averse, unfavorable, antagonistic, inimical, at variance.

3. Offensive, distasteful, repellent, repulsive, detestable.

Repulse, *n.* 1. Repelling, driving back, repulsion.

2. Refusal, denial.

3. Failure, disappointment.

——, *v. t.* 1. Repel, beat back, drive back.

2. Refuse, reject.

Repulsion, *n.* Repulse, rejection, discarding, spurning, rebuff; aversion, antipathy, repugnance, dislike, hatred, loathing, disgust, abhorrence; antagonism, hostility.

Repulsive, *a.* 1. Repelling, repellent.

2. Cold, frigid, reserved, repellent, forbidding, harsh, unpleasant, disagreeable, offensive, odious, hateful, disgusting, loathsome, nauseating, nauseous, sickening, revolting, repugnant, abhorrent.

Reputable, *a.* Respectable, creditable, honorable, worthy, estimable, in good odor.

Reputation, *n.* 1. Repute, name, mark, note, account, character, fame.

2. Credit, repute, regard, respect, estimation, esteem, renown, honor, fame, celebrity; prestige, distinction, éclat, report, glory.

Repute, *v. t.* Regard, consider, esteem, estimate, account, reckon, hold, deem, think, judge.

——, *n.* See REPUTATION.

REQUEST, *n.* Petition, prayer, entreaty, beseechment, importunity, suit, solicitation, supplication, asking, invitation, call, demand, requisition, claim.

——, *v. t.* Solicit, ask, entreat, beg, desire, beseech, beg for, petition for, ask for.

Require, *v. t.* 1. Demand, claim, request, beg, beseech, crave, sue, pray, importune, dun, requisition, invite, bid, summon; call on.

2. Need, want, call for, make necessary.

3. Enjoin, prescribe, direct, order, exact, insist on.

Requirement, *n.* 1. Demand, claim, requisition, need, want, requisite; needfulness, exigency, urgency, indispensability, stress, pinch, call, request, market.

2. Command, mandate, order, precept, charge, bidding, decree, behest, exaction, injunction, charge, claim.

Requisite, *a.* Needful, needed, necessary, essential, indispensable, imperative, called for, in demand.

Requisition, *n.* 1. Demand, claim, exaction, requirement, call.

2. Request, demand.

Requital, *n.* 1. Reward, recompense, compensation, remuneration, satisfaction, payment.

2. Retribution, retaliation, punishment; return, revenge, reprisal.

Requite, v. t. 1. Reward, recompense, compensate, remunerate, reciprocate, satisfy, pay, repay.

2. Retaliate, avenge, punish, revenge.

Rescind, v. t. 1. Cut off, cut short, remove.

2. Annul, abrogate, abolish, revoke, recall, repeal, cancel, reverse, countermand, quash, set aside, do away, vacate, void.

Rescission, n. Rescindment, abrogation, repeal, revocation, annulling, cancelling, abolition.

Rescript, n. Edict, decree, mandate, law.

Rescue, v. t. Liberate, free, deliver, save, redeem, extricate, release, ransom, set free, bring off, retake, recapture, preserve, recover.

——, n. Liberation, release, redemption, ransom, salvation, deliverance, extrication.

Research, n. Investigation, inquiry, scrutiny, analysis, examination, exploration, study, careful search.

Resemblance, n. 1. Similarity, likeness, similitude, semblance, analogy, agreement, affinity.

2. Representation, image, counterpart, facsimile, likeness, similitude.

Resemble, v. t. 1. Be like, bear likeness or resemblance to, simulate, "favor," look like, parallel, agree with.

2. Liken, compare.

3. Imitate, counterfeit, copy.

Resent, v. t. Take ill, take amiss, take offence at, take umbrage at, be offended at, be indignant at, be provoked at.

——, v. i. Be angry, take offence, take umbrage, harbor resentment, be indignant, bridle, bristle.

Resentful, a. Angry, irritable, irascible, choleric, revengeful, malignant; huffy, touchy, hurt, bitter, sore, in high dudgeon.

Resentment, n. Indignation, anger, irritation, annoyance, vexation, gall, rage, fury, choler, ire, wrath, displeasure, grudge, umbrage, dudgeon, pique, acrimony, bitterness, spleen, soreness, sulks, huff, heart-burning.

Reservation, n. 1. Concealment, suppression, reserve.

2. Reserve, appropriation, something reserved, restriction, exception, saving.

3. Salvo, proviso.

4. Custody.

Reserve, v. t. 1. Keep, hold, retain, husband, set by, lay by, lay up, store up, withhold.

2. Except, make an exception of.

——, n. 1. Reservation, something reserved; store, fund, supply, savings, provision.

2. Constraint, restraint, backwardness, cautious behavior, coldness, closeness, reservedness, self-control, distance, aloofness, retention, uncommunicativeness, unresponsiveness, reticence, concealment, suppression.

3. Exception, something excepted.

4. Reservation, restriction.

5. Shyness, coyness, taciturnity, modesty, demureness.

Reserved, a. 1. Retained, kept, withheld, excepted, set apart, bespoken, taken, booked, held.

2. Restrained, backward, cautious, cold, incommunicative, unsociable, unsocial, distant, reticent, self-controlled, aloof, offish.

3. Shy, coy, taciturn, modest, demure.

Reservoir, n. 1. Basin, cistern, tank, pond, standpipe; magazine.

2. Receiver, receptacle.

Reside, v. i. 1. Dwell, inhabit, live, abide, lodge, room, remain, domiciliate, domicile, sojourn.

2. Inhere.

Residence, n. 1. Habitancy, inhabitancy, legal settlement, domiciliation, stay, sojourn, stop, tarrying.

2. Habitation, dwelling, domicile, abode, lodging, mansion, house, place of residence, home.

Resident, a. 1. Abiding, dwelling, residing, inhabiting.

2. Fixed, firm.

——, n. 1. Inhabitant, dweller, resider, inhabiter, sojourner.

2. Tenant, occupant, dweller.

Residual, a. Remaining.

Residue, n. 1. Remainder, rest, remnant, residuum, remains, leavings.

2. (Law.) Surplus (of a testator's estate), excess, overplus.

Residuum, n. 1. Residue, remainder.

2. Surplus.

Resign, v. t. 1. Yield, surrender, relinquish, abjure, disclaim, wash one's hands of, forego, abandon, quit, forsake, abdicate, leave, give up, assign back, give back, commit.

2. Withdraw, give up, throw up, renounce.

3. Yield, submit, hand over, confide.

——, v. i. Abdicate, relinquish office, tender one's resignation.

Resignation, n. 1. Surrender, relinquishment, abandonment, renunciation, abdication, retirement.

2. Endurance (*with a submissive, religious spirit*), submission, acquiescence, compliance, patience, sufferance, forbearance, fortitude, long-sufferance, long-suffering.

Resigned, *a.* 1. Surrendered, given up.

2. Submissive, unresisting, complying, acquiescent, passive, meek, patient, yielding, uncomplaining; reconciled, philosophical.

Resilient, *a.* Rebounding, recoiling, elastic, buoyant, springy.

Resist, *v. t.* Oppose, withstand, impugn, confront, assail, attack, strive against, counteract, neutralize, stop, stem, block, rebuff, stand against, hinder, check, thwart, baffle, obstruct, frustrate, impede, disappoint; repulse.

——, *v. i.* Stand fast, stand; rebel, stand at bay.

Resistance, *n.* Opposition, renitency, non-conductivity. See also RESIST.

Resistless, *a.* Irresistible, invincible, overpowering, unconquerable.

Resolute, *a.* Firm, determined, steady, decided, resolved, stanch, steadfast, fixed, constant, persevering, earnest, sturdy, tenacious, relentless, pertinacious, unflinching, unwavering, inflexible, unyielding, unbending, unalterable, undaunted, hardy, unshaken, bold, stout, stout-hearted, strong-willed, game.

Resolution, *n.* 1. Disentanglement, explication, unravelling.

2. Firmness, determination, steadiness, constancy, inflexibility, courage, energy, pluck, "grit," backbone, "sand," stamina, hardihood, decision, manliness, tenacity of purpose, earnestness, tenacity, relentlessness, resolvedness, resoluteness, perseverance, steadfastness, fortitude, boldness, purpose, resolve, intention, fixed purpose.

3. (*Math.*) Solution, explanation, analysis, separation.

4. (*Med.*) Disappearance, dispersion, decomposition, dissolution, solution, termination, breaking up, removal.

Resolvable, *a.* 1. Decomposable.

2. Solvable.

Resolve, *v. t.* 1. Analyze, separate, reduce, disperse, scatter, split up.

2. Dissolve, melt, liquefy, reduce, change, transform.

3. Disentangle, interpret, decipher, unravel, elucidate, explain, unfold, solve.

4. Determine, decide, fix in purpose; confirm, fix in resolution.

5. (*Legislation.*) Declare, determine on, express.

——, *v. i.* 1. Dissolve, melt, liquefy, become fluid.

2. Intend, purpose, decide, determine, will, fix, persevere in, go the limit, stick at nothing, conclude, form a resolution, make up one's mind, come to a determination.

3. Determine by vote.

4. Be convinced, be settled in opinion.

——, *n.* 1. Intention, resolution, determination, fixed purpose, will, decision, conclusion.

2. Declaration (*by a legislature* or *an organized body*), resolution, determination.

Resonant, *a.* Resounding, sonorous, ringing, reverberating, vibrant, roaring, booming, thundering, deep-mouthed, clangorous.

Resort, *v. t.* Frequent, haunt.

——, *v. i.* 1. Go, repair, convene, congregate, assemble; take refuge.

2. Have recourse, betake one's self, apply.

——, *n.* 1. Recourse, application, expedient.

2. Haunt, retreat, place frequented, rendezvous, "dive," "joint"; spa, vacation place.

3. Concourse, meeting, confluence, assembling.

4. Company, intercourse.

Resound, *v. t.* 1. Echo, re-echo, reverberate, ring.

2. Sound, extol, celebrate, praise.

——, *v. i.* Echo, reverberate, ring.

Resource, *n.* 1. Resort, dependence.

2. Means, expedient, device, contrivance, resort, appliance, instrumentality.

Resources, *n. pl.* Money, wealth, funds, capital, property, reserve, income, pecuniary means, supplies, available means.

Respect, *v. t.* 1. Esteem, reverence, regard, admire, honor, revere, venerate, value, prize, think highly of, have a high opinion of, look up to, defer to; spare, treat with consideration.

2. Relate to, refer to, bear upon, pertain to, be concerned with.

3. Heed, consider, notice, observe.

——, *n.* 1. Esteem, reverence, veneration, homage, estimation, consideration, regard, honor, deference; politeness, civility, courtesy, attention, notice, recognition; [*pl.*] compliments, greetings, devoirs, regards.

2. Favor, good-will, kind consideration.

3. Relation, reference, regard, connection, bearing, aspect, matter, feature, point, particular, point of view.

Respectability, *n.* Estimableness, reputableness, respectableness.

Respectable, *a.* 1. Estimable, honorable, worthy, proper, reputable, presentable, upright, considerable.

2. Mediocre, moderate, considerable, fair.

Respectful, *a.* Deferential, courteous, dutiful, civil, decorous, polite, complaisant, ceremonious, formal.

Respective, *a.* 1. Relative.

2. Particular, own, several, individual.

Respects, *n. pl.* Compliments, regards, greetings, devoirs, commendations.

Respiration, *n.* Breathing.

Respire, *v. i.* Breathe, exhale, live.

Respite, *n.* 1. Delay, pause, rest, interval, stop, break, recess, intermission, cessation, stay, breathing-time.

2. Reprieve, suspension of punishment.

3. Postponement, delay, forbearance.

——, *v. t.* 1. Delay, postpone.

2. Reprieve, suspend the punishment of.

3. Relieve (*by pause*).

Resplendent, *a.* Brilliant, splendid, shining, radiant, lustrous, luminous, beaming, effulgent, bright, lucid, glorious, gorgeous, glittering.

Respond, *v. i.* 1. Answer, reply, rejoin.

2. Correspond, suit, be agreeable to, accord.

Response, *n.* Answer, reply, replication, rejoinder, retort.

Responsibility, *n.* 1. Accountableness, accountability, responsibleness, trustworthiness, liability, obligation, bounden duty.

2. Trust, duty.

Responsible, *a.* Answerable, liable, accountable, amenable; trustworthy.

Responsive, *a.* 1. Answering.

2. Suited, correspondent, sympathetic, sensitive.

REST, *n.* 1. Repose, quiet, motionlessness, fixity, immobility, calm, quiescence, ease, comfort.

2. Peace, tranquillity, peacefulness, security, stillness, quietness, quiet, hush, relief.

3. Pause, cæsura, intermission, stop, stay, cessation, interval, respite, relaxation, lull, let-up, breathing space.

4. Sleep, slumber, siesta.

5. Death, the grave.

6. Support, stay, brace, prop.

7. Remainder, residue, remnant, residuum, balance.

8. Overplus, surplus.

——, *v. i.* 1. Stop, pause, halt, hold, repose, desist, cease, come to a stand, stand still, come to a stand-still, keep quiet.

2. Repose, relax, breathe, unbend, take rest, be tranquil, take one's ease, be at ease, be quiet.

3. Sleep, slumber, repose.

4. Lie, recline, lean, ride, perch, lounge.

5. Acquiesce, confide, trust, be satisfied.

6. Stand on, be supported, be based on.

7. Lean, trust, rely, confide.

——, *v. t.* 1. Quiet, lay at rest, give rest to, refresh, relieve.

2. Lay, place, repose, settle, set, put.

Restaurant, *n.* Eating-house, chophouse, *café,* cafeteria.

Restitution, *n.* 1. Restoration, return.

2. Indemnification, reparation, rehabilitation, recompense, amends, compensation, requital, remuneration, satisfaction, repayment.

Restive, *a.* 1. Stubborn, mulish, restiff, obstinate, stopping, unwilling.

2. Uneasy, impatient, restless, ill at ease, unquiet, recalcitrant.

Restless, *a.* 1. Unquiet, uneasy, unresting, disquieted, disturbed, restive; sleepless.

2. Unsteady, inconstant, changeable, unstable, unsettled, vacillating, irresolute.

3. Roving, wandering, in motion, active, astatic, transient, on the move, unsettled.

4. Turbulent, agitated, fretful, fidgety.

Restoration, *n.* 1. Replacement, reinstatement, restitution, reddition, recall, recovery, reparation, re-establishment, return.

2. Renewal, revival, resuscitation, redemption; renovation, redintegration, renewal, repair, reconstruction.

3. Cure, convalescence, recovery, recruitment, recuperation.

Restorative, *a.* Restoring, curative, remedial, invigorating, recuperative, stimulating.

——, *n.* Cure, remedy, medicine, curative, stimulant, healing, reparative, corrective.

Restore, *v. t.* 1. Return, give back, bring back, render up, refund, repay.

2. Replace, re-establish, redintegrate, repair, mend, emend, heal, patch, splice, caulk, cobble, tinker, retrieve, repristinate, rehabilitate, reinstate, renew.

3. Cure, heal, revive, recover.

4. Revive, resuscitate.

5. Compensate, make amends for.

Restrain, *v. t.* 1. Check, curb, bridle, shackle, trammel, hobble, picket, tie, fasten, confine, muzzle, gag, leash; snub, limit, repress, bind, cramp, "bottle up," suppress, withhold, constrain, coerce, keep, hold, govern, rule, control.

2. Hold back, hold in, keep under, check, arrest, stay, hinder, prevent, debar, bar, stop, prohibit, inhibit, interdict.

3. Restrict, confine, abridge, hinder, circumscribe, narrow.

4. Withhold, forbear.

Restraint, *n.* 1. Check, curb, control, discipline, repression, bridle, suppression, constraint, coercion, compulsion.

2. Hindrance, prevention, limitation, arrest, stop, stay, repression, inhibition, deterrence, restriction, prohibition.

3. Imprisonment, confinement, detention, shackles.

4. Stiffness, constraint, unnaturalness, reserve.

Restrict, *v. t.* Limit, bound, restrain, confine, circumscribe, hedge in, straiten, qualify.

Restriction, *n.* 1. Limitation, confinement.

2. Restraint, constraint.

3. Reservation, reserve.

Result, *v. i.* 1. Proceed, come, follow, flow, issue, arise, spring, rise, originate, ensue, accrue, be the effect, be derived.

2. End, terminate, eventuate.

——, *n.* 1. Consequence (*from a certain combination of causes* or *from premises*), inference, conclusion, deduction, outcome.

2. Issue, event, effect, termination, end, fruit, sequel, corollary, eventuality, product, consequence, outcome.

3. Decision, resolve, determination, resolution, finding, verdict, conclusion.

Resume, *v. t.* 1. Take back, take again, reassume.

2. Recommence, renew, begin again, continue, take up again; summarize.

Résumé, *n.* [Fr.] Summary, abstract, recapitulation, summing up, epitome, synopsis, condensed statement.

Resurrection, *n.* Rising, revival, revivification, renewal, resuscitation.

Resuscitate, *v. t.* Revivify, reanimate, renew, revive, quicken, restore to life, recall to life, bring back to life.

Retail, *v. t.* 1. Sell in small quantities, hawk, peddle.

2. Mention one by one, narrate, relate, recount.

Retain, *v. t.* 1. Hold, keep, reserve, husband, save, withhold, preserve, detain,

keep in possession; remember, recall, recollect, bear in mind.

2. Engage (*by fee paid*), hire, employ, maintain, keep in pay.

Retainer, *n.* 1. Attendant, adherent, dependant, follower, hanger-on, servant.

2. Retaining fee, preliminary fee.

Retaliate, *v. t.* Return (*by giving like for like, as an injury*), repay, requite, revenge, retort, turn, pay back, match, avenge.

——, *v. i.* Take revenge, return like for like, give *quid pro quo*, give a Roland for an Oliver.

Retaliation, *n.* Requital (*of evil*), reprisal, retribution, repayment, revenge, punishment, counterstroke, boomerang, Roland for an Oliver, measure for measure, eye for an eye.

Retard, *v. t.* 1. Check, obstruct, clog, impede, slacken, hinder.

2. Delay, defer, postpone, adjourn, procrastinate, put off.

Retch, *v. i.* Heave, strain, keck, gag, try to vomit.

Retention, *n.* 1. Reservation, holding, keeping, maintenance, grasp, tenacity, retaining, detention.

2. Reserve, restraint.

3. Memory, remembrance, retentiveness.

Retentive, *a.* Tenacious, unforgetting.

Reticence, *n.* Reserve, taciturnity, uncommunicativeness.

Reticent, *a.* Reserved, taciturn, silent, dumb, secretive, close, mum, uncommunicative.

Reticular,
Reticulated, } *a.* Meshy, retiform, netted.

Reticulation, *n.* Net-work.

Reticule, *n.* Hand-bag.

Retinue, *n.* Train, suite, followers, tail, "people," entourage, ménage; bodyguard, escort, body of attendants, *cortège*.

Retire, *v. t.* Withdraw from circulation (*as currency*), remove, shelve, superannuate, discharge.

——, *v. i.* 1. Withdraw, depart, retreat, remove, leave; go to bed.

2. Recede, retrocede, fall back, beat a retreat.

Retired, *a.* 1. Withdrawn, removed, abstracted.

2. Secret, private, secluded, apart, sequestered, solitary.

3. Superannuated.

Retirement, *n.* 1. Withdrawal, departure, abdication, regression.

2. Privacy, seclusion, retreat, solitude, loneliness, isolation.

Retiring, *a.* 1. Withdrawing, retreating.

2. Reserved, shy, demure, diffident, modest, coy.

Retort, *n.* 1. Repartee, smart *or* witty reply.

2. Vial, jar, vessel, alembic, crucible.

Retouch, *v. t.* Repair, touch up, improve; revise, brighten.

Retract, *v. t.* 1. Withdraw, draw back, draw in, draw away, pull back, abduce.

2. Recall, revoke, recant, abjure, disavow, cancel, take back, withdraw, unsay, disown, rescind, recall.

——, *v. i.* Take back, unsay.

Retraction, *n.* Recantation, abjuration, revocation, disavowal.

Retreat, *n.* 1. Departure, withdrawal, recession, recoil, departure, retirement.

2. Retirement, seclusion, privacy, solitude.

3. Asylum, refuge, shelter, cove, recess, niche, alcove; haunt, habitat, den, resort.

——, *v. i.* 1. Withdraw, retire, give way, recoil.

2. Recede, fall back, move back, retire.

Retrench, *v. t.* 1. Curtail, cut, lop, dock, delete, mutilate, prune, pare, clip, cut short, cut off, lop off.

2. Diminish, lessen, decrease, abridge, curtail.

3. Confine, limit.

——, *v. i.* 1. Economize.

2. Encroach, make inroad.

Retrenchment, *n.* Curtailment, reduction, diminution, abridgment, lessening.

Retribution, *n.* Repayment, requital, recompense, reward, compensation, return, retaliation, vengeance, revenge, nemesis, desert, penalty, judgment.

Retrieve, *v. t.* 1. Regain, recover, restore, recoup, recruit, repair, re-establish, get again.

2. Repair, make amends for.

3. Recall, bring back.

Retroaction, *n.* Recoil, reaction, rebound.

Retroactive, *a.* 1. Reflex.

2. Retrospective, that affects the past, regressive.

Retrocede, *v. i.* Retire, recede, retrograde, go back, give place.

Retrocession, *n.* Retrogression, retrogradation, going back.

Retrograde, *a.* Backward, unprogressive, inverse, retrogressive.

——, *v. i.* Retrocede, recede, retire, go *or* move backward, retrace one's steps; decline, degenerate.

Retrogression, *n.* Retrogradation, decline, degeneration.

Retrospect, *n.* Review, survey, re-examination, re-survey, recollection, reminiscence.

Retrospection, *n.* Looking back.

Retrospective, *a.* 1. Looking back.

2. Retroactive, that affects the past.

Return, *v. i.* 1. Go *or* come back, get back, retreat, turn back.

2. Recur, revert, recoil, reappear.

3. Answer, reply, respond.

4. Retort, recriminate.

5. Revisit, come again.

——, *v. t.* 1. Restore, give back, send back, volley, reflect, echo.

2. Repay, refund, give, reciprocate, requite, recompense, communicate, tell, render, report, remit, send, transmit, convey.

3. Elect.

——, *n.* 1. Repayment, reimbursement, remittance, payment.

2. Recompense, reward, requital, repayment, restitution, recovery, restoration; recurrence, renewal.

3. Advantage, benefit, profit, interest, rent, yield.

Reunion, *n.* Assembly, meeting, festive gathering; reconciliation.

Revamp, *v. t.* Rehabilitate, reconstruct, vamp, mend, patch up again.

Reveal, *v. t.* 1. Disclose, discover, unveil, unmask, unseal, uncover, publish, announce, open, expose, divulge, tell, declare, impart, confess, communicate, display, make known, lay open, show, betray.

2. Disclose, discover, make known.

Revel, *n.* Festivity, merry-making, feast, carousal, spree, Saturnalia.

——, *v. i.* 1. Carouse, tipple, make merry, disport, roister, riot.

2. Indulge, delight, luxuriate, wanton.

Revelation, *n.* 1. Discovery, disclosure, divulgence, exposé, exposure, detection, unveiling.

2. Divine communication of truth, oracle, gospel.

3. The Apocalypse.

Reveller, *n.* Carouser, bacchanal, bacchanalian, merry-maker, mænad, roisterer.

Revelry, *n.* Carousal, carouse, revel, riot, jollity, festivity, orgy, bacchanal, saturnalia, wassail, rout, debauch, jollification, drinking-bout, noisy festivity.

Revenge, *v. t.* 1. Retaliate, requite, take vengeance for.

2. Avenge, vindicate by punishment.

——, *n.* Retaliation, requital, vengeance, vindictiveness, rancor, malevolence.

Revengeful, *a.* Vindictive, malicious, malignant, spiteful, resentful, implacable, vengeful, rancorous, malevolent.

Revengefulness, *n.* See REVENGE.

Revenue, *n.* 1. Income, receipts.

2. Return, reward.

Reverberate, *v. t.* 1. Echo, re-echo, send back, return.

2. Reflect, send back, cast back.

——, *v. i.* Resound, echo, re-echo.

Reverberation, *n.* Echoing, re-echoing, echo, reflected sound.

Revere, *v. t.* Venerate, reverence, adore, honor, esteem, worship, hallow.

Reverence, *n.* 1. Veneration, honor, adoration, awe.

2. Homage, courtesy, bow.

Reverend, *a.* Venerable.

Reverential, *a.* Respectful, deferential, reverent, submissive, humble.

Reversal, *n.* Repeal, revocation, annulment, abrogation, change, overthrowing.

Reverse, *v. t.* 1. Invert, transpose, turn upside down, turn end for end, turn topsy-turvy.

2. Overturn, overthrow, overset, subvert, undo, unmake.

3. Change to the opposite.

4. Annul, repeal, revoke, rescind, retract, countermand, overthrow, make void.

——, *a.* Opposite, converse, back, contrary, verso, turned backward.

——, *n.* 1. Contrary, opposite, counterpart, back, tail, other side.

2. Change, vicissitude.

3. Misfortune, mischance, mishap, misadventure, trial, hardship, affliction, reverse of fortune, adversity, set-back, comedown, calamity, check, defeat.

Reversion, *n.* 1. Succession, inheritance, escheat.

2. Atavism, throwback.

3. Return, revulsion.

Revert, *v. t.* 1. Reverse, turn back.

2. Repel, drive back, turn back.

——, *v. i.* Return, escheat, recur, come back, turn back; relapse, backslide.

Revery, *n.* Musing, a waking dream, abstraction, absorption, inattention, preoccupation, absence of mind, daydream, brown study, reverie.

Review, *v. t.* 1. Revise, reconsider, re-examine, survey, inspect, overlook, retrace, go over again, pass in review.

2. Criticise, notice critically, discuss, edit, analyse, comment upon, write a critical notice of.

——, *n.* 1. Retrospect, re-survey, re-examination, survey, reconsideration.

2. Synopsis, digest, analysis.

3. Criticism, critique, reviewal, critical notice, commentary.

4. Military *or* naval inspection; parade.

Revile, *v. t.* Vilify, defame, reproach, slander, execrate, calumniate, asperse, traduce, upbraid, malign, abuse, backbite, speak ill of.

Revise, *v. t.* 1. Review, re-examine, reconsider.

2. Alter, amend, review, edit, overhaul, polish, correct.

Revision, *n.* Review, revisal, revise, re-examination, editing, correcting.

Revival, *n.* 1. Resuscitation, revivification, restoration, recovery, renascence, rebirth, renaissance, reawakening, reanimation, quickening.

2. Reproduction, restoration.

Revive, *v. t.* 1. Resuscitate, reanimate, revivify, revitalize, reinvigorate, reinspirit, bring to life again.

2. Rouse, quicken, animate, refresh, renovate, restore, reawaken, strengthen, reinspire, invigorate, cheer, recomfort, renew, recover.

3. Reawake, recall, bring to mind.

4. Recover, bring back, bring into use.

——, *v. i.* 1. Be resuscitated *or* reanimated, return to life, recover life, live again, rise.

2. Be invigorated, refreshed, *or* roused, recover strength.

Revocation, *n.* Retraction, recall, recantation, reversal, repeal, abjuration.

Revoke, *v. t.* Recall (*what has been said*), recant, retract, repeal, reverse, annul, cancel, rescind, countermand, abrogate, abolish, make void.

——, *v. i.* Renege.

Revolt, *v. i.* 1. Desert, fall off.

2. Rebel, mutiny, rise, renounce allegiance.

——, *v. t.* Repel, shock, do violence to, disgust, nauseate, sicken.

——, *n.* 1. Desertion, inconstancy, faithlessness, change of sides, defection.

2. Rebellion, insurrection, mutiny, sedition, outbreak, strike, disobedience, uprising.

Revolting, *a.* 1. Shocking, disgusting, sickening, objectionable, nauseating, nauseous, repulsive, offensive, obnoxious, hateful, horrible, abominable, monstrous, abhorrent.

2. Mutinous, insurgent.

Revolution, *n.* 1. Rotation, whirling, circular motion, turn, round, circuit, whirl, gyration.

2. Change (*in the political constitution of a country*), organic change, successful revolt *or* rebellion, overturn, overthrow,

reversal; uprising, mutiny, insurrection, *coup d'état.*

Revolutionize, *v. t.* Remodel, reform, refashion, recast, model anew, change completely.

Revolve, *v. i.* 1. Rotate, wheel, turn, swing, circulate, roll round an axis, turn round, circle, move round a center.

2. Pass away in cycles.

3. Fall back, return, devolve.

——, *v. t.* 1. Cause to turn round, circulate, roll, wheel.

2. Consider, meditate, ponder, study, reflect upon, ruminate upon, brood over.

Revolving, *a.* Turning, rolling, moving round, gyral, gyratory.

Revulsion, *n.* 1. Withdrawal, drawing back, shrinking, violent separation, abstraction.

2. Reaction, change, transition.

Reward, *v. t.* Recompense, compensate, gratify, remember, indemnify, requite, remunerate, pay, punish.

——, *n.* 1. Recompense, compensation, guerdon, requital, remuneration, pay, indemnity.

2. Premium, bonus, bounty, remembrance, meed, honorarium, prize, emolument, hire; perquisite, gratuity, fee, tip.

3. Retribution, punishment.

Rhapsodical, *a.* Unconnected, broken, confused, ecstatic, rambling, like a rhapsody.

Rhapsody, *n.* Rambling composition, medley of thoughts, sentences, *or* passages; effusion, rapture.

Rhetoric, *n.* 1. Art of composition, art of discourse.

2. Oratory, elocution, eloquence, diction, science of oratory.

3. Declamation, artificial eloquence, grandiloquence.

Rhetorical, *a.* 1. Oratorical.

2. Declamatory, highly wrought.

Rhetorician, *n.* 1. Adept in rhetoric, proficient in rhetoric.

2. Public speaker, declaimer.

Rhomb, *n.* Rhombus, lozenge, oblique-angled parallelogram (*with equal sides*).

Rhymester, *n.* Versifier, poetaster, rhymer, poor poet, rhymist.

RHYTHM, *n.* 1. Periodical emphasis, regular *or* melodious movement, harmonious flow, cadence, pulsation, lilt, swing.

2. Rhyme, metre, verse, number, measure.

Rhythmical, *a.* Measured, regular, *or* melodious in movement.

Ribald, *a.* Base, low, mean, obscene, vile, filthy, lewd, gross, coarse, loose, indecent.

Ribaldry, *n.* Obscenity, indecency; low, vile, *or* vulgar language.

RICE, *n.* (*Basic Eng.*) Staple grain-food.

Rich, *a.* 1. Wealthy, opulent, affluent, moneyed, prosperous, well-to-do, flush.

2. Splendid, precious, costly, sumptuous, luxurious, valuable, estimable, highly valued.

3. Savory, delicious, luscious.

4. Plentiful, plenteous, abundant, copious, abounding, ample, full, well-supplied; enough, sufficient.

5. Fruitful, fertile, luxuriant, productive, prolific.

6. Vivid, bright, gay; dark, deep.

7. Sweet, mellow, soft, harmonious, melodious.

8. Funny, laughable, humorous, comical.

Riches, *n. pl.* Wealth, opulence, affluence, fortune, plenty, abundance, richness, wealthiness, money, fortune, ample means, ample store.

Richly, *adv.* 1. Gayly, splendidly, magnificently.

2. Plenteously, abundantly, amply, fully.

3. Truly, really, abundantly, fully, highly, strongly.

Richness, *n.* 1. Abundance, plenty, fulness, copiousness, luxuriance, exuberance, profusion.

2. Fertility, fruitfulness, productiveness.

3. Excellence, value, costliness.

4. Brightness, vividness, brilliancy.

5. Sweetness, melodiousness, harmoniousness.

Rick, *n.* Stack, pile, heap (*of corn* or *hay*).

Rickets, *n. pl.* (*Med.*) Rachitis, inflammation of the spine.

Rickety, *a.* 1. Affected with the rickets.

2. Shattered, broken, weak, imperfect, frail, tumbledown, shaky, tottering, approaching ruin.

Rid, *v. t.* 1. Free, deliver, set free, release.

2. Free, clear, disencumber, disburden, scour, sweep.

3. Finish, despatch, dispose of; divorce, sever, cut off, disinherit, dissolve.

4. Destroy, make away with, remove by violence.

Riddance, *n.* Freedom, escape, relief, disencumberment, extrication, release, deliverance.

Riddle, *v. t.* Solve, explain, unriddle; sift, perforate.

——, *n.* Enigma, puzzle, dark problem, puzzling question, mystery.

Rider, *n.* 1. Equestrian, horseman.

2. Jockey, postilion, courier.

3. Additional clause (*to a legislative act*), corollary, codicil.

Ridge, *n.* Extended elevation, long crest *or* summit, spine, rib, wrinkle, weal, chine, hogback, ledge, saddle, watershed.

Ridged, *a.* Porcate, furrowed, crested.

Ridicule, *n.* Derision, mockery, game, "roasting," squib, persiflage, quip, chaff, *badinage*, raillery, satire, sarcasm, gibe, jeer, sneer, banter, wit, burlesque, irony.

——, *v. t.* Deride, mock, scout, satirize, lampoon, jeer, taunt, rally, banter, burlesque, laugh at, scoff at, make game of, make fun of, "guy," sneer at, disparage, chaff, "josh," "roast," "rag," make a butt of.

Ridiculous, *a.* Ludicrous, laughable, droll, funny, preposterous, farcical, comical, absurd, risible; waggish, amusing; odd, fantastic, queer, outlandish, eccentric; nonsensical.

Rife, *a.* Prevailing, prevalent, current, general, abundant, common; replete, abounding in, well supplied, plentiful, numerous.

Riff-raff, *n.* 1. Refuse, sweepings.

2. Rabble, populace, the masses, dregs of the people, swinish multitude, scum of society, ignoble vulgar, lower classes, rough-scuff, *canaille*.

Rifle, *v. t.* 1. Seize, snatch away, carry off.

2. Rob, pillage, plunder, strip, despoil, fleece.

Rift, *n.* Cleft, fissure, crack, rent, breach, fracture, break, gap, opening, chink, crevice, cranny, reft.

——, *v. t.* Burst open, cleave, rive, split.

——, *v. i.* Split, burst open.

Rig, *v. t.* 1. Dress (*particularly in a fanciful manner*), clothe, accoutre, put on.

2. Furnish with gear, fit with tackling.

——, *n.* 1. Dress (*odd* or *fanciful*), costume, garb.

2. Sportive trick, frolic.

3. Team, equipment.

Rigging, *n.* Tackle, gear, ropes of a ship.

RIGHT, *a.* 1. Straight, direct, rectilinear, not crooked.

2. Upright, erect, not oblique, perpendicular, plumb.

3. Just, lawful, legitimate, legal, equitable, fair, rightful, honest, square, even-handed; justifiable, in accordance with duty, unswerving, upright.

4. Fit, suitable, seemly, proper, becoming, appropriate, as it should be, *comme il faut*, conventional, reasonable, meet, fitting, orderly, well-regulated, well-performed, well-done, correct.

5. Real, true, actual, unquestionable, genuine.

6. Correct, true, not erroneous, not mistaken, accurate.

7. Right-hand, dextral, dexter.

——, *adv.* 1. Directly, in a direct line.

2. Uprightly, equitably, fairly, lawfully, rightfully, rightly, justly.

3. Fitly, suitably, properly, correctly, truly.

4. Very, extremely, in a great degree.

5. Actually, truly, really, exactly, just.

——, *n.* 1. Rectitude, uprightness, integrity, probity, honor, virtue, justice, equity, fairness, goodness, lawfulness, legality, "square deal," fitness, propriety, what ought to be, what should be.

2. Truth, correctness.

3. Prerogative, privilege, grant, legal power, license, authority, exemption, immunity, due, just claim, legal title, ownership.

——, *v. t.* 1. Set upright, make straight, regulate, correct, adjust.

2. Do justice to, relieve from wrong, see one righted, see justice done to one, vindicate.

Righteous, *a.* 1. Pious, holy, virtuous, godly, God-fearing, saintly, religious, honest, good, incorrupt, upright, just, devout.

2. Equitable, fair, right, rightful.

Righteousness, *n.* 1. Piety, godliness, holiness, sanctity, purity, virtue, goodness, integrity, honesty, justice, uprightness, equity, rightfulness, faithfulness.

2. Rectitude of conduct, practice of right, doing right, acting from principle, uprightness, equity, rightfulness, faithfulness.

Rightful, *a.* 1. Legitimate, true, lawful.

2. Just, equitable, fair, lawful, legitimate, legal, licit, suitable, proper, deserved, merited, due, fitting, correct, meet, appropriate, right, reasonable, true, honest.

Rightly, *adv.* 1. Uprightly, equitably, fairly, lawfully, rightfully, honestly.

2. Fitly, suitably, properly, appropriately.

3. Correctly, truly, exactly.

Rigid, *a.* 1. Stiff, stiffened, inflexible, unpliant, firm, hard, unbending, unyielding.

2. Stiff, bristling, erect, precipitous, steep.

3. Sharp, severe, strict, stern, rigorous, harsh, formal, conventional, correct, precise, austere, inflexible, exact, unmitigated.

4. Sharp, cruel.

Rigidity, *n.* 1. Stiffness, inflexibility, rigidness, firmness, want of pliability.

2. Severity, rigor, harshness, strictness, formality, austerity, rigidness.

3. Ungracefulness, want of ease, stiffness.

Rigmarole, *n.* Nonsense, jargon, gibberish, verbiage, trash, balderdash, twaddle, palaver, flummery, foolish talk.

Rigor, *n.* 1. Stiffness, rigidity, rigidness, inflexibility, hardness.

2. Severity, austerity, harshness, sternness, asperity.

3. Strictness, exactness.

4. Inclemency, severity.

Rigorous, *a.* 1. Severe, austere, harsh, stern, rigid, hard, strict, stringent, inflexible, unyielding, stiff.

2. Exact, accurate, precise, scrupulously nice, strict.

3. Inclement, severe.

Rile, *v. t.* 1. Stir up, roil, render turbid.

2. (*Colloq.*) Vex, anger, irritate.

Rilievo, *n.* Projection, prominence, relief.

Rill, *n.* Streamlet, rivulet, runnel, small brook.

Rim, *n.* Border, edge, margin, brim, brink, verge, ring, flange, girdle, curb, border, skirt, confine.

Rime, *n.* 1. Hoar-frost, congealed dew.

2. Rhyme.

Rimple, *n.* 1. Wrinkle, fold, rumple, crease, gather, corrugation, pucker, plait.

2. Ripple, undulation, little wave.

Rind, *n.* Skin, peel, bark, husk, hull, shell, integument, crust, coating, glume, outer covering.

RING, *n.* 1. Circle, hoop, round, circlet, whorl, girdle; finger ring.

2. Race-course, racing-ground, arena, lists, prize-ring.

3. Circular group of persons.

4. Resonance, reverberation.

5. Clique, junto, cabal, coterie, set, combination, league, confederacy, gang, machine.

——, *v. i.* Sound, resound, tingle, keep sounding, jingle, peal, clang, tintinnabulate, toll, knell, chime.

——, *v. t.* Encircle, enclose, circle, girdle.

Ringlet, *n.* 1. Small ring.

2. Curl, tress, lock.

3. Circle, fairy ring.

Rinse, *v. t.* Wash (*lightly*), lave.

Riot, *n.* 1. Tumult, uproar, disturbance, row, commotion, broil, brawl, outbreak, fray, affray, altercation, squabble, quarrel, strife, *mêlée*, pandemonium.

2. Luxury, excess, revelry, wild festivity, excessive feasting, merry-making, dissipation.

——, *v. i.* 1. Revel, carouse, luxuriate.

2. Be excited, be tumultuous.

3. Raise an uproar, riot, *or* sedition.

Riotous, *a.* 1. Revelling, luxurious, wanton, merry, boisterous, unrestrained.

2. Tumultuous, seditious, turbulent, insubordinate, mutinous, rebellious, disorderly, lawless, violent, ungovernable, unruly, refractory.

Rip, *v. t.* 1. Tear open, tear apart, split.

2. Tear out, discover, disclose.

——, *n.* 1. Tear, rent, laceration.

2. Scamp, cheat, libertine, debauchee, worthless person.

Ripe, *a.* 1. Mature, mellow, soft, grown, advanced, seasoned, perfected by growth.

2. Fit, prepared, ready, in readiness.

3. Consummate, finished, perfect, perfected, complete, accomplished.

Ripen, *v. i.* 1. Grow ripe, be matured; gather, head.

2. Be fitted, be prepared.

——, *v. t.* 1. Mature, bring to maturity, make ripe, bring to perfection.

2. Mature, fit, prepare.

Ripeness, *n.* 1. Maturity, matureness, full growth, completeness, perfection.

2. Fitness, preparation, readiness, qualification.

Ripple, *v. i.* Purl, play, lap, ruffle, babble, gurgle.

——, *v. t.* Fret, dimple, curl.

——, *n.* Rimple, undulation, little wave, fretting, ruffling (*of water*).

Rise, *v. i.* 1. Ascend, mount, arise, levitate, clamber, climb, go *or* move upward.

2. Appear, come forth, come into view.

3. Get up, arise.

4. Revive, come to life, be raised from death.

5. Grow, spring up, kindle, wax.

6. Tower up, be heaved up, spring up.

7. Be advanced, be promoted, gain a position, succeed, excel.

8. Increase, swell, enlarge, become greater, heighten, thrive, prosper.

9. Spring, take rise, have source *or* origin, proceed, originate, be produced, head, flow from, start, begin.

10. Become hostile, take up arms, go to war, mutiny, rebel, revolt.

11. Happen, occur, come by chance.

——, *n.* 1. Ascent, rising, ascension.

2. Elevation, elevated place, rising ground, hill, grade, slope.

3. Source, origin, spring, beginning, flow, emergence.

4. Increase, advance, augmentation, expansion.

Risible, *a.* 1. Laughable, ridiculous, droll, ludicrous, comical, funny, farcical, amusing.

2. Producing laughter (*as certain muscles*).

Rising, *a.* Eastern, ortive, ascendant.

Rising, *n.* 1. Ascent, rise.

2. Reviving, resurrection.

3. Insurrection, rebellion, sedition.

4. Swelling, tumor, boil.

Risk, *n.* Danger, hazard, chance, venture, jeopardy, peril, exposure to harm.

——, *v. t.* 1. Hazard, peril, endanger, jeopard, jeopardize, put in peril, put to hazard, wager, stake, bet, expose to danger.

2. Venture, dare to undertake, speculate in.

Rite, *n.* Ceremony, form, observance, ritual, ministration, rubric, usage, ordinance, solemnity, ceremonial formulary, sacrament.

Ritual, *a.* Ceremonial, formal.

——, *n.* Liturgy, formulary of worship.

Rival, *n.* Competitor, antagonist, opponent, emulator.

——, *a.* Competing, contending, emulating, emulous, opposing.

——, *v. t.* 1. Oppose, compete with, contend with, vie with.

2. Emulate, try to equal *or* excel.

3. Match, equal, be equal to.

Rivalry, *n.* Competition, emulation, rivalship, strife, contention, race, contest.

Rive, *v. t.* Rend, split, cleave, tear *or* rend asunder.

RIVER, *n.* 1. Stream, reach, affluent, tributary, current.

2. Large stream, copious flow, abundance.

Rivet, *v. t.* Fasten, fix, make firm.

Rivulet, *n.* Brook, streamlet, runnel, rill, runlet, creek, riverlet, small stream, burn.

ROAD, *n.* 1. Path, way, lane, street, route, course, roadway, avenue, pathway, track, passage, highway, thoroughfare, highroad, turnpike.

2. Roadstead, anchorage.

Roadstead, *n.* Anchorage, road.

Roadster, *n.* Horse (*fitted for the road*), pad.

Roam, *v. i.* Ramble, stroll, wander, range, rove, prowl, jaunt, stray, straggle.

——, *v. t.* Wander *or* range over, stray about.

Roamer, *n.* Wanderer, rover, stroller, vagrant.

Roar, *v. i.* 1. Bellow (*as a beast*).

2. Bawl, shout, vociferate, yell, howl, cry, cry aloud, laugh loudly.

3. Boom, resound, thunder, rattle, peal.

——, *n.* 1. Bellow, bellowing, roaring.

2. Loud noise (*as of the wind* or *the sea*), resonance, thunder; storm, rage.

3. Shout, cry, outcry.

4. Laugh (*loud and long*), laughter, shout.

Rob, *v. t.* 1. Plunder, strip, despoil, fleece, pilfer, pillage, rook.

2. Take from, deprive, appropriate, embezzle, plagiarize.

Robber, *n.* Plunderer, pillager, thief, despoiler, desperado, depredator, highwayman, footpad, brigand, bandit, marauder, freebooter, rifler, pirate.

Robbery, *n.* Depredation, peculation, theft, larceny, spoliation, despoliation, despoilment, plundering, pillage, freebooting, piracy, embezzlement, plagiarism.

Robe, *n.* Gown, dress, garment, habit, attire, costume.

——, *v. t.* Dress, clothe, invest, array.

Robust, *a.* Strong, athletic, brawny, stout, seasoned, sinewy, muscular, stalwart, hale, hearty, hardy, lusty, sturdy, firm, sound, vigorous, energetic, self-assertive, powerful, forceful, able-bodied, iron.

Rock, *n.* 1. Stone, crag, cliff, boulder, reef.

2. Defence, support, refuge, protection, strength, asylum.

3. Distaff.

——, *v. t.* 1. Move backward and forward (*as something that rests on a support*), sway.

2. Lull, quiet, calm, tranquillize, soothe, still, cradle, put to sleep.

——, *v. i.* Reel, totter, teeter, wabble, move backward and forward.

Rocky, *a.* 1. Hard, stony, flinty, craggy, rugged, rough.

2. Obdurate, stubborn, hard.

ROD, *n.* 1. Twig, shoot, slender stem.

2. Wand, slender stick, cane, shaft, ferule, sceptre, staff.

3. Switch, scourge, birch, cudgel.

4. Pole, perch.

5. Shoot, branch (*of a family*), tribe, race.

Rodent, *a.* Gnawing.

Rodomontade, *n.* Blustering, bluster, boasting, bragging, rant, vain-glory, gasconade.

——, *v. i.* Boast, brag, bluster, rant, swagger, gasconade.

Rogation, *n.* Litany, supplication.

Rogue, *n.* 1. Vagrant, sturdy beggar, vagabond.

2. Knave, villain, swindler, sharper, cheat, mischief maker, trickster, rascal, scamp, scoundrel, scapegrace, caitiff, picaroon.

3. Mischievous fellow, wag, sly fellow, playful knave.

Roguery, *n.* 1. Knavery, rascality, villainy, fraud, cheating, dishonest practices, knavish tricks, trickery, swindling.

2. Waggery, mischief, arch tricks.

Roguish, *a.* 1. Knavish, dishonest, fraudulent, rascally, scoundrelly, trickish, tricky.

  2. Sportive, arch, mischievous, puckish, waggish, wanton.

Roil, *v. t.* 1. Make turbid, rile, muddy.

  2. Vex, disturb, plague, anger, rile, irritate, worry, annoy, bother; perplex.

Roily, *a.* Turbid, rily, disturbed, muddy.

Roisterer, *n.* Swaggerer, bully, rioter, blustering fellow, reveler.

Rôle, *n.* [Fr.] Part, character (*in a play*), impersonation; function, task.

Roll, *v. t.* 1. Turn, make revolve.

  2. Whirl, wheel, revolve.

  3. Revolve, turn about (*in one's mind*).

  4. Wrap round (*one part on another*), curl, wind, muffle, swathe.

  5. Bind, involve, inwrap, infold, enroll, envelop.

  6. Press, level, smooth, flatten, spread.

  7. Drive, impel forward, bowl.

  8. Emit, give expression to.

  9. Wheel, trundle.

——, *v. i.* 1. Revolve, rotate, turn, wheel, whirl, gyrate, whirl round, go round, turn round.

  2. Run on wheels.

  3. Revolve, perform a revolution, gyrate.

  4. Turn, move circularly.

  5. Rock from side to side, sway, stagger, lean, reel, lurch, yaw, gybe, be tossed about.

  6. Undulate, swell, billow.

  7. Fluctuate, move tumultuously.

  8. Fall over and over, tumble.

  9. Wallow, welter, tumble about.

  10. Run, flow, glide.

ROLL, *n.* 1. Volume, scroll, document.

  2. Chronicle, record, history, annals, rota.

  3. List, register, catalogue, inventory, schedule, official document.

  4. Loaf of bread (*small, and rolled up while in the dough*), biscuit, twist.

  5. Rocking (*as of a vessel in a heavy sea*).

  6. Reverberation, booming, resonance, thunder.

  7. Cylinder, roller.

Rollicking, *a.* Frolicsome, jolly, frolicking, playful, sportive, lively, frisky, full of frolic, swaggering, jovial.

Roman, *a.* 1. Of Rome, of the Romans.

  2. Of the Latins, of ancient Rome.

  3. Noble, distinguished, brave, hardy, patriotic.

  4. Roman Catholic, of the Roman Catholic religion.

Romance, *n.* 1. Novel, tale, story, work of fiction; fanciful exaggeration.

  2. Falsehood, lie, fiction, fable.

  3. Romanza, ballad, song.

Romanism, *n.* Roman Catholic religion, "popery," Catholicism.

Romanist, *n.* Roman Catholic, Romist.

Romanize, *v. t.* 1. Latinize.

  2. Convert to Romanism.

Romantic, *a.* 1. Fanciful, imaginative, ideal, sentimental, extravagant, fantastic, wild.

  2. Fictitious, improbable, chimerical, imaginary, fantastic, wildly picturesque.

Romany, *n.* Gypsy.

Romp, *n.* 1. Rude girl.

  2. Rude play, rude frolic.

——, *v. i.* Frisk, sport, caper, gambol, frolic (*rudely*), play boisterously.

Rood, *n.* 1. Forty square rods, fourth part of an acre.

  2. Rod, pole, perch.

  3. Cross, crucifix.

ROOF, *n.* 1. Cover (*of a house* or *of a building*), thatch, slate, shingles, roofing.

  2. Cover, canopy, arch, vault, ceiling.

  3. House, dwelling, home, shelter.

——, *v. t.* 1. Cover (*with a roof*).

  2. Shelter, enclose in a house.

Rook, *n.* 1. Castle (*in chess*).

  2. Cheat, trickish fellow, sharper.

——, *v. i.* 1. Cheat, defraud, rob, ruck, cower.

  2. Squat, sit close.

ROOM, *n.* 1. Space, extent, expanse, scope, capacity, accommodation, compass, field, range, sweep, swing, play, leeway, elbowroom, latitude.

  2. Place, stead.

  3. Apartment, chamber, lodging.

  4. Chance, opportunity, occasion.

  5. Unoccupied space, unoccupied place.

Roomy, *a.* Spacious, capacious, large, wide, extensive, ample, broad, commodious, comfortable; expansive, extensive.

Roost, *n.* Perch.

——, *v. i.* 1. Perch.

  2. Lodge, settle.

ROOT, *n.* 1. Bottom, base, foundation, lower part.

  2. Cause, origin, source, occasion, reason, motive.

  3. Radical, radix, etymon, primitive word, stem.

——, *v. i.* Take root, strike.

——, *v. t.* 1. Implant, embed, place, settle, set, fix, fasten.

  2. Establish, confirm, sink deep, plant deeply.

  3. Eradicate, tear out, exterminate, extirpate, uproot, unearth, destroy utterly, remove utterly.

4. Dig, burrow with the snout, grub.

5. (*Colloq.*) Applaud, encourage, cheer.

Rooted, *a.* Fixed, deep, radical, confirmed, established, chronic.

Rootlet, *n.* Radicle, small root.

Rope, *v. t.* 1. Draw as by a rope, fasten, tie, bind.

2. Pull, curb in, restrain.

——, *v. i.* Be ropy *or* viscous.

——, *n.* Line, stay, cable, cord.

Rope-dancer, *n.* Acrobat, funambulist, rope-walker.

Ropy, *a.* Viscous, viscid, glutinous, tenacious, stringy, adhesive.

Rosary, *n.* 1. Chaplet, garland.

2. Rose-garden, rosery.

3. String of beads for counting prayers.

Roseate, *a.* 1. Rosy, blushing, blooming, rose-colored; hopeful.

2. Full of roses.

Rostrum, *n.* Platform, stage, tribune, stand.

Rosy, *a.* Blooming, ruddy, blushing, roseate, rose-colored, red, flushed; hopeful, auspicious, sanguine, favorable.

Rot, *n.* Putrefaction, corruption, decomposition, decay.

——, *v. i.* 1. Putrefy, corrupt, decompose, decay, spoil, taint, degenerate.

2. Moulder, rust.

Rotary, *a.* Whirling, rotating, rotatory, turning, circular, revolving.

Rotate, *v. i.* Revolve, wheel, whirl, spin, twirl, turn, go round, turn round; alternate.

Rotation, *n.* 1. Revolution, turn, round, roll, whirling, spinning, gyration.

2. Succession, alternation, sequence, round, order, series.

Rote, *n.* 1. Repetition.

2. Rut (*of the sea*).

Rotten, *a.* 1. Putrid, corrupt, carious, decomposed, putrefied, decaying, decayed, fetid, putrescent, foul; ill-smelling, rank.

2. Unsound, defective.

3. Treacherous, deceitful, untrustworthy, immoral, corrupt, unsound.

Rotund, *a.* 1. Round, spherical, globular; plump, full, chubby, obese, stout, buxom.

2. Grandiloquent, mouth-filling, fluent.

Rotundity, *n.* Roundness, sphericity, rotundness, globosity.

Roué, *n.* [Fr.] Rake, debauchee, profligate, libertine, dissolute man.

ROUGH, *a.* 1. Uneven, irregular, bumpy, rugged, craggy, cragged, jagged, scraggy, scabrous, stubby, scratchy.

2. Unhewn, unwrought, unfashioned, formless, shapeless; vague, crude, incomplete, sketchy, approximate; unpolished, cross-grained, knotty, roughhewn, uncut, unfinished.

3. Shaggy, hairy, coarse, hirsute, bristly, bushy, unkempt, ragged, disordered.

4. Coarse, indelicate, rude, uncivil, impolite, surly, brusque, ungracious, bearish, churlish, gruff; rugged, harsh, austere, uncourteous, unpolished, blunt, bluff, unrefined, burly.

5. Harsh, sharp, severe, violent.

6. Tart, sour, crabbed, hard, astringent.

7. Inharmonious, discordant, jarring, raucous, unmusical, scabrous, grating.

8. Tempestuous, boisterous, stormy, inclement, foul, severe, violent, turbulent, tumultuous.

9. Wild, boisterous, untamed.

10. Severe, uncivil, unfeeling, hard, acrimonious, ungentle, brutal; riotous, disorderly, rowdy, cruel.

——, *n.* Rowdy, ruffian, bully, coarse fellow, "roughneck."

Rough draught. Sketch, outline, rude sketch.

Roughness, *n.* 1. Unevenness, ruggedness.

2. Harshness, rudeness, coarseness, incivility, gruffness, bluntness, impoliteness.

3. Acerbity, unsavoriness, astringency, harshness.

4. Storminess, boisterousness, tempestuousness, inclemency, violence.

5. Violence, severity.

6. Inelegance, coarseness.

ROUND, *a.* 1. Circular; spherical, globular, orbicular, rotund, orbed, bulbous; cylindrical.

2. Full, complete, entire, unbroken, whole; large, great, considerable.

3. Plump, chubby, corpulent, stout, full, swelling.

4. Smooth, continuous, flowing, full, harmonious.

5. Quick, brisk, full.

6. Plain, fair, candid, open, upright, honest, blunt, frank.

——, *n.* 1. Cycle, revolution, rotation, succession; turn, bout, game, lap.

2. Circular dance; catch, canon.

3. Circle, sphere, cylinder, globe, ball; circumference.

4. Circuit, compass, perambulation, tour, routine, watch.

5. Rung (*of a ladder*).

——, *adv.* 1. Around, on all sides.

2. Circularly, in a circle, in a circuit.

3. Not directly, circuitously.

4. In circumference.

5. From first to last.

Round, *prep.* 1. Around, circularly, about.

2. All over, in all parts of.

——, *v. t.* 1. Make circular, make spherical, make cylindrical, curve.

2. Surround, encircle, encompass, circuit.

3. Make full, finish off, make complete, smooth.

4. Move about, go round, traverse.

Roundabout, *a.* 1. Indirect, tortuous, circuitous, circumlocutory.

2. Ample, extensive, broad.

3. Encompassing, encircling.

Roundly, *adv.* 1. Openly, plainly, boldly, without reserve, peremptorily.

2. Briskly, swiftly, speedily.

3. Completely, vigorously, in earnest, to the purpose.

Roundness, *n.* 1. Sphericity, circularity, rotundness, rotundity, globosity, globularity, globularness, orbicularness, cylindricity, fulness, plumpness.

2. Fulness, smoothness of flow.

3. Openness, plainness, boldness, positiveness.

Rouse, *v. t.* 1. Awaken, wake, waken, arouse, raise, shake.

2. Animate, kindle, enkindle, stimulate, excite, provoke, stir up, stir, bestir, inspire, rally, brace, whet.

3. Put in commotion, agitate.

4. Startle, surprise, drive from cover.

——, *v. i.* 1. Rise, stand up, stand erect.

2. Awake, wake, get up, start up, move, stir.

Rout, *n.* 1. Defeat, discomfiture, ruin, flight, complete overthrow.

2. Concourse, rabble, multitude, tumultuous crowd, clamorous multitude.

3. Fashionable assembly, evening party.

4. Uproar, brawl, disturbance, noise, roar.

——, *v. t.* 1. Defeat, discomfit, overthrow, overcome, vanquish, overpower, beat, conquer.

2. Dispel, chase away, drive away, chase, scatter, disperse, rout out, turn out, search thoroughly.

Route, *n.* Way, path, passage, course, road, itinerary, circuit.

Routine, *n.* Practice, custom, round, path, rut, groove, beat, ordinary way, wont, course, method, procedure; order.

Rove, *v. i.* Roam, ramble, stroll, range, prowl, wander, stray, straggle.

Rover, *n.* 1. Rambler, wanderer, straggler, bird of passage.

2. Robber, pirate, freebooter.

3. Fickle person, inconstant person.

Row, *n.* Rank, line, file, series, string, queue, tier, range; street, alley.

——, *n.* (*Pron.* rou. *Colloq.*) Broil. tumult, uproar, riot, commotion, squabble, outbreak, quarrel, affray, disturbance, altercation, brawl.

Rowdy, *n.* (*Colloq.*) Rough, bully, ruffian, desperado, "tough," "hoodlum," roisterer, brawler, coarse fellow.

——, *a.* (*Colloq.*) 1. Disreputable, blackguard, rough.

2. Flashy, coarsely showy.

Rowel, *n.* Goad, spur.

Rowen, *n.* Aftermath, eddish, lattermath, rowett.

Royal, *a.* Kingly, regal, imperial, sovereign, monarchical; magnificent, princely, august, courtly, majestic, kinglike, grand, splendid, superb; noble, generous, dignified, magnanimous.

Royalty, *n.* 1. Kingship, sovereignty, monarchy.

2. Kingliness; majesty.

3. Percentage (*as on copyright*), share.

4. Kingdom, domain, sphere, province.

Rub, *v. t.* 1. Abrade, scrape, chafe, grate, graze.

2. Wipe, clean, scour, polish, burnish; massage.

3. Chafe, fret, gall, touch hard.

4. Spread, put, apply, smear.

——, *v. i.* Grate, chafe, fret, make friction.

RUB, *n.* 1. Rubbing, friction.

2. Collision, obstruction, hindrance.

3. Obstacle, difficulty, embarrassment, perplexity, dilemma, pinch, hardship.

4. Taunt, gibe, sarcasm, jeer, severe rebuke.

Rubber, *n.* 1. Caoutchouc, india-rubber, gum-elastic.

2. Masseur.

Rubbing, *n.* Attrition, abrasion, friction.

Rubbish, *n.* 1. Ruins, fragments, refuse, *débris*, detritus, waste.

2. Litter, lumber, trash, orts, dross, dregs, scum, scoria, sweepings, refuse; trumpery.

3. Confusion, mingled mass.

Rubicund, *a.* Ruddy, reddish, red, florid, erubescent.

Rub off. Abrade, wear away.

Rub out. Efface, erase, obliterate, expunge, cancel, wipe out.

Ruck, *v. i.* Squat, cower, crouch, lie close, take shelter, rook.

——, *v. t.* Wrinkle, crease.

——, *n.* Mob, heap, crowd.

Ruddy, *a.* Reddish, florid, of a red color.

Rude, *a.* 1. Rough, rugged, coarse, uneven, shapeless, unfashioned, unformed, unwrought, crude, ill-formed.

2. Artless, unpolished, raw, inelegant, crude, rustic.

3. Coarse, uncouth, vulgar, clownish, loutish, boorish, ungraceful, uncivilized, untrained, unskilful, unskilled, untutored, untaught, undisciplined, ignorant, barbarous, illiterate, savage.

4. Uncivil, uncourteous, brusk, rough, coarse, blunt, bluff, impolite, impudent, impertinent, saucy, insolent, insulting, ill-bred, surly, currish, gruff, churlish, brutal, uncivilized, unrefined, barbarous, savage.

5. Violent, fierce, impetuous, inclement, boisterous, tumultuous, harsh, severe, discordant, turbulent.

Rudeness, *n.* 1. Roughness, ruggedness, unevenness.

2. Artlessness, inelegance.

3. Ignorance, uncouthness, barbarousness, clownishness.

4. Coarseness, incivility, impoliteness, insolence, impertinence, pertness, sauciness, surliness, gruffness, churlishness, currishness, presumption, effrontery, face, assurance, brass, ill-breeding.

5. Violence, boisterousness, severity, inclemency, tempestuousness, storminess.

6. Violence, impetuosity, fierceness.

Rudiment, *n.* 1. Embryo, rude state, beginning, germ, root, seed, starting point.

2. Element, first principle, essential point.

Rudimental, *a.* 1. Embryonic, rudimentary.

2. Elementary, primary, initial.

Rue, *v. t.* Regret, deplore, lament, repent of, be sorry for, grieve for.

Rueful, *a.* 1. Doleful, mournful, woful, sorrowful, lamentable, regretful, penitent.

2. Melancholy, sad, sorrowful, piteous, pitiful, grievous, lugubrious, dismal.

Ruff, *n.* Ruffle, collar.

Ruffian, *n.* Villain, miscreant, caitiff, rascal, scoundrel, wretch, monster, robber, cut-throat, murderer; rowdy, roisterer, bully, hoodlum.

——, *a.* Savage, brutal, savagely boisterous, tumultuous, raging, violent, ruffianly, scoundrelly, blackguardly.

Ruffle, *v. t.* 1. Disarrange, damage, disorder, ripple, roughen, dishevel, muss, rumple, derange.

2. Discompose, disquiet, trouble, vex, torment, molest, plague, worry, harass, disturb, agitate, perturb, irritate, confuse, excite.

3. Gather into folds, wrinkle, cockle, pucker, plait, flounce.

——, *v. i.* 1. Flutter, play loosely.

2. Swagger, put on airs.

——, *n.* 1. Ruff, frill, edging.

2. Bustle, disturbance, excitement, commotion, contention, fight, tumult, confusion, perturbation, flutter, flurry, agitation, fluster, hurry-skurry.

Rugged, *a.* 1. Rough, craggy, cragged, uneven, wrinkled, seamed, irregular, scraggy, ragged; bristly, unkempt, shaggy; crabbed, austere, hard, hardy, robust, robustious; coarse, rude, severe.

2. Tempestuous, turbulent, stormy, rude, violent, tumultuous, boisterous, inclement.

3. Harsh, inharmonious, grating, unmusical, scabrous.

Ruggedness, *n.* 1. Roughness, unevenness, asperity.

2. Harshness, severity, rigor, roughness, coarseness, rudeness, surliness.

3. Boisterousness, storminess, inclemency, turbulence, tempestuousness.

Rugose, *a.* Wrinkled, rugous.

Ruin, *n.* 1. Destruction, demolition, devastation, desolation, decay, discomfiture, overthrow, defeat, wreck, wrack, rack, loss, perdition, ruination, damnation, fall, downfall, prostration, subversion, undoing, shipwreck.

2. Bane, pest, mischief, destruction.

——, *v. t.* 1. Destroy, demolish, devastate, desolate, shatter, smash, crush, overthrow, subvert, overturn, overwhelm, defeat, ruinate, damn, wreck; violate, seduce.

2. Impoverish, bring to want, beggar, reduce to poverty.

Ruination, *n.* Demolition, destruction, subversion, overthrow, ruin.

Ruinous, *a.* 1. Decayed, dilapidated, demolished.

2. Destructive, disastrous, calamitous, pernicious, damnatory, baneful, noxious, noisome, calamitous, wasteful, mischievous, subversive.

Ruins, *n. pl.* Remains, débris.

RULE, *n.* 1. Command, control, domination, dominion, lordship, mastership, mastery, regency, reign, regnancy, governance, government, empire, sway, direction, authority, jurisdiction.

2. Behavior, conduct.

3. Method, regularity, order, habit, system, custom, routine.

4. Precept, law, canon, maxim, aphorism, axiom, guide, formula, test, criterion, standard, touchstone, convention, precedent, model.

5. Order, ruling, prescription, regulation, decision.

Rule, *v. t.* 1. Govern, command, control, judge, conduct, manage, bridle, restrain, direct, lead.

2. Guide, advise, persuade, prevail on.

3. Settle, establish, pass upon, determine, decide.

——, *v. i.* 1. Command, govern, have command, domineer, reign, have control, exercise supreme authority.

2. Prevail, obtain, predominate.

3. Settle, decide, establish, decree, adjudicate.

Ruler, *n.* 1. Governor, sovereign, monarch, king, potentate, regent, chief, lord, master.

2. Director, manager, head, president.

3. Rule, controller, guide, straight-edge.

Ruling, *a.* 1. Governing, controlling, reigning, regnant, regent, chief.

2. Predominant, prevailing, prevalent; natural, habitual.

Ruminate, *v. i.* 1. Chew the cud.

2. Muse, meditate, ponder, cogitate, think, reflect, "thinksay."

——, *v. t.* Meditate, chew, muse on, reflect upon, ponder upon, think about, brood over, chew the cud upon.

Rumination, *n.* Musing, meditation, reflection, cogitation, pondering.

Rummage, *v. t.* Search, examine, explore, ransack.

——, *v. i.* Make a search.

——, *n.* Search, examination, exploration.

Rumor, *n.* 1. Report, talk, bruit, gossip, hearsay.

2. Flying report, common voice, town talk, scandal.

3. Report, story, news, tidings, bruit.

4. Fame, reputation, celebrity, repute.

——, *v. t.* Report, tell, bruit, circulate, spread abroad, noise abroad.

Rump, *n.* Buttocks, croup; remnant.

Rumple, *v. t.* Wrinkle, crumple, disarrange, dishevel, muss, ruffle, crease, crush, pucker, corrugate.

——, *n.* Wrinkle, crumple, pucker, rimple, crease, corrugation, fold.

Rumpus, *n.* (*Colloq.*) Riot, brawl, confusion, tumult, uproar, squabble, outbreak, quarrel, feud, affray, disturbance, altercation, row.

Run, *v. i.* 1. Race, step quickly, move swiftly; haste, hasten, hie, hurry, scud, scamper, sprint, scorch, scurry, scuttle, lope, bolt, course, career, gallop, scour, speed, post, trip.

2. Flow, glide, move, go, proceed, stream, roll on, move on.

3. Fuse, melt, become fluid, be fusible, liquefy.

4. Pass, proceed, advance, elapse, vanish.

5. Spread, extend; stretch, lie.

6. Continue, proceed, go, pass, press, circulate.

7. Tend, incline, make transition, average, trend.

8. Steal away, depart privately, flee.

——, *v. t.* 1. Pierce, stab.

2. Push, thrust, put with force; force, drive, propel, turn.

3. Fuse, melt.

4. Shape, form, mould, cast.

5. Incur, be liable to, fall into, be exposed to, encounter.

6. Pursue, follow, perform, take.

7. Pour forth, emit, let flow, discharge.

8. Cause to ply, maintain, manage, direct.

RUN, *n.* 1. Running; race.

2. Current, progress, course, flow, passage, wont, way, motion.

3. Continued course, continued success, continuance, currency, popularity.

4. Trip, excursion, journey; gallop, trot.

5. Pressure, demand, urgent application.

6. Generality, people *or* things as they are, people *or* things of average quality, average, trend, rule.

7. Brook, streamlet, runlet, runnel, rivulet, flow, rill, small stream, burn.

Run after. 1. Follow, pursue, chase, course.

2. Search for, try to find, hunt.

Run away. Flee, fly, escape, elope.

Runaway, *n.* Fugitive, deserter, eloper.

Run down. 1. Catch by chasing, chase to weariness.

2. Run against and sink.

3. Crush, overthrow, overbear, overwhelm.

4. Decry, disparage, depreciate, condemn, traduce, cry down.

Rung, *n.* Round (*of a ladder*), roundle.

Runlet, *n.* Brook, run, runnel, rivulet, small stream.

Runner, *n.* 1. Racer.

2. Messenger, courier.

Run out, *v. t.* 1. Extend, thrust out, push out.

2. Waste, exhaust, expend.

——, *v. i.* 1. Expire, be at end, be exhausted.

2. Spread, expatiate.

Run through. 1. Pierce, penetrate, stab.

2. Waste, expend, exhaust, dissipate.

Run together. Unite, mingle.

Rupture, *n.* 1. Breach, split, fracture, disruption, break, burst.

2. Quarrel, feud, faction, schism, contention, hostility.

——, *v. t.* Break, burst.

Rural, *a.* Rustic, pastoral, bucolic, country, agrarian.

Ruralize, *v. i.* Rusticate.

Ruse, *n.* Stratagem, trick, artifice, wile, hoax, manœuvre, fraud, deceit, deception, imposture, chouse, sham, fetch, crafty device.

Rush, *n.* Onrush, onset, dash, plunge, tear, precipitancy, stampede, rout.

——, *v. i.* Career, push on, press on, charge, sweep, dash, drive, hurtle, gush, surge, tear, precipitate.

Rush out. 1. Issue, flow, flow out.

2. Press out, hurry out, go out with a rush.

Russet, *a.* 1. Reddish-brown.

2. Coarse, rustic, homespun.

Rust, *n.* Mildew, blight, must, mustiness, mould.

——, *v. i.* 1. Gather rust, become rusty, be oxidized, corrode.

2. Decay, degenerate, grow dull, become sluggish.

Rustic, *a.* 1. Rural, country.

2. Countrified, unpolished, uncouth, clownish, loutish, rough, awkward, untaught, rude, outlandish, boorish, "clodhopping."

3. Simple, plain, coarse, unadorned, homely, countrified.

4. Simple, artless, honest, unsophisticated.

——, *n.* Swain, peasant, clown, boor, bumpkin, "hayseed," hind, countryman, yokel.

Rusticate, *v. i.* Dwell *or* reside in the country.

Rusticity, *n.* Rudeness, coarseness, artlessness, simplicity, boorishness, clownishness.

Rustle, *n.* Rustling, swish, susurrus.

Rustling, *a.* Whispering, susurrous.

Rusty, *a.* 1. Covered with rust, affected with rust, corroded.

2. Musty, fusty, mildewed, rubiginous.

3. Dull, sluggish, time-worn.

4. Rough, hoarse, grating, unmusical.

Rut, *n.* 1. Track of a wheel, furrow, channel, groove.

2. Rote (*of the sea*).

Ruth, *n.* Mercy, pity, compassion, tenderness.

Ruthful, *a.* Merciful, compassionate, pitiful, tender.

Ruthless, *a.* Merciless, pitiless, cruel, uncompassionate, unpitying, unmerciful, relentless, unrelenting, unsparing, inexorable, barbarous, fell, savage, ferocious, inhuman, hard-hearted, truculent.

S

Sabbath, *n.* 1. [With *The* prefixed.] Lord's day, Sunday, the day of rest.

2. Rest, repose, time of rest.

Sable, *a.* Dark, dusky, sombre, ebon, black.

Sabre, *n.* Cavalry sword, dragoon's sword, falchion.

Sabulous, *a.* Sandy, gritty.

Sac, *n.* Pocket, cyst, vesicle.

Saccharine, *a.* Sugary, sweet.

Sacerdotal, *a.* Priestly.

Sacerdotalism, *n.* Priest-craft, clericalism.

Sachem, *n.* American Indian chief, sagamore.

Sack, *n.* 1. Bag, pouch.

2. Spoliation, destruction, desolation, devastation, havoc, waste, ravage, sackage, despoilment.

3. Booty, spoil, plunder.

4. Sherry, sherry wine.

——, *v. t.* Ravage, despoil, devastate, spoil, plunder, pillage, take by storm.

Sacrament, *n.* 1. Rite, ceremony, solemnity.

2. [With *The* prefixed.] Eucharist, communion, Lord's Supper.

Sacred, *a.* 1. Hallowed, holy, consecrated, divine, dedicated, devoted.

2. Inviolable, inviolate.

3. Venerable, sainted.

Sacredly, *adv.* Inviolably, strictly, religiously.

Sacredness, *n.* 1. Holiness, sanctity.

2. Inviolableness, inviolability.

Sacrifice, *v. t.* 1. Immolate, offer up.

2. Surrender, give up, forego.

——, *n.* 1. Offering, oblation, immolation.

2. Surrender, destruction, loss, devotion with loss.

Sacrilege. *n.* Profanation, desecration, violation.

Sacrilegious, *a.* Irreverent, impious, profane, desecrating.

Sacristan, *n.* Sexton, sacrist, vestry-keeper.

Sacristy, *n.* Vestry, vestry-room.

SAD, *a.* 1. Serious, sedate, grave, staid, sober, pensive, sombre, saturnine.

2. Sorrowful, melancholy, mournful, downcast, afflicted, heavy, disconsolate, despondent, depressed, dejected, unhappy.

3. Gloomy, dismal, doleful, dreary, mirthless, cheerless, mournful, lugubrious, woe-begone, dull.

4. Grievous, afflictive, calamitous, disastrous, dire, deplorable.

5. Bad, naughty, vexatious, wicked, troublesome, mischievous.

6. Dark, sombre, dull (*as of colors*).

Sadden, *v. t.* Deject, depress, grieve.

Saddle, *v. t.* 1. Put a saddle on.

2. Load, burden, encumber, clog, charge.

Saddle-cloth, *n.* Housing.

Saddle-horse, *n.* Palfrey.

Sadly, *adv.* 1. Sorrowfully, mournfully, miserably, grievously.

2. Badly, afflictively, calamitously.

3. Darkly.

4. Seriously, soberly, gravely.

Sadness, *n.* 1. Sorrow, despondency, sorrowfulness, mournfulness, melancholy, depression, dejection.

2. Gloominess, mournfulness, heaviness, grief, sorrow, dolefulness.

3. Seriousness, sedateness, gravity.

SAFE, *a.* 1. Unharmed, undamaged, unscathed, unhurt.

2. Protected, guarded, secure, snug, unexposed, under lock and key.

3. Trusty, trustworthy, reliable, dependable, certain, sure.

4. Sound, whole, good.

——, *n.* 1. Place of safety, secure place.

2. Coffer, chest, strong box.

Safe-conduct, *n.* 1. Escort, convoy, safeguard, protection.

2. Pass, passport, warrant of security, safeguard.

Safeguard, *n.* 1. Defence, protection, security.

2. Convoy, escort, safe-conduct, guard.

3. Pass, passport, safe-conduct.

——, *v. t.* Guard, protect.

Safe-keeping, *n.* Preservation, guardianship, custody, charge, care, ward.

Safely, *adv.* 1. In safety.

2. Securely, carefully, in close custody.

Safety, *n.* 1. Security, safeness.

2. Preservation; close custody.

Saffron, *a.* Yellow.

——, *v. t.* Gild, make yellow.

Sag, *v. i.* Bend (*by force of gravity*), settle, swag, give way.

Saga, *n.* Scandinavian legend, tradition, tale, history, geste.

Sagacious, *a.* 1. Discerning, intelligent, rational, judicious, sage, shrewd, acute, apt, astute, keen, able, penetrating, perspicacious, wise, sharp-witted, keen-witted, keen-sighted, clear-sighted, long-headed.

2. Sage, wise, enlightened, gifted, sapient.

3. Intelligent (*said of animals*).

Sagacity, *n.* 1. Sagaciousness, quickness of scent.

2. Shrewdness, acuteness, sharpness, astuteness, penetration, ingenuity, discernment, perspicacity, sense, insight, mother-wit, quickness, readiness, wisdom.

Sage, *a.* 1. Wise, sagacious, sapient, discerning, shrewd, acute, intelligent, sensible, prudent.

2. Prudent, judicious, well-judged.

3. Serious, grave, solemn.

——, *n.* Philosopher, wise man, savant, pundit.

Said, *a.* 1. Declared, uttered, reported, related.

2. Aforesaid, before-mentioned.

SAIL, *v. i.* [*The noun is Basic Eng.*] 1. Make sail, put to sea, get under way, set sail, begin a voyage.

2. Pass by water, navigate.

3. Fly smoothly, scud.

4. Glide, float.

——, *v. t.* Navigate.

Sail-cloth, *n.* Duck, canvas.

Sailor, *n.* Seaman, mariner, seafarer, sea dog, seafaring man, old salt, "Jack Tar."

Sail round. Circumnavigate.

Saint, *n.* Holy person, devotee.

Sainted, *a.* 1. Consecrated, sacred, holy, hallowed.

2. Canonized.

3. Holy, pious, virtuous.

Saintly, *a.* Holy, devout, pious, religious, godly, heavenly-minded.

Saint Vitus's dance. Chorea.

Sake, *n.* 1. Reason, purpose, end, final cause.

2. Score, account, regard, respect, consideration, reason, cause, interest.

Salable, *a.* 1. Vendible, marketable, merchantable, fit for sale.

2. In demand, of ready sale, staple.

Salacious, a. Lewd, lustful, carnal, lecherous, lascivious, wanton, libidinous, lickerish, concupiscent, loose, prurient, unchaste, incontinent.

Salary, n. Stipend, pay, wages, hire, allowance.

Sale, n. 1. Demand, market, vent, vendition, opportunity to sell.

2. Auction.

Salient, a. 1. Leaping, bounding, jumping.

2. Springing, beating, throbbing, shooting up.

3. Projecting, jutting, prominent, standing out, in relief.

4. Striking, remarkable, conspicuous, prominent.

Saline, a. Briny, salt.

Saliva, n. Spittle, spit, drool, slobber.

Sallow, a. Yellow (as from illness), yellowish; muddy, of a pale, sickly color.

Sally, n. 1. Sortie.

2. Digression, excursion, trip, run.

3. Frolic, escapade, wild gayety.

4. Jest, joke, quip, quirk, crank, witticism, sprightly fancy, flash of wit, jeu d'esprit.

——, v. i. Rush out, issue suddenly.

Salmagundi, n. Medley, olio, miscellany, mixture, farrago, jumble, hodge-podge, hotch-potch, mish-mash, gallimaufry, pot-pourri, mélange.

Saloon, n. 1. Spacious room, reception room.

2. Bar room, bar, dramshop, "grog-shop," sample room.

SALT, n. 1. Chloride of sodium, muriate of soda, common salt.

2. Taste, smack, savor, flavor, seasoning, relish.

3. Wit, piquancy, pungency, sarcasm, humor, smartness, poignancy.

4. See SAILOR.

Salt, a. 1. Saline, salty, brackish.

2. Sharp, bitter, pungent.

Saltation, n. 1. Leaping, jumping, hopping, springing, bounding, vaulting.

2. Palpitation.

Saltatory, a. Leaping, jumping, skipping, hopping, dancing.

Saltish, a. Brackish, somewhat salt.

Salubrious, a. Healthy, healthful, salutary, wholesome, salutiferous.

Salubriousness, ⎫ n. Healthiness, health-
Salubrity, ⎭ fulness, salutariness, wholesomeness.

Salutary, a. 1. Healthy, healthful, salubrious, wholesome, salutiferous, helpful, safe.

2. Advantageous, beneficial, serviceable, good, useful, profitable.

Salutation, n. Greeting, salute, address; hail, Ave, salaam.

Salutatory, a. Greeting.

Salute, v. t. Greet, hail, address, accost, welcome, congratulate.

——, n. Salutation, greeting, address.

Salvation, n. Preservation, deliverance, rescue, escape from danger.

2. Redemption, deliverance.

Salve, n. 1. Healing ointment, cerate.

2. Help, remedy, corrective, antidote.

——, v. t. 1. Anoint, heal, cure.

2. Help, remedy, mend, gloss over.

Salver, n. Waiter, tray.

Salvo, n. Volley, general discharge (of firearms), fusillade, broadside.

SAME, a. 1. Identical, self-same, ditto.

2. Similar, like, corresponding; of like kind, sort, or degree.

Sameness, n. 1. Identity, identicalness, selfsameness, oneness.

2. Similarity, resemblance, correspondence, likeness.

3. Monotony, want of variety.

Sample, n. 1. Specimen, illustration, exemplification, instance.

2. Example, pattern, model.

Sanable, a. Curable, remediable, healable.

Sanative, ⎫ a. Healing, curative, curing,
Sanatory, ⎭ remedial, therapeutic.

Sanctification, n. 1. Justification, absolution, remission of sin.

2. Consecration.

Sanctified, a. 1. Consecrated, hallowed.

2. Sanctimonious, affectedly holy.

Sanctify, v. t. 1. Make holy, cleanse from sin.

2. Consecrate, hallow, purify.

3. Sanction, justify, ratify.

Sanctimonious, a. Pharisaical, affectedly holy, hypocritically devout.

Sanctimoniousness, n. Pharisaism, hypocrisy, cant, formalism, pietism, sanctimony, assumed piety.

Sanctimony, n. Affected holiness, hypocritical devoutness, pretence of holiness, sanctimoniousness.

Sanction, n. 1. Confirmation, ratification, countenance, support, authority, warranty, authorization, endorsement, allowance.

2. Penalty, punishment.

——, v. t. Ratify, confirm, countenance, support, authorize, endorse, warrant, allow, legalize, bind.

Sanctity, n. 1. Purity, holiness, godliness, saintliness, goodness, piety, grace, devotion, religiousness.

2. Sacredness, inviolability, solemnity.

Sanctuary, n. 1. Sacred or holy place, shrine, consecrated spot, holy ground, holy of holies, *sanctum sanctorum, penetralia, adytum*.

2. Temple, church, place of worship, consecrated building, consecrated ground.

3. Asylum, refuge, shelter.

SAND, *n.* Gravel, small pebbles, comminuted silica.

——, *v. t.* Cover *or* sprinkle with sand.

Sand-blast, *n.* Sand-jet.

Sandy, *a.* 1. Sabulous, gritty.

2. Unstable, shifting, arenaceous.

3. Yellowish-red, sand-colored.

Sane, *a.* 1. Sound (*especially in mind*), sober, lucid, rational.

2. Reasonable.

Saneness, *n.* See SANITY.

Sang-froid, *n.* [Fr.] Coolness, unconcern, indifference, calmness.

Sangreal, *n.* Grail, holy dish.

Sanguinary, *a.* 1. Bloody, gory, murderous.

2. Cruel, blood-thirsty, savage, inhuman, barbarous, ruthless, pitiless, fell, truculent.

Sanguine, *a.* 1. Red, crimson.

2. Warm, ardent, lively, animated, cheerful.

3. Confident, hopeful, enthusiastic, optimistic, buoyant.

4. Plethoric, full-blooded.

——, *v. t.* 1. Ensanguine, stain with blood.

2. Stain red, varnish blood color.

Sanitary, *a.* Hygienic, health-promoting.

Sanitation, *n.* Hygiene, sanitary measures *or* provisions.

Sanitory, *a.* Therapeutic, remedial, curative, healing, curing. See SANATORY.

Sanity, *n.* Saneness, soundness, rationality, mental balance.

Sans-culotte, *n.* [Fr.] 1. Ragamuffin, tatterdemalion, ragged fellow.

2. Jacobin, radical, republican.

Sans souci. [Fr.] Without care, with unconcern, free and easy.

Sap, *n.* Juice (*of a plant*); vital juice.

——, *v. t.* Mine, undermine.

Sapid, *a.* Savory, relishing, tasteful, palatable.

Sapidness, *n.* Savoriness, savor, taste, sapidity, tastefulness.

Sapience, *n.* Wisdom, sageness, knowledge, sagacity, shrewdness, intelligence, sense.

Sapient, *a.* Wise, sage, sagacious, sensible, discerning, shrewd, acute, intelligent, knowing.

Sapless, *a.* 1. Without sap, destitute of sap.

2. Decayed, dry, old, withered.

Saponaceous, *a.* Soapy.

Sapor, *n.* Taste, flavor, savor, relish, smack.

Sapphire, *a.* Blue, sapphirine.

Sappiness, *n.* Juiciness, succulence.

Sappy, *a.* 1. Juicy, succulent.

2. Young, weak, soft.

3. Weak, silly, foolish.

Saracen, *n.* 1. Arabian, Arab.

2. Mussulman, Mahometan, Moslem.

Sarcasm, *n.* Taunt, gibe, jeer, fling, satire, irony, ridicule, cutting jest, sneer, flout.

Sarcastic, *a.* Severe, cutting, taunting, acrimonious, satirical, sharp, biting, mordacious, mordant, sardonic.

Sarcophagus, *n.* Stone coffin.

Sardonic, *a.* Sarcastic, derisive, malignant, bitterly ironical.

Sash, *n.* Girdle, band, belt, scarf.

Satan, *n.* Belial, Apollyon, Devil, the Evil One, the Arch-fiend, the Tempter, the Old Serpent, the Prince of Darkness, the Foul Fiend.

Satanic, *a.* Diabolical, infernal, hellish, devilish, malicious, malignant, evil, false, fiendish.

Satchel, *n.* Bag, little sack.

Sate, *v. t.* See SATIATE.

Satellite, *n.* 1. Moon, secondary planet.

2. Attendant, follower, dependant, retainer, vassal, hanger-on.

Satiate, *v. t.* 1. Sate, satisfy, suffice, fill.

2. Cloy, gorge, overfill, glut, overfeed, surfeit, pall, sate.

Satiety, *n.* Repletion, satiation, surfeit, fulness, glut, cloyment.

Satire, *n.* Ridicule, sarcasm, invective, irony, philippic, diatribe, fling, squib, lampoon, pasquinade, burlesque, skit.

Satirical, *a.* Sarcastic, severe, taunting, censorious, cutting, biting, sharp, keen, poignant, invective, mordacious, bitter, reproachful, abusive, ironical.

Satirize, *v. t.* Censure, ridicule, abuse, lampoon, lash.

Satisfaction, *n.* 1. Gratification.

2. Contentment, content, satiety; enjoyment, ease, comfort, pleasure; complacency.

3. Compensation, amends, requital, remuneration, indemnification, reparation, redress, appeasement, atonement, recompense, reward.

4. Discharge, payment, fulfilment, settlement.

Satisfactory, *a.* 1. Gratifying, pleasing.

2. Sufficient, adequate, conclusive, convincing, decisive.

3. Compensating, atoning, that makes amends.

Satisfy, *v. t.* 1. Please, gratify, content, appease, satiate, sate, fill, suffice.

2. Recompense, requite, indemnify, pay, liquidate, compensate, remunerate.

3. Pay, discharge, settle.

4. Convince, persuade, assure.

5. Fulfil, answer, meet.

Satisfy, *v. i.* 1. Give satisfaction.

2. Atone, make payment.

3. Feed full, supply to the full.

Satrap, *n.* [Persian.] 1. Governor, viceroy, ruler.

2. Prince, petty despot.

Satrapy, *n.* Principality, princedom.

Saturate, *v. t.* Drench, fill full, imbue thoroughly, soak. Cf. IMPREGNATE.

Saturation, *n.* Repletion, fulness.

Saturnalia, *n. pl.* [L.] Revels, orgies, feasts.

Saturnalian, *a.* Riotous, licentious, sportive, loose, dissolute.

Saturnian, *a.* 1. Of Saturn.

2. Palmy, joyous, halcyon, golden, happy, innocent, simple, pure.

Saturnine, *a.* 1. Dull, heavy, grave, sad, gloomy, sedate, morose, phlegmatic, sombre.

2. Leaden, dull.

Sauce, *n.* Seasoning, relish, condiment, appetizing compound.

Saucily, *adv.* Pertly, boldly, impertinently, impudently.

Sauciness, *n.* Impertinence, insolence, impudence, pertness, malapertness, rudeness.

Saucy, *a.* Impertinent, impudent, pert, insolent, cavalier, rude, forward, bold, flippant, malapert, disrespectful.

Saunter, *v. i.* 1. Loiter, linger, lounge, stroll, move slowly.

2. Dawdle, dilly-dally, loiter, lag, delay, linger.

Saunterer, *n.* 1. Loiterer, lounger, stroller.

2. Lagger, laggard, dawdler.

Saurian, *n.* Lizard.

Savage, *a.* 1. Uncultivated (*as a forest*), wild, rough, sylvan.

2. Uncivilized (*like an inhabitant of the woods*), untaught, rude, unpolished.

3. Wild, untamed, fierce, ferocious, rapacious, ravenous, ferine, blood-thirsty.

4. Inhuman, beastly, brutal, brutish, brute.

5. Cruel, barbarous, atrocious, fell, pitiless, ruthless, merciless, heathenish, relentless, hard-hearted, sanguinary, bloody, murderous, truculent, vandalic.

——, *n.* Barbarian, vandal, Hun.

Savagely, *adv.* Cruelly, inhumanly, barbarously, fiercely.

Savagery, *n.* 1. Savagism, barbarism.

2. Cruelty, barbarity.

Savanna, *n.* Meadow, plain, plateau, prairie, open country, champaign.

Savant, *n.* Scholar, pundit, learned man, erudite person, one of the literati, man of science.

Save, *v. t.* 1. Rescue, keep, preserve.

2. Redeem, salvage, recover.

3. Deliver, rescue, keep clear.

4. Reserve, keep, hold, husband, lay up, lay by, gather, hoard, store, economize.

5. Spare, prevent, hinder, obviate, insure against.

——, *prep.* Except, leaving out, not including, deducting, excepting.

Saver, *n.* Rescuer, deliverer, saviour, preserver.

Saving, *a.* 1. Preserving, sparing, redemptory.

2. Economical, frugal, sparing, thrifty, careful.

3. Reserving.

——, *prep.* 1. With exception, excepting, in favor of.

2. Without disrespect to.

——, *n.* 1. Exception, reservation.

2. Preservation, keeping.

Savingness, *n.* Frugality, parsimony, economy, thrift.

Savior, } *n.* 1. Rescuer, saver, deliverer, **Saviour,** } preserver, protector, defender, guardian.

2. [With *The* or *Our* prefixed.] Christ, Jesus, Immanuel, the Messiah, the Redeemer, the Mediator, the Intercessor, the Advocate, the Judge, the Anointed, the Word, the Son of God, the Son of Man, the Lamb of God, Shiloh.

Savor, *n.* 1. Taste, flavor, relish, gust, smack, *goût.*

2. Odor, scent, smell, fragrance.

3. Characteristic property, distinctive temper.

——, *v. i.* 1. Taste, smack.

2. Partake, have a touch of, betoken, smack.

——, *v. t.* Like, relish, enjoy, appreciate, affect.

Savorless, *a.* Tasteless, insipid, vapid, stale, flat, without savor *or* relish.

Savory, *a.* Relishing, piquant, luscious, palatable, delicious, flavorous, nice, well-tasted.

Saw, *n.* Saying, maxim, adage, proverb, aphorism, apothegm, dictum, by-word, sententious precept, axiom.

Saw-toothed, *a.* Serrated.

SAY, *v. t.* 1. Speak, utter, tell, declare, pronounce, express.

2. Argue, allege, affirm.

3. Repeat, rehearse, recite.

4. Suppose, presume, assume, take for granted.

5. Decide, judge.

SAY, *v. i.* Declare, speak, assert, tell.

——, *n.* 1. Affirmation, declaration, statement, speech.

2. (*Colloq.*) Decision, voice, vote.

Saying, *n.* 1. Expression, observation, remark, declaration, statement, speech.

2. Proverb, saw, maxim, aphorism, adage, apothegm, dictum, *mot,* by-word, sententious precept.

Scabbed, *a.* Mean, paltry, vile, shabby, sorry, worthless.

Scabious, *a.* Rough, itchy, scabby, scabbed, leprous.

Scabrous, *a.* 1. Rough, rugged, scraggy, cragged, uneven.

2. Harsh, unmusical, rough.

Scaffold, *n.* Stage, frame, scaffolding, staging.

Scald, *v. t.* Burn (*with a hot liquid*).

——, *a.* Scurvy, paltry, poor.

SCALE, *n.* 1. Dish (*of a balance*), pan, basin.

2. Balance.

3. Gradation, progressive series.

4. Lamina, layer, flake, plate, lamella.

——, *v. t.* Climb, ascend, escalade, mount, clamber up.

Scaled, *a.* Squamose, squamous, scaly.

Scale off. Exfoliate, shell off, peel off, fall off in scales.

Scall, *n.* Scab, scurf, scabbiness, leprosy.

Scallop, *v. t.* Indent, notch.

Scaly, *a.* 1. Flaky, lamelliform, squamous, imbricate, scutate. Cf. SCHISTOSE.

2. Mean, scurvy, stingy, contemptible, paltry, scald.

Scamp, *n.* Rogue, rascal, cheat, knave, swindler, sharper, trickster, scoundrel, villain, scapegrace, worthless fellow.

Scamper, *v. i.* Scud, run, trip, hie, haste, hasten, speed.

Scan, *v. t.* 1. Recite metrically, divide into feet.

2. Scrutinize, examine, investigate, sift, inquire into, look into.

Scandal, *n.* 1. Defamation, aspersion, calumny, backbiting, slander, detraction, traducement, reproach, obloquy.

2. Disgrace, dishonor, shame, infamy, offence, reproach, discredit, disrepute, ignominy, odium, opprobrium, ingloriousness.

——, *v. t.* Defame, traduce, libel, asperse.

Scandalize, *v. t.* 1. Offend, give offence to, shock.

2. Vilify, asperse, defame, backbite, traduce, decry, calumniate, slander, reproach, libel, revile, satirize, lampoon, inveigh against.

3. Disgrace, bring disgrace on.

Scandalous, *a.* 1. Opprobrious, defamatory, libellous, slanderous.

2. Disgraceful, shameful, infamous, disreputable, ignominious, atrocious, odious, inglorious, opprobrious.

Scant, *v. t.* 1. Limit, straiten, stint.

2. Grudge, keep back, be niggard of, cut short.

——, *a.* See SCANTY.

Scantiness, *n.* Insufficiency, meagreness, narrowness, deficiency, short supply, short measure.

Scantly, *adv.* 1. Penuriously, narrowly, illiberally, sparingly.

2. Scarcely, hardly.

Scantness, *n.* Narrowness, smallness, scantiness.

Scanty, *a.* 1. Insufficient, narrow, meagre, scant, small.

2. Hardly sufficient, scarce, short.

3. Sparing, skimp, scrimpy, niggardly, parsimonious, penurious.

Scapegrace, *n.* Careless fellow, idle fellow.

Scaphoid, *a.* (*Anat.*) Boat-shaped, cymbiform, navicular.

Scapula, *n.* Shoulder-blade, omoplate, shoulder bone.

Scar, *n.* 1. Cicatrix, cicatrice, seam.

2. Blemish, mark, injury, disfigurement, flaw, defect.

3. Cliff, precipitous bank, detached rock.

——, *v. t.* Wound, hurt, mark.

Scarab, *n.* Beetle, scarabee.

Scaramouch, *n.* 1. Buffoon, harlequin, clown, zany.

2. Poltroon, braggadocio, braggart.

Scarce, *a.* 1. Deficient, wanting, not plentiful, not abundant. Cf. SCANTY.

2. Rare, uncommon, infrequent.

Scarce, } *adv.* Hardly, barely, but just,
Scarcely, } with difficulty, scantly.

Scarcity, *n.* 1. Deficiency, dearth, want, insufficiency, lack.

2. Rareness, rarity, uncommonness, infrequency.

Scare, *n.* Fright, panic, sudden terror.

——, *v. t.* Frighten, affright, fright, intimidate, daunt, appall, terrify, make afraid, put in fear.

Scarfskin, *n.* Cuticle, epidermis.

Scarify, *v. t.* 1. Deface, scratch, scar, disfigure, cover with scars.

2. (*Surg.*) Cut, incise, puncture.

Scathe, *v. t.* Injure, harm, blast, destroy, damage, waste.

——, *n.* Damage, injury, waste, harm, mischief.

Scathless, *a.* Uninjured, unhurt, intact, undamaged, whole, sound, unharmed, untouched, unscathed.

Scatter, *v. t.* 1. Strew, sprinkle, broadcast, throw about loosely.

2. Dissipate, disperse, diffuse, separate, spread, disseminate, distribute.

3. Disunite, distract, confound, harass.

4. Dispel, frustrate, disappoint, overthrow.

——, *v. i.* 1. Disperse, straggle, go at random, dissipate.

2. Disband, break up.

Scatter-brain, *n.* Giddy, thoughtless person.

Scatter-brained, *a.* Giddy, thoughtless, inattentive, heedless.

Scattered, *a.* 1. Strewn, sprinkled.

2. Diffused, dispersed, spread about, dissipated, separated.

3. Sporadic, occurring here and there, infrequent, sparse.

Scatteringly, *adv.* Thinly, loosely, sparsely, dispersively.

Scene, *n.* Spectacle, exhibition, show, pageant, sight, view, display, representation.

Scenery, *n.* Landscape, prospect, view.

Scenic, *a.* Theatrical, dramatic.

Scent, *n.* 1. Odor, smell, perfume, fragrance, redolence, balminess.

2. Smell, sense of smell.

3. Track, course of pursuit.

——, *v. t.* 1. Smell, get scent of.

2. Perfume, fill with odor, give odor to, imbue with odor.

Scentless, *a.* Inodorous, odorless.

Sceptic, *n.* See Skeptic.

Sceptical, *a.* See Skeptical.

Scepticism, *n.* See Skepticism.

Sceptre, *n.* 1. Royal mace, royal baton.

2. Royal power, sovereign authority.

Sceptred, *a.* Regal, royal, imperial.

Schedule, *n.* 1. Scroll, document.

2. Inventory, list, record, roll, table, catalogue, register.

Schema, *n.* Form, arrangement, plan, design, system.

Schematist, *n.* Projector, schemer, planner, designer, systematizer.

Scheme, *n.* 1. Plan, system, theory.

2. Device, design, plan, project, contrivance, plot, stratagem, conspiracy, intrigue, cabal, machination.

3. Draught, outline, diagram, arrangement.

——, *v. t.* Plan, contrive, project, plot, devise, design, imagine, frame, excogitate.

——, *v. i.* Intrigue, plot, plan, contrive.

Schemer, *n.* Planner, projector, contriver, plotter.

Scheming, *a.* 1. Planning, contriving.

2. Artful, intriguing, designing, calculating.

Schism, *n.* 1. Division (*in a church*), split, separation.

2. Disunion, discord, faction, separation, division.

Schismatic, *n.* Sectary, heretic, non-conformist, dissenter, separatist.

Schismatical, *a.* Discordant, dissentient, heterodox.

Schistose, *a.* Lamellate, lamellated, laminar, laminated, foliated, foliaceous, scaly, flaky.

Scholar, *n.* 1. Disciple, pupil, student, learner.

2. *Savant*, man of letters, philomath, pundit, learned man, erudite person.

Scholarly, *a.* Scholar-like, befitting a scholar.

Scholarship, *n.* 1. Learning, erudition, knowledge, attainments, acquirements, accomplishments, acquired knowledge.

2. Maintenance for a student, foundation for support.

Scholastic, *a.* 1. Academic, literary, lettered, bookish.

2. Pedantic, formal.

——, *n.* Schoolman.

Scholiast, *n.* Commentator, annotator, glossarist.

Scholium, *n.* Annotation, comment, remark, observation, note, elucidation, gloss.

SCHOOL, *n.* 1. Seminary, academy, institute, gymnasium, place of education.

2. Sect, denomination.

——, *v. t.* 1. Instruct, teach, educate, train, drill, exercise, indoctrinate.

2. Tutor, discipline, control, govern, chide, admonish, reprove, bring under subjection.

Schooling, *n.* 1. Tuition, instruction, education, teaching, training, nurture, discipline.

2. Reproof, reprimand, lecture.

Schoolman, *n.* Scholastic.

School-master, *n.* Instructor, preceptor, teacher, tutor, master.

SCIENCE, *n.* 1. Knowledge, information, learning, discipline. Cf. Art.

2. System of knowledge, body of knowledge, philosophical knowledge, knowledge of principles *or* general laws.

3. Branch of knowledge.

Scientific, *a.* Philosophical, according to principles *or* general laws.

Scientist, *n.* *Savant*, scientific man, researcher.

Scintilla, *n.* [L.] Spark, glimmer, jot, shadow, trace, iota, whit, tittle, bit, ace, grain, atom, particle, scrap, mite.

Scintillate, *v. i.* 1. Sparkle, twinkle, glitter, flash, coruscate.

2. Emit sparks.

Scintillation, *n.* 1. Sparkling, flashing, coruscation; intellectual splendor.

2. Twinkling, sparkling.

Sciolism, *n.* Smattering, shallowness, superficialness, imperfect knowledge, superficial knowledge, slight knowledge.

Sciolist, *n.* Smatterer, ignoramus, novice, greenhorn, pretender to science.

Scion, *n.* 1. Sprout, shoot, twig, branch, cion, graft, slip.

2. Descendant, heir.

Scission, *n.* Division, split, fission.

SCISSORS, *n.* Shears.

Scissure, *n.* Cleft, rent, fissure.

Scoff, *v. t.* Mock, deride, jeer, rail at, taunt, flout, ridicule.

——, *v. i.* Mock, jeer, gibe, sneer, fleer.

——, *n.* 1. Sneer, gibe, jeer, taunt, flout, biting jest, mock.

2. Derision, ridicule, mock, reproach.

Scoffer, *n.* Scorner, mocker, ridiculer, railer, derider, despiser, jeerer.

Scold, *v. t.* Berate, rate, censure, reprimand, reprove, blame, chide, find fault with, brawl, rebuke rudely, "dress down."

——, *v. i.* Rate, reprimand, vituperate, brawl, rail, chide with rudeness.

——, *n.* 1. Vixen, shrew, termagant, virago.

2. Scolding, brawl.

Scold at. Rebuke, chide, reprimand, reprove, censure, condemn, denounce, blame, declaim against, inveigh against, exclaim against, rail at.

Scolding, *a.* Chiding, berating, abusive, vituperative, railing, clamorous.

——, *n.* Railing, vituperation, abuse, rating.

Sconce, *n.* 1. Cover, shelter, protection.

2. Candle-holder, candelabrum.

3. Bulwark, fort, defence, block-house, fortification.

4. Helmet, head-piece.

5. Skull, head.

6. Brains, sense, judgment, discretion.

7. Mulct, fine, poll-tax.

Scoop, *v. t.* 1. Empty with a scoop; lade out.

2. Excavate, hollow out, dig out.

3. Remove, leave hollow.

Scope, *n.* 1. Purpose, drift, tendency, aim, mark, intention, intent, design, object, view, end.

2. Room, space, field, vent, opportunity, margin, range, liberty, latitude, amplitude, purview, sphere, free course, free play, full play.

3. Length, extent, span, stretch, sweep.

Scorch, *v. t.* 1. Burn superficially, singe, char, roast, parch, sear, shrivel.

2. Burn, blister.

Scorched, *a.* Burned, adust, parched, browned, shrivelled.

Score, *n.* 1. Mark, incision, notch.

2. Account, charge, bill, debt, reckoning.

3. Reason, motive, ground, consideration, sake, account.

——, *v. t.* 1. Mark, notch, furrow, cut, scratch.

2. Record, note, charge, set down.

3. Note, impute, charge.

4. Enter, register.

Scoria, *n.* Dross, slag, recrement.

Scoriæ, *n. pl.* Volcanic cinders, slaggy lavas.

Scorn, *v. t.* Contemn, despise, disdain, scout, spurn, disregard, slight, hold in contempt.

——, *n.* 1. Contempt, disdain, derision, mockery, slight, sneer.

2. Mockery, derision, scoff.

Scorner, *n.* Scoffer, derider, despiser, contemner, ridiculer, jeerer, mocker.

Scornful, *a.* 1. Contemptuous, disdainful, insolent.

2. Defiant, regardless, disdainful, contemptuous.

Scot, *n.* 1. Tax, contribution, custom.

2. Payment, fine, mulct, contribution, reckoning, shot.

3. Scotchman, native of Scotland.

Scotch, *v. t.* 1. Cut (*slightly*), wound (*superficially*), score, notch, scot, jag.

2. Stop (*as a wheel, to prevent it from rolling back*), block, prop, support.

——, *a.* Scottish, Scots, Caledonian.

Scotchman, *n.* Scot, Scotsman, native of Scotland.

Scot-free, *a.* 1. Untaxed, without payment, without expense, shot-free.

2. Unhurt, uninjured, clear, safe, shot-free.

Scoundrel, *n.* Knave, rogue, villain, rascal, scamp, cheat, trickster, swindler, sharper, caitiff, vile wretch, miscreant, reprobate.

Scoundrelism, *n.* Knavery, roguery, villainy, rascality, turpitude, baseness.

Scoundrelly, *a.* Base, mean, unprincipled, villainous, disgraceful, knavish.

Scour, *v. t.* 1. Clean (*by friction*), scrape, brighten, polish, rub hard, scrub, cleanse.

2. Range over, brush along, pass swiftly over.

3. Rake, search closely.

4. Obliterate, efface, cleanse away, remove.

5. Overrun, sweep clear, drive away.

——, *v. i.* 1. Clean (*by rubbing*).

2. Clean, cleanse.

3. Course, career, scamper, range, run swiftly.

Scourge, *n.* 1. Whip, lash, thong, strap, cowhide, cord.

2. Punishment, affliction, curse, pest, bane, plague, annoyance, infliction, nuisance.

——, *v. t.* 1. Lash, whip.

2. Punish, chastise, chasten, correct, afflict.

3. Harass, torment, afflict.

Scout, *v. t.* Ridicule, deride, disdain, despise, contemn, scorn, spurn, scoff at, laugh at, sneer at, hold in contempt, hoot at.

Scowl, *v. i.* Frown, look angry, sour *or* sullen, lower, glower.

Scrabble, *v. t.* Scribble, scrawl, scratch.

——, *v. i.* Scribble, scrawl.

——, *n.* Scramble, struggle.

Scragged, *a.* Rough, scraggy.

Scragginess, *n.* Leanness, ruggedness, roughness, scraggedness.

Scraggy, *a.* 1. Rough, rugged, uneven, broken, craggy, scabrous, scragged.

2. Lean, thin, bony, lank, meagre, gaunt, angular, skinny, emaciated, attenuated, scranny, scrawny.

Scramble, *v. i.* 1. Struggle (*as in climbing*), scrabble, clamber, climb (*with difficulty*).

2. Struggle, strive.

——, *n.* Struggle, contest, scrabble.

Scranny, *a.* (*Local.*) Thin, lank, meagre, scraggy, scrawny.

Scrap, *n.* 1. Fragment, bit, little piece, small part, scantling.

2. Crumb, morsel, bite, mouthful, bit, fragment.

Scrap-book, *n.* Album.

Scrape, *v. t.* 1. Rub *or* abrade (*with something edged*), grate harshly over, rasp, grind, scuff, bark.

2. Gather, collect, accumulate, acquire, save.

3. Remove, erase.

4. Clean (*by rubbing*), scour.

——, *n.* Difficulty, perplexity, distress, embarrassment, predicament.

Scratch, *v. t.* 1. Mark with a scratch *or* with scratches, scarify.

2. Wound slightly (*as with the nails*).

3. Scribble, write carelessly.

4. Obliterate, expunge, erase, rub out.

——, *n.* 1. Incision (*slight and ragged*), laceration, slight wound.

2. Slight furrow, score, striation.

3. Scratch-wig, small wig, periwig, peruke.

Scrawl, *v. t.* and *v. i.* Scribble, scrabble, scratch, write carelessly.

——, *n.* Scribble, scratch, inelegant writing.

Scrawny, *a.* (*Colloq.*) Thin, lank, meagre, scraggy, scranny, wasted, raw-boned.

Scream, *v. i.* Shriek, screech, cry out (*in a shrill voice*), squall, ululate.

——, *n.* Shriek, screech, yell, outcry, shrill cry, ululation.

Screech, *v. i.* Shriek, scream, scritch.

Screed, *n.* [*Scotch.*] 1. Rent, tear.

2. Fragment, shred.

3. Harangue, tirade.

Screen, *n.* 1. Curtain, blind, partition, lattice.

2. Protection, guard, defence, shield.

3. Veil, disguise, cloak, cover.

4. Sieve, riddle.

——, *v. t.* 1. Hide, shelter, cover, conceal, shroud, mask, cloak, protect, fence, defend.

2. Riddle, sift.

SCREW, *n.* 1. Threaded nail for holding fast.

2. Miser, niggard, curmudgeon, skinflint, extortioner, churl, codger, scrimp, hunks, lick-penny, muckworm, sordid wretch, mean fellow.

Screw, *v. t.* 1. Wrench, squeeze, press, twist, force.

2. Rack, raise extortionately, oppress.

3. Distort.

Screw-shaped, *a.* Cochleary, cochleated, spiral, helical, winding.

Scribble, *v. i.* Scrawl, scrabble, scratch.

Scribbler, *n.* 1. Scrawler.

2. Petty author, hack.

Scribe, *n.* 1. Writer, penman, chirographer, chirographist.

2. Clerk, secretary, notary, amanuensis, copyist, scrivener.

Scrimmage, *n.* Skirmish, scuffle, brawl, riot, *mêlée*.

Scrimp, *a.* Scanty, narrow, contracted, deficient, "skimpy."

——, *v. t.* Scant, contract, curtail, pinch, limit, straiten, reduce, shorten.

Scrip, *n.* 1. Wallet, satchel, small bag.

2. Certificate, schedule.

Scriptural, *a.* Biblical, Scripture, of the Scriptures, of the Bible.

Scripture, *n.* 1. Writing, document, inscription, manuscript, book.

2. The Scriptures, the Bible, Holy Writ, the word of God.

Scrivener, *n.* Writer (*by profession*), scribe.

Scroll, *n.* 1. Schedule, list, roll of paper *or* parchment.

2. Flourish, paraph.

3. Volute, spiral ornament.

Scrub, *v. t.* Scour, cleanse, clean, rub hard.

Scrub, *n.* 1. Mean fellow.

2. Brushwood, underwood, underbrush.

——, *a.* Mean, niggardly, contemptible, scrubby, shabby.

Scrubby, *a.* 1. Vile, mean, pitiful, poor, shabby, sorry, miserable, despicable, worthless, small, insignificant.

2. Small, diminutive, puny, stunted, dwarfed, dwarfish, pygmy, pygmean.

Scrunch, *v. t.* 1. Crush, crunch, scranch.

2. Grind down, oppress.

Scruple, *n.* 1. Hesitation, hesitancy, perplexity, qualm, nicety, delicacy.

2. Twenty grains.

——, *v. i.* Hesitate, doubt, waver.

Scrupulosity, *n.* Nicety, niceness, delicacy, conscientiousness, punctiliousness, scrupulousness, preciseness, caution, nice regard to propriety, tenderness of conscience.

Scrupulous, *a.* 1. Conscientious, punctilious, rigorous, strict, nice, precise, fastidious.

2. Cautious, careful, exact, vigilant, circumspect.

Scrutinize, *v. t.* Examine, investigate, search, canvass, study, sift, explore, overhaul, probe, dissect, look into, search into, pry into, inquire into.

Scrutiny, *n.* Search, examination, investigation, inquisition, exploration, sifting, inspection, searching *or* careful inquiry, close search, critical examination.

Scud, *v. i.* 1. Flee, run, speed, trip, hie, post, scamper, haste, hasten, fly.

2. (*Naut.*) Drive before a gale.

Scuddle, *v. i.* Scuttle, hurry, bustle, run about (*in affecting to be busy*).

Scuff, *v. i.* Shuffle.

Scuffle, *v. i.* Struggle (*in a disorderly manner*), contend, fight, strive (*as in a close embrace*).

——, *n.* Contest (*of a disorderly kind*), struggle, fight, rencounter, encounter, broil, fray, brawl, quarrel, squabble, wrangle, altercation, set-to.

Scull, *n.* 1. Boat, cock-boat.

2. Short oar.

Scullery, *n.* Back-kitchen.

Scullion, *n.* Mean fellow, worthless fellow.

Sculpture, *n.* 1. Statuary, plastic art.

2. Carved work.

——, *v. t.* 1. Carve, chisel, cut, sculp.

2. Engrave, grave.

Scum, *n.* Froth, dross, refuse, recrement, *scoria*.

Scurf, *a.* 1. (*Med.*) Miliary scab.

2. Soil, stain, foul remains.

Scurfy, *a.* Scabby, scabbed, scurvy, scaly, lentiginous, furfuraceous.

Scurrile, *a.* Low, mean, scurrilous, grossly opprobrious, lewdly jocose.

Scurrilous, *a.* 1. Abusive, scurrile, reproachful, opprobrious, vituperative, insulting, insolent, contumelious, ribald, blackguard, indecent, offensive, infamous, foul, foul-mouthed.

2. Low, mean, vile, foul, coarse, vulgar, gross, obscene.

Scurry, *v. i.* Hurry, hasten, move rapidly, scutter.

——, *n.* Haste, hurry, impetuosity.

Scurvily, *adv.* Meanly, basely, coarsely, vilely.

Scurviness, *n.* Meanness, vileness, baseness.

Scurvy, *a.* 1. Scurfy, scabbed, scabby.

2. Vile, mean, low, vulgar, base, bad, sorry, contemptible, despicable, worthless, pitiful, abject.

3. Offensive, mischievous, malicious.

Scutate, *a.* Clypeiform, shield-shaped, buckler-shaped.

Scutcheon, *n.* Shield, escutcheon, ensign armorial, emblazoned shield.

Scutter, *v. i.* Scurry, run, hurry.

Scuttle, *v. i.* Hurry, bustle, scuddle, run (*affecting to be busy*).

SEA, *n.* 1. Ocean, main, the deep, the briny deep.

2. Wave, billow, surge, flood.

Sea-coast, *n.* Sea-board, beach, strand, shore, coast.

Seafarer, *n.* See SEAMAN.

Seal, *n.* 1. Stamp.

2. Wax, wafer, fastening.

3. Attestation, authentication, confirmation, ratification, assurance, pledge.

——, *v. t.* 1. Close, fasten, secure.

2. Confirm, ratify, establish, sanction, authenticate, attest.

3. Keep close, keep secret, shut close, make fast.

4. Enclose, confine, imprison.

Seam, *n.* 1. Suture, commissure, joint, line of juncture.

2. Fissure, crevice.

3. (*Mining.*) Thin layer, stratum, *or* bed; narrow vein.

4. Scar, cicatrice, cicatrix.

——, *v. t.* 1. Unite, join together.

2. Scar, mark with a cicatrix, line.

Seaman, *n.* Sailor, mariner, seafarer, seafaring man, tar.

Seamstress, *n.* Sempstress, needle-woman.

Séance, *n.* [Fr.] Session, sitting.

Sear, *v. t.* 1. Dry, wither, blight.

2. Cauterize, burn with a hot iron, burn with cautery, scorch, brand.

3. Make callous, make insensible.

——, *a.* Dry, withered, sere.

Search, *v. t.* 1. Examine, explore, ransack, scrutinize, investigate, overhaul, sift, inspect, look into, search into, pry into, peer into, ferret, probe.

2. Inquire after, seek, look for.

——, *v. i.* 1. Seek, look, make search, hunt, explore, forage, rummage, delve.

2. Inquire, make inquiry.

——, *n.* Examination, inquiry, scrutiny, hunt, research, exploration, investigation, quest, pursuit, inspection, seeking.

Searcher, *n.* Seeker, explorer, examiner, inquirer, investigator.

Searching, *a.* 1. Penetrating, trying, close, keen.

2. Exploring, examining, inquiring, seeking, investigating, probing.

Searchless, *a.* Unsearchable, inscrutable.

Seared, *a.* 1. Cauterized, burnt on the surface.

2. Hardened, callous, impenitent, unrepentant, obdurate, graceless, incorrigible, shameless, irreclaimable.

Sea-robber, *n.* Pirate, corsair, buccaneer, picaroon, sea-rover, sea-thief.

Sea-shore, *n.* Beach, strand, shore, sea-coast.

Sea-sickness, *n.* Nausea (*caused by the ship's motion*), *mal-de-mer.*

Season, *n.* 1. Period of the year.

2. Time, conjuncture, fit time, convenient time, suitable time.

3. While, time, spell, term, interval, period.

——, *v. t.* 1. Habituate, accustom, acclimatize, mature, inure, harden, form, train, fit by habit.

2. Make palatable, give relish to, spice, flavor.

3. Moderate, temper, qualify.

——, *v. i.* Be seasoned, become seasoned.

Seasonable, *a.* Timely, opportune, fit, convenient, suitable, appropriate.

Seasonably, *adv.* In due time, sufficiently early, in season, opportunely.

Seasonal, *a.* Periodic.

Seasoning, *n.* Condiment, relish, flavoring, sauce, salt.

SEAT, *n.* 1. Place, station, site, situation.

2. Abode, dwelling, residence, mansion, capital, house.

3. Bottom, fundament.

——, *v. t.* 1. Place, station, locate, establish, fix, set, settle, situate.

2. Cause to sit.

3. Fix, set firm.

Sebaceous, *a.* Fat, fatty, unctuous, greasy, oily, oleaginous, adipose.

Secant, *a.* Cutting, dividing.

Secede, *v. i.* Withdraw, apostatize, retire, draw off.

Seceder, *n.* Sectary, separatist.

Secession, *n.* 1. Withdrawal, apostasy, separation.

2. Departure.

Seclude, *v. t.* 1. Separate (*from society*), sequester, keep apart.

2. Shut out, exclude, repel.

Secluded, *a.* Retired, withdrawn, removed, covert, close, sequestered, isolated, private, screened, embowered.

Seclusion, *n.* Separation, retirement, privacy, secrecy, obscurity, solitude, withdrawment.

SECOND, *a.* 1. Next to the first (*in place* or *in time*).

2. Other, another.

3. Secondary, second-rate, inferior.

——, *n.* Maintainer, supporter, helper, assistant, backer.

——, *v. t.* 1. Support, help, forward, assist, aid, promote, back, encourage, abet, further, sustain, advance, stand by, side with, take part with.

2. Approve, favor, support.

Secondary, *a.* Subordinate, collateral, subsidiary, inferior, minor.

——, *n.* Deputy, delegate, proxy.

Second-sight, *n.* Prophetic vision.

Secrecy, *n.* 1. Concealment, stealth, clandestineness, furtiveness, surreptitiousness, "hugger-mugger."

2. Seclusion, retirement, privacy, hiddenness, solitude, separation.

SECRET, *a.* 1. Hidden, hid, concealed, covert, privy, close, covered, shrouded, veiled, unseen, unknown, unrevealed, mysterious, cryptic.

2. Clandestine, sly, underhand, underhanded, furtive, surreptitious, covert, concealed, hidden, privy, stealthy.

3. Secluded, retired, private, unseen, hid, concealed, privy, confidential.

4. Occult, mysterious, latent, obscure, recondite, abstruse, unknown, hidden.

——, *n.* 1. Something concealed.

2. Mystery.

SECRETARY, *n.* 1. Scribe, clerk, writer.

2. Escritoire, writing-desk.

Secrete, *v. t.* 1. Hide, conceal, shroud, bury, disguise.

2. Separate (*as from blood* or *sap*), secern.

Secretive, *a.* Reserved, reticent, close, uncommunicative, cautious, wary, taciturn.

Secretly, *adv.* Privately, privily, underhand, clandestinely.

Sect, *n.* Denomination, school, faction, schism.

Sectarian, *a.* Party, schismatical, denominational, exclusive, narrow, intolerant.

——, *n.* Sectary, partisan, schismatic.

Sectary, *n.* 1. Dissenter, non-conformist.

2. Separatist, schismatic, seceder, sectarian.

Section, *n.* Division, cutting, segment, slice, piece, portion, part.

Sectional, *a.* Partial, exclusive, narrow, provincial, local.

Secular, *a.* Temporal, worldly, profane, lay, laic, laical.

Secularity, *n.* Worldliness, secularism, secularness, worldly-mindedness.

Secure, *a.* 1. Certain, sure, assured, confident.

2. Safe, free from danger, protected, insured.

3. Fixed, fast, firm, stable, immovable.

4. Careless, unsuspecting, undisturbed, easy.

5. Over-confident, incautious, careless, inattentive, heedless, negligent.

——, *v. t.* 1. Guard, protect, make safe.

2. Insure, assure, ensure, guarantee, make sure, make certain, make sure of.

3. Fasten, make fast.

4. Get, acquire, gain, procure, obtain, get possession of.

Security, *n.* 1. Safety.

2. Protection, safeguard, defence, shelter, guard, bulwark, palladium.

3. Pledge, pawn, deposit, collateral, surety, stake, gage, guarantee, warranty, bond.

4. Carelessness, heedlessness, overconfidence, negligence.

5. Certainty, assuredness, confidence, ease, assurance.

Sedate, *a.* Calm, composed, collected, quiet, placid, serene, tranquil, still, unruffled, undisturbed, settled, imperturbable, sober, serious, staid, demure, cool, philosophical, contemplative, grave, thoughtful.

Sedative, *a.* Soothing, tranquillizing, allaying, composing, anodyne, calming, assuasive, assuaging, lenient, lenitive, demulcent, balmy.

——, *n.* Opiate, anodyne, narcotic, anæsthetic, hypnotic.

Sedentary, *a.* Inactive, motionless, sluggish, torpid.

Sedge, *n.* Reed, flag.

Sediment, *n.* Dregs, lees, settlings, grounds, precipitate.

Sedition, *n.* Insurrection, insurgence, riot, rising, rebellion, treason, revolt, tumult, mutiny, uproar.

Seditious, *a.* Rebellious, mutinous, refractory, insurgent, tumultuous, factious, riotous, incendiary, turbulent.

Seduce, *v. t.* Allure, decoy, entice, betray, attract, tempt, inveigle, mislead, lead astray, ensnare, corrupt, debauch, deceive.

Seduction, *n.* 1. Enticement, allurement, betrayal, seducement, violation; solicitation, attraction, temptation, witchery.

2. Lure, decoy, bait, temptation.

Seductive, *a.* Enticing, alluring, tempting, attractive.

Sedulous, *a.* Diligent, assiduous, industrious, laborious, active, busy, notable, persevering, painstaking, unremitting, untiring, diligently employed, busily engaged.

Sedulousness, *n.* Assiduity, assiduousness, industry, diligence, sedulity.

See, *n.* 1. Diocese.

2. Papal court.

SEE, *v. t.* 1. Behold, descry, look at, glimpse, view, survey, contemplate.

2. Perceive, notice, espy, observe, discern, distinguish, know, remark, comprehend, understand, conceive.

3. Regard, look to, care for, give attention to, consider, envisage, attend to, beware.

4. Attend, escort, wait upon, accompany.

5. Experience, feel, suffer, know, meet with.

——, *v. i.* 1. Look.

2. Inquire, examine, notice, mark, observe, distinguish, consider.

3. Take heed, take care, be careful, beware, be attentive, pay attention.

4. Perceive, penetrate, discern, understand, look.

——, *interj.* Look, lo, behold, observe.

SEED, *n.* 1. Semen, sperm.

2. (*Bot.*) Embryo (*with its envelope* or *pericarp*), matured ovule, kernel, grain.

3. Original, first principle, germ.

4. Progeny, offspring, descendants, children.

5. Race, generation, birth.

Seeded, *a.* 1. Matured, full-grown.

2. Sown, sprinkled with seed.

Seed-vessel, *n.* Pericarp, pod, case, capsule, legume.

Seedy, *a.* (*Colloq.*) 1. Old, worn, faded, shabby.

2. Poor, needy, destitute, indigent, distressed, penniless, pinched, out of money, short of money, out of pocket, out of cash, out at the elbows, in need, in want, in distress.

Seeing, *n.* 1. Sight, vision.

2. Perception.

——, *conj.* Considering, since, because, inasmuch as, for the reason that, it being so.

See into. } Comprehend, understand,
See through. } see with half an eye, penetrate.

Seek, *v. t.* 1. Search for, seek for, look for, hunt, go in quest of, look after, try to find.

2. Solicit, ask, inquire for, try to get, endeavor to gain.

3. Solicit, pursue, court, prosecute, follow.

4. Go to, resort to, have recourse to.

5. Aim at, attempt, pursue, strive after.

——, *v. i.* 1. Search, make search, look.

2. Try, strive, endeavor, attempt.

Seek after. Seek, search for, seek for, look for, look after, try to find, make pursuit of, attempt to find.

Seeker, *n.* Inquirer.

Seel, *v. t.* Close, blind, hoodwink.

SEEM, *v. i.* Appear, look, appear to be, present the appearance, have the appearance, strike one as being.

Seeming, *n.* Show, appearance, semblance, look, color, guise.

——, *a.* 1. Apparent, specious, ostensible.

2. Appearing.

Seemingly, *adv.* Apparently, ostensibly, in show, in semblance, in appearance.

Seemliness, *n.* 1. Fitness, propriety, decency, decorum.

2. Comeliness, beauty, grace.

Seemly, *a.* 1. Fit, fitting, befitting, becoming, proper, suitable, convenient, expedient, appropriate, congruous, meet, decent, decorous, right.

2. Comely, fair, good-looking, beautiful, handsome, pretty, well-favored, graceful.

Seer, *n.* Prophet, foreteller, predictor, diviner, soothsayer, vaticinator.

Seethe, *v. t.* 1. Boil.

2. Steep, soften, soak.

——, *v. i.* Boil, be hot.

Segment, *n.* Portion, section, sector, part, division.

Segregate, *v. t.* Separate, dissociate, part, insulate, isolate, set apart.

Segregation, *n.* Separation, disconnection, insulation, isolation, detachment, parting, dispersion.

Seigniory, *n.* Lordship, manor.

Seine, *n.* Large fishing-net.

Seize, *v. t.* 1. Gripe, grab, grip, grasp, snatch, clutch, catch, capture, grapple, lay hold on, lay hold of, fasten upon, lay hands on, take hold of (*forcibly and suddenly*).

2. Confiscate, impress, impound, sequestrate.

3. Come upon suddenly (*as attacks of disease*), attack, take hold of.

4. Comprehend, apprehend.

5. Take, capture, arrest, apprehend.

Seizure, *n.* 1. Taking, catching, griping, grasping, capture, appropriation, prehension.

2. Retention, possession, hold, grasp, gripe.

3. Impressment, sequestration, confiscation.

Seldom, *adv.* Rarely, infrequently, semi-occasionally.

Select, *v. t.* Choose, pick, cull, prefer, pick out, single out, pitch upon, fix upon.

——, *a.* 1. Selected, chosen, picked, rare, choice, good, excellent, exquisite.

2. Preferable.

SELECTION, *n.* Choice, pick, election, preference.

SELF, *n.* Ego, the I.

Self-abasement, *n.* Humiliation, humility, humbleness, meekness, lowliness.

Self-abnegation, *n.* See SELF-DENIAL.

Self-abuse, *n.* Onanism, masturbation, self-pollution.

Self-asserting, *a.* Bold, forward, presuming, "bumptious."

Self-command, *n.* See SELF-CONTROL.

Self-conceit, *n.* Vanity, conceit, self-sufficiency, egotism, self-complacency, self-esteem, self-opinion.

Self-conceited, *a.* Vain, egotistical, conceited, self-complacent, opinionated, self-sufficient, self-satisfied.

Self-contained, *a.* Reserved, reticent, taciturn.

Self-control, *n.* Self-command, self-government, self-mastery, self-restraint, self-possession, equanimity, poise, stoicism.

Self-deception, *n.* Illusion, delusion, hallucination, monomania.

Self-denial, *n.* Self-abnegation, self-sacrifice, unselfishness, devotion, disinterestedness.

Self-denying, *a.* Self-sacrificing, devoted, generous, unselfish, disinterested.

Self-esteem, *n.* See SELF-CONCEIT.

Self-government, *n.* See SELF-CONTROL.

Self-importance, *n.* Pride, vanity, conceit, pomposity, consequentialness, "cockiness."

Self-important, *a.* Pompous, vain, proud.

Selfish, *a.* Illiberal, mean, "hoggish," ungenerous, narrow, narrow-minded, self-seeking, egoistic.

Selfishness, *n.* Undue love of self, self-interest, egoism, private interest, illiberality, meanness, self-love.

Self-mastery, *n.* See SELF-CONTROL.

Self-pollution, *n.* Onanism, masturbation, self-abuse.

Self-possessed, *a.* Calm, placid, composed, collected, unruffled, unexcited, cool, undisturbed, sedate.

Self-possession, *n.* Calmness, composure, coolness, self-command, self-control, equanimity.

Self-reliance, *n.* Confidence (*in one's own powers*), self-confidence, resolution, assurance, firmness, courage, intrepidity.

Self-respect, *n.* Pride, dignity.

Self-restraint, *n.* See SELF-CONTROL.

Self-sacrifice, *n.* See SELF-DENIAL.

Self-same, *a.* Same, identical, the very same, exactly the same.

Self-seeking, *a.* Selfish, illiberal, mean.

Self-styled, *a.* Pretended, would-be, self-dubbed, *soi-disant*.

Self-sufficiency, *n.* Conceit, conceitedness, smugness, pride, haughtiness, self-complacency, self-conceit, self-esteem, self-confidence.

Self-sufficient, *a.* Proud, haughty, over-bearing, assuming, over-weening, consequential, lordly.

Self-willed, *a.* Wilful, dogged, pig-headed, obstinate, uncompliant, contumacious, headstrong, stubborn.

Sell, *v. t.* 1. Vend, barter, exchange, market, hawk, peddle, put up to sale.

2. Betray, take a bribe for.

Selvage, } *n.* List, strip of cloth (*forming*
Selvedge, } *an edge*).

Semblance, *n.* 1. Likeness, resemblance, similarity.

2. Show, appearance, seeming, figure, form, exterior, air, mien, aspect, bearing.

3. Likeness, image, similitude, representation.

Semen, *n.* [L.] Sperm, seed.

Semi-barbarous, *a.* Half-civilized, semi-barbarian, semi-savage, half-barbarous, semi-barbaric.

Seminal, *a.* Germinal, original, rudimental, radical.

Seminary, *n.* School, academy, high-school, institute, gymnasium, college, university, place of education.

Sempiternal, *a.* Everlasting, endless, perpetual, ever-during, unending, eternal.

SEND, *v. t.* 1. Throw, hurl, cast, fling, impel, drive, propel, emit, project, toss, launch, lance, jaculate.

2. Despatch, delegate, depute, send forth, send out.

3. Transmit, forward.

4. Give, bestow, grant, confer.

Senile, *a.* 1. Aged, superannuated, doddering.

2. Imbecile, doting.

Senility, *n.* 1. Old age, caducity.

2. Dotage, second childhood.

Senior, *a.* 1. Older, elder.

2. Higher, more advanced.

——, *n.* Elder, dean.

Seniority, *n.* 1. Eldership.

2. Priority, superiority.

Sensation, *n.* 1. Feeling (*without perception or reference to any object that causes the feeling*), sense, perception.

2. Excitement, thrill, impression.

SENSE, *n.* 1. Faculty of perception.

2. Feeling, sensation, perception.

3. Intellect, mind, understanding, reason, brains, thinking principle.

4. Discernment, perception, apprehension, understanding, appreciation, feeling, recognition, tact.

5. Opinion, judgment, notion, idea, view, sentiment.

6. Signification, meaning, import, purport, interpretation.

7. Reason, understanding, judgment, good mental capacity, soundness, sagacity, wisdom.

Senseless, *a.* 1. Inert, not sentient, without perception.

2. Insensible, insensate, unfeeling, apathetic.

3. Unreasonable, foolish, nonsensical, ill-judged, unwise, absurd, unmeaning, silly.

4. Stupid, foolish, doltish, silly, simple, witless, weak-minded.

Sensibility, *n.* 1. Feeling, sensitiveness, susceptibility, impressibility.

2. Delicacy of feeling, tender feeling, quick emotion.

Sensible, *a.* 1. Perceptible (*by any of the senses* or *by the mind*), apprehensible, that makes an impression.

2. Cognizant, observant, aware, conscious, convinced, persuaded, satisfied.

3. Judicious, wise, discreet, sage, sagacious, reasonable, intelligent, rational, sober, sound, understanding.

4. Sensitive, impressible.

Sensitive, *a.* 1. Sentient, perceptive.

2. Impressible, impressionable, susceptible, responsive, alive to, easily affected.

Sensitize, *v. t.* (*Photography.*) Make sensitive to light.

Sensual, *a.* 1. Carnal, fleshly, unspiritual, animal, earthy.

2. Voluptuous, luxurious, sensuous.

3. Lewd, dissolute, licentious.

Sensualist, *n.* Voluptuary, epicure, sybarite, free-liver, man of pleasure.

Sensuous, *a.* 1. Affecting the senses (*mediately* or *immediately*), that concerns sensible objects *or* impressions derived from the senses, sensory, material.

2. Pleasurably stirring the senses, luscious, delicious.

Sentence, *n.* 1. Decision, judgment, determination, opinion.

2. Dogma, doctrine, tenet, opinion.

3. (*Common Law*.) Condemnation, doom, judgment passed on a criminal.

4. Period, proposition.

5. Maxim, axiom, apothegm.

——, *v. t.* Doom, condemn, pass judgment upon.

Sententious, *a.* Pithy, terse, laconic, succinct, concise, compendious, didactic, pointed, compact, full of meaning, very expressive, to the point, short and energetic.

Sentient, *a.* Perceiving, perceptive, sensitive, sensate, feeling.

Sentiment, *n.* 1. Feeling, sensibility, tenderness, emotion, tender susceptibility.

2. Thought (*prompted by feeling*), opinion, notion, judgment.

3. Saying, maxim, striking remark.

4. Thought, feeling, disposition, state of mind.

Sentimental, *a.* Tender, impressible, romantic; responding with excess of sentiment, overemotional.

Sentimentalism, *n.* Sentimentality, affectation of sentiment, affected sensibility.

Sentinel, *n.* Watchman, guard, patrol, picket, sentry, guardsman.

Sentry, *n.* 1. See SENTINEL.

2. Watch, guard, watch and ward.

Separable, *a.* Divisible, discerptible.

Separate, *v. t.* 1. Disjoin, disunite, part, divide, sever, dissever, detach, disconnect, disengage, dissociate, divorce, sunder, hold apart.

2. Withdraw, remove, eliminate, set apart.

——, *v. i.* 1. Part, divide, be divided, be disunited, be separated, sunder.

2. Cleave, open, be divided.

SEPARATE, .*a.* 1. Disjoined, disconnected, dissociated, detached, disjointed, disunited, parted, divided, severed.

2. Unconnected, distinct, dividual, discrete.

3. Alone, withdrawn, segregated.

Separately, *adv.* Distinctly, singly, apart.

Separation, *n.* 1. Disjunction, dissociation.

2. Disunion, disconnection, division, divorce.

3. Analysis, decomposition.

Separatist, *n.* Sectary, schismatic, dissenter, seceder, non-conformist, "come-outer."

Sept, *n.* Tribe, clan, race, family, generation.

Septentrional, *a.* Northern.

Sepulchral, *a.* Funereal, mournful, sombre, sad, woeful, gloomy, dismal, lugubrious, melancholy, deep, grave, hollow.

Sepulchre, *n.* Tomb, grave, ossuary, charnel-house, burial vault, burial-place, sepulture.

Sepulture, *n.* 1. Burial, interment, inhumation.

2. Grave, burial-place, sepulchre, tomb.

Sequel, *n.* 1. Continuation, succeeding part.

2. Close, conclusion, termination, *dénouement*.

3. Consequence, event, issue, upshot, result.

Sequence, *n.* 1. Succession, following, progression, gradation.

2. Order of succession, arrangement, series, train.

Sequester, *v. t.* 1. Separate, set aside, sequestrate.

2. Remove, put aside, separate, set apart.

——, *v. i.* Withdraw, seclude, retire.

Sequestered, *a.* 1. (*Law*.) Seized and detained.

2. Private, retired, secluded, withdrawn, hidden, unfrequented.

3. Separated, set apart.

Sequestrate, *v. t.* 1. Sequester, set aside.

2. (*International Law*.) Confiscate.

Sequestration, *n.* Separation, seclusion, retirement.

Seraphic, *a.* 1. Angelic, celestial, heavenly, sublime.

2. Pure, refined, holy.

Sere, *a.* Dry, withered. See SEAR.

Serene, *a.* 1. Calm, quiet, placid, tranquil, unruffled, peaceful, composed, undisturbed, unperturbed, collected, sedate.

2. Clear, fair, bright, calm, unclouded.

Serenely, *adv.* 1. Calmly, quietly.

2. Coolly, deliberately.

Serenity, *n.* 1. Calmness, peacefulness, tranquillity, collectedness, sedateness, imperturbability, composure, coolness, calm, peace.

2. Clearness, fairness, brightness, calmness, stillness, quietness, peace.

3. Peace, quietness, tranquillity, calm.

Serf, *n.* Slave (*attached to the soil*), bondman, thrall, bond-servant, villein.

Serfdom, *n.* Enslavement, slavery, servitude, bondage, thraldom, enthralment, subjection, serfage.

Serial, *a.* Successive, consecutive, continuous, continued.

——, *n.* Periodical.

Seriatim, *adv.* [L.] In a series, in order, successively, one after another.

Series, *n.* Succession, order, sequence, progression, course, line, concatenation, chain, train.

SERIOUS, *a.* 1. Grave, solemn, sedate, staid, sober, earnest, demure.

2. Important, weighty, great, momentous, grave.

3. In earnest.

4. See DANGEROUS.

Sermon, *n.* Homily, exhortation, religious discourse, sermonette.

Sermonize, *v. i.* Preach, discourse.

Serous, *a.* Thin (*as parts of animal fluids*), watery, serose.

Serpent, *n.* Snake.

Serpentine, *a.* Winding, meandering, crooked, anfractuous, spiral, tortuous, undulating, sinuous, twisted.

Serrate, } *a.* Notched, indented, toothed,
Serrated, } denticulated, jagged.

Serried, *a.* Close, compacted, crowded.

SERVANT, *n.* 1. Servitor, attendant, retainer, henchman, underling, understrapper, subaltern, dependant, subordinate, helper, "help," factotum.

2. Menial, domestic, drudge, lackey, "flunky," scullion, slave.

Serve, *v. t.* 1. Work for, labor for, be under the orders of, be subservient to, obey, subserve.

2. Aid, assist, help, succor, attend, oblige, wait on, minister to.

3. Promote, advance, forward, benefit, contribute to, be of use to, conduce to, assist, be sufficient for.

4. Satisfy, content, be sufficient for.

5. Treat, behave toward, requite, act toward.

6. Manage, manipulate, handle, work.

7. Wait on, attend, supply (*with food*).

8. Place, arrange, bring forward, deal, distribute.

9. Be in lieu of, answer, do duty for.

——, *v. i.* 1. Be a servant, be a slave, be in bondage, be in subjection.

2. Obey, be dutiful, perform duty.

3. Answer, do, be sufficient, suffice, be of use.

4. Suit, be convenient, be suitable.

5. Attend, wait on.

6. Act, discharge the requirements of, officiate, minister.

Service, *n.* 1. Labor (*for another*), ministration, work, menial duties.

2. Duty, office, business, employment, employ, attendance.

3. Benefit, advantage, profit, gain, good.

4. Use, utility, avail, useful office, purpose.

5. Office of devotion, religious rite.

6. Spiritual obedience, reverence, love.

Serviceable, *a.* Useful, helpful, handy, profitable, advantageous, convenient, beneficial, available, operative.

Service-book, *n.* Missal, prayer-book, mass-book.

Servile, *a.* 1. Dependent, menial, held in bondage, held in slavery, held in subjection.

2. Slavish, mean, base, cringing, obsequious, truckling, fawning, supple, grovelling, sycophantic, abject, low, beggarly, sneaking, base-minded, low-minded, meanly submissive.

Servility, *n.* 1. Slavery, bondage, dependence.

2. Slavishness, baseness, meanness, abjectness, abjection, obsequiousness, fawning, sycophancy.

Servitor, *n.* Servant, attendant, dependant, retainer, squire, lackey, valet, waiter, footman.

Servitude, *n.* Slavery, bondage, thraldom, enthralment, enslavement, serfdom, service.

Session, *n.* Sitting (*of a court, of a legislature, etc.*), assize.

Set, *v. t.* 1. Put, place, plant, station, locate, lay, mount, stand.

2. Fix, establish, settle, appoint, determine.

3. Stake, wager, risk.

4. Regulate, adjust, adapt.

5. Stud, variegate, adorn.

6. Place, place upright, cause to sit, put, rest.

7. Arrange, dispose, post, pose.

8. Prescribe, appoint, assign, predetermine.

9. Value, estimate, rate, prize.

10. Embarrass, perplex, pose.

11. Offer for sale, expose.

12. Contrive, produce.

——, *v. i.* 1. Decline, sink, go down (*as the sun*).

2. Concrete, congeal, solidify, harden, consolidate.

3. Flow, run, tend, incline.

——, *a.* 1. Regular, formal, established, prescribed, settled, appointed, ordained.

2. Determined, firm, unyielding, obstinate, fixed, stiff, positive.

3. Predetermined, fixed beforehand.

4. Immovable, fixed.

5. Placed, put, located, fixed.

6. Regular, well-arranged.

——, *n.* 1. Suit, assortment, collection, "kit."

2. Group, school, class, sect, party, knot, division, cluster, company, clique, coterie, circle, "gang."

3. Attitude, position, posture.

Set about. Begin, commence, take in hand, apply one's self to, take the first steps in.

Set apart. Reserve (*for a particular use*), appropriate, dedicate, consecrate, devote, set aside.

Set aside. 1. Reserve, set apart.

2. Omit, leave out of the account.

3. Reject.

4. Abrogate, annul.

Set at ease. Quiet, tranquillize.

Set at naught. 1. Contemn, despise, disregard, undervalue.

2. Break, infringe, transgress, violate.

Set before. Exhibit, display.

Set down. Register, record, state, put in writing, chronicle, make a note of, jot down, take down, make a memorandum of.

Set fire to. Kindle, inflame, ignite, set on fire.

Set forth. 1. Manifest, exhibit, display, show, put forward.

2. Publish, promulgate, make appear.

3. Explain, expound, represent, show, make known.

Set forward. Advance, promote, further.

Set free. Liberate, release, emancipate, disenthrall, clear, acquit.

Set off, *v. t.* 1. Portion off, define the boundaries of.

2. Adorn, decorate, embellish.

Set-off, *n.* 1. Decoration, ornament, embellishment, adornment.

2. Counter-claim, counter-balance, equivalent.

Set on. 1. Incite, instigate, prompt, encourage, spur, urge, impel, influence, actuate.

2. Attack, assault, set upon.

Set on foot. Originate, begin, set in motion, start, set going.

Set out, *v. t.* 1. Publish, proclaim, issue.

2. Show, display, recommend.

3. Show, prove.

Set right. Correct, put in order.

Set store by. Esteem highly, regard much, place a high value on, think a good deal of.

Settle, *n.* Bench, seat, stool.

——, *v. t.* 1. Fix, establish.

2. Decide, determine, make clear, free from doubt, confirm.

3. Adjust, regulate, arrange, compose.

4. Colonize, people.

5. Liquidate, pay, discharge, close up, finish, balance, adjust.

6. Clarify, defecate, fine, clear.

7. Compose, quiet, tranquillize, calm, still, allay, pacify.

8. Place, establish, plant, domicile, make permanent.

——, *v. i.* 1. Subside, sink, fall, gravitate.

2. Rest, repose, be quiet, be tranquil, be composed.

3. Dwell, abide, inhabit, reside, plant one's self, get established.

4. Account, reckon, square accounts, pay up, satisfy all demands.

Settled, *a.* 1. Fixed, established, stable.

2. Deep-rooted, unchanging, steady, decided, firmly seated.

3. Arranged, adjusted.

4. Quiet, orderly, methodical.

5. Established, ordinary, common, wonted, usual, customary, every-day.

Settlement, *n.* 1. Adjustment, arrangement.

2. Reconciliation, pacification.

3. Liquidation, payment, discharge.

4. Colonization.

5. Colony, post.

6. Ordination, installation, establishment, fixture.

Settle on. 1. Fix on, fix upon, determine on.

2. Establish one's habitation upon.

Settler, *n.* Colonist, immigrant, squatter.

Settling, *n.* 1. Planting, colonizing.

2. Subsidence.

Settlings, *n. pl.* Lees, dregs, sediment.

Set-to, *n.* (*Colloq.*) Fight, combat, contest, conflict.

Set to rights. Adjust, regulate, put in order, put to rights.

Set up, *v. t.* 1. Erect, raise, elevate, exalt.

2. Institute, establish, found.

Set upon. Attack, assault, assail, have at, fly at, rush upon.

Sevenfold, *a.* Septuple.

Sever, *v. t.* 1. Part, divide, separate, sunder, rend.

2. Disjoin, disunite, detach, disconnect.

Several, *a.* 1. Separate, distinct, independent, exclusive.

2. Single, individual, particular.

3. Various, manifold, different, diverse, distinct.

4. Sundry, divers.

Severally, *adv.* Separately, distinctly.

Severance, *n.* Separation, partition.

Severe, *a.* 1. Rigid, stern, sharp, harsh, bitter, austere, rigorous, stiff, straitlaced, hard, dour (*Scot.*), unrelenting, relentless, inexorable, bitter, morose.

2. Strict, exact, accurate, methodical.

3. Simple, plain, unadorned, chaste, restrained.

4. Caustic, satirical, sarcastic, keen, cutting, stinging, biting, sharp, harsh, bitter, cruel, trenchant.

5. Distressing, afflictive, acute, violent, extreme, intense, sharp, stringent.

6. Serious, earnest, sedate, grave, austere, sober.

7. Exact, critical, rigorous, hard.

Severely, *adv.* 1. Harshly, sharply, sternly, rigidly.

2. Strictly, rigorously.

3. Painfully, fiercely, extremely, distressingly, afflictively.

Severity, *n.* 1. Sternness, harshness, rigor, austerity, gravity, seriousness, strictness.

2. Strictness, exactness, accuracy, niceness, rigorousness.

3. Simplicity, plainness, chasteness.

4. Sharpness, keenness, causticity, acrimony.

5. Extremity, afflictiveness, violence, keenness, stringency.

6. Harshness, cruel treatment.

Sew, *v. i.* Work with needle and thread, stitch.

——, *v. t.* Stitch, tack, bind.

Sewage, *n.* 1. Contents of a sewer, refuse.

2. Drainage, sewerage.

Sewer, *n.* Drain, cloaca, subterranean canal.

Sewerage, *n.* 1. Drainage, sewage.

2. Sewage, contents of a sewer.

SEX, *n.* Gender, sexuality, masculinity, femininity.

Shabby, *a.* 1. Ragged, worn, faded, threadbare, seedy, worn out, poor, mean.

2. Mean, penurious, stingy, beggarly, paltry, unhandsome, ungentlemanly.

Shackle, *n.* Fetter, gyve, chain, handcuff, manacle.

——, *v. t.* 1. Fetter, chain, manacle, hamper, gyve.

2. Trammel, embarrass, obstruct, clog, impede, restrict, bind, confine, cumber.

SHADE, *n.* 1. Shadow, umbrage.

2. Darkness, obscurity, dusk, duskiness, gloom.

3. Screen, curtain, veil, awning, blind, shutter.

4. Protection, shelter, cover.

5. See Hue, Tint.

6. Degree, kind, variety, minute difference.

7. Ghost, spirit, apparition, spectre, phantom, manes, shadow.

——, *v. t.* 1. Obscure, cloud, darken, eclipse, dim, obfuscate.

2. Screen, cover; ensconce, hide, protect, shelter.

Shades, *n. pl.* Hades, spirit-world, *sheol.*

Shadiness, *n.* Umbrageousness.

Shadow, *n.* 1. Shade, umbrage, umbra, penumbra.

2. Darkness, obscurity, gloom.

3. Shelter, cover, protection, security.

4. Image, adumbration, representation, prefiguration, foreshowing.

5. Spirit, ghost, shade, phantom, apparition.

6. Image, portrait, reflection, silhouette.

——, *v. t.* 1. Shade.

2. Darken, obscure, cloud, becloud.

3. Typify, adumbrate, foreshadow.

4. Protect, shroud, screen, cover, conceal, hide.

5. Typify, symbolize.

Shadowy, *a.* 1. Shady, umbrageous.

2. Dark, obscure, dim, murky, gloomy.

3. Unreal, unsubstantial, impalpable, intangible, visionary, imaginary, spectral, ghostly.

Shady, *a.* Shadowy, umbrageous.

Shaft, *n.* 1. Arrow, missile, weapon.

2. Handle, helve.

3. Thill, pole, tongue.

4. Trunk (*of a column*).

5. Axis, spindle, arbor.

6. Spire, pinnacle.

7. Stem, stalk, trunk.

Shaggy, *a.* 1. Rough (*with long hair or wool*).

2. Rough, rugged.

Shake, *v. t.* 1. Agitate, convulse, jar, jolt, stagger, make to tremble *or* quiver.

2. Intimidate, frighten, daunt.

3. Endanger, weaken, move, make less firm, threaten to overthrow.

4. Wave, oscillate, vibrate.

5. Move, remove, throw off, rid one's self of, put away.

——, *v. i.* Tremble, quake, quiver, quaver, totter, shudder, shiver.

——, *n.* Agitation, concussion, jar, jolt, shaking, tremor, flutter, shock, trembling, shivering, quaking.

Shaky, *a.* Shaking, trembling, quaky, tottering, "jiggly."

Shallow, *a.* 1. Shoal, fleet (*dial.*).

2. Superficial, empty, silly, slight, unintelligent, simple, ignorant.

3. Flimsy, trivial, frivolous, trifling, foolish, puerile, trashy.

——, *n.* Shoal, flat shelf, sand-bank.

Shallow-brained, *a.* Simple, ignorant, foolish, empty-headed, shallow-pated, silly.

Sham, *v. t.* 1. Feign, pretend, make pretence of, imitate, ape.

2. Trick, cheat, delude, dupe.

3. Impose, obtrude by fraud.

——, *v. i.* Deceive, feign, impose, pretend.

Sham, *n.* Imposture, imposition, trick, fraud, feint, delusion, humbug, pretence, clap-trap.

——, *a.* Pretended, false, assumed, feigned, counterfeit, mock, spurious, clap-trap, make-believe.

Shamble, *v. i.* Hobble, shuffle.

Shambles, *n. pl.* Slaughter-house, *abattoir.*

Shame, *n.* 1. Abashment, mortification, chagrin, confusion, humiliation.

2. Disgrace, dishonor, opprobrium, derision, reproach, ignominy, infamy, obloquy, contempt, odium, scandal, degradation, discredit, disrepute.

3. Reproach, disgrace, scandal, dishonor.

4. Decency, decorum, propriety, modesty.

——, *v. t.* 1. Abash, mortify, confuse, confound, disconcert, discompose, humiliate, humble, make ashamed.

2. Disgrace, dishonor, degrade, debase, discredit, sully, taint, stain, tarnish.

3. Deride, jeer, ridicule, mock at, sneer at, point at, flout.

Shame-faced, *a.* Bashful, diffident, overmodest.

Shameful, *a.* 1. Disgraceful, scandalous, dishonorable, disreputable, infamous, outrageous, ignominious, opprobrious, base, vile, villainous, nefarious, heinous, atrocious, wicked, dark.

2. Indecent, unbecoming, degrading, scandalous.

Shameless, *a.* 1. Impudent, unblushing, unabashed, immodest, frontless, assuming, brazen, brazen-faced, bold-faced, insolent, audacious, cool, indecent, indelicate.

2. Depraved, vicious, sinful, unprincipled, corrupt, profligate, dissolute, reprobate, abandoned, graceless, obdurate, hardened, incorrigible, irreclaimable, lost.

Shanty, *n.* Hut, hovel, shed, mean cabin, mean dwelling.

Shape, *v. t.* 1. Form, create, make, produce.

2. Mould, fashion, model, form.

3. Regulate, adjust, direct, frame.

4. Image, conceive, conjure up, figure, imagine.

——, *n.* 1. Form (*with especial reference to what is visible*), figure, make, guise, appearance, outward aspect.

2. Figure, image, appearance, apparition.

3. Mould, model, fashion, cut, pattern, build, cast, form.

Shapeless, *a.* 1. Amorphous, formless.

2. Unsymmetrical, rude, irregular, uncouth, grotesque.

Shapely, *a.* Symmetrical, comely, well-formed, trim.

Shard, *n.* Fragment, potsherd.

Share, *v. t.* 1. Divide, distribute, apportion, parcel out, portion.

2. Partake, participate in, have a portion of.

3. Experience, receive.

——, *v. i.* Participate, have part, have a portion.

——, *n.* 1. Part, portion, certain quantity, quantum.

2. Allotment, dividend, quota, interest, contingent, proportion, apportioned lot, deal, allowance.

Sharer, *n.* Partaker, participator, communicant.

Shark, *n.* Sharper, cheat, swindler, blackleg, knave, trickster, artful fellow.

SHARP, *a.* 1. Acute, keen, keen-edged, cutting, trenchant.

2. Pointed, needle-shaped, acuminate, peaked, ridged.

3. Sagacious, apt, shrewd, astute, acute, canny, penetrating, subtle, perspicacious, discerning, discriminating, ingenious, inventive, witty, quick, clever, ready, smart, shrewd, keen-witted, sharp-witted, clear-sighted, cunning.

4. Biting, pungent, hot, burning, stinging, mordacious, acrid, sour, bitter, acid, poignant, piquant, high-flavored, high-seasoned.

5. Severe, harsh, acrimonious, keen, sarcastic, caustic, cutting, tart, pointed, biting, mordant, trenchant.

6. Rigid, cruel, hard, severe.

7. Distressing, poignant, intense, very painful, afflicting, severe, violent, sore, acute, keen, shooting, lancinating, piercing, subtile, excruciating.

8. Pinching, piercing, nipping, biting.

9. Strong, eager, fierce, ardent, violent, fiery, fervid, impetuous.

10. Shrill, high, piercing.

11. Keen, penetrating, piercing, severe; attentive, vigilant.

12. Shrewd, exacting, close.

Sharp-cut, *a.* Clear, distinct, well-defined.

Sharpen, *v. t.* 1. Edge, make keen, point.

2. Make eager.

3. Sharp, make shrill.

4. Intensify, make more intense.

Sharper, *n.* Cheat, rogue, swindler, trickster, shark, knave, blackleg, tricky fellow, defrauder, deceiver.

Sharply, *adv.* 1. Severely, rigorously, roughly.

2. Vigorously, acutely, keenly.

3. Vehemently, violently.

4. Minutely, exactly, accurately.

5. Wittily, acutely, trenchantly.

6. Steeply, abruptly.

Sharpness, *n.* 1. Acuteness, keenness, trenchancy; acuity, spinosity.

2. Sagacity, shrewdness, ingenuity, wit, cleverness, quickness, smartness, acuteness, discernment, acumen.

3. Pungency, piquancy, acridity, acidity, tartness, sting.

4. Severity, sarcasm, satire, pungency, incisiveness, causticness.

5. Poignancy, intensity, painfulness, keenness, pungency, severity, afflictiveness.

6. Fierceness, violence, ardor.

7. Shrillness, highness.

8. Eagerness, keenness.

Sharp-sighted, *a.* Keen, keen-eyed, keen-sighted, clear-sighted.

Sharp-witted, *a.* Acute, shrewd, quick, sharp, discerning, sagacious, ingenious, intelligent, keen, clear-sighted, keen-sighted, long-headed, cunning.

Shatter, *v. t.* 1. Shiver, burst, break in pieces, dash into fragments, rend, crack, split, smash to bits.

2. Disorder, derange, overthrow, break up, render unsound.

Shave, *v. t.* 1. Cut off (*close to the surface*), make smooth or bare (*as by cutting off hair closely*), pare close, crop, mow.

2. Slice, cut in thin slices.

3. Graze, skim, touch lightly (*in passing over*).

Shaver, *n.* 1. Youngster, child, little fellow, boy.

2. Sharper, extortioner, hard bargainer.

Shear, *v. t.* 1. Cut, clip.

2. Strip, fleece, plunder.

——, *v. i.* 1. Cut, penetrate.

2. Deviate, swerve, turn aside. See SHEER.

Sheath, *n.* Case (*as for a sword*), scabbard, casing, envelope.

Sheathe, *v. t.* 1. Put into a sheath, enclose in a sheath.

2. Cover, case, incase.

Sheathing, *n.* Casing, covering, sheath.

Shed, *v. t.* 1. Spill, effuse, pour out, let fall.

2. Spread, diffuse, scatter, emit, give out.

3. Cast, throw off, put off, let fall, slough.

——, *n.* Hut, hovel, cot, cabin, out-house, shack.

Sheen, *n.* Brightness, splendor, shine, gloss.

SHEEP, *n.* Lamb, ewe, ram.

Sheepcot, } *n.* Sheepfold, sheep-pen.
Sheepcote, }

Sheepish, *a.* Timid, shame-faced, over-modest, very bashful, excessively diffident, timorous.

Sheer, *a.* 1. Pure, clear.

2. Mere, simple, unmixed, unmingled, downright, pure, unqualified, unadulterated, clear, utter.

3. Perpendicular, precipitous, vertical.

——, *v. i.* Deviate, decline, move aside. See SHEAR.

SHELF, *n.* Ledge, bracket, console, mantelpiece.

Shell, *n.* 1. Case, outer covering, shard, carapace.

2. Bomb, grenade, shrapnel.

3. Framework.

——, *v. t.* 1. Take out of the shell, strip the shell from, hull.

2. Bombard.

——, *v. i.* Exfoliate, fall off, peel off, shell off.

Shelter, *n.* 1. Asylum, refuge, retreat, cover, covert, sanctuary, harbor, haven.

2. Protection, shield, screen, defence, security, safety, cover.

3. Guardian, protector.

——, *v. t.* Shield, screen, hide, shroud, protect, defend, cover, house, harbor, ensconce.

Shelve, *v. t.* Put on the shelf, put aside, dismiss.

——, *v. i.* Slope, incline.

Shepherd, *n.* 1. Herdsman (*of sheep*), herder.

2. Pastor, minister, clergyman.

Shibboleth, *n.* Criterion, watchword, test.

Shield, *n.* 1. Buckler, ægis, targe.

2. Safeguard, protection, defence, shelter, guard, cover, security, bulwark, rampart, palladium.

3. Escutcheon, ensign armorial, emblazoned field.

——, *v. t.* 1. Defend, protect, guard, shelter, cover.

2. Ward off, repel, defend against.

3. Forbid, forefend, avert.

Shield-shaped, *a.* Scutate, clypeiform, peltate, peltated.

Shift, *v. t.* Change, alter, move.

——, *v. i.* 1. Move, veer, swerve, chop, dodge, gybe, change place, change about.

2. Alter, change, vary, fluctuate.

3. Contrive, manage, plan, scheme, shuffle, devise ways and means.

——, *n.* 1. Change, turn, substitution.

2. Expedient, contrivance, resort, resource, means.

3. Evasion, artifice, fraud, trick, stratagem, subterfuge, mask, wile, craft,

device, dodge, chicane, chicanery, artful contrivance, *ruse.*

4. Chemise, smock.

Shiftiness, *n.* Changeableness, variableness, unreliability.

Shiftless, *a.* Improvident, imprudent, unresourceful, negligent, slack, thriftless.

Shifty, *a.* Wily, tricky, undependable.

Shillalah, *n.* Club, cudgel, oak sapling.

Shilly-shally, *v. i.* Hesitate, waver.

——, *n.* Irresolution, hesitation, foolish trifling, wavering.

Shimmer, *v. i.* Glimmer, glisten, flash, shine faintly.

Shin, *n.* Fore part of the lower leg, tibia, shinbone.

——, *v. i.* Swarm, climb (*with hands and knees*).

Shindy, *n.* (*Colloq.*) Row, spree, riot, disturbance, uproar, "rough-house."

Shine, *v. i.* 1. Beam, radiate, give light, lighten, blaze, flare, glimmer, glitter, glisten, sparkle, gleam, glow, glare, coruscate, be bright, be brilliant.

2. Be eminent, be distinguished, be conspicuous, excel.

——, *n.* Brightness, luster, brilliancy, polish, gloss, glaze, sheen.

Shining, *a.* 1. Beaming, gleaming.

2. Radiant, bright, splendid, glistening, lustrous, brilliant, glittering, resplendent, effulgent, glowing, luminous.

3. Illustrious, splendid, conspicuous, distinguished.

Shiny, *a.* 1. Bright, clear, sunshiny, unclouded, luminous.

2. Glossy, brilliant, burnished, glassy, polished.

SHIP, *n.* Boat, craft, steamer, vessel, argosy.

Ship-builder, *n.* 1. Naval architect, naval constructor.

2. Ship-carpenter, shipwright.

Ship-shape, *a.* Well-arranged, neat, trim, tidy.

Shipwreck, *n.* Wreck, ruin, perdition, destruction, miscarriage, overthrow, subversion, demolition.

——, *v. t.* Wreck, strand, cast away.

Shirk, *v. t.* 1. Avoid unfairly, evade, dodge, get off from, slink away from.

2. Cheat, trick, shark.

——, *v. i.* Evade one's task, blink, malinger, soldier, be a slacker or quitter.

Shiver, *v. t.* Shatter, break in pieces, dash to fragments.

——, *v. i.* Shudder, quake, tremble, quiver, shake.

——, *n.* 1. Sliver, slice, fragment, bit, piece.

2. Tremor, tremulous motion, shivering, shaking, shuddering.

Shivery, *a.* Friable, brittle, frangible, incompact.

Shoal, *n.* 1. Crowd, throng, multitude, swarm, horde.

2. Shallow, sand-bank, bar.

——, *v. i.* 1. Crowd, throng.

2. Grow shallow.

SHOCK, *n.* 1. Concussion, collision, shog, clash, blow, stroke, impact, percussion.

2. Brunt, onset, assault, hostile encounter, conflict.

3. Blow, stroke, agitation, offence.

4. Stook, hattock.

——, *v. t.* 1. Shake, strike against, jar, jolt, collide with.

2. Encounter, meet.

3. Offend, disgust, disturb, disquiet, nauseate, sicken, scandalize, revolt, outrage.

4. Stun, astound, stagger.

5. Appall, horrify.

——, *a.* Shaggy, matted, shagged.

Shocking, *a.* 1. Repulsive, offensive, hateful, detestable, execrable, obnoxious, odious, disgusting, revolting, repugnant, disgraceful, loathsome, foul, abominable.

2. Dreadful, terrible, horrid, horrible, fearful, frightful, dire, horrific, awful, hideous, monstrous, ghastly, appalling.

SHOE, *n.* Footwear, boot, sandal, slipper.

Shoemaker, *n.* Crispin, cordwainer.

Shoot, *v. t.* 1. Let fly, propel, expel, catapult, hurl.

2. Fire, discharge, let off.

3. Hit *or* kill by a missile, pelt.

4. Protrude, dart forth, thrust forward.

5. Extend, put forth, thrust forth, send forth.

6. Dart, emit.

——, *v. i.* 1. Fire, discharge a missile.

2. Pass, fly, dart.

3. Bud, sprout, germinate.

4. Project, jut, stretch, push, protuberate.

——, *n.* Sprout, branch, twig, scion, offshoot.

Shoot up. Grow, increase, spring up, run up, grow up, start up.

Shop, *n.* 1. Store, market, mart, emporium.

2. Workshop.

Shopkeeper, *n.* Tradesman, shopman, retail trader, storekeeper.

Shore, *n.* 1. Coast, beach, brim, strand, sea-board, sea-side, waterside.

2. Prop, support, stay, brace, buttress.

Shorn, *a.* 1. Cut off.

2. Deprived.

SHORT, *a.* 1. Brief, curtailed.

2. Near, direct, straight.

3. Compendious, succinct, concise, condensed, terse, pithy, sententious, laconic, brief, summary.

4. Abrupt, sharp, pointed, petulant, curt, snappish, uncivil.

5. Deficient, defective, inadequate, scanty, niggardly, "scrimpy," insufficient.

6. Limited, contracted, lacking, wanting, "minus," destitute.

7. Dwarfish, squat, undersized.

8. Brittle, friable, crumbling, crisp.

Short, *adv.* Suddenly, abruptly, at once, forthwith.

Short-coming, *n.* 1. Deficiency.

2. Slip, fault, error, failing, delinquency, remissness, defect, weakness, deficiency, imperfection, failure.

Shorten, *v. t.* 1. Abbreviate, abridge, cut short, curtail.

2. Lessen, diminish, contract, reduce, abridge, retrench.

3. Curtail, cut off, lop, dock, trim.

4. Confine, restrain, restrict, hinder.

Shortening, *n.* Abbreviation, curtailment, abridgment, contraction, reduction, retrenchment, diminution.

Short-hand, *n.* Stenography, brachygraphy, tachygraphy.

Short-lived, *a.* Transient, ephemeral, mushroom, transitory.

Shortly, *adv.* 1. Soon, quickly, in a short time, in a little time.

2. Briefly, concisely, tersely, succinctly, in a few words.

Shortness, *n.* 1. Brevity, conciseness, terseness.

2. Deficiency, deficit, shortage, insufficiency, imperfection, poverty.

Short-sighted, *a.* 1. Myopic, purblind, nearsighted.

2. Imprudent, indiscreet.

Shot, *n.* 1. Discharge.

2. Ball, bullet, missile, projectile.

3. Marksman, shooter.

——, *a.* 1. Chatoyant, iridescent, irisated.

2. Interwoven, interspersed, intermingled.

Shoulder, *n.* Projection, protuberance.

Shoulder-blade, *n.* Shoulder-bone, blade-bone, omoplate, scapula.

Shout, *v. i.* Exclaim, vociferate, halloo, cheer, clamor, whoop, bawl, roar, yell.

——, *n.* Halloo, huzza, hoot, outcry, clamor, vociferation. See the verb.

Shove, *v. t.* 1. Push, propel.

2. Jostle, push aside, press against.

Shove off. Thrust away, push away.

Show, *v. t.* 1. Exhibit, display, present to view, parade, flaunt, blazon.

2. Indicate, point out.

3. Disclose, divulge, proclaim, publish, explain, unfold, reveal, discover, make known, make clear.

4. Prove, manifest, demonstrate, evidence, verify.

5. Conduct, guide, usher.

6. Teach, instruct, inform, direct.

7. Explain, expound, interpret, make clear, elucidate.

——, *v. i.* 1. Appear, become visible.

2. Appear, look, seem.

——, *n.* 1. Spectacle, exhibition, array, sight, representation.

2. Parade, ostentation, demonstration, flourish, dash, bravery, blazonry, pomp, pageantry, splendor, display, "splurge," ceremony.

3. Semblance, resemblance, likeness, external appearance.

4. Pretence, pretext, color, mask, simulation, speciousness, plausibility, illusion.

Show off. 1. *v. t.* Exhibit (*ostentatiously*), display, make a parade of, set off.

2. *v. i.* Make a show, display one's self, put on airs.

Show up. Expose.

Showy, *a.* 1. Gaudy, flashy, gay, loud, glaring, garish, flaunting, gorgeous, splendid, fine, dressy, "swanky," smart, ornate, bedizened, pranked out, tinsel.

2. Grand, stately, ostentatious, pompous, pretentious, magnificent, sumptuous.

Shred, *n.* 1. Strip.

2. Scrap, fragment, bit, piece, flitter, tatter, rag, strip.

Shrew, *n.* Brawler, scold, spitfire, termagant, vixen, virago, fury, turbulent woman.

Shrewd, *a.* 1. Artful, cunning, sly, wily, subtle, crafty, arch, astute, Machiavelian.

2. Sagacious, acute, sharp, canny, discriminating, astute, sharp-sighted, penetrating, keen, ingenious, discerning, knowing.

Shrewdness, *n.* 1. Cunning, archness, artfulness, subtlety, craft, astuteness, slyness, art, address, skill, policy.

2. Sagacity, acumen, acuteness, perspicacity, sharpness, keenness, ingenuity, discernment, penetration, mother-wit.

Shrewish, *a.* Froward, peevish, petulant, scolding, brawling, clamorous, vixenish.

Shriek, *v. i.* Scream, screech, squeal, yelp, yell.

——, *n.* Scream, screech, yell, shrill cry.

Shrill, *a.* Acute, sharp, high, high-toned, high-pitched, piercing, piping.

Shrine, *n.* 1. Reliquary, sacred tomb.

2. Altar, sacred place, sacred object, hallowed place.

Shrink, *v. i.* 1. Shrivel, contract, decrease, dwindle, wither.

2. Recoil, blench, flinch, quail, wince, balk, withdraw, retire, swerve, draw back, give way.

Shrivel, *v. t.* Parch, dry, dry up.

——, *v. i.* Shrink, contract, dwindle, wither, decrease, wrinkle.

Shroud, *n.* 1. Garment, covering.

2. Winding-sheet, grave-clothes, cerement.

——, *v. t.* Cover, hide, veil, mask, cloak, screen, bury, muffle, protect, shelter, conceal.

Shrub, *n.* Bush, low tree, dwarf-tree.

Shrubby, *a.* Bushy.

Shrunk, *a.* Shrivelled, withered, dwindled, contracted.

Shudder, *v. i.* Tremble, shake, quake, quiver, shiver.

——, *n.* Tremor, shuddering, shaking, trembling.

Shuffle, *v. t.* Confuse, jumble, mix, shift, intermix, throw into disorder.

——, *v. i.* 1. Prevaricate, quibble, equivocate, cavil, dodge, palter, evade, sophisticate.

2. Struggle, shift, make shift.

——, *n.* Trick, quibble, prevarication, cavil, sophism, evasion, artifice, fraud, shuffling, subterfuge, pretence, pretext, *ruse.*

Shun, *v. t.* Avoid (*in a positive sense* or *denoting positive exertion*), evade, escape, elude, eschew, get clear of.

Shunt, *v. t.* [*Eng.*] Switch (*from one set of rails to another*).

SHUT, *v. t.* [*The adjective is Basic Eng.*]
1. Close, close up, stop.

2. Enclose, confine, imprison, shut up, coop up, lock up, close the door upon.

3. Close to, slam, clap to.

Shut in. Enclose, confine.

Shut off. Exclude, bar, intercept.

Shut up. 1. Shut, close up.

2. Confine, lock up, enclose, imprison, lock in, fasten in.

Shy, *a.* 1. Timid, coy, reserved, diffident, bashful, sheepish, retiring, shrinking.

2. Cautious, wary, heedful, chary, distrustful.

——, *n.* 1. Sudden start (*as of a horse*).

2. (*Colloq.*) Fling, throw.

——, *v. t.* Fling, throw, jerk, cast, toss, flirt, hurl, chuck, pitch, "sling."

——, *v. i.* Sheer, start aside, boggle.

Sibilant, *a.* Hissing, sibilous, buzzing.

Sibyl, *n.* Prophetess, sorceress, fortune-teller, witch.

Siccative, *a.* Drying.

Sick, *a.* 1. Ill, indisposed, ailing, unwell, laid up.

2. Nauseated, affected with nausea, sick at the stomach, queasy.

3. Disgusted, tired, weary.

4. Diseased, weak, morbid, unsound, distempered, disordered, feeble.

5. Pining, languishing, longing.

Sicken, *v. t.* 1. Disease, make sick.

2. Nauseate, make sick, turn one's stomach, make qualmish.

3. Disgust, weary.

——, *v. i.* 1. Become sick, fall sick, fall ill, ail, droop, pine.

2. Be disgusted, feel disgust, become qualmish.

3. Decay, languish, become weak, become distempered.

Sickening, *a.* 1. Nauseating, nauseous, sickish, palling.

2. Disgusting, distasteful, repulsive, revolting, foul, loathsome, offensive.

Sickle-shaped, *a.* Falcate, falcated, hooked.

Sickliness, *n.* Unhealthiness, insalubrity, pining, ailing.

Sickly, *a.* Weak, languid, faint, feeble, ailing, languishing, unhealthy, diseased, infirm, weakly, morbid, valetudinary.

Sickness, *n.* 1. Illness, disease, disorder, distemper, malady, complaint, ail, ailment, indisposition, morbidity, invalidism.

2. Nausea, qualmishness, queasiness.

SIDE, *n.* 1. Verge, margin, edge, border, flank.

2. Party, sect, faction, interest, cause.

——, *a.* 1. Lateral, flanking, skirting.

2. Indirect, oblique.

Side-board, *n.* Buffet, dresser.

Side by side. Abreast, alongside, by the side (*of one another*).

Sideling, *a.* Sloping, inclined, oblique.

Sidelong, *a.* Lateral, oblique.

——, *adv.* 1. Laterally, obliquely.

2. On the side.

Sidereal, *a.* Starry, stellar, astral.

Sidewalk, *n.* Footway (*at the side of a street*), footpath.

Sidewise, *adv.* Laterally, sideways, sideling.

Siege, *n.* Beleaguerment, investment, blockade.

Siesta, *n.* [Sp.] Nap (*after dinner*), doze.

Sift, *v. t.* 1. Bolt, screen, winnow.

2. Separate, part.

3. Scrutinize, probe, fathom, sound, try, analyze, investigate, canvass, discuss, examine critically, look into, follow up, inquire into.

Sigh, *n.* Long breath, suspiration, sough.

Sigh, *v. i.* Grieve, mourn, complain, lament.

Sight, *n.* 1. Perception, view, ken, cognizance.

2. Vision, eyesight, beholding, seeing.

3. Spectacle, prospect, scene, show, exhibition, representation.

4. Knowledge, view, estimation, consideration.

5. Inspection, examination.

——, *v. t.* See, perceive, get sight of.

Sightless, *a.* Blind, eyeless, unseeing.

Sightly, *a.* Comely, handsome, beautiful.

SIGN, *n.* 1. Token, mark, note, indication, proof, signification,' index, symptom, manifestation, symbol, emblem.

2. Signal, beacon.

3. Prodigy, wonder, miracle, portent, augury, presage, prognostic, auspice, foreboding, omen.

4. Symbol, type.

5. Countersign, password.

——, *v. t.* 1. Signify, indicate.

2. Subscribe, indorse, countersign, put one's name to, affix one's signature to.

Signal, *n.* Token, mark, indication, sign, cue.

——, *a.* Eminent, memorable, extraordinary, remarkable, notable, noteworthy, conspicuous.

Signalize, *v. t.* Distinguish, celebrate, make memorable.

Signature, *n.* 1. Stamp, mark, sign.

2. Sign-manual, autograph, hand.

Signet, *n.* Seal (*especially of a sovereign*).

Significance, *n.* 1. Meaning, import, implication, purport, sense.

2. Importance, consequence, weight, moment, portent.

3. Expressiveness, impressiveness, force, emphasis, energy.

Significant, *a.* 1. Betokening, indicative, expressive, signifying, significative.

2. Important, weighty, momentous, portentous.

3. Forcible, eminently expressive, emphatic, telling.

Signification, *n.* 1. Expression.

2. Meaning, sense, import, purport, acceptation.

Signify, *v. t.* 1. Express, communicate, intimate, indicate, betoken.

2. Denote, betoken, mean, imply, purport, import, suggest.

3. Declare, proclaim, impart, announce, give notice of, manifest, utter, make known.

4. Indicate, betoken, portend, augur, foreshadow, suggest as being in prospect, represent.

5. Weigh, matter, import.

——, *v. i.* Import, matter, be of importance, be of consequence.

Silence, *n.* 1. Stillness, noiselessness, hush, soundlessness, quiet, quietude, lull, calm, peace.

2. Taciturnity, muteness, dumbness, "mumness," reticence.

——, *v. t.* 1. Still, hush, put to silence, muzzle.

2. Allay, quiet, calm, put to rest, put an end to.

——, *interj.* Hush, whist, soft, tush, chut, tut, be still, be silent, hold your tongue.

Silent, *a.* 1. Still, noiseless, soundless, hushed, quiet, calm.

2. Mute, dumb, speechless, nonvocal, tacit, "mum," inarticulate.

3. Taciturn, reticent, uncommunicative.

SILK, *n.* (*Basic Eng.*)

Silken, *a.* Silky, soft, flossy.

Silkiness, *n.* Smoothness, softness.

Sill, *n.* 1. Lower piece of a frame (*as of a door* or *a window*).

2. Ground-sill, ground-plate, threshold.

Silly, *a.* 1. Senseless, witless, stupid, foolish, simple, childish, inept, weak-minded, brainless, shallow.

2. Absurd, trifling, frivolous, extravagant, preposterous, nonsensical, unwise, indiscreet, imprudent.

Silt, *n.* Sediment, deposit, alluvium.

SILVER, *a.* [*The noun is Basic Eng.*]

1. Silvery, of silver, silvern, argent.

2. White, bright, of the color of silver, silvery.

3. Soft and clear (*as sound*), mellifluous.

Similar, *a.* 1. Like, resembling, analogous, duplicate, twin.

2. Homogeneous, uniform.

Similarity, *n.* Likeness, resemblance, parallelism, analogy, correspondence, agreement, parity, similitude, sameness, semblance.

Simile, *n.* Similitude, comparison, metaphor.

Similitude, *n.* 1. Likeness, resemblance, image.

2. Simile, comparison, metaphor.

Simmer, *v. i.* Boil (*gently*), seethe, stew, bubble.

Simmering, *a.* Boiling, piping.

Simper, *v. i.* Smile (*affectedly*), smirk.

SIMPLE, *a.* 1. Single, uncombined, unmingled, unalloyed, uncompounded, unmixed, homogeneous, elementary, bare, mere, incomplex, unblended.

2. Plain, homespun, unadorned, inornate, unstudied, unaffected, unpreten-

tious, unvarnished, natural, chaste, neat, unembellished.

3. Artless, undesigning, guileless, sincere, unaffected, unconstrained, frank, open, downright, inartificial, plain, single-minded, unsophisticated, ingenuous, straightforward, true, simple-hearted, simple-minded, *naïve*.

4. Silly, foolish, fatuous, weak, credulous, shallow, unwise.

5. Unmistakable, clear, intelligible, understandable, plain, uninvolved.

Simple-hearted, *a.* Ingenuous, frank, open, artless, single-hearted, simple.

Simpleton, *n.* Fool, ninny, "greenhorn," "nincompoop."

Simplicity, *n.* 1. Plainness, homeliness, naturalness, chasteness, neatness.

2. Artlessness, simplesse, sincerity, frankness, openness. See the adjective, 3.

3. Plainness, clearness.

4. Silliness, folly, weakness.

Simply, *adv.* 1. Plainly, artlessly, sincerely, unaffectedly.

2. Alone, absolutely.

3. Merely, barely, solely, of itself.

Simulate, *v. t.* Feign, counterfeit, act, ape, mimic, sham, affect, pretend, assume.

Simulation, *n.* Feigning, counterfeiting, personation, pretence.

Simultaneous, *a.* Concomitant, concurrent, coincident, synchronous, contemporaneous, coeval.

Sin, *n.* 1. Offence (*against the divine law*), transgression, iniquity, unrighteousness, guilt, wickedness, moral depravity, wrong, delinquency.

2. Offence, transgression, misdeed.

——, *v. i.* Trespass, do wrong, transgress, err.

Since, *conj.* Because, as, considering, seeing that, because that, inasmuch as.

——, *adv.* 1. Ago, before this.

2. From that time.

——, *prep.* After, from the time of, subsequently to.

Sincere, *a.* 1. Pure, unmixed.

2. True, real, unfeigned, genuine, unaffected, unvarnished, inartificial, honest.

3. Honest, ingenuous, open, frank, candid, straightforward, whole-hearted, hearty, undissembling, artless, guileless, single, truthful, true, upright, direct, plain.

Sincerely, *adv.* 1. Perfectly, purely.

2. Honestly, unfeignedly.

Sincerity, *n.* Honesty, ingenuousness, candor, frankness, artlessness, unaffectedness, guilelessness, probity, veracity, truth, truthfulness, genuineness, earnestness.

Sinew, *n.* 1. Tendon, ligament.

2. Muscle, nerve, brawn, strength.

Sinewy, *a.* Muscular, brawny, wiry, nervous, vigorous, firm, stalwart, strapping, robust, powerful, sturdy, strong, Herculean, able-bodied, made of iron.

Sinful, *a.* Wicked, unrighteous, peccant, transgressive, iniquitous, unholy, wrong, immoral, depraved, criminal, mischievous, bad.

Sinfulness, *n.* Wickedness, depravity, unrighteousness, iniquity, unholiness, criminality, ungodliness, irreligion, moral corruption.

Sing, *v. i.* Carol, chant, lilt, troll, yodel, warble.

——, *v. t.* Carol, chant, intone, cantillate, warble, hum, hymn, celebrate in song.

Singe, *v. t.* Scorch, burn (*slightly*), sear.

Singer, *n.* Chanter, songster, caroler, cantor, gleeman, psalmodist, prima donna, vocalist, minstrel.

Single, *a.* 1. Sole, one only, alone, solitary, isolated.

2. Particular, individual, separate.

3. Unmarried, unwedded, celibate.

4. Pure, simple, unmixed, uncompounded.

5. Sincere, uncorrupt, unbiassed, upright, ingenuous, simple, honest.

Single-handed, *a.* Alone, unaided, unassisted, by one's self.

Single-minded, *a.* Ingenuous, guileless, sincere, candid, artless.

Singleness, *n.* 1. Unity, individuality.

2. Purity, simplicity.

3. Sincerity, integrity, uprightness, ingenuousness.

Single out. Choose, select, single, pick.

Singular, *a.* 1. Single, individual.

2. Single, uncompounded, not complex.

3. Unusual, uncommon, exceptional, eminent, rare, unwonted, strange, extraordinary, remarkable.

4. Particular, exceptional, unexampled, unparalleled, remarkable, unprecedented.

5. Unaccountable, strange.

6. Peculiar, odd, eccentric, queer, fantastic, *bizarre*.

Singularity, *n.* 1. Uncommonness, rareness, rarity, strangeness, oddness, abnormity, aberration, irregularity.

2. Peculiarity, particularity, idiosyncrasy, individuality.

3. Eccentricity, oddity, queerness, strangeness.

Sinister, *a.* 1. Left, on the left hand.

2. Unlucky, inauspicious, ominous, boding ill.

3. Baleful, untoward, injurious.

Sink, *v. i.* 1. Fall (*gradually*), subside, submerge, founder, descend, go down, go to the bottom.

2. Fall slowly, drop, droop.

3. Penetrate, enter.

4. Be depressed, be overwhelmed, collapse, fail.

5. Decline, decrease, decay, dwindle, languish, lose strength, give way.

——, *v. t.* 1. Merge, submerge, submerse, immerse, engulf.

2. Dig, excavate, scoop out.

3. Depress, degrade, lower, abase, debase, diminish, lessen, bring down, let down.

4. Ruin, destroy, waste, overthrow, overwhelm, swamp.

5. Depress, overbear, crush.

6. Reduce, bring low.

——, *n.* Drain, sewer, cloaca.

Sinless, *a.* 1. Guileless, innocent, spotless, unspotted, faultless, immaculate, impeccable, unblemished, untarnished, undefiled, unsullied.

2. Pure, perfect, holy.

Sinner, *n.* Offender, delinquent, criminal, reprobate, wrong-doer, evil-doer, wicked person.

Sinuosity, *n.* Curvature, flexure, crook, winding, tortuosity, sinus.

Sinuous, *a.* Winding, crooked, curved, curvilinear, sinuate, sinuated, serpentine, tortuous, flexuous, bending in and out, undulating, wavy.

Sinus, *n.* [L.] 1. Bay, recess.

2. Hollow, opening, bending, sinuosity.

3. (*Conch.*) Groove, cavity.

Sip, *v. t.* 1. Drink (*a little at a time*), sup, suck up.

2. Absorb, drink in (*in small quantities*).

——, *n.* Taste, small draught.

Sire, *n.* Father, progenitor, male parent.

Siren, *n.* 1. Mermaid.

2. Tempter, seducer, Circe, bewitching *or* fascinating woman.

——, *a.* Alluring, seducing, tempting, bewitching, fascinating.

SISTER, *n.* Soror (*Lat.*), sibling; nun.

Sit, *v. i.* 1. Be seated, have a seat.

2. Perch (*as a bird*).

3. Stay, be, rest, remain, repose, abide.

4. Lie, bear on, rest.

5. Dwell, settle, rest, abide, be placed, have a seat.

6. Brood (*as fowls*), incubate.

7. Fit, be adjusted, suit, become, be suited.

Site, *n.* See SITUATION, 1.

Sitting, *n.* Session.

Situation, *n.* 1. Place, locality, station, location, whereabouts, site, position, seat, ground, spot.

2. Condition, state, plight, case, predicament, juncture, category, circumstances.

3. Post, station, office, employment, place.

SIZE, *n.* Bigness, greatness, magnitude, amplitude, mass, bulk, volume, dimensions, largeness, expanse.

Sizing, *n.* Size, weak glue.

Skeleton, *n.* 1. Framework.

2. Sketch, outline, draught, rough draught.

Skeptic, *n.* 1. Doubter, questioner, Pyrrhonist.

2. Deist, infidel,, unbeliever, freethinker.

Skeptical, *a.* Doubting, unbelieving, incredulous, questioning.

Skepticism, *n.* 1. Doubt, incredulity, Pyrrhonism, agnosticism.

2. Unbelief, infidelity, free-thinking.

Sketch, *n.* Outline, drawing, delineation, plan, skeleton, rough draught, first draught, design in outline.

——, *v. t.* 1. Draw (*in outline*), chalk out, make a rough draught of, design, draught.

2. Depict, delineate, represent, portray, paint.

Sketchy, *a.* Incomplete, unfinished, crude.

Skilful, *a.* Skilled, well-versed, versed, conversant, proficient, cunning, "feat," deft, ingenious, competent, able, clever, qualified, practised, trained, accomplished, expert, adept, dexterous, adroit, apt, handy, ready, quick, masterly.

Skill, *n.* 1. Skilfulness, dexterity, deftness, aptness, adroitness, readiness, facility, expertness, cleverness, quickness, knack, address, ingenuity, ability, art, aptitude.

2. Discrimination, discernment, understanding, wit, knowledge.

Skim, *v. i.* Pass lightly *or* superficially.

SKIN, *n.* 1. Hide, pelt, derm, *cutis*, integument, epidermis, cuticle, pellicle.

2. Husk, hull, peel, rind.

——, *v. t.* Flay, excoriate, decorticate, pare, peel.

Skinflint, *n.* Miser, niggard, churl, hunks, scrimp, screw, curmudgeon, lick-penny, sordid wretch.

Skinny, *a.* Lean, poor, thin, lank, shrunk, emaciated, shrivelled.

Skip, *n.* and *v. i.* Leap, jump, bound, spring, hop, caper, frisk, gambol.

——, *v. t.* Disregard, omit, intermit, neglect, miss, skip over, pass without notice.

Skipper, *n.* Master (*of a small vessel*), sea-captain.

Skirmish, *n.* Fight (*of slight consequence*), battle, collision, conflict, combat, brush, affair, contest, encounter.

SKIRT, *n.* 1. Flap, loose part (*of a garment below the waist*), kilt, overskirt.

2. Petticoat.

3. Edge, border, margin, verge, rim, extreme part.

——, *v. t.* Border, lie *or* move along the edge of.

Skittish, *a.* 1. Shy (*as a horse*), timid, timorous, easily frightened.

2. Hasty, volatile, wanton.

3. Changeable, inconstant, fickle.

Skulk, *v. i.* Lurk, hide, sneak, slink, lie hid.

Skulker, *n.* 1. Lurker, sneak, mean fellow.

2. Shirk, malingerer, "slacker."

Skull, *n.* Cranium, brain-pan.

SKY, *n.* Firmament, heavens, empyrean, canopy of heaven, celestial expanse, welkin.

Sky-blue, *a.* Cerulean, azure, sky-colored, sapphire.

Skylarking, *n.* Frolicking, sporting, carousing.

Slab, *a.* Thick, viscous, slimy.

——, *n.* Slime, puddle, mud.

Slabber, *v. t.* Slaver, slobber.

——, *v. i.* 1. Slaver, drivel.

2. Shed, spill, drop, let fall.

Slabby, *a.* 1. Viscous, sticky, glutinous, thick.

2. Wet, slimy, muddy, sloppy, miry.

Slack, *a.* 1. Backward, remiss, careless, lax, negligent.

2. Slow, tardy, dilatory, lingering, abated, diminished.

3. Loose, relaxed.

4. Dull, idle, quiet, inactive, sluggish.

Slacken, *v. i.* 1. Slack, abate, become less intense, be diminished.

2. Become loose *or* slack, be made less tight *or* tense, relax.

3. Neglect, be remiss, be backward, fail.

4. Slow down, flag.

——, *v. t.* Retard, slack, moderate, make slower.

2. Loosen, relax, make less tight *or* tense, lessen the tension of.

3. Lessen, diminish, abate, mitigate, remit, relieve.

4. Relax, neglect, be remiss in, defer, put off.

5. Abate, lower, make less.

6. Repress, check, restrain, curb, bridle, control.

Slackness, *n.* 1. Looseness.

2. Remissness, negligence, inattention.

3. Slowness, tardiness, want of effort.

Slag, *n.* Refuse, dross, recrement, cinder, clinker, scoria.

Slake, *v. t.* 1. Quench, extinguish, allay, abate, sate, satiate, decrease, slacken.

2. Slack (*as lime*).

——, *v. i.* 1. Desist, fail, go out, be quenched, become extinct.

2. Abate, decrease, become less decided.

Slam, *v. t.* Bang, shut with noise.

Slander, *v. t.* 1. Defame, calumniate, vilify, scandalize, decry, reproach, malign, traduce, brand, blacken, asperse, backbite, libel, belie.

2. Disparage, detract from.

——, *n.* Defamation, aspersion, detraction, calumny, backbiting, scandal, libel, obloquy, vilification.

Slanderous, *a.* Calumnious, defamatory, maligning, libellous, false and malicious.

Slang, *n.* Cant, jargon, argot, lingo, low language, inelegant expression.

Slant, *n.* Slope, inclination, steep, tilt.

——, *v. i.* Slope, lean, incline, lie obliquely, list.

Slanting, *a.* Inclining, sloping, oblique, slant.

Slap, *n.* Blow (*with something broad*), clap.

——, *adv.* With a slap, plumply, quickly, instantly.

——, *v. t.* Strike (*with something broad*), dab, smack, clap, pat, spank.

Slap-dash, *adv.* (*Colloq.*) In a hurry-skurry, without forethought, at haphazard, precipitately.

Slash, *v. t.* Slit, gash.

——, *n.* Slit, long cut.

Slashed, *a.* 1. Slit, cut.

2. (*Bot.*) Laciniate, multifid, jagged.

Slattern, *n.* Slut, drab, draggletail, sloven, trollop.

——, *a.* Slovenly, slatternly, sluttish.

Slatternly, *a.* Slovenly, slattern, untidy, uncleanly, dirty, sluttish.

——, *adv.* Negligently, carelessly, sluttishly, untidily, in a slovenly manner.

Slaty, *a.* Laminated, laminar, schistous, schistose.

Slaughter, *n.* Massacre, murder, carnage, bloodshed, butchery, havoc, killing, slaying.

——, *v. t.* Massacre, slay, kill, murder, butcher.

Slaughterer, *n.* Murderer, assassin, slayer, killer, butcher, cut-throat, destroyer.

Slave, *n.* 1. Bondman, bond-servant, bond-slave, helot, captive, vassal, henchman, dependant, peon, serf, thrall.

2. Drudge, menial.

——, *v. i.* Drudge, toil, moil.

Slavery, *n.* 1. Bondage, servitude, serfdom, thraldom, enthralment, enslavement, captivity, bond-service, vassalage, villeinage.

2. Drudgery, mean labor.

Slavic, *a.* Slavonic, Slavonian.

Slavish, *a.* 1. Servile, low, mean, base, cringing, obsequious, fawning, supple, grovelling, abject, beggarly.

2. Drudging, laborious, menial, servile.

Slay, *v. t.* 1. Kill, slaughter, murder, massacre, dispatch, butcher, assassinate.

2. Destroy, ruin, put an end to.

Slayer, *n.* Killer, murderer, destroyer, slaughterer, assassin.

Sledge, *n.* 1. [*Eng.*] Sled, drag.

2. Sleigh, cutter, pung.

Sleek, *a.* Smooth, glossy, silken, silky, satin.

Sleekly, *adv.* Smoothly, glossily, nicely, evenly.

Sleep, *v. i.* 1. Slumber, rest, repose, doze, "snooze," drowse, nap.

2. Rest, be still, be motionless.

SLEEP, *n.* 1. Slumber, dormancy, lethargy, hypnosis, repose, rest.

2. Drowse, dose, nap, catnap, siesta.

Sleepily, *adv.* 1. Drowsily.

2. Lazily, dully, stupidly, heavily.

Sleepiness, *n.* Drowsiness, somnolence, doziness, dormancy, inclination to sleep.

Sleeping, *a.* Dormant, inactive, quiescent.

Sleep-walker, *n.* Somnambulist, nightwalker, noctambulist.

Sleep-walking, *n.* Somnambulism.

Sleepy, *a.* 1. Drowsy, somnolent, dozy, heavy, lethargic, nodding, comatose, inclined to sleep.

2. Somniferous, soporiferous, narcotic, soporific, somnific, slumberous, opiate.

3. Sluggish, inactive, heavy, lazy, dull, torpid, slow.

Sleight, *n.* 1. Sly artifice, artful trick.

2. Adroitness, dexterity, manoeuvring, dexterous management.

Sleight of hand. Legerdemain, hocuspocus, jugglery, prestidigitation.

Slender, *a.* 1. Slim, thin, narrow, lank, lithe, spindling, skinny, slight.

2. Weak, feeble, slight, tenuous, fragile, flimsy, fine.

3. Small, inconsiderable, moderate, trivial.

4. Meagre, scanty, exiguous, inadequate, small, insufficient, pitiful, lean.

5. Spare, sparing, abstemious, light, meagre, simple.

Slice, *v. t.* 1. Cut (*into thin pieces*), skive, pare.

2. Cut, divide, part, section.

3. Cut off, sever.

——, *n.* Collop, chop, thin piece.

Slick, *a.* [*Dial.*] Smooth, sleek.

Slide, *v. i.* Glide, slip, move smoothly.

——, *n.* Glide, slip, skid, glissade.

Sliding, *a.* Slippery, uncertain, gliding.

——, *n.* Lapse, falling, backsliding, transgression, fault.

Slight, *a.* 1. Small, little, trifling, inconsiderable, trivial, petty, paltry, insignificant, unimportant, unsubstantial.

2. Weak, feeble, frail, delicate, gentle.

3. Cursory, hasty, hurried, desultory, superficial, scanty, careless, negligent.

4. Perishable, flimsy.

5. Slim, slender.

——, *n.* Neglect, disregard, inattention, discourtesy, disrespect, indignity.

——, *v. t.* 1. Neglect, disregard, disdain, cold-shoulder, snub.

2. Overlook.

3. Do negligently, scamp, slur over.

Slightingly, *adv.* Disrespectfully, scornfully, contemptuously, slightly, with contempt, with scorn.

Slightly, *adv.* 1. Little, inconsiderably, somewhat.

2. Weakly, feebly, slenderly.

3. Cursorily, negligently, hastily, superficially.

Slim, *a.* 1. Slender, spare, thin, narrow, lank, lithe, skinny, gaunt.

2. Weak, slight, trivial, trifling, paltry, unsubstantial, inconsiderable, poor.

3. Insufficient, meager.

Slime, *n.* Mud, ooze, mire, sludge.

Slimy, *a.* 1. Miry, muddy, oozy.

2. Ropy, clammy, viscous, viscid, glutinous, gummy, mucilaginous, gelatinous, lubricous, mucous, slabby.

Sling, *v. t.* 1. Throw, cast, hurl, fling.

2. Hang up, suspend.

Slink, *v. i.* Sneak, skulk, steal away, slip away.

Slip, *v. i.* 1. Glide, slide.

2. Err, trip, mistake, fall into error, commit a fault.

——, *v. t.* 1. Put stealthily, convey secretly.

2. Omit, allow to escape, lose by negligence.

3. Throw off, disengage one's self from.

4. Loose, loosen, let loose, let go.

SLIP, *n.* 1. Slide, glide, slipping.

2. Error, mistake, blunder, fault, peccadillo, misstep, trip, oversight.

3. Transgression, impropriety, indiscretion, backsliding, error, fault.

4. Cutting, twig, shoot, scion.

5. Strip, long and narrow piece, streak.

6. Leash, strap, string, cord.

7. Escape, desertion.

8. Case, covering, wrapper.

Slipperiness, n. 1. Lubricity, smoothness.

2. Uncertainty, mutability, changeableness, unsteadiness, instability.

3. Lubricity, untrustworthiness, shiftiness.

Slippery, a. 1. Smooth, glib, slithery.

2. Unstable, uncertain, changeable, mutable, unsteady, shaky, insecure, perilous, unsafe.

3. Treacherous, perfidious, faithless, knavish, dishonest, false, cunning, shifty, elusive.

Slipshod, a. Careless, slovenly, shuffling, untidy.

Slit, v. t. 1. Cut (lengthwise).

2. Sunder, divide, rend, slash, split.

——, n. Long cut.

Slobber, v. t. 1. Slabber, slaver, drivel, drool.

2. Daub, stain, obscure, darken, smear, slaver.

——, v. i. Slabber, slaver, drivel, drool.

Slobbery, a. Moist, muddy, sloppy, wet, dank, floody.

Slop, v. t. Spill.

SLOPE, n. 1. Obliquity, oblique direction, direction downward by degrees.

2. Inclination, incline, ramp, gradient, grade, pitch, cant, glacis, acclivity or declivity.

——, v. i. Incline, slant, tilt, take an oblique direction.

Sloping, a. Inclining, slanting, aslant, bevel, declivitous, shelving, oblique.

Sloppy, a. Plashy, splashy, muddy, slobbery, wet, slabby.

Sloth, n. 1. Slowness, tardiness, dilatoriness.

2. Inactivity, inaction, laziness, indolence, idleness, inertness, sluggishness, torpor, lumpishness, supineness, slothfulness.

Slothful, a. Lazy, idle, inert, sluggish, indolent, dronish, inactive, lumpish, supine, torpid, slack.

Slouch, n. 1. Lubber, clown, awkward fellow, lout.

2. Clownish gait, stoop.

Slouching, a. Awkward, uncouth, clownish, lubberly, loutish, ungainly.

Slough, n. 1. Quagmire, morass, marsh, bog, fen.

2. Crust, scab, eschar.

3. Spoil, cast skin, tegument.

Sloughy, a. 1. Miry, boggy, queachy, marshy.

2. Foul, mortified, suppurated.

Sloven, n. "Slouch," "slob," slattern, slut.

Slovenly, a. 1. Untidy, unclean.

2. Disorderly, loose, untidy, unkempt, "sloppy," blowzy, frowzy, slatternly, "tacky," dowdy.

3. Perfunctory, heedless, careless, lazy, negligent.

SLOW, a. 1. Not fast, deliberate of movement, gradual.

2. Dull, heavy, dead, inert, inactive, sluggish, stupid, "logy."

3. Tardy, behindhand, unready, late.

4. Dilatory, delaying, lingering, slack.

Sludge, n. 1. Slosh, slush.

2. Mud, mire.

Slug, n. 1. Snail (without a shell).

2. See SLUGGARD.

Sluggard, n. Drone, lounger, idler, laggard, slug, dawdler.

Sluggish, a. 1. Indolent, idle, lazy, slothful, inactive, drowsy, inert, dronish, lumpish, listless, languid, torpid, phlegmatic.

2. Slow.

3. Dull, tame, stupid, supine.

Sluggishness, n. Phlegm, apathy, insensibility, dulness, indifference, inertness, indolence, slothfulness, laziness, supineness, torpor, sloth.

Sluice, n. Opening, vent, flood-gate.

Slumber, v. i. Sleep (lightly). See the noun.

——, n. 1. Sleep (not deep or profound), repose, rest, doze, nap, light sleep, siesta,

2. Sleep, repose, rest.

Slumberous, a. Soporific, somniferous, somnific, drowsy.

Slump, v. i. Sink (as in walking on snow), fall through.

Slur, v. t. 1. Reproach, traduce, asperse, disparage, depreciate, calumniate, speak of slightingly or disrespectfully.

2. Disregard, slight, pass by, pass over, gloss over, obscure, conceal.

——, n. 1. Mark, stain.

2. Reproach, stigma, stain, brand, disgrace.

3. Innuendo.

4. (In printing.) Blur, double, macule.

Slush, n. Slosh, sludge.

Slushy, a. Sloshy, sludgy, sloppy, plashy.

Slut, n. See SLATTERN.

Sluttish, a. Untidy, careless, disorderly, uncleanly, dirty.

Sly, a. 1. Cunning, artful, crafty, wily, subtle, insidious.

2. Cautious, shrewd, astute.

3. Arch, knowing.

4. Secret, underhand, clandestine, stealthy.

Smack, v. i. 1. Taste, have a taste, have a flavor.

2. Have a tincture, have a quality *or* trace, have a savor.

3. Kiss (*loudly*), buss.

Smack, *v. t.* 1. Kiss (*loudly*), buss.

2. Crack, snap, slash.

3. Slap (*loudly*).

——, *n.* 1. Taste, savor, flavor, tang, tincture.

2. Tincture, touch, tinge, dash, spice, infusion, sprinkling, little, small quantity, *soupçon*.

3. Buss, loud kiss.

4. Smattering, superficial knowledge.

5. Crack, snap, slash; loud slap.

SMALL, *a.* 1. Little, diminutive, tiny, *petite*, miniature, minikin, pygmy, Liliputian, "wee."

2. Minute, microscopic, infinitesimal, fine.

3. Petty, trifling, trivial, inconsiderable, inappreciable, insignificant, unimportant.

4. Slender, scanty, paltry, moderate.

5. Feeble, weak, faint, slight, puny.

6. Mean, sordid, selfish, illiberal, ungenerous, narrow, narrow-minded, paltry, unworthy.

Smallpox, *n.* Variola.

Small-talk, *n.* Gossip, chat, light conversation.

Smart, *n.* Pungent *or* sharp pain, lancinating pain.

——, *v. i.* 1. Feel sharp pain.

2. Suffer, be punished.

——, *a.* 1. Sharp, stinging, keen, severe, poignant, pungent, pricking, painful.

2. Vigorous, forcible, effective, energetic, efficient.

3. Brisk, fresh, quick, lively, agile, nimble, spry, active, sprightly, spirited.

4. Expert, dexterous, clever, quick, active, alert, adroit, intelligent, stirring.

5. Witty, acute, apt, pertinent, ready.

6. Spruce, trim, fine, showy, dapper, *chic*, "natty."

Smartness, *n.* 1. Sharpness, keenness, poignancy, pungency, acuteness, severity.

2. Vigor, force, energy, efficiency.

3. Liveliness, briskness, vivacity, agility, nimbleness, spryness, sprightliness.

4. Expertness, dexterity, cleverness, quickness, activity, intelligence, alertness.

5. Wit, wittiness, acuteness, aptness, pertinency.

6. Spruceness, trimness, etc. See the adjective, 6.

Smash, *v. t.* Crush, mash, shatter, dash to pieces, break in pieces.

SMASH, *n.* 1. Ruin, destruction, *débâcle*, crash.

2. Failure, bankruptcy.

Smattering, *n.* Smatter, dabbling, sciolism, slight *or* superficial knowledge.

Smear, *v. t.* 1. Daub, bedaub, besmear, plaster, begrime, smudge.

2. Contaminate, soil, stain, pollute, smirch, smut, tarnish, sully.

——, *n.* Daub, stain, blot, blotch, patch, smirch, smudge, spot.

Smeary, *a.* Adhesive, viscous, viscid, glutinous, dauby, sticky, splotchy.

Smell, *v. t.* Scent, get scent of.

——, *v. i.* Have an odor, have a scent.

SMELL, *n.* 1. Scent, odor, perfume, fragrance, aroma, bouquet, redolence, fume, stench, stink.

2. Sniff, snuff.

Smelt, *v. t.* Fuse (*as ore*), melt.

SMILE, *n.* Simper, grin, smirk.

Smirk, *n.* Affected smile, soft look, smickering (*Scot.*).

——, *v. i.* Smile (*affectedly*), simper.

Smite, *v. t.* 1. Strike, beat, box, cuff, buffet, "whack," "wollop."

2. Kill, slay, destroy.

3. Afflict, chasten, punish.

4. Blast, destroy.

——, *v. i.* Strike, collide, knock.

Smith, *n.* Metal-worker; blacksmith.

Smithy, *n.* Smithery, stithy, smith's shop, forge.

Smitten, *p. a.* 1. Struck, smit.

2. Killed, slain, destroyed.

3. Afflicted, chastened, punished.

4. Charmed, captivated, fascinated, attracted, taken, enamoured.

Smock, *n.* 1. Chemise, shift, slip.

2. Blouse, gabardine, smock-frock.

SMOKE, *n.* 1. Sooty vapor, smudge, fumigation.

2. Reek, steam, exhalation, effluvium, fume, mist, smother, vapor.

Smoke, *v. t.* 1. Fumigate, expose to smoke, smudge.

2. Smell out, find out, discover.

——, *v. i.* Emit smoke, reek, steam, exhale, emit vapor.

Smoky, *a.* 1. Of the nature of smoke.

2. Fumy, fuliginous, fumid, smudgy.

3. Sooty, begrimed, blackened, tanned, reeky, black, dark.

SMOOTH, *a.* 1. Even, level, flat, plane, polished, unruffled, unwrinkled.

2. Sleek, glossy, glabrous, silky, satiny, velvet, soft.

3. [*Of sounds*] Liquid, flowing, euphonious, mellifluent.

4. Voluble, fluent, glib.

5. Bland, mild, soothing, insinuating, soft, suave, oily, flattering, unctuous, courtier-like, fair-spoken, smooth-spoken, smooth-tongued, ingratiating, "slick."

6. Equable, calm, serene, unruffled.

Smooth, *v. t.* 1. Level, flatten, make smooth, plane.

2. Ease, make easy, lubricate.

3. Palliate, soften, extenuate.

4. Calm, allay, assuage, mollify, mitigate, alleviate.

Smoothly, *adv.* 1. Evenly.

2. Readily, easily, unobstructedly.

3. Blandly, softly, gently, mildly, soothingly, pleasantly, flatteringly.

Smooth-tongued, *a.* Plausible, flattering, cozening, adulatory, smooth, smooth-spoken, fair-spoken.

Smother, *v. t.* 1. Stifle, suffocate, choke.

2. Suppress, repress, conceal, stifle, extinguish, deaden, hide, keep back, keep down.

——, *v. i.* 1. Smoulder, smoke.

2. Be stifled, suffocate.

Smudge, *v. t.* Smear, besmear, stain, blacken, spot, smutch, soil.

Smug, *a.* 1. Nice, spruce, trim, neat.

2. Self-satisfied, complacent.

Smuggler, *n.* Contrabandist, "runner."

Smut, *n.* 1. Dirt, soot, smutch, smudge.

2. Obscenity, ribaldry, smuttiness, nastiness, obscene language.

3. Mildew, blight, dust-brand.

——, *v. t.* 1. Soil, tarnish, sully, taint, stain, blacken, smouch, smudge.

2. Mildew, mould, decay, blight.

Smutty, *a.* 1. Dirty, foul, soiled, stained, nasty.

2. Obscene, ribald, indecent, indelicate, immodest, gross, coarse, loose, impure, nasty.

Snack, *n.* 1. Share, snip.

2. Luncheon, slight meal, hasty repast.

Snag, *n.* Knot, knarl, knob, projection, jag, protuberance, snub.

Snail, *n.* 1. Slug.

2. Drone, idler, sluggard, laggard, slug.

SNAKE, *n.* Serpent, ophidian, viper.

Snaky, *a.* 1. Serpentine, winding, snakish.

2. Sly, cunning, artful, deceitful, insinuating, subtle.

Snap, *v. t.* 1. Break short, break short off, fracture.

2. Bite, seize, catch at, snatch at, snip.

3. Crack (*as a whip*).

——, *v. i.* 1. Break short.

2. Crackle, decrepitate, crepitate, pop.

3. Bite suddenly, dart and bite.

——, *n.* 1. Bite, nip, catch, seizure.

2. Clasp, fastening, catch, small lock.

3. Crack (*as of a whip*), smack, flip, flick, fillip.

4. (*Colloq.*) Energy, vim, briskness, "ginger," verve.

Snappish, *a.* Touchy, testy, crabbed, cross, crusty, irascible, waspish, petulant, perverse, froward, pettish, snarling, currish, peevish, captious, churlish, splenetic, acrimonious, ill-tempered, surly, tart.

Snare, *n.* Gin, noose, net, trap, springe, toil, catch, wile.

——, *v. t.* Entrap, entangle, catch, ensnare.

Snarl, *v. i.* Growl, gnarl, grumble, "girn," murmur.

——, *v. t.* 1. Entangle, complicate, knot, involve in knots.

2. Entangle, embarrass, confuse, ensnare.

——, *n.* 1. Entanglement, tangle, complication.

2. Intricacy, complication, embarrassment, difficulty.

Snatch, *v. t.* Grasp, clutch, gripe, wring, wrest, twitch, pluck, seize suddenly, pull, catch, snip.

——, *n.* 1. Bit, fragment, portion, small part.

2. Catch, short effort.

Sneak, *v. i.* 1. Skulk, lurk, slink, steal.

2. Crouch, truckle.

——, *n.* Shirk, lurker, mean fellow.

Sneaking, *a.* 1. Skulking, slinking, furtive.

2. Grovelling, crouching, mean, abject.

3. Secret, underhand, clandestine, concealed, hidden, covert, sly.

Sneer, *v. i.* Scoff, gibe, jeer, flout, mock, fleer, rail, turn up the nose.

——, *n.* Scoff, jeer, gibe, fling.

Sneer at. Deride, ridicule, scorn, disdain, scout, scoff, spurn, despise, contemn, mock, look down upon, laugh at, rail at, turn up the nose at.

SNEEZE, *n.* (*Basic Eng.*)

Sneezing, *n.* Sternutation.

Snicker, *v. i.* Laugh (*under restraint*), titter, snigger, giggle.

Sniff, *v. i.* Snuff.

——, *v. t.* 1. Snuff, inhale, breathe, breathe in.

2. Snuff, smell, scent.

Snip, *v. t.* 1. Clip, cut, nip, nip off.

2. Snap, snatch.

——, *n.* 1. Clip, cut.

2. Piece, shred, fragment, bit, particle.

3. Share, snack.

Snivel, *v. i.* Cry (*as a child*), blubber, whimper, weep, fret, sniffle, whine.

Snivelly, *a.* 1. Snotty.

2. Whining, pitiful.

Snob, *n.* Toady, climber; one who over-values social pretensions.

Snooze, *v. i.* (*Colloq.*) Slumber, drowse, sleep, nap, doze.

Snout, *n.* 1. Nose (*of a beast*), muzzle.

2. Nozzle.

SNOW, *n.* (*Basic Eng.*)

Snowy, *a.* White, pure, spotless, unblemished, immaculate, unsullied, unstained.

Snub, *v. t.* 1. Nip, clip, dock, prune, cut short, cut down, check, stunt.

2. Abash (*as a pretentious person*), cut, cold-shoulder, slight, humble, humiliate, mortify, discomfit, take down, teach (one) to keep his distance.

——, *n.* Check, rebuke, slight.

Snuff, *v. t.* 1. Inhale, breathe, sniff, breathe in.

2. Smell, scent.

——, *v. i.* 1. Snort (*as a horse*).

2. Sniff.

Snuffle, *v. i.* Sniffle.

Snuff out. Extinguish, annihilate, obliterate, efface, destroy.

Snug, *a.* 1. Close, concealed.

2. Comfortable, convenient, compact, neat, trim.

Snuggle, *v. i.* Nestle, nuzzle, cuddle, snug, lie snug, lie close.

SO, *adv.* 1. Thus, in like manner, for a like reason, with equal reason, in the way that.

2. To such a degree, in such a manner.

3. Likewise, in the same manner, in such a manner, in this way.

4. Such, in the same state *or* condition, as it is, as it was.

5. Therefore, for this reason, on this account.

6. Be it so, thus be it, it is well, so let it be, it is good, it is all right, well.

——, *conj.* Provided that, on condition that, in case that.

Soak, *v. t.* 1. Steep, macerate, imbrue.

2. Drench, wet, saturate.

3. Imbibe, absorb.

——, *v. i.* Steep, be soaked.

Soaked, *a.* Soggy, steeped, soppy, sodden, saturated, drenched, moist, wet.

SOAP, *n.* (*Basic Eng.*)

Soapy, *a.* Lathery, saponacious.

Soar, *v. i.* Tower, mount, rise, ascend, fly aloft.

Sob, *v. i.* Weep, cry, sigh convulsively.

Sober, *a.* 1. Unintoxicated.

2. Temperate, abstemious, abstinent.

3. Sane, sound, reasonable, rational.

4. Calm, moderate, cool, composed, regular, unruffled, unimpassioned, dis-passionate, steady, rational, collected, well-regulated, temperate, reasonable.

5. Grave, solemn, serious, sedate, demure, staid, quiet, sombre.

6. Quiet, dull-looking, sad, dark, drab, subdued, sombre.

Sobriety, *n.* 1. Temperance, abstemiousness, abstinence, soberness.

2. Calmness, coolness, sedateness, soberness, thoughtfulness, gravity, sober-mindedness, staidness.

3. Seriousness, gravity, solemnity, sedateness.

Sobriquet, *n.* [Fr.] Nickname, by-name, fanciful appellation.

Sociability, *n.* Sociableness, companionableness, comradeship, sociality, good-fellowship.

Sociable, *a.* Companionable, social, friendly, familiar, neighborly, conversable, communicative, accessible, affable, genial.

Social, *a.* 1. Civil, civic.

2. See SOCIABLE.

3. Convivial, festive.

Socialism, *n.* Communism, collectivism.

SOCIETY, *n.* 1. Association, fellowship, company, social sympathy, companionship, converse.

2. Association, union, partnership, copartnership, club, fellowship, company, sodality, fraternity, brotherhood, corporation, body.

3. The élite, *monde*, fashionable world, high life.

4. The community, the public, the world.

SOCK, *n.* Half-hose, ankle-hose.

Sod, *n.* Turf, sward, greensward.

Sodality, *n.* Fraternity, brotherhood, society, fellowship.

Sodden, *a.* 1. Boiled, decocted, stewed, seethed.

2. Soaked, steeped, drenched, thoroughly wet (*so as to be soft*), saturated.

Sodomy, *n.* Buggery, unnatural carnal intercourse.

Sofa, *n.* Couch, seat to recline on, davenport, divan, ottoman, settee.

SOFT, *a.* 1. Impressible, yielding, plastic, pliable, easily moulded, malleable.

2. Yielding to touch; downy, fleecy, velvety; mushy, pulpy, squashy.

3. Compliant, submissive, irresolute, facile, weak, undecided.

4. Mild, gentle, bland, kind, lenient, tender.

5. Delicate, tender.

6. Gentle, steady, even, smooth-going, easy, quiet.

7. Effeminate, unmanly, luxurious.

8. Mellifluous, dulcet, smooth, gentle, fluty, melodious.

Soft, *interj.* Hold, stop, not so fast.

Soften, *v. t.* 1. Intenerate, melt, mellow, make tender, make soft.

2. Assuage, appease, mitigate, balm, moderate, milden, alleviate, soothe, mollify, quiet, calm, still, quell, allay, relieve, ease, abate, temper, attemper, qualify, dull, lessen, blunt, make easy.

3. Palliate, qualify, modify, extenuate.

4. Enervate, weaken, make effeminate.

——, *v. i.* 1. Grow soft, become soft, mellow, melt.

2. Relent, mollify.

3. Grow gentle, milden.

Soil, *v. t.* Foul, dirty, stain, smirch, pollute, sully, tarnish, defile, taint, contaminate, daub, bedaub, begrime, besmear, bespatter, make foul, bemire.

——, *n.* 1. Dirt, filth, foulness, foul matter.

2. Stain, blot, spot, tarnish, defilement, taint, blemish.

3. Mould, loam, earth, ground.

4. Land, country.

Sojourn, *v. i.* Abide (*temporarily*), stay, tarry, lodge, rest, remain, live, dwell, reside, stop, take up one's quarters, put up, take lodgings, have lodgings.

——, *n.* Stay, temporary abode, residence.

Solace, *n.* Comfort, consolation, cheer, relief, alleviation.

——, *v. t.* 1. Cheer, comfort, soothe, console.

2. Allay, assuage, soften, mitigate, relieve.

Soldier, *n.* 1. Warrior, fighting man, man at arms.

2. Private, common soldier, "doughboy."

Soldierly, *a.* 1. Warlike, marshal, military.

2. Valiant, brave, gallant, intrepid, courageous, heroic, honorable.

Soldiery, *n.* Soldiers, the military, the army, forces, troops, militia, gendarmery.

Sole, *a.* Single, only, individual, unique, alone, solitary, one.

Solecism, *n.* 1. Impropriety (*in the use of language*), error, mistake, slip, blunder, incongruity, barbarism.

2. Breach of form, *faux pas.*

Solemn, *a.* 1. Formal, ritual, ceremonial.

2. Sacred, religious, devout, reverential, devotional.

3. Serious, grave, sober, earnest.

4. Awful, august, venerable, imposing, grand, stately, majestic, awe-inspiring, impressive.

Solemnity, *n.* 1. Rite (*religious*), ceremonial observance, ceremony, celebration, office.

2. Awfulness, sacredness, sanctity.

3. Seriousness, gravity, impressiveness.

Solemnize, *v. t.* Celebrate (*with solemn ceremonies*), commemorate, observe, do honor to, honor, keep.

Solemnly, *adv.* 1. Reverently, devoutly, religiously.

2. Seriously, gravely, soberly.

3. Ceremoniously, formally, regularly.

Solicit, *v. t.* 1. Ask (*earnestly*), request (*urgently*), entreat, beg, pray, implore, crave, importune, beseech, supplicate, petition, conjure, press, urge, appeal to.

2. Invite, summon, awake to action, excite, awaken, arouse.

3. Seek, endeavor to obtain, canvass.

Solicitant, *n.* 1. Solicitor, petitioner, asker.

2. Aspirant, candidate.

Solicitation, *n.* 1. Entreaty, importunity, supplication, imploration, appeal, petition, address, insistence, urgency, suit, request, asking.

2. Invitation, summons, bidding, call, excitement.

Solicitor, *n.* 1. Asker, petitioner, solicitant, canvasser, "drummer."

2. Attorney, law agent.

Solicitous, *a.* Anxious, careful, concerned, apprehensive, troubled, uneasy, eager, disturbed.

Solicitude, *n.* Anxiety, care, carefulness, concern, trouble, perplexity.

SOLID, *a.* 1. Hard, firm, congealed, impenetrable.

2. Dense, massed, compact, impermeable.

3. Cubic.

4. Strong, substantial, stable, sound, stout, firm.

5. Real, true, valid, just, weighty, firm, strong, sound, substantial.

6. Well-established, reliable, trustworthy, sound, safe.

Solidarity, *n.* Consolidation (*of interests and responsibilities*), community (*in whatever befalls*), close fellowship, joint interest, mutual responsibility, communion of interests.

Solidify, *v. t.* Consolidate, compact, make solid, petrify, harden.

——, *v. i.* Become solid, become compact, congeal, harden.

Solidity, *n.* 1. Hardness, firmness, solidness, density, compactness, consistency.

2. Density, compactness, fulness.

3. Strength, stability, massiveness.

4. Reality, truth, weight, validity, justice, gravity, firmness, soundness, strength.

5. (*Geom.*) Volume, solid contents, cubic contents.

Soliloquy, *n.* Monologue.

Solitariness, *n.* 1. Retirement, seclusion, isolation, reclusion, privacy.

2. Loneliness, solitude.

Solitary, *a.* 1. Lone, lonely, alone, unaccompanied, companionless, separate.

2. Isolated, secluded, unfrequented, retired, deserted, desolate, remote, lonely, desert.

3. Single, sole, individual.

——, *n.* Hermit, eremite, anchorite, anchoret, recluse, solitarian, *solitaire.*

Solitude, *n.* 1. Loneliness, isolation, seclusion, solitariness, retiredness, recluseness, retirement, privacy.

2. Desert, wilderness, waste, lonely place, deserted region.

Solution, *n.* 1. Disruption, breach, disjunction, disconnection, discontinuance.

2. Explanation, explication, clue, key, answer, resolution, disentanglement, elucidation, unraveling, unriddling.

3. Liquefaction, dissolution, melting.

4. Dissolution, disintegration, separation, resolution.

Solvability, *n.* Solubility.

Solvable, *a.* Resolvable, solvable.

Solve, *v. t.* Explain, unfold, expound, disentangle, interpret, elucidate, clear, make plain, resolve, clear up.

Solvent, *n.* Menstruum, diluent, dissolvent.

Somatic, *a.* Corporeal, bodily.

Somber, *a.* 1. Shady, dusky, cloudy, murky, dark, dull, darksome, rayless, sunless, unilluminated, overcast, dismal, sombrous, gloomy.

2. Melancholy, sad, mournful, doleful, lugubrious, funereal, grave, sober.

SOME, *a.* 1. More *or* less, a certain quantity of, a certain number of.

2. One (*indefinitely*), a, an, any, a certain.

3. About, near.

4. Several, a considerable number.

5. Some people, some persons, certain.

6. A part, a portion.

7. A little, moderate.

Somebody, *n.* 1. One, some person, some one.

2. Something, a person of consequence.

Somehow, *adv.* In some way, somehow or other.

Somersault, *n.* Somerset.

Something, *n.* 1. A thing (*indefinitely*).

2. A part, a portion.

3. Somebody, a person of consequence.

4. A thing, matter, affair, event.

Sometime, *adv.* 1. Once, formerly.

2. Now and then, at one time or other, sometimes.

——, *a.* Former, late, whilom.

Sometimes, *adv.* 1. At times, at intervals, now and then, somewhiles, occasionally.

2. Once, formerly, at a past period.

Somewhat, *adv.* Something, in some degree, more or less, rather, a little.

——, *n.* 1. Something.

2. A little, more or less, a part.

Somewhere, *adv.* In some place, in one place or another, here and there.

Somnambulism, *n.* Sleep-walking, somnambulation.

Somnambulist, *n.* Sleep-walker, nightwalker, noctambulist, somnambulator, somnambule.

Somniferous, *a.* Soporific, soporiferous, slumberous, somnific, narcotic, opiate.

Somnolence, *n.* Sleepiness, drowsiness, doziness, somnolency.

Somnolent, *a.* Sleepy, drowsy, dozy.

SON, *n.* Heir, cadet, junior, scion.

SONG, *n.* 1. Ballad, ditty, canticle, carol, canzonet, lay, aria, lullaby, glee, snatch.

2. Descant, melody.

3. Lay, strain, poem, hymn, psalm, anthem.

4. Poetry, poesy, verse, numbers.

Sonorous, *a.* 1. Sounding, resonant, resounding, ringing, full-toned.

2. High-sounding, loud.

Soon, *adv.* 1. Shortly, presently, anon, before long, pretty soon, by and by, in a short time.

2. Early, at so early an hour, betimes, quick, forthwith, promptly.

3. Lief, willingly, readily, gladly.

Soot, *n.* Crock, black dust, carbon.

Soothe, *v. t.* 1. Cajole, humor, flatter.

2. Assuage, calm, quiet, appease, tranquillize, compose, pacify, sober, still, lull, mollify, soften, balm.

3. Moderate, alleviate, mitigate, palliate, lessen, allay, repress, check, temper, soften, deaden, qualify, relieve, ease, dull, blunt.

Soothsayer, *n.* Seer, foreteller, predictor, prophet, diviner, vaticinator, sorcerer, necromancer, augur.

Sooty, *a.* Dark, dusky, murky, fuliginous, black, sable.

Sophism, *n.* Fallacy, paralogism, paralogy, casuistry, quibble, specious argument. See SOPHISTRY.

Sophist, *n.* Quibbler, captious reasoner, fallacious reasoner, artful logician.

Sophistical, *a.* Fallacious, illogical, quibbling, casuistical, trickily subtle, unsound.

Sophistry, *n.* Paralogy, paralogism, fallacy, shift, equivocation, cavil, chicane, trick, quibble, speciousness, false logic, fallacious reasoning.

Soporific, *a.* Somniferous, somnific, slumberous, dormitive, soporiferous, narcotic, hypnotic, opiate, soporous.

Soppy, *a.* Sopped, soaked, saturated, drenched.

Soprano, *n.* (*Mus.*) Treble, descant, discant.

Sorcerer, *n.* Magician, conjurer, juggler, enchanter, necromancer, thaumaturgist, shaman, charmer, wizard, exorcist, diviner, seer, soothsayer.

Sorcery, *n.* Divination (*by evil spirits*), magic, enchantment, witchcraft, necromancy, thaumaturgy, voodoo, charm, spell, black art.

Sordid, *a.* 1. Mean, base, vile, low, degraded.

2. Covetous, avaricious, stingy, miserly, niggardly, close, illiberal, ungenerous, penurious, close-fisted.

Sore, *n.* 1. Ulcer, fester, abscess, imposthume, gathering, boil, pustule.

2. Pain, trouble, grief, affliction, sorrow.

——, *a.* 1. Painful (*from inflammation*), tender, irritated, raw, ulcerated.

2. Pained, hurt, grieved, tender, galled, aggrieved, vexed, irritable.

3. Violent, severe, sharp, afflictive, distressing.

Sorely, *adv.* Grievously, severely, violently, greatly.

Sorrily, *adv.* Meanly, pitiably, despicably, poorly, wretchedly.

Sorrow, *n.* Grief, sadness, affliction, dolor, heartache, mourning, trouble, woe.

——, *v. i.* Grieve, mourn, be sad, weep, lament, bemoan, bewail.

Sorrowful, *a.* 1. Grieved, afflicted, heartsore, grieving, in sorrow, in mourning, sad, depressed, dejected.

2. (*Of the occasion.*) Sad, mournful, grievous, lamentable, distressing, painful, melancholy, baleful.

3. Dismal, disconsolate, drear, dreary, rueful, woebegone, woeful, doleful, dolorous, melancholy, piteous, lugubrious.

Sorry, *a.* 1. Grieved, afflicted, pained, sorrowful, dejected.

2. Vexed, chagrined, mortified, pained, regretful, remorseful.

3. Mean, vile, base, poor, miserable, wretched, pitiful, abject, beggarly, contemptible, despicable, shabby, low, paltry, worthless.

SORT, *n.* 1. Kind, species, description, class, type, denomination, character, nature, order, race, rank.

2. Manner, way.

——, *v. t.* 1. Distribute (*into sorts*), assort, class, classify, arrange.

2. Order, reduce to order, arrange.

3. Conjoin, join, put together.

4. Select, choose, elect, pick out.

——, *v. i.* 1. Associate, consort, fraternize.

2. Suit, fit, accord, be in harmony with, agree with, be adapted to.

Sortie, *n.* Sally.

So-so, *a.* Indifferent, mediocre, tolerable, middling, passable, ordinary.

Sot, *n.* 1. Blockhead, dolt, dullard, dunce, simpleton, fool, snipe, malt-horse.

2. Toper, tippler, drunkard, wine-bibber, dram-drinker.

So that. In order that, to the end that.

Sottish, *a.* 1. Dull, stupid, senseless, doltish, foolish, simple.

2. Besotted (*from intemperance*), foolish, senseless, insensate, befuddled, drunken, tipsy.

Sotto voce. [It.] Softly, in a low voice, in an under-tone.

Sough, *n.* 1. Sigh, murmur, murmuring sound.

2. Waft, breath, gentle breeze.

Soul, *n.* 1. Mind, spirit, psyche.

2. Essence, vital principle, spirit.

3. Active power, energy.

Soulless, *a.* Lifeless, dead, unfeeling, expressionless.

Sound, *a.* 1. Whole, entire, unbroken, uninjured, intact, unhurt, unmutilated, unimpaired.

2. Healthy, hearty, hale, hardy, vigorous.

3. Perfect, undecayed, good.

4. Firm, strong, stable, solvent.

5. Sane, well-balanced, perfect.

6. Correct, valid, solid, well-founded, orthodox, established in reason, rationally grounded.

7. Legal, valid.

8. Profound, unbroken, undisturbed, fast, deep.

9. Lusty, stout, severe, forcible.

SOUND, *n.* 1. Strait, narrows, channel.

2. Noise, tone, note, voice, whisper, etc. (Many imitative words — bang, blare, boom, etc.)

——, *v. i.* 1. Resound, make a noise, give out a sound.

2. Appear by the sound, seem.

——, *v. t.* 1. Cause to sound, play on.

2. Utter, express audibly, pronounce.

3. Celebrate (*by sounds*), publish, proclaim, announce, spread abroad.

4. Measure, fathom, try the depth of, take soundings, test, gauge.

5. Examine, test, try, search, probe.

Sounding, *a.* 1. Sonorous, ringing, resounding, resonant, audible.

2. Imposing, significant.

Soundless, *a.* 1. Silent, noiseless, dumb.

2. Unfathomable, unsounded, bottomless, very deep, very profound, abysmal.

Soundly, *adv.* 1. Thoroughly, satisfactorily, well.

2. Healthily, heartily.

3. Severely, lustily, smartly, stoutly, forcibly.

4. Truly, correctly, rightly.

5. Firmly, strongly.

6. Fast, deeply, profoundly.

Soundness, *n.* 1. Wholeness, entireness, integrity, entirety.

2. Healthiness, vigor.

3. Saneness, sanity.

4. Correctness, truth, rectitude, validity, orthodoxy.

5. Firmness, strength, solidity, validity, truth.

SOUP, *n.* Broth, consommé, purée.

Sour, *a.* 1. Acid, tart, pricked, sharp, acetous, acetose, vinegary, astringent.

2. Cross, crabbed, acrimonious, currish, surly, crusty, fretful, peevish, petulant, pettish, glum, ill-humored, snarling, ill-tempered, ill-natured.

3. Bitter, unpleasant, disagreeable.

4. Gloomy, sad, dismal, morose, sullen, austere.

5. Rancid, musty, spoiled, bad, coagulated, turned, curdled, loppered.

——, *v. t.* 1. Make acid, acidulate, turn sour.

2. Imbitter, make unpleasant.

——, *v. i.* Turn sour, become acid.

Source, *n.* 1. Origin, spring, fountain, head, rise, root, beginning, fountain-head, well.

2. Cause, original.

Sourish, *a.* Acidulous.

Sourness, *n.* 1. Acidity, tartness, sharpness.

2. Acrimony, asperity, moroseness, harshness, crabbedness, churlishness, peevishness, discontent, crossness.

Souse, *v. t.* 1. Pickle.

2. Plunge, dip, immerse, submerge, douse, put under water (*or other liquid*).

SOUTH, *a.* Southern, southerly.

Southern, *a.* 1. Meridional.

2. Southerly, south.

Southerner, *n.* Southron, southern.

Souvenir, *n.* [Fr.] Remembrancer, reminder, memento, keepsake.

Sovereign, *a.* 1. Supreme, regal, royal, imperial, monarchical, princely.

2. Chief, predominant, principal, supreme, paramount, excellent, commanding, monarch, utmost, highest.

3. Efficacious, effectual.

——, *n.* 1. Monarch, autocrat, suzerain, supreme ruler.

2. King, emperor, prince, lord, potentate, ruler.

Sovereignty, *n.* 1. Dominion, supremacy, sway, empire, supreme power, supreme rule, absolute authority.

2. Supremacy, supreme excellence.

Sow, *v. t.* 1. Scatter, strew, spread.

2. Disseminate, disperse, propagate, spread abroad.

3. Plant, put seed in.

4. Besprinkle, scatter over.

——, *v. i.* Plant, scatter seed, put in seed.

SPACE, *n.* 1. Extension, extent, proportions, spread, expansion.

2. Capacity, room, accommodation.

3. Distance, interval, interspace.

Spacious, *a.* 1. Wide, extended, extensive, vast.

2. Roomy, broad, ample, capacious, commodious, wide, large.

SPADE, *n.* Spud, shovel.

Span, *n.* 1. Nine inches, eighth of a fathom.

2. Brief period, spell.

3. Pair, team, yoke of animals.

——, *v. t.* Compass, measure, cross, overlay.

Spank, *v. t.* Strike (*with the open hand*), slap.

Spar, *v. i.* 1. Box, contend with fisticuffs.

2. Dispute, wrangle, quarrel, bicker, squabble, "spat."

——, *n.* Pole, beam, boom, sprit, yard.

Spare, *v. t.* 1. Reserve, save, lay by, lay aside, set apart, set aside.

2. Dispense with, do without, part with.

3. Withhold, omit, forbear, refrain from.

4. Withhold from, keep from, exempt.

5. Give, grant, afford, allow, give up.

6. Preserve (*from anything dreaded*), save.

——, *v. i.* 1. Be frugal, be parsimonious, economize, pinch.

2. Forbear, refrain, be scrupulous.

3. Be lenient, be merciful, be tender, forgive.

——, *a.* 1. Scanty, sparing, frugal, stinted.

2. Parsimonious, chary, sparing.

3. Lean, meagre, thin, poor, lank, gaunt, skinny, scraggy, raw-boned, emaciated.

4. Supernumerary, extra, additional.

Sparing, *a.* 1. Scanty, little, scarce.

2. Spare, abstemious, meagre, scanty.

3. Frugal, saving, chary, parsimonious, economical.

4. Merciful, compassionate, forgiving, lenient.

Sparingly, *adv.* 1. Frugally, parsimoniously, abstinently, moderately, temperately.

2. Seldom, infrequently, rarely.

Spark, *n.* 1. Sparkle, scintillation, particle of fire, scintilla.

2. Germ, element, active principle, seed, beginning.

3. Buck, beau, dashing fellow, dandy, gallant.

Sparkle, *v. i.* 1. Shine (*with intermissions*), glitter, glisten, glister, twinkle, scintillate, coruscate, flash, radiate, gleam.

2. Effervesce, bubble, foam, froth.

——, *n.* 1. Spark, scintillation, glint.

2. Luminosity, lustre.

Sparkling, *a.* 1. Glittering, glistening, twinkling, flashing, brilliant.

2. Bubbling, foaming, effervescing, frothing, mantling.

3. Lively, glowing, brilliant, spirited, piquant, nervous, racy.

Sparse, *a.* Scattered, spread here and there, infrequent, sporadic, dispersed, thin.

Spartan, *a.* Brave, courageous, hardy, undaunted, daring, intrepid, dauntless, fearless, bold, valiant, valorous, doughty, chivalric, heroic, lion-hearted.

Spasm, *n.* 1. Twitch, sudden contraction (*as of the muscles*), cramp, crick.

2. Fit, paroxysm, throe, seizure.

Spasmodic, *a.* Convulsive, spasmodical, paroxysmal, fitful, violent and short-lived.

Spat, *v. i.* Dispute, wrangle, quarrel, spar, bicker, jangle, squabble, have words, have an altercation.

Spatter, *v. t.* Sprinkle, besprinkle, bespatter, splash, plash.

——, *v. i.* Sputter, spit.

Spawn, *n.* 1. Eggs (*of fish* or *of frogs*), hard roe.

2. Product, offspring, fruit.

3. (*Bot.*) Mycelium, filaments (*from which fungi originate*).

——, *v. t.* [*In contempt.*] Generate, produce, bring forth.

Speak, *v. i.* 1. Articulate, enunciate, talk with articulate sounds.

2. Talk, dispute, argue, converse, say.

3. Plead, "spout," hold forth, make a speech, "orate," discourse, harangue, declaim.

4. Treat, make mention, discourse, tell.

——, *v. t.* 1. Utter, express, deliver, pronounce, articulate.

2. Tell, say, declare, disclose, announce.

3. Announce, make known, spread abroad, proclaim, declare, celebrate.

4. Talk, converse in.

5. Accost, address, greet; hail (*Naut.*).

6. Exhibit, declare, make known.

Speaker, *n.* 1. Discourser, orator, spokesman, elocutionist, prolocutor.

2. Chairman, presiding officer.

Speaking, *n.* 1. Talk, discourse, utterance.

2. Elocution, declamation, oratory.

Spear, *n.* 1. Lance, javelin, pike, gaff, dart, harpoon.

2. Shoot, spire.

Spear-shaped, *a.* Hastate, hastated, lanceolate.

SPECIAL, *a.* 1. Specific, specifical.

2. Particular, peculiar, especial, individual, unique.

3. Extraordinary, uncommon, particular, marked, exceptional.

4. Appropriate, peculiar, especial, express.

Specialty, *n.* 1. Particularity.

2. Speciality, object of special attention, particular object of pursuit, pet subject.

Specie, *n.* Coin, cash, metallic money, hard money, stamped money.

Species, *n.* 1. Group (*subordinate to a* genus), class, collection, assemblage.

2. Kind, sort, description, variety.

3. (*Law.*) Form, figure, fashion, shape.

Specific, *a.* 1. Peculiar, particular, especial, characteristic.

2. Definite, precise, specified, limited.

Specification, *n.* 1. Designation (*of properties*), characterization.

2. Particularization, detailed statement.

Specify, *v. t.* Designate, particularize, indicate, define, individualize, detail, show clearly, name with precision.

Specimen, *n.* Pattern, sample, model, copy, example.

Specious, *a.* 1. Obvious, showy, manifest, open.

2. Fair (*apparently, but not really*), plausible, sophistical, colorable, ostensible, showy, flimsy, illusory.

Speck, *n.* 1. Stain, spot, speckle, flaw, blemish, blot.

2. Bit, mite, mote, atom, particle, corpuscle, scintilla, small thing.

Spectacle, *n.* 1. Show, exhibition, sight, scene, representation, display, pageant, parade, review, gazing-stock.

2. Curiosity, wonder, marvel, phenomenon, sight.

Spectacles, *n. pl.* Glasses, goggles.

Spectator, *n.* Beholder, observer, bystander, looker-on, on-looker, witness.

Specter, *n.* Apparition, ghost, spirit, shade, banshee, sprite, phantom, shadow, goblin, hobgoblin, wraith.

Spectral, *a.* Ghostly, phantomlike, ghostlike, eerie, shadowy, "spooky," wraithlike, weird.

Spectrum, *n.* Image, appearance, representation.

Speculate, *v. i.* 1. Meditate, contemplate, cogitate, reflect, ponder, muse, ruminate, think, consider, theorize.

2. Trade (*hazardously*), take a "flyer."

Speculation, *n.* 1. Contemplation, intellectual examination, mental view.

2. Theory, scheme, hypothesis, supposition, conjecture, view, *a priori* reasoning, reflection.

Speculative, *a.* 1. Contemplative, unpractical, Platonic, philosophical, speculatory.

2. Theoretical, ideal, imaginary.

Speculator, *n.* Theorizer, speculatist, theorist.

Speech, *n.* 1. Articulate utterance, verbal expression, language, words.

2. Language, tongue, dialect, idiom, locution.

3. Talk, parlance, verbal intercourse, oral communication, conversation.

4. Observation, remark, talk, mention, saying.

5. Oration, discourse, address, declamation, harangue, palaver.

Speechless, *a.* Mute, dumb, inarticulate, silent, gagged.

Speed, *v. i.* 1. Make haste, hasten, hurry, scurry, rush.

2. Succeed, prosper, thrive, flourish.

——, *v. t.* 1. Despatch, send away quickly, send away in haste.

2. Hasten, expedite, accelerate, hurry, despatch, quicken, urge *or* press forward, urge *or* press on.

3. Despatch, execute, carry through.

4. Assist, help, aid, help forward, advance.

5. Prosper, favor, make successful.

——, *n.* 1. Haste, hurry, despatch, celerity, swiftness, fleetness, velocity, quickness, rapidity, expedition, acceleration.

2. Success, prosperity, good fortune, good luck, favorable issue, event.

3. Impetuosity, headlong violence.

Speedy, *a.* 1. Swift, rapid, quick, fleet, hasty, hurried, flying, nimble, hurrying, fast.

2. Quick, prompt, expeditious.

3. Near, approaching, early.

Spell, *n.* 1. Charm, witchery, "hoodoo," "jinx," incantation, exorcism.

2. Turn (*at work*).

3. Season, term, period, round, interval, fit.

——, *v. t.* 1. Represent by letters.

2. Read, interpret, decipher, unfold, unriddle, unravel, discover by characters (often with *out*).

3. Fascinate, charm, bewitch, allure, captivate, entrance.

Spell-bound, *a.* Enchanted, charmed, bewitched, transported, fascinated, under a spell, under magic influence.

Spelling, *n.* Orthography.

Spend, *v. t.* 1. Expend, disburse, lay out, dispose of, part with.

2. Waste, consume, exhaust, squander, dissipate, lavish, use up.

3. Employ, devote, bestow, apply, pass.

4. Waste, wear away, exhaust of force.

——, *v. i.* Lay out money, incur expense.

Spendthrift, *n.* Prodigal, squanderer, waster, spender.

Spent, *a.* Exhausted, played out, worn out, fatigued, wearied.

Sperm, *n.* Semen, seed.

Spermatic, *a.* Seminal.

Spew, *v. t.* 1. Vomit, puke, cast up, throw up.

2. Eject, cast forth.

——, *v. i.* Vomit, puke.

Spheral, *a.* Symmetrical, complete, perfect.

Sphere, *n.* 1. Globe, ball, orb, spheroid.

2. Circuit, circle, orbit, ambit, range, bound, compass, province, department, walk, beat, function, office.

3. Rank, standing, order.

4. Region, realm, domain, quarter, country.

Spherical, *a.* 1. Globular, orbicular, globated, bulbous, globous, globose, rotund, round, spheroid.

2. Planetary.

Sphericity, *n.* Rotundity, roundness, globosity, globularity.

Spice, *n.* 1. Flavoring, flavor, relish, taste, savor.

2. Admixture, sprinkling, tincture, dash, infusion, grain, particle, small quantity, smack, *soupçon*.

Spiciferous, *a.* Spicated, eared, spicose, spicous.

Spicily, *adv.* Pungently, wittily.

Spicy, *a.* 1. Aromatic, fragrant, balmy, racy.

2. Pungent, sharp, piquant, pointed, keen, racy.

Spigot, *n.* Spile, stopper, stopple, spill, faucet, plug.

Spike, *n.* 1. Ear (*of grain*), head.

2. Large nail *or* pin.

Spill, *v. t.* Shed, effuse, pour out.

Spin, *v. t.* 1. Twist (*into thread*).

2. Extend, draw out.

3. Protract, spend, lengthen, prolong, draw out.

4. Twirl, whirl.

Spindle, *n.* (*Mech.*) Axis, shaft, arbor.

Spindle-shaped, *a.* Fusiform.

Spine, *n.* 1. Thorn, prickle, barb.

2. Backbone, spinal column, vertebral column.

3. Ridge.

Spinet, *n.* Virginal, clavichord.

Spinose, *a.* Thorny, spiny, spinous, briery.

Spiny, *a.* 1. Thorny, spinose, spinous, briery, prickly.

2. Thorny, difficult, troublesome, perplexed.

Spiracle, *n.* Aperture (*especially in animal and vegetable bodies*), blowhole, vent, orifice, pore.

Spiral, *a.* Winding (*like the thread of a screw*), curled, cochlear, cochleated, spiry, helical, screw-shaped.

——, *n.* Helix, worm, winding.

Spire, *n.* 1. Spiral, curl, twist, wreath.

2. Steeple.

3. Shoot, spear, stalk, blade.

4. Summit, apex.

Spirit, *n.* 1. Life, vital essence (*apart from matter*), immaterial substance.

2. Soul, person.

3. Apparition, ghost, specter, shade, phantom, demon, genius, sprite, fairy, elf, angel.

4. Disposition, temper, humor, mood, spirits, frame of mind, turn of mind.

5. Courage, ardor, fire, energy, force, vivacity, cheerfulness, enterprise, vigor, vim, mettle, earnestness, enthusiasm, zeal, resolution, elevation of soul.

6. Liveliness, animation, *ésprit*, spice, "ginger," "spunk," piquancy, warmth, glow, vivacity, cheerfulness, enterprise.

7. Meaning, significance, purport, intent, drift, gist, tenor, sense.

8. Nature, character, complexion, characteristic quality, essential part, essence, quintessence.

9. Alcohol, distilled liquor.

10. [With *The* prefixed.] Holy Ghost, Paraclete, Comforter.

——, *v. t.* 1. Excite, encourage, animate, inspirit.

2. Kidnap, carry off (*secretly*).

Spirited, *a.* Animated, lively, vivacious, brisk, frisky, sprightly, ardent, earnest, active, bold, courageous, alert, high-strung, mettlesome, high-mettled, high-spirited, full of life.

Spiritless, *a.* 1. Lifeless, breathless, extinct, dead.

2. Dejected, depressed, discouraged, dispirited, low-spirited.

3. Dull, torpid, sluggish, cold, apathetic, phlegmatic, languid, soulless, feeble, unenterprising.

4. Heavy, stupid, dull, frigid, tame, prosaic, prosy, insipid, uninteresting.

Spirits, *n. pl.* 1. Disposition, temper, mood, humor, spirit, frame of mind, turn of mind.

2. Distilled liquors, ardent spirits.

Spiritual, *a.* 1. Immaterial, incorporeal, supersensible, ethereal, psychical, ghostly.

2. Moral, ideal, unworldly.

3. Holy, divine, pure, sacred.

4. Ecclesiastical.

Spiritualize, *v. t.* Purify, elevate, etherealize, refine, make spiritual.

Spirituous, *a.* Alcoholic, ardent, spiritous.

Spirt, *v. i.* Gush, jet, spout. See SPURT.

——, *v. t.* Spout, throw out.

Spiry, *a.* 1. See SPIRAL.

2. Pyramidal, tapering.

Spit, *v. t.* 1. Pierce, thrust through, transfix, impale.

2. Eject, throw out.

——, *v. i.* Spawl, splutter, drivel, drool, expectorate, salivate, slobber.

——, *n.* Spittle, saliva, spawl, *sputum.*

Spite, *n.* Malice, malevolence, rancor, venom, gall, malignity, maliciousness, hate, grudge, pique, ill-nature, ill-will, hatred, vindictiveness, spleen.

——, *v. t.* 1. Mortify, thwart, injure, treat maliciously.

2. Offend, annoy, vex.

Spiteful, *a.* Malicious, malignant, malevolent, malign, ill-disposed, evil-minded, ill-natured, hateful, rancorous.

Spittoon, *n.* Spit-box, cuspidor.

Splash, *n.* 1. Water, dirty water.

2. Blot, daub, spot.

——, *v. i.* Plash, dabble in water, spatter, swash, swish, splurge.

——, *v. t.* Dash, spatter, plash.

Splay, *a.* Wide, broad, spreading out, turned out.

Spleen, *n.* 1. (*Anat.*) Milt.

2. Anger, spite, animosity, gall, rancor, pique, malevolence, malignity, grudge, hatred, malice, ill-humor, peevishness, irascibility, chagrin.

3. (*Archaic.*) Melancholy, despondency, hypochondria, dejection, depression, dumps, megrims, the dismals, the blues, blue devils, vapors, *hypochondriasis.*

Spleeny, *a.* 1. Angry, fretful, peevish, ill-tempered, irritable, spleenish, spleenful, splenetic.

2. Melancholy, hypochondriacal, low-spirited.

Splendid, *a.* 1. Shining, glowing, resplendent, effulgent, refulgent, bright, lustrous, radiant, beaming, brilliant.

2. Showy, magnificent, gorgeous, sumptuous, pompous, superb, kingly, dazzling, imposing.

3. Illustrious, conspicuous, eminent, distinguished, pre-eminent, remarkable, famous, celebrated, glorious, brilliant, noble, signal.

4. Grand, heroic, sublime, lofty, noble.

Splendor, *n.* 1. Luster, brilliance, brilliancy, brightness, refulgence, radiance.

2. Magnificence, pomp, stateliness, show, gorgeousness, pompousness, display, parade, showiness, grandeur, *éclat*.

3. Eminence, celebrity, fame, glory, grandeur, renown.

4. Grandeur, sublimity, loftiness, nobleness.

Splenetic, *a.* 1. Irascible, irritable, fretful, peevish, touchy, testy, pettish, waspish, petulant, choleric, snappish, cross.

2. Morose, sullen, sulky, churlish, sour, crabbed.

3. Melancholy, despondent, moping, gloomy, melancholic, hypochondriacal, jaundiced.

Splice, *v. t.* Braid together (*as the ends of ropes*), connect, knit, mortise, join together.

Splinter, *v. t.* Split (*into thin pieces*), shiver, sliver, rend.

——, *v. i.* Be split (*into thin pieces*), shiver.

Splinters, *n. pl.* Flinders, fragments.

Split, *v. t.* 1. Cleave, rive.

2. Burst, rend, splinter.

3. Divide, sunder, separate, part.

——, *v. i.* 1. Burst, be riven, be rent, be split, splinter.

2. Be broken, be dashed to pieces.

3. Separate, divide, break.

——, *n.* 1. Crack, fissure, rent.

2. Division, separation, breach.

Splotch, *n.* Spot, stain, smear, daub, blot.

Splutter, *v. i.* (*Colloq.*) Stammer (*through haste*), sputter, stutter.

Spoil, *v. t.* 1. Plunder, rob, despoil, loot, fleece, strip, ravage, waste.

2. Injure, harm, disfigure, mar, impair, damage, ruin, vitiate, corrupt, destroy.

——, *v. i.* 1. Steal, pilfer, rob.

2. Decay, decompose, be corrupted.

——, *n.* 1. Booty, pillage, plunder, prey, loot.

2. Robbery, waste, pillage, rapine, spoliation.

Spoiler, *n.* 1. Plunderer, robber, pillager.

2. Destroyer, corrupter.

Spokesman, *n.* Speaker, prolocutor, mouthpiece.

Spoliate, *v. t.* Rob, plunder, spoil, despoil, loot, destroy, pillage.

Spoliation, *n.* 1. Robbery, destruction, deprivation, despoliation.

2. Robbery, pillage, plundering, rapine, devastation, destruction.

SPONGE, *v. t.* [*The noun is Basic Eng.*] 1. Wipe (*with a sponge*), cleanse.

2. Efface, obliterate, wipe out, expunge, rub out.

3. Drain, squeeze, plunder.

Sponger, *n.* Parasite, hanger-on.

Spongy, *a.* 1. Porous, spongeous, absorbent.

2. Wet, rainy, showery.

3. Drenched, saturated, soaked, wet, marshy.

Sponsor, *n.* 1. Surety, guarantor.

2. Godfather *or* godmother.

Spontaneity, *n.* Spontaneousness.

Spontaneous, *a.* Voluntary, instinctive, uncompelled, unbidden, unconstrained, willing, gratuitous, free, impulsive, improvised, self-moving, self-acting.

Spool, *n.* Bobbin, reel, "pirn."

SPOON, *n.* (*Basic Eng.*) Scooping implement.

Sporadic, *a.* Scattered, separate, dispersed, infrequent.

Sport, *n.* 1. Play, diversion, amusement, pastime, game, fun, frolic, gambol, prank, recreation, gayety, entertainment, merriment, mirth, jollity, joviality, pleasantry, merry-making.

2. Jest, joke.

3. Mockery, derision, mock, ridicule, contemptuous mirth, jeer.

4. Monstrosity, *lusus naturæ*.

——, *v. i.* 1. Play, frolic, disport, wanton, skip, frisk, romp, caper, make fun, make merry.

2. Trifle.

——, *v. t.* (*Colloq.*) Exhibit, display, make a show of.

Sportive, *a.* 1. Gay, frolicsome, playful, lively, merry, gamesome, sprightly, frisky, tricksy, rollicking, hilarious, wanton, prankish, full of fun.

2. Jocose, jocular, waggish, humorous, comic, ludicrous, frolicsome, playful, gamesome, facetious, funny, merry, vivacious, lively, sprightly, jocund, mirthful.

Spot, *n.* 1. Speck, blot, mark, speckle, fleck, mottle, freckle, dapple, pip, maculation, patch.

2. Blemish, blotch, splotch, pock, stain, taint, flaw.

3. Disgrace, reproach, fault, blemish, flaw.

4. Place, locality, site.

Spot, *v. t.* 1. Make spots on, dapple, speck, stud, dot, besprinkle, variegate.

2. Stain, sully, soil, tarnish, blemish, splotch; (*fig.*) disgrace.

Spotless, *a.* 1. Unspotted, undefaced, perfect.

2. Immaculate, unstained, untainted, unblemished, untarnished, blameless, stainless, innocent, pure, irreproachable.

Spotted, *a.* Speckled, bespeckled, bespotted, dotted, freckled, flecked, spotty, maculated, ocellated.

Spousal, *a.* Matrimonial, conjugal, connubial, hymeneal, bridal, marital, nuptial, wedded.

Spouse, *n.* Husband *or* wife, married person, consort, mate, partner, companion.

Spout, *n.* 1. Ajutage, tube, conduit.

2. Nozzle, nose, beak, waterspout, gargoyle.

——, *v. t.* 1. Spirit, pour out (*through a narrow orifice*), squirt, jet.

2. (*Colloq.*) Utter (*pompously*), mouth, declaim, speak.

——, *v. i.* 1. Gush, issue, spirt.

2. (*Colloq.*) Declaim, rant, make a speech, hold forth, speechify.

Sprain, *v. t.* Strain (*as a joint*), twist, wrench, rick, overstrain.

Spray, *n.* 1. Twig, shoot, sprig, branch, bough.

2. Foam, froth, spume.

Spread, *v. t.* 1. Extend, expand, mantle, stretch, dilate.

2. Disperse, scatter, distribute, diffuse, radiate, strew, sprinkle.

3. Publish, divulge, propagate, disseminate, broadcast, circulate, promulgate, make known, make public, spread abroad.

4. Unfold, unfurl, open.

5. Cover, overspread, extend over.

——, *v. i.* 1. Extend, be expanded.

2. Be dispersed, be scattered, diffuse.

3. Circulate, be circulated, be spread abroad, go the rounds.

——, *n.* 1. Extent, reach, compass, range, scope, stretch.

2. Extension, expansion.

3. Dissemination, circulation, propagation.

4. Cover, cloth.

Spree, *n.* (*Colloq.*) Carousal, revel, revelry, frolic, jollification, bacchanals, saturnalia, debauch, compotation, wassail, orgies, carouse, cups, drinking-bout.

Sprig, *n.* 1. Twig, shoot, spray.

2. Youth, lad.

Sprightliness, *n.* Liveliness, life, briskness, nimbleness, vivacity, animation, cheerfulness, gayety, frolicsomeness, vigor, activity.

Sprightly, *a.* Lively, mercurial, animated, vigorous, vivacious, buoyant, brisk, blithe, blithesome, gay, airy, cheerful, joyous, frolicsome, buxom, debonair.

Spring, *v. i.* 1. Leap, bound, jump, vault, hop, prance.

2. Arise, proceed, issue, put forth, shoot forth, make its appearance, emerge.

3. Originate, emanate, flow, take its source, have its origin, rise, start, come forth.

4. Rebound, fly back, recoil.

5. Warp, bend, become warped.

6. Grow, thrive, wax.

SPRING, *n.* 1. Leap, bound, jump, vault, saltation, hop.

2. Elasticity, resiliency, springiness, elastic force.

3. Fountain, well, geyser, fountainhead, fount, spring-head.

4. Source, original, origin, principle, cause.

5. Vernal season, spring-tide, seedtime.

Springe, *n.* Snare, gin, noose, net, toil, trap.

Springiness, *n.* 1. Elasticity, resilience, spring.

2. Wetness, sponginess.

Springy, *a.* Elastic, resilient, rebounding.

Sprinkle, *v. t.* 1. Scatter, strew.

2. Bedew, besprinkle, powder, spatter, sand, dust.

3. Wash, cleanse, purify.

Sprinkler, *n.* Watering-pot, sprinkle, atomizer.

Sprinkling, *n.* Affusion, bedewing.

Sprite, *n.* Fairy, fay, pixy, elf, spirit, ghost, specter, apparition, shade, phantom, goblin, hobgoblin.

Sprout, *v. i.* 1. Shoot, germinate, vegetate, push, grow, pullulate, put forth, shoot forth, burst forth, bourgeon.

2. Ramify, shoot into branches.

——, *n.* 1. Acrospire, plumule.

2. Shoot, ratoon, young branch.

Spruce, *a.* Neat, trim, nice, trig, fine, smart, jaunty, natty, foppish, dandyish, tidy.

——, *v. i.* Prink, dress finically, preen.

——, *v. t.* Trim, deck, dress, smarten.

Spry, *a.* (*Colloq.*) Active, lively, brisk, nimble, supple, agile, sprightly, quick, smart, prompt, alert, stirring, ready, dapper.

Spume, *n.* Foam, froth, spray, scum.

Spumy, *a.* Foamy, frothy, spumous.

Spur, *n.* 1. Goad, prick, point, rowel.

2. Incitement, stimulus, incentive, impulse, inducement, instigation, provocation, motive, fillip, whip, goad.

3. Snag, point, knot, gnarl, knob, projection.

——, *v. t.* 1. Prick (*with the spur*).

2. Stimulate, incite, rouse, arouse, goad, induce, instigate, impel, urge forward, drive, animate.

——, *v. i.* Prick, gallop, hasten, press forward, press on.

Spurious, *a.* 1. Illegitimate, bastard.

2. Counterfeit, supposititious, meretricious, deceitful, sham, false, mock, pretended, feigned, claptrap, fictitious, unauthentic, make-believe, adulterate, bogus, pinchbeck, brummagem.

Spurn, *v. t.* 1. Kick, drive back, drive away.

2. Contemn, scorn, scout, despise, disdain, make light of, look down upon, hold in contempt.

Spurt, *n.* 1. Jet, sudden gushing.

2. Sudden effort, short exigency.

——, *v. i.* [Written also *Spirt*.] Gush, spring out, stream out suddenly, jet, well, spout.

Sputter, *v. i.* 1. Spit, spawl.

2. Splutter, stammer.

Spy, *n.* Scout, emissary (*in disguise*), detective, undercover agent.

——, *v. t.* 1. See, behold, discern, espy, detect.

2. Discover, search out, detect.

3. Explore, view, inspect *or* examine secretly, discover by artifice.

——, *v. i.* Scrutinize, search narrowly.

Squab, *a.* 1. Fat, plump, stout, dumpy, squabbish, squabby, thick, bulky, heavy, short, thickset, chunky, fleshy.

2. Unfledged, unfeathered.

Squabble, *v. i.* 1. Quarrel, wrangle, fight, scuffle, struggle, brawl.

2. Dispute, contend, jangle, brawl, bicker, altercate, wrangle.

——, *n.* Brawl, wrangle, dispute, petty quarrel, broil, scrimmage, rumpus.

Squad, *n.* Gang, band, crew, relay, set, knot, bevy, lot, small company.

Squalid, *a.* Dirty, foul, unclean, slovenly, unkempt, mucky.

Squalidness, *n.* Foulness, filthiness, squalidity, squalor.

Squall, *v. i.* Cry (*as an infant*), bawl, yell, scream, cry out.

——, *n.* 1. Cry, bawl, yell, scream, outcry.

2. Storm (*sudden and brief*), blast, gust, flurry, brief gale, little tempest, brief hurricane.

Squally, *a.* Gusty, blustering, stormy, tempestuous, intermittently windy.

Squamose, *a.* (*Bot. and Anat.*) Scaly, squamate, squamated, squamous. Cf. LAMELLAR.

Squander, *v. t.* Spend (*profusely*), lavish, expend, waste, lose, dissipate, throw away, muddle away, scatter, misuse.

Squanderer, *n.* Spendthrift, prodigal, waster, lavisher.

Square, *a.* 1. Quadrilateral and equiangular, four-square, quadrate.

2. Just, honest, fair, equitable, upright, exact, equal.

3. Adjusted, balanced, settled, even.

4. True, just, exactly suitable.

SQUARE, *n.* 1. Four-sided figure (*with equal sides and angles*), quadrate, rectangle, tetragon.

2. Open area (*in a city or town*), plaza, parade.

——, *v. t.* 1. Make square, quadrate.

2. Regulate, adapt, fit, suit, accommodate, mould, shape.

3. Adjust, settle, close, balance, make even.

——, *v. i.* Suit, fit, accord, harmonize, quadrate, comport, cohere, chime in, fall in.

Squarrose, *a.* Ragged, rough, jagged.

Squash, *v. t.* Crush, mash.

Squashy, *a.* Soft, pulpy.

Squat, *v. i.* 1. Crouch, cower, sit close to the ground.

2. [*Modern.*] Settle (*without title to the land*), plant one's self, take up one's quarters, pitch one's tent.

——, *a.* 1. Crouching, cowering.

2. Dumpy, stubby, stocky, stumpy, short and thick, thickset, pudgy.

Squeal, *v. i.* Cry (*as a pig*), yell.

Squeamish, *a.* Fastidious, nice, delicate, finical, particular, hypercritical, dainty, priggish, over-nice, hard to please.

Squeeze, *v. t.* 1. Compress, constrict, gripe, pinch, nip, press closely, clutch in a vise.

2. Force (*between close bodies*), drive.

3. Harass, oppress, crush.

——, *v. i.* Press, crowd, force a way, urge one's way.

Squeeze out. Press out, force out, extract.

Squelch, *v. t.* Suppress, silence, crush, quash.

Squib, *n.* Lampoon, pasquinade, satire, fling.

Squint, *v. i.* Look askant, look askance, look obliquely.

Squint-eyed, *a.* 1. Cock-eyed, cross-eyed, squinting, strabismic.

2. Oblique, sinister, indirect, malignant.

Squinting, *n.* Strabism, strabismus.

Squirarchy, *n.* Gentlemen, gentry, gentlefolk.

Squire, *v. t.* Attend, escort, gallant, accompany, wait on.

——, *n.* Esquire, armiger.

Squirm, *v. i.* Writhe, wriggle, twist.

Squirt, *v. t.* Eject (*through a syringe*), spirt.

Stab, *v. t.* 1. Pierce, transfix, gore, spear, transpierce, pink, broach, "jab," "stick."

2. Wound, wound maliciously.

——, *n.* 1. Thrust, cut, prick, "jab."

2. Wound, blow, dagger-stroke.

3. Injury, malicious thrust, covert wound.

Stability, *n.* 1. Fixedness, durability, firmness, permanence, stableness, steadiness, immovability.

2. Constancy, steadiness, firmness, stableness.

Stable, *a.* 1. Fixed, established, permanent, immovable, immutable, unalterable, unchangeable, invariable.

2. Constant, steady, firm, steadfast, unwavering, stanch.

3. Durable, lasting, enduring, abiding, permanent, secure, perpetual, sure, fast.

Stable-man, *n.* Groom, hostler.

Staff, *n.* 1. Stick, pole, rod, baton, wand, cane.

2. Partisan, truncheon, quarter-staff, club, mace, cudgel, bludgeon, shillelah, bat.

3. Support, prop, stay.

4. Personnel, force, body of employees.

STAGE, *n.* 1. Platform, scaffold, staging, dais, rostrum, stand.

2. Theatre, playhouse.

3. Arena, place of exhibition, field, platform, boards, theatre.

4. Step, degree, point.

5. Stage-coach, omnibus, *diligence.*

Stagey, *a.* (*Colloq.*) Ranting, declamatory, bombastic, theatrical, stage-like, dramatic, melodramatic, fustian, pompous.

Stagger, *v. i.* 1. Reel, sway, totter, vacillate.

2. Hesitate, waver, falter.

——, *v. t.* Shock, astonish, astound, amaze, confound, dumfound, pose, surprise, nonplus, strike with wonder, take by surprise.

Stagnant, *a.* 1. Motionless, standing, close, quiet.

2. Sluggish, inactive, inert, torpid, dormant, dull, heavy.

Stagnate, *v. i.* 1. Be stagnant, stand still.

2. Be dull, be inactive, vegetate.

Staid, *a.* Sober, grave, steady, serious, composed, demure, solemn, calm, settled, sedate.

Stain, *v. t.* 1. Soil, sully, tarnish, spot, ensanguine, crock, blot, blotch, splotch, smirch, blemish, discolor, maculate.

2. Dye, tinge, color.

3. Disgrace, pollute, corrupt, defile, dishonor, debase, deprave, contaminate, taint, blot, soil, tarnish, sully, befoul.

——, *n.* 1. Blemish, tarnish, spot, blot, imperfection, discoloration.

2. Disgrace, dishonor, contamination, taint, reproach, tarnish, pollution, blemish.

3. Shame, disgrace, infamy, cause of reproach, reproach.

Stainless, *a.* 1. Spotless, untarnished, unspotted.

2. Unsullied, faultless, innocent, uncorrupted, guiltless, pure, blameless, spotless.

Stairs, *n. pl.* Staircase, stairway, flight of steps, flight of stairs, pair of stairs, set of steps.

Stake, *n.* 1. Stick (*pointed for driving into the ground*), picket, pale, palisade.

2. Wager, bet, pledge.

3. Risk, hazard, venture, adventure.

——, *v. t.* Risk, venture, hazard, peril, imperil, jeopardize, wager, pledge, put at stake, put at hazard.

Stale, *a.* 1. Vapid, tasteless, insipid, mawkish, flat, flashy, musty, mouldy, fusty, sour.

2. Old, decayed, faded, effete, timeworn, worn out.

3. Trite, common, hackneyed, commonplace, threadbare, old, vapid, stereotyped.

Stalk, *v. i.* 1. Walk (*stealthily*).

2. Stride, strut, pace, march.

——, *n.* Stem, petiole, pedicel, peduncle, culm, spire.

Stall, *n.* 1. Stable.

2. Compartment (*as in a stable*), cell, recess.

3. Stand (*where things are sold*), shop, booth, *étalage.*

——, *v. t.* 1. Put in a stable, keep in a stable.

2. Set fast (*as in mire*), fix in a slough, stick fast.

Stall-fed, *a.* Stable-kept, fatted.

Stallion, *n.* Stud-horse, breeding-horse, stockhorse, stone-horse.

Stalwart, *a.* 1. Strong, stout, sinewy, brawny, muscular, athletic, lusty, robust, sturdy, strapping, vigorous, powerful, puissant, able-bodied, Herculean, gigantic, stalworth.

2. Brave, bold, manly, valiant, valorous, gallant, intrepid, daring, resolute, firm, indomitable, redoubtable, redoubted.

Stamina, *n. pl.* 1. Firm parts (*that give strength*), principal elements.

2. Strength, vigor, force, stoutness, sturdiness, lustiness, power.

Stammer, *v. i.* Stutter, hesitate (*in speaking*), falter, hem and haw.

——, *n.* Stutter, falter, hesitant utterance.

Stamp, *v. t.* Impress, imprint, print, mark, brand, put a stamp on.

STAMP, *n.* 1. Mark, impress, print, impression, brand.

2. Make, cast, mould, form, fashion, cut, character, complexion, description, kind, type, sort.

Stampede, *n.* Sudden flight (*as of horses from fright*), rush, pellmell running.

Stanch, *v. t.* Stop the flow of, stop from running.

——, *a.* 1. Strong, sound, stout, firm.

2. Steady, firm, constant, steadfast, resolute, stable, unwavering, hearty, strong, zealous, faithful, loyal, trusty.

Stanchion, *n.* Prop, support, shore.

Stand, *v. i.* 1. Be erect, continue erect, remain upright.

2. Remain, continue, abide, be fixed, endure, hold good, be permanent.

3. Stop, halt, pause.

4. Stay, be firm, be resolute, keep one's position, maintain one's ground, stand one's ground, be fixed, be steady.

5. Be valid, have force, have validity.

6. Rest, depend, have support.

——, *v. t.* 1. Endure, sustain, bear, brook, suffer, weather, bear up against.

2. Abide, await, submit to, yield to, tolerate, put up with, admit.

3. Put, place, set upright, fix.

——, *n.* 1. Place, post, station, standing-place, position.

2. Stop, halt, stay.

3. Platform, raised station, rostrum.

4. Resistance, opposition.

5. Stall, booth.

Stand against. Oppose, resist, withstand.

Standard, *n.* 1. Ensign, banner, flag, streamer, gonfalon, pennon, colors.

2. Criterion, rule, model, norm, canon, test, type.

3. Gauge, model, measure, scale.

4. Support, upright.

Standard-bearer, *n.* Ensign (*of infantry*), cornet (*of cavalry*), color-sergeant.

Stand by. 1. Stand near, be near, be present.

2. Support, assist, aid, help, defend, side with, stand for.

3. Defend, maintain, vindicate, make good, justify, support.

4. (*Naut.*) Attend, be ready.

Stand fast. Be fixed, be unshaken, be immovable.

Stand for. 1. Signify, mean, represent.

2. Defend, support, aid, help, side with, stand by, maintain.

Standing, *a.* 1. Established, settled, fixed, immovable.

2. Lasting, permanent, durable.

3. Stagnant, motionless.

——, *n.* 1. Stand, station, position.

2. Duration, existence, continuance.

3. Footing, hold, ground, power to stand.

4. Position, rank, condition, reputation, estimation, *status.*

Stand in stead. Benefit, profit, be of use, be of service, be advantageous.

Stand off. 1. Keep off, keep at a distance, keep aloof.

2. Not to comply.

Stand one's ground. Stand, stay, be firm, be resolute, keep one's position, maintain one's ground.

Stand out. 1. Project, jut, protrude, be prominent, jut out.

2. Persist (*in resistance*), not yield, not comply.

Standpoint, *n.* Point of view, view-point.

Standstill, *n.* Stand, stop, interruption, cessation; deadlock.

Stand up for. Defend, justify, uphold, support, sustain.

Stand with. Be consistent with, agree.

Stanza, *n.* Stave, staff, strophe.

Staple, *n.* 1. Chief commodity (*of a country* or *a district*), principal production.

2. Fibre (*of cotton, wool, etc.*), pile, filament, thread.

3. Raw material, unmanufactured material.

4. Bulk, mass, body, substance, principal part, greater part, chief ingredient.

——, *a.* Chief, principal.

STAR, *n.* 1. Heavenly body, luminary.

2. Asterisk, pentagram, pentacle.

3. Fate, fortune, destiny, lot, doom.

Starboard, *n.* (*Naut.*) Right-hand side (*of a vessel, to a person looking forward*).

——, *a.* (*Naut.*) Right.

Starched, *a.* Stiff, precise, formal, prim, rigid, punctilious, ceremonious, starchy, affectedly exact.

Stare, *v. i.* Gaze, gape, look intently, gaze earnestly.

Stark, *a.* 1. Stiff, rigid.

2. Mere, simple, sheer, bare, downright, gross, pure, entire, absolute.

STARK 504 STAY

Stark, *adv.* Wholly, entirely, completely, fully, absolutely.

Star-like, *a.* 1. Bright, lustrous, twinkling.
2. Radiated, stellate, stellated, stellular.

Starry, *a.* 1. Full of stars, star-spangled, stellar.
2. Stellar, stellary, astral, sidereal.
3. Brilliant, shining, sparkling, twinkling, lustrous.

Start, *v. i.* 1. Shrink, flinch, wince, startle.
2. Depart, set out, set off, take off, begin going.
3. Arise, come into existence suddenly.
4. Move suddenly, spring, startle.

——, *v. t.* 1. Rouse, alarm, startle, disturb, fright, scare.
2. Evoke, raise, call forth.
3. Begin, initiate, inaugurate, institute, set on foot.
4. Discover, invent.
5. Move (*suddenly*), dislocate.

START, *n.* 1. Startle, sudden motion, jump.
2. Fit, spasmodic effort, twitch, spasm.
3. Beginning, outset, setoff, "getaway."
4. Sally, sudden effusion, impulse.

Startle, *v. i.* Shrink, wince, flinch, start.

——, *v. t.* 1. Frighten, fright, affright, alarm, scare, shock.
2. Strike with wonder, surprise, astonish, astound, amaze.

Startling, *a.* Shocking, alarming, sudden, unexpected, unforeseen, surprising, astonishing, unheard of, abrupt.

Starvation, *n.* Famishment.

Starve, *v. i.* 1. Famish, perish (*with hunger*).
2. Lack, want, be in need.

——, *v. t.* 1. Kill with hunger, starve to death.
2. Subdue by famine.

Starveling, *a.* Lean, meagre, lank, emaciated, gaunt, skinny, scraggy, raw-boned, hungry, thin, attenuated, ill-fed, ill-conditioned.

——, *n.* Pauper, mendicant, beggar.

State, *n.* 1. Condition, situation, position, plight, posture, phase, predicament, pass, case, status, circumstances.
2. Rank, condition, quality, mode, guise.
3. Commonwealth, civil community, body politic.
4. Pomp, parade, dignity, splendor, pageantry, grandeur, magnificence.

——, *v. t.* Express (*with particularity*), explain, specify, set forth, narrate, recite, represent fully, declare, affirm, assert.

——, *a.* National, public.

State-craft, *n.* Statesmanship, state management, diplomacy, political subtlety.

Stated, *a.* 1. Settled, established, regular, fixed.
2. Detailed, set forth, specified.

Stately, *a.* 1. Lofty, dignified, majestic, imperial, magnificent, grand, noble, princely, royal, elevated, august, imposing.
2. Pompous, ceremonious, solemn, formal, magisterial, dignified, lofty, majestic, elevated.

STATEMENT, *n.* 1. Specification, mention, declaration, allegation, announcement, report, account, recital, relation, narration, narrative, description, exposition.
2. Proposition, predication, assertion, thesis, pronouncement.

Statesman, *n.* Statist, politician, Solon.

STATION, *n.* 1. Place, position, post, location, situation, seat.
2. Office, function, business, employment, sphere of duty, occupation.
3. Rank, standing, footing, character, state, degree, dignity, condition, *status*.
4. Station-house, railway station, depot, stop, terminal.

——, *v. t.* Place, locate, post, fix, establish, set.

Stationary, *a.* Fixed, stable, permanent, standing, still, quiescent, motionless, at rest, at a stand, standing still.

Stationery, *n.* Pens, ink, paper, etc.

Statuary, *n.* 1. Sculpture, carving.
2. Statues (*collectively*).
3. Sculptor, artist in stone.

Statue, *n.* Image (*in stone, metal, etc.*), statuette, figurine.

Stature, *n.* Height, tallness, size.

Status, *n.* [L.] Standing, footing, position, caste, rank, station, condition.

Statute, *n.* Law, act, enactment, ordinance, edict, decree, regulation.

Stave, *v. t.* Burst, break a hole in, stave in.

Stave off. Defer, delay, postpone, adjourn, procrastinate, put off, lay over, let lie over, waive, shift off.

Stay, *v. i.* 1. Sojourn, tarry, abide, dwell, lodge, rest, take up one's quarters, pitch one's tent.
2. Remain, continue, stop, halt, be fixed, stand still.
3. Wait, attend, delay, linger.

——, *v. t.* 1. Stop, restrain, arrest, check, hold, withhold, curb, keep in, rein in, prevent.
2. Delay, obstruct, hinder, detain.
3. Support, sustain, uphold, prop, hold up, shore up.

Stay, *n.* 1. Sojourn, delay, rest, repose.

2. Stand, stop, halt.

3. Hindrance, obstruction, interruption, obstacle, impediment, check, bar, restraint, curb, stumbling-block.

4. Support, prop, staff, dependence, supporter, buttress.

Stead, *n.* Place, room.

Steadfast, *a.* 1. Fixed, fast, established, firm, stable.

2. Resolute, firm, steady, stanch, constant, stable, pertinacious, unwavering, unhesitating, unshaken, unreserved, implicit, faithful, resolved, persevering.

Steadiness, *n.* 1. Steadfastness, firmness, constancy, resolution, persistence, perseverance.

2. Stability, firmness, fixedness.

Steady, *a.* 1. Fixed, firm, stable.

2. Regular, undeviating, unremitting, uniform, constant, equable.

3. Constant, resolute, stanch, steadfast, stable, unwavering, persevering, unchangeable.

Steak, *n.* Collop, slice, broiling-piece.

Steal, *v. t.* 1. Purloin, pilfer, filch, "crib," poach, peculate, embezzle, plagiarize, make off with, come unlawfully by.

2. Take secretly, accomplish secretly.

——, *v. i.* 1. Pilfer, purloin, peculate, shoplift, thieve, practise theft, take feloniously.

2. Pass stealthily, slip, creep, sneak, go unperceived, withdraw privily.

Stealing, *n.* Theft, robbery, larceny, shoplifting, thievery, peculation.

Stealth, *n.* Stealthiness, secrecy, slyness.

Stealthy, *a.* Sly, secret, private, clandestine, furtive, underhand, sneaking, skulking, surreptitious.

STEAM, *n.* 1. Vapor (*especially of water*), water in a gaseous state.

2. Mist, fume, reek, smoke, exhalation, effluvium.

——, *v. i.* 1. Emit vapor, fume.

2. Evaporate, pass off in vapor.

Steamboat, *n.* Steamer, steamship.

Steamy, *a.* Vaporous, misty, moist.

Steed, *n.* (*Poetical.*) Horse (*especially a war-horse*), charger, mount.

STEEL, *n.* 1. Knife, sword, dagger, dirk, poniard, claymore, sabre, falchion, rapier, hanger, blade.

2. Hardness, sternness, vigor, mercilessness.

——, *v. t.* 1. Case-harden, edge *or* point with steel.

2. Harden, strengthen, fortify, nerve, brace, make firm.

Steep, *a.* Precipitous, abrupt, sheer, sudden, declivitous, sharply sloping.

——, *n.* Precipice, abrupt declivity.

——, *v. t.* Soak, macerate, imbrue, drench, saturate, digest, imbue.

Steeple, *n.* Spire, tower, turret, pointed belfry.

Steer, *n.* Young ox.

——, *v. t.* Direct (*as a vessel by the helm*), guide, pilot, conduct, govern, have *or* take the direction of.

——, *v. i.* 1. Direct one's course, point.

2. Be directed, be governed.

Steersman, *n.* Helmsman, pilot, guide, conductor.

Stellar, *a.* 1. Astral, starry, stellary.

2. Full of stars, starry, star-spangled.

Stellate, *a.* Star-like, radiated, stellular, stellated, stellulate.

STEM, *n.* 1. Trunk (*of a tree*), main stock, stipe, axis.

2. Peduncle, pedicel, petiole, stalk.

3. Branch, shoot, scion, descendant, progeny, offspring.

4. Stock, race, pedigree, descent, family, generation, lineage, line, ancestry.

5. (*Naut.*) Forepart (*of a ship*), prow, beak, bow, cutwater.

6. Lookout, leading position, helm.

7. Root, origin, radical, radix, primitive word, etymon.

——, *v. t.* 1. Oppose (*as a current*), resist, breast, withstand, bear up against, make head against.

2. Stop, check, oppose, stay.

Stench, *n.* Stink, fetor, bad smell, offensive odor.

Stenography, *n.* Shorthand, tachygraphy, brachygraphy.

Stentorian, *a.* Loud-voiced, sonorous, powerful, thundering, trumpet-like.

STEP, *n.* 1. Pace, stride, footstep.

2. Stair, tread.

3. Degree, grade, gradation, interval.

4. Advancement, progression, advance.

5. Action, act, deed, proceeding, procedure.

6. Footprint, track, trace, vestige.

7. Gait, walk, pace, footfall.

8. Measure, means, method, expedient.

9. Round (*of a ladder*), rundle, rung.

——, *v. i.* Walk, stride, tread, pace, tramp.

Steppe, *n.* Prairie, pampa, savanna.

Sterile, *a.* 1. Barren, unfruitful, unproductive, unprolific, infecund, unfruitful.

2. Poor, bare, dry, empty.

3. (*Bot.*) Acarpous, staminate, male.

Sterility, *n.* Barrenness, unfruitfulness, fruitlessness, unproductiveness, infecundity.

Sterling, *a.* Genuine, pure, true, real, substantial, positive, standard, sound.

Stern, *a.* 1. Forbidding, austere, dour, grim, severe.

2. Harsh, cruel, severe, bitter, rigorous, strict, hard, unrelenting, inflexible, rigid.

3. Steadfast, immovable, incorruptible, uncompromising.

——, *n.* Hinder part (*of a vessel*), poop.

Sternness, *n.* 1. Severity, austerity, rigidity.

2. Harshness, asperity, rigor, inflexibility, cruelty.

Sternum, *n.* (*Anat.*) Breastbone, sternon.

Sternutatory, *a.* Sternutative, errhine, that produces sneezing.

Stertoreous, } *a.* Snoring, hoarsely breath-
Stertorous, } ing.

Stew, *v. t.* Boil (*slowly*), seethe, simmer, stive.

——, *n.* 1. Hot-house, bagnio, hot bath-house, sudatory.

2. Ragout, stewed meat.

3. (*Colloq.*) Confusion,· difficulty, scrape, mess.

Steward, *n.* 1. Major-domo, chamberlain, seneschal.

2. Manciple, purveyor.

Stew-pan, *n.* Saucepan, kettle, skillet.

Stews, *n. pl.* Brothel, bagnio, bawdy-house, whore-house, house of prostitution, house of ill fame.

STICK, *n.* 1. Rod, switch, birch.

2. Club, bludgeon, cudgel, shillelah, bat.

3. Cane, staff, walking-stick.

4. Stake, pole, spar, cue.

5. Stab, thrust, prick.

——, *v. t.* 1. Pierce, penetrate, puncture, transfix, stab, spear, gore.

2. Insert, thrust, infix.

3. Attach, paste, glue, cement.

4. Set, fix in.

——, *v. i.* 1. Adhere, cleave, cling, hold, stay affixed.

2. Abide, remain, persist, stop, stay, hold fast, be infixed.

3. Hesitate, waver, doubt, scruple, stickle.

Stick by. Adhere to, be faithful to, be true to, stick to, be constant, be firm.

Stickiness, *n.* Adhesiveness, viscousness, glutinousness, tenacity, viscosity.

Stickle, *v. i.* 1. Struggle (*pertinaciously and on trifling grounds*), contend, altercate, contest.

2. Hesitate, waver, doubt, scruple, stick.

STICKY, *a.* Adhesive, clinging, gummy, glutinous, viscous, viscid, tenacious, gluey, mucilaginous.

STIFF, *a.* 1. Rigid, unbending, unyielding, inflexible, stark, subrigid.

2. Firm, tenacious, thick, inspissated.

3. Stubborn, obstinate, pertinacious, tenacious, strong.

4. Rigorous, severe, strict, strait-laced, stringent, peremptory absolute, positive, austere, dogmatic, uncompromising, inexorable.

5. Formal, constrained, ceremonious, punctilious, prim, starch, stilted, stately, chilling, frigid.

6. Inelegant, cramped, harsh, crude, graceless, abrupt.

Stiff-necked, *a.* Stubborn, obstinate, obdurate, dogged, mulish, headstrong, contumacious, cross-grained, unruly, intractable.

Stiffness, *n.* 1. Rigidity, inflexibility, rigidness, rigor, hardness, starkness.

2. Thickness, spissitude, density, compactness, denseness, consistence.

3. Stubbornness, obstinacy, pertinacity, contumaciousness, inflexibility.

4. Severity, rigor, strictness, harshness, rigorousness, austerity, sternness.

5. Formality, precision, constraint, tenseness, primness, frigidity.

Stifle, *v. t.* 1. Smother, choke, suffocate.

2. Suppress, repress, check, deaden, stop, destroy, extinguish, quench.

3. Still, hush, silence, muffle, muzzle, gag, conceal, smother.

Stigma, *n.* Stain, blot, disgrace, reproach, dishonor, shame, spot, blur, brand, tarnish, taint.

Stigmatize, *v. t.* Disgrace, reproach, dishonor, vilify, defame, discredit, brand, post, slur, hold up to shame.

Stiletto, *n.* 1. Dagger, dirk, ·poniard, stylet.

2. Bodkin, piercer, eyeleteer.

Still, *v. t.* 1. Silence, stifle, muffle, hush, lull.

2. Calm, compose, quiet, allay, appease, pacify, tranquillize, smooth, lull.

3. Stop, immobilize, check, restrain, subdue, suppress, calm, quiet.

——, *a.* 1. Silent, noiseless, hushed, mute, mum.

2. Quiet, calm, tranquil, placid, serene, stilly, unruffled.

3. Motionless, quiescent, at rest, inert, stagnant, stationary.

4. Soft, gentle, mild, low, quiet.

STILL, *adv. or conj.* 1. Yet, till now, to this time.

2. However, nevertheless, notwithstanding.

3. Always, ever, continually, habitually, uniformly.

4. After that, after what is stated, in continuance, again.

Still, *n.* 1. Distillery, still-house.

2. Distillatory, distilling vessel, alembic, retort, stillatory.

Stilted, *a.* Pompous, swelling, inflated, bombastic, turgid, pretentious, grandiloquent, magniloquent, high-sounding, fustian, stilty, tumid, high-flown, grandiose.

Stimulant, *a.* Stimulating, exciting, stimulative.

——, *n.* 1. Stimulating medicine, cordial, tonic, "bracer," "pick-me-up."

2. Incentive, stimulus, fillip, provocative, spur.

Stimulate, *v. t.* Incite, excite, instigate, animate, awaken, brace, rally, energize, encourage, inspirit, urge, prompt, goad, rouse, arouse, whet, foment, spur, impel, inflame, fire, kindle, stir up, set on, work up, prick, fillip, provoke, pique.

Stimulus, *n.* Incentive, spur, goad, fillip, incitement, stimulant, provocative, provocation, motive, encouragement.

Sting, *v. t.* 1. Prick, nettle, wound, hurt.

2. Afflict, pain, cut to the quick, go to one's heart.

——, *n.* Prick, act of stinging.

Stinging, *a.* 1. Piercing, painful, acute.

2. Pungent, nipping, biting, tingling.

Stingy, *a.* Niggardly, penurious, parsimonious, grudging, miserly, close, mean, covetous, avaricious, sordid, close-fisted, narrow-hearted.

Stink, *v. i.* Smell bad, smell ill, emit a stench.

——, *n.* Stench, fetor, offensive odor, bad smell.

Stint, *v. t.* 1. Limit, bound, restrain, confine.

2. Straiten, pinch, scant, scrimp, skimp, begrudge, put on short allowance.

——, *v. i.* Stop, cease, desist.

——, *n.* 1. Limit, bound, restraint.

2. Quantity assigned, allotted portion, quota, task.

Stipend, *n.* Salary, wages, allowance, pay, hire, compensation, remuneration, emolument, fee, *honorarium.*

Stipulate, *v. i.* Bargain, agree, contract, engage, condition, covenant, provide, settle terms.

Stipulation, *n.* Bargain, agreement, contract, engagement, obligation, covenant, indenture, concordat, pact, convention.

Stir, *v. t.* 1. Move, set in motion.

2. Agitate, disturb, prod, bestir.

3. Discuss, argue, moot, start, raise, agitate, bring into debate.

4. Instigate, incite, excite, rouse, arouse, awaken, prompt, stimulate, provoke, animate, quicken, goad, spur, stir up, set on.

——, *v. i.* 1. Move, budge, go, change place, change one's position, move one's self.

2. Be active, be in motion.

3. Appear, happen, turn up, come into notice.

4. (*Colloq.*) Rise (*from bed in the morning*), get up.

——, *n.* 1. Agitation, tumult, bustle, excitement, confusion, hurry, movement, activity, flurry, ado, fidget, fuss.

2. Disorder, tumult, uproar, commotion, public disturbance, seditious commotion.

Stirring, *a.* 1. Active, lively, brisk, smart, industrious, diligent.

2. Animating, arousing, awakening, stimulating, quickening, exciting.

Stir up. Incite, instigate, animate, put in action, excite, quicken, awaken, move, rouse, provoke, stimulate.

STITCH, *v. t.* [*The noun is Basic Eng.*] 1. Sew, sew together.

2. Make stitches in.

Stithy, *n.* Smithy, smithery, smith's shop, forge.

Stive, *v. t.* 1. Stow, stuff close.

2. Make hot, close, *or* sultry.

3. Stew, seethe, boil gently.

Stock, *n.* 1. Trunk (*of a tree*), stipe, stalk, stem.

2. Post, pillar, block, log, stake.

3. Dolt, dullard, dunce, blockhead, fool, block, stick, dunderhead, numskull, loggerhead, clod.

4. Handle (*of an instrument*), haft, butt.

5. Cravat, neckcloth.

6. Race, breed, strain, lineage, pedigree, parentage, ancestry, family, line, descent, house.

7. Capital, fund, invested property, principal.

8. Store, supply, accumulation, provision, hoard, reserve.

——, *v. t.* 1. Store, supply, furnish, fill.

2. Reserve, save, garner, hoard, reposit, accumulate, lay in, treasure up, lay by, lay up.

——, *a.* Standard, permanent, standing.

Stockholder, *n.* Shareholder.

STOCKING, *n.* Hose, sock.

Stock-jobber, *n.* Speculator in stocks, trader in stocks.

Stock-market, *n.* 1. Stock-exchange.

2. Cattle-market.

Stocks, *n. pl.* 1. Funds (*invested in joint-stock enterprises* or *in the obligations of a Government*), public funds, public securities.

2. Shares (*in joint-stock companies,* or *in the obligations of a Government*).

Stock-still, *a.* Stone-still, perfectly still, motionless, still as a post.

Stocky, *a.* (*Colloq.*) Stout, plump, chubbed, "chunky," dumpy, stubby, short and thick, thickset.

Stoic, *n.* Follower of Zeno, Stoical philosopher.

Stoic, ⎫ *a.* Passionless, apathetic, unim-
Stoical, ⎭ passioned, imperturbable, philosophic, cold-blooded, impassive, patient.

Stoicism, *n.* 1. Stoical philosophy, philosophy of Zeno.

2. Apathy, insensibility, coolness, indifference, coldness, phlegm, cold blood, impassibility, nonchalance.

Stolen, *a.* 1. Purloined, pilfered, filched, taken wrongfully.

2. Furtive, stealthy, surreptitious, clandestine, secret, sly.

Stolid, *a.* Stupid, dull, heavy, doltish, slow, stockish, foolish, blockish, obtuse.

Stolidity, *n.* Stupidity, dulness, foolishness, doltishness, obtuseness, stolidness.

STOMACH, *n.* Appetite, inclination, keenness, desire, taste, liking, relish.

——, *v. t.* (*Colloq.*) Brook, endure, bear, tolerate, abide, swallow, stand, submit to, suffer, put up with.

Stomachic, ⎫ *a.* 1. Of the stomach, gas-
Stomachical, ⎭ tric.

2. Stomachal, cordial, wholesome, tonic, salutary, good for the stomach.

STONE, *n.* 1. Rock, pebble, bowlder, cobble, gravel.

2. Gem, jewel, precious stone.

3. Gravestone, tombstone, monument, cenotaph, monumental tablet.

4. Nut (*of a drupe*), pit.

5. Adamant, flint, marble, etc.

——, *v. t.* 1. Pelt with stones.

2. Face with stone, line with stone.

3. Free from stones, stein.

Stone-pit, *n.* Quarry, stone-bed, stone-quarry.

Stone's throw. Stone's cast, short distance, few steps.

Stony, *a.* 1. Hard, petrous, gritty, rocky, lapidose, lithic.

2. Obdurate, inflexible, hard, adamantine, flinty.

3. Cruel, unfeeling, pitiless, unrelenting, stony-hearted, hard-hearted, inexorable.

Stook, *n.* Shock (*of corn*), hattock, stuckle.

Stool, *n.* 1. Seat (*without a back*), footstool, hassock, tabouret.

2. Discharge (*from the bowels*), evacuation, excrement.

Stool pigeon, *n.* 1. Decoy-pigeon, decoy (*for game*).

2. Decoy, inveigler, decoyer, inveigling accomplice, cat's-paw.

Stoop, *v. i.* 1. Couch, bend forward, bend down, lean forward, lean.

2. Yield, submit, succumb, surrender, give in, cower, cringe.

3. Condescend, descend, deign, vouchsafe.

4. Swoop, descend, come down, bear down.

5. Sink, fall.

——, *v. t.* Lower, abase, bow, bend down, bend forward, sink.

——, *n.* 1. Inclination, bend, act of stooping.

2. Condescension, descent.

3. Swoop, descent.

4. Flagon, bowl, cup, mug, tankard.

5. [*U. S.*] Doorsteps, porch, perron, steps, outer stair.

Stop, *v. t.* 1. Close, close up, obstruct, occlude, render impassable, block, blockade.

2. Bring to a standstill, stay, check, arrest, block, stall, halt, hold, bring to a close.

3. Hinder, repress, restrain, suppress, obstruct, stanch, stay, intercept, preclude, bar, thwart, impede, interrupt, lay an embargo on, prevent, delay.

4. Leave, cease from, desist from, refrain from, leave off, make an end of, discontinue, have done with, give over.

5. Suspend, arrest, intermit, discontinue, quiet, put an end to, end, terminate.

——, *v. i.* 1. Be at a standstill, come to a standstill, come to a deadlock, cease progress, halt, pause, stall.

2. Cease, desist, forbear, leave off, break off.

3. (*Colloq.*) Tarry, stay, lodge, take lodgings, have lodgings.

STOP, *n.* 1. Pause, rest, intermission, stoppage, suspension, halt, respite, truce.

2. Interruption, repression, cessation, obstruction, hindrance, block, check.

3. Impediment, obstacle, obstruction, bar.

4. Point, mark of punctuation.

Stopcock, *n.* Cock, tap, faucet.

Stoppage, *n.* Obstruction, block, check, closure, arrest, hindrance, interruption, prevention.

Stopper, *n.* Stopple, plug, cork.

STORE, *n.* 1. Stock, supply, fund, hoard, treasure, treasury, provision, accumulation, reserve, cache, deposit.

2. Abundance, plenty, great quantity, great number.

3. See STOREHOUSE.

4. Shop, emporium, market.

Store, *v. t.* 1. Garner, hoard, husband, deposit, save, reserve, treasure up, lay in, lay up, lay by, put by, accumulate, amass, heap up, store up, stow away.

2. Supply, furnish, stock, replenish, provide.

Storehouse, *n.* Magazine, warehouse, repository, store, depot, godown.

Storm, *n.* 1. Tempest, gale, hurricane, tornado, typhoon, squall, whirlwind, violent wind (*usually accompanied with rain, hail*, or *snow*), blizzard.

2. Disturbance, agitation, commotion, tumult, turmoil, clamor, sedition, insurrection, outbreak.

3. Calamity, adversity, distress, affliction.

4. Attack, assault, onslaught, onset, brunt.

5. Violence, tumultuous force.

——, *v. t.* Attack (*with violence, as a fortification*), assault, assail.

——, *v. i.* 1. Blow violently (*with* or *without rain, hail*, or *snow*).

2. Rage, rave, rampage, fume, rant, tear.

Storminess, *n.* Tempestuousness, inclemency, roughness.

Stormy, *a.* 1. Tempestuous, windy, gusty, squally, boisterous, blustering.

2. Violent, passionate, rough, riotous, turbulent, wild.

3. Furious, agitated, blustering.

STORY, *n.* 1. History, chronicle, annals, record.

2. Narration, narrative, recital, relation, rehearsal, account, statement, tale, record, report.

3. Fiction, fable, romance, novel.

4. Anecdote, incident, tale, legend.

5. (*Colloq.*) Falsehood, untruth, lie, fib, fabrication, invention, fiction, figment, fable, *canard*.

6. Floor, loft.

Story-teller, *n. Raconteur.*

Stout, *a.* 1. Strong, sinewy, brawny, athletic, lusty, robust, sturdy, stalwart, vigorous, able-bodied.

2. Brave, valiant, valorous, intrepid, bold, manful, manly, resolute, gallant, firm, indomitable, hardy, courageous, dauntless, doughty.

3. Proud, resolute, obstinate, stubborn, contumacious.

4. Firm, strong, solid, strongly built, hardy, compact, sturdy, stanch.

5. Large, corpulent, obese, strapping, bouncing, portly, chubby, jolly, burly, plump, fat, in good case, thick-set.

Stout-hearted, *a.* Fearless, heroic, redoubtable. See STOUT, 2.

Stow, *v. t.* Pack, stuff, stive, wedge in, put in compactly.

Strabismus, *n.* Squinting, strabism, cast of the eye, obliquity of vision.

Straddle, *v. t.* Bestride.

Straggle, *v. i.* 1. Rove, wander.

2. Ramble, stroll, range, roam, wander, deviate, stray, rove, digress, gad about, go out of the way, go astray.

Straggler, *n.* 1. Wanderer, rover.

2. Rambler, strayer, stroller, vagrant, vagabond, nomad, bird of passage.

Straggling, *a.* 1. Roving, rambling, straying, strolling, wandering.

2. Scattered, occurring here and there.

STRAIGHT, *a.* 1. Rectilinear, direct, short, near, right, undeviating, unswerving.

2. Vertical, upright, erect, perpendicular, plumb, right.

3. Just, fair, square, honorable, straightforward, honest, equitable.

——, *adv.* Immediately, directly, forthwith, straightway, at once, without delay.

Straighten, *v. t.* Make straight.

Straightforward, *a.* 1. Direct, undeviating, straight, not turning to right or to left.

2. Truthful, veracious, reliable, trustworthy.

3. Honest, honorable, equitable, fair, just, square, even-handed, upright, straight, conscientious.

4. Artless, ingenuous, frank, sincere, candid, honest, guileless, outspoken, true-hearted.

Straightway, *adv.* Immediately, directly, suddenly, speedily, without delay, straight, at once, forthwith.

Strain, *v. t.* 1. Stretch, draw tightly, make tense, make tight, tighten.

2. Wrench, sprain, injure by stretching.

3. Exert (*to the utmost*), put to the utmost strength, overexert, overtax, rack.

4. Pervert (*from the true intent*), push too far.

5. Squeeze, press, embrace, hug, fold tightly in the arms.

6. Force, constrain, compel.

7. Filter, purify (*by filtration*), filtrate, percolate, separate, drain, dilute, distill.

8. Fatigue, over-exert, tire, over-task, tax, task, over-work.

——, *v. i.* 1. Try hard, make great efforts.

2. Percolate, filter, be filtered, be strained, ooze.

——, *n.* 1. Extreme tension, stress, tensity, tenseness.

2. Over-exertion, violent effort, great exertion, force; burden, tax, task.

3. Sprain, wrench.

4. Tune, melody, movement, snatch, stave; lay, song.

5. Style, manner, vein, tone.

6. Turn, tendency, disposition, inborn disposition.

7. Stock, race, descent, family, lineage, pedigree, extraction.

Strait, *a.* 1. Narrow, close, contracted, constricted, constrained, confined.

2. Strict, rigorous, rigid, severe.

3. Difficult, distressful, straitened, grievous.

——, *n.* 1. Narrow pass (*especially between two seas*), gut, narrows.

2. Distress, difficulty, perplexity, dilemma, embarrassment, pinch, exigency, emergency, critical situation, distressing necessity, pass.

Straiten, *v. t.* 1. Confine, limit, constrict, contract, constrain.

2. Narrow.

3. Stretch, straighten, make tight *or* tense.

4. Distress, perplex, pinch, embarrass, press.

Straitened, *a.* Distressed, perplexed, embarrassed, pinched, limited.

Strait-laced, *a.* Strict, rigid, formal, stiff, stern, rigorous, austere, uncompromising.

Straitness, *n.* 1. Strictness, rigor, severity, narrowness.

2. Difficulty, distress, trouble.

3. Want, scarcity, insufficiency, narrowness.

Strand, *n.* Beach, shore, coast.

——, *v. i.* Run aground, get ashore, be wrecked, be cast away.

Stranded, *a.* Aground, ashore, wrecked, shipwrecked, cast away, lost.

STRANGE, *a.* 1. Foreign, outlandish, exotic, alien, far-fetched, remote.

2. New, novel.

3. Unusual, uncommon, irregular, odd, singular, peculiar, particular, exceptional, rare, extraordinary, curious, surprising.

4. Unnatural, abnormal, anomalous, extraordinary, wonderful, inexplicable, unbelievable, inconceivable, incredible, marvellous, preternatural, unaccountable, mysterious, unique, unheard of, out of the way.

5. Odd, eccentric, queer, peculiar, *bizarre*, quaint, droll, grotesque.

6. Unacquainted, unknown, unfamiliar, inexperienced; bashful, distrustful, shy, distant, reserved, uncommunicative.

Strangeness, *n.* 1. Foreignness.

2. Distance, reserve, coldness, shyness, bashfulness, uncommunicativeness.

3. Uncouthness, oddness, uncommonness, singularity, eccentricity, grotesqueness.

Stranger, *n.* 1. Foreigner, alien, outsider, immigrant; newcomer.

2. Guest, visitor, visitant.

Strangle, *v. t.* 1. Choke, throttle, suffocate, tighten, contract, squeeze, stifle, smother.

2. Suppress, repress, still, quiet, keep back.

Strap, *n.* 1. Thong.

2. Strop, razor-strap, razor-strop.

3. Ligature, tie, band, strip.

——, *v. t.* 1. Whip (*with a strap*), thrash.

2. Bind (*with a strap*), fasten.

3. Strop, sharpen (*on a strap*).

Strapping, *a.* (*Colloq.*) Large, burly, stout, tall, strong, big, lusty, stalwart.

Stratagem, *n.* Artifice, device, manœuvre, intrigue, wile, trick, fetch, dodge, crafty device, machination, plot, plan, scheme, artful contrivance, stroke of policy, finesse, *ruse*, cunning.

Strategist, *n.* Skilful general, adroit tactician, expert manœuvrer.

Strategy, *n.* Generalship, strategetics, tactics, manœuvring, military science, art of war.

Stratified, *a.* In strata, in layers, laminate, foliated.

Stratum, *n.* [L. *pl. Strata.*] Layer, bed.

Straw, *n.* 1. Stalk, stem *or* culm (*of grain after being thrashed*).

2. Fig, pin, button, rush, penny, farthing, snap.

Stray, *v. i.* Wander, rove, ramble, range, meander, roam, straggle, stroll, deviate, digress, go out of the way, go astray, swerve, err, transgress.

——, *a.* (*Colloq.*) Strayed, wandering, gone astray.

Streak, *n.* Stripe, vein, band, thread, line, trace, bar.

Streaky, *a.* Striped, streaked.

Stream, *n.* 1. Current, course, flow, rush, tide, confluent, affluent, tributary, race, flood.

2. River, rivulet, brook, run.

3. Current, drift, tendency.

4. Effusion, gush.

——, *v. i.* 1. Flow, run, glide, pour, spout.

2. Shed, pour out, emit.

3. Issue, radiate, go forth, emanate.

4. Extend, stretch out, float, wave.

Streamer, *n.* Pennon, banner, flag, ensign, standard, colors.

Streamlet, *n.* Rill, brook, rivulet, runlet, runnel, trickle, run, small stream, burn.

STREET, *n.* Road, highway, public way, way, avenue.

Street-walker, *n.* Common prostitute.

Strength, *n.* 1. Power, might, force, potency, main, puissance, nerve, vigor.

2. Solidity, toughness, hardness.

3. Impregnability, proof.

4. Lustiness, brawn, robustness, stoutness, sinews, muscle, stamina, stalwartness, thews, grit.

5. Fortitude, courage, spirit, animation, firmness, resolution, determination.

6. Validity, cogency, efficacy, soundness.

7. Vigor (*of style*), energy, nervous diction, nerve, force, emphasis.

8. Support, security, stay.

9. Intensity, brightness, brilliance, clearness, vitality, vividness.

10. Spirit, virtue, excellence, potency, body.

11. Vehemence, force, impetuosity, violence.

12. Energy, boldness, vigor.

Strengthen, *v. t.* 1. Make strong, make stronger, reinforce, buttress, recruit, give strength to, add strength to.

2. Fortify.

3. Harden, brace, nerve, steel, indurate, stimulate, energize, reman.

4. Intensify, make more intense.

5. Invigorate, impart health to, freshen, vitalize.

6. Animate, encourage, fix in resolution.

7. Confirm, corroborate, clench, clinch, establish, justify, sustain, support, fix.

Strengthening, *a.* 1. Fortifying, bracing.

2. Invigorating, roborant, tonic.

Strenuous, *a.* 1. Zealous, ardent, earnest, active, vigorous, resolute, energetic, eager.

2. Vigorous, spirited, bold, valiant, intrepid, strong, determined, resolute, doughty.

Strenuously, *adv.* 1. Earnestly, ardently, eagerly, vigorously, zealously, resolutely, energetically, actively, with might and main, tooth and nail, through thick and thin, through fire and water, hammer and tongs, *pugnis et calcibus.*

2. Boldly, courageously, valiantly, intrepidly, bravely.

Stress, *n.* 1. Force, strain, effort, pull, tension, tug.

2. Violence, inclemency, boisterousness, severity.

3. Pressure, urgency.

4. Importance, significance, weight, force.

5. Emphasis, accent, accentuation.

Stretch, *v. t.* 1. Strain, tighten, make tense, brace, screw.

2. Extend, lengthen, elongate, draw out, pull, protract.

3. Reach, stretch forth, hold out, extend, put forth.

4. Spread, expand, distend, widen, unfold, display.

5. Strain, sprain.

6. Exaggerate, misrepresent, distort, extend too far, strain.

——, *v. i.* Extend, reach, be drawn out, straggle.

STRETCH, *n.* 1. Extent, extension, reach, compass, scope, range.

2. Effort, struggle, strain, exertion.

3. Course, direction.

Stretcher, *n.* Litter.

Strew, *v. t.* 1. Scatter, spread, strow, sprinkle.

2. Cover, overspread.

Striate, } *a.* Channelled, grooved, furrowed, streaked.
Striated, }

Stricken, *a.* 1. Struck, smitten, wounded, afflicted, blighted.

2. Advanced (*in years*), far gone, worn out, aged, venerable, time-worn.

Strict, *a.* 1. Tight, strained, tense, close.

2. Exact, accurate, literal, precise, very nice, careful, scrupulous, particular, close.

3. Severe, rigorous, rigid, stringent, stern, austere, unyielding, inflexible, orthodox, harsh, uncompromising, straitlaced, puritanical, "blue."

4. Confined, limited, restricted, exact.

Stricture, *n.* 1. Animadversion, censure, criticism, critical remark, denunciation.

2. Contraction, compression, constriction.

Stride, *n.* Long step; step, gait.

——, *v. i.* Take long steps, stalk.

Stridor, *n.* [L.] Grating, creaking, jarring, harsh sound.

Stridulous, *a.* Grating, harsh, creaking.

Strife, *n.* 1. Contention, contest, conflict, fight, battle, combat, warfare, struggle, quarrel, discord.

2. Contrariety, opposition, disagreement, dissension, dispute.

3. Emulation, competition.

Strike, *v. t.* 1. Beat, hit, knock, pound, give a blow to, impinge, slap, smite, buffet, thump, thwack, bang, box, belabor, punch, rap, slug, cudgel, lash, whip, cuff.

2. Impress, imprint, stamp.

3. Deal, inflict, give; punish, afflict, smite, chastise.

4. Impress (*suddenly*), affect, stun, electrify, astonish.

5. Make, ratify, conclude.

——, *v. i.* 1. Deal a blow.

2. Hit, clash, dash, collide, touch, come in contact.

3. Yield, surrender, strike the flag.

4. Rebel, mutiny, rise, quit work.

Strike, *n.* 1. Stroke.

2. Strickle, straight-edge, strikle.

3. Suspension of work (*in support of labor demands*), walkout, shutdown, mutiny, revolt.

Strike off. 1. Cut off (*by a blow*), separate.

2. Erase (*from an account*), strike out, remove, delete.

3. Print (*as copies of a book*), impress.

Strike out, *v. t.* 1. Produce (*by a blow*), force out.

2. Erase, efface, expunge, delete, blot out, strike off.

3. Devise, contrive, invent, plan.

4. Bring to light.

——, *v. i.* Rove, wander, make a sudden excursion.

Strike up. 1. Begin to beat (*as drums*), cause to sound.

2. Begin to play *or* sing.

Striking, *a.* Affecting, impressive, noticeable, surprising, astonishing, wonderful, extraordinary, forcible; percussive.

String, *n.* 1. Line, cord, thread, twine, cordon, lace, leash, lead, wire, twist, filament, ribbon, fillet.

2. Row, file, series, concatenation, chain.

——, *v. t.* 1. File, put on a string.

2. Set in a row, put in line.

3. Strengthen, fortify, make firm, make tense.

4. Hoax.

Stringent, *a.* 1. Binding, contracting.

2. Strict, rigid, severe, rigorous.

Stringy, *a.* 1. Fibrous, filamentous.

2. Ropy, viscid, viscous, glutinous, adhesive, sticky, smeary, dauby, gluey, tough, tenacious.

Strip, *v. t.* 1. Tear off, pull off, strip off, uncover, denude, peel, lay bare, skin, hull.

2. Divest, deprive, bereave, shave, make destitute, unrig, dismantle, disfurnish, disarm, deforest, disrobe, expose.

3. Rob, plunder, pillage, spoil, sack, ransack, loot, devastate, desolate, lay waste, fleece, despoil.

——, *v. i.* Undress, uncover, disrobe, take off the clothes.

——, *n.* Piece (*long and narrow, torn off*), slip, tape, lath, ribbon, shred.

Stripe, *v. t.* Streak.

——, *n.* 1. Streak, band.

2. Stroke (*with a lash*), blow, lash; wale, mark of the lash.

3. Kind, color.

Stripling, *n.* Lad, boy, youth.

Strive, *v. i.* 1. Labor, endeavor, toil, struggle, strain, attempt, try, aim, exert one's self, make an effort, do one's best, lay one's self out.

2. Contend, contest, fight, have a contest, tussle, wrestle.

3. Compete, cope, strive together, contend, struggle, vie.

Stroke, *n.* 1. Blow, knock, rap, pat, hit, thump, glance, switch, lash, shot, impact, percussion; caress.

2. Attack, shock; paralysis.

3. Affliction, reverse, calamity, hardship, misfortune, visitation, hurt, damage, injury.

4. Touch, dash, sudden effort, sudden effect; masterstroke, feat.

——, *v. t.* Rub gently (*with the hands, in one direction*).

Stroll, *v. i.* Wander, ramble, rove, roam, straggle, stray, range, wander about, stray about, saunter, loiter, lounge.

——, *n.* Ramble, walk, promenade, excursion, trip, tour, wandering, rambling, roving.

Stroller, *n.* Wanderer, rambler, rover, strayer, straggler, vagrant, vagabond, boulevardier, nomad, bird of passage.

STRONG, *a.* 1. Vigorous, robust, sturdy, athletic, brawny, sinewy, muscular, stalwart, Herculean, "husky," tough, ablebodied, hardy, stout, lusty, powerful.

2. Hale, sound, robust, firm, solid, able to endure, healthy, hardy, stout.

3. Able, capable, efficient, mighty, potent, masterful, powerful, puissant.

4. Firm, solid, compact, impregnable, secure, substantial, well fortified.

5. Energetic, vivid, intense, forcible, bold, violent, impetuous, vehement.

6. Pungent, piquant, biting, sharp, racy, spicy, gamy, high, hot, highflavored, rank, strong-smelling, rancid, fetid.

7. Tenacious, tough, cohesive, resisting, stubborn, firm, compact, stout, stanch, sound.

8. Cogent, forcible, impressive, conclusive, persuasive, powerful, influential.

9. Ardent, eager, zealous, hearty, earnest, strenuous, stanch.

10. Vivid, intense, brilliant, dazzling.

11. Alcoholic (*in a high degree*), intoxicating, happy, bodied, hard, spirituous.

12. Valid, confirmed, binding.

Strong-box, *n.* Coffer (*for money*), safe, money-chest.

Stronghold, *n.* Fort, fortress, castle, citadel, fortification, fastness, keep, bulwark, donjon, muniment, fortified place; refuge.

Strop, *n.* Strap, razor-strap, razor-strop.

Strop, *v. t.* Strap, sharpen (*on a strap*).

STRUCTURE, *n.* 1. Construction, make, form, organization, build, frame, arrangement, conformation, configuration, make-up, constitution, mode of building, manner of making.

2. Formation, composition, anatomy, arrangement of parts, texture.

3. Edifice, fabric, building, erection, pile, framework.

Struggle, *v. i.* 1. Strive, labor, toil, endeavor, try, aim, exert one's self, make an effort, do one's best.

2. Contend, contest, fight, have a contest.

3. Writhe, be in agony, labor in distress, agonize, flounder.

——, *n.* 1. Labor, endeavor, effort, exertion, pains.

2. Contest, contention, conflict, strife, fight.

3. Contortions, agony, distress.

Strum, *v. t.* Thrum, play, play upon.

Strumpet, *n.* Harlot, prostitute, whore, courtesan, punk, wench, drab, Cyprian, street-walker, woman of the town, woman of ill fame.

Strut, *v. i.* Walk (*pompously*), swell, peacock, swagger, prance.

——, *n.* 1. Pompous walk, swagger.

2. (*Arch.*) Brace, stretching-piece.

Stub, *n.* 1. Stump, end; counterfoil.

2. Log, block.

——, *v. t.* 1. Eradicate, grub up, extirpate, clear.

2. Strike (*as the toes, against a stump, stone, etc.*).

Stubbed, *a.* Blunt, obtuse, truncated, stubby, short and thick.

Stubborn, *a.* 1. Obstinate, unyielding, obdurate, inflexible, positive, contumacious, refractory, perverse, headstrong, wilful, dogged, mulish, unruly, unmanageable, ungovernable, intractable, indocile, heady, cross-grained.

2. Persevering, persistent, steady, constant, unremitting; hardy, firm, enduring, stoical, uncomplaining.

3. Stiff, unpliant, inflexible, firm, tough, hard, strong.

Stubby, *a.* Blunt, obtuse, truncated, stubbed, stocky, short and thick.

Stucco, *n.* Plaster (*for covering walls and ceilings*), mortar, cement.

Stud, *n.* 1. Post, prop, support.

2. Knob (*for ornament*), boss.

Student, *n.* 1. Scholar, pupil, learner.

2. Scholar, bookish man, philomath.

3. Close examiner, observer.

Studied, *a.* 1. Well-versed, learned, qualified by study, skilled.

2. Premeditated, deliberate, elaborate, studious, predetermined, wilful.

Studio, *n.* Workshop (*of an artist*), atelier.

Studious, *a.* 1. Meditative, reflective, contemplative, given to study, thoughtful.

2. Diligent, assiduous, eager, zealous, attentive, desirous; scholarly, lettered.

Studious of. Careful of, attentive to, interested in.

Study, *n.* 1. Research, inquiry, investigation, reading, close attention, application of mind, exercise.

2. Meditation, thought, reflection, cogitation, lucubration, studious mood, contemplation, consideration.

3. Subject of attention, object, model, sketch, representation.

4. Studio, den, office, library.

——, *v. i.* 1. Meditate, muse, reflect, cogitate, lucubrate, think, ponder, apply the mind; "dig," "cram."

2. Be eager, be zealous, try hard, do one's best.

——, *v. t.* 1. Learn, apply the mind to.

2. Investigate, examine, scrutinize, contemplate, ponder, weigh, sift, search into, probe, analyze, meditate on, think about, reflect upon, inquire into, consider attentively, revolve in the mind.

3. Con, commit to memory, learn, get by heart *or* rote, pore over.

Stuff, *n.* 1. Material, matter, substance, raw material.

2. Cloth, textile fabric.

3. Essence, elemental part.

4. Mixture, medicine, potion.

5. Trash, nonsense, absurdity, folly, moonshine, twaddle, balderdash, fudge, inanity, platitude, flummery.

——, *v. t.* 1. Cram, stow, pack, fill full, wad, press, crowd, squeeze.

2. Fool, "sell," humbug.

——, *v. i.* Cram, eat greedily, feed, gorge, gormandize.

Stuffing, *n.* Filling, packing, wadding; dressing, force-meat.

Stuffy, *a.* Musty, close, confined, mouldy-smelling.

Stultify, *v. t.* Make foolish, prove foolish, besot, duncify, make a fool of.

Stumble, *v. i.* 1. Trip, miss one's footing, falter, lurch, stagger, pitch, make a false step.

2. Err, do wrong, blunder, slip.

3. Happen, chance.

——, *n.* 1. Trip, false step.

2. Error, blunder, failure.

Stumble upon. Fall upon by chance, light upon, strike upon without design.

Stumbling-block, *n.* Hindrance, obstruction, snag, obstacle, check bar, barrier, difficulty, impediment, lion in the way, stumbling-stone; offense, scandal.

Stump, *n.* Stub, remnant, fag-end; log, scrag, block.

Stun, *v. t.* 1. Make senseless (*by a blow*), make dizzy, shock, deafen.

2. Stupefy, confound, bewilder, overcome, dizzy, dumfound, astonish, electrify, overwhelm, overpower.

Stunning, *a.* 1. Deafening, stentorian, very loud.

2. Stupefying, dumfounding.

3. (*Colloq. exaggeration.*) Striking, astonishing, wonderful.

Stunt, *v. t.* Dwarf, stint, stop the growth of, check, nip, cramp, hinder from growth.

Stunted, *a.* Undersized, dwarfish, dwarfed, checked, nipped, runty, diminutive, small, little, tiny, Lilliputian, pygmean.

Stupefacient, *n.* Stupefactive, narcotic, opiate, sedative, anodyne, anæsthetic, sleeping-draught.

Stupefaction, *n.* 1. Lethargy, stupor, numbness.

2. Insensibility, dulness, obtuseness, torpor, stupidity, bewilderment, confusion, petrifaction, paralysis.

Stupefy, *v. t.* Dull, blunt, benumb, muddle, hebetate, make stupid, make dull, make torpid; confuse, confound, obfuscate, bewilder, stun, daze, paralyze, petrify, deaden, drug, hypnotize.

Stupendous, *a.* 1. Astonishing, surprising, amazing, wonderful, wondrous, marvellous, overwhelming, astounding.

2. Huge, vast, prodigious, tremendous, immense, enormous, towering, monstrous.

Stupid, *a.* 1. Senseless, witless, dull, brainless, weak-headed, addle-pated, muddle-headed, beef-witted, fat-headed, shallow-brained, lack-witted, short-witted, dull-witted, blunt-witted, shallow-pated, clod-pated, thick-skulled, wooden-headed, dunderheaded, bull-headed, slow, doltish, stolid, obtuse, "thick," foolish, sluggish, insensate, muddy-headed, sottish, "dumb."

2. Unentertaining, prosaic, pointless, prosy, vacant, inept, fatuous, inane, asinine, crass, flat, heavy, insipid, tame, vapid, bald, uninteresting, humdrum, dull, foolish, tiresome, tedious, idiotic, imbecile.

3. Stupefied, drowsy, torpid, heavy, comatose, lethargic, morbidly sleepy.

Stupidity, *n.* 1. Dulness, obtuseness, insensibility, sottishness, blockishness, doltishness, senselessness, sluggishness of understanding, slowness of apprehension.

2. Lifelessness, heaviness, insipidity, tameness, vapidness, want of interest, stupidness.

3. Stupor, lethargy, torpor, stupefaction, morbid drowsiness, coma.

Stupor, *n.* Lethargy, *narcosis*, torpor, numbness, coma, stupefaction, daze, confusion, dazement, torpidity.

Sturdy, *a.* 1. Bold (*from coarseness* or *rudeness*), obstinate, dogged, stubborn, pertinacious, determined, resolute, sturdy, firm, stiff, hardy, persevering.

2. Strong, lusty, robust, stout, stalwart, athletic, brawny, muscular, vigorous, powerful, forcible, well-set, thickset.

Stutter, *v. i.* Stammer, hesitate, falter, halt, stumble.

Sty, *n.* 1. Hog-sty, pig-sty, swine-pen.

2. Filthy place, den, sink, lair, Augean stable, slum, rookery.

Stygian, *a.* 1. Hellish, infernal, diabolical.

2. Dark, Cimmerian, tenebrous, sunless, sombre, gloomy, murky.

Style, *n.* 1. Diction, phraseology, mode of expression, mode of speech, turn of expression, choice of words, literary artistry.

2. Manner, method, mode, way, form, genre, kind, make, shape, character, taste, model, vogue, fashion, cast, pattern.

3. Title, appellation, name, designation, denomination, mode of address.

4. Gnomon (*of a dial*), pin, pen, point; stylus, graver, etching-needle.

——, *v. t.* Denominate, name, designate, call, term, dub, christen, characterize, entitle.

Stylet, *n.* 1. Stiletto, poniard, dagger.

2. (*Surgery.*) Specillum.

Stylish, *a.* (*Colloq.*) Fashionable, modish, elegant, genteel, "high-toned," "dressy," smart, courtly, in fashion, in vogue, *à la mode*.

Styptic, *n.* Astringent (*to stop bleeding*).

Styptic, } *a.* Astringent, binding, con-
Styptical, } tracting.

Suave, *a.* Pleasant, agreeable, gracious, delightful, courteous, amiable, sweet, debonair, urbane, affable, mild; smooth, bland, glib, fair-spoken, unctuous, oily.

Suavity, *n.* Sweetness (*of temper* or *of manner*), urbanity, amenity, civility, politeness, courtesy, decorum, gentleness, mildness, pleasantness, agreeableness, complaisance, affability, amiability, conciliatoriness, obliging manner, good manners, good-breeding, blandness.

Subaltern, *a.* Inferior, subordinate, subalternate.

Subdivision, *n.* 1. Division, dividing, ramification.

2. Part, portion, piece, fraction, section, share.

Subdue, *v. t.* 1. Conquer, subjugate, subject, overcome, overpower, vanquish, overbear, beat, crush, defeat, rout, discomfit, worst, overwhelm, master, quell, surmount, foil, get the better of, down, break, bend, bow, get the upper hand of, put down, beat down.

2. Reduce, curb, temper, restrain, moderate, mellow, mollify, soften, allay, choke, choke down, suppress, repress.

3. Tame, subject, control, make submissive, bring under rule, break, make tractable, discipline.

Subject, *v. t.* 1. Subdue, control, bring under rule, make submissive, make subordinate, master, subjugate, overcome, tame, break in, reduce.

2. Enslave, enthrall, tread down, lead captive.

3. Expose, make liable.

4. Submit, refer, make accountable, surrender, abandon.

5. Cause to undergo, treat.

——, *a.* 1. Underneath, beneath, placed under, subjacent.

2. Subservient, subjected, subordinate, servile, slavish, enslaved, dependent, inferior, in bondage, under the lash, under one's thumb, at one's command, at one's beck *or* call, at one's mercy.

3. Submissive, obedient, conditional.

4. Exposed, liable, prone, disposed, obnoxious.

——, *n.* 1. Dependent, subordinate, person owing allegiance, slave, liegeman, henchman.

2. Topic, theme, thesis, point, matter, subject-matter, matter in hand, object-matter.

3. (*Gram.* and *Log.*) Subject-term, leading term, nominative, premise.

4. Recipient, object, case, patient.

5. Mind, thinking being, conscious being, conscious subject, self, ego, me.

Subjection, *n.* 1. (Act of) subjecting, subduing, controlling, putting down *or* under, subjugation, conquest, subordinating.

2. Dependence, subordination, subserviency, submission, obedience, subordinacy; slavery, serfdom, bondage, thrall, thralldom, servitude, vassalage, yoke.

Subjective, *a.* 1. Belonging to *or* characteristic of the subject (*as contrasted with the object*), in the mind, within the self, individual, immanent.

2. Merely mental, limited to the subject, in the mind only, unreal, non-objective, not actual, inner, inherent, interior, internal, non-external; ideal.

3. Imagined, fancied, imaginary, illusory.

4. Introversive, introspective, contemplative, inward-looking, dealing with one's own feelings, colored by one's own states.

Subjoin, *v. t.* Add (*at the end*), annex, affix, attach, suffix, postfix, append, join.

Subjugate, *v. t.* Conquer, vanquish, subdue, enslave, enthrall, overcome, overpower, overbear, overthrow, master, subject.

Subjugation, *n.* Conquest, mastery, subjection.

Subjunctive, *a.* Subjoined, annexed, added, joined.

Sublet, *v. t.* Underlet, sublease.

Sublimate, *v. t.* 1. (*Chem.*) See SUBLIME.

2. Refine, exalt, elevate, heighten, idealize, purify.

Sublimation, *n.* 1. Vaporization (*of a solid, to be again condensed*).

2. Refinement, exaltation, elevation.

Sublime, *a.* 1. High, elevated, aloft, sacred.

2. Exalted (*in excellence* or *dignity*), great, noble, grand, lofty, eminent.

3. Stately, majestic, eminent, grand, solemn, august, noble, magnificent, glorious.

4. Elate, elevated, raised, exhilarated.

——, *v. t.* 1. Vaporize (*as a solid, to be again condensed*), sublimate.

2. Refine, exalt, elevate, heighten, improve, purify.

3. Dignify, ennoble, exalt, elevate, greaten, idealize.

Sublimity, *n.* 1. Elevation, lofty height.

2. Grandeur, greatness, nobleness, loftiness, exaltation, nobility, sublimeness.

3. Exaltation, elevation.

4. Loftiness, grandeur, greatness.

Sublunary, *a.* Earthly, mundane, terrestrial, subastral, subcelestial, sublunar.

Submarine, *a.* Subaqueous, subaquatic, underwater.

Submerge, *v. t.* 1. Immerse, plunge, sink, submerse.

2. Deluge, flood, overflow, overwhelm, inundate, cover with water, drown.

——, *v. i.* 1. Plunge, sink, submerse, duck, engulf.

2. Be merged, be incorporated, be included.

Submission, *n.* 1. Surrender, cession, yielding, relinquishment, capitulation.

2. Obedience, resignation, compliance, acquiescence.

3. Submissiveness, deference, lowliness, humility, meekness, humiliation, self-abasement, state of being submissive, passiveness, non-resistance; homage, obeisance, prostration.

4. Endurance, sufferance, long-sufferance, forbearance, fortitude, patience.

5. Acknowledgment, confession, penitence, contrition.

Submissive, *a.* 1. Yielding, tractable, pliant, docile, compliant, amenable, tame.

2. Obedient, resigned, uncomplaining, unrepining, patient, long-suffering, passive, acquiescent, unassertive.

3. Humble, meek, lowly, obsequious, prostrate, deferential, self-abasing.

Submissiveness, *n.* 1. Pliancy, docility.

2. Obedience, submission, resignation, compliance, passiveness, non-resistance.

3. Humility, humbleness, meekness, lowliness, self-abasement.

Submit, *v. t.* 1. Yield, surrender, resign, subject, give up, defer, cede.

2. Refer, commit.

3. Propone, offer.

——, *v. i.* 1. Yield, surrender, succumb.

2. Yield, surrender, succumb, give up, knock under, lower one's flag, kiss the rod, lick the dust, eat humble pie, draw in one's horns, acquiesce, comply, resign oneself, bend, capitulate, come to terms, be subject.

Submit to. Endure, tolerate, put up with, bear with, reconcile one's self to, be reconciled to, make the best of.

Subordinate, *a.* Inferior, subservient, subject, ancillary, minor, secondary, subsidiary, dependent.

——, *n.* 1. Inferior, dependent.

2. Inferior, subject, underling.

——, *v. t.* Subject, make subordinate, make subservient.

Subordination, *n.* 1. Subjection, act of subordinating, submission.

2. Inferiority, subjection, subserviency, servitude.

Suborn, *v. t.* 1. Procure indirectly.

2. (*Law.*) Bribe (*to commit perjury*), bribe to take a false oath, induce.

Sub rosa. [L.] Privately, secretly, confidentially, in confidence, under the rose, between ourselves, between you and me, *entre nous.*

Subscribe, *v. t.* Sign, set one's name to, affix one's signature to, underwrite, endorse, attest; promise to contribute.

——, *v. i.* 1. Sign one's name (*in token of consent*).

2. Agree, consent, assent, give consent, accede, approve, yield assent.

3. Enter one's name (*for a newspaper, etc*).

4. Promise to contribute.

Subsequent, *a.* Following, succeeding, posterior, sequent, latter, attendant, ensuing, later, after.

Subserve, *v. t.* Promote, forward, further, serve, aid, assist, help forward, be subservient to, pander to, minister to.

Subservient, *a.* 1. Subordinate, inferior, subject; obsequious, servile.

2. Useful, helpful, serviceable, conducive, contributory, aiding, auxiliary, accessory, subsidiary, ancillary, instrumental.

Subside, *v. i.* 1. Sink, settle.

2. Decrease, diminish, lessen, lull, wane, ebb, fall, drop, lapse, abate, intermit, grow less.

Subsidence, *n.* 1. Sinking, settling.

2. Decrease, diminution, lessening, abatement, ebb.

3. Descent, sinking.

Subsidiary, *a.* Assistant, auxiliary, aiding, helping, adjuvant, corroborative, cooperating, subordinate, subservient.

Subsidize, *v. t.* Supply with a subsidy, aid, finance.

Subsidy, *n.* Support, aid, government aid, subvention, underwriting, bounty, grant.

Subsist, *v. i.* 1. Exist, be, live, breathe, inhere, consist, prevail.

2. (*Rare.*) Remain, abide, continue, persist, endure.

3. Be supported, obtain a livelihood, get a living, live.

——, *v. t.* Feed, victual, ration, support, maintain.

Subsistence, *n.* 1. Real being, life, entity.

2. Support, livelihood, maintenance, aliment, nourishment, nutriment, sustenance, living, food, provision, meat, rations.

3. Inherence, inherency.

Subsistent, *a.* 1. Substantial, really existing.

2. Inherent.

SUBSTANCE, *n.* 1. Substratum, groundwork, reality, hypostasis, substantiality, actuality, element, essential nature, real being, real existence.

2. Meaning, import, significance, essence, sum, heart, core, content, sense, drift, burden, pith, gist, soul, chief part, essential part, vital part; weight, gravamen, solidity.

3. Body, matter, material, texture, stuff.

4. Property, wealth, means, estate, resources, income.

5. (*Theol.*) Divine essence, divine being.

Substantial, *a.* 1. Real, actual, existent, hypostatic, subsistent, actually existing, having substance, considerable, essential, virtual, potential, pithy.

2. True, positive, solid, not imaginary, concrete, tangible.

3. Corporeal, material, bodily.

4. Strong, stout, solid, firm, stable, sound, heavy, well-made, massive, bulky; sizable, goodly, large, notable, significant.

5. Weighty, valid, just, cogent, efficient, influential.

6. Responsible (*pecuniarily*), moderately wealthy.

Substantiate, *v. t.* Establish, verify, prove, confirm, corroborate, ratify, make good, actualize.

Substantiation, *n.* Confirmation, corroboration, establishment, evidence, proof, ratification.

Substantive, *n.* (*Gram.*) Noun, name.

Substitute, *v. t.* Exchange, commute, change, shift. duplicate, act for, alternate, put in the place of.

——, *v. i.* Alternate, change, "pinch-hit," understudy.

——, *n.* 1. Proxy, lieutenant, agent, deputy, *locum tenens*, vicar, understudy, representative, alternate, "pinch-hitter."

2. Makeshift, temporary expedient, stopgap, apology; equivalent.

Substitution, *n.* Exchange, commutation, shift, supplanting, replacement.

Substratum, *n.* 1. Principle, element, groundwork, underlying substance, fundamental *or* primordial substance.

2. (*Agric.*) Subsoil.

Substructure, *n.* Foundation, under-building.

Subterfuge, *n.* Evasion, excuse, expedient, shift, artifice, trick, quirk, shuffle, pretence, pretext, mask, sophistry.

Subterranean, } *a.* Underground.
Subterraneous, }

Subtile, *a.* See Subtle.

Subtilize, *v. t.* 1. Make thin.

2. Rarefy, etherealize.

3. Refine excessively, make over-nice.

——, *v. i.* Refine, be over-nice.

Subtilty. See Subtlety.

Subtle, *a.* 1. Crafty, cunning, artful, sly, wily, arch, astute, designing, intriguing, insinuating, crooked, tricky, diplomatic, Machiavelian, sophistical, Jesuitical.

2. Cunningly devised, artful, cunning, clever, ingenious.

3. Acute, keen, shrewd, sagacious, deep, discerning, discriminating, profound.

4. Rare, thin, light, airy, ethereal, volatile, sublimated, delicate, subtile, slender, nice, refined.

Subtlety, *n.* 1. Craft, craftiness, cunning, artifice, astuteness, artfulness, subtleness, guile, slyness.

2. Acuteness, acumen, keenness, shrewdness, astuteness, sharpness, discernment, intelligence, cleverness, sagacity.

3. Refinement, nicety, fineness; rareness, subtileness, subtilty, attenuation, delicacy.

Subtract, *v. t.* Deduct, withdraw, take, take away.

Subtraction, *n.* Deduction, abstraction.

Suburbs, *n. pl.* Environs, outskirts, purlieus, neighborhood, vicinage, border, limit, confines, *faubourg*.

Subvention, *n.* See Subsidy.

Subversion, *n.* 1. Overturn, inversion.

2. Overthrow, destruction, demolition, ruin.

Subversive, *a.* Destructive, tending to the overthrow, upsetting.

Subvert, *v. t.* 1. Overturn, overset, overthrow, reverse, upset, invert, turn upside-down.

2. Destroy, ruin, overthrow, demolish, raze, extinguish, overturn, upset.

3. Pervert, corrupt, confound, destroy, injure.

Succeed, *v. t.* 1. Follow, come after, be subsequent to.

2. Take the place of, replace, assume the office of, follow in order.

——, *v. i.* 1. Follow, ensue, come afterward, come subsequently, inherit.

2. Prosper, flourish, prevail, thrive, hit, make a hit, come on, be successful, meet with success, win, gain, go on well, go on swimmingly, have a run of luck, hit the right nail on the head, turn up trumps, have the game in one's hands.

Succeeding, *a.* Following, subsequent.

Succeed to. 1. Follow, succeed, come after, inherit.

2. Take the place of, assume the authority of.

Success, *n.* 1. Issue, result, attainment.

2. Prosperity, luck, good fortune, good luck, lucky hit, fortunate hit, prosperous issue, masterstroke, "ten-strike," victory, triumph.

Successful, *a.* Prosperous, fortunate, lucky, auspicious, felicitous, happy; booming, victorious, winning.

Successfully, *adv.* Favorably, prosperously, luckily, fortunately.

Succession, *n.* 1. Sequence, consecution, following, rotation, round, procession, cycle, series, suite, progression, chain, concatenation.

2. Lineage, descent, race, line of descendants, inheritance, reversion, entail.

Successive, *a.* Consecutive, sequent, following.

Successor, *n.* Follower, heir.

Succinct, *a.* Short, brief, concise, laconic, terse, compact, compendious, condensed, pithy, summary, curt.

Succor, *v. t.* 1. Aid, assist, help, relieve.

2. Cherish, foster, encourage, nurse, comfort.

——, *n.* Relief, aid, assistance, help, support, helping hand.

Succulent, *a.* Juicy, sappy, lush, full of juice, succulous, nutritive.

Succumb, *v. i.* Yield, submit, surrender, capitulate, give in, give way; die.

SUCH, *a.* 1. Like, similar, of that kind, of the like kind.

2. So, in the same state *or* condition, as it is, as it was.

Suck, *v. t.* Draw into the mouth, drink, imbibe, absorb, swallow up, engulf.

Sucker, *n.* 1. One who sucks.

2. Embolus, piston.

3. (*Ich.*) Lump-sucker, lump-fish.

4. (*Bot.*) Stole, stolon.

Suckle, *v. t.* Nurse, give suck to, feed at the breast.

Suckling, *n.* Infant, babe, baby, nursling, chit, brat, bantling, little child, little one.

Sudatory, *n.* Hot-house, sweating-bath, vapor-bath, sweating-room, stew, bagnio, Turkish bath, Russian bath, warm bath, *tepidarium*.

——, *a.* Sweating, perspiring.

SUDDEN, *a.* 1. Unexpected, abrupt, precipitate, instantaneous, immediate, unforeseen, unanticipated, unlooked for, unusual.

2. Quick, rapid, quickly prepared; brief, momentary.

Suddenly, *a.* Unexpectedly, abruptly, pop, on a sudden, "slap," "plump," forthwith, immediately, at once.

Sue, *v. t.* 1. Prosecute, follow up, seek after, woo, court, solicit.

2. Prosecute, bring an action against, indict, commence a suit against.

——, *v. i.* 1. Beg, petition, entreat, plead, appeal, supplicate, implore, pray, demand, seek by request.

2. Bring an action, make legal claim, prosecute.

Suet, *n.* Tallow (*with adhering membranes*), beef-fat, mutton-fat.

Suffer, *v. t.* 1. Undergo, feel, meet with, experience, go through.

2. Endure, sustain, support, tolerate, bear, bear up under, put up with, stand, pocket, stomach.

3. Undergo, sustain, receive, be affected by, be acted upon.

4. Permit, allow, indulge, admit, let, give permission to, give leave to.

——, *v. i.* 1. Feel pain, smart, agonize, ache, groan.

2. Be put to inconvenience.

3. Be punished, undergo punishment, pay.

4. Be injured, be impaired, sustain loss *or* damage.

Sufferance, *n.* 1. Suffering, endurance, pain, misery, inconvenience.

2. Patience, moderation, long-suffering, submission.

3. Permission, allowance, toleration.

Suffering, *n.* 1. Endurance, sufferance.

2. Pain, inconvenience, distress, discomfort, misery, sufferance, passion.

3. Poverty, want.

Suffice, *v. i.* Be enough, be sufficient, do, satisfy, serve, avail, be adequate, pass muster.

——, *v. t.* Satisfy, content, be enough for.

Sufficiency, *n.* 1. Adequacy.

2. Ability, qualification, capacity.

3. Competence, enough.

4. Plenty, supply, ample stock, adequate resources.

5. Conceit, self-confidence, self-sufficiency.

Sufficient, *a.* 1. Adequate (*to supply a want*), competent, ample, enough, full, satisfactory, up to the mark, commensurate.

2. Qualified, fit, able, competent, responsible, equal.

Suffix, *n.* Affix, postfix, termination, ending, addition.

——, *v. t.* Append, add, annex, postfix, affix.

Suffocate, *v. t.* 1. Stifle, smother, choke, strangle, kill (*by stopping respiration*), asphyxiate.

2. Destroy, extinguish.

Suffragan, *n.* Bishop (*as subject to an archbishop*), assistant bishop, suffragan bishop.

Suffrage, *n.* 1. Vote, voice, ballot, franchise.

2. Approval, witness, attestation, testimonial.

Suffuse, *v. t.* Overspread, spread over, cover, bathe, fill.

SUGAR, *n.* (*Basic Eng.*)

Sugary, *a.* Sweet, saccharine, honeyed; flattering, complimentary.

Suggest, *v. t.* Hint, intimate, insinuate, move, propose, present, propound, indicate, prompt, give an inkling of, refer to, glance at, allude to, put in mind of, remind of, recommend, advise, counsel.

SUGGESTION, *n.* Hint, intimation, insinuation, allusion, prompting, presentation, reminder.

Suicide, *n.* 1. Self-murder, self-slaughter, self-homicide, self-destruction.

2. Self-murderer, *felo de se.*

Sui generis. [L.] Peculiar, individual.

Suit, *n.* 1. Request, solicitation, petition, entreaty, prayer, supplication, appeal, invocation, suing; courtship, wooing, addresses.

2. (*Law.*) Prosecution, process, trial, action, cause, case.

3. Clothing, costume, habit.

——, *v. t.* 1. Fit, adapt, adjust, fashion, accommodate, level, match, make suitable *or* proper.

2. Become, befit, beseem; be suited, fitted, *or* adapted to; be suitable for, be appropriate for.

3. Please, gratify, make content, satisfy.

——, *v. i.* Agree, accord, harmonize, comport, tally, correspond, match, fit, serve, conform, answer.

Suitable, *a.* Fit, proper, meet, apt, appropriate, expedient, seemly, becoming, due, just, apposite, applicable, fitting, befitting, worthy, relevant, eligible, adapted, accordant, consonant, conformable, congruous, pertinent, agreeable, answerable, correspondent, decent, convenient, to the point, to the purpose, ready.

Suitableness, *n.* Fitness, propriety, agreeableness, correspondence, congruity, compatibility, consistency, consonance.

Suite, *n.* 1. Train (*of attendants*), staff, retinue, escort, convoy, bodyguard, court, followers, *cortège.*

2. Set (*particularly of apartments*), series, collection, suit.

Suitor, *n.* 1. Solicitor, petitioner, applicant, suppliant, supplicant, litigant.

2. Wooer, lover, gallant, beau, "steady," admirer, sweetheart.

Sulcate,
Sulcated, } *a.* Furrowed, grooved, scored.

Sulk, *v. i.* Be sullen, be sulky, be out of humor, pout, mope, frown, scowl.

Sulkiness, *n.* See SULLENNESS.

Sulky, *a.* Cross, morose, sour, sullen, spleeny, spleenish, splenetic, perverse,

wayward, surly, moody, dogged, churlish, mumpish, cross-grained, grouchy, ill-tempered, ill-humored, in the sulks, out of humor, out of temper, out of tune, unsociable.

Sullen, *a.* 1. Cross, ill-tempered, glum, grumpy, mumpish, splenetic, crusty, sore, morose, sulky, sour, moody.

2. Gloomy, dismal, sombre, dark, funeral, mournful, foreboding, lowering, cheerless, cloudy, melancholy, depressing.

3. Heavy, dull, sluggish, slow, gloomy.

4. Obstinate, intractable, stubborn, refractory, perverse, vexatious.

5. Malignant, baleful, unpropitious, evil, inauspicious, malign, sinister, unlucky.

Sullenness, *n.* 1. Moroseness, moodiness, sourness, churlishness, spleen, sulkiness, ill-temper, bad blood.

2. Gloominess, sombreness, dismalness.

3. Sluggishness, slowness, heaviness.

4. Obstinacy, intractableness, stubbornness, intractability.

Sully, *v. t.* Soil, stain, tarnish, spot, blemish, smirch, blot, dirty, contaminate, deface, foul; dishonor, disgrace, defame, slur.

Sulphur-colored, *a.* Yellow, lemon-colored, primrose-colored, citrine, citron-colored, greenish-yellow.

Sulphurous, *a.* Sulphureous, sulphury.

Sultan, *n.* Padishah, grand-seignior, soldan, grand Turk, Ottoman sovereign.

Sultana, *n.* Sultaness, sultan's wife.

Sultriness, *n.* Moist heat, mugginess, oppressiveness, closeness, humidity.

Sultry, *a.* Hot and close, warm and damp, close, stuffy, humid, stifling, oppressive, muggy, sweltering.

Sum, *n.* 1. Aggregate amount, total, totality, the whole, sum total, gross amount, entirety, all.

2. Quantity of money, any amount.

3. Summary, compendium, amount, substance, sum and substance.

4. Height, completion, summit, acme.

5. Question (*in arithmetic*), problem.

——, *v. t.* 1. Add, add together, sum up, cast up, compute, calculate, reckon.

2. Condense, summarize, sum up, state in brief, collect, comprehend, epitomize, put in a nutshell.

Summarily, *adv.* 1. Briefly, concisely, compendiously, in a few words.

2. Without delay, by a short method.

Summary, *a.* 1. Short, brief, concise, compendious, synoptical, succinct, laconic, curt, terse, pithy, compact, condensed.

2. Brief, rapid, quickly performed, quick.

Summary, *n.* Abridgment, compend, brief, compendium, abstract, epitome, digest, synopsis, syllabus, conspectus, sum and substance, the short and the long, *résumé*, *précis*, capitulation.

Summation, *n.* 1. Computation, addition.

2. Aggregate.

SUMMER, *n.* (*Basic Eng.*)

Summerhouse, *n.* 1. Arbor, gardenhouse, kiosk, bower.

2. Country-seat.

Summit, *n.* 1. Top, highest point.

2. Top, apex, vertex, acme, pinnacle, zenith, crown, peak, crest, cap, tip-top, climax, utmost height, culminating point.

Summon, *v. t.* 1. Bid, cite, call, invite, call for, send for, order to appear, notify to appear, invoke.

2. Give notice to, command to appear, "summons," subpoena, convene, convoke; (*Mil.*) demand the surrender of.

Summons, *n.* Citation, official call *or* notice, call, bid, invocation, subpoena.

Summon up. Raise, rouse, arouse, call up, excite, pluck up, call into action.

Sumptuous, *a.* 1. Costly, expensive, dear; magnificent, splendid, gorgeous, stately, splendid, rich, superb, grand, showy, pompous, luxurious, munificent, lavish, prodigal.

SUN, *n.* 1. Day-star, orb of day, luminary.

2. Sunshine, light, sunny place, sunlight, sunrise.

Sunburnt, *a.* Tanned, brown, bronzed, blowzy, ruddy, blowzed, ruddy-faced, brown as a berry.

Sunday, *n.* The Lord's day, the Christian Sabbath, the day of rest, the first day of the week.

Sunder, *v. t.* Disunite, disjoin, dispart, disconnect, part, separate, dissociate, divide, sever, dissever, break, part, tear asunder.

Sundry, *a.* Several, divers, various, more than one or two, not a great many, many.

Sunless, *a.* 1. Shaded, shady, unillumined, unlighted.

2. Rayless, beamless, dark, darksome, black, dismal, pitchy, Cimmerian, Stygian.

Sunlight, *n.* Daylight, sunshine, day, light of day, light of heaven.

Sunny, *a.* 1. Bright, shining, brilliant, clear, unclouded, fine, sunshiny, luminous, radiant.

2. Warm, mild, genial, pleasant; cheerful, joyful, happy, smiling, optimistic.

Sunrise, *n.* 1. Dawn, sunrising, daybreak, sun-up, cockcrow, peep of day, break of day, aurora, first blush of the morning.

2. East, Orient.

Sunset, *n.* 1. Evening, sundown, curfew, close of the day, sunsetting, eve, eventide, nightfall, going down of the sun.

2. West, Occident.

Sunshade, *n.* Parasol, sun-umbrella.

Sunshine, *n.* 1. Sunlight.

2. Illumination, warmth, light.

Sunstroke, *n.* Insolation, stroke of the sun, siriasis, *coup de soleil.*

Sup, *v. i.* Take supper.

——, *v. t.* Drink (*a little at a time*), sip.

——, *n.* Sip, taste, small mouthful.

Superable, *a.* 1. Surmountable, conquerable, vincible, that may be overcome.

2. Possible, achievable, feasible.

Superabundance, *n.* Excess, overflow, exuberance, luxuriance, superfluity, redundance, swarming, teeming, plethora, surfeit.

Superabundant, *a.* Exuberant, superfluous, excessive.

Superannuated, *a.* Decrepit, anile, aged, imbecile, doting, antiquated, effete, rusty, time-worn, disqualified, retired, unfit for service, on the retired list, on the pension list, *passé.*

Superb, *a.* Grand, stately, august, majestic, noble, magnificent; sumptuous, rich, splendid, elegant, beautiful, exquisite; showy, pompous, gorgeous, imposing.

Supercilious, *a.* 1. Haughty, overbearing, domineering, dictatorial, arrogant, proud, high, lofty, overweening, consequential, lordly, intolerant, insolent, vainglorious, magisterial, imperious, high and mighty.

2. Haughty, disdainful, contemptuous, proud, arrogant, lordly, consequential, scornful.

Supereminence, *n.* Pre-eminence, transcendence, marked superiority, superexcellence.

Supereminent, *a.* Pre-eminent, transcendent.

Superficial, *a.* 1. External, exterior, outer, on the surface, outward, outside.

2. Shallow, slight, meretricious, frivolous.

Superficies, *n.* Surface, exterior, outside.

Superfine, *a.* Excellent, choice, prime, first-rate, very good, very fine, superior, the best, unexceptionable; subtle.

Superfluity, *n.* Superabundance, excess, redundance, redundancy, exuberance, surfeit, more than enough, enough and to spare; fifth wheel.

Superfluous, *a.* Excessive, superabundant, redundant, exuberant, unnecessary, needless, useless, expletive, more than enough, spare, *de trop*.

Superhuman, *a.* 1. Divine, godlike, angelic, seraphic.

2. Supernatural, preternatural, preterhuman, miraculous, hyperphysical, Herculean.

Superimpose, *v. t.* Superpose.

Superinduce, *v. t.* Superadd, bring on, cause.

Superintend, *v. t.* Supervise, oversee, overlook, direct, conduct, manage, control, administer, have charge of, have the direction of, have the oversight of, preside over.

Superintendence, } *n.* Supervision, in-
Superintendency, } spection, oversight, care, direction, control, charge, management, guidance, surveillance.

Superintendent, *n.* Overseer, supervisor, master, conductor, inspector, curator, warden, guardian, custodian, intendant, director.

Superior, *a.* 1. High, higher, upper, paramount, finer, better, greater, supreme, ultra, more elevated.

2. Of higher rank, more exalted, more dignified, chief, principal, foremost.

3. Surpassing, noble, more eminent, pre-eminent, "topping," distinguished, more excellent, preferable, matchless, unrivalled, unsurpassed, sovereign, incomparable.

4. Predominant, prevalent.

Superiority, *n.* 1. Pre-eminence, ascendency, predominance, supremacy, preponderance, lead, transcendence, advantage, prevalence, odds.

2. Excellence, worthiness, nobility.

Superlative, *a.* Supreme, most eminent, greatest, most excellent, surpassing, transcendent, consummate, pre-eminent, peerless, incomparable.

Supernal, *a.* Heavenly, celestial, divine.

Supernatural, *a.* Miraculous, marvellous, unearthly, otherworldly, metaphysical, preternatural, above nature, beyond the powers of nature, that exceeds the laws of nature.

Supernumerary, *a.* Odd, redundant, in excess, excessive, above the regular number, left over (*from a specified number*), superfluous.

Superpose, *v. t.* Superimpose, lay upon, impose.

Superscription, *n.* Inscription, direction.

Supersede, *v. t.* 1. Suspend, annul, overrule, set aside, make void, obviate, neutralize.

2. Displace, replace, supplant, succeed, remove.

Superstition, *n.* 1. Bigotry, fanaticism.

2. False religion, worship of false gods, irrational worship.

3. Belief in omens.

4. Excessive nicety, scrupulous exactness.

Supervene, *v. i.* Occur (*with reference to something that precedes*), happen, take place, be added, come as an accessory, follow upon.

Supervise, *v. t.* See SUPERINTEND.

Supervision, *n.* See SUPERINTENDENCE.

Supervisor, *n.* See SUPERINTENDENT.

Supine, *a.* 1. On the back, prostrate, recumbent.

2. Indolent, sluggish, lazy, slothful, idle, inert, spineless, torpid, languid, dull, lumpish, listless, careless, thoughtless, inattentive, negligent, heedless, drowsy, indifferent, otiose, lethargic, apathetic, sleepy.

Supper, *n.* Tea, evening meal.

Supplant, *v. t.* 1. Undermine, overthrow, overpower, force away.

2. Displace (*by stratagem*), replace, remove, supersede.

Supple, *a.* 1. Pliant, pliable, flexible, flexile, limber, lithe, lithesome, easily bent, elastic.

2. Yielding, compliant, submissive, humble, soft.

3. Servile, obsequious, cringing, slavish, fawning, grovelling, sycophantic, flattering, supple-chapped, adulatory, oily, parasitical.

Supplement, *n.* 1. Addition (*to supply something wanting*), appendix, addendum, postscript, complement, sequel, continuation.

2. Counterpart, correlative.

——, *v. t.* Supply, add to, fill up, supplete.

Supplementary, *a.* Additional, supplemental, accessory.

Suppliant, *a.* Supplicating, beseeching, entreating, imploring, begging, praying, suing, precatory.

——, *n.* Petitioner, supplicant, applicant, solicitor, suitor.

Supplicate, *v. t.* Beg, implore, pray, entreat, beseech, importune, petition, crave, solicit, call upon, pray to, appeal to, prefer a request to.

——, *v. i.* Entreat, beg, pray, petition, plead, sue, implore, put up a prayer, prefer a request *or* petition.

Supplication, *n.* 1. Prayer, orison, invocation, petition.

2. Entreaty, petition, solicitation, prayer, request.

Supplicatory, *a.* Petitionary, humble, submissive.

Supplies, *n. pl.* Stores, stock.

Supply, *v. t.* 1. Provide, furnish, equip, outfit, minister, replenish, stock, store, endue, endow, invest, fill up.

2. Give, grant, afford, accommodate with, contribute, yield, furnish.

3. Serve instead of, take the place of.

——, *n.* Stock, store, reserve, provision, hoard, fund.

Support, *v. t.* 1. Sustain, uphold, prop, brace, bear up, hold up, shore up, cradle, pillow.

2. Endure, bear, undergo, suffer, tolerate, submit to, put up with, go through.

3. Cherish, nourish, maintain, provide for, keep, nurture.

4. Have, hold, keep up, maintain, sustain, carry on, preserve.

5. Perform, play, act, take the part of, sustain, assume, carry, represent.

6. Substantiate, confirm, make good, verify, bear out, corroborate, accredit.

7. Assist, aid, help, second, patronize, champion, abet, befriend, back, countenance, encourage, back up, strengthen, reinforce, float, succor, relieve, uphold, favor, shield, protect, defend; further, forward, advocate, vindicate, approve, maintain, stay.

SUPPORT, *n.* 1. Prop, stay, shore, supporter, brace, substructure, foothold, purchase, hold, underpinning, bolster, guy, buttress; groundwork, mainstay, staff.

2. Base, basis, bed, foundation.

3. Sustenance, maintenance, subsistence, livelihood, living, keeping, sustentation; nutriment, sustenance, food, bread.

4. Confirmation, evidence.

5. Aid, help, assistance, succor, favor, championship, approval, advocacy, strengthening, backing, behalf, countenance, encouragement, patronage, comfort.

Supportable, *a.* 1. Endurable, tolerable.

2. Maintainable, defensible.

Supporter, *n.* 1. See SUPPORT, *n.* 1.

2. Sustainer, comforter.

3. Maintainer, defender, aider, assistant, partisan, adherent, follower, upholder, seconder, patron, "stand-by," champion, partisan.

Suppose, *v. t.* 1. Presume, conceive, apprehend, believe, imagine, consider, deem, think, judge, presuppose, conjecture, conclude.

2. Imply, assume, presuppose, take for granted, predicate, posit, hypothesize.

3. Imagine, believe, receive as true, think.

——, *v. i.* Think, imagine, fancy, believe, speculate, theorize, surmise, conjecture, divine, suspect, opine, ween.

Supposition, *n.* 1. Surmise, conjecture, presumption, guess, guesswork, "shot."

2. Hypothesis, postulate, assumed position, assumption, theory, thesis.

3. Doubt, uncertainty.

Supposititious, *a.* Spurious, counterfeit, sham, feigned, pretended, pseudo, deceptive, forged, mock, false, foisted in, subditious; conjectural, supposed.

Suppress, *v. t.* 1. Crush, overpower, subdue, quell, overthrow, stifle, choke, smother, put down, destroy, overwhelm, quench, quash, withhold.

2. Restrain, repress, keep back, stop, check, inhibit, arrest, obstruct.

3. Conceal, keep secret, retain, strangle, stifle, extinguish, silence, keep down, keep out of sight, keep secret, restrain from disclosure, hush up.

Suppression, *n.* 1. Overthrow, crushing, quelling.

2. Restraint, repression, check, stoppage, obstruction, detention.

3. Concealment, retention.

Suppurate, *v. i.* Fester, maturate, generate pus, gather, ripen, putrefy.

Suppuration, *n.* 1. Festering, maturation, generation of pus, purulence.

2. Virulent matter, matter.

Supremacy, *n.* Domination, predominance, predominancy, lordship, mastership, headship, mastery, sovereignty, supreme authority, upper hand, supremeness, primacy, ascendancy.

Supreme, *a.* 1. Highest, greatest, paramount, dominant, predominant, principal, chief, leading, first, sovereign, preeminent.

2. Highest, greatest, superlative, utmost, greatest possible.

Surbase, *n.* Skirting-board, mop-board, baseboard, skirting, washboard.

Surcharge, *v. t.* Overload, overburden, overcharge.

Surcharged, *a.* Overcharged, overloaded, overburdened, surfeited, plethoric, overfull.

Surcingle, *n.* Girth, girt, girdle, belt, band.

Surd, *a.* 1. (*Math.*) Radical, incommensurable.

2. (*Orthoepy.*) Aspirate, toneless, unintonated, atonic, unheard, without vocality, pronounced with a simple breathing.

Sure, *a.* 1. Certain, confident, positive, assured, fully convinced.

2. Safe, secure, stable, firm, steady, reliable, trustworthy.

3. Infallible, unfailing, never-failing, strong, permanent, enduring, abiding, fast, indisputable, unquestionable, certain.

4. Certain, unerring.

Surely, *adv.* 1. Certainly, infallibly, undoubtedly, assuredly, sure, without doubt.

2. Safely, securely, firmly, steadily.

Surety, *n.* 1. Certainty, indubitableness, confidence, sureness, certitude, assurance.

2. Safety, security.

3. Support, foundation; witness, evidence, ratification, confirmation.

4. Guaranty, pledge; bondsman, bail; guarantor, sponsor, voucher; substitute, hostage.

Surf, *n.* Breakers, breaking waves.

SURFACE, *n.* Superficies, exterior, outside, face, top, area, external part; finish, covering, appearance.

Surfeit, *v. t.* 1. Satiate, glut, gorge, sate, cram, overfeed.

2. Cloy, pall, nauseate.

——, *v. i.* Be surfeited, feed to satiety, cram, gorge.

——, *n.* Excess; fulness, oppression, repletion, plethora, satiety; satiation, disgust; glut, superabundance, over-abundance, redundance, superfluity, nimiety, oversupply.

Surge, *n.* Wave, billow, breaker, roller, white horse.

——, *v. i.* Swell, rise high, billow, sweep, rush, swirl; rise, tower.

Surly, *a.* 1. Morose, cross, crabbed, testy, touchy, crusty, fretful, peevish, petulant, perverse, pettish, snappish, waspish, snarling, froward, uncivil, discourteous, rude, rough, harsh, grumpy, sullen, ill-tempered, ill-natured, sour, gruff, churlish, ungracious.

2. Rough, sullen, dark, tempestuous.

Surmise, *v. t.* Imagine, suspect, conjecture, suppose, guess, divine, fancy, believe, think, presume.

——, *n.* Conjecture, suspicion, supposition, guess, doubt, imperfect notion.

Surmount, *v. t.* 1. Rise above, climb, scale, top, crown, overtop, tower above; vault, clear.

2. Overcome, conquer, subdue, overpower, vanquish, master, triumph over, rise above, get the better of.

3. Surpass, exceed, go beyond, pass, overpass, transcend.

Surmountable, *a.* Conquerable, superable, that may be surmounted.

Surname, *n.* Cognomen, family name, patronymic.

Surpass, *v. t.* Excel, exceed, outdo, outstrip, outmatch, outnumber, surmount, outrun, override, transcend, cap, overtop, beat, go beyond, distance; overshadow, outshine, eclipse.

Surpassing, *a.* Excellent, supreme, incomparable, transcendent, pre-eminent, peerless, fine, superlative.

Surplus, *n.* Overplus, residue, excess, surplusage, remainder, superplus.

SURPRISE, *n.* Wonder, astonishment, amazement; blow, shock.

——, *v. t.* 1. Take unawares, take by surprise, take off one's guard, attack.

2. Astonish, astound, stun, dumfound, amaze, startle, strike with wonder, take aback.

Surprising, *a.* Extraordinary, remarkable, wonderful, unexpected, startling, astonishing, astounding, strange, marvellous.

Surrender, *v. t.* 1. Cede, yield, give up, give over, deliver up, render, sacrifice.

2. Resign, relinquish, forego, abdicate, abandon, part with, renounce, waive.

——, *v. i.* Yield, capitulate, comply, give up, fall, succumb, give over, give in, give one's self up, strike one's flag *or* colors, cry quarter, cry quits.

——, *n.* Relinquishment, renunciation, cession, resignation, abandonment, capitulation, yielding, delivery.

Surreptitious, *a.* Fraudulently introduced, foisted in, done by stealth, hidden, secret, stealthy.

Surreptitiously, *adv.* Fraudulently, by stealth, secretly, without authority.

Surrogate, *n.* Deputy, delegate, substitute, proxy, lieutenant, representative, *locum tenens.*

Surround, *v. t.* Encircle, environ, encompass, compass, hem, girdle, circumscribe, enclose, invest, hem in, fence about, beset, loop.

Surroundings, *n. pl.* [*Recent.*] External circumstances, *entourage*, neighborhood.

Surtout. *n.* Overcoat, great-coat.

Surveillance, *n.* [Fr.] Superintendence, inspection, oversight, supervision, care, watch, charge, control, direction, management, surveyorship.

Survey, *v. t.* 1. View, observe, overlook, scan, reconnoiter, scout, contemplate, review, take a view of.

2. Inspect, examine, scrutinize.

3. Measure and estimate (*as lands or buildings*), plot.

4. Oversee, supervise, inspect.

Survey, *n.* 1. View, sight, prospect, retrospect.

2. Inspection, examination, scrutiny, review, reconnoissance.

3. Mensuration (*to determine areas, contours, etc.*), surveying.

4. Conspectus, prospectus.

Surveyor, *n.* 1. Overseer, superintendent, supervisor; inspector.

2. Land-measurer; cartographer, topographer, geodesist.

3. (*Customs.*) Gauger, custom-house officer.

Survive, *v. i.* Remain alive, continue to live, live on, abide, last, endure, persist, subsist.

——, *v. t.* Outlive, live longer than, outlast, outwear.

Susceptibility, *n.* Sensitiveness, impressibility, susceptibleness, susceptivity, excitability.

Susceptible, *a.* Susceptive, impressible, sensitive, excitable, receptive, capable; inclined, predisposed.

Suspect, *v. t.* 1. Surmise, imagine, fancy, judge, believe, conjecture, guess, suppose, think.

2. Distrust, mistrust, doubt, misdoubt, have no confidence in, "smell," scent, be jealous of.

3. Believe to be guilty.

——, *v. i.* Be suspicious, have suspicion, imagine guilt.

Suspend, *v. t.* 1. Hang, swing, append, sling.

2. Make to depend.

3. Interrupt, intermit, stay, delay, hinder; discontinue, arrest, leave off, give over, stop, break off; defer, delay, postpone, adjourn, withhold, lay over, stave off.

4. Debar (*as from an office*) temporarily, dismiss, rusticate.

——, *v. i.* Stop payment, become bankrupt, go into bankruptcy.

Suspended, *a.* Hanging, pendent, pendulous, pensile.

Suspenders, *n. pl.* Braces, gallowses.

Suspense, *n.* 1. Uncertainty, indetermination, incertitude.

2. Hesitation, hesitancy, irresolution, doubt, perplexity, indecision, vacillation, wavering, scruple, misgiving; excited curiosity.

3. Suspension, intermission, remission, interruption, cessation, stoppage, stop, respite, pause, rest, stay, quiescence, discontinuance, abeyance.

Suspension, *n.* 1. Hanging, pendency.

2. Interruption, intermission, suspense, stay.

3. Delay, postponement.

4. Temporary deprivation (*as of an office*).

Suspicion, *n.* 1. Surmise, conjecture, supposition, assumption, guess, inkling, hint, trace, dash, suggestion.

2. Distrust, mistrust, doubt, misgiving, jealousy, want of confidence, apprehension, fear.

Suspicious, *a.* 1. Distrustful, jealous, inclined to suspect, given to suspicion, mistrustful.

2. Liable to suspicion, doubtful, questionable.

Sustain, *v. t.* 1. Bear, support, uphold, hold up, strengthen, fortify, prop, bolster, keep from falling.

2. Nourish, maintain, support, perpetuate, preserve, keep alive, supply with food.

3. Aid, comfort, relieve, assist.

4. Suffer, undergo, endure, bear, brave.

5. Sanction, approve, confirm, ratify, validate.

6. Justify, prove, establish, confirm.

7. (*Mus.*) Continue, hold.

Sustenance, *n.* 1. Subsistence, support, maintenance.

2. Food, victuals, provisions, bread, supplies, aliment, nutriment, nutrition, nourishment, *pabulum.*

Sustentation, *n.* 1. Support, preservation from falling.

2. Maintenance, support of life, subsistence, sustenance.

Susurrus, *n.* Whispering, whisper, murmuring.

Suture, *n.* Line of junction, seam.

Suzerain, *n.* Feudal lord, liege lord, lord paramount.

Suzerainty, *n.* Lordship, sovereignty, seigniory.

Swab, *n.* Mop, wipe up.

Swaddle, *v. t.* Swathe.

Swag, *v. i.* Bend (*by force of gravity*), settle, sag, give way, lean

Swagger, *v. i.* Bluster, bully, vapor, brag, be insolent, boast, strut, swell, ruffle, flourish.

——, *n.* Bluster, boastful manner, boastfulness, ruffling, strut, airs, arrogance, braggadocio, "side," pretentiousness.

Swaggerer, *n.* Blusterer, bully, braggart, boaster, braggadocio, Gascon, swashbuckler, fire-eater.

Swaggering, *n.* Bravado, bluster, gasconade, flourish, fanfaronade, swagger.

Swain, *n.* 1. Rustic, hind, peasant, countryman, clown.

2. Country gallant, rustic lover, wooer, suitor, adorer, inamorato, *amoroso*.

Swale, *v. i.* Melt (*as a candle*), waste, consume, waste away, sweal.

Swallow, *v. t.* 1. Take into the stomach, gulp, imbibe, gorge, engorge, englut, ingurgitate, bolt, gobble, eat, drink.

2. Absorb, engulf, devour, swallow up, submerge; appropriate, arrogate; occupy, employ, use up, consume; engross, engage completely, involve.

3. Believe (*without scruple*), receive implicitly, accept as true, credit.

4. Brook, stomach, pocket, endure, bear, put up with, stand, submit to, digest.

5. Renounce, retract, recant, take back.

6. Consume, exhaust, waste, use up.

——, *n.* 1. Throat, gullet, œsophagus.

2. Voracity, gluttonous appetite.

3. Taste, relish, inclination, liking, palate.

4. Mouthful, taste, little drink, draught; gulp, ingurgitation, deglutition.

Swamp, *n.* Bog, fen, quagmire, morass, marsh, slough, marish, spongy land, soft and wet ground.

——, *v. t.* 1. Engulf, sink, whelm, overwhelm, swallow up.

2. Upset, overset, sink, whelm, capsize; plunge into difficulties, sink, wreck, ruin, run aground, embarrass.

Swampy, *a.* Boggy, fenny, marshy, undrained, wet and spongy.

Sward, *n.* Turf, sod, lawn, grass, greensward.

Swarm, *n.* Multitude (*especially of winged insects*), crowd, throng, concourse, mass, press, flock, shoal, host, drove, horde, cloud, hive.

——, *v. i.* 1. Crowd, throng, gather in a swarm; climb.

2. Be crowded, be thronged, be filled, abound, be abundant.

Swarthy, *a.* Dark, dark-skinned, dark-hued, swart, brown, tawny, of a dark complexion, dusky.

Swash, *v. i.* 1. Swagger, bluster, vapor, brag, boast, bully.

2. Flow noisily, dash, splash.

Swash-buckler, *n.* Bully, braggadocio, swaggerer, blusterer, roisterer, rough, fanfaron, Captain Bobadil.

Swathe, *v. t.* Swaddle, bind, bandage, clothe.

——, *n.* Bandage, swaddling clothes.

Sway, *v. t.* 1. Move, wield, swing, wave, brandish, poise, balance, roll, rock.

2. Bias, bend, turn, urge, persuade, influence.

3. Rule, govern, direct, guide, control, dominate, manage.

4. (*Naut.*) Hoist, raise.

——, *v. i.* 1. Swing, wave, rock, reel, totter, wobble, fluctuate, vibrate, oscillate.

2. Govern, bear rule, reign; have weight, have influence, prevail.

3. Incline, lean, lurch, yaw.

——, *n.* 1. Power, dominion, control, empire, domination, command, rule, government, sovereignty, ascendency, authority, predominance, mastership, mastery, supreme power, omnipotence.

2. Influence, weight, authority, direction, bias.

3. Preponderation, preponderance.

4. Swing, sweep, wave, wag, oscillation.

Sweal, *v. i.* 1. Melt (*as a candle*), swale.

2. Blaze away.

——, *v. t.* Dress, singe, swale, burn the hair off.

Swear, *v. i.* 1. Utter an oath, take oath, take an oath.

2. Declare (*solemnly*), avow, affirm, depose, depone, attest, testify, state, say, vow, promise.

3. Use profane language, take the name of God in vain, curse, blaspheme.

——, *v. t.* Administer an oath to, put under oath, bind, promise.

Sweat, *n.* 1. Perspiration, exudation, excretion, sweating, cutaneous excretion.

2. Labor, toil, drudgery.

3. Ooze, reek, exuding moisture.

——, *v. i.* 1. Perspire, exude, emit moisture.

2. Toil, labor, drudge, work.

——, *v. t.* 1. Exude, emit by the pores.

2. Put into a perspiration.

Sweaty, *a.* 1. Perspiring, sweating.

2. Laborious, toilsome, difficult.

Sweep, *v. t.* 1. Clean (*with a broom*), brush.

2. Graze, touch (*in passing*), brush, rub over.

3. Traverse, pass over; rake, scour.

4. Carry off, sweep off, sweep away, clear.

5. Carry with pomp, flourish.

——, *n.* 1. Range, compass, scope, reach, movement, drive, amplitude.

2. Swipe, swape, well-sweep.

3. Destruction, havoc, ravage, devastation.

4. Sweeper, chimney-sweep.

5. Curve, curvature, flexure, bend.

Sweep away. 1. Clear away (*by a broom*), brush away.

2. Dislodge, remove, expel, drive off, sweep off.

3. Destroy, overwhelm, carry off.

Sweeping, *a.*   1. Destructive.

2. Wholesale, extensive, broad, general, comprehensive; unqualified, exaggerated, extravagant.

Sweepings, *n. pl.*   Refuse, offscourings, dirt, rubbish.

Sweep off.   Sweep away, sweep, brush off, brush away.

Sweep out.   1. Eject.

2. Clean, brush out, clear out.

Sweepstakes, *n.*   1. Winner (*in gaming* or *in horse-racing*).

2. Total stakes (*at a horse-race*).

SWEET, *a.*   1. Sugary, honeyed, saccharine, candied, luscious, cloying, nectareous.

2. Redolent, fragrant, balmy, odorous, sweet-smelling, spicy.

3. Soft, melodious, harmonious, mellifluous, pleasant, dulcet, musical, mellow, tuneful, silvery, silver-toned.

4. Beautiful, fair, lovely.

5. Delightful, agreeable, pleasant, charming, grateful, gratifying.

6. Mild, gentle, engaging, winning, attractive, affectionate, amiable, lovable.

7. Soft, gentle, benignant, serene.

8. Wholesome, sound, pure, fresh, clean.

——, *n.*   1. Sweetness, sweetest part.

2. Perfume, fragrance, redolence.

3. Dear, darling.

4. Joy, blessing, enjoyment, pleasure, gratification, delight.

5. See SWEETMEAT.

Sweeten, *v. t.*   1. Make sweet, dulcify, disembitter, candy, mull.

2. Soften, make mild, make tender, make kind, mollify, dulcify, milden.

3. Give zest to, give a relish to, revive, renew.

4. Soothe, relieve, solace.

5. Freshen, disinfect, ventilate, fumigate, purify, cleanse, deodorize.

Sweetheart, *n.*   1. Lover, beau, wooer, admirer, suitor, follower, adorer, swain, flame, love, spark, true-love, inamorato, betrothed, *fiancé*.

2. Flame, mistress, lady-love, dulcinea, inamorata, dear, darling, *cara sposa*.

Sweetly, *adv.*   Gratefully, pleasantly, agreeably.

Sweetmeat, *n.*   Confection, comfit, junket, sugar-plum, sweet, candy, confiture, confectionery, preserve, conserve.

Sweetness, *n.*   1. Dulcitude, sugariness, saccharinity.

2. Agreeableness, pleasantness; melody; fragrance, redolence; beauty, fairness, loveliness.

3. Amiableness, gentleness, mildness, suavity.

Sweet-scented, *a.*   Fragrant, redolent, balmy, sweet-smelling, aromatic, spicy, perfumed.

Sweet-sounding, *a.*   Melodious, harmonious, symphonious, tuneful, dulcet, musical.

Sweet-tempered, *a.*   Amiable, kind, gentle, mild, equable.

Sweet-toned, *a.*   Euphonious, euphonic, mellifluous.

Swell, *v. i.*   1. Dilate, expand, tumefy, distend, fill out, intumesce, grow larger *or* bigger (*by expansion*), belly, inflate, bulge, protuberate, puff, bloat.

2. Increase (*by outward addition*), augment, enlarge.

3. Rise (*as waves*), heave, surge.

4. Strut, look big, put on airs, be puffed up, swagger, ride a high horse, carry with a high hand; be turgid *or* bombastic, rise into arrogance.

5. Glow, expand, warm, thrill, heave, throb, grow big; be elated.

——, *v. t.*   1. Dilate, expand, inflate, enlarge.

2. Enhance, heighten, aggravate.

3. Puff up, make arrogant.

——, *n.*   1. Swelling.

2. Augmentation, protuberance, excrescency.

3. Elevation, rise, hill, ascent.

4. Force, intensity, power, *crescendo*, volume, boom.

5. Waves, billows, surge, undulation.

6. (*Colloq.*)   Fox, coxcomb, dandy, beau, exquisite, jackanapes, popinjay, blade, buck, fine gentleman, spark, jack-a-dandy, dandiprat, man milliner, man of dress, vain fellow.

Swelling, *a.*   1. Bombastic, pompous, turgid, inflated, tumid, stilted, grandiloquent, pretentious, high-flowing, high-sounding, rhetorical, declamatory, grandiose.

2. Protuberant, tumescent, inflated, surging, swollen, bloated, puffing.

——, *n.*   Swell, protuberance, bump, prominence, rise, inflation; gathering, tumor, boil, etc.

Swell out.   Bulge, protuberate.

Swelter, *v. i.*   Be oppressed with heat, be overcome by heat, be hot, glow, perspire, sweat.

Swerve, *v. i.*   1. Deviate, depart, diverge, deflect, turn aside, go astray.

2. Bend, incline, yield, give way.

3. Climb, move upward, swarm, wind.

Swift, *a.* 1. Quick, fast, fleet, rapid, speedy, expeditious, flying.

2. Ready, prompt, eager, zealous, forward, alert.

3. Sudden, instant, speedy.

Swift-footed, *a.* Fleet, nimble, agile, light-footed.

Swiftly, *adv.* Quickly, speedily, expeditiously, trippingly, apace, posthaste, rapidly, fleetly, at full speed, with speed, under press of canvas, by forced marches, on eagle's wings, in double-quick time, in seven-league boots.

Swiftness, *n.* Quickness, celerity, velocity, rapidity, speed, fleetness.

Swill, *v. t.* 1. Drink (*greedily*), guzzle, quaff, swallow.

2. Inebriate, intoxicate, fuddle.

——, *n.* 1. Potations, large drams, greedy draughts of liquor.

2. Hogwash, swillings, garbage.

Swiller, *n.* Drunkard, sot, toper, tippler, toss-pot, hard drinker, soaker.

SWIM, *v. i.* [*The noun is Basic Eng.*] 1. Float, be borne up (*on a liquid*).

2. Be borne along (*as on water, by a current*), float with the tide.

3. Propel one's self through the water, buffet the waves.

4. Glide, skim.

5. Be flooded, be inundated.

6. Be dizzy (*as the head*), be giddy.

7. Overflow, abound, have abundance.

Swimming, *n.* 1. Floating.

2. Dizziness, vertigo.

Swimmingly, *adv.* Smoothly, successfully, prosperously, easily.

Swindle, *v. t.* Cheat, cozen, deceive, dupe, gull, hoax, trick, defraud, overreach, victimize, chouse, diddle, impose upon, practise upon, take in; steal, embezzle, forge.

——, *n.* Cheat, fraud, imposition, deception, chouse, piece of knavery.

Swindler, *n.* Rogue, knave, cheat, fraud, faker, peculator, forger, embezzler, defaulter, impostor, trickster, sharper, blackleg, jockey.

Swindling, *n.* Knavery, cheating, rascality, roguery, imposture, default, embezzlement, forgery.

Swine, *n. sing. and pl.* 1. Hog, pig, porker, "grunter."

2. Hogs (*collectively*).

Swing, *v. i.* 1. Oscillate, vibrate, wave, sway, move to and fro, move backward and forward.

2. Depend, hang, dangle, hang loose.

3. (*Colloq.*) Be hanged, hang.

——, *v. t.* 1. Cause to swing, wave, *or* vibrate.

2. Wave, flourish, brandish, move to and fro, whirl.

3. Manage, administer, run.

——, *n.* 1. Oscillation, vibration, waving motion, fluctuation, undulation, pendulation, sway.

2. Scope, range, play, margin, free play, freedom, rhythm, full play, elbow-room, free course, sweep.

3. Bias, tendency, inclination.

Swinge, *v. t.* Beat, whip, scourge, flog, lash, bastinade, switch, chastise, punish.

Swinish, *a.* Hoggish, piggish, porcine; gross, sensual, brutish, beastly.

Swipe, *n.* Sweep, swape, well-sweep.

Swirl, *v. t. and v. i.* Whirl, eddy.

——, *n.* Eddy, whirl, gyration.

Switch, *n.* 1. Rod, twig, stick, birch, withe, rattan, whip.

2. Slash, cut, stroke.

3. Shunt, by-pass.

——, *v. t.* 1. Beat, whip, lash, swinge, flog, cut, slash, birch, cane.

2. Sidetrack, shunt, turn, shift, divert.

Swivel, *n.* 1. Caster.

2. Turning link (*in a chain*).

3. Swivel-gun.

Swoon, *v. i.* Faint, faint away.

——, *n.* Syncope, fainting, fainting fit.

Swoop, *v. t.* 1. Seize (*as a hawk its prey*), catch while on the wing, descend.

2. Catch up, pounce upon, seize, clutch.

——, *v. i.* Stoop, descend, come down, bear down, pounce.

——, *n.* 1. Clutch, seizure, pounce.

2. Stoop, descent.

Sword, *n.* 1. Sabre, broadsword, cutlass, falchion, cimeter, rapier, claymore, hanger, steel, blade, brand, bilbo, skean, Toledo, tuck.

2. Emblem of vengeance, emblem of justice.

3. Destruction by the sword.

Sybarite, *n.* Voluptuary, epicure, man of pleasure, sensualist, votary of Epicurus.

Sybaritic, } *a.* Voluptuous, luxurious,
Sybaritical, } wanton.

Sycophancy, *n.* Servility, obsequiousness, fawning, gross flattery, sycophantism.

Sycophant, *n.* Parasite, fawner, toady, wheedler, cringer, flunky, spaniel, lick-spittle, pick-thank, toad-eater, time-server, hanger-on, mean flatterer.

Sycophantic, *a.* Fawning, cringing, servile, slavish, parasitic, obsequious, adulatory, supple, grovelling, meanly submissive.

Syllabus, *n.* Abstract, abridgment, outline, epitome, summary, compend, digest, compendium, synopsis, breviary, brief, sum and substance.

Sylph, *n.* Fairy, fay, peri, sylphid.

Sylvan, *a.* 1. Forest-like.

2. Woody, shady.

——, *n.* Satyr, faun.

Symbol, *n.* Emblem, type, sign, token, figure, representative, representation, badge, picture, exponent.

Symbolic, } *a.* Emblematical, typical,
Symbolical, } hieroglyphical, representative, significative, figurative, ideographic.

Symbolization, *n.* Representation, indication, prefigurement.

Symbolize, *v. t.* Prefigure, typify, emblematize, represent, signify, mean, symbolify, imply, show, denote, illustrate, be symbolical of.

Symmetrical, *a.* Proportional (*in the several parts*), regular, shapely, harmonious, congruent, balanced, parallel, even, corresponding; shapely, beautiful, eurhythmic, well-proportioned, well-set, well-formed.

Symmetry, *n.* Proportion, harmony, shapeliness, evenness, balance, congruity, parallelism, regularity, order, regular arrangement.

Sympathetic, *a.* Compassionate, sympathizing, commiserating, pitiful, tender, kind, affectionate, loving, with the heart in the right place; harmonious, consonant.

Sympathize with. Feel sympathy with, feel for, enter into the feelings of, have pity for, condole with, fraternize with, make common cause with, have a common feeling; harmonize with.

Sympathizer, *n.* Favorer, patron, advocate, champion, partisan, well-wisher, friend; condoler, compassionator, pitier.

Sympathy, *n.* 1. Fellow-feeling.

2. Agreement, harmony, accord, correspondence, correlation, affinity, union, reciprocity, congeniality, concord, communion, concert.

3. Compassion, commiseration, condolence, pity, tenderness, kindliness, fellow-feeling, bowels of compassion.

Symphonious, *a.* Harmonious, consonant, accordant, concordant, musical, symphonic.

Symphony, *n.* Consonance, harmony, music, concert.

Symposium, *n.* Feast, drinking together, compotation, revel, banquet, festival.

Symptom, *n.* Indication, sign, mark, note, prognostic, diagnostic, token.

Symptomatic, } *a.* Indicative.
Symptomatical, }

Synagogue, *n.* 1. Jewish temple, Jewish house of worship.

2. Sanhedrin, great synagogue.

Synchronal, *a.* Synchronical, synchronous, coincident, contemporaneous.

Synchronize, *v. i.* Be simultaneous, agree in time, concur in time, coexist.

Synchronism, *n.* Simultaneousness, coincidence, coexistence, concurrence.

Syncopate, *v. t.* Contract, elide.

Syncope, *n.* 1. (*Gram.*) Elision (*in the middle of a word*).

2. (*Med.*) Swoon, fainting, fainting fit.

Synergetic, *a.* Co-operating, co-operative, synergistic, working together.

Synod, *n.* 1. Council of ecclesiastics.

2. Meeting, convention, council, assembly.

Synonym, *n.* Equivalent word (*of the same language*), word of nearly the same meaning.

Synonymous, *a.* Equivalent, interchangeable, equipollent, of similar meaning, that express the same idea; tantamount.

Synopsis, *n.* Abridgment, epitome, abstract, outline, compend, compendium, summary, syllabus, digest, sum and substance, general view.

Synthesis, *n.* Combination (*of elements*), composition, putting together.

Syringe, *n.* Squirt.

Syrinx, *n.* Pandean pipes, shepherd's pipes, Pan.

SYSTEM, *n.* 1. A whole (*viewed with reference to the interdependence of its parts*), combination of parts to form a whole, organism, organization, universe.

2. Scheme, body, plan, theory, connected view, hypothesis, classification, arrangement.

3. Order, method, regularity, rule, routine, custom.

Systematic, } *a.* 1. Methodical, orderly,
Systematical, } regular.

2. Cosmical.

Systematize, *v. t.* Methodize, arrange, harmonize, regulate, order, reduce to order, organize, regiment, standardize, put into a systematic form.

T

Tabby, *n.* 1. Watered silk.

2. Brindled cat, tabby-cat.

3. Gossip, tale-bearer, news-monger, tattler, chatterer.

——, *v. t.* Water, sprinkle and calender.

Tabefaction, *n.* Emaciation (*by tabes*), wasting away.

Tabernacle, *n.* 1. Tent, pavilion, habitation.

2. The Jewish temple; temple, church, chapel, cathedral, minster, meeting-house, place of worship, sacred place.

3. Pyx, reliquary, shrine.

——, *v. i.* Dwell (*temporarily*), sojourn, be housed.

Tabid, *a.* Consumptive, phthisical.

TABLE, *n.* 1. Slab, tablet, plate.

2. Stand (*to take food from*), board, counter, desk.

3. Food, diet, provision, fare, repast, victuals, entertainment, *cuisine*, menu.

4. Index, list, catalogue, syllabus, chart, tabulation, schedule, compendium, record, file; synopsis, condensed statement.

Tableau, *n.* [Fr.] Picture, scene, representation; *tableau vivant*.

Table-land, *n.* Elevated plain, plateau.

Tablet, *n.* 1. Small table, slab, tablature, plaque.

2. Pocket memorandum-book, pad.

3. Lozenge, troche, wafer, cake.

Taboo, *n.* [Written also *Tabu*.] Interdict, prohibition.

——, *v. t.* Interdict, forbid, prohibit, put under taboo, put under an interdict, forbid to be used *or* touched.

——, *a.* Forbidden, prohibited, inviolable.

Tabouret, *n.* Fr.] Stool; embroidery-frame.

Tabular, *a.* 1. Of a table, tabulate, tabulary.

2. Flat, plane.

3. Laminated, lamellar, lamelliform, foliated, scaly, flaky.

Tabulate, *v. t.* Put into tabular form, tabularize.

Tacit, *a.* Implied, understood, inferred, silent, unexpressed (*by words*), implicit, unspoken.

Taciturn, *a.* Silent (*by habit*), reserved, uncommunicative, close, unconversable, reticent, reserved, laconic, sententious, of few words, sparing of words, close-tongued, mute, mum, dumb, close-mouthed.

Taciturnity, *n.* Reserve, closeness, reticence, habitual silence, uncommunicativeness, muteness, dumbness, laconicism.

Tack, *v. t.* Fasten (*slightly*), attach, append, add, affix, tag.

——, *v. i.* (*Naut.*) Go about, tack ship, gybe, yaw; zigzag.

——, *n.* Course, leg, trip, route, road, gybe.

Tackle, *n.* 1. Pulley.

2. Equipment, gear, rigging, tackling, cordage, furniture, implements, apparatus, harness, weapons, instruments of action, tools.

——, *v. t.* (*Colloq.*) Attack, seize, lay hold of, seize upon, grapple; attempt, try, undertake.

Tact, *n.* Adroitness (*in appreciating circumstances and acting accordingly*), skill (*in saying or doing what is most appropriate to the occasion*), quick judgment, nice perception, insight, discernment, cleverness, dexterity, knack, *savoir faire*, address, diplomacy, finesse.

Tactician, *n.* Manœuvrer, wire-puller, adroit manager; military strategist.

Tactics, *n.* 1. Strategy, military science, generalship, art of war.

2. Management, manœuvring, policy, diplomacy.

Tactile, *a.* Tangible, palpable, tactual.

Tædium, *n.* [L.] Wearisomeness, irksomeness, tiresomeness, tediousness.

Tag, *n.* 1. Metal point (*at the end of a string*).

2. Label, card, tab, pendant; tail, tip, stub.

3. Cue, catchword, stock phrase, *cliché.*

4. Game of tag, tig.

——, *v. t.* 1. Attach a tag to, fit with a tag.

2. Fasten, attach, append, affix, tack, join, add to, follow.

TAIL, *n.* 1. Caudal appendage, hinder part.

2. Back part, lower part, inferior part.

3. End, extremity, fag-end, conclusion, appendage, tag, stub.

4. Skirt, flap.

5. Catkin, cattail.

6. Train, retinue, queue.

——, *a.* (*Law.*) Limited, abridged, reduced, curtailed.

Taint, *v. t.* 1. Imbue, impregnate.

2. Corrupt, infect, contaminate, defile, poison, make noxious, make putrid, pollute, spoil, touch, mildew, flyblow, disease, vitiate.

3. Tarnish, stain, sully, blot.

——, *n.* 1. Tincture, tinge, stain, touch.

2. Infection, corruption, depravation, contamination, defilement.

3. Fault, blemish, defect, flaw, spot, stain.

TAKE, *v. t.* 1. Receive, accept; get, procure, obtain.

2. Seize, grasp, gripe, grip, clutch, snatch, clasp, lay hold of, get hold of.

3. Filch, purloin, steal, pilfer, misappropriate.

4. Entrap, ensnare, capture, catch, "collar," bag, arrest, apprehend, make prisoner of, pocket, appropriate.

5. Come upon, befall, smite, fasten on, attack.

6. Conquer, capture, cause to surrender; gain, win.

7. Captivate, delight, please, interest, attract, allure, engage, fascinate, bewitch, enchant, charm.

8. Understand, interpret; regard, consider, hold, suppose.

9. Choose, select, elect, espouse, be in favor of.

10. Use, employ, make use of, expend, avail one's self of.

11. Demand, require, need, be necessary, necessitate, claim, call for.

12. Experience, feel, perceive, be sensible of, entertain, be conscious of; bear, endure, tolerate, submit to.

13. Draw, derive, deduce, discover, detect.

14. Conduct, lead, convey; carry, transfer.

15. Clear, surmount, leap over.

——, *v. i.* 1. Catch, be fixed, fix, stick.

2. Please, be well received, be welcomed.

3. Succeed, have the intended effect, work.

4. Go, proceed, resort, direct one's course.

——, *n.* Catch of fish, haul of fish.

Take aback. Astonish, surprise, take by surprise, startle.

Take advantage of. 1. Turn to account, profit by, make use of.

2. Impose upon (*by some advantage of superior knowledge* or *of opportunity*), catch by surprise, outwit.

Take after. 1. Copy, imitate.

2. Resemble, be like.

Take amiss. Take ill, take in bad part.

Take back. 1. Take again.

2. Recall, revoke, recant, withdraw, retract, retire, disavow, abjure.

Take breath. Rest, stop to rest.

Take care. Be careful.

Take care of. Oversee, superintend, take charge of, care for.

Take courage. Be encouraged, take heart.

Take down. 1. Take from above.

2. Reduce, lower, depress.

3. Humble, abash, humiliate.

4. Pull to pieces, pull down.

5. Swallow, take.

6. Record, note, make a note of, write down.

Take effect. 1. Be efficacious.

2. Go into operation.

Take exception. 1. Object, dissent, make objection.

2. Take it ill, be displeased, be offended.

Take fire. Be ignited, catch fire, be inflamed, be kindled.

Take flight. Fly, take to one's heels, run, flee, scamper off, make off.

Take for. Mistake for.

Take for granted. Admit, allow, concede.

Take heart. Be encouraged, take courage, gain confidence.

Take heed. Beware, be cautious, be careful.

Take in. 1. Receive, admit, entertain, accommodate.

2. Comprise, embrace, comprehend, include, encompass, enclose.

3. Comprehend, understand, discern, grasp.

4. Lessen, contract, make smaller, diminish, reduce, furl.

5. Impose upon, defraud, cheat, deceive, trick, fool, hoax.

Taking, *a.* 1. Pleasing, alluring, captivating, attractive.

2. Infectious, catching.

Take in good part. Receive kindly, take without offence.

Take in hand. 1. Undertake, engage in, set the hand to.

2. Deal with (*in the way of correction* or *discipline*).

Take into account. Consider, remember.

Take in tow. Tow, draw, drag, haul, pull.

Take it. Think, suppose, presume, believe, imagine, conclude.

Take it ill. Be offended, be displeased, take exception.

Take leave. Bid adieu, bid farewell, take one's departure.

Take notice. Observe, remark, pay attention.

Take-off, *n.* Imitation, caricature.

Take off. 1. Remove, divest one's self of, take away, carry off.

2. Destroy, kill.

3. Imitate, personate, mimic; copy, reproduce.

Take on, *v. t.* Assume, be willing to bear, take upon, take up.

Take one's chance. Venture, tempt fortune, try one's fortune, try one's luck.

Take one's choice. Choose, select, pick and choose.

Take one's fancy. Please, afford pleasure, charm.

Take one's own course. Act one's pleasure, do as one chooses.

Take out. Remove, withdraw, draw out, extract.

Take part. 1. Share, partake.

2. Unite, join.

Take place. 1. Happen, occur, come to pass.

2. Prevail, have effect.

Take root. Be rooted, be firmly established.

Take sides. Favor one side, take up the cause of one side, be partisan.

Take the lead. Lead the way, go before, go ahead, go in the van.

Take the place of. Supply the place of, be a substitute for, stand in the shoes of.

Take to. Apply to, be fond of.

Take to flight. Flee, fly, run away, take to one's heels.

Take to heart. Feel keenly, be greatly grieved at, be much affected by, take on about, be much troubled by, lay to heart.

Take to one's heels. Flee, fly, run away, take to flight.

Take to task. Reprove, reprimand, chide, take to do, call to account, rebuke.

Take up. 1. Raise, lift, hoist, gather up, pick up.

2. Begin (*especially where another has left off*), resume; set about, undertake.

3. Engross, engage, employ, occupy, fill, cover, absorb, monopolize.

4. Arrest, seize, catch, take prisoner, take into custody.

5. Assume, adopt, pay (*as a note*), discharge, settle.

Take upon one's self. 1. Assume, undertake.

2. Incur, appropriate to one's self.

Take up with. Be contented with.

Tale, *n.* 1. Oral relation, story, account, recital, that which is told, rehearsal, narrative, story, fable, legend, yarn, relation, apologue, parable, novel, romance.

2. Information, anything disclosed.

3. Account, count, reckoning, numbering, tally, enumeration.

Tale-bearer, *n.* Tell-tale, tattler, mumble-news, gossip.

Talent, *n.* Gift, faculty, capacity, genius, endowment, ability, ableness, power, parts, cleverness, turn, aptitude, aptness, knack, forte.

Talented, *a.* Gifted, of talent, of brilliant parts, able.

Talisman, *n.* Charm, amulet, phylactery, mascot, fetish.

Talismanic, *a.* Magical.

Talk, *v. i.* 1. Speak, converse, palaver, "jaw," parley, prattle, prate, chat, gossip.

2. Confer, reason, deliberate, consult, discuss.

——, *v. t.* 1. Speak, use for conversing.

2. Speak, utter, say, mention in speaking.

TALK, *n.* 1. Conversation, converse, colloquy, speech, utterance, parlance, discourse, conference, communication, dialogue, confabulation, palaver, chat, parley, oral intercourse; address, lecture.

2. Report, rumor, bruit, town talk, scandal, gossip.

Talkative, *a.* Loquacious, garrulous, voluble, "glib," fluent, chatty, conversational, cozy, long-tongued, windy, leaky.

Talker, *n.* 1. Converser, conversationalist, speaker, orator.

2. Prattler, loquacious person, chatterer, chatter-box, babbler, magpie, *moulin à paroles*, windbag, gossip.

3. Boaster, braggart, gascon.

TALL, *a.* High (*in stature*), lofty, elevated, soaring, towering; lank; exaggerated.

Tallness, *n.* Height (*of stature*).

Tallow, *n.* Suet (*freed from adhering membranes*).

Tally, *n.* Mate, match, counterpart; check; rollcall, muster.

——, *v. i.* Match, agree, accord, conform, correspond, harmonize, square, coincide, suit.

Talon, *n.* Claw (*of a bird*), nail.

Tame, *a.* 1. Domesticated, domestic, mild, gentle, docile, reclaimed.

2. Subdued, crushed, broken, unresisting, submissive, meek.

3. Spiritless, dull, flat, feeble, lean, vapid, insipid, jejune, barren, languid, prosing, prosy, prosaic, uninteresting, poor, tedious, commonplace.

——, *v. t.* 1. Domesticate, make tame, make docile, reclaim, meeken, gentle, train.

2. Subdue, repress, conquer, overcome, overthrow, subjugate, break in, master.

Tamper, *v. i.* 1. Meddle, intermeddle, interfere, dabble, have to do (*in a tentative way*).

2. Intrigue, deal secretly, use bribery, seduce, suborn.

Tan, *v. t.* 1. Convert into leather, impregnate with tannin.

2. Imbrown, make tawny, imbrown by exposure.

Tan-colored, *a.* Leather-colored, tawny.

Tang, *n.* 1. Smack, taste, flavor, savor, relish, aftertaste.

2. Sting, nip, keenness.

Tangency, *n.* Contact, touching.

Tangent, *a.* Touching.

Tangible, *a.* 1. Tactile, touchable, palpable, corporeal, material.

2. Real, certain, positive, substantial, stable, solid, actual, embodied, perceptible, sensible, open, plain, evident, obvious.

Tangle, *v. t.* 1. Interweave (*confusedly*), intertwine, complicate, perplex, snarl, entangle, mat.

2. Entrap, ensnare, catch, trap, involve.

3. Embroil, embarrass, perplex.

——, *n.* 1. Complication, intricacy, perplexity, snarl, disorder, jumble.

2. Perplexity, embarrassment, dilemma, quandary.

Tank, *n.* Cistern, reservoir, boiler.

Tanned, *a.* Imbrowned, sunburnt, ruddy, blowzy, blowzed, ruddy-faced.

Tantalize, *v. t.* Torment (*by exciting hopes and refusing to gratify them*), vex, tease, irritate, provoke, disappoint, balk, frustrate.

Tantamount, *a.* Equivalent, equal.

Tantamount to. The same as, equal to, as good as.

Tantrum, *n.* (*Colloq.*) Burst of ill-humor, fit, paroxysm, outburst.

Tap, *v. t.* 1. Broach, draw off.

2. Rap, strike (*lightly*), pat, tip, touch.

——, *v. i.* Rap.

——, *n.* 1. Gentle blow, light stroke, touch, pat, tip, rap.

2. Spigot, plug, stopper, stopple, spile.

3. Tap-room, bar, tap-house.

Taper, *a.* Conical, pyramidal, tapering.

——, *v. t.* Make taper, make conical, narrow, diminish, point.

——, *v. i.* Take a conical form, have a conical shape.

Tapering, *a.* Conical, taper, pyramidal, diminishing, narrowing, pointed.

Tapestry, *n.* Arras, drapery.

Tap-house, *n.* Ale-house, public-house, tavern.

Tapis, *n.* Carpet.

Tapped, *a.* Abroach, broached, on tap.

Tap-room, *n.* Tap, bar-room.

Tar, *n.* (*Colloq.*) Sailor, seaman, mariner, seafarer, seafaring man, tarpaulin.

Tardiness, *n.* Slowness, dilatoriness, delay, slackness, lateness.

Tardy, *a.* 1. Slow, snail-like, sluggish, slow-paced.

2. Dilatory, slack, late, behindhand, overdue, backward, slow.

Target, *n.* Mark (*to be shot at*), butt, aim, shield.

Tariff, *n.* Schedule of duties (*on imports or on exports*), charge, scale of prices.

Tarn, *n.* 1. Pool (*among mountains*), pond, lake, mere.

2. Bog, marsh, fen, swamp, morass, marish.

Tarnish, *v. t.* Soil, stain, sully, slur, defame, smear, smudge, deface, dim, discolor, dull, blemish.

——, *n.* Soil, stain, spot, blemish, blot.

Tarry, *v. i.* 1. Wait, linger, delay, loiter, dally, remain, stay, stop.

2. Delay, put off, defer.

3. Stay, sojourn, abide (*temporarily*), lodge, rest, take up one's quarters, pitch one's tent, have lodgings, take lodgings, continue, stop, halt.

Tart, *a.* 1. Sour, acid, acidulous, sharp, acrid, astringent.

2. Severe, harsh, caustic, crabbed, sharp, snappish, testy, petulant, acrimonious, sarcastic, curt, ill-tempered, ill-humored, keen.

Tartan, *n.* Plaid.

Tartar, *n.* Ill-tempered person.

Tartarean, *a.* Infernal, hellish, tartareous.

Tartarus, *n.* Hades, Erebus, hell, the lower world, the infernal regions, shades below, purgatory, pandemonium, realms of Pluto.

Tartness, *n.* 1. Sourness, acidity.

2. Acrimony, harshness, asperity, sourness, sarcasticness, severity, piquancy, sharpness, keenness, acerbity, crabbedness.

Tartuffe, *n.* Hypocrite, hypocritical devotee.

Tartuffish, *a.* Formal, hypocritical.

Task, *n.* 1. Work, labor, toil, drudgery.

2. Employment, business, undertaking, enterprise, work, labor, stint, chore, job, duty, mission, charge.

3. Lesson, exercise, assignment.

——, *v. t.* 1. Impose a task on.

2. Burden, oppress, tax, strain, overwork.

Taskmaster, *n.* Overseer, tasker.

Taskwork, *n.* Piece-work, job-work.

Taste, *v. t.* 1. Try the flavor of, test by the tongue.

2. Experience, perceive, feel, undergo.

3. Partake of, participate in.

——, *v. i.* 1. Try the flavor.

2. Smack, savor, be tinctured, relish, have a smack *or* flavor.

TASTE, *n.* 1. Gustation, act of tasting.

2. Flavor, relish, savor, goût, gusto, smack, piquancy.

3. Dash, infusion, admixture, sprinkling, hint, suggestion, shade, sip, bite,

fragment, tincture, *soupçon;* bit, morsel, mouthful, sample.

4. Sense of taste, tooth.

5. Fondness, liking, partiality, predilection, desire, appetite.

6. Discernment (*of beauty* or *excellence*), judgment (*of propriety*), nice perception, discrimination, acumen, refinement, delicacy, fine feeling, culture, cultivation, elegance, polish, grace.

7. Manner, style.

8. Narrow ribbon.

Tasteful, *a.* 1. Savory, toothsome, delicious, palatable, flavorsome, appetizing.

2. Tasty, elegant, in good taste, æsthetic, artistic, attractive.

Tasteless, *a.* 1. Insipid, flat, without relish, savorless, stale, watery.

2. Dull, flat, insipid, uninteresting, vapid, mawkish.

Tasty, *a.* 1. (*Colloq.*) Elegant, refined, tasteful.

2. Toothsome, palatable, savory, relishing.

Tatterdemalion, *n.* Ragamuffin, ragged fellow, wretch, *sans-culotte.*

Tattered, *a.* Torn, ragged, flittered.

Tatters, *n. pl.* Rags.

Tattle, *v. i.* 1. Prate, prattle, chatter, chat, jabber, babble, talk idly *or* thoughtlessly, talk at random, spin a long yarn.

2. (*Colloq.*) Blab, gossip, tell tales, inform, "peach," tell secrets.

——, *n.* Prate, prattle, gossip, twaddle, gabble, idle talk, tittle-tattle.

Tattler, *n.* Prattler, babbler, chatterer, prater, gossip, gadabout, gadder, rattlehead, idle talker, news-monger, talebearer, informer, whisperer, magpie.

Tattoo, *n.* Beat of drum (*to summon soldiers to quarters at night*), tapto.

Taunt, *v. t.* Mock, flout, chaff, ridicule, revile, reproach, upbraid, censure, deride, jeer, twit, scoff at, sneer at, rail at, make game of, make fun of, treat with scorn, make a butt of, make merry with.

——, *n.* Ridicule, derision, scoff, censure, reproach, insult, jeer, gibe, quip, quirk, caustic remark.

Taut, *a.* Tight, tense, stretched, strained.

Tautological, *a.* Repetitious, repetitional, redundant, pleonastic.

Tautology, *n.* Repetition (*of the same idea in different words*), redundancy, iteration, reiteration, verbosity, wordiness, pleonasm.

Tavern, *n.* Inn, public-house, hostelry, eating-house.

Tawdry, *a.* Showy (*without elegance*), gaudy, flashy, glittering, in bad taste, meretricious, tinsel, garish, loud.

Tawny, *a.* Fulvous, fulvid, yellowish-brown, dull yellow.

TAX, *n.* 1. Impost, duty, custom, toll, excise, taxation, tithe, tribute, assessment, rate, levy.

2. Demand, burden, charge, requisition, strain.

3. Charge, accusation, censure.

——, *v. t.* 1. Put a tax upon, assess tribute upon, rate.

2. Burden, load, task, make demands upon, strain, overtax, require, exact.

3. Accuse, charge, lay upon, censure.

Tea, *n.* (*Colloq.*) Supper, evening meal.

Teach, *v. t.* 1. Instruct, inform, educate, edify, enlighten, train, discipline, drill, school, tutor, "coach," "cram," "prime," catechize, ground, indoctrinate, initiate, give instruction to, give lessons to, give lessons in.

2. Communicate, impart, inculcate, instil, infuse, disseminate, propagate, implant, preach, interpret, explain, expound.

3. Admonish, counsel, show, guide, direct, tell, advise, signify, suggest to, indicate to, point out to.

4. Direct as an instructor, manage as a preceptor, guide the studies of.

——, *v. i.* Act as teacher, practise teaching, profess.

Teachable, *a.* Docile, apt, apt to learn, tractable.

Teacher, *n.* 1. Instructor, tutor, coach, preceptor, informant, pedagogue, inculcator, trainer, educator, master, schoolmaster.

2. Guide, mentor, adviser, counselor.

3. Preacher, minister of the gospel, pastor.

TEACHING, *n.* Education, instruction, tutelage, tuition, grounding, discipline, drill, pedagogy, pedagogics, didactics, indoctrination, inculcation.

Tear, *v. t.* 1. Rend, pull apart, separate by pulling, rip, shred, burst, slit, rive.

2. Lacerate, laniate, lancinate, mangle, rend, claw, shatter, wound.

3. Sever, sunder.

4. Break away, force away, rend away, snatch away.

——, *v. i.* 1. Rush with violence, move with violence, dash, fly, race.

2. Rage, rave, fume, rant.

——, *n.* Rent, fissure, wrench, rip, laceration.

Tearful, *a.* Weeping, shedding tears, lachrymose, mournful, maudlin.

Tease, *v. t.* Worry, vex, plague, annoy, torment, molest, irritate harass, tantalize, badger, chafe, hector, harry, pester, bother, trouble, disturb, chagrin, provoke; haze, "rag"; beg, importune.

Tea-set, *n.* Tea-service, tea-things.

Teat, *n.* Dug, nipple, pap.

Techy, *a.* [Written also *Tetchy.*] Peevish, fretful, irritable, touchy.

Te Deum. Hymn of thanksgiving.

Tedious, *a.* 1. Wearisome (*in consequence of being prolonged*), tiresome, operose, irksome, dull, uninteresting, fatiguing, too long, monotonous, trying.

2. Slow, sluggish, tardy, dilatory.

Tediousness, *n.* Wearisomeness, tiresomeness, ennui, monotony, irksomeness, tedium.

Teem, *v. i.* 1. Bring forth, produce, bear, generate; conceive, be pregnant, engender young.

2. Abound, be full, be prolific, be stocked, swarm, exuberate.

Teeming, *a.* Fraught, replete, full, prolific, pregnant, overflowing, swarming, abounding.

Teeter, *v. i.* [*U. S.*] Seesaw, titter, titter-totter.

Teetotalism, *n.* (*Colloq.*) Total abstinence, strict temperance.

Tegument, *n.* 1. Covering, cover, integument, capsule, case.

2. Skin.

Telegram, *n.* Telegraphic despatch, radiogram, marconigram, "wire," cable.

Telegraph, *v. t.* Convey by telegraph, announce by telegraph, "wire," wireless, radio.

Telescope, *n.* Spyglass, fieldglass.

Tell, *v. t.* 1. Number, count, enumerate, compute, reckon, run over, sum up, take an account of, mention one by one.

2. Relate, recount, rehearse, narrate, describe, report, give an account of.

3. Disclose, reveal, divulge, confess, betray, acknowledge, own, declare, make known, announce.

4. Acquaint, teach, inform, apprise, make known to, explain to, instruct, communicate to.

5. Discern, discover, make out, distinguish, find out.

6. Express, utter, speak, state, mention, communicate, publish, speak of, make mention of.

——, *v. i.* 1. Give account, make report.

2. (*Colloq.*) Take effect, be effective, weigh, count.

Telling, *a.* Effective, powerful.

Tell of. Speak of, mention, narrate *or* describe.

Tell off. Count off, detach, distribute.

Telltale, *a.* Babbling, tattling, blabbing, tale-bearing.

Telluric, *a.* Terrestrial, earthly.

Temerity, *n.* Recklessness (*of disposition*), rashness, heedlessness, venturesomeness, hastiness, incautiousness, precipitancy, inconsiderateness, presumption, foolhardiness, precipitation, impetuosity, over-confidence, audacity.

Temper, *v. t.* 1. Modify, qualify, mix in due proportion.

2. Soften, mollify, assuage, soothe, calm, moderate, restrain, pacify, attemper, appease, mitigate.

3. Adapt, fit, suit, adjust, accommodate.

4. Bring to the right degree of hardness (*as iron, by sudden cooling*).

5. Anneal.

——, *n.* 1. Due mixture, just combination.

2. Constitution, temperament, nature, character, type, quality, structure, organization.

3. Disposition, humor, frame, mood, grain, tone, vein, spirits.

4. Calmness, moderation, equanimity, composure, tranquillity.

5. (*Colloq.*) Anger, passion, irritation, heat of mind, spleen, ill-temper.

Temperament, *n.* Constitution, temper, nature, disposition, organization, idiosyncrasy, habit.

Temperance, *n.* 1. Moderation, sobriety, soberness, self-control, abstinence, frugality, forbearance; teetotalism, prohibition.

2. Patience, calmness, sedateness, contentment, moderation.

Temperate, *a.* 1. Moderate, abstemious, frugal, sparing, chaste, continent, self-denying, self-controlled, austere, ascetic.

2. Cool, calm, dispassionate, sedate, sober, mild.

Tempest, *n.* 1. Storm, hurricane, gale, squall, blizzard, cyclone, tornado, violent wind (*usually accompanied with rain, hail, or snow, and sometimes with thunder and lightning*).

2. Excitement, tumult, disturbance, commotion, turmoil, perturbation, violent outbreak.

Tempestuous, *a.* 1. Stormy, windy, breezy, squally, gusty, blustering, boisterous.

2. Violent, turbulent, tumultuous, impetuous, stormy.

Temple, *n.* Fane, sanctuary, tabernacle, conventicle, church, house of worship, house of God, meeting-house, holy place.

Tempo, *n.* (*Mus.*) Time, rate of movement.

Temporal, *a.* 1. Worldly, terrestrial, mundane, secular, of this world, of this life; lay, profane, civil, political.

2. Transient, fleeting, temporary, transitory, short-lived, ephemeral.

Temporary, *a.* Transitory, transient, fleeting, momentary, brief, evanescent, ephemeral, short-lived, temporal, brief, for a time, of short duration.

Temporize, *v. i.* Trim, comply with occasions, hedge, diplomatize, yield to circumstances, fall in with current opinion, act the time-server, be on the fence, wait to see which way the cat will jump.

Temporizer, *n.* Trimmer, time-server, hedger, opportunist.

Tempt, *v. t.* 1. Try, test, prove, put to trial.

2. Entice (*especially to evil*), allure, seduce, decoy, induce, inveigle, persuade, prevail upon, attract, fascinate, draw on, bring over, lure.

3. Incite, instigate, provoke, incline, dispose, prompt, endeavor to persuade, lead.

4. Attempt, venture on, essay, try.

Temptation, *n.* 1. Enticement (*especially to evil*), allurement, attraction.

2. Bribe, bait, lure, decoy, golden apple, voice of the tempter, song of the sirens.

Tempter, *n.* 1. Seducer, prompter, instigator, coaxer, siren, Circe.

2. Satan, the Devil, Lucifer, Belial, Beelzebub, Prince of Darkness, the Arch-fiend, Apollyon, Abaddon, the Evil One, the Author of Evil, the Old Serpent, the Prince of this World, the Foul Fiend.

Tempting, *a.* Alluring, attractive, seductive, enticing.

Tenable, *a.* Defensible, maintainable, capable of being held *or* defended.

Tenacious, *a.* 1. Retentive, apt to retain, unforgetful.

2. Adhesive, sticky, glutinous, viscous, gummy, cohesive, smeary, dauby, clinging, tough, resisting, firm, strong, holding, fast, unyielding.

3. Stubborn, obstinate, pertinacious, persistent, dogged, resolute, unwavering; opinionated, opinionative, positive.

Tenaciousness, *n.* See TENACITY.

Tenacity, *n.* 1. Retentiveness, tenaciousness.

2. Adhesiveness, cohesiveness, glutinousness, gumminess, stickiness, viscidity, toughness, strength.

3. Stubbornness, obstinacy, pertinacity, firmness, persistency, perseverance, doggedness, resolution.

Tenancy, *n.* Holding, tenure, temporary possession, occupancy.

Tenant, *n.* Occupier, occupant, resident, dweller, lessee, renter.

Tenantable, *a.* Habitable.

Tend, *v. t.* 1. Watch, guard, keep, protect, shepherd, graze, attend, accompany, nurse, take care of, wait on, look after; minister to, serve.

2. Attend to, be attentive to, note carefully, mind.

——, *v. i.* 1. Attend, wait, serve, be attendant.

2. Incline, lean, verge, trend, make, be directed, aim, exert influence, head, lead, point, gravitate, work towards.

3. Conduce, contribute.

4. Tend to, attend, mind.

TENDENCY, *n.* Inclination, leaning, direction, determination, bearing, bent, bias, warp, turn, twist, drift, course, set, *penchant*, gravitation, aim, scope, proclivity, aptitude, proneness, predisposition, propensity, turn, disposition, liability, susceptibility.

Tender, *a.* 1. Soft, delicate; weak, feeble, fragile; callow, immature, young, infantile, youthful; effeminate, feminine, womanly, delicate.

2. Sensitive, easily pained.

3. Compassionate, kind, humane, loving, affectionate, sympathetic, pitiful, merciful, lenient, gentle, mild, tender-hearted.

4. Pathetic, affecting, touching; painful (*to speak of* or *treat of*), unpleasant, disagreeable.

5. Dear, precious, valuable.

——, *v. t.* Offer, proffer, present, volunteer, propose, suggest.

——, *n.* Offer, proffer, proposal.

Tender-hearted, *a.* Affectionate, kind, compassionate, sympathetic, merciful, tender, pitiful.

Tenderly, *adv.* Mildly, gently, softly, kindly.

Tenderness, *n.* 1. Softness, delicacy, want of firmness; weakness, feebleness; effeminacy, womanly quality.

2. Soreness, sensitiveness, sensibility, susceptibility.

3. Compassion, kindness, sympathy, affection, pity, love, gentleness, benevolence, leniency, clemency, sensibility, mildness, benignity, humanity, loving-kindness.

4. Pathos, softness.

5. Caution, carefulness, scrupulousness, cautious care.

Tendon, *n.* Sinew, ligament.

Tendril, *n.* (*Bot.*) Filament, cirrus.

Tenebrous, *a.* Dark, dusky, darksome, gloomy, tenebrious, caliginous, shady, shadowy, obscure, murky, sombre.

Tenement, *n.* House, dwelling, habitation, abode, domicile; flat, apartment; slum.

Tenet, *n.* Doctrine, dogma, opinion, notion, principle, position, belief, creed, way of thinking.

Tenor, *n.* 1. Course, manner, fashion, mood, nature, form, cast, cut, stamp, tone, tendency, trend, character.

2. Meaning, intent, purport, import, sense, spirit, drift, gist, significance.

Tense, *a.* Tight, stretched, strained, rigid, stiff, taut; excited, high-strung, nervous; intent, rapt.

Tensile, *a.* Tensible, ductile.

Tension, *n.* 1. Stretching, straining.

2. Stiffness, tenseness, rigor, tensity, tightness.

3. Strain, rigor, severe effort.

4. Nervousness, excitement.

5. (*Phys.*) Expansive force, elastic force.

Tent, *n.* Pavilion, portable lodge, marquee, wigwam, tepee.

Tentacle, *n.* Feeler.

Tentative, *a.* Trying, essaying, experimental, provisional, probationary, makeshift, temporary, empirical, probative.

Tenth, *n.* Tithe.

Ten thousand. Myriad.

Tenuity, *n.* 1. Thinness.

2. Slenderness, fineness.

3. Rarity, rareness, thinness.

Tenuous, *a.* 1. Thin, slender, small, minute.

2. Rare, subtle, rarefied, unsubstantial.

Tenure, *n.* 1. (*Law.*) Manner *or* principle of holding (*lands and tenements*).

2. Holding, use, occupation, occupancy, tenement, tenancy, possession (*for the time*).

Tepid, *a.* Lukewarm, slightly warm, moderately warm; moderate, mild.

Tergiversation, *n.* Evasion, shift, subterfuge, shifting, vacillation, veering, fickleness, instability, inconstancy, change of mind.

Term, *n.* 1. Limit, boundary, bound, confine, bourn, mete, terminus.

2. Time, season, spell, duration, termination, span, space of time, period of time; semester.

3. Word (*considered as having a definite meaning; particularly a technical word*), expression, name, denomination, phrase, locution.

4. Member (*of a syllogism, of an equation, of a fraction, of a proportion, etc.*).

——, *v. t.* Designate, denominate, name style, entitle, call, phrase, dub, christen.

Termagant, *n.* Scold, shrew, vixen, virago, hag, beldam, Xantippe, brawling woman, turbulent woman.

Terminal, *a.* 1. Limiting, bounding.

2. Final, ultimate, terminating.

——, *n.* 1. Termination, extremity, end.

2. Termination, limit, bound.

Terminate, *v. t.* 1. Bound, limit, set bounds to.

2. End, conclude, complete, close, finish, bring to an end, put an end to.

3. Bring to completion, finish, complete.

——, *v. i.* 1. End, cease, close, be limited, stop short, come to an end.

2. Eventuate, issue, prove, turn out.

Termination, *n.* 1. Ending; suffix.

2. Limit, bound, extent.

3. End, conclusion, outcome, completion, issue, result, consequence, effect.

Terminative, *a.* Terminating, determining, absolute, definitive.

Terminology, *n.* Nomenclature, technology, glossology.

Terminus, *n.* [L. *pl. Termini.*] 1. Boundary, border, limit, term, mete.

2. Term, terminal figure.

3. End, destination.

Terms, *n. pl.* Conditions, stipulations, provisions, articles of agreement.

Ternary, *a.* Triplicate, threefold.

——, *n.* Ternion, number three, three.

Terrace, *n.* Plateau, esplanade.

Terra firma. [L.] Firm earth, solid ground.

Terrene, *a.* 1. Earthy, of earth.

2. Earthly, terrestrial, worldly.

Terrestrial, *a.* Earthly, sublunary, mundane, worldly, terrene, tellurian, subastral, subcelestial, sublunar.

Terrible, *a.* 1. Frightful, horrible, dreadful, formidable, fearful, terrific, dire, tremendous, appalling, shocking, grewsome, horrid, hideous.

2. Awful, awe-inspiring, dreadful, dread, alarming.

3. (*Colloq.*) Excessive, extreme, severe, great.

Terribly, *adv.* 1. Dreadfully, horribly, formidably.

2. (*Colloq.*) Violently, very much.

Terrific, *a.* Frightful, tremendous, fearful, alarming, dreadful, formidable, terrible.

Terrify, *v. t.* Frighten, fright, affright, alarm, scare, horrify, appall, daunt, strike with terror, petrify with terror, shock, dismay, startle.

Territory, *n.* Country, domain, dominion, district, quarter, region, place, tract, division, section, province, land.

Terror, *n.* Consternation, fright, alarm, affright, panic, horror, dismay, intimidation, terrorism, great fear, extreme dread.

Terrorism, *n.* 1. Government by terror.

2. State of terror, reign of terror.

Terse, *a.* Concise (*with elegance*), brief, compact, short, laconic, neat, pithy, sententious, succinct, free from superfluity, polished, smooth.

Tessellated, *a.* Checkered, inlaid, mosaic.

TEST, *n.* 1. Experiment, trial, proof, ordeal, examination, essay, attempt.

2. Criterion, standard, touchstone.

3. Proof, exhibition, example.

4. Ground of admission *or* exclusion, discriminative characteristic.

5. Judgment, distinction, discrimination.

——, *v. t.* 1. Try, prove, examine, subject to trial, put to the proof, experiment upon, make trial of, make an experiment with, give a trial to.

2. Assay.

Testament, *n.* Will, last will and testament; Old Testament, New Testament.

Tested, *a.* Tried, pure, assayed.

Testify, *v. i.* Depose, state, affirm, declare, swear, attest, evidence, avow, asseverate, certify, bear witness, depone.

Testimonial, *n.* 1. Credential, certificate, recommendation, voucher.

2. Monument, remembrancer, record.

Testimony, *n.* 1. Affirmation, declaration, deposition, attestation; confirmation, corroboration; profession, confession.

2. Proof (*by a witness*), evidence, witness, ground of belief.

3. Manifestation, expression.

Testiness, *n.* Fretfulness, peevishness, petulance, irascibility, irritability, hastiness, techiness, touchiness.

Testudinated, *a.* Vaulted, roofed, arched.

Testy, *a.* Peevish, petulant, fretful, pettish, touchy, cross, waspish, snappish, choleric, splenetic, irascible, irritable, captious, hasty, quick, peppery.

Tetanus, *n.* [L.] (*Med.*) Spasm, spasmodic contraction of the muscles.

Tête-à-tête. [Fr.] 1. (*Adverbially.*) Face to face, cheek by jowl, privately, confidentially, familiarly, *vis-à-vis*.

2. (*As a noun.*) Close conversation, private conversation, familiar conference, private interview.

Tether, *n.* Tedder; fastening.

——, *v. t.* Fasten, tie, chain, picket, stake.

Tetrachord, *n.* (*Mus.*) Diatessaron, fourth.

Tetrad, *n.* Four, quaternion.

Tetrahedral, *a.* Four-sided.

Text, *n.* 1. Body (*of a literary work, as distinguished from comments*), true copy.

2. Verse (*of Scripture*), passage, sentence, wording, words, clause, paragraph.

3. Topic, subject, theme, thesis.

Textile, *a.* 1. Woven.

2. Textorial, pertaining to textrine weaving.

Textual, *a.* 1. Textuary, contained in the text.

2. Authoritative.

Texture, *n.* 1. Fabric, web, weft.

2. Manner of weaving, make, intertexture.

3. Structure, make, organization, constitution, composition, character, fineness, coarseness, fibre, nap, tissue, grain, contexture, make-up.

THAN, *conj.* (*Basic Eng.*)

Thank, *v. t.* Return thanks to, make acknowledgments to, express gratitude, bless.

Thankful, *a.* Grateful (*with a desire to give thanks*), obliged, beholden, indebted, appreciative, under obligation.

Thankfulness, *n.* Gratitude (*with a desire to acknowledge it*), gratefulness, appreciation, sense of obligation, feeling of obligation.

Thankless, *a.* 1. Ungrateful, unthankful, ingrate.

2. Unpleasant (*as a service not likely to be repaid by thanks*), disagreeable, undesirable, unacceptable, ungracious.

Thanks, *n. pl.* Acknowledgments (*for favors*), expressions of gratitude, blessing, grace; thank-you.

THAT, *conj.* and *pron.* (*Basic Eng.*)

Thaumaturgics, *n.* Legerdemain, prestidigitation, sleight of hand.

Thaumaturgist, *n.* Necromancer, sorcerer, magician, conjurer, juggler, seer, wizard, prestidigitator, wonder-worker.

Thaumaturgy, *n.* Necromancy, magic, sorcery, witchcraft, theurgy, wonder-working, the black art, feats of magic, occult art.

Thaw, *v. i.* Melt (*after freezing*), dissolve, liquefy, become fluid, fuse, run; soften, unbend.

——, *v. t.* Melt (*something frozen*), dissolve, liquefy.

THE, *art.* (*Basic Eng.*)

Theatre, *n.* 1. Playhouse.

2. Scene, stage, field, arena, seat.

3. Drama.

Theatrical, *a.* 1. Dramatic, scenic, histrionic, dramaturgical, spectacular.

2. Ostentatious, showy, pompous, ceremonious, stagy, affected, unnatural, stilted.

Theatricals, *n. pl.* Dramatic performances, amateur dramatics, charades.

Theft, *n.* Larceny, robbery, stealing, pilfering, purloining, thievery, peculation, embezzlement, fraud, swindling, depredation, thieving.

Theme, *n.* 1. Subject, topic, text, thesis, treatise, short dissertation, essay, composition (*as a school exercise*).

2. (*Gram.*) Radical verb, stem.

THEN, *adv.* 1. At that time.

2. Afterwards, afterward, soon afterward; at another time, hereafter, sooner or later.

3. Therefore, for this reason, on that account, consequently, in that case.

Thence, *adv.* 1. From that place.

2. Thenceforth, from that time.

3. Therefore, then, for that reason, on that account.

Thenceforth, *adv.* Thence, thenceforward, from that time.

Theocracy, *n.* Thearchy, government by God.

Theologian, *n.* Divine, theologist, "theolog."

Theology, *n.* Divinity, theologics, science of God and His relations to man, scientific statement of the facts of religion, divine wisdom, hagiography; creed, dogma, articles of faith.

Theorem, *n.* Proposition (*to be demonstrated*), rule, position, dictum, thesis.

Theoretic, ⎫ *a.* Speculative, conjectural,
Theoretical, ⎬ hypothetical, abstract, unapplied, pure, ideal; doctrinaire.

Theorize, *v. i.* Speculate, form theories, guess, doctrinize.

Theorizer, *n.* Speculator, theorist, man of abstractions, philosopher.

THEORY, *n.* 1. Speculation, hypothesis, surmise, principle, assumption, conjecture, postulate, plan, scheme, system, "ism."

2. Science, philosophy, doctrine, abstract principles.

3. Exposition, rationale, philosophical explanation.

Therapeutic, ⎫ *a.* Curative.
Therapeutical, ⎬

THERE, *adv.* In that place.

Thereabout, ⎫ *adv.* 1. Nearly, about that,
Thereabouts, ⎬ somewhere about that.

2. Near that place, thereat.

Thereafter, *adv.* 1. Afterward, subsequently, after that.

2. Accordingly, according to that.

Thereby, *adv.* By that means, in consequence of that.

Therefore, *conj.* and *adv.* 1. Thence,

hence, then, for that reason, on that account, for that, so, *ergo.*

2. Consequently, accordingly, by consequence.

3. In return *or* recompense for this *or* that, in consideration of.

Therefrom, *adv.* From this *or* that.

Therein, *adv.* In that, in this, in that particular.

Thereof, *adv.* Of that, of this.

Thereon, *adv.* On that, on this.

Thereto, *adv.* To that, to this.

Thereupon, *adv.* 1. Upon that, upon this.

2. In consequence of that, on account of that.

3. Immediately, at once, without delay.

Therewith, *adv.* With that, with this.

Thermal, *a.* 1. Warm, hot.

2. As respects heat.

Thesaurus, *n.* [L.] 1. Treasury, storehouse.

2. Repository (*especially of knowledge*); dictionary, glossary.

Thesis, *n.* 1. Proposition, affirmation, position, dictum, doctrine.

2. Theme, subject, topic, text.

3. Essay, dissertation, composition, treatise.

Theurgy, *n.* Necromancy, witchcraft, sorcery, magic, thaumaturgy, wonderworking, the black art.

Thews, *n. pl.* Muscles, sinews, ligaments, brawn, muscular strength, nerve.

Thewy, *a.* Muscular, sinewy, brawny, strong.

THICK, *a.* 1. Not thin (*in measure*).

2. Dumpy, squab, squat, plump, chunky, stubby, thickset; bulky, solid.

3. Dense, gross, crass, heavy, inspissate, inspissated, viscous, clotted, grumous.

4. Misty, cloudy, foggy, hazy, obscure, blurred, indistinguishable, dirty, vaporous, vapory.

5. Turbid, muddy, roiled, sedimental.

6. Abundant, frequent, numerous, multitudinous.

7. Compact, crowded, close, closely set, thickset.

8. Indistinct, inarticulate, confused, guttural, hoarse.

9. Dull, not quick, dim, indistinct, weak.

10. (*Colloq.*) Intimate, familiar, neighborly, well-acquainted, friendly, hand and glove.

——, *n.* Thickest part.

——, *adv.* 1. Frequently, fast, quick.

2. Densely, closely, thickly.

3. To a great depth.

Thicken, *v. t.* 1. Inspissate, make dense, stiffen, inviscate, condense, coagulate, curdle, jelly, congeal, set, cake, petrify.

2. Make close, make compact, deepen, intensify, make frequent.

3. Roil, bemire, befoul.

——, *v. i.* 1. Grow thick, become inspissated, become solid, be consolidated, condense, solidify.

2. Become obscure, become dark, become dim, cloud.

3. Press, crowd, become close, become compact, increase.

Thicket, *n.* Grove, copse, wood, forest, coppice, jungle, brake, *bocage*, shrubbery, undergrowth, underbrush, covert, canebrake, boskage, bosket.

Thick-lipped, *a.* Blobber-lipped.

Thickly, *adv.* 1. Closely, densely, compactly.

2. Deeply, to a great depth.

3. Quickly.

Thickness, *n.* 1. The third dimension.

2. Denseness, density, compactness, crassness, heaviness; crowdedness; diameter, bore.

3. Consistence, grossness, spissitude, stiffness, coagulation, clot, coagulum, jellification, concentration, viscosity.

4. Indistinctness.

Thickset, *a.* 1. Close-planted, dense.

2. Stout, massive, strongly built.

Thick-skinned, *a.* Dull, obtuse, insensible, unsusceptible, callous.

Thief, *n.* 1. Pilferer, petty robber, filcher, stealer, purloiner, lifter, marauder, depredator, shark.

2. Swindler, peculator, embezzler, defrauder, sharper, defaulter, pickpocket, cutpurse, pick-purse, poacher, kidnapper, pirate, privateer, corsair, burglar, housebreaker, cracksman (*cant*), footpad, highwayman.

Thieve, *v. i.* 1. Steal, pilfer, purloin.

2. Swindle, peculate, shark.

3. Plagiarize.

Thievery, *n.* 1. Theft, larceny, stealing, thievishness, thieving, pilfering, filching, petty robbery, petty larceny.

2. Peculation, embezzlement, theft, fraud, swindling.

3. Plagiarism.

Thievish, *a.* 1. Given to stealing, inclined to theft, light-fingered, larcenous, predatory, burglarious.

2. Sly, secret, stealthy, underhand, like a thief, furtive.

Thievishness, *n.* Kleptomania, klopemania, propensity to steal, mania for stealing.

Thills, *n. pl.* Shafts.

Thimbleful, *n.* 1. As much as a thimble holds.

2. Sip, sup, drop, swallow, mouthful, spoonful, taste.

THIN, *a.* 1. Not thick (*in measure*).

2. Slender, slim, meagre, lean, poor, gaunt, spare, pinched, pindling, peaked, "spindly," lank, lanky, haggard, bony, fleshless, scraggy, skinny, scrawny, shrunk, emaciated, not well-grown.

3. Fine, slender, small, tenuous, delicate, sensitive, thread-like, fine-spun, slight, flimsy, light, gossamery, unsubstantial.

4. Rare, rarefied, watery, subtile, attenuated, dilute, tenuous.

5. Sparse, scanty.

6. Small, fine, faint, low, feeble, slight, light.

——, *v. t.* 1. Make thin.

2. Rarefy, attenuate, dilute, make less dense, extenuate.

THING, *n.* 1. Being (*animate* or *inanimate*), entity, monad, something, creature, substance, body, object, created being; production, contrivance.

2. Inanimate object, lump of matter, lifeless substance, article.

3. Event, transaction, deed, act, action, affair, arrangement, concern, occurrence, circumstance, matter.

4. [*pl.*] Furniture, appurtenances, chattels, goods, effects, movables, commodities.

Think, *v. i.* 1. Cogitate, reflect, meditate, dream, ponder, muse, contemplate, exercise the mind, ruminate, speculate.

2. Deliberate, consider, reason, understand.

3. Conclude, determine, judge, suppose, imagine, fancy, believe, deem, opine, ween, reckon, hold, surmise, presume, have an opinion, be of opinion, take it, conceive, apprehend.

4. Purpose, intend, design, mean, have in mind.

——, *v. t.* 1. Imagine, conceive, entertain an idea of, cherish a thought of, ideate.

2. Consider, regard, hold, believe, judge, suppose, esteem, deem, account, count, reckon, look upon.

3. Plot, plan, compass, contrive, design.

Thinkable, *a.* Cogitable, conceivable, possible, imaginable.

Thinking, *a.* Reasoning, rational, cogitative, reflecting, reasonable.

——, *n.* 1. Reflection, meditation, cogitation, musing, contemplation, thought, brainwork, ratiocination, intellection.

2. Judgment, opinion, thought, belief, mind.

Thinness, *n.* 1. Slenderness, slimness, meagreness, leanness, gauntness, emaciation, lankness, poorness.

2. Tenuity, fineness, attenuation, flimsiness, lightness, slenderness, delicacy, exiguity, rareness, rarity, subtilty, etherealness.

3. Sparseness, scantiness, paucity, fewness, scarcity.

Thin-skinned, *a.* (*Colloq.*) Sensitive, irritable, touchy.

Third estate. Commons, commonalty.

Thirst, *n.* 1. Desire for drink, dipsomania.

2. Desire, longing, craving, hankering, yearning, appetite, hunger.

3. Dryness, drought, aridity.

——, *v. i.* 1. Desire to drink.

2. Desire, long, crave, hanker, yearn.

Thirsty, *a.* 1. Suffering from thirst, dipsetic, athirst.

2. Dry, parched, arid, without moisture.

3. Longing, craving, greedy, eager.

THIS, *pron.* (*Basic Eng.*)

Thither, *adv.* 1. To that place, there.

2. To that point, to that end, to that result.

Thole, *n.* Dome, cupola, tholus.

Thong, *n.* Strap, strip of leather, leathern string.

Thorax, *n.* 1. Chest, trunk (*of the body*).

2. Breast-plate, corselet, cuirass.

Thorn, *n.* 1. Spine, prickle.

2. Annoyance, plague, nuisance, care, infliction, trouble, scourge, torment, bitter pill, curse, gall and wormwood, evil, bane, nettle.

Thorny, *a.* 1. Spiny, spinose, spinous, prickly, briery.

2. Pricking, sharp, pointed, acuminated, picked, spiky, barbed.

3. Troublesome, vexatious, annoying, harassing, perplexing, difficult, rugged, trying.

Thorough, *a.* Complete, entire, total, perfect, finished, arrant, "regular," out-and-out, downright, radical, unmitigated, sweeping, absolute, exhaustive.

Thorough-bred, *a.* 1. Instructed, accomplished, finished, practised, qualified, trained, proficient, able, well-educated, well-versed, *au fait.*

2. Of full blood (*as horses*).

Thoroughfare, *n.* Passage (*free from obstruction*), street, road, way, highway, avenue.

Thorough-going, *a.* Very thorough, complete, unqualified, radical, extreme.

Thorp, *n.* Hamlet, small village, dorp.

THOUGH, *conj.* 1. Although, granting, admitting, if, allowing, notwithstanding that.

2. However, yet, nevertheless.

THOUGHT, *n.* 1. Cogitation, reflection, rumination, reverie, brown study, engrossment, absorption, meditation, musing; contemplation, thinking, intelligence, thoughtfulness, brainwork, lucubration, cerebration, ratiocination, intellection.

2. Idea, conception, consideration, speculation, study, deliberation, pondering, application.

3. Imagination, consciousness, intellect, understanding, perception; conceit, fancy, notion.

4. Judgment, conclusion, opinion, notion, fancy, supposition, idea, view.

5. Deliberation, consideration, attention, care, solicitude, anxiety, concern.

6. Design, purpose, intention, expectation.

Thoughtful, *a.* 1. Contemplative, reflective, musing; absorbed, engrossed, lost in thought; pensive, speculative, deliberative, sedate, reflecting, introspective, philosophic.

2. Careful, heedful, regardful, mindful, kindly, kind-hearted, neighborly, friendly, attentive, considerate, circumspect, wary, watchful, discreet, prudent.

3. Studious, serious, sober, quiet, promoting thought.

Thoughtfulness, *n.* 1. Deep meditation.

2. Serious attention, anxiety, solicitude.

Thoughtless, *a.* 1. Heedless, regardless, careless, neglectful, negligent, inattentive, inconsiderate, unthinking, unreflective, unmindful, unobservant, remiss, casual, unwatchful, inadvertent, flighty, reckless, hare-brained, giddy-brained, light-headed, giddy.

2. Stupid, dull, insensate, unthinking, vacant, vacuous, blank, blockish.

3. Dissipated, gay, giddy, loose.

Thoughtlessness, *n.* Inattention, heedlessness, carelessness, absence of mind, inadvertence, neglect, oversight, lack of consideration.

Thousand, *n.* 1. Ten hundred, milliad.

2. Great number, many, multitude, myriad.

Thraldom, *n.* Slavery, servitude, subjection, bondage, vassalage, serfdom, enslavement, enthralment, thrall.

Thrall, *n.* 1. Slave, bondman, vassal, serf.

2. See THRALDOM.

——, *v. t.* Enslave, enthrall.

Thrash, *v. t.* 1. Thresh.

2. Drub, maul, trounce, punish, pommel, beat, flog, whip, lash, bruise, thwack, wallop; conquer, defeat.

Thrasonical, *a.* Boastful, bragging, vainglorious, ostentatious, pretentious.

THREAD, *n.* 1. Filament, fibre, small string, yarn, twist, hair, slender cord; streak, line.

2. Filament, fibre, pile, staple.

3. Course, tenor, drift.

——, *v. t.* Thrid, go through, pass through, file through, reeve, trace.

Threadbare, *a.* 1. Napless, worn, seedy.

2. Trite, hackneyed, stale, worn out, common, commonplace.

Thread-shaped, *a.* Filiform, filamentous.

Threat, *n.* Menace, denunciation; fulmination, thunderbolt, thunder, defiance, intimidation, commination.

Threaten, *v. t.* 1. Menace, denounce, comminate, thunder, fulminate, look daggers, shake the fist.

2. Portend, presage, forebode, augur, foreshadow, prognosticate, indicate, warn.

——, *v. i.* 1. Use threats, use menaces.

2. Impend, be near at hand, be imminent, overhang, lour, lower, stare one in the face.

Threatening, *a.* 1. Menacing, minatory, minacious, comminatory, black, dark, sinister, abusive, defiant, denunciatory, direful, ominous, ill-boding, forbidding, baneful, lowering.

2. Impending, impendent, imminent.

Three-leaved, *a.* (*Bot.*) Triphyllous, trifoliate.

Threescore, *a.* Sixty, thrice twenty.

Threnody, *n.* Song of lamentation, lament, mourning, requiem, dirge.

Thresh, *v. t.* See THRASH.

Threshold, *n.* 1. Doorsill, sill.

2. Entrance, gate, door, vestibule.

3. Entrance, outset, beginning, commencement, start, opening.

Thrift, *n.* 1. Success, prosperity, gain, profit, luck, good fortune; vigor, growth.

2. Frugality, thriftiness, economy, good-husbandry, economical management, savingness.

Thriftless, *a.* Extravagant, profuse, lavish, prodigal, wasteful, unthrifty, shiftless, too free, over-liberal, improvident.

Thrifty, *a.* 1. Frugal, sparing, economical, saving, careful, provident.

2. Thriving, prosperous.

3. Vigorous, growing well, flourishing, thriving.

Thrill, *v. t.* Penetrate, pierce, move, touch, affect, strike, agitate, stir, inspire, rouse, electrify.

——, *v. i.* Pass with a tremulous motion, tremble, vibrate; tingle.

——, *n.* Sensation, shock, tremor, tingling, excitement, "kick."

Thrive, *v. i.* 1. Prosper, succeed, get on, come on, become wealthy, get rich.

2. Grow, increase, advance, flourish, improve, make improvement, boom, batten, bloom.

3. Grow, flourish, increase in bulk.

Thriving, *a.* 1. Prosperous, successful, thrifty, flourishing.

2. Growing, flourishing.

THROAT, *n.* 1. Pharynx, swallow, gullet, œsophagus, gorge, maw.

2. (*Bot.*) Faux.

Throb, *v. i.* Beat, palpitate, pulsate.

——, *n.* Beat, beating, pulsation, palpitation, throbbing.

Throbbing, *n.* Beating, pulsating, palpitating, act of pulsating.

Throe, *n.* Paroxysm (*of extreme pain, especially in childbirth*), fit, spasm, anguish, pang, agony.

Throne, *n.* 1. Chair of state, royal seat.

2. Sovereignty, sovereign power, sway.

——, *v. t.* 1. Enthrone, place on a royal seat.

2. Exalt, give an elevated place.

Throng, *n.* Crowd, multitude, horde, press, congregation, mob, assemblage, host.

——, *v. i.* Crowd, press, flock, congregate.

Throttle, *n.* Windpipe, trachea, throat, weasand.

——, *v. t.* Choke, strangle, suffocate, silence.

THROUGH, *prep.* 1. From one side, end, *or* part of to the other.

2. Between the sides of, between the walls of, within.

3. By means of, by the agency of, in consequence of, by the aid of.

4. Over the whole surface of.

5. Among, in the midst of.

6. From beginning to end, to the end, throughout, during.

——, *adv.* 1. From one side *or* part to the other.

2. From beginning to end, to the end.

Throughout, *prep.* Over, completely through, quite through, through every part of, from one extremity to the other of.

——, *adv.* From beginning to end, from first to last, in every part, everywhere, from end to end, from head to foot, from top to toe.

Throw, *v. t.* 1. Whirl, cast in a winding direction, hurl.

2. Cast, hurl, launch, fling, send, toss, pitch, "chuck," pitchfork, sling, dart,

lance, propel, jaculate, project, shy, let fly, precipitate, plunge.

3. Wind, twist, twist together.

4. Put, spread.

5. Overturn, prostrate, throw down, lay flat, fell, unhorse.

Throw, *v. i.* Make a cast, cast dice.

——, *n.* 1. Fling, cast, toss, projection, delivery, pitch, lob.

2. Jigger, potter's wheel.

Throw in. Inject, put in; relinquish, give up.

Throw off. 1. Discard, reject, repudiate, renounce.

2. Expel, drive off, drive away, clear from.

3. Put off, lay aside, cast off.

Throw out. 1. Reject, exclude, cast out, discard, expel.

2. Speak, utter, express.

Throw up. 1. Resign, lay down, give up, demit.

2. Emit, eject, send up; vomit, disgorge.

Thrum, *v. t.* 1. Play (*as an instrument*), strum, play upon, drum.

2. Fringe, knot, tuft.

Thrust, *v. t.* Push, drive, impel, propel, stick, run, plunge, ram, jab, jam, force, clap, poke, shove, dig.

——, *v. i.* Make a thrust, lunge.

——, *n.* 1. Push, shove, pass, stab, allonge, propulsion, plunge, jab, dig, poke, lunge, tilt.

2. Assault, attack, charge.

Thud, *n.* 1. Shock, impetus.

2. Stroke, blow, thump, knock.

THUMB, *n.* Digit, pollex.

Thump, *n.* Blow, knock, stroke.

——, *v. t.* Beat, knock, strike, belabor, thwack, punch, whack, batter.

Thumping, *a.* 1. Heavy, knocking, striking.

2. (*Colloq.*) Stout, fat, large, big, overgrown.

THUNDER, *n.* 1. Reverberating report (*of a discharge of atmospheric electricity*).

2. Loud noise, roar, rumbling, boom, detonation.

3. Alarming threat, startling denunciation, fulmination.

——, *v. i.* 1. Sound, rattle, roar, roll, peal, rumble, boom.

2. Make a loud noise, detonate, resound, crash, crack.

——, *v. t.* Utter threateningly, fulminate, hurl.

Thunderbolt, *n.* 1. Thunderclap, thunderstroke; thunder.

2. Fulmination, denunciation.

Thunder-storm, *n.* Tempest (*accompanied with thunder and lightning*), thundershower.

Thunder-struck, *a.* Astonished, amazed, astounded, dumfoundered.

Thurible, *n.* Censer.

Thus, *adv.* 1. In this manner, in this wise; so, to this degree.

2. Consequently.

Thwack, *v. t.* (*Colloq.*) Strike, beat, thump, belabor, whack, rap, bang, thrash.

——, *n.* Blow, stroke, thump, pat, knock, rap.

Thwart, *v. t.* 1. Traverse, cross, intersect, lie across, move across.

2. Hinder, oppose, oppugn, obstruct, contravene, counteract, disconcert, cross, frustrate, defeat, balk.

Tiara, *n.* Triple-crown (*of the Pope*).

Tic, *n.* Twitching, vellication.

Tick, *n.* 1. Click, beat, tap; mark, check.

2. Bed-tick, ticking.

3. Trust, credit.

——, *v. i.* Click, beat.

——, *v. t.* Score, check, check off, mark off.

TICKET, *n.* Billet, coupon, label, voucher.

Ticking, *n.* Bed-ticking, tick, ticken.

Tickle, *v. t.* 1. Titillate.

2. Please (*by trifles*), delight, gladden, rejoice, divert, amuse, enliven, gratify, make glad, give joy to, take one's fancy, do one's heart good.

Tickling, *n.* Titillation.

Ticklish, *a.* 1. Easily tickled.

2. Unsteady, unstable, tottering, uncertain, dangerous, risky, precarious.

3. Delicate, nice, critical, difficult.

Tidbit, *n.* Titbit, dainty, delicacy, nice bit, choice morsel, delicate morsel, delicious mouthful.

Tide, *n.* 1. Rise and fall of the sea.

2. Current, stream, flow; flood.

3. Course, tendency of events, direction of influences, concurrence of influences.

Tide over. 1. Float over, get over by waiting, surmount *or* pass by caution and patience, escape *or* evade by the favor of circumstances, avoid by delay.

2. Escape the shoals, avoid by a little, get over without scraping *or* sinking, keep one's head above water.

Tidily, *adv.* Neatly.

Tidiness, *n.* Neatness.

Tidings, *n. pl.* News (*of special interest*), message, intelligence, word, advice, information.

Tidy, *a.* Neat, orderly, trim, trig, spruce, shipshape.

Tie, *v. t.* 1. Bind, fasten (*with a cord or string*), knot, confine, manacle, shackle, fetter; knit, interlace, complicate, entangle.

2. Unite, join, connect, link, fasten, hold, bind, knit, lock, yoke.

3. Oblige, constrain, restrain, confine.

Tie, *v. i.* Be equal, divide the honors, come out even, draw.

——, *n.* 1. Knot, fastening, band, ligature, (*mus.*) slur; link.

2. Bond, obligation, allegiance.

3. Equal number (*on both sides, as of votes*); drawn game, draw, dead heat.

4. Necktie, bow, cravat.

5. Beam, sleeper, railroad-tie.

Tier, *n.* Row, rank, series.

Tiff, *n.* Pet, miff, rage, passion, fume, fit of anger, petty quarrel, angry mood.

Tiffin, *n.* Luncheon.

TIGHT, *a.* 1. Compact, firm, firmly held together; close, fast, not open, not leaky, close-fitting, not loose.

2. Tense, stretched, taut.

3. Narrow, impassable, strait.

4. (*Colloq.*) Fuddled, boozy, disguised, mellow, in liquor, high, in one's cups, somewhat intoxicated.

5. (*Colloq., U. S.*) Parsimonious, stingy, penurious, hard, close-fisted; stringent.

Tighten, *v. t.* Make tight, straiten, lace up, draw.

Tights, *n. pl.* Close-fitting pantaloons.

Tike, *n.* See TYKE.

Till, *n.* Money-drawer.

TILL, *conj.* or *adv.* Until, to the time when.

——, *v. t.* Cultivate, dress the ground, plow, harrow.

——, *prep.* Until, to the time of, up to.

Tillable, *a.* Arable.

Tillage, *n.* Culture (*of land*), cultivation, husbandry, agriculture, farming, geoponics.

Tiller, *n.* 1. Husbandman, cultivator, ploughman.

2. Rudder-bar, helm.

3. Cross-bow handle.

4. Till, small drawer, money-box.

Tilt, *n.* 1. Covering overhead, tent, awning, canopy.

2. Thrust, pass, allonge, lunge.

3. Encounter, combat (*as a practice of arms*), joust.

4. Slant (*as of a barrel for discharging a liquor*), slope, inclination, cant, tip.

——, *v. t.* 1. Slant, slope, incline, cant, tip.

2. Forge (*with a tilt-hammer*), hammer.

3. Point, thrust.

——, *v. i.* 1. Joust, rush (*as in combat*), make a rush, make a tilt.

2. Lean, incline, tip.

3. Float, toss, ride unsteadily.

Timber, *n.* 1. Wood (*for building*), lumber, raff, stumpage.

2. Beam, squared stick.

3. Rib (*of a ship's frame*).

4. Trunk, stem, body (*of a tree*).

5. Material, stuff, stock.

6. [*Western U. S.*] Woods, forest-trees, timberland.

Timbered, *a.* 1. Wooded.

2. Furnished with timber.

Timbre, *n.* (*Mus.*) Quality (*of tone*), clang, resonance, tone color.

TIME, *n.* 1. Duration.

2. Spell, season, interval, term, interim, meanwhile, while, span, space of time.

3. Period, age, era, epoch, eon, date, term, stage; reign, cycle, dynasty.

4. Delivery, parturition, confinement, hour of travail, period of childbirth.

5. Fit season, proper time, opportunity, season.

6. Allotted period, appropriated time.

7. Occasion, particular period, moment, instant, point, hour.

8. Life, lifetime, duration of one's life; present life, existence in this world.

9. Leisure, vacant time, unoccupied time, opportunity, ease, freedom, liberty, chance.

——, *v. t.* 1. Adapt to the occasion, adjust, harmonize with.

2. Regulate (*as to time*).

3. Note the rate of (*with respect to speed*), keep time.

Time-honored, *a.* Venerable, worthy of honor by reason of antiquity, ancient, old, of long standing.

Timeliness, *n.* Seasonableness.

Timely, *a.* Seasonable, appropriate, acceptable, apropos, well-timed, opportune, early, punctual, prompt.

——, *adv.* Early, soon, in good season.

Timepiece, *n.* Clock, watch, water glass, hour glass, chronometer, timekeeper, horologue.

Times, *n. pl.* 1. Seasons, spells.

2. Periods, epochs, ages.

3. State of things (*at a particular period*), general condition of affairs.

Time-server, *n.* Trimmer, temporizer, time-pleaser, opportunist.

Time-serving, *a.* Trimming, temporizing, truckling, obsequious, fawning, servile, supple, mean, selfish, ambidextrous, tricky, worldly-wise, self-seeking, pliant, unscrupulous, crooked, slippery, untrustworthy.

Time-worn, *a.* Impaired by time, superannuated, old, antiquated, dilapidated.

Timid, *a.* 1. Timorous, fearful, skittish, nervous, afraid, cowardly, pusillanimous, faint-hearted, chicken-hearted, easily frightened, inadventurous, meticulous, irresolute.

2. Diffident, bashful, retiring, coy, shrinking, demure, shy, blushing, shamefaced, modest.

Timidity, *n.* 1. Timorousness, fearfulness, skittishness, shyness, cowardice, pusillanimity, meticulousness, want of courage, timidness.

2. Diffidence, bashfulness, coyness, sheepishness, shamefacedness.

Timorous, *a.* 1. Fearful, timid, destitute of courage.

2. Scrupulous, full of scruples, indicating fear.

TIN, *n.* Tin-plate, tinned iron, white iron.

Tincture, *n.* 1. Tinge, stain, tint, hue, tone, shade, grain.

2. Flavor, taste, smack, spice.

3. Infusion, admixture, touch, dash, tinge, spice, seasoning, sprinkling, *soupcon*.

4. Alcoholic solution.

——, *v. t.* 1. Tinge, stain, dye, color, tint, shade.

2. Flavor, season.

3. Imbue, impress, infuse, impregnate.

Tine, *n.* Spike of a fork, prong.

Tinge, *v. t.* 1. Dye, stain, color, tint, tincture.

2. Imbue, impress, infuse, impregnate.

——, *n.* 1. Tint, stain, color, dye, tincture, shade (*of color*), cast, hue.

2. Taste, flavor, smack, spice, quality.

Tingle, *v. i.* Have a pricking sensation, sting, thrill, prickle.

Tinker, *n.* Mender (*of old pans, kettles, etc.*).

——, *v. t.* Mend (*as old pans, kettles, etc.*), cobble, patch up, repair, vamp, put in repair.

Tinkle, *v. i.* Jingle, clink, ring, ting, chink.

Tinkling, *n.* Tinkle, jingle, jingling, clinking, tintinnabulation, ringing.

Tinsel, *n.* Frippery, finery, gewgaw, tawdriness, spangle, glitter, paste, pinchbeck, sham, pretense, worthless ornament.

——, *a.* Showy, glittering, gaudy, specious, garish, flaunting, flashy, superficial, worthless.

Tinsmith, *n.* Tinner, tinman, worker in tin.

Tint, *n.* Tinge, color, hue, tincture, stain, dye, shade, grain.

——, *v. t.* Dye, stain, tinge.

Tiny, *a.* Little, small, diminutive, minute, miniature, wee, microscopic, minikin,
pygmean, pygmy, puny, Liliputian, dwarfish.

Tip, *n.* 1. End, point, extremity; pinnacle, peak, apex, vertex.

2. Donation, gift, *douceur*, fee, gratuity, reward, perquisite.

3. Inclination, slant.

4. (*Colloq.*) Pointer, hint, suggestion.

——, *v. t.* 1. Top, cap, put a point on.

2. Tap, strike (*lightly*).

3. Incline (*to one end, as a cart*), cant, tilt.

4. Fee.

——, *v. i.* Lean, incline, tilt.

Tip over, *v. t.* Overturn, turn over.

——, *v. i.* Fall over.

Tipple, *v. i.* Tope, guzzle, drink hard, be addicted to strong drink.

Tippler, *n.* Toper, hard drinker.

Tipsy, *a.* 1. Intoxicated, inebriated, drunk, drunken, in one's cups, boozy, fuddled, muddled, disguised, mellow, in liquor.

2. Reeling, staggering.

Tip-top, *a.* (*Colloq.*) Perfect, first-rate, excellent, capital, picked, choice, first-class, superfine, very best.

Tirade, *n.* Strain of invective, series of violent declamation, diatribe, harangue.

Tire, *v. t.* 1. Fatigue, weary, jade, fag, exhaust, "tucker," knock up, tire out.

2. Irk, bore, bother.

——, *v. i.* Be fatigued, become weary, flag, sicken, grow weary.

TIRED, *a.* Fatigued, wearied.

Tiresome, *a.* 1. Wearisome, fatiguing, irksome, fagging, monotonous, tedious, humdrum, dull.

2. Laborious, arduous, hard, toilsome, troublesome, difficult, uphill.

Tissue, *n.* 1. Fabric, cloth, woven stuff (*especially cloth interwoven with gold or silver or figured colors*).

2. Texture, structure, web, membrane, network.

3. Combination, series, accumulation, set, collection, conglomeration, mass, network, chain.

Titanic, *a.* Gigantic, huge, Herculean, Cyclopean, enormous, monstrous, stupendous, vast, immense, colossal, prodigious, mighty.

Tit for tat. Give and take, blow for blow, a Roland for an Oliver, measure for measure, diamond cut diamond, equivalent (*in retaliation*), quid pro quo.

Tithe, *n.* Tenth, tenth part.

——, *v. t.* Tax (*to the amount of one tenth*).

Titillate, *v. t.* Tickle, please.

Titillation, *n.* 1. Tickling.

2. Slight pleasure, pleasurable sensation.

Title, *n.* 1. Inscription.

2. Inscription in the beginning of a book, heading, head, caption, legend, name.

3. Name, appellation, designation, epithet, application, cognomen, compellation, denomination.

4. Appellation of dignity, style *or* honor, "handle to one's name."

5. Right, ground of claim, claim, ownership, possession, due, prerogative, part, privilege.

Titter, *v. i.* 1. Laugh (*under restraint*), snicker, snigger, giggle, chuckle.

2. Teeter, see-saw.

Tittering, *n.* Suppressed laughter, giggling.

Tittle, *n.* Jot, iota, whit, bit, particle, atom, grain, scrap, mite, ace, corpuscle, scintilla, speck.

Tittle-tattle, *n.* Prate, prattle, gabble, chatter, idle talk, trifling discourse, babble, cackle, gossip, prittle-prattle.

Titular, *a.* Nominal, titulary, only in name.

TO, *prep.* (*Basic Eng.*)

Toast, *v. t.* 1. Brown, dry (*in order to make more palatable, as bread or cheese*); warm (*thoroughly*), heat.

2. Pledge, drink a health to, drink the health of, drink in honor of, drink to, propose, honor.

——, *n.* 1. Toasted bread.

2. Health (*in drinking*), pledge.

3. Sentiment (*uttered at a convivial meeting*).

Tocsin, *n.* Alarm, alarum, alarm-bell.

Today, *n.* This day, the present day.

Toddle, *v. i.* Tottle, walk unsteadily (*as a child*).

Toddy, *n.* Spirit and water (*sweetened*).

To-do, *n.* (*Colloq.*) Ado, bustle, commotion, tumult, turmoil, confusion, stir, flurry, pother, noise, fuss.

TOE, *n.* Foot digit.

TOGETHER, *adv.* 1. Unitedly, in union, in company, conjointly, collectively, mutually, reciprocally; hand in hand, side by side, cheek by jowl, arm in arm, in concert.

2. Simultaneously, in the same time, contemporaneously.

Toil, *v. i.* Labor (*hard*), work, strive, drudge, moil, exert one's self, take pains.

——, *n.* 1. Labor (*that fatigues*), work, exertion, exhaustion, grinding, pains, effort, drudgery, hard work, travail.

2. Snare, net, trap, springe, noose, gin.

Toiler, *n.* Drudge, laborer, hard worker.

Toilet, *n.* 1. Dressing-table, toilet-table.

2. Dress, attire, costume, mode of dressing.

Toilsome, *a.* Laborious, fatiguing, wearisome, arduous, onerous, operose, tedious, hard, difficult, painful, severe.

Token, *n.* 1. Mark, sign, indication, evidence, note, badge, symbol, index, manifestation, trace, trait.

2. Memorial (*of friendship*), souvenir, memento, keepsake, reminder.

Tolerable, *a.* 1. Endurable, sufferable, bearable, supportable.

2. Passable, ordinary, middling, so-so, fair, indifferent, pretty good, not very bad.

Tolerance, *n.* Endurance, sufferance, toleration, receptivity. See also TOLERATION.

Tolerant, *a.* Forbearing, indulgent, liberal.

Tolerate, *v. t.* 1. Permit (*as something unpleasant*), allow, admit, indulge, receive.

2. Suffer, endure, abide, brook, put up with, bear with, take patiently *or* easily.

Toleration, *n.* 1. Endurance, sufferance, tolerance, concession.

2. License (*for free opinion in religious matters*), permission, allowance, indulgence, lenity, clemency.

3. Catholicity, liberality, impartiality, candor, magnanimity, high-mindedness, largeness of mind, open-mindedness.

Toll, *n.* Tax (*especially on travellers, as in crossing bridges, ferries, etc.*), duty, impost, custom.

——, *v. t.* 1. Allure, draw, draw on.

2. Ring, knell.

Tomb, *n.* Sepulchre, sepulture, mausoleum, charnel house, vault, crypt, catacomb, grave, house of death, narrow house, long home.

Tomboy, *n.* (*Colloq.*) Romp, hoyden, romping girl, tomrig.

Tome, *n.* 1. Volume.

2. Book, work.

Tomentous, *a.* (*Bot.*) Downy, nappy, hairy.

Tomfoolery, *n.* (*Colloq.*) Nonsense, folly, fooling, vagary, mummery, buffoonery, absurd trifling, monkey-tricks, escapade.

TOMORROW, *n.* The day after the present, the morrow, the next day.

Ton, *n.* (*Com.*) 1. Twenty hundred gross, 2,240 pounds.

2. Forty cubic feet.

3. *Naut.* One hundred cubic feet — *a unit of internal capacity.*

Tone, *n.* 1. Sound, note.

2. Accent, intonation, emphasis, cadence, modulation, inflection.

3. Temper, mood, state of mind, strain, key, spirit.

4. Vigor, strength, energy, force, tension, elasticity, health.

5. Prevailing color (*of a picture*), hue, color, shade, tint, general effect, style, manner, cast.

6. Tenor, drift, prevailing character.

Tone down. 1. Give a lower tone to.

2. Moderate, relax, diminish, weaken, soften.

3. (*Painting.*) Soften, bring colors into harmonious relations.

Toneless, *a.* Unintonated, aspirated, atonic, surd, pronounced with a simple breathing, without tone, without vocality, not sonant.

Tone up. Make more intense, heighten, strengthen, give a higher tone to.

Tong, *n.* Tongue, catch of a buckle.

TONGUE, *n.* 1. Language, vernacular, accent, utterance, dialect; talk, discourse, speech.

2. Nation, race.

3. Projection, projecting part, pole.

Tonic, *n.* 1. Strengthening medicine, stimulant, roborant.

2. (*Mus.*) Key, key-note, first note of the scale, fundamental note.

——, *a.* Stimulating, invigorant, bracing.

Tonight, *n.* The present night, the night after the present day.

Tonsilitis, *n.* Quinsy, inflammation of the tonsils.

Tonsured, *a.* 1. Having the tonsure, shaven, shorn, clipped.

2. Bald.

Too, *adv.* 1. Overmuch, over.

2. Also, likewise, moreover, in addition, additionally.

Tool, *n.* 1. Instrument, implement, utensil, device, machine; vehicle, medium.

2. Hireling, instrument, cat's-paw, puppet, pawn.

Toot, *v. t.* Blow (*as a horn*), sound.

TOOTH, *n.* Fang, incisor, molar, tusk.

Tooth and nail. (*Colloquial expression used adverbially.*) 1. Biting and scratching, using every means of attack and defence.

2. Strenuously, energetically, with might and main, hammer and tongs, *pugnis et calcibus.*

Toothsome, *a.* Palatable, delicious, savory, nice, luscious, dainty, agreeable to the taste.

TOP, *n.* 1. Summit, apex, acme, pinnacle, zenith, vertex, utmost height, culminating point, crest, meridian; upmost degree; head, crown of the head, upper part.

2. Surface, upper side, superficies.

3. Head, highest rank, most honorable position, highest place; chief, most prominent one.

——, *a.* Highest, uppermost, topmost, culminating, apical, chief.

——, *v. t.* 1. Cap, tip, cover on the top, crown, head.

2. Rise above, surmount, ride.

3. Rise to the top of, reach the summit of.

4. Outgo, surpass.

5. Crop, lop, take the top off.

Top-coat, *n.* Overcoat, outer coat, upper coat.

Tope, *v. i.* Tipple, drink hard, be addicted to strong drink.

Toper, *n.* Tippler, drunkard, sot, dram-drinker, wine-bibber, toss-pot, hard drinker.

Topic, *n.* 1. Subject, theme, *Motiv, Leitmotiv,* text, thesis, question, moot-point, point at issue, point, field of inquiry, matter, subject-matter, matter in hand, business.

2. Head, division, subdivision.

3. Commonplace (*of argument* or *oratory*), general truth, general idea, maxim, dictum, rule, proposition, precept, principle, general statement.

4. Scheme, arrangement, method of arrangement, principle of arrangement.

5. (*Med.*) External local remedy, plaster, blister, poultice, vesicatory, epispastic.

Topical, *a.* 1. Local, limited, particular, restricted.

2. Probable, not demonstrative.

3. Consisting of topics.

Topmost, *a.* Uppermost, highest, chief, head, supreme, leading.

Top off. Complete, finish.

Topographer, *n.* Topographist.

Topping, *a.* 1. Surpassing, rising above, eminent.

2. Fine, gallant.

Topple, *v. i.* Fall (*top foremost*), tumble down, topple over, topple down, tumble over.

Top-shaped, *a.* Cone-shaped, turbinate.

Topsy-turvy, *adv.* Upside down, bottom upward, inverted, the wrong side up, top side t'other way, keel upward.

Torch, *n.* Flambeau, blazing brand, link, light, firebrand.

Torment, *n.* Anguish, agony, torture, rack, pang, extreme pain, excruciating pain, acute distress.

——, *v. t.* 1. Torture, distress, agonize, rack, excruciate, pain extremely, put to the rack, put to torture, harass with anguish, afflict.

2. Tease, vex, plague, harass, worry, harry, badger, fret, irritate, nettle, provoke, tantalize, trouble, annoy.

Tornado, *n.* Storm (*of great violence and with a whirling motion*), hurricane, whirlwind, tempest, cyclone, blizzard.

Torose, *a.* (*Bot.*) Knobby, torous.

Torpid, *a.* 1. Numb, benumbed, motionless, lethargic.

2. Sluggish, inert, dull, inactive, indolent, apathetic, stupid; dormant, listless, sleepy.

Torpify, *v. t.* Numb, benumb, make torpid.

Torpor, *n.* 1. Numbness, torpidity, torpescence, lethargy, insensibility, stupor, coma.

2. Sluggishness, inertness, dulness, inactivity, stupidity, inaction.

Torrefy, *v. t.* 1. Dry (*by fire*).

2. Roast, scorch, parch.

Torrent, *n.* 1. Rapid stream, strong current.

2. Rapid flow, flood.

Torrid, *a.* 1. Dried, parched, scorched, burnt, arid.

2. Burning, parching, scorching, violently hot, fiery, tropical.

Torsion, *n.* Twisting.

Torso, *n.* Trunk (*of a statue*), body.

Tort, *n.* (*Law.*) Wrong, injury, wrongful act.

Tortuosity, *n.* Crookedness, sinuosity, curvature, bend, crook, winding, tortuousness.

Tortuous, *a.* 1. Crooked, sinuous, curved, curvilinear, curvilineal, sinuate, sinuated, winding, serpentine, bending in and out, wreathed, twisted, mazy, flexuous.

2. Perverse, circuitous, roundabout, indirect, deceitful, crooked, ambiguous.

Torture, *n.* Anguish, agony, torment, rack, pang, extreme pain, excruciating pain, acute distress; martyrdom, impalement, rack, screws, inquisition.

——, *v. t.* 1. Torment, distress, agonize, rack, excruciate, pain extremely, put to extreme pain; martyr, impale.

2. Garble, misrepresent, distort, pervert, misapply, twist.

Tory, *n.* (*Eng. politics.*) Conservative, adherent of the crown, supporter of royal and ecclesiastical authority.

Toss, *v. t.* 1. Throw (*by the hand and upward*), throw up, lift up suddenly, raise violently, fling, pitch, cast, hurl.

2. Agitate, shake, rock.

3. Try, harass, disquiet, make restless.

4. Keep in play, bandy; tumble over.

——, *v. i.* 1. Roll, writhe, fling, tumble about, pitch, heave, be uneasy, be in violent commotion.

2. Be agitated, be tossed, be moved tumultuously.

Total, *a.* 1. Whole, complete, full, entire, absolute.

2. Integral, entire, undivided.

——, *n.* Whole, totality, aggregate, gross, lump, mass, amount, sum, sum total, gross amount, all.

Tote, *v. t.* (*Southern U. S.*) Carry, bear, transport, lead.

Totter, *v. i.* 1. Stagger, reel, vacillate, falter.

2. Shake, tremble, oscillate, rock, threaten to fall, reel, lean, waver, titubate, wabble, sway; flag, fail, fall.

Touch, *v. t.* 1. Hit (*lightly*), strike against, impinge.

2. Perceive by the sense of feeling, handle, finger, feel of, paw, thumb.

3. Meet, be contiguous to, abut on, reach, come to, arrive at, attain to, join, adjoin.

4. Graze, glance, kiss, brush, come in contact with (*in passing over*).

5. Delineate (*lightly*), sketch, mark out, touch off.

6. Handle, speak of, deal with, allude to, mention in passing.

7. Concern, regard, relate to, refer to, pertain to, appertain to, belong to, affect, bear upon, treat of, have to do with.

8. Affect, impress, strike, come home to, smite, stir; move, melt, work upon, soften, mollify, strike mentally; distress, hurt, injure, afflict, molest, wound, sting.

9. Strike, play on.

——, *v. i.* Meet, hit, be contiguous, be in contact, abut on one another, impinge, kiss, brush, adjoin, border, neighbor.

TOUCH, *n.* 1. Contact, impact, tangency, palpability.

2. Feeling, tact, sense of feeling, sensation.

3. Power of exciting the affections; emotion, affection.

4. Stroke, kiss, glance, brush, caress; quality of touch, technique.

5. Tinge, tincture, cast, shade, grain, smack, trace, taste, savor, flavor, spice, dash, sprinkling, seasoning, infusion, little, small quantity, soupçon.

6. Hint, suggestion, slight notice; twinge.

7. Communication, intercourse, sympathy, accord, understanding.

Touchiness, *n.* Peevishness, snappishness, testiness, irritability, irascibility, petulance, fretfulness, spleen, pettishness.

Touching, *a.* Affecting, moving, melting, pathetic, impressive, heart-rending, pitiable, tender; adjacent, bordering, tangent, abutting.

Touching, *prep*. Concerning, regarding, respecting, with regard to, with respect to, in relation to, relating to, about.

Touch off. 1. Delineate lightly, touch, sketch, mark out hastily.

2. Discharge, apply the match to.

Touchstone, *n*. Test, criterion, proof, ordeal, assay, touch.

Touch up. Repair, improve by slight touches, mend, rub up.

Touchy, *a*. Peevish, snappish, waspish, cross, testy, irritable, fretful, splenetic, techy, irascible, petulant, choleric, peppery, hot-tempered, quick-tempered, like tinder, like touchwood.

Tough, *a*. 1. Adhesive, tenacious, cohesive, flexible, without brittleness; coriaceous, leathery; viscous, clammy, ropy, stringy, sticky.

2. Stiff, rigid, inflexible, intractable.

3. Strong, firm, hardy.

4. Refractory, stubborn, obdurate, callous, hard.

5. (*Colloq.*) Difficult, hard, hard to deal with, troublesome, formidable.

Tour, *n*. Journey (*in a circuit*), excursion, trip, expedition, pilgrimage, circuit, round, perambulation, course.

Tourist, *n*. Traveller, voyager, wayfarer, pilgrim, excursionist.

Tournament, *n*. Tourney, joust, combat, contest.

Tow, *n*. 1. Refuse flax, hards.

2. Pull, drag, lift.

——, *v. t.* Draw (*as a vessel, through the water*), haul, drag, pull, take in tow, tug.

Toward, ⎫ *prep*. 1. In the direction of.
Towards, ⎭ 2. Regarding, respecting, with respect to, with regard to.

3. Nearly, almost, near about, nigh, about, near.

——, *adv*. Near at hand, advancing, in a state of preparation.

Toward, *a*. Ready, docile, apt, towardly.

Towardly, *a*. Docile, apt, tractable, toward, compliant with duty, ready to do, manageable, pliant.

Towboat, *n*. Tug, steam-tug.

Tower, *n*. 1. Minaret, spire, steeple, belfry, bell-tower, *campanile*, column, turret.

2. Citadel, fortress, castle, stronghold; rock, pillar, refuge, tower of strength, support.

——, *v. i.* Soar, mount, rise, transcend, overtop.

Towering, *a*. 1. Lofty, elevated, very high.

2. Extreme, violent, very great, excessive, prodigious.

To wit. To know, namely, *videlicet*.

TOWN, *n*. 1. Place, borough, burgh, village, "burg," hamlet, thorp.

2. City, metropolis.

Town-hall, *n*. 1. Town-house.

2. City residence.

Township, *n*. Town territory, district of a town.

Townsman, *n*. 1. Inhabitant of a town, burgher, citizen, burgess.

2. [*New Eng.*] Selectman.

Toy, *n*. 1. Plaything, bawble, gewgaw, trinket, knick-knack, gimcrack, kickshaw, doll, puppet.

2. Trifle, petty commodity, small matter, bubble, *bagatelle*.

3. Folly, wild fancy, odd conceit, trifling opinion.

4. Play, sport, amorous dalliance.

——, *v. i.* Trifle, dally, sport, wanton, play, bill and coo.

Trace, *n*. 1. Footprint, footmark, footstep, track, trail, wake, vestige, evidence, mark, sign, token, remains, impression.

2. Record, memorial.

3. Bit, hint, *soupçon*, suggestion, dash, flavor, tinge, streak, "suspicion."

——, *v. t.* 1. Follow (*by a track* or *mark*), track, trail.

2. Delineate, draw, sketch, mark out, trace out, copy, describe; derive, deduce.

3. Traverse, go over, walk over.

Tracing, *n*. Copy (*of a drawing on tracing-paper*).

Track, *n*. 1. Footprint, footmark, footstep, trace, vestige, spoor.

2. Trail, wake, trace; course, way, road, path, pathway, beaten path, runway, rails.

——, *v. t.* Follow (*by a track*), trace, trail, pursue, chase, scent, draw.

Trackless, *a*. Untrodden, pathless.

Tract, *n*. 1. Region, district, territory, quarter, area.

2. Piece (*of land*), part, portion, parcel, plot, patch.

3. Treatise, dissertation, pamphlet, essay, thesis, tractate, written discourse, disquisition, sermon, homily.

4. Length, extent, continued duration.

Tractable, *a*. Docile, manageable, governable, submissive, yielding, willing; plastic, tractile, readily wrought, adaptable.

Tractableness, *n*. Docility, tractability.

Tractarian, *n*. Puseyite, Tractite, writer of the Oxford tracts.

Traction, *n*. 1. Drawing, pulling, draught, hauling, haulage, towage.

2. Tension, contraction.

3. Attraction, drawing toward.

Tractive, *a*. Pulling, attracting; tractile, ductile.

TRADE, *n.* 1. Traffic, commerce, barter, dealing, business, purchase and sale, buying and selling, bargaining, exchange of commodities.

2. Manual occupation, mechanical employment, handicraft.

3. Occupation, employment, business, calling, pursuit, vocation, craft, office, avocation, profession.

——, *v. i.* Traffic, deal, bargain, barter, interchange, chaffer, carry on commerce, buy and sell, drive a trade, drive a bargain.

——, *v. t.* 1. Sell, exchange in commerce.

2. Exchange, barter.

Trader, *n.* Tradesman, dealer, shop-keeper, merchant, retailer.

Trading, *a.* Commercial, mercantile.

Tradition, *n.* 1. (*Law.*) Transfer (*of possession*), delivery.

2. Usage, custom, unwritten law, oral report (*from generation to generation*), traduction.

Traditional, *a.* Orally transmitted (*from age to age*), traditionary, traditive, customary.

Traduce, *v. t.* Vilify, defame, revile, slander, malign, calumniate, asperse, abuse, decry, disparage, depreciate, blemish, brand, run down, speak ill of, wilfully misrepresent, expose to contempt.

Traducer, *n.* Slanderer, calumniator, defamer, detractor, vilifier.

Traffic, *n.* Trade, commerce, exchange *or* sale of commodities, business, truck, chaffer, barter; transportation.

——, *v. i.* 1. Trade, barter, deal, bargain, chaffer, carry on commerce, buy and sell, exchange.

2. Trade meanly, trade mercenarily.

Trafficker, *n.* Trader, merchant.

Tragedian, *n.* Actor (*of tragedy*), tragic actor, tragedienne, Thespian.

Tragedy, *n.* 1. Dramatic poem, drama, play.

2. Calamity, disaster, catastrophe, shocking event.

Tragic, } *a.* 1. Of tragedy, of the nature
Tragical, } of tragedy, after the manner of tragedy; dramatic, buskined.

2. Shocking, dreadful, calamitous, mournful, sorrowful, fatal, disastrous, dire.

Trail, *v. t.* 1. Draw, drag along.

2. Track, trace, follow, hunt.

——, *v. i.* 1. Drag, be drawn along, be drawn out; hang, flow, float.

2. Run (*as a plant*), climb, grow to great length, creep.

——, *n.* 1. Train.

2. Track, trace, mark, footprint, footmark, footstep.

3. Footpath.

TRAIN, *n.* 1. Trail, wake.

2. Retinue, suite, staff, followers, entourage, body of attendants, *cortège.*

3. Orderly company, procession, line of connected cars, railroad train.

4. Series, set, succession, consecution, chain, sequel.

5. Course, process, method, order.

6. Persuasion, artifice, enticement, allurement, device, stratagem; trap, lure.

——, *v. t.* 1. Trail, draw, drag, haul, tug.

2. Entice, allure, draw by persuasion.

3. Educate, discipline, instruct, drill, form by practice, school, exercise, teach.

4. Break in, accustom, habituate, inure, use, rehearse, prepare, familiarize.

——, *v. i.* Drill, exercise, do military duty.

Trained, *a.* Experienced, practised, skilled, disciplined, educated, qualified, fitted, brought up, reared, thoroughpaced.

Training, *n.* Instruction, teaching, education, drilling, drill, discipline, schooling, breeding, tuition, nurture.

Trait, *n.* 1. Stroke, touch, mark, line.

2. Feature, lineament, characteristic, quality, particularity, peculiarity, mark.

Traitor, *n.* 1. Betrayer (*especially of one's country*), deceiver, renegade, apostate, perfidious person, turncoat, Judas, serpent, snake in the grass.

2. Rebel, insurgent, revolter, deserter, conspirator, mutineer.

Traitorous, *a.* 1. Treacherous, perfidious, faithless, false, recreant.

2. Treasonable, treacherous, seditious, perfidious, insidious.

Trammel, *n.* 1. Net; impediment, fetter, shackle, clog, bond, chain, restraint, hindrance.

2. Pot-hook.

——, *v. t.* Shackle, hamper, clog, fetter, confine, restrain, hinder, cramp, cumber, tie, curb, restrict.

Tramontane, *a.* 1. Foreign, barbarous, outlandish, alien, strange, heathenish.

2. Ultramontane, beyond the mountains *or* the Alps.

Tramp, *v. i.* (*Colloq.*) Travel (*on foot*), trudge, walk, march (*heavily*), jog on, plod, hike.

——, *n.* 1. Journey (*on foot*), excursion, walk, march.

2. Heavy walk, heavy tread.

3. Stroller, tramper, vagabond, vagrant, loafer, beggar, landloper.

Tramper, *n.* Hiker, walker, pedestrian.

Trample, *v. t.* 1. Tread upon, tread under foot, trample on, crush.

2. Tread down, prostrate by treading.

3. Treat with scorn, spurn, defy, set at naught.

Tram-way, *n.* Tram-road, plate-railway, track-way.

Trance, *n.* 1. Ecstasy, rapture, dream, hypnosis.

2. (*Med.*) Catalepsy, coma.

Tranquil, *a.* Calm, still, quiet, serene, placid, unperturbed, unruffled, unmoved, untroubled, peaceful, undisturbed.

Tranquillity, *n.* Quiet, quietness, peace, stillness, serenity, calmness, placidness, tranquilness, peacefulness.

Tranquillize, *v. t.* Calm, quiet, silent, still, compose, lull, hush, quell, lay, allay, pacify, soothe, appease, assuage, moderate, make tranquil.

Transact, *v. t.* Do, perform, manage, conduct, carry on, execute, enact, despatch.

——, *v. i.* Treat, manage, negotiate, conduct.

Transaction, *n.* 1. Doing, act, action, conduct, performance, management, negotiation.

2. Affair, proceeding, occurrence, incident, event, procedure, business, job, "deal," dealing, matter.

Transcend, *v. t.* 1. Exceed; transgress, overstep, pass, overpass, go beyond, pass over, overleap.

2. Surmount, rise above, surpass, excel, outstrip, overtop, outdo, exceed, outvie, outrival, be superior.

Transcendence, ⎫ *n.* Supereminence, supe-
Transcendency, ⎭ rior excellence, marked superiority.

Transcendent, *a.* 1. Pre-eminent, surpassing, supereminent, unequalled, unparalleled, peerless, unrivalled, inimitable, very superior, consummate, unsurpassed, supreme in excellence.

2. Transcendental, above *or* dominating the (*Aristotelian*) categories.

3. Transcending the scope of knowledge, supersensible, metempirical, noumenal, transcending the limits of possible experience, beyond the range of reason *or* of the transcendental (or *a priori*) principles of knowledge.

Transcendental, *a.* 1. Supereminent, transcendent, pre-eminent, surpassing, supreme, consummate.

2. (*Colloq.*) Obscure, dark, vague, indefinite, speculative, mystic, mystical, fantastic, filmy, thin, abstruse, abstract, indistinct, rarefied, attenuated, unreal, intangible, impalpable, recondite.

3. (*Math.*) Non-algebraic, extra-algebraic, involving other than the four fundamental operations.

4. (*Met.*) *a.* *A priori*, pure, organic, primordial, original, aboriginal, formal, formative, constitutive, relating to form as distinguished from matter, non-empirical.

b. Synthetical, combinative, unitive, unifying, unificatory, colligative, constructive of system in experience, warranting inference from the past to the future.

c. Non-transcendent, immanent, limited to experience, applicable to phenomena alone, inapplicable to the absolute, to noumena, to the supersensible, *or* to things in themselves.

Transcribe, *v. t.* Copy, write a copy of, decipher, decode.

Transcriber, *n.* Copier, copyist.

Transcript, *n.* 1. Written copy, transcription, engrossment, duplicate, rescript.

2. Copy, imitation.

Transcription, *n.* 1. Copying, transcribing.

2. (*Mus.*) Adaptation (*to one instrument of a piece intended for another,* or *for the voice*), rearrangement, reproduction.

3. Copy, transcript.

Transfer, *v. t.* 1. Transport, carry over, convey, send, dispatch, transmit, remove, translate.

2. Remove, transplant.

3. Alienate, abalienate, consign, convey, cede, grant, devise, hand over, make over, forward, relegate, assign, deed, pass on, deliver over, pass, confer, pass over, transmit.

——, *n.* Transferring, traduction, removal, copy, cession, grant, assignment, devisal, bequest, gift, transmission, shift, change, displacement, relegation, transportation, carriage, shipment, transit, alienation, abalienation, demise, conveyance, transference.

Transference, *n.* 1. Transmission, transmittal, transfusion.

2. Alienation, conveyance, transfer.

Transfiguration, *n.* Transformation, metamorphosis, change of form.

Transfigure, *v. t.* Transform, metamorphose, dignify, idealize.

Transfix, *v. t.* Transpierce, penetrate, perforate, pierce through, impale, spear, broach, stake, pin, skewer.

Transform, *v. t.* 1. Transfigure, metamorphose, change the form of.

2. Transmute, change into another substance, translate, transmogrify, resolve, convert.

3. Change, change the nature of, convert.

4. Transubstantiate (*Roman Catholic Church*).

Transformation, *n.* 1. Metamorphosis, transfiguration, change of form.

2. Transmutation, conversion, change.

3. Change, conversion.

4. Transubstantiation.

Transfuse, *v. t.* Transfer (*as by pouring, instilling,* or *injecting*), convey, transmit, pour.

Transfusion, *n.* Transference, transmission.

Transgress, *v. t.* 1. Exceed, transcend, pass, overstep, overpass, go beyond, pass over.

2. Disobey, infringe, break, contravene, set at naught, violate.

——, *v. i.* Err, sin, offend, do amiss, trespass, slip, intrude.

Transgression, *n.* 1. Infringement, encroachment, violation, infraction, breach, non-observance, disobedience, transgressing.

2. Sin, offence, crime, misdemeanor, misdeed, slip, delinquency, iniquity, misdoing, fault, trespass, evil deed, error, wrongdoing.

Transgressive, *a.* Faulty, culpable, wrong.

Transgressor, *n.* Offender, trespasser, culprit, delinquent, sinner, evil-doer, wrong-doer, misfeasor, misdemeanant, malefactor.

Transient, *a.* 1. Passing, fleeting, temporary, transitory, impermanent, volatile, ephemeral, evanescent, short-lived, meteoric, diurnal, mortal, perishable, soon past, soon passing, flying, flitting, brief, fugitive.

2. Hasty, momentary, imperfect, short.

Transit, *n.* 1. Passage through, passage over, act of passing, change; conveyance, passage.

2. Line of passage, line of conveyance.

Transition, *n.* Change, shifting, passage, passing, transit.

Transitional, *a.* Transitionary, passing.

Transitive, *a.* (*Gram.*) 1. Active.

2. Transitional.

Transitory, *a.* Transient, passing, fleeting, flitting, flying, temporary, evanescent, ephemeral, momentary, short, brief, fugacious, short-lived, of short duration, here to-day and gone to-morrow.

Translate, *v. t.* 1. (*Archaic*). Remove, transport, transfer.

2. Render, construe, interpret, turn, decipher, decode.

3. Transform, change into another form.

Translation, *n.* 1. Removal, transportation, conveyance, carriage.

2. Transfer, transferring, transference.

3. Interpretation, rendering, rendition, version, deciphering, decoding, key.

4. (*Med.*) Metastasis, change in the seat of a disease.

Translucency, *n.* 1. Semi-transparency, translucence, pellucidity, pellucidness, diaphaneity.

2. See TRANSPARENCY.

Translucent, *a.* 1. Semi-transparent (*admitting rays of light, but not capable of being distinctly seen through*), pellucid, diaphanous, semi-opaque, translucid.

2. See TRANSPARENT.

Transmigrate, *v. i.* 1. Migrate.

2. Transanimate.

Transmigration, *n.* 1. Migration.

2. Metempsychosis, transanimation, Pythagorean theory.

Transmission, *n.* Transference, transmittal, transmittance, conveyance, traduction, circulation, communication.

Transmit, *v. t.* 1. Send, remit, forward, send on, send forward; communicate, conduct, radiate.

2. Transfer, convey, carry, bear, hand over.

Transmittal, *n.* See TRANSMISSION.

Transmittible, *a.* Transmissible.

Transmutable, *a.* Changeable.

Transmutation, *n.* 1. Transformation, metamorphosis, transfiguration.

2. (*Geom.*) Change, reduction, conversion.

Transmute, *v. t.* Change (*from one form* or *nature into another*), transform.

Transom, *n.* Window, ventilator.

Transparence, } *n.* Clearness, lucidity,
Transparency, } limpidness, translucency.

Transparent, *a.* 1. Clear, lucid, bright, limpid, diaphanous; gauzy, flimsy, thin; pellucid, serene, unclouded, hyaline, crystalline, transpicuous, translucent, that may be seen through.

2. Open, porous, transpicuous.

3. Clear, lucid, open, perspicuous, unambiguous, explicit, unequivocal, evident, manifest, patent, obvious, transpicuous.

Transpire, *v. i.* 1. Evaporate (*through the pores*), exhale, pass off in vapor.

2. Become known, be disclosed, come to light, come out, be made public, get abroad, leak out, escape, appear.

Transplant, *v. t.* 1. Plant in a new place, replant, repot, graft.

2. Remove, transfer, transpose, transport, carry.

Transplendent, *a.* Transcendently splendid, radiant, brilliant, glittering, scintillant, resplendent.

Transport, *v. t.* 1. Carry (*from one place to another*), convey, bear, fetch, remove, transfer, take, conduct, cart, truck, ship.

2. Banish (*to a penal colony*), carry into banishment, expel.

3. Enrapture, ravish, enravish, entrance, beatify, put into ecstasy, make very happy, delight, carry away (*by excitement of any kind*).

TRANSPORT, *n.* 1. Conveyance, transportation, carriage, transporting, movement.

2. Transport-ship, transport-vessel.

3. Convict (*sentenced to banishment*), felon.

4. Rapture, ravishment, beatitude, ecstasy, beatification, bliss, happiness, felicity.

5. Warmth, vehemence, violent manifestation, passion, frenzy.

Transportation, *n.* 1. Transporting, conveyance, carriage, transmission, removal, movement, moving, portage, shipment, transference.

2. Banishment, forced exile, expulsion.

Transporting, *a.* Passionate, ecstatic, ravishing.

Transpose, *v. t.* Change the order of (*by putting one in place of the other*, or *substituting one for the other*), reverse, interchange, shift.

Transposition, *n.* Transposal.

Transubstantiation, *n.* Change of substance, transformation.

Transude, *v. i.* Exude, ooze, filter, percolate, strain, pass by pores.

Transverse, *a.* Cross, oblique, thwart.

Transversely, *adv.* Crosswise, in a cross direction.

Trap, *n.* 1. Snare, gin, pitfall, springe, toil, trapfall, deadfall, net.

2. Ambush, stratagem, artifice, pitfall, trepan, toil, wile.

3. Trap-ball.

4. Trap-rock.

——, *v. t.* 1. Ensnare, entrap, springe, noose, catch, snare.

2. Trepan, ensnare, take by stratagem, tangle, enmesh.

Trappings, *n. pl.* 1. Dress, ornaments, embellishments, decorations, frippery, paraphernalia, rigging, gear, livery, adornments.

2. Equipments, accoutrements, caparisons, gear.

Traps, *n. pl.* (*Colloq.*) Goods, things, stuff, luggage, effects, small articles (*of household use*).

Trash, *n.* Dross, refuse, rubbish, trumpery, waste matter, worthless stuff; nonsense, balderdash.

Trashy, *a.* Worthless, trifling, trumpery, flimsy, paltry, insignificant, unimportant, poor, useless.

Traumatic, *a.* Vulnerary, good for wounds.

Travail, *n.* Childbirth, parturition, labor, delivery, bringing forth.

Travel, *v. i.* 1. Walk, go on foot.

2. Journey, ramble, rove, roam, take a journey, take a trip, make a tour, make an excursion, itinerate.

3. Pass, go, move, make progress.

——, *n.* 1. Journeying, traveling, locomotion.

2. Journey, tour, excursion, trip, expedition.

Traveler, *n.* 1. Wayfarer, voyager, itinerant, excursionist, sightseer, globe-trotter, "tripper," journeyer, *voyageur*, trekker, explorer, tourist, passenger, pilgrim, wanderer, rover.

2. Salesman, drummer, representative.

Traveling, *n.* Journeying, travel, wandering, peregrination.

Traverse, *a.* Lying across, cross, crosswise, athwart.

——, *v. t.* 1. Cross, lay athwart, thwart.

2. Thwart, obstruct, cross in opposition, counteract, frustrate, defeat, contravene.

3. Pass, travel over, wander over, ford, overpass, cross in traveling, go across, pass through, ply, range.

4. Pass over and view, survey carefully, examine thoroughly, scour, measure.

Travesty, *v. t.* Parody, imitate, take off, turn into burlesque.

——, *n.* Parody, burlesque, caricature, imitation, take-off.

TRAY, *n.* 1. Small trough, wooden vessel, trencher.

2. Waiter, salver, coaster, shallow box.

Treacherous, *a.* Traitorous, traitor, untrue, recreant, perfidious, faithless, unfaithful, false, deceitful, insidious, disloyal, recreant, treasonable, betraying, untrustworthy; unreliable, unsafe.

Treachery, *n.* Perfidiousness, perfidy, faithlessness, double-dealing, foul play, infidelity, recreancy, betrayal, treason, disloyalty, breach of faith, Punic faith, insidiousness, deceitfulness.

Tread, *v. i.* 1. Set the foot.

2. Walk, go, pace, dance, step, march, tramp.

——, *v. t.* 1. Set the foot on, walk on, step on.

2. Stamp upon, press down with the foot, beat with the foot.

3. Crush under foot, trample.

4. Subdue, subject.

Tread, *n.* 1. Step, stepping.

2. Gait, manner of stepping.

Tread upon. 1. Trample, tread under foot, tread on, spurn, crush, subdue.

2. Follow closely.

Treason, *n.* Treachery (*to a sovereign or a Government*), disloyalty, breach of allegiance, lese-majesty, sedition, perfidy, betrayal.

Treasonable, *a.* Treacherous, traitorous, disloyal.

Treasure, *n.* 1. Money (*hoarded up*), funds, savings, hoardings, cash, wealth, accumulated riches.

2. Stock, store, reserve, abundance.

3. Precious thing, thing of great value, jewel, valuable.

——, *v. t.* 1. Hoard, store, garner, save, husband, lay in, lay by, lay up, treasure up, collect and reposit.

2. Remember, cherish in memory.

3. Value.

Treasurer, *n.* Bursar, cash-keeper, receiver, trustee, banker, purser.

Treasure-trove, *n.* Windfall, godsend, unexpected good fortune, "velvet."

Treasury, *n.* Till, strong-box, money-box, money-bag, exchequer, coffer, chest, safe, fisc, bursary, bank, purse; purse-strings.

Treat, *v. t.* 1. Use, behave to, behave toward, deal with, deal by.

2. Entertain, feast, gratify, refresh.

3. Handle, manage, serve, doctor, prescribe for, dose, attend.

4. Discourse on, treat of, discuss.

——, *v. i.* 1. Negotiate, bargain, come to terms, make terms, deal, parley, temporize, covenant.

2. Discourse.

——, *n.* 1. Entertainment, feast, banquet.

2. Pleasure, entertainment, luxury, delight, refreshment, enjoyment, gratification.

Treatise, *n.* Disquisition, dissertation, tractate, discourse, commentary, monograph, formal essay, paper tract.

Treatment, *n.* 1. Usage, use.

2. Handling, management, manipulation, dealing.

3. Handling, management, method of treating, therapy, doctoring, medical care.

Treat of. Discuss, handle, discourse upon, descant upon, deal with.

Treaty, *n.* 1. Negotiation, act of treating.

2. Agreement (*between nations*), league, contract, compact, pact, convention, concordat, covenant, alliance.

Treble, *a.* Triple, threefold.

——, *v. t.* Triple, make threefold.

——, *n.* (*Mus.*) Highest part (*for a woman's voice*), soprano.

Trebuchet, *n.* Tumbrel, castigatory, ducking-stool, cucking-stool, trebucket.

TREE, *n.* Sapling, pollard; stand.

Trellis, *n.* Lattice, lattice-work, *treillage.*

Tremble, *v. i.* 1. Quake, shake, shudder, shiver, quiver, quaver.

2. Shake, totter, oscillate, rock, quake.

Tremendous, *a.* 1. Terrible, dreadful, fearful, horrible, horrid, horrific, frightful, terrific, alarming, awful, appalling.

2. Immense, monstrous.

Tremor, *n.* Trembling, shaking, quaking, quivering, trepidation, agitation, tremulousness, vibration.

Tremulous, *a.* Shaking, trembling, quivering, shivering, shaky, quavering, tottering, vibrating.

Trench, *v. t.* 1. Cut, carve.

2. Furrow, intrench.

3. Ditch, dig into ditches, channel.

4. Intrench, fortify with a ditch and parapet.

——, *v. i.* Encroach, intrude, infringe, trespass, intrench.

——, *n.* Ditch, fosse, moat, drain, sewer, furrow, water-course, pit, gutter, channel, trough; intrenchment, fortification, dugout.

Trenchant, *a.* 1. Cutting, sharp, keen.

2. Cutting, sharp, incisive, unsparing, severe, biting, sarcastic, pointed, acute, keen, caustic, sententious, crisp, pungent, piquant.

Trencher, *n.* 1. Platter (*of wood*), large plate.

2. Table, board.

Trencher-friend, *n.* Sponger, parasite, trencher-fly, trencher-mate.

Trend, *v. i.* Turn, run, drift, gravitate, stretch, tend, incline, sweep.

——, *n.* Tendency (*to a certain direction*), bent, drift, inclination, trending, direction, set.

Trepan, *v. t.* 1. Trephine.

2. Ensnare, trap, entrap, trapan.

Trepidation, *n.* 1. Shaking, trembling, quaking, quivering, tremor, agitation, tremulousness.

2. State of terror, fear, agitation, excitement, dismay, perturbation, alarm, fright, terror, consternation.

Trespass, *v. i.* 1. Encroach, infringe, intrude, make inroad *or* invasion, trench, enter unlawfully.

2. Transgress, offend, sin, commit an offence.

Trespass, *n.* 1. Injury, infringement, encroachment, intrusion, invasion.

2. Transgression, crime, fault, sin, misdeed, misdemeanor, offence, delinquency, error, wrong-doing.

Trespasser, *n.* 1. Intruder, invader.

2. Offender, sinner, transgressor, misdoer, delinquent.

Tress, *n.* Lock, curl, ringlet.

Trestle, *n.* Frame (*for supporting a table, bridge, etc.*).

Trial, *n.* 1. Testing, examination, experiment.

2. Experience, experimental knowledge.

3. Attempt, endeavor, effort, essay, exertion, struggle, aim.

4. Test, criterion, proof, touchstone, ordeal, probation, assay.

5. Suffering, trouble, affliction, infliction, grief, sorrow, distress, tribulation, misery, woe, burden, pain, dolor, mortification, chagrin, heartache, unhappiness, wretchedness, vexation, hardship.

6. Suit, case, cause, action, hearing.

Triangle, *n.* Three-sided figure, trigon.

Triangular, *a.* Trigonal, triquetral, deltoid.

Tribal, *a.* Tribual, tribular.

Tribe, *n.* 1. Family, race, lineage, clan, sept.

2. Class (*of persons* or *things*), order, division, distinct portion.

Tribulation, *n.* Distress, suffering, trouble, affliction, grief, sorrow, trial, misery, woe, wretchedness, unhappiness, pain, vexation of spirit, adversity.

Tribunal, *n.* 1. Bench, judgment-seat.

2. Court, judicatory, judicature, bar, court of justice; sessions, assizes.

Tribunate, *n.* Tribuneship.

Tributary, *a.* 1. Paying tribute, subject to tribute, contributing.

2. Subject, subordinate, inferior.

Tribute, *n.* 1. Tax, subsidy.

2. Tax, impost, duty, excise, custom, toll.

3. Grant, contribution, offering.

Trice, *n.* Moment, instant, second, jiffy, flash, twinkling.

Trick, *n.* 1. Artifice, stratagem, wile, cheat, shift, device, "game," "fake," "dodge," doubling, fraud, chicane, blind, feint, manœuvre, deceit, imposition, imposture, deception, juggle, reach, shuffle, hocus-pocus, swindle, jape, chouse, fetch, humbug, hoax, cog, gammon, cunning contrivance, sharp practice, *ruse.*

2. Sleight, juggle, craft, deftness, antic, caper, gambol.

3. Mischievous behavior, annoying conduct, prank.

4. Habit, practice, peculiarity, particular manner, mannerism.

——, *v. t.* 1. Cheat, defraud, deceive, cozen, fob, jockey, hoax, dupe, delude, circumvent, gull, chouse, diddle, overreach, impose upon.

2. [Often followed by *up, off,* or *out.*] Dress, decorate, set off, adorn fantastically, bedizen, bedeck.

Trickery, *n.* Deception, fraud, artifice, deceitfulness, knavery, chicane, chicanery, stratagem, claptrap, bunkum, hocus-pocus.

Trickish, *a.* Knavish, artful, deceitful, wily, dishonest, roguish, unprincipled, tricky, fraudulently cunning, mischievously subtle.

Trickle, *v. i.* Drop, drip, flow gently, trill, dribble, distil.

Trickster, *n.* Deceiver, cheat, rogue, knave, shifter, "faker," sharper, tricker, impostor, double-dealer, hocus-pocus, swindler.

Tricksy, *a.* Trickish, artful.

Tricuspid, *a.* Three-pointed, tricuspidate.

Tridentate, *a.* Three-toothed, tridented.

Trifid, *a.* Three-cleft.

Trifle, *n.* Triviality, small matter, bawble, nothing, bubble, thing of little value *or* consequence, thing of no moment, drop in the bucket, shadow of a shade, *bagatelle,* fig, bean; trace, particle, modicum, iota, jot.

——, *v. i.* 1. Act with levity, be busy about trifles, toy, dally, play, dawdle, palter, potter; fribble, fool, frivol.

2. Talk idly *or* frivolously, toy, wanton.

Trifler, *n.* Idler, fribbler, dallier, potterer.

Trifle with. Play the fool with, treat without respect, mock.

Trifling, *a.* Trivial, petty, frivolous, frippery, worthless, inconsiderable, nugatory, slight, unimportant, insignificant, immaterial, piddling, finicking, of little value *or* consequence, of no moment, of small importance; foolish, idle, silly.

Trifoliate,
Trifoliated, } *a.* Three-leaved.

Trifurcate,
Trifurcated, } *a.* Three-pronged.

Trig, *a.* (*Local.*) Trim, neat, spruce, smart, tidy.

Trigraph, *n.* Triphthong, trigram.

Trill, *n.* Shake, quaver, tremulo, warbling.

——, *v. t.* Shake, sing with a trill, warble.

——, *v. i.* 1. Quaver.

2. Trickle.

Trim, *a.* 1. Snug, neat, nice, compact, well-adjusted, well-ordered, tidy, shapely.

2. Spruce, finical, smart, elegant, *chic.*

Trim, *n.* 1. Dress, gear, ornaments, trimmings, trappings.

2. State, condition, order, case, plight.

——, *v. t.* 1. Adjust, arrange, put in order, set right, make trim, prepare; equalize, balance, fill.

2. Dress, decorate, ornament, embellish, adorn, garnish, deck, bedeck, set out, array, set off, trick out.

3. Clip, lop, shear, prune, curtail, shave, shear, cut, mow, poll, barber.

4. (*Colloq.*) Rebuke, chide, reprove sharply, reprimand, trounce, berate, chastise.

——, *v. i.* Fluctuate, vacillate, balance, be on the fence, veer round, change sides, be a timeserver, shift, shuffle, play fast and loose, blow hot and cold, hedge, temporize.

Trimmer, *n.* Time-server, time-pleaser, timist, Janus, weather-cock.

Trimmings, *n. pl.* 1. Ornaments, trappings, dress, gear, trim.

2. Relish, garnish.

Trinity, *n.* 1. Triunity.

2. [With *The* prefixed.] The Holy Trinity, the Godhead, Triune God.

Trinket, *n.* Toy, bawble, knick-knack, gewgaw, *bijou*, gaud, gimcrack, whim-wham, trifle, *bagatelle*.

Trinkets, *n. pl.* Jewels, jewelry, bijoutry, trifling ornaments.

Trip, *v. i.* 1. Skip, hop, step quickly, dance, foot it, caper, frisk.

2. Stumble, lose footing, make a false step, misstep, make a false movement.

3. Fail, mistake, err, be at fault, come short, commit an offence, bungle, blunder.

——, *v. t.* 1. Supplant, throw off the balance, trip up.

2. Overthrow, cause to fail, supplant, upset.

3. Detect, catch, convict.

——, *n.* 1. Skip, hop, light step.

2. Stumble, false step, misstep, loss of balance, lurch.

3. Slip, lapse, failure, mistake, oversight, bungle, error, blunder, fault, miss, stumble.

4. Jaunt, excursion, tour, ramble, stroll, circuit, route, expedition, journey.

Triphthong, *n.* Trigraph.

Triphyllous, *a.* Three-leaved.

Triple, *a.* 1. Threefold, triplicate.

2. Treble, three times repeated, three-ply, ternary, triplex.

——, *v. t.* Treble, make threefold, cube.

Triplicate, *a.* Threefold, treble.

Tripping, *a.* Quick, nimble, agile, nimble-footed.

Trite, *a.* Common, stale, threadbare, hackneyed, beaten, worn out, common-place, stereotyped.

Triturate, *v. t.* 1. Grind, bruise, rub, thrash, bray, pound, beat.

2. Levigate, comminute, grind to powder, pulverize.

Trituration, *n.* Pulverization, comminution, levigation.

Triumph, *n.* 1. Ovation, celebration, jubilee, jubilation, exultation, flourish of trumpets, joy.

2. Conquest, victory, success, accomplishment.

——, *v. i.* 1. Exult, rejoice, hold a triumph, celebrate a victory.

2. Prevail, succeed, get the mastery, obtain a victory, meet with success, win, succeed.

3. Be prosperous, flourish, thrive, prosper.

4. Boast, crow, swagger, brag, vaunt, exult, gloat, boast insolently.

Triumphant, *a.* 1. Triumphing, rejoicing for victory, exultant, elated, jubilant.

2. Exultant, jubilant, exulting.

3. Victorious, successful, crowned with success, graced with conquest.

Triumph over. Subdue, conquer, vanquish, overcome, subjugate, overpower, beat, master, get the better of, obtain victory, prevail over.

Triune, *a.* Trinal.

Trivial, *a.* Trifling, petty, small, frivolous, slight, light, little, slim, "picayunish," six-penny, nugatory, paltry, unimportant, inconsiderable, insignificant, immaterial, of little value, gimcrack, trumpery, of little consequence.

Triviality, *n.* 1. Trivialness, unimportance, insignificance, indifference.

2. Trifle, small matter, bawble, nothing, bubble, thing of little value *or* consequence, thing of no moment, *bagatelle*.

Trivialness, *n.* 1. Commonness, triviality.

2. See TRIFLE, *n.*

Trochlear, *a.* Pulley-shaped.

Troglodyte, *n.* Wretch, outcast, pilgarlic, pariah, miserable fellow, castaway.

Troll, *v. t.* 1. Send about, circulate, pass round.

2. Sing loudly.

3. Angle with a trolling line; allure, entice, lure, draw on.

——, *v. i.* 1. Sing a catch *or* round.

2. Fish with a trolling line.

——, *n.* 1. Catch, round.

2. Dwarf, kobold, elf, gnome, goblin.

Trollop, *n.* Slattern, slut.

Troop, *n.* 1. Throng, multitude, company, number, crowd, herd, flock.

2. Band, company, squad, body, party.

3. Company (*of stage-players*), troupe.

Troop, *v. i.* 1. Throng, gather in crowds, collect in numbers, muster, flock, crowd.

2. March in a company.

3. March in haste.

Trooper, *n.* Horse-soldier, horseman, cavalryman, hussar, dragoon.

Troops, *n. pl.* 1. Throngs, gangs.

2. Army, soldiers, soldiery, forces, legions, armed force, military force, body of troops.

Trope, *n.* Figure of speech, metaphor.

Trophy, *n.* Memorial of conquest, evidence of victory; prize, palm, laurels, wreath, medal, blue ribbon.

Tropical, *a.* 1. Of the tropics, blazing, torrid, fiery.

2. Figurative, metaphorical.

Troth, *n.* 1. Truth, verity, veracity, sincerity, honesty, candor.

2. Fidelity, faith, belief, allegiance, word.

Trot out. 1. Lead out, bring out.

2. Bring forward, exhibit, lead out, produce, display.

Trouble, *v. t.* 1. Agitate, disturb, derange, disorder, put out of order, disarrange, put in commotion, confuse.

2. Afflict, distress, grieve, annoy, vex, fret, ail, plague, torment, harass, worry, pester, badger, disquiet, concern, make anxious, make uneasy, disturb, perplex, molest, perturb.

3. Inconvenience, incommode, give occasion for labor to.

TROUBLE, *n.* 1. Affliction, distress, dolor, suffering, calamity, grief, tribulation, adversity, hardship, misfortune, sorrow, woe, misery, pain.

2. Annoyance, perplexity, vexation, embarrassment, plague, torment, irritation, worry, care, pains, anxiety, inconvenience, bother, pother, fuss, discomfort, ado; disturbance, row.

3. Perplexity, embarrassment, bewilderment, disquietude, uneasiness.

4. Matter, cause of distress, ailment, curse, bane, care, burden, pest.

Troublesome, *a.* 1. Vexatious, annoying, perplexing, harassing, galling, painful, grievous, distressing, disturbing, worrisome, "tough."

2. Burdensome, wearisome, tiresome, irksome.

3. Importunate, teasing, intrusive.

4. Hard, difficult, trying, arduous, inconvenient, unwieldy.

Troublous, *a.* 1. Tumultuous, agitated, disturbed, turbulent, perturbed, disquieted.

2. Full of trouble, tumultuous, full of affliction, troublesome.

Trough, *n.* 1. Long tray, wooden channel, manger, hutch.

2. Channel, depression, furrow, hollow.

TROUSERS, *n. pl.* Pantaloons, breeches, "pants."

Trousseau, *n.* [Fr.] Outfit (*of a bride*).

Truant, *a.* Wandering from business, loitering, idling, shirking.

——, *n.* Idler, loiterer, shirk, laggard, lounger, run-away, quitter, absentee, deserter.

Truce, *n.* 1. Armistice, suspension of hostilities, cessation of arms.

2. Intermission, cessation, short rest, short quiet, pause, respite, interval of rest, reprieve, delay, lull, recess, temporary peace, breathing-time.

Truck, *v. i.* Barter, deal, trade, traffic.

——, *v. t.* Barter, exchange, traffic, give in exchange, trade.

——, *n.* 1. Barter, exchange.

2. (*Colloq.*) Small commodities, merchandise, wares, goods; luggage.

3. Wheel, roller; delivery wagon, motor lorry.

Truckage, *n.* 1. Exchange, barter.

2. Freight, charge for carriage.

Truckle, *v. t.* Trundle, roll.

——, *v. i.* Cringe, stoop, crouch, submit, knuckle, yield (*obsequiously*), bend the knee, knock under, be servile, bend obsequiously, fawn upon, curry favor with.

Truculent, *a.* 1. Savage, fierce, ferocious, barbarous.

2. Savage, fierce, relentless, ferocious, malevolent, cruel, brutish.

3. Cruel, destructive, ruthless, fatal, deadly.

Trudge, *v. i.* 1. Travel (*on foot*), tramp, go.

2. March (*heavily*), jog on, travel with labor, walk heavily, lumber, drag, shamble, plod.

TRUE, *a.* 1. Real, genuine, veritable, actual, pure, sincere, legitimate, rightful, sound, authentic.

2. Truthful, veracious, substantial, conformable to fact.

3. Faithful, constant, steady, loyal, stanch.

4. Honest, honorable, upright, just, equitable, virtuous, trusty, trustworthy.

5. Exact, accurate, correct, right, even, undeviating, straight, conformable to a rule.

——, *adv.* Yes, ay, good, well, very well, well and good, granted.

True-blue, *a.* (*Colloq.*) Honest, faithful, stanch, loyal, true, incorruptible.

True-hearted, *a.* Honest, sincere, faithful, loyal, constant, trusty, guileless, trustworthy.

True-love, *n.* Lover, sweetheart, beloved, darling, dear, love.

Truism, *n.* Axiom, self-evident truth, evident proposition, necessary truth.

Trull, *n.* Drab, strumpet, prostitute, harlot, whore, courtesan, bawd, punk, trollop, Cyprian, street-walker, night-walker, woman of the town.

Truly, *adv.* 1. Really, verily, in truth, with truth, assuredly, forsooth, in reality, in fact, indeed, actually.

2. Truthfully, veraciously; honestly, candidly, plainly, sincerely, really, faithfully, in good earnest, in sober earnest, sooth to say, without equivocation, in plain English, without mincing the matter.

3. Faithfully, constantly, steadfastly, sincerely.

4. Correctly, exactly, strictly, accurately, justly, precisely.

Trump, *n.* 1. (*Poetical.*) Trumpet.

2. Trump-card, winning card.

——, *v. t.* 1. Lay a trump on, win with a trump.

2. Trick, impose on, obtrude, impose unfairly.

——, *v. i.* Play a trump.

Trumpery, *n.* 1. Falsehood, deceit, imposture, humbug, deception.

2. Trash, rubbish, stuff, frippery, worthless finery, trifles.

——, *a.* Worthless, good for nothing, trifling, trashy, rubbishy, pinchbeck.

Trumpet, *n.* 1. Horn, clarion, bugle, cornet.

2. Celebrator, praiser.

——, *v. t.* Proclaim, publish, announce, herald, promulgate, advertise, blazon, blaze abroad, spread abroad, noise abroad, make known, blare, blow.

Trumpet-call, *n.* Bugle-call, alarm, rallying cry, summons to arms, rappel.

Trumpet-tongued, *a.* Loud, sonorous, powerful, stentorian, vociferous.

Trump up. Devise, fabricate, collect with unfairness, forge.

Truncate, *v. t.* Lop, maim, lop off, cut off, dock.

Truncheon, *n.* 1. Club, cudgel, short staff, partisan.

2. Staff (*of command*), wand, *bâton*.

3. Bolling, pollard.

Trundle, *n.* 1. Roller, castor, little wheel.

2. Rolling motion.

3. Wallower, lantern-wheel.

——, *v. t.* Roll, bowl, roll along, truckle, wheel, revolve, spin.

Trundle-bed, *n.* Truckle-bed.

Trunk, *n.* 1. Stem, stock, stalk, body, bole, shaft, butt, torso.

2. Main body, main part.

3. Box, chest, coffer.

Trunnel, *n.* Treenail, wooden pin.

Truss, *n.* 1. Bundle, package, packet.

2. Bandage (*for hernia*), support, apparatus.

——, *v. t.* 1. Bind, pack close, pack up, bind up, put up, cram.

2. Keep tight, make fast, hold fast.

3. Skewer, hold together, make fast.

4. Hang, hang up, execute by hanging.

Trust, *n.* 1. Confidence, reliance, faith, belief, credence.

2. Credit, "tick."

3. Charge, deposit.

4. Commission, errand, duty, charge.

5. Faith, hope, expectation, belief, assured anticipation, confidence, assurance.

6. Merger, corporation, combination.

——, *v. t.* 1. Rely on, depend upon, confide in, put confidence in, trust to, place reliance on.

2. Give credit to, sell to on credit.

3. Believe, give credence to, credit.

4. Intrust, commit, confide.

——, *v. i.* 1. Expect, hope, be confident, feel sure.

2. Be confiding, be credulous, be won to confidence.

——, *a.* Held in trust, fiduciary.

Trustee, *n.* Depositary, fiduciary.

Trustful, *a.* 1. Trusting, confiding, unsuspecting, unquestioning.

2. Faithful, trusty, trustworthy.

Trustily, *adv.* Honestly, faithfully, with fidelity.

Trust in. Confide in, trust, place confidence in, rely on.

Trustless, *a.* Unfaithful, false, untrustworthy, unreliable.

Trustworthy, *a.* Honest, credible, true, faithful, upright, straightforward, uncorrupt, trusty, confidential, responsible, dependable, constant, reliable, stanch.

Trusty, *a.* 1. See TRUSTWORTHY.

2. Strong, firm.

Truth, *n.* 1. Fact, reality, verity.

2. Conformity to fact *or* reality; authenticity, actuality, realism.

3. Principle, law, canon, oracle.

4. Veracity, truthfulness, right.

5. Honesty, sincerity, integrity, frankness, ingenuousness, candor, probity, fidelity, honor, virtue.

6. Faithfulness, fidelity, constancy, loyalty, steadfastness, devotion, fealty, faith.

7. Exactness, accuracy, correctness, trueness, exactitude, regularity, nicety, precision, conformity to rule.

Truthful, *a.* 1. Correct, true, veracious, reliable, trustworthy.

2. Sincere, honest, candid, frank, open, ingenuous, artless, guileless, true, straightforward, single-hearted, trustworthy, trusty.

Truthless, *a.* 1. False.

2. Faithless, disingenuous, insincere, unfair, dishonest, hollow, hypocritical, pharisaical, canting, treacherous.

Try, *v. t.* 1. Examine, test, prove, make experiment of, make trial of, put to the test, put to proof, prove by experiment.

2. Experience, have knowledge of (*by trial*).

3. Attempt, essay.

4. (*Law.*) Hear, examine judicially, adjudicate, adjudge.

5. Purify, refine.

6. Subject to trial, put to the test, sound, smell, sift, taste, sample.

——, *v. i.* Attempt, endeavor, strive, aim, seek, strain, make an effort, make essay, do one's best, do all that in one lies, strain every nerve.

——, *n.* Attempt, experiment, trial, act of trying, effort, endeavor.

Trying, *a.* 1. Irksome, wearisome, tiresome, fatiguing, difficult, hard.

2. Severe, painful, afflictive, afflicting, grievous, calamitous, hard, distressing, sad, dire, deplorable, hard to bear.

Tryst, *n.* Appointment (*to meet*), appointed meeting, assignation, rendezvous.

Tube, *n.* Pipe, hollow cylinder, duct, bore, main, tunnel, hose, worm, pipette, bronchus; tuba.

Tubular, *a.* Fistular, tube-like, pipe-like, tube-shaped, tubiform, capillary, tubulate, tubate, cannular.

Tuck, *n.* 1. Small sword, rapier, bilbo.

2. Tuck-net.

3. Pull, lugging.

4. Fold, plait, pleat, doubling, lap.

——, *v. t.* 1. Pack, stow, fold under, press together.

2. Press in bed-clothes, wrap, infold.

3. Fold, pleat, wimple, double, lap.

Tuft, *n.* 1. Knot, bunch, brush, feather, plume, topknot, crest, pompon; tussock.

2. Cluster, group, clump. ·

3. (*Bot.*) Capitulum.

Tuft-hunter, *n.* Lion-hunter.

Tug, *v. t.* Pull (*with great effort*), draw, haul, tow, drag.

——, *v. i.* 1. Pull hard, pull with great effort.

2. Labor, struggle, strive.

——, *n.* 1. Hard pull, great effort.

2. Tow-boat.

3. Trace, drawing-strap.

Tuition, *n.* Instruction, teaching, education, training, schooling.

Tumble, *v. i.* 1. Roll, toss, heave, pitch about, wallow.

2. Fall, be precipitated, fall over, roll down, sprawl, trip, fall suddenly, topple.

3. Play mountebank tricks.

——, *v. t.* 1. Precipitate, throw headlong.

2. Turn over, throw about.

3. Disturb, derange, rumple, put in disorder, disorder, disarrange, dishevel, tousle.

Tumble-down, *a.* Tottering, ready to fall, rickety, dilapidated.

Tumbler, *n.* 1. Acrobat, juggler, posturemaster.

2. Glass.

Tumbrel, *n.* 1. Dung-cart, muck-cart, rough cart.

2. Trebuchet, castigatory, ducking-stool, cucking-stool.

Tumefaction, *n.* Tumor, swelling, intumescence.

Tumefy, *v. i.* Swell, inflate, distend, puff up, enlarge.

Tumid, *a.* 1. Swollen, swelled, enlarged, bloated, distended, puffed up, turgid.

2. Protuberant, swelling.

3. Bombastic, turgid, swelling, pompous, inflated, stilted, grandiloquent, declamatory, rhetorical, high-flown, puffy, falsely sublime, grandiose, fustian, turgent.

Tumidity, *n.* Tumidness, turgidity.

Tumor, *n.* Swelling, tumefaction, boil, carbuncle.

Tumult, *n.* 1. Uproar, affray, fray, brawl, feud, row, altercation, squabble, turbulence, bluster, riot, hubbub, fracas, quarrel, outbreak, strife, general riot, *mêlée.*

2. Violent commotion, turbulence, noisy agitation, confusion, disturbance, stir, breeze, turmoil, ferment, huddle, pother, ado, bustle, flurry, noise, fuss, confused noise, hurly-burly, bluster, hubbub, racket, disorder, "to-do."

3. Ferment, state of high excitement, agitation, perturbation.

Tumultuous, *a.* 1. Uproarious, riotous, turbulent, tumultuary, violent, lawless, seditious, wild.

2. Disturbed, agitated, restless, uneasy, unquiet, tumultuary.

3. Irregular, obstreperous, confused, disorderly, noisy, boisterous.

4. Full of tumult, disorderly, wild, stormy.

Tumulus, *n.* Barrow, artificial mound, artificial hillock.

Tun, *n.* 1. Large cask, hogshead.

2. Two pipes, four hogsheads, 252 gallons.

——, *v. t.* Barrel, cask.

Tunable, *a.* 1. That may be tuned.

2. Harmonious, musical, tuneful, melodious, sweet.

Tune, *n.* 1. Air, melody, strain, aria.

2. Concord, harmony, harmonious accordance, agreement, concert of parts.

3. Order, harmony, concord, accord, fit disposition, proper mood.

——, *v. t.* 1. Harmonize, accord, modulate, attune, put in tune.

2. Put into order, put into a proper state.

3. Attune, adapt, adjust.

4. Sing.

5. Play harmoniously.

Tuneful, *a.* Musical, harmonious, melodious, dulcet.

Tunnel, *n.* 1. Funnel.

2. Subterranean passage, underground thoroughfare, tube; drift, gallery, shaft.

Tunnel-shaped, *a.* (*Bot.*) Infundibular, infundibuliform.

Turbid, *a.* Roiled, roily, unsettled, feculent, dirty, dreggy, muddy, thick, cloudy, foul; unsettled, confused, muddled, disordered.

Turbinate,
Turbinated, } *a.* Top-shaped.

Turbulence, *n.* 1. Tumult, uproar, disturbance, excitement, turmoil, commotion, disorder, confusion, agitation, tumultuousness, unruliness.

2. Riot, sedition, mutiny, insurrection, rebellion, insubordination.

Turbulent, *a.* 1. Disturbed, agitated, restless, tumultuous, wild.

2. Tumultuous, disorderly, blustering, obstreperous, boisterous, uproarious, blatant, brawling, vociferous.

3. Riotous, seditious, mutinous, insubordinate, refractory, insurgent, rebellious, revolutionary, factious, disorderly, wild, violent, stormy, raging.

4. Producing commotion.

Tureen, *n.* Soup-dish.

Turf, *n.* 1. Sod, sward, greensward, grass.

2. Peat.

3. Race-course, race-ground; horse-racing.

Turfy, *a.* Cespitose, turf-like, grassy.

Turgent, *a.* 1. Swelling, tumid, protuberant.

2. Inflated, tumid, bombastic, turgescent.

Turgescence, *n.* 1. Swelling, tumefaction, distention.

2. See TURGIDITY.

Turgid, *a.* 1. Swelled, swollen, bloated, distended, tumid, puffed up.

2. Pompous, bombastic, tumid, puffy, inflated, digressive, diffuse, stilted, grandiloquent, declamatory, rhetorical, ostentatious, turgent, grandiose, fustian, high-flown.

Turgidity, *n.* 1. Swelling, distention, turgescence, turgidness.

2. Bombast, inflation, turgidness, grandiloquence, pompous style.

Turmoil, *n.* Tumult, agitation, disturbance, disorder, turbulence, confusion, commotion, uproar, activity, ferment, bustle, huddle, hurly-burly, trouble, harassing labor.

Turn, *v. t.* 1. Revolve, move round, turn round, rotate, make go round.

2. Cause to deviate, cast, deflect, inflect, bend, round, sway, swivel, spin, twirl, twist, wheel; grind, crank, wind, incline differently, change the direction of.

3. Divert, deflect, slew, warp, transfer.

4. Reverse the position of, turn over, subvert, invert.

5. Shape (*as in a lathe*), form, mould, fashion.

6. Adapt, fit, suit, manœuvre.

7. Change, alter, transmute, metamorphose, vary, transform, convert.

8. Change opinion, alter belief, persuade, convert, prejudice.

9. Translate, construe, render.

10. Direct, apply.

11. Direct the look to, change position to see.

——, *v. i.* 1. Revolve, rotate, whirl, turn round, have a circular motion, wheel round.

2. Be directed, have direction.

3. Deviate, incline, bend, be deflected, veer, shift, swerve, sway, swing, roll.

4. Be changed, be transformed, be converted, be altered, become transmuted.

5. Grow, become; become sour, become acid, curdle, ferment, acidify.

6. Depend, hinge, pivot, hang, be dependent.

7. Result, terminate, come about, eventuate, issue.

8. Become giddy, grow dizzy.

TURN, *n.* 1. Revolution, rotation, cycle, movement about a center, act of turning, gyration, round.

2. Change of direction, alteration of course, new tendency, deviation, deflec-

tion, flexion, retroversion, counter turn, diversion, slew, bend, swing, swivel, doubling, twist, coil, whirl, twirl, swirl, spin, reel, flexure, bending, sweep, winding, turning.

3. Change, alteration, vicissitude, variation.

4. Winding, bend, brief walk, short excursion; round, circuit, stroll, run, ramble, drive.

5. Successive course, due chance, appropriate time, hand, shift, spell, inning, bout, round, opportunity.

6. Opportune deed, occasional kindness, act, action, deed, office.

7. Convenience, occasion, purpose, exigence.

8. Form, cast, shape, manner, fashion, phase, mould, guise.

9. Form of expression, mode of signifying.

10. Aptitude, talent, bias, proclivity, gift, faculty, bent, tendency, inclination, genius, propensity, proneness.

Turncoat, *n.* Apostate, renegade, backslider, deserter.

Turn in, *v. i.* (*Colloq.*) Retire, go to bed.

Turning, *n.* 1. Winding, bending course, flexure, meander.

2. Deviation from the way, direction.

3. Turnery.

Turning-point, *n.* Crisis, decisive moment, juncture, climacteric.

Turn off, *v. t.* 1. Dismiss, discard, turn away.

2. Deflect, divert.

3. Accomplish, perform, execute, do.

4. Give over, resign.

Turn one's stomach. Nauseate, sicken.

Turn out, *v. t.* 1. Expel, drive out, turn adrift.

2. Put to pasture, put out to pasture.

3. Produce, furnish, manufacture, make, accomplish, do.

——, *v. i.* 1. Bend outward, project.

2. Issue, result, prove, eventuate.

3. Get up, rise from bed.

Turn-out, *n.* 1. Siding, short side-track (*on a railway*), shunt.

2. Equipage.

Turn over, *v. t.* 1. Turn, reverse the position of, roll over.

2. Transfer, hand over.

3. Open and examine page by page.

4. Overset, overturn.

——, *v. i.* Roll over, tumble, turn from side to side.

Turn round. Revolve, whirl, turn.

Turn tail. (*Colloq.*) Flee, run away, make off, cut and run, retreat ignominiously.

Turn the head. Infatuate, make giddy, make insane, make wild, overthrow the judgment of.

Turn the scale. Change the preponderance, give success, give superiority.

Turn the tables. Reverse positions, reverse circumstances.

Turn to. Have recourse to, refer to.

Turn to account. Utilize, take advantage of, make use of.

Turn topsy-turvy. Upset, disorder, confuse.

Turn up. 1. Bend upward.

2. Occur, happen, come to pass.

3. Come to light, transpire.

Turpitude, *n.* Baseness, depravity, wickedness, degradation, vileness.

Turret, *n.* Minaret, pinnacle, small tower, tourelle, cupola.

Turtle, *n.* 1. Turtle-dove, turtle-pigeon.

2. Sea-tortoise, marine tortoise.

Tusk, *n.* Tush, fang, pointed tooth.

Tussle, *n.* Scuffle, struggle, conflict, contest.

Tutelage, *n.* Protection, guardianship, tutorship, teaching.

Tutelar, ⎫ *a.* Protecting, protective, guard-
Tutelary, ⎭ ian, guarding.

Tutor, *n.* 1. (*Law.*) Guardian.

2. Teacher, instructor, master, preceptor, school-master, coach.

——, *v. t.* 1. Teach, instruct, coach.

2. Discipline, train, bring under control, treat with authority.

Twaddle, *n.* Prate, prattle, chatter, tattle, twattle, gabble, gossip, balderdash, moonshine, nonsense, jargon, flummery, rigmarole, gibberish, stuff, platitude, wishwash, senseless talk, idle talk, frothy discourse, twaddling, twaddy.

——, *v. i.* Prate, prattle, maunder, twattle, gabble, chatter.

Twang, *n.* 1. Nasal tone, nasality.

2. Harsh, quick sound; vibrating sound.

——, *v. t.* Twank, twangle.

Tweak, *v. t.* Twitch, twinge, pinch, pull rudely, jerk.

Tweedle, *v. t.* Allure (*by some slight influence as by fiddling*), coax, entice, drib, decoy, toll, troll, lure, lead, draw over, bring over, prevail upon.

Tweezers, *n. pl.* Nippers, pincers.

Twelve, *a.* Dozen, duodecimal, duodenary.

Twice, *adv.* Two times, bis, doubly, once more, over again, encore.

Twiddle, *v. t.* Play with, touch lightly, tweedle, twirl with the fingers, wiggle, fidget, twirl.

Twig, *n.* Shoot, sprig, spray, branch, stem, stick, switch, slip; offshoot.

Twilight, *n.* 1. Crepuscular light, dusk, gloaming, nightfall.

2. Dim light, faint light.

——, *a.* Obscure, dim, shaded, crepuscular.

Twin, *a.* Doubled, geminate, in pairs; double, duplex, twain, fellow, second, like, similar.

Twine, *v. t.* 1. Twist together.

2. Encircle, surround, embrace, entwine, interlace, wind about, wind around, wreathe.

——, *v. i.* 1. Unite closely.

2. Wind, bend, make turns, meander.

3. Twist, ascend in spiral lines, coil.

——, *n.* 1. Twist, convolution, coil.

2. Winding, twining, embrace.

3. Cord, string, small cordage.

Twinge, *v. t.* Tweak, twitch, pinch, pull rudely.

——, *n.* 1. Pinch, tweak, twitch.

2. Gripe, pang, sharp pain.

Twinkle, *v. i.* 1. Blink, wink, twink.

2. Sparkle, flash, scintillate, glimmer.

Twinkling, *n.* 1. Flashing, sparkling, twinkle.

2. Instant, moment, second, jiffy, trice, flash, twinkling of an eye, time of a wink.

Twins, *n. pl.* (*Astron.*) [With *The* prefixed.] Gemini.

Twirl, *v. t.* Whirl, revolve, rotate, turn rapidly, turn round, twist.

——, *n.* Whirling, circular motion, revolution, turn, quick rotation, convolution, twist.

Twist, *v. t.* 1. Twine, twist together, spin, purl, rotate.

2. Writhe, contort, distort, pervert; complicate, convolve, crook spirally, twine, screw, wring, coil.

3. Wind, wreathe, encircle.

4. Form, weave, make up.

5. [*Used reflexively.*] Wind in, insinuate.

TWIST, *n.* Convolution, writhing, contortion, tortion, twirl, winding, flexure, kink, turn, tangle, bending, bight, spiral, coil; cord, thread; distortion, perversion.

Twit, *v. t.* Reproach, blame, upbraid, taunt, fling at.

Twitch, *v. t.* Pull suddenly, snatch, jerk, yerk, pluck.

——, *n.* 1. Jerk, quick pull.

2. Spasm, twitching, quiver, sudden contraction (*as of the muscles*).

Twitter, *v. i.* 1. Chirp, chirrup, peep, cheep.

2. Flutter, be agitated, be flurried, be excited.

3. Titter, giggle.

——, *n.* 1. Twittering, chirping, chirp, chirruping.

2. Trembling, agitation, tremor, flutter.

3. Titter, giggle, half-suppressed laugh.

Twit with. Reproach for, cast in the teeth, fling at.

Two, *n.* 1. Sum of two units.

2. Pair, couple, brace, twain, yoke, couplet; deuce.

Two-faced, *a.* Hypocritical, double-dealing, deceitful, double-faced.

Twofold, *a.* Double, duplicate.

Two-lipped, *a.* (*Bot.*) Bilabiate.

Two-parted, *a.* Bipartite.

Two-ply, *a.* Double.

Two-tongued, *a.* Double-tongued, deceitful.

Two-valved, *a.* Bivalve, bivalvular.

Tyke, *n.* 1. Dog, cur.

2. (*Scot.*) Country bumpkin, rustic, clown, hind, churl.

Tympan, *n.* (*Arch.*) Panel, tympanum.

Type, *n.* 1. Stamp, impressed sign, emblem, mark.

2. Emblem, symbol, sign, token, shadow, ideal, image, representative, representation, adumbration.

3. Original, model, pattern, prototype, standard, archetype, exemplar, protoplast.

4. Stamp, form, kind, sort, nature, character.

5. Printing character; letter, figure, text, typography.

6. Representative, aggregate of characteristic qualities.

Typhoon, *n.* 1. Tornado in the Chinese seas.

2. Simoom.

Typical, *a.* Figurative, emblematical, emblematic, indicative, representative, exemplary, symbolic, true, ideal, model; illustrative, normal, true-to-type.

Typify, *v. t.* Figure, indicate, betoken, denote, represent, stand for, shadow forth, symbolize, exemplify, image, embody, signify.

Typographer, *n.* Printer.

Typography, *n.* Art of printing, printing.

Tyrannical, *a.* 1. Despotic, arbitrary, imperious, domineering, high, absolute, tyrannous, irresponsible, bound by no law.

2. Cruel, severe, oppressive, grinding, galling, inhuman.

Tyrannize, *v. i.* Domineer, act the tyrant, despotize, dictate, be despotic, exercise arbitrary power, lord it, rule with a rod of iron, carry matters with a high hand.

Tyranny, *n.* 1. Despotism, absolutism, dictatorship, arbitrary power, despotic rule, autocracy.

2. Oppression, iron rule, reign of terror, arbitrariness, harshness, cruel government.

Tyrant, *n.* 1. Despot, absolute ruler, autocrat, dictator.

2. Oppressor, cruel master.

Tyro, *n.* 1. Beginner, novice, learner, neophyte.

2. Sciolist, smatterer, dabbler, half-scholar.

U

Ubiquitous, *a.* Omnipresent, ubiquitary, universally present.

Ubiquity, *n.* Omnipresence, universal presence.

Udder, *n.* 1. Bag (*of a cow, etc.*).

2. Teat, dug, nipple, pap.

Udometer, *n.* Rain-gauge, pluviometer, ombrometer.

Ugh, *interj.* Faugh, foh.

Ugliness, *n.* 1. Want of beauty, homeliness, uncomeliness, plainness, unsightliness, deformity; eyesore, blemish, disfigurement.

2. Turpitude, depravity, loathsomeness, wickedness, enormity.

3. Ill-nature, crossness, ill-temper, viciousness, bad temper, spitefulness.

Ugly, *a.* 1. Unsightly, plain, homely, ordinary, unshapely, ill-shapen, crooked, deformed, ill-looking, ill-favored, unprepossessing, uncomely, unlovely, unbeautiful, evil-looking.

2. Frightful, horrible, hideous, horrid, shocking, terrible, grewsome, loathsome, monstrous; forbidding, repellent, repulsive.

3. Cross, ill-tempered, ill-natured, quarrelsome, surly, cantankerous, churlish, cross-grained, spiteful, vicious, bad-tempered.

Ulcer, *n.* Sore (*discharging pus*), fester, imposthume, gathering, boil, pustule.

Ulcerate, *v. i.* Fester, suppurate, turn to an ulcer.

Ulterior, *a.* 1. Beyond, on the farther side, distant, farther, remoter, more distant.

2. Unavowed, indirect, not manifest.

Ultimate, *a.* 1. Last, final, farthest, extreme, eventual, most remote; conclusive.

2. Constituent, incapable of further analysis, elemental.

——, *v. t.* and *v. i.* 1. Eventuate, end, terminate, issue, conclude.

2. Bring into use, carry into practice.

Ultimately, *adv.* Finally, at last, in the end.

Ultima Thule. [L.] Farthest limit.

Ultimatum, *n.* Final condition, final proposition, last offer.

Ultimo. In *or* of last month.

Ultra, *a.* 1. Beyond.

2. Extreme, radical, advanced.

Ultramarine, *a.* Beyond the sea, foreign.

Ultramontane, *a.* Tramontane, beyond the mountains *or* the Alps.

Ultramundane, *a.* Beyond the world, beyond the limits of our world *or* system.

Ululation, *n.* Howl, howling, wailing, cry, crying, yelp, bellowing, hoot.

Umbilical cord. Navel-string.

Umbrage, *n.* 1. Shade, shadow.

2. Offence, resentment, suspicion of injury, dudgeon, pique, grudge.

Umbrageous, *a.* 1. Shading, shady, affording shade.

2. Shady, dark, shadowy, shaded.

UMBRELLA, *n.* Parasol.

Umpire, *n.* Arbitrator, arbiter, referee, judge; linesman.

Unabashed, *a.* Undaunted, bold, brazen, shameless, barefaced, unblushing, undismayed, unflinching, unshrinking.

Unabated, *a.* Undiminished.

Unable, *a.* Incapable, incompetent, impotent, weak, powerless.

Unacceptable, *a.* Unpleasant, disagreeable, displeasing, offensive, unwelcome, unpopular, undesirable, distasteful.

Unaccommodating, *a.* Disobliging, ungracious, unfriendly, noncompliant, uncivil.

Unaccompanied, *a.* Unattended, alone, solitary.

Unaccomplished, *a.* 1. Unfinished, incomplete, unexecuted, unperformed, undone, unachieved.

2. Uncultivated, ill-educated, unpolished.

Unaccountable, *a.* 1. Strange, inexplicable, mysterious, incomprehensible, unintelligible.

2. Irresponsible, unanswerable.

Unaccredited, *a.* Unauthorized.

Unaccustomed, *a.* 1. Unused, uninitiated, unskilled.

2. New, unfamiliar, strange, foreign, unusual, unwonted.

Unacknowledged, *a.* 1. Ignored, unrecognized, unavowed.

2. Unrequited, unthanked.

Unadapted, *a.* Unsuited, unfit.

Unadorned, *a.* Simple, plain, severe, unornamented, unembellished.

Unadulterated, *a.* Unmixed, undiluted, neat, genuine, pure, clear, real, true, sincere, honest.

Unadvisable, *a.* Inexpedient, improper, unfit, unsuitable, objectionable, inappropriate, impolitic, undesirable.

Unadvised, *a.* Imprudent, indiscreet, inconsiderate, rash, thoughtless.

Unaffected, *a.* 1. Simple, plain, natural, artless, ingenuous, honest, *naïve*, sincere, real, genuine, unfeigned.

2. Simple, plain, natural, chaste, pure, unadorned.

3. Unmoved, untouched, insensible, unstirred, unchanged, unimpressed.

Unaided, *a.* Unassisted, unsupported, unseconded, single-handed, alone; helpless.

Unalloyed, *a.* Pure, unmixed, genuine, unadulterated, absolute.

Unalterable, *a.* Unchangeable, immutable, stable, constant.

Unambiguous, *a.* Plain, clear, explicit, certain, unequivocal, perspicuous, intelligible, distinct, unmistakable.

Unamiable, *a.* Unkind, ungracious, ill-natured, ill-tempered, unlovely.

Unanimity, *n.* Agreement, harmony, accord, unison, unity, concert, union, unanimousness.

Unanimous, *a.* Concordant, agreeing, united, harmonious, like-minded, of one mind, consentient; solid.

Unanswerable, *a.* Irrefutable, irrefragable, incontrovertible, unquestionable, incontestable, unconfutable, irresistible, conclusive.

Unanticipated, *a.* Unexpected, sudden, abrupt, startling, unthought of, unlooked for, unforeseen, unhoped for.

Unappalled, *a.* Undismayed, unawed, undaunted, dauntless, unscared, fearless, intrepid, daring, bold, unflinching, resolute.

Unappeasable, *a.* 1. Insatiable, insatiate, that cannot be appeased, inexpiable, inextinguishable.

2. Irreconcilable, implacable.

Unappreciated, *a.* Unvalued, unprized.

Unapprised, *a.* Uninformed, ignorant, unacquainted, unaware.

Unapproachable, *a.* Inaccessible.

Unapt, *a.* 1. Inappropriate, unsuitable, unfit, inapposite, inapplicable, irrelevant.

2. Unqualified, incompetent, inapt, ill-qualified, dull, unskilful.

Unarmed, *a.* Defenceless, naked, unprotected, weaponless, unguarded.

Unassailable, *a.* Impregnable, inexpugnable, invulnerable, secure from assault, not to be taken by assault *or* by storm, tenable against all odds, unassaultable.

Unassorted, *a.* Promiscuous, confused, mingled, mixed, indiscriminate, miscellaneous.

Unassuming, *a.* Modest, humble, unpretending, reserved, unpresuming, unpretentious, unobtrusive, unostentatious.

Unatonable, *a.* Inexpiable, unpardonable, inexcusable, irremissible, that admits of no satisfaction.

Unattainable, *a.* Unobtainable, out of reach, inaccessible, unachievable, unreachable, insuperable.

Unattempted, *a.* Untried, unproved.

Unattended, *a.* Unaccompanied, alone.

Unattended to. Neglected, unheeded, unregarded.

Unattractive, *a.* Unalluring, uninviting, undesirable, uninteresting, without charm.

Unauthentic, *a.* Spurious, counterfeit, supposititious, false, sham, pretended, feigned, fictitious, make-believe, uncanonical.

Unauthorized, *a.* Unwarranted, unjustified, undue, unlicensed, unlawful, lawless, illegal, illegitimate, unsanctioned, unconstitutional.

Unavailing, *a.* Ineffectual, fruitless, useless, bootless, abortive, vain, futile, inept, nugatory, to no purpose, inutile, of no avail, thrown away, unsuccessful.

Unavoidable, *a.* Inevitable, necessary, that must be suffered, certain, ineluctable, unpreventable, irresistible.

Unaware, *a.* Inattentive, heedless, unconscious, ignorant, insensible; unknowing, unwarned, non-expectant.

Unawares, *adv.* Unexpectedly, suddenly, abruptly, without warning.

Unbalanced, *a.* 1. Not poised, not balanced.

2. Unadjusted (*as accounts*), unsettled.

3. Unsteady, unsound, not sane, deranged.

Unbar, *v. t.* Unfasten, open, unclose, unbolt.

Unbearable, *a.* Intolerable, insufferable, unendurable, insupportable, that cannot be borne *or* endured.

Unbecoming, *a.* Indecorous, unsuitable, improper, indecent, unseemly, unbeseeming, unmeet, inappropriate, unfit, unbefitting.

Unbelief, *n.* 1. Incredulity, distrust, miscreance, incredulousness, disbelief, dissent, non-conformity, want of belief, doubt.

2. Scepticism, infidelity, disbelief, freethinking, refusal to believe, heresy.

Unbeliever, *n.* 1. Doubter, incredulous person.

2. Sceptic, infidel, disbeliever, deist, agnostic, heathen, free-thinker.

Unbend, *v. t.* 1. Straighten, make straight.

2. Relax, slacken, remit, recreate, take recreation, be diverted, be amused.

3. (*Naut.*) Unfasten, untie; cast loose.

Unbending, *a.* 1. Inflexible, unyielding, stiff, rigid, unpliant.

2. Unyielding, resolute, rigid, inflexible, firm, obstinate, stubborn.

3. Formal.

Unbiased, *a.* Unprejudiced, impartial, uninfluenced, disinterested, neutral, indifferent, unwarped.

Unbidden, *a.* 1. Unordered, uncommanded.

2. Spontaneous.

3. Uninvited, unasked, unsolicited, unsought.

Unbind, *v. t.* 1. Untie, unloose, loose, unfasten, undo.

2. Unchain, set free, set at liberty, unfetter, release, unshackle.

Unblamable, *a.* Blameless, inculpable, irreprovable, irreprehensible, faultless, unexceptionable, irreproachable, guiltless, innocent.

Unblemished, *a.* Pure, spotless, stainless, sinless, guileless, innocent, faultless, impeccable, intact, perfect, unspotted, immaculate, unsullied, undefiled, untarnished, without a stain.

Unblessed, *a.* Unhappy, wretched, accursed.

Unblushing, *a.* Bold-faced, impudent, shameless, brazen-faced, brazen-browed.

Unbolt, *v. t.* Unbar, undo, unfasten, unlock.

Unborn, *a.* Future, to be born, still to appear; uncreated, unconceived, unbegotten.

Unborrowed, *a.* Native, original, genuine.

Unbosom, *v. t.* Reveal, disclose, open, divulge, unburden, unfold, communicate, lay bare.

Unbought, *a.* 1. Unpurchased.

2. Unpaid, gratuitous.

Unbound, *a.* 1. Untied, unfastened, loose.

2. Without a cover (*as a book*).

3. Untrammelled, uncontrolled, unrestrained, unchecked, unconfined, unrestricted, free.

Unbounded, *a.* 1. Infinite, interminable, unlimited, boundless, immeasurable, vast, endless, immense, measureless, illimitable, absolute.

2. Unrestrained, unrestricted, uncontrolled, unbridled, immoderate.

Unbrace, *v. t.* 1. Loosen, remit.

2. Relax, enervate, enfeeble, weaken, debilitate, prostrate.

Unbridled, *a.* Unrestrained, licentious, reinless, licensed, lax, violent, uncontrolled, ungovernable, unruly, intractable.

Unbroken, *a.* 1. Round, full, complete, entire, even, level, unimpaired, intact.

2. Sound, profound, undisturbed, fast, uninterrupted, continuous, constant, successive.

3. Inviolate, unbetrayed, unviolated.

Unbuckle, *v. t.* Unfasten, loose, unloose.

Unburden, *v. t.* Relieve, unload, rid of a load, free, unencumber.

Unbury, *v. t.* Disinter, disentomb, dig up, exhume, uncharnel.

Uncandid, *a.* Disingenuous, unfair, insincere.

Uncanny, *a.* 1. [*Scotch.*] Unpropitious, unsafe, inopportune.

2. Weird, unnatural, "spooky," unearthly, ghostly, eery.

Uncanonical, *a.* Unauthentic, legendary, apocryphal, of doubtful authority.

Uncared for. Neglected, unattended to, unprovided for, unheeded.

Uncautious, *a.* Incautious, indiscreet, unwary, heedless.

Unceasing, *a.* Incessant, constant, continual, perpetual, uninterrupted, unremitting, unintermitting, unending, endless, eternal.

Unceremonious, *a.* 1. Ungracious, blunt, bluff, abrupt, brusque, curt, gruff, rough, plain, homely, rude, coarse.

2. Informal, familiar, unconstrained, offhand, casual.

Uncertain, *a.* 1. Equivocal, doubtful, dubious, unsettled, indistinct, ambiguous, indeterminate, mistakable, indefinite, questionable.

2. Unreliable, insecure, precarious, problematical.

3. Not sure, not confident, doubtful, dubious.

4. Irregular, unpunctual, capricious, desultory, fitful, variable, changeable, mutable, slippery, shaky, unsettled.

Uncertainty, n. 1. Doubt, dubiousness, incertitude, doubtfulness, ambiguity, obscurity, indecision, hesitation, suspense, indefiniteness, confusion, vagueness, insecurity, precariousness.

2. Contingency.

3. Doubtfulness, dubiousness, doubt.

4. Irregularity, variableness, changeableness, vacillation, wavering, capriciousness.

Unchain, v. t. Unbind, unshackle, set free, liberate, set at liberty.

Unchallenged, a. Undisputed, uncontradicted, unquestioned, uncontroverted.

Unchangeable, a. Changeless, immutable, unalterable, invariable, irrevocable.

Unchanged, a. Unaltered, unvaried.

Unchanging, a. Unvarying.

Uncharitable, a. Harsh, censorious, unkind, illiberal, severe.

Unchaste, a. Dissolute, libidinous, lascivious, licentious, lecherous, incontinent, loose, lewd, indecent, immoral, wanton, obscene.

Unchastity, n. Dissoluteness, libidinousness, incontinence, lewdness, wantonness, lechery.

Unchecked, a. Unrestrained, unhampered, untrammelled, unobstructed, unhindered, unprevented, uncurbed.

Unchristian, a. 1. Infidel, unchristianized.

2. Irreligious, unholy, ungodly, unchristianlike, unkind, uncharitable, unrighteous, evil, wicked, sinful, unbecoming a Christian.

Uncircumspect, a. Imprudent, unguarded, unwary, inconsiderate, careless, heedless, thoughtless, headlong, reckless, indiscreet, incautious, giddy, flighty, unsteady, wild, giddy-brained, hare-brained.

Uncivil, a. Rude, impolite, uncourteous, discourteous, unmannerly, ungentle, unmannered, ungracious, disrespectful, rough, irreverent, blunt, gruff, bearish, ill-mannered, ill-bred, unseemly, uncouth, boorish, clownish, churlish, uncomplaisant, brusque.

Uncivilized, a. Rude, barbarous, savage, barbarian, barbaric, low, heathenish.

Unclean, a. 1. Foul, dirty, filthy, offensive, abominable, beastly, repulsive, purulent, nasty, grimy, lutose, muddy, soiled, miry, grubby, uncleanly.

2. (*Jewish Law.*) Ceremonially impure, needing ritual cleansing, impure.

3. Sinful, morally impure, foul with sin, unholy, polluted, indecent, obscene,

indecorous, gross, lewd, smutty, *risque*, off-color.

Uncleanly, a. 1. Foul, filthy, unclean, dirty, nasty.

2. Unchaste, indecent, impure, obscene.

Uncleanness, n. 1. Foulness, defilement, impurity, dirtiness, filthiness, nastiness, pollution, abomination, uncleanliness, squalor; contamination, dirt, filth.

2. (*Jewish Law.*) Impurity, pollution.

3. Moral impurity, defilement by sin, sinfulness, unholiness, pollution, obscenity, smut.

Unclench, v. t. Unclinch, open.

Unclose, v. t. 1. Open, break the seal of.

2. Open, disclose, lay open.

Unclothed, a. Undressed, uncovered, naked, bare, stark naked, in a state of nature, *in puris naturalibus.*

Unclouded, a. Clear, bright, sunny, cloudless, unobscured.

Uncoil, v. t. Unwind.

Uncolored, a. Colorless, untinged, unstained, hueless, achromatic, free from color.

Uncomfortable, a. 1. Disagreeable, displeasing, distressing, restless, disquieted, disturbed, unpleasant, uneasy.

2. Close (*as the weather*), oppressive.

3. Dismal, miserable, unhappy, cheerless, uneasy.

Uncommon, a. Rare, scarce, unfamiliar, unusual, odd, unwonted, infrequent, strange, queer, singular, remarkable, original, out of the way, exceptional, unexampled, extraordinary, noteworthy.

Uncommonly, adv. Unusually, remarkably, singularly, particularly, peculiarly, notably.

Uncommunicative, a. Reserved, taciturn, close, inconversable, unsociable, reticent, incommunicative, sparing of words, of few words.

Uncompassionate, a. Ruthless, merciless, pitiless, unkind, unfeeling, stony, relentless, fierce, hard-hearted, cruel, unpitying, unmerciful, harsh.

Uncompelled, a. Spontaneous, voluntary, unbidden, unconstrained, willing, gratuitous, free, of one's own accord.

Uncomplaining, a. Patient, long-suffering, meek, tolerant, resigned.

Uncomplaisant, a. Uncivil, disagreeable.

Uncomplimentary, a. Blunt, brusk, frank, candid, plain-spoken, unflattering.

Uncomplying, a. Unbending, unyielding, stubborn, rigid, stiff, inflexible.

Uncompounded, a. Unmixed, incomposite, simple, single.

Uncompromising, *a.* Unyielding, obstinate, inflexible, stiff, rigid, strict, narrow, orthodox.

Unconcealed, *a.* Open, plain, manifest, evident, public, overt, patent, obvious, naked.

Unconcern, *n.* Indifference, carelessness, coolness, nonchalance, *insouciance.*

Unconcerned, *a.* Indifferent, uninterested, careless, cool, unsolicitous, unmoved, apathetic, listless, easy in mind, nonchalant.

Unconditional, *a.* 1. Unrestricted, unlimited, free, complete, absolute, unqualified, unreserved, full, entire, positive, categorical.

2. (*Log.*) Categorical, positive, explicit, non-hypothetical.

Unconditioned, *a.* 1. Not conditioned.

2. Infinite, inconceivable, incogitable.

Unconfined, *a.* Unrestrained, uncontrolled, unenclosed, unrestricted, free, unchecked, unhampered, unbridled, unbound, untrammelled.

Unconformable, *a.* Irregular, dissimilar, unlike, incongruous, aberrant, exceptional, erratic, abnormal, exceptionable, anomalous, heterogeneous.

Uncongenial, *a.* Unharmonious, ill-assorted, unsuited, discordant, unsympathetic, antagonistic, mismatched, incompatible, displeasing.

Unconnected, *a.* Disconnected, inconsequent, disjoint, irrelevant, unrelated, illogical, inconsequent.

Unconquerable, *a.* Invincible, indomitable, irresistible, resistless, impregnable, insuperable, insurmountable.

Unconscionable, *a.* 1. Unreasonable, inordinate, excessive, exorbitant, extravagant, preposterous.

2. Enormous, vast, immense, monstrous, prodigious.

Unconscious, *a.* 1. Insensible, senseless, brute.

2. Imperceptible, imperceivable.

3. Ignorant, unaware, uninformed, incognizant.

4. Artless, natural, ingenuous, simple, *naïve.*

Unconsciously, *adv.* Unwittingly, ignorantly.

Unconsciousness, *n.* 1. Insensibility, senselessness.

2. Ignorance.

3. Artlessness, ingenuousness, absence of consciousness, simplicity.

Unconstitutional, *a.* Illegal, unwarrantable, unauthorized by the constitution, unlawful.

Unconstrained, *a.* 1. Uncompelled, unforced.

2. Free, easy, natural, spontaneous, voluntary.

Uncontrollable, *a.* Ungovernable, incontrollable, unrestrainable, wild, rampageous, irrepressible, rampant, headstrong, violent, unruly, unmanageable.

Unconventional, *a.* Informal, unorthodox, unusual, peculiar, odd, lawless, eccentric, untrained, original, erratic.

Unconversable, *a.* See UNCOMMUNICATIVE.

Unconvincing, *a.* Inconclusive, indecisive, weak.

Uncooked, *a.* Raw.

Uncorrupt, *a.* Upright, honest, true, virtuous, innocent, honorable, impartial, even-handed, straightforward.

Uncourteous, *a.* Impolite, uncivil, disrespectful, unmannerly, rude, uncourtly, discourteous, inurbane, bearish, ill-mannered, ill-bred, ill-behaved.

Uncourtly, *a.* 1. Rustic, awkward, unrefined, homely, homespun, provincial, inelegant, countrified, unpolished.

2. See UNCOURTEOUS.

Uncouth, *a.* 1. Rustic, awkward, boorish, clownish, loutish, clumsy, unseemly, unrefined, unpolished, uncourtly, lubberly, rude, rough, gawky, inelegant, ungainly.

2. Unfamiliar, unusual, strange, odd, outlandish.

Uncover, *v. t.* 1. Strip, lay bare, lay open, divest of covering, denude.

2. Disclose, reveal, discover, unmask, expose, unfold, unveil.

3. Bare, take the cover off, doff.

4. Open, unclose, unseal.

——, *v. i.* Take off the hat (*in token of respect*), bare the head.

Uncrown, *v. t.* Discrown, dethrone, depose.

Unction, *n.* 1. Anointing, aneling, smearing, rubbing.

2. (*Rare.*) Unguent, ointment.

3. Fervor, warmth, ardor, fervency, earnestness, passion, enthusiasm, power, force, spirit, gusto, energy, *verve,* zest, emotion, devotional feeling.

Unctuous, *a.* 1. Greasy, oily, fatty, fat, oleaginous, adipose, adipous, sebaceous, pinguid, butyraceous, unguinous.

2. Smooth, bland, slippery, lubric, lubricous.

3. (*In a bad or offensive sense.*) Smooth, bland, suave, over-complaisant, oily, plausible, smooth-spoken, glib, sycophantic, sycophantish, parasitic, obsequious, adulatory, fawning, servile.

4. (*Also in a bad sense.*) Fervid, over-fervid, full of unction, gushing, of affected warmth.

Unctuousness, *n.* 1. Oiliness, greasiness, fatness, unctuosity, fattiness.

2. Oiliness, smoothness, fulsomeness, suavity, blandness, complaisance.

Uncultivable, *a.* Sterile, barren, uncultivatable.

Uncultivated, *a.* 1. Untilled, uncultured, wild, unreclaimed, fallow.

2. Rude, uncivilized, unlettered, illiterate, unfit, unready, untaught, unread, ignorant, unpolished, uneducated, uncultured, unrefined, homely.

3. Wild, savage, rough, sylvan, uncouth.

Undamaged, *a.* Uninjured, unhurt, unimpaired.

Undaunted, *a.* Bold, intrepid, fearless, brave, plucky, courageous, resolute, undismayed, unterrified, unappalled, unawed, dauntless.

Undebased, *a.* Unadulterated, pure, unalloyed.

Undecaying, *a.* Enduring, unfading, lasting, undying, amaranthine, imperishable, perennial, immortal, ever-vernal, ever-blooming.

Undeceive, *v. t.* Set right, correct, open the eyes of, disabuse, free from mistake, disengage from fallacy, disillusion.

Undecided, *a.* 1. Undetermined, unsettled, pending, in suspense, open, drawn; tentative, problematical.

2. Uncertain, irresolute, undetermined, unresolved, doubtful, dubious.

Undecipherable, *a.* Illegible, indistinct, puzzling, unintelligible.

Undeclared, *a.* Tacit, implied, silent, understood, unproclaimed.

Undefended, *a.* Unprotected, unguarded, naked, guardless, exposed.

Undefiled, *a.* 1. Pure, spotless, stainless, unblemished, unspotted, unsullied, immaculate, untarnished, without a stain, clean.

2. Innocent, pure, stainless, inviolate, unstained, clean, unblemished, uncorrupted, unpolluted, unspotted, honest, honorable, unsullied.

Undefined, *a.* 1. Unbounded, limitless, boundless.

2. Indistinct, indeterminate, indefinite.

Undemonstrative, *a.* Reserved, quiet, modest, impassive, tranquil, staid, sober, demure, sedate, placid, calm, composed.

Undeniable, *a.* Indisputable, indubitable, incontrovertible, unquestionable, incontestable, irrefutable, irrefragable, evident, obvious, beyond all question, beyond a doubt, past dispute, unimpeachable, conclusive, certain.

UNDER, *prep.* 1. Beneath, below, underneath.

2. Subordinate to, subject to, in subordination to.

3. In a less degree than.

4. For that which is less than.

5. Below, less than, with less than.

6. By means of.

7. Inferior to, in a state of inferiority to.

8. While burdened with, under the load of.

9. When exposed to, while suffering.

10. In a state of being liable to, subject to.

11. In, in the state *or* condition of.

12. Attested by, authorized by, signed by.

13. Subjected to, being the subject of.

14. Not having reached *or* arrived at.

——, *a.* Lower in rank *or* degree, subject, subordinate, inferior, in a lower position.

——, *adv.* In subjection.

Underbred, *a.* Unmannerly, uncivil.

Underbrush, *n.* Undergrowth, underwood, thicket, brake, coppice, scrub, brushwood.

Underdone, *a.* Rare, done *or* cooked rare, moderately cooked.

Underestimate, *v. t.* Undervalue, underrate, underprize, belittle, "knock," " run down," make light of, minimize, set little store by, misprize, rate below the true value, rate too low.

Undergo, *v. t.* Bear, suffer, endure, sustain, experience, pass through, go through, meet with, be exposed to, be subjected to, spend.

Underground, *a.* Subterranean, subterraneous.

Undergrowth, *n.* See UNDERBRUSH.

Underhand, *adv.* 1. Secretly, privately, clandestinely, underhandedly, in a clandestine manner, by secret means, slyly, surreptitiously, unfairly, stealthily.

2. Fraudulently, by fraudulent means, surreptitiously, unfairly.

——, *a.* Secret, sly, clandestine, hidden, stealthy, deceitful, disingenuous, unfair, fraudulent, underhanded, surreptitious.

Underived, *a.* 1. Original, primeval, aboriginal, primary, first.

2. Radical, primitive.

Underlet, *v. t.* Sublet, let *or* lease at second hand.

Underlie, *v. t.* 1. Lie under, rest beneath, be situated under.

2. Support, be at the basis of.

Underline, *v. t.* Underscore, draw a line under.

Underling, *n.* Understrapper, fag, servant, inferior agent, subordinate.

Undermine, *v. t.* 1. Sap, mine, excavate, tunnel.

2. Ruin secretly, sap the foundations of, underwork, demoralize, weaken; frustrate, thwart, foil.

Undermost, *a.* Lowest, bottom.

Underneath, *prep.* Under, beneath, below.

——, *adv.* Below, under, beneath.

Underplot, *n.* 1. Subordinate plot.

2. Secret plot, clandestine scheme.

Underprop, *v. t.* Support, uphold, sustain.

Underrate, *v. t.* See UNDERESTIMATE.

Underscore, *v. t.* Underline, draw a line under.

Undersell, *v. t.* Sell cheaper than.

Undersign, *v. t.* Subscribe, underwrite.

Undersized, *a.* Small, dwarfish, little, diminutive, stunted, scrub, undergrown.

Undersoil, *n.* Subsoil.

Understand, *v. t.* 1. Apprehend, conceive, perceive, know, penetrate, discern, see, comprehend, catch, grasp, seize, have knowledge of, see through, realize, sense, "twig," "tumble to," get to the bottom of, fathom, make out.

2. Be informed, be apprised, learn.

3. Interpret, take, suppose to mean, assume.

4. Mean, imply.

——, *v. i.* 1. Be an intelligent being, have understanding.

2. Learn, hear, be apprised, be informed.

Understanding, *n.* 1. Intellect, mind, reason, sense, brains, thinking principle, reasoning faculty, rational faculty, discursive faculty, intellectual powers, intellectual faculties.

2. Intelligence, apprehension, comprehension, perception, knowledge, discernment, judgment, sense, conception, "head," insight, penetration, notion, idea.

3. Agreement, accord, unanimity.

Understandingly, *adv.* Intelligibly, intelligently, with full knowledge, with the eyes open.

Understrapper, *n.* See UNDERLING.

Undertake, *v. t.* Attempt, set about, engage in, take up, assume, begin, embark in, enter upon, take in hand, take upon one's self, take on one's shoulders.

——, *v. i.* Engage, agree, guarantee, contract, covenant, stipulate, bargain, promise, be bound, be sworn, pledge one's self, pledge one's word, plight one's word, pass one's word, take upon one's self.

Undertaking, *n.* Enterprise, emprise, venture, task, move, business, affair, project, engagement, essay, attempt, adventure, endeavor, effort.

Under the weather. Ill, sick, unwell, indisposed, ailing, out of sorts, on the sick list, laid on the shelf.

Undervalue, *v. t.* 1. Underrate, misprize, rate below the true value, rate too low.

2. Despise, depreciate, esteem lightly, underestimate, make light of, minimize, hold in low estimation.

Underwood, *n.* See UNDERBRUSH.

Underwrite, *v. t.* 1. Subscribe, undersign.

2. Insure.

Underwriter, *n.* Insurer.

Undeserved, *a.* Unmerited, not deserved.

Undesigned, *a.* Unintentional, unintended, unpremeditated.

Undesigning, *a.* Sincere, upright, artless, simple, straightforward, unsophisticated, ingenuous, guileless.

Undesirable, *a.* 1. Inexpedient, inadvisable.

2. Unwelcome, distasteful, disliked, unpleasant, objectionable, unacceptable, unsatisfactory.

Undetermined, *a.* 1. Unsettled, undecided, uncertain, problematical.

2. Wavering, hesitating, irresolute.

3. Unbounded, undefined, unlimited, indeterminate.

Undeveloped, *a.* Latent, in embryo, primordial, rudimentary, embryonic, immature, "half-baked."

Undeviating, *a.* 1. Straight, straightforward, unchanging, direct, unswerving.

2. Steady, regular, steadfast, constant.

Undigested, *a.* Crude, raw.

Undignified, *a.* 1. Unbecoming, unbefitting, unseemly, indecorous, ungentlemanly, unladylike, ill-bred.

2. Without dignity.

Undiminished, *a.* Unlessened, unimpaired, unabated.

Undimmed, *a.* Clear, bright.

Undiscernible, *a.* Invisible, imperceptible, undiscoverable, indiscernible.

Undiscerning, *a.* 1. Blind, purblind.

2. Stupid, dull, unintelligent, unenlightened, unattentive, unheeding.

Undisciplined, *a.* 1. Untrained, unpractised, undrilled, inexperienced, raw.

2. Untrained, untaught, unschooled, untutored, uninstructed.

Undiscouraged, *a.* Undismayed, undispirited, undisheartened.

Undiscoverable, *a.* 1. See UNDISCERNIBLE.

2. Inscrutable, unsearchable, hidden, unfathomable, unknowable, occult, mysterious, past *or* above comprehension.

Undisguised, *a.* Open, ingenuous, unreserved, plain, frank, sincere, honest, true, genuine, real, pure, unadulterated.

Undismayed, *a.* Undaunted, unawed, unappalled, fearless, bold, courageous, brave, intrepid.

Undissembling, *a.* Sincere, honest, ingenuous, artless, guileless, open, frank, candid, hearty, straightforward, open-hearted, unaffected.

Undistinguishable, *a.* Indistinct, indeterminate, confused, indistinguishable, that cannot be distinguished.

Undisturbed, *a.* Calm, placid, quiet, tranquil, serene, peaceful, unmoved, unruffled, composed, unmolested, unagitated, motionless.

Undivided, *a.* 1. Whole, entire, complete, intact.

2. United, one.

Undo, *v. t.* 1. Annul, invalidate, reverse, neutralize, nullify, frustrate, bring to naught, cancel, offset.

2. Loose, unfasten, untie, disengage, open, unfold, disentangle, unravel, unmake.

3. Ruin, destroy, crush, overturn.

4. Impoverish, bring to poverty.

Undoing, *n.* Ruin, destruction.

Undomesticated, *a.* Wild, not tame.

Undoubted, *a.* Indisputable, indubitable, undisputed, incontrovertible, unquestionable, unquestioned.

Undoubting, *a.* Sure, confident.

Undress, *v. t.* Disrobe, dismantle, denude, unclothe, unrobe, strip, peel, divest of clothes.

——, *n.* Dishabille, loose dress, ordinary dress, disarray, negligée, mufti.

Undrilled, *a.* Untrained, unpractised, undisciplined, unschooled, inexperienced.

Undue, *a.* 1. Improper, illegitimate, unsanctioned, illegal, unlawful.

2. Unsuitable, improper, excessive, extreme, inordinate, immoderate, disproportioned.

3. Unfit, unsuitable.

Undulate, *v. i.* Wave, fluctuate, move up and down, billow, ripple, roll, pulsate.

Undulating, *a.* Waving, wavy, undulatory, rolling.

Undulation, *n.* Wave, fluctuation, ripple, rimple, billowing, pulsation, wave-like motion.

Unduly, *adv.* Excessively, in an undue manner, improperly.

Undutiful, *a.* Disobedient, unfilial, disloyal, disrespectful, remiss, unfaithful, unworthy.

Undying, *a.* Deathless, imperishable, immortal, never-dying, ever-living, endless.

Unearth, *v. t.* 1. Uncover, draw from the earth, exhume, disinter.

2. Bring to light, disclose, discover, expose, bring out from concealment, ferret out, find out, draw out.

3. Extirpate, uproot, eradicate.

Unearthly, *a.* Supernatural, preternatural, weird, uncanny.

Uneasiness, *n.* Disquiet, restlessness, inquietude, anxiety, disquietude, perturbation, trouble, perplexity.

Uneasy, *a.* 1. Restless, restive, unquiet, disquieted, worried, perturbed, discomposed, troubled, disturbed, impatient, ill at ease, fidgety, twitchy.

2. Constrained, stiff, awkward, ungraceful, ungainly.

3. Disagreeable, unpleasing, constraining, cramping, uncomfortable.

Uneducated, *a.* Illiterate, unlettered, unlearned, unschooled, untrained, untaught, uncultivated, uninstructed, unenlightened, ignorant, rude, uninformed.

Unembarrassed, *a.* 1. Unencumbered, unburdened, untrammelled.

2. Easy, unconstrained, *dégagé.*

Unemployed, *a.* 1. Unoccupied, doing nothing, disengaged, out of employment, loafing, resting, idle, unexercised, unapplied.

2. Disused.

Unending, *a.* Everlasting, ever-enduring, eternal, perpetual, endless, sempiternal, unceasing, interminable, ceaseless, never-ending.

Unendurable, *a.* Insufferable, intolerable, insupportable, unbearable.

Unenviable, *a.* Undesirable, disagreeable, unpleasant.

Unequal, *a.* 1. Uneven, not alike.

2. Inferior.

3. Disproportioned, ill-matched, disparate, inadequative.

4. Irregular, not equable, not uniform, rough.

5. Inadequate, insufficient.

6. (*Bot.*) Inequilateral.

Unequaled, *a.* Unmatched, matchless, unparalleled, unexampled, unparagoned, peerless, unapproached, unsurpassed, unrivalled, exceeding, surpassing, nonpareil, superlative, transcendent, unique, incomparable, inimitable, paramount, preeminent.

Unequivocal, *a.* 1. Indubitable, incontestable, clear, plain, evident, certain, positive, definite, absolute.

2. Unmistakable, unambiguous, explicit.

Unerring, *a.* 1. Infallible, incapable of error.

2. Certain, sure, exact, accurate, dead.

Unessential, *a.* Unimportant; meaningless, irrelevant, inapposite; immaterial, non-essential, of no account, of no consequence, of no moment, unnecessary, dispensable; secondary, accessory.

Uneven, *a.* 1. Rough, ragged, jagged, rugged, lumpy, stony, hilly, etc.

2. Unequal, variable, variegated, motley.

3. Odd, not exactly divisible by 2.

Uneventful, *a.* Quiet, commonplace, uninteresting, uncheckered, dull, monotonous, smooth, humdrum, eventless.

Unexampled, *a.* Unprecedented, unparalleled.

Unexcelled, *a.* Unsurpassed, unrivalled.

Unexceptionable, *a.* Unobjectionable, good, excellent, faultless, irreproachable.

Unexpected, *a.* Sudden, abrupt, unanticipated, unlooked for, unthought of, unforeseen.

Unexpensive, *a.* Cheap, moderate, low-priced, inexpensive.

Unexperienced, *a.* Inexperienced, unpractised, untrained, unschooled, uninitiated, raw, unversed, undisciplined, unskilled, green, without experience.

Unexpressive, *a.* Inexpressive, characterless, blank, unmeaning.

Unfading, *a.* Perennial, undecaying, lasting, fresh, fast, permanent, enduring, amaranthine.

Unfailing, *a.* Inexhaustible, exhaustless, certain, reliable, infallible, constant, never-failing.

Unfair, *a.* Unjust, inequitable, partial, dishonest, dishonorable, disingenuous, one-sided, unequal, insincere, uncandid, false, hypocritical, faithless, oblique, truthless.

Unfaithful, *a.* 1. Faithless, treacherous, dishonest, perfidious, unreliable, derelict, false, deceitful, disloyal, recreant, treasonable, undutiful, false-hearted, untrustworthy.

2. Negligent, careless, untrustworthy, unreliable.

3. Fickle, untrue, inconstant, changeable, faithless.

Unfaltering, *a.* Firm, resolute, steadfast, determined, unwavering, unhesitating, unswerving, steady.

Unfamiliar, *a.* 1. Unusual, uncommon, strange, novel, new, bizarre, outlandish, foreign, new-fangled, singular, queer, unheard of, out of the way.

2. Unaccustomed, unacquainted, inconversant.

Unfashionable, *a.* Obsolete, disused, antiquated, old-fashioned, out of use, out of fashion, out of date, fallen into desuetude; unconventional, unmodish.

Unfasten, *v. t.* Loose, unloose, untie, unbind, unclasp, unlace, undo, unfix, etc.; liberate, set loose.

Unfathomable, *a.* 1. Fathomless, bottomless, unplumbed, soundless, very deep, very profound, abysmal.

2. Inscrutable, unsearchable, impenetrable, mysterious, unintelligible, inexplicable.

Unfavorable, *a.* 1. Adverse, contrary, indisposed, malign, sinister, disadvantageous, untimely, inopportune, unpropitious, unfriendly, inauspicious, discouraging, inimical, ill, unlucky.

2. Inclement, foul.

Unfeasible, *a.* Impracticable, infeasible, that cannot be accomplished *or* done.

Unfeathered, *a.* Unfledged, callow.

Unfeeling, *a.* 1. Insensible, unconscious, torpid, numb, apathetic, callous, insensate, without sensibility, obdurate, unimpressionable, heartless.

2. Cruel, unkind, unsympathizing, unsympathetic, hard, hard-hearted, cold-blooded, cold-hearted, merciless, pitiless, unmerciful, inhuman, stony, adamantine, insensate.

Unfeigned, *a.* Real, sincere, sterling, true, undisguised, genuine, unaffected, honest.

Unfeminine, *a.* 1. Unwomanly, mannish, bold.

2. Unwomanly, indelicate, rude, coarse.

Unfetter, *v. t.* Unshackle, unbind, set free, loose, set at liberty, extricate, disengage.

Unfettered, *a.* Free, unrestrained, unshackled, untrammelled.

Unfilial, *a.* Undutiful, disobedient, ungrateful.

Unfinished, *a.* 1. Incomplete, unexecuted, unaccomplished, unperformed.

2. Imperfect, sketchy, raw; inelegant.

Unfit, *a.* 1. Not fit, not in suitable condition, unready, unripe.

2. Inapposite, inapt, unsuitable, inappropriate, irrelevant.

3. Improper, unbecoming, unbefitting, objectionable, unseemly, unsuitable.

4. Unqualified, incapable, unequal, inefficient, inexpert, incompetent.

——, *v. t.* Disqualify, make unfit, incapacitate, disable.

Unfix, *v. t.* 1. Unsettle, unhinge, detach.

2. Loosen, take off, undo.

Unflagging, *a.* Untiring, unremitting, unwearied, indefatigable, persevering, undrooping, never-tiring, unfaltering, constant, steady.

Unflattering, *a.* Frank, candid, uncomplimentary, blunt, plain-speaking, brusque.

Unfledged, *a.* 1. Unfeathered, callow.

2. Inexperienced, raw, green, untried.

Unflinching, *a.* Resolute, firm, steady, unshrinking.

Unfold, *v. t.* 1. Expand, open, unroll, spread out, display, unfurl, separate.

2. Reveal, disclose, declare, divulge, tell.

3. Decipher, unravel, unriddle, explain, develop, resolve, disentangle, interpret, evolve, illustrate, make known, set forth, make clear.

4. Display, spread out, set to view.

5. Release, dismiss from a fold.

Unforced, *a.* 1. Willing, unconstrained, uncompelled.

2. Free, unurged, nothing loath.

3. Natural, unfeigned, spontaneous.

4. Easy, ready, voluntary, willing.

Unforeseen, *a.* Unexpected, unlooked for, unanticipated.

Unforgiving, *a.* Implacable, inexorable, relentless, hard, stony-hearted, unrelenting, unappeasable, merciless, pitiless, rancorous.

Unforgotten, *a.* Remembered, recollected, cherished in the memory.

Unformed, *a.* Shapeless, unfashioned, unshaped.

Unfortunate, *a.* 1. Unsuccessful, unprosperous, unhappy, unlucky, luckless, ill-fated, ill-starred, hapless.

2. Disastrous, calamitous, unhappy, deplorable.

3. Infelicitous, inappropriate, inopportune, inexpedient.

Unfounded, *a.* 1. Unestablished, unbuilt, unproven.

2. Baseless, idle, vain, groundless, false, erroneous, untrue, ungrounded, unsubstantial.

Unfrequent, *a.* Uncommon, rare, infrequent.

Unfrequented, *a.* Uninhabited, unoccupied, deserted, lone, lonely, abandoned, forsaken, solitary, rarely visited.

Unfriended, *a.* Friendless, forlorn, solitary, desolate.

Unfriendliness, *n.* Disfavor, unkindness.

Unfriendly, *a.* Unkind, hostile, inimical, enemy, malevolent, antagonistic, opposed, adverse, ill-disposed, unfavorable.

Unfruitful, *a.* 1. Barren, fruitless, acarpous, sterile.

2. Barren, unprolific, sterile, infecund.

3. Fruitless, unprofitable, unproductive, barren.

4. Unproductive, barren, unprolific, sterile, unfertile, fruitless.

Unfulfilled, *a.* Unaccomplished, unperformed, neglected, unobserved, unredeemed.

Unfurl, *v. t.* Open, display, spread out, give to the breeze, expand, unfold.

Unfurnished, *a.* Empty, bare, unsupplied, unequipped, ungarnished.

Ungainly, *a.* Clumsy, awkward, uncouth, uncourtly, inelegant, clownish, boorish, gawky, loutish, lubberly, lumbering, slouching, ungraceful, stiff.

Ungallant, *a.* Unchivalrous, ungentle, ungracious, uncourtly, unhandsome, churlish.

Ungenerous, *a.* 1. Illiberal, stingy, mean, shabby, close, miserly, sordid, selfish.

2. Ignoble, ignominious, unkind, base, churlish.

Ungentle, *a.* Harsh, rude, impolite, uncourteous, uncivil.

Ungentlemanly, *a.* Uncivil, impolite, uncourteous, discourteous, rude, rough, coarse, bearish, boorish, ungentle, illbred, ill-mannered, unmannerly, churlish.

Ungodly, *a.* 1. Wicked, impious, sinful, unrighteous, godless, profane, reprobate.

2. Unhallowed, unsanctified, unholy, polluted.

Ungovernable, *a.* Unruly, refractory, uncontrollable, intractable, unmanageable, irrepressible, rebellious, mutinous, wild, unbridled, rampant, headstrong, infuriate, mad, frantic, furious, violent, impetuous, vehement.

Ungoverned, *a.* 1. Without government.

2. Uncontrolled, unbridled, uncurbed, licentious.

Ungraceful, *a.* Stiff, constrained, awkward, graceless, clumsy, inelegant, ungainly, uncouth, gawky.

Ungracious, *a.* 1. Uncivil, unkind, impolite, unmannerly, rude, rough, unfriendly, disobliging, churlish, unamiable.

2. Unpleasing, disagreeable, ungrateful, offensive, unacceptable, unpleasant, thankless.

Ungrammatical, *a.* Incorrect, inaccurate, faulty, unidiomatic, without regard to the rules of grammar.

Ungrateful, *a.* 1. Unthankful, thankless, ingrate, without gratitude.

2. Unpleasing, offensive, disagreeable, unacceptable, unwelcome, thankless.

Ungratefulness, *n.* 1. Ingratitude, unthankfulness, thanklessness.

2. Unacceptableness, disagreeableness.

Ungrounded, *a.* Unfounded, baseless, without foundation, groundless.

Ungrudgingly, *adv.* Heartily, cheerfully, willingly, freely, generously, unsparingly.

Ungual, *a.* Ungueal, unguical, unguicular.

Unguarded, *a.* 1. Undefended, unprotected, unwatched, uncared for, defenceless, naked.

2. Careless, incautious, thoughtless.

Unguent, *n.* Ointment, unction, *unguentum*.

Unguinous, *a.* Oily, unctuous, oleaginous, fat.

Ungulate, *a.* Hoof-shaped; hoof-bearing.

Unhackneyed, *a.* Fresh, new, recent, novel.

Unhallowed, *a.* Unsanctified, unholy, profane, impure, polluted, wicked.

Unhandsome, *a.* 1. Plain, ugly, ill-looking, uncomely, homely.

2. Unbecoming, unsuitable, ungraceful, undignified.

3. Unfair, illiberal, disingenuous, ungenerous.

4. Uncivil, impolite, churlish.

Unhandy, *a.* 1. Awkward, unskilful, clumsy, bungling, maladroit, inexpert, inapt, *gauche*.

2. Inconvenient, uncomfortable, awkward.

Unhappily, *adv.* 1. Unfortunately, unluckily, as luck would have it.

2. Miserably, wretchedly, calamitously.

Unhappiness, *n.* 1. Wretchedness, misery, distress, affliction, woe, infelicity.

2. Misfortune, calamity, disaster.

Unhappy, *a.* 1. Unfortunate, unlucky, infelicitous.

2. Wretched, miserable, distressed, afflicted, disconsolate, comfortless, dejected, sad, sorrowful, heart-sick.

3. Grievous, disastrous, calamitous, severe, joyless, dismal, trying, painful, unfortunate, unlucky, sad, afflicting, afflictive, distressing, deplorable, dire.

4. Unpropitious, infelicitous, unblest, unlucky, malign, inauspicious, sinister, evil.

Unharmed, *a.* Uninjured, unhurt, unscathed, scatheless, scot-free, immune, undamaged.

Unharmonious, *a.* 1. Discordant, dissonant, unmusical, inharmonic, inharmonical, inharmonious, out of tune.

2. Discordant, dissonant, disagreeing, at variance.

Unhealthy, *a.* 1. Unsound, diseased, ailing, sickly, out of health, valetudinary, valetudinarian.

2. Unsound, diseased, sickly, ailing, unwell, "poorly," "seedy," indisposed, infirm, feeble, weak.

3. Unwholesome, insalubrious, deleterious, poisonous, morbific, unhealthful, noxious, unsanitary, noisome, pestiferous, pestilential, toxic, septic, venomous, unfavorable to health.

4. Morbid, indicative of disease.

Unheard of. 1. Obscure, unknown to fame, hidden, concealed.

2. Novel, unexampled, unprecedented, unusual, uncommon, exceptional, abnormal, unwonted, improbable, unbelievable, inconceivable, singular, surprising, out of the way, strange.

Unheeded, *a.* Disregarded, unnoticed, ignored, unobserved, unregarded, overlooked, neglected.

Unheedful, *a.* Careless, negligent, disregardful.

Unheeding, *a.* Careless, heedless, unmindful, regardless.

Unhelped, *a.* Unaided, unassisted.

Unhesitating, *a.* Prompt, ready, immediate, forthright.

Unhindered, *a.* Unobstructed, unimpeded, unchecked.

Unhinge, *v. t.* 1. Remove from the hinges.

2. Disorder, confuse, derange, unsettle, shatter.

3. Displace, unfix, upset, unbalance.

Unhitch, *v. t.* Unfasten, loose.

Unholy, *a.* 1. Unhallowed, unsanctified, profane, ungodly.

2. Undevout, irreligious, ungodly, impious, irreverent, wicked, sinful, profane, evil.

Unhonored, *a.* Inglorious, renownless.

Unhorse, *v. t.* Dismount, throw from a horse, buck.

Unhurt, *a.* Uninjured, unharmed, safe and sound, safe.

Unideal, *a.* Real, actual, material, substantial.

Unification, *n.* Union, junction (*so as to become one*), incorporation.

Uniflorous, *a.* (*Bot.*) One-flowered.

Unifoliate, *a.* (*Bot.*) One-leaved.

Uniform, *a.* 1. Undeviating, unvarying, unvaried, unchanged, regular, constant, steady, even, smooth, unbroken, undiversified, equable, alike.

2. Consonant, consistent, monotonous, stable.

Uniformity, *n.* 1. Sameness, regularity, uniformness, even tenor, constancy, evenness, stability, permanence, continuity.

2. Consonance, conformity, unanimity, accordance, agreement, consistency.

3. Similitude between the parts of a whole, homogeneity.

4. Continued sameness, unvaried likeness, monotony, routine.

Unify, *v. t.* Cause to be one, make into a unit, unite, view as one.

Unilluminated, *a.* Unenlightened, obscure, dark, rayless, darksome, dusky, gloomy, sombre, lurid, shadowy, dim, murky, shady, sunless, dismal.

Unimaginable, *a.* Inconceivable, that cannot be imagined *or* conceived, impossible, unthinkable.

Unimaginative, *a.* Literal, practical, unpoetical, unromantic, prosaic, matter-of-fact, pedestrian.

Unimpaired, *a.* Uninjured, undiminished.

Unimpassioned, *a.* Calm, cool, cold, tranquil, quiet, dispassionate, passionless, unemotional, impassive, sober, placid.

Unimpeachable, *a.* Blameless, unexceptionable, irreproachable, irreprehensible, unchallengeable.

Unimportant, *a.* Insignificant, inconsequent, inconsequential, trivial, trifling, inconsiderable, small, slight, petty, paltry, of no consequence, of no moment, immaterial, non-essential, unessential, inappreciable, mediocre, fair, indifferent, minor.

Unimposing, *a.* Unimpressive, ineffective, nugatory.

Unimpressible, *a.* Unsusceptible, impassive, impassible, passionless, apathetic, phlegmatic, stoical, Platonic, cold, tame, obtuse, torpid, callous, dead, cold-blooded, without sensibility, destitute of feeling.

Unimproved, *a.* 1. Untaught, untutored, unenlightened, uneducated, undeveloped.

2. Unused, unemployed.

3. Uncultivated, untilled, unoccupied.

Unincumbered, *a.* Unburdened, untrammelled.

Uninfluenced, *a.* Unmoved, untouched, unaffected, impartial, unbiased, unswayed, unprejudiced.

Uninformed, *a.* Uninstructed, unenlightened, ignorant, unapprised.

Uninhabited, *a.* Deserted, unfrequented, solitary, lone, secluded, without inhabitants, abandoned, desolate, lifeless, unsettled, unpeopled, untenanted, waste, forsaken.

Uninitiated, *a.* See UNINFORMED.

Uninjured, *a.* Unharmed, unhurt, undamaged, whole, unimpaired, sound.

Uninspired, *a.* Unstirred, unmoved, untouched, unaffected, uninfluenced.

Uninstructed, *a.* Untaught, unenlightened, uneducated, uninformed, ignorant.

Unintellectual, *a.* Stupid, dull, obtuse, stolid, doltish, blockish, stockish, heavy, shallow, foolish, simple, soft, sappy, unintelligent, dull-witted, blunt-witted, weak-minded, feeble-minded, half-witted, shallow-brained.

Unintelligent, *a.* Stupid, dull, obtuse, unintellectual, unenlightened.

Unintelligible, *a.* Incomprehensible, meaningless, illegible, undecipherable, mumbled, confused, puzzling, enigmatic, insoluble, intricate, inexplicable, inscrutable, baffling.

Unintentional, *a.* Undesigned, unpurposed, unmeant, inadvertent, unthinking, unpremeditated, involuntary, spontaneous, accidental, fortuitous, casual.

Uninteresting, *a.* Dull, tiresome, tedious, wearisome, wearying, stupid, dry, dreary, jejune, flat, featureless.

Uninterrupted, *a.* Incessant, unceasing, unintermitted, continual, constant, perpetual, unbroken, continuous, solid.

Uninvited, *a.* Unbidden, unasked, uncalled for.

Uninviting, *a.* Unattractive, unpleasant, disagreeable.

Union, *n.* 1. Junction, combination, coalition, coalescence, conjunction, unification, incorporation, uniting, joining, fusion, coupling.

2. Harmony, concord, agreement, concert, unison, unanimity, unity, concurrence.

3. Confederacy, alliance, league, association, federation, guild, club.

4. Marriage.

Unique, *a.* Single (*in kind* or *excellence*), sole, only, unmatched, unexampled, singular, peculiar, uncommon, rare, exceptional, *sui generis*.

Unison, *n.* Agreement, accordance, accord, concord, harmony, homophony.

UNIT, *n.* One, unity, monad, item, point, integer.

Unite, *v. t.* 1. Join, combine, connect.

2. Incorporate, amalgamate, confederate, embody, consolidate, centralize, blend, merge, fuse, cement, attach, weld.

3. Associate, couple, conjoin, connect, link, marry.

4. Reconcile, harmonize.

——, *v. i.* 1. Concur, agree, co-operate, join forces, pull together, act in concert, harmonize, fraternize, mate.

2. Coalesce, combine, league, confederate, amalgamate, form a league, form an alliance.

3. Be consolidated, be cemented, become one, grow together.

Unity, *n.* 1. Oneness, singleness, individuality, undividedness, integrality, organic totality.

2. Sameness, self-sameness, identity, uniformity.

3. Concord, harmony, agreement, accordance, uniformity, unanimity, unison, concert, union, solidarity.

Universal, *a.* 1. Unlimited, all-reaching, catholic, general, cosmic, encyclopedic, pandemic, without exception.

2. Total, whole, entire, complete.

3. All, comprising all particulars.

4. Ecumenical, general, world-wide.

——, *n.* (*Log.*) 1. General notion *or* conception, concept, notion, idea (*in the Platonic sense*).

2. Universal proposition.

Universality, *n.* Generality, catholicity, unlimited application.

Universally, *adv.* Without exception, uniformly, invariably, in all cases, in every instance.

Universe, *n.* World, cosmos, nature, whole creation, all created things, system.

University, *n.* Seminary of learning (*of the highest class*), literary institution, universal school.

Unjust, *a.* 1. Inequitable, unequal, partial, unfair, wrong, unwarranted, wrongful, injurious.

2. Unrighteous, wicked, wrong, iniquitous, nefarious, flagitious, heinous.

3. Unfair, partial, uncandid, prejudiced, biased, one-sided.

Unjustifiable, *a.* 1. Unwarrantable, indefensible, unreasonable, wrong, unjust.

2. Inexcusable, unpardonable.

Unkind, *a.* Unfriendly, ungracious, unsympathizing, ungenial, unamiable, disobliging, harsh, cruel, unfeeling.

Unkindly, *a.* 1. Unkind, harsh, hard.

2. Unfavorable, malignant.

Unknowingly, *adv.* Ignorantly, unwittingly.

Unknown, *a.* 1. Unascertained, unperceived.

2. Unexplored, uninvestigated, undiscovered.

3. Mysterious, mystic, hidden, dark, concealed, enigmatical.

4. Without the knowledge of.

5. Obscure, undistinguished, unheralded, ignored, nameless, incognito, anonymous, unnoted, unhonored, renownless, inglorious.

Unlace, *v. t.* Loose, loosen, unloose, untie, unfasten, unbind.

Unlade, *v. t.* 1. Unload, take out the cargo of.

2. See Unload.

Unladylike, *a.* Ungentle, ill-bred, unmannerly, rude, uncivil, impolite, ungracious.

Unlamented, *a.* Unwept, unmourned, unregretted, undeplored.

Unlawful, *a.* 1. Illegal, illicit, unlicensed.

2. Illegitimate, bastard, spurious, misbegotten.

3. Undue, unauthorized, unwarranted, unjustified, unconstitutional, prohibited, usurped.

Unlearned, *a.* 1. Uneducated, unlettered, illiterate, ignorant, uninstructed; stupid, thick-headed.

2. Unknown, unstudied.

3. Unscholarly.

Unless, *conj.* Except, if not, supposing that not.

Unlicensed, *a.* Unlawful, illicit, forbidden, prohibited, unauthorized.

Unlike, *a.* Dissimilar, different, heterogeneous, diverse, diversified.

Unlikelihood, *n.* Improbability, unlikeliness.

Unlikely, *a.* 1. Improbable.

2. Unpromising.

Unlikeness, *n.* Dissimilarity, dissimilitude.

Unlimited, *a.* 1. Boundless, measureless, interminable, unbounded, limitless, infinite, illimitable.

2. Unrestricted, unconstrained, unconfined, absolute, full.

3. Undefined, indefinite.

Unload, *v. t.* Discharge, unlade, disburden, unburden, disencumber, lighten, free from, empty, dump, transfer.

Unlock, *v. t.* 1. Unfasten, unbolt.

2. Open, lay open.

Unlodge, *v. t.* Dislodge.

Unlooked for. Unexpected, unforeseen.

Unloose, *v. t.* Unbind, loose, loosen, untie, unfasten, unbuckle.

Unlovely, *a.* 1. Unlovable, unamiable, disagreeable, unpleasant.

2. Unattractive, plain, homely, ugly, uncomely, ill-favored.

Unluckily, *adv.* Unfortunately, as ill-luck would have it, in an evil hour.

Unlucky, *a.* 1. Unfortunate, unsuccessful, unprosperous, baleful, disastrous, luckless, ill-starred, ill-fated, misadventurous.

2. Inauspicious, ill-omened.

3. Unhappy, miserable.

Unmaidenly, *a.* Immodest, bold, forward, indelicate.

Unman, *v. t.* 1. Emasculate, castrate, geld, deprive of virility.

2. Dishearten, discourage, make despondent, deject.

3. Weaken, debilitate, effeminate, emolliate, enfeeble, unnerve, make effeminate.

Unmanageable, *a.* 1. Not easily governed, ungovernable.

2. Unwieldy, unhandy, cumbersome, cumbrous, awkward, incommodious, inconvenient.

3. Intractable, unworkable, unruly, refractory, vicious.

4. Difficult, impracticable.

Unmanly, *a.* 1. Effeminate, womanish, weak.

2. Base, ignoble, mean, ungenerous, cowardly, dastardly.

Unmannerly, *a.* Impolite, uncivil, uncourteous, ungracious, rude, rough, rustic, unmannered, mannerless, ill-mannered, ill-bred, caddish.

Unmarried, *a.* Single, spouseless, unwedded, lone, celibate.

Unmask, *v. t.* Expose, lay open, strip of disguise, disclose.

Unmatched, *a.* 1. Unequalled, unparalleled, matchless, unexampled, unrivalled, unparagoned, without an equal, consummate, incomparable, peerless.

2. Odd, single (*of a pair or set*).

Unmeaning, *a.* Meaningless, insignificant, expressionless, nonsensical, senseless, inexpressive, unintelligent.

Unmeasured, *a.* 1. Unsparing, unstinted, unstinting, lavish.

2. Measureless, immense, infinite.

Unmeet, *a.* Improper, unfit, unbecoming, unseemly.

Unmelodious, *a.* Harsh, unmusical, discordant, inharmonious.

Unmentionable, *a.* Scandalous, infamous, disreputable; indescribable.

Unmerciful, *a.* 1. Merciless, cruel, inexorable, inhuman, pitiless, unpitying, unfeeling, ruthless, unrelenting, unsparing.

2. (*Colloq.*) Exorbitant, extravagant, unconscionable, excessive.

Unmerited, *a.* Undeserved.

Unmethodical, *a.* Immethodical, planless, disorderly.

Unmindful, *a.* Careless, inattentive, heedless, regardless, unobservant, negligent, forgetful, mindless, oblivious.

Unmistakable, *a.* Clear, evident, palpable, plain, sure, certain, manifest, obvious, patent, open, visible, unequivocal, positive, unambiguous, pronounced, decided, notorious.

Unmitigated, *a.* Complete, thorough, absolute, unredeemed, perfect, utter, sheer, stark, consummate, unqualified.

Unmixed, *a.* Unmingled, pure, clear; straight, simple, sheer, solid, incomposite; sincere, unalloyed.

Unmolested, *a.* Undisturbed, untroubled.

Unmourned, *a.* Unwept, unlamented, unregretted, undeplored.

Unmoved, *a.* 1. Firm, steadfast, unwavering, unswerving, unfaltering, constant.

2. Calm, collected, self-possessed, cool, undisturbed, quiet.

3. Indifferent, insensible, unaffected, untouched, unstirred, with dry eyes, without a tear.

Unmurmuring, *a.* Uncomplaining, patient, long-suffering.

Unmusical, *a.* Discordant, harsh, rude, inharmonic, inharmonical, unharmonious.

Unnatural, *a.* 1. Unusual, uncommon, anomalous, irregular, abnormal, aberrant, foreign, exceptional, monstrous, preternatural, prodigious.

2. Heartless, brutal, stony-hearted, inhuman, cold, unfeeling.

3. Forced, strained, stilted, affected, constrained, artificial, insincere, self-conscious.

4. Factitious, artificial.

Unnecessary, *a.* Needless, useless, superfluous, inessential, supererogatory, dispensable, extra, spare, uncalled for.

Unneighborly, *a.* 1. Unfriendly, unkind, unkindly, inconsiderate.

2. Unsociable.

Unnerve, *v. t.* Weaken, enfeeble, upset.

Unnoted, *a.* 1. Unheeded, disregarded, overlooked, unobserved.

2. Unhonored, slighted.

Unnoticed, *a.* Unobserved, neglected, overlooked, unnoted, unperceived, unremarked, disregarded, unregarded, unseen, undescried, slighted, ignored, unheeded.

Unnumbered, *a.* Innumerable, numberless, countless, untold.

Unobjectionable, *a.* Unexceptionable, inoffensive, harmless.

Unobservant, *a.* Heedless, careless, inattentive, unmindful, unobserving, disregardful.

Unobserved, *a.* See UNNOTICED.

Unobstructed, *a.* Unhindered, unimpeded, open, fair, free, clear.

Unobtainable, *a.* Unattainable.

Unobtrusive, *a.* Modest, retiring, unostentatious, unpretending, unpretentious, unassuming.

Unoccupied, *a.* 1. Vacant, empty, tenantless, unpossessed, untenanted, uninhabited, deserted, abandoned.

2. Vacant, unthinking, thoughtless.

3. Spare, leisure, unemployed, idle.

Unoffending, *a.* Harmless, blameless, inoffensive, innocent.

Unofficial, *a.* Private, unprofessional.

Unofficious, *a.* Retiring, modest, backward.

Unopened, *a.* Shut, closed.

Unorganized, *a.* Inorganic, inorganical, without organs, without organization.

Unorthodox, *a.* Heterodox, heretical.

Unostentatious, *a.* 1. See UNOBTRUSIVE.

2. Quiet, subdued, inconspicuous.

Unowned, *a.* 1. Ownerless.

2. Unacknowledged, unadmitted, unavowed.

Unpaid, *a.* Unsettled, owing, due, outstanding, unsatisfied, unliquidated.

Unpalatable, *a.* 1. Vapid, savorless, unsavory, untoothsome.

2. Disagreeable (*to the taste*), unpleasant, disgusting, nauseous, offensive.

3. Bitter, sour, distasteful, disagreeable, unpleasant.

Unparalleled, *a.* Unexampled, unequalled, unrivalled, unmatched, matchless, peerless, unique, inimitable, unparagoned, unprecedented, without a parallel, incomparable.

Unpardonable, *a.* Inexcusable, indefensible, unforgivable, unjustifiable, irremissible, inexpiable, unatonable.

Unperceived, *a.* See UNNOTICED.

Unpitying, *a.* Relentless, unrelenting, pitiless, uncompassionate, cruel, ruthless, merciless, unmerciful, savage, implacable, unsparing.

Unpleasant, *a.* Unpleasing, disagreeable, displeasing, unwelcome, unacceptable, unpalatable, distasteful, unlovely, repulsive, obnoxious, offensive, ungrateful.

Unpliant, *a.* Stiff, inflexible, rigid, unbending, unyielding.

Unpoetic, ⎫ *a.* Prosy, prosaic, common-
Unpoetical, ⎭ place, matter-of-fact.

Unpolished, *a.* 1. Rough, not polished.

2. Rude, uncivilized, unrefined, illbred, crude, ungraceful, untrained, untaught, undisciplined, barbarous, illiterate, rustic.

Unpolluted, *a.* Pure, undefiled, uncorrupted, unvitiated, immaculate.

Unpopular, *a.* Disliked (*by the people*), obnoxious (*generally*), out of favor, unacceptable, unapproved.

Unpractical, *a.* 1. Theoretical.

2. Speculative, contemplative, Platonic, philosophical, given to speculation.

Unpractised, *a.* Untrained, inexperienced, unskilled, raw, unaccustomed, inexpert.

Unprecedented, *a.* Unexampled, novel, new, exceptional.

Unprejudiced, *a.* Unbiassed, unprepossessed, uninfluenced, unwarped, impartial, fair, judicial.

Unpremeditated, *a.* Unstudied, extemporaneous, undesigned, unintentional, extempore, impromptu, spontaneous, off-hand.

Unprepared, *a.* Unready, unqualified, unfitted, incompleted.

Unprepossessing, *a.* Unattractive, repulsive, ugly, uncomely.

Unpresuming, *a.* Modest, humble, retiring, unpresumptuous.

Unpretentious, *a.* Modest, unassuming, retiring, simple, unambitious, unpretending, unobtrusive, unostentatious.

Unprevented, *a.* Unhindered.

Unprincipled, *a.* Immoral, wicked, vicious, bad, knavish, roguish, dishonest, trickish, iniquitous, lawless, fraudulent, thievish, rascally, profligate, villainous, tricky, crooked, unscrupulous.

Unproductive, *a.* 1. Unfruitful, fruitless, unyielding, arid, unprolific, issueless, infecund, fallow, barren, sterile, unprocreant.

2. Unprofitable, unremunerative.

3. Inefficient, ineffectual, without effect, futile, otiose, nugatory, unsuccessful, inefficacious.

Unprofitable, *a.* 1. Worthless, sterile, poor, unproductive, unfruitful, barren, profitless.

2. Useless, futile, bootless, fruitless, unavailing.

3. Worthless, unremunerative, useless, poor.

4. Barren, unfruitful, unserviceable, unbeneficial, unhelpful.

Unpromising, *a.* 1. Inauspicious, unpropitious, unfavorable, unlucky, untoward, ill-omened, not encouraging, not promising.

2. Unlikely.

Unpropitious, *a.* Unfavorable, inauspicious, unpromising, adverse, sinister, minatory, ill-omened, untimely.

Unprosperous, *a.* Unfortunate, luckless, unlucky, unsuccessful, ill-starred.

Unprotected, *a.* Defenceless, unguarded, exposed, naked, undefended, unshielded.

Unprovided with. Without, destitute of, devoid of, unsupplied with, unfurnished, unequipped.

Unpunctual, *a.* Tardy, dilatory, behindhand, late.

Unpurified, *a.* Unclean, defiled, uncleansed, unsanctified, unhallowed.

Unqualified, *a.* 1. Incompetent, unfit, unadapted, unsuited; disqualified, ineligible.

2. Absolute, unconditional, unmeasured, unrestricted, thorough, plump, outright, out-and-out, straight, consummate, unmitigated, thorough-going, full, direct, downright, decided, certain.

3. Exaggerated, sweeping.

Unquenchable, *a.* Inextinguishable, quenchless, slakeless, unslakable, that cannot be quenched.

Unquestionable, *a.* Indisputable, incontrovertible, indubitable, undeniable, irrefragable, unimpugnable, unmistakable, incontestable, irrefutable, certain, sure, conclusive, evident, obvious, beyond all question, beyond a doubt, past dispute.

Unquestioned, *a.* 1. Undoubted, undisputed.

2. Unexamined, having no questions asked.

3. Indisputable, not to be opposed.

Unquiet, *a.* 1. Uneasy, restless, fidgety.

2. Disturbed, agitated, unpeaceful, restless, uneasy.

Unravel, *v. t.* 1. Disentangle, extricate, ravel, untwist.

2. Unfold, develop, evolve, decipher, interpret, understand, resolve, solve, explain, read, clear up, make out, disclose.

Unreadable, *a.* Illegible.

Unready, *a.* 1. Unprepared.

2. Unfit, unqualified.

3. Slow, slack, awkward, clumsy, unhandy.

Unreal, *a.* Insubstantial, flimsy, unsubstantial, imaginary, shadowy, visionary, spectral, ghostly, vaporous, illusory, illusionary, dreamlike, fanciful, chimerical, nebulous.

Unreasonable, *a.* 1. Irrational, illogical, unreasoning, foolish, unwise, absurd, silly, preposterous, senseless, stupid, injudicious, nonsensical, unphilosophical, ill-judged, impracticable, unwarrantable, unjustifiable.

2. Exorbitant, extravagant, unfair, unjust, extortionate, excessive, vast, immoderate.

3. Bigoted, stubborn, obstinate.

Unrecognized, *a.* 1. Ignored, overlooked, disregarded.

2. Unknown, unacknowledged.

Unredeemed, *a.* 1. Unransomed, forfeited.

2. Unfulfilled, unperformed.

Unreflecting, *a.* Heedless, thoughtless.

Unregarded, *a.* Disregarded, neglected, unheeded.

Unregenerate, *a.* Unconverted, natural.

Unrelenting, *a.* 1. Inexorable, implacable, pitiless, relentless, merciless, ruthless, unmerciful, uncompassionate, hard, cruel, unpitying, stern, harsh, bitter, austere, rigorous, remorseless, unsparing.

2. Rigid, severe, inflexible, inexorable.

Unreliable, *a.* Untrustworthy, irresponsible, unstable, fickle, not to be depended upon, uncertain, unsure, treacherous, fallible, inauthentic.

Unremitting, *a.* Unceasing, continual, persevering, constant, unabated, incessant, assiduous, sedulous, diligent, indefatigable, unwearied.

Unremunerative, *a.* Unprofitable, unproductive.

Unrepentant, *a.* Impenitent, seared, hardened, callous, incorrigible, irreclaimable, obdurate, abandoned, lost, graceless, shameless, profligate, recreant.

Unrequited, *a.* Unreturned, unrewarded, unanswered.

Unreserved, *a.* 1. Full, entire, unlimited, absolute.

2. Frank, communicative, open, candid, ingenuous, undesigning, undissembling, artless, guileless, sincere, honest, fair, single-minded, above-board.

3. Demonstrative, emotional, open-hearted.

Unresisting, *a.* Submissive, patient, passive, long-suffering, non-resistant, yielding, compliant, obedient.

Unresponsive, *a.* Unsympathetic, irresponsive.

Unrestrained, *a.* 1. Unchecked, unhindered, unreserved, unobstructed, unfettered, uncurbed, unbridled.

2. Licentious, loose, dissolute, incontinent, inordinate, wanton, broad, lewd, lax.

3. Wild, lawless.

Unrestricted, *a.* 1. Unrestrained, unlimited, unconditioned, unqualified, free, unconfined, unbridled, unfettered, independent.

2. Unobstructed, open, public, clear.

Unrevealed, *a.* Secret, hidden, unknown, undiscovered, occult.

Unrewarded, *a.* Unpaid, unrecompensed.

Unriddle, *v. t.* Solve, explain, expound, unfold, unravel.

Unrighteous, *a.* 1. Wicked, ungodly, unholy, sinful, wrong, evil, vicious.

2. Unjust, unfair, iniquitous, inequitable, nefarious, heinous.

Unripe, *a.* 1. Immature, premature, green, hard, sour, crude.

2. Incomplete, unfinished.

Unrivalled, *a.* Unequalled, unparalleled, peerless, matchless, incomparable, inimitable, of the best, without a rival, of the first water.

Unrobe, *v. t.* Undress, disrobe.

Unroll, *v. t.* 1. Unfold, open.

2. Display, lay open.

3. Develop, evolve, unfold, open.

Unromantic, *a.* Literal, prosaic, matter-of-fact.

Unroot, *v. t.* Extirpate, eradicate, uproot, root out, pull up by the roots.

Unruffled, *a.* 1. Calm, tranquil, quiet, still, placid, peaceful, serene, smooth.

2. Placid, peaceful, philosophical, collected, serene, unmoved, imperturbable, composed, cool, undisturbed, calm, tranquil.

Unruly, *a.* 1. Turbulent, ungovernable, fractious, refractory, disobedient, insubordinate, mutinous, riotous, seditious, rebellious, disorderly, headstrong, obstreperous, wanton.

2. Refractory, vicious, stubborn, obstinate, unmanageable, ungovernable, rebellious, lawless.

Unsafe, *a.* Dangerous, perilous, hazardous, precarious, uncertain, treacherous, risky, unprotected, insecure, full of risk.

Unsaid, *a.* Unuttered, unmentioned, unspoken, tacit.

Unsanctified, *a.* Unholy, unhallowed, profane.

Unsated, *a.* See UNSATISFIED.

Unsatisfactory, *a.* 1. Insufficient.

2. Disappointing.

3. Lame, poor, weak, feeble, imperfect, faulty.

Unsatisfied, *a.* 1. Unsated, unsatiated, insatiate, unstanched.

2. Dissatisfied, discontented, displeased, malcontent.

3. Unpaid, undischarged, unperformed, unrendered.

Unsavory, *a.* 1. Unpalatable, unflavored, tasteless, insipid, flat, vapid, savorless, mawkish.

2. Unpleasing, disgusting, nauseous, offensive, distasteful, disagreeable, uninviting, sickening, nauseating, nasty, revolting, rank.

Unsay, *v. t.* Retract, recall, recant, take back.

Unscathed, *a.* Uninjured, unharmed.

Unschooled, *a.* 1. Uneducated, uninstructed, ignorant.

2. Undisciplined, untrained.

Unscrupulous, *a.* Unprincipled, unrestrained, ruthless, reckless, unconscientious, without scruples, regardless of principle, dishonest.

Unsealed, *a.* Open, without a seal, unclosed.

Unsearchable, *a.* Inscrutable, incomprehensible, mysterious, hidden, that cannot be found out *or* known by searching, past finding out.

Unseasonable, *a.* 1. Inopportune, untimely, ill-timed, inappropriate, out of season.

2. Late, too late.

3. Ill-timed, unfit, untimely, unsuitable, unwelcome, ungrateful, inappropriate.

4. Premature, too early.

Unseasonably, *adv.* Untimely, at an unsuitable time, unsuitably, malapropos.

Unseasoned, *a.* 1. Unqualified, inexperienced, unaccustomed, untrained.

2. Irregular, inordinate, immoderate.

3. Green.

4. Fresh, unsalted.

Unseeing, *a.* Blind, sightless.

Unseemly, *a.* Improper, indecorous, unbecoming, uncomely, unmeet, unfit, unbefitting, indecent, unsuitable, inappropriate.

Unseen, *a.* 1. Unperceived, unobserved, undiscerned, undiscovered.

2. Invisible, indiscoverable, imperceptible, latent.

Unselfish, *a.* Disinterested, generous, liberal, magnanimous, high-minded, self-forgetful, self-sacrificing, altruistic, selfless, self-denying, devoted, impersonal.

Unserviceable, *a.* 1. Useless, unsound, ill-conditioned.

2. Unprofitable, useless, profitless.

Unsettle, *v. t.* Derange, disturb, disconcert, unfix, disarrange, upset, trouble, confuse, disorder, throw into disorder, unhinge, unbalance.

Unsettled, *a.* 1. Wavering, restless, vacillating, fickle, unsteady, unstable, changeable, inconstant, transient, not steady.

2. Unequal, changeable, inequable.

3. Turbid, roily, roiled, feculent, muddy.

4. Uninhabited, without inhabitants; homeless, unestablished, adrift, afloat.

5. Undetermined, open, unadjusted, pending, undecided, tentative.

6. Unpaid, owing, due, outstanding.

7. Unnerved, troubled, perturbed.

Unshackle, *v. t.* Unfetter, unchain, unbind, loose, liberate, emancipate, set free, set at liberty, release.

Unshaken, *a.* Unmoved, firm, steady, resolute, steadfast, constant.

Unshapen, *a.* Deformed, misshapen, shapeless, ill-formed, ill-made, ill-shaped, grotesque, ugly, uncouth.

Unsheltered, *a.* Exposed, unprotected.

Unshrinking, *a.* Unblenching, persisting, determined, unflinching, firm, resolute.

Unshroud, *v. t.* Uncover, discover, expose, reveal.

Unsightly, *a.* Ugly, deformed, disagreeable to the sight, hideous, repulsive, repellent.

Unskilful, *a.* Awkward, bungling, unhandy, clumsy, maladroit, unversed, rough, rude, unskilled, inapt, inexpert, without dexterity.

Unskilled, *a.* 1. Inexperienced, undrilled, unexercised, unpractised, undisciplined, uneducated, unschooled, unprepared, raw.

2. See UNSKILFUL.

Unslaked, *a.* Unslacked, unquenched.

Unsleeping, *a.* Wakeful, watchful, vigilant, unslumbering.

Unsmirched, *a.* Unpolluted, undefiled, unspotted.

Unsociable, *a.* Reserved, retiring, shy, stand-offish, distant, segregative, taciturn, unsocial, solitary, uncompanionable, ungenial, uncommunicative, averse to society; morose, misanthropic, inhospitable.

Unsoiled, *a.* Untarnished, unstained, unsullied, unspotted, spotless, clean.

Unsophisticated, *a.* 1. Pure, unadulterated, genuine.

2. Guileless, undepraved, good, unpolluted, unvitiated, innocent.

3. Artless, simple, natural, unaffected, unstudied, *naïve*, sincere, ingenuous, straightforward, honest, undesigning.

Unsought, *a.* 1. Unrequested, unasked, unsolicited.

2. Avoided, shunned, eschewed.

Unsound, *a.* 1. Defective, imperfect, impaired, wasted, thin, weak, decayed, rotten; disturbed, restless, light, broken.

2. Diseased, sickly, weakly, poorly, infirm, unhealthy, morbid, feeble.

3. Erroneous, wrong, false, fallacious, incorrect, deceitful, sophistical, illogical, defective, untenable, invalid, unsubstantial, faulty, hollow, questionable.

4. Deceitful, dishonest, untrustworthy, insincere, false, unfaithful, untrue.

5. Insubstantial, unreal.

6. Heterodox, heretical, unorthodox, defective.

Unsparing, *a.* 1. Liberal, profuse, lavish, bountiful, generous, ungrudging.

2. Unmerciful, unforgiving, severe, harsh, rigorous, inexorable, relentless, ruthless, uncompromising.

Unspeakable, *a.* Inexpressible, unutterable, ineffable, indescribable, beyond expression.

Unspiritual, *a.* Sensual, carnal, fleshly, bodily.

Unspotted, *a.* 1. Unstained, unsoiled, untarnished, unsullied, spotless, clean.

2. Pure, uncorrupted, untainted, unblemished, untarnished, unsullied, spotless, stainless, clean, undefiled, immaculate.

Unstable, *a.* 1. Unsteady, insecure, unsafe, infirm, topheavy, unbalanced, unballasted, precarious.

2. Inconstant, changeable, unsteady, fickle, weak, vacillating, irresolute, wavering, erratic, variable.

Unstained, *a.* 1. Untinged, undyed, uncolored, colorless.

2. See UNSPOTTED.

Unsteady, *a.* 1. Unsettled, fluctuating, oscillating.

2. Inconstant, fickle, unstable, changeable, desultory, irresolute, wavering, mutable, variable, ever-changing.

3. Tottering, wavering, vacillating, wabbly, drunken, tipsy, jumpy.

Unstinted, *a.* Abundant, ample, plentiful, large, full, lavish, bountiful, profuse, prodigal.

Unstrung, *a.* Unnerved, weak, shaken, overcome.

Unstudied, *a.* 1. Unpremeditated, spontaneous, extempore, extemporaneous, impromptu, off-hand.

2. Unskilled, inexpert, unversed.

Unsubdued, *a.* Unbroken, untamed, unconquered, unbowed.

Unsubmissive, *a.* Disobedient, uncomplying, refractory, obstinate, contumacious, unruly, perverse, unyielding, indocile, insubordinate, ungovernable, unmanageable.

Unsubstantial, *a.* 1. Light, flimsy, gossamery, slight, gaseous, tenuous, vaporous, airy, thin.

2. Unreal, imaginary, chimerical, visionary, bodiless, imponderable, vague, moonshiny, dreamlike, empty, spectral, apparitional, cloudbuilt, ideal, illusory, fantastical.

3. Unsound, unsolid, ungrounded, groundless, without foundation, unfounded, untenable, weak, flimsy, fallacious, erroneous, illogical.

Unsuccessful, *a.* 1. Unavailing, ineffectual, abortive, fruitless, bootless, profitless, vain, futile, in vain.

2. Luckless, unfortunate, unlucky, unprosperous, ill-starred, ill-fated, unhappy.

Unsuitable, *a.* 1. Unfit, inappropriate, malapropos, unsatisfactory, unsuited, ill-adapted.

2. Improper, unbecoming, unbeseeming, inapplicable, inexpedient, unfitting, incongruous, out of keeping, out of character, out of place, in bad taste, inapt, infelicitous.

Unsuited, *a.* Unfitted, unqualified, unadapted.

Unsullied, *a.* See UNSPOTTED.

Unsupplied, *a.* Unprovided, unfurnished, destitute.

Unsupported, *a.* 1. Unassisted, unaided.

2. Unseconded, unsustained, unupheld, unbacked.

Unsurpassed, *a.* Unexcelled, matchless, unequalled, unmatched, unparalleled, unrivalled, unexampled, peerless, unparagoned, without an equal.

Unsusceptible, *a.* Unimpressible, unimpressionable, impassive, apathetic, cold, phlegmatic, stoical, insusceptible.

Unsuspecting, *a.* Unsuspicious, credulous, trusting, confiding.

Unsuspicious, *a.* Unsuspecting, having no suspicion, simple, trustful, confiding, credulous, childlike, gullible.

Unsustainable, *a.* 1. Insupportable, intolerable.

2. Erroneous, unmaintainable, untenable, controvertible.

Unswerving, *a.* 1. Undeviating, straight, direct.

2. Firm, determined, resolute, steady, steadfast, stanch, stable, constant, unwavering.

Unsymmetrical, *a.* Disproportionate, irregular, out of proportion, without symmetry, asymmetric, unbalanced, amorphous, formless.

Unsystematic, } *a.* Irregular, disorderly,
Unsystematical, } immethodical, casual, haphazard, planless.

Untainted, *a.* 1. Pure, clean, wholesome, fresh, sweet, healthy.

2. See UNSPOTTED.

Untamable, *a.* Unconquerable.

Untamed, *a.* Unbroken, wild, fierce.

Untangle, *v. t.* Disentangle, explain, explicate.

Untarnished, *a.* See UNSPOTTED.

Untaught, *a.* Uninformed, unenlightened, unlettered, illiterate. See UNTUTORED, 1.

Untaxed, *a.* 1. Scot-free, without payment, without expense.

2. Exempt from reproach.

Unteachable, *a.* Indocile, untractable.

Untenable, *a.* 1. Unmaintainable, indefensible, unsound.

2. Weak, hollow, fallacious, unjustifiable, indefensible, illogical, insupportable.

Untenanted, *a.* Unoccupied, tenantless, uninhabited, empty, deserted.

Unterrified, *a.* Undaunted, unscared, undismayed, unappalled, unawed, fearless.

Unthankful, *a.* Ungrateful, thankless, without gratitude.

Unthinking, *a.* Thoughtless, heedless, careless, unreasoning, inconsiderate, unreflecting; automatic, mechanical.

Unthoughtful, *a.* Thoughtless, inconsiderate, heedless, careless.

Unthrifty, *a.* Thriftless, wasteful, lavish, profuse, prodigal, improvident, extravagant.

Untidy, *a.* Slovenly, disorderly, unneat, dowdy, mussy, frumpy, slatternly, careless, unkempt.

Untie, *v. t.* 1. Loose, loosen, unfasten, unbind, unloose, unknot, free.

2. Resolve, solve, clear, unfold.

Until, *adv.* or *conj.* 1. Till, to the time when *or* that.

2. To the place, point, state, *or* degree that.

——, *prep.* To, till.

Untimely, *a.* Ill-timed, unseasonable, mistimed, inopportune, out of season, immature, premature, unsuitable, inconvenient; inauspicious, unfortunate, ill-considered, uncalled for.

——, *adv.* Unseasonably, unsuitably, at an unsuitable time, in an evil hour.

Untinged, *a.* Uncolored, undyed, unstained, colorless, hueless, achromatic.

Untiring, *a.* Unwearied, indefatigable, unfatiguable, unwearying, persevering, unflagging, unremitting, unceasing, incessant, tireless, patient.

Untold, *a.* 1. Unnumbered, uncounted, countless, innumerable, incalculable.

2. Unrelated, unrevealed.

Untouched, *a.* 1. Not touched.

2. Intact, uninjured, unhurt, scathless, unharmed.

3. Unmoved, unaffected, unstirred, insensible.

Untoward, *a.* 1. Froward, perverse, intractable, stubborn, refractory, adverse, unfortunate.

2. Inconvenient, ill-timed, unmanageable, annoying, troublesome, vexatious.

3. Awkward, ungainly, ungraceful, uncouth.

Untrained, *a.* Undisciplined, uninstructed, untaught, uneducated, untutored, inexperienced, undrilled, unpractised, unskilled, ignorant, raw, green, unbroken.

Untrammelled, *a.* Unhampered, free.

Untravelled, *a.* 1. Not travelled over, unfrequented by travellers.

2. Not experienced as a traveller, never having travelled.

Untried, *a.* 1. New, fresh, unattempted, unassayed, unattested, maiden, virgin, unexperienced.

2. Undecided.

Untrodden, *a.* Pathless, trackless, unbeaten.

Untroubled, *a.* Peaceful, calm, serene, tranquil, unvexed, undisturbed, composed, smooth, careless.

Untrue, *a.* 1. False, contrary to fact, wrong, inaccurate.

2. Faithless, treacherous, recreant, false, disloyal, unfaithful, perfidious.

Untrustworthy, *a.* Unreliable, inaccurate, deceitful, treacherous, rotten, not to be depended on, slippery, dishonest; false, disloyal; deceptive, illusive, fallible, questionable.

Untruth, *n.* 1. Falsehood, treachery, want of fidelity, incorrectness, error, inveracity, falsity, faithlessness.

2. Falsehood, lie, fiction, fabrication, story, forgery, invention, misstatement, misrepresentation, deception, deceit, error, fib, imposture.

Untutored, *a.* 1. Uninstructed, uneducated, untaught, undisciplined, inexperienced, uninitiated, undrilled, ignorant.

2. Artless, natural, simple, unsophisticated.

Untwist, *v. t.* Disentangle, ravel, unravel, disentwine, unwreathe.

Unused, *a.* 1. Unemployed, idle, untried.

2. Unaccustomed, new, unfamiliar.

Unusual, *a.* Uncommon, rare, *recherché*, unwonted, unaccustomed, singular, remarkable, strange, curious, extraordinary, odd, queer, peculiar, out of the way, abnormal, exceptional.

Unutterable, *a.* Inexpressible, ineffable, unspeakable, indescribable, that cannot be uttered, beyond expression, incommunicable.

Unvarnished, *a.* 1. Unpolished.

2. Unembellished, plain, unadorned, candid, simple, true.

Unvarying, *a.* Unchanging, invariable, constant.

Unveil, *v. t.* Disclose, uncover, expose, show, reveal, unmask.

Unveracious, *a.* Mendacious, false, lying, untruthful.

Unversed, *a.* See UNSKILLED.

Unviolated, *a.* Unbroken, inviolate, unbetrayed.

Unwarlike, *a.* Peaceful, pacific.

Unwarped, *a.* Impartial, unbiased, unprejudiced, undistorted.

Unwarrantable, *a.* Indefensible, unjustifiable, improper.

Unwary, *a.* Imprudent, hasty, incautious, indiscreet, uncircumspect, careless, remiss, unguarded, reckless, precipitate, heedless, rash.

Unwavering, *a.* Constant, steadfast, steady, unhesitating, firm, settled, determined, fixed, stanch, resolute.

Unwearied, *a.* 1. Not fatigued.

2. Indefatigable, persevering, persistent, constant, continual, incessant, unremitting, unceasing, untiring.

Unwelcome, *a.* Unpleasing, ungrateful, unacceptable, disagreeable, unpleasant.

Unwell, *a.* Ill, ailing, sick, indisposed, diseased, delicate, out of sorts, out of health, on the sick list, laid on the shelf, under the weather.

Unwept, *a.* Unlamented, unmourned, unregretted.

Unwholesome, *a.* 1. Insalubrious, unhealthy, unhealthful, noxious, noisome, deleterious, baneful, poisonous, injurious to health.

2. Pernicious (*to the mind*), injudicious, unsound.

3. Unsound, corrupt, tainted.

Unwieldy, *a.* Unmanageable (*from size or weight*), ponderous, bulky, weighty, heavy, massy, clumsy, large, cumbrous, cumbersome, lubberly, "hulking," elephantine.

Unwilling, *a.* Loath, disinclined, opposed, averse, reluctant, backward, indisposed, recalcitrant, laggard; forced, grudging.

Unwind, *v. t.* 1. Wind off, unreel, untwine, unravel.

2. Disentangle.

Unwise, *a.* Foolish, injudicious, indiscreet, unwary, inexpedient, impolitic, imprudent, ill-advised, ill-judged, weak, senseless, silly, brainless, stupid.

Unwitnessed, *a.* Unknown, unseen, unspied.

Unwittingly, *adv.* Inadvertently, unconsciously, ignorantly, undesignedly, unintentionally, without knowing it.

Unwomanly, *a.* Unfeminine, unbecoming a woman.

Unwonted, *a.* 1. Unusual, uncommon, rare, infrequent.

2. Unaccustomed, unused.

Unworkmanlike, *a.* Unskilful, inartistic, not workmanlike *or* workmanly, unbecoming a workman.

Unworldly, *a.* Spiritual-minded.

Unworthy, *a.* 1. Undeserving.

2. Worthless, base, bad, blameworthy.

3. Unbecoming, base, shameful, bad, vile.

4. Mean, contemptible, despicable, reprehensible, derogatory, discreditable, shabby, paltry.

Unwrap, *v. t.* Open, unfold.

Unwrinkled, *a.* Unfurrowed, smooth.

Unwritten, *a.* Oral, traditional.

Unwrought, *a.* Unfashioned, unformed, rude, crude, rough.

Unyielding, *a.* 1. Inflexible, constant, steady, resolute, steadfast, stanch, pertinacious, determined, indomitable, uncompromising, unwavering, tenacious.

2. Stubborn, stiff, obstinate, wilful, headstrong, self-willed, intractable, perverse, wayward.

3. Stiff, rigid, stubborn, hard, firm, unbending, adamantine, implastic, immovable, inexorable, grim, relentless.

Unyoke, *v. t.* 1. Loose from a yoke.

2. Part, disjoin, disconnect, separate.

Unyoked, *a.* 1. Not yoked.

2. Unrestrained, loose, licentious.

UP, *prep.* and *adv.* (*Basic Eng.*)

Upbraid, *v. t.* Reproach, reprove, blame, chide, condemn, twit, taunt, find fault with, scold, denounce, revile, accuse.

Upheave, *v. t.* Elevate, raise, lift, lift up, heave up.

Uphill, *a.* 1. Ascending, upward.

2. Difficult, hard, arduous, toilsome, laborious, strenuous, wearisome.

Uphold, *v. t.* 1. Raise, elevate, lift on high.

2. Support, sustain, hold up, bear up.

3. Maintain, defend, vindicate, justify, aid, advocate, champion, countenance, support, sustain.

Up in arms. 1. Stirring, bustling, at work, astir, up and doing.

2. Alert, ready, on the alert, vigilant, prepared, wide awake, in readiness, booted and spurred, in harness.

3. At daggers drawn.

Upland, *n.* High land, ridge, down, fell, plateau.

Uplift, *v. t.* Raise, upraise; animate, inspire, refine, elevate, lift aloft.

Upon, *prep.* 1. On, over, on top of.

2. About, concerning, on the subject of, relating to.

3. With, immediately after.

Upper-hand, *n.* Superiority, advantage, ascendency, dominion, rule, pre-eminence, supremacy, mastery, mastership, whip-hand, control.

Uppermost, *a.* Highest, loftiest, topmost, upmost, foremost, supreme.

Uppish, *a.* (*Colloq.*) Proud, arrogant, haughty, assuming, smart, perk, perky.

Upright, *a.* 1. Erect, perpendicular, vertical, on end.

2. Honest, just, honorable, conscientious, square, incorruptible, righteous, upstanding, virtuous, good, pure, straightforward, faithful, true, trustworthy.

3. Virtuous, just, honorable.

Uprightness, *n.* 1. Erectness, perpendicularity, verticality.

2. Honesty, integrity, probity, rectitude, squareness, justice, equity, fairness, incorruptibility, righteousness, goodness, virtue, honor, trustworthiness, trustiness, worth, dignity of character.

Uproar, *n.* Tumult, disturbance, commotion, confusion, turmoil, hubbub, hurly-burly, riot, pandemonium, clamor, racket, din, vociferation, noise, *fracas*.

Uproarious, *a.* Boisterous, riotous, tumultuous, loud, noisy, clamorous, obstreperous.

Uproot, *v. t.* Eradicate, extirpate, pull up by the roots.

Upset, *v. t.* 1. Overturn, capsize, tip over, overtumble, overthrow.

2. Turn upside down, invert.

3. Disconcert, disturb, discompose, throw off one's center, agitate, perturb, startle, fluster, embarrass, shock, excite, overwhelm; defeat, checkmate, subvert.

Upshot, *n.* Conclusion, end, termination, consummation, issue, event, result, outcome, effect, conclusion.

Upside down. Topsy-turvy, in confusion, in complete disorder.

Upstart, *n.* Snob, mushroom, pretentious fellow, pretender to gentility, *parvenu, nouveau riche.*

Upturned, *a.* Turned up, directed upward, raised, uplifted; *retroussé.*

Upward, *a.* 1. Ascending, uphill.

2. Directed to a higher place.

Urbane, *a.* Polite, civil, courteous, mannerly, complaisant, refined, polished, elegant, well-bred, well-mannered, well-behaved.

Urbanity, *n.* Politeness, civility, courtesy, complaisance, amenity, suavity, good-breeding, good manners.

Urchin, *n.* Child, brat, " shaver."

Urge, *v. t.* 1. Push, press, impel, drive, crowd, force onward, push on, press on.

2. Solicit, importune, beg, entreat, beseech, press, tease, exhort, ply, implore, conjure.

3. Incite, animate, encourage, instigate, egg on, stimulate, goad, spur, hurry, quicken.

4. Press upon attention, present in an urgent manner.

Urgency, *n.* 1. Pressure, press, exigency, push, drive, haste, emergency, stress, necessity, pressing want.

2. Importunity, entreaty, insistence, solicitation, instance, clamorousness.

3. Incitement, stimulus, spur, goad.

Urgent, *a.* Pressing, cogent, importunate, instant, exigent, critical, crucial, pertinacious, earnestly solicitous, imperative, clamant, crying, insistent.

Urinal, *n.* Chamber-pot, jorden.

Urinate, *v. i.* Piddle, piss, stale, urine, make water, void urine.

Ursa Major. [L.] (*Astron.*) Charles's Wain, the Wain, the Great Bear, the Dipper.

Ursa Minor. [L.] (*Astron.*) The Little Bear, the Lesser Bear.

Ursine, *a.* Bear-like.

Usage, *n.* 1. Treatment.

2. Practice (*long continued*), custom, use, fashion, consuetude, mode, habit, prescription, method.

3. Customary use.

USE, *n.*   1. Employment, employ, utilization, application, appliance, exercise, practice, conversion to an act *or* purpose, consumption, disposal.

2. Advantage, benefit, utility, service, profit, usefulness, avail, convenience, adaptability, wear, usufruct.

3. Occasion, need, necessity, exigency, want, requisiteness, indispensability.

4. Usage, custom, habit, method, treatment, handling, way, customary employment, practice, exercise.

——, *v. t.*   1. Employ, apply, make use of, handle, manipulate, wield, avail one's self of, take advantage of, turn to account, improve, occupy, put into action, work, drive, administer, operate, ply, make the most of, put in requisition, bring into play.

2. Practise, exercise, put to use, utilize, exploit, exert, profit by.

3. Expend, consume, waste, exhaust, swallow up, absorb, wear out.

4. Accustom, habituate, inure, harden, familiarize, train, render familiar by practice.

5. Treat, deal with, act *or* behave toward, handle, manage.

——, *v. i.*   Be accustomed, be wont.

Useful, *a.*   1. Advantageous, profitable, remunerative, gainful, utilitarian, beneficial, serviceable, helpful, available, good, salutary, convenient, practical, commodious, suitable, instrumental, effective, availing, active, operative.

2. Serviceable, helpful, valuable, available.

Usefulness, *n.*   Utility, serviceableness, value, advantage, profit.

Useless, *a.*   1. Unavailing, fruitless, bootless, profitless, unprofitable, unproductive, unserviceable, valueless, worthless, futile, abortive, of no use, ineffectual, inutile, idle, nugatory, null.

2. Unserviceable, worthless, valueless, waste, good for nothing, of no use.

Usher, *n.*   Sub-master, assistant teacher.

——, *v. t.*   Introduce, forerun, herald, precede, induct, announce.

Usual, *a.*   Customary, ordinary, common, familiar, regular, general, frequent, habitual, wonted, accustomed, prevailing, prevalent, every-day, normal.

Usurp, *v. t.*   Seize (*without right*), arrogate, assume, appropriate unlawfully.

Usurpation, *n.*   Seizure, assumption, infringement on the rights of others, dispossession.

Usury, *n.*   Illegal interest, exorbitant interest.

Utensil, *n.*   Implement, tool, instrument.

Utility, *n.*   1. Usefulness (*in an abstract sense*), advantageousness, benefit, avail, profit, service, use.

2. Happiness, welfare, public good.

Utilize, *v. t.*   Put to use, make use of, make useful, turn to account, take advantage of, exploit.

Utmost, *a.*   1. Extreme, farthest, last, highest, main, most distant, most remote.

2. Greatest, uttermost.

——, *n.*   Best, most, greatest effort, highest endeavor, the most that can be done.

Utopian, *a.*   Ideal, visionary, fanciful, imaginary, chimerical, unreal, air-drawn, air-built.

Utricle, *n.*   Vesicle, cyst, bladder, sac.

Utter, *a.*   1. Total, complete, entire, perfect.

2. Absolute, peremptory, unconditional, unqualified, sheer, blank, stark, downright, diametric, total.

——, *v. t.*   1. Speak, articulate, enunciate, pronounce, express, give forth, give expression to, emit, voice, breathe, tell, deliver, reveal, disclose, divulge.

2. Put into circulation, put off, cause to pass in trade, issue, announce, circulate, publish, declare.

Utterable, *a.*   Pronounceable, expressible.

Utterance, *n.*   Pronunciation, expression, delivery, emission, articulation, speech, pronouncement, publication, disclosure.

Uttermost, *a.*   1. Extreme, farthest.

2. Greatest, utmost.

Uxoriousness, *n.*   Philogyny, connubial dotage.

V

Vacancy, *n.*   1. Emptiness, vacuum, void, vacuity, empty space.

2. Freedom from employment, intermission, leisure, idleness, listlessness.

3. Inanity, unintelligence.

4. Chasm, gap, space.

5. Unemployed time, interval of leisure, time of intermission.

6. Unoccupied office, unfilled place; opportunity, opening.

Vacant, *a.* 1. Empty, void, unfilled, blank, hollow.

2. Disengaged, unoccupied, unemployed, unencumbered, free, leisure.

3. Thoughtless, unthinking, unreflecting, unmeaning.

4. Unfilled, unoccupied, empty, uninhabited, untenanted.

Vacate, *v. t.* 1. Make vacant, leave empty, quit possession of, resign, surrender, depart from, relinquish, abandon, evacuate, disoccupy.

2. Annul, disannul, nullify, rescind, cancel, quash, invalidate, abrogate, abolish, overrule, make void, set aside, do away with, deprive of force.

Vacation, *n.* 1. Intermission, recess.

2. Holidays.

Vaccinate, *v. t.* Inoculate with vaccine matter.

Vacillate, *v. i.* 1. Sway, rock, move to and fro, have an unsteady motion, waver, oscillate.

2. Waver, fluctuate, hesitate, be inconstant, be unsettled, be unsteady, play fast and loose, blow hot and cold, box the compass, run with the hare and hunt with the hound, be a weathercock.

Vacillating, *a.* Wavering, fluctuating, unsteady, shilly-shally, inconstant.

Vacillation, *n.* 1. Swaying, reeling, staggering, rocking.

2. Wavering, fluctuation, hesitation, unsteadiness, inconstancy, faltering, indecision, irresolution.

Vacuity, *n.* 1. Emptiness, vacancy, inanity, inanition.

2. Void, vacuum, empty space, emptiness, vacancy.

3. Inanity, nihility, want of reality, unintelligence, poverty of intellect, expressionlessness.

Vacuum, *n.* Void, empty space, vacuity.

Vagabond, *a.* Wandering, homeless, landlouping, truant.

——, *n.* Vagrant, outcast, castaway, loafer, lounger, nomad, land-louper, idle wanderer, strolling beggar, tramp.

Vagary, *n.* Whim, freak, whimsey, crotchet, whimsicality, caprice, fancy, humor.

Vagrancy, *n.* Roving, wandering, vagabondage.

Vagrant, *n.* See VAGABOND.

——, *a.* Strolling, wandering, roving, roaming, unsettled, nomadic, itinerant, erratic.

Vague, *a.* 1. Uncertain, ambiguous, dim, doubtful, obscure, undetermined, indefinite, indistinct, ill-defined, confused, unsettled, loose, lax, unfixed.

2. Unauthorized, unwarranted, flying, loose, discursive.

Vain, *a.* 1. Unreal, shadowy, unsubstantial, supposititious, dreamy, delusive, deceitful, false, baseless, imaginary, empty, void.

2. Unavailing, useless, bootless, ineffectual, fruitless, profitless, futile, nugatory, abortive, unprofitable, without avail, idle, to no purpose, to no end.

3. Worthless, unsatisfying, unsatisfactory, vapid, unimportant, trivial, unessential, useless.

4. Conceited, vain-glorious, inflated, arrogant, proud, egotistical, overweening, ostentatious, high, self-sufficient, flushed, opinionated, self-satisfied, self-confident, self-admiring, self-opinioned, self-flattering, high-flown, puffed up, wise in one's own conceit.

5. Showy, ostentatious, gaudy, glittering, gorgeous.

Vain-glorious, *a.* 1. Conceited, vain, proud beyond desert.

2. Boastful, vaunting, braggart, pretentious.

Vain-glory, *n.* 1. Vanity, empty pride, show, pride without merit.

2. Rodomontade, empty boasting.

Vainly, *adv.* 1. Without effect, ineffectually, in vain, to no purpose, in a vain manner.

2. Proudly, arrogantly, boastingly, vauntingly.

3. Idly, foolishly.

Vale, *n.* (*Poetical.*) Valley, dingle, dell.

Valediction, *n.* Farewell, adieu, leave-taking, goodby.

Valedictory, *a.* Farewell.

Valet, *n.* [Fr.] Groom, servant, servingman, waiting-servant, waiter, lackey, attendant, flunky.

Valetudinarian, *n.* Invalid, valetudinary.

——, *a.* Weak, infirm, sickly, feeble, ailing, weakly, frail, invalid, valetudinary.

Valiant, *a.* 1. Brave, courageous, intrepid, valorous, gallant, chivalrous, chivalric, heroic, daring, dauntless, bold, fearless, doughty, undaunted, Spartan, lion-hearted, stout-hearted, redoubtable.

2. Brave, gallant, heroic, chivalrous.

Valid, *a.* 1. Efficacious, efficient, sound, weighty, powerful, conclusive, logical, cogent, good, just, solid, important, grave, sufficient, strong, well-grounded, substantial.

2. (*Law.*) Having legal strength *or* force, efficacious, executed with the proper formalities, supportable by law *or* right, good in law.

Validity, *n.* 1. Soundness, justness, efficacy, cogency, weight, strength, goodness, force, gravity, importance.

2. (*Law.*) Legal force *or* strength, quality of being good in law.

Valise, *n.* Portmanteau, travelling bag.

Valley, *n.* Dale, bottom, dell, dingle, ravine, canyon, dene, glen, vale; hollow, basin, pocket.

Valor, *n.* Bravery (*especially in war*), courage, prowess, boldness, spirit, daring, gallantry, intrepidity, heroism.

Valorous, *a.* Brave, courageous, stout, intrepid, bold, dauntless, doughty.

Valuable, *a.* 1. Precious, useful, serviceable, profitable, advantageous.

2. Precious, costly, expensive, rich.

3. Worthy, estimable, prizable, admirable.

——, *n.* Thing of value, treasure, precious possession.

Valuation, *n.* 1. Appraisement, estimation, estimate, assessment, appreciation.

2. Value, worth.

VALUE, *n.* 1. Worth, utility, importance (*value in use*), usefulness, avail.

2. Price, cost, rate, equivalent (*value in exchange*).

3. Estimation, valuation, merit, worth, excellence, importance.

4. Precise signification, import, worth.

5. (*Mus.*) Relative length, duration.

6. (*Art.*) Shade, tone, color.

Value, *v. t.* 1. Appraise, rate, estimate, account, apprize, price, assess, set a value on.

2. Esteem, appreciate, regard, prize, treasure, set a high value on, rate highly, hold in high esteem, set store by.

Valueless, *a.* Worthless, miserable, of no value, of no use.

Vamp, *v. t.* Repair, mend, piece, patch, tinker, refit, retouch, vamp up, patch up.

Vampire, *n.* 1. Parasite, bloodsucker, ghoul.

2. Extortioner, vulture, "vamp," temptress.

Van, *n.* 1. Front (*of an army or a fleet*), forerank, head.

2. Covered wagon, dray, truck, lorry.

Vandal, *n.* Barbarian, savage, destroyer.

——, *a.* Barbarous, savage, Vandalic, rude.

Vandalism, *n.* Barbarity, savagery; destruction, barbarism.

Vane, *n.* 1. Weather-cock.

2. Blade (*of a windmill, propeller, etc.*), beard (*of a feather*).

Van-guard, *n.* Advance-guard, first line, van, front rank.

Vanish, *v. t.* 1. Disappear, go out of sight, be lost to view, become invisible.

2. Disappear, dissolve, fade away, melt away, evaporate, fly, sink, die, pass away, be lost, be no more, pass, fade, be annihilated, "vamose."

Vanity, *n.* 1. Emptiness, hollowness, triviality, inanity, foolishness, unreality, worthlessness, futility, unrealness, unsubstantialness, falsity, *vanitas vanitatum.*

2. Conceit, conceitedness, egotism, self-conceit, vaingloriousness, *amour propre,* self-sufficiency, petty pride, self-complacency, self-approbation, self-admiration, pretension, affectation, arrogance.

3. Idle show, ostentation, display, vain pursuit, unsubstantial enjoyment, fruitless effort, fruitless desire.

Vanquish, *v. t.* 1. Conquer, defeat, overcome, subdue, subjugate, overpower, overthrow, outwit.

2. Overpower, overbear, master, crush, worst, rout, discomfit, foil, quell, put down, get the upper hand of, get the better of.

3. Confute, disprove, silence, confound.

Vanquisher, *n.* Conqueror, subduer, victor.

Vapid, *a.* 1. Insipid, tasteless, flat, savorless, lifeless, spiritless, stale, dead.

2. Tame, dull, meagre, jejune, languid, feeble, prosing, prosy, prosaic, insipid, spiritless, flat.

Vapor, *n.* 1. Gaseous state (*of a substance ordinarily fluid or solid*), aeriform state.

2. Fume, steam, reek, exhalation, smoke, fog, cloud, mist, rack.

3. Phantom, fantasy, whim, whimsey, vagary, day-dream, vain imagination, unreal fancy, dream, vision.

——, *v. i.* 1. Boast, brag, bluster, swagger, bully.

2. Evaporate, reek, steam, fume.

Vaporer, *n.* Boaster, blusterer, braggart, swaggerer, vaunter, bully, braggadocio.

Vaporish, *a.* Splenetic, hypochondriacal, peevish, petulant, humorsome, vapory.

Vaporize, *v. t.* Evaporate, convert into vapor, atomize, spray, sublimate, volatilize, gasify, fumigate.

Vaporous, *a.* 1. Foggy, vapory, full of vapor, steaming, reeking, moist.

2. Unreal, unsubstantial, vain.

Vapors, *n. pl.* Hypochondriasis, spleen, melancholy, dejection, blues, depression of spirits, blue devils, dumps, *tædium vitæ.*

Variable, *a.* 1. Changeable, mutable, shifting.

2. Inconstant, unsteady, fickle, vacillating, capricious, changing, floating, aberrant, protean, wavering, fluctuating, fitful, mutable, mobile, alterable, versatile, shifting.

Variance, *n.* 1. Alteration, change of condition.

2. Disagreement, difference, discord, dissension, jarring, strife, incompatibility.

3. (*Law.*) Variation, want of conformity (*as between the writ and the declaration,* or *between the allegation and the proof*).

Variation, *n.* 1. Alteration, mutation, change, modification.

2. Deviation, departure, difference, diversity, innovation, discrepancy.

3. Contrariety, discordance.

Variegate, *v. t.* Diversify, vary, streak, checker, counterchange, variate, varify, mottle, streak, spot, fret, diaper, stripe, fleck, speckle, dapple, figure, mark with different colors.

Variegated, *a.* Party-colored, motley, mottled, diversified, multicolored, dappled, pied, many-colored, many-hued, divers-colored, polychromatic, kaleidoscopic, pepper-and-salt, spotted, striped, checkered, flecked, of all manner of colors.

Variety, *n.* 1. Diversity, difference, variation, dissimilarity, variance.

2. Varied assortment.

3. Kind, species, class, phylum, race, genus, group, sort, type, brand.

4. Multiplicity, multiformity, multifariousness.

Various, *a.* 1. Diverse, different, manifold, several, sundry, numerous, many, divers.

2. Changeable, mutable, uncertain, unfixed.

3. Multiform, diverse, unlike each other.

4. Variegated, diversified.

Varlet, *n.* Scoundrel, rascal, rogue, knave, scapegrace, low fellow.

Varnish, *n.* 1. Lacquer, stain, shellac, enamel.

2. Glossy appearance.

3. Outside show, gloss, cover, palliation, extenuation, mitigation.

——, *v. t.* 1. Lacquer, japan, glaze, shellac, enamel.

2. Polish, adorn, decorate, garnish, gild, embellish.

3. Palliate, gloss, extenuate, excuse, gloze, glaze over, disguise.

Vary, *v. t.* 1. Alter.

2. Transform, transmute, metamorphose, change, make some change in.

3. Exchange, alternate, rotate, change to something else.

4. Diversify, variegate, modify.

——, *v. i.* 1. Alter, change, be changeable, fluctuate, veer.

2. Differ, be unlike, be different.

3. Alter, alternate, change in succession, range, succeed, rotate.

4. Deviate, depart, swerve.

5. Disagree, be at variance, be in dissension.

Vassal, *n.* 1. Feudatory, feudal tenant, liegeman, thrall.

2. Subject, dependant, retainer.

3. Servant, bondman, slave.

Vassalage, *n.* Subjection, dependence, servitude, slavery, enslavement.

Vast, *a.* 1. Very spacious, very extensive, infinite, boundless, measureless, wide.

2. Very great, huge, enormous, immense, colossal, gigantic, prodigious, stupendous, monstrous; mighty, tremendous.

3. Remarkable, extraordinary.

Vaticinate, *v. t.* (*Rare.*) Foretell, predict, soothsay, prophesy, presage, prognosticate, augur, divine, forebode.

Vaticination, *n.* Prophecy, prediction, prognostication, augury, divination.

Vaudeville, *n.* [Fr.] Ballad, street song, trivial strain, light song.

Vault, *n.* 1. Arched ceiling, arched roof, continued arch, curvet, dome, cupola.

2. Cell, cellar, dungeon; tomb, crypt, catacomb, repository for the dead.

3. Leap, bound, jump.

——, *v. t.* Arch, cover with an arch, arch over.

——, *v. i.* 1. Leap, bound, jump, spring.

2. Tumble, turn, exhibit feats of jumping, play the posture-master.

Vaulted, *a.* 1. Arched, domed, cupolar, concave.

2. (*Bot.*) Fornicate, fornicated.

Vaulter, *n.* Leaper, jumper, tumbler, acrobat.

Vaulting, *a.* Aspiring, eager, impatient, overeager.

Vaunt, *v. i.* Brag, boast, exult, "blow."

——, *v. t.* Brag of, boast of, make a display of, make a boast of, show off, display with ostentation.

——, *n.* Boast, brag.

Vaunter, *n.* Boaster, braggart, braggadocio, drawcansir, roisterer, huff, vaporer, noisy fellow.

Veer, *v. i.* Shift, turn, change course, deviate, gybe, change direction, change about, come round, turn about.

Veering, *n.* 1. Shifting, turning, change of course.

2. Tergiversation, flickleness, instability, vacillation.

3. Trimming, temporizing, time-serving, shifting.

Vegetable, *n.* Plant, truck, produce.

Vegetate, *v. i.* 1. Shoot, germinate, spring, pullulate, grow (*as a plant*), shoot up, spring up, put forth, swell, sprout, increase, develop, blossom, flower, flourish.

2. Bask, idle, hibernate, do nothing, be inactive, luxuriate, become rooted, stagnate.

Vegetation, *n.* 1. Vegetable growth, plant life, process of vegetating.

2. Plants, vegetables, the sum of vegetable life.

3. Stagnation, inertia.

Vehemence, *n.* 1. Impetuosity, violence, impetuous force.

2. Ardor, fervor, fervency, eagerness, earnestness, keenness, warmth, zeal, enthusiasm, passion, heat.

3. Force, might,.intensity.

Vehement, *a.* 1. Impetuous, violent, furious, rampant, passionate, high, hot, high-wrought.

2. Ardent, zealous, eager, keen, earnest, fervid, enthusiastic, sanguine, passionate, burning, fiery.

3. Strong, forcible, powerful, mighty, very great.

Vehicle, *n.* 1. Carriage, conveyance.

2. Medium, instrument, agency, intermediary.

Veil, *n.* 1. Screen, shade, curtain, cover, film.

2. Cover, disguise, mask, visor, blind, cloak, muffler, screen.

——, *v. t.* Screen, cover with a veil, throw a veil over, cover, invest, envelop; hide, mask, conceal, disguise, gloze, curtain, cloak, shroud.

Vein, *n.* 1. Blood-vessel.

2. Rib (*of a leaf*), nerve.

3. Seam (*in a mine*), lode, ledge, leader.

4. Stripe, streak, wave, variegation.

5. Current, course, thread, train.

6. Bent, humor, disposition, mood; talent, faculty, genius, quality, strain, turn of mind, peculiar temper.

——, *v. t.* Stripe, streak.

Vellicate, *v. t.* Twitch, pluck, stimulate, cause to twitch.

Velocity, *n.* 1. Swiftness, speed, celerity, fleetness, quickness, rapidity, haste, acceleration, expedition.

2. (*Mech.*) Rate of motion.

Velvet, *a.* Soft, smooth, delicate, velvety, velutinous, downy.

Venal, *a.* 1. Mercenary, purchasable, hireling, mean, sordid, prostitute, corrupt, vendible.

2. Venous, contained in the veins.

Venality, *n.* Mercenariness.

Venary, *a.* Venatical, venatorial.

Vend, *v. t.* Sell.

Vendee, *n.* [Correlative of *Vendor*.] Purchaser, buyer.

Vendible, *a.* Salable, merchantable, that may be sold.

Vendition, *n.* Sale, selling.

Vendor, *n.* [Correlative of *Vendee*.] Seller, vender, hawker, peddler.

Vendue, *n.* Auction, cant, public auction, auction sale, public sale, sale by outcry.

Veneer, *v. t.* Overlay, cover thinly, coat, face, gloze, disguise.

Venerable, *a.* 1. To be venerated, worthy of veneration, grave, respected, revered, time honored.

2. Dread, awful, dreadful.

3. Old, aged, patriarchal.

Venerate, *v. t.* Reverence, revere, respect, esteem, adore, honor, regard highly.

Veneration, *n.* Reverence, high respect, respect mingled with awe, devotion, worship, admiration, esteem.

Venery, *n.* Hunting, the chase.

Venesection, *n.* Bleeding, phlebotomy, blood-letting.

Vengeance, *n.* 1. Avengement, retribution.

2. Revenge, retaliation.

3. Vindictiveness, revengefulness.

Vengeful, *a.* Vindictive, revengeful, rancorous.

Venial, *a.* Excusable, pardonable; allowed, permitted.

Venom, *n.* 1. Poison (*naturally secreted by certain animals*), virus.

2. Malignity, maliciousness, malice, spite, spitefulness, gall, rancor, rankling, grudge, bitterness, acerbity, acrimony, malevolence, hate, ill-will, virulence.

Venomous, *a.* 1. Poisonous, noxious to animal life, virulent, toxic, septic, deadly.

2. Malignant, malicious, spiteful, mischievous, noxious, envenomed, caustic.

Venous, *a.* 1. Venal.

2. (*Bot.*) Reticulated, netted, veiny, venose.

Vent, *n.* 1. Opening, hole, vent-hole, orifice, mouth, airhole.

2. Spiracle, air-tube, air-pipe, blow-hole, bunghole, plug, hydrant, spout, tap.

3. (*Arch.*) Crenelle, loop-hole.

4. Emission, passage, outlet, escape, effusion.

5. Discharge, utterance, expression.

6. Market, sale, opportunity to sell.

——, *v. t.* 1. Emit, pour forth, let out.

2. Utter, give vent to, express.

Venter, *n.* 1. (*Anat.*) Abdomen, belly.

2. Uterus, womb, matrix.

Ventilate, *v. t.* 1. Air, oxygenate, aërate; freshen, purify.

2. Winnow, fan.

3. Examine, sift, scrutinize, discuss, canvass, comment, review, publish.

Ventilation, *n.* 1. Airing.

2. Winnowing, fanning.

3. Examination, scrutiny, discussion, public exposure.

Ventose, *a.* Windy, flatulent.

Ventral, *a.* Abdominal, stomachal.

Ventricose, *a.* (*Bot.*) Distended, bellied, inflated.

Ventriloquist, *n.* Polyphonist.

Venture, *n.* 1. Hazard, risk, danger, jeopardy, peril.

2. Chance, hap, luck, contingency.

3. Stake, adventure, risk.

4. Speculation, flyer, gamble.

5. Enterprise, project, work.

——, *v. t.* Hazard, risk, jeopardize, jeopard, expose to hazard, presume, dare, undertake, speculate, try, test.

——, *v. i.* 1. Dare, adventure, hazard one's self.

2. Run the risk, tempt fortune, take one's chance.

3. Presume, make bold, take the liberty, have the presumption.

Venturesome, *a.* Adventurous, daring, intrepid, rash, foolhardy, presumptuous, bold, courageous, venturous, enterprising, doughty, fearless.

Veracious, *a.* 1. Truthful, observant of truth, truth-telling, true, truth-loving, straightforward, trustworthy, reliable.

2. True, credible, reliable, trustworthy, honest, genuine, unfeigned.

Veracity, *n.* Truthfulness, truth, ingenuousness, sincerity, probity, love of truth, fidelity, trueness, exactness, correctness, honesty, candor, frankness.

Verbal, *a.* 1. Oral, spoken, unwritten, parol, nuncupative, expressed in words.

2. Literal, word for word.

Verbally, *adv.* 1. Orally, by word of mouth.

2. Word for word, *verbatim.*

Verbatim, *adv.* [L.] Literally, word for word, in the same words.

Verbiage, *n.* Wordiness, verboseness, verbosity, prolixity, diffuseness.

Verbose, *a.* Wordy, prolix, diffuse, talkative, loquacious.

Verbosity, *n.* Wordiness, macrology, prolixity, verboseness, perissology, redundancy, pleonasm.

Verdancy, *n.* 1. Greenness, viridity, verdantness.

2. (*Colloq.*) Inexperience, rawness, liability to be imposed upon.

Verdant, *a.* 1. Green, fresh, verdurous.

2. (*Colloq.*) Raw, inexperienced, green, green in knowledge, unsophisticated.

Verdict, *n.* 1. (*Law.*) Decision, finding.

2. Decision, judgment, opinion, sentence.

Verdure, *n.* Greenness, green, viridity, freshness (*of vegetation*), foliage, vegetation.

Verge, *n.* 1. Rod, staff, mace.

2. Edge, brink, border, margin, rim, brim, boundary, confine, limit, extreme, skirt.

3. Eve, brink, edge, point.

4. Arbor (*of a watch-balance*), spindle.

——, *v. i.* 1. Tend, incline, slope, lean, trend, bear.

2. Border, approach, skirt, be near, tend, incline, tend toward.

Verification, *n.* Authentication, attestation, confirmation, corroboration.

Verify, *v. t.* Prove to be true, prove to be correct, establish the truth of, confirm, corroborate, attest, substantiate; identify, authenticate, make good.

Verily, *adv.* 1. In a true manner, in truth, in fact, certainly, indeed.

2. Truly, really, absolutely, confidently, positively, actually, indeed.

Verisimilitude, *n.* Likelihood, probability, appearance of truth.

Veritable, *a.* True, real, actual, genuine, positive, absolute.

Verity, *n.* 1. Truth, truthfulness, true *or* real nature, reality, consonance to the reality of things.

2. True statement, true assertion, fact, true tenet.

Vermicular, *a.* 1. Sinuous, tortuous, undulating, flexuous, waving, serpentine, meandering, winding, twisting, convoluted, vermiform, worm-like, worm-shaped.

2. Peristaltic.

Vermiculate, *a.* 1. Worm-like, worm-shaped.

2. Crawling, creeping, twisting, sinuous.

3. Creeping, insinuating, sophistical.

Vermiform, *a.* Worm-like, worm-shaped, vermiculate.

Vermifuge, *n.* Anthelmintic, helminthagogue.

Vermilion, *n.* Cochineal, bright red.

Vermin, *n. sing.* and *pl.* 1. Noxious insects *or* animals (*of small size*).

2. Off-scourings, riff-raff, off-scum, rabble, scum.

Vermivorous, *a.* Worm-eating, worm-devouring.

Vernacular, *a.* Native, indigenous, mother, vulgar.

——, *n.* Vernacular language, native language, mother tongue; dialect.

Verrucose, *a.* Warty, knobby.

Versatile, *a.* 1. Changeable, variable, mobile, kaleidoscopic, capricious, erratic.

2. Inconstant, unsteady, fickle, mercurial.

3. Varied, many-sided, plastic, ready, protean, adaptable.

VERSE, *n.* 1. Line (*metrically arranged*), line of poetry, stich, stave, number.

2. Versification, poetry, poesy, metrical composition, metrical language.

3. Passage (*of Scripture*), text, sentence.

Versed, *a.* Skilled, skilful, practised, accomplished, conversant, acquainted, qualified, trained, proficient, clever, able, good at, at home in, *au fait*.

Versemonger, *n.* Poetaster, manufacturer of poetry, writer of verses (*used humorously* or *in contempt*).

Verses, *n. pl.* Numbers, poetry, song.

Versification, *n.* Verse, metrical composition, prosody, orthometry, scansion.

Versify, *v. t.* Turn into verse, rhyme *or* rime, metrify.

——, *v. i.* Make verses.

Version, *n.* 1. Translation, rendering, interpretation, reading, lection.

2. Translation, rendition.

Versus, *prep.* (*Law.*) Against.

Vertebrate, *n.* Vertebral, back-boned animal.

Vertex, *n.* 1. Point.

2. Top, summit, crown.

3. Crown of the head.

4. Zenith.

Vertical, *a.* Perpendicular (*to the horizon*), upright, plumb, erect, steep.

Verticle, *n.* Axis, hinge, joint.

Vertiginous, *a.* 1. Whirling, rotary, rotatory.

2. Dizzy, giddy.

Vertigo, *n.* Dizziness, giddiness, swimming of the head.

Verve, *n.* [Fr.] Enthusiasm, rapture, spirit, ardor, animation, force, energy, excitement of the imagination.

Very, *a.* 1. True, real, actual.

2. Same, self-same.

VERY, *adv.* Highly, exceedingly, absolutely, vastly, hugely, enormously, "terribly," excessively, extremely, remarkably, surpassingly, to a high degree, quite, "jolly."

Vesicle, *n.* Cell, cyst, utricle, bladder, follicle, blister.

Vespers, *n. pl.* Evening service, evening song, evensong (*in the Catholic Church*).

VESSEL, *n.* 1. Utensil (*for holding anything*), receptacle, jar, vase, etc.

2. Bottom, sailing craft, ship.

3. Tube, duct, canal, vein, artery, blood-vessel.

Vest, *n.* 1. Vesture, garment, vestment, robe, dress.

2. Waistcoat (*for men*).

——, *v. t.* 1. Clothe, dress, surround, robe, enrobe, envelop, cover.

2. Endow, furnish, put in possession, invest.

3. (*Law.*) Clothe with possession.

Vestal, *a.* Pure, chaste, immaculate, stainless; maidenly.

Vested, *a.* Fixed, established, legalized; clothed, robed, furnished.

Vestibule, *n.* 1. Porch, entrance-way.

2. Hall, lobby, ante-room, passage.

Vestige, *n.* Footprint, footstep, token, sign, mark, record, trace, track, evidence, relic.

Vestment, *n.* Garment, dress, robe, vest, habiliment, garb, vesture.

Vestry, *n.* Sacristy, vestry-room.

Vesture, *n.* 1. Garment, dress, robe, vestment, vest.

2. Clothes, clothing, apparel, covering, attire, habit, garb, costume, habiliment, raiment, dress.

Veteran, *a.* Old (*in experience*), experienced (*especially in war*), long exercised, long practised, aged, grayheaded, seasoned, disciplined.

——, *n.* 1. Old soldier, old campaigner; old man, graybeard, old timer, oldster.

2. Expert, adept, proficient, old stager, old hand, practised hand.

Veterinarian, *n.* Farrier, horse-doctor, horse-leech, veterinary surgeon, "vet."

Veto, *n.* 1. Prohibition (*of a legislative act by the Executive*), refusal to sanction, interdiction, restriction.

2. Authoritative prohibition, forbidding.

——, *v. t.* Prohibit, forbid, negative, withhold assent to.

Vex, *v. t.* 1. Tease, torment, plague, spite, roil, "rile," harass, worry, harry, hector, distress, annoy, trouble, perplex, persecute, cross, pother, gall, chafe, molest, pester, bother, badger.

2. Fret, irritate, provoke, displease, offend, irk, nettle, try the patience of, affront, enchafe.

3. Disturb, disquiet, agitate, put in commotion.

Vexation, *n.* 1. Irritation, chagrin, displeasure, pique, mortification, trouble, disquiet, agitation, affliction, uneasiness, grief, sorrow, distress, discomfort.

2. Torment, plague, trouble, annoyance, nuisance, curse, affliction.

3. Harassing by law, vexing, troubling, damage.

Vexatious, *a.* 1. Troublesome, irritating, pestilential, pestiferous, provoking, annoying, unpleasant, disagreeable, aggravating.

2. Distressing, harassing, troublesome, afflictive, painful, grievous, disturbing.

3. Troubled, anxious, uneasy, distressed, uncomfortable, comfortless, galling, burdensome, irksome.

Vexed, *a.* 1. Irritated, plagued, worried, harassed, annoyed, troubled, provoked, disquieted.

2. Disputed, contested, in dispute, causing contention.

Via, *adv.* [L.] By way of.

Vial, *n.* Small bottle, phial.

Viands, *n. pl.* Food, victuals.

Vibrant, *a.* Vibrating, resonant, undulous, oscillating.

Vibrate, *v. i.* 1. Oscillate, swing, move to and fro, move backward and forward, undulate, sway, shake, tremble, thrill.

2. Impinge, sound, quiver, produce a vibratory effect.

3. Vacillate, hesitate, waver, fluctuate.

——, *v. t.* 1. Brandish, swing, move to and fro.

2. Cause to quiver, undulate, affect with vibratory motion.

3. Measure by swinging.

VIBRATION, *n.* Oscillation, swinging, nutation.

Vibratory, *a.* Vibrating, oscillating, vibrative, vibratile, oscillatory, swinging.

Vicarious, *a.* 1. Deputed, delegated, commissioned.

2. Substituted.

Vice, *n.* 1. Defect, fault, blemish, imperfection, failing, short-coming, besetting sin, infirmity.

2. Wickedness, sin, iniquity, depravity, depravation, immorality, laxity, evil, error, corruption, badness, wrongdoing, evildoing, obliquity, viciousness, the old Adam.

Vice-consul, *n.* Deputy-consul, assistant-consul.

Vicegerent, *n.* Deputy, lieutenant, representative, agent, vicar.

Viceroy, *n.* Vice-king.

Vice versa. [L.] Conversely, reversely, contrariwise, turn about.

Vicinity, *n.* 1. Nearness, proximity, propinquity.

2. Neighborhood, vicinage.

Vicious, *a.* 1. Faulty, defective, imperfect.

2. Wicked, mischievous, depraved, degenerate, immoral, unrighteous, evil, evil-minded, sunk in iniquity, shameless, atrocious, flagrant, devilish, diabolical, demoniac, hellish, sinful, corrupt, unprincipled, abandoned, demoralized, bad, worthless, profligate, iniquitous.

3. Spiteful, malicious, venomous.

4. Foul, bad, impure.

5. Impure, debased, faulty, corrupt.

6. Unruly, refractory, contrary.

Vicissitude, *n.* 1. Alternation, interchange, regular change, mutual succession.

2. Variation, mutation, revolution, change, fluctuation.

Victim, *n.* 1. Sacrifice, martyr.

2. Prey, sufferer.

3. (*Colloq.*) Dupe, gull, cull, cully, prey, puppet, cat's-paw, gudgeon.

Victimize, *v. t.* (*Colloq.*) Cheat, dupe, trick, defraud, deceive, swindle, cozen, chouse, gull, overreach, befool, fool, beguile, circumvent, diddle, hoax, "bamboozle," hoodwink, jockey, impose upon, put upon, practise upon, play upon, take in.

Victor, *n.* Conqueror, vanquisher, champion, winner.

Victorious, *a.* Triumphant, conquering, winning, successful.

Victory, *n.* Conquest, triumph, mastery, achievement; palm.

Victual, *v. t.* Provide with food, supply with provisions, store with sustenance, supply with victuals.

Victualler, *n.* 1. Tavern-keeper, innkeeper, publican.

2. Provision-ship.

3. [*Scotch.*] Corn-factor.

Victuals, *n. pl.* Food, meat, sustenance, provisions, cooked provisions, viands, comestibles, eatables.

Videlicet, *adv.* [L. Usually represented by *viz.*] Namely, to wit, that is, that is to say, to particularize, to be more explicit, in other words.

Vie, *v. i.* Contend, compete, strive (*for superiority*), rival, emulate.

View, *v. t.* 1. Survey, scan, eye, see, witness, behold, inspect, explore, contemplate, look on *or* upon, turn the eyes to, have in sight.

2. Consider, regard, inspect, study, contemplate, think about, reflect upon, survey intellectually, examine with the mental eye.

VIEW, *n.* 1. Sight, survey, inspection, regard, observation, examination by the eye.

2. Mental survey, intellectual examination, review.

3. Sight, reach of the sight.

4. Prospect, scene, vista, perspective, outlook, range, conspectus, panorama.

5. Sketch, picture.

6. Design, purpose, object, aim, intent, intention, scope, drift.

7. Opinion, judgment, notion, belief, theory, impression, idea, sentiment, conception.

8. Appearance, show, aspect.

Vigil, *n.* 1. Watch, sleeplessness, abstinence from sleep.

2. Devotional watching, waking for religious exercises.

3. Wake.

Vigilance, *n.* Watchfulness, lookout, caution, activity, circumspection, incessant care, scrupulous attention.

Vigilant, *a.* Watchful, circumspect, careful, cautious, wakeful, unslumbering, unsleeping, sharp, jealous, on the lookout, wide-awake, on the alert.

Vigor, *n.* 1. Strength, force, might, power, physical force, activity, spirit, potency, efficacy.

2. Energy, strength, intellectual force.

3. Health, haleness, soundness, robustness, heartiness, "pep," "vim," vitality, "punch," bloom, elasticity, tone, thriftiness, flourishing condition.

4. Liveliness, raciness, piquancy, strenuousness, vehemence, freshness, intensity, ardor, fire, verve, enthusiasm.

Vigorous, *a.* 1. Strong, powerful, lusty.

2. Strong, powerful, energetic, forcible, active, strenuous, cordial, hearty, virile, alert, vivid, vehement.

3. Healthy, hale, robust, sturdy, sound, hardy, buxom, brisk, hearty, in health, in good health.

4. Thrifty, flourishing, growing well, fresh.

5. Nervous, robust, spirited, lively, sparkling, sharp, severe, bold, trenchant, emphatic, racy, pointed, piquant, impassioned.

Vile, *a.* 1. Base, mean, low, despicable, paltry, contemptible, beggarly, grovelling, slavish, brutish, beastly; odious, repulsive, disgusting, pitiful, ugly, ignoble, abject, scurvy, shabby, sorry.

2. Sinful, wicked, bad, base, impure, obscene, lewd, foul, gross, evil, vicious, iniquitous.

3. Worthless, of poor quality, linseywoolsey, cheap, valueless, mean, sorry, miserable, wretched.

Vileness, *n.* 1. Baseness, meanness, despicableness, foulness, abasement, shabbiness, abjectness, abjection.

2. Wickedness, sinfulness, turpitude, baseness, depravity, badness.

3. Worthlessness, poor quality.

Vilify, *v. t.* Defame, traduce, revile, slander, brand, libel, asperse, calumniate, scandalize, malign, abuse, blacken, blemish, slur, vituperate, backbite, lampoon, disparage, berate, run down, speak ill of, accuse falsely, decry.

Villa, *n.* Country house, country seat, country residence, rural mansion.

Village, *n.* Hamlet, town, settlement, thorp.

Villain, *n.* Rascal, knave, scoundrel, rogue, scamp, reprobate, scapegrace, blackguard, slip-halter, ruffian, evildoer, miscreant, caitiff, vile wretch; "heavy."

Villainous, *a.* 1. Base, mean, vile.

2. Wicked, depraved, knavish, ruffianly, corrupt, unprincipled.

3. Heinous, sinful, nefarious, outrageous, very bad, atrocious.

4. (*Familiar.*) Sorry, mischievous, mean, vile.

Villainy, *n.* 1. Wickedness, sinfulness, depravity, turpitude, atrocity, criminality, infamy.

2. Depraved discourse, infamous speech.

3. Roguery, rascality, knavery, knavishness, miscreancy, dishonesty, trickery, crime, sin, iniquity.

Vindicable, *a.* Justifiable, warrantable, fit, defensible, right, proper.

Vindicate, *v. t.* 1. Justify, defend, uphold.

2. Assert, maintain, support, stand by, make good, advocate, right, avenge.

Vindication, *n.* 1. Justification, defence, excuse, apology.

2. Assertion, maintenance, support.

Vindicator, *n.* 1. Assertor, pleader, advocate.

2. Defender, champion, justifier.

Vindictive, *a.* Revengeful, unforgiving, unrelenting, implacable, vengeful, rancorous, malevolent, malicious, malignant, spiteful, retaliative, grudgeful, avenging.

Vinegar, *a.* Sour, acid.

Vinery, *n.* Grapery.

Viola, *n.* Tenor-viol, alto-viol, *bratsche.*

Violate, *v. t.* 1. Injure, hurt.

2. Break, infringe, transgress, invade, break through, trench upon, encroach upon, disregard, set at naught, disobey.

3. Profane, desecrate, pollute, do violence to, dishonor, defile.

4. Abuse, outrage, ravish, deflower, debauch, constuprate, defile, commit rape upon.

Violation, *n.* 1. Interruption.

2. Infringement, transgression, breaking, breach, non-observance.

3. Profanation, desecration, pollution, dishonor.

4. Ravishment, ravishing, rape, constupration, defloration, defilement, stupration, pollution, debauchment.

Violence, *n.* 1. Vehemence, impetuosity, boisterousness, force, might, brute force, ferocity.

2. Passion, fury, fierceness, wildness, rage, turbulence, uproar, tumult, riot.

3. Outrage, injustice, injury, wrong, violation, profanation.

4. Sharpness, acuteness, severity, poignancy, intensity.

5. Ravishment, rape, constupration.

VIOLENT, *a.* 1. Boisterous, furious, impetuous, forcible, forceful, stormy, vehement, turbulent, tumultuous, wild, insane, demented, frenzied.

2. Fierce, fiery, fuming, raging, ungovernable, rapid, rampant, rank, roaring, rough, tearing, towering, infuriate, passionate, high, hot, strong, heady, heavy, obstreperous, refractory.

3. Unnatural, effected by force, accidental, by violent means.

4. Unjust, outrageous, extreme, desperate.

5. Sharp, severe, acute, poignant, intense, exquisite.

Violin, *n.* Fiddle, kit.

Viper, *n.* 1. Poisonous snake.

2. Wretch, reptile, serpent, snake, adder, scorpion.

Viperous, *a.* Malignant, poisonous, venomous, viperish.

Virago, *n.* 1. Female warrior, amazon.

2. Termagant, vixen, shrew, Tartar, brawler, scold, Xantippe, fury.

Virgate, *a.* (*Bot.*) Wand-shaped.

Virgin, *n.* Maid, maiden, girl, lass, damsel, vestal, spinster, celibate.

——, *a.* 1. Chaste, pure, undefiled, unpolluted, virginal, vestal, stainless, maidenly, modest.

2. Fresh, unused, untouched, new, maiden.

Virginity, *n.* Maidenhood.

Viridescent, *a.* Greenish, slightly green, virescent.

Viridity, *n.* Greenness, verdancy, verdure, viridness.

Virile, *a.* 1. Of a man.

2. Manly, masculine, vigorous, masterful, forceful, robust.

Virility, *n.* 1. Manhood, maturity.

2. Masculinity, masculineness, male energy, manliness, manly vigor, masculine force.

Virtual, *a.* Substantial, constructive, practical, essential, equivalent, tantamount, implied, implicit, indirect.

2. Potential, in essence *or* effect.

Virtually, *adv.* In effect, potentially, substantially, practically, to all intents and purposes.

Virtue, *n.* 1. Force, efficacy, effectiveness, potentiality, power, strength, potency, energy, inherent power.

2. Natural excellence, worth, merit, value, grace, desert.

3. Goodness (*that comes from self-discipline*), honor, honesty, uprightness, probity, integrity, rectitude, morality, worth, moral excellence.

4. Excellence, good quality.

5. Virginity, purity, female chastity, innocence.

Virtuoso, *n.* [It.] Connoisseur, amateur, *dilettante*, man devoted to *virtu*, person skilled in the fine arts; master, expert.

Virtuous, *a.* 1. Upright, honest, good, righteous, noble, exemplary, worthy, excellent, blameless, morally right, equitable.

2. Chaste, modest, pure, innocent, continent, immaculate, undefiled.

3. Efficacious, powerful.

Virulence, ⎫ *n.* 1. Poisonousness, venom-
Virulency, ⎭ ousness.

2. Acrimony, malignancy, malignity, bitterness, malevolence.

Virulent, *a.* 1. Poisonous, venomous, malignant, deadly, toxic, highly noxious.

2. Acrimonious, bitter, acrid, caustic.

Virus, *n.* Poison (*of a morbid nature*), venom.

Visage, *n.* Face, countenance, physiognomy; guise, semblance, aspect.

Viscera, *n. pl.* [L.] Entrails, intestines, bowels, "insides," inwards, guts.

Viscid, *a.* See VISCOUS.

Viscosity, *n.* 1. Glutinousness, ropiness, tenacity, viscidity.

2. Glutinous substance.

Viscous, *a.* Glutinous, clammy, slimy, mucilaginous, sticky, adhesive, tenacious, viscid, ropy, sizy.

Visibility, *n.* 1. Perceptibility, discernableness, apparentness, clearness, distinctness, exposure to view.

2. Conspicuousness.

Visible, *a.* 1. Perceptible, perceivable, visual, discernible, in view, in sight, to be seen, perceivable by the eye, seeable.

2. Apparent, manifest, evident, open, obvious, conspicuous, clear, plain, palpable, patent, unhidden, discoverable, revealed, distinct, in focus, well-defined, unmistakable, noticeable, observable.

Vision, *n.* 1. Sight, seeing, eyesight, faculty of seeing.

2. Eyeshot, ken, range of vision.

3. Apparition, ghost, spectre, phantom, phantasm, chimera, illusion, supernatural appearance, dream, hallucination.

Visionary, *a.* 1. Imaginative, romantic, given to revery, impractical, quixotic.

2. Unreal, fanciful, fancied, ideal, fantastic, wild, imaginary, chimerical, illusory, shadowy, dreamy, romantic, unsubstantial, air-built, utopian.

——, *n.* Dreamer, enthusiast, zealot, castle-builder, fanatic, utopian, optimist.

Visit, *v. t.* 1. Go to see, call upon, pay a visit to.

2. Inspect, examine, survey.

3. Frequent, haunt; afflict, affect.

——, *v. i.* Drop in, call, stop, tarry, stay.

Visitant, *n.* See VISITOR.

Visitation, *n.* 1. Dispensation (*especially of retributive evil*), calamity, disaster, affliction, misfortune, trial, blow, stroke, trouble, hardship, sorrow, ill-luck, ill-fortune, infliction, retribution; attack, seizure, paroxysm.

2. (*Law.*) Visiting (*in order to examine*), inspection, official visit.

Visitor, *n.* 1. Guest, company, visitant; caller, sojourner, stranger, newcomer; *habitué,* frequenter.

2. Inspector, examiner, censor, critic.

Vista, *n.* View (*especially through an avenue*), prospect, perspective.

Visual, *a.* Optic, optical, ocular, of the eye, of the sight *or* vision.

Vital, *a.* 1. Essential, indispensable, cardinal, radical, basic.

2. Necessary to life, life-supporting.

3. Living, alive, having life, animate, existing.

4. Very necessary, highly important, essential, paramount.

Vitality, *n.* Life, animation, vital power, vigor, virility.

Vitalize, *v. t.* Vivify, animate, quicken, strengthen, make alive, give life to, furnish with vital principle.

Vitals, *n. pl.* 1. Seat of life, vital organs.

2. Parts essential to life.

Vitiate, *v. t.* 1. Impair, invalidate, spoil, deteriorate, degrade, debase, deprave, corrupt, pollute, adulterate, injure, contaminate, infect, defile, poison, render defective, make vicious.

2. Make void, destroy, cause to fail of effect.

Vitiation, *n.* Deterioration, degeneration, debasement, degradation, degeneracy, depravation, impairment, injury, corruption, perversion, pollution, adulteration, prostitution, invalidation.

Vitreous, *a.* Glassy.

Vitriform, *a.* Hyaloid, transparent, like glass.

Vituperate, *v. t.* Find fault with, berate, scold, denounce, censure, overwhelm with abuse, abuse, vilify, revile, reproach, rate, upbraid, rail at, objurgate.

Vituperation, *n.* Abuse, blame, reproach, reviling, upbraiding, railing, objurgation, invective, scolding, severe censure.

Vituperative, *a.* Abusive, reproachful, scolding, scurrilous, opprobrious, condemnatory, damnatory, contemptuous, insulting.

Vivacious, *a.* Lively, sprightly, brisk, animated, active, breezy, spirited, gay, sportive, frolicsome, jocund, merry, bright, light-hearted, cheerful, mirthful, pleasant, full of life, buxom.

Vivacity, *n.* 1. Life, animation, spiritedness, vivaciousness, activity, *élan,* energy.

2. Liveliness, sprightliness, cheerfulness, gayety, cheer, good humor, good spirits, high spirits.

Vive, *interj.* [Fr.] Live, long live, success.

Vivid, *a.* 1. Lively, living, sprightly, vigorous, animated, quick, active, strong, bright, clear, lucid, brilliant, intense, fresh.

2. Telling, graphic, striking, expressive.

Vivify, *v. t.* Animate, vitalize, awake, arouse, quicken, make alive, give life to, endue with life.

Vixen, *n.* Scold, termagant, shrew, Tartar, brawler, spitfire, Xantippe.

Vocable, *n.* Word, term, name.

Vocabulary, *n.* 1. Dictionary, glossary, lexicon, word-book, list of words.

2. Language, words, terms; range of language.

Vocalist, *n.* Singer, songstress, melodist, warbler, cantatrice, caroller, chanter.

Vocation, *n.* 1. Call, summons, citation, injunction.

2. Occupation, employment, calling, business, pursuit, profession, trade, avocation.

Vociferate, *v. i.* 1. Cry, bawl, roar, cry out, bellow, howl, yell, clamor, exclaim, cry out with vehemence.

2. Rant, mouth.

——, *v. t.* Cry aloud, roar out, utter loudly *or* vehemently.

Vociferation, *n.* Clamor, outcry, loud utterance, hue and cry.

Vociferous, *a.* Noisy, clamorous, loud, blatant, open-mouthed, stunning, uproarious, obstreperous.

Vogue, *n.* Fashion, mode, style, usage, custom, practice, repute, favor.

VOICE, *n.* 1. Spoken sound, utterance, tongue, speech, articulate sound.

2. Sound, noise, notes.

3. Vote, suffrage, choice expressed, say, option, preference, opinion, wish.

4. Tone, mode of speaking, distinctive character *or* quality of tone, intonation, inflexion, enunciation, pronunciation, articulation, modulation, accent.

5. Language, words, expression, signification of feeling.

Void, *a.* 1. Empty, vacant, blank, vacuous, hollow.

2. Free, destitute, clear, without, wanting, devoid, lacking.

3. Unoccupied, unfilled, unsupplied, untenanted.

4. Null, invalid, nugatory, ineffectual, of no effect, of no binding force, inept.

5. Unsubstantial, vain, unreal, imaginary.

——, *n.* Vacuum, empty space, emptiness, blank, hole, abyss, chasm.

——, *v. t.* 1. Suit, leave.

2. Throw out, emit, eject, clear, empty, send out, evacuate, pour out.

3. Vacate, annul, nullify, make null.

Volant, *a.* 1. Flying.

2. Current.

3. Nimble, rapid, quick, light, active.

Volatile, *a.* 1. Evaporable, incoercible, gaseous, vaporific, vaporizable, vaporable.

2. Airy, gay, lively, jolly, sprightly, vivacious, frivolous, buoyant, full of spirit, jocund.

3. Fickle, changeable, giddy, inconstant, mercurial, flyaway, light-headed, flighty, reckless, capricious, unsteady, whimsical, humorsome, wild, harebrained.

Volatility, *n.* 1. Evaporableness, disposition to evaporate.

2. Airiness, liveliness, gayety, vivacity, sprightliness, cheerfulness.

3. Changeableness, fickleness, flightiness, giddiness, inconstancy, levity, frivolity, want of seriousness, mutability.

Volition, *n.* 1. Will, choice, preference, option, discretion, determination, freewill, free-agency, power of willing, purpose, elective preference.

2. Act of willing, act of determining, exercise of the will.

Volley, *n.* 1. Flight of shot, salvo, round, fusillade, shooting.

2. Discharge, emission, burst, explosion, blast, outbreak, report, storm, shower.

Volubility, *n.* Fluency, glibness, copiousness of speech, command of language, facility of expression.

Voluble, *a.* 1. Fluent, glib, loquacious, talkative, of a ready tongue, ready in speech, nimble of speech.

2. (*Bot.*) Twining, volubile.

Volume, *n.* 1. Convolution, turn, contortion, whirl.

2. Book, tome.

3. Dimensions, bulk, mass, amplitude, compass, body, substance, size, vastness.

4. Solid contents, content.

5. (*Mus.*) Power, quantity, fulness.

Voluminous, *a.* 1. Of many volumes.

2. Large, bulky, ample, big, full, great.

3. Copious, diffuse, flowing, discursive.

Voluntarily, *adv.* Spontaneously, freely, of one's own accord, purposely, intentionally, deliberately.

Voluntary, *a.* 1. Volitional.

2. Spontaneous, free, unforced, unconstrained, without compulsion, freewill, unasked, unbidden.

3. Willing, from inclination.

4. Designed, intended, intentional, purposed, deliberate.

5. Optional, discretional.

6. (*Law.*) *a.* Free, without compulsion.

b. Gratuitous, without consideration.

Volunteer, *v. t.* Offer, proffer, tender, present, come forward with.

Voluptuary, *n.* Sensualist, epicure, man of pleasure, Sybarite, softling.

Voluptuous, *a.* Luxurious, epicurean, sensual, Sybaritic, effeminate, fleshly, carnal.

Voluptuousness, *n.* Sensuality, luxury, luxuriousness, epicurism, pleasure, animal gratification.

Vomit, *v. i.* Puke, spew, throw up.

——, *v. t.* 1. Disgorge, throw up (*from the stomach*), puke up, cast up.

2. Eject, emit, throw forth, belch forth.

——, *n.* Emetic, puke, vomitory.

Voracious, *a.* Ravenous, greedy, rapacious, devouring, ravening, edacious, hungry.

Voracity, *n.* Ravenousness, greediness, voraciousness, gluttonous appetite, insatiate hunger.

Vortex, *n.* 1. Whirl, whirlpool, eddy.

2. Whirlwind, eddy.

3. Whirl, whirlwind, whirlpool, maelstrom, dizzy round.

Vortical, *a.* Whirling, turning.

Votary, *n.* Devotee, votarist, zealot, adherent, enthusiast.

——, *a.* Devoted, promised, consecrated by a vow.

Vote, *n.* 1. Suffrage, voice, "say," judgment, choice, franchise.

2. Ballot, plebescite, poll, election.

Votive, *a.* Devoted, given by vow, dedicated.

Vouch, *v. t.* 1. Obtest, call to witness.

2. Warrant, declare, affirm, avouch, attest, evidence, maintain by affirmations, guarantee.

3. Support, back, follow up, answer for, confirm.

Vouch, *v. i.* Bear witness, give attestation.

Vouchsafe, *v. t.* Concede, grant, accord, deign to grant, condescend to grant, allow.

——, *v. i.* Condescend, deign, yield, descend, stoop.

Vow, *n.* 1. Promise (*solemnly made*), pledge.

2. Promise of fidelity, pledge of love.

——, *v. t.* 1. Consecrate, dedicate, devote.

2. Assert solemnly, asseverate.

——, *v. i.* Promise (*solemnly*), pledge one's word, swear.

Voyage, *n.* Journey by water, passage by sea, crossing, cruise; trip, excursion.

——, *v. i.* Cruise, sail, take a voyage, take a cruise, travel by sea, take ship, plough the waves, plough the deep.

Vulgar, *a.* 1. Plebeian, common, ignoble, mean, lowly, low-born, base-born.

2. Homespun, rustic, boorish, unrefined, common, uncultivated, coarse, cheap, ill-bred, discourteous, inelegant, in bad taste, tawdry, flashy, showy, garish, gaudy, loud.

3. General, common, ordinary, popular, public.

4. Low, mean, base, gross, coarse, vile, raffish, ribald, broad, loose.

5. Unauthorized, inelegant, cant.

6. (*Rare.*) Vernacular, native, in general use.

Vulgarism, *n.* Vulgar expression, vulgar phrase, vulgar idiom.

Vulgarity, *n.* Grossness, coarseness, rudeness, vileness, meanness, want of refinement.

Vulnerability, *n.* Vulnerableness.

Vulnerable, *a.* 1. Capable of being wounded.

2. Assailable, liable to injury, weak, defenceless, exposed, accessible.

Vulnerary, *a.* Healing.

Vulpine, *a.* 1. Of a fox.

2. Cunning, crafty, artful, sly, foxlike, wily, foxy.

Vulture, *n.* Bird of prey, harpy.

Vulturine, *a.* Rapacious, ravenous.

W

Waddle, *v. i.* Toddle, tottle, waggle.

Waft, *v. t.* Bear (*through a buoyant medium*), convey, transport, carry, transmit.

——, *v. i.* Float, be wafted.

Wag, *v. t.* Shake, waggle, shake to and fro, sway.

——, *v. i.* 1. Vibrate, move to and fro, oscillate, waver, be shaken to and fro.

2. (*Colloq.*) Move, progress, stir, advance.

——, *n.* 1. Wit, humorist, joker, jester, droll, humorous fellow, droll fellow.

2. Shake, swing, sway, jerk.

Wage, *v. t.* 1. Bet, stake, pledge, lay, wager, hazard.

2. Undertake (*as war*), carry on, engage in, conduct.

Wager, *n.* Bet, stake, pledge, gamble, risk.

——, *v. t.* Bet, stake, pledge, lay, wage, back.

——, *v. i.* Bet, lay a wager, plunge, gamble.

Wages, *n. pl.* Hire, salary, pay, payment, compensation, remuneration, stipend, allowance, earnings, reward, emolument.

Waggery, *n.* Jocularity, facetiousness, drollery, pleasantry, humor, fun, waggishness, mischievous merriment, sport, roguery, jocosity, jocoseness.

Waggish, *a.* 1. Mischievous, roguish, frolicsome, gamesome, tricksy.

2. Jocular, jocose, humorous, sportive, merry, facetious, droll, funny, comical.

Waggle, *v. i.* Tottle, toddle, waddle.

——, *v. t.* Wag, shake, move one way and the other, sway.

Wagon, *n.* Wain, lorry, truck.

Waif, *n.* Estray, foundling.

Wail, *v. t.* Lament, moan, bemoan, bewail, deplore, mourn over, grieve for (*audibly*).

——, *v. i.* Moan, lament, cry, weep, howl.

——, *n.* Moan, lamentation, complaint, plaint, lament, wailing, cry, loud weeping.

Wailing, *n.* Moaning, howling, wail, loud lamentation, audible expression of sorrow.

Waist, *n.* 1. Middle part (*as of the human body* or *a ship*), body.

2. *Corsage,* bodice, basque

Waistcoat, *n.* Vest, doublet.

Wait, *v. i.* 1. Stay, tarry, delay, remain, linger, rest, bide one's time.

2. Watch, look, be expectant.

3. Serve, minister, attend.

——, *v. t.* Await, abide, stay for, wait for, look for.

Waiter, *n.* 1. Attendant, servant, servitor, lackey, valet; steward, *garçon.*

2. Tray, salver.

WAITING, *n.* [*The adj. is Basic Eng.*]

1. Staying, delaying, tarrying.

2. Expectation, abeyance, attendance.

Wait on. ⎫ 1. Attend (*as a servant*), per-
Wait upon. ⎭ form services for, attend to, serve.

2. Attend, go to see, visit, call upon, pay attendance.

3. Follow (*as a consequence*), await.

4. Attend to, perform.

5. Accompany, escort, squire.

Waive, *v. t.* 1. Relinquish, renounce, surrender, remit, give up, forego, give up claim to.

2. Throw away, cast off, reject, desert.

3. (*Law.*) Throw away, relinquish voluntarily.

Wake, *v. i.* 1. Watch, be awake, continue awake.

2. Awake, waken, be awakened, be roused from sleep, cease from sleep.

3. Revel, carouse, feast, sit up late for festive purposes.

4. Be excited, be roused up, be active.

——, *v. t.* 1. Awaken, waken, rouse from sleep.

2. Arouse, rouse, excite, kindle, stimulate, provoke, stir up, put in motion, animate, put in action, summon up, reanimate, revive, bring to life again.

3. Watch, attend in the night.

——, *n.* 1. Vigil, watching.

2. Track (*of a vessel*), trail, wash, train, path, rear.

Wakeful, *a.* 1. Sleepless, indisposed to sleep, waking, restless, awake.

2. Watchful, vigilant, observant, wary, alert.

Wakefulness, *n.* 1. Sleeplessness, want of sleep, indisposition to sleep, *insomnia.*

2. Watchfulness, vigilance, wariness, alertness.

Waken, *v. t.* 1. Wake, awake, awaken, rouse from sleep, arouse.

2. Excite to action, put in motion, arouse.

3. Excite, stir up, rouse to action, call forth.

Wale, *n.* 1. [Written also *Weal.*] Ridge (*made by stripes on the skin*), welt, whelk, stripe, streak, mark of the lash.

2. Ridge, streak.

Walk, *v. i.* 1. Go on foot, advance by steps, step, march, pace, tramp, tread, saunter, stroll.

2. Be stirring, be abroad, go about.

3. Depart, move off.

4. Behave, conduct one's self, pursue a course of life, act, demean one's self.

——, *v. t.* 1. Perambulate, traverse.

2. Cause to walk, move.

WALK, *n.* 1. Step, gait, carriage, manner of walking; amble.

2. Sphere, beat, career, course, frequented track, habitual place of action, field, province, department.

3. Conduct, behavior, course of action, procedure.

4. Avenue, path, alley, way, footpath, pathway, range; cloister, promenade, ambulatory, esplanade.

5. Promenade, stroll, excursion, hike, tramp, saunter, turn, ramble, constitutional.

Walking-stick, *n.* Cane, staff, walking-staff, stick, crutch.

WALL, *n.* Upright plane, escarp, parapet.

Wallet, *n.* Bag, sack, knapsack, pouch, pocket-book, purse.

Wallow, *v. i.* 1. Flounder, roll, toss, welter, tumble.

2. Grovel, live in filth.

Wallower, *n.* Trundle, lantern-wheel.

Wall-paper, *n.* Paper-hangings.

Wan, *a.* Pale, pallid, cadaverous, ashen, colorless, of a sickly hue, haggard, bloodless.

——, *v. i.* Turn pale, grow pale.

Wand, *n.* 1. Rod, stick.

2. *Bâton*, mace, truncheon, staff of authority, caduceus, scepter.

3. Divining-rod.

Wander, *v. i.* 1. Ramble, roam, rove, stroll, prowl, "traipse," forage, range, range about, gad about, straggle.

2. Deviate, swerve, stray, digress, turn aside, go astray, straggle.

3. Be delirious, be crazed, rave, ramble, moon.

Wanderer, *n.* Rambler, rover, stroller, land-louper, nomad, traveller, vagrant, straggler, itinerant, runagate, gadabout, strayer.

Wandering, *n.* 1. Roving, rambling, travelling, straying, travel, peregrination, excursion, range, roaming.

2. Aberration, deviation from rectitude, mistaken way, error, divagation.

3. Aberration of mind, delirium, raving, rambling of the mind.

Wane, *v. i.* 1. Decrease, diminish, grow less, abate, subside, ebb.

2. Decline, fail, sink.

——, *n.* 1. Diminution, decrease, lessening.

2. Decline, declension, decay, failure, falling off, decrease.

Want, *n.* 1. Deficiency, absence, lack, dearth, default, defect.

2. Inadequacy, scarcity, scarceness, scantiness, meagreness, shortness, defectiveness, failure, insufficiency, deficiency, paucity, poverty.

3. Need, necessity, requirement, desideratum.

4. Desire, wish, craving, longing.

5. Poverty, indigence, penury, need, necessity, destitution, distress, straits, privation.

Want, v. t. 1. Lack, be without, be destitute of, be in need of.

2. Require, need, have need of, have occasion for, stand in need of, cannot do without, cannot dispense with.

3. Desire, wish, crave, wish for, long for, covet.

4. Fall short in, lack, be lacking in respect of.

——, v. i. 1. Lack, fail, be deficient, fall short, come short, be lacking.

2. Be missed, not to be present.

3. Omit, neglect, fail.

Wanting, a. 1. Deficient, defective, lacking, absent.

2. Slack, deficient, backward, lacking.

Wanton, a. 1. Wandering, loose, unrestrained, unchecked, free.

2. Luxuriant, exuberant, abounding, rank, rampant, overgrown.

3. Sportive, frolicsome, playful, gay, frisky, coltish, airy, skittish, capricious.

4. Dissolute, licentious, irregular, loose.

5. Incontinent, prurient, lustful, lewd, lascivious, lecherous, carnal, salacious, libidinous, concupiscent, lickerish, unchaste, immoral, light, loose.

6. Reckless, heedless, careless, inconsiderate, wayward, perverse, froward, needless, groundless, gratuitous, wilful.

——, n. Lewd person, flirt, baggage, light-o'-love.

——, v. i. 1. Revel, frolic, sport, play, disport, frisk, romp, caper.

2. Luxuriate, live luxuriously, live in clover.

3. Toy, trifle, play, sport, dally amorously, flirt.

War, n. 1. Enmity, hostility, state of opposition, strife, contention.

2. Declared hostilities, fighting, warfare, arbitrament of the sword, contest of nations, armed conflict of powers.

——, v. i. 1. Make war, carry on war, campaign, crusade.

2. Contend, fight, strive, battle, combat, engage.

Warble, v. t. 1. Sing (with turns or trills like a bird), trill, yodel.

2. Hymn, carol, chant, hum, utter musically, modulate.

3. Cause to quaver, vibrate.

Warbler, n. Singer, songster.

War-cry, n. Whoop, war-whoop, battle-cry, slogan.

Ward, v. t. 1. Watch, guard.

2. Defend, protect, parry, fend, stave off, repel.

——, v. i. Parry, act on the defensive.

——, n. 1. Watch, guard, guardianship, care, charge.

2. Warden, keeper, defender, protector, guardian.

3. Custody, confinement.

4. Defence, protection, garrison, means of guarding.

5. (Law.) Pupil, minor (under guardianship).

6. Division, district, precinct, quarter (of a town).

7. Division, apartment, room.

Warden, n. Keeper, guardian, warder, custodian, curator, superintendent; church warden; ranger; gamekeeper.

Warder, n. 1. Keeper, guardian, warden, guard, gatekeeper; jailer, turnkey.

2. Truncheon, mace, staff of command.

Ward off. Fend off, repel, turn aside, parry, stave, avert, forefend, keep off.

Wardrobe, n. 1. Portable closet (for clothes).

2. Apparel, raiment, clothes, clothing, dresses, garments, vestments, habiliments, attire.

Wardship, n. 1. Guardianship, right of guardianship.

2. Pupilage, minority, pupilarity.

Warehouse, n. Store, storehouse, magazine, repository, depot.

Wares, n. pl. Goods, commodities, merchandise, movables.

Warfare, n. 1. Hostilities, war, state of war, fighting, military operations, art of war, tactics, strategy, battle.

2. Contest, struggle, strife, discord, battle, onslaught, conflict, combat, fray, engagement.

War-horse, n. Charger.

Warily, adv. Cautiously, carefully, heedfully, circumspectly, watchfully, vigilantly, charily.

Wariness, n. Caution, cautiousness, care, circumspection, watchfulness, forethought, vigilance, foresight, scrupulousness.

Warlike, a. 1. Fit for war.

2. Military, martial, militant, stratonic, bellicose, combative; soldierly.

3. Inimical, unfriendly, hostile, disposed for war, belligerent, pugnacious, truculent.

WARM, *a.* 1. Not cold, thermal, tepid, calid, lukewarm.

2. Sunny, mild, genial, pleasant.

3. Close, muggy, oppressive.

4. Zealous, ardent, fervent, earnest, fervid, hot, glowing, enthusiastic, hearty, cordial, affectionate, eager.

5. Excited, lively, vehement, passionate, furious, violent, fiery, flushed, quick, hasty, keen.

——, *v. t.* 1. Heat (*moderately*), make warm, tepify, toast, roast.

2. Animate, excite, rouse, waken, stir up, chafe, foment.

——, *v. i.* 1. Become warm.

2. Become ardent, become animated.

Warm-hearted, *a.* Kind, affectionate, hearty, cordial, tender, kind-hearted.

Warmth, *n.* 1. Glow, moderate heat, tepidity.

2. Ardor, zeal, fervor, fervency.

3. Enthusiasm, earnestness, eagerness, heat, fire, flush, fever, animation, excitement, vehemence, fervency, passion, intensity, spirit, cordiality.

Warn, *v. t.* 1. Caution (*against danger*), premonish, forewarn, exhort to take heed, put on one's guard.

2. Admonish (*with respect to some duty*), advise.

3. Inform, notify, apprise, disclose to, mention to, communicate to, make aware, make acquainted, give notice to, give warning, sound the alarm.

4. Summon, bid, call.

Warning, *n.* 1. Caution (*against danger*).

2. Admonition, advice, monition, caveat.

3. Notice, notification, information.

4. Omen, presage, portent, prognostic, augury, intimation, indication, symptom, sign.

5. Summons, call.

6. Example, sample, lesson.

——, *a.* Admonitory, monitory, cautionary, cautioning.

Warp, *v. i.* 1. Twist *or* be twisted out of shape (*by drying*), spring, bend.

2. Deviate, swerve, turn.

3. Wind along.

——, *v. t.* 1. Twist out of shape (*by drying*).

2. Pervert, distort, bend, bias, turn aside, cause to swerve, twist.

3. Prejudice, influence.

Warrant, *v. t.* 1. Guarantee, secure, answer for, make secure, certify.

2. Assure, vouch, avouch, declare, affirm, state, justify, attest, give assurance to.

3. Maintain, support, sanction, authorize, justify, support by authority *or* proof, sustain, uphold, license, attest.

——, *n.* 1. Guarantee, security, surety, pledge, warranty.

2. Authority, commission, verification, authentication.

3. Permit, order, pass, writ, summons, subpoena, voucher.

Warrantable, *a.* Justifiable, allowable, permissible, admissible, lawful, proper, defensible, vindicable, right.

Warranty, *n.* 1. Stipulation, agreement.

2. Guaranty, security, surety, pledge, warrant, authority.

Warrior, *n.* Soldier, captain, military man, man at arms, fighting man.

Wart, *n.* Morbid excrescence, fungous growth.

Wary, *a.* Cautious, heedful, careful, watchful, vigilant, circumspect, prudent, discreet, guarded, scrupulous, chary.

Wash, *v. t.* 1. Cleanse by ablution; purge, purify.

2. Wet, moisten, fall on and moisten.

3. Wet, moisten, bathe, lave, rinse, irrigate, flush, sluice, lap, lick.

4. Overflow, fall on, dash against, break against.

5. Waste, abrade, wash away.

6. Stain, tint, color.

——, *v. i.* 1. Perform ablution, bathe, splash.

2. Cleanse clothes in water.

WASH, *n.* 1. Ablution, lavation, washing, bathing, cleansing.

2. Bog, marsh, fen, quagmire, slough, morass, swamp.

3. Lotion, bath, embrocation.

4. Thin coating.

5. Laundry, buck, washing.

Washboard, *n.* 1. Skirting-board, mopboard, base-board, surbase.

2. (*Naut.*) Wasteboard.

Washerwoman, *n.* Laundress.

Washing, *n.* Ablution, immersion, lavation, bathing; wash, laundry, buck.

Washy, *a.* 1. Watery, damp, moist, oozy, wet, sloppy.

2. Weak, thin, dilute, watery.

3. Vapid, trashy, spiritless, pointless, feeble, poor, unmeaning, trumpery, worthless, jejune, "wishy-washy."

Waspish, *a.* 1. Irritable, irascible, petulant, snappish, pettish, snarly, peevish, captious, testy, fretful, splenetic, touchy, choleric.

2. Slender, small-waisted, slim.

Wassail, *n.* Carousal, revelry, revels, saturnalia, debauch, orgies, potation, compotation, convivial entertainment, jollification, drunken bout.

Waste, *v. t.* 1. Decrease, diminish, wear, corrode, use up, prey upon, wear away, consume, enfaciate, wear out, impair gradually, diminish by constant loss.

2. Consume (*foolishly*), spend, expend, scatter, use up, absorb, devour, exhaust, empty, deplete, drain, squander, dissipate, lose, misspend, misuse, fool away, fritter away, muddle away, use prodigally, burn the candle at both ends.

3. Spend in vain, expend uselessly, lavish, squander, dissipate.

4. Destroy, desolate, ravage, pillage, plunder, strip, ruin, spoil, devastate, sack, devour, demolish, dilapidate, lay waste, harry, scour.

5. (*Law.*) Damage, impair, injure.

——, *v. i.* 1. Dwindle, wither, pine, perish, decay, be diminished, waste away.

2. Swale, melt (*as a candle*), sweal, consume, run to waste, disappear, vanish, run dry.

——, *a.* 1. Destroyed, ruined, ravaged, spoiled, devastated, desolated, stripped, bare, void, empty.

2. Dreary, dismal, forlorn.

3. Wild, uncultivated, bare, untilled, unoccupied, unimproved, barren, uninhabited, abandoned.

4. Worthless, refuse, valueless, useless.

5. Superfluous, exuberant.

WASTE, *n.* 1. Consumption, loss, diminution, decrement, expenditure, wasting, dissipation, exhaustion, wear and tear.

2. Squandering, dispersion, prodigality, ineconomy, extravagance, wanton destruction, loss.

3. Devastation, ravage, ruin, decay, rapine, destruction, desolation, pillage, havoc.

4. Refuse, worthless matter, rubbish, wastrel, detritus, débris, trash, spilth, dross, junk, husks, chaff, offal.

5. Wild, wilderness, desert, solitude, lonely place, deserted region, dreary void, expanse, Sahara, barren.

Wasteful, *a.* 1. Destructive, ruinous.

2. Lavish, prodigal, profuse, extravagant, squandering, thriftless, unthrifty, too free, too liberal, improvident.

Waster, *n.* Squanderer, prodigal, spendthrift, wastrel.

Wasting, *n.* Decay, decline, consumption, marasmus, emaciation, atrophy, *tabes*, phthisis.

WATCH, *n.* 1. Vigil, watching, wakefulness, watchfulness, outlook, guard, ward, espial.

2. Inspection, observation, attention, surveillance, oversight.

3. Guard, sentry, watchman, sentinel, picket.

4. Pocket timepiece, "ticker."

——, *v. i.* 1. Wake, be awake, keep awake, not be asleep, keep vigil.

2. Keep guard, keep watch and ward, stand guard, be on guard, be on the watch, act as sentinel, be on the lookout, look sharp, keep a sharp lookout, have all one's eyes about one, take care.

3. Wait, look, be expectant, seek opportunity, gaze, stare.

——, *v. t.* 1. Guard, tend, attend, have in keeping, patrol, scout; oversee, superintend.

2. Mark, observe, eye, keep the eye on, keep an eye upon, keep in view, not lose sight of, spy, follow.

Watchful, *a.* Vigilant, attentive, observant, awake, alive, heedful, careful, wary, cautious, prudent, circumspect, guarded, on one's guard, on the alert, with the eyes open, wide-awake, on the lookout, wakeful.

Watchman, *n.* Guard, sentinel, picket, sentry, guardsman, watch, patrol, scout, lookout, warden.

Watchword, *n.* Countersign, password, catchword, shibboleth, cry, word.

WATER, *v. t.* [*The noun is Basic Eng.*] 1. Irrigate, moisten, wet, drench, soak, steep.

2. Supply with water (*for drink*), furnish with water, give water to.

3. Sprinkle and calender (*as cloth, to give it an undulating or wavy appearance*), damp.

4. Attenuate, dilute, adulterate, thin, weaken.

——, *v. i.* 1. Shed water.

2. Take in water, get water, cloud.

Water-closet, *n.* Privy, backhouse, necessary, toilet, jakes.

Water-course, *n.* 1. Stream, brook, river, waterway, run.

2. Canal, drain, trench, ditch, channel, fosse, moat, sewer, leat.

Water-cure, *n.* Hydropathy.

Waterfall, *n.* Cataract, cascade, fall, linn.

Waterish, *a.* 1. Aqueous, moist, wet, watery, humid, liquid.

2. Thin, diluted, weak, like water, watery, tasteless, insipid, flat.

3. Lachrymose, tearful.

Waterman, *n.* Boatman, ferryman.

Water-nymph, *n.* Naiad.

Watery, *a.* 1. Aqueous, of water.

2. Thin, weak, diluted, waterish, like water.

3. Tasteless, insipid, vapid, spiritless.

4. Wet, moist.

Wattle, *n.* Hurdle (*of twigs*), withe, switch.

WAVE, *n.* 1. Undulation, billow, breaker, surge, swell, ripple, bore, roller, comber; eagre, sea, water; tide, flush, flood.

2. Wave of vibration.

3. Sway, flourish, gesture.

4. Unevenness, inequality of surface; convolution, curl, roll.

——, *v. i.* 1. Undulate, float, play loosely, play to and fro, heave, wallow; shake, sway, flutter.

2. Be moved (*as a signal*).

——, *v. t.* 1. Brandish, flourish, flaunt, swing, sway, shake.

2. Beckon, signal.

Waveless, *a.* Smooth, calm, placid, undisturbed.

Wavelike, *a.* Undulating.

Waver, *v. i.* 1. Wave, undulate, float, flicker.

2. Totter, reel, be in danger of falling.

3. Vacillate, hesitate, fluctuate, oscillate, falter, be in suspense, be undetermined, be unsettled, be in doubt.

Wavering, *n.* 1. Vacillation, fluctuation.

2. Indecision, indetermination, hesitancy, uncertainty, irresolution, vacillation, fluctuation.

——, *a.* Unsettled, vacillating, fickle, unsteady, unstable, changeable, fluctuating.

Wavy, *a.* Undulating, undulate, undulant, billowy, choppy, flickering, waving, playing to and fro; sinuous, curly.

WAX, *v. t.* [*The noun is Basic Eng.*] Cere, smear with wax.

——, *v. i.* 1. Increase (*as the moon*), become larger, become fuller, rise.

2. Grow, become, come to be, get to be.

Waxen, *a.* 1. Wax-like, waxy, ceruminous; of wax.

2. Soft, yielding, tender.

3. Wax-covered.

Waxy, *a.* 1. Viscid, adhesive, tenacious.

2. Yielding, pliable.

WAY, *n.* 1. Passage, march, advance, trend, transit, journey, progression.

2. Road, path, route, course, track, street, beat, pathway, trail, alley, channel, avenue, artery, highway, highroad, room for passing, opportunity to pass, passage, approach, access.

3. Method, mode, manner, fashion.

4. Space, distance, interval, stretch.

5. Custom, usage, habit, habitude, practice, wont, second nature, regular course, habitual method, plan of conduct, mode of dealing, manner, form, wise, guise, fashion, style, behavior.

6. Scheme, device, plan, means by which anything is reached.

7. Course, direction of motion, tendency of action.

8. Determined course, step, resolved mode of action.

9. (*Naut.*) Progress.

Wayfarer, *n.* Traveller, passenger, pilgrim, itinerant, rambler, voyager.

Wayfaring, *a.* Travelling, passing.

Waylay, *v. t.* Lie in wait for (*with evil intent*), lie in ambush for.

Ways and means. 1. Methods, resources, facilities.

2. (*Legislation.*) Means for raising money, resources for revenue.

Wayward, *a.* Perverse, froward, wilful, obstinate, headstrong, stubborn, intractable, unruly, cross-grained, refractory, capricious, self-willed, contrary, captious.

Wayworn, *a.* Wearied by travelling, travel-stained, footsore, weary, fatigued.

Weak, *a.* 1. Feeble, languid, weakly, sickly, debilitated, unhealthy, unsound, enfeebled, wasted, spent, exhausted, enervated, shaky, faint, languishing, strengthless, infirm, tender, valetudinary, valetudinarian, invalid, frail, delicate, fragile.

2. Defenceless, unguarded, exposed, vulnerable, assailable, accessible, unprotected.

3. Soft, unstressed, unaccented, light.

4. Pliable, pliant, pusillanimous, easily influenced, weak-kneed, vacillating, wavering, undetermined, infirm, unstable, unsteady, undecided, unsettled, without any backbone, invertebrate, boneless, sinewless, nerveless, irresolute.

5. Shallow, simple, silly, senseless, witless, stupid, foolish, childish, imbecile, weak-minded, shallow.

6. Unwise, injudicious, indiscreet, erring, peccable, foolish, imprudent.

7. Low, faint, small, feeble, piping, womanish, effeminate, gentle, indistinct.

8. Thin, watery, diluted, waterish, insipid, attenuated, adulterated, vapid, tasteless.

9. Sleazy, flimsy, slight, poor, trifling, feeble, frivolous.

10. Poor, inconclusive, unconvincing, unsustained, unsupported, ineffectual, unsatisfactory, lame, illogical, vague; ineffective, inefficient, inefficacious, futile, unavailing, vain.

11. Unsound, unsafe, untrustworthy, frail, unsubstantial.

12. Powerless, impotent, helpless, impuissant.

13. Delicate, frail, fragile, breakable, frangible, brittle.

14. Small, slight, slender, inconsiderable, puny.

Weaken, *v. t.* 1. Enfeeble, enervate, unstring, debilitate, unnerve, make weak, sap, undermine, stagger, shake, unman, effeminize, devitalize, relax, cripple, cramp.

2. Invalidate, make of less effect.

3. Reduce, depress, debase, lower, impair, attenuate, adulterate, dilute, exhaust, impoverish.

Weakly, *a.* Feeble, weak, infirm.

Weak-minded, *a.* Shallow, weak, soft, sappy, feeble-minded, short-witted, half-witted, weak-headed, doting.

Weakness, *n.* See WEAK, under its various senses.

Weal, *n.* 1. Welfare, prosperity, good, advantage, happiness, interest, utility, profit.

2. Streak, welt, ridge, wale, stripe.

Wealth, *n.* Affluence, opulence, abundance, richness, fortune, independence, competence, riches, mammon, pelf, money, gold, moneybags, treasure, funds, cash, lucre, property, substance, capital.

Wealthy, *a.* Affluent, opulent, rich, moneyed, flush, well-off, well-to-do.

Wean, *v. t.* 1. Put from the breast.

2. Withdraw, disengage, alienate, detach, reconcile to the loss of anything.

Weapons, *n. pl.* Arms.

Wear, *v. t.* 1. Carry (*upon the person*), bear, don, put on, have on.

2. Bear, have an appearance of, exhibit in appearance, display, "sport."

3. Impair (*by use*), waste, consume by use, use up, wear away, wear out; diminish, consume gradually, eat away, spend, cause to disappear.

4. Cause by friction, occasion by wasting, fray.

5. Affect by degrees, bring about gradually.

6. (*Naut.*) [Written also *Ware.*] Veer, yaw; gybe.

——, *v. i.* 1. Be wasted, wear away.

2. Endure use, last under employment.

3. Suffer injury by use, be wasted, be consumed, be diminished by use.

4. Be tediously spent, be consumed by slow degrees.

Wear away, *v. t.* 1. Waste, consume, impair, diminish, destroy by gradual attrition, wear.

2. Consume, spend tediously, use up.

——, *v. i.* Be consumed, be wasted.

Wearied, *a.* Tired, fatigued, bored, *ennuyé*, jaded, fagged, exhausted, weary, worn.

Weariness, *n.* Fatigue, lassitude, exhaustion, prostration, languor, languidness, boredom, tedium, *ennui*, monotony, sameness.

Wearisome, *a.* Tedious, tiresome, fatiguing, toilsome, burdensome, arduous, laborious, annoying, weary, vexatious, trying, humdrum, prosy, monotonous, uninteresting, irksome, boring, prolix, stupid, slow, difficult.

Wear off, *v. t.* 1. Obliterate, rub off.

2. Diminish by attrition, rub off.

——, *v. i.* Pass off by degrees *or* gradually.

Wear out. 1. Consume, render useless, waste.

2. Consume tediously, bore, fatigue.

3. Harass, tire.

4. Waste the strength of.

Weary, *a.* 1. Fatigued, tired, exhausted, careworn, toilworn, drowsy, used up, worn out, wearied, impatient, discontented, dispirited, *blasé*, *ennuyé*.

2. Tiresome, irksome, wearisome.

——, *v. t.* 1. Fatigue, tire, jade, fag, exhaust, tire out, wear out.

2. Make impatient by continuance, surfeit, glut, bore.

3. Harass, irk, dispirit.

WEATHER, *v. t.* [*The noun is Basic Eng.*] 1. (*Naut.*) Pass to windward of, pass between the wind and.

2. Endure, sustain, bear, stand, bear up against, get the better of, overcome, resist, encounter and sustain.

——, *v. i.* 1. Disintegrate, tan, bleach, toughen.

2. Gain *or* accomplish anything against opposition.

Weather-cock, *n.* 1. Vane, weather-vane, cock.

2. Trimmer, time-server, fickle person, chameleon.

Weave, *v. t.* 1. Interlace, lace, twine (*as the threads of a fabric*), intwine, plait, plat, braid, mat.

2. Unite intimately, unite by close connection *or* intermixture.

3. Compose, design, form into a fabric, fabricate, construct, make.

——, *v. i.* Work a loom, practise weaving.

Weazen, *a.* Thin, sharp, lean, withered, shrunken, dried, shrivelled, wizened.

Web, *n.* 1. Texture, tissue, structure, textile fabric.

2. Cobweb, gossamer.

Wed, *v. t.* 1. Marry, espouse, couple.

2. Join in marriage, give in wedlock.

3. Attach firmly, unite closely in affection.

4. Unite forever, connect indissolubly.

Wed, *v. i.* Marry, contract matrimony.

Wedding, *n.* Marriage, nuptials, espousals, bridal, marriage ceremony, nuptial rites.

Wedge-shaped, *a.* Cuneiform.

Wedlock, *n.* Matrimony, nuptial state, marriage, nuptial tie.

Wee, *a.* Little, small, diminutive, tiny, minikin, minute, microscopic, pygmy, pygmean, Lilliputian.

Weed, *v. t.* 1. Rid of weeds, free from noxious plants.

2. Root out, extirpate, take away, remove, eliminate, eradicate, free, rid.

3. Weed out, segregate, separate.

Weeds, *n. pl.* Mourning, symbol of sorrow, sables, sack cloth.

WEEK, *n.* (*Basic Eng.*) Sevennight.

Weekly, *a.* Hebdomadal, hebdomadary.

Ween, *v. i.* (*Poetical.*) Fancy, imagine, think, suppose.

Weep, *v. i.* 1. Cry, sob, shed tears, wail, blubber, "boohoo."

2. Lament, complain.

3. Flow in drops, run in drops.

4. Drip, drop water.

——, *v. t.* 1. Lament, bewail, bemoan.

2. Shed, pour forth, drop, shed drop by drop.

Weft, *n.* Woof.

Weigh, *v. t.* 1. Bear up, raise, swing up, "heft," lift so that it hangs in the air.

2. Try in the balance, find the weight of, poise, determine the heaviness of.

3. Counterbalance, be equivalent to in weight, have the heaviness of.

4. Pay, allot, take by weight.

5. Examine, ponder, balance in the mind, consider, meditate upon, estimate deliberately, balance.

6. Regard, esteem as worthy of notice.

——, *v. i.* 1. Gravitate, be heavy, carry weight, count, tell.

2. Bear, press, bear heavily, press hard.

Weigh down, *v. t.* 1. Overbalance.

2. Oppress, overburden, depress, load, cumber.

——, *v. i.* Sink by its own weight.

WEIGHT, *n.* 1. Heaviness, heft, tonnage, gravity, ponderousness, ponderosity.

2. Pressure, burden, load.

3. Importance, influence, power, prominence, value, efficacy, consequence, moment, significance, impressiveness, import, pith; emphasis, burden.

4. Scale, mode of estimating weight, measure, system of weighing.

Weight, *v. t.* Load, lead, make heavy, load down, ingravidate, plumb.

Weightily, *adv.* 1. Heavily, ponderously.

2. Forcibly, impressively, significantly.

Weightiness, *n.* 1. Ponderousness, gravity, heaviness.

2. Solidity, force, impressiveness.

3. Importance, gravity, consequence, moment.

Weighty, *a.* 1. Heavy (*intrinsically*), massive, unwieldy, ponderous, onerous.

2. Important, influential, efficacious, forcible, determinative, significant, considerable, momentous, grave, serious, of consequence.

Weir, *n.* Dam.

Weird, *n.* 1. Fate, destiny.

2. Spell, charm.

3. Prediction.

——, *a.* 1. Skilled in witchcraft.

2. Supernatural, unearthly, wild, uncanny, eerie, eldritch, witching, spooky.

Weird Sisters. [*Scotch.*] The Fates, the Sisters Three, *Parcæ.*

Welcome, *n.* 1. Greeting, salutation.

2. Kind reception, entertainment.

——, *v. t.* Greet, receive, bid welcome, gratulate, embrace, hail.

——, *a.* 1. Gladly received *or* entertained, admitted with pleasure.

2. Acceptable, pleasing, agreeable, pleasant, grateful, gratifying.

3. Free to have, free to enjoy gratuitously.

Welfare, *n.* Prosperity, happiness, success, weal, affluence, thrift, well-being, advantage, benefit, profit.

Welkin, *n.* (*Poetical.*) Sky, empyrean, firmament, heaven, the heavens, canopy of heaven, vault of heaven, starry heavens.

Well, *n.* 1. Spring, fountain, font, reservoir, well-head, well-spring.

2. Source, origin.

3. Hole, shaft, pit.

——, *v. i.* Issue, spring, flow, jet, gush, pour.

WELL, *adv.* 1. Rightly, justly, in a proper manner, first-rate.

2. Properly, suitably, correctly, accurately, finely, "famously," "splendidly," excellently, thoroughly, skilfully, not amiss.

3. Sufficiently, abundantly, amply, fully, thoroughly, adequately.

4. Favorably, commendably, with praise, agreeably, worthily.

5. Highly, very much.

6. Far, considerably, not a little, quite.

7. Conveniently, easily, fortunately.

——, *a.* 1. Healthy, hale, hearty, in health, wholesome, sound, in good health.

2. Fortunate, happy.

3. Profitable, convenient, beneficial, expedient, good, useful, advantageous, for one's advantage, for one's interest.

4. Favored, fortunate, being in favor.

Well-behaved, a. Courteous, civil, polite, well-bred, well-mannered, polished, of good manners, orderly, decorous.

Well-born, a. Gentle, high-born, of good descent, of a good stock, thoroughbred.

Well-bred, a. Refined, polished, polite, courteous, cultivated, genteel, gentlemanly, ladylike.

Well-known, a. Proverbial, notorious, renowned, recognized, familiar.

Well-nigh, adv. Almost, nearly.

Well-off, a. Prosperous, thriving, flourishing, rich, wealthy, influential, propertied, forehanded, beforehand, in easy circumstances, well-to-do, possessed of a competence, in good condition.

Wellspring, n. Spring, fountain, well, well-head, source of continual supply.

Well-timed, a. Opportune, seasonable, timely, felicitous, happy.

Well-to-do, a. Well off, affluent.

Welter, v. i. 1. Wallow, tumble about, roll, toss.

2. Rise and fall (as waves), tumble over (as billows).

Wench, n. 1. Strumpet.

2. Peasant girl, maid, serving-woman.

Wend, v. i. Go, pass, betake one's self.

——, v. t. Direct, betake.

Werewolf, n. Man-wolf, lycanthrope, changeling, loup-garou.

Wesleyanism, n. Methodism.

West, n. Occident, sunset.

WEST, a. Western, westerly, occidental.

Westerly, a. Western, west, westward.

Western, a. 1. West, occidental, Hesperian.

2. See WESTERLY.

WET, a. 1. Damp, moist, humid, dank, dewy, dripping, sloppy, clammy.

2. Rainy, showery, sprinkly, very damp.

——, n. 1. Humidity, moisture, dampness, wetness.

2. Rainy weather, foggy or misty weather.

Wet, v. t. Moisten, damp, dampen, sprinkle, soak, water, dip, dabble, drench, saturate.

Wetness, n. 1. Moisture, humidity.

2. Fogginess, mistiness, wet.

Whalebone, n. Baleen, whale-fin.

Whale-oil, n. Train-oil.

Wharf, n. Quay, dock, pier, landing.

What, pron. 1. That which.

2. The sort of, the kind of.

3. Which (out of many, or of many kinds).

4. How, how great, how remarkable.

5. In part, partly.

6. Whatever, whatsoever, what thing soever.

Whatever, pron. 1. Anything, be it what it may, anything soever, whatsoever.

2. All that, the whole that.

Wheedle, v. t. 1. Flatter, cajole.

2. Inveigle, humor, court, fawn upon, coax, lure, pay court to.

Wheedler, n. 1. Flatterer, coaxer.

2. Sycophant, parasite, fawner, toady, flunky, spaniel, lick-spittle, pick-thank, toad-eater, time-server, hanger-on, mean flatterer.

WHEEL, v. i. [The noun is Basic Eng.]

1. Move on wheels, roll.

2. Revolve, rotate, turn, roll, turn on an axis.

3. Gyrate, turn round, move round.

4. Revolve, move round, move in a circle, wind, twist, turn, double, countermarch.

5. Fetch a compass.

6. Deviate, deflect, diverge, turn aside, alter one's course.

7. Move forward, roll forward.

——, v. t. 1. Whirl, twirl, spin, roll, revolve, put into a rotatory motion.

2. Move on wheels, convey on wheels, transport.

Wheeze, v. i. Breathe hard, breathe audibly.

Whelk, n. 1. Protuberance, pustule.

2. Stripe, streak, mark, wale.

Whelm, v. t. 1. Overwhelm.

2. Cover completely, immerse deeply, submerge, overwhelm, overburden.

Whelp, n. 1. Cub, young beast.

2. Puppy, pup, young dog.

WHEN, adv. 1. At the time, at the time that, at what time.

2. Whenever, at what time.

3. While, whereas.

4. Which time, then, as soon as.

Whence, adv. 1. From what place, wherefrom.

2. From what cause, from what source, how.

Whenever, adv. At whatever time, whensoever.

WHERE, adv. 1. At which place, in which place, wherever.

2. At what place, in what place.

3. Whither, to what, to which place (recent), where to.

Whereabouts, adv. Near what place, about where, near what.

——, n. (Colloq.) Residence, location.

Whereas, *conj.* 1. Since, considering that, it being the case that.

2. When in fact, while on the contrary.

Wherefore, *adv.* and *conj.* 1. Why, for what cause *or* reason, on what account.

2. Why, for what reason.

3. For which reason.

Wheresoever, *adv.* In what place soever, in whatever place, wherever.

Whereupon, *adv.* Upon which, in consequence of which.

Wherewithal, *n.* (*Colloq., used with* The *prefixed.*) The means (*with which to accomplish any purpose*).

Whet, *v. t.* 1. Sharpen (*by rubbing*), grind.

2. Stimulate, excite, arouse, rouse, awaken.

3. Stir up, excite, provoke, make angry.

4. Animate, warm, kindle, quicken, inspire.

Which, *pron.* 1. What one.

2. That.

Whiff, *n.* Puff, blast, sudden gust.

——, *v. t.* Puff.

Whiffle, *v. i.* Veer (*as by change of wind*), turn about, waver, shake, shift, turn, prevaricate, be fickle, be unsteady.

While, *n.* Time, season, space of time.

WHILE, *adv.* 1. During the time that, whilst.

2. As long as.

3. At the same time that.

4. Under which circumstances, in which case, though, although, whereas.

While away. Pass away (*as time*), spend pleasantly.

Whim, *n.* Freak, fancy, vagary, humor, caprice, notion, bent, wish, fantasy, crotchet, quirk, whimsey, kink, "wrinkle."

Whimper, *v. i.* Cry (*in low and broken tones*), whine.

Whimsey, *n.* See WHIM.

Whimsical, *a.* 1. Capricious, freakish, odd, singular, strange, fanciful, fantastical, notional, erratic, crotchety, queer, quaint.

2. Singular, curious, odd, fantastic, grotesque, outlandish, quaint.

Whimsicality, *n.* 1. Whimsicalness, singularity, freakishness, odd disposition.

2. Oddity, whim, caprice, freak.

Whine, *v. i.* 1. Cry (*plaintively*), moan (*in a childish way*), snivel, whimper, mule, cant, wail.

2. Complain meanly, grumble.

——, *n.* 1. Plaintive tone.

2. Mean *or* affected complaint.

Whinny, *v. i.* Neigh.

WHIP, *v. t.* [*The noun is Basic Eng.*] 1. Lash, strike (*with a cord*), beat.

2. Drive with lashes, cause to rotate, spin.

3. Flog, beat, punish with the whip, flagellate, scourge, lash, rawhide, horsewhip, slash, smite, goad.

4. Lash, hurt, sting.

5. Strike, thrash, beat out (*as grain*).

6. Stitch, baste, sew lightly, overcast.

7. Wrap, inwrap, overlay with cord.

8. Snatch, jerk, whisk, snap, take by a sudden motion.

Whip-hand, *n.* Advantage, upper-hand, better.

Whipping, *n.* Flogging, beating, castigation, flagellation, dusting, bastinado, breeching, thrashing.

Whirl, *v. i.* Twirl, revolve, rotate, spin, pirouette.

——, *v. t.* Twirl, spin, wheel, turn round.

——, *n.* Gyration, rotation, vortex, eddy, swirl, twirl, spin, pirouette; flutter, flurry.

Whirlpool, *n.* Vortex, eddy, maelstrom, gurge, swirl.

Whirlwind, *n.* Cyclone, tornado, typhoon, windstorm.

Whirring, *n.* Whiz, buzzing noise.

Whisk, *v. i.* 1. Trip, speed, hasten, hie, post, rush, scud, brush, move nimbly, push on, dash on, cut along.

2. Brush.

Whisper, *v. i.* Speak under the breath, speak softly.

——, *v. t.* Breathe, murmur, sigh, utter softly; divulge, reveal, hint, intimate, disclose.

——, *n.* 1. Whispering, *susurrus.*

2. Low, soft voice, gentle utterance.

3. Murmur, sibilant sound (*as of the wind*).

4. Hint, intimation, inkling.

Whist, *interj.* Hush, silence, be still, be silent, keep quiet, make no noise.

WHISTLE, *n.* (*Basic Eng.*) Shrill pipe.

Whit, *n.* Iota, jot, tittle, particle, bit, atom, grain, scrap, mite, ace, scintilla.

WHITE, *a.* 1. Of a white color, snowy, frosty, hoary, hoar, milky, argent, silvery, silver, ivory, chalky, marmoreal, canescent.

2. Pale, wan, destitute of color, pallid, gray.

3. Pure, clean, spotless, unblemished, candid, immaculate, chaste, innocent.

4. Shining, bright.

5. Happy, fortunate, innocent.

6. (*Colloq.*) True-blue, honest, square, just, upright.

Whiten, *v. t.* 1. Bleach, blanch, etiolate, make white, frost, silver, albify.

2. Cover with white, make white.

Whiten, *v. i.* Bleach, blanch, etiolate, blench, become *or* grow white.

Whitsuntide, *n.* Whit-Sunday, Pentecost.

Whiz, *v. i.* Buzz, whir, hum.

——, *n.* Whirring, buzzing, buzzing noise, humming.

WHO, *pron.* (*Basic Eng.*)

Whole, *a.* 1. All, total.

2. Entire, undivided, integral, complete, intact.

3. Uninjured, unimpaired, unbroken, undivided, unsevered, perfect, faultless, good, firm, strong.

4. Sound, well, healthy; restored, healed.

——, *n.* All, total, totality, aggregate, gross, entirety, ensemble, integrity, amount, sum, sum total.

Wholesome, *a.* 1. Healthy, healthful, salubrious, salutary, salutiferous, helpful, nourishing, nutritious, strengthening, invigorating, roborant.

2. Beneficial, salutary, helpful, improving, good.

3. Sound, healthy, uncorrupt, fresh, sweet.

4. Rational, sane.

Wholly, *adv.* 1. Totally, altogether, utterly.

2. Entirely, completely, fully, perfectly, clean, quite, outright.

Whoop, *n.* Shout, halloo, hoot, yell.

——, *v. i.* Shout, halloo, hollo, holla, yell, cry out.

Whopper, *n.* (*Colloq.*) Falsehood, monstrous lie, bounce, bouncer.

Whore, *n.* Harlot, prostitute, strumpet, courtesan, bawd, punk, drab, demirep, street-walker, night-walker, Cyprian, woman of the town, woman of ill fame.

WHY, *adv.* 1. Wherefore, for what cause *or* reason, on what account.

2. For what purpose, with what intent, to what end.

Wicked, *a.* 1. Sinful, vicious, depraved, unprincipled, immoral, impious, irreligious, unrighteous, unprincipled, ungodly, godless, unholy, devilish, abominable, infamous, profane, irreverent, worthless, graceless, vile, abandoned, corrupt.

2. Bad, evil, unjust, ill, atrocious, iniquitous, heinous, flagitious, nefarious, criminal, outrageous, monstrous, villainous, dark, black.

Wickedness, *n.* 1. Sin, evil, depravity, vice, immorality, unrighteousness, sinfulness, crime, turpitude, perversity, corruption, unregeneracy, deviltry, malignity, impiety, criminality, villainy.

2. Atrocity, iniquity, enormity, flagitiousness.

Wicker, *n.* Twig, osier, withe.

WIDE, *a.* 1. Broad.

2. Spacious, vast, large, ample, extensive, roomy, comprehensive, inclusive, general, expansive, expanded.

3. Remote, distant.

4. Widespread, prevalent, rife.

Wide-awake, *a.* Watchful, vigilant, attentive, keen, astute, shrewd, observant, heedful, careful, wary, cautious, circumspect, on the alert, with the eyes open, knowing.

Width, *n.* Breadth, broadness, wideness, beam, span, amplitude, diameter.

Wield, *v. t.* 1. Handle, brandish, flourish, manipulate, work, ply.

2. Manage, use, control, make use of, sway.

Wife, *n.* Married woman, matron, helpmate, consort, spouse, mate, partner, better half, wife of one's bosom, gray mare.

Wig, *n.* Peruke, periwig, scratch, toupee.

Wight, *n.* [*In irony or burlesque.*] Creature, being, person.

Wigwam, *n.* Hut (*of an American Indian*), cabin, tepee.

Wild, *a.* 1. Undomesticated, untamed, feral.

2. Uncultivated, native, waste, desert, rough, rude, desolate.

3. Uncivilized, savage, rude, ferocious, fierce, outlandish, barbarous, unrefined, untamed.

4. Dense, luxuriant, rank.

5. Impetuous, turbulent, irregular, violent, ungoverned, unrestrained, disorderly, furious, raving, mad, distracted, uncontrolled, frantic, frenzied, outrageous.

6. Giddy, reckless, thoughtless, harebrained, flighty, incorﾃerate, heedless, light-headed, "harum-scarum"; fast, dissipated; unwise, foolish, ill-advised.

7. Stormy, boisterous, rough.

8. Fanciful, imaginary, extravagant, visionary, crazy, grotesque, strange, *bizarre*.

——, *n.* Desert. See WILDERNESS.

Wilderness, *n.* Wild, desert, waste.

Wild-goose chase. Foolish pursuit, foolish enterprise, wool-gathering.

Wile, *n.* Trick, trickery, plot, stratagem, cheat, fraud, chicane, chicanery, artifice, chouse, imposture, deceit, imposition, deception, ruse, dodge, fetch, manœuvre, cunning contrivance, crafty device.

Wilful, *a.* 1. Obstinate, stubborn, perverse, contumacious, refractory, headstrong, unruly, intractable, mulish, dogged, unyielding, inflexible, heady, self-willed, pig-headed, obdurate, cantankerous.

2. Self-willed, arbitrary, capricious.

3. Deliberate, intentional, planned, intended, premeditated.

Will, *n.* 1. Power of determination, power of choosing, faculty of volition, volition, free-will.

2. Resolution, resoluteness, determination, decision, self-reliance, force of will, will-power, "grit," moral courage, strength of purpose.

3. Wish, desire, inclination, disposition, pleasure, intent, purpose.

4. Command, behest, order, direction, requirement, request, demand, decree.

5. Testament, last will and testament.

WILL, *v. i.* Exercise volition, desire, choose, elect, be disposed, be inclined, be pleased, have a mind, intend.

——, *v. t.* 1. Determine, decree, enjoin, command, direct.

2. Bequeath, devise, demise, leave, convey, give by will.

Willing, *a.* 1. Inclined, disposed, desirous, minded, compliant, adaptable, amenable, easily persuaded, ready, of a mind, nothing loath, not averse.

2. Intentional, voluntary, free, deliberate, spontaneous, unasked, unbidden.

3. Prompt, ready, eager, forward, cordial.

Willingly, *adv.* 1. Cheerfully, readily, gladly, with all one's heart.

2. Voluntarily, of one's own accord, freely, spontaneously.

Will-o'-the-wisp, *n.* 1. Friar's lantern, Jack-with-a-lantern, Jack-o'-lantern, *ignis fatuus*, St. Elmo's fire.

2. Illusion, mirage, dream, shadow.

Willow, *n.* Osier.

Wilt, *v. i.* Droop, wither.

Wily, *a.* Insidious, artful, cunning, sly, crafty, subtle, arch, designing, deceitful, treacherous, trickish, tricky, intriguing, politic, foxy, snaky, crooked, diplomatic, Machiavelian.

Win, *v. t.* 1. Get (*by mastery* or *in competition*), make, gain, obtain, procure, acquire, gather, earn, achieve, catch, recover, reclaim, accomplish, reach.

2. Bring over, gain over, get the compliance of, carry, conquer, conciliate, induce, sway, influence, persuade, prevail upon.

——, *v. i.* 1. Succeed, be successful, gain the victory, surpass, triumph.

2. Reach, get, arrive.

Wince, *v. i.* Flinch, shrink, startle, start back, quail, blench, shy.

WIND, *n.* 1. Air (*in motion*), draught, breeze, blast, gust, hurricane, whiff, zephyr, puff of air, breath of air.

2. Breath, respiration, afflatus, inspiration, expiration, breathing.

3. Flatulence, windiness, gas.

Wind, *v. t.* 1. Coil, twine, twist, wreathe, involve, crank, turn, roll, reel, encircle.

2. Turn in and out.

3. Blow, sound.

——, *v. i.* 1. Twine, coil, twist, turn and twist, take a spiral course.

2. Meander, turn in and out, bend, curve, be devious, be tortuous, zigzag.

Windfall, *n.* Godsend, unexpected gift, stroke of luck *or* good fortune, good luck, run of luck, piece of good fortune, piece of good luck; unexpected legacy.

Winding, *n.* Flexure, turning, meandering, twisting, twist, convolution, contortion, sinuosity, curvature, tortuosity, bend, crook, kink, crookedness, circuit, filature, insinuation.

——, *a.* Flexuous, sinuous, meandering, serpentine, bending, curving, crooked, twisted, twining, turning, devious, tortuous, circuitous.

WINDOW, *n.* Casement, dormer, oriel, fenestration.

Windpipe, *n.* Trachea, weasand, throttle, throat, airpipe.

Wind up. 1. Wind into a ball, coil, coil up, roll up.

2. Settle, close, close up, end, bring to a close *or* conclusion.

Windy, *a.* 1. Breezy, gusty, squally, stormy, blowy, drafty, tempestuous, blustering, boisterous.

2. Empty, airy, hollow, inflated.

3. Flatulent.

WINE, *n.* (*Basic Eng.*)

Wine-bibber, *n.* Toper, tippler, drunkard, dram-drinker, hard drinker, intemperate man.

WING, *n.* 1. Pennon, pinion, arm, sail.

2. Side-piece, extension, ell, adjunct, ramification.

3. (*Mil.*) Flank.

Winged, *a.* 1. With wings, having wings, pennate, alar.

2. Swift, rapid, fleet, fast, speedy, nimble, agile, flying.

3. Aspiring, soaring, lofty, inspired.

Wink, *v. i.* Blink, nictate, squint, twinkle.

Wink at. Connive at, overlook, pretend not to see, shut one's eyes to, condone, excuse, ignore, humor, pass over.

Winning, *a.* Attractive, alluring, pleasing, charming, bewitching, engaging, captivating, fascinating, prepossessing, enchanting, delightful, lovely, persuasive.

Winnow, *v. t.* 1. Fan, clear of chaff, ventilate.

2. Separate, part, divide, sift, glean, cull, select.

Winsome, *a.* Cheerful, merry, gay, lively, sportive, blithe, bonny, lovable, pleasant, blithesome, buoyant, jocund, light-hearted, debonair, charming, winning.

WINTER, *v. i.* [*The noun is Basic Eng.*] Hibernate.

Wintry, *a.* Hyemal, brumal, cold, icy, frosty, arctic, boreal, brumous.

Wipe, *v. i.* Rub (*as with a cloth, in order to clean or dry*), mop, clean, dry.

——, *n.* 1. Wiping.

2. (*Colloq.*) Blow, stroke, hit.

3. (*Slang.*) Sneer, gibe, taunt, jeer, sarcasm.

Wipe out. Efface, obliterate, erase, expunge, cancel, raze, scratch out, rub out.

WIRE, *n.* Metallic thread, cable; telegraph, telephone; (*colloq.*) telegraphic message.

Wire, *v. t.* 1. Put upon a wire.

2. Bind with wire.

3. Ensnare by wires.

4. (*Colloq.*) Telegraph, convey by electric telegraph, report by telegram.

Wire-puller, *n.* Tactician, manœuvrer, diplomatist, adroit manager, pipe-layer.

Wisdom, *n.* 1. Sense, understanding, sagacity, wiseness, sapience, judgment, judiciousness, prescience, insight, discernment, depth, profundity, solidity, good sense, enlarged views, reach *or* compass of thought, good judgment, prudence, foresight, knowledge how to live, judgment of ends.

2. Knowledge, erudition, learning, attainment, scholarship, lore, information, enlightenment.

3. Reasonableness, reason, right *or* just view, sense.

4. Advisability, policy, expediency.

WISE, *a.* 1. Sensible, sage, judicious, sagacious, sapient, penetrating, deep, profound, discerning, reasonable, rational, intelligent, enlightened, sound, solid, philosophical, of good judgment.

2. Erudite, learned, informed, scholarly, knowing.

3. Subtle, cunning, crafty, sly, foxy, wily, politic, knowing, designing, long-headed, wary.

4. Advisable, expedient.

Wise, *n.* Manner, way, mode, fashion.

Wish, *v. i.* Desire, long, hanker, list.

——, *v. t.* 1. Bid, direct, want, desire, intend, mean.

2. Desire, want, long for, hanker after, set one's heart upon.

——, *n.* 1. Desire, want, will, pleasure, behest, hest (*poetical*), mind, intention.

2. Longing, want, desire, hankering, yearning, craving, inclination, liking.

Wishful, *a.* Desirous, longing, eager, hankering, wistful.

Wishy-washy, *a.* (*Colloq.*) Thin, feeble, weak, diluted, watery, flat.

Wistful, *a.* 1. Contemplative, meditative, reflective, musing, thoughtful, pensive.

2. Longing, eager, desirous. See WISHFUL.

Wit, *n.* 1. Intellect, understanding, mind, sense, intelligence, reason, genius, mental power, intellectual faculties, thinking principle, mother-wit.

2. Quick perception (*as of partial resemblance in things mostly unlike*), felicitous discernment of unexpected associations between words or ideas.

3. Facetiousness, humor, fun, drollery, waggery, waggishness, jocularity, sparkle, readiness, cleverness, brightness, *esprit*, whim, point, piquancy, quickness at repartee, Attic salt.

4. Sally, repartee, witticism, joke, epigram, conceit, *bon mot*, pleasantry, quip, quirk, word play.

5. Humorist, wag, bright man, bright woman, bright person.

Witch, *n.* Sorceress, enchantress, fascinator, charmer; crone, hag, sibyl.

——, *v. t.* Charm, enchant, fascinate, enamour, captivate, ravish, bewitch.

Witchcraft, *n.* Sorcery, necromancy, magic, witchery, thaumaturgy, theurgy, wonder-working, enchantment, incantation, conjuration, charm, spell, the black art.

Witchery, *n.* 1. Sorcery. See WITCHCRAFT.

2. Fascination, spell, entrancement, enchantment, ravishment, enravishment, captivation.

WITH, *prep.* 1. Through (*as the immediate agent or instrument*), by *or* with the help of, by the agency of, by means of. See BY.

2. Attending, accompanying, in company with, among, amidst, along with, beside, plus.

3. In the opinion of, in the estimation of, according to.

4. By the side of, in contrast with, notwithstanding.

5. Upon, immediately after.

Withdraw, *v. t.* 1. Remove, subduct, subduce, separate, sequester, sequestrate, retire, deduct, abstract, subtract, take away, draw out, draw back.

2. Wean, disengage, draw off.

3. Retract, recall, recant, disavow, revoke, relinquish, resign, abjure, take back.

Withdraw, *v. i.* Retire, retreat, secede, depart, shrink, dissociate, vacate, abdicate, decamp, go away, be off, go off, "welsh."

Withdrawal, *n.* 1. Abduction, withdrawing, retraction, separation, recall, revocation, abstraction, removal, subduction, subtraction, withdrawment.

2. Departure, exit, retirement, leave, recession, retreat, going away.

Withe, *n.* Twig, osier, wicker.

Wither, *v. i.* 1. Shrivel, dry, wilt, dry up, fade, sear, wizen, contract, droop, lose freshness.

2. Waste, decay, droop, languish, wane, decline, pine, pine away, waste away.

Withhold, *v. t.* 1. Restrain, check, detain, hinder, hold back, suppress, repress, keep in, rein in.

2. Retain, suppress, keep back, conceal, reserve.

——, *v. i.* Forbear.

Within, *prep.* 1. In the inside of, inside of, inside.

2. In the compass of, in the limits of, during, enclosed by, not beyond, not above, not more than.

3. In the reach *or* influence of.

——, *adv.* 1. Inwardly, internally, in the mind *or* heart.

2. Indoors, in the house, at home.

Without, *prep.* 1. Out of, on the outside of, outside of, beyond.

2. In the absence of, independently of, exclusively of.

3. Destitute of, lacking.

4. Free from *or* of, unburdened *or* unharmed by.

——, *adv.* Exteriorly, externally; outside, outdoors.

Withstand, *v. t.* Resist, oppose, face, confront, defy, strive against, stand against, make a stand against.

Witless, *a.* Silly, foolish, stupid, dull, shallow, senseless, obtuse, daft (*Scotch*), unintelligent, feeble-witted, short-witted, half-witted, dull-witted, muddy-headed, muddy-brained, slow of apprehension, fat-witted.

Witling, *n.* Pretender to wisdom, man of small wit, "smart Alec." See DUNCE.

Witness, *n.* 1. Testimony, evidence, attestation, corroboration, proof, confirmation.

2. Deponent, corroborator, testifier, eye-witness, observer, beholder, bystander, onlooker, spectator.

——, *v. t.* 1. Attest, be a witness of, bear witness to, testify to, confirm, corroborate.

2. Observe, see, mark, note, notice, take cognizance of.

Witticism, *n.* Joke (*made by one who affects wit*), jest, conceit, quip, quirk, crank, *bon mot,* sally, flash of wit.

Witty, *a.* 1. Facetious, humorous, jocular, jocose, waggish, droll, funny, pleasant, bright, clever.

2. Sprightly, sparkling, alert, quick, penetrating, apt at repartee.

Wizard, *n.* Conjurer, enchanter, sorcerer, magician, soothsayer, necromancer, charmer, diviner, seer, wonder-worker.

Wizened, *a.* Dried, shrivelled, shrunken, thin, sharp, lean, weazen.

Woe, *n.* Sorrow, grief, distress, tribulation, affliction, anguish, agony, torture, bitterness, misery, wretchedness, unhappiness, trouble, dole, disconsolateness, melancholy, depression, heartache, heavy heart, bleeding heart, broken heart, mental suffering, pain of mind.

Woe-begone, *a.* Wretched, miserable, pitiable, disconsolate, comfortless, sad, forlorn, sorrowful, melancholy, downcast, desponding, cheerless, crestfallen, chapfallen, cast down.

Woeful, *a.* 1. Sorrowful, mournful, distressed, sad, afflicted, unhappy, grieved, anguished, agonized, miserable, piteous, wretched, melancholy, disconsolate, troubled, burdened. See WOE-BEGONE.

2. Grievous, distressing, afflicting, afflictive, disastrous, calamitous, dreadful, tragical, deplorable, piteous, pitiable, depressing, sorrowful, lamentable, saddening.

3. Wretched, paltry, mean, pitiful.

WOMAN, *n.* (*Basic Eng.*)

Woman-hater, *n.* Misogynist.

Womanhood, *n.* 1. Womanliness, high feminine quality, femininity, matronhood.

2. Maturity (*in the human female*), ripeness, adult age, muliebrity.

3. Muliebrity, feminality, femineity, feminine sexual quality.

4. Women (*collectively*), womankind.

Womanish, *a.* Feminine (*in a bad sense*), effeminate, petticoat, soft, weak; unmanly.

Womanly, *a.* Feminine (*in a good sense*), becoming a woman, womanlike, matronly, ladylike; gentle, tender, motherly.

Womb, *n.* 1. Uterus, matrix, *venter.*

2. Hollow, interior recess, depth, deep, abyss, arcanum, cavern.

Wonder, *n.* 1. Astonishment, awe, amazement, wonderment, stupefaction, surprise, bewilderment. See ADMIRATION.

2. Curiosity, curious awe, inquiring surprise, awed curiosity.

3. Prodigy, marvel, miracle, portent.

4. Curiosity, phenomenon, spectacle, rarity, sight.

——, *v. i.* 1. Marvel, admire, gape, be surprised, be amazed, be astonished *or* astounded, be wonderstruck, be struck with wonder, be taken aback, hold one's breath, stand amazed, stand agog, look blank, open one's eyes, open one's mouth.

2. Ponder, meditate, conjecture, speculate, query, question, be curiously doubtful.

Wonderful, *a.* Astonishing, astounding, stupendous, surprising, amazing, startling, awe-inspiring, awful, awesome, marvellous, wondrous, miraculous, portentous, prodigious, extraordinary, very strange.

Wonder-worker, *n.* Conjurer. See WIZARD.

Wonder-working, *n.* Thaumaturgy, magic, sorcery. See WITCHCRAFT.

Wont, *n.* Custom, habit, use, practice, usage.

Wonted, *a.* Accustomed, usual, habitual, customary, conventional, familiar, common, frequent, regular, ordinary, everyday.

Woo, *v. t.* Court, solicit in love, make love to, pay one's addresses to, address, importune, sue, pursue.

——, *v. i.* Court, make love.

WOOD, *n.* 1. Forest, grove, copse, thicket, bosk, covert, coppice, spinny, greenwood, woodland, forest-land, timber-land.

2. Timber, lumber.

Woodcut, *n.* Wood-engraving, cut.

Wooded, *a.* Timbered, covered with woods, forest-covered, forest-crowned, overgrown.

Wooden, *a.* 1. Made of wood.

2. Woody, ligneous.

3. Awkward, clumsy, ungainly, stiff, rigid, expressionless, hard, unpliant, unpliable, unplastic.

Woodland, *n.* Woods, forest, grove, forest-land, timber-land.

Woody, *a.* 1. Ligneous, wooden, xyloid.

2. See WOODED.

3. Sylvan, shady, bosky, umbrageous, leafy, woodsy, bowery.

Wooer, *n.* Lover, suitor, gallant.

Woof, *n.* Weft.

Wooing, *n.* Suit, courtship, addresses.

WOOL, *n.* (*Basic Eng.*)

Woolen, *a.* Made of wool, of wool.

——, *n.* Cloth of wool, woolen cloth.

Wool-gathering, *n.* Vagary, idle fancy, foolish enterprise, useless pursuit, wild-goose chase.

Woolly, *a.* 1. Downy, like wool, lanated, lanate, lanose, fleecy.

2. Downy, covered with wool, nappy, fluffy, flocculent.

3. (*Bot.*) Lanuginous, downy.

WORD, *n.* 1. Vocable, expression, term, name, utterance, phrase.

2. Report, tidings, account, advice, intelligence, information, news, message.

3. Statement, affirmation, declaration, avowal, assertion, averment.

4. Conversation, speech.

5. Promise, pledge, assurance, engagement, agreement, plight, parole, word of honor.

6. Order, command, behest, bidding, direction, precept.

7. Signal, watchword, password, countersign.

8. Scripture, Word of God.

Word for word. Literally, *verbatim*, exactly, in the exact words, verbal.

Words, *n. pl.* 1. Language, accents, tongues, talk, discourse, conversation, speech, intercourse, parley, chat.

2. Dispute, wrangling, bickering, altercation, contention, argument, jangle, logomachy, war of words.

Wordy, *a.* Verbose, prolix, diffuse, tedious, garrulous, talkative, loquacious, rambling, periphrastic, circumlocutory, lengthened, inflated, windy, long-winded.

Work, *v. i.* 1. Act, operate, be in action, "take," be effective.

2. Labor, toil, moil, drudge, grind, slave, fag, grub, sweat, be *or* keep at work, be diligent, be industrious, practise, exercise.

3. Move, perform, succeed, get on.

4. Strive, endeavor, aim, attempt, try, exert one's self.

5. Ferment, effervesce, leaven, rise.

6. Heave, be tossed, be agitated.

——, *v. t.* 1. Labor upon, operate upon, ply, manipulate, wield.

2. Produce, originate, accomplish, effect, cause, engender, beget, lead to, manage, bring about; shape, forge, mould.

3. Keep at work, keep employed.

4. Exert, strain.

5. Embroider, broider, stitch, decorate with the needle.

WORK, *n.* 1. Toil, labor (*that fatigues*), exertion, drudgery, "elbow grease," pain, grind.

2. Occupation, employment, business, task; office, function.

3. Product (*of labor*), opus, composition, performance, production, fruit, achievement, accomplishment, handiwork, deed, action, feat.

4. Fabric, structure, manufacture.

5. Leaven, ferment.

6. Management, treatment.

Work against. Resist, oppose, antagonize, try to thwart.

Workbag, *n.* Reticule, hussy.

Worker, *n.* 1. Laborer, workman, operative, toiler, artificer, craftsman, handicraftsman, artisan; drudge, grubber, grind, fag.

2. Doer, performer.

3. Working-bee.

Workhouse, *n.* 1. Manufactory.

2. Penitentiary, jail, prison, bridewell, house of correction.

3. Poor-house.

Working, *a.* 1. Laboring.

2. Moving, operating, acting, in operation *or* action; practical.

3. On duty, at work.

4. Fermenting.

——, *n.* Motion, operation, action.

Workman, *n.* 1. Laborer, operative, hand, worker, workingman, journeyman, wright.

2. Artisan, mechanic, craftsman, handicraftsman, artificer.

3. Skilful artificer, master in his art, skilled workman, master workman.

Workmanlike, *a.* Skilful, workmanly, masterly, shipshape, thorough.

Workmanship, *n.* Handiwork, handicraft, craftsmanship, manufacture, manipulation, execution, work, achievement.

Work out. Accomplish, effect, perform, realize, bring to pass.

World, *n.* 1. Universe, cosmos, creation, nature.

2. Earth, globe, sphere, terrestrial ball, terraqueous globe *or* ball.

3. Planet, heavenly body.

4. Life, things, human affairs, secular affairs, material matters, mundane interests, affairs of life, social life, society, worldly people, *haute monde*, fashionable world, ways of men, course of things, stream of time.

5. Public, society, people, men, mankind, humanity, human kind, human race.

6. Natural order, unspiritualized order, natural man, unregenerate man *or* order.

7. Sphere, division, department, realm, kingdom.

8. Multitude, infinite number.

Worldly, *a.* 1. Earthly, mundane, terrestrial, terrene, sublunary, human, common.

2. Secular, temporal, profane, carnal, fleshly.

3. Sordid, grovelling, selfish, ambitious, proud, anxious for power, place, *or* wealth, worldly-minded, earth-born, irreligious, unspiritual, unregenerate, unsanctified.

WORM, *v. t.* [*The noun is Basic Eng.*] Work slowly, secretly, and gradually (*like a worm*), insinuate, writhe, wriggle, crawl, creep.

Wormlike, *a.* Worm-shaped, vermicular, vermiform.

Worm out. Find out (*as a secret*).

Worn, *a.* Impaired (*by use*), wasted, abraded, exhausted, consumed, decayed, threadbare, worn out, used up, worn to a thread, worse for wear, shabby, dilapidated.

Worry, *v. t.* Tease, vex, plague, pain, harass, annoy, trouble, torment, pester, bother, bore, persecute, molest, harry, irritate, badger, bait, haze, fret, chafe, hector, infest, beset, gall, disturb, disquiet.

——, *v. i.* (*Colloq.*) Fret, chafe, fidget, fume, fuss, be vexed, be troubled, worry one's self.

——, *n.* Anxiety, vexation, trouble, annoyance, perplexity, solicitude, care, disquiet, concern, uneasiness, fear, apprehension, misgiving.

Worship, *n.* 1. Adoration, idolizing, respect, esteem, devotion, homage, reverence.

2. Aspiration, supplication, invocation, prayer, praise, laud, exaltation.

——, *v. t.* 1. Adore, venerate (*with religious rites*), revere, reverence, honor, admire extravagantly, esteem.

2. Idolize, deify.

——, *v. i.* Aspire, pray, lift up the heart, bow down, attend church service.

Worshipful, *a.* 1. Venerable, reverend, honorable, worthy of honor, estimable, esteemed, respected.

2. Adoring, devout, reverent, prayerful, solemn.

Worst, *v. t.* Defeat, conquer, foil, overcome, overpower, overthrow, subdue, subjugate, vanquish, beat, rout, discomfit, crush, choke, quell, master, get the better of, put down.

Worth, *n.* 1. Merit, desert, worthiness, nobleness, excellence, virtue, credit, character, integrity, importance, account.

2. Value, price, cost, estimation.

Worthless, *a.* 1. Useless, valueless, meritless, nugatory, unproductive, unsalable, unserviceable, futile, miserable, poor, wretched, of no account *or* value, good-for-nothing, of no use.

2. Base, vile, unworthy, ignoble, abject, depraved, profligate, abandoned, graceless, ne'er-do-well, good-for-nothing.

3. Refuse, waste, riff-raff.

4. Tinsel, showy, glittering, gaudy, superficial, trashy, trumpery, flimsy.

5. Trifling, trivial, paltry, frivolous, slight, inane, empty, piddling, of no moment, of small importance.

Worthy, *a.* 1. Deserving, meritorious, suitable, fit.

2. Estimable, excellent, good, virtuous, exemplary, honest, righteous, upright, honorable, reputable.

Would-be, *a.* Self-styled, pretended, *soidisant*.

Wound, *n.* 1. Hurt, injury (*for example, a cut, laceration, stab, bruise, etc.*), blow.

2. Injury, hurt, damage, detriment, harm.

3. Pain (*of the mind or feelings*), pang, torture, grief, anguish.

——, *v. t.* 1. Hurt, injure, damage, harm (*with some weapon or such agency*).

2. Pain, irritate, gall, lacerate, prick, harrow, pierce, stab, cut, etc.

3. Annoy, mortify, offend, pain, give pain to, hurt the feelings of.

Wraith, *n.* Apparition, vision, spectre, ghost, unreal image.

Wrangle, *v. i.* Quarrel, bicker, spar, spat, jangle, cavil, dispute, brawl, argue, jar, squabble, tiff, have words, fall out, be at variance, have an altercation.

——, *n.* Quarrel, squabble, jangle, brawl, altercation, jar, bickering, contest, contention, controversy, wrangling, angry dispute, "scrap" (*slang*).

Wrangler, *n.* 1. Disputant, controversialist, jangler, quarrelsome fellow.

2. [*Cambridge University, Eng.*] Honor man, superior scholar (*especially in mathematics*).

Wrangling, *n.* Altercation. See WRANGLE, *n.*

Wrap, *v. t.* 1. Fold, lap, roll together, wrap up.

2. Envelop, cover (*by winding or folding*), infold, muffle, involve, swathe, wind, furl, cloak; hide, conceal.

——, *n.* Overcoat, cloak, cape, shawl; blanket, cover, coverlet.

Wrapper, *n.* 1. Envelope, cover, covering, wrapping.

2. Dressing-gown, loose gown, kimono.

Wrath, *n.* Anger, ire, indignation, exasperation, irritation, rage, fury, choler, passion, heat, resentment, offence.

Wrathful, *a.* Angry, mad, furious, infuriate, raging, rageful, wroth, indignant, passionate, resentful, exasperated, provoked, incensed, irritated, hot, irate, ireful, in a passion, out of temper, out of tune.

Wreak, *v. t.* Inflict (*as wrath or vengeance*), work, execute, exercise, indulge, give rein to.

Wreath, *n.* 1. Curl, ring.

2. Garland, chaplet, festoon, crown, coronet, bays, laurel.

Wreathe, *v. t.* 1. Twist, interweave, intwine, twine, garland, festoon.

2. Encircle, surround, infold.

Wreck, *n.* 1. Destruction, perdition, undoing, prostration, ruin, desolation, shipwreck, smash, crash.

2. Stranded vessel, shipwrecked vessel; ruins.

——, *v. t.* 1. Strand, founder, shipwreck, cast away.

2. Ruin, destroy, shipwreck, break, shatter, blight, blast.

Wrench, *v. t.* 1. Wrest, wring, twist, distort; pervert.

2. Sprain, strain.

3. Extort, extract.

——, *n.* 1. Twist, wring.

2. Sprain, strain.

3. Screw-key, monkey-wrench, spanner.

Wrest, *v. t.* 1. Twist. See WRENCH.

2. Pervert, strain, turn out of its true meaning, put a violent construction on.

Wrestle, *v. i.* Contend, strive, struggle, grapple, contest.

Wrestling, *n.* Struggle, contention, throwing, grappling.

Wretch, *n.* 1. Pilgarlic, pariah, vagabond, outcast, troglodyte, miserable being, unhappy being, victim, sufferer.

2. Miscreant, villain, knave, rogue, rascal, hound, beggar, "cur," "skunk," scoundrel, scapegrace, caitiff, ruffian, criminal.

Wretched, *a.* 1. Unhappy, unfortunate (*on account of outward condition*), forlorn, comfortless, sad, woe-begone, afflicted, distressed. See MISERABLE.

2. Calamitous, afflictive, afflicting, pitiable, deplorable, shocking, depressing, saddening, sad, sorrowful.

3. Bad, poor, vile, sorry, shabby, pitiful, beggarly, worthless, paltry, contemptible, mean.

Wretchedness, *n.* Unhappiness, distress, misery, affliction. See WOE.

Wriggle, *v. i.* Squirm, writhe, worm.

Wring, *v. t.* 1. Twist (*violently*), wrench, contort.

2. Force, extort, wrest.

3. Harass, distress, torture, anguish, torment, rack, pain.

Wrinkle, *n.* 1. Furrow, crease, fold, plait, gather, pucker, rumple, corrugation, rimple, ridge, cockle, crumple, crimp, crinkle, crow's-foot.

2. (*Colloq.*) Notion, whim, fancy, whimsey, caprice, crotchet, vagary, freak, quirk, maggot.

——, *v. t.* Corrugate, crease, rumple, cockle, pucker, crumple.

Wrinkled, *a.* 1. Rugose, rugous. See WRINKLE, 1.

2. Shrivelled, bent, aged.

Writ, *n.* 1. Writing, scripture, Holy Writ, precept.

2. (*Law.*) Decree, order, written order, brieve.

Write, *v. t.* 1. Inscribe, pen, pencil, scrawl, scribble, scratch, engross.

2. Compose, indite, produce, frame, draft, draw up.

3. Set down, set down in writing, set down in black and white, jot down, commit to paper *or* writing, put on paper, record.

——, *v. i.* 1. Compose, invent (*in a literary way*), make books, practise authorship.

2. Write a letter, send a letter.

3. Tell (*in writing*), give account.

4. Use the pen, take pen in hand.

Writer, *n.* 1. Penman, calligraphist.

2. Scribe, scribbler, clerk, secretary, amanuensis, quill-driver, scrivener, clerk.

3. Author, scribbler, composer; correspondent.

Writhe, *v. t.* Twist, distort, contort, make awry, wring.

——, *v. i.* Wriggle, squirm, be distorted.

WRITING, *n.* 1. Chirography, calligraphy, penmanship, handwriting, hand, "fist," "quill-driving."

2. Document, instrument, manuscript, script, writ.

3. Book, work, publication, piece, literary production, composition, opus; authorship.

4. Inscription, title, engrossment, legend.

Writing-desk, *n.* Secretary, *escritoire.*

WRONG, *a.* 1. Unjust, inequitable, unfair, wrongful.

2. Bad, wicked, evil, improper, immoral, sinful, criminal, iniquitous, blameworthy, reprehensible, guilty, vicious.

3. Unfit, inapposite, inappropriate, unsuitable, amiss, improper.

4. Incorrect, inaccurate, erroneous, mistaken, faulty, false, untrue, wide of the mark.

Wrong, *n.* 1. Injustice, unfairness, inequity, injury, trespass, grievance, foul play, violation of right, tort (*law*).

2. Sin, wickedness, evil, immorality, vice, crime, villainy, unrighteousness, wrong-doing, transgression, iniquity, blame, guilt, misdoing, misdeed.

3. Falsity, error.

——, *adv.* Erroneously, incorrectly, inaccurately, falsely, amiss, improperly, wrongly, faultily.

——, *v. t.* Injure, abuse, maltreat, oppress, encroach, impose upon, treat unjustly, do a wrong to, do an injury to.

Wrong-doer, *n.* Delinquent, offender, sinner, culprit, evil-doer, criminal.

Wrong-headed, *a.* Perverse, stubborn, obstinate, intractable, crotchety, mulish, headstrong, cross-grained, dogged, wayward, pig-headed.

Wroth, *a.* Angry. See WRATHFUL.

Wrought. (*Imperfect and participle of work.*) Performed, done, worked, effected.

Wrought up. Maddened, excited, fired, worked up, beside one's self.

Wry, *a.* Distorted, twisted, contorted, crooked, askew, awry, on one side, turned to one side.

X

Xanthic, *a.* Yellowish, tending to yellow, fulvous, fulvid.

Xanthous, *a.* 1. Fair, blond(e), light-complexioned, fair-complexioned.

2. Fair-haired, blond-haired, yellow-haired.

Xiphoid, *a.* (*Anat.*) Ensiform, sword-shaped, gladiate, swordlike.

Xylograph, *n.* Wood-cut, wood-engraving, cut, engraving on wood.

Xylographer, *n.* Wood-engraver.

Xylography, *n.* 1. Wood-engraving, woodgraver's art, woodcutting, engraving on wood.

2. Decorative printing on wood, printed wood-decoration.

Xylophagous, *a.* Wood-eating, living on wood, feeding on wood, wood-nourished.

Y

Yard, *n.* 1. Enclosure, compound, court, close.

2. Three feet, thirty-six inches.

Yarn, *n.* 1. Woolen thread, worsted, spun wool.

2. (*Colloq.*) Story, tale, narrative, anecdote, "fish story," boasting; untruth, fabrication, romancing.

Yaup, *v. i.* Yelp, yap, cry (*as a child or a bird*).

Yawn, *v. i.* 1. Gape, oscitate.

2. Open wide, gape, threaten to engulf.

Yea, *adv.* Yes, ay, aye.

Yean, *v. i.* Lamb, bring forth a lamb.

YEAR, *n.* Twelvemonth.

Yearly, *a.* Annual, anniversary.

——, *adv.* 1. Annually, once a year, every year.

2. By the year, per annum.

Yearn, *v. i.* Long, be eager, feel a strong desire, covet, hanker, crave, long fondly, long pityingly.

Yeast, *n.* Barm, ferment, rising, leaven.

Yeasty, *a.* Barmy, fermenting, foaming.

Yell, *v. i.* Screech, shriek, scream, bawl, squeal, howl, roar, cry out (*as with pain or horror*), shout, halloo, bellow.

YELLOW, *a.* 1. Golden, fulvous, fulvid, gold-colored, aureate.

2. Jaundiced, jealous.

3. Sensational, hysterical, jingoistic.

4. (*Colloq.*) Cowardly, craven, despicable.

Yellow-eyed, *a.* Jaundiced, jealous, green-eyed.

Yelp, *v. i.* Yaup, yap, bark, cry (*as a dog*).

Yeoman, *n.* Freeholder, commoner, farmer; beef-eater, guardsman.

Yeomanry, *n.* Body of yeomen, yeomen.

YES, *adv.* Yea, ay, aye; it is so; granted, true.

YESTERDAY, *n.* Yestermorn, yestereve.

Yet, *conj.* Nevertheless, notwithstanding, however, still, at the same time.

——, *adv.* 1. Besides, further, in addition, over and above.

2. Still, to this time, now, even now.

3. Hitherto, thus far, up to the present time.

Yield, *v. t.* 1. Produce, bear, furnish, fetch, sell for, bring in, bring forth, supply, afford, impart, render, bestow, confer, communicate.

2. Permit, grant, allow, give, accord, concede, acknowledge.

3. Relinquish, surrender, abandon, cede, resign, abdicate, forego, waive, deliver up, give up, part with, make over, let go.

——, *v. i.* 1. Submit, surrender, succumb, give in, give up, resign one's self, relent, capitulate.

2. Bend, relax, bow, be pliant, give way.

3. Assent, comply, acquiesce, give consent, obey.

4. Give place, give way, make way.

——, *n.* Product, crop.

Yielding, *a.* 1. Submissive, complying, obedient, compliant, accommodating, unresisting, non-resistant, acquiescent, passive, facile, complaisant, affable, easy, manageable.

2. Pliable, pliant, supple, flexible, flexile, tractable, soft, plastic.

3. Productive, fertile.

Yoke, *n.* 1. Bond, chain, link, tie, ligature, union.

2. Bondage, servitude, service, dependence, enslavement, subjection, thraldom, vassalage.

3. Couple, pair.

——, *v. t.* Join, couple, link, interlink, conjoin, bracket, harness, connect, associate; marry.

Yonder, *adv.* 1. At a distance (*within view*), yon.

2. There.

YOU, *pron.* (*Basic Eng.*)

YOUNG, *a.* Youthful, juvenile, not old, in one's teens; green, immature, inexperienced; recent.

Younger, *a.* Junior.

Youngster, *n.* (*Colloq.*) Youth, boy, lad, adolescent, stripling, schoolboy, younker, young man.

Youth, *n.* 1. Juvenility, adolescence, juniority, childhood, immaturity, wardship, pupilage, leading strings, minority, teens, bloom, nonage, youthfulness, prime of life, flower of life, heyday, springtime.

2. Boy, stripling, sprig, slip, adolescent, schoolboy, lad, youngster.

3. Young men, young women, young persons, the rising generation.

Youthful, *a.* 1. Young, in one's teens, under age, beardless.

2. Childish, juvenile, boyish, callow, adolescent, juvenescent, immature.

3. Early, green, maiden.

Youthfulness, *n.* Juvenility, juvenescence, youth.

Yule, *n.* 1. Christmas, yuletide.

2. Lammas, Lammas-tide.

Z

Zany, *n.* Buffoon, clown, jester, droll, merry-andrew, harlequin, punch, punchinello, scaramouch, fool, jack-pudding, pickle-herring; half-wit, simpleton.

Zanyism, *n.* Buffoonery, clownishness, drollery, harlequinism, foolery.

Zeal, *n.* Ardor, eagerness, alacrity, engagedness, fervor, fervency, warmth, glow, feeling, energy, earnestness, devotedness, devotion, intentness, intensity, jealousness, heartiness, cordiality, enthusiasm, passion, soul, spirit; zealotry, fanaticism.

Zealot, *n.* 1. Fanatic, bigot, devotee, partisan.

2. Enthusiast, visionary, dreamer.

Zealous, *a.* Ardent, eager, keen, earnest, fervent, fervid, warm, glowing, burning, fiery, passionate, jealous, enthusiastic, devoted, swift, prompt, ready, forward.

Zenith, *n.* Summit, top, apex, pinnacle, acme, utmost height, highest point, culminating point; climax, culmination, prime, heyday, flower.

Zephyr, *n.* 1. West wind.

2. (*Poetical.*) Gentle, mild, *or* soft breeze, light wind.

Zero, *n.* Naught (*or* nought), nothing, nothingness, nullity, cipher, nil, "nix," nadir, lowest point, point of commencement.

Zest, *n.* 1. Relish, gust, gusto, appetite, enjoyment, liking, exhilaration, thrill, "kick."

2. Relish, flavor, savor, taste, smack, twang, salt, edge, piquancy.

3. Relish, appetizer, sauce.

Zone, *n.* 1. (*Poetical.*) Belt, girdle, cincture, girth, baldric, band.

2. Region, clime, climate; circuit.

3. (*Geom.*) Surface bounded by parallel circles (*on a sphere*), belt.

Zymotic, *a.* Infectious (*as if by the action of a ferment*), germinating, diffused by germs, originating from decomposition, bacterial, fermentative.